PUBLIC PAPERS OF THE PRESIDENTS

OF THE UNITED STATES

PUBLIC PAPERS OF THE PRESIDENTS

OF THE UNITED STATES

Lyndon B. Johnson

Containing the Public Messages, Speeches, and

Statements of the President

1963–64

(IN TWO BOOKS)

BOOK II—JULY 1 TO DECEMBER 31, 1964

UNITED STATES GOVERNMENT PRINTING OFFICE

WASHINGTON : 1965

PUBLISHED BY THE
OFFICE OF THE FEDERAL REGISTER
NATIONAL ARCHIVES AND RECORDS SERVICE
GENERAL SERVICES ADMINISTRATION

For sale by the Superintendent of Documents, U.S. Government Printing Office
Washington, D.C. 20402 · Price $7.00

CONTENTS

Book I

Book II

LIST OF ITEMS, Book I

[List of Items, Book II, starts on page XLI]

List of Items, Book I

XIII

List of Items, Book I

LIST OF ITEMS, Book II

Page

List of Items, Book II

Lyndon B. Johnson

July 1–December 31, 1964

442 Remarks at the Swearing In of John T. McNaughton, Daniel Luevano, Solis Horwitz, and Robert W. Morse as Key Officials in the Department of Defense. *July 1, 1964*

THIS IS a very proud and satisfying moment, I am sure, for each of you men who have weathered the perils of the United States Senate and find yourself duly approved and confirmed here today.

I know it must be a matter of great satisfaction for your family and for your friends.

I want each of you to know that this is a very proud and satisfying moment for your President as well. We Presidents have many responsibilities. Unfortunately, Presidents have no more hours in the day than other men, but when able and brilliant and dedicated men are willing to help bear those burdens with little hope of glory, any President would feel as I do that we should give recognition to it and congratulate you.

You men assembled here this morning come from many regions of our country— from New England, from the west coast, from metropolitan centers of the East, and from a small town in the Midwest. Each of you in your respective fields has established a most distinguished and impressive record. The country is fortunate to have your services in this critically important work of this period when the first purpose of America in the eyes of every citizen of the world is keeping the peace.

So, I congratulate you. I thank you for coming aboard to help us carry forward the great task of these times. All of you have demonstrated the experience, the judgment, and the dedication to public service worthy of the recommendation of the most distinguished Secretary of Defense, and I think worthy of the nominations that I have made and the confirming action the Senate has taken.

So, it is a great pleasure to be here and be present when you are sworn in and when you assume your new responsibilities.

NOTE: The ceremony was held at 1 p.m. in the Rose Garden at the White House. Mr. McNaughton and Mr. Horwitz were sworn in as Assistant Secretaries of Defense, Mr. Luevano, as an Assistant Secretary of the Army, and Mr. Morse, as an Assistant Secretary of the Navy.

443 Joint Statement Following Discussions With the President of Costa Rica. *July 2, 1964*

THE PRESIDENT of Costa Rica, Francisco Orlich, and President Johnson, have concluded friendly discussions on matters of mutual concern.

The two Presidents discussed the Alliance for Progress and the contribution it is making toward the economic and social development of the Hemisphere. They expressed their satisfaction with its achievements in Central America and the Hemisphere since President Kennedy's visit to San José, and reaffirmed their faith in the goals of the Alliance. They noted especially the intimate relationship which exists between the practice of effective representative democracy and the achievement of social and economic progress, and they renewed their determination to encourage democratic ideals throughout the Hemisphere. President Johnson expressed his admiration for the leadership which Costa Rican people have given over the years, by their example, to the accomplishment of this objective.

President Orlich reviewed the efforts of the Central American countries to promote their economic well-being through the Central American Common Market. President Johnson expressed gratification that these efforts had already made a significant contribution to the economic development of Central America. The two Presidents discussed the participation of private enterprise in the Central American Common Market, and the fundamental importance of cooperation between the public and private sectors in creating sound and healthy conditions in which each can make its most effective contribution. They agreed that a responsible and vigorous private sector is an essential element of a free and democratic society, and is indispensable to the success of the Central American Common Market and the Alliance for Progress.

President Orlich outlined the economic situation in his country, and expressed appreciation for the understanding and friendly cooperation of the United States. He gave special praise to the United States Navy Seabees, who are cooperating with Costa Rica to relieve flood conditions, which have been seriously aggravated by the eruption of Irazu Volcano. President Johnson assured President Orlich of the continued and sympathetic cooperation of the United States in the present natural disaster afflicting Costa Rica, and of the desire of the United States to help Costa Rica achieve further economic and social progress in keeping with the Charter of Punta del Este.

The Presidents noted the continued efforts of subversive agents trained in Cuba and other Communist countries to create unrest and undermine democratic governments in Latin America. They agreed that each country must adopt effective measures to defend itself against such activities, and that the Organization of American States should take meaningful steps to demonstrate the collective will of the American Republics to resist such aggression.

The Presidents concluded their talks by expressing satisfaction that relations between their two countries had reached a high level of mutual understanding and respect. They pledged themselves to continued cooperation within the Organization of American States to achieve the objectives of the Alliance for Progress.

444 Remarks Upon Signing Bill Broadening the Prevailing Wage Section of the Davis-Bacon Act. *July 2, 1964*

I WANT to express my satisfaction that the leaders of the workers of this country could be here with the Members of Congress who have been so devoted to their welfare throughout the years.

I am very happy this morning to sign this legislation, H.R. 6041. I am especially glad that this measure has support from such a broad consensus among all the groups that are affected by it.

We have come a long ways since the original Davis-Bacon Act became law. That act provided wage protection for workers that were employed locally on construction which was financed with Federal funds. Congress and the people recognized that principle as just and sound. I think the record through the years confirms the wisdom and the value of that act.

This bill basically brings the law up to date. Thirty years ago fringe benefits were unknown. Today such provisions are standard practice in most employer-employee relationships.

The new law sensibly provides that wage determinations shall, in addition to cash wages, take account of prevailing benefits such as medical and hospital care, pensions and workmen's compensation, unemployment insurance, vacations, holidays, and other such factors.

Our American prosperity today, we are glad to say, is unparalleled. Our prospects for the future seem to us to have never been brighter. So it is very reassuring to me to know that the great majority of Americans want to keep moving forward, not backward. Few want to reopen the old and the settled debates. Few want to stir up the old divisions and suspicions of class. We don't want to set labor and management at bitter odds with one another. We don't want to have Government take over everything or ignore everything.

I believe that all of us want to clear off our agenda, put the past behind us, and get on with building a better America.

I know that this is a glad day for a great leader of American labor, Mr. George Meany, and Mr. Haggerty, of the Building Trades group, that this legislation affects so vitally. I am happy that Senator McNamara, Senator Morse, Senator Kuchel, members of both parties, Congressman Roosevelt and members of both parties of the House, are here to show that this is an American measure and not just a party measure.

I am gratified to think that we are making progress toward these goals every day by working together in unity and putting the past behind us, hoping to leave this a better world than we found it.

NOTE: The President spoke shortly before noon in the Cabinet Room at the White House. In his closing remarks he referred to George Meany, President, AFL–CIO, Cornelius J. Haggerty, President, Building and Construction Trades Department, AFL–CIO, Senator Pat McNamara of Michigan, Senator Wayne Morse of Oregon, Senator Thomas H. Kuchel of California, and Representative James Roosevelt of California.

As enacted, H.R. 6041 is Public Law 88–349 (78 Stat. 238).

445 Remarks at the Swearing In of General Taylor as Ambassador to Viet-Nam. *July 2, 1964*

Ladies and gentlemen, General Taylor, Secretary Rusk:

General Taylor, on behalf of all of your countrymen, I want to congratulate you and express a very deep gratitude for the example of unselfish citizenship that you offer to the world today.

On many occasions in both war and peace, Maxwell Taylor has responded to his country's call without any thought of self.

Today you undertake still another demanding task. There are no illusions about the difficulty of the challenge. There are likewise no illusions about the responsibility or the importance of this assignment.

As you leave, Mr. Ambassador, the prayers and the hopes of all the American people are with you.

We are fortunate as a Nation that in this post to the highest duty one great American follows another great American. We are likewise fortunate to have in our military officers of the highest rank who respect with every fiber in their bodies the civilian tradition of our democratic society. And we are fortunate that they are willing to serve that tradition without any hesitation.

Our first purpose, our constant purpose in everything we seek to do, is honorable peace. We stand with those who stand in defense of their own freedom and independence. We work with those who work in support of peace for the world and progress under freedom for human mankind.

I know that as our Ambassador to Viet-Nam you will, Mr. Ambassador, communi-cate to the Vietnamese people and their leaders the resolve, the determination, and the continuing support of the American people.

General Taylor, we wish you Godspeed on your journey and in your service.

NOTE: The ceremony was held in the early afternoon in the Rose Garden at the White House. In his opening words the President referred to Gen. Maxwell D. Taylor, formerly Chairman of the Joint Chiefs of Staff, and Dean Rusk, Secretary of State.

The text of General Taylor's response was also released.

446 Radio and Television Remarks Upon Signing the Civil Rights Bill. *July 2, 1964*

[Broadcast from the East Room at the White House at 6:45 p.m.]

My fellow Americans:

I am about to sign into law the Civil Rights Act of 1964. I want to take this occasion to talk to you about what that law means to every American.

One hundred and eighty-eight years ago this week a small band of valiant men began a long struggle for freedom. They pledged their lives, their fortunes, and their sacred honor not only to found a nation, but to forge an ideal of freedom—not only for political independence, but for personal liberty—not only to eliminate foreign rule, but to establish the rule of justice in the affairs of men.

That struggle was a turning point in our history. Today in far corners of distant continents, the ideals of those American patriots still shape the struggles of men who hunger for freedom.

This is a proud triumph. Yet those who founded our country knew that freedom would be secure only if each generation fought to renew and enlarge its meaning. From the minutemen at Concord to the soldiers in Viet-Nam, each generation has been equal to that trust.

Americans of every race and color have died in battle to protect our freedom. Americans of every race and color have worked to build a nation of widening opportunities. Now our generation of Americans has been called on to continue the unending search for justice within our own borders.

We believe that all men are created equal. Yet many are denied equal treatment.

We believe that all men have certain unalienable rights. Yet many Americans do not enjoy those rights.

We believe that all men are entitled to the blessings of liberty. Yet millions are being deprived of those blessings—not because of their own failures, but because of the color of their skin.

The reasons are deeply imbedded in history and tradition and the nature of man. We can understand—without rancor or hatred—how this all happened.

But it cannot continue. Our Constitution, the foundation of our Republic, forbids it. The principles of our freedom forbid it. Morality forbids it. And the law I will sign tonight forbids it.

That law is the product of months of the most careful debate and discussion. It was proposed more than one year ago by our late and beloved President John F. Kennedy. It received the bipartisan support of more than two-thirds of the Members of both the House and the Senate. An overwhelming majority of Republicans as well as Democrats voted for it.

It has received the thoughtful support of tens of thousands of civic and religious leaders in all parts of this Nation. And it is supported by the great majority of the American people.

The purpose of the law is simple.

It does not restrict the freedom of any American, so long as he respects the rights of others.

It does not give special treatment to any citizen.

It does say the only limit to a man's hope for happiness, and for the future of his children, shall be his own ability.

It does say that there are those who are equal before God shall now also be equal in the polling booths, in the classrooms, in the factories, and in hotels, restaurants, movie theaters, and other places that provide service to the public.

I am taking steps to implement the law under my constitutional obligation to "take care that the laws are faithfully executed."

First, I will send to the Senate my nomination of LeRoy Collins to be Director of the Community Relations Service. Governor Collins will bring the experience of a long career of distinguished public service to the task of helping communities solve problems of human relations through reason and commonsense.

Second, I shall appoint an advisory committee of distinguished Americans to assist Governor Collins in his assignment.

Third, I am sending Congress a request for supplemental appropriations to pay for necessary costs of implementing the law, and asking for immediate action.

Fourth, already today in a meeting of my Cabinet this afternoon I directed the agencies of this Government to fully discharge the new responsibilities imposed upon them by the law and to do it without delay, and to keep me personally informed of their progress.

Fifth, I am asking appropriate officials to meet with representative groups to promote greater understanding of the law and to achieve a spirit of compliance.

We must not approach the observance and enforcement of this law in a vengeful spirit. Its purpose is not to punish. Its purpose is not to divide, but to end divisions—divisions which have all lasted too long. Its purpose is national, not regional.

Its purpose is to promote a more abiding commitment to freedom, a more constant pursuit of justice, and a deeper respect for human dignity.

We will achieve these goals because most Americans are law-abiding citizens who want to do what is right.

This is why the Civil Rights Act relies first on voluntary compliance, then on the efforts of local communities and States to secure the rights of citizens. It provides for the national authority to step in only when others cannot or will not do the job.

This Civil Rights Act is a challenge to all of us to go to work in our communities and our States, in our homes and in our hearts, to eliminate the last vestiges of injustice in our beloved country.

So tonight I urge every public official, every religious leader, every business and professional man, every workingman, every housewife—I urge every American—to join in this effort to bring justice and hope to all our people—and to bring peace to our land.

My fellow citizens, we have come now to a time of testing. We must not fail.

Let us close the springs of racial poison. Let us pray for wise and understanding hearts. Let us lay aside irrelevant differ-ences and make our Nation whole. Let us hasten that day when our unmeasured strength and our unbounded spirit will be free to do the great works ordained for this Nation by the just and wise God who is the Father of us all.

Thank you and good night.

NOTE: The Civil Rights Act of 1964 is Public Law 88–352 (78 Stat. 241).

447 Statement by the President Upon Making Public the Names of the 1964 Recipients of the Presidential Medal of Freedom. *July 4, 1964*

THESE individuals add distinction to this high award. Each person we honor has previously honored his fellow man by set-ting for himself a standard of excellence only he was able to achieve.

Collectively, they have made man's world safe, his physical body more durable, his mind broader, his leisure more delightful, his standard of living higher, and his dignity important.

They are creators; we are the beneficiaries.

NOTE: The statement is part of a White House re-lease announcing the President's selection of the 1964 recipients of the Presidential Medal of Free-dom, the highest civil honor the President of the United States can bestow. For the names of the recipients and for the President's remarks upon presenting the awards, see Item 568.

The Presidential Medal of Freedom was estab-lished by President Kennedy on February 22, 1963 (Executive Order 11085, 28 F.R. 1759; 3 CFR, 1959–1963 Comp., p. 719. See also "Public Papers of the Presidents, John F. Kennedy 1963," Item 76). The awards are given for "exceptionally meritorious contributions to the security or national interest of the United States, to world peace, or to cultural or other significant public or private endeavors." The 1963 awards were presented by President Johnson on December 6, 1963 (see Item 27, above).

448 Remarks to the Members of the President's Committee on Equal Employment Opportunity Upon Receiving Their Report. *July 7, 1964*

Secretary Wirtz, Mr. Taylor, members of the Committee, ladies and gentlemen:

This is a doubly gratifying privilege for me. I am satisfied that this is a report of success, a report of steady and substantial success in a most challenging field.

I am gratified personally that I had the privilege of working with you as your Chairman during a part of the period covered by this report when I was your Vice President.

In 1960, immediately after the election, President Kennedy asked me to devote some time to this work and no assignment that I received from him was ever closer to my heart or my interests.

The ideal of equal opportunity, I believe, is the bedrock ideal of our society and of our system. I am grateful for the opportunity I had to work for that ideal's greater realization.

There have been other Presidential committees that have operated in this field from time to time. I believe it is fair and, I hope, objective to say that no committee has ever written anything like the substantial record that you have written that is incorporated in these pages.

Since March of 1961, when you were formally organized, your activities have helped unite in this country management and labor, church and school, organizations and individuals, and they have commonly supported national ideals and national goals.

I believe the work of this Committee has done much to lay the groundwork for the responsible and, I believe, peaceful acceptance of the Civil Rights Act of 1964.

I have been especially pleased with the many leaders from business and labor in our communities who have been working with this Committee's program who have come forward and offered their valuable leadership in response to this new law of the land. I have been hearing from them from all parts of the Nation in the last few hours. Our Nation's progress and the progress of all humankind toward equality of rights and toward opportunity is a steady climb and not just a big, quick leap.

The challenge continues, the need for patience and perseverance continues, the need for responsible leadership from responsible citizens continues, and we must be grateful and glad that we are moving forward and that we have the unified leadership of all sectors of our national life.

You members of this Committee have set a notable example for others to follow. You have made it clear that we are not working in any one region or in any one industry or to benefit any one group of Americans alone. This is a national program to the benefit of all the people. This shall continue to be the guiding star and the prevailing standard in all the work that we do to expand the horizons of every American regardless of race or religion or region.

We started on a very modest basis. We had a few individuals get together and outline a plan that would bring equality in employment. That plan has now grown to where it covers companies that employ more than 7 million people. The President's Committee on Equal Employment Opportunity is known to most of the leaders of industry and leaders of labor in this country, and to the church and educational leaders in this country.

This Committee, wherever it is known, has been accepted and has been rewarded with the support of our people. Your service has been a great contribution, and I have not the slightest doubt that we would not be where we are today except for the leadership that you have given.

To those of you who are in public service, you can take real pride in pointing to the achievements of your Government.

To those of you who are in private life, you see a law that has been passed by more than two-thirds of the Congress and is now being accepted in every State of the Union. That is the most comprehensive set of guidelines for the preservation of human rights and for the protection of individual freedom that has been written in this country in the last century.

So, you must be proud of the part that you have played in that achievement.

We are just beginning. The people of this country have a long, hard road to travel before we will have achieved all of our objectives. But if we make progress in the next year as we have made in the last year, if we move forward in the next 4 years as we have moved in the last 4 years, we will see a new nation, a better nation and a stronger nation—a land in which all of us can take increased pride.

Thank you so much for your help.

NOTE: The President spoke shortly after noon in the Rose Garden at the White House. His opening words referred to Secretary of Labor W. Willard Wirtz, Vice Chairman of the President's Committee on Equal Employment Opportunity, who presented the report to the President, and Hobart Taylor, Jr., Executive Vice Chairman of the Committee.

The Committee's "Report to the President," cov-

ering the period March 1961–November 1963, is dated November 26, 1963 (150 pp., Government Printing Office).

The President's Committee on Equal Employment Opportunity was established on March 6, 1961, to eliminate discrimination because of race, creed, color, or national origin in employment by the Federal Government, by government contractors, and on federally assisted construction projects (see Executive Orders 10925, 11114, 3 CFR, 1959–1963 Comp., pp. 448, 774). In addition the Committee developed "Plans for Progress," voluntary agreements covering manufacturers and other businesses which do not fall within the scope of the Executive orders. The Committee's report pointed out that more than 200 corporations, employing more than 7 million persons, were participating in these voluntary agreements.

449 Telephone Remarks on the Occasion of the Keel-Laying of the U.S.S. *Vallejo*. July 7, 1964

CITIZENS of Vallejo, while I cannot be with you, I am proud to participate in this way in these unique and very historic ceremonies.

With this new Polaris submarine, we honor a great American hero. Like so many of our Nation's heroes, his is a name of Mexican ancestry. As a soldier and as a statesman, General Vallejo was one of the first of the long line of courageous Mexican-Americans who fought so bravely for freedom and who worked so tirelessly for peace in the world.

In honoring him, we honor the citizens of your city which bears his great name. For 100 years you have built more than 500 vessels to fulfill the Mare Island slogan: "Our

sole mission is to serve the Fleet."

I am sure that in building the *Vallejo* you will surpass all of your own past records. The mission of this vessel will be a mission of peace.

We today live in peace with our good neighbor and our good friend, the Republic of Mexico.

We of America work for a world in which all men of all lands may live side by side without fear, without suspicion, without war. To that goal we now dedicate this vessel.

NOTE: The President spoke early in the evening from the Cabinet Room at the White House to participants in the ceremony at the Mare Island Naval Shipyard in California.

450 Statement by the President on the Death of Roy E. Davidson. July 8, 1964

I WANT to express my deep sorrow at the passing of Roy E. Davidson. Last winter, when this Nation faced a critical time in the railroad dispute, I asked Mr. Davidson and

the other men of both sides to help preserve collective bargaining in America. He accepted that challenge, as he did others in his long and accomplished career. He was a fine man, a good citizen, an honest leader of men. His union and his Nation both benefited from the achievements of his life.

NOTE: The statement was read by the Press Secretary to the President, George E. Reedy, at his news conference held at the White House at 11:16 a.m. on July 8, 1964.

451   Statement by the President on New York City's Mobilization for Youth Program. *July 8, 1964*

JOBLESSNESS among young men and women today is the bitter root of tomorrow's poverty. While unemployment among young workers has always been higher than among the the more mature, it has been worsening in recent years. Almost 1 million young men and women are today without work. The unemployment rate for teenagers is 18 percent.

I am especially concerned about the plight of those young people who are growing into adulthood in areas of poverty and depression. There unemployment is not just a temporary hiatus between school and work. It is too often the beginning of an enduring disqualification from opportunity. It is a turning onto a road that leads nowhere. Lack of skill, language difficulty, ignorance of work discipline, and poor academic backgrounds enforce discrimination's hand. The result is a generation without a future.

The program announced today is the latest and one of the most promising in a variety of efforts we are making to bring opportunity to neighborhoods where it has long been absent. The road before us is long, but it lessens with each step. The Mobilization for Youth program has my deep interest and support.

NOTE: The statement was read by the Press Secretary to the President, George E. Reedy, at his news conference held at the White House at 11:16 a.m. on July 8, 1964.

The Press Secretary stated that the program was developed to provide training for some 2,000 unemployed, out-of-school, and disadvantaged youth in New York City's Lower East Side area. It was to be financed by funds from the Ford Foundation and from the Federal Government under the Manpower Development and Training Act, and to be operated by Mobilization For Youth, a nonprofit organization formed in 1962 to combat delinquency and youth unemployment.

452   Remarks at a Meeting With United States Attorneys. *July 8, 1964*

Mr. Attorney General and Mrs. Kennedy, ladies and gentlemen:

With your wives and children here this morning this almost has the appearance of another White House press conference. As for those of you who left your families at home, maybe you can get a good lawyer to defend you when you return.

We are very proud and very glad to have you, and I am greatly honored to welcome you here to your house.

Someone once said that lawyers are like bread—they are best when they are young and fresh. I know that this country is very fortunate to have so many unusually able young lawyers giving their fresh talents and their energies to the cause of justice in this country today.

At the same time, I know that you are fortunate, too.

You are serving in an unusually creative, landmark era. Our society's concepts of justice are undergoing a historic advance and substantial enlargement. Your own contributions in this field are both significant and substantial.

Many trends of these times seem to be submerging the identity and the dignity of the individual. On the one hand, the trend in our laws, in our courts, and in the administration of justice is to serve and to save that identity and dignity.

We welcome that trend. I applaud the courage of those who are helping to help make and break new ground in this regard.

In the courtrooms of the United States, you represent no individual but you represent the Government of your country. Yet, in the strictest sense, you are not the Government's attorneys but you are always the peoples' advocates. That is why your service is so vital and so decisive to the quality of freedom our people are to enjoy in the years that are ahead of us.

In your conferences here in Washington, I know you are discussing and considering many matters of immediate concern to your official responsibilities. If I may, I would like to express this morning some personal thoughts to you in regard to how I feel about your leadership.

First, I hope that both as public officials and as private citizens you will be restless champions of the cause of equal justice for the poor as well as for the rich. Our outstanding Attorney General, Mr. Robert Kennedy, has performed a most remarkable service for our Nation in awakening our national conscience in this regard. No one knows better than you the disadvantage of the underprivileged in our courtrooms. So I hope that you will join the Attorney General and give all of us your strong support in helping to overcome this outstanding inequity.

Second, I want you to know that we look to you to be leaders outside, as well as inside, the courtroom in helping to achieve the full value and the full meaning of the new Civil Rights Act passed by more than two-thirds of the votes of the Congress of the United States and signed by the President.

In our times there has been no greater challenge to responsible, articulate citizens than to make this law the landmark of human justice that it deserves to be. The task cannot be discharged perfunctorily, and certainly it cannot be discharged in any punitive spirit. All of you have a great opportunity as Americans as well as United States Attorneys to participate in this new undertaking.

Third, I would like to say to you this morning—at least express the hope—that as you are steadfast in the defense of civil rights that you will be equally steadfast in defense of civil liberties. We do not seek and we do not want—and the conscience of the American people will never tolerate—a concept of justice which seeks convictions at the expense of human decency and at the expense of liberty and at the expense of privacy. The American system of justice can never serve a free state by borrowing from the techniques of the totalitarian state.

These are three points that I would like to leave with you as a result of our brief meeting here.

There is much more that I would like to take the time to say to you, but I was once told by an old lawyer friend of mine that two thousand years ago Plato said that a lawyer is always in a hurry, so I think I will just say we are pleased to have you here; we are proud of your achievements. In the long period of Government service that it has been my opportunity to participate in, I have never known a time when I thought we had more dedicated personnel representing the interests of all of our people in the courtrooms than we have now, better prepared, better qualified, or better led.

So, if the lawyer is always in a hurry, I will let you hurry on with your remaining schedule, and I thank you very much for coming here.

NOTE: The President spoke in the East Room at the White House to a group of U.S. Attorneys and their families, in Washington for an annual meeting, and officials of the Department of Justice. His opening words referred to Attorney General and Mrs. Robert F. Kennedy. The Attorney General introduced the President to the group.

453   Remarks Upon Signing the Urban Mass Transportation Act.   *July 9, 1964*

Ladies and gentlemen:

I am very pleased to be able to sign today the Urban Mass Transportation Act of 1964.

This is by any standard one of the most profoundly significant domestic measures to be enacted by the Congress during the 1960's.

I very especially want to congratulate all of you who have done so much to assure the passage of this long-needed, long-awaited, landmark legislation.

Our Constitution empowered Congress to provide for post roads. Since that time, congressional support of transportation has been a major constructive influence on the progress and development of our American society and our American economy.

In the last century, such support of transcontinental railroads and canals and river navigation gave immeasurable impetus to our expansion. Now, in this century, sound congressional policies in support of both highways and airways for automobile and airplane travel has given incalculable momentum to American progress.

This new act that all of you have contributed to passing remains faithful to this tradition of vision.

Only a very short time ago, six out of ten Americans lived in rural areas—six out of ten Americans in rural areas. As we meet here today, seven out of ten live in urban areas. The change has come rapidly and has come dramatically, and today urban congestion is an unpleasant fact of everyday life for too many millions of Americans.

All of us recognize that the curses of congestion in commuting cannot be wiped away with the single stroke of a pen, or 50 pens that we have here. But we do know that this legislation that we are coming to grips with faces the realities of American life and attempts to put in motion a movement to do something about it.

It is symbolic of the challenge facing us that most Americans today travel to and from work over city street patterns that were originally laid out by the horses which pulled our grandfathers' carriages.

We face a great task, publicly and privately, of catching up with our full potential and making life as good as it can be and making life as good as it should be for this generation of Americans.

This is a many sided challenge. We cannot and we do not rely upon massive spending programs as cure-alls. We must instead look to closer cooperation among all levels of government and between both public and private sectors to achieve the prudent progress that Americans deserve and that they expect.

I am very proud this morning to see some of America's most progressive mayors, who speak for large segments of our population, sufficiently interested and determined to provide vision and leadership in this field to come from faraway to participate in these ceremonies.

It is inspiring to me to know that some of the ablest chief executives of some of our best States have joined those mayors to come here in a local State-Federal undertaking that will provide leadership and provide vision for the people who have entrusted us with these responsibilities. I hope and I expect that this milestone measure will serve us as a beneficial forerunner of many other steps forward in meeting the present challenges of metropolitan life in America.

I remember regularly in the Congress we had an anniversary when we celebrated the first signing of the highway act. We brought rural free delivery to our people. I think in the years to come that you and your descendants will be very proud that you were part of the vision that provided this legislation.

For the fine work that the Congress has done, I want to commend them all. I especially want to commend Senator Sparkman and Congressman Rains and Senator Williams and Congressman Widnall of New Jersey. All of you have earned the special gratitude of your countrymen, especially those who live in urban areas, large or small, and I just want to make this prediction that when we sign this act today we will be taking one step—but only one of several—that this administration is prepared to take in the days ahead to face up to the problems of the urban areas of this country. We are determined that we will provide the vision and the leadership necessary and that they will no longer be a stepchild and be neglected by their Government in Washington.

Thank you for coming, and I hope we have enough pens here to serve you all.

NOTE: The President spoke shortly before noon in the Cabinet Room at the White House. In his closing remarks he referred to Senators John Sparkman of Alabama and Harrison A. Williams, Jr., of New Jersey, and to Representatives Albert Rains of Alabama and William B. Widnall of New Jersey.

The Urban Mass Transportation Act of 1964 is Public Law 88–365 (78 Stat. 302).

454 Remarks Upon Presenting the Distinguished Service Medal to Admiral Felt. *July* 10, 1964

Secretary McNamara, Admiral Felt, ladies and gentlemen:

We have come here this morning to pay honor to an outstanding officer and his outstanding career of honorable and faithful service to our country and to the cause of freedom in the world.

A few months after the end of the First World War the United States Naval Academy enrolled Midshipman Harry D. Felt. From that day in 1919 to this day in 1964, he has given 44 years of his life to the

service of this Nation. I know of no way in which such devotion and such dedication could ever be rewarded fully or honored adequately, but I am sure that the personal knowledge of what he has done to make our freedom more secure is reward enough for Admiral Felt.

In many respects this long career of service around the world symbolizes the role of our Nation during this century. Over the span of nearly 5 decades, we have asked our sons and all our people to bear burdens which citizens of no other nation have ever borne. We have waved no flag of conquest. We have shouted no cries of national pride. But we have mustered great armies and we have floated great fleets and we have rallied our great resources to defend human freedom and world peace.

In all the history of humankind no other peoples have ever sought to exercise such an influence for responsibility among nations.

As this distinguished officer can be proud of the individual contribution that he has made, all of the American people can together be proud of the contribution that they and their Nation have made in the affairs of men. This great effort has not been for naught. We have not in 50 years changed the ways of the world for the last 5,000 years. But we have sown the seeds of decency, and I believe that we shall reap a harvest of victory if we continue on our course of preparedness and prudence and firm purpose.

The world in which Admiral Felt retires from active duty is much smaller than the world in which his duty and our destiny began, but the cause which we uphold is a much larger cause now for independent, freedom-loving men and women on every continent today. They stand with us, and our cause is the cause of free men everywhere. In the support of that cause, Admiral Felt has won the admiration and the respect of men from many free nations on both sides of the globe. For the past 6 years he has borne the responsibility for the largest joint military command in the world, acting as our Commander in Chief for the Pacific.

As your colleagues in uniform know, and as your country knows, Admiral Felt, you have met the challenges of this duty skillfully, prudently, and with a telling effect. You have been a lifelong credit to the traditions of your service and to the traditions of our country.

It is my privilege now, and a very great honor for me, on behalf of the Government and the people of the United States to add another honor to the many that you have received already in war and in peace—the Distinguished Service Medal.

I have asked Secretary McNamara to be present this morning and to read this citation.

NOTE: The President spoke at 10:55 a.m. in the Cabinet Room at the White House. Following the reading of the citation by Secretary of Defense Robert S. McNamara, Admiral Felt responded briefly. The text of his remarks was also released.

Admiral Felt served as Commander in Chief, Pacific, from July 31, 1958, to June 30, 1964.

455 The President's News Conference of July 10, 1964

THE PRESIDENT. I have some announcements and some appointments to make and then I would be glad, if you desire, to follow up with any questions, to attempt to answer them.

[1.] With the passage of the foreign assistance appropriation bill on July 1, the House of Representatives completed its work on the regular 1965 appropriation bills—all of them. I want to express my appreciation and that of the Nation for the efficiency and the speed with which the House acted upon the 1965 budget. Not in 4 years has the House completed its work on the regular money bills as early as the first day of the new fiscal year.

We owe a special debt of gratitude to the Members of the House Appropriations Committee, who labored long hours to meet a tight schedule, and to the two forceful and effective leaders of the Committee, the late Congressman Cannon, and his distinguished successor, Congressman Mahon.

The scorecard of House action on the regular 1965 money bills shows a total reduction from the budget request of 3 percent, as compared with a reduction of 7.4 percent last year. The size of the House reductions, less than half as deep as last year, is welcome confirmation of our belief back in January that we were submitting a budget that would be hard to cut.

When Congress completes its action on the budget, we are going to look upon the appropriations as a ceiling—not as a mandate to spend. Wherever we can get by with less money than Congress has given us, we are going to do just that. The money we save through our drive to improve management and to cut costs we will return to the Treasury next June.

Within a week or, I hope, at most 10 days, I want to announce the final figures for the fiscal year which ended June 30. Some early and incomplete reports on expenditures, the deficit, and Government employment lead me to hope that I will have some good news for you at that time.

[2.] I have a brief statement on the midyear review of the economy that has been given—gone over with the Council of Economic Advisers yesterday.

At midyear we have all seen many glowing reports on our recent economic advances in employment, sales, profits, and income. In this midyear review, let us look at these advances in human terms. What do they mean to people? You will have a copy of this available to you if you care to use it when you leave.

First, more jobs. Today, 1,200,000 more people have jobs than 6 months ago; 1,600,000 more people are at work than a year ago.

Two, higher wages. Average weekly earnings in manufacturing hit a new high of $103 in May, $3.74 more than a year earlier.

Higher profits. Great gains in profits are being translated into rising investments and new highs in the Dow-Jones average of stock prices. The Dow-Jones average of stock prices were around 700 when we came in on November 22d; they are now 840-plus.

Rising dividends for the country's nearly 20 million stockholders. These dividends are 11 percent higher in May than they were last year, a year earlier.

Bigger incomes. The tax cut and prosperity are boosting incomes to new peaks. The estimated after-tax incomes of the American people in the second quarter of this year, which has just ended, were running at a rate of about $19 billion above the fourth quarter of last year—and $30 billion above a year earlier.

This is a very important fact for all of us, and one that we can take great pleasure in observing. The average American family of four has gained about $500 of annual income after taxes in the past year, a rate of advance matched only once before in America's peacetime history, in 1948. A family of four gained about $500 of annual income after taxes in the past year.

Stable prices. These gains were not eaten away by inflation. The wholesale price level is right where it was a year ago, and 3 years ago, and it is lower than 6 years ago, which is quite a remarkable record. Consumer prices in May were only two-tenths of 1 percent above December and 1½ percent above a year earlier.

A special news note on retail sales in June. The advance report on the whole month, seasonally corrected: Sales maintained the strong May rate, despite a few apparently slower weeks, and were 6.2 percent above last June. Retail sales in the week ending July 4 spurted up 11 percent above the comparative week a year earlier.

Now, looking ahead. We look for continued strong gains in the second half of the year as the benefits of the tax cut flow through the economy. This is partly based on surveys of 1964 business capital spending plans which now show a rise of nearly $5 billion, or 12 percent above 1963. Consumer spending surveys show buying intentions near a record high.

Even more impressive is the calm confidence that we find in the consuming public and in the business community. People know that times are good and that they are getting better, and they are responding by consuming wisely, investing soundly, and showing restraint in price and wage policies. There is a growing response to the challenge of cooperation and respect for the public interest on the part of business in setting prices, and unions in pursuing wage increases, and workers and managers in finding ways to raise efficiency and to cut costs.

In that spirit, the economic horizon will be bright not only in 1964, but I am informed by the Council of Economic Advisers, as far as the trained eye can see, into 1965.

[3.] I have a brief statement on the auto negotiations. The auto industry is one of the Nation's largest industries and plays a significant role in our national economy. The importance of the current auto negotiations is obvious. The results of this collective bargaining will have a profound impact upon our future price stability and, therefore, on our economic prospects at home and abroad.

The negotiators in autos on both sides are experienced and responsible men. They do not want governmental intervention in these negotiations—nor do I. We are of one mind, that the collective bargaining process should be conducted and completed in accordance with the pattern of free collective bargaining that we are determined to maintain in this country.

I am confident that the parties to the auto negotiations by free, private collective bargaining will work out a responsible settlement consistent with both their private needs and their public responsibilities, a settlement which will reinforce and extend the excellent noninflationary record which has characterized our vigorous economic expansion.

[4.] Mr. Bertrand Harding is being appointed today as Acting Commissioner of the Internal Revenue Service.

Q. What is his name again, sir?

THE PRESIDENT. Bertrand Harding is being appointed today as Acting Commissioner of the Internal Revenue Service. Mr. Harding is a 23-year veteran of the Federal service and a recipient in 1962 of the National Civil Service League's award for top career achievement. I am completely confident that Mr. Harding will carry on in an efficient and fair manner the work of the Internal Revenue Service.

[5.] I have today designated Mr. Michael Forrestal to replace Mr. William Sullivan as chairman of the interdepartmental committee which supports the U.S. country team in Viet-Nam. Mr. Forrestal, the son of the late Secretary of Defense, Mr. James Forrestal, will work under the supervision of Secretary Rusk. As you know, Mr. Forrestal has been associated with the staff of the Security Council here in the White House. This is a further step in the series of appointments which have been made in support of Ambassador Taylor.[1]

[6.] I intend to appoint Mr. Lucius D. Battle, the Assistant Secretary of State for Educational and Cultural Affairs and a career Foreign Service officer, as U.S. Ambassador to the United Arab Republic. He will succeed Mr. John S. Badeau, who is assuming a position at Columbia University. The background biographical sketch will be available to you in the press office.

[7.] I am announcing today two additional members of the National Food Marketing Commission: Mr. Albert K. Mitchell, a distinguished businessman, and expert in certain aspects of food marketing; Mr. Mitchell is Republican National Committeeman from New Mexico. I am also appointing to the Commission Mr. William M. Batten, president of the J. C. Penney Company. Mr. Batten has had a broad background in retail trade, and I am sure he will make a valuable contribution to the work of this Commission. Mr. Batten is a Republican. Although the statute does not require membership in either party, we are trying to make appointments from both parties. As of now we have two Democrats, Judge Jones and former Congressman Marshall, who is a dirt farmer in Minnesota, and two Republicans, Mr. Mitchell and Mr. Batten.

[8.] I am also pleased to announce my intention to appoint Mr. Manuel Cohen as Chairman of the Securities and Exchange Commission, when Mr. William Cary, the present Chairman, leaves that position late in the summer. Mr. Cary plans to leave as soon as we complete action on certain legislation. Mr. Cohen, who is now a member of the Commission, has an enviable record in the securities field and an outstanding reputation at the bar. I know that he shares

completely my own philosophy of regulation, which is to be fair and equitable, applying the law with vigor and commonsense. I look forward to an era of creative leadership in the Securities and Exchange Commission under Mr. Cohen.

I am also appointing to the existing Democratic vacancy on the SEC Mr. Frank Wheat of California. Mr. Wheat is a distinguished member of the California Bar, chairman of the Los Angeles Bar Association's Committee on Corporations, and a member of the American Bar Association's Committee on Federal Regulation of Securities. Mr. Wheat is a cum laude graduate of the Harvard Law School and a graduate of Pomona College. Mr. Wheat is married and has three children, and is currently practicing law in Los Angeles.

I will be glad to answer any questions.

[9.] Q. Mr. President, can you tell us anything about Mr. J. Edgar Hoover's mission to Mississippi, what he is down there for? There has been some speculation that there might be a break in the making on these three missing civil rights workers, or is he down there just to coordinate the overall FBI program?

THE PRESIDENT. The information I have on Mr. Hoover's visit is that he has recently added additional FBI personnel to his force in Mississippi, some additional 50 agents. After a survey of the situation he has decided that he should establish a headquarters office in that State, that he is transferring a director from out of State, an assistant director to take charge of that office, that they have made arrangements for the new office to be opened, and that he will officially open it sometime today.

Of course, I am told that while he is there he will confer with the responsible people from his service who have been stationed there for some time, and get a complete re-

---

[1] Gen. Maxwell D. Taylor, Ambassador to Viet-Nam.

port and give any instructions that he may think are indicated to the people under his jurisdiction.

[10.] Q. Mr. President, the Attorney General said recently that the only thing he has going for him in the vice presidential nomination is the fact that the big city bosses in the North, the party bosses in the North, are for him. Do you think this is a factor in his favor in getting the nomination?

THE PRESIDENT. I think that the delegates to the convention, after they nominate the President, will act on the vice presidential nomination, and I plan to make recommendations to them in that connection, as is customary, if I am the nominee. At that time I believe the convention will select the man that is available who has the best qualifications to occupy the office of Vice President and President, if he should be called upon to do that.

Q. Mr. President, do you plan to see Mayor Daley of Chicago when he is in town today?

THE PRESIDENT. Yes.

Q. Would you be discussing this vice presidential question with him?

THE PRESIDENT. I have no plans to.

Q. What was the answer, sir?

THE PRESIDENT. I have no plans to.

[11.] Q. Mr. President, do you plan to reappoint Mr. Ross to the Federal Power Commission?

THE PRESIDENT. I am giving consideration to that now. I have not made a decision on it.

[12.] Q. Mr. President, Mr. Tshombe was sworn in today as Premier of the Congo with the pledge that he would bring peace and unity. What, sir, do you believe the prospects are for that, and what will the United States do to help bring it about?

THE PRESIDENT. Everything that we can. We are very anxious to make a contribution

in the direction of peace whenever and wherever possible. Where we are offered that opportunity we will certainly exercise it.

[13.] Q. Mr. President, do you have any comment on Senator Goldwater's charge of fiscal irresponsibility in your administration?

THE PRESIDENT. I don't know what the Senator may have said about this, or all that he may have said about it, but I have been interested in the comments of some of those who are in authoritative positions to determine the fiscal responsibility of this administration without any other motives. For instance, the American Bankers Association said only yesterday that the unusual length of the current upswing could be attributed to the reduction in taxes, the stability of costs and prices, which I have just referred to, and the maintenance of monetary and credit conditions which preserve international confidence in the dollar.

I saw a very interesting column on that that went into some detail yesterday.

Mr. Henry Ford is quoted in the Wall Street Journal as saying that "our economy is now healthier than it has been in many years. Part of the credit must go to Government policies which, on the whole, have been well calculated to stimulate economic growth without inflation. Part of the credit must go to the recent tax cut."

The National Research Bureau's report to business executives yesterday said, "Just about any place you look you find evidence of the boom and signposts that point to a continuation of good times."

"The tax cut is still the major factor in the business boom."

Miss Porter [2] said yesterday that "the United States dollar is winning new popularity. The comeback of the dollar is an enormous tribute to our economy's inherent

---

[2] Sylvia Porter, financial columnist.

power, and to the policies of recent years."

The Morgan Guaranty Trust Company in its latest survey of current economic conditions lists this main reason for continuing optimism: "The excellent business news of the past month indicate that the nourishment of the tax reduction is reaching the muscles of the economy."

And, finally, the New York Times says, "This has been and still is a truly phenomenal epoch in the Nation's economic history. The sustained advance is notable not only for its unusual longevity, but even more for the absence of excesses."

[14.] Q. Mr. President, you have signed a bill for the International Roosevelt Campobello Memorial.[3] Will you ask the Governor of Maine to make suggestions for any one of the three American Commissioners?

THE PRESIDENT. I will be looking into that, pursuant to your suggestion.

Q. The bill suggests it, but does not direct it, I understand.

THE PRESIDENT. I will be glad to talk to him about it.

[15.] Q. Mr. President, the National Space Administration is apparently going to get considerably less funds than it asked for the space program this year. Do you think that this is going to preclude our landing on the moon in this decade?

THE PRESIDENT. I think the funds that we requested are necessary. I hope the Congress will act on this appropriation soon. The Committee has not acted on the appropriation yet. I don't know how to gauge the exact way it will exercise its judgment. I have every reason to believe that they are sympathetic with our national objectives, and I would hope that they will be as generous in their response to our request as possible.

---

[3] Public Law 88–363 (78 Stat. 299), approved July 7, 1964.

[16.] Q. Mr. President, can you tell us anything about your meetings, series of meetings, with the Latin American ambassadors last week and this?

THE PRESIDENT. Yes. We have divided up the meetings into small meetings made up of six or seven of the ambassadors from Latin American countries in each meeting. There will be a series of three meetings. We have had two already. In addition to the Latin American ambassadors, we have the presence of the Secretary of State and Mr. Walt Rostow of the State Department, and Mr. Tom Mann, my Special Assistant, Assistant Secretary for Latin America.

We have an hors d'oeuvre, relax, and start around the room in a conversational, informal manner, and ask the ambassador from each country—Panama, Mexico, whatever country it may be—to give us his evaluation of the problems that exist between our two countries, any suggestions that he has regarding hemispheric solidarity, any criticism he may have to make concerning actions of our agencies with whom he is dealing, or delays that may be present; any suggestions that he could offer that should be considered for the hemisphere, with particular reference to the streamlining and the speedup techniques that we have brought into focus in the Alliance for Progress program.

Our people, Mr. Ball, Mr. Rostow, Mr. Mann, and in instances the President himself, have not only made comments on these suggestions but have outlined this Government's views, this Government's hope, and this Government's ideals. We have talked about the foreign aid bill, the Alliance for Progress funds, pending before the Senate; the action of the Senate Foreign Relations Committee and the possible action of the Appropriations Committee on our foreign aid bill.

We have talked about the visits of the

President from Costa Rica. We have welcomed new ambassadors from some of the countries. We spend about an hour and a half to two hours near the close of the working day, 6 to 8 generally, in that area. We will be having meetings of that type from time to time so that the executive branch can keep better informed on the needs of the area and the hemisphere, and the problems of it, and so that the ambassadors themselves can report to their government on our approaches, our procedures, and our attitudes.

I am glad to report that they have been very stimulating meetings and much good has come from them. The reports we have received from not only ambassadors but heads of state in that area express appreciation for some of the steps that we have taken to centralize functions, to combine functions, to eliminate red tape, give a direct line of authority, and be able to make prompt decisions.

[17.] Q. Mr. President, a couple of months ago your oratorical propensities were officially recognized by the National Forensic Society.[4] Will this in any way influence your decision to debate your opponent in the upcoming election?

THE PRESIDENT. No, I don't think so.

[18.] Q. Mr. President, on Latin America, again, what do you expect or hope would come out of this meeting of inter-American foreign ministers that is taking place here in July?

THE PRESIDENT. I would think that we would have a very constructive meeting, judging from the expressions of the ambassadors, and the conversations that I have had with OAS officials. I would not want to prejudge the actions or deliberations in advance. I don't know of any particular re-

_____
[4] See Item 343.

ward in the offing for so doing. I would just say let's follow the meeting closely and report accurately its deliberations.

[19.] Q. Mr. President, how do you size up the political activity of Governor Wallace of Alabama? Will his candidacy hurt the Democrats more than the Republicans, or the Republicans more than the Democrats, in your opinion?

THE PRESIDENT. I haven't conducted any study of the Governor's activities or evaluated the effect of those activities. I am not in the polling business, but I did, I believe, read this morning a poll on the front page of the Washington paper, and I think there is a copy there in my office if you want to look at it.

[20.] Q. Mr. President, Senator Goldwater has gotten into considerable controversy in the Republican Party in the last couple of days by saying that as of now you could beat any Republican. Do you think he was right or wrong in saying that?

THE PRESIDENT. I think the Republican Party has enough problems already without my adding to them in any way.

[21.] Q. Mr. President, have you any comment on the Baker report which has come out of the Senate Rules Committee now?

THE PRESIDENT. The report has been filed. Undoubtedly it will be read and thoroughly considered and such action as the Senate feels justified will be taken.

[22.] Q. Mr. President, Premier Castro has recently had a long interview in which he is offering to negotiate peace with the United States. What is your attitude or your response to that?

THE PRESIDENT. I have seen newspaper reports purporting to reflect his attitude. I am much more interested in the deeds than the words, and I shall carefully watch for any actions or any deeds that would carry into effect the actions that I think would be in the best interest of the people of Cuba and the people of the world. I am much more interested in deeds than words.

Merriman Smith, United Press International: Thank you, Mr. President.

NOTE: President Johnson's twenty-first news conference was held in the Cabinet Room at the White House at 11:10 a.m. on July 10, 1964.

456 Letter to Dr. Killian in Response to Report: "Toward Better Utilization of Scientific and Engineering Talent." *July* 12, 1964

[Released July 12, 1964. Dated July 7, 1964]

Dear Dr. Killian:

In completing such a broad analysis of problems concerned with the utilization of scientific and technical talent and making recommendations for their solution, your Committee has rendered a significant public service.

Your report deals with issues which are important in carrying out this Nation's commitment to deploy science and technology boldly and effectively in the interest of the Nation's welfare. Your counsel is especially timely because of the intensified interest this Administration is taking in providing rewarding employment opportunities and education to all our citizens, and because of the need to strengthen the relationships between Government, industry, and colleges and universities.

The higher salaries at the upper levels of Government service which your Committee supports would help redress the persistent imbalance between Governmental and private salaries that penalize the Government in meeting competition for talent. The Administration's bill is a major step toward that end.

The Federal Government has a special responsibility to conduct its affairs with an enlightened concern for the critical part it now plays in the utilization of the Nation's

manpower. I am thus asking that Dr. Donald F. Hornig, my Science Advisor, and Secretary of Labor Willard Wirtz, as Chairman of my Committee on Manpower, report to me on further steps that the Government should take in light of your Committee's recommendations.

Please extend to all of those who have given generously of their time in the conduct of this study my sincere appreciation for their contributions.

Sincerely,

LYNDON . B. JOHNSON

[Dr. James R. Killian, Jr., Chairman of the Corporation, Massachusetts Institute of Technology, Cambridge 39, Massachusetts]

NOTE: The letter was part of a White House release making public the report "Toward Better Utilization of Scientific and Engineering Talent, A Program for Action" (193 pp., National Academy of Sciences), prepared by the Committee on Utilization of Scientific and Engineering Manpower, under the chairmanship of Dr. James R. Killian, Jr.

The Committee was appointed by the National Academy of Sciences following a request of President Kennedy in 1961 that the Academy undertake a study on the utilization of the existing supply of technical manpower. At the same time the President's Science Advisory Committee and the Federal Council for Science and Technology were asked to study requirements for the development of new scientists and engineers.

In its report the Committee's recommendations called for action by and cooperation among the Federal Government, industry, and the universities to:

1. Strengthen the management of research in all sectors, through improved contracting procedures and efforts to identify and train more project managers and engineers who combine understanding of a complex, changing technology with mastery of the art of leadership.

2. Achieve a balance in the allocation of scarce scientific and engineering talent between "big science" and large development projects on the one hand, and the individual investigator (or scholar-teacher) and the manpower requirements of the civilian economy on the other.

3. Greatly expand the opportunities open to individual scientists and engineers to renew, update, and extend their skills throughout their professional careers.

Other Committee recommendations called for the development of statistical information on scientific and technical manpower resources to permit the Government to assess the impact of major new technological ventures on employment and manpower utilization before reaching a decision to proceed, and urged a continuing assessment of the total impact of Government policies and practices on the deployment and utilization of manpower.

The text of Dr. Killian's letter of transmittal, dated June 22, was also released.

---

457 Statement by the President Upon Accepting Report of the Committee on Public Higher Education in the District of Columbia. *July 12, 1964*

THE recommendations in this report should have the immediate attention of the Congress. Less than a month ago I said that if our society is to move higher, higher education must be made a universal opportunity for all young people. There is no more urgent need today than to provide the educational opportunities which will permit every young person to develop to his maximum potential. The report shows that this opportunity is not now available to many District high school graduates. The Nation's Capital, which should set an example for the Nation, has instead lagged behind.

I am asking the District Commissioners to prepare a draft of appropriate legislation for submission to the Congress. In the meantime, I commend the report for study by all interested groups.

NOTE: The President's statement was made public as part of a White House release summarizing "A Report to the President, Public Higher Education in the District of Columbia," dated June 1964 (44 pp., Government Printing Office).

The President's Committee on Public Higher Education in the District of Columbia, of which Dr. Francis S. Chase, Dean, Graduate School of Education, University of Chicago, served as chairman, was appointed by President Kennedy on September 23, 1963.

The Committee's recommendations are summarized in the report as follows:

1. The immediate creation of a comprehensive community (or junior) college, publicly supported, that will put within reach of all high school graduates opportunities for technical and vocational training and for general education leading both to greater personal and civic effectiveness and to further study in a 4-year college or university for those who qualify and seek it.

2. The immediate creation of a college of liberal arts and sciences, also publicly supported, authorized to confer both baccalaureate and the master's degrees, with a special concern with teacher education (a function it should assume from the D.C. Teachers College) and prepared to offer specialized courses of study as need and feasibility are established.

3. The prompt establishment of a system of noncompetitive scholarships, publicly supported, enabling qualified District students who wish, after 2 years' work in the community college, to pursue special courses of study not offered at the outset by the proposed public college of liberal arts and sciences at an institution where such curriculums are available.

4. The early development in the District of a center or centers for high-level graduate and postdoctoral studies, with a Presidential review undertaken within 3 to 5 years to make specific recommendations, if desirable, with respect to ways in which the Federal Government might be helpful in the attainment of this goal.

859

458   Statement by the President on Narcotic and Drug Abuse.   *July 15, 1964*

NARCOTIC and other drug abuse is inflicting upon parts of the country enormous damage in human suffering, crime, and economic loss through thievery. The Federal Government, being responsible for the regulation of foreign and interstate commerce, bears a major responsibility in respect to the illegal traffic in drugs and the consequences of that traffic. That responsibility is shared by several departments of the Government and by a number of divisions, bureaus, etc., within them.

I now direct those units to examine into their present procedures, to bring those procedures into maximum activity, and, wherever necessary, put into effect additional programs of action aimed at major corrections in the conditions caused by drug abuse. I desire the full power of the Federal Government to be brought to bear upon three objectives: (1) the destruction of the illegal traffic in drugs, (2) the prevention of drug abuse, and (3) the cure and rehabilitation of victims of this traffic. Attention is called to the program described in the report of the President's Advisory Commission on Narcotic and Drug Abuse.

For the purpose of coordinating the steps to be taken by the several units of the Government in this matter I designate Lee White of the White House Staff to act as liaison agent between them, with instructions to implement the foregoing directive.

NOTE: The "Final Report of the President's Advisory Commission on Narcotic and Drug Abuse" is dated November 1963 (123 pp., Government Printing Office). For the President's letter to Judge E. Barrett Prettyman in response to the Commission's final report, see Item 159.

459   Statement by the President on the Second Quarter Advance in Gross National Product and Income.   *July 17, 1964*

NOTABLE advances in gross national product and personal income in the second quarter bear further witness to our strong and balanced economic expansion.

GNP rose to a rate of $618.5 billion

—nearly $10 billion above the first-quarter GNP (which was itself revised upward).

—$41 billion above the year-earlier rate, the best year-to-year gain in over 2 years.

—a rise fully consistent with our January forecast of $623 billion for 1964 as a whole.

The personal income of all Americans, after taxes, rose faster than we had expected.

It reached a rate of $431.4 billion for the second quarter.

This is a near-record advance of $11.4 billion over the first quarter.

It is an all-time record advance of $32.3 billion over a year earlier.

This means that the average American today is getting $139 more after-tax income annually than he did a year ago—the equivalent of $556 for a family of four—a remarkable advance.

The second-quarter performance set the stage for continued strong advances the rest of the year:

Consumers stepped up their saving, putting them in a better position to buy more in the months ahead.

Merchants and manufacturers prudently held their inventories down, so further rises in demand will be quickly reflected in higher production.

Businessmen spent more for plant and equipment, and their plans call for a continued vigorous rise in the months ahead.

On the basis of this fine record—and with the tax cut's major impact yet to come—we fully expect the gains in the second half of the year to be even greater than the first.

460   Message to President Nasser Extending Greetings to the Conference of African Heads of State.   *July 17, 1964*

I EXTEND, through you, to the representatives of the nations and peoples of Africa gathered in Cairo, the friendly greetings of the Government and people of the United States of America.

As the Heads of State and of Government meet again one year after creating the Organization of African Unity at that historic Addis Ababa gathering, we are impressed with the striking progress which has been made toward African unity in peace and freedom.

Africa through the OAU has shown its capacity to deal through peaceful means with African problems, including such disputes as have arisen among its members. In this way, within the framework of the United Nations Charter, African nations are making a vital contribution to world peace.

As the OAU moves into its second year of activity, it will face new challenges which, I am sure, it will meet in the same spirit it has already demonstrated in the momentous year just past. I and the people of the United States extend to this Organization our best wishes for continued progress toward your high aims.

LYNDON B. JOHNSON

[President Gamal Abdel Nasser, Cairo, United Arab Republic]

461   Statement by the President Upon Signing the Water Resources Research Act.   *July 17, 1964*

THE Water Resources Research Act of 1964, which I have approved today, fills a vital need.

Abundant, good water is essential to continued economic growth and progress. The Congress has found that we have entered a period in which acute water shortages are hampering our industries, our agriculture, our recreation, and our individual health and happiness.

Assuming a continuation of current practices, by the year 2000 there will not be enough usable water to meet the water requirements of parts of the States of Arizona, California, Colorado, Delaware, Idaho, Illinois, Indiana, Iowa, Kansas, Louisiana, Michigan, Minnesota, Montana, Nebraska, Nevada, New Jersey, New Mexico, New York, North Dakota, Ohio, Oklahoma, Oregon, Pennsylvania, South Dakota, Texas, Utah, Wisconsin, and Wyoming.

This legislation will help us solve this problem. It will create local centers of water research. It will enlist the intellectual power of universities and research institutes in a nationwide effort to conserve and utilize our water resources for the common benefit. The new centers will be concerned with municipal and regional, as well as with national water problems. Their ready accessibility to State and local officials will permit each problem to be attacked on an individual basis, the only way in which the complex characteristics of each water deficiency can be resolved. The bill contemplates a high degree of interstate cooperation, and I urge that this be encouraged.

In large measure, this legislation is a tribute to the vision and wisdom of Senator Clinton P. Anderson of New Mexico. He has long recognized the problems. He developed the program. He guided it through Congress. He has been in the forefront of the effort to see that adequate supplies of water are available in all parts of the Nation.

One provision of the bill, however, causes me serious concern, and I request its deletion. The Secretary of the Interior, in administer-

ing the program is required, in effect, to obtain the approval of the committees of the House and Senate for each water research grant or contract. Although this legislation is so phrased that it is not technically subject to constitutional objection, it violates the spirit of the constitutional requirement of separation of power between the executive and legislative branches. It is both inappropriate and inefficient for committees of the Congress to participate in the award of individual contracts or grants. Apart from the question of the relationship between the executive and legislative branches, the delays which would ensue from the suggested procedure would be detrimental to both scientific research and the timely achievement of the important mission of the legislation.

NOTE: The Water Resources Research Act of 1964 is Public Law 88–379 (78 Stat. 329).

462 The President's News Conference at the LBJ Ranch. *July* 18, 1964

THE PRESIDENT. Good morning. You are mighty welcome here. I hope you enjoy your visit to the hill country as much as I anticipate that we will.

I had a very refreshing couple of hours here before the sun went down yesterday. After lunch we plan to take a ride through the ranch to see the cattle, do some horseback riding, and probably go over to the lake later in the afternoon.

[1.] Next week I have asked a group of businessmen to meet with me on Thursday, July 23d, for lunch at the White House; a group of labor leaders to meet with me on July 24th, at a reception later in the afternoon. These meetings will be an exchange of views on the state of the economy and the

state of the world. I have carried them on periodically in the 7 months that I have been in the Presidency. I seek the advice and counsel of these leaders in American industry and labor. I think it is important to the future of our economy and to our relations with the other nations in the world.

[2.] As I told you earlier this week, the Budget Bureau has been assembling the data that came in on the fiscal year that ended June 30th. I now have the closing figures on the budget expenditures, receipts, and Federal civilian employment for the fiscal year 1964 which ended last June 30th. As far as I know, none of you are in a hurry this morning, so we will take ample time, we will have our usual 15 or 20 questions, whatever you want, afterwards, and we don't have any deadlines. There are printed copies of this statement, so you don't have to take everything by notes. They will be available to you. We have a chart here. It may be helpful to you in working it out. I am very happy that on every count the news is good this Saturday.

Our expenditures for the fiscal year which just ended June 30th were $97 billion 700 million. President Kennedy estimated those expenditures when he asked the Congress to give him money for that year. He estimated those expenditures at $98.8 billion, so we are down more than $1 billion from the original 1964 budget estimate. We have spent $1 billion less than we estimated we would spend.

When I came in in January and put some new ceilings on and called the Cabinet and independent agencies together and asked them to effect economies and to curtail every possible expenditure, we revised the estimate to $98.4 billion. We placed quarterly ceilings on employment. We asked each department to become cost conscious. We had Secretary McNamara review with others some of the efforts that he had made in that figure, and we revised our estimate in the second quarter, after we placed our ceilings, to $98.3 billion. That is down $700 million from the original January estimate.

We have just concluded expenditures on June 30th. The first few days in July we tabulated them, and we now find that our expenditures were $97.7, from the $98.3 estimate that was made in May. So the net of it is that we are down $1 billion 100 million from our estimate.

That accounts for the spending process during this fiscal year that just ended and this is the first definite, accurate figure that we have on the actual expenditures that were certified to me. These charts were made up yesterday evening. They are the source of the material from the Director of the Budget, Mr. Gordon.

Now we will go over the receipts as estimated and actual. We do not have a chart. The receipts as estimated were $89 billion 400 million.

Q. That was in January?

THE PRESIDENT. Yes. Up $2.5 billion from the original 1964 budget estimate— $89.4 billion is what we took in. That is up $2.5 billion from the original 1964 budget estimate, up $1 billion from the revised estimate in last January's budget while most of the same is $89.5 billion reestimate that we made 2 months ago.

So, summarizing, we took in $89 billion 400 million. We estimated that we would take in about $87 billion; we are up $2.5 billion over that, $86.9 billion. That gives you a figure for your deficit for the year. The deficit was $8.3 billion actual. We estimated in January that it would be $11.9——

Q. January 1963?

THE PRESIDENT. ——when President Kennedy submitted it. You will remember the record budget deficit during the Eisenhower administration was approximately that. We had a $12 billion figure for Mr. Eisenhower, and for President Kennedy—you will recall a great deal of publicity about it—at about $11.9 billion.

From November until January, the 37 days that we all went through in that cost-conscious program and budget preparation, we reduced that estimate, and we announced it at $10 billion. In May, when we got in our reports, again, after meeting with the Cabinet, we cut it to $8.8, and the actual expenditure is $8.3 billion. The details on these receipts and expenditures will be available next week when the Treasury completes its work and issues the June Treasury statement.

Federal civilian employment in the executive branch on June 30th totaled 2,468,700 employees. This is a subject on which you get reports from Senator Byrd's committee from time to time. All of us are interested in it, and we have attempted to make every department head very conscious of it. That means that we are down actually from the January estimate submitted to the Congress for the budget to 101,800 employees. We are down 43,700 from the revision carried in the budget last January. I believe this is 59 that was cut out from January ('63) to January ('64) and 43 from January to now. We are down 28,500 from our latest employment ceiling. We are down 21,600 from the actual number on the rolls 1 year ago. We are down 15,900 by actual number on the rolls 2 years ago.

That is a very interesting chart, but the net of it is from the day we sent our budget until we completed it, we are down 101,800 from what we estimated, and we are actually 15,900 lower than the actual number that we had on the payroll 2 years ago, notwithstanding the fact that this budget was about $5 billion over the preceding budget and up until this year, the last 3 years our budgets have been increasing at the rate of about $5 billion a year because of increased schools and roads and health and unfilled needs that an increased population requires from time to time.

The dollar outflow abroad resulted in Federal programs—was reduced in fiscal '64 as a result of vigorous action taken by the executive branch. The estimated '64 overseas payments by the Federal Government dropped $380 million, and regular receipts rose by $116 million, compared with the previous year. This means that the net

dollar outflow from Federal programs decreased in fiscal year 1964 by $500 million, about 18 percent. This is a net improvement of $300 million since I sent the budget to Congress last January.

I thought maybe you would be interested in some of the productivity gains in some of the Government agencies and how we have helped to reduce Government employment since last year, and I have some specific illustrations.

The Treasury's Division of Disbursement improved employee output by more than 14 percent over 1963 due to electronic data processing improvements, consolidation of many field offices, streamlining procedures, elimination of red tape. This is the equivalent of the work of over 200 employees.

The Veterans Administration insurance program increased the productivity of its manpower by 24 percent. That is the equivalent of 600 employees.

The Federal Aviation Agency's Systems Maintenance Service achieved a 6 percent increase which results in a saving of about 600 man-years.

The decisions to close or reduce field installations were taken by the Tennessee Valley Authority—52 installations.

Department of Interior closed 6.

Treasury Department closed 35 throughout the country.

The Post Office Department closed 469 post offices.

The Treasury Department closed 20 local operations.

Federal Aviation Agency closed 3 manned facilities and eliminated intermediate airfields and consolidated air traffic control.

The Department of State closed 13 unneeded consulates.

We will continue the drive to close down or curtail any installation which is not necessary to perform essential functions, much as we have done in the closing down of the obsolete military installations throughout the country.

We have inaugurated a drive to lessen the burden placed on private industry by Government requests for reports. The annual number of responses will be reduced by 2,-851,000. One hundred and ninety-five forms involving almost two million responses were eliminated entirely. Ninety-five new reports were started in this period so that the net result of this drive has been either to discontinue or to simplify 320 reports representing a net reduction in annual responses of 2.5 million.

Small savings are not being neglected either. A review of Government publications has produced savings of nearly $2 million. Two hundred and forty existing publications were eliminated; 130 proposed publications were canceled; 50 were consolidated.

In our foreign aid program we have effected substantial economies and improved the administration.

As you will recall, the Executive asked the Congress for $4.9 billion for foreign aid in last year's budget. We reduced that request by $1.4 billion to $3.5, although in fairness General Clay [1] reduced it from $4.9 to $4.5 billion after his review.

We have insisted on rigorous self-help standards, saving, in two cases alone, $30 million.

By diligent efforts to maximize the participation of other free-world lenders, in one case we required other donors to contribute $21 million more than the plans submitted to us.

By strong efforts to use local currency instead of dollars, we have saved $16.5 million on another program.

By improving AID procurement practices, including use of excess U.S. Government property instead of buying new equipment, we have saved $32 million.

This cost reduction has the priority concern of every department and agency, and it will continue to be. Each one of them will have delivered to them today a copy of this report.

Secretary McNamara's cost reduction program in the Department of Defense actually realized savings of $2.5 billion compared with the initial forecast of $1.5.

The Space Agency reduction goal of $81 million, which was established in the fiscal year 1964, has been exceeded by $128 million.

In the Post Office, June 1964, the goal was 3,164 less than June 1962, while mail volume was 3,760,000 pieces more than in 1962. So with 3,164 less people they handled 3.7 billion more pieces of mail. If output per postal worker today were the same as 1961, the cost of operating the Post Office would have had to be $140 million more.

In concluding, I want to say that few if any of these accomplishments were easy to come by. It took hard work and in many cases courage, and was due a great deal to the thinking, initiative, and the imagination of a good many of our career employees, led by people in the Budget Bureau and in the departments themselves who are determined to get these expenditures under control and to save everything possible, primarily to get a dollar's worth of value out of every dollar spent. Saving money is always hard. Spending it is always easy.

[3.] I have a statement here on economic facts which I will distribute to you.[2] It has some new information which I think will be of great interest considering what is happening in the automobile field in Detroit and their employment gains.

---

[1] General Lucius D. Clay, Chairman of the Committee to Strengthen the Security of the Free World.

[2] See Item 463.

Their unemployment was 15.5 percent in 1961. That has been reduced to 4.6 in May of this year.

The retail sales figures, the after-tax income, as revised, will be available to you and you can say that I used it, and if you want it for sound, I will be glad to repeat it, but I won't take your time to go over it now.

[4.] I have a brief announcement that the United States and the United Kingdom tested a low-yield British nuclear device underground at the U.S. Atomic Energy Commission's test site in Nevada yesterday.

The test was requested by the British Government and was conducted under the Agreement for Cooperation on the Uses of Atomic Energy for Mutual Defense Purposes.

Both governments were satisfied that substantial technical and military benefits could be obtained. The test was carried out within the framework of the limited nuclear test ban treaty of August 1963.

I will have that statement distributed to you so you don't need to copy it.[3]

[5.] Some of the factual reports which I read daily have recently given me cause for concern regarding organized violence by small groups who mask their identity. I

---

[3] The statement, dated July 18, reads as follows:

The United States and the United Kingdom tested a low-yield British nuclear device underground at the U.S. Atomic Energy Commission's test site in Nevada yesterday (July 17).

The test was requested by the British Government and was conducted under the Agreement for Cooperation on the Uses of Atomic Energy for Mutual Defense Purposes, which has been in effect between the two countries since August 4, 1958.

Both governments were satisfied that substantial technical and military benefits could be obtained by testing a British nuclear device underground as part of a continuing nuclear research program. The test was carried out within the framework of the limited nuclear test ban treaty of August 1963.

condemn as do most Americans the use of violence and terror by clandestine hate organizations. Savagery of this or any other kind is completely alien to the entire moral and political tradition of the United States.

The effort to force, bully, and intimidate American citizens—to prevent them from claiming their rights under the Constitution—must be stopped. State and local governments have been working to halt such terrorism. I urge them to continue this work and I assure them and all Americans that if local enforcement is inadequate, the Federal Government will always promptly assist local authorities to maintain order as long as the lives and security of our fellow citizens are in danger.

In fact, I would like to say something about the entire subject of effective political action to secure human rights.

To those seeking to secure their rights, the Constitution provides a hallowed and an effective path. That is the path of peaceful petition and legal recourse; that, of course, is free speech and free election. Along that road have come, throughout our entire history, the great warriors in the battle to extend human freedom. Where their cause was just, they have prevailed. As long as that road is open to those who wage daily struggles for civil rights, they have an obligation to follow it. And most of them, I believe, are following it. Any other course will place in question the entire, centuries-old tradition of peaceful settlement of man's just claims to liberty. Once we have destroyed the fabric of this tradition, then the liberties of all of us are in danger.

And where we have had reports of violence such as we have had in Philadelphia, Miss., and such as we have had of the killing of a lieutenant colonel on Federal travel returning from his training course this summer,[4] the Federal Government has immediately sent to the scene investigative forces to cooperate with the bureau of investigation of the State and the local officials, and we are going to leave no stone unturned until we find the answers to those heinous crimes.

I am now ready for questions.

[6.] Q. Mr. President, your mention of hate organizations leads to another question. In the wake of the Republican Convention in San Francisco, Governor Rockefeller last night issued a statement in which he took issue with Senator Goldwater's references to extremism and moderation, and Governor Rockefeller said that the extremism of communism, the Ku Klux Klan and the John Birch Society, for example, had always been claimed by these groups to be in the defense of liberty.

When you speak of hate organizations, sir, are you referring, say, specifically to the Ku Klux Klan or the Birch Society, and how did you react to the way this subject was treated in San Francisco?

THE PRESIDENT. I refer to all hate organizations under whatever name they mask and prowl and spread their venom. I am not one who believes that the end justifies the means.

Q. Mr. President, referring back to Mr. Smith's question, Governor Rockefeller and also Governor Brown of California said they were disturbed that the effect of the statement by Senator Goldwater would be to encourage these extremist groups who think of their own cause as in pursuit of liberty as they see it. Are you concerned about such an effect?

THE PRESIDENT. I have stated it as clearly as I know how, my viewpoint in connection with the terror and with hate organizations, and with the theory that the end justifies the means.

I have stated it on the floor of the Senate. I criticized Senator McCarthy[5] for the practices he employed. I voted to censure him, as did every Democrat who was present at that time, for some of the practices along that line. And I have tried to make known my record clearly in the statements I have made this morning.

I condemn, as most Americans do, anyone taking the law in their hands or anyone organizing for the purpose of hate and dividing his fellow man and practicing upon the prejudices and playing upon the prejudices of the people of this country.

I am not going to start passing personal opinions on the expressions of the other party and the other candidate at this point because I think the American people are perfectly careful and prudent people and they can very well judge those matters themselves.

I certainly don't want to get into any argument between the members of the other parties. They have their own problems, as I told you before, and I am not going to spread any hate or any rumor about them.

[7.] Q. Mr. President, even though Senator Goldwater said he would not indulge in personalities in the campaign, you have already been called a phony and a faker and Governor Brown has declared that the stench of Fascism is in the air. Are you looking forward to a real dirty campaign?

THE PRESIDENT. No, I don't anticipate, so far as the Democratic Party is concerned, that there will be anything about our campaign that is dirty or there'll be any mudslinging. I think we will try to present a positive program to the American people and let them judge the proposals presented

---

[4] Lt. Col. Lemuel A. Penn of the Army Reserve, a Negro educator, was shot while driving along the highway near Athens, Ga., on July 11, while returning to Washington after 2 weeks' training at Fort Benning, Ga.

[5] Former Senator Joseph R. McCarthy of Wisconsin.

to them by the other party and then choose which party they think is best for their country.

[8.] Q. Mr. President, can you give us any indications when the Warren report might be released, sir?

THE PRESIDENT. No. That is a Presidential commission. I asked the Chief Justice and other members to serve on it. They have been at it for a good while. They are very insistent that they pursue every possible lead. When their report is completed, I assume they will submit it to the President and at that time I will be very glad to review it carefully and make such decision as I may feel the national interest requires.

[9.] Q. Mr. President, have you been in further communication with Senator Goldwater about possible intelligence briefings now that he has the nomination?

THE PRESIDENT. No, I have not, but they are available to him, as I stated before, and I think from time to time he has received certain briefings in his capacity as a major general. But I will be very happy for Mr. McCone, the Director of CIA, to brief him at any time that he cares to be briefed.

[10.] Q. Mr. President, Senator Goldwater said the issue of crime and violence in the streets should be a major campaign issue. Do you regard this as a proper area of Federal responsibility?

THE PRESIDENT. Well, I think that I should remind all of you that the United States is one of the few nations which does not have a national police force. The Constitution provides that responsibility for law and order should be vested in the States and in the local communities, for the protection of the individual.

I would be interested in seeing the other party spell out what some of you seem to feel is a serious takeover of local law enforcement, because I think all of us realize it has

the gravest implications. I think it would be of utmost concern to those who believe that the Federal Government's general police power should be limited to interstate matters and situations where the States' ability to maintain law and order has broken down.

If we were to give the Federal Government the responsibility for all law enforcement, in the cities and towns, even here in the hill country, I would think that the people would believe that it would do more than anything else to concentrate power in Washington. I read from some of my columnist friends, and some of the front pages of the newspapers, and I see on TV, where some people are very much opposed to concentrating any further power in Washington.

So far as we are concerned, we are going to urge State and local governments to halt terrorism and to continue their law enforcement, and where it is inadequate, the Federal Government will always promptly assist local authorities to maintain order as long as the lives and the security of our fellow citizens are in danger.

[11.] Q. Mr. President, in view of the political campaigns coming up, what future do you foresee for the rest of your legislative program if the Republicans engage in any footdragging?

THE PRESIDENT. We will have our difficulties ahead, without any doubt. We have had a very good year, however. We have a good deal of our program behind us.

When we last met here at the ranch before this session of Congress, we all felt at that time that if we could pass a good tax bill it would help our economy along, and if we could pass the civil rights bill that we would consider that we had a pretty good session.

We have passed the tax bill; we have finally passed the civil rights bill. We have passed the farm bill. We have passed the International Development Act—the idea that had such great difficulty and was defeated on the first go-round.

Before we adjourn, I hope to conclude many other bills that are now in conference. There are some six or eight in conference.

I would hope that we can get action on the food stamp plan, and the pay bill, the poverty bill, the Appalachia bill, and I believe that already we have one of the best records of any Congress.

I am planning to ask the Members of Congress and their wives to come to the White House before the convention just to give a salute to the Congress and honor this Congress for the fine work it has done. I hope by the time we have that meeting we will have some additional measures to tack up on the wall.

[12.] Q. Mr. President, I wonder if you feel, sir, that Senator Goldwater's rather bellicose statements on attitude toward the Communists and our foreign policy in general has increased the difficulties of this Government in its relations with its allies abroad?

THE PRESIDENT. My experience has been that we must be very cautious in formulating the policy of our country in relation to the other some 130 nations in the world. And I think that we are going to have a simple issue this year that the American people can decide which men and which party can best meet the the responsibilities of conducting the Nation's foreign relations. I think you will find that there will be a very different viewpoint expressed in that regard.

I am not in a position to honestly and accurately estimate what reaction other people may have to what some folks say. My experience has been that what men say is always more revealing about themselves than it is about other people. But I have every confidence that the Democratic Party will talk about its record and will explain fully,

through the President, the Secretary of State, and all the facilities of this Government, what it proposes to do about meeting the issues that concern our relations with other nations.

I would hope that the other party will campaign in the same spirit, because I want to point out that what Democrats think about Republicans, and what I might think about Senator Goldwater, is of secondary importance and impresses very few people, I think, except the partisans.

What is important, I think, is what each party thinks about America and what the leadership of each party offers to the American people and to the rest of the world. I believe the American people will take the recommendations and the various statements made by both candidates, weigh them carefully, and determine which man they think will be the more responsible, more constructive, more enlightened, and more intelligent in trying to bring peace to this world.

I have not the slightest doubt but what the uppermost problem in the mind of every American and in the mind of most people of the world is how to learn to live with our fellow man and how to achieve peace in this period in which we live. As long as I am permitted to hold the office that I now occupy, no single statement of mine and no single act of mine is going to be in the direction of provoking war. I am going to utilize every resource at the command of the Federal Government and all of its people, and command the intelligence of all the people of both parties to try to find the road to peace.

We have difficulties that appear every day in our relations with 100-odd other nations, just as we do in relations with our neighbors here up the road and down the road and down the river. But I prefer to try to reason out those problems, talk them out be prepared to defend ourselves at all times. But I would hope that no other nation would think that we are a nation of warmongers and that we have any evil designs on conquest or domination.

Reporter: Thank you, Mr. President.

THE PRESIDENT. Did you get in your full 15 or 20 questions?

Q. If you have some answers that we don't have questions for——

THE PRESIDENT. I don't want any of you to feel left out.

Q. We think you did very well.

NOTE: President Johnson's twenty-second news conference was held at the LBJ Ranch, Johnson City, Tex., at 10:03 a.m. on Saturday, July 18, 1964.

463 Statement by the President on the U.S. Economy. *July 18, 1964*

1. *After-tax income*

—Because of some revisions in the 1st quarter, the advance in after-tax income in the 2d quarter turns out to be $12 billion, the biggest gain of any quarter in history.

—So both the quarter-to-quarter gain of $12 billion and the year-to-year gain of $32½ billion are all-time records. This year-to-year gain in after-tax income breaks down into $556 per family of 4.

2. *Weekly retail sales*

—Retail store sales for the week ended July 11 were up 8 percent from a year ago.

—The rise over a year ago averaged 9½ percent for the 2 weeks ending July 11, bettering the 6.2 percent year-to-year rise for the month of June, and the 5.4 percent year-to-year rise for the first half of 1964.

3. *Housing starts*

Private nonfarm starts, after declining for 2 months, rose in June to a seasonally adjusted rate of 1.5 million units.

—4.8 percent above May,

—making June the 11th month out of the last 12 that starts have been at, or above a strong 1½ million rate.

4. *Detroit employment gains*

The city of Detroit has had such good employment gains that it is now off the depressed areas list.

Estimated unemployment for the city fell to 4.6 percent (not seasonally corrected) in May, down from 6.0 percent last May.

Detroit is a striking example of our expansion of the past 3 years. Their unemployment was

—15.5 percent for 1961, against 6.7 percent for the U.S.

—9.6 percent for 1962, against 5.6 percent for the U.S.

—7.0 percent for 1963, against 5.7 percent for the U.S.

—4.6 percent for May 1964, against 4.9 percent for the U.S.

So rising demand (mainly for autos) can and does create jobs—stronger markets and incentives generated by the tax cut are bringing the national unemployment rate down too (as Secretary Wirtz's new figures made so clear yesterday).

5. *Manufacturers' new orders*

New orders for durable goods in June:

—fell 1.3 percent from May (seasonally corrected),

—but were 12.2 percent above last June.

6. *Real GNP and our fine price stability*

To get a picture of how much real GNP advances, an overall price index used for this purpose is called the "GNP deflator." It rose only 0.3 percent in the 2d quarter, as against an average of 0.5 percent in the previous 4 quarters.

This means that the advance in real GNP from a year ago was 5.2 percent, the best advance in nearly 2 years.

This is one piece of evidence that there's no overheating, or inflation, in response to the tax cut.

—From February to June, the wholesale price index fell 0.4 percent.

—From February to May, the consumer price index rose only 0.2 percent.

—Both our own surveys and private surveys show very little expectation of price increases by businessmen.

464   The President's Toast at a Luncheon for Prime Minister Holyoake of New Zealand.   *July 20, 1964*

Mr. Prime Minister, distinguished guests:

It is a great pleasure to welcome to this house of the American people one of their very good friends—and also one of the free world's most stalwart citizens and leaders.

Many miles of ocean separate our two lands.

But many bonds of common purpose have made our two peoples one in devotion and dedication to freedom.

I am sure that no one will misread the meaning of the unity expressed by New Zealand, Australia, and the United States in the ANZUS Council meeting which brought our friend, the Prime Minister, to our country.

On all matters of concern, we stand together as one.

I need not reaffirm what is not in doubt or in question.   But I would repeat, Mr. Prime Minister. that the United States will keep its commitments in the Southwest Pacific. We will keep our commitments around the world.   We will stand firm until freedom is secure and until peace is assured.

I congratulate you, Mr. Prime Minister, and all the participants in the ANZUS meeting on the achievements of this vital and vigorous alliance.

We are especially grateful that the occasion of that meeting brings you back to Washington after an interval of nearly 2

years.   I know that you must be reluctant to leave your beautiful land—and your farm on which so much of your life has been spent.

Having just returned from my own farm after 2 days there, I assure you that I understand your feelings.   Much as I should like to talk to you today about agriculture, there are other subjects on which I think I might learn from you just now.

The Prime Minister—like myself—spent some 25 or 26 years in his country's Parliament before coming to his present post in 1960.   What is of particular interest to me—in an academic sense, of course—is his record last year.   When he stood for a second elective term, he was returned to office with a Parliamentary majority only one vote less than in the first term.

Mr. Prime Minister, we are very proud to welcome you today as a friend, as the great leader of a staunch and valued ally for freedom, and as an untiring coworker in the quest for peace on this earth.

So I ask my friends who have gathered here with me today to join me in a toast— to our eminent friend, the Right Honorable Keith Holyoake, the Prime Minister of New Zealand.

NOTE: The President proposed the toast at a luncheon in the State Dining Room at the White House.   The text of Prime Minister Holyoake's response was not released.

465 Remarks to the American Field Service Students.
July 20, 1964

I SUPPOSE I should introduce myself. Well, I am the father of Lynda and Luci Johnson—and I am known as the man who is the White House dogs' best friend.

It is good to have you here at the White House with us this evening. We have been very much in doubt all afternoon about whether the weather would permit.

Nothing makes a house happier than young people—and this house is a very happy home right now with all of you here on our lawn.

I know that during the past year each of you has made life much happier, much more rewarding for the American families with whom have lived. I hope that you will take back to your own lands even half as much enrichment as you are leaving behind in our land.

You have been in the United States during a year that history will never forget—and that I think you will always remember. You have seen our system—and our people— tested by a terrible tragedy. But you have also seen that system and this people respond nobly—respond with great courage and with great commonsense.

I believe there is an example in this for all the rest of the world.

People in other countries sometimes forget what we in America can never forget: that America has been built by sons and daughters of every continent and every country.

Men may try to tell you that peace among nations and neighbors is not possible—that old animosities can never be forgotten—that old suspicions and prejudices can never be overcome—that old rivalries and struggles can never be laid aside.

When any tell you that, then you tell them of America.

Because here in this diverse land of 190 million people—people with the blood of your own ancestors in their veins—have forgotten and have overcome and have laid aside the divisions of the past.

We live together today in 50 States as one people—one people, united and indivisible.

If such unity can be accomplished here, it can be accomplished everywhere. And we believe that you will—in your own times— be leaders for peace and justice around the world.

I don't know what impressions you may have brought here—or what impressions you may be taking away now.

But I do hope that you will convey to your families and your friends and your fellow countrymen one fact about America. That almost nobody in America thinks that much in America is as good as it should or could be—even, sometimes, including its President!

Free expression, self-criticism, constant self-examination are the great strengths of free peoples—and are the great sources of the energy from which progress comes.

You have seen this process at work this year. We have been dealing with problems in our society which have existed 100 years or more. But we are making progress—toward fulfilling the rights of all the people, toward opening greater opportunity, toward building better cities, toward building a more prosperous economy, toward making life better for people.

So America is not an old, contented, complacent land—ready to stand still. America is young—as you are young—with its future before it, as your future is before you.

Your land and this land have much to do together.

I am sure you will be leaders in those great works.

On this happy evening, I know there is in the hearts of all of us one note of sadness. One week ago today the man who had done so much for 40 years to foster and to nurture this program passed away in his sleep—Director General Stephen Gallati.

Mr. Gallati was a most remarkable American—and quite a remarkable citizen of the world. Through the fruits of this program, his influence will live on for many generations yet to come.

And so tonight, before I conclude, I would like to announce that I am conferring upon Mr. Stephen Gallati, Sr., a Presidential Citation. The citation reads as follows:

"Trusted Counselor, Friend, and Inspiration for Young People Throughout the World, he selflessly devoted his life to the cause of Peace by laboring tirelessly to foster understanding today among the youth who will lead the nations of the world tomorrow."

If Mr. Gallati's son, Stephen, Jr., will come forward, I would like to present this Presidential Citation to him at this time.

NOTE: The President spoke on the South Lawn at the White House. The group was composed of some 3,000 exchange students, representing 59 countries, who had completed their senior year in high schools in the United States and were preparing to return to their homes.

466   Letter to the Speaker Transmitting Supplemental Appropriations Request for Civil Rights.   *July* 20, 1964

Sir:

I have the honor to transmit herewith for the consideration of the Congress proposed supplemental appropriations for the fiscal year 1965 in the amount of $13,088,000 to support programs authorized by the Civil Rights Act of 1964.

The details of these proposed appropriations are set forth in the attached letter from the Director of the Bureau of the Budget, with whose comments and observations thereon I concur.

Passage of the Civil Rights Act will earn for the 88th Congress a place of honor among those who have fought for human dignity in our history. By enacting this Charter, the Congress has assured that we shall achieve ultimate victory in the long struggle to guarantee the fundamental rights of every American citizen.

I am sure that the Congress which enacted this Charter will wish promptly to provide the funds necessary to implement it. Though some activities can and will be started immediately without additional financing, money is needed to support programs to increase popular understanding of the law, to provide help in coping with the problems caused by its initial impact, and to increase the Federal Government's capacity to enforce it. The modest request I make today will allow us to begin these vital tasks.

I wish to emphasize the importance I attach to early action on this request. The more promptly we are able to make effective the Act's protections, the sooner justice will be provided to all our citizens in the manner prescribed by the Constitution. To delay that justice would be to deny it.

Respectfully yours,

LYNDON B. JOHNSON

[The Speaker of the House of Representatives]

NOTE: The Supplemental Appropriations Act, 1965, was approved by the President on October 7, 1964 (Public Law 88–635, 78 Stat. 1023).

The letter from the Director of the Bureau of the Budget was also released.

467 Remarks at the Defense Department Cost Reduction Week Ceremony. *July 21, 1964*

Secretary McNamara, Secretary Vance, Service Secretaries, valued members of the Joint Chiefs of Staff, devoted employees of the United States Government:

When Secretary McNamara invited me here several weeks ago, I don't know what he knew that I didn't know at that time, but needless to say I am happy to arrive at the Pentagon on the day after the Senate unanimously approved the military pay increase bill.

We expect the House to act favorably shortly, but we will withhold our "well done" to the Congress until that bill is signed by the President.

It is good to see all of you and to be with you here today. I want to express my gratitude to your computers for giving you time off to attend these ceremonies.

The Secretary is under instructions to watch costs closely these days, but I will use what influence I have to see that this hour is not charged against your annual leave.

Last December I attempted to impress upon all the officers of the Cabinet that I expected each of them to personally do his full share in holding the line on Government spending. Specifically, I said at that time: "Your budgets should reflect economies from better management and higher productivity, resulting from improved methods, procedures, organization, and employee incentive."

A good manager can do all of this. The response throughout the Government has more than justified my belief that our Federal Government is staffed with many very good managers, both civilian and military.

The line has been held on spending. It is still being held today and nowhere was that challenge more difficult than here in your Defense Department. Nowhere has that challenge been met more effectively or more responsibly.

Secretary McNamara's report to me a few days ago tells an impressive story.

In the fiscal year of 1964 your Department realized savings of $2½ billion, and those savings are at least $1 billion more than had been forecast.

But that is not the whole story. Our military muscle has grown while budgetary fat has been trimmed away.

As Secretary McNamara reported to me, in the last 3 years we have attained the following:

First, 150 percent increase in the number of nuclear warheads in the Strategic Alert Force.

Second, a 60 percent increase in the tactical nuclear forces deployed in Western Europe.

Third, a 45 percent increase in the number of combat ready Army divisions.

Fourth, a 75 percent increase in airlift capability.

Fifth, a 100 percent increase in general ship construction and conversion to modernize our Navy; and

Sixth, an 800 percent increase in the special forces trained to deal with threats of counterinsurgency.

This is by every standard a record of which each of you can be proud and for which all of your Nation is grateful.

But this record has not been achieved and could not have been achieved merely by orders and edicts from the top. That is the real reason that I came over here this morning. I believe that the other departments and agencies and the people of this country should all know what your able Secretary, Mr. McNamara, has emphasized to me on many occasions.

In 1962 and again in 1963 many of the very substantial cost savings came from the upper echelons of this Department.

In 1964 he tells me the reverse is true. Cost consciousness has permeated throughout the Pentagon and throughout all of our Commands.

We are today being literally flooded with thousands of suggestions from individual military and civilian personnel in the Commands in the lower units. This is a wholesome and very hopeful development.

So, I came here this morning to thank you and to congratulate you for the example you are offering the Nation and the record that you are making for your country.

I have tried to set an example. I shall continue to do so.

I remember what the head of another government once said long ago, and I quote: "I would rather have the people laugh at my economies than weep for my extravagance."

Budget levels cannot be changed drastically overnight either by cutting out the lights or waving a wand. Every thinking citizen knows this, but attitudes can be changed, and attitudes toward budgeting and attitudes toward public spending, and every thinking citizen in or out of our Government knows that it is time for many old attitudes to be changed.

We are the richest nation in the history of the world. We can afford to spend whatever is needed to keep this country safe and to keep our freedom secure. And we shall do just that.

But we cannot afford to spend one dollar more than is absolutely necessary, because we have other needs to meet with those dollars—public needs and private needs.

We of the United States keep a courageous vigil of peace around the world, but there are also vigils of justice and vigils of progress and vigils of decency that we must keep here at home.

If we are to do that, you and I and all of us who hold the public trust must keep a closer vigil and a more courageous vigil on the public purse.

I think now we have come to the point to present the awards to the men and women of the Defense Department who have kept that vigil and have done just that and thereby have set an example for all of us.

[*After the presentation of the awards the President resumed speaking.*]

This has been a most refreshing and stimulating morning for me. I am proud to meet and to congratulate some of those who are responsible for the very great economies that have been reflected in this report.

One aspect of that report gave me very special pleasure, and that is the goal that you have set for the future: your goal of saving $4,600 million a year, each year, every year. That goal may seem unattainable. Not too many months ago the prospect of saving an extra $1 billion would have seemed unattainable for fiscal 1964. But I believe that you will reach that goal, and I believe you will exceed it.

Soft budgets do not build a strong America. Flabby fiscal practices are enemies not only of our muscle and our might; they are enemies of mental capabilites and moral concepts.

I thank you and all who worked with you for the great job that you are doing to defend freedom and to preserve peace.

Now I must go back across the river to see what I can do to secure some other things—both the military and civilian pay bill—through the Congress.

NOTE: The President spoke in midmorning on the concourse at the Pentagon building. In his opening words he referred to Secretary of Defense Robert S. McNamara and Deputy Secretary of Defense Cyrus R. Vance.

As announced by the White House on July 13, Defense Cost Reduction Week (July 20–25) had a twofold purpose: (1) to recognize the efforts of civilian and military personnel in the Defense establishment throughout the world who had contributed to the $2.5 billion savings accomplished in fiscal year 1964, and (2) to concentrate attention on the actions required to attain in the coming months the savings goal of $4.6 billion.

At the ceremony 4 military officers and 15 civilian employees of the Defense establishment were honored with special recognition Certificates of Merit, the first to be presented following a White House announcement on May 21 that special Presidential citations would be awarded during the year to Federal employees and governmental units responsible for achieving significant cost reduction or other improvements in Government operations. Marking the 10th year of the Federal Employees' Incentive Awards system, the awards offered additional recognition and a tangible symbol of the President's personal appreciation.

468   Statement by the President on the Riots in New York City. *July 21, 1964*

FOR THE past 3 days the Nation has been shocked by reports of rioting and disorder in the streets of our largest and one of our proudest cities.

The immediate overriding issue in New York City is the preservation of law and order and the right of our citizens to respect for their property and to be safe in their person as they walk or drive through the streets. In the preservation of law and order there can be no compromise—just as there can be no compromise in securing equal and exact justice for all Americans.

I have called the acting mayor of New York City. I have told him of my willingness to cooperate in every way possible to help him in this time of agony. Law enforcement is basically the responsibility of the Governor, State and local officials. The acting mayor informs me that he is aware of all his responsibilities and is determined to discharge them including the full application of impartial justice.

It must be made clear once and for all that violence and lawlessness cannot, must not, and will not be tolerated. In this determination, New York officials shall have all of the help that we can give them. And this includes help in correcting the evil social conditions that breed despair and disorder.

American citizens have a right to protection of life and limb—whether driving along a highway in Georgia, a road in Mississippi, or a street in New York City.

I believe that the overwhelming majority of Americans will join in preserving law and order and reject resolutely those who espouse violence no matter what the cause.

Evils acts of the past are never rectified by evil acts of the present. We must put aside the quarrels and the hatreds of bygone days; resolutely reject bigotry and vengeance; and proceed to work together toward our national goals.

I have directed Mr. J. Edgar Hoover, Director of the Federal Bureau of Investigation, to contact Commissioner Michael J. Murphy and the Governor of New York and to inform them that we are conducting a complete investigation of the possibility of violation of Federal laws in connection with the recent disturbances and offering them our complete cooperation.

NOTE: For a statement by the President upon making public an FBI report on recent urban riots, see Item 600.

469 Remarks at the Swearing In of George H. Hearn as a Member of the Federal Maritime Commission. *July 22, 1964*

Mr. Hearn, ladies and gentlemen:

There are two methods for entering public office—by appointment or by election. I was just reflecting here, Commissioner, that the method you have followed has a great deal to commend it. Whether elected or appointed, the individual entering public service assumes a very great trust, a very sacred trust.

I know that Commissioner Hearn and all those who serve in positions such as this are acutely aware of that responsibility— their responsibility to all the people and certainly in this instance to all the free world.

This position on the Maritime Commission is one of far greater responsibility than many public positions. As long as there has been a United States of America, our maritime capabilities have been a vital part of our Nation's success and our prosperity and our Nation's influence throughout the world.

Today the maritime world is a highly competitive world. I want to say that I am looking to Commissioner Hearn and to his colleagues to offer us real leadership in that competitive world. I very much want us all to do all we can to strengthen the thrust of this Nation's competitiveness, its competitiveness on the sealanes of the world's oceans.

I think we are making some progress in increasing our trade. We are encouraged by the gains last year that we made, and this year, but those of us who give some thought to these fields know that we must do a great deal more and we are going to. One place where more can be done is to improve the efficiency of the Maritime Commission, to cut through delays that impede the competitiveness of our shippers, to make decisions fairly, justly, and most importantly, promptly.

You have a big job to do, Mr. Commissioner. Needless to say, you would not have been selected for this office of trust if your outstanding record in private and public life had not convinced me that you were the man to do the job.

Congratulations, and we will now administer the oath.

NOTE: The ceremony was held at 11:15 a.m. in the Fish Room at the White House.

470 Remarks of Welcome at the White House to Prime Minister Rahman of Malaysia. *July 22, 1964*

Mr. Prime Minister, ladies and gentlemen:

It is my great personal pleasure and my privilege on behalf of the people of America to welcome you this morning to the United States.

We remember happily your visit to our country 4 years ago. We are very proud to welcome you back again today, this time as the leader of the new nation of Malaysia.

Our two countries are far removed from

one another, but we here in the United States are very much aware of the outstanding leadership that you have offered during these midcentury decades. We have greatly admired the courage with which you led your native land to a decisive victory over Communist terrorism. We have no less admired and applauded the vision with which you have worked to secure the blessings of liberty for all of your people.

In times of trial and in times of hope, you have manifested the highest order of responsibility and foresight toward the best interests of your people. The impressive mandate of your recent elections is a great tribute from your people to you.

For myself, I welcome this opportunity to add through personal conversation to the understanding already achieved by our personal correspondence.

Mr. Prime Minister, we in America share with you and your people the same hopes for the future and the same devotion to peace and the same desire to see the lot of mankind made better throughout the world. I am hopeful and I am confident that our discussions together will be to the profit of the great cause in which both of our countries earnestly labor together.

NOTE: The President spoke just before noon on the South Lawn at the White House where Prime Minister Tunku Abdul Rahman was given a formal welcome with full military honors. The Prime Minister responded as follows:

Mr. President:

Thank you very much, indeed, for your warm and cordial welcome. I have looked forward to this moment for some time, because I am very happy to have the chance at last to meet you personally. It is always a privilege to meet the President of the greatest democracy in the world, particularly when you have heard so much of his work in the cause of freedom and peace.

In the past we have had contacts through the normal diplomatic channels, but as you have rightly said, there is a world of difference between the correspondence and the pleasure of having personal conversations.

Remembering with heartfelt pleasure my last visit to the United States, I have always cherished the hope of returning some day, so when your invitation reached me I was very happy, indeed, to accept.

I know that you are rather preoccupied with national affairs at present, but in spite of that you were good enough to ask me to come at this time. It was a considerate move on your part and I appreciate it most sincerely.

I most heartily endorse the sentiments you have expressed of our mutual hopes of peace and happiness in the world. I come from an area of the world that is beset with all kinds of troubles. To the north there is trouble, to the east there is trouble, and now there is trouble coming from the south of my country. These troubles threaten to encircle the two countries in southeast Asia that have so far remained free.

To us small nations, America forever stands out as a pillar of hope, a guarantor of our rights as free nations. Therefore, Mr. President, I believe there should be no embargoes on friendship and good will between men and nations.

I wish to thank both you and the American people, and at the same time to convey the very warm good wishes of the nations and people of Malaysia to our American friends.

471 Toasts of the President and Prime Minister Rahman.
July 22, 1964

Mr. Prime Minister, Mr. Secretary, Mr. Ambassador, Governor Harrison, ladies and gentlemen:

In this house none are so welcome as those leaders who have chosen the path of freedom and democracy. Our guest today is such a leader. He guided his native Malaysia to independence. He led his people to a decisive victory over Communist guerrillas.

He took the lead in the formation last year

of the nation of Malaysia. In all of this, he has kept faith with democracy.

He has sought for his people food instead of bullets, clothes instead of uniforms, homes instead of barracks.

Malaysia's success shines as an example for many lands.

Mr. Prime Minister, you and your people have our respect and our faith. We are very glad that you are here today. There are many choices for the world today. There is the choice of perpetual war or permanent peace. There is the choice of order or chaos. There is the choice of the rule of law or the rule of the jungle.

The American people have made their choice—for peace, for order, and for the rule of law.

We are proud to support those whose choices are the same. We support our friends with all the resources of our Nation. We of this generation are determined that men shall live in a world where aggression will not go unpunished, where terror will not go unchallenged, where irresponsibility will not be left to run rampant.

Our course—the course of the United States—has been chosen freely. It will not be lightly changed.

The people of Malaysia have likewise made their choice freely and it likewise will not be changed.

Your Excellency, we of the United States extend to you our congratulations. We wish for your people a future of peace and progress.

Now I should like to ask all of you to join me in a toast to His Majesty, the King of Malaysia, and to the friendship between the Malaysian and American people—long may it endure. To His Majesty.

NOTE: The President proposed the toast at a luncheon in the State Dining Room at the White House. Prime Minister Rahman responded as follows:

"Mr. President, Mrs. Johnson, Your Excellencies, ladies and gentlemen:

"I wish to thank you, Mr. President, very much indeed for the glowing compliments you have paid to the nation and the people of Malaysia and to me, sir. This is a most pleasant luncheon in my honor.

"It is always heartwarming to know that the successes we have achieved during the short years of independence both in overcoming the Communist terrorism that plagued our country for nearly 12 long years and in being able to build a democratic and, as you say, a prosperous nation are admired and appreciated by other countries of the free world. To win praise from the United States—the redoubtable champion of democracy, the bastion of strength in the free world—is to me praise indeed.

"Malaysia may be small—and it is small in size and population—but our people, as you know, are great in heart.

"We know, however, that success cannot feed upon itself; otherwise, it dwindles and dies. So, success must always be with basic ground for greater efforts, and that is what we are endeavoring to do in Malaysia today despite external difficulties and troubles.

"We are well aware that although we have won the struggle against communism in our own country, the menace still exists and may strike us again.

"I think it is true to say that Malaysia has proved two important truths: first, that through unity and cooperation democracy can and does work in Asia; second, that a truly successful democracy, prosperous and progressive, thinking first and always of the welfare and well-being of the people is the only effective answer to insidious intrusion of communism.

"From our own experience we have learned that it is not practical to be neutral in this struggle. In our view the state is made for men and not men for the state. That is why we are proud to belong to the free world.

"My last visit to the United States coincided with the election campaign. This time I have arrived between national conventions and at a time when you are so preoccupied.

"I can only thank my stars that Malaysia's elections are not on so vast a scale as yours. Nevertheless, we have just emerged from the elections and are not quite yet recovered from the effects of it. I can well understand that with your huge country and with voters by the millions what you will have to go through in the next few months.

"When I was here last I came to know what American presidential elections mean, and all I can say is that I am a happy man that I don't have to stand for the elections.

"I wish you all the luck. However, the whole world will be waiting and watching the elections in the United States. I shall say no more for fear of treading on dangerous ground, so I will content myself by wishing every success to the voters.

"The great interest the United States has shown in our progress and development in Malaysia is a source of satisfaction to us. I appreciate very deeply the help that you have given us in various ways and in various forms such as providing technical assistance in the form of experts under the Colombo plan and for the excellent work being done by dedicated men and women of the Peace Corps.

"In fact, I would like to see more members of the Peace Corps serving in Malaysia, especially doctors and engineers. Those whom I have had the pleasure of meeting have said to me, and I think they are sincere, that they are very happy to be in Malaysia—so why not, Mr. President, send more of them?

"We were getting on very well indeed with our tremendous plans for development since the struggle against the Communists, and the help we obtained from our friends has proved most valuable to us.

"As you said, Malaysia has been a beacon to other lands and a beacon that does shine but, unfortunately, it can also attract insects and pests. Some of these are harmless but others are very harmful. Unfortunately, the glow from our beacon has attracted quite the wrong kind of attention as well where both the Communists and now our next door neighbors, the Indonesians, who plainly consider us a tasty morsel to tempt the appetites of the giants. I think they are doing just a little bit more than just that, but I would not like to bore you, sir, in our pleasant company by telling all that was happening.

"As far as I am concerned we have done everything humanly possible to humor them, but nothing can satisfy them until, I am afraid, they have devoured us.

"But I know I can trust you to stop them from devouring us and getting the help from our friends in the free world. I hope that the beacon can then continue to shine in order to guide others to safety, security, peace, and happiness.

"In the meantime we must push ahead with development, because this is an essential element in our effort to provide higher standards of life and a richer future for our Nation.

"So, we look to freedom-loving people for understanding and support, and that is why I am so especially glad to hear your warm praise today.

"Mr. President, in conclusion, I do most sincerely appreciate both your kindness and your hospitality and all of the nice things you have said about my country.

"Your Excellencies, to the President, Mrs. Johnson, I ask you, ladies and gentlemen, to join me in a toast to the President of the United States and to the lasting friendship between America and the Malaysian people."

The President's opening words referred to Prime Minister Rahman, Secretary of State Dean Rusk, the Malaysian Ambassador to the United States, Dato Ong Yoke Lin, and Governor Albertis S. Harrison, Jr., of Virginia.

472 Remarks at a Luncheon for a Group of Businessmen. *July 23, 1964*

I HAVE ASKED you here to review the position and prospects of America.

Such a meeting is especially important now—as we approach a national election. For I believe that all of us—whatever our political views—can agree the demands of politics should not lead us to any acts which might damage the health of the economy or interrupt our steady expansion. Far too much is at stake—for our country and for its people—to permit that to happen.

As long as I am President I will continue these meetings with leaders of the American economic community. I will review our progress, discuss our plans, and seek your counsel. No President, no government, no nation can hope for meaningful progress without constant communication and contact with those who lead the great decision making machinery of our democratic economy.

I believe in the importance of these meetings because today more than ever we share a broad common purpose.

The business of government is people. Its job is the prosperity and safety, the welfare and freedom of all Americans.

These are also the essential conditions to the growth of American business. For American business is like no other in the history of the world. It is not the property of a few. It is not a tool for exploitation of the many. It is owned by millions. It is shaped by the demands and needs of an entire nation. It draws its strength from the fact that nearly 190 million people can desire and choose and share in the enormous abundance which our genius has created. And it flourishes best in the atmosphere of freedom, and peace, and confidence in the future which is the business of government to ensure.

The object of business is production and profit and progress. And government knows that your success in realizing these goals is essential to the people which it serves.

There is another thread of common purpose which we too often neglect. Government and business are not abstract and isolated empires. Government officials and businessmen—you and I—are Americans; sharing love of country, pride in achievements, faithfulness to freedom. We are, many of us, parents; sharing hope for the education and careers and safety of our children. We are moral human beings; sharing compassion for the helpless, belief in justice, hope for the brotherhood of man. This common purpose will always transcend any other considerations.

I believe we are entering a new era of cooperation between government and business and labor and the many groups which form this Nation. This does not mean we will always agree. It does mean we have created an economy which has never existed before, and which some said could never exist.

It is an economy where the health of business benefits all the people. It is an economy where the prosperity of the people benefits the health of business. It is an economy where, in large measure, the fortunes of each are tied to the fortunes of all.

Over the years the effort of millions has laboriously built our American economy. It rests, in all essentials, on the private decisions of private individuals and organizations and groups. It is not neat. It is not orderly. It does not fit into a preconceived plan. But it works. And it works better than any other system ever shaped by the mind of man or the force of events.

In this system government is not a dictator or a master planner. Government is the great moderator—adjusting those differences and injustices which require its effort. Government is the public servant—carrying forward those public tasks which its people require. Government is an agent of prosperity—carefully and prudently using its influence and scope in the cause of economic progress.

Let me tell you how well this partnership is working.

For the past 41 months we have enjoyed the longest and largest peacetime expansion in our history. Our 5.3 percent unemployment and 87 percent industrial operating rate remind us that we have not yet made full use of our potential. But we are on the way.

You, and others, are employing nearly 5 million more people than in February 1961. Total jobs now number 72 million, an all-time peak. And payrolls are expanding.

Work stoppages due to strikes during the past 3½ years have been at their postwar low. In the past 8 months the country has solved all of its major national labor disputes—including the 5-year dispute in the railroad industry—without strikes.

Corporate profits after taxes were running

almost $12 billion, or 60 percent higher, in the first quarter of this year than 3 years ago. And they are still rising.

The total value of shares in your companies, and others, is up $100 billion since I assumed the Presidency 8 months ago.

Wholesale prices in June were down almost 1 percent since early 1961. This is part of a price and cost stability over the past 3½ years unmatched by any other country.

With your business leadership, and your help—and the help of the labor leadership I will meet with tomorrow—the years 1961–1964 have been the most prosperous in American peacetime history. The Council of Economic Advisers informed me today that this will be the first peacetime administration in a century unmarred by economic recession or depression. This is in sharp contrast with the three recessions we unfortunately suffered in the 1950's.

And I am also proud to report to you that we turned the corner on our external payments position about a year ago.

This year's payment deficit will be below last year's. Next year's should be even lower. Our record on costs and prices—our monetary and tax policies to check capital outflow—on conserving defense and foreign aid dollars through buying goods at home—and your cooperation in our export drive—will all bring increased strength to the dollar.

Nor need we fear that a European inflation will weaken our defense of the dollar. The reasons for confidence are simple.

First, the Europeans are acting responsibly to hold prices in check. We wish them well, even though rising prices overseas improve our competitive position.

Second, new methods of cooperation in OECD, IMF, the group of Ten, and the Bank for International Settlements are a great force for international stability.

Third, we have across-the-board bipartisan support—here at home—of policies to defend the dollar.

As a result of this effort we have restored the full meaning of "sound as a dollar" across the world.

This combination of rapid expansion and real stability is not only a great achievement. It is a great lesson. It teaches us that if we eliminate fear, and hostility, and distrust, among ourselves—if we work together in a partnership of moderation—then the history of these years can be only the first page in a new era of American abundance.

While working to expand the economy, we have also worked to bring about the most prudent and efficient use of every tax dollar collected by the United States Government.

We have done this in the spirit of the man who said, "it is every American's duty to support his government, but not necessarily in the style to which it has been accustomed."

I have some charts here to show you how that effort is coming along.

That concludes the report I wish to make to you as businessmen. That is the state of the American economy and the national budget in the summer of 1964.

But I did want to take a moment to talk to you as Americans—Americans who are also leaders of the Nation, shapers of opinion, molders of events. I wish to talk to you not only about fiscal responsibility but about moral responsibility.

Our Constitution and our laws place upon us a duty to provide equal justice to all Americans. To fail to observe this duty attacks the entire structure of ordered liberty on which the life of this Nation depends.

I ask you to use the influence and position and respect—which you possess in such abundant measure—to persuade others that the law of the land must be obeyed.

I did not become President to preside over mounting violence and deepening disorder. I fully intend to use all the resources I have to make sure that those who claim rights— and those who deny them—bend their passions to peaceful obedience to law.

I intend to work to ensure that every person enjoys the full constitutional rights and equal opportunity that are his birthright as an American citizen.

But this cannot be done from the White House alone. I need the help of every American. I ask you to do this not just because it is good for business or for economic stability. I ask you to do this because it is vital for the America you and I know and believe in.

Much of the work of my great office is devoted to preserving the freedom and health of this country. No day goes by without problems whose wise resolution is important to our liberties and the strength of our people.

Government is not a business. Its success or failure cannot be gauged in statements of profit and loss. But it requires the same qualities as any great human enterprise—the qualities you bring to your work— moderation in the conduct of affairs, re-

sponsible innovation to meet rapid change, the imagination to find new solutions to new needs.

The Presidency is not just a place to protect the present. It is a focus for the possibilities of the future. It is often said that a President must have a vision of the America and world he wants to see. I believe that to be so. But the President does not put his purely personal stamp upon the future. His vision is compounded of the hopes and anxieties and values of the people he serves. He can help guide them toward the highest and most noble of their desires. He cannot take them where they do not want to go. Nor can he hope to move ahead without the help of all those who share a common purpose.

I believe that in this room are Americans who share with me a common dedication to American greatness. Each of you contributes to that purpose each day in the conduct of our economy. I hope that we will always be able to match shared beliefs to shared actions in the interests of all the people of this land.

NOTE: The President spoke in the State Dining Room at the White House. The luncheon was attended by more than 200 of the Nation's leading businessmen.

As printed, this item follows the prepared text released by the White House.

473   Remarks in Valley Forge at the Boy Scout Jamboree. *July 23, 1964*

Mr. Watson, Scout leaders, members of the Boy Scouts of America:

The America that you will build and live to see will be far different from the America of today.

In 50 years there will be 400 million Americans instead of 190 million Americans. Man will have reached into outer space and

probed the inner secrets of human life. And some of you will take those journeys. New inventions will have changed the way in which you live, just as the automobile and the airplane and the television have brought changes to my life. Fast planes and satellites will make neighbors of distant lands.

You will see wonders and participate in

achievements of which we older Americans can only dream.

This is an exciting challenge. I envy you the great adventures which await you.

But it was an American President, Woodrow Wilson, who said, "A nation which does not remember what it was yesterday does not know what it is today nor what it is trying to do."

If you are to do great things, you must remember also what America has been.

For this country of ours is not just a collection of factories and banks. It is not simply 190 million people, or crowded cities, or broad highways.

This country of ours is a community built on an idea. Its history is the history of an idea. And its future will be bright only so long as you are faithful to that idea.

It all began right here where we are standing tonight. In 1777, in Valley Forge, a few thousand men suffered and starved through the freezing cold of the harsh winter. They did not have, as you have, regular meals, a decent place to sleep, protection from harm.

But they did have an idea, an idea and a dream. That idea gave them the strength to survive the winter, and when their ordeal was over, George Washington led them forth to liberate and to create the United States of America.

Throughout our history, most Americans have shared the common purpose which gave strength to the soldiers at Valley Forge. Most Americans share those purposes tonight.

The American idea is, first of all, the belief in freedom and the rights of man. Government was to be chosen and directed by the people. And every individual citizen was to have the right to speak his views, to worship as he wanted, and to be safe from the arbitrary acts of Government. Even if a single man stood alone against the entire Nation, that single man was to be protected in his beliefs and in his right to voice those beliefs.

This dedication to freedom was founded on the great moral truth that all men were created equal. This was a recognition that all men were equal in the eyes of God. Being equal, the poorest and the most oppressed among us had the same right as all others to share in Government, to enjoy liberty, to pursue happiness as far as his abilities would take him.

It will be up to you to carry this idea forward. For it is not yet a reality for all in this land.

If Government was to be chosen by the people, it must exist to serve the needs of the people. This, too, is part of the American idea.

As a result, in America we have a Government which exists to protect the freedom and enlarge the opportunities of every citizen. That Government is not to be feared or to be attacked. It is to be helped as long as it serves the country well, and it is to be changed when it neglects its duty.

I know that to many of you the Government in Washington must often seem far away, must often seem very difficult to understand.

But your Government is made up of people, people like those you know in your own hometowns, people who are chosen by your parents and your neighbors and sent to Washington to serve your towns and your States.

Government is an Irish boy from Boston who grew up to become President of the United States.

Government is the son of a German immigrant from Pekin, Ill., who became a leader of the American Senate.

Government is a rancher from Montana,

a banker from New York, an automobile maker from Detroit.

Yes, Government is the son of a tenant farmer from Texas who is speaking to you tonight.

And I am sure that here tonight within the sound of my voice are others who will grow up to work for this country in the councils of Government.

The American idea is also the belief in expanding opportunity and in progress. This was not to be a country where a few were rich and most were deprived. It was to be a country where every citizen had the chance, through his own work and skill, to provide for his family and to enrich his life. And that is the kind of country that we have built.

In the early days a man needed only an axe and a gun to build a new life in the open spaces of the West. Today it takes knowledge and skill. Today they must have that in order to have a chance to find a job, in order to take a rewarding place in the life of our country.

But because we have been faithful to this idea, more men have greater opportunity in America than in any other country in the history of civilization.

These ideas are as old as your country, but they are not old-fashioned ideas. They are as alive and as vital as America itself.

I have no doubt that if you remain true to them, you will remember these days of scout-ing as only the beginning of a lifetime of useful service to America.

The qualities you will require for this task are those contained in your Boy Scout oath. Its pledge has meaning not only for you but has great meaning for all of our citizens.

What that pledge really means is the theme of this jamboree. It means "This Is My Country," and "I must prepare myself to serve it well."

Be faithful to it. And your life and the life of your country will be the richer for it.

It is wonderful to come here and be with you this evening, and to look into your smiling, optimistic faces. It will give me strength that I need in the lonely hours that I spend in attempting to lead this great Nation.

It is wonderful that you could be here in this peaceful atmosphere of one of the great States in our Union and at such an historic site.

You have much to be thankful for. Yes, we have much to preserve and much to protect.

I am grateful that your great leader, Mr. Tom Watson, Jr., asked me to come here to be with you tonight, and I want to thank you from the bottom of my heart for receiving me so warmly.

God bless you all.

NOTE: The President spoke in the evening at the sixth National Scout Jamboree at Valley Forge, Pa. His opening words referred to Thomas J. Watson, Jr., president of the Boy Scouts of America.

474   Joint Statement Following Discussions With the Prime Minister of Malaysia. *July 23, 1964*

THE PRESIDENT of the United States and the Prime Minister of Malaysia met on July 22 and 23 to discuss matters of mutual interest and recent developments in Southeast Asia.

President Johnson and Prime Minister

Tunku Abdul Rahman welcomed this, their first meeting, and the opportunity it presented to become personally acquainted and to review major problems in Southeast Asia. The President and the Prime Minister discussed the Communist threat to and activities in Laos and Vietnam and reaffirmed their support of the cause of freedom in those countries. The President noted with appreciation the contribution Malaysia has made to the common cause in Vietnam by providing equipment, training and advice based on her own experience in combating Communist terrorism. In turn the President made clear that all Southeast Asian countries, including Malaysia, could rely on the firm intent of the United States to resist Communist aggression against Free Asian nations.

The Prime Minister reviewed developments in Malaysia with the President and progress made thus far in furthering the economic and social progress of its people. The Prime Minister also expressed appreciation for the contribution of American Peace Corps Volunteers in this task.

The President informed the Prime Minister of his special interest in Malaysia's impressive achievements in the fields of education, economic growth and rural development. The President noted with admiration the Prime Minister's objective of a happy and prosperous nation upholding the principles of justice, freedom and democracy.

The Prime Minister outlined for the President the origins of the Malaysia concept and the history of its formation, and in this context reviewed the current activities by a neighboring state in violation of the territorial integrity of Malaysia.

The Prime Minister recounted his determined and various efforts to seek an amicable and honorable solution to the problem including the recent tripartite meeting in Tokyo. He also informed the President of the discussions at the recent Commonwealth Prime Ministers Conference in London.

The President re-affirmed the support of the United States for a free and independent Malaysia, and for Malaysia's efforts to maintain her security, preserve her sovereignty and continue her development in peace and harmony.

The President agreed to provide military training in the United States for Malaysian personnel, and to consider promptly and sympathetically credit sales, under existing arrangements, of appropriate military equipment for the defense of Malaysia.

The President expressed his strong hope that a peaceful and honorable way out of the current and dangerous situation could be found, and his appreciation for the earnest endeavors of the Prime Minister to this end. The President and the Prime Minister agreed that, while firmness in self-defense is indispensable, it is better to talk than fight.

The President and the Prime Minister found in the common devotion of the United States and Malaysia to the principles of democratic government and individual freedom a bond of understanding which is certain to bring their two countries into a constantly closer relationship, and agreed to maintain close contact on problems of mutual interest.

475   The President's News Conference of *July 24, 1964*

THE PRESIDENT. Good afternoon, ladies and gentlemen.

[1.] I would like to announce the successful development of a major new strategic manned aircraft system, which will be employed by the Strategic Air Command. This system employs the new SR–71 aircraft, and provides a long-range, advanced strategic reconnaissance plane for military use, capable of worldwide reconnaissance for military operations.

The Joint Chiefs of Staff, when reviewing the RS–70, emphasized the importance of the strategic reconnaissance mission. The SR–71 aircraft reconnaissance system is the most advanced in the world. The aircraft will fly at more than three times the speed of sound. It will operate at altitudes in excess of 80,000 feet. It will use the most advanced observation equipment of all kinds in the world.

The aircraft will provide the strategic forces of the United States with an outstanding long-range reconnaissance capability. The system will be used during periods of military hostilities and in other situations in which the United States military forces may be confronting foreign military forces.

The SR–71 uses the same J–58 engine as the experimental interceptor previously announced, but it is substantially heavier and it has a longer range. The considerably heavier gross weight permits it to accommodate the multiple reconnaissance sensors needed by the Strategic Air Command to accomplish their strategic reconnaissance mission in a military environment.

This billion dollar program was initiated in February of 1963. The first operational aircraft will begin flight testing in early 1965.

Deployment of production units to the Strategic Air Command will begin shortly thereafter.

Appropriate Members of Congress have been kept fully informed on the nature of and the progress in this aircraft program. Further information on this major advanced aircraft system will be released from time to time at the appropriate military secret classification levels.

[2.] I am pleased to announce today that in the year ending July 30th American exports of farm products broke all records, reaching an all-time high of $6 billion 151 million. This represents a 20 percent increase in farm exports in a single year—a $1 billion and a 35 percent gain over the level for the year 1960. Once again American agriculture has demonstrated its ability to succeed in highly competitive world markets.

The trade surplus in agriculture last year was over $2 billion, the highest in 50 years. This represents a substantial contribution to the plus side of our balance-of-payments ledger.

Farm exports contribute to the increased prosperity of our farm economy. The latest revised estimates from the Department of Agriculture show that net farm income in 1963 was $12 billion 518 million, more than a quarter of a billion dollars higher than we had estimated 6 months ago. The net income per farm increased from $2,961 in 1960 to $3,504 in 1963, an increase in this period, from 1960 to 1963, of more than 18 percent.

[3.] I think I should comment briefly on a number of international problems.

First, I think most Europeans know that

the United States has never had any interest whatever in trying to dominate Europe or any other area of the world. On the contrary, the United States has constantly supported the strengthening of the free nations of Europe. We believe that Europe and the United States have great common interests, common purposes, and common obligations. So we have never supposed that any European country would need to choose between its ties to the United States and its ties to Europe.

We believe that any effort to force such a choice would be bad for Europe, bad for the alliance. And I have found, I might say, general agreement on this view in my talks with Prime Minister Home, Chancellor Erhard, President Segni, and many other European leaders who have been here this year.

Second, I should like to call your attention to the excellent series of meetings which we have had in Washington this last week with the leaders of Australia, New Zealand, and Malaysia. These meetings have allowed the United States to underscore its support for the freedom and independence of three most important Pacific states; and our friendship and understanding with these governments, I feel, has been greatly strengthened.

Third, in the continuing discussion of Southeast Asia, let me state American policy once more. We are determined to support the freedom and the independence of South Viet-Nam, where Prime Minister Khanh and Ambassador Taylor have established the closest understanding with each other. They are in continual consultation and the policies of the two nations are the same; namely, to increase the effectiveness of the whole program in that country—political, social, economic, and military.

It is true that there is danger and provocation from the North, and such provocation could force a response, but it is also true that the United States seeks no wider war. Other friends suggest that this problem must be moved to a conference table and, indeed, if others would keep the solemn agreements already signed at a conference table, there would be no problem in South Viet-Nam.

If those who practice terror and ambush and murder will simply honor their existing agreements, there can easily be peace in Southeast Asia immediately. But we do not believe in a conference called to ratify terror, so our policy is unchanged. For 10 years, and in three different administrations, the United States has been committed to the freedom and the independence of South Viet-Nam, helping others to help themselves.

In those 10 years, we have taken whatever actions were necessary, sending men and supplies for different specific purposes at different times. We shall stick to that policy and we shall continue our effort to make it even more effective. We shall do the same in our support for the legitimate Government of Laos.

Fourth, this week I have conferred with the foreign ministers of this hemisphere at the White House and our eyes turned to Latin America. Down in Mexico there has been a highly successful meeting of the Inter-American Committee on the Alliance for Progress. The foreign ministers are working here to meet a challenge to our peace and freedom.

That meeting is still in session, so I must announce to you that I shall confine myself to the hope that in the spirit of the hemisphere, a sound and, I believe, an effective answer will be found.

These four problems are not the only ones that we have to deal with in the world today.

There are many, many others, such as dangers in Cyprus, and disturbances in the Congo, and difficulty in the Kennedy Round. But we still work for peace in Cyprus and in the Congo and for progress in the Kennedy Round.

We are a steadfast people in the United States, and in the larger sense the world is less dangerous, and we are stronger than we were 4 years ago, so our work for peace must go on and will go on with success, I believe.

I understand that we have with us today a group of journalists from Latin America who are here to cover the meeting of the foreign ministers. I want to extend to them a very cordial welcome.

Now I am ready to answer any questions you may have.

[4.]   Q. Mr. President, how do you feel about the statements that have come from various officials in New York City, including the mayor and the deputy mayor, to the general effect that there are indications of Communist involvement in the recent racial violence in New York City, and have you received any such evidence that would back up such indications?

THE PRESIDENT. I receive detailed reports at the close of each day with regard to the investigations that have been carried on by the Federal Bureau of Investigation. I do not care to comment in detail on those reports until some conclusions have been reached and some recommendations made, and until I think it is more appropriate to do so. I would not hesitate to say that the impression I gain from reading those reports is that there are extremist elements involved, and at the appropriate time I think that their identity will be made known.

[5.]   Q. Mr. President, would you comment on what you hope or what you feel might be accomplished in your meeting with Senator Goldwater this afternoon?

THE PRESIDENT. Senator G o l d w a t e r, through the facilities of his office, asked the legislative representative of the White House for an opportunity to meet with the President, and on an unpublicized basis. We informed the White House representative that we would be glad to meet with Senator Goldwater. We have met with Senators every day, and we would certainly be glad to meet with him any time that he thought a meeting would be useful. The 5:30 arrangement today was made.

I cannot anticipate all the subjects that will come up, but I am very glad to talk to him and will try to be responsive and make the meeting as fruitful as possible.

[6.]   Q. Mr. President, in elaboration of your statement on South Viet-Nam, President de Gaulle yesterday called for France, Communist China, the Soviet Union, and the United States all to get out of Indochina and leave them to settle their problems themselves. Would you address yourself to that proposal, sir?

THE PRESIDENT. I think I have already done that. I pointed out that we had already had one conference, and that we would carry out the agreements reached at that conference table, that there would be no need of our presence there, but until there is demonstrated upon the part of those who are ignoring the agreements reached at the conference table, some desire to carry out their agreement, we expect to continue our efforts in Viet-Nam.

[7.]   Q. Mr. President, after Senator Goldwater said last week that if he were President he would give at least the NATO Commander more latitude in the utilization of nuclear weapons, the Republican Convention rejected an amendment to the platform restating the traditional civilian authority over the military. What is your reaction to these actions, and could you give us your philosophy of civilian-military relationships in this particular area of nuclear weapons?

THE PRESIDENT. Well, I think there should be complete understanding and confidence in this country and among all our friends abroad. The control of nuclear weapons is one of the most solemn responsibilities of the President of the United States—the man who is President can never get away from that responsibility and can never forget it. The American people rely on his good judgment. They want that authority vested in a civilian. They do not expect to abandon this duty to military men in the field, and I don't think they have ever seriously considered that since the Founding Fathers drafted our Constitution.

I, myself, give close and continual attention to maintaining the most effective possible command and control over these awesome weapons. I believe that the final responsibility for all decisions on nuclear weapons must rest with the civilian head of this Government—the President of the United States—and I think and reiterate that I believe that is the way the American people want it.

[8.] Q. Mr. President, in view of the opposition that your administration has shown in the past to Mr. Tshombe, how do you plan to deal with him now that he has returned and taken over control of the Congolese Government?

THE PRESIDENT. We are going to be as cooperative and as helpful as we can in an attempt to see that the people of that area have as good a government as is possible, and we have every intention of being understanding and cooperative.

[9.] Q. Mr. President, to go back to your meeting with Senator Goldwater, do you and Senator Goldwater intend to enter into a pact to take the issue of civil rights out of the campaign?

THE PRESIDENT. Well, I would say to the architect of this meeting this afternoon that I do not believe that any issue which is before the people can be eliminated from the campaign in a free society in an election year. After all, that is the purpose of elections, is to discuss the issues. If candidates differ on important questions, it is up to the electors who must choose between them and in order to be able to satisfactorily choose between them, they must hear their views.

Now, I believe that all men and women are entitled to their full constitutional rights, regardless of their ancestry or their religion or the region of the country in which they may live. I believe that disputes, no matter how bitter, should be settled in the courts and not in the streets. I made that statement many times in press conferences and speeches over the country in the last several years. That is the reason that after more than two-thirds of the Democrats in the Congress approved the civil rights bill, and some 80 percent of the Republicans in the Senate supported the civil rights bill, I signed the civil rights bill.

I believe that all men and women are entitled to equal opportunity so that they can be judged according to their merits and not according to some artificial barrier. Now, to the extent that Senator Goldwater differs from these views, or the Republican Party differs, there will, of course, be discussion. I intend to carry on some of it, if I am a candidate.

The test of a free society is that it discusses and resolves these issues intelligently. It doesn't sweep them under the rug when they become difficult. I propose to discuss and debate the hard and difficult issues in the spirit of attempting to resolve them, and on the assumption that the American people are willing to listen and are intelligent and are unafraid.

No word or deed of mine, that I am aware of, has ever—or I hope will ever—lend any aid or any comfort to this small minority who would take the law into their own hands for whatever cause or whatever excuse they may use.

If Senator Goldwater and his advisers, and his followers, will follow the same course that I intend to follow, and that I expect the Democratic Party to follow, which is a course of rebuffing and rebuking bigots and those who seek to excite and exploit tensions, then it will be most welcome and I think it will be a very fine contribution to our political life in America.

[10.] Q. Mr. President, to return to the trouble in southeast Asia for a moment——

THE PRESIDENT. Can you speak a little louder?

Q. To return to your statement 3 in your opening statement on southeast Asia, do you and the Defense Department foresee a possible withdrawal of our military wives and children from Saigon or other southeast Asian command posts in the foreseeable future?

THE PRESIDENT. No, we have no plans along that line. Over the past several years I have heard rumors to that effect, and have seen news stories making predictions along that line, but we have no plans at the present time for any such action.

[11.] Q. Mr. President, recently in San Francisco some rather rough language was directed at you as being President, by the Republican opposition. I wondered if you felt this might be some sort of a signal as to a rather rough campaign for the Presidency that is coming up.

THE PRESIDENT. Most campaigns are rough campaigns. I am an old campaigner. I

have been at it 30 years. One of the first things I learned, at least so far as I am concerned, is the people are not much interested in my personal opinion of my opponent.

[12.] Q. Mr. President, your statement that the meeting with Senator Goldwater was to be unpublicized suggests that you are unhappy at the publicity about it. Was there any breach of faith by Senator Goldwater in announcing that he was going to meet you?

THE PRESIDENT. Well, you have asked two questions there. First, there is no such suggestion at all. I am not unhappy. I hope I don't look unhappy. I don't feel unhappy. I don't know who suggested that to you. But the question was raised that it was unpublicized, and knowing the initiative and ingenuity of the American press, I didn't think it would be unpublicized very long.

I just suggested that it was rather difficult for a fellow to take a glass of water at the White House, or even go out to the hydrant and get a drink, without it being adequately publicized. I can't even visit with my dogs without a lot of publicity. So I am not unhappy about it at all. I just explained that I thought it would be better to put it on the record, and so far as I know, Senator Goldwater is perfectly happy with it.

There is no breach of faith on his part and certainly none on my part. I realize that someone might indicate, because the suggestion in all its entirety wasn't carried out, there might be some difficulty between us, but my object in life has always been to not provoke fights, but to prevent them, if possible.

[13.] Q. Mr. President, without regard to the inter-American conference now underway here, I take it you don't want to discuss the topic under negotiation, but I wonder if you could tell us what your interpretation of the viewpoint of the American people is on the Cuban problem, and what should be done about it?

THE PRESIDENT. I think that their viewpoint is the same as the viewpoint of their Government. I think, generally speaking, that viewpoint is being considered by the foreign ministers who are meeting here now. I believe that they all recognize the challenge to peace and freedom which exists, and the necessity for not only being aware of that challenge but attempting to combat it with every reasonable and wise means available.

I believe out of this meeting the hemisphere will find a sound and effective answer, and I think that there are some indications now that the policies that we have pursued heretofore and the ones that we are suggesting be followed now are being effective.

[14.] Q. Mr. President, assuming you are not ready to name him yet, sir, could you describe for us your ideal running mate in terms of his characteristics and attributes?

THE PRESIDENT. The convention will meet in Atlantic City and select a candidate for President, and nominate him. I assume he will make his recommendations and then the delegates will act. I think that for me to make any announcement at this time as to my personal preferences—and I have none, I have made no decision in the matter—would be premature.

[15.] Q. Mr. President, Senator Goldwater has said that he will make an important issue out of what he views as increasing lawlessness and violence in the streets of our major cities. Are you willing to take this on as a campaign issue?

THE PRESIDENT. Well, I am against sin, and I am against lawlessness, and I am very much opposed to violence. I think we have to put a stop to it.

To the extent that we have the power to do so, in the Federal Government, we are doing so. We are exerting every action we

know to keep violence to a minimum.

We do not have a national police force in this country, we have not assumed power that we do not have, and we do not intend to. But wherever there is violence, we respond to it within the limits of our power and our authority.

We do have confidence in the local authorities. We do respect the sovereign States and the executives of those States. We have communicated with the mayors and the Governors and have made available to them all the facilities of the Federal Government to cooperate with them and work effectively with them. We will continue to do so.

We deplore men taking the law into their own hands and men disregarding the law, wherever it takes place. We treat them all alike.

I don't think there is any doubt in anyone's mind in the United States that the President of the United States, the power of the Presidency and the people of the United States are going to do everything within their power and within their authority to stop violence wherever it appears. But our judgment is that it is not up to us to take over the authority of all the local governments and not up to us to take over the authority of all the State governments.

I seem to have read and heard that other people, too, are opposed to the Federal Government usurping the rights of the States.

[16.] Q. Mr. President, are there differences of opinion between the United States and South Vietnamese officials on the question of attacking North Viet-Nam, and if there are differences, what are they, please?

THE PRESIDENT. The answer is no. I stated that earlier, but I repeat it.

[17.] Q. Mr. President, how do you assess your opponent this November, Barry

Goldwater, and do you anticipate a close race?

THE PRESIDENT. I think what I think about Senator Goldwater and my prediction as to the outcome of the race is not very important. I think that is a matter for the American people to decide. I think what the people want to know is how I stand on issues, and what my policies will be, and what my party stands for. They are much more interested in what the Democratic nominee advocates than what he thinks about his opponent or his chances of winning.

I have every confidence that the Democratic Party will adopt a good platform, will select good candidates, and that they will present their views to the people without regard to personalities, and the people, in their wisdom, will make a good decision.

Q. Mr. President, about 10 days ago Senator Goldwater used some very strong personal epithets to challenge your own sincerity of purpose in the civil rights issue. Now, would you sit down this afternoon to discuss civil rights without clearing that matter up first?

THE PRESIDENT. Yes. Yes, I am not concerned with Senator Goldwater's opinion of me. Of course, I would like for it to be a good opinion, but if it is not, that is a matter for him. He is entitled to his view and he has the right to express it, if he thinks it is a proper thing to do and a wise thing to do.

The American people will make their judgments of the various statements that he may make from time to time. I am perfectly willing to leave his opinion of me to the judgment of the people of this country.

[18.] Q. Mr. President, could you give us your assessment of the effect Governor Wallace's withdrawal from the Presidential race will have?

THE PRESIDENT. I have been rather busily engaged the last few days and I haven't spent a great deal of time evaluating that situation. I don't know how much support Governor Wallace had. I don't know how it would affect the platforms and the nominees of the two parties. All I know is that he decided to withdraw. I had heard and anticipated that he would do that. He confirmed it. But what effect it will have in November, I don't know.

[19.] Q. Mr. President, how active a campaign do you plan to conduct this fall?

THE PRESIDENT. Whatever I think is wise and necessary, and I expect to appear in various parts of the country and be very concerned with seeing that my party and my platform and the views of my candidates are properly presented. I will make whatever contribution I can, consistent with discharging my other duties, and try to be as helpful to the ticket as possible at all times.

[20.] Q. Mr. President, can you tell us if you plan any further action, any further Federal action, in New York City? And can you give us some elaboration of what you meant by extremist elements involved in the disorders?

THE PRESIDENT. No, I said that we get reports from there every evening. I don't think there is any question but what there are some extremist elements involved in the violence that takes place there. I think that must be evident to everyone who reads the newspapers. So far as we are concerned, we are prepared to take whatever action may be necessary and desirable. We have Mr. Hoover keeping very close watch on it. He has an adequate supply of manpower available to him. He has them assigned on specific investigations at the moment, and we will follow it very closely and do whatever needs to be done.

[21.] Q. Mr. President, in presenting your views this fall and discussing the issues that you want to present, would you be willing to debate Senator Goldwater on television?

THE PRESIDENT. Well, we will cross that bridge when we get to it.

[22.] Q. Mr. President, sir, there has been the claim in the campaign of an across-the-board attack on the foreign policy of the United States during recent years. This has raised questions here and abroad as to whether this wholesale kind of attack could cause your administration to trim its foreign policy in any major way. Could you answer these questions, sir?

THE PRESIDENT. I think foreign policy is an appropriate subject for discussion. I think the people of this country really need no advice from anyone else in other parts of the world about the decision they should make, but I think they will certainly want to be sure that the foreign policy of their country is a proper one, and I am prepared to present the views of my party on that subject and will do so at such time and at such length as may be desirable.

[23.] Q. Mr. President, sir, in response

to an earlier question, you said you hoped neither candidate's words or deeds would encourage extremists. Do you feel that anything Senator Goldwater has said of late would encourage extremists?

THE PRESIDENT. I will leave that up to the judgment of the people and you. I don't want to be passing personal judgment on the acts of another individual. I have given you my viewpoint on it. That is a little mission you will have to do for yourself.

Q. Mr. President, would you give us your reaction, please, to the attacks that were made on Senator Goldwater by foreign officials in the foreign press?

THE PRESIDENT. I think that the American people are perfectly capable of making their own decision with regard to the parties and the candidates, and I think that they will do that without the necessity of advice from anyone abroad.

Merriman Smith, United Press International: Thank you, Mr. President.

NOTE: President Johnson's twenty-third news conference was held in the State Department Auditorium at 3:30 p.m. on Friday, July 24, 1964.

476 Remarks of Farewell to General Prapass Charusathiara of Thailand. *July 24, 1964*

I HAVE had a very delightful and enjoyable visit with the General and it brought back many pleasant memories of my visit to your wonderful country in 1961 when I was Vice President and was out there.

I asked about some friends that I met. We talked about our problems. We regard your friendship very highly.

We are very grateful for the contribution that you have made to our efforts in that area to resist aggression for the people there who love their freedom.

We are participating to the extent we can

in helping in the economic development of your wonderful country, and we are very proud of the advancements and the contributions you have made.

I thank you, General, for coming in to see me.

I am happy to know that his visit to Walter Reed has been a success, and I will look forward to meeting him again.

NOTE: The President spoke shortly after 6 p.m. from the West Wing at the White House upon the departure of General Prapass and his party. General Prapass, Deputy Prime Minister of Thailand, had undergone eye surgery at Walter Reed Hospital in Washington.

477   Remarks at a Reception for a Group of Labor Leaders.
July 24, 1964

RESPONSIBLE leaders of labor are part of the responsible leadership of our American economy and society—and that is why you are here.

I believe the Presidency was conceived as an office of domestic persuasion more than domestic power. That is how I have tried to use the office since it was thrust upon me that tragic day last November.

The response of all sectors convinces me this is the right course. All Americans, working together, have written a most impressive record these last 7 months.

Since November, GNP is up nearly $20 billion. Personal income is up $15½ billion. After-tax income is up $20 billion. In this short span the typical family of four has gained almost $370 more after taxes—to save or to spend.

I am especially gratified that last month there were 72 million Americans at work—2,628,000 more than last November. Some of that increase is seasonal. But when adjustment is made, there is still a gain of 1,165,000 jobs in just 7 months.

Unemployment is still too high. But it has dropped—from 5.9 percent for November to 5.3 percent for June.

This is progress we have made together.

We can view the record through business eyes or the eyes of labor. Either way, the record of the past 41 months is the best American eyes have ever beheld.

For 41 consecutive months we have enjoyed the longest and largest peacetime expansion in our history.

Five million more Americans are at work in nonfarm jobs than in February 1961.

Average weekly earnings in manufacturing reached $103.50 last month—an all-time high.

I announced yesterday—and I repeat today: The Council of Economic Advisers informs me this will be the first peacetime administration in a century unmarred by economic recession or depression.

We have come a long way—up—from the bottom of the last of the three recessions during the preceding 7 years.

In 3½ years industrial production is up 27½ percent. Average weekly earnings are up $14.56. Personal income is up by $83 billion—or one-fifth. That typical family of four has gained $1,200 in after-tax take-home income.

This is the profile of the most prosperous years in American peacetime history—because that is what the 1961–1964 years have been.

We do not have—the free world does not have—any stronger asset than this solid, steady economic well-being for the American system.

I want to preserve it—and we shall by relying on cooperation, not by experimenting with compulsion.

I want to continue it—and we shall by trusting our tradition of compassion, not by toying with the expedients of coercion.

I remember—and you have not forgotten—other days when American men, old and young, were idle in the streets. They had no homes—no help—no hope. We faced a fundamental crisis.

We made a basic national choice. We chose compassion. We put our faith in man—in the dignity and decency of individual man. We committed our system, then and there, to offer jobs for the jobless, not jabs; provide homes for the homeless not hate; give love for the children, no lectures.

Our prosperity today is the harvest of those seeds of compassion sown not so long ago. Compassion gave us the impetus. From then until now, we have moved straight and sure toward our present level of well-being.

If we are to live in a decent society, there is no substitute for compassion. But compassion must go hand-in-hand with courage.

As we keep a vigil for freedom around the world with our allies, so we must keep a vigil for well-being at home among ourselves. We must be as courageous against threats to our civilian supply of jobs as we would be against threats to our military lines of supply. We must be as alert to conditions on the perimeter of our society as to those on the perimeter of the free world. We must be as resolute in keeping our commitments to our own people as we are in keeping our commitments to others.

We have a commitment to full employment. We must keep it—and we shall.

We have a commitment to equal rights and equal opportunity. We must keep it—and we shall.

We have a commitment to universal education. We must keep it—at every level.

We have a commitment to security for the aged. We must keep it—and we shall, when they are ill as well as when they are in good health.

We have embedded in our national policies—and our national character—a commitment to compassion. We must keep that commitment and keep it fully.

We have peace—and prosperity. Times are good. But all through our society there are signs and signals which tell us we cannot be complacent or callous.

There are Americans at the top of the ladder—more than ever before. We want to keep them there.

There are Americans at the bottom of the ladder—far more than we can tolerate. We want to help them move up.

We must go to war on poverty—and all its causes.

Poverty at home is an enemy of our society as much as aggressors abroad. Poverty amid plenty can subvert our prosperity and undermine our stability. A war on poverty is a war to redeem human life, not destroy it—and it is a war this generation of Americans must wage and win.

As there are Americans at the top and at the bottom, there are also Americans in the middle. This great majority must be served.

The father with a steady job and steady bills must know his job is secure and that his bills can be paid. The mother of growing children who lives with growing worries must know that her concerns are not hers to bear alone.

America's families have just concerns—for their cities and their neighborhoods, for old debts and new rooms, for the approaching costs of college and the eventual expenses after retirement. Our system must respect those concerns—and respond to them.

Our challenge—yours and mine and all Americans—is to sustain the prosperity we have achieved and enlarge its meaning for all Americans.

We must press our attack on unemployment. The tax cut has been a stimulus. It will continue to bear much fruit. But we cannot—and must not—rest on that alone.

We must continue our attack on unnecessary spending in government. But I believe as Thomas Jefferson put it we should always have a "wise and frugal Government" which "shall not take from the mouth of labor the bread it has earned." While we continue to press the cause of frugality, we shall see to it that the economy receives the stimulus it needs to sustain prosperity and narrow unemployment.

We must continue our balance-of-payments improvement and to strive for continuing price stability.

America's agenda is long. But at the head of it now is one imperative—assuring the rights of all our people under the law and assuring respect for the law from all our people.

I would repeat to you as I said yesterday: I intend to work to ensure that every person enjoys the full constitutional rights and equal opportunity that are his birthright as an American citizen.

I intend to use all the resources I have to make sure those who claim rights—and those who deny them—bend their passions to peaceful obedience of the law of the land.

But the man in the White House—whoever he may be—cannot do that job alone. I need your help—and the help of every American.

You are leaders. I ask you to exercise that leadership.

America's labor movement won its great strength and freedom and respect through the law. You who pursued that long struggle can serve your country and your cause now by urging your communities to trust the law of the land and help it to prevail.

A united America has come to a place and posture of greatness in the world.

We must not slip from that position into the depths of division and lose the greatness we have won together.

NOTE: The President spoke at 4:10 p.m. in the East Room at the White House. Included in the group were some 280 of the Nation's labor leaders.

On July 25 the White House released a list of "Ten Key Economic Gains" showing comparative gains since November 1963 and since January 1961. In addition to those mentioned by the President in his remarks, the list shows an estimated gain in corporate profits (after taxes) of $3.5 million (12 percent) since 1963, and $12.2 billion (62.5 percent) since 1961, also a gain in stock values of 19 percent since 1963 and 34 percent since 1961.

Also released on July 25 was a list of "Presidents and Recessions Since 1837" listing 21 Presidents and the months of recession during their administrations. The periods of recession ranged from 1 month during the Kennedy-Johnson administrations to 43 months during President Hoover's administration.

As printed, this item follows the prepared text released by the White House.

478 Remarks of Welcome at the White House to President Tsiranana of the Malagasy Republic. *July 27, 1964*

Mr. President:

Your country and my country are both young, but friendship between our peoples is old.

Even before we gained our independence, Americans were engaged in peaceful commerce with your people. We are proud to welcome you here today in friendship and in independence.

Independence is the great trust of this century. Never before have so many men had in their own hands the privilege and the responsibility of determining their own destiny.

We of the United States rejoice in this. We rejoice especially, Mr. President, when nations such as yours and leaders such as you emphasize the responsibility of independence as well as the privilege of independence.

In our 188 years of independence we have learned that liberty is not license; freedom is not a favor; security is not to be had without sacrifice.

In your nation's 4 years of regained independence, you have impressed these same lessons upon those that you lead. Your statesmanship speaks eloquently as an example of the new leaders of the new nations on both continents between which your country is an ancient bridge. In Africa and in Asia the will for independence, freedom, and peace runs strong. We welcome and we applaud the courage of men on every continent who stand against the efforts of any to turn that tide or stem its flow.

Mr. President, the United States does not seek to dominate any friend and does not seek to destroy any foe. But where men stand up for their own freedom, we will stand with them. Where men strive to make life better for their children, we will strive with them. Where men are ready to seek sincerely after peace, we welcome them to join with us genuinely in its pursuit.

In the 1860's our two countries solemnly declared that peace and friendship should exist between them forever. In these 1960's, 100 years later, it gives me great pleasure to reaffirm that declaration.

It is my high privilege this morning to welcome you here, to welcome you as the leader of free and independent friends of these free and independent people of the United States for whom I speak.

NOTE: The President spoke at 11 a.m. on the South Lawn at the White House where President Philibert Tsiranana was given a formal welcome with full military honors. President Tsiranana responded as follows:

Mr. President, Mrs. Johnson:

I am most grateful to you for welcoming us, my wife, the members of my party, and myself, in this very high and lofty place of the American history.

I am most grateful to you also for giving me the occasion to get better acquainted with your huge country. Up to now I had only visited New York City and Washington.

Owing to the very close relations which have already existed between our two peoples and owing to the present international situation, it behooves me to meet with you at this point and to have meetings and talks with the high officials of your government.

These considerations were not the only ones which caused me to decide to accept your friendly invitation. The feelings of Madagascar toward the United States as well as my own personal feelings led us very naturally to strengthen the already important action of our respective embassies in the field of friendship.

Lately, the Government of the United States has been of great service to Madagascar and has effectively contributed to our development policy. But the Government of the United States has done even more in preparing and in enacting the bill on civil rights, and I was most happy to be able to congratulate personally Secretary G. Mennen Williams on the very day of the enactment of this historic bill after sending a telegram of personal congratulations to you, Mr. President.

The administration which was led first by the much beloved President Kennedy and which was led then by Your Excellency, Mr. President, has displayed itself as a human and courageous administration. The Nation which you are leading is favored among all nations, and it has the greatest of destinies promised to it.

The Malagasy people will never forget the unity displayed in this noble endeavor by the representatives of the American people and by its leaders.

On behalf of the Parliament and of the people of Madagascar, and on behalf of our Government, I salute you, Mr. President and Mrs. Johnson, and I bring you the assurances that the great Malagasy Island counts firmly the United States of America among its greatest friends. Long live the United States and long live Madagascar.

479   Toasts of the President and President Tsiranana. *July 27, 1964*

Mr. President, ladies and gentlemen:

Four years ago the land of our guest regained its independence. As head of the new republic the President asked his legis-

lative branch to impose an independence tax upon the people. The purpose was not to raise revenue but to impress upon the people that independence was not a gift. As sometimes happens even in Washington, the legislative branch was not too receptive to the suggestion.

But we honor the President for all he has done to make it clear that independence means taking up new responsibilities, not laying them down.

The American people have taken up many responsibilities these days around the world. Those burdens are not light. The way we have chosen is neither short nor smooth. But we entertain no thought of casting off those responsibilities and leaving them at the roadside of history.

We in America have only one policy, only one purpose, and one pursuit, and that is victory for freedom. When that victory for freedom is won, it will be a victory for responsibility among nations, young and old, small and large.

We in the United States take great encouragement from the model of moderate and mature leadership that our guest and other leaders like him offer the newly independent nations.

We welcome the close relationship between us. We are especially grateful that our countries can be associated in the great efforts of space exploration for the good of all mankind.

The President and I met all too briefly 3 years ago in Dakar. Today that friendship has deepened and grown.

We discovered that we were both born in cattle country of parents with meager means. In the 1930's we were both teachers. We both entered public service in the legislative branch.

There is one difference: the President is not up for election until next year.

The road of opportunity under freedom and democracy is a road that all men may walk on all sides of the world. It is a road that we intend to keep open and to keep it

wide open for all men whatever their race, their region, their faith, or their flag.

So, this is a happy privilege to be gathered here this evening under the sky and the stars with many of our friends from throughout the Nation and some of the leaders in all forms of public life in this country.

And to our friends who have come to pay honor to this leader, I should now like to ask you to join with me in a toast to the President of the Malagasy Republic—to the friendship between our peoples, to the victory for freedom toward which we all work together—Mr. President.

NOTE: The President proposed the toast at a state dinner held in the Rose Garden at the White House. President Tsiranana responded as follows:

Mr. President, Mrs. Johnson, Members of the Cabinet and Members of Congress:

I shall speak since I feel it is incumbent upon me to do so, but I know that I shall not be as eloquent as you, Mr. President.

I speak as a duty and perhaps as a responsibility of being a chief of state, as you pointed out.

I should like to thank you on behalf of the Malagasy people and on behalf of the Malagasy Government and in my own name, in the name of my wife. We thank you, your wife, the American people, and the American Government for receiving us here tonight and for conferring such great honor and such friendship upon us, because it is indeed a very great honor for us to come and visit your great country.

As I was telling Secretary Rusk today at lunch, we are happy and proud to be in a country which was once a colony and which, today, is the greatest country in the world. We take great pride in this even though we only have been independent for 4 years and you have been independent for close to 200 years.

We know how glorious your history is. We know that the American people love freedom, and we recognize how the American people love freedom, and I shall tell you very simply how I came to recognize and understand that the American people love freedom.

I was here in 1959 and I noticed most of all that even the small houses in the country had no fences around them. I understood then that the American people were very fond of freedom when I saw there were no fences around any of the houses. I saw a school and my reaction was the same. I asked about this and the reply which came to me was, "We want the children to feel free, so there are no fences around the school."

This is a small thing perhaps, but it denotes a state of mind—the love of freedom in the American people, a freedom for which the American people have struggled hard. And we also know that the American people love democracy. The two cannot be divided, and this is a wonderful example which has been given to us young nations.

I very often speak against some self-styled free countries. For instance, I do not care for the regime in the eastern part of the world. When I was in Berlin and looked at the wall, I knew that there was no freedom there.

So, my dear Mr. President, there is much that we can take from you, our elder sister nation, in the struggle that you have waged for freedom. The Malagasy people are also much attached to freedom.

I should not like to sound here as if I were boasting, but if in the whole world of today there are only two countries which love freedom and independence, then Malagasy is the second. If there is only one such country in the world, then perhaps that country is my own country.

You have said, Mr. President, that we are very much alike. In a sense, we are. You came from a cattle-raising family and I myself was herding cows as a child. My parents were raising cattle and, later

on, I became a teacher and then deviated into politics, and I am caught in the public of my small country.

But there is indeed something that we have very much in common. Since you have referred to the elections, Mr. President, let me say that the Malagasy people love freedom very much and that we admired your predecessor, President Kennedy, very much. We sensed his love of freedom and we sense that you also, Mr. President, love freedom.

We know that you have displayed much courage in your support of the entire segregation legislation. The Malagasy people have followed your efforts very closely, and we thank you for all you have done even though we ourselves are not American, but anything that is done anywhere to promote the cause of mankind is very dear to us.

You stand in the forefront of liberty and human brotherhood. My wish is that you shall succeed in the forthcoming election, and I shall make a special prayer that the good Lord be with you and help you to carry the success that that wish shall be yours and also that there shall be peace in the whole world and in the United States.

I invite you, ladies and gentlemen, to join with me in a toast to the success of the President in the forthcoming election, to his health, and to peace in the world.

Long live America and long live Madagascar.

480   White House Statement on the Desalting of Sea Water. *July 27, 1964*

THE President has requested the Department of the Interior to collaborate with the Atomic Energy Commission, in consultation with the Office of Science and Technology, to develop a plan for "an aggressive and imaginative program" to advance progress in large-scale desalting of sea water.

The President, in making his request, noted that the Federal saline water conversion program has concentrated thus far on research, and development efforts have been limited. Substantial progress has been made, the President said, but much remains to be done and the greatest necessity is to advance the technology of large-scale desalting plants.

The President requested that the Interior Department submit a report to the Budget

Bureau by September 11.

The President also announced that a three-man team from the Department of the Interior and the Atomic Energy Commission is leaving for Israel to begin joint discussions with Israeli representatives in Tel Aviv on July 27 on the desalting of sea water. This team is the outgrowth of a two-day meeting held in Washington on June 2 between President Johnson and Israeli Prime Minister Eshkol. A group will investigate the technical and economic feasibility of building a combined nuclear power and sea water desalting plant in Israel.

The United States representatives will be Milton Chase and Stewart Mulford of the Interior Department and Irving Spiewak, a nuclear reactor expert from the Atomic Energy Commission laboratory at Oak Ridge, Tenn.

The President also announced that a one-week long international symposium on desalting of water will be held in Washington beginning October 3, 1965. The symposium will be sponsored by the Department of the Interior and the Department of State with the cooperation of the Agency for International Development and the United Nations Educational, Scientific, and Cultural Organization.

In his request to the Interior Department, the President said that every means should be explored to increase the momentum of desalting progress by exploiting the now best developed technology (evaporators), using conventional or nuclear fuels or both and by pursuing other alternatives. He said the plan should provide for the full use of existing research and development facilities.

The President pointed out that a recent study made under the auspices of the Office of Science and Technology indicates that a combination of large-scale nuclear power plants and large-scale desalting plants could produce power and water at competitive costs by about 1975 in many water short coastal areas. He said the plan should propose the best strategy and time schedule for relating the development of large-scale nuclear power technology to the development of large-scale desalting technology.

The President also requested that full recognition should be given to the importance of sharing the benefits of American desalting technology with other nations.

NOTE: On July 16 the White House announced that representatives of the United States and the Soviet Union had met in Washington July 14–16 to explore the possibilities of mutually beneficial scientific cooperation in the development of methods for desalting sea water, including the use of nuclear energy. Dr. Donald F. Hornig, Special Assistant to the President for Science and Technology, headed the U.S. delegation. The Soviet delegation was headed by Aleksandr I. Churin, Chief Administrator of the State Committee on Coordination of Scientific Work. The text of the joint memorandum released following the meeting and the list of delegates are printed in the Department of State Bulletin (vol. 51, pp. 144–145).

For the President's statement upon making public the requested report on desalinization, see Item 715. For a further statement concerning joint U.S.-Israel studies, see Item 672.

481   Remarks Upon Signing Bill Authorizing Grants for the Publication of Historical Documentary Source Material. *July 28, 1964*

I APPRECIATE very much you gentlemen coming here this morning.

I am very proud to be able to sign this valuable legislation.

Through the years Americans have been too busy making history to read it carefully or to record it, but we cannot steer a sure course to the future without a sure knowledge of the past. As has been said, people who do not know their past are doomed to repeat its mistakes.

The lessons of this century about our responsibilities at home and abroad are etched indelibly in our minds and in our memories, but it is vital and valuable for those who come after us that we preserve in orderly fashion those historic documents which recount this period and its lessons.

This bill will be a major step forward in assisting both public and private groups to preserve the records of our times.

I want to thank Congressman Brooks for

suggesting that we come together today and to express appreciation to him and all those associated with the legislation for having rendered the future of our country a great service by helping to hold to our past.

NOTE: The President spoke in midmorning in the Cabinet Room at the White House. In his closing remarks he referred to Representative Jack Brooks of Texas.

On February 5 the President wrote to the General Services Administrator, Bernard L. Boutin, concerning the bill as follows:

"I am glad to note that the bill (HR 6237) to authorize the National Historical Publications Commission to make small grants to encourage the preservation, compilation and publication of the original documents of our history is now before the Senate. I agree fully with the letter President Kennedy wrote last year in support of this project.

"America has had a proud history, and the American people are entitled to have the documentary record of our past and the papers of our great statesmen and leaders compiled and published in easily available form. Federal participation in the program will help support and stimulate our archival agencies, historical societies, research libraries and related educational institutions to share their documentary holdings with universities and colleges throughout the land and with the American people. I look forward particularly to the completion of the projects to publish the papers of the Adamses, Franklin, Hamilton, Jefferson and Madison.

"This bill supplements and, in the field of American history, is an essential adjunct to, the major legislation in aid of education enacted by Congress last session.

"It is my hope that the Senate will complete action on the bill early in the new session. I would like it to be in time to permit the necessary appropriations for the coming year and to allow the National Historical Publications Commission to make its plans with this in mind."

For President Kennedy's letter in support of the project see 1963 volume, this series, Item 26. See also Item 245, 1963 volume.

The bill (H.R. 6237), as enacted, is Public Law 88-383 (78 Stat. 335).

482 Remarks to the Delegates to the Conference on International Rural Development. *July 28, 1964*

Mr. Bell, ladies and gentlemen:

You are in the city—and on the grounds of your house—in what some now call our "summer of discontent."

Before you return to your homes and duties, I would like to share with you some thoughts about this season.

In the long view of history, these years of the 1960's are the early summer of America. Our land is young. Our strength is great. Our course is far from run.

Yet there is among our people a deep discontent.

It is not the discontent of a single segment—or a single section. It reaches through the whole of our society. The most prosperous, the best housed, the best fed, the best read, the most intelligent, and the most secure generation in our history—or, for that matter, in all history—is discontent.

Why?

It seems to me that we can find answers from our history.

In our national character, one trait has run unbroken. That is the trait of putting the resources at hand to the fullest use—to make life better tomorrow for those who follow.

Since World War II we have multiplied our capabilities as never before, but we have not put them to the fullest use.

We have the capacity to abolish hunger. We have the capacity to end poverty and to eliminate most diseases. We even have the capacity to unsnarl our traffic—except possibly around the typical college campus.

We face no new problems in our society this summer—only old problems which we have for too long refused to face up to and have failed to meet.

We have not put our capacities to work.

Our cities show it.   Our schools show it. Our rural areas show it.   Our rivers and our streams show it.   The edges of our society show it.

This is the source of our discontent.

We haven't been keeping faith with tomorrow—or with ourselves—and we ought to realize it.

If we are learning anything from our experiences, we are learning that it is time for us to go to work, and the first work of these times and the first work of our society is education.

Without compromise—without favor— we must demand and we shall maintain respect for law and order in this country. But democracy never has and democracy never will solve its problems at the end of a billy club.

We—no less than generations of Americans before us—must put our faith in education at all levels for all the people.

The institutions you represent are the foundation stones of our society today.   Yet those foundations were put in place long ago—by the Northwest Ordinance of 1787, by the Land Grant Act of 1862, by the State support of their universities in the 1870's.

Dr. Harry Ransom of my own University of Texas not long ago told the people of our State that "the early frontiersmen thought more of us 100 years ago than we think of those who will be living in the year 2064."

In our States and Nation we just simply must not let that indictment stand.   We must rest our faith and our hopes for America on education—not for some but education for all.

I am proud to say that we are trying to do just that.

The 88th Congress has written its name in history as the education Congress on the basis of the legislation that you already know well.

We are very proud that it is going to be also the conservation Congress—more comprehensive conservation legislation will be passed this Congress than any Congress in our history, except perhaps for a period during Theodore Roosevelt's administration.

But the real important point I want to make is that this is an education Congress for all.

The first 60 days I was in office I signed three far-reaching educational pieces of legislation.   More meaningful progress has been made this year than in any other single year in this century.

This is good, but there is much more that we can do.

To meet the needs of an urban Nation, I am directing that we push forward with discussions of what can be done to bring our city people those benefits that were long available to rural families through extension service.

Likewise, we intend to continue and strengthen the effective relationship between the Federal Government and your institutions in support of research in all of your regions.

I want to dwell on that in just a moment. But I have in the last 10 days seen the membership of 10 task forces from throughout this Nation who represent what we believe to be the best brains that are available in the Nation, because we think the best brains ought to be available to the President, and we have asked them to come here to study some of these vital subjects: the relation of Federal, State, and local governments; education, transportation, many of the things that will determine whether we have a Great Society or not.   And they will burn some midnight oil in these task forces from now until the first of the year in preparation for the course that we will recommend that the Nation follow next year in the legislation to the Congress and the people on the country-side.

I would like to point out to you this morning that since the end of 1961 the number of AID-financed contracts with universities in this country has increased already 35 percent. The number of universities participating in those contracts has already increased 36 percent. The total amount of Federal contracts with universities is already up 44 percent.

The Federal role in relationships with institutions of higher learning is not a role of control, as you men know. The record of the institutions you represent is a record of real partnership in moderation between universities and colleges of this country and between the agencies of Government at all levels—Federal, State, and local.

In a short time we will have another group of educators from not only all the public school systems, to get a representative group, but also the State universities from each State in the Nation to get their views and their recommendations and exchange ideas with them as to what we can do to make tomorrow better living than yesterday.

We do not want centralized control of our society because experience has taught us that the surest way to prevent such centralization is to support strong institutions of higher learning in every State. And that is what we are trying to do.

This has been our Nation's course and it is the course that I am trying to steer today.

But our Nation faces great challenges here at home and many serious problems abroad—challenges of military security and challenges of economic stability, and these challenges cannot be met by Government alone or by business, that I conferred with last week, alone, or by labor, that met with me last Friday, alone, or by agriculture alone. What we must do is bring our great capabilities to bear on our problems and on our needs.

We have learned and we do know that those capacities can be focused most effectively for us by reliance upon the leadership of our institutions of higher learning of which you are an integral part.

So, ladies and gentlemen, you have a great trust to our society. We look to you for leadership. We plead with you to keep us moving. We vest in you great confidence, believing that a new age—an age of greater service, of greater influence, of greater contribution—is opening for all America and particularly for your institutions.

Our generation has spent most of its time and efforts, energies and talents on trying to preserve Western civilization. And because we have been successful and we now have the preparedness that is essential to preserve that civilization, we now have an opportunity to develop it and cultivate it and enjoy it and share some of its blessings.

Our Defense Department has spent $30 billion more than would have been spent if we had spent the same amount the last 4 years as we did the last year of the other administration. We were spending $43 billion a year. Now we are spending about $51 billion—about $7.5 billion more each year—but that is buying us more missiles, more bombers, more combat units, more paratroopers, and more power—power that we pray we will never have to use but power that protects us.

So, we are preserving that civilization in order to be able to develop this society, and you must be the bellwethers, the sheep that go through that fence first where others can follow you.

A great President of the Republic of Texas said in another generation, in another century, that education is the guardian genius of democracy. It is the only dictator that free men recognize and the only ruler that free men desire.

So, I thank you for honoring us here with your presence this morning. You are always welcome in this House as long as I am permitted to occupy it.

NOTE: The President spoke shortly before noon in the Rose Garden at the White House. His opening words referred to David E. Bell, Administrator of the Agency for International Development.

The conference, held in Washington July 27–28, was sponsored by the Agency for International Development, the Department of Agriculture, and the Association of State Universities and Land-Grant Colleges in a joint effort toward improving the effectiveness of U.S. assistance to rural development in the less-developed countries.

483 Joint Statement Following Discussions With the President of Malagasy. *July 28*, 1964

THE PRESIDENT of the Malagasy Republic, Philibert Tsiranana, and the President of the United States, Lyndon B. Johnson, have held very cordial discussions on matters of interest to both countries.

President Tsiranana described the economic matters of concern in his country and the efforts of his government to promote the advancement of the Malagasy people. He expressed appreciation for the understanding and friendly cooperation of the United States in assisting the economic development of Madagascar, and received assurances that the United States Government will contribute to the realization of the Malagasy 5-year plan.

President Johnson recalled the long-standing friendly relations that have existed between Americans and Malagasy and expressed his conviction that this visit would serve to further cement these ties.

President Tsiranana praised the efforts of the late President Kennedy carried on by President Johnson in the quest for better understanding between the peoples of the world and recognition of the integral rights of man and of his dignity.

The two Presidents reviewed the situation existing in the world today and stressed the necessity of maintaining peace and security in conformity with the Charter of the United Nations. They considered the difficulties confronting the developing nations of the world and discussed ways in which the industrial nations might assist in overcoming these problems.

The two Presidents discussed foreign private investments and the measures taken by the Malagasy Government to encourage them, and they spoke of ways in which trade between the United States and Madagascar can be expanded.

The two Presidents have stated they are quite satisfied with the relations existing between their two countries. They pledged themselves to continue cooperation and friendship.

484 Remarks to the Members of the National Agricultural Advisory Commission. *July 29*, 1964

WHAT is good news for the farmer is always good news for the country. The farmer and the country have been getting some good news about agriculture lately.

Farm exports for the year ending June 30 were up to $6.1 billion—nearly 1 billion better than the best year on record previously.

Farm net income reached $12.5 billion in 1963 by the latest estimates. That is a quarter billion better than earlier estimates indicated.

For the third year in a row, farm profits have exceeded the 1960 levels by nearly a billion dollars.

This is good news. We welcome it. We wish it were even better—but we believe it will be.

In agriculture we are beginning to realize the benefit from keeping our whole economy on a stable, steady, recession-free, and non-inflationary course.

Since February 1961 we have had 41 consecutive and uninterrupted months of recession-free economic expansion—the longest and largest in history. In contrast, in the 7 years prior to that point we experienced three closely-spaced recessions.

Using that date as the break-off point, the record is significant.

Since 1960, gross farm income is up 10 percent to $41.7 billion—in stable dollars. Cash marketing receipts are up 9 percent to $36.9 billion. Farm net income is up nearly 9 percent—to $17.5 billion.

Reduced to individual human terms the gains are even more encouraging. The per capita income of the farm population during the 1961–63 years has averaged one-third higher than over the 7 previous years.

You gentlemen of this Commission can be proud of your own solid contribution to this. Your recommendations have been welcomed and put to use. But more than that, you have by your example, shown a kind of leadership agriculture sorely needs—nonpartisan, unbiased, unprejudiced, and genuinely statesmanlike.

You have had disagreements. But you have done what some in agriculture seem to have forgotten how to do. You have

reasoned together, worked together, and reached agreements together in the public interest.

I applaud you—I congratulate you—and I thank you.

We can make progress in agriculture. We can if we lay aside partisanship, lay aside organizational prejudices and positions, and serve the Nation's interest and the public's welfare.

If you won't mind—and I don't think you will—I would like to speak very frankly with you for a moment.

Before I knew where or what the White House was, I was plowing a straight furrow. I don't know farmers or farming from the bloc viewpoint, or the pressure group viewpoint, or the what-do-we-do-for-them-this-year viewpoint. I know farm people and farm problems as a farm boy and farm owner myself.

In this perspective, I happen to believe that the time has come for this country to find and put to use some better answers to farm policy than we have had in many years.

Partisanship won't do the job.

Pettiness and peevishness won't do the job.

Prettily packaged programs won't do the job.

We need an approach to agriculture that serves all the people.

We need both some plain old-fashioned candor—and some plain old-fashioned courage.

On our commodity programs, we need the candor to admit that criticism of some is accurate and appropriate—and the courage to say that criticism of other programs is aimless and absurd.

We need the candor and the courage to agree that the needs of rural America won't be met by commodity programs alone.

We must have community programs, to build up small town America.

We must have consumer programs, to serve growing family America.

We need not—we must not—assign rural America to the scrapheap of history. We must not—and we will not—tell the American consumer, rural or urban, to stand at the foot of the line.

Our need—our urgent and pressing need today—is to preserve the stability of our economy as a whole.

Sharp and sudden turns from the course of the past are unthinkable.

Prosperity for our people is not less important than security for our people.

Whatever our goals, whatever our will, whatever our politics or prejudices, we must proceed with prudence, with patience, with perseverance.

America is prospering. Our goal and our guide must be to make sure that America's farmers prosper in proportion, too.

NOTE: The President spoke at 12:15 p.m. in the Fish Room at the White House. As printed, this item follows the prepared text released by the White House.

485   Statement by the President on Announcing a White House Meeting of the Presidents of State Universities.   *July 29, 1964*

THE White House meeting will be an intellectual convocation of the States. Its object will be to get underway in each State a study group of the highest expertness—consisting of men and women drawn from all the faculties in the State and of experts outside the universities—which at a specific time will be ready to report on the problems and possibilities of that particular State and region during the coming decades.

Our American system is the happy one of federalism. Both the Federal Government and the States have always exercised leader-

ship in solving the problems of the Nation. Through this conference, I hope to lend whatever help I can to the exciting process of revitalization now going on in our 50 States.

NOTE: The statement was not made public in the form of a White House press release. It was read by the Press Secretary to the President, George E. Reedy, at his news conference held at the White House at 4:25 p.m. on July 29, 1964, at which time he announced that a meeting of presidents of leading State universities would be held at the White House on August 13.

For the President's remarks at the meeting, see Item 513.

486   The President's News Conference of *July 30, 1964*

THE PRESIDENT. I am rushed a little bit this morning, but I thought I had a few items you might be interested in. I will get these statements distributed for you as soon as they can be copied.

[1.] First, a year ago this week the nuclear test ban treaty was signed and agreed upon. Today, a year later, more than 100 nations have joined the three original sign-

ing countries. We have also seen a U.N. Resolution Banning Weapons of Mass Destruction in Outer Space, and steps to cut back production of fissionable materials.

A year without atmospheric testing has left our air cleaner. This is a benefit to every American family, and to every family everywhere, since all radiation, however small, involves some possibility of biological risk to us or to our descendants.

At the same time we have taken every precaution to insure the security of the United States. To this end we have put into full effect the program of safeguards originally approved by President Kennedy on the advice of the Joint Chiefs of Staff. I can report that the Chiefs have reviewed the present program and agree that satisfactory progress is being made under it. Indeed, the safeguards program leaves us much safer against surprises than we were in the period of moratorium begun in 1959.

Even if this treaty should end tomorrow, the United States would be safer and stronger than before.

We owe the test ban treaty, and this year of progress, to the determined and dedicated leadership of a great President, and the Senate of the United States. This leadership toward peace has had no partisan tinge. Four-fifths of the Democrats and three-fourths of the Republicans in the Senate voted for this treaty. It is therefore right that all Americans without regard to party should give thanks in this anniversary week for what the President and the Senate achieved last year.

This thankfulness can be traced to the deep desire that all of us have for a world in which terror does not govern our waking lives. We should think of a world in which we need not fear the milk which our children drink; in which we do not need engage in agonizing speculation on the future generations and whether they will be deformed or scarred.

We can live in strength without adding to the hazards of life on this planet. We need not relax our guard in order to avoid unnecessary risks. This is the legacy of the nuclear test ban treaty and it is a legacy of hope.

Q. You say we will get that statement, Mr. President?

THE PRESIDENT. It will be copied and gotten to you as soon as possible.

[2.] I have recently had reports from several Government groups dealing with the hard problems of minimizing the adverse impact of shifts in our defense programs.

The Atomic Energy Commission has reported to me on the steps it has been taking to cushion the impact of scheduled reductions in the production of fissionable materials at such sites as Hanford, Wash., and Aiken, S.C.

The AEC has set up an Office of Economic Impact and Conversion, similar to the Defense Department office set up by Secretary McNamara, to work with communities affected by base closings or contract terminations. AEC is bringing in new contractors at its Hanford plant. They are expected to undertake private work along with their Government contracts, thus helping to diversify the local economy. And Congress has just passed legislation we requested to make Government land and facilities more readily available for diversification programs.

I have also had an informal progress report from the group I set up last December under the chairmanship of Gardner Ackley of the Council of Economic Advisers to study how we can best adjust to shifts in our defense programs.[1]

Some areas—such as Long Island, Boston, southern California, and Seattle—have already lost many jobs by defense cutbacks. But the overall problem has been greatly relieved by our general prosperity.

South Bend, Ind.—which has been hit by the closing of an automobile factory rather

---

[1] Committee on the Economic Impact of Defense and Disarmament, established December 21, 1963. See Item 62.

than defense cutbacks—is an example of what vigorous Government programs, aided by a strong economy, can do. The rate of unemployment in South Bend—which rose to almost twice the national average—has now been cut to 6½ percent.

South Bend has provided a test case for stepped-up Government programs of placement, retraining, relief, and help to local authorities in attracting new industries. These programs are available for other communities which might be hit by closing of a defense facility or ending of a defense contract. But additional measures may be needed.

Some new measures have already been taken, for example, a change in defense procurement regulations, to allow defense contractors to count civilian product planning as cost in defense contracts, and new Defense Department surveys to pinpoint the regional and industrial impact of defense subcontracts.

The committee expects to report to me within the next 2 or 3 months. This report will include its first set of recommendations for further actions to relieve problems of economic adjustment. The problem is a complex one, and will not be solved in 1 month or 1 year. But I am sure that the intensive work of the committee will lead to constructive measures.

[3.] Here is a brief statement, a copy of which will be given to you, on the OAS meeting.

The inter-American system demonstrated once again this week its effectiveness and vitality by dealing resolutely with Cuban aggression against Venezuela. The speeches at the meeting showed general agreement on a verdict condemning Cuban aggression, and the final resolution made it abundantly clear that the hemisphere will not tolerate aggression by subversion.

There was a genuine concern, which we shared, that although Venezuela was the target of Communist aggression today, another country might be the target tomorrow, and that we must stand all for one and one for all. Many able diplomats contributed to this encouraging result, but we Americans can be proud of our own Secretary Rusk, and of Secretary Tom Mann and Ambassador Bunker who backed him up.[2]

[4.] I had a meeting yesterday which I would like to make a comment on that may be of interest to you. It was with my economic and financial advisers. We reviewed economic prospects, problems, and policies. We can, and do, take great pride in our record-breaking prosperity on the home front and the restored prestige and strength of our dollar abroad.

But it is a President's constant duty to focus on areas where we still fall short of our goals; to foresee and forestall problems that may arise in the future.

We took a close look at the further impact of the tax cut in creating jobs and putting idle machines to work, and what fiscal and monetary policies will get us to our goal of full employment.

We took a close look at methods of assuring continued improvement in our export surplus, our balance of payments, and our gold flows.

We took a closer look at prospects for maintaining our excellent price and cost record—the world's best—and preventing any renewal of the price-wage spiral.

We took a close look at warding off any threats of slow-down or recession that may arise to endanger our record-breaking expansion in 1965 or 1966.

---

[2] Secretary of State Dean Rusk, Assistant Secretary of State for Inter-American Affairs Thomas C. Mann, and the U.S. Representative on the Council of the Organization of American States, Ellsworth Bunker.

With the aid of able and experienced men like Secretary Dillon, Chairman William Martin, Budget Director Gordon, and Economic Adviser Heller [3]—all of whom have been here since the Democratic administration and economic expansion got under way early in 1961—I know that the Government, in partnership with labor and business and all the private economy, will do its part to maintain our unparalleled economic advance.

[5.] I wish to report that the number of direct hire civilian employees of the Department of Defense has been reduced to less than 1 million for the first time since the Korean war buildup of the early 1950's.

The Department's civilian personnel strength on July 1, 1964, was 997,864, some 6,600 less than the goal of 1,004,467 set for that date. The Department has not had less than 1 million civilian employees since December 1950.

The breakdown by Departments is:

Army 337,670
Navy 332,678
Air Force 289,720
Other Agencies................. 37,796

These reductions in civilian personnel are attributable mainly to base closings, improvements in productivity, and a reduction of direct hire foreign nationals as part of the Department's program to reduce the unfavorable balance of payments.

Secretary of Defense McNamara, while pleased that the goal for July 1, 1964, has been exceeded, expects to achieve additional reductions before the end of the year. The figure for November 22, 1963, was 1,011,939,

so we have had a reduction of about 14,000 or 15,000 in that period.

[6.] I have a brief statement on Senator Engle which you can pick up.

Clair Engle was set apart by qualities of intelligence, compassion, and integrity which made him an unusual person and an exceptional public servant. His life was given to the pursuit of high goals and to the service of just causes. He was the servant of millions and the friend of many, but none held him in greater affection than Lady Bird and I did.

[7.] I have sent up two additional budget messages. I think you got one yesterday—George gave you—on the breakthrough in a new era of cooperation between public and private power in this country. The great city of Los Angeles public plant received a surplus of power there.[4]

I have today sent to the Congress a $19.8 million budget amendment to maintain schedules on four projects now under construction by the Corps of Engineers. We would lose $11 million by setting back a year the Arkansas River navigation project. The States interested in this one are Oklahoma, Arkansas, and Kansas.

Now I will take any questions.

[8.] Q. Mr. President, do you see anything to be gained by the candidates or by the voters by having televised debates such as the one in 1960?

THE PRESIDENT. I will repeat it every day for the record, if you want me to. I haven't been nominated yet. We haven't

---

[3] Secretary of the Treasury Douglas Dillon, Chairman of the Board of Governors of the Federal Reserve System William McC. Martin, Jr., Director of the Bureau of the Budget Kermit Gordon, and Chairman of the Council of Economic Advisers Walter W. Heller.

[4] On July 29 the President requested that $45.5 million be appropriated to begin construction of a power transmission network in the Far West which would tie together public and private power systems and would make possible the transmission of surplus power wherever needed from Seattle to western Texas. For further remarks on the new power intertie see Item 578.

selected our candidate. We have a convention. When that is done, we will carefully review any suggestions that any of you have and give attention to them and act in the national interest on them.

[9.] Q. Mr. President, there have been reports that you plan to announce your vice presidential preference within 10 days.

THE PRESIDENT. I know of no such reports. Who is reporting it?

Q. The New York Herald Tribune had a story that you plan to do it within 10 days, August 15th they say.

THE PRESIDENT. As far as I know, they have had no contact from me. Anyone here from the Herald Tribune?

Q. Yes, sir; but I didn't write the story.

THE PRESIDENT. Who did?

Q. Andrew Glass.

Q. It said you would make up your mind by August 15th and not announce it until the convention. Is that a fact?

THE PRESIDENT. I would say that I haven't seen the story. I haven't talked to the author and I haven't discussed the subject with anyone else. While I would not want to reflect on the accuracy of his speculations, I would say it was written right off the top of someone's head without any consultation with the President.

Q. Mr. President, just so——

THE PRESIDENT. I wouldn't want to forego the privilege of announcing it at any time that I reached a conclusion, but I would say for your protection, so you don't think the President has given someone some inside stuff.

Q. Have you reached a decision, Mr. President?

THE PRESIDENT. No.

Q. What was your answer to that, sir?

THE PRESIDENT. No.

Q. I would like to know just when to start alerting myself about when do you think there might be some announcement on your decision.

THE PRESIDENT. When I feel something like that coming on, I will let you know. My high regard for you will give me a chance to give you warning and I hope you have adequate notice so you can interpret it and analyze it properly for the country.

Q. A fellow could get a bloody nose on that story, Mr. President.

THE PRESIDENT. He could.

Q. Mr. President, could you tell us what criteria you might be thinking of in the selection of a running mate?

THE PRESIDENT. Yes, I think so. I think that we want the person that is equipped to handle the duties of the Vice Presidency, and the Presidency, if that awesome responsibility should ever fall upon him—I think he should be a man that is well received in all the States of the Union among all of our people. I would like to see a man that is experienced in foreign relations and domestic affairs. I would like for him to be a man of the people who felt a compassionate concern for their welfare and who enjoyed public service and was dedicated to it.

I would like for him to be attractive, prudent, and progressive. I would like him to be one who would work cooperatively with the Congress and with the Cabinet and with the President. I would expect him to be one that would meet with overwhelming approval of the delegates who have the responsibility for passing upon him.

Q. What was that last, Mr. President?

THE PRESIDENT. —who have the responsibility for passing upon him. I think that is enough. Helen?

Helen [5] has a question she wanted to ask.

[10.] Q. I just wanted to know if you thought elective office was sort of a——

THE PRESIDENT. I don't think I want to get

----

[5] Helen Thomas, United Press International.

into that. You might place the wrong con-struction on something like that. I am doing my best to keep you all active.

[11.] Q. Mr. President, of your own var-ied experience, what did you find the most useful after you succeeded to the Presidency?

THE PRESIDENT. I needed all I had and a good deal more, too, and I don't think one ever has too much. I doubt that many Presi-dents have ever felt that they have had enough experience. My administrative ex-perience in the executive branch of the Gov-ernment served me in very good stead. I use it every day now in directing other agencies of Government. I had only brief experience, less than 2 years, but it has been helpful to me.

My 12 years in the House of Representa-tives has given me a background that was helpful on a lot of things, particularly meas-ures like the farm bill, mass transit, and problems of that kind that we have had there.

My 12 years in the Senate has been a mat-ter of assistance to me in connection with treaty matters for foreign relations and pro-cedures in the Senate, difficulties like we worked out yesterday with this new era of cooperation which can mean much to our Nation between all of the private power companies and the public power companies.

My 10 years of leadership, 2 as whip and 2 as minority leader, and the rest as majority leader, helped me some in knowing the per-sonalities and leadership of Democrats and Republicans.

I am glad to say that on some of our key measures like civil rights, over 80 percent of the Republicans supported that measure, and on key measures like taxes we got the support of them, and I think that my meet-ing with their leaders in the Minority from time to time might not have been done if

I hadn't worked with them and had some association and experience with them.

My travels as a Vice President to more than 30 countries have resulted in acquaint-ances with people of Latin America and Scandinavia and Western Europe, and most of these men I have known, whether it is the Shah of Iran or Prime Minister of Britain or Chancellor of Germany, the President of France—all of these men I have met and talked and exchanged views with, and that has all been helpful.

[12.] Q. If you are elected, Mr. Presi-dent, will you see that your Vice President is equipped as much as you can help him to be after the election?

THE PRESIDENT. I haven't been nominated and I haven't been elected and I don't want to be presumptuous by telling you what is going to happen in the event that those things arise. But it is my view that the Vice President ought to be a very intimate, close part of the Chief Executive's responsi-bilities, and work with him in discharging them. He ought to be available to do any-thing the Chief Executive wants him to do and he ought to be competent to do it.

[13.] Q. Mr. President, we have been reading a lot of stories lately about the kind of campaign you are going to run. Some say you are going to sit in this chair and go out only on weekends.

THE PRESIDENT. I saw one story, and some-one thought I held a backgrounder on it, and I did not. I never talked to him, don't know him, never had a discussion, and whoever talked to him did it without my authority and knowledge. I don't know who it was. So I would say it was another story off the top of his head. I thought it was favorable and I liked it, but it was with-out research and authorization. I don't want you to think I left you out.

Q. That is why I am asking. Can you tell us about your plans after the convention?

THE PRESIDENT. I think it will be better to talk to you about it after the convention.

Q. Do you think it will be a vigorous campaign?

THE PRESIDENT. I said I think it will be better to talk to you about it after the convention.

[14.] Q. In reviewing your economic policies yesterday, did you inaugurate any new policy changes or alter any old ones to reach these goals?

THE PRESIDENT. No, we analyzed what is taking place. We tried to anticipate what it is down the road. We made some new assignments and some new studies. We are watching certain factors. We have a group of men in addition to these studying ways and means of preserving the prosperity we enjoy, because we don't think you can sit and enjoy the status quo and not anticipate what will happen a year from now. And we are trying to prepare for it by having the best minds in the country look at the problem, anticipate and prepare for it, and evaluate and analyze it.

[15.] Q. Mr. President, just yesterday six civil rights leaders called for a period of quiet in racial demonstration. Do you think a period of cooling off will be beneficial to the Nation during the campaign?

THE PRESIDENT. I haven't read the text of that statement. I have some thoughts in that general field which I will be glad to give you and I will have a copy of it made a little later, if you want it in more detail.

I don't want to be in a position of intervening in the decisions of any private organization as long as it stays within the law. But as a general matter, it seems to me that there are some general propositions for our people which all of us should consider.

When machinery does not exist to redress grievances, it is understandable that those who are aggrieved will take to the streets, whether rightly or wrongly. Their judgment might be wrong as to how justice could be obtained, but they would be less or more than human if they did not seek justice.

The Civil Rights Act was established to provide machinery—to transfer the area of conflict from the streets and highways to the courts and the conciliation chambers, and the weapons of conflict from the club and the brick to the presentation of evidence and reasoned argument. This is in accord with our traditional concepts of a society that is both stable and free.

The enactment of the law—which was passed by better than a two-thirds vote of each branch of Congress, voted for by over 80 percent of the Members of the Republican Party in the Senate and over 60 percent of the Members of the Democratic Party in the Senate—imposes upon us both the obligation of obedience and the obligation of use. And above all, it instills the obligations of conformance to all the laws, even to some of those which remain in effect but which have become somewhat dusty over the years.

So I commend all of those who are willing to give all the laws a chance to work, whether we are talking about the civil rights statutes or local ordinances against disorder or individual brutality, personal or authoritative. I have a deep and abiding faith in the ability of a free society to work through the ballot and through established judicial machinery, and I do not believe that those who walk those roads will be disappointed.

I might add that I would not argue with anyone who chose to pursue a policy of registration in lieu of demonstration.

One of the reasons for urging the civil rights law was so that we would have the yardstick. Now that we have this law, I would hope that all of our citizens will follow its observance and none of our citizens would do anything to encourage, incite, or inflame disputes.

[16.] Q. Mr. President, I don't mean for this question to be facetious, but in your prescription for a Vice Presidential running mate, were you thinking of an ideal, or did you have some living person in mind?

THE PRESIDENT. No, I don't have any prescription. I was attempting to be helpful and courteous to one of the questioners who wondered what are the things that you would consider in evaluating the type of person you thought you would like to be associated with on the ticket. I had prepared no brief on the subject. I tried to be open and frank about it. But I do not want to set standards for anybody else, but just some of the things that have come to my mind in talking about it.

I have had many conferences with many people who, like you, have interest as to who that person will be. I am very proud that they do have an interest. I am very happy that we have gotten away from the feeling that John Adams had about the frustrations that accompanied the Vice Presidency. I see so many people today who just a few months ago were talking about what was happening to Lyndon Johnson. I read some of those articles with people coming from downtown up to the Hill to get information on it.

I am glad that you have a renewed interest in the Vice President, and a great concern about his equipment and his qualifications, and that you have moved along past John Adams' comment to a more fertile field and a more modern base. I better stop here.

Q. Mr. President, may I go back a moment to the question of the Vice Presidency? You made a remark that sounds significant.

THE PRESIDENT. I did not intend for it to be.

Q. That is it. The question is whether you meant it to sound significant.

THE PRESIDENT. Well, it was not.

Q. I understood you to say, Mr. President, that the number two man should be well received in all parts of the United States. I can think of some possibilities, what some men regard as possibilities, who might not be well received in all parts.

THE PRESIDENT. I would think that would apply to all of them. I don't think that anyone that I have ever heard mentioned would be perfectly received everywhere. There is no significance whatever. It applies to every person. For instance, we are really in the minority party in this century, the Democrats. We have had several million less votes cast for Democrats than for Republicans. I don't imagine any of them mentioned for the Vice Presidency would be well received in some of these Republican precincts—wherever they may be—or other sections. That has no significance of any kind. It must not have.

I have made no decision. I have told you that. There are still many people that are being considered. Whoever is selected, I would hope would be well regarded, at least by some people.

Q. You have saved me from "experting" on something, Mr. President. Thank you.

Alvin A. Spivak, United Press International: Thank you, Mr. President.

NOTE: President Johnson's twenty-fourth news conference was held in his office at the White House at 12:05 p.m. on Thursday, July 30, 1964.

487   Remarks Upon Presenting the Distinguished Service Medal to General McKee.   *July 30, 1964*

General McKee, and members of your family, Secretary McNamara, members of the Defense Department, Senator Symington, Members of the Congress who are responsible for the defense of the Nation, Chairman Vinson, ladies and gentlemen:

This is a kind of ceremony that I enjoy. We are not here to say goodby. We are here to say, "Well done on your first career, General McKee; and good luck on your second career, General McKee."

For 35 years General McKee has written a record as one of America's most distinguished officers. He is that rarest and most valuable of men, a genuinely good manager. He has made our resources stretch further and our dollars buy more, and our strength have more meaning and effect. I know him, and Members of Congress know him, and his fellow officers know him, as one of the chief architects of the modern Air Force.

He has earned all that a grateful Nation can bestow upon him, except one thing—retirement. I was pleased to announce earlier that his services will not be lost. The General will become Assistant Administrator for Management of our Space Agency, and America will be the beneficiary.

Since time began, all men have honored the courage of those who have faced death, and now in our times we honor no less the courage of those who help us face life, and all of life's changes. The test of courage for citizens of this age is not how fast we hold the past, but how unflinchingly we face up to the future. General McKee has faced a lifetime of change without ever flinching.

Born 1 year after the first aircraft flew at Kitty Hawk 852 feet in 59 seconds, today he leaves the Air Force with this country building an aircraft to fly at more than 80,000 feet, more than 2,000 miles per hour. Over this span, this officer's courage in challenging old concepts and testing new concepts must have given men like Tooey Spaatz of the military, and Stu Symington, both of whom are adventuresome fellows, a great deal of pride, because he has helped us build, and he has helped us organize, and he has helped us maintain the world's greatest air arm which has preserved peace through all these years.

His good management has helped us control events instead of allowing events to control us. We honor him for that. We look to him for more such leadership in new duties.

One day recently, some of us here were going over General McKee's record. I asked, I believe, Secretary McNamara, to look up what the General's father used to do. Punctual as always, brief as always, accurate as always, Secretary McNamara came back and he said, "Used to do? Why, the General's father is only 91 years old and he is still practicing medicine!"

Well, on that basis, the way I calculate it, some other President may have the General around here in 1990 to present him another award for his civilian career. Then I guess he will have truly earned retirement.

So today, on behalf of a grateful Nation, I am proud and I am privileged to present to this most valuable American his third Distinguished Service Medal. Our beloved Secretary of Defense will now read the citation. Mr. McNamara.

[*Following the reading of the citation by Secretary McNamara, the President resumed speaking.*]

One thing that I learned about the General, and I promised the new Chairman of the Armed Services Committee, Chairman Rivers, of the House, and Chairman Stennis, that I would keep as classified information at least until he retired, his nickname and I have not divulged that. But from now on, we can start calling him "Bozo."

NOTE: The President spoke at 1 p.m. in the Rose Garden at the White House. In his opening words he referred to General William F. McKee, retiring Vice Chief of Staff of the Air Force, Secretary of

Defense Robert S. McNamara, Senator Stuart Symington of Missouri, and Representative Carl Vinson of Georgia, Chairman of the House Armed Services Committee. Later he referred to Gen. Carl (Tooey) Spaatz (USAF, retired), Representative L. Mendel Rivers of South Carolina, and Senator John Stennis of Mississippi.

Following the President's remarks, General McKee responded briefly. The text of his remarks was also released.

General McKee served as Vice Chief of Staff of the Air Force from August 1, 1962, to July 31, 1964.

488   Remarks to a Group of State and Local School Officials. *July 30, 1964*

Mr. Secretary, ladies and gentlemen:

The honor is mine to meet with you today.

This house is your house. This office is your office.

The trust I bear is a trust you share. You and I are servants of the American people. Together, we are trustees of the American promise.

That is why I have asked you here today.

The American promise has never been so great. We are prosperous. We are strong. We live in peace. The roots of freedom run deep in our society's soul.

By every measure—and in every view—we have our greatest works yet to do.

This moment we hold must not be lost. This is the call—this is the challenge—to all who are leaders in America today. Other generations, in other times, have been summoned to serve their communities by answering the call of our Nation. Our generation, in these times, is summoned to serve our Nation by answering the call of our communities.

The challenges of our society are no longer far away.

The cures for our society can no longer come from far away.

What America is to be for our children will be decided and be determined by how we work—by what we do—by where we live today.

I know that you know this.

If I had continued on the course I first began in life, I might be sitting where you sit now—as one of you. If I have an understanding of the work and the worries and the wishes of any Americans, I believe I understand what you face each day in your offices of trust and responsibility.

That is why I say to you that no Americans have an opportunity—or an obligation—so great as yours now to serve and to help us shape the future of our country.

We are what we are in this land of ours—and what we have become in the rest of the world—because we have placed our faith as a nation in public education.

Onto my desk each day come the problems of 190 million men and women. When we consider those problems, when we study them, when we analyze them, when we evaluate what can be done, the answer almost always comes down to one word: education.

This is true for economic problems, this is true for social problems. This is true for the challenges of peace as well as for the challenges of preparedness.

The simple and sure truth of our times is that America in this decade must enlarge, must broaden, must deepen its commitment to the classroom as the central core of our society and of our success.

I am proud, and I am deeply gratified, that the record of the 88th Congress clearly confirms that just such a commitment is being made by the American people.

This Congress has set in motion what I believe are the grandest measures for American education of any Congress in all of our history.

When you begin your school year this fall, you will have support America's educators have never had before, support to help your systems, support to serve your communities. Because in the past year, this education Congress has passed legislation:

—for vocational and technical education
—for higher education facilities
—for teaching handicapped children
—for preventing juvenile delinquency
—for medical education
—for public community libraries
—for college libraries
—for graduate schools
—for technical institutes
—for public community colleges
—for student college loans
—for guidance and counseling and training
—for science and mathematics and foreign language instruction
—for schools in federally-impacted areas
—for educational media
—for educational research
—for manpower development and retraining.

And there are still being debated before the Congress:

—the antipoverty bill; its major objectives are for education,

—the nurse training act,
—the extension and expansion of the National Defense Education Act, and,
—the extension and expansion of the Vocational Rehabilitation Act.

I believe that this Congress has truly earned from you—and from the Nation— a long round of applause. And let's give it to them!

These measures and this activity represent what I believe is a new maturity among Americans.

We cherish our liberty.

We are jealous of our freedom.

We resent—and we would resist—inroads upon either from an all-powerful central government.

But we have come to one profound realization today.

The greatest guardian against centralization of power is the diffusion of knowledge throughout the world—and particularly to our own people.

Men who neglect their schools neglect their liberty.

The challenge of our times is to end the neglect of all on which our society stands— our classrooms, our cities, our countryside, and our family fireside.

I am conscious—and I know you are— of how much greater is the responsibility imposed upon our schools today than when my own teaching career began 35 years ago.

Our schools are bearing many burdens that were once borne only within the family home. Upon you and upon the teachers of America rests today the responsibility of passing to tomorrow's leaders the values and the standards by which America has been led in all of her past.

The soul of our society is in your hands this year.

This same Congress which has reaffirmed

America's faith in education has also re-affirmed—before the world—America's fidelity to the rights of man.

After 100 years the ugly cloud of division has been rolled away from America's horizon—and a brighter future beckons to us than any generation has ever known.

This is the moment that we must not lose.

This is a moment when the best in America must rise up to put down the worst in the nature of man. This is a moment when America seeks—when America needs—when America will receive the best from those who are America's real leaders.

I will say to you what I said last week to the leaders of business in this country and the captains of industry and the leaders of labor.

As President of all the people, I intend to work to ensure that every human being enjoys the full constitutional rights and equal opportunity that are his birthright as an American citizen.

I intend to use all the resources that I have to make sure those who claim rights—and those who deny them—bend their passions to peaceful obedience of the law of the land.

No man could attain a higher honor than to occupy this office I now hold. No man would be worthy of that honor who thought of self. No man would be worthy who thought of any success except America's success.

That is the only thought I have in this house today.

If the man who lives in this house is not free to stand for right, no man in any house in America is free from the injury of wrong.

The task before our Nation in this hour—the challenge before our system and our so-ciety—cannot be met by the man in the White House alone, whoever he may be.

I need your help—I need the help of every American.

You are leaders from every State in the Union. I ask you to exercise that leadership in every State in the Union.

You are respected in your communities. You are looked up to and emulated by those who must lead America tomorrow. Your respect for law and order—your respect for human rights—will live long after you in the lives of those who look to your example now.

This is a great and golden moment for America—a moment to lay aside the burdens of the past, a moment to look forward and to move ahead.

As your President, I wanted you to come here and talk to your servants, to exchange viewpoints, to share ideas, to determine how we can close ranks to prevent our society from being divided, to keep our brothers from being separated, and to keep our Nation united.

I trust to your leadership to help us hold that course.

I hope your deliberations are successful. I am going to leave you to the tender mercies of some of the men who work for you. And I leave with the thought, that because of your visit, America will be stronger tomorrow than it is today. And that is the purpose and the objective of all who really care.

Thank you very much.

NOTE: The President spoke in the late afternoon in the East Room at the White House. His opening words referred to Secretary of Health, Education, and Welfare Anthony J. Celebrezze.

Attending the reception were more than 300 public school superintendents and other State and local school officials.

489   Statement by the President Relating to the Selection of a Vice Presidential Candidate. *July 30, 1964*

IN REFERENCE to the selection of a candidate for Vice President on the Democratic ticket, I have reached the conclusion that it would be inadvisable for me to recommend to the convention any member of the Cabinet or any of those who meet regularly with the Cabinet. In this regard, because their names have been mentioned in the press, I have personally informed the Secretary of State, Mr. Rusk; the Secretary of Defense, Mr. McNamara; the Attorney General, Mr. Kennedy; the Secretary of Agriculture, Mr. Freeman, of my decision.

I have communicated this to the United States Ambassador to the United Nations, Mr. Stevenson, and the head of the Peace Corps, Mr. Shriver. In this manner, the list has been considerably narrowed. I shall continue to give the most thoughtful consideration to the choice of the man that I will recommend to the convention and I shall make my decision known in due course.

NOTE: The President read the statement shortly after 6 p.m. to reporters in the Fish Room at the White House.

490   Statement by the President on Receiving a Progress Report of the Council on Physical Fitness. *July 30, 1964*

THE FITNESS of our Nation for the tasks of our times can never be greater than the general physical fitness of our citizens. A people proud of their collective heritage will take pride in their individual health, because we cannot stay strong as a country if we go soft as citizens.

In the past few years there has been a wholesome and welcome reawakening of pride and self-respect among us about our individual fitness. Our greater leisure is not leading to a greater lethargy—and this is reassuring. A nation cannot be both a leader and lazy.

The progress report of the President's Council on Physical Fitness shows impressively that America's abundance is not encouraging apathy and our self-sufficiency is not breeding self-indulgence.

Since the Council's program began 3 years ago under the inspiration of President Kennedy, there has been remarkable response and imposing progress toward instilling in

our youth the good habits of physical fitness.

—Nine million more pupils in grades 4–12 took part in school physical activity programs in the last school year than in 1961–62.

—Eight out of 10 of our 31 million school children in the primary and secondary grades participated in physical activity programs during the 1963–64 school year.

—Three years ago less than half (47 percent) of our high school juniors and seniors participated in school physical activity programs. In 1963–64 the level of participation reached 84 percent.

—Since the beginning of the Council's efforts, 68 percent of the Nation's schools have strengthened their physical activity programs. Seventeen States have raised their physical education requirements. Twelve States have improved the criteria for accrediting health and physical education.

—Interest in personal and home exercise

programs is rising. Since publication on August 22, 1963, more than 385,000 copies of the Council's home exercise plan have been purchased, and orders average 5,000 per week at present.

These are solid and substantial gains. The cooperation of the States and local school districts is most encouraging and reflects the growing awareness of this key responsibility.

We have more to do. One out of seven school children do not participate in any physical activity program. Another 27 percent take part only once or twice a week. I believe that interested and responsible parents should and will work with their local schools to strengthen physical activity programs.

In all our communities we ought to come to grips with the challenge of increasing the use and availability of the recreation facilities of our schools—for more hours each day, more days each year, for more members of the families in the neighborhood.

Our Nation pays a tangible and measurable price each year for neglect of the fitness of our people, young and old. I would hope that in the year ahead at least one of our civic organizations in each city and community will dedicate its effort to constructive leadership for fitness. Our minimum goal should certainly be 100 percent participation by our school children in physical activity programs during the 1964-65 school year.

In his new role Stan Musial is starring once again and the country can be grateful for the leadership he is offering.

NOTE: The statement is part of a White House release making public a progress report of the President's Council on Physical Fitness dated July 10, 1964 (11 pp. processed).

In closing his remarks the President referred to Stan Musial, Consultant to the President on Physical Fitness.

491   Remarks Upon Signing a Proclamation to Commemorate the 20th Anniversary of the Warsaw Uprising. *July 31, 1964*

Friends:

I want to say to each of you, and especially to the Members of Congress who have indulged me, that I regret very much I have been delayed. I had about 50 newspapermen in my office and I couldn't evict them as quickly as I should have, perhaps, but I thank you for your understanding and for your tolerance and I hope you didn't get too hot.

There are some compensating advantages. Maybe the sunburn will make you look better.

In any event, this is a very special occasion for me and I want to genuinely extend to you a warm welcome as a participant in this historic occasion. I want to thank you for coming. I want to review with you some of my thoughts, very briefly.

Twenty years ago tomorrow, in the city of Warsaw, there occurred a demonstration of human courage that the world will never forget. The courageous people of a captive city challenged the chains of their captors. Three hours after the start of what is known as "Operation Tempest," the flag of the Polish Republic was flying in the heart of Warsaw, for the first time in 5 years. For 63 days proud Poles fought to liberate their beloved capital from the occupying army.

On October 2, 1944, a decision to cease the valiant fight was dictated and required by lack of food, a lack of water, a lack of ammunition, and a desire to save the remaining civilian population from systematic destruction. Eighty percent of Warsaw had been destroyed. Twenty thousand Polish soldiers had been killed, or seriously wounded. The toll among civilians was too high to even count.

But as the Polish forces marched past on that final day, the citizens in the streets sang to them, "Poland is not yet lost, while we still live." We, in America, know that kind of spirit well. It attended us at the birth of our Nation. We have seen it shine from the Polish character time and time again. We see it, again, now in Warsaw rebuilt from the ashes and the rubble.

We see it in the steadfast faith of the Polish people. We see it gratefully in our fellow citizens of Polish ancestry and I visited only a few months ago in Chicago with hundreds of thousands of them. They live among us now as patriots of the cause of freedom for all mankind. The congressional district from which I come is inhabited by hundreds and thousands of people of Polish ancestry.

So, we know the Polish spirit well. We know the unswerving dedication of the Polish people to the goals of liberty and equality and independence. That is why our policy is designed to help the Polish

people so they may increasingly help themselves. We have done much toward this goal in many fields.

Today all Americans are proud to join with the Poles of Poland, the Poles abroad, and the Polish-Americans to commemorate the 20th anniversary of the Warsaw Uprising. We repeat with them now the motto of the Polish struggle for independence: For Your Freedom and Ours.

I want to acknowledge the presence in our audience this morning of the former Commander in Chief of the Underground, General Tadeusz Bor-Komorowski, from Warsaw.

And now it is my pleasure to present the President of the Polish-American Congress, Mr. Charles Rozmarek.

NOTE: The President spoke at noon in the Rose Garden at the White House. Following Mr. Rozmarek's remarks the President read and signed a proclamation which proclaimed August 1, 1964, as Warsaw Uprising Day (Proclamation 3603, 29 F.R. 11255; 3 CFR 1964 Supp.).

Included in the group were representatives of Polish-American organizations and presidents of Polish-American fraternal societies. Other Americans of Polish ancestry attending the reception included Government officials, Congressmen, veterans of military units who served during World War II, editors of Polish-American newspapers, and representatives of State legislatures.

492   Statement by the President Upon the Successful Flight of Ranger VII. *July 31, 1964*

ON BEHALF of the whole country, I want to congratulate you and those associated with you in NASA and the Jet Propulsion Laboratory and in the industrial laboratories. All of you have contributed the skills to make this Ranger VII flight the great success that it is. We are proud of the tremendous technical achievement which this successful flight represents.

This is a basic step forward in our orderly program to assemble the scientific knowledge necessary for man's trip to the moon.

The pictures obtained of the lunar surface should prove extremely useful. They will be a guide in constructing the lunar excursion module and in planning the trip. We shall now be able to better map out our descent route. We'll be able to build our lunar landing equipment with greater certainty and knowledge of the conditions which our astronauts will encounter on the moon.

I recognize that this great success has come only after a number of failures and partial failures in our efforts to send probes to the moon. This success should spur us on to added effort in the future.

The fact that our Soviet competitors have had many unpublicized failures to the moon

and the planets also confirms the complexity of today's success.

On behalf of a grateful Nation let me again congratulate you on this magnificent achievement. All of you today have helped further the peaceful exploration of space.

NOTE: The President read this statement during a telephone conversation with Dr. William H. Pickering, Director of the Jet Propulsion Laboratory, Pasadena, Calif., and Dr. Homer E. Newell, Associate Administrator for Space Science and Application, National Aeronautics and Space Administration.

493 Remarks Following a Briefing With Space Scientists on the Successful Flight to the Moon. *August 1, 1964*

I WANT to say that all Americans are very proud of you today. We are proud of this historic extension of man's knowledge. We are proud of our scientists, and our engineers, and all the great team, under the leadership of one of the greatest of all Americans, Jim Webb, who are responsible for this success. We can be duly proud of our free and open society, our system of government.

We started behind in space. We were making many apologies just a few years ago. We had our failures, but we kept our faith in the ways of freedom, and we did not follow the easy or the inexpensive course.

We know this morning that the United States has achieved fully the leadership we have sought for free men. But we do not claim this as an American triumph alone. In the brief period of time that I have occupied the office of the Presidency, I have visited with the leaders of many countries, more than 25 and less than 50, some 30 of them, big countries and small countries, densely populated peoples, sparsely populated regions, but I have found a deep and exciting interest among all these leaders in cooperating with us and extending their

hands to us to supplement the work that we are doing.

I thank them for their tracking stations. I thank them for their joint participation with us. We have considered this adventure a truly peace weapon, rather than a military might.

I think we can say this morning that this is a victory for peaceful civilian international cooperation in this hour of frustration, when so many people are getting upset at some minor disappointments.

I think we can all take great pride in this development. More than 60 countries all around the world work for us and work for peaceful progress and work for peaceful uses of outer space. It is good to learn from this event that we are on the right course.

We know that if we can continue on that course, and if you great scientists, most of whom know no party and no political allegiance, who are concerned with freedom first and America second—if we continue to give you support without any tinge of partisanship, you will give us the leadership and ultimately the supremacy in an area that is essential to the prolongation of civilization itself.

If we could only supplant the fear and the hate, the bitterness and the division, the poison and the venom that our fellow man contains, with the hope and the optimism and the achievements represented by this venture here, how much better our world will be for ourselves, our children, and our grandchildren.

I want to say this in conclusion. In this century in which we live, all my life we have been either preparing for war or fighting a war or protecting ourselves from war. When I grew up as a kid, one of my first real memories was hearing the powder go off on an anvil on Armistice Day.

I remember the terror that flowed from the sinking of the *Lusitania*. I remember seeing the boys come marching home, and the welcome we gave them at our little schoolhouse. I remember leaving, the day after I voted, to go to Pearl Harbor and crossing the Pacific, and later the Atlantic, and all the men who gave their lives that we could win World War II.

I have seen the billions and billions of dollars that we have spent in the 17 years since that war to protect Western civilization. Now I think it is the most powerful Nation in the world, and I would remind you that we spent $30 billion more in the last 4 years on defense alone than was being spent 4 years ago.

We were spending about $42 billion a year then, and we are spending $51 billion now. So $7.5 billion extra a year for 4 years is $30 billion. That has bought a good many more missiles, and that has bought a good many more combat-fit men. That has bought a good many more antisubmarine weapons, and it has bought a great deal more research.

But now, today, as the most powerful nation in the world, why do we have satisfaction from that? Not just because it protects our scalps and allows us to sleep at night knowing that we are safe, but (2) it gives us the opportunity to enjoy the fruits of this society and to develop this land, not just with parks and recreational areas, highways and swimming pools, things of that kind, but all the blessings that are going to flow from these scientific discoveries and achievements.

Hundreds of lives, millions of dollars were saved in Hurricane Carla in my State alone because they gave them hours of advance notice to get ready: "This is coming, and your lives will be snuffed out if you don't get out of the way." They rode bumper to bumper for dozens of miles getting out of there, 48 hours before it hit. That is what it means to you and to your neighbors.

These men don't wear a DSM this morning, and we are not presenting them any Congressional Medal of Honor. But they do have—they and all of their associates from Mr. Webb down to the fellow who sweeps out the dust in the remote test laboratory, deserve the gratitude and the admiration of all Americans of all faiths, of all parties, of all regions.

You are welcome to the White House. The people who live here are mighty proud of you.

NOTE: The President spoke at 10 o'clock in the Cabinet Room at the White House. Among those present for the briefing were Donald F. Hornig, Special Assistant to the President for Science and Technology, and the following officials of the National Aeronautics and Space Administration: James E. Webb, Administrator, Homer E. Newell, Associate Administrator for Space Science and Application, and William H. Pickering, Director of the Jet Propulsion Laboratory, Pasadena, Calif.

494 Statement by the President in Response to a Request for Mediation in the Shipping Industry Negotiations. *August 1, 1964*

I HAVE been advised by Secretary of Labor W. Willard Wirtz that both the New York Shipping Association and the International Longshoremen's Association, AFL–CIO, have jointly requested the appointment of a board of neutrals to assist them in their current contract negotiations. Secretary Wirtz has been instructed by me to respond to this joint and voluntary request of the parties.

NOTE: The current contracts in the maritime industry, negotiated after a long strike in 1962–3 (see 1962 volume, this series, Items 421, 428; 1963 volume, Item 18) would expire on September 30, 1964. On that date, voluntary attempts at mediation having failed, the President issued Executive Order 11181 (29 F.R. 13557; 3 CFR, 1964 Supp.) creating a board of inquiry under the Taft-Hartley Act.

See also Item 614.

495 Letter to Manlio Brosio on His Appointment as Secretary General of NATO. *August 1, 1964*

Dear Mr. Secretary General:

I extend my warm congratulations on the occasion of your assumption of duties as Secretary General of NATO. I have long admired the dedication and wisdom of your predecessors and am confident that with your appointment, the North Atlantic Organization is assured of continued wise and imaginative leadership.

Since the North Atlantic Treaty was signed some 15 years ago, NATO not only has proved to be a defensive military Alliance sufficiently strong to deter aggression but it has also provided a most effective forum for political discussion and consultation between the member governments. Indeed it has encouraged all of us to think in terms of mutual assistance and interdependence. And I assure you that in your efforts to strengthen the Alliance you will always be able to depend upon the fullest support and cooperation by the United States.

Sincerely,

LYNDON B. JOHNSON

[His Excellency Manlio Brosio, Secretary General, North Atlantic Treaty Organization, Paris, France]

NOTE: Manlio Brosio, of Italy, succeeded Dirk U. Stikker of the Netherlands, who served as Secretary General of NATO from April 21, 1961, to August 1, 1964.

496 Remarks to Foreign Language Newspaper Publishers on Their Role in Building American Unity. *August 3, 1964*

THIS IS your House—the House of all the people.

I am honored to welcome you here—as free men and fellow Americans.

Your publications represent one of the most American of all our American institutions.

Four hundred newspapers and magazines—published in 30 languages other than English—reach into more than five million American homes.

You and your predecessors have done much to unify us, to bring us together—as one people and one Nation.

That is why I have asked you here today.

This is a great hour in our national history.

We have come far together.

We have the opportunity to move far ahead.

That opportunity must not be lost.

This is your challenge—and mine.

America's leadership at every level is called now to work for America's unity—and to work against America's division.

This is not new work.

This is our oldest work.

This is the work we must always put first—if we are to keep faith with those who have come to these shores from across the seas.

Forty-three million have come—from 70 lands.

They have brought much to us.

They have found much for themselves—and their heirs.

But—for every group—the difference has been made by the American will and work for unity.

Unity closed the doors of sweatshops and opened the doors of opportunity.

Unity shut down the slums of the early century and opened the suburbs of the mid-century.

Unity said "No" to second-class citizenship and said "Yes" to one-class citizenship for all our people—without regard to origins or ancestry, flag or faith, religion or race.

Unity still is—and unity will always be—the genius of our greatness.

That is why we must work today to perfect our unity.

A divided America cannot be a prosperous America—or a peaceful America—or a progressive America. A divided America cannot fulfill its promise at home—or accomplish its purposes abroad.

On each of us, rests a great trust.

Around the world, men who love freedom look to this land for the will and the wisdom to win the victory of this century for freedom.

If we are to fulfill that trust, we must hold our course.

We must work—with high resolve and high responsibility—for the unity of our society, the prosperity of our people, the honorable and just peace of men everywhere under freedom.

Our forefathers left the lands of their birth because cries for justice fell upon deaf ears—cries for peace fell upon closed and willful minds—cries for opportunity fell upon stony hearts.

We do not want to turn back toward what we left behind.

That is why we move with confidence, with courage and with compassion to perfect our unity—to overcome our divisions—to fulfill the great promise of this hour in American history.

And that is why I have asked you here.

The challenge of unifying America—of holding our land on a straight and sure course of success—cannot be met by the man in the White House alone.

I need your help—and the help of every American.

I will say to you what I have said to leaders of every sector of American life—business and labor and education.

As President of all the people, I intend to work to ensure that every person enjoys the full constitutional rights and equal opportunity that are his birthright as an American citizen.

I intend to use all the resources I have to make sure those who claim rights—and those who deny them—bend their passions to peaceful obedience of the law of the land.

But there is more work—there is other

work—we must continue to do.

Beyond this moment, beyond this hour, beyond this year, we must work for a better America—for all Americans.

We must work against poverty—and against prejudice.

We must work for more and better jobs, better schools, better cities, better neighborhoods, better futures for our young and our old alike.

This is the work we must always do.

This is the work that will fulfill the dreams of those who have chosen to come and live in our land—and contribute their great talents to the success of the American ideal.

This is the work we can only do in unity and in peace.

Standing here—talking with you—I am very proud of America and what our unity has wrought for us.

Your presence here has a special meaning for me.

Thirty years ago, I began my public life in a district where families had come from many lands to find peace—and freedom.

Newspapers were published there in seven or eight languages. My neighbors then spoke—and still speak—the tongues of many ancestries.

What I know of the mind and heart of such Americans, I knew long before coming here. No memory of my boyhood is more vivid than the memory of my father's own example.

In a time when emotions ran strong—when some sought to turn upon those from other lands—my father served in the legislature.

There he took his stand—to say "No."

No, you shall not deny the children of these Americans access to our public schools. No, you shall not discriminate against these Americans because of their ancestry. No, you shall not reduce them to second-class citizenship.

My father stood alone at first. But he stood steadfastly.

In the end, his courage and his compassion prevailed.

In this house—in the task that is mine now for all Americans—I pray to be worthy as his son, to stand as he stood for the rights, the dignity, the honor of all Americans.

The challenge is great—but it is not mine alone.

It is your challenge, too.

You are respected in your communities—by those you serve. Your example is the example others will follow. Your effort is effort others will emulate.

Your respect for law and order—your respect for human rights—will live long after you in the lives of those who look to your leadership today.

This is a great moment for America—an hour of great opportunity. It is a moment to unite—and in that unity move ahead together to win the victory for freedom and justice throughout the world.

NOTE: The President spoke in the late afternoon in the East Room at the White House.

As printed, this item follows the prepared text released by the White House.

497 Statement by the President Upon Instructing the Navy To Take Retaliatory Action in the Gulf of Tonkin. *August 3, 1964*

I HAVE instructed the Navy

(1) to continue the patrols in the Gulf of Tonkin off the coast of North Viet-Nam,

(2) to double the force by adding an additional destroyer to the one already on patrol,

(3) to provide a combat air patrol over the destroyers, and

(4) to issue orders to the commanders of the combat aircraft and the two destroyers (a) to attack any force which attacks them in international waters, and (b) to attack with

the objective not only of driving off the force but of destroying it.

NOTE: The statement was issued following an attack on the U.S. destroyer *Maddox* by Communist PT boats as it patrolled the Gulf of Tonkin. See also Items 498, 499.

498   Radio and Television Report to the American People Following Renewed Aggression in the Gulf of Tonkin.   *August* 4, 1964

[Delivered from the Fish Room at the White House at 11:36 p.m., e.d.t.]

My fellow Americans:

As President and Commander in Chief, it is my duty to the American people to report that renewed hostile actions against United States ships on the high seas in the Gulf of Tonkin have today required me to order the military forces of the United States to take action in reply.

The initial attack on the destroyer *Maddox,* on August 2, was repeated today by a number of hostile vessels attacking two U.S. destroyers with torpedoes. The destroyers and supporting aircraft acted at once on the orders I gave after the initial act of aggression. We believe at least two of the attacking boats were sunk. There were no U.S. losses.

The performance of commanders and crews in this engagement is in the highest tradition of the United States Navy. But repeated acts of violence against the Armed Forces of the United States must be met not only with alert defense, but with positive reply. That reply is being given as I speak to you tonight. Air action is now in execution against gunboats and certain supporting facilities in North Viet-Nam which have been used in these hostile operations.

In the larger sense this new act of aggression, aimed directly at our own forces, again brings home to all of us in the United States the importance of the struggle for peace and security in southeast Asia. Aggression by terror against the peaceful villagers of South Viet-Nam has now been joined by open aggression on the high seas against the United States of America.

The determination of all Americans to carry out our full commitment to the people and to the government of South Viet-Nam will be redoubled by this outrage. Yet our response, for the present, will be limited and fitting. We Americans know, although others appear to forget, the risks of spreading conflict. We still seek no wider war.

I have instructed the Secretary of State to make this position totally clear to friends and to adversaries and, indeed, to all. I have instructed Ambassador Stevenson to raise this matter immediately and urgently before the Security Council of the United Nations. Finally, I have today met with the leaders of both parties in the Congress of the United States and I have informed them that I shall immediately request the Congress to pass a resolution making it clear that our Government is united in its determination to take all necessary measures in support of freedom and in defense of peace in southeast Asia.

I have been given encouraging assurance by these leaders of both parties that such a resolution will be promptly introduced, freely and expeditiously debated, and passed with overwhelming support. And just a few minutes ago I was able to reach Senator Goldwater and I am glad to say that he has expressed his support of the statement that I am making to you tonight.

It is a solemn responsibility to have to order even limited military action by forces whose overall strength is as vast and as awesome as those of the United States of America, but it is my considered conviction, shared throughout your Government, that firmness in the right is indispensable today for peace; that firmness will always be measured. Its mission is peace.

NOTE: The President began speaking at 11:36 p.m., eastern daylight time.

For the President's special message to Congress, see Item 500. For his remarks upon signing the joint resolution in support of freedom and in defense of peace in southeast Asia see Item 507.

499 Remarks at Syracuse University on the Communist Challenge in Southeast Asia. *August 5, 1964*

Dr. Newhouse, Chancellor Tolley, Governor and Mrs. Rockefeller, Members of the Congress, distinguished guests, members of the faculty, ladies and gentlemen:

I know that you share with me the great admiration and pride that the generosity of Dr. Newhouse has made possible for this area of our Nation and for this great institution. We all are in his debt, and in the years and generations and centuries to come, we will see the products of this great adventure.

On this occasion, it is fitting, I think, that we are meeting here to dedicate this new center to better understanding among all men. For that is my purpose in speaking to you.

Last night I spoke to the people of the Nation.

This morning, I speak to the people of all nations—so that they may understand without mistake our purpose in the action that we have been required to take.

On August 2 the United States destroyer *Maddox* was attacked on the high seas in the Gulf of Tonkin by hostile vessels of the Government of North Viet-Nam.

On August 4 that attack was repeated in those same waters against two United States destroyers.

The attacks were deliberate.

The attacks were unprovoked.

The attacks have been answered.

Throughout last night and within the last 12 hours, air units of the United States Seventh Fleet have sought out the hostile vessels and certain of their supporting facilities. Appropriate armed action has been taken against them. The United States is now asking that this be brought immediately and urgently before the Security Council of the United Nations.

We welcome—and we invite—the scrutiny of all men who seek peace, for peace is the only purpose of the course that America pursues.

The Gulf of Tonkin may be distant, but none can be detached about what has happened there.

Aggression—deliberate, willful, and systematic aggression—has unmasked its face to the entire world. The world remembers—the world must never forget—that aggression unchallenged is aggression unleashed.

We of the United States have not forgotten.

That is why we have answered this aggression with action.

America's course is not precipitate.

America's course is not without long provocation.

For 10 years three American Presidents—President Eisenhower, President Kennedy, and your present President—and the American people have been actively concerned with threats to the peace and security of the peoples of southeast Asia from the Communist government of North Viet-Nam.

President Eisenhower sought—and President Kennedy sought—the same objectives that I still seek:

That the governments of southeast Asia honor the international agreements which apply in the area;

That those governments leave each other alone;

That they resolve their differences peacefully;

That they devote their talents to bettering the lives of their peoples by working against poverty and disease and ignorance.

In 1954 we made our position clear toward Viet-Nam.

In June of that year we stated we "would view any renewal of the aggression in violation of the 1954 agreements with grave concern and as seriously threatening international peace and security."

In September of that year the United States signed the Manila pact on which our participation in SEATO is based. That pact recognized that aggression by means of armed attack on South Viet-Nam would endanger the peace and the safety of the nations signing that solemn agreement.

In 1962 we made our position clear toward Laos. We signed the Declaration of Neutrality of Laos. That accord provided for the withdrawal of all foreign forces and respect for the neutrality and independence of that little country.

The agreements of 1954 and 1962 were also signed by the government of North Viet-Nam.

In 1954 that government pledged that it would respect the territory under the military control of the other party and engage in no hostile act against the other party.

In 1962 that government pledged that it would "not introduce into the Kingdom of Laos foreign troops or military personnel."

That government also pledged that it would "not use the territory of the Kingdom of Laos for interference in the internal affairs of other countries."

That government of North Viet-Nam is now willfully and systematically violating those agreements of both 1954 and 1962.

To the south it is engaged in aggression against the Republic of Viet-Nam.

To the west it is engaged in aggression against the Kingdom of Laos.

To the east it has now struck out on the high seas in an act of aggression against the United States of America.

There can be, there must be no doubt about the policy and no doubt about the purpose.

So there can be no doubt about the responsibilities of men and the responsibilities of nations that are devoted to peace.

Peace cannot be assured merely by assuring the safety of the United States destroyer *Maddox* or the safety of other vessels of other flags.

Peace requires that the existing agreements in the area be honored.

Peace requires that we and all our friends stand firm against the present aggressions of the government of North Viet-Nam.

The government of North Viet-Nam is today flouting the will of the world for peace. The world is challenged to make its will against war known and to make it known

929

clearly and to make it felt and to make it felt decisively.

So, to our friends of the Atlantic Alliance, let me say this, this morning: the challenge that we face in southeast Asia today is the same challenge that we have faced with courage and that we have met with strength in Greece and Turkey, in Berlin and Korea, in Lebanon and in Cuba. And to any who may be tempted to support or to widen the present aggression I say this: there is no threat to any peaceful power from the United States of America. But there can be no peace by aggression and no immunity from reply. That is what is meant by the actions that we took yesterday.

Finally, my fellow Americans, I would like to say to ally and adversary alike: let no friend needlessly fear—and no foe vainly hope—that this is a nation divided in this election year. Our free elections—our full and free debate—are America's strength, not America's weakness.

There are no parties and there is no partisanship when our peace or the peace of the world is imperiled by aggressors in any part of the world.

We are one nation united and indivisible. And united and indivisible we shall remain.

NOTE: The President spoke at the dedication of the new journalism building, the first unit of the Newhouse Communications Center to be constructed at Syracuse University. In his opening words he referred to Dr. Samuel I. Newhouse, owner and publisher of a chain of newspapers, Dr. William P. Tolley, chancellor of the University, and Governor and Mrs. Nelson A. Rockefeller of New York. The Communications Center is a gift from Dr. and Mrs. Newhouse.

Following his address, the President received an honorary degree of doctor of laws from the University.

500   Special Message to the Congress on U.S. Policy in Southeast Asia.   *August 5, 1964*

To the Congress of the United States:

Last night I announced to the American people that the North Vietnamese regime had conducted further deliberate attacks against US naval vessels operating in international waters, and that I had therefore directed air action against gun boats and supporting facilities used in these hostile operations. This air action has now been carried out with substantial damage to the boats and facilities. Two US aircraft were lost in the action.

After consultation with the leaders of both parties in the Congress, I further announced a decision to ask the Congress for a Resolution expressing the unity and determination of the United States in supporting freedom and in protecting peace in Southeast Asia.

These latest actions of the North Vietnamese regime have given a new and grave turn to the already serious situation in Southeast Asia. Our commitments in that area are well known to the Congress. They were first made in 1954 by President Eisenhower. They were further defined in the Southeast Asia Collective Defense Treaty approved by the Senate in February 1955.

This Treaty with its accompanying protocol obligates the United States and other members to act in accordance with their Constitutional processes to meet Communist aggression against any of the parties or protocol states.

Our policy in Southeast Asia has been consistent and unchanged since 1954. I summarized it on June 2 in four simple propositions:

1. *America keeps her word.* Here as elsewhere, we must and shall honor our commitments.

2. *The issue is the future of Southeast Asia as a whole.* A threat to any nation in that region is a threat to all, and a threat to us.

3. *Our purpose is peace.* We have no military, political or territorial ambitions in the area.

4. *This is not just a jungle war, but a struggle for freedom on every front of human activity.* Our military and economic assistance to South Vietnam and Laos in particular has the purpose of helping these countries to repel aggression and strengthen their independence.

The threat to the free nations of Southeast Asia has long been clear. The North Vietnamese regime has constantly sought to take over South Vietnam and Laos. This Communist regime has violated the Geneva Accords for Vietnam. It has systematically conducted a campaign of subversion, which includes the direction, training, and supply of personnel and arms for the conduct of guerrilla warfare in South Vietnamese territory. In Laos, the North Vietnamese regime has maintained military forces, used Laotian territory for infiltration into South Vietnam, and most recently carried out combat operations—all in direct violation of the Geneva Agreements of 1962.

In recent months, the actions of the North Vietnamese regime have become steadily more threatening. In May, following new acts of Communist aggression in Laos, the United States undertook reconnaissance flights over Laotian territory, at the request of the Government of Laos. These flights had the essential mission of determining the situation in territory where Communist forces were preventing inspection by the International Control Commission. When the Communists attacked these aircraft, I responded by furnishing escort fighters with instructions to fire when fired upon. Thus, these latest North Vietnamese attacks on our naval vessels are not the first direct attack on armed forces of the United States.

As President of the United States I have concluded that I should now ask the Congress, on its part, to join in affirming the national determination that all such attacks will be met, and that the U.S. will continue in its basic policy of assisting the free nations of the area to defend their freedom.

As I have repeatedly made clear, the United States intends no rashness, and seeks no wider war. We must make it clear to all that the United States is united in its determination to bring about the end of Communist subversion and aggression in the area. We seek the full and effective restoration of the international agreements signed in Geneva in 1954, with respect to South Vietnam, and again in Geneva in 1962, with respect to Laos.

I recommend a Resolution expressing the support of the Congress for all necessary action to protect our armed forces and to assist nations covered by the SEATO Treaty. At the same time, I assure the Congress that we shall continue readily to explore any avenues of political solution that will effectively guarantee the removal of Communist subversion and the preservation of the independence of the nations of the area.

The Resolution could well be based upon similar resolutions enacted by the Congress in the past—to meet the threat to Formosa in 1955, to meet the threat to the Middle East in 1957, and to meet the threat in Cuba in 1962. It could state in the simplest terms the resolve and support of the Congress for action to deal appropriately with attacks against our armed forces and to defend freedom and preserve peace in southeast Asia in accordance with the obligations of the United States under the southeast Asia Treaty. I urge the Congress to enact such a Resolution promptly and thus to give convincing evidence to the aggressive Communist nations, and to the world as a whole, that our policy in southeast Asia will be carried forward—and that the peace and security of the area will be preserved.

The events of this week would in any event have made the passage of a Congressional Resolution essential. But there is an additional reason for doing so at a time when we are entering on three months of political campaigning. Hostile nations must understand that in such a period the United States will continue to protect its national interests, and that in these matters there is no division among us.

Lyndon B. Johnson

NOTE: A joint resolution "to promote the maintenance of international peace and security in southeast Asia" was approved by the President on August 10 (see Item 507).

501 Remarks of Welcome at the White House to the Secretary General of the United Nations.   *August 6, 1964*

Mr. Secretary General, Congressman Halleck, Members of the Senate, ladies and gentlemen:

On behalf of the American people, I am very privileged this morning and very proud to welcome you, Mr. Secretary General, to our Capital City.

Our honor today is not honor alone for the office you hold or just the organization that you serve. It is rather an expression of our esteem and our respect for you and for your achievement as the faithful public servant of the entire world.

The world has lived through difficult hours during your tour as Secretary General. Your wise and willing search for reason during those seasons of unreason has served us all well. The people of my country are grateful.

The United Nations lives today as evidence of the wish and the will of men everywhere for peace. That wish and that will runs nowhere stronger in all the world than in the United States of America.

In all that we do, America's purpose is to prevent war and to prevent others from provoking war.

This Nation has acted and this Nation will always act when necessary in self-defense.

Our actions have been and will be consistent with the principles and the purpose of the Charter of the United Nations.

Our Nation has great strength and, with it, a sense of great trust. Our strength supports all men who cherish their independence and stand up for their freedom and respect the rights of others to govern themselves.

Likewise, our strength opposes those who would abridge the independence, those who would breach the peace, those who would violate the rights of other men or other nations.

These convictions are deep in the character of my country, and that is why American Presidents and American Congresses and the American people support and will continue to support the United Nations.

That is why the United States believes in—and the United States works for—a stronger United Nations.

We want a United Nations that is better able to help keep the peace wherever and whenever and by whomever the peace is threatened.

We want a United Nations that is better able to arrive at peaceful solutions, to help settle world problems through negotiation and mediation and conciliation, arbitration, and adjudication.

We want a United Nations that is better able to foster and to expand and to respect the rights of man.

We want a United Nations that is better able to serve as a center for growing co-operation among nations in the sciences and the arts and in all the works of human progress.

Yes, Mr. Secretary General, we want in our country a United Nations that is better able to serve the world community by virtue of being solvent.

We stand ready today as we always have in the past to pay our fair share of the necessary cost. The pledges we make to the support of the United Nations are pledges that we shall keep.

So it makes me very happy this morning to be able to welcome you here to Washington, to the White House, to our Rose Garden where many of the leaders of this Nation have come to greet you and to express their personal welcome.

Our Nation is honored to have you as our guest, and we are so pleased that you can spend the next few hours with us.

NOTE: The President spoke shortly before noon in the Rose Garden at the White House, where Secretary General U Thant was given a formal welcome. The Secretary General responded as follows:

"Mr. President, Mrs. Johnson, Your Excellencies, and friends:

"I am, you may be sure, deeply appreciative of your kindness in asking me to come to Washington at this time.

"I recall most soberly my visit here last fall when all the world shared your Nation's grief at the tragic loss of your highly distinguished predecessor.

Permit me, Mr. President, to mention now the profound admiration I had for the remarkable strength you, Mr. President, demonstrated at that critical juncture which did so much to restore the confidence of a shaken world in this great country.

"I feel that my visit here now is especially fitting and timely since, as you know, I have only just recently completed an extended journey more than halfway around the world.

"During that trip, I had talks with the leaders of three states which are permanent members of the Security Council as well as with a number of heads of African states in Cairo, and with leaders of my own country.

"I am certain that my talks with you and your associates in the United States Government will be equally useful and constructive to the further strengthening of the United Nations so that it may more effectively serve the cause of peace and good neighborliness amongst nations as provided for in the Charter.

"May I express on this occasion the profound gratitude I feel for your Government's long-standing and unwavering support of the United Nations and and the support which was just reiterated by you, Mr. President, and here I may stress the United Nations peace-keeping activities throughout the world. I am quite convinced that you share with me, Mr. President, as well as with the leaders of other member states with whom I have talked recently a mutual desire to see the United Nations develop into an ever more viable instrument of peace and human advancement in freedom, in rights, and in general well-being.

"I am looking forward today to our discussions which will certainly touch upon some important aspects of the overriding issues of these times.

"While I was traveling at jet speed across three continents a few days ago, I learned of the incredible technological feat that was achieved by the space scientists and engineers of the United States in obtaining through the marvelous performance of Ranger VII the first truly close-up photographs of the surface of the moon. I extend to you, Mr. President, heartiest congratulations and also to your Government and to the American people, on this remarkable achievement in the peaceful application of science and technology which unquestionably constitutes a major contribution to man's knowledge.

"Again, let me thank you, Mr. President, and to you, Mrs. Johnson, for having bestowed upon me and my colleagues who have accompanied me this morning the high honor of being your guests in the Capital of your country and for your warm welcome here at the White House.

"Let me also offer my very sincere thanks to you, Mr. President, for your very gracious words, not only about the United Nations to which you and your Government have been dedicated, but also to me in particular.

"Thank you once again."

In the President's opening words he referred to the Secretary General of the United Nations, U Thant, and Representative Charles A. Halleck of Indiana, House minority leader.

502   Toasts of the President and Secretary General U Thant. *August 6, 1964*

Mr. Secretary General, distinguished guests:

This has been a very gratifying and a very satisfying day in this house of the American people.

Mr. Secretary General, we have from many of the States of this Union from coast to coast some of our most distinguished citizens who have come here to pay their respects and their tribute to you.

I should like to have the opportunity to present each of them to you but, instead, I am going to ask only for the privilege of presenting three or four of your old friends who, I think, are representative of all that is best in our country.

First, I want to ask to stand for you, and so that all the people here may have a chance to see him, the articulate and understanding Chairman of the Foreign Relations Committee of the United States Senate, Mr. Fulbright.

Next, the eloquent minority leader of the United States Senate whose loyalty to the country knows no party bounds, Mr. Everett Dirksen.

One of the most talented and dedicated public servants that America has produced, the Ambassador to the United Nations, Mr. Adlai Stevenson.

And a young and distinguished former Member of the United States Senate who left his seat in that body to ride a tank in World War II, a former Ambassador of this Nation to the United Nations, a former Ambassador to Viet-Nam and a present counselor to the President and the Secretary of State, Ambassador Lodge.

I know that those of you who are here this evening feel as I do that we are privileged to receive and to welcome the man who is the public servant of the world.

For me, this day has been quite a particular personal pleasure. The Secretary General and I have a few things in common. We are very nearly the same age. We both began life as teachers. We both have spent many years in the public service of our countries. There are some differences, of course.

Before coming to the United Nations, the Secretary General was in charge of information for his government in Burma. That type position would be very appealing at times to most Presidents in this country.

But there is another and a much more serious bond between us. Both the Secretary General and I serve in our present offices as successors to men whom the world will always honor and whom the world will always remember as champions of peace.

When we look back upon them, the first 3 years of this decade took a cruel toll of leadership. The world still mourns tonight the loss of Dag Hammarskjold. The world will always sorrow for the loss of John Fitzgerald Kennedy.

But I think it is a commentary upon their work and upon the world itself that their tragic and untimely deaths have not deterred us for a moment in our quest for peace.

934

The will for peace in the world is a will that springs from the soul of the human race. That will is stronger tonight, stronger in this decade, I think, than ever before in the history of the human race.

Willful men may still design willful schemes for war, but they will meet today the strong and the steadfast will of men everywhere who reject war as an acceptable instrument of national policy.

In this century there has formed a new and resolute morality among mankind. That morality rejects both the immorality of war as well as the immorality of indifference and inaction toward all threats of war.

This new morality of mankind is nowhere more manifest than in the growing respect for the peacekeeping and the peacemaking purposes of the United Nations.

We here in the United States take great satisfaction from the success of the United Nations. It is the embodiment and the fulfillment of an old American vision.

We are so proud, Mr. Secretary General, to have the United Nations on these shores, and we are so proud to be privileged to participate in its work.

So, tonight, to those of us who are privileged to be here together in this peaceful hour, when so many are troubled throughout the world, I should like to ask each of you to join with me now in a toast to the Secretary General, to the organization which he so ably serves, and to the cause of peace on earth for which we all work together—Mr. U Thant.

NOTE: The President proposed the toast at a dinner in the State Dining Room at the White House. Secretary General U Thant responded as follows:

Mr. President, Your Excellencies, ladies and gentlemen:

I am suddenly overwhelmed by the very gracious words of you, Mr. President, not only about the United Nations but also about me.

Of course, it is not news to me when you say that the Government of the United States and the people of this great country are dedicated to the ideas and ideals of the Charter of the United Nations, and you have a very distinguished record of consistent support and cooperation with all United Nations activities since its inception in 1945.

You have also, Mr. President, rightly pointed out the horrors of war and the dedication of the great American people to avert war and to maintain peace. This is in strict conformity with the Charter of the United Nations which I have the privilege to represent here tonight.

I think it is what we are calling one of the primary purposes of the United Nations when it was established in San Francisco 19 years ago—to prevent war which twice in our lifetime had brought untold sorrow to mankind. That was the original provision in the Charter of the United Nations to save succeeding generations from the scourge of war. That is the text of the Charter—to save succeeding generations from the scourge of war which twice in our lifetime has brought untold sorrow to mankind.

To achieve this objective, among others, the founding fathers 19 years ago asked all member states to practice tolerance and to live with one another in peace as good neighbors and to unite our common strength to achieve common objectives. These also were the original texts of the Charter provisions.

So long as I am performing the functions of the Secretary General of the United Nations, Mr. President, I can assure you, and assure all these ladies and gentlemen who are present here tonight, that it shall be my constant endeavor to do my utmost to bring about a state of affairs by which the member states, which number at present 112, will be in a position to practice tolerance and life together with one another in peace as good neighbors and unite our common strength for the achievement of the common objectives outlined in the Charter.

There is also another very important provision in the Charter; that is, the founding fathers in 1945 had one very pertinent observation in the Charter. They wanted to see the United Nations as a center to harmonize the actions of states for the achievement of the common objectives.

It seems to me, Mr. President, that this particular objective of trying to see the United Nations as a center for harmonizing the actions of states in order to achieve the common objective is, to me, the most significant and the most important provision in the Charter of the United Nations.

Then, how are we to practice tolerance? How are we to see the United Nations develop into a real center for harmonizing the actions of member states so diverse for the achievement of common objectives?

For the achievement of this objective, it seems to me, as I have stated on previous occasions, that we should give a little thought to our concepts and to our attitudes toward problems. Perhaps it will not be news to most of you, I am sure, but I beg your indulgence to deal with this aspect for a couple of minutes.

It seems to me, Mr. President, that in many societies, particularly in technological societies, there has been too much stress on the development of the intellect. The primary objective of education in many countries in the second half of the 20th century has been and still is to create doctors and scientists and engineers, to discover outer space, to go to the Moon and Mars and to the stars. That has been the primary objective of modern education.

It seems to me that pure intellectual development unaccompanied by a corresponding moral and spiritual development is sure to lead humanity from one crisis to another.

To my way of thinking, the development of man must be fully integrated in all three aspects—intellectual, moral, and spiritual.

In my part of the world, as you are no doubt aware, Mr. President, the stress has been the other way around. The primary aim has been a monastic education, the moral and spiritual development aspects of men at the expense of the intellectual aspect of men. As a result, the traditional monastic education in Burma or China or Japan or Thailand, I stress, has been traditional, has been the discovery of what has been happening inside of us.

We try to understand the thought processes. We try to understand the moral and spiritual values like tolerance, like patience, the philosophy of live and let live, the desire to understand the other man's point of view. These we tried to develop for centuries and, at the same time, the intellectual aspect of man has been ignored.

As the result, the traditional concept of education and culture in Asia is now an anachronism in the second half of the 20th century. At the same time, the pure intellectual development which has been stressed in technological societies at the expense of ignoring the moral and spiritual aspects of men is also lopsided.

I feel very strongly that in the second half of the 20th century, under the shadow of the hydrogen bomb, it is very necessary for all of us, particularly leaders of thought and leaders of men to realize the imperative need for the development of men in all three aspects—intellectual, moral, and spiritual. Then only, Mr. President, do I feel that the world will be a much better place for all of us to live in.

Once again, Mr. President, thank you very much for the extraordinary warmth of reception accorded to me and my colleagues during our very brief stay in this beautiful Capital of your great country. I shall always retain very happy memories of my present visit and particularly your very gracious words with me, and may I request you ladies and gentlemen to join me in a toast to the health of the President of the United States and Mrs. Johnson.

503 Statement by the President on the Passage of the Joint Resolution on Southeast Asia. *August 7, 1964*

THE 414-to-nothing House vote and the 88-to-2 Senate vote on the passage of the Joint Resolution on Southeast Asia is a demonstration to all the world of the unity of all Americans. They prove our determination to defend our own forces, to prevent aggression, and to work firmly and steadily for peace and security in the area.

I am sure the American people join me in expressing the deepest appreciation to the leaders and Members of both parties, in both Houses of Congress, for their patriotic, resolute, and rapid action.

NOTE: This statement was read by the Press Secretary to the President, George E. Reedy, at his news conference held at the White House at 1:40 p.m. on August 7, 1964.

504 The President's News Conference at the LBJ Ranch.
August 8, 1964

THE PRESIDENT. [1.] First, I am glad to see so many of you made the bus this morning. When we set this early hour last evening, I asked George Reedy if he thought the eastern press that is traveling with us would interpret this as extremism. He assured me that the press regards moderation in pursuit of the eastern daylight deadlines as no virtue.[1]

Last Saturday we all met together and I think you were interested in photographs of the surface of the moon. This Saturday I suppose some of you may be more interested in photographs of the surface of Granite Shoals Lake.

But I thought I would tell you as President of all of the press photographers as well as reporters I want you to be able to catch up on your rest after you file, so I will just tell you about this afternoon. I may be on the lake, but there won't be any story over there.

[2.] For several days at the White House, I spoke of our "summer of discontent." There has been discontent and there has been dissatisfaction, but it seems to me that these last 7 days deserve very special consideration in contemplation of every thinking citizen. All week long the Americans have been doing what Americans do best—working together.

The results have been highly gratifying. The week has been deeply reassuring. Wherever we have faced them, we have been meeting our challenges—at the Gulf of Tonkin, the Halls of Congress, in distant space of our universe, and all sections of our Nation.

Only a week ago we saw a steady, stable, straightforward national course yield an important national success in the mission of Ranger 7. Only a few days later we saw that same kind of steadiness and stability and straightforwardness permit us to make America's peaceful purpose unmistakably clear when we were challenged by an act of aggression in the Tonkin Gulf.

Today, both adversaries and allies have the basis for new respect and understanding of America's resoluteness. In the unity of nonpartisanship and commonsense which Americans rallied together for, we have the basis for new confidence in the continuing strength of our own society, but there are other reassurances, too.

I find it reassuring in this week, while we faced challenges abroad, our Congress faced up to challenges at home—facing them with an active answer to them.

You will see the fruits of their labors signed into law, a good many of them, next week. We have several signing ceremonies scheduled.

This has been one of the most constructive weeks within my memory in the Congress, and it is a fitting climax to one of the most constructive sessions that I witnessed in my 33 years.

[3.] In addition, I think we may properly note with reassurance another development at home.

I have just talked to Mr. J. Edgar Hoover, head of the Federal Bureau of Investigation. He assures me that the investigation in Mississippi is going exceedingly well; that substantive results can be expected in a very short period of time.

Murder in any State, whether Mississippi

---

[1] The conference was held at 10:05 a.m., central standard time.

or Georgia or New York, and civil disorder in any region—North or South, East or West—cannot and will not be condoned in this country.

Perpetrators of these crimes and these law violators are being apprehended and will be brought to justice. We must not allow violence and lawlessness to go unpunished. No person can be allowed to attack the right of every American to be secure in this land.

Under our system of government, local authorities have the basic responsibilities for civil peace. We look to the Governors and local officials to keep the peace and to protect the citizens. It is essential to our Federal system that they keep that responsibility. I am in constant communication with Governors where these problems appear.

A Federal police force is inconsistent with the tradition of this country, and I do not believe we must create such a force to keep the peace and enforce the laws. But inaction on the part of the Government when Federal laws are violated and assistance is needed is equally repugnant to our traditions. We intend to do our part when it is necessary and right to do so.

[4.]   I have been in communication with the Secretary of State, the Secretary of Defense, Mr. McGeorge Bundy,[2] and other officials in Washington, and I have a brief statement to make on southeast Asia.

The situation created by unprovoked aggression against our naval forces on the high seas remains serious, but there have been no further incidents in the last 24 hours. We, of course, remain fully alert against any attempt to renew or widen the attacks from any source.

It is important for us all to understand that these attacks at sea are only part of a basic pattern of aggression which had already shown itself against the people and Government of South Viet-Nam and the people and the Government of Laos. Our actions this week make clear not only our determination to give a clear and positive reply to aggression at sea, but our general determination to resist and repel aggression in the area as a whole. That is the meaning also of the resolution adopted yesterday by the Congress with almost complete unanimity.

The most encouraging fact of the week, indeed, was the unity, calmness, and strength of purpose shown by our own people, together with the understanding and support which our actions have received from our friends around the world.

Ambassador Lodge,[3] pursuant to my request and in accordance with my directions, will proceed at an early date to communicate in more detail with our friends in other parts of the world.

Our friends who are defending their freedom and independence in the area can take new courage from this unity and this support as they carry on, with our help, in the continuing work of repelling aggression by terror and by infiltration.

Finally, let me repeat again and again that in all our actions, our purpose is peace.

[5.]   Another situation which is a matter of grave concern is the renewed fighting on Cyprus between the Greek and Turkish cypriots. We are intently watching this development, and I don't wish to comment on it further except to say that we are in very close touch with the situation through our embassies, that we strongly support the efforts of the U.N. peace force to achieve a cessation of fighting so that movements toward a peaceful solution can continue.

---

[2] Secretary of State Dean Rusk, Secretary of Defense Robert S. McNamara, and McGeorge Bundy, Special Assistant to the President.

[3] Henry Cabot Lodge, former United States Ambassador to Viet-Nam.

As I am sure you know, the Turks have asked for an emergency meeting of the United Nations Security Council.

[6.] The Air Force will proceed immediately with the program to orbit 24 satellites for an interim, independent Defense Satellite Communications System. This system will provide reliable, worldwide circuits, highly resistant to jamming and physical attack, for carrying essential military communications in time of crisis.

Further details of it can be in a statement, and George [4] can give it to you.

[7.] I have approved a proposal by Secretary Wirtz to survey job vacancies in 20 labor market areas across the Nation.

For more than a year the Labor Department has been studying the feasibility of collecting information from employers on vacant jobs that could be filled if qualified workers were available.

Experimental surveys, research, and the investigation of job-vacancy information activities in other countries indicate that such a program would be of tremendous value in combating unemployment.

I have a letter here from the Secretary describing the project, which I won't go into, which you can take.[5]

We are greatly encouraged by the success

---

[4] George E. Reedy, Press Secretary to the President.

[5] In a letter to the President, released by the White House on August 8 at Austin, Tex., Secretary Wirtz proposed that pilot surveys be conducted in 20 labor market areas of different sizes, industrial composition, and labor market conditions, with a view toward the eventual establishment of a job-vacancy identification system in each major labor market area. The surveys would measure the extent and nature of unfilled job openings by occupation so that manpower training and retraining programs could be geared to local labor market conditions. Mr. Wirtz added that the surveys would provide needed information for the prompt placement of skilled workers and also provide employers with a systematic method of assessing their own training needs.

of breaking through the 5 percent barrier on unemployment, getting it down to 4.9. We believe if we get the bill that was voted on yesterday—dilatory tactics required us to carry over until today for final vote—if we pass that bill today,[6] we expect to make strong inroads into the largest group of unemployed that we have; namely, the young people. We have reduced that from 16 down to 13 percent. We expect thousands of young people to be able to obtain useful training in employment as a result of this bill in all parts of the Nation.

I will be glad to take any questions.

[8.] Q. Mr. President, when you said that you expect substantive results in the Mississippi investigation in a very short time, do you mean, sir, you are expecting something today or within days? Could you pin it down slightly?

THE PRESIDENT. I would say a very short time. I don't want to get down to minutes or hours. I would just leave it at that.

Q. That is, arrests?

THE PRESIDENT. I would say substantive results.

[9.] Q. Mr. President, Mr. Lodge told us yesterday he was going to allied capitals. Are you planning to send anyone to neutralist capitals?

THE PRESIDENT. We are in touch with most capitals most of the time. I don't think that there is any clear line of demarcation that would divide one capital from the other, although I think early in his schedule he will be discussing some joint efforts that would not apply to the neutralists that are going on now in southeast Asia. I would say that he would not be precluded from visiting any capital whether it was our ally or a neutral, but I would say probably the first ones he will visit will be allied capitals because of

---

[6] Economic opportunity bill, passed by the House of Representatives on August 8. See Item 505.

some of the plans that some of them have announced for their increased efforts there.

[10.] Q. Mr. President, last week Senator Goldwater said it appeared to him that as of now Viet-Nam is dead as a campaign issue this year but that it probably could be revived later. Do you agree with this?

THE PRESIDENT. I prefer to treat it as a problem of free people without association in a political campaign. I think that all Americans are going to support their country in defending our interests in the world.

I have seen no evidence that our action in Viet-Nam should be made a partisan matter. I am exceedingly pleased with the unanimity with which the Congress and the people—and, if you will pardon me, the press—supported this movement.

[11.] Q. Sir, have you been able to better establish the motives in the Vietnamese two attacks?

THE PRESIDENT. You had better find out about their motives from them.

Q. Do you have any ideas or do you assume why?

THE PRESIDENT. The same answer would go to that same question. I am unable to speak with any accuracy on the imaginations or motives or ideas they may have had in mind on what they did. It would be pure speculation and I don't care to indulge in that.

Q. Mr. President, there has been some criticism of your timing on the announcement of the attack. Can you give us any feeling about this thing?

THE PRESIDENT. I haven't paid much attention to it. I don't know what you referred to, but I think that our conduct is going very well there, and I didn't know there had been any criticism from any responsible source. It looks like the votes have been pretty uniform and pretty unanimous.

Q. I was thinking of the criticism by Congressman Foreman yesterday in the House.[7]

THE PRESIDENT. I didn't see that. Did he think we shouldn't have done it?

Q. He suggested you were acting irresponsibly by announcing the attack before it started.

THE PRESIDENT. Before what?

Q. Before the attack started.

THE PRESIDENT. Of course that didn't happen.

Q. Didn't it?

THE PRESIDENT. No.

Q. Before the planes got to the target is what he was saying.

Q. Before the strike actually began.

THE PRESIDENT. When the strike got off the carrier they were in their radar and the Defense Department and the Secretary of Defense and the Chairman of the Joint Chiefs of Staff thought it was very important that we say to the American people what was happening before Hanoi said it to them, and that we say to all peoples what kind of an attack it was without any description. I don't think any well-informed or reasonable person would feel that we did not act properly and successfully.

Q. Mr. President, have you talked with former President Eisenhower about the air strikes?

THE PRESIDENT. No, I haven't. I think it is fair to say that I have had General Eisenhower fully briefed, and I have received his reactions, and I have asked for any opinions or suggestions he might have at any time, and I have received them in this connection. I have suggested that Ambassador Lodge talk to him about my suggestions of the last couple of days with the Ambassa-

---

[7] Representative Ed Foreman's remarks appear in the Congressional Record, August 7, 1964, p. 17962.

dor. He has done that and he has reported back to me—not me personally.

Q. The Ambassador said the General was pleased that he had told him.

[12.] Q. Mr. President, have you been in communication with Premier Khrushchev in the past week either through the "hot line" or through regular diplomatic channels?

THE PRESIDENT. We are in communication with most of the governments of the world most of the time. The specific method and timing I don't go into.

[13.] Q. Sir, in connection with some other communications, there have been some conflicting and some confusing reports as to whether you did or did not ask the Attorney General to be your campaign manager or director this year. Have you made any such request of him?

THE PRESIDENT. I would just leave that up to your description. I don't think anything I could say would change it in any way. It would be conflicting and confusing as long as all of you speculate, and I would say that I am not going to take any active part in any campaign until after the convention.

[14.] Q. Mr. President, I want to ask a question about Adam Yarmolinsky,[8] if I pronounce it correctly. He had been with the Department of Defense——

THE PRESIDENT. He still is.

Q. I thought he had been working for the Peace Corps and working on the poverty bill.

THE PRESIDENT. No, your thoughts are wrong. He is still with the Department of Defense.

Q. I was also asked to ask you, sir, if he was going back to the Pentagon, but you say he is still there.

THE PRESIDENT. He never left.

[15.] Q. Mr. President, by drawing Chinese power southward, as they appeared

---

[8] Assistant to the Secretary of Defense.

---

to be doing, Mr. McNamara said they appeared to be bringing planes into South Viet-Nam. Are we reducing the potentiality of friction between China and the Soviet Union?

THE PRESIDENT. I would not care to go even so far as Mr. McNamara in speculating on what other people are going to do. That involves a great many imponderables, and I don't see any useful purpose being gained by speculation.

[16.] Q. Mr. President, would you care to comment on any of those recent rumors about a possible price increase in steel?

THE PRESIDENT. If the reports had any basis, it would be a matter of very serious concern because steel is very important in our economy. We follow all of these problems very closely. We would be surprised if steel raised prices in light of the information we have; namely, declining costs and rising profits, increased volume, favorable Government actions that we have taken on depreciation and taxes, interest rates, and our Government policies in connection with all of these. It seems to us that the steel industry has been getting steadily healthier.

It is now engaged in a major modernization program, and we have been told from time to time that they have been very successful in cutting their costs.

We all know that the volume of steel output is setting a new record. Increases in hourly labor costs have apparently been exceeded by good productivity gain.

As I said before, profits have been steadily rising. The first half of 1964 steel profits were up 17 percent over the first half of 1963.

Now, if you had a price increase, it would strongly conflict with our national interest in price stability. We think that stability is essential to sustain a strong expansion of jobs and output, to sustain the improvement in our balance of payments.

941

I am confident that leaders of the steel industry will act responsibly in the national interest. I have had no indication whatever that there is going to be any other action.

Q. Mr. President, you did not mean to imply, sir, any criticism——

THE PRESIDENT. I did not mean to imply any. I don't want to imply anything.

Alvin A. Spivak, United Press International: Thank you, Mr. President.

NOTE: President Johnson's twenty-fifth news conference was held in his office at the LBJ Ranch, Johnson City, Tex., at 10:05 a.m. on Saturday, August 8, 1964.

505   Statement by the President Following House Action on the Economic Opportunity Bill.   *August 8, 1964*

ALL Americans can be proud of the action taken today by the House of Representatives in committing the strength and talents of our nation to war on poverty.

The goal is high. We shall not reach it easily or swiftly.

We have by this compassionate commitment kept faith with the morality of our society and I congratulate the members of both parties in Congress who have supported this historic measure.

The struggle of this century between freedom and tyranny has been a struggle among men in many lands to find a system which would relieve them from the oppression of poverty.

I believe we can and should be proud that it is our free society—and our system of responsible capitalism—which is first able and willing to make a credible commitment to eradicate poverty among its own people.

This bill gives us the tools with which to begin our work.

Success in this depends upon the quality of response citizens offer in every community. Our objective is national—but realization of it will come through local effort, local leadership, local vision. I call upon all who share concern for the character of their own communities to enlist in this war against the blight and blemish of the poverty which exists amid plenty.

The program implemented by this legislation presents a particularly challenging opportunity to young Americans. As other generations have gone to war abroad to protect our Nation's values, today's generations will have through the war on poverty a rare opportunity to serve those values in peace.

We are opening the door of opportunity a little wider for more of our people and that is what has always made our country stronger and more successful.

NOTE: For the President's remarks upon signing the Economic Opportunity Act, see Item 528.

506   Remarks at a Luncheon for Businessmen.   *August 10, 1964*

THIS house in which you are visiting today is not a personal residence. And it must never be a political prize.

This house is the house of all the people.

For so long as I am your tenant—and your servant—I shall use this house as we are using it today: use it to bring together America's leaders from all walks of American life, to think together, to plan together, to work together for the future of America.

As President, I would much rather explain why leaders of labor—or leaders of business—are in their White House, than to try to explain why either are not here or weren't invited.

As I conceive it, a President's first role and first responsibility is to help perfect the unity of the people, not to perpetuate their divisions.

The last 10 days have reminded us anew of just how vital our unity has come to be. Far away—and near at home—grim and grave challenges have confronted us. Those challenges continue to come. But so long as our land is strong and free, those challenges will not cease.

In this period we have been able to meet our challenges steadily and surely and swiftly. Our friends have not misunderstood—our adversaries have not mistaken—our purpose has remained unchanged, because we in America have been united. A united America has never been—and, I think, will never be—a misunderstood America.

In these days, among many thoughts in my own mind, one has been impressed strongly upon me. How different America's response might have been—how different America's role might be—if we were today a nation divided by struggles of class or strife, a nation split between capital and labor.

In your lifetime and mine, we have moved beyond those dangerous shoals. Our responsibility together now is to steer the course of this system, steer the course of this economy, and this society to the high and hopeful and happier seas of a more perfect unity.

And that is why I asked you to come here today.

Around the world—throughout our times—men of business have lived in dread and fear of the governments of their lands. They live with fear in many lands today—wondering if what they have accumulated will be taken away or taxed away or foolishly thrown away.

That is why I wanted you to know something about how your Government is operating. That is why I want all American businessmen to understand that your Government is devoted to your success, not dedicated to your enslavement.

American business is like no other in history.

It is owned by millions, it employs millions more, it serves all 190 million of our people. The promise for their lives rests upon the performance of your enterprise. While some of you may not be interested in our success, I can assure you that we here in Washington are greatly interested in your success.

I am glad I can say today that no businessmen anywhere have ever at any time enjoyed the measure of success that American businessmen are enjoying now.

For 42 consecutive months, we have had the longest and the largest peacetime expansion of our economy on record. These years from 1961 through 1964 are going into the record books as the most prosperous years of our history. It is prosperity not just for businessmen—it is prosperity for all the people of this Nation.

Last month 72.4 million Americans were at work—a new high in the history of the Republic. Unemployment declined to 4.9 percent. It has not been below this figure since November 1957—almost 7 years ago.

Since early 1961, our gross national product is up $117 billion.

Industrial production is up 27.6 percent.

I might also mention that your stocks are up almost $100 billion since November 22d last year.

Many other figures could be cited to you. Every week new reports bring more good news.

The Council of Economic Advisers tells me just today that—

—initial reports from 1,100 nonfinancial corporations indicate that second quarter profits set an all-time quarterly record in the history of the Nation.

—the full year of 1964 will set a new annual record.

This news is mighty welcome here in Washington—as it must be to you.

But there is more.

The Council of Economic Advisers informs me that in the past 6 months the purchasing power of the average American consumer has expanded by 3½ percent. Over the whole period since early 1961 buying power has averaged a 3.4 percent gain per year.

Now contrast this with the average gain of only 1.6 percent per year during the 1952 to 1960 period.

Gains in jobs and profits are going hand in hand.

Workers are gaining in purchasing power through fuller employment, through longer hours, through higher wages. But on the average, higher wages have not increased the cost of doing business. Why? Because productivity has risen to match the wages.

Profits are gaining through higher volume and lower costs and lower taxes—thanks to the help of a good many men in this room. But on the average the gains are not coming through higher prices.

So long as this is the pattern, we can use our fiscal and our monetary policies to stimulate business activity and not to restrain it.

Both business and labor are making their economic gains by enlarging the size of the economic pie. They are not making—and they cannot continue to make—gains by taking bigger slices at the expense of one another or at the expense of the American consumer.

So I say today: the times are good.

Our prospects are bright.

Your Nation's strength is great.

The promise before us all is bright.

But one fact stands out above all the rest.

What we have, what you have accumulated, what all American families hope to accumulate can be lost if we do not continue on the course of perfecting our unity.

Our prosperity today is not a one-time phenomenon. This is a solid, stable, steady prosperity—achieved by the confidence and the certainty of a climate that's free of doubt and division and bitter contention.

Our dollar is strong because the world has new confidence in our responsibility.

Our consumer market is strong because Americans at home have confidence in our future course.

Our enterprise system is functioning successfully because we have been doing here in Washington many of the things so long needed to lift off burdens of the past.

Taxes have been cut.

Spending has been curbed.

Earnest and honest efforts have been made to put to work in Government today's new tools and new concepts to produce more efficient management of your public business.

Your Government seeks to be not a dictator but a moderator—not a master planner but a faithful public servant—not an agent for your control but a vehicle for your freedom.

What I have said to all others I want to repeat to you before we leave today.

As a man who wants to be President of all the people, I intend to work to ensure that every person enjoys the full constitutional rights and equal opportunity that are his birthright as an American citizen.

I intend to use all the resources I have to make sure those who claim rights—and those who deny them—bend their passions to peaceful obedience of the law of the land.

No man could attain a higher honor than to occupy this office I now hold. No man would be worthy of that honor who thought of self. No man would be worthy who thought of any success except America's success. And that is the only thought I have in this house today.

If the man who lives in this house is not free to stand for right, no man in any house in America is free from the injury of wrong.

When I came into this office very suddenly 8 months ago, confronted with all the problems and obstacles that faced me at that time, I tried to look about America and draw all the strength that was available to me. And a great deal of that is in this room today.

President Eisenhower and President Truman immediately headed for Washington to give me their counsel and to try to help me lead this Nation at that critical time.

Since that time I have met with thousands of leaders of our free enterprise system. I met with the capitalists of the Nation, with the managers of that capital, with the workers employed by that management. I have gone to them with my problems. I have asked for their counsel. I have profited from their advice.

So I have asked you today to come here to visit with me, to have a chance to know you.

Charles Lamb was once reading a book. And when he finished the book, he threw it on the floor. And he said, "I don't like that man," speaking of the author. And his old maid sister said, "Do you know him?" And he said, "No. If I knew him, I would like him."

I have said this to a good many of you before in our other conferences, but I think it is worth repeating. I believe if we prevail in this world and if we survive, it will be primarily due to the efficiency and the strength of our system of government.

I think our system of government is better than the system of our adversaries. And I think in time we will demonstrate it and it will prevail.

I think that we can do a job better and more efficient and more satisfactory for the capitalist who sends his dollar out hoping to get a small return on it, the manager who gets up at daylight and works until midnight to put that dollar and the men together and develops stomach ulcers in the process but looks forward to the bonus that he may get from the board of directors at the end of the year, to the worker who tries to produce a better mousetrap at lower costs. And when all these three are put together, I believe that they can do a better job than any slaves can do for any commissars. And I have faith that that system will prevail.

So I want to say to you gentlemen here today that I realize the concern that businessmen feel for their Government. Most of them, as I said earlier in my statement, have been afraid of governments wherever they were, at whatever time in history they existed.

Mr. Rayburn used to say to me—and he stayed here over 50 years—that it had been his experience that the most frightened man in American society was the average businessman. He said sometimes he has cause for it, but he goes around being constantly scared about what his Government is going to do. First of all, he doesn't know a great deal about his Government because he's so busy making his own business operate. He's concentrating there on his own problems that he doesn't have time to become a political expert and understand all the intricacies of our governmental system. So he is constantly frightened about it. And if he can't get his blood pressure up high enough on his own, he'll go hire him a lawyer and pay him to keep him scared.

Well, I want you to know more about your Government. And I want your Government to know more about you.

These men on this row are part of this country—very vital and very important parts of this country. But a few weeks ago and maybe a few weeks from now they will be back occupying some of the chairs that you now occupy.

So we wanted you to come here today, to tell you that we need your help. And we need the help of every American. You are the leaders of this country. And we want you to exercise that leadership. We have faith and confidence in our system. We want to develop it. We want to strengthen

it. We want to promote it. In short, we are going to perform our responsibilities, to give you the best Government of which we are capable. And we are going to ask you in return not to agree with us, not to support us, but to give us the leadership that you are capable of giving us and help us to unite this country instead of divide it.

All the world looks to this Nation for its future, for the leadership that is required at this moment. And we cannot give that leadership and we cannot offer it if we are split up in guerrilla groups chewing on each other.

We hope that in the months to come that we will have another opportunity to meet and talk and grow together because I think we have the greatest system of government ever devised by man. And I am going to contribute all I can to strengthen it and, more important, to perpetuate it.

Thank you very much.

NOTE: The President spoke in the State Dining Room at the White House. The luncheon was attended by 192 leading business and industrial executives, and by members of the Cabinet and other key Government officials.

507 Remarks Upon Signing Joint Resolution of the Maintenance of Peace and Security in Southeast Asia. *August* 10, 1964

My fellow Americans:

One week ago, half a world away, our Nation was faced by the challenge of deliberate and unprovoked acts of aggression in southeast Asia.

The cause of peace clearly required that we respond with a prompt and unmistakable reply.

As Commander in Chief the responsibility was mine—and mine alone. I gave the orders for that reply, and it has been given.

But, as President, there rested upon me

still another responsibility—the responsibility of submitting our course to the representatives of the people, for them to verify it or veto it.

I directed that to be done last Tuesday.

Within 24 hours the resolution before me now had been placed before each House of Congress. In each House the resolution was promptly examined in committee and reported for action.

In each House there followed free and serious debate.

In each House the resolution was passed on Friday last—with a total of 502 votes in support and 2 opposed.

Thus, today, our course is clearly known in every land.

There can be no mistake—no miscalculation—of where America stands or what this generation of Americans stand for.

The unanimity of the Congress reflects the unanimity of the country.

The resolution is short. It is straightforward. I hope that it will be read around the world.

The position of the United States is stated plainly. To any armed attack upon our forces, we shall reply.

To any in southeast Asia who ask our help in defending their freedom, we shall give it.

In that region there is nothing we covet, nothing we seek—no territory, no military position, no political ambition.

Our one desire—our one determination—is that the people of southeast Asia be left in peace to work out their own destinies in their own way.

This resolution stands squarely within the four corners of the Constitution of the United States. It is clearly consistent with the principles and purposes of the Charter of the United Nations.

This is another new page in the outstanding record of accomplishments the 88th Congress is writing.

Americans of all parties and philosophies can be justly proud—and justly grateful. Proud that democracy has once again demonstrated its capacity to act swiftly and decisively against aggressors. Grateful that there is in our National Government understanding, accord, and unity between the executive and legislative branches—without regard to partisanship.

This is a great strength that we must always preserve.

This resolution confirms and reinforces powers of the Presidency. I pledge to all Americans to use those powers with all the wisdom and judgment God grants to me.

It is everlastingly right that we should be resolute in reply to aggression and steadfast in support of our friends.

But it is everlastingly necessary that our actions should be careful and should be measured.

We are the most powerful of all nations—we must strive also to be the most responsible of nations.

So, in this spirit, and with this pledge, I now sign this resolution.

NOTE: The President spoke in the East Room at the White House. The joint resolution is Public Law 88–408 (78 Stat. 384).

508   Remarks at a Ceremony Marking the Issuance of the "Register and Vote" Stamp. *August 11, 1964*

Chairman Bailey and Chairman Burch, ladies and gentlemen:

I welcome you to this house which is your house. We come together at a time when we are preparing to test our differences. But on some things Americans have no disagreement. You have come, not because you are Republicans, not because you are Democrats, but because you are citizens deeply conscious of your civic responsibilities.

During the recent days we have been very attentive to the preservation of peace and the preservation of freedom in far-off countries. Yet we all know that we cannot be less attentive to the freedom that we cherish here in our own country. We preach the virtues of democracy abroad. We must practice its duties here at home.

Voting is the first duty of democracy. Yet, in our Nation too many citizens too often disregard their duty. Almost 40 million eligible men and women are not registered to vote, as we meet here today. In the last national elections when there was a record turnout, almost 35 percent of the electorate failed to vote.

I think that these are shocking statistics. They measure the magnitude of the job that is before us. Some countries make it a crime not to vote. But the answer does not lie in herding people to the polls. A free democracy can no more order a citizen to vote than it can tell him how to vote. Yet democracy must never neglect its obligation to provide every encouragement to every citizen to exercise his right to vote.

And that is why we work to remove the barriers which limit a man's franchise, because of the color of his skin. That is why we need a voluntary citizens movement to make certain that no one fails to register and fails to vote, because he failed to understand.

It is this unfinished business on the agenda of democracy that brings you patriotic men and women here today. The mandate of November's election must be by vote of the people; never by default of the people. As representatives of the two great parties in America, we come here today to renew our common faith that voting itself is more important than the way people vote.

The time has come, the time is here, the time is now to make a concerted effort to reduce the no-shows on election day. So,

as President of all Americans, I call on your help to go out and register more Americans than have ever been registered before and to work to get more Americans to the polls this November than have ever gone before.

It gives me a great deal of pleasure and pride to be joined by a great President, Dwight Eisenhower, in commending the American Heritage Foundation for its leading role in democracy's great drama. This is a non-partisan enterprise and, as such, you men have worked tirelessly to give vitality to our electoral system.

This year you have joined as partners with the Advertising Council and nearly 100 national organizations to carry your campaign through the mass media out to the grass roots. This campaign deserves the wholehearted support of every living American. Much more is at stake than the coming election.

As more and more Americans come of voting age, you are helping get them ready to share in what has been called, "Democracy's ceremonial, its feast, its great function." You could have no more important mission to perform. How well you perform it may well determine how well your descendants live.

Thank you very much.

NOTE: The President spoke shortly after noon in the East Room at the White House at the launching of a bipartisan campaign, sponsored by the American Heritage Foundation and the Advertising Council, to encourage more Americans to register and vote. His opening words referred to John M. Bailey, Chairman of the Democratic National Committee, and Dean Burch, Chairman of the Republican National Committee.

509   Remarks to Members of the National Association of Counties.
      August 11, 1964

Ladies and gentlemen:

We are honored that you have come here this afternoon. You represent what we in Washington are here to serve, to protect, and to defend. And that is the right of men around the world to govern themselves—at the local level.

Only one week ago, at about this same hour, we were very conscious of that responsibility. At that time we were faced with the challenge of a direct, deliberate, and unprovoked act of aggression. That act was committed by a government which is a relentless and ruthless enemy of local self-government.

That government sends its guerrillas into, neighboring free lands with orders to seek out, with orders to kill, local officials and their families like you and your families.

When that challenge was laid down, there was no delay, there was no hesitation, there was no divided counsel here in your White House.

The United States delivered a firm and unmistakable reply and delivered it promptly.

The world understands that the United States' only purpose is peace. But the world also understands that this generation of Americans has only one policy. Our resources are committed, our sacrifices are made, our vigil is maintained so that there shall be no win for aggression in our times.

At this time last week, we could not know what the consequences of our course would be. But as we could be confident that our cause was right, we could also be confident of our might.

Since 1961 we have worked very hard to strengthen the hopes for peace. That is and that must always be the first work of our land. We have also worked to strengthen our preparedness, for only the strong can be brave in the pursuit of peace.

We have increased by $28 billion our expenditures, our investment in preparedness, in the last 4 fiscal years over what we were spending the year we came in.

I could take some time to tell you how much additional preparedness we bought with these $30 billion, but I can assure you it is there and I can assure you that the world knows it is there. And because of it, all Americans can know tonight that the United States is the strongest nation in all history. I want you to know, and I want the world to know, that all of our plans and all of our work now going on will keep it that way.

But you know, I think, and I know that our strength is never just the strength of arms alone. And that is why we must work in many ways to make this Nation stronger in every way.

We are harvesting the fruits of those labors now.

Our economy has never been more prosperous. For 42 consecutive months there have never been so many Americans at work, 72,400,000 are on the payroll now, and their average weekly pay has never been higher in our history. American business is on its way to the most profitable year that business has ever had in the record of this country.

All of that is good and all of us want to keep it that way. Unemployment is down below 5 percent and we are going to drive it still lower. Purchasing power is up and we are going to send it higher.

Taxes have been cut. Federal spending has been held down. We intend to make every effort to keep the budget below $100 billion again next year. If prices remain stable, as they have, and prosperity continues as it is, we want to cut some of our excise taxes at least and before too long to cut income taxes once more.

We are making the effort to reduce expenditures. You men and women out there today have made budgets of your own. No one knows better than you the work and the long hours and the care and the thought and the sweat that economizing requires. But it can be done.

We have saved $1 billion more than anticipated in our Defense expenditures this year as a result of the cost consciousness program of Secretary McNamara. We will, within a few years, be saving more than $4.6 billion in this area of our budget alone. Our course is steady. Our course is sure—at home and in the world. And if I know anything about the American people, I think I know that they want to hold to this sure and steady course.

We have problems at home.

No one is more aware than I am of how many of our problems must be met, must be answered, and must be solved at the local level. But I look, America looks, and even the world looks to you as our local leadership to supply the leadership that these times require.

Your local burdens are many and they are growing. Since 1948, Federal spending has increased 168 percent, but State and local spending has increased 268 percent. Federal debt is up 21 percent. State and local debt is up 365 percent.

Some may want to have Washington impose more burdens upon you by transferring responsibilities to your level of government. For myself, my first interest, my only interest, is to see the 91,000 units of government in the United States working together arm in arm, shoulder to shoulder, for the good of all the people all the time.

I didn't ask you over here this afternoon to frighten you or to threaten you. I did ask you to come, because I want to tell you that I am proud of our country. I am proud of what our country has done. I am proud of what our country is doing. I am proud of what we are capable of doing, if we trust each other, if we work together with each other, and if we love each other, instead of hate each other.

All that I ever want to do, and all that I think you ever want to do, is to preserve in this land, and in all free lands, the right of 'men and women to govern themselves. Now, how can we do that?

We can do it by serving that cause, by working for unity, and by not prolonging our divisions. We can serve that cause by working for the rights of men in every region of America and by working for the rights of men in every region of the world.

We are happy that you came here. We hope you enjoyed your visit to Washington. We trust that you will have a pleasant journey home. I received some invitations from some of you that I may just accept between now and the first of the year.

NOTE: The President spoke in midafternoon at a reception on the South Lawn at the White House for a group composed of some 2,000 members of the National Association of Counties. The Association was holding its County Information Congress at the Sheraton-Park Hotel in Washington.

510 Remarks Upon Signing the Military Pay Bill.
August 12, 1964

Mr. Secretary, Members of the Congress, ladies and gentlemen:

One hundred sixty-three years ago, in his first message to Congress, President Thomas Jefferson said, "We should at every session of Congress continue to amend the defects . . . in the laws for regulating the militia . . ." And, he added, "until we can say we have done everything for the militia which we could do were an enemy at our door."

This 88th Congress, like the 87th Congress, has followed that advice. In 1961 and 1962, last year and now this year, much has been done to show our uniformed citizens a fuller measure of the respect that they have earned. Quarters allowances were increased. Management of military family housing has been completely reorganized. Less than 1 year ago, for the first time in 5 years, military pay was increased by more than 14 percent.

By this bill, which I am signing today, still another increase will go into effect September 1. These efforts reflect our historic trust of our professional military men.

For 188 years the American in uniform has been bent upon peace and the preservation of democracy. The world respects him as a fighting man. His fellow countrymen respect him as a thinking man.

This measure is an answer to those who would libel his loyalty to our civilian society or slander his sense of responsibility for the trust he bears to all mankind.

We need and we want our most able men at all grades to make the military a profession. We want them to be able to know

their service to America's defense will not be a disservice to their families' dignity.

We cannot promise, and they do not ask, assurance of comfort. None can know what tomorrow may require of any of us or all of us. But we can promise, and our citizens in uniform may expect, that we shall provide them with:

—the best and most modern arms available in this world,

—the support of the most stable free Government and successful united society in the world,

—the strength of the most prosperous and vigorous free economy in the world, and

—the incalculable asset of responsible national policies and purposes which inspire other peace-loving nations to send their sons to stand beside ours in the common cause of freedom around the world.

I am pleased to be able to in person congratulate many of the Members of Congress who are responsible for this legislation and certainly some of the leaders in formulating it.

I am proud that they could come here this morning to meet with the representatives of the services, the Joint Chiefs, the distinguished Secretaries of the Services, the Under Secretary of Defense, and Secretary McNamara himself.

I am proud now, in their presence to sign into law at this time this bill which I think the services so deserve.

NOTE: The President spoke at 10 a.m. in the Cabinet Room at the White House. In his opening words he referred to Secretary of Defense Robert S. McNamara.

The military pay bill as enacted is Public Law 88–422 (78 Stat. 395).

511   Remarks in New York City Before the American Bar Association.   *August 12, 1964*

Mr. President, Ambassador Stevenson, members of the American Bar Association:

Today I speak to you in the midst of a troubled week in a turbulent world.

Since the end of World War II, America has been found wherever freedom was under attack, or wherever world peace was threatened.

The stage has shifted many times.

The stakes have grown as man's capacity for destruction grew. But America's role has not changed. With constancy we have pursued the defense of freedom and we have prevented nuclear destruction. We have patiently labored to construct a world order in which both peace and freedom could flourish.

We have lived so long with crisis and danger that we accept, almost without division, the premise of American concern for threats to order.

Yet this is a unique responsibility—unique for America, and unique in history.

We accepted this responsibility, first, because at one time no other nation could do it. For the last 20 years, only under the shadow of our strength could friends keep their freedom and build their nation. Now that our allies have been restored to strength, they must share our responsibility in the pursuit of common purpose.

We have done this because we have, at painful cost, learned that we can no longer wait for the tides of conflict to touch our shores. Aggression and upheaval, in any part of the world, carry the seeds of destruction to our own freedom and perhaps to civilization itself.

We have done this, lastly, for a reason that is often difficult for others to understand. We have done it because it is right that we should.

Friendly cynics and fierce enemies alike often underestimate or ignore the strong thread of moral purpose which runs through the fabric of American history.

Of course, our security and welfare shape our policies. But much of the energy of our efforts has come from moral purpose.

It is right that the strong should help the weak defend their freedom.

It is right that the wealthy should help the poor emerge from their hunger.

It is right that help and understanding should flow from friendship and loyalty.

It is right that nations should be free from the coercion of others.

That these truths may coincide with interest does not make them less true.

There is another value which guides America's course. It is the deep American belief in the peaceful process of orderly settlement.

I would like this afternoon to briefly discuss two very different places where we are working at this hour for this principle—Cyprus and Viet-Nam.

The conflict in Cyprus comes from causes that are deeply rooted in the history and the circumstances of that troubled little island. We do not know the final result of that conflict. We do know the United States should not stand idly by while two of its best friends are at the edge of kicking off a big war.

Both Greece and Turkey are fellow members of the NATO Alliance. They are both courageous and dedicated members of the free world community. They have both been closely associated with us for the 17 years since the Truman Doctrine.

It is our duty to the Alliance to help prevent its disruption. It is our duty to help settle any conflict which might erupt into a wider arena. It is our duty to help avoid large-scale loss of life among the peoples of Cyprus, whose true interests really lie in peace. It is our duty to work toward the acceptance of the principle that disputes should be settled without force. For, if orderly process is not accepted among friends, it will not be possible between adversaries.

In the pursuit of these responsibilities, I have sent our Under Secretary of State to all the capitals concerned.

We invited the heads of government of Greece and Turkey to come to see me at the White House for long and serious talks.

I have sent a distinguished former Secretary of State, Mr. Acheson, to Geneva to work for peaceful agreement.

We have kept in close touch with Athens and Ankara and Nicosia by repeated personal messages from the President.

In this spirit, we have welcomed the efforts of the United Nations to arrange a cease fire.

In Viet-Nam, too, we work for world order.

For 10 years through the Eisenhower administration, the Kennedy administration, and this administration, we have had one consistent aim—observance of the 1954 agreements which guaranteed the independence of South Viet-Nam. That independence has been the consistent target of aggression and terror.

For 10 years our response to these attacks has followed a consistent pattern. First, that the South Vietnamese have the basic responsibility for the defense of their own freedom. Second, we would engage our strength and our resources to whatever ex-

tent needed to help others repel aggression.

Now, there are those who would have us depart from these tested principles. They have a variety of viewpoints. All of them, I am sure, you have heard in your local community.

Some say that we should withdraw from South Viet-Nam, that we have lost almost 200 lives there in the last 4 years, and we should come home. But the United States cannot and must not and will not turn aside and allow the freedom of a brave people to be handed over to Communist tyranny. This alternative is strategically unwise, we think, and it is morally unthinkable.

Some others are eager to enlarge the conflict. They call upon us to supply American boys to do the job that Asian boys should do. They ask us to take reckless action which might risk the lives of millions and engulf much of Asia and certainly threaten the peace of the entire world. Moreover, such action would offer no solution at all to the real problem of Viet-Nam. America can and America will meet any wider challenge from others, but our aim in Viet-Nam, as in the rest of the world, is to help restore the peace and to reestablish a decent order.

The course that we have chosen will require wisdom and endurance. But let no one doubt for a moment that we have the resources and we have the will to follow this course as long as it may take. No one should think for a moment that we will be worn down, nor will we be driven out, and we will not be provoked into rashness. But we will continue to meet aggression with firmness and unprovoked attack with measured reply.

That is the meaning of the prompt reaction of our destroyers to unprovoked attack. That is the meaning of the positive reply of our aircraft to a repetition of that attack. That is the meaning of the resolution passed by your Congress with 502 votes in favor and only 2 opposed. That is the meaning of the national unity that we have shown to all the world last week.

There is another consideration wherever the forces of freedom are engaged. No one who commands the power of nuclear weapons can escape his responsibility for the life of our people and the life of your children.

It has never been the policy of any American President to sympathetically or systematically place in hazard the life of this Nation by threatening nuclear war. No American President has ever pursued so irresponsible a course. Our firmness at moments of crisis has always been matched by restraint—our determination by care. It was so under President Truman at Berlin, under President Eisenhower in the Formosa Straits, under President Kennedy in the Cuba missile crisis. And I pledge you that it will be so as long as I am your President.

In Viet-Nam, in Cyprus, and in every continent, in a hundred different ways America's efforts are directed toward world order. Only when all nations are willing to accept peaceful procedures as an alternative to forceful settlement will the peace of our world be secure.

While we work for peaceful process among nations, we must also maintain law and order among our own citizens.

No person whatever his grievance can be allowed to attack the right of every American to be secure in his home, his shop, and in his streets. We will not permit any part of America to become a jungle, where the weak are the prey of the strong and the many.

Such acts must be stopped and punished, whether they occur in Mississippi or in the State of New York. Under our Constitution, the local authorities have the central responsibility for civil peace. There is no place in our Federal system for a national police force. But where help is needed, or Federal law is violated, we shall be there. We will work together to punish all such lawbreakers, wherever they may be, whether they are hooded night-riders on our highways, or whether they are hoodlums in the city streets or parks.

Fulfillment of rights and prevention of disorder goes hand in hand.

Resort to violence blocks the path toward racial justice.

The denial of rights invites increased disorder and violence.

Those who would hold back progress toward equality and, at the same time, promise racial peace are deluding themselves and deluding the people. Orderly progress, exact enforcement of law, are the only path to an end of racial strife.

The Emancipation Proclamation was signed more than 100 years ago. But as we all know, emancipation was a proclamation and not a fact. After a century of wanting and waiting, a compassionate and comprehensive law came into being. It was passed by more than two-thirds of all the Members of both parties of the Congress under the leadership of both Republican and Democratic leader sponsorship. This is a Government of laws and not men. The Congress has passed the law, the President has signed the law, and the President will enforce the law.

I believe that our citizens will and must observe it. Neither demonstrations in the streets nor violence in the night can or will restrain us from seeing to it that laws rightly passed will be justly observed. That is the path along which I intend to lead this Nation.

And I am convinced that the same dedication to legal order, which will keep the peace in this land, will bring us nearer to peace among all lands.

I have hopes, despite crisis and conflict, that that day may be coming nearer.

It was 19 years ago—19 years ago this month—that President Truman announced: "The force from which the sun draws its power has been loosed."

When he heard the news Albert Einstein exclaimed: "The world is not yet ready."

But unprepared or not, the reality was there and we have struggled together to master it.

Today, as we meet in freedom here, free-dom is much stronger. For despite the difficulty and the danger, no nation—no single nation—has fallen to communism since Cuba in 1959. War has been prevented. Danger has been receding. If we can continue that course, the future will perhaps some day say of us: "They became the masters and not the victims of the age."

NOTE: The President spoke early in the afternoon at the Waldorf Hotel in New York City. In his opening words he referred to Walter E. Craig, president of the American Bar Association, and Ambassador Adlai Stevenson, U.S. Representative to the United Nations. Later he referred to George W. Ball, Under Secretary of State, and Dean Acheson, former Secretary of State.

512   Remarks Upon Signing the Highway Bill. *August* 13, 1964

Members of the Congress, the Cabinet, ladies and gentlemen:

This is a very welcome occasion for me. With this legislation, we are helping to do justice for the most important but often the most neglected member of our society—the American motorist.

For much too long, the man who owns and drives an automobile has been treated like a stepchild. We require him to pay for the highways he uses and we require him to pay in advance. We divert his taxes to other uses but we delay the building of the roads that he deserves. We denounce him for getting snarled in traffic jams not of his own making. We complain about what he costs us but we never thank him for what he adds to the worth and the wealth of our economy. We could not get along without him, but we often talk as though we can't live with him.

I hope and I believe that our attitudes are changing. Today, as never before, the Federal, State, and local governments are working together to meet the highway needs of this Nation on wheels.

They are working together largely because of the leadership of dedicated men of both parties whom you see around this Cabinet table this morning.

I hope you picture men get a good picture of everyone in this room because I think this is a red-letter day in the lives of a good many of us.

Eight years ago, in 1956, we set out on a 16-year program to catch up with ourselves—catch up through the Federal Interstate Highway System. This has been described as the most ambitious highway program since the days of ancient Rome. It was my privilege then to guide that program to passage as Senate majority leader. In every respect it has met our hopes. It has put more than one million Americans to work. It is already saving 3,000 lives a year and by 1972 it will be saving 8,000 lives a year.

It is saving dollars—$6 billion in user benefits last year; $11 billion a year 8 years from now; and the program is not costing the General Fund of the United States Treasury a single cent.

This legislation here today serves still another need. It helps to provide us better primary and secondary highways on a 50/50 basis with the States. In addition, it will support needed efforts to improve forest highways, public land roads and national park roads, and other such purposes.

The American people have never been compromised, have never been contaminated by riding over roads and highways that are partially financed by Federal aid.

This is one of our best investments, and I think most of the informed leaders of this country will agree on that point.

I might just mention this one additional point. If we add together all the tangible assets of this Government of the United States, including our share of investment in public highways and roads, that balance sheet would show that our assets far exceed our national liabilities.

Republicans as well as Democrats are working for and with a solvent, sound, and successful institution here at the seat of the Government of these United States.

I say this, this morning, because I want the American motorist to know that things aren't so bad that we must sell off our public roads to the highest bidder in order for Uncle Sam to stay liquid.

NOTE: The President spoke shortly after 10 a.m. in the Cabinet Room at the White House.

The Federal-Aid Highway Act of 1964 is Public Law 88–423 (78 Stat. 397).

513 Remarks at a Luncheon for a Group of State University Presidents. *August* 13, 1964

I AM very proud of our State universities and colleges, and all that they have come to mean in this country. In the last 100 years we have refuted the idea that higher education belongs only to what other societies have called "the higher classes."

At many of our State institutions we have achieved genuine excellence, and I think there is no better proof that what Government does, what is done with public funds, does not have to be mediocre, does not have to be massive, does not have to be content with the mean. The Government of the people can serve the best within the people, and I hope that we can in the next decade, bring all of Government up to the standards of excellence and selectivity and superiority.

One thing I would like to ask each of you to do for me and for your country today is this: I wish you would keep us advised at the White House, by writing me or by calling Mr. Dungan, of your really excellent, outstanding students who you think might be drawn into tours of public service.

We have not completed our responsibilities until we make public service something for our best young people to seek. I am afraid from what some of you may have been teaching them, and what they may have heard from some of us politicians out on the stump, they may now be seeking to avoid it.

If nobody else can persuade them to enter Government careers, I will talk to them myself, although I know they are a little harder to persuade than some other folks around here, but I do think that we should concentrate on bringing the best people that our institutions produce to the Capital of this country where they can set an example, where they can provide leadership not only for this Nation but for all the world. And

I think that you might be proud of your participation if you could, during your lifetime, make a contribution of just one or two Abraham Lincolns or Oliver Wendell Holmes, or Arthur Vandenbergs or Sam Rayburns, and I hope you will be on the lookout for them and will give us a note, and we will try to see where we can fit them in.

I also have a number of regulatory agencies, have a number of high administrative posts, have a number of difficult personnel assignments, and when you find someone who is unusually objective and judicious and able and talented and dedicated that could profit from his experience here, and that we could learn from, I would like for you to drop a note to Dr. Ralph Dungan over here, who is on my staff—stand up Ralph—I think he is the best personnel officer in the United States. I don't want any of you to hire him.

In recent days I have had the pleasure of meeting here with a wide variety of Americans. I have had presidents of the leading businesses in this country, most of the large employers of the Nation. I have met with the heads of all of the international labor unions—Mr. Meany, Mr. Reuther, and all of the national officers. I have met with the school superintendents from throughout the land, and many American publishers. I have met with the publishers of the foreign language newspapers and all of these meetings have meant much to me. I think I have gained strength from them.

All Presidents want, and I think all Presidents need, to get out among the people. I can't move as freely as I would like. So I am particularly grateful that you were good enough to visit with me today in this house which, as long as I am here, will always be your house.

You gentlemen are reminders of one of the most exciting achievements of our American democracy. The idea of a college education for all young people of capacity, provided at nominal cost by their own States, is very peculiarly American. We in America invented the idea. We in America have developed it with remarkable speed. It is hard to remember that so many of your institutions were established within the lifetime of many people in this room. We have come a long way—we are going farther. We have just begun to move.

In 1880 James Bryce wrote about the Western swing of his visit through the United States. He came upon a State university president who was named, of all things, Johnson. Incidentally, Johnson is the second most numerous family name in America. It is not far below Smith. That is good to know—very good to know so close to November.

Well, it seems that Mr. Johnson was a very vigorous young college president when Bryce visited him, and he kept talking about how the faculty—what he was going to do and what he was contemplating doing and plans ahead and so forth, and Bryce said, "How many professors are there on your faculty?" The president said in a tone which I suspect some of you will understand, "Well, just at present the faculty is below its full strength." Bryce pressed him a little bit and he said, "How many do you really have present on your faculty?" This young fellow Johnson, like Johnsons frequently have to do, said, "Well, at present the faculty consists of Mrs. Johnson and myself."

Now, today, our State universities comprise the largest and the most productive educational system in the history of the world. Our State universities have a combined faculty of more than 140,000 people, a combined annual budget of nearly $3 billion, and they enroll about 60 percent of our college students in this country. So your

957

institutions are the chief suppliers of intellectual talent for the strongest nation in the world.

You grant more than half of the Ph. D. degrees—those of you here. You would never think so when you walk around the White House and see where these folks come from. That is why I want to give you an opportunity to compete with them and supply some good staff members that can hold their own with the Bundys of Harvard, the Shrivers of Yale, the Goldmans of Princeton, and the Hellers of Minnesota.

You have educated more than 50 percent of all living American Nobel prize winners, and whether you are proud of it or not, you have trained 60 percent of our Senators and 44 percent of our Congressmen and 29 of our 50 Governors. You have educated the heads of AT&T and General Motors. One of them spends $16 billion a year, the president of General Motors told me the other day, the other one spends $10 billion a year as head of AT&T. You have also educated the heads of General Electric, Prudential Life, U.S. Steel, Gulf Oil, RCA, CBS, American Airlines, and five of the seven original Mercury astronauts. Your graduates discovered streptomycin and the blue-baby operation.

Another aspect of your work has particularly impressed me, and that is your role in providing expert knowledge and guidance for the people of your States. There has been much loose talk about the Federal Government versus the States. They talk about it often as if we were enemies, as if we were foreign powers.

The American system is the fortunate one of federalism. James Madison called it the happy combination. The Founding Fathers in their wisdom set up both the States and the National Government.

His purpose, his intention, was for each to do what it could do best. The Government was not, as some would have it, an alien invention.

Both the Federal Government and the States have always exercised leadership in solving the problems of the Nation. They are not, they must not be, rivals for the citizens' taxes and loyalty. They are separate agencies, each with special resources, each with special capabilities, but both joined in a united attack on the enemies of our country and on our common problems.

At times one or another has not pulled its full weight. You know that as well as I do.

Early in the 20th century the Federal Government was doing far too little to protect and to advance the welfare of the general public. When we look back on really how little it was doing, we wonder how we avoided a more serious revolution.

Then you remember, under President Theodore Roosevelt who, if you will pardon the expression, was a Republican—apologies to Dr. Hannah, Dr. Flemming, and others I have seen here today—and under a series of Democratic Presidents, the Federal Government began to assume its proper responsibilities. Today we are clearly moving into another period of the history of our Federal system. I think the signs are everywhere you go. This is an era of revitalization for our States, and there is much you can do about that.

A fresh generation of energetic Governors and reactivated legislatures are on the move. They are thinking about and doing something about what they think their people need.

One statistic suggests the whole trend, I think. From 1952 to 1963, Federal expenditures have increased by one-third—1952 to 1963, up one-third, Federal.

But State and local expenditures have more than doubled.

Throughout the history of our Federal system, State universities have played a very special role. They were always there to serve as a brain reservoir for the Governor, for the legislature, and for citizens groups. If I had my one wish, I would hope that in every State capital the Governor made as much use of educators and college brainpower as the President does here.

Our Cabinet is manned by men who are or were educators. Bob McNamara, the man who buys three-fourths of everything the Federal Government buys and handles a budget of $52 billion of his own and influences greatly the budget of every department, was a former professor, as was Dean Rusk, the Secretary of State; as was Mac Bundy, the head of the Security Council; as was Walter Heller who is responsible for our lack of inflation, for our stable prices, and for our great prosperity.

No man contributes more to the work I do every day or the success of this country than Dr. Goldman, who just put on his hat when I came in here and saw I needed help— and he has been giving it to me without quarreling ever since, at great sacrifice to himself.

Your State universities are playing a very critically important role in the revitalization of these States. I hope you play more. I hope that you just shovel up your knowledge to where that Governor chokes on it and where that information is available to his administrators who need your help.

You have established groups that are thinking and studying ahead. They are asking pointed questions. I have 15 task forces that are now working. One of them is working on how can we maintain prosperity after next July—not how we are going

to avoid the recessions that always come. We have gone longer than any period in history, for 42 months, without having a dip, but we know we just can't sit in a rocking chair with a Panama hat on and look out and let the rest of the world go by.

Harry Hopkins got criticized one time for saying we planned it that way. But a fellow without a plan is a man who may go off a cliff mighty easy.

Now, how is our State likely to develop economically and socially during the next 20 years or so? We have to determine that with plans. We have to do that with thinkers. We have to work on it. What old problems will continue during this period? What new ones will emerge? How can these problems be most sensibly met by State action—by States cooperating as regions, or by improving relations between Federal and State programs.

I think the best government we can have is the government that is closest to the people, that can get the job done. I never would want my county commissioner to recommend the plan for the Tonkin Gulf. I would much prefer to have some centralization of authority and have a few products from West Point sitting at my elbow before I send those planes out to destroy the nests that those PT boats are hiding in. But I wouldn't necessarily want the Chairman of my Joint Chiefs of Staff to grade the road that leads to my schoolhouse.

So I am intensely interested in these efforts of determining who can best do the job, and how. To me, this is democracy functioning in its most effective way—citizens calling their own experts from their own communities to solve their own problems.

So I have invited you men to come here today to meet in this house so that we can encourage the forward movements of such efforts. Your White House has not the slightest direct interest in directing or controlling or influencing such efforts. Your Federal Government today has no appetite for power. We have really more power than we know how to wisely use. That is what I debate about most of my waking hours.

But we do hunger for the application and the use of principle, including the real principles of federalism. We live by the belief that this Federal Government exists not to grow larger, but to encourage and permit the people to grow larger than any or all of their governments. This Federal Government exists not to subordinate the sovereign States. We exist to support them, and as long as I am here we are going to serve them and work with them and cooperate with them.

This Federal Government exists not to corrupt the character of men, but to give that character opportunity for full and for pure fulfillment. I don't have to look out at this brilliant, intellectual convocation of the States very long before I realize that you do not need us. But I do believe that we here in Washington need you very much.

All of us are Americans. All of us are free men. All of us are citizens of the state, and all of us take pride in the community in which we live. Woodrow Wilson once remarked—you can see who worked on this speech, can't you?—President Wilson said, "Our slow world spends its time catching up with the ideas of its best minds." So you represent what we believe are our best brains. You train the majority of our best young minds. In your hands the catching up is going to be a good deal more speedy, I trust. It is you that we look forward to and expect to educate men and women who think.

If I may be pardoned for another sugges-

tion, which I hope you won't forget, I also hope you teach them not just to think. I hope you educate them, too, to feel and to care.

I want people with compassion, and people who feel, and people who care around me, just as much as I want people who think. So maybe when you go back home without saying you got any Federal orders, I would like for you to whisper to your wife that the thing that I pointed out in my talk with you was how much it means to us to have men like you teaching our young minds to think, and how much I want you to teach them also to feel and to care. You educate the young to earn a livelihood. I hope you also educate them to care about the rights of others. I hope you educate them to care about the aspirations of others.

You educate young people to be good citizens of your States. I hope you educate them to be good citizens of their country and their world and their time.

What America is today and what it is tomorrow will rest largely upon you. The trust that you bear, and the trust that is borne here in this house, in this body, is a mutual trust that we share together, which we share to the same people. We have that obligation to the same nation, the same country, to the same cause. Our Founding Fathers in the original States recognized that trust was not divisible by 13. I hope we all realize now that it is not divisible by 50.

History teaches us many lessons about the follies and the failures of over-centralized government. In our own American history we have learned that the greatest protection against centralization of power is the diffusion of knowledge throughout the land. The diffusion of knowledge gives you protection and insurance against power. That responsibility is one that you bear well.

I believe that Federal-State relations should rest upon the faith. Dr. Ransom will pardon me if I lift a quotation from a former President of our Republic of Texas, "that an educated mind is the guardian genius of democracy. It is the only dictator that free men recognize and the only ruler that free men desire," said President Lamar of the Texas Republic.

So, gentlemen, you are men of courage and individualism and character and you know what I am saying is true; that we can work together. We must not work apart. I hope that you will carry that message to those that you lead. We can work for the same objective, not for 50 different objectives.

That is the reason I asked you to come here today. That is why you are here. You will, this afternoon, in this room, meet with the leaders of your Government in many fields. While they report to you, both they and I look to you for counsel and guidance on how we can better serve our trust, and we hope help you to better serve your trust, and to help you better meet your trust.

Yours is a great opportunity. I didn't bring you here to either stimulate you or to inspire you. Charles Lamb once said, when he finished reading a book, that he didn't like that man—speaking of the author. His old maid sister said to him, "Do you know him?" and he said, "No, if I knew him, I would like him." So much of our talent is wasted in this country because we don't know each other. So much consternation comes from our lack of understanding and our lack of realizing the other man's problem.

So I really envy you on this afternoon here in the first house of this land. I want you to go back and train some more Dr. Hornigs for me, my science adviser, some more Dr. Bundys, some more Dr. Hellers, some more

Dr. Dungans, Dr. Cater over there. I jerked him out of school. Stand up here, Doug. There is Douglass Cater, a young man on my staff that I brought out of school up here.

Now you are going to hear from some men who have visited your campus before, and some other leaders in Government.

But before I leave, I want to tell you one of the great satisfactions that comes to me as President is when, with the help of some of the men in this room, particularly some of the Republicans in this room, we passed the poverty program that will permit us to help educate thousands and thousands of young men who would drop out of school except for this program.

A young working boy that had to make his own way through college has inspired the Nation and the world by his leadership in the Peace Corps, and now he is devising the first real, organized, centralized attack on poverty in this country.

Franklin Roosevelt talked of the third that were ill-clothed and ill-fed and ill-housed. That was 30 years ago. In 30 years, we have moved that one-third down to one-fifth—33 percent to 20 percent. Now we are making a determined attack, under the leadership of men like Dr. Keppel over here, and Dr. Hornig, and others that I have already named, but under the generalship of Dr. Shriver. I call him "Doctor" because I really don't know how many doctors' degrees he actually earned, but I read in the paper that he is the only man who was awarded more of them this year than the President.

NOTE: The President spoke in the East Room at the White House at a luncheon meeting of about 80 college and university presidents from the United States and Puerto Rico. In the course of his remarks he referred to, among others, Ralph A. Dungan, Special Assistant to the President, George Meany, president of the AFL–CIO, Walter Reuther, president, United Automobile Workers, AFL–CIO, John A. Hannah, president, Michigan State University, Arthur S. Flemming, president, Oregon University, Robert S. McNamara, Secretary of Defense, Dean Rusk, Secretary of State, McGeorge Bundy, Special Assistant to the President for National Security Affairs, Walter Heller, Chairman, Council of Economic Advisers, Dr. Eric F. Goldman, professor of history at Princeton University and Special

Consultant to the President, Dr. Harry Ransom, chancellor, University of Texas, Mirabeau Buonaparte Lamar, the second President of the Republic of Texas, S. Douglass Cater, Jr., Special Assistant to the President, Francis Keppel, Commissioner of Education, Department of Health, Education, and Welfare, Donald Hornig, Special Assistant to the President for Science and Technology, and Sargeant Shriver, Director of the Peace Corps.

514 Remarks Upon Signing the Government Employees Pay Raise Bill. *August 14, 1964*

Members of Congress, ladies and gentlemen:

For many reasons, this is both a proud and a very gratifying occasion for me. There have been 16 Presidents in the 20th century. Only one of that number has had the opportunity to sign his name to more major legislation from one session of Congress than I will sign this year.

In fact, I think it can be said that "While there were a few exceptions, this Congress has displayed a greater freedom from mere partisanship than any other peacetime Congress since the administration of President Washington himself."

Those words are not my own. As some may recognize, that was the tribute paid to the second session of the 73d Congress on June 28, 1934, by President Franklin D. Roosevelt. That session produced 32 major legislative accomplishments. This session of the energetic, even-handed, and effective 88th Congress has produced 25 major measures already. Since none of us are in a hurry to get home, there may be many more.

There is one indelible lesson from this. Our American system functions best when it functions as the Founding Fathers intended, without divisive partisanship, with a united will to put the country and the people first. We don't have to have stalemates. We don't have to have issues carry-

ing over from session to session, generation to generation, or even century to century. We can make this system work and that is what members of both parties in both houses of the Congress are doing.

Of the many measures enacted this year, this legislation ranks near the top of the list in importance to the entire country. This is much more than just a pay bill. It is, as the title says, a reform measure, the Government Employees Salary Reform Act of 1964. For the first time this gives us the tools to identify and inspire, to reward and retain excellence in our Federal service.

This is one of the most profound advances in the last 30 years or longer. We are very sensibly putting behind us in this country the concept that the Federal service can be treated indifferently as a massive, mindless, faceless, anonymous bureaucracy.

America's challenges cannot be met in this modern world by mediocrity at any level, public or private. All through our society we must search for brilliance, welcome genius, strive for excellence. And this measure will help us to do that in our Federal Government.

This legislation provides both the flexibilities and the incentives to recognize differences between marginal, competent, and superior performance. I hope that every responsible manager will use these tools fully, use them equitably, and use them conscientiously.

Our continuing goal is to fulfill the mandate of making Federal salaries reasonably comparable with those of private life. Alongside that goal is the parallel objective of expecting and achieving high productivity. Everyone in the Federal Service, from the lowest grade to the highest, has the responsibility of assuring the American taxpayer full value for every dollar spent and that no dollar will be spent unnecessarily.

The United States Government has great responsibilities as our largest employer. This legislation helps us set a better example. I might note especially that the salary in-

creases, when averaged across the years of no increase, are within the range of the wage guideposts suggested for private enterprise.

I congratulate the Congress, the Federal employees, and the leaders of their groups who are here this morning, and I might say a special thanks to three outstanding journalistic "Congressmen" the gentlemen from the Washington Post, Star, and News, Mr. Kluttz, Mr. Young, and Mr. Cramer.

NOTE: The President spoke in midmorning in the Rose Garden at the White House. In his concluding remarks he referred to Jerry Kluttz, Joseph Young, and John F. Cramer, columnists for the Washington Post, the Washington Star, and the Washington Daily News, respectively.

The Government Employees Salary Reform Act of 1964 is Public Law 88–426 (78 Stat. 400).

515   Remarks by Telephone on the Occasion of the Commissioning of the U.S.S. *Casimir Pulaski.*   *August 14, 1964*

I AM proud to participate today in these ceremonies. We are adding a name, that all Americans honor, to our nuclear fleet which all free men so greatly trust. Our birth as a nation was attended by many brave men from many lands. Their names we shall never forget and never cease to revere.

On the scroll of freedom no name is written larger than that of General Pulaski. In his native Poland and on these shores he fought with a valor always so much a part of the Polish people. He reached our country saying, "I came to hazard all for the freedom of America." On October 11, 1779, at the Battle of Savannah he gave his all, laying down his life that our nation might be born in freedom.

In this century, America has sent her sons to hazard all for freedom around the world. Many have not returned, but our sacrifice has not been in vain. In our times

the world is safer and freedom is more secure. The hope for peace is brighter and the confidence and ultimate victory for our cause has never been greater than it is now.

In all the history of man, few peoples have been privileged to bear the responsibilities for all mankind which are borne now by this generation of Americans. Those responsibilities require us to run a responsible course through the perilous seas of our times. The U.S.S. *Pulaski,* which we commission today, is part of our great effort to uphold the trust for peace which rests in our hands.

Today no nation on earth is so strong as ours. That strength is committed to peace and that commitment is both irrevocable and unhesitating. Any who choose to be enemies of peace can trust that America's strength will be ready for use as the ally of peace. All who choose to be friends of peace can likewise trust that America's great strength will be used responsibly by a nation that is deeply conscious of its responsibilities to all mankind.

NOTE: The President spoke in midafternoon by telephone from the Cabinet Room at the White House.

His remarks were carried by loudspeakers on the vessel and at dockside to several thousand persons attending the commissioning of the Polaris-carrying nuclear submarine at the yards of the Electric Boat Division of the General Dynamics Corporation in Groton, Conn.

516   The President's News Conference of
August 15, 1964

THE PRESIDENT. [1.] I have signed a joint resolution and issued a proclamation calling on all Americans and our friends in other lands to see more of our great country, to visit and to enjoy our historic shrines and our scenic wonders.[1]

This resolution and proclamation are important for several reasons:

First, we Americans and our friends abroad need to discover and visit the many great places in our own land. In July of 1963, when President Kennedy sent his balance-of-payments message to Congress, he urged that private industry launch a drive to encourage Americans "to learn more about their own country and the glory of their heritage." This private industry effort is already underway, and this resolution and this proclamation, I hope, will make a contribution to it.

Second, travel within the United States provides the opportunity to keep abreast of the changes which are constantly occurring across the land, and to appreciate more fully the diverse characteristics possessed by the different regions of this lovely country. This diversity which has contributed to the strength and to the broad appeal of America includes not only the many sections of our mainland, but our newest States of Alaska

and Hawaii, as well as the Commonwealth of Puerto Rico and the Virgin Islands and the Caribbean and the Pacific Ocean territories.

Third, I would urge that Americans enjoy the recreational opportunities which this country offers. Life is at its best when balanced between work and play, and our land provides limitless opportunities for both. I am sure Lady Bird will attest to this wherever she may be as I speak.

Americans are now enjoying an income in excess of twice that of 1929. Much of this increased income is going as it should, to increased recreation and to increased enjoyment of the out-of-doors. New jobs that are being generated in restaurants and hotels, motels and resorts, and recreational centers of the country contribute to the expansion of our national well-being, providing an important contribution, therefore, to our total economy. Tourism is an important industry for many parts of our land and can be a powerful factor in building the economy of such areas as Appalachia.

And fourth, all Americans can gain a richer sense of the Nation's history and traditions by visiting our historic sites. I am confident that the "See the United States" program will be successful and I urge both American citizens and citizens of other countries to travel whenever they can throughout our beautiful country.

I am happy to say to you this morning

---

[1] Public Law 88–416 (78 Stat. 388), approved on August 11, 1964, and Proclamation 3607 "See the United States in 1964 and 1965," issued on August 15, 1964 (29 F.R. 11883, 3 CFR 1964 Supp.).

that Mrs. Johnson and Lynda Bird and Luci are practicing what I am preaching. They are touring the countryside today, visiting, seeing new people, enjoying some of the historic shrines and scenic wonders of our great country, from the far West in Montana, Idaho, Utah, and Wyoming, where Mrs. Johnson is, to Wisconsin where Luci is in the afternoon, to Long Island where Lynda is now.

[2.] Now to another subject that may interest you. Because all matters relating to nuclear weapons are matters of great gravity, I think it is quite important to have the record absolutely straight on this matter of the orders to the commanders in the Gulf of Tonkin that I issued last week.

On Wednesday, at a Governors' Conference, peace conference, at Hershey, Pa., Senator Goldwater, the Republican candidate, said repeatedly that the President had given an "admonition" to the commanders to use "any weapons." He admitted that he had not seen the orders; that he had not read the orders; that he did not know what was in the orders. But he said that he had read of this "admonition" in some newspaper.

The truth and the record show, and show plainly: (1) that I gave no such admonition in public or in private; (2) that our orders to the commanders plainly specified conventional ordnance weapons only; (3) that Secretary of Defense McNamara made this fact entirely plain again in a public press conference one-half hour after my speech, and it, too, was carried by both radio and television on August 4th; and (4) no magazine or daily, or even weekly newspaper that we can locate contains any such report of any such "admonition."

There was, therefore, no justification whatever for Senator Goldwater's initial statements, and it was both necessary and proper, I think, for the Secretary of State and for the Secretary of Defense to call the Republican candidate's interpretation "unjustified and irresponsible."

So yesterday, Senator Goldwater took back the charges he made on Wednesday. He now says he did not mean what he said on Wednesday. It is said, instead, that it was not so much what I said, as he speaks in retrospect, but what Secretary McNamara said. And then he charges we used fuzzy language.

This appears clearly in the Philadelphia Enquirer, the front page, this morning.

But in this discussion, it is not our language that has been fuzzy. The Senator has repeated the charge that we said "all weapons," whereas in fact we said the opposite, and the record proves it.

The Senator has thus suggested again that we gave field commanders authority to use nuclear weapons. This suggestion is preposterous, because we had carefully, explicitly, and publicly ruled out the use of nuclear weapons and stated so on the radio and on the television the day the attack was ordered.

The Senator points to no language of mine which justifies any of his many different interpretations. He has not cited the name of any paper in the United States, or any press service in the country, or has not even told any reporter where he heard or where he saw any such language. He does not do so because he cannot do so. His running mate now speaks in a corridor of a Government building of the President having authorized "complete, full retaliation," and this assertion is equally false and reckless.

From the beginning the language that responsible Government officials have used in this crisis has been most carefully chosen. Our position has been explained not only in repeated public statements but in working sessions with the leaders of both parties, and with at least three committees of the Congress, including the Armed Services Committee, of which Senator Goldwater is a member, but which he did not attend. No one has misunderstood this matter except the Republican candidates.

The control of nuclear weapons is one of the gravest of all the responsibilities of the Commander in Chief, the President of the United States. Loose charges on nuclear weapons without any shadow of justification by any candidate for any office, let alone the Presidency, are a disservice to our national security, a disservice to peace, and, as for that matter, a great disservice to the entire free world.

So it seems to me that even at the price of some reflection the Republican candidate ought to keep his lenses in his glasses, at least on the subject of nuclear warheads.

[3.] The Secretary of Defense has reported to me this morning that he has approved a program for the development of an aircraft designed specifically for air support of counterinsurgency, and limited war operations, and the Department of the Navy to contract for the building of seven prototype aircraft at a cost of about $18 million.

This counterinsurgency (COIN) aircraft will be an airborne equivalent of the "jeep." It will be able to perform peacetime emergency functions such as disaster relief, medical missions, or riot control, as well as military missions to include light armed reconnaissance, helicopter escort and attack, and support of ground troops.

The aircraft will have the capability to operate from rough clearings, primitive roads, and waterways, in addition to prepared airfields and aircraft carriers.

This aircraft has been extensively studied by the military services. The Marine Corps initially stated the formal requirement for a light armed reconnaissance aircraft and the

Air Force confirmed the need for such an aircraft. The Marine Corps supplied the specifications. The Navy was designated as the developing agency.

The first flight of the new aircraft will be in about 1 year. I am sure if you are interested the Defense Department will give you further details.

[4.] I shall send to the Senate on Monday the nomination of Mr. Sargent Shriver to head the poverty program. I have talked to Mr. Shriver about this, and I have carefully reviewed all the people that could be available for this very important assignment. I am making my recommendation of Mr. Shriver. I think he has done an excellent job during the time he has been in public service, and I hope the Senate will take prompt action.

In addition, we are tentatively selecting some 22 job corps conservation camps to be opened this year in the States of Arizona, Arkansas, California, Idaho, Maryland, Massachusetts, Montana, New Mexico, New York, North Carolina, Oregon, Pennsylvania, Utah, Virginia, Washington, and Wyoming. Further details on the camps will be made available to you by Mr. Shriver's office, when the negotiations have proceeded further.

I will be glad now to take any questions.

[5.] Q. Mr. President, do you feel any sort of concern about the situation in Congress where the redistricting thing or reapportionment may threaten adjournment?

THE PRESIDENT. Yes, I am always interested in any matter that concerns the country and the Congress. I will talk to the congressional leaders about their schedule, when we meet again on Tuesday, and I am sure that we will discuss this subject and others rather fully.

[6.] Q. Mr. President, there has been some question about as to why you felt it necessary to specify conventional ordnance in your instructions to the fleet. The commanders would not have instructions to use other than conventional ordnance, would they?

THE PRESIDENT. Well, we may have anticipated that some people would be asking that question and we wanted to be sure the record was clear. But we have made a very clear record on it, and we think we were justified in doing so, and we think that the American people would be glad that we had done so, at least if it served no other purpose. It brought out on the table what had happened and made it clear that unsubstantiated charges would not stand up for long.

Q. Mr. President, do you think that the Senator's comments on this matter have caused us harm abroad with other nations?

THE PRESIDENT. I am unable to evaluate that. I want to be sure that the people of my own country and the people of the world know that we speak and act with responsibility.

[7.] Q. Mr. President, as Senate majority leader, you always sought consensus on legislation. If the consensus of the State Democratic leaders, convention delegations, labor leaders, Negro leaders, points toward one man as your running mate, would you be bound or guided by it?

THE PRESIDENT. I would only say now that I am carefully and conscientiously and earnestly considering the availability of various individuals, and at the appropriate time when I have reached a conclusion that I think is a good one and a sound one, and one worthy of the Presidency, I will make my recommendations.

[8.] Q. Mr. President, are you in favor of the candidacy of Robert Kennedy for the U.S. Senate seat in New York State?

THE PRESIDENT. I explained that to you yes-

terday. I have no desire to repeat it, unless you failed to get it the first go-round. I never interfere in primaries of any kind. I think you know, and I think those present realize, that I have a very high regard for the ability of the Attorney General. He has performed outstanding public service in very important posts in this administration and before this administration in the legislative branch of the Government. I have worked closely with him and admired his performance.

I made it clear, however, that he had not consulted me when we talked here in the White House about any desires he might have. He has not asked me to make any recommendations. I have not made any recommendations. I will not intervene in New York, or Massachusetts, or Texas in a primary. I have repeated that time and time again. I have no desire to repeat the speech, but if any of you have any doubt that same rule has applied to my entire public life. Who the Democratic Party selects as a nominee in New York, or Massachusetts, or Texas, is a matter for the Democrats of that State.

As close as I was to Mr. Rayburn and as long as we served together, I never even intervened when he had a hot congressional race. And he did not intervene in my primaries either. I hope that makes clear that, first, I have great admiration for the Attorney General; second, the matter of whether he is a candidate in New York or not is a matter for him to decide and for the people of New York to decide. And when they make that decision, I am sure it will be a good one.

[9.] Q. Mr. President, sir, there is a report published this morning that the administration is now supporting a modified version of the medicare bill rather than the original King-Anderson bill. Is this correct?

Could you help us out on that?

THE PRESIDENT. The administration strongly favors the King-Anderson bill. No one speaking for the administration has ever made any statement at variance with that. I do not want to assume the responsibility for keeping accuracy in reporting, but this is the first question that has been raised since that report about the administration's attitude, and if I had been consulted by the reporter who made the report, I would have answered him as I am answering you.

We favor the King-Anderson bill. The administration has favored it for several years. We will continue to favor it and do everything we can to get it enacted.

[10.] Q. Mr. President, you say you feel Senator Goldwater has performed a disservice to the national security and to world peace. Do you feel he should now publicly recant what he said and join you in setting the record straight?

THE PRESIDENT. That is a matter for the Republican candidate and his own conscience.

[11.] Q. Mr. President, in this same connection, sir, do you plan to renew your offer to make intelligence files available to Senator Goldwater so they can be of use to him in the campaign?

THE PRESIDENT. I don't see any necessity or requirement to renew it or restate it. It still exists. We made the briefings available to all the candidates. Governor Scranton accepted them, Ambassador Lodge had them available to him and utilized them, and even Governor Stassen came here and was thoroughly briefed. We have made that offer to the Republican nominee. If he does not care to have the information or the knowledge that would be contained in those briefings, that is a matter for him. I would say it is a matter entirely for his judgment and for his conscience.

The administration's record is clear that we want every person seeking the office of the Presidency, every responsible candidate, to have responsible and accurate information, and full knowledge, on the position of our Government and conditions in the world. If he does not desire to receive that knowledge, that is entirely a matter for him.

[12.] Q. Mr. President, there have been some public comments that Mr. Yarmolinsky [2] had been offered as a sort of a sacrifice to the southerners in exchange for support of the poverty program. I wonder if you would care to make any further comment on that?

THE PRESIDENT. I don't want to get into another running discussion here like we are in on nuclear weapons. What public comment? Who said what, so I will know what I am answering and what I am saying.

Q. Sir, I believe there were some published columns from various sources.

THE PRESIDENT. I would think that probably you ought to seek the columnist and see what the source of his information is. Mr. Yarmolinsky is employed by the Defense Department. And the Defense Department, the Labor Department, the Health, Education, and Welfare Department, and the Justice Department are jointly interested in the poverty program, so they all shared a part in preparing it. No one, to repeat, to emphasize, no one, at any time, any place, anywhere, suggested to me anyone for any of these places. The first information that I had that Mr. Yarmolinsky was, in effect, appointed to one of these places that did not exist was the columnist rumor that you talked about.

I was informed by the leader of this task force, Mr. Shriver, that he had made no recommendations to anyone, that he had

---

[2] Adam Yarmolinsky, Assistant to the Secretary of Defense.

not recommended Mr. Yarmolinsky to anyone associated with me, or with me, and did not plan to. I have asked Mr. Shriver, now that the bill has passed and we plan to start selecting our personnel, to review the four other Presidential appointments and submit his recommendations to me. I would not be able to say in advance whether I would embrace all those recommendations or not, but I would certainly be inclined to.

We do not plan to give any assignment, necessarily, to any person who participated in the drafting of it, and that may have been the reason for the report being given out. Nor do we plan to make any assignment because some columnists think we ought to.

[13.] Q. Mr. President, the question has been raised from time to time on the possibility of a defense slip in the presidential campaign debate.

THE PRESIDENT. Defense what?

Q. Of a defense slip in a presidential campaign debate. In other words, if you were to debate with Senator Goldwater, he has raised the question, himself, that the President shouldn't debate on TV because there might be a defense slip.

THE PRESIDENT. We will get into that after our convention when we make a decision in the matter. I don't quite follow what you are saying now. But after the convention, if I am the nominee, we will go into all manners of how we will conduct the campaign and we will give you due and adequate notice.

[14.] Q. Mr. President, we have been told that the Senate-House conferees on the beef import restrictions are trying to work out a compromise acceptable both to the cattle industry and to the White House. Could you tell us what might be acceptable to you along this line?

THE PRESIDENT. The Secretary of State is working with the appropriate leadership in both Houses in connection with this very important subject, and I am hopeful that we will be able to reach some meeting of the minds that will be satisfactory to all.

[15.] Q. Mr. President, do you anticipate that Mrs. Johnson will be campaigning this year?

THE PRESIDENT. She is and will be.

[16.] Q. Mr. President, Mayor McKeldin of Baltimore yesterday had lunch with Mr. Jenkins. Is there any indication that he is going to play a role in the campaign with you?

THE PRESIDENT. I didn't know that they had lunch together, so I wouldn't be able to tell you what happened. This is the first information I had about it.

[17.] Q. Mr. President, do you favor a Secret Service guard now for Senator Goldwater?

THE PRESIDENT. I haven't explored that subject. If the Senator felt that he was in danger in any way and felt the necessity of protection and felt that we ought to carefully consider adopting a policy of protecting candidates, I would be glad to review it carefully and try to work out some kind of an agreement that would be satisfactory to him. He has not told me of his views on the matter. All I know about it is what I have seen about the suggestion of the Vice Presidential candidate.

[18.] Q. Mr. President, the Wall in Berlin was just 3 years old. Do you see any chances for tearing it down?

THE PRESIDENT. We are constantly concerned with improving the conditions of the free world. We are very proud of our relationship with the Federal Republic of Germany. We are going to continue in cooperation with them to do everything that is humanly possible to bring about the unification of the great people of Germany at the earliest possible date.

[19.] Q. Mr. President, what are the issues in this campaign, as you see them?

THE PRESIDENT. We plan, after our convention in Atlantic City, to release to the country the platform we have adopted, and that
platform will be an affirmative, positive declaration of the problems, the issues, and the
matters that we think are of most concern
to the American people.

Hearings on that platform will begin
Monday. I think the appearance of those
witnesses gives some indication of the subjects that we think are most important.
The Secretary of State will lead off and will
discuss conditions in the world, our viewpoint pertaining to those conditions, what
this administration has done in connection
with our relations with other nations and
in our attempt to prevent the spread of
communism and the enslavement of free
people.

I think Secretary Rusk will point out, as I
did at the Bar Association a few days ago,[3]
that peace in the world is the primary objective of our party and our country, and we
have had many difficult problems but we are
quite proud that communism has not en-
veloped any single nation and taken it over
since Cuba in 1959. We do have several
spots in the world that create serious problems, but we will try to outline our approach
to the problems of peace.

That will be followed by our preparedness efforts, the strength of our Nation, and
how important it was that we improve our
defenses as we did when President Kennedy
came into office. He has recommended
the expenditure of $30 billion over and above
what would have been recommended in
the last year of the last Republican administration. So, we think that peace and
preparedness are very important.

We will discuss economic conditions at
some length in this platform, working
conditions, agricultural conditions. We are
sure that peace and preparedness and prosperity will all be subjects of discussion and
will more or less resolve themselves into
the presentation of opposite viewpoints.
You might refer to these as some of the principal issues.

[20.] Q. Mr. President, Congressman
Albert[4] this morning seemed a little uncertain as to at what point you would review
the platform. Could you tell us at what
point you will review it?

THE PRESIDENT. I haven't worked out that
agenda, that date. Whenever it is available and they would care to review it with
me or discuss it, I would try to find the time
to do so.

[21.] Q. Mr. President, you've mentioned responsibility in government a great
deal in the last week or two. Is this going
to be an issue in the campaign?

THE PRESIDENT. No, I had not felt that I
was overstressing any particular thing, and
I had not intended to indicate that. I observe that when I say our country is strong
that it is usually interpreted as a reply or a
jab. When I say something about responsibility, that may have sudden implications,
but they must be your implications. I don't
intend them to imply anything other than
what I say.

I do believe that I want my administration
to be constructive, affirmative, forward-
looking, progressive, and always, of course,
responsible.

Merriman Smith, United Press International: Thank you, Mr. President.

NOTE: President Johnson's twenty-sixth news conference was held in the Rose Garden at the White
House at 1:10 p.m. on Saturday, August 15, 1964.

---

[3] See Item 511.

[4] Representative Carl Albert of Oklahoma, Majority Floor Leader.

517 Remarks to Members of the Communications Satellite Corporation Board. *August* 17, 1964

ONLY 18 months ago you of this Board were handed the skeleton of an idea. In this short time you have fleshed that skeleton and brought that idea to life.

You have won the confidence of 130,000 stockholders and the congratulations of 190 million Americans. I am personally gratified by the job you have done.

I believed at the time—and I believe more strongly now—that President Kennedy and the Congress were right in the concept of this Communications Satellite Corporation.

The law creating this corporation reaffirms our devotion to private enterprise and private initiative. But it does more. This law reiterates our resolve to protect and preserve private ownership as the partner—not the victim—of Government's current role in research and development.

Whatever tides run in the world, there is no tide of nationalization or socialization running in the United States. Your Government is determined to support our private sector—not subjugate it. We want to stimulate private initiative—not suppress it.

Our private economy is responding to this confidence and certainty—with 42 consecutive months of the longest, largest, and most stable prosperity ever known in peacetime.

Some may talk of radical changes in our policies—of greater governmental intervention in the economy or abrupt governmental withdrawal from our commitments to our own people. For myself, I do not believe the American people are interested in economic radicalism and recklessness.

We are going to hold our course and preserve our prosperity.

Several years ago I expressed the view that the communications satellite program would produce "one of the most dramatic advances in human history."

You are on the leading edge of that dramatic advance.

In 3 years you will have a worldwide communications system in operation. Even sooner, operations will be established with many nations, particularly our European friends.

The practical benefits ahead are too numerous to count—for business, trade, education, research, and other fields. Above all, we know better communication means better understanding and better understanding is the doorway to world peace.

The communications technology of space will open many new doors to understanding.

For the first time, we will have 24-hour-a-day telephone service to all areas of the world.

For the first time it will be possible to publish and deliver daily newspapers worldwide—provide worldwide photo facsimile services—transmit hundreds of written messages per second continent to continent.

We will be able to transmit entire contents of valuable books from our oldest and largest libraries to our newest and smallest libraries in less than a minute. All the human knowledge stored in computers will be available in seconds to help solve problems half-a-world away.

You are helping pioneer this exciting new advance for all mankind.

You can be proud of your public service—just as I am proud of your public spirit in handling this vital organizational task.

NOTE: The President spoke at 6:35 p.m. in the Cabinet Room at the White House.

The Communications Satellite Corporation was established by act of Congress approved August 31, 1962 (76 Stat. 423). See also "Public Papers of the Presidents, John F. Kennedy 1962," Item 476.

518 Statement by the President Upon Sending Copies of the Moon Photographs to Leaders of 110 Nations. *August 17, 1964*

IN THE NAME of the people of the United States, as an expression of their desire that human knowledge be used for human betterment, I am sending to the leaders of 110 nations a set of photographs of the moon taken by the cameras of the Ranger VII on its historic mission of July 31, 1964. Each set includes five photographs taken at distances from the lunar surface varying from 480 miles down to 100 feet.

The success of the Ranger VII exploration has been greeted with enthusiasm and interest around the world. Men of all nations recognize this is one of the greatest extensions of human knowledge about the lunar surface to occur in many centuries.

The American people can be justly proud. We started behind in the space age. But we placed our trust in our open society and free system. Our achievements in peaceful exploration of space give us all cause to be proud, grateful, and confident.

Since the beginning of our space effort, the United States has invited and urged all nations to make this vital new exploration a joint venture of international cooperation. More than 60 countries now work together voluntarily in this pursuit. We continue to hope that the extent of such international cooperation will be enlarged and that all nations will join through the United Nations to place the peaceful realms of space off-limits to the designs of aggressors on earth.

The responsibility placed upon us by our role is great and continuing. I am sure the American people will continue to support what is necessary to assure leadership. In return they will rightfully expect that our program hold to the orderly and responsible course which has brought such outstanding success in such a short period.

519 Statement by the President Upon Issuing Memorandum on the Staffing of International Organizations. *August 17, 1964*

I HAVE issued a memorandum which seeks to assure that the very highest caliber of Americans will be available for staffing the international organizations in which the United States plays a role.

Over the years, United States participation in such organizations has been constantly increasing. We have sponsored many of them and we contribute financially to all of them. At the present time we belong to more than 50 such groups.

It seems to me to be the part of wisdom to back our stake in such groups with the very highest caliber of people available. The capacity and effectiveness of these organizations depend upon the quality of those who administer them. And even though I have a great deal of respect for the efforts of those Americans already working in them, I do not feel we have done enough to help these agencies secure the services of highly qualified American men and women from private life and from Government agencies.

Final responsibility for selecting people rests quite properly with the appropriate agencies themselves. But it is our duty, not only to the international agencies but to our own country, to be certain that in recruiting their personnel, these agencies have ready access to talented and dedicated Americans who are qualified by every prudent test.

With that thought in mind, I have approved the attached memorandum.

MEMORANDUM TO THE HEADS OF EXECUTIVE DEPARTMENTS AND AGENCIES

It is the policy of this government to do its full share to assist in the development of sound, efficient international organizations to keep the peace, to resolve disputes, to promote peaceful change, to conduct a world war against poverty, to exchange technology, and for other purposes.

At the present time we belong to more than half a hundred such organizations. We have sponsored many of them. We contribute financially to all of them.

But the capacity and efficiency of these organizations depend, in the end, upon the quality and the motivations of the international civil servants who administer them. These organzations—and our national interest in their fortunes—deserve the services of some of the ablest citizens of the United States. In past years we have not done enough to help these agencies secure the services of highly qualified men and women from private life and from government agencies.

Final responsibility for selection of personnel to staff international organizations rests, of course, with the appropriate officers of those organizations. But we must make sure that recruitment of their personnel is supported by ready access to talented citizens of this country who are qualified for positions in the international agencies.

It is my desire that:

(1) All Executive Departments and Agencies take affirmative and continuing steps to assist international organizations to obtain properly qualified United States candidates for employment.

(2) All Executive Departments and Agencies encourage their able employees to accept assignments with international organizations in accordance with the authority of Public Law 85–795, and give positive recognition to the government's interest in the training and career advancement advantages of such employment.

(3) All Executive Departments and Agencies continue employer contributions toward Federal retirement and insurance benefits for employees serving international organizations in accordance with the authority of Public Law 85–795, in the absence of arrangements for such contributions by the employing international organization.

(4) All Executive Departments and Agencies assist actively in finding qualified candidates in their fields of specialization when requested to do so by the Agencies having primary responsibility.

(5) The Secretary of State provide leadership and coordination of this effort and develop policies and procedures to advance it, including the seeking of assistance from the state and local governments and from non-governmental organizations in locating qualified candidates in private employment.

(6) The Secretary of State report annually on the effectiveness of the recruitment program in behalf of international organizations established herein.

This memorandum shall be published in the Federal Register.

LYNDON B. JOHNSON

August 15, 1950

520   Remarks Upon Signing Bill Extending the Hill-Burton Act.
August 18, 1964

Members of the Congress, ladies and gentlemen:

Americans have always been great hospital builders. At home our first general hospital was built 25 years before the signing of the Declaration of Independence—and both events occurred in the same city, Philadelphia.

Abroad, the men in many lands have first met America, and first understood the character of the American people, in hospitals that were built by American hands.

Since World War II the Federal Government and the States, working together under the Hill-Burton program, have made long studies to keep up with our growing needs.

I deeply regret that Senator Hill cannot be with us this morning. He is in the hospital and I think we should all send him our best wishes for an early return to the Senate and our deep gratitude for the efforts that he has made throughout the years in connection with this great program.

We have added more than 300,000 hospital and nursing home beds and have added nearly 2,000 other health facilities. Today, for every 10 hospital beds our growing population requires, 8 are already in place and available for use.

We have many new hospitals today in cities that are large and small. But many of our most important hospitals are too old. The hospitals which serve more than two-thirds of our population in nearly 200 metropolitan areas are obsolete, are out of date, are desperately in need of modernization. This legislation that I am signing today will help us get started on that long overdue job.

Our record on hospital beds is good. The record on nursing home beds is not so good. For every 10 nursing home beds that are needed to provide long-term care for older citizens, only 4 beds are in service now. With our population over 65 increasing by 1,000 every 24 hours, we need to catch up and this legislation that your Congressmen have passed will help us do that.

Good medical practice and good facilities are inseparable. America's families—old, young, and middle-aged—deserve the most modern hospital facilities.

We are meeting this demand. The 88th Congress, is not only the education Congress, it is, I am happy to say, the better health Congress. It has done more than any other Congress to provide the health facilities and the health manpower that the American people ought to have.

The Hill-Burton hospital construction program has been extended another 5 years, but Congress has also provided assistance for constructing mental health facilities, mental retardation facilities, the medical and dental schools that we need.

And Congress has helped to meet our health manpower needs by a program to overcome our critical shortage of nurses, a program to train more graduate public health personnel, and by providing assistance to students attending medical and dental and nursing schools.

We are supporting, as no nation on earth has ever supported, the strength of our medical profession. We are supporting them with modern facilities, with more and better trained manpower, and productive research in more and more fields. I believe that we are pursuing a sensible and yet a most responsible course.

Americans have no patience with mixing politics and medicine and there is going to be none of that.

Our American medical profession is the best that the world has ever known. Our only purpose is to help that profession, never to harass it. We are casting our vote for the medical profession's effectiveness, regardless of how that profession casts its own votes in our election.

So I want to congratulate all the Members of the Congress who are here this morning and the others who couldn't be here for their contributions on this bill. I want to especially congratulate my two old and dear friends and colleagues, Senator Lister Hill, about whom I spoke earlier, and my neighbor and friend for many years, Congressman Oren Harris.

NOTE: The President spoke in midmorning in the Cabinet Room at the White House. In the course of his remarks he referred to Senator Lister Hill of Alabama and Representative Oren Harris of Arkansas.

The Hospital and Medical Facilities Amendments of 1964 is Public Law 88–443 (78 Stat. 447).

521   The President's News Conference of *August* 18, 1964

THE PRESIDENT. [1.] I have a moment here, before I have some recordings I want to do and I have a 12 o'clock meeting. George [1] told me that a suggestion that I made to him earlier might be helpful, if I carried it out. So I thought I would review with you some of the things we are going to do the rest of the week, so you can have some advance notice of it.

I have some real news for you this morning. I can announce positively that the husband and father in this house has not, repeat *not,* seen a moose all day and is mighty happy to have his family back with him.

As a friend observed this morning, he said he had read about some of my problems and he believed the White House is the one place where the grass is greener on the other side of the fence. We have been doing something more than watering the lawn around here, though, and we have some other plans. We put in a busy time over the weekend seeing all the press and going to church Sunday.

[2.] For your information, guidance,

---
[1] George E. Reedy, Press Secretary to the President.

and background, I want to tell you about some of the plans in the days ahead. As you know, we have been conducting a number of meetings with leadership of all segments of our national life, Congress, business, labor, public school superintendents, State university presidents, women's groups, foreign language publishers, chiefs of bureaus, members of the press, and so forth. A number of other such meetings are in the planning stages.

We will have some women's organizations in, leaders of other organizations and trade associations in various fields, leaders of Negro groups throughout the country, with whom we want to talk especially about observance, compliance, and enforcement of laws of particular concern to civil rights groups. These meetings will be announced as the plans are completed and as soon as we can get confirmation on the invitations.

This week we have a number of sessions scheduled at the White House that may be of interest to you and to the country. On Tuesday, at 5 o'clock, that is today, we will meet with the Community Relations Citizens Committee from all sections of the Nation and Governor Collins.[2] One of the members stayed all night with me last night, Mr. Palmer Hoyt of the Denver Post, and got me up early this morning.

On Wednesday, August 19, at 11:30 a.m. we will have 5,000 young people on the White House lawn as part of the White House seminar program. Let me say that our Nation's leadership challenge knows no age. Our young citizens have very great responsibilities in these times for active community leadership, wherever they live or attend school.

On Wednesday, August 19, in the evening, we have invited all Members of Congress, from both parties, to the White House for a richly deserved "Salute to Congress." When the record of this Congress is completed, it will place the 88th Congress in the record books as the most productive and, I think, the most constructive in the 20th century. Executive and congressional relationships could hardly have been better.

Before Members return home, I want to congratulate them personally, salute them, have them all to the White House once again. As you will remember, they were here a short time after I assumed the Presidency.

On Thursday, August 20, at 4:30 p.m., we have a broad cross section of small business leaders coming from throughout the Nation for a meeting at the White House on the general subjects we have followed before. We want to discuss economic opportunity for American enterprise. We want to explore a subject of first importance, the continued growth of job opportunities for all of our people. We will discuss the fiscal policy of the Government. We want to discuss

law observance, law enforcement.

On Saturday, August 22, we are inviting the Democratic Governors from 34 States to come to the White House for a working session in the afternoon and to stay with us for dinner that night, if they can. We are inviting all the Governors, although we know some of them are unable to come to the convention and some may be unable to come to Washington, may be out of the country.

In this administration we have given, and expect to continue to give, unusual attention to the constructive potential of the Federal-State relations. As I indicated last week in my remarks to the State university presidents, I feel a new era of resurgence and vitality is coming among the States. We want the Federal and State relations to enter a new era, too, and we are confident that it is possible.

One of the first meetings that I held after assuming office—after assuming office in November, I held the meeting in December—was with the Governors. Since then, I have had well over 100 meetings with at least 37 of our Governors, either here or in their States. We have met with 85 percent of the Democratic Governors and 50 percent of the Republican Governors. I hope to meet with them all and often.

Earlier this year the Republican Governors met here in Washington. I invited them to the White House. Unfortunately, they were not able to come. This week, for the first time this year, the Democratic Governors will be in this vicinity. So that is why we have asked them to come to the White House, if they can.

There is much we will talk about. Our programs are set now. Most of our appropriation bills have passed the House and the Senate and have been signed or are in con-

---

[2] LeRoy Collins, Director of the Community Relations Service, Department of Commerce, and former Governor of Florida.

ference. So we want to review with the Governors the impact of Federal activities on their State economies over the next 12 months. We will have a complete discussion and will review with them the impact of our defense and space programs and where we will be developing; the new opportunities for Federal and State cooperation in education and health programs—the Hill-Burton Act was signed this morning—the three educational bills we signed the latter part of last year; the mass transit program, and what it means for our metropolitan areas, just enacted; what we can all do together to increase the growth of plants and payrolls, new jobs and new opportunities.

[3.] We have gotten below the 5 percent barrier on unemployment and we want to keep moving. We will make to them a private report of a little survey that we are doing on the capital expenditures that are being made, capital investment that is providing jobs out in the States to help us break through that 5 percent unemployment figure.

As an illustration, one man told me if we could get the tax bill passed that his company could add 20,000 new people. He told me the other day that he had broken through and added 22,000 so far. So we are working with a good many companies asking them to do that, to help reduce the heavy youth unemployment.

We brought that down from 16 to 13, and the total unemployment is down for the first time, under 5 percent, in several years. We will review the full range of the record number of major legislative accomplishments and what these bills mean in helping our State governments meet their responsibilities.

[4.] The economic health and prosperity of the Nation today requires closer understanding and, I think, much closer cooperation among all our levels of Government. I believe it is in the interest of all the people for the White House and the State houses to work together with a new outlook, with a new trust, a new creativity, and this is our objective now in all that we do.

[5.] I just might add, for your information, that we have been meeting with various Governors who have been coming in and have been talking about problems in their State and politics in their States. A number of them spent the weekend with me at the White House. The same thing has been true of mayors who have come to the White House, mayors from the Midwest, Mayor Daley of Chicago, Mayor Wagner from New York, various mayors. We had the Midwest Governors in 2 or 3 weeks ago and we had Governor Brown and some of the Midwest Governors, the Governor of Indiana, and others in for dinner and they spent the weekend with us.[3]

So this time we will add to that by inviting them all. That is all I have to say, except that we are going to continue every week bringing people in from over the Nation to exchange viewpoints with and to discuss our problems with and to ask for their help.

[6.] If you have any questions on this schedule, or these points, I will be glad to have you ask them. I cannot spend the time on detailed questions, because the Prime Minister of Iceland has landed and is enroute to the White House now. He is going to come in the southwest gate and I will greet him and take him into the office for a

---

[3] The President referred specifically to Mayor Richard J. Daley of Chicago, Mayor Robert F. Wagner of New York, Governor Edmund G. Brown of California, and Governor Matthew E. Welsh of Indiana.

meeting. If you want to, I will take him on a little walk. I haven't had one and you can go with us.[4]

[7.] Q. That meeting with the Governors is Saturday afternoon of this week, sir?

THE PRESIDENT. Yes.

[8.] Q. Mr. President, can you tell us anything about your plans for next week?

THE PRESIDENT. No, but maybe Jack Valenti[5] can. With regard to the convention, I expect to go up later Thursday evening—I don't know what time—if I go at all.

[9.] Q. Mr. President, will you entertain a question about your schedule this morning?

THE PRESIDENT. Yes.

Q. Did you have a long visit with Senator Humphrey this morning, or can you tell us about it?

THE PRESIDENT. No, I didn't have a long one. After the signing there he wanted to report to me on a little situation there on the Hill, and he did. We discussed it a little earlier at breakfast. We didn't get to finish it.

[10.] Q. With respect to what you are saying about the economy, I don't know whether it is too early to ask this, but I was wondering how seriously the Government looks at the status of the automobile problem.

THE PRESIDENT. I don't want to get into a general press conference. I just said that.

This man is on his way here. There is nothing to say at this stage of the game. They are going through their routine.

[11.] Q. Mr. President, you said you talked politics with Governors and mayors. Did they give you an outlook on the situation throughout the country in November?

THE PRESIDENT. Yes.

Q. Can you tell us about that?

THE PRESIDENT. I don't think we ought to take time right now to talk about that. It is good.

[12.] Q. Mr. President, in relation to next week's schedule, have you decided how you will communicate with the convention on your vice presidential choice—how or when?

THE PRESIDENT. No.

Q. Mr. President, did I understand that you might not go to Atlantic City at all?

THE PRESIDENT. No.

Q. I misunderstood.

THE PRESIDENT. Evidently. I didn't say I would, or I wouldn't.

Q. You will go, if you are asked?

THE PRESIDENT. We will announce that, when we know definitely what we are going to do.

[13.] Q. Are there going to be any special ceremonies for the signing of the antipoverty bill on the 20th, I believe it is?

THE PRESIDENT. Yes. I believe there is a signing schedule arranged for and it seems to me it is on Thursday.

Alvin A. Spivak, United Press International: Thank you, Mr. President.

NOTE: President Johnson's twenty-seventh news conference was held in his office at the White House at 11:45 a.m. on Tuesday, August 18, 1964.

---

[4] Immediately after his news conference the President greeted Prime Minister Bjarni Benediktsson of Iceland and walked with him through the White House grounds. They were accompanied by members of the press.

[5] Jack Valenti, Special Consultant to the President.

522   Remarks to Members of the National Citizens Committee for Community Relations.   *August 18, 1964*

Governor Collins, Ambassador Dean, Mr. Manger, Mr. Wheeler, ladies and gentlemen:

On this occasion you come to begin work as important as any that has ever been undertaken by any Americans—in any time. You deserve the fullest gratitude of your President.

I believe that the occasion deserves, and the times require, that what is said now be spoken without thought of favor or without fear of consequence.

From long habit we speak too often in whispers, when we speak of race. We cannot evade our responsibilities now by speaking evasively, or softly, or illusively of what has become the central challenge of our society and its success.

Our national house stands strong and secure today. In that house, 190 million of us live together as no people of any nation have ever lived before—well paid, well clad, well housed, well schooled, well endowed in all things material and all things spiritual.

We cannot believe, and we cannot conceive, that life in our national house could ever be other than it is today. But we would do well, always, to recall the words spoken in another time by another President, "A house divided against itself cannot stand." That was true a century ago. It is no less true today.

Across our national house a long shadow is being cast. At the high noon of our success, the sun is being dimmed by the darkness of division, division that need not be, division that must not prevail. And that is what requires some frank speaking.

The shadow falling across America is not the shadow of race itself. It is the darker shadow of indefensible counsel about what America's response should be, about what our responsibilities are, and what are the challenges which race presents.

In the white community, and in the Negro community, counsel is being offered today which has no place in this land of ours. In both communities men are being told that no answer is better than any answer, that no progress is better than any progress, that no peace is better than any peace.

Whatever our race, whatever our region, we of this generation must understand what this counsel means and we must understand where this counsel leads. For, if we follow the logic of this counsel to its irresponsible conclusion, we would come inevitably to agree that no house is better than any house, that no America is better than any America in which our own wishes and will do not prevail alone.

This is not the course that we choose.

Division is not our destiny.

Failure at home is not to be the fate of our Nation which has succeeded so nobly in the world.

A time has come to cease telling ourselves and the world that the destiny and the fate of this Nation will be decided by street rioters and night riders.

A time has come to cease this cynical guessing of who will be helped and who will be hurt by disorders and disobedience and disrespect for the decency of our society.

All will be hurt, none will be helped, if responsible citizens sit on the sidelines regarding the stability of our society as a spectator sport.

So, then, let us together soberly face the facts before us. A problem older than any of us, older even than our Nation, as old as the history of man, himself, has come upon us to test our system and to challenge our society.

There are two courses open to us. We can meet the challenge, or we can turn away from it. We can master the problem, or we can leave it to master us.

Well, we have made our decision. We have chosen to meet it by the answer of law.

The law enacted by the Congress says simply that voting booths and classrooms, that public parks and public places, programs supported by public funds, shall be open to the public, all the public, on an equal basis.

This is not a law to select neighbors, or to dictate associates, or to control human relations. This is not a law to impose the power of the central Government upon the State governments of the land.

The provisions of this law merely validate for all people the national provisions of law already in force. And laws of this kind are in force with regard to public accommodations in all but 19 of our 50 States already. In most of the States, the State law that has been enacted, in many instances a long, long time ago, is much more comprehensive than the national law that was passed a few weeks ago.

The provisions of this law represent not the views of one party, but of both parties; not the views of one philosophy, but of all responsible philosophies.

The Civil Rights Act of 1964 would not be on our books today, except for the support that it received from the members of both parties: the Republican Party and the Democratic Party in both the Senate and the House. Conservatives voted for it, liberals voted for it. So we demand, and we are going to have, respect for law and order in this land. That respect begins with the law which is the law of our land today.

But respect for the law requires respect for ourselves. Self-respecting Americans will not—and must not—permit the destiny and the direction of their Nation to fall into the hands of those who seek our division.

And this means one thing: If we are to keep our system secure and our society stable, we must all begin to work where all of us work best. And where is that? That is in the communities where we all live today.

So that is the real challenge before us, as we meet here this afternoon in the shadow of the White House in this lovely Rose Garden.

Wherever we live, we must ask ourselves:

Are we prepared to give up our prosperity and our peace and let our prejudices make paupers of us all?

Are we of this generation to be remembered for allowing America's progress to run aground on the shoals of race?

The answers are "no."

A nation of courage and compassion, a nation of commonsense, must not and will not allow its greatness to be degraded by those who work only for its division.

The question before our Nation is not how whites will vote, or Negroes will vote, next November. The question is, how shall we work together and succeed together for the next 100 Novembers to come?

We all know that the Emancipation Proclamation was signed 100 years ago, but emancipation was a proclamation, it was not a fact. So, upon you in your own communities fall the great task of these times, the task of fostering understanding, the task of securing observation and compliance, the task of assuring justice for all Americans. And that is a very great task.

I wish you well. I pray for our success together; that this house in which we live shall stand and shall endure for all times to come. And let us, in our understanding and our tolerance and our patience, forgive those that know not what they do. Let's turn our cheek to those who would spread smear and fear and try to create problems that should not be developed.

Let us look at this land we love and be constantly reminded that the spotlight of the world is upon us and we are under that microscope and we are living in a goldfish bowl.

Let us ask ourselves if our every act, our every public declaration and exhibition, is being guided by the Golden Rule, "Do unto others as you would have them do unto you."

I secure the strength that permits me to endure the responsibilities that are mine from associating with good and great men and women who are willing to do what you are doing today, giving your very all to try to preserve the unity of this Nation.

I shall never cease to be grateful for men like Governor Hodges and Governor Collins who feel and who care and who love humanity, and who made great personal sacrifices in order to come here and work in the vineyard with us to try to heal the wounds and to avoid the pitfalls that they could see in this atmosphere.

I shall always be proud that I am a citizen of a country that can produce an Arthur Dean who, without any hesitancy, could leave a great law practice and say, "Where my country needs me, I will be." And to Mr. Manger and Mr. Wheeler and to each of you I again express my deep gratitude for all that you have done and all you are going to do on behalf of all the people of this country. I want to say "thank you" from a grateful heart.

NOTE: The President spoke at 5:10 p.m. in the Rose Garden at the White House. His opening words referred to LeRoy Collins, Director of the Community Relations Service, Department of Commerce, and former Governor of Florida, Arthur H. Dean, chairman of the National Citizens Committee for Community Relations and former head of the U.S. delegation to the disarmament negotiations in Geneva with rank of Ambassador, Julius Manger, executive vice chairman of the Committee and president of the Manger Hotels, and John H. Wheeler, vice chairman of the Committee and president of the Mechanics and Farmers Bank, Durham, N.C. Later in his remarks the President referred to Secretary of Commerce Luther H. Hodges, former Governor of North Carolina.

At the invitation of the President, the National Citizens Committee for Community Relations—a committee composed of national leaders in business, labor, education, and religion, working toward a broad national consensus in support of the Civil Rights Act—met in Washington with officials of the Department of Commerce to discuss methods of encouraging voluntary compliance with the law.

523   Remarks to the United States Marshals.
August 18, 1964

General Kennedy, Mrs. Kennedy, ladies and gentlemen:

I am honored to welcome you to this house this evening. I thought it best that we not assemble in the Cabinet Room. It looks something like a jury room—and some of you might try to keep us from talking to anyone on the outside. That would be quite a considerable handicap for Cabinet officers or Presidents in this election year!

The marshals' service and the Presidency are sharing a common anniversary. For both offices, this is the 175th year of existence.

We still have only one President. But where President Washington nominated 13 United States marshals, Presidents today nominate 91 of the 92 marshals.

The first task of the first marshal is still your task today—the task of maintaining respect for law and order on which our democratic system stands.

Our system and our society are made stronger by free expression, free petition, free and full debate. But no cause of liberty is ever license for disregard of the law or disrespect for those who serve as responsible agents of this system of justice of ours.

All who wear the badge bear a proud trust. Their conduct, their attitudes, their actions—off duty as well as on duty—personifies the dignity and the equity and the essential nobility of our society's highest values.

We demand much, and we receive much, from all such men as you. But our demands upon you and your families, and all who serve law enforcement, are not a one-way street.

Our society must always demand and must always require respect for the person of those who personify the majesty of the law. Any who defy, or defame, or do injury to law enforcement officers defame and do injury to all the people.

This is an exacting season in our national life, because we strive toward the exacting standards of free men: equal rights and equal responsibilities, equal opportunity and equal obligation, equal justice under law and equal respect for that law.

We have raised our standards high. We will maintain them without compromise. As Thomas Jefferson once put it, "Laws made by common consent must not be trampled on by individuals."

So we should never forget that lawlessness is found in many places and found in many forms. Sophisticated syndicates which systematically evade the law are no more tolerable to a law-abiding society than spontaneous street demonstrations which degenerate into disregard for the law.

I am determined that we shall use every resource of our Federal Government, in cooperation with State and local authorities, to eradicate organized crime in all of its forms. That extends from shakedown racketeers who prey on business and labor to smut peddlers who prey upon our youth.

You are doing high honor to a long tradition. In your honor this afternoon, I am issuing a proclamation designating your service's 175th anniversary—on September 24, 1964—as United States Marshals' Day, to be observed throughout all the States in this land.

I am particularly glad that our able Attorney General would call these meetings and institute a practice of regularly asking you to come here to meet with us and to counsel with us. I am happy about the high quality of personnel that make up the marshals in the United States.

I am very pleased to have in our company this afternoon a marshal who served his country in another capacity on a PT boat with our late beloved President Kennedy.

So, we are glad that you came here. We honor you for the fine work that you are doing. We thank you for the indulgence that you have given us in the critical days in many civil rights situations in the last few weeks.

We look forward, with great hope and expectancy, to the same high quality of dedicated service in the future that has so characterized your past.

Thank you very much.

NOTE: The President spoke at 6 p.m. in the Rose Garden at the White House at a reception for the U.S. Marshals and their families. His opening words referred to Attorney General and Mrs. Robert F. Kennedy. Later he referred to U.S. Marshal John E. Maguire, Sr., who served as a radioman on a PT boat with President Kennedy in the Asiatic theater in World War II.

On the same day the President issued Proclamation 3608 proclaiming September 24, 1964, as United States Marshal Day (29 F.R. 11995, 3 CFR, 1964 Supp.).

524   Letter to the Speaker in Support of the Establishment of a National Council on the Arts.   *August 18, 1964*

Dear Mr. Speaker:

I am glad to learn that H.R. 9586, which provides for the establishment of a National Council on the Arts, is scheduled for floor action today. The principles expressed in this legislation are sound and have my whole-hearted support.

There has been an encouraging growth of interest in the arts. For example, 85 cities and states have either formed or are in the process of forming arts councils, the number of symphony orchestras and the number of people who play musical instruments have virtually doubled in the last 25 years, and in the last 30 years the number of museums has grown from 1500 to 5000.

But there are many problems in the fields of the arts which not only are limiting their development, but threaten their very existence. Private initiative is, and should undertake the major responsibility for resolving these problems. However, they are also of vital concern to the Federal Government.

The formation of a council of outstanding representatives of the arts fields, as provided in the bill on the House floor, will help us express that concern and provide a method of cooperation with private groups that will have lasting benefits for all the people. In addition, this council will provide the much needed recognition of the artist, assure his place in society, and stimulate audience participation.

History has shown that, if we are to achieve The Great Society for which we are all working, it is essential that the arts grow and flourish.

Sincerely,

LYNDON B. JOHNSON

[Honorable John W. McCormack, Speaker of the House of Representatives, Washington 25, D.C.]

NOTE: On September 3, 1964, the President approved H.R. 9586 providing for the establishment of a National Council on the Arts (Public Law 88–579, 78 Stat. 905).

The membership of the Council was announced on February 23, 1965. Roger L. Stevens, Special Assistant to the President, was nominated as Chairman.

525   Remarks Upon Signing Bill Creating the National Commission on Technology, Automation, and Economic Progress.   *August 19, 1964*

Members of Congress, representatives and spokesmen for labor, captains of industry, business, ladies and gentlemen:

This office has many concerns. None receives more earnest attention or greater effort than the challenge of creating more jobs, creating better jobs for more people.

More Americans are working today than ever in history. Congress deserves the fullest share of credit. Members of both

Houses, Members of both parties have rejected make-work and handout answers to unemployment.

First things have been put first to enlarge private payrolls—not public relief rolls.

The record is reassuring. The President and the Government is deeply grateful for the cooperation demonstrated between the leaders of labor and the leaders of business.

The disturbing trend of the 1950's has

been reversed. Unemployment is no longer growing 10 percent a year as it did from 1952 to 1960. Instead, unemployment is shrinking at an average annual rate of 6.2 percent since 1961. Unemployment is below the 5 percent level because, in the last 4 years, our economy has created more than 4 million new jobs.

One of the best pieces of statistical information that the President has received in his first 8 months in office is the assurance by one of our leading businessmen that if the tax bill passed he would, in the first year, employ 20,000 additional workers.

At a luncheon the other day in the White House, he leaned over and whispered in my ear, "I put on 22,000 as I promised."

Since January 1961 we have created more new jobs in America than the total of the populations of nearly half the countries of the world. That is a remarkable and very reassuring record.

Our challenge now is to do even better this year, even better throughout this decade, even better throughout this century.

This legislation creating a National Commission on Technology, Automation, and Economic Progress will help us meet our responsibility.

Technology is creating both new opportunities and new obligations for us—opportunity for greater productivity and progress—obligation to be sure that no workingman, no family must pay an unjust price for progress.

Automation is not our enemy. Our enemies are ignorance, indifference, and inertia. Automation can be the ally of our prosperity if we will just look ahead, if we will understand what is to come, and if we will set our course wisely after proper planning for the future.

That is the purpose of this commission.

I hope and I expect that its work will benefit the workingman and benefit the businessman, and serve the interests of the farmer and the professionals and all of our people in America.

The techniques of automation are already permitting us to do many things that we simply could not do otherwise. Some of our largest industries, some of our largest employers would not exist and could not operate without automation, and some of those employers are here this morning.

We could not provide our great shield for the security of this country and the shield for the security of the free world if we did not have automation in the United States. If we understand it, if we plan for it, if we apply it well, automation will not be a job destroyer or a family displacer. Instead, it can remove dullness from the work of man and provide him with more than man has ever had before.

In all we do in this country, our objective first and last is to serve man and his greatness.

To those of you who are gathered around me this morning who contributed so much to bringing this bill to the stage that it is in today, I want to say thank you. I know that when the history of this country is written, you will be proud of the part you played in passing this act that will contribute so much to our Republic.

NOTE: The President spoke in midmorning in the Cabinet Room at the White House.

As enacted, the bill (H.R. 11611) is Public Law 88–444 (78 Stat. 462).

On November 14 the White House made public the names of 14 citizens appointed by the President to serve as members of the Commission, of which Dr. Howard R. Bowen, president of the University of Iowa, was nominated Chairman. The release stated that the membership was broadly representative of business, labor, and the public, and that it included experts in economics, engineering, sociology, industrial relations, and law.

526 Remarks to the White House Seminar Students.
August 19, 1964

IF I COULD ask your indulgence for a moment, I would like to present to you some participants in my seminar. Mrs. Johnson.

[*Mrs. Johnson responded briefly, telling the students they were doing "exactly what I would have liked to have done when I was your age." She expressed the hope that through their experience they would understand their Government better and would want to have a part in it to make it better in their time.*
[*The President then introduced his daughters Lynda Bird and Luci. Lynda Bird spoke briefly welcoming the students to the White House. The President then resumed speaking.*]

I hope that none of you will assume from the sign over there that Congress was going to come down here and be with us this morning. We know when Congress is coming. The big question is—when will they be leaving?

This is a nonpolitical occasion, I regret very much to say. It must be that way because you are bipartisan. Out of the 5,000 here, one lady spent the summer working in the office of Senator Goldwater. I am told that she was a Democrat when she came and I trust she has not moderated her convictions.

Personally and as your President, I am proud of you. I am proud to see you. I am glad that you are members of both parties. I am happy that you are taking an active and constructive interest in your Government which is served well by members of both parties.

I stand before you this morning as an example of what can happen to someone who is your age who comes to Washington to work for awhile, and then carries it to an extreme.

This city is your city. Wherever you go, whatever you do, I hope Washington will mean to you what Paris meant to Ernest Hemingway, as he describes it in the book which many of you are reading. May the memories of your Capital be always for you a "Moveable Feast" of constant delight and continuing pride.

You will carry with you the memories of libraries and museums, concerts and coffee hours, folk festivals and, by all means, discotheques. But my wish for you is that from this experience you will carry for the rest of your years a stronger and a surer faith in the role and the worth of the individual.

Your Government is large. You are sons and daughters of a massive age, an age when men and nations have been much concerned with massive force and massive power and massive struggles.

But I hope that your experiences and your observations have instilled into you a new and lasting faith in the fact that is paramount.

On this earth, there is no force so strong, none so powerful, none so finally decisive as the influence for good or evil of the committed man or the committed woman.

The course of this Nation, the contest of this world, will finally be decided not by the force of the atom, not by the strength of arms, not by the weight of industrial production. The future will finally fall to those that are most committed to their cause.

I know there are those who say of your generation that you are apathetic, that you are indifferent, that you are cold, hard, unfeeling, and uncaring security chasers seeking only a sports car, a split level, and an annuity.

Well, this I do not believe.

I know there are those who consider it correct to play it cool—right to remain reserved—not good form to show great faith.

But for myself, I believe that this generation of young Americans is a committed generation, anxious and asking to be permitted to fulfill that commitment. Where other generations of Americans have had a rendezvous with war, I believe that your generation, God willing, will keep a rendezvous with peace.

Whether at home or faraway, I believe it will be your destiny to fight wars men have never fought before—wars against poverty, wars against disease, against illiteracy, against discrimination, against all those things which blight the lives and the hopes of our fellowman.

As you are committed, I want you to know that your President is committed, too—committed to the future and not to the past, because we live in an age when the times men know in their youth are old history before men themselves have grown old.

The times of my generation's youth are old history now.

I came here—I was schooled here—in exciting and memorable years of our national history. None whoever knew those times can ever really forget them.

Your generation has no memory—as mine does—of Franklin Roosevelt and the New Deal. Your generation did not know—and I pray will never know—the Great Depression and the experience of the Great Recovery.

With due respect, but without regret, we leave behind 1934 and turn to work for the promise of 1964. For the answers of the Roosevelt years and the answers of the Coolidge years, and the answers of the Wilson and McKinley years do not serve as replies to the questions of our age or the answers of our time or the replies to today.

No man of our times understood this so well as John Fitzgerald Kennedy. He un-

derstood, as we must all understand, that in these times the Government of the United States must be lean and trim and not large and soft. He understood that power must be principled—that when nations acquire the capacity to destroy human life they must assert the courage to redeem human life; that when nations are sure of their strength they must never be unsure of their search for peace.

This is the course that we follow in our land today.

No man can say that the road ahead will be easy, that our footing will always be sure, that there will be no obstacles, no perils. Wherever the strong and the free may walk, danger will stalk their trail.

I believe that—30 years from now when you are nearing the age that I have attained—you will look back upon these 1960's as the time of the great American breakthrough—toward the victory of peace over war, toward the victory of prosperity over poverty, toward the victory of human rights over human wrongs, toward the victory of enlightened minds over darkness.

Thomas Wolfe has written: "The true discovery of America is before us . . . the true fulfillment of our spirit, of our people, of our mighty land is yet to come."

Come, give us what youth alone can give us, and together let us make that discovery.

Thank you for coming here.

NOTE: The President spoke shortly before noon on the South Lawn at the White House. The group was composed of more than 5,000 college students, summer employees of the Government.

Early in his remarks the President referred to the temporary stage and backdrop that had been erected on the South Lawn for a "Salute to Congress" ceremony to be held later in the day (see Item 527).

527 Remarks at the President's Salute to the Congress. *August* 19, 1964

Mr. Speaker, Senator Mansfield, Members of the House and Senate, ladies and gentlemen:

On behalf of the Congress and the Cabinet, I want to say well done to Mr. Cronkite, Mrs. Dickerson, and Mr. Smith. I know that upon this occasion at least I can speak for all of you when I thank this cast this evening for a most delightful and entertaining evening.

Originally we scheduled this evening as an end-of-Congress get-together. In view of the developments at your end of Pennsylvania Avenue, we have redesignated tonight as a night of mid-session hospitality.

Perhaps we will be able this year to combine our farewell to Congress party with the annual Christmas Tree lighting ceremony.

We are very glad that you could come here tonight. The privilege is mine to welcome you to this house—the house of all the people.

If this occasion is unprecedented, it is no more than the year deserves.

This has been a year without precedent in the history of relations between the executive and the legislative branches of our Government.

This session of Congress has enacted more major legislation, met more national needs, disposed of more national issues than any other session of this century or the last. This record of cooperation and accomplishment should give heart to all who stand with this great Nation and should give pause to all who oppose the cause that we champion.

This is why you have been invited here this evening.

I want to, first of all, thank all of you for myself. More than that—much more than

that—I want the American people to be aware of the record that you have written and the relationship that exists between us.

That record and that relationship testify to the reassuring fact that there has been this year no stalemate in our system, no deadlock in our democracy.

For myself, I believe that this is the way our system was intended to function—not with Presidents and Congresses locked in battle with each other—but locked arm in arm instead, battling for the people that we serve together.

I believe in and I try to practice the philosophy of a great Republican President, Theodore Roosevelt. He once put it this way: "I have a very strong feeling that it is a President's duty to get on with Congress if he possibly can, and that it is a reflection upon him if he and Congress come to a complete break."

This second session of the 88th Congress is distinguished most by the simple fact that at no time has there been—or is there now—a question of the President and the Congress "getting on" together.

This has been a constructive Congress. It has passed a test ban treaty, a tax-cut bill, a series of education measures, hospital legislation, the mass transit bill.

This has been a compassionate Congress. It has passed the Civil Rights Act, a food stamp plan, and approved a program to attack poverty.

I am very happy tonight to say that this has been a cooperative Congress. For these measures and many others have been brought into being by the votes from both parties.

So, let none suggest—let none suppose—that debate has been suspended, that princi-

987

ples have been laid aside, or that convictions have been diluted.

The opposite is much more nearly the case.

But from full debate, from advocacy of principles, from devotion to convictions, strength has been forged into the laws that have been enacted. This Congress has expressed on the record the commitment of the American people to the pillars on which our system and our society stand.

Our economic system of private enterprise has received the most significant vote of confidence in our times with the enactment of the legislation reducing taxes for both individuals and corporations. Eleven and one-half billion dollars have been returned to the pockets of American families and American enterprise—in the confidence that private initiative would put these dollars to work creating jobs, creating opportunity, and creating greater effectiveness in competition with the world.

For 100 years, emancipation was a proclamation but it was not a fact.

This Congress with the help and the support and the votes from both sides of the aisle brought into being the most comprehensive Civil Rights Act in the last century. This act wrote into the book of law the equality of opportunity for all of our people.

Our Nation's great commitment to universal education has received more support from this Congress than from any other.

The 88th Congress will be always remembered as the Education Congress.

And I know how much pride and satisfaction that our late, beloved President John F. Kennedy would get tonight if he could only be here and see you and thank you for helping him to see that his dreams came true.

You have responded to the needs of our cities with the mass transit legislation. The beauty and the values of our countryside will be conserved by the wilderness bill, and many more measures.

For classroom, city, and countryside, you have made long strides toward meeting the needs of our times and toward building a great society.

As your former colleague, as your President now, as an American first and a partisan second, I am proud and privileged tonight to salute the Congress one and all.

Mrs. Johnson and I are indeed privileged to have a chance to say thanks to all of you this evening.

Thank you.

NOTE: The President spoke in the evening on the South Lawn at the White House at a reception for Members of the 88th Congress. In his opening words he referred to Representative John J. McCormack of Massachusetts, Speaker of the House, and Senator Mike Mansfield of Montana, Majority Leader of the Senate. Early in his remarks he also referred to Walter Cronkite of the Columbia Broadcasting System, Mrs. Nancy H. Dickerson of the National Broadcasting Company, and Howard K. Smith of the American Broadcasting Company, who had served as narrators for a musical program featuring songs used in earlier political campaigns.

528 Remarks Upon Signing the Economic Opportunity Act. *August* 20, 1964

My fellow Americans:

On this occasion the American people and our American system are making history.

For so long as man has lived on this earth poverty has been his curse.

On every continent in every age men have

sought escape from poverty's oppression.

Today for the first time in all the history of the human race, a great nation is able to make and is willing to make a commitment to eradicate poverty among its people.

Whatever our situation in life, whatever our partisan affiliation, we can be grateful and proud that we are able to pledge ourselves this morning to this historic course. We can be especially proud of the nature of the commitments that we are making.

This is not in any sense a cynical proposal to exploit the poor with a promise of a handout or a dole.

We know—we learned long ago—that answer is no answer.

The measure before me this morning for signature offers the answer that its title implies—the answer of opportunity. For the purpose of the Economic Opportunity Act of 1964 is to offer opportunity, not an opiate.

For the million young men and women who are out of school and who are out of work, this program will permit us to take them off the streets, put them into work training programs, to prepare them for productive lives, not wasted lives.

In this same sound, sensible, and responsible way we will reach into all the pockets of poverty and help our people find their footing for a long climb toward a better way of life.

We will work with them through our communities all over the country to develop comprehensive community action programs—with remedial education, with job training, with retraining, with health and employment counseling, with neighborhood improvement. We will strike at poverty's roots.

This is by no means a program confined just to our cities. Rural America is afflicted deeply by rural poverty, and this program will help poor farmers get back on their feet and help poor farmers stay on their farms.

It will help those small businessmen who live on the borderline of poverty. It will help the unemployed heads of families maintain their skills and learn new skills.

In helping others, all of us will really be helping ourselves. For this bill will permit us to give our young people an opportunity to work here at home in constructive ways as volunteers, going to war against poverty instead of going to war against foreign enemies.

All of this will be done through a program which is prudent and practical, which is consistent with our national ideals.

Every dollar authorized in this bill was contained in the budget request that I sent to the Congress last January. Every dollar spent will result in savings to the country and especially to the local taxpayers in the cost of crime, welfare, of health, and of police protection.

We are not content to accept the endless growth of relief rolls or welfare rolls. We want to offer the forgotten fifth of our people opportunity and not doles.

That is what this measure does for our times.

Our American answer to poverty is not to make the poor more secure in their poverty but to reach down and to help them lift themselves out of the ruts of poverty and move with the large majority along the high road of hope and prosperity.

The days of the dole in our country are numbered. I firmly believe that as of this moment a new day of opportunity is dawning and a new era of progress is opening for us all.

And to you men and women in the Congress who fought so long, so hard to help bring about this legislation, to you private citizens in labor and in business who lent us a helping hand, to Sargent Shriver and that band of loyal men and women who made up this task force that brings our dream into a reality today, we say "Thank you" for all the American people. In the days and years to come, those who have an opportunity to participate in this program will vindicate your thinking and vindicate your action.

Thank you very much.

NOTE: The President spoke in midmorning in the Rose Garden at the White House. Among those attending the ceremony were Members of Congress who sponsored the bill and other supporters of the antipoverty program. The President specifically referred to Sargent Shriver, Director of the Peace Corps, who was later appointed Director of the Office of Economic Opportunity.

As enacted, the bill (S. 2642) is Public Law 88–452 (78 Stat. 508).

Earlier, on August 12, the White House released the text of a letter from the President to the Speaker of the House requesting appropriations to support activities authorized by the Economic Opportunity Act, together with a letter from the Director of the Bureau of the Budget outlining details of the appropriation. The Supplemental Appropriation Act, 1965 (Public Law 88–635, 78 Stat. 1023), authorizing the appropriations, was approved by the President on October 7, 1964.

529 Special Message to the Congress on U.S. Participation in the United Nations. *August* 20, 1964

To the Congress of the United States:

Pursuant to the provisions of the United Nations Participation Act, I transmit herewith the eighteenth annual report covering United States participation in the United Nations during 1963.

This report describes in detail the day-to-day, month-to-month work of the United Nations system of agencies on behalf of peace and security, economic and social development, the trust territories, human rights and legal and constitutional developments. It also reports on administrative and financial matters.

The 18th General Assembly was concerned with many of the most urgent problems of our times: peace and disarmament, national independence and human rights, and international cooperation along a broad spectrum of human endeavor.

As in other years and with other institutions, the U.N. record for 1963 was an amalgam of progress and problems as the Organization sought to cope with many of the world's most basic and difficult issues. This report is a factual accounting of what was accomplished on the United Nations agenda for mankind—and of its unfinished business.

In transmitting this report to the Congress I should like to add two observations which go beyond the scope of the objective record of U.N. activities during the year.

First, the extraordinary importance which this Government attaches to the United Nations was underscored by the fact that two Presidents of the United States addressed the same Assembly.

On September 20, President Kennedy went to the rostrum of the General Assembly to tell the delegates of more than a hundred countries that:

". . . the badge of responsibility in the modern world is a willingness to seek peaceful solutions.

". . . if either of our countries [the United States and the Soviet Union] is to be fully secure, we need a much better weapon than the H-bomb—a weapon better than ballistic missiles or nuclear submarines—and that better weapon is peaceful cooperation."

When tragedy struck two months later, the General Assembly convened a special plenary meeting in honor of President Kennedy. Speaker after speaker rose to pay solemn tribute to the great qualities of my predecessor—and above all to the U.S. commitment to the United Nations which he both symbolized and strengthened.

When Ambassador Stevenson expressed the gratitude of our people to all the peoples who shared our grief, he also assured the delegates, on my behalf, that ". . . there will be no Johnson policy toward the United Nations, any more than there was a Kennedy policy. There was—and is—only a United States policy."

By this time the work of the United Nations for 1963 was drawing rapidly to a close. Christmas was approaching. My own schedule was crowded by the extraordinary pressures of the first weeks in office.

Yet I asked to go to the United Nations in the closing days of its work to address the General Assembly. I wanted to demonstrate to the world that neither tragedy nor transition could cause this country's support for the United Nations to waver. I wanted to confirm personally that international cooperation lies at the heart of U.S. foreign policy regardless of who sits in the office of President and regardless of what party label he wears.

I told the assembled delegates at that moment:

"The greatest of human problems, and the greatest of our common tasks, is to keep the peace and save the future. . . . If there is one commitment more than any other that I would like to leave with you today, it is my unswerving commitment to the keeping and to the strengthening of the peace."

"Now, on the world scale the time has come, as it came to America 30 years ago, for a new era of hope—hope and progress for that one-third of mankind that is still beset by hunger, poverty, and disease."

". . . And more than ever we support the United Nations as the best instrument yet devised to promote the peace of the world and to promote the well-being of mankind."

Second, the work of the United Nations reflected the often harsh and sometimes hopeful political and economic realities of the world in which it operates, and thus demonstrated once again its relevance to contemporary international affairs.

We see this relevance in the stepped-up activities of the Security Council over the past months, particularly in the peacekeeping field.

We see it in the dialogue on trade and economic policies now beginning between developed and developing countries.

We see it in the Assembly debates over the final steps in the process of decolonization.

We see it in the universal relief and overwhelming acceptance which greeted Assembly resolutions endorsing the limited nuclear test ban agreement, the new communications link between Moscow and Washington, the expressed intent of the United States and the Soviet Union not to place weapons of mass destruction in outer space, and renewed efforts by the Eighteen-Nation Disarmament Committee to seek agreement "with energy and determination."

We see it in the Assembly resolution setting forth certain legal principles to govern the use of outer space—and in calls for continuing cooperation in scientific exploration, weather forecasting, and communications in outer space.

And we see it, finally, in the peacekeeping efforts which continued in the Congo and along the armistice lines between Israel and the United Arab Republic. In these efforts, as more recently in Cyprus, the members of the United Nations reaffirmed their commitment to the increasingly vital task of helping to keep the peace—a task of growing importance to this nation and to the world.

In short, the General Assembly was a faithful mirror of political reality, which is another way of saying that it was useful because it dealt in an intensely practical way with current human events.

I take this occasion to remind the Congress of these points because they are not all recorded in the following report, and because they illustrate how closely we associate our future hopes for world peace and progress with the fortunes of the United Nations.

LYNDON B. JOHNSON

NOTE: The report, "U.S. Participation in the UN," is printed as House Document 188 (88th Cong., 2d sess.), and as Department of State Publication 7675 (433 pp., Government Printing Office, 1964).

530 Remarks Upon Signing Bill Amending Securities and Exchange Act. *August 20, 1964*

Members of the Congress, distinguished guests, members of the Securities and Exchange Commission and other related financial organizations in town, ladies and gentlemen:

This is a very gratifying day for me in this house. This morning I signed into law legislation committing our society and our system to a war on poverty and all its causes. This afternoon, I am signing a measure designed to protect the prosperity of our people.

In a few moments I will meet with leaders of small business from throughout this great Nation to talk with them about the opportunities and the obligations of leadership in order to assure our system's continuing success in America.

All Americans and all the world can take new inspiration and fresh faith from the example that this day presents.

Our Nation is diverse. The interests of our people are many. But it is reassuring that the strongest, the richest, and the most successful Nation ever fashioned by men anywhere can be concerned with the prosperity of the many without ever forgetting the poverty of the few.

Capitalism in the United States today is not the capitalism known anywhere at any time in the past. The angry slogans of communism are archaic when directed against the capitalism of the American people, for under our system the worker is also the investor. The people are also the owners of our productive system.

Capitalism in America is what it is today because of the initiative, the enterprise, and the responsibility of our free system.

But it is also what it is because of the course that we have chosen for this Government to follow.

We rejected the idea that the role of government is either coercion or control. On the contrary, the proper function of government is to meet its responsibilities wisely so that the people may have confidence in their future, in their system, and in themselves.

I would say a good example, exhibit A, in this system is Mr. William Martin of the Federal Reserve who is here today. He is a man who understands the proper function of government. He meets his responsibilities wisely. The people of this country and the people of the world have confidence in our system and in themselves because of that type of leadership.

Few more dramatic demonstrations of this exist than the record of the Securities and Exchange Commission also. Less than a lifetime ago this country's confidence in the securities market was very small. On July 31 this year the market value of stocks listed on the New York Stock Exchange reached a new high of $465 billion in contrast to a value of $23 billion prior to the enactment of the first Federal securities law in 1933 of which my very dear, beloved friend, the late Sam Rayburn, was the author.

Investors' confidence is due to many factors. High on the list is the factor of confidence in the common-sense attitude taken in the administration of our laws by our Government, and in this instance particularly by the Securities and Exchange Commission.

The law signed today should further strengthen the securities market and public confidence in them.

Industry and government have worked together in the writing of these laws. Industry and government will work together in making these measures succeed.

For my part, I believe the President's first

responsibility in this sector is the quality of men chosen to discharge the duties of the SEC. We deeply regret that we are losing the Chairman of that great Commission. He is returning to private life to help prepare others to follow in his footsteps. But I am very proud of the men who have accepted the sensitive trust to carry on and I am most especially proud of the able trusted public servant who has agreed to accept the duties of Chairman, my friend Manuel Cohen.

I want all of you here today to share with us the pleasure of seeing Mr. Cohen take the oath of his new office. A new era of regulatory relationship is coming, a relationship sincerely devoted to confidence, to understanding, to a responsible role on the part of Government in helping and not harassing our American capitalistic system.

Mr. Cohen will be given his order designating him Chairman as soon as I have completed this little mission of signing this bill.

NOTE: The President spoke in midafternoon in the Cabinet Room at the White House. In the course of his remarks he referred to William McC. Martin, Jr., Chairman, Board of Governors of the Federal Reserve System, William L. Cary, retiring Chairman of the Securities and Exchange Commission, and Manuel F. Cohen, Chairman-designate of the Commission.

Mr. Cary served as Chairman of the Securities and Exchange Commission from March 27, 1961, to August 21, 1964.

531   Remarks at a Reception for Small Businessmen.
August 20, 1964

Good afternoon, ladies and gentlemen:

I'm very pleased that you could come here to be with us this afternoon. This is your house and the house of all the people of this great Nation. For so long as I live here, the door through which you have come will

be open to all—except those who demand that it be closed to any.

I do not know your politics. I have not asked about your politics. I do not care about your politics.

Some believe our great question today is

who we choose for our political leadership this fall.

Well, I am not entirely disinterested in that choice.

But I do believe that the greater question—this year and the greater question every year, as a matter of fact—is how well and how wisely our nonpolitical, nonoffice-holding leadership leads us all.

And that is why you are here.

Your business may be small. But in every community where you live, your opportunity—and your responsibility—for leadership is large.

Small business bears big responsibilities under our economy.

Of the 4.8 million businesses in the United States, 4.6 million of them are classified as "small businesses." These firms generate 40 percent of the entire Nation's economic business activity—they provide livelihood for 75 million Americans, they provide jobs for 40 percent of all jobs in this country.

But that is not all the role of the small businessmen. It is much larger than that. Every American community draws its base of leadership, draws its stability, its continuity, and its drive for progress from responsible, energetic, forward-looking, progressive business people.

Today—in this land of yours and mine—the future of our system and our society is being determined. What kind of a future we will have will not be determined here in this city, nor in this house, nor even on Capitol Hill. The quality of the America that you and your children and my children will know is being determined in the communities where Americans live and where Americans lead.

Your responsibilities—as well as mine—in this 20th century are very great responsibilities.

America cannot afford for us to stand apart. America cannot afford to let us go in different directions. Our political leadership, our business leadership—our leadership in labor, in agriculture, in education, and in the professions—must be united in understanding, must be united in mutual trust, must be united in common purpose.

I have made no contribution that I am aware of, at any single moment, in arraying class against class. I don't want to be a labor President or a business President or a bureaucratic President. I want to be an American President, President for all the people of this country, and a President that all the people of this country can have confidence in.

Today, as we meet here, we all have together more than any of us separately can afford to lose. Together we have achieved a pinnacle of peace—together we have achieved a pace of prosperity—never enjoyed before by any men in any land in any time in the world.

These years from 1961 to 1964 are the most prosperous years that any people have ever known. For 42 consecutive months we have had the longest and the largest and the most stable peacetime expansion of American economy that's on record in this country.

I guess I shouldn't make this observation, but—to show you that there is not anything partisan about that economy—we are very proud of what our country is doing with your help. Someone laughed at me the other day and said, "I don't guess the fact that you are saving all this money could have anything to do with the fact that you have a Republican Secretary of Defense." And I think that it is proper to add that in this period of price stability, in this great era of prosperity, when we have done so well—I would like to also point out we have a Republican Secretary of the Treasury.

Last month 72.4 million Americans were at work—72,400,000 Americans were working on their jobs. That's a new record in this country.

Unemployment declined below the 5 percent mark. It has not been lower for the last 7 years.

The worker is doing better. The American family is doing better than it's ever done before. The American businessman has never done so well for so long.

For the third year in a row corporate profits are rising. Only once before since World War II have they risen even 2 years in a row. Since the beginning of 1961, corporate profits have increased by more than 60 percent after taxes.

The total income of unincorporated businesses is up 14 percent over these same years—an alltime record in this country.

The slump in fixed investment by business has been broken. Investment today is higher as a percentage of our gross national product than in any of the past 6 years.

American business is modernizing—American business is making new investments to become even more competitive in the market places at home and around the world.

One of the businessmen that met here in this room with me shortly after I became President said to me, "If you will express your confidence in us by helping us pass a new tax bill, we will express our confidence in our country by taking this money and going out and making capital investments—my company alone will produce 20,000 new jobs for you." I sat next to him at lunch the other day and he whispered in my ear and said, "I have kept my promise. We have added 22,000 new jobs since the tax bill was signed."

I might also mention—as a matter of some little interest to you—that your stocks are worth $175 billion more today than when this expansion began. They are worth $100 billion more than they were when I became President last November.

So times are good—and you know it and I know it.

But times are never easy—and I know it.

And we must look ahead. For that reason yesterday I had President Eisenhower's Chairman of his Economic Council come to visit with me. I had President Truman's Chairman of Economic Council come to visit with me—his Council of Economic Advisers. I had President Kennedy's Council come visit with me and my own Chairman. And we all met in that room together. We all love this system. We want to preserve it. We all know that we can't just sit back with our hands in our pockets, chewing gum in our mouth, and rocking in a rocking chair, and let the rest of the world go by, and enjoy the status quo.

Our thinking, our looking ahead, our planning may well determine whether the middle of next year we have a dropoff, whether we have a curve that's downward. And we don't want to study how to avoid a recession. We want to plan to keep our prosperity where it is and advancing. And all of these able men yesterday agreed that things look good for this year and at least for a substantial part of next year. And we discussed at some length what we could do to meet our problems as they appear.

Most of you have worked most of your lives—you have worked the longest hours of anyone in your organization—you have worked to build what you have built, you have resisted a great many efforts—to save what you have saved.

But you understand, as Lord Chesterfield once advised his son, that "few people do business well who do nothing else."

And that is why men who are the most successful business-builders are almost always the most active in their community affairs. You know men do not protect or perpetuate what they have built only by watching over the books—or reading over the stock market reports.

The fruits of your labor are secure only as the lives of the people in your community are secure. Your businesses prosper only as the people themselves are prosperous. You are successful only as the community where you live is successful.

Your Nation, as well as your community, needs the best of your leadership now.

If life in this land is to have meaning for all of us, full and equal participation in it, then its promise cannot be denied to any of us.

But if we are to progress together, we must preserve together the values and the standards which make this life worthwhile for all of us.

Wherever we live, responsible Americans must never allow community leadership to pass by default to the night riders, to the men who travel down the highways with shotguns in their cars and shoot innocent people driving along the road to their Capital, to the street rioters who break the plate-glass windows and take the law into their own hands.

Well, I am here to say to you—and to say through you to all the American people—and ask your help in saying that we shall preserve respect for law and order in this country.

We preserve respect for law by making laws responsive to the people's needs. For men who are poor, for men who are under-educated and undertrained, for men whose rewards are small and whose hope is scarce, preachments of respect for law will never be as persuasive as demonstrations of law's respect for them.

So here in your city—and in your Government—we have been attempting to do many things that are long needed to lift off of your business the burdens of the past.

As I told you, taxes have been cut.

As I told you, spending has been curbed. As I told you, economy is the watchword.

Earnest and honest efforts are being made to put to work in Government new concepts to produce more efficiency and to give you better management of the public business that you pay for.

I believe that Government must never be either an enemy of business nor a parasite in business. I believe that Government must not remain neutral or unconcerned with business success or the success of the workingman.

Government should actively promote and welcome the gains that business makes in the public interest—just as Government should foster and welcome the gains the people make.

Our one purpose here is freedom of opportunity for your business and freedom of opportunity for the people of this country.

So we ask of you—we urge upon you—we say to you this afternoon here in the first house of this land, the use of your freedom and your business prosperity to continue to promote the growth and the expansion of this economy is essential. We ask of you the use of your time and your initiative in the leadership of your country when you go back home, and the leadership of your community.

Your leadership at the local level will decide the quality of our cities. It will decide the quality of our classrooms. It will decide what kind of a countryside we have. It will decide the quality of life in our Nation for a century to come.

The trust of all that has gone before us rests now upon you and in your hands.

So I wanted to say to you this afternoon that I want you to know that I need, and the Nation needs, the best from you to keep America on its course and to make tomorrow better for all than the past has been for any.

We have so much in this country to preserve. We have so much to protect. And, in all of our lavishness and in our luxury, sometimes we take these things as a matter of fact.

A friend of mine that I worked for when I first came to this town—33 years ago—came in my office a few weeks ago to talk to me about a great big ranch that he once owned in Cuba. I hope that none of you ever come to talk to me about property that you once owned in the United States.

But whether we are Democrats or Republicans, we all believe in this system. We are all Americans first. And we know that in this world in which we live and all of its uncertainties and the pitfalls that we may face tomorrow—as Secretary Rusk described those days when we sat across that table with Russian missiles 90 miles from our shores ready to be launched, I thought of the agonizing evaluations that we had to make, and that last day when we left our house not knowing whether we would come back that night or not.

So as we meet here in this beautiful city on the banks of the Potomac, in this Capital of the free world, we realize that there are two philosophies at each other's jugular in the world.

The Russian people have a desire for peace, in my judgment; but they have a different philosophy from ours. They have more people. They have more land. They have more acreage. They have more of many resources than we have.

And if we are not to be buried, if we are to survive, it's going to be not because of the number of our people or the wealth of our resources or the measurement of our acres. It's going to be because we have a better system of government—the free enterprise system. A system where a man can take his dollar and invest it with the hope of getting back a small additional return; where the manager will get up at daylight and work 'til midnight and develop stomach ulcers trying to avoid a strike and to get the most out of those men and match that management and men and money to produce a better mousetrap at a smaller cost; where the worker is worthy of his hire and is not so concerned about his retirement or his social security at the moment as he is about doing a good day's work and producing what needs to be produced in order to compete with his neighbor.

And those three working together—the capitalist, the manager, the worker—I believe can produce more, faster, cheaper than any commissar or any slave labor in all the world.

Now I'm through.

I don't believe that labor has to hate business. I don't believe that business has to snipe at labor. I know that Government, which is supported by both of them, oughtn't to be fighting with either of them. And that's why, in the few months that I have had in this house—we've had two governments in the last 8 months and we may have another one—I know that I want these people in each segment of our society to know that they are welcome here, that their constructive ideas and their constructive criticism are needed here.

And with the help of God we will perpetuate this system. And we will preserve it. And we'll leave this world a better place for our children than we found it for ourselves.

NOTE: The President spoke in midafternoon in the East Room at the White House. In the course of his remarks he referred to Secretary of Defense Robert S. McNamara, Under Secretary of Defense Cyrus R. Vance, Chairman of the Council of Economic Advisers Walter W. Heller, Small Business Administrator Eugene P. Foley, Secretary of Commerce Luther H. Hodges, and Secretary of State Dean Rusk.

532 Statement by the President on the Agreements for the Establishment of a Global Communications Satellite System. *August* 20, 1964

OVER THE YEARS of man's history on this earth, men have undertaken many explorations of distant horizons. But, in all this long span, no new horizon has so clearly beckoned for nations to work together as the horizons of space.

Today it is a cause of gratification among men everywhere that 11 nations are this afternoon joining together to lay the foundation for an immeasurably valuable new use of space as medium for international communications.

The two agreements signed today provide for the establishment of a global commercial communications satellite system. These agreements are firm expressions of the policy written into the law of our land by the will of our people.

The United States—from the beginning of the age of space—has sought and encouraged cooperation among all nations for peaceful and practical uses of this new dimension. These agreements fulfill that objective.

We will continue to seek—as we have sought—the fullest measure of cooperation by all nations on this earth for the peaceful use of the realms of space around us.

These agreements are open for signatures by all countries that are members of the International Telecommunication Union. Countries that do not sign the agreements will be able to use the global system.

The prospects for development of communications systems in space outrun our imagination. In the future, the voices, messages, and pictures will span the barriers of distance on earth and bring men and nations closer together in understanding and cooperation.

By 1965 an experimental operational satellite is expected to link North America and Europe. In 1966 and 1967 a system will be launched to provide global coverage—for the first time.

The benefits will be many to all of mankind.

We mark this day with pride and confidence—pride that nations are working together and we work with them—confidence that from such cooperation will come sure progress toward fulfillment of man's great hope for finding in our times the basis of honorable and universal peace.

NOTE: The agreements were reached at the International Conference to Establish Interim Arrangements for a Global Commercial Communication Satellite System, held in Washington, July 21–24, 1964. The meeting was the culmination of a series of conferences and discussions held during the previous year, and was attended by representatives of 18 nations. The U.S. delegation was headed by G. Griffith Johnson, Assistant Secretary of State for Economic Affairs, who served as chairman.

The text of the agreements and of a communique issued at the close of the conference is printed in the Department of State Bulletin (vol. 51, p. 281).

533   Remarks at the Convocation of the National War College and the Industrial College of the Armed Forces.   *August* 21, 1964

Secretary Vance, my fellow Americans:

On this occasion, I am privileged to speak before an audience of men who know their country's strength and its full meaning to this age.

You have come from duty in Viet-Nam and Korea, from the Disarmament Agency and SAC, and one of you from our National Security Council staff at the White House. You are here because your Nation recognizes in each of you the presence and promise of excellence in leadership.

For the years ahead, you are thinking ahead. You will be studying the basis of our military policy, the broad context of our Nation's widest objectives, and the total world environment.

As you begin this year let me call upon each of you to challenge yourself to the fullest. In a course like this you must be your own pacemaker, and only your best will repay the honor of being chosen for this service.

For your profession—and for mine—these are new and challenging times.

The next 20 years will demand more of America's military men, America's diplomats, and America's political leadership than the last 200 years of our professions. Together we shall continue to face, as we face now, a world in contest—freedom against totalitarianism, the sovereignty of the many against a sovereign few, the rule of law against the rule of men. In this contest America's objectives will not change.

Abraham Lincoln once said: "Our defense is in the preservation of the spirit which prizes liberty as the heritage of all men, in all lands, everywhere."

Our purpose in this contest is to serve our rightful interests while we keep the peace with honor. But it is our purpose also to nourish in other peoples "the spirit which prizes liberty"—and to help where we can when their liberty is in danger.

These purposes are unchanging. But the responsibilities of our Nation and the responsibilities of our professions are changing even now.

Our responsibilities are changing in dimension and in depth both at home and abroad. And our most basic responsibilities are here at home.

The world respects America's strength. The world reacts and responds to America's success. Everywhere that America's military men have been sent in this century, the way has been made easier for them by the world's knowledge and the world's understanding of the triumphant record of America's free society.

What a nation is in the world depends on what a nation is at home. This is true not only for the United States but true almost universally among nations of both West and East.

Military and diplomatic policies and performances are being influenced and are being dominated by policies and performances at the center of the political systems. This is true for free Europe and Eastern Europe. This is true for Soviet Russia. This is true for Communist China. This is clearly and conspicuously true for the United States.

The strengthened role of the United States in the world today depends directly on the improvement achieved in the performance of our whole system since the beginning of 1961.

You know—and I do not need to repeat before you—the facts of the increase in our military strength. We have spent more than

$30 billion in the last 4 years attempting to achieve a better defense strength than would have been spent had we followed the last appropriation bill of 1960. We are today stronger in every aspect of our defense than we were 3½ years ago.

But the effectiveness of that strength, the faith in it among our allies, the respect for it among those who have ambitions of aggression, rests on other sources as well.

The 43 consecutive months of economic expansion—the record of the fullest employment in American history, the stability of our prices—wholesale prices have actually dropped during the greatest economic expansion in our history—the success of our space program, the legislative response to both long-standing and recently developing needs of our society—all of these are major factors in the influence we now exert for freedom and that we exert for peace around the world.

The point I am making is vital for your profession.

The military man is many persons. He is the great captain who commands fleets and air forces and armies. He is the dedicated professional in school, on patrol, on guard. He is the draftee taking his turn at freedom's watch. He is the reservist or the guardsman leaving his home to go to summer training. He is also in a sense the civilian who devotes his mind and his energy to public service.

Whoever he is, wherever he serves, the man is a product of our whole society, and he means more to peace today than he ever meant before.

As Secretary Vance observed, for more than 30 years my association with the military has been an intimate one—as a member of many congressional committees, for a brief period on active duty in World War II, as a member of the National Security Council when I was Vice President. And today as Commander in Chief nothing is more gratifying, nothing more reassuring than to see, as I do every day, the quality of the new generations of military men.

Our officers and our enlisted men have no true counterparts in military history. In a time of our Nation's greatest affluence they and their families willingly and courageously undertake the most Spartan sacrifices and hardships for us all.

Around the globe they are, in Emerson's words, the "brave men who work while others sleep, who dare while others shy."

They are fighting men—the best in the world today. But they are also thinking men, men whose mission is peace, men who are devoted to peace, stern in their respect for our democratic values.

The military career today demands a new order of talent and training and imagination and versatility. Our military men have these qualities and they have them in abundance. Seventy percent of our commissioned officers are college graduates compared to 49 percent in 1952. Seventy-three percent of all of our enlisted men are high school graduates compared to 53 percent in 1952.

I believe, as I have often said, that our country justly must and safely can accord to our American military men a place in our society long denied to soldiers throughout our history.

I very much want our uniformed citizens to be first-class citizens in every respect. I want their wives and their children to know only first-class lives.

I am in this regard directing the Secretary of Defense to speed up his present review of such matters as housing and medical care, pay and allowances, so that we can at the earliest possible moment take whatever steps both human equity and national defense may require to enhance the standing and the morale of those who defend us.

I am also directing the Secretary of Defense to review the educational systems and major schools within the services and the opportunities now offered to continue civilian education while still in service in order to broaden and strengthen these programs.

One thing more:

I know and you know that in our system there is no more sensitive relationship than that between the military and the political, the military and the civilian sectors. Enemies of our system have always and will always make this relationship a point of their attack in their efforts to divide us or to implant distrust among us.

I want the whole world to know that in this land there is today a strong mutual confidence between military men and civilian political leaders. This is true at every level.

I have myself the highest sense of personal trust for great officers like General Wheeler and the other members of the Joint Chiefs of Staff. I have seldom if ever in my life been so inspired as by the unselfishness of Gen. Maxwell Taylor who gave up the highest post of his profession to leave here alone to serve freedom in far-off Viet-Nam simply because I indicated and implied that he might be useful there.

I am proud of the service to our national defense which has been rendered since 1961 by dedicated civilian officials too, under the brilliant and driving leadership of a great Secretary of Defense, Robert McNamara, and an Under Secretary of Defense, Cyrus Vance. Our soldiers and our civilians are one team.

In our country's history, the oldest article of faith is the principle that we pursue today. Many others have said it since, but President Washington, our first President, said it first a long, long time ago:

"To be prepared for war is one of the most effectual means of preserving peace."

This morning America's military men stand vigil for peace and freedom—in West Berlin and in South Viet-Nam, at Guantanamo and in the 7th Fleet, in nuclear submarines under the sea and in SAC planes high in the skies.

Wherever they patrol, our Nation's heart is with them—our Nation's life is in their hands. We pray God to keep them and to speed them home in a day of peace that they will have won.

Thank you.

NOTE: The President spoke in midmorning in the auditorium of the Industrial College of the Armed Forces at Ft. Lesley J. McNair, in Washington. His opening words referred to Cyrus R. Vance, Deputy Secretary of Defense. Later in his remarks he referred to Gen. Earle G. Wheeler, Chairman of the Joint Chiefs of Staff, Gen. Maxwell D. Taylor, Ambassador to Viet-Nam and former Chairman, Joint Chiefs of Staff, and Robert S. McNamara, Secretary of Defense.

---

534   Statement by the President on the Fifth Anniversary of Statehood for Hawaii. *August* 21, 1964

PRESIDENT JOHNSON today noted the fifth anniversary of Statehood for Hawaii by hailing the Nation's newest State as "a symbol to people everywhere of what it is possible to achieve within the American system of Government."

The President observed that Hawaii's five years of Statehood have been marked by unprecedented growth and prosperity and he called attention to the fact that in this period it has risen from 22d in per capita income to 17th among the 50 States.

The President also applauded Hawaii for its position on civil rights.

The President disclosed that the Bureau of the Budget has determined that 285 additional acres of U.S. Government property on the island of Oahu in Hawaii are no longer needed by the Federal Government and arrangements are being made to transfer title to the State. All the land being returned to the State was originally donated to the United States by Hawaii.

NOTE: The statement was made public as part of a White House release announcing the completion

of the Budget Bureau's review of Federal lands to be conveyed to Hawaii under the Statehood Act of 1959 (73 Stat. 4).

The release added that in the course of its review the Bureau of the Budget had thoroughly analyzed and assessed Federal needs for land in Hawaii. A major consideration in this review, the release noted, was the disposition of thousands of acres of State lands which were used under license by the Armed Forces. The Statehood Act authorized setting such lands aside in Federal ownership. However, by negotiating satisfactory long-term leases for these lands it was possible to leave ownership of more than 30,000 acres with the State.

Another major result of the review, the release further stated, was the enactment of Public Law 88-233 of December 23, 1963, which would overcome an inequity created by provisions of the Hawaii Statehood Act by recognizing Hawaii's claim to certain lands which the Republic and Territory of Hawaii had given to the United States without charge.

535   Remarks Upon Awarding the Silver Star Posthumously to Sgt. Harry A. Walling.   *August 22, 1964*

Mrs. Walling, ladies and gentlemen:

On the 19th day of June, this year, a young and brave American set out into the jungles of a distant land—half-a-world away. He walked at the side of a patrol of young and brave Vietnamese. Their purpose—and his—was to defend freedom against its aggressors.

The name of that American was Harry A. Walling.

He was a sergeant of the United States Army—a proud member of the proud Special Forces who wear the green beret.

When the Vietnamese patrol came under attack, the only thought of Sergeant Walling was for the patrol—and for its success. He gave no thought to safety or to self. Those who recovered his body found that—before he died—Sergeant Walling had fired his every round of ammunition.

We have come today to bestow upon Sergeant Walling one of our country's highest

honors. No medal, no words, no eulogy of ours can honor him so highly as he has honored our country and our cause. But we can—and we must always—honor ourselves by working everywhere we can, in every way we can, for a world of peace in which the young and the brave need not die in war.

When Sergeant Walling fell, he left behind his young widow and three young children—the oldest age 3, the youngest now 4 months old. Mrs. Walling's bravery is no less than her husband's.

Two nights after she learned her husband would never return, Mrs. Walling wrote out a message to the other wives of her husband's unit. That remarkable letter has deeply touched all who have read it—including the Commander in Chief. I would like to read these lines from it:

"I know that you are all afraid for your husbands and you love them as much as I loved my husband. He loved me just as your husbands do you, and he didn't want to die. He had so much to live for. But he was a brave man and a fighting man. . . . My husband died for what he believed in, and if he had a choice of where and how he would die, he would choose the same place—fighting for a decent world for his children to grow up in. . . .

"So don't let the world, the loneliness, the despair and the fear get you down. Stand as tall as that man of yours who wears the beret and thank God you got him. . . . My prayers are that all of your husbands

come home to you safe and well."

I am proud now on behalf of the Nation to bestow the Silver Star, posthumously, upon Sergeant Harry A. Walling.

The distinguished Acting Secretary of Defense, Mr. Vance, will read the citation.

NOTE: The President spoke shortly after noon in the Rose Garden at the White House. His opening words referred to Mrs. Harry A. Walling, who accepted the award on behalf of her husband. Among others present were Maj. Gen. William P. Yarborough, Commanding General of the John F. Kennedy Special Warfare Center at Ft. Bragg, N.C., and a group of 13 Special Forces sergeants he brought with him for the ceremony.

536   Remarks to a Group of Democratic Governors. *August 22, 1964*

Distinguished Governors, ladies and gentlemen:

On this day 9 months ago at very nearly this same hour in the afternoon, the duties of this office were thrust upon me by a terrible moment in our national history.

I pledged then to continue the work that had been begun by the great and gallant American who fell on that tragic day—John Fitzgerald Kennedy.

The work of this Nation is not complete. But when this session of Congress is ended, I believe that we shall be able to say that that pledge of last November has been redeemed.

In a world of peril America has kept the peace. We have widened no war. We have embarked on no expeditions. When aggression has been unleashed against us, we have given it reply.

Today, all nations know—no nation doubts—America's resolve and determination to defend freedom and to keep the peace in the world.

For 43 consecutive months, we have en-

joyed the longest and the largest economic gain in American history. These years from 1961 to 1964 have been the most prosperous American families have ever known and the most prosperous that the system of American free enterprise has ever known.

But, more than that, we have in these short months found answers to issues which have perplexed and troubled generations of Americans since the last century.

The second session of the 88th Congress has been the most productive and the most constructive in our Nation's life.

This is patriotism—for men never serve their nation more nobly than when they serve the success of their nation's system. This we have done these 9 months as one nation and as one people undivided and indivisible.

Others may believe and others may say that the people of America want to pursue some other way, but I do not and I cannot agree. I do not believe the people of this country want to turn aside from this course of sure success—to risk war or to gamble with peace—to place their prosperity in peril or their well-being in doubt—to reopen old questions that are now resolved or to fail to face new questions that are now imposed— and that is why I believe it is fitting today for you and I as chief executives of the majority of the States and as chief executive of the Nation to spend these moments now looking ahead.

What are the opportunities of our times and what are our obligations?

What is required of us all if we are to keep the public trust which is ours?

I find myself recalling what John Adams once wrote to Thomas Jefferson many long years ago: "While all of the sciences have advanced, that of Government is still at a standstill—little better understood, little better practiced than 3,000 or 4,000 years ago."

Well, that, I believe, is our challenge today.

If this new Nation, this new population, this new economy, America's new position in the world are to be served, we must have and we must practice a new politics, a new kind, a new quality of public service, and I think a new kind and character of partisanship.

Labels won't serve us—and labels won't save us. "Isms" will not make America stronger and "isms" will not make peace more secure. A time has come for public servants to be just that—servants of all the people, solving the peoples' problems instead of exploiting the peoples' troubles, bringing the people together instead of dividing them apart.

Our responsibilities—yours and mine— seem to me to be clear.

We have a duty—wherever we work—to lighten the load that our people must bear for the costs of the public programs by making sure that we receive a dollar's worth of value for every dollar we spend. We are doing that in your Federal Government.

We have a duty—wherever we work—to maintain in our Government compassion and concern and always the highest order of competence.

We have a duty—wherever we serve—to maintain respect for law and order, to summon up the best in our people, to put down the worst that would divide us and destroy us all.

We have a duty—wherever we serve—to maintain, as our forefathers did, a decent respect for the opinions of mankind.

We must make sure that none abroad and none at home misunderstand the will of American mothers and fathers that this generation of their sons shall fight the battles of peace and not the battles of unnecessary wars.

We must likewise make sure that none misunderstand in our land or in any other land that the strength that we have is strength that we shall use to keep the freedom and to make it secure in our times.

Since that day last November, I have been very, very proud of the people of your land and mine. From the moment of deep tragedy they have risen to new heights of triumph. Fate has placed upon me great responsibilities for their success, for their security and, yes, finally, for their safety.

I have sought with all that is within me to serve that trust and to serve it to the fullest. So long as I am their servant, I shall work in no other way than for their peace, their prosperity, and their progress toward a new day, a finer day, and a better day.

In that work I am pleased to be joined by the able chief executives of more than 30 of our sovereign States here in the East Room of the White House this afternoon.

In this coming week, our party—your party and mine—will meet in convention to express its will. I do not know what decisions the delegates will reach, but it is my hope and it is my expectation that they will pledge our party to freedom, to peace, to freedom for all nations, to peace for all peoples.

The goals of our party should be the goals of our Nation. Those are the unchanging goals of our Nation in these times and in this changing era.

Thank you very much.

NOTE: The President spoke early in the afternoon in the East Room at the White House.

Earlier in the day the White House released a list of the 30 Democratic Governors who were expected to meet with the President.

537   Letter to the Attorney General on a Program To Combat Juvenile Delinquency in the District of Columbia. *August 22, 1964*

[Released August 22, 1964. Dated August 18, 1964]

Dear Mr. Attorney General:

Thank you for your letter on behalf of the Committee on Juvenile Delinquency and Youth Crime and the program proposed by Washington Action for Youth for an attack on juvenile delinquency in the District of Columbia.

I am pleased to know that the program prepared by the citizens of the District and approved by the Committee will attack the underlying causes of delinquency as well as try to improve the methods of dealing with children already in trouble with the law. I am also pleased that the program is designed to stimulate all parts of the community to join in this battle, for it cannot be won unless the total community is willing and enabled to help. In addition, I believe it makes sense to coordinate the juvenile delinquency program through the United Planning Organization with the work already being done in the Washington area by the Ford Foundation and the work which can be undertaken here to attack poverty under the Economic Opportunity Act of 1964.

The Federal Government has properly been concerned, through your Committee, with the preparation of this program. It must be no less concerned that it cooperate fully in implementing it. To this end, I request that you, together with the Secretaries of Commerce, Labor, and Health, Education, and Welfare, and the Administrator of the Housing and Home Finance Agency, each appoint one or two persons from your respective staffs to a group that will see to it that every possible Federal aid is given to the Washington program. I have asked Mr. Charles Horsky, my Advisor for National Capital Affairs, to serve as chairman of the group, and to keep me personally advised as to the progress of the program.

May I take this occasion to extend my gratitude to the members of the Committee on Juvenile Delinquency and Youth Crime, and to all who are working for and with the Committee, for the efforts you have made in this vital area.

Sincerely,

LYNDON B. JOHNSON

[Honorable Robert F. Kennedy, The Attorney General, Washington, D.C.]

NOTE: The Attorney General's letter, also made public, stated that the program was prepared by District of Columbia citizens and officials under a planning grant from the President's Committee on Juvenile Delinquency and Youth Crime, and that the program had been approved by the Committee.

The letter further stated that the Committee believed that the Nation's capital could and should be a leader in demonstrating that juvenile delinquency is not an incurable social cancer. "To this end," the letter continued, "we have taken steps to insure that the experience already available from demonstration programs in other cities has been fully exploited in the preparation of this . . . program for the District. We are encouraged to know that the Congress shares our view, and has authorized an appropriation of $5,000,000 to carry out the District program."

The letter concluded by stating that the program was designed for a target area, the Cardozo area, in the inner city, and that it would form a vital part of a larger program financed under the poverty bill and a grant from the Ford Foundation which would extend throughout the entire metropolitan area.

538   Remarks Upon Signing Bill Permitting Private Ownership of Nuclear Materials.   *August 26, 1964*

Chairman Seaborg, ladies and gentlemen:

The measure before me now represents the most significant amendment to the atomic energy legislation that has been passed since 1954.

For the first time, it will allow private ownership in the United States of special nuclear materials—the materials used as fuels for nuclear plants.

We have made the most substantial progress in this Nation since 1954 in developing peaceful application of atomic energy particularly in the generation of electric power with nuclear reactors.

The new law recognizes that great advance and that progress. We are eliminating the statutory requirement that the Federal Government own all special nuclear material within the United States—a requirement that we feel is no longer appropriate for our growing civilian industry.

At the same time, we continue to insure the necessary control of nuclear material by the Government to meet present and future responsibilities abroad and here at home.

The legislation that we are acting upon this morning involves the very finest teamwork between the executive branch and the Congress. I am pleased that it enjoyed complete bipartisan support.

I am happy to see many of my friends from the Congress here this morning, and

I especially wish that Senator Pastore, Chairman of the Joint Committee on Atomic Energy, could be here, for he deserves a substantial share of the credit for our legislation. I trust that you may forgive him for performing another mission and understand his absence on this occasion.

I am very glad, however, that Congressman Holifield who performed diligently 4 years ago in a similar capacity is here with us this morning and others who have worked on this legislation are also present.

The new law will fully protect the national and international interests of the United States. It will meet the needs and the desires of private enterprise at the same time. By any measure, this legislation demonstrates the highest order of responsibility within our system. It is a compliment to all men and women of both parties who contributed to its passage.

I believe that this law represents still another major step in this Nation's efforts to achieve full use of the force of the atom for peaceful purposes to the benefit of all mankind. That is our objective and our prayer, and all of our efforts will be directed along those lines. I welcome you here for this signing ceremony, and this is a very eventful day for all of us.

NOTE: The President spoke shortly before noon in the Cabinet Room at the White House. His opening words referred to Glenn T. Seaborg, Chairman of the Atomic Energy Commission. Later he referred to Senator John O. Pastore of Rhode Island and Representative Chet Holifield of California.

As enacted, the bill (S. 3075) is Public Law 88–489 (78 Stat. 602).

539   The President's News Conference Before Departing for Atlantic City for the National Convention.   *August 26, 1964*

THE PRESIDENT. I am sorry to have delayed you. We are going over and get a little hors d'oeuvre and sandwich, in a moment, and then we are going to Atlantic City. Those who want to go, talk to George,[1] and if we have room in our plane I will be glad to have you go with us under the regular rules that you follow.

I was delayed in getting to you. I thought we would be out of here before, but I had to visit with Secretary Rusk, Secretary McNamara, and Mr. Bundy on another matter.[2] That held us some.

I have this afternoon talked to some people and have others in to see me. That is one reason why I am running a little bit late. We will have our hors d'oeuvres and we will cut our birthday party short.

My reason for going up there is to make an announcement which I expect I will make sometime between 9 and 10 o'clock.

Q. When?

THE PRESIDENT. Between 9 and 10 o'clock. That announcement will be my recommendation to the convention on a running mate.

[*At this point the President spoke off the record.*]

Q. How will you make that recommendation, sir?

THE PRESIDENT. I will point out what I have considered, who I have talked to, the factors that have entered into it, and then I will make my suggestion.

I expect to do that in an open convention after they nominate, if they nominate and make the nomination speeches for me, and after they take action on those nominations.

Q. Will this be at the Convention Hall?

THE PRESIDENT. This will be at the convention tonight.

Q. Will you return tonight?

THE PRESIDENT. Yes, and we will be back in the salt mines tonight.

Q. Privately, before you make any announcement in Atlantic City, will you advise the person whom you will recommend to be your running mate?

THE PRESIDENT. I have not gone into that. I have not thought of it. I will think of it and you will be on the plane, so you can ask me, and I will let you know what I decide— if you are available. I don't know whether I can reach him.

Q. You don't know?

THE PRESIDENT. I will make the announcement between 9 and 10 o'clock.

Q. But you have made up your mind?

THE PRESIDENT. Yes, I have. This is the first time I have said it.

Q. What time did you make up your mind, Mr. President?

THE PRESIDENT. I just stand on the previous statement. I found out today that you ask real tough questions. That little clarifying statement of yours got me into trouble.

Q. Mr. President, what time do you plan to take off for Atlantic City?

THE PRESIDENT. After we get an hors d'oeuvre and get some planes, and get me there in time for 9:15. If we work it out,

---

[1] George E. Reedy, Press Secretary to the President.

[2] Secretary of State Dean Rusk, Secretary of Defense Robert S. McNamara, and McGeorge Bundy, Special Assistant to the President.

we will go in Air Force One. If there are too many, I will go in the Jet Star and you can go in a second plane, but you will have to reimburse the Air Force. Does anyone know how many we can haul in Air Force One? See if we can't have a followup plane. How many want to go? Hold up those hands and somebody count them.

Mr. Valenti: [3] About 35.

THE PRESIDENT. I would ask them to have a followup plane, and those who go up with me can come back on the followup plane, and those who are going up in the other plane can come back with me. I don't want to make anybody go with me both ways.

[3] Jack Valenti, Special Consultant to the President.

Tell the Secret Service, Jack. If they can satisfy this many, they will have to be very special people.

Reporter: Thank you, Mr. President.

NOTE: President Johnson's twenty-eighth news conference was held in his office at the White House at 7 p.m. on Wednesday, August 26, 1964.

Earlier in the day the White House released the following statement, signed by four examining physicians:

"President Lyndon B. Johnson has no symptoms. His exercise tolerance continues to be superb. Physical examination, including the examination of the eyes, lungs, heart, abdomen, lower intestinal tract, and reflexes, is normal. His blood pressure is normal. . . .

"There is no health reason why he should not continue an active vigorous life."

540 Remarks Before the National Convention Upon Recommending the Nomination of Hubert Humphrey as Vice President. *August 26, 1964*

Mr. Chairman, my fellow Americans, my fellow Democrats, columnists and commentators:

It is wonderful to be here with you tonight, but do we really need all of these lights on?

I thank the convention for the honor it has done me. I will be with you tomorrow to begin the march toward an overwhelming victory for our party and for our Nation.

Four years ago one of our greatest Americans stood before this Democratic Convention, John F. Kennedy of the State of Massachusetts. We grieved at his loss, but we carried on, and we have fulfilled his program without flinching for one moment.

In the last 3 days, the noble Democrats who are delegates to this convention have made a great start toward a great Democratic victory. You have built a platform on which I am proud to stand, a platform built on solid performance and framed for a future of prosperity and peace.

In your settlement of the problems of credentials, you have found a fair answer to honest differences among honorable men. You have struck a magnificent keynote through the eloquence of the gifted Senator from Rhode Island, John Pastore. You have reaffirmed our enduring values through your wise and beloved permanent Chairman, Mr. Rayburn's friend and his worthy successor, Speaker John McCormack of the State of Massachusetts.

No chairman of any Platform Committee ever guided a committee better or a party better than the Honorable Carl Albert of the State of Oklahoma.

Well, I, too, have been working to carry out my obligations under a very old American tradition, for it is the traditional task of your Presidential nominee to recommend for your deliberation a candidate for Vice President of the United States.

I have such a recommendation. I have

reached it after consultations with the leaders of the Democratic Party in every section of this Nation, and at every level of our Government. I have reached it after discussions with outstanding Americans in every area of our national life. I have reached it after long and prayerful private thought, consulting my own experience of that office, and the burdens that it brings.

All of this has had a single guide—to find a man best qualified to assume the office of President of the United States should that day come. I have found such a man.

He has been tested and proven in our Democratic process of political campaign and election. He has had long and distinguished experience in public life as an executive and as a legislator. And every step has been marked by excellence and achievement.

He knows the problems of all of our people in every part of our Nation. He knows the world and he knows its problems, and he has shown understanding and a deep concern for the strength of our country and for the peace of the world. He matches energy in the right with compassion for the needs of others. He matches strong convictions with understanding of the convictions of others.

If you select him, you can proudly say to the American people, "This is not a sectional choice." This is not just merely the way to balance the ticket. This is simply the best man in America for this job.

The qualities that he brings to office will help make the Vice Presidency an important instrument of the executive branch. From that office he can help connect Congress to the White House, and he can help carry America around the world.

I want to say to you that I will feel strengthened knowing that he is at my side at all times in the great work of your country and your Government.

Nothing has given me greater support in the past 9 months than my knowledge of President Kennedy's confidence that I could continue the task that he began. I have found a man that I can trust in the same way. This confidence and this recommendation are not mine alone. They represent the enthusiastic conviction of the great majority of the Democratic Party in the United States.

They will, I believe—they will, I am sure, receive the overwhelming support of the American people. I hope that you will choose as the next Vice President of the United States my close, my longtime, my trusted colleague, Senator Hubert Humphrey of Minnesota.

NOTE: The President spoke at the Democratic National Convention in Convention Hall at Atlantic City, N.J. In his opening words he referred to Speaker of the House John W. McCormack of Massachusetts, permanent chairman of the Convention. Later he referred to Senator John O. Pastore of Rhode Island, keynote speaker at the Convention, and House Majority Leader Carl Albert of Oklahoma, platform chairman.

541   Remarks Before the National Convention Upon Accepting the Nomination. *August 27, 1964*

Chairman McCormack, my fellow Americans:

I accept your nomination.

I accept the duty of leading this party to victory this year.

And I thank you, I thank you from the bottom of my heart for placing at my side the man that last night you so wisely selected to be the next Vice President of the United States.

I know I speak for each of you and all of you when I say he proved himself tonight in that great acceptance speech. And I speak for both of us when I tell you that from Monday on he is going to be available for such speeches in all 50 States!

We will try to lead you as we were led by that great champion of freedom, the man from Independence, Harry S. Truman.

But the gladness of this high occasion cannot mask the sorrow which shares our hearts. So let us here tonight, each of us, all of us, rededicate ourselves to keeping burning the golden torch of promise which John Fitzgerald Kennedy set aflame.

And let none of us stop to rest until we have written into the law of the land all the suggestions that made up the John Fitzgerald Kennedy program. And then let us continue to supplement that program with the kind of laws that he would have us write.

Tonight we offer ourselves—on our record and by our platform—as a party for all Americans, an all-American party for all Americans. This prosperous people, this land of reasonable men, has no place for petty partisanship or peevish prejudice. The needs of all can never be met by parties of the few. The needs of all cannot be met by a business party or a labor party, not by a war party or a peace party, not by a southern party or a northern party.

Our deeds will meet our needs only if we are served by a party which serves all our people.

We are members together of such a party, the Democratic Party of 1964.

We have written a proud record of accomplishments for all Americans.

If any ask what we have done, just let them look at what we promised to do. For those promises have become our deeds. And the promises of tonight I can assure you will become the deeds of tomorrow.

We are in the midst of the largest and the longest period of peacetime prosperity in our history. And almost every American listening to us tonight has seen the results in his own life.

But prosperity for most has not brought prosperity to all. And those who have received the bounty of this land—who sit tonight secure in affluence and safe in power—must not now turn from the needs of their neighbors.

Our party and our Nation will continue to extend the hand of compassion and the hand of affection and love to the old and the sick and the hungry. For who among us dares to betray the command: "Thou shalt open thine hand—unto thy brother, to thy poor, and to thy needy, in thy land."

The needs that we seek to fill, the hopes that we seek to realize, are not our needs, our hopes alone. They are the needs and hopes of most of the people.

Most Americans want medical care for older citizens. And so do I.

Most Americans want fair and stable prices and decent incomes for our farmers. And so do I.

Most Americans want a decent home in a decent neighborhood for all. And so do I.

Most Americans want an education for every child to the limit of his ability. And so do I.

Most Americans want a job for every man who wants to work. And so do I.

Most Americans want victory in our war against poverty. And so do I.

Most Americans want continually expanding and growing prosperity. And so do I.

These are your goals. These are our goals. These are the goals and will be the achievements of the Democratic Party. These are the goals of this great, rich Nation. These are the goals toward which

I will lead, if the American people choose to follow.

For 30 years, year by year, step by step, vote by vote, men of both parties have built a solid foundation for our present prosperity. Too many have worked too long and too hard to see this threatened now by policies which promise to undo all that we have done together over all these years.

I believe most of the men and women in this hall tonight, and I believe most Americans, understand that to reach our goals in our own land, we must work for peace among all lands.

America's cause is still the cause of all mankind.

Over the last 4 years the world has begun to respond to a simple American belief: the belief that strength and courage and responsibility are the keys to peace.

Since 1961, under the leadership of that great President, John F. Kennedy, we have carried out the greatest peacetime buildup of national strength of any nation at any time in the history of the world.

I report tonight that we have spent $30 billion more on preparing this Nation in the 4 years of the Kennedy administration than would have been spent if we had followed the appropriations of the last year of the previous administration.

I report tonight as President of the United States and as Commander in Chief of the Armed Forces on the strength of your country, and I tell you that it is greater than any adversary. I assure you that it is greater than the combined might of all the nations, in all the wars, in all the history of this planet. And I report our superiority is growing.

Weapons do not make peace. Men make peace. And peace comes not through strength alone, but through wisdom and patience and restraint.

And these qualities under the leadership of President Kennedy brought a treaty banning nuclear tests in the atmosphere. And a hundred other nations in the world joined us.

Other agreements were reached and other steps were taken. And their single guide was to lessen the danger to men without increasing the danger to freedom.

Their single purpose was peace in the world.

And as a result of these policies, the world tonight knows where we stand and our allies know where we stand, too. And our adversaries have learned again that we will never waver in the defense of freedom.

The true courage of this nuclear age lies in the quest for peace.

There is no place in today's world for weakness. But there is also no place in today's world for recklessness. We cannot act rashly with the nuclear weapons that could destroy us all. The only course is to press with all our mind and all our will to make sure, doubly sure, that these weapons are never really used at all.

This is a dangerous and a difficult world in which we live tonight. I promise no easy answers. But I do promise this. I pledge the firmness to defend freedom, the strength to support that firmness, and a constant, patient effort to move the world toward peace instead of war.

And here at home one of our greatest responsibilities is to assure fair play for all of our people.

Every American has the right to be treated as a person. He should be able to find a job. He should be able to educate his children, he should be able to vote in elections and he should be judged on his merits as a person.

Well, this is the fixed policy and the fixed determination of the Democratic Party and the United States of America.

So long as I am your President I intend to carry out what the Constitution demands—and justice requires—equal justice under law for all Americans.

We cannot and we will not allow this great purpose to be endangered by reckless acts of violence. Those who break the law—those who create disorder—whether in the North or the South—must be caught and must be brought to justice.

And I believe that every man and woman in this room tonight join me in saying that in every part of this country the law must be respected and violence must be stopped.

And wherever a local officer seeks help or Federal law is broken, I have pledged and I will use the full resources of the Federal Government.

Let no one tell you that he can hold back progress and at the same time keep the peace. This is a false and empty promise. To stand in the way of orderly progress is to encourage violence.

And I say tonight to those who wish us well—and to those who wish us ill—the growing forces in this country are the forces of common human decency, and not the forces of bigotry and fear and smear.

Our problems are many and are great. But our opportunities are even greater.

And let me make this clear. I ask the American people for a mandate—not to preside over a finished program—not just to keep things going, I ask the American people for a mandate to begin.

This Nation—this generation—in this hour, has man's first chance to build the Great Society—a place where the meaning of man's life matches the marvels of man's labor.

We seek a nation where every man can find reward in work and satisfaction in the use of his talents. We seek a nation where every man can seek knowledge, and touch beauty, and rejoice in the closeness of family and community.

We seek a nation where every man can, in the words of our oldest promise, follow the pursuit of happiness—not just security—but achievements and excellence and fulfillment of the spirit.

So let us join together in this great task.

Will you join me tonight in rebuilding our cities to make them a decent place for our children to live in?

Will you join me tonight in starting a program that will protect the beauty of our land and the air that we breathe?

Won't you join me tonight in starting a program that will give every child education of the highest quality that he can take?

So let us join together in giving every American the fullest life which he can hope for. For the ultimate test of our civilization, the ultimate test of our faithfulness to our past, is not in our goods and is not in our guns. It is in the quality—the quality of our people's lives and in the men and women that we produce.

This goal can be ours. We have the resources; we have the knowledge. But tonight we must seek the courage.

Because tonight the contest is the same that we have faced at every turning point in history. It is not between liberals and conservatives, it is not between party and party, or platform and platform. It is between courage and timidity. It is between those who have vision and those who see what can be, and those who want only to maintain the status quo. It is between those who welcome the future and those who turn away from its promises.

This is the true cause of freedom. The man who is hungry, who cannot find work or educate his children, who is bowed by want—that man is not fully free.

For more than 30 years, from social security to the war against poverty, we have diligently worked to enlarge the freedom of man. And as a result, Americans tonight are freer to live as they want to live, to pursue their ambitions, to meet their desires, to raise their families than at any time in all of our glorious history.

And every American knows in his heart that this is right.

I am determined in all the time that is mine to use all the talents that I have for bringing this great, lovable land, this great Nation of ours, together—together in greater unity in pursuit of this common purpose. I truly believe that we someday will see an America that knows no North or South, no East or West—an America that is undivided by creed or color, and untorn by suspicion or strife.

The Founding Fathers dreamed America before it was. The pioneers dreamed of great cities on the wilderness that they crossed.

Our tomorrow is on its way. It can be a shape of darkness or it can be a thing of beauty. The choice is ours, it is yours, for it will be the dream that we dare to dream.

I know what kind of a dream Franklin Delano Roosevelt and Harry S. Truman and John F. Kennedy would dream if they were here tonight.

And I think that I know what kind of a dream you want to dream.

Tonight we of the Democratic Party confidently go before the people offering answers, not retreat; offering unity, not division; offering hope, not fear or smear.

We do offer the people a choice, a choice of continuing on the courageous and the compassionate course that has made this Nation the strongest and the freest and the most prosperous and the most peaceful nation in the history of mankind.

To those who have sought to divide us they have only helped to unite us.

To those who would provoke us we have turned the other cheek.

So as we conclude our labors, let us tomorrow turn to our new task. Let us be on our way!

NOTE: The President spoke in late evening at the Democratic National Convention in Convention Hall at Atlantic City, N.J. In his opening words he referred to Speaker of the House John W. McCormack of Massachusetts, permanent chairman of the Convention.

The nomination took place on the President's 56th birthday. A birthday party in his honor was held in the ballroom at Convention Hall.

542   Remarks in Atlantic City Before the Democratic National Committee. *August* 28, 1964

Mr. Chairman, Mr. Vice President, ladies and gentlemen:

All of us are planning to go home—but not Senator Humphrey.

All of us are planning to get out and relax a little bit—but not Senator Humphrey!

All of us think Hubert Humphrey is the ideal nominee for Vice President. But—I hate to tell you this, Hubert—so does Senator Goldwater, or at least that is what he told the press before your speech last night.

I am happy to be permitted to come here and visit with you this morning, particularly to thank you for your service to the Democratic Party. Hubert and I are leaving shortly for a session this weekend, and it is not going to be an organizational one. We came to the Senate back in 1949 together, and he and I have had very little difficulty getting organized.

But with your support, and the support of the leading Democrats in every State of the Union, the support of many people who have never before supported the Democratic Party, the American people are going to win one of their finest victories this November.

We have two problems that we will deal with when we get back home, and we will deal with nationally from time to time. One is the so-called backlash. That backlash according to the three national pollsters, plus some 15 or 20 State polls that we have, indicates that there will be somewhere between 10 and 15 percent of the Democrats or those who allege to be Democrats or those who have called themselves Democrats at some time or other in their lives who do not plan to vote for the Democratic ticket this year.

A smart publicity man has latched onto a—coined a new explanation of that defection that we have come to experience in Democratic conventions and in Democratic elections from time to time, and he calls it backlash.

But the plain fact is that in some States you have very little, if any, defection. In other States it runs up to 20 or 30 percent. In certain areas of the South it runs 26 percent. But the average of the Democrats that for one reason or another, because they don't like my accent or that I am too tall or I am too short or they don't like the tax bill or they don't like the Viet-Nam policy or they don't like the civil rights bill, for some of those reasons they plan to vote otherwise. They run from 10 to 15 percent. So, we are going to deal with that problem. We are going to try to get that 10 percent back if we can.

[*At this point there was a commotion in the room.*]

It seems we still have some of these—some of these fellows who were out in San Francisco have evidently come in here!

So much for Democratic defection.

Let's welcome them back. Let's do what we can to persuade them of the errors of their ways without being offensive. Let's try to reason with them. Let's give them a little time and hope that by November we can improve on that situation, and while we may not have 100 percent of the Democrats we can have over 90 percent of the Democrats.

Now, Mr. Nixon, when he started out to run in 1960, I don't want to use him as an example, but he had 92 percent of the Republicans the day he was nominated.

Now, Mr. Roper shows that the present Republican nominee has got 50 percent of the Republicans and Mr. Gallup and Mr. Harris show that ranges from a little above 50 to a little above 60. But the point is he has 2 out of 3, and they have what you would call a frontlash of about 30 percent.

Now, for the life of me I can't understand why a fellow who is interrogating or interviewing someone is not just as concerned with the 30 percent frontlash as he is with the 10 percent backlash, and I hope between now and November to discuss frontlash around the country if I can get the cooperation of some of my commentator friends.

I talked to one of the publishers late yesterday. I believe he is going to be a part of that frontlash this year. He is going to endorse the Democratic ticket and I said, "Why don't you get your people to inquire about the frontlash because it is 30 percent compared to 10 percent, and it is a lot more serious and it should be of a great deal more concern?"

Now, our problem with the frontlash is to hold that frontlash right where it is. That frontlash is made up of liberal Republicans. Some of them are out organizing independent tickets now, some of them are running on their own. Some of them are divorcing themselves from their candidate, some of them are waiting until he makes some further explanation. Some of them are saying, "Well, what did you mean last Saturday?"

Then we have the so-called moderate Republicans, and there are a good many in that group, and they say for various reasons they are not going to vote Republican this year. We have a good many business people— I understand that Hubert has just had a couple of organizational meetings with them; he has got some others scheduled—but a good many of the business people whose attachment to the Republican Party is well known, are very happy with economic conditions in this country, with the fiscal policy of this Government, with our sound, prudent management of our fiscal affairs, and a goodly number of them have indicated to us and indicated to their associates that they are part of the frontlash.

So, whether you take it nationwide, whether you take it in New York or Indiana or Wisconsin or Hawaii, all of those States we have polled, Pennsylvania, you will find this: that for every backlash that the Democrats lose, we pick up 3 frontlash.

And when you can get 3 to 1 it is always satisfying.

But it is particularly satisfying when you realize that the 1 you are losing, you are losing because they don't want to treat people alike and they don't want to treat all people as Americans. And the ones that we are winning, we are winning because they have confidence in our leadership and confidence in our management and they want peace on earth and good will toward men.

We have got a great system in this country. We can worship God according to the dictates of our conscience. We have free speech. We have free press, and we—it

never gets quite as free as it does during convention time.

I almost put off my physical examination the other day because I watched these commentators and I read these various analytical pieces by some of the ablest men in the country that I had known well for many years. I was afraid my blood pressure would be too high to have an examination at that time.

But this has been a happy convention. It has been a historic convention. I heard a few questions asked from time to time that I thought were calculated to provoke a fight, and I saw men almost come to blows a time or two, but thank goodness it really didn't happen.

We have had 164 years of the Democratic Party, and I think that it has really come alive this year. Back in 1800 we founded it and that was a year of bitter and extreme partisanship. Our Nation was torn by division, but when the campaign was over, when the dust had settled, when the victory was won, Thomas Jefferson's instinct was to heal and not to hate. He went before his countrymen in speaking to them all and he said, "We are all Democrats. We are all Republicans."

Of course, I am taking a little liberty with the names because there really wasn't a Republican Party then. But the equivalent that did exist, the equivalent to the Republican Party, soon faded away because Americans became tired of their extreme partisanship.

Now, comparisons are odious and none is implied although some may be inferred!

I deeply believe this, this year: I believe in the year 1964 we are going before the wisest and before the best informed and the most intelligent and the most independent electorate that any candidates ever faced in the history of America. The American families in their homes across the land want and expect and deserve something better of politics and politicians than they have ever been offered before. This convention has affirmed what this Congress and this administration have already made clear, and that is that the Democrats of this day and age are providing this Nation with the kind of leadership that the world requires.

Ours is a party that is responsible and is responsive, that is progressive and is prudent. It is a party of vision, and a party of commonsense.

It is a party where all expect full hearing, and all receive fair play. We let people talk and we don't boo them when they speak. We do not fear to expose ourselves to their words and we don't contribute to smearing their character.

Ours is a party that respects and trusts our electorate, and I think it can be trusted by all Americans of all sections and of all segments. The Nation sees this clearly and the opportunity is yours to build upon the broadest base of our history, to fashion a true national party for national leadership.

This fall and in the seasons to come, let us go forth to build a stronger party, to carry on with the work of building a stronger society so that we can have a stronger civilization.

The doors of the Democratic Party are and must always be open to all people—to the humble and to the proud, to the weak and to the strong, to those who need help and to those who are willing to give it, and we invite them to enter in and to work with us.

We mean to do the work that America needs to have done. We mean to work for unity and we mean to obtain it, but we mean to do much more than that. We mean to work for peace in the world, and peace in the lives of the average American family. We mean to keep our Nation strong and we mean

to help each American to rise to his full strength.

We are determined that compassion shall not pass from the character of this Nation's soul; that America shall never cease to care, care for the needy and the sick, and care for the young and the old, and to care for the family farmer, and care for the family of the workingman. We aim to conserve the values of America, and to perpetuate the vitality of the American system, and we welcome all who believe in that system.

We welcome all from both sides. We welcome the backlash to come back, and the frontlash to come forward.

We do not want big government or small government. What we want is good government.

We do not want spendthrift government or stingy government. We do want sensible government—saving every place it can but serving every place that it's needed.

We who have assembled in this room this morning and those of us who wear the proud honor that you have given us, are inheritors of a very long and very proud trust, from Jefferson to Jackson, from Grover Cleveland to Woodrow Wilson, from Franklin Delano Roosevelt to Harry S. Truman to John Fitzgerald Kennedy.

And I always want to conduct myself, and I hope that you will do likewise, just as though they were sitting there on the pedestal watching our every act. And when I walked out of the hall last night I looked up to three great men who had played a great part in some of the years that I had lived and somehow or other I felt good because I felt that they would approve what you had done at this convention.

We are not going to be remembered for what we stopped. We are going to be remembered for what we started and what we executed.

We are not going to be remembered for where we have been. We are going to be remembered for where we are going.

We are not going to turn the clock back and roll the carpet back to the 18th century. We are going forward to build a new life.

We are going to finish the work that Jack Kennedy left us, but we have a mandate to begin a new program of our own. And it is going to be a program that is prudent but progressive. It is going to be a program that is fashioned for all the people of all parties, but it is not going to be one that is built on the past.

Yes, the torch is passed to us, and the responsibility is ours. The burdens of preserving peace and defending freedom are challenges to us and let our glory shine in the hope and health and happiness of every American home because I predict that when the record shall have been written and you return to the next Democratic Convention you can look back upon your work and your endeavors of the last 4 years and point with pride instead of view with alarm.

Now, I don't want to be suggestive or arbitrary but I have found that the officers of your committee and those that they have employed and surrounded themselves with have been very cooperative, have been very dedicated to the interests of our party, have brought us to the position this morning of being in the best shape that I have ever known the Democratic Party to be in, in the 30 years that I have been an active participant in the Democratic Party.

The first time that I remembered that we ever launched a campaign and nominated two candidates without a single no.

The first time that I know that we ever met and started a campaign with a surplus instead of a debt.

The first time that I ever have known that you can have a real rumpus in the Cre-dentials Committee and say all the ugly things that were said there for 3 or 4 days and then Dave Lawrence comes out and makes such a persuasive report they don't even have a roll call.

One of my youthful idealistic naïve friends raised a question in one of his columns the other day about some of the folks that were running this convention, and they pointed out about the professional experience of the distinguished Speaker, and the fact that the majority leader of the House had been in Congress several years, and the parliamentarian was not a schoolboy. He had been around a few places, and the distinguished chairman of the credentials committee was not without experience.

Well, I never wanted or never needed or never was happier to have around me professionals more than I was this week.

So, if you will not consider it presumptuous, I see no reason for a change. And I can think of—nothing would do them greater honor or would please me more than to have you elect every officer the same way you nominated your President and your Vice President.

[*After certain intervening proceedings of the Democratic National Committee, the President resumed speaking.*]

Could I have your attention for just a moment?

I was just handed the official backlash-frontlash figures, if any of you are interested in them, from Mr. Roper, Mr. Gallup, and Mr. Harris, the three national pollsters.

Mr. Roper shows that 78 percent of the Democrats are still Democrats and 13 percent plan to vote for another candidate, and Mr. Gallup shows that 85 percent to 11, as compared to 78 to 13, and Mr. Harris shows 78 to 22. He gives the undecided to the other side. That is an average of about 15 percent.

The Republicans, Mr. Roper shows that 50 percent will vote for their own candidate and 27 percent will vote for the Democratic candidate.

So just so you can remember that in case some of these folks inquire about the backlash, the same man says it is 27 percent Republican frontlash to 13 percent Democratic backlash.

Come on, get your picture and let me go ahead.

The next one is Dr. Gallup. He shows it is 65 to 26, so he shows this 26 percent frontlash to 11 percent backlash. I wonder why that is not as attractive to them as the backlash, the frontlash.

Then Mr. Harris shows 33 percent backlash, 67 to 33. So, whatever poll you take, one of them has 27, one has 26, and one has 33 backlash.

Voices: Frontlash.

THE PRESIDENT. Frontlash, yes.

Minnesota, 22 percent Republicans will vote Democratic, California poll, 25 percent of the Republicans vote Democratic, Iowa, 31 percent of the Republicans vote Democratic, New Jersey, 35 percent of the Republicans, and in New York, 37 percent of those who voted for Richard Nixon in 1960 in the poll completed by Oliver Quayle this week say 37 percent of those who voted for Nixon say they will vote for the Democratic ticket this year.

Thank you very much.

Goodby, and when you go back to your homes I hope you will give our very deep thanks and sincere, genuine appreciation to all the good Democrats that have worked so hard to make possible what happened this week. And I want you to know that if the good Lord will give us strength, that Hubert and I will be as many places as we can between now and next November, and we will give you a margin of victory that will make even the most downcast of you feel real proud.

NOTE: The President spoke to the members of the Democratic National Committee in Room 20 at Convention Hall in Atlantic City, N.J. In his opening words he referred to John M. Bailey, chairman of the Democratic National Committee, and Senator Hubert H. Humphrey of Minnesota, Democratic nominee for the Vice Presidency. Later in his remarks he referred to Richard M. Nixon, Republican candidate for the Presidency in 1960, national pollsters Elmo Roper, George Gallup, Louis Harris, and Oliver Quayle, David L. Lawrence, chairman of the credentials committee at the Democratic National Convention and former Governor of Pennsylvania, Speaker of the House John W. McCormack of Massachusetts, permanent chairman of the Convention, Majority Leader of the House Carl Albert of Oklahoma, platform chairman, and Representative Hale Boggs of Louisiana, parliamentarian of the Convention.

543   Telephone Remarks Opening the "Parade of Progress" in Cleveland. *August 28, 1964*

Mayor Locher, my good friends in Cleveland:

I am very happy and proud to be speaking to you this morning from Atlantic City where I have some good friends meeting here.

This is a very happy day for us. I know this is also a happy and proud day for the citizens of Cleveland. Cleveland has made many contributions to the advancement and the adventure of what we call the American spirit.

I am particularly grateful for one specific contribution that Cleveland has made to the strength and character of my administration, that is your own Anthony Celebrezze, the Secretary of Health, Education, and Welfare.

You in Cleveland are beginning your celebration of the Parade of Progress, but it is much more than just a local celebration. All Americans can be proud and all inspired by Cleveland's example of imagination and initiative which are really the genius of our Nation's progress.

Your city and your State and your Nation are all still young as we measure history, but we have come to a time when there is both an opportunity and an obligation to renew our cities and our States and to assure new strength for our Nation, and that is what you are doing today. You are building a new tomorrow on yesterday's foundations, and this is what Americans have been doing throughout the life of this great country.

Few developments of our times are more encouraging than this rebirth of Cleveland's local initiative and local enterprise and local pride which we see not only in your great city but we see throughout the country. You are investing $250 million in downtown Cleveland, but you are investing much more than that in the lives of your children by assuring them a better city, by assuring those children a greater opportunity, by assuring them that a city they will know as you have known it, has the best location in the Nation.

Progress requires courage but courage always pays the highest return. I understand, for example, that your Erie View Plaza Building will provide tax revenues 32 times greater than the buildings it replaced and that Cleveland's share of that revenue could pay the salaries of more than 90 public schoolteachers. You are building a more beautiful city. You are building a more prosperous city. You are building a city of more jobs for more workingmen and more profit for businessmen.

You are making the free enterprise system work where the capitalist with his dollars, where the manager, with his effort and his talents, where the worker can all combine into a three-way partnership, with each taking their appropriate and proper slice of the pie. This is work that our generation must do everywhere. We must build a second America. We must build a great society of our vision. So, I want to say thank you to the people of Cleveland.

I want to congratulate you.

Now, I want to participate in helping you to dedicate your Parade of Progress by pushing the button to start the mall fountains.

NOTE: The President spoke by telephone from Room 20 at Convention Hall in Atlantic City, N.J., to those attending the opening of a public plaza in downtown Cleveland, Ohio. His opening words referred to Ralph S. Locher, Mayor of Cleveland.

At the close of his remarks the President pressed a button to activate a group of 40 fountains in the plaza.

544   Remarks at a Barbecue in Stonewall, Texas.
August 29, 1964

Mr. Stehling, Reverend Clergy, Senator and Mrs. Yarborough, Congressman Pickle, Mrs. Stehling, Mrs. Weinheimer, the next Vice President of the United States and Mrs. Humphrey, ladies and gentlemen, boys and girls:

This is a very nice thing for you to do for us, and we appreciate it very much. We have had a long and an exciting week. It is nice to end it here at home among friends that we have known for 56 years. I know that a lot of hard work has gone into this effort that makes this such a pleasant evening for all of us. I want to thank all of you who served on the committee that brought us this barbecue, the fine singing, the good band, the excellent speaker that you will hear a little later, and these distinguished guests.

I need not take any of your time to tell you how much this State and this particular area of the State means to me. I do want to take this opportunity to tell you how proud I am of the people that you send to Washington to help us there do the work that needs to be done for you here.

I am particularly proud of Congressman Jake Pickle, who serves the 10th District, beginning down here at the Blanco County line, whose district runs almost to Houston. He has been in Congress only a short time, but he has caught on. He knows his way around Washington; he is doing a good job; he is genuinely and sincerely interested in making life better for our people; and he has contributed a great deal to the program that we have passed this year that we think will do just that.

Now if I can have a few more words, I want to take this chance to tell you how proud I am and how grateful I am for the steadfast, courageous support that I have received from Senator Yarborough and his wife, Opal Yarborough.

You have heard and you have read that Senator Yarborough and I have had differences at times. I have read a good deal more about them and I have heard a good deal more about them than I was ever aware of.

But I do want to say this, that I don't think that Texas has had a Senator during my lifetime whose record I am more familiar with than I am with Senator Yarborough's. And I don't think Texas has had a Senator that voted for the people more than Senator Yarborough has voted for them. And no Member of the United States Senate has stood up and fought for me or fought for the people more since I became President than Ralph Yarborough. He is the Democratic nominee of the good Democrats of this State for the 6-year assignment of United States Senator.

We have one Republican Senator from Texas already, and I hope that all of you who claim to be Democrats, all of you who pretend to be Democrats, all of you who want to be Democrats, all of you who are really good Americans will go out, come election day, and send to Washington to help Hubert Humphrey and me in the program for all the people of this Nation, Senator Ralph Yarborough.

Thank you very much for this nice party. I want to assure you that we are going to have a long and rough campaign. It is not going to be any new adventure for us or any new experience because we have cut our teeth on campaigns for 30 or 40 years around this place. We are not afraid of what we face. We will not indulge in any fear or any smear. We will put the searchlight on and the spotlight out there and we will tell the people what we stand for.

In very brief terms, we stand for them. We want prosperity here at home where the laborer is worthy of his hire and where he gets a chance to get decent wages for his work; where the farmer can have stable income, and can enjoy the fruits of this rich land, and educate his children and provide them with clothes and food and some of the luxuries of life; we want a place where business can prosper and earn a fair return on their investment and a fair profit on the capital that they have put into their venture; we want to build a Nation of peace lovers, who do not seek war, but who yearn for peace, but who realize that we cannot build fortress America and put our heads in the sand, and let the rest of the world go by.

We do not covet the acreage of anyone else. We seek to dominate no other people. All we try to do is promote peace and harmony in the world, and we like peace so much that we want everybody to have some of it.

We don't question the motives of our adversaries; we don't spend the time talking about the people that oppose us. We don't think you are really interested in my personal opinion of the man who may be on the Republican ticket in various places. What you are interested in is what we stand for, what we are going to do about it, how prepared we are to accept the challenge, how experienced we are to render the judgment that will preserve for you the kind of a land that you want to live in.

I spent a good many serious evenings studying the problems of this land, and what could confront us the next 4 years. After doing that to the best of my ability, I came to the conclusion that the man and woman on this platform tonight could do more to help us to do what you need to have done for you than anyone else that was available.

So I recommended to the Democratic National Convention for their consideration Senator Humphrey. I did this after reviewing the recommendations made by the various Presidents that preceded me for their running mates. I observed that a few Presidents didn't have the privilege of recommending their running mates and, generally speaking, where they didn't they had very poor running mates.

So I was glad that after I made my recommendation at the Democratic Convention, made up of more than 2,000 delegates, there wasn't one single "no" in that hall.

I think that is a great tribute to Senator Humphrey and Mrs. Humphrey, and the kind of life they have led.

Now we bring you no readymade answers and we don't know the answers to all the problems we have. We have them in various parts of the world tonight. We have serious problems in Viet-Nam. We have serious problems on the continent of Africa. We have serious problems on the little island of Cyprus that Lady Bird and I visited just a few weeks ago.

Any one of those problems can turn into serious events that would bring great shock to our country. We are doing our dead level best to find the solutions to those problems, and we appreciate the support we have from the people of America.

I particularly appreciate the faith of my homefolks. I can't tell you that every decision I make will be the right one. But I can tell you that when I had to issue the order the other day to send the boys off of that carrier with the bombs in their planes to destroy the nests of those PT boats that had fired on our destroyer, that it was an order that I didn't want to give. It was an act that I realized was a very serious act. But I felt that it was in the best interest of this Nation and it was the only course I could follow if I really wanted peace, to let them know that we meant what we said and said what we meant, and we were prepared to back it up. And we did that.

We didn't bomb any cities. As a matter of fact, we carefully refrained from doing that. We didn't kill any women and children. We didn't invade any metropolitan areas. We didn't provoke any great nations. We said to them, "You must leave your neighbors alone and you mustn't ever shoot at United States destroyers without expecting a reply."

I get a lot of advice and I need a lot, and

I seek it all the time. I am very happy that the men on this platform with me tonight are the kind of men that I can counsel with and I can trust. I have had advice to load our planes with bombs and to drop them on certain areas that I think would enlarge the war and escalate the war, and result in our committing a good many American boys to fighting a war that I think ought to be fought by the boys of Asia to help protect their own land.

And for that reason, I haven't chosen to enlarge the war. Nor have I chosen to retreat and turn it over to the Communists. Those are two alternatives that we have to face up to. The third alternative is neutralization in Viet-Nam. We have said that if anyone was willing to come forward and guarantee neutralization, in other words guarantee the independence of these free people and guarantee them security from their neighbors who are trying to envelop them, we would be the first to stand up to the table and say to them, "Show us that you can guarantee their independence and we will salute you and we will be very proud of you."

But there is no country that is willing to do that, that we know of, so neutralization is not very practical at this stage of the game. There are three alternatives we considered.

The fourth alternative is to do what we are doing, to furnish advice, give counsel, express good judgment, give them trained counselors, and help them with equipment to help themselves. We are doing that. We have lost less than 200 men in the last several years, but to each one of those 200 men—and we lose about that many in Texas in accidents on the 4th of July—to each one of those 200 men who have given their life to preserve freedom, it is a war and a big war and we recognize it.

But we think that it is better to lose 200 than to lose 200,000. For that reason we have tried very carefully to restrain ourselves and not to enlarge the war. We have had a good many difficulties that could have sprung into major events. We had four of our soldiers killed in Panama, and some of our people thought I ought to send in paratroopers, and that we ought to launch a strong force against the small group of folks that live in Panama.

But we told them that they couldn't behave this way, and that they would have to sit down and reason with us across the table, that we could not make any precommitments and we wouldn't sign a blank check to a treaty that we didn't know what was in it, but that we would do what was fair, what was right, and what was just.

It took us 60 days to work out an agreement with them, but they finally came to us and said, "We think that is fair enough," and so we worked out an agreement. Now we have rather peaceful relations and we are on the way to making amendments and modifications in the arrangements between the two nations that will be satisfactory.

Mr. Castro sought to cut our water off at Guantanamo. He notified us in a hasty moment in his own impulsive way that he would not supply water to our base. I had some military experts, some generals here and there, that hollered at me right loudly and said, "Please send in the Marines immediately."

I didn't see any reason to send in the Marines to cut the water off. I just sent in one admiral to turn it off and kept the Marines at home. I didn't start any war, although I would like very much to see the free people of Cuba be able to govern themselves without the dictations of Mr. Castro.

We are going to do everything that we consistently can in our policies to see that the people of Cuba are free people, and can govern themselves. But I would remind you that Mr. Castro came to power before Mr. Kennedy came to power. He came to power in 1959. All these people that give you solutions to Cuba today—ask them where they were in 1959.

So we have had in Viet-Nam in less than a year, three different governments. That is pretty difficult, to carry on the resistance that must be carried on when you are changing governments very often. As a matter of fact, I know how difficult it is to change governments at all, because notwithstanding the experience that we had, the transition following the tragedy in Dallas has been a very difficult one that required the cooperation of all good people, Republicans, Democrats, and independents for the last 8 months.

We just had two governments in the United States. I hope we don't have another one in November. But we do have some of our people, a rather hard core people, they make up a rather small minority, I think, of our total population.

But some of them are frustrated, some of them are overalarmed, some of them have their blood pressure worked up, some of them are excited and think our country is not doing at all well, and everything is being mismanaged, and we have a lot of woes and a lot of troubles and a lot of headaches that we could do without.

Well, we do have troubles and we do have problems, any great nation has them. When you are the leader of the world, when you are the richest nation in the world, when you are the most prosperous people in the world, you do have difficulties.

I don't know of any people anywhere that don't look up to the United States of America and really wish that they had some of the things that we have. In all of the travels of more than 40 countries that I have

had, I have had impressed upon me the great faith that the people have in our system of government and in our fairness and our justice as people. And most of them like what we have so well they would like to have a little of it themselves.

So I say to you tonight, engage in a little introspection, and ask your wife when you go home, ask your children, talk to your family about it, and see just what country you would like to live in that you think is better than this one.

Try to figure out what people you think have as high a standard of living as you have. Try to figure out the group of citizens anywhere that enjoys the freedom that you enjoy here in America.

Think about how your ancestors came across the water in risky, dangerous adventure, seeking the liberty that you now enjoy. Ask yourself what you are really doing to preserve that liberty, and to be worthy of that liberty, and to justify that liberty and that freedom.

All I can say to you is that I have talked much longer than I intended to, but I am proud of the opportunity that you have given me to try to wrestle with your safety and your security, and your future, and the future of the little ones that are here in the front row. I accepted that challenge when I accepted that nomination.

As long as the Good Lord gives me life, I am going to do my dead level best with all the energy I have, and with any talent that I may have, and with any experience and any judgment that I may have, to leave this world better than I found it. And to leave it prepared always to defend itself; to leave it willing always to meet any neighbor halfway and do him justice; leave it a prosperous Nation, where every child has an opportunity to get an education, where every man has an opportunity to get a job, where every family can worship God according to the dictates of their own conscience, and where we have the right of free speech and we do not discriminate against our own people, and that we try to make this one happy family made up of 200 million people in this country that can be an example for all the rest of the world to follow.

Thank you and good night.

NOTE: The President spoke in the local rodeo arena in Stonewall, Tex. In his opening words he referred to, among others, Arthur Stehling, an attorney of Fredericksburg, Tex., who helped in arrangements for the barbecue celebration, and Mrs. Stehling, Senator and Mrs. Ralph Yarborough of Texas, Representative J. J. Pickle of Texas, Mrs. Tom Weinheimer, Secretary to the Gillespie County Democratic Executive Committee, and Senator and Mrs. Hubert H. Humphrey of Minnesota. Later he referred to Thomas C. Ferguson, a former District Judge of Burnet County, Tex., who spoke during the program.

The barbecue, sponsored by the Gillespie County Democratic Executive Committee, was planned in honor of the President's 56th birthday anniversary.

545   Filmed Message to Delegates of the Third International Conference on the Peaceful Uses of Atomic Energy. *August 30, 1964*

I WOULD like to extend my best wishes to all the delegates at this Third International Conference on the Peaceful Uses of Atomic Energy.

A great challenge confronts you. You can hasten the day when the atom will be harnessed to hard labor for man's welfare. You can reduce the risk that the atom will be used for man's destruction.

We stand at the threshold of the age of nuclear power but whether nuclear power will meet our needs tomorrow depends on our work and our wisdom today.

In the United States we have been working and learning. We have now learned how to build large-scale reactors whose electric power will be economically competitive in many parts of our country and the world.

Our utility companies now aim to build or purchase reactors producing electricity at between 4 and 6 mils per kilowatt hour. This achievement has come from 15 years of concentrated research and development. The United States Government has spent more than $1,600 million on this effort. American private enterprise has spent an additional $500 million. These expenditures are an investment of our people, an investment in the future of all mankind.

Through our Government and through private enterprise we are prepared to use this vast new technology to help other countries meet their energy needs.

At present the large-scale reactor offers the best hope of economic production of electricity. Not every country and not every community can use this large size, but our rapid rate of progress should soon lead to economic production in smaller reactors, too.

A further application of nuclear energy will be large-scale desalting of water. The time is coming when a single desalting plant powered by nuclear energy will produce hundreds of millions of gallons of fresh water and large amounts of electricity every day.

Our Government is proceeding with an aggressive program of nuclear desalting. What we learn in this program will be shared with other nations. Already we have begun cooperative exchanges with Mexico, with Israel, and with the Soviet Union.

Today I invite all of you to join with us in this enterprise. As we move ahead we look to the International Atomic Energy Agency to play an ever larger role in these peaceful efforts. Already it has set standards for the care and for the keeping of nuclear materials. This achievement has raised our hopes for a workable system of world law on nuclear energy.

For almost 20 years we have known the atom's terror as a weapon of war. Today we begin to know its hope as a powerhouse of peace.

Today at last we really have good reason for believing that the atom can be made the servant and not the scourge of mankind.

NOTE: The message was filmed on August 22 in the Cabinet Room at the White House. The film was shown at the opening of the U.S. Technical Exhibit in Geneva on August 30. It was viewed by Secretary General U Thant of the United Nations, and some 3,000 scientists and engineers from 71 countries who had gathered in Geneva for the Third United Nations International Conference on the Peaceful Uses of Atomic Energy, held August 31–September 9.

The Chairman of the U.S. Atomic Energy Commission, Glenn T. Seaborg, headed the U.S. delegation to the conference. Other U.S. delegates are listed in the Department of State Bulletin (vol. 51, p. 412).

546 Remarks Upon Signing the Food Stamp Act.
August 31, 1964

Members of the Congress, ladies and gentlemen:

I am proud to sign the Food Stamp Act of 1964 because it is a realistic and responsible step toward the fuller and wiser use of our agricultural abundance.

I believe the Food Stamp Act weds the best of the humanitarian instincts of the American people with the best of the free enterprise system. Instead of establishing a duplicate public system to distribute food surplus to the needy, this act permits us to use our highly efficient commercial food distribution system.

It is one of many sensible and needed steps we have taken to apply the power of America's new abundance to the task of building a better life for every American.

In 1961 President Kennedy's first Executive order doubled the quantity and variety of foods to be distributed to the needy. Today nearly 6 million people enjoy a better share of our food abundance through this program and up to 15 different food items are now available.

Likewise, this year we anticipate that 17 million children—3.2 million more than in 1960—will enjoy hot lunches in their schools, many of them for the first time. This is because of the sustained effort made to help our schools provide student lunches.

For 3 years we have conducted pilot operations for the food stamp program in both urban and rural areas. These tests have exceeded our best expectations. They have raised the diets of low-income families substantially while strengthening markets for the farmer and immeasurably improving the volume of retail food sales.

As a permanent program, the food stamp plan will be one of our most valuable weapons for the war on poverty.

It will enable low income families to increase their food expenditures, using their own dollars.

Our efforts to make better use of abundance are not limited to domestic programs. Hunger is a worldwide challenge. Through the Food for Peace program, we are sharing 17 percent more of our food with other peoples than in 1960. Our food abundance is being used constructively not only to combat hunger but also to help other nations to control inflation, generate funds for financing development projects, and to help provide lunches for some 40 million school children throughout the developing world.

The support given the food stamp plan illustrates the willingness of thoughtful Americans to find better uses for our food abundance. I wish to compliment those who have played a role in the passage of this legislation, including the distinguished chairmen of the House and Senate Committees on Agriculture, Senator Ellender and Representative Cooley.

Special tribute is also due Congresswoman Sullivan and Senator Aiken, both of whom have long supported a Federal food stamp program effectively.

Finally, I wish to convey my personal note of thanks to all agencies of State and local governments and to those bankers, food retailers, and wholesalers who have cooperated with the United States Department of Agriculture in this program during its 3-year pilot trial, and, finally, to the majority of the Members of the House and Senate who made it possible for this bill to be on my desk tonight.

NOTE: The President spoke in the Cabinet Room at the White House. During the course of his remarks he referred to Senator Allen J. Ellender of Louisiana, Representative Harold D. Cooley of North Carolina, Representative Leonor K. Sullivan of Missouri, and Senator George D. Aiken of Vermont.

The Food Stamp Act of 1964 is Public Law 88–525 (78 Stat. 703).

547 Telephone Remarks to the Convention of the Plasterers' Union. *August 31, 1964*

President Leonard and members:

I am proud to be able to join today in congratulating you as you celebrate the 100th anniversary of your union.

Over these last 100 years, we have made much progress in this country toward fulfilling the promise of freedom for our people and of all mankind. It is symbolic, I think, that your union was founded at a time when Americans were fighting other Americans in a terrible war that divided our Nation. For the gains all of us have made—whether in labor or business or agriculture—have come because of our Nation's growing unity since that era of tragic division.

We are a happier people, we are a stronger Nation because we have avoided the division of class against class and creed against creed and color against color.

Today, great opportunities open before us to make this life better for all of us. The right of the workingman to be recognized—and to bargain collectively—must not and will not be compromised as long as I sit in the White House. The same is true for the rights and attainments of all sectors of our society—business as well as labor, farmers as well as consumers, the old as well as the young.

Our challenge is not to turn back or to look aside—but to go ahead to the work that will make this a better and finer land for all of us.

We want to assure that every child born in this land will in the future have the opportunity for a full education—to the full extent of his abilities. We want our citizens who enjoy a longer life to know that the savings of their productive years will not be wiped away by hospital costs in their later years. We want the heads of every family to know that when they need work and want to work there will be jobs available to them—good jobs at decent pay.

Devotion to goals such as these has made America what it is today. And I don't think there is one of you at that convention this morning that would choose any other of the 120 countries in lieu of America. For I believe the American people know in their hearts that the course we are following is the right course.

We have the wisdom and the will to build a great society in the United States. All of you are builders of America and in these next years ahead I believe that you will be building—both on the job and in your participation as citizens of this republic.

Our generation is privileged to bear the burdens of defending freedom and preserving peace around the world. This is a great and noble task. None of us would turn away from it.

But if we are to stand as the strong center of the free world—and the hopes of man— we must always work to assure the success, stability, progress, and unity of our democratic system and our society here at home.

That is why we work as we do to protect the equal rights and equal opportunity of

all—to assure the progress of all families in our land.

Let those of us who are well-fed, well-clothed, and well-housed never forget and never overlook those who live on the outskirts of hope. Most of us have lived that way ourselves at some time in our lives. Let us not forget the Golden Rule of do unto others as we would have them do unto us. And while we work to maintain peace in the world, let us not forget that here at home we are locked in battle against poverty and ignorance and disease and violence.

In the year 2064, when your convention meets to celebrate your 200th anniversary, it is my earnest hope, my genuine prayer, and your wish that your heirs in your trade union will be able to say that this, the year 1964, was the time when all Americans began the work of our greatest construction project—the building of the Great Society in America where the fruits of that society would be distributed to all the people.

Thank you and goodby.

NOTE: The President spoke by telephone from the LBJ Ranch in Johnson City, Tex., to the delegates to the 100th Anniversary Convention of the Operative Plasterers' and Cement Masons' International Association of the United States and Canada, held at the Sheraton Hotel in Philadelphia, Pa. His opening words referred to Edward J. Leonard, general president of the association.

The text of the President's remarks was released at Austin, Tex.

548   Remarks to the General Board of the AFL–CIO. September 1, 1964

I THANK YOU for your endorsement. I will carry it proudly during this campaign. I will remember it fondly in January as we begin 4 more exciting years of progress.

Twenty-five years ago today Hitler's tyranny struck at helpless Poland. The

world as we knew it was never to be the same.

Americans of all parties can share a moment of pride in our achievements in those 25 years. In the factories, and in the field of battle, we won the victory. And in the dangerous years that followed we never wavered in the defense of freedom or the pursuit of peace. As a result we are closer than ever to making the Second World War the last world war.

At home we have seen depression become boom, idle men find rewarding toil, and our country climb to heights of prosperity beyond our most daring dreams.

In 1960 men of little faith said the climb was over—America had reached its peak. But you did not believe them. The Democratic Party did not believe them. And the American people did not believe them.

America chose to move forward. And the result has been a steady, uninterrupted, expanding prosperity for all Americans. Since 1961, 5 million nonfarm jobs have been added to the economy. Unemployment in July dropped to 4.9 percent. The average family of four earns today, after taxes, $1,200 more than in 1961. Average manufacturing wages have gone up more than 15 percent.

This prospertity is not an accident. It is not good luck. It is the result of tested policies. It is the result of the hard work and cooperation of business and labor. It is a result of the unmatched vitality of our free enterprise system—the envy of all the world.

Today again men of faulty vision cry, "Halt . . . we have done all we can do." And today again the American people will reject these fear-filled slogans.

We are on the edge of an abundance which can tower over all the gains of the past. I predict, if we continue on our course, the growth of the next 4 years will be the greatest in all our history. And every person in this country will benefit from expanding prosperity.

Let no one mistake our aims. Neither pressure nor protest, danger or difficulty will move us one inch from the historic principles which have brought us to today's heights. Nor will we neglect the poor, the sick, the aged—those who have not shared in our abundance. Medical care for the old, increased minimum wages, the war on poverty are parts of a program with a single goal: to give every American a place of dignity in our national life.

And this is only the beginning. The country is changing. Population is growing and technology is expanding. We must move to meet these challenges or be overwhelmed by them. They will require the same courage and confidence we have brought to the challenges of the past.

With these as our tools, we can build a nation which will enlarge and enrich the life of every citizen. We have the knowledge and the resources. And this November, the American people will confirm that this country has the determination to keep moving forward.

I ask you to be at my side in this great task.

I will be at yours.

NOTE: The President spoke at 3:40 p.m. in the East Room at the White House. In his opening remarks he referred to a resolution adopted earlier in the day by the executive council of the AFL–CIO unanimously endorsing the nomination of the President and Senator Humphrey.

549   Remarks Upon Signing the Housing Act. September 2, 1964

Members of the Congress, ladies and gentlemen:

I am pleased today to approve the Housing Act of 1964. I believe that we have a commitment to assure every American an opportunity to live in a decent home, in a safe and a decent neighborhood.

This milestone measure will help us to honor that commitment. This bill carries forward our continuing efforts to eradicate slums and blight in our cities; to assure decent housing for those least able to find it—the poor, the elderly, the severely handicapped—and those in our rural areas; to help our communities grow in orderly directions and avoid future blight and assure lasting beauty.

This bill does more than to continue the successful programs that we have had in operation in the past. It provides new support for greater success in the future. The plight of property owners in urban renewal areas is recognized in this measure. Provision is made so that they can rehabilitate their homes and businesses instead of having to move from the path of the bulldozers.

Looking ahead, this measure assists local communities in enforcing housing codes so blight does not develop or persist in the future. It also provides for training local urban development administrators and to produce the city planners that we shall need in the future to guide in the growth that we expect.

This is by no means a bill just for the cities of America alone. A key new program provides for the construction of low-cost rental housing for our farmworkers in the Nation. This is a most needed and a most welcome step.

Nor is this bill a bill solely for the housing of those that are in unfortunate circumstances. It provides expanded benefits to builders and to lenders, and to families in good circumstances.

By every standard we think this bill benefits all Americans, and if we are to continue to keep our commitments in the world, then I believe it is fundamental that we must consider keeping our commitments here at home. And that is what we are trying to do with this legislation.

For our generation, courage is not confined to meeting the challenges faraway from us. Courage is also required to meet the problems and the obligations and the challenges that are nearest to us.

This Congress deserves, I believe, very special commendation for the foresight and the courage that it has shown in meeting our problems here at home and in our own country, with our own people. The Urban Mass Transportation Act, the highway aid bill, the Hill-Burton extension, the many education measures all represent, together, the most constructive attack by any Congress on the challenge of keeping America fit and a fine place for our families.

I believe it is noteworthy that all of these programs represent a new spirit of cooperation between the Federal and the State and local governments; likewise, I think it is significant that a strong spirit of trust between the public sector and the private sector is present. We reject the thought of our families living in a faceless, regimented, monotonous America. We intend to preserve the role of private enterprise, the force of private initiative, and the right of private choice in our life as free men.

May I express my very special congratulations this morning to both Senator Sparkman and Congressman Rains of Alabama. Certainly for Albert Rains this Housing Act of 1964 is a crowning achievement for a highly constructive career of great public service. I know that I express the thought of all of us when I say we regret that he has not chosen to run again for the Congress. We do hope that he will see fit to honor us in other fields of public service in the years ahead.

I want to thank all the Members of the Congress who have come here this morning, and applaud their efforts in passing this most constructive and helpful piece of legislation that is designed to benefit all Americans.

NOTE: The President spoke in midmorning in the Cabinet Room at the White House. The Housing Act of 1964 is Public Law 88–560 (78 Stat. 769).

550 Remarks at the Swearing In of Dr. Otto Eckstein as a Member of the Council of Economic Advisers. *September 2, 1964*

Dr. and Mrs. Eckstein, ladies and gentlemen:

I know that the Ivy League takes a dim view of recruiting athletes. But I hope that they will be more favorable toward our recruiting economists. We have had a "Big Ten" team on the Council, from Minnesota, Michigan, and Indiana. Walter Heller and Gardner Ackley may have the height on you, Dr. Eckstein, but we do expect you to add depth worthy of both Harvard and Princeton.

Eighteen years ago the Council of Economic Advisers was established by the Employment Act of 1946. At that time there were many predictions that the Council would become either an aloof academic supreme court of academic policy or a sinister scheming cell of master planners. Under both Republican and Democratic administrations it has become neither. Instead, the Council is one of the most effective and one of the most successful instruments of responsible policy guidance that has been created in modern times.

I am both proud and grateful for its services and for the leadership offered by Chairman Heller and Acting Chairman Ackley.

In 1946 our Nation faced considerable uncertainty about employment in postwar America. I remember, as a Member of the House of Representatives at that time, our concern for the facts of prewar America.

In 1938 unemployment stood at 19 percent. Even in 1941 unemployment was 10 percent. But in the Employment Act of 1946 we made a bold new national commitment. We committed the Federal Government to use all practical means to create and maintain conditions under which there would be afforded useful employment opportunities for those that were able and willing and seeking work. The facts today tell the story of our success.

This summer, 72,400,000 Americans have been at work, more than have ever been at work in our history. Unemployment has dropped below 5 percent. We are enjoying together the longest and the strongest uninterrupted prosperity in the Nation's history.

Well, this is a great record, and credit is wisely due. Our success is not the success of Government alone, or labor alone, or business alone. But it is the success of all of these parts of our general system, and all working together in our system.

One factor in that success is the greater use in all sectors of reliable, responsible guidance from our economics profession. I suppose that professors, like politicians, will always be the target of critics. But I do think it is healthy for America that we no longer look down our noses at trained men with trained minds. Our policies, public and private, are wiser and more successful today because we do respect and we do accept the counsel of our academic community.

Today, unlike 1946, we face the future with strong confidence, with solid expectations. We are hopeful the time may come when recessions as we have known them will become not merely milder and less frequent but even become a relic of the past.

We are confident that this resourceful and resolute economy can meet its responsibilities for creating the jobs that are required by a growing population. Maximum employment is not the only answer to the war on poverty. Most of the poor have jobs but their jobs are poor because they are unprepared for good jobs. Many of the rest are simply not in the labor force because of age or disability, or family status.

Victory in the war on poverty requires more than jobs. It requires a strong and a vigorously growing economy as the environment for progress on all fronts and that is the target that is in our sights today.

Dr. Eckstein, we want to welcome you aboard. It is good to have you. I want to welcome to the White House not only you under these circumstances, but your wonderful family who is present to see you sworn in.

NOTE: The ceremony was held in the Cabinet Room at the White House. During the course of his remarks the President referred to Walter W. Heller, Chairman, Council of Economic Advisers, and Gardner Ackley, member of the Council. The text of brief remarks by Dr. Eckstein was also released.

551   Special Message to the Congress Transmitting Report on U.S. Policy and International Cooperation in Antarctica. *September 2, 1964*

To the Congress of the United States:

I am pleased to transmit to the Congress this special report on United States Policy and International Cooperation in Antarctica.

Men and nations alike tend to concentrate their energies on unsolved problems. In foreign affairs, disagreements all too often distract public attention from accords and agreements.

But preoccupation with world problems should not obscure situations like Antarctica where this country and others work together harmoniously to construct the prototypes of peace.

The Treaty provides for freedom of scientific investigation in Antarctica and for carrying on undiminished the cooperation started during the International Geophysical Year. It prohibits nuclear explosions in Antarctica and the disposal there of radioactive waste.

To see that the Treaty is complied with, national Observers may be sent at any time to any part of Antarctica to inspect various national installations. In late 1963, the United States sent two such inspection teams to examine facilities of six other countries. In January 1964 they reported that no Treaty violations were observed in any of the installations visited.

Since the Treaty came into force in 1961, the parties have held periodic meetings in a rare spirit of frankness and cooperation to find acceptable ways to carry out various provisions of the Treaty.

On Antarctica's icy wastes, scientists visit freely between their various national installations, sometimes spending an entire year working with their counterparts from other countries. Many important expeditions have been completed and lives saved in time of danger because of timely assistance from other national stations.

Thus the Antarctic Treaty to which the Senate of the United States gave its advice and consent to ratification on August 10, 1960, serves not only as a pact guaranteeing freedom of scientific inquiry in the Continent of Antarctica but, more importantly, as an outstanding example of practical cooperation between nations and a positive step toward a peaceful world.

LYNDON B. JOHNSON

NOTE: The report "United States Policy and International Cooperation in Antarctica," dated May 1964, is printed in House Document 358 (88th Cong., 2d sess.).

For the text of the Antarctic Treaty, see "United States Treaties and Other International Agreements" (12 UST (pt. 1) 794, TIAS 4780).

552   Statement by the President Following Senate Passage of the Medicare Bill.   *September 2, 1964*

THE VOTE in the Senate was a victory not only for older Americans but for all Americans. The health of every citizen— old and young, rich and poor—is vital to our strength as a nation.

This is the first time either House of Congress has endorsed health care for the aged under the social security system. I congratulate the Senate and hope that the Congress will not long delay final action on this constructive, fair, and wise proposal.

In a free and prosperous society there is no need for any person, especially the elderly, to suffer personal economic disaster and become a tragic burden upon loved ones or the State through major illness when, by prudently setting aside the employers and employees contributions this can be avoided.

553   Statement by the President on the Death of Sergeant York.   *September 2, 1964*

SERGEANT Alvin Cullum York has stood as a symbol of American courage and sacrifice for almost half a century. His valor, above and beyond the call of duty, in World War I was recognized with the Nation's highest award, the Medal of Honor. As the citizen-soldier hero of the American Expeditionary Forces, he epitomized the gallantry of American fighting men and their sacrifices in behalf of freedom.

As Commander in Chief, I know that I express the deep and heartfelt sympathy of the American people to his wife and family.

554   Remarks Upon Signing the Wilderness Bill and the Land and
      Water Conservation Fund Bill. *September 3, 1964*

*Members of the Cabinet and the Congress,
ladies and gentlemen:*

This is a very happy and historic occasion for all who love the great American outdoors, and that, needless to say, includes me. The two bills that I am signing this morning are in the highest tradition of our heritage as conservators as well as users of America's bountiful natural endowments.

The wilderness bill preserves for our posterity, for all time to come, 9 million acres of this vast continent in their original and unchanging beauty and wonder.

The land and water conservation bill assures our growing population that we will begin, as of this day, to acquire on a pay-as-you-go basis the outdoor recreation lands that tomorrow's Americans will require.

I believe the significance of this occasion goes far beyond these bills alone. In this century, Americans have wisely and have courageously kept a faithful trust to the conservation of our natural resources and beauty. But the long strides forward have tended to come in periods of concerted effort.

The first, I think, was under the leadership of a great Republican President, Theodore Roosevelt. This brought passage of the Reclamation Act. This brought the creation of the national forests. This brought the development of a new concept of national stewardship.

The second period came under a great Democratic President, Franklin Delano Roosevelt. He led this Nation in rebuilding the land and developing the resources for improving the life of all of us. He did it through the TVA, through the CCC, through the Soil Conservation Service, through the water conservation projects.

Anyone that objectively studies the rec-ord of the 88th Congress I think would have to conclude that another historic era has begun this year. If the 88th had not earned already so many honorable titles, such as the education Congress, the health Congress, the full prosperity Congress, it would be remembered as the conservation Congress, because in addition to the measures before me this morning, Congress has wisely this year passed the Ozark Rivers National Riverway bill, which I signed last week; the Fire Island National Seashore bill, which is awaiting action; the Canyonlands National Park legislation, which I expect to sign shortly, creating our first new national park on this continent in 17 years.

But Congress has done even more. Action has been taken to keep our air pure and our water safe and our food free from pesticides; to protect our wildlife; to conserve our precious water resources. No single Congress in my memory has done so much to keep America as a good and wholesome and beautiful place to live.

I think it is significant that these steps have broad support not just from the Democratic Party, but the Republican Party, both parties in the Congress. For example, the wilderness bill has been before the Congress since 1957, but it passed this year 73 to 12 in the Senate, and 373 to 1 in the House. So it seems to me that this reflects a new and a strong national consensus to look ahead, and, more than that, to plan ahead; better still, to move ahead.

We know that America cannot be made strong by leadership which reacts only to the needs or the irritations or the frustrations of the moment. True leadership must provide for the next decade and not merely the next day. That is the kind of leadership that this Congress is providing.

I am very proud of the leadership and the wisdom and the vitality and the vigorous approach that the distinguished and able Secretary of Interior has made, and the leadership that he has provided from coast to coast in this field. For their leadership on these bills, I am especially grateful to Senator Anderson, who has been in the forefront of conservation legislation since he first came to the House; to Senator Jackson; to Congressman Aspinall; and to Members of both parties on these important committees that reported these bills.

So it is with a great deal of pride and pleasure and hope for the future that we enact into law today by signing these bills

some of the most far-reaching conservation measures that a farsighted nation has ever coped with.

NOTE: The President spoke at 10:30 a.m. in the Rose Garden at the White House. In the course of his remarks he referred to Secretary of the Interior Stewart L. Udall, Senator Clinton P. Anderson of New Mexico, Senator Henry M. Jackson of Washington, and Representative Wayne N. Aspinall of Colorado.

As enacted, the wilderness bill (S. 4) is Public Law 88–577 (78 Stat. 890); the land and water conservation fund bill (H.R. 3846) is Public Law 88–578 (78 Stat. 897).

In his comments on the record of the 88th Congress in the field of conservation the President referred to the Ozark National Scenic Riverways bill (78 Stat. 608), the Fire Island National Seashore bill (78 Stat. 928), and the Canyonlands National Park bill (78 Stat. 934).

---

555 Remarks to Members of the National Independent Committee for Johnson and Humphrey. *September 3, 1964*

I AM GRATEFUL that the record and conduct of this administration have earned your vote of confidence this afternoon—as independent Americans. And, I might add, so is Senator Humphrey.

Our American system was not intended to be controlled by the rigid disciplines of party. On the contrary, it was founded on the belief that in political decisions affecting the fate and fortune of their country, all Americans would be, as you are, proudly and patriotically independent.

This year independent Americans, of all walks of life, have a choice: the choice of the kind of country they want America to be.

They can choose an America which sails a straight and sure course, steered by experience, confident in its strength, steadfast in its purposes. They can choose an America devoted, as America has always been devoted, to peace in the world and progress for mankind.

Or they can choose quite a different America—an America tacking sail and turning about to retrace its course. They can choose an America whose purposes will not be understood by the people of the world, or even by the people at home.

Yes, the independent American has a choice, and with that choice goes a responsibility: the responsibility to stand up and be counted.

In this year of 1964, we are not determining the future of our parties. But we are determining the fate and fortune of America itself—and of the cause we are privileged to lead.

I commend all of you not only on the choice you have made for your country, but on your courage in now assuming the responsibility of your convictions.

Ten months ago, it fell to me to become the 36th man—in 188 years—to take up the burdens of this office I hold. I entered these duties with the same determination that guides me now: to strive to be—always and only—President of all the people.

I did not, I do not, I shall never seek to be a labor President or a business President, a President for liberals or a President for conservatives, a President for the North or a President for the South—but only President for all the people.

In these 10 months, as you well know, the record of our Nation's progress tells the story of what Americans can do together in unity.

Our GNP is up nearly $20 billion.

Our industrial production is up 5.2 percent.

Personal income after taxes is up $20 billion.

Corporate profits are up more than $3½ billion.

Your stock values are up more than $100 billion.

In all our history, business has never been better than in these last 43 months of uninterrupted prosperity and the families of our land have never been more prosperous.

Times are good, but never easy. There is still work to be done—hard work, demanding work, but infinitely rewarding work—here at home as well as across the seas. It is this work that I want a united America, a progressive America, a prudent America, to be doing in the years to come.

I want the world to know beyond doubt that America stands for peace and that we are prepared to protect it. I also want the people of America to know that their Government, here in Washington, stands for the people's progress and is determined to continue it.

In all the world and in all history, no men have ever had so much to conserve as we. You know, I know—all thoughtful Americans know—that we do not conserve the goodness of our life or the nobility of our values by abruptly changing our national character or course.

Our national history for 188 years has been a history of liberal and conservative working together. Liberalism and conservatism are partners, not enemies—and it must always be so.

We have a heritage to preserve from our ancestors. But we also have trust to keep with our posterity.

In this year of national decision, I am confident that responsible and independent Americans will play a decisive role in holding America on course, so that we may keep faith with those before us and those who shall come after us.

NOTE: The President spoke in the Cabinet Room at the White House. In his opening remarks he referred to a resolution adopted by the National Independent Committee for Johnson and Humphrey at its organization meeting earlier in the day expressing confidence in the President's leadership. The Committee, a group of 45 business and financial leaders—many of them former supporters of the Republican Party—was formed to sponsor "a collective public endorsement of President Johnson and Senator Humphrey by outstanding people throughout the country who are well known for their accomplishments in nonpartisan and nonpolitical activities."

As printed, this item follows the prepared text released by the White House.

556 Letter Accepting Resignation of Robert F. Kennedy as Attorney General. *September 3, 1964*

Dear Bob:

It is with regret that I have received your resignation. You have played a very vital role in the conduct of public affairs.

Both President Kennedy and I sought your counsel on a wide range of matters going far beyond the usual concerns of the Department of Justice. For four years you have shared in deliberations on major matters of national security, and your contributions have been significant.

You must also share my special satisfaction at your conduct of the office of Attorney General. Under your administration the Department of Justice achieved new standards of excellence and has come to symbolize this government's insistence on the vigorous and impartial assurance of equal justice to all Americans. It has been an administration worthy in every way of the grand tradition of justice on which American liberty rests.

My regret at your leaving is tempered by satisfaction in the knowledge that you intend to continue your service to your country. You will soon be back in Washington where I can again call upon your judgment and counsel.

With best regards,

Sincerely,

LYNDON B. JOHNSON

[Honorable Robert F. Kennedy, Department of Justice, Washington, D.C.]

NOTE: Mr. Kennedy served as Attorney General from January 21, 1961, through September 3, 1964. His letter of resignation, dated September 3, was released on the same day.

557 Remarks Upon Signing the Nurse Training Act of 1964. *September 4, 1964*

Members of the Congress, ladies and gentlemen:

The best of health for all Americans is a primary national goal for all of us. Today we are moving a long step nearer that objective. The Nurse Training Act of 1964 is the most significant nursing legislation in the history of our country. I believe that it will enable us to attract many more of our most qualified young people to this great and noble calling.

Nurses today are essential members of our Nation's health team. The health needs of a growing population cannot be met without their help. Blessed with the gifts of healing and with a wise and understanding heart, nurses perform a vital role in maintaining and strengthening America's health services and our national well-being. Yet we are critically short of the nurses that we need.

Far too many people today suffer needlessly, or go without the attention they require, simply because we do not have enough well-trained nurses. About 20 percent of positions for professional nurses in hospitals are today unfilled. The shortage of nurses has forced some hospitals to close wards and entire sections. Others have been obliged to fill vacancies with people who are poorly, or at least incompletely, trained.

By the year 1970 we will need 850,000 nurses. That is a startling figure, but that is 300,000 more than we have today. At their present strength, our nursing schools can graduate only 30,000 a year. Clearly the capacity to train additional thousands of nurses must be increased, if we are to improve or even maintain America's national health standards.

The Nurse Training Act of 1964, which we have met this morning to finally sign and complete, represents the response of an enlightened Congress to the urgent need. The act contains four principal elements. It authorizes a program of grants to build and renovate nursing schools; it establishes a program to help schools of nursing strengthen and improve their training programs and to help diploma schools of nursing meet the costs which will come with increased enrollment; it expands the existing program of advanced training of professional nurses; it establishes a loan program which will enable many talented but needy students to undertake the professional training for a nursing career.

All of this has very special meaning for the young women of our Nation; by removing some of the financial barriers to training it will enable many more deserving and talented young women to enter the proud profession of nursing.

A century has passed since Florence Nightingale and Clara Barton brought the art of nursing on to the world's stage. We owe a great debt of gratitude to these courageous and dedicated women, and to the many other women who have served humanity throughout our long history. Today's nurse must be both humanitarian and scientist. Her great compassion must be matched by much greater competence.

So the Nurse Training Act of 1964 is recognition of the new needs of the profession, as well as the growing needs of all of our people. We feel a very special debt to those whose legislative effort and dedication and energy and hard work made this legislation possible.

I particularly appreciate the efforts of Congressman Oren Harris, who is the author of much good legislation; and my dear friend Senator Lister Hill, who is unable to be with us this morning; Congressman Kenneth Roberts, who chaired the subcommittee which held the detailed hearings; and the other Members of the House and Senate committees that pioneered this legislation and are responsible for bringing it safely through both bodies.

You see them on the platform this morning. I am sorry that they are not outdoors people and they all like to get up in the shade, but they are here to receive what is properly theirs, a tribute for their pioneering effort in this field where we need this legislation so much.

This is truly a notable achievement toward raising the standards of health care in the United States. I predict that down through the years to come that every person here this morning will be proud that they were permitted to be a participant in this historic legislation that will do so much to keep our Nation healthy and that will permit our suffering to at least be endurable as a result of a compassionate and concerned nurse.

Thank you very much.

NOTE: The President spoke in midmorning in the Rose Garden at the White House. During his remarks he referred to Representative Oren Harris of Arkansas, and to Senator Lister Hill and Representative Kenneth A. Roberts of Alabama.

The Nurse Training Act of 1964 is Public Law 88–581 (78 Stat. 908).

558   Statement by the President: Labor Day.
September 4, 1964

ON MONDAY, our Nation will observe Labor Day for the 70th year.

In 1894, when Congress first designated this day, our labor force consisted of approximately 25 million persons—including children as young as 10 years of age—working, when work was to be found, 60 hours each week at wages averaging only 20¢ an hour.

In this year of 1964, we have reached a new record of 72.4 million Americans at work, laboring one-third fewer hours each week at wages tenfold greater than on the first Labor Day.

The greater gains of these years are not measurable in material terms.

The life of the workingman and his family in our society today is a world away from 70 years ago.

Then, in the lingering tradition of centuries past, the worker in America was a citizen of second class—often excluded, too often exploited, regarded as unequal, and treated as inferior.

Now, the worker in America is a full citizen of the first class—accorded a place of dignity in our society, a role of participation in our affairs, and a trust of high responsibility for the success of our system. A compassionate society cares for the life he leads as well as for the labor he performs.

Today we travel a road of well-being together.

In the service of our well-being, the American trade union movement serves an invaluable role. It was founded in time of social crisis to give the individual the strength of many in his contest with the power of the privileged few. Today, in a time of the privileged many, that movement speaks on behalf of the forgotten few.

American unions consistently advance and support programs to increase the welfare of all.

Such work is today the work of us all.

For if we have come far, we still have far to go.

Our purpose and our policy must be to create more jobs, open more doors of opportunity, shelter and safeguard the rights which have been won and seek to assure rights not yet secure.

On this Labor Day of 1964, let us as a people take pride not only in what we have done but in what we are privileged now to undertake.

Let us, in particular, continue to strive to serve the stability and success of our society by:

—assuring the prosperity and competitiveness of American enterprise,

—maintaining free collective bargaining as the basic means of economic decision,

—making the development of our manpower a priority piece of public business,

—and by increasing the well-being of workers and security of their organizations in all that we do.

In these times responsibility is required of our Nation in the world, but that responsibility begins at home.

For if we are to keep our commitments to freedom in all lands, we must faithfully keep our commitments to our families in this land.

559   Statement by the President on the North Pacific Fisheries Negotiations.   *September 4, 1964*

THE THIRD round of negotiations with Canada and Japan on North Pacific fisheries problems is scheduled to begin in Ottawa on September 9. I have just received a report on the issues involved from Ambassador Benjamin A. Smith II, who will head the United States delegation in these negotiations. The major problem with which the negotiations will deal is the revision of the existing international arrangements for the conservation and rational utilization of the fishery resources in the North Pacific Ocean.

Two earlier rounds of negotiations were held in Washington and Tokyo last year. They made substantial progress toward full agreement. I hope the negotiations can be completed during the new round of discussions.

The primary objective of the United States in these negotiations is to protect the interests of Alaska and the Pacific Northwest in the North Pacific fisheries, which consist principally of salmon and halibut. The economy of these regions is heavily dependent upon the U.S. fisheries supported by these resources.

The interests of the United States in these fishery stocks have been advanced by the International Convention for the High Seas Fisheries of the North Pacific Ocean. Basic to that convention is the concept that in special situations, such as those exemplified by the North American salmon and halibut fisheries, where the countries participating in the fisheries have built up and maintained the resources through major research and regulatory programs, other countries should exercise restraints on their fishing of the type provided for in that convention.

This concept provides the incentives necessary to the establishment and continuation of the conservation measures essential to the attainment, both now and in the future, of the maximum harvest of food for mankind. This will insure the conservation of important marine resources and prevent irreparable damage to them through overexploitation. This is in the common interest of Japan, Canada, and the United States.

Over the years we have made major contributions to the restoration and maintenance of the salmon and halibut fisheries. For this reason, we have a special interest in them. We are determined to protect that interest, while giving every consideration to the legitimate interests of the other parties to the convention. I am confident that Ambassador Smith, who was the United States representative during the earlier discussions, will effectively present our point of view.

I urge that the three delegations work out a solution that will permit the conservation of these resources for future generations, taking into account the unique circumstances surrounding the convention and the interests of all parties to it.

NOTE: The International Convention for the High Seas Fisheries of the North Pacific Ocean is published with related papers in "United States Treaties and Other International Agreements" (4 UST (pt. 1) 380, TIAS 2786; 14 UST (pt. 1) 953, TIAS 5385).

560 The President's News Conference of September 5, 1964

THE PRESIDENT. [1.] I have just signed a proclamation designating the week of September 6th as College Students Registration Week.[1] I won't take any of your time going into it, but it may interest you. Only 52 percent of these young people cast ballots in recent presidential elections compared with 82 percent of the men and women in their 60's.

The American Heritage Foundation, the group that met with us once before with the chairman of both parties, in the White House, are interested in this matter and they have conducted this poll. It was at their suggestion that we are issuing this proclamation. Get Mac[2] to get you a copy of it.

[2.] The first thing I want to say this morning is about the Chilean election, that it was an internal matter in which the people of Chile were the only judges of the issues. The election reminds us once more, however, of the strength of democracy in Chile and throughout the Western Hemisphere.

It reminds us that the last 6 months have been good for democracy and progress in the Americas. Prospects in a number of important countries are more hopeful now than they were 6 months ago, and the prospects for those who are hostile to freedom are weaker.

The Chilean election reminds us of the advances which the Alliance for Progress is making throughout the hemisphere. Mr. Frei, in the campaign, expressed his intention to work for the economic and social development of his country within a democratic framework which emphasizes personal liberty. These are our goals and the goals of the Alliance for Progress.

We wish the Chilean people well. We look forward to cooperating with their newly selected leader just as we have in the past with his distinguished predecessor. We hope that the next 6 years will be a period of peace and prosperity and a period of continued progress in economic and social reform.

Let me say again that I see yesterday's events in Chile in the context of Latin American affairs generally. In that context, the Chilean election seems to me to reinforce our hopes for a very bright future in the Americas. Each country in the hemisphere must work for progress and democracy by its own methods. We have a long road to travel, but we are on our way.

[3.] Another item that may interest you: General Taylor[3] is coming back, in accordance with the plans which we previously made, but which he delayed last week because of the political situation in Viet-Nam. I look forward to meeting with him early next week, and also with Ambassador Lodge,[4] who has done an outstanding job abroad in explaining our policy and purpose in Viet-Nam to our allies in Europe.

These meetings, like other meetings which we have had in the past on Viet-Nam, will be devoted to a careful review of our programs, and the reaffirmation of our simple basic purpose which is to help the free people of that country in their struggle for progress against the Communist subversion and terror.

[4.] I think you should know also that I

---

[1] Proclamation 3614 (29 F.R. 12817; 3 CFR, 1964 Supp.).

[2] Malcolm M. Kilduff, Assistant Press Secretary.

[3] Gen. Maxwell D. Taylor, U.S. Ambassador to Viet-Nam.

[4] Henry Cabot Lodge, former U.S. Ambassador to Viet-Nam.

plan to have a talk with Mr. Dean Acheson, former Secretary of State, who has returned from 8 weeks of the most delicate and diplomatic talks.[5] He is in the country today, and he will be in the early part of the week, perhaps Monday or Tuesday.

Although the situation in Cyprus has not yet been removed and the situation there remains full of danger, all Americans can be very proud of Mr. Acheson's patient and skillful efforts to help find the honorable and peaceful solution. I believe when such a settlement is found, it will be clear that his work was a major constructive element in the process.

The United States continues to have an intimate interest in finding such a settlement because of its close ties with all parties and its commitment to freedom and peace for this eastern wing of the great alliance.

[5.] A couple of other matters that might interest you:

[*Reading*] "I have been advised by Secretary of Defense McNamara that a new and significantly improved weapon—the Polaris A–3 missile—will soon become part of our strategic missile force. The new A–3 will be deployed for the first time aboard the nuclear submarine U.S.S. *Daniel Webster* when she begins her first patrol later this month.

"The A–3 missile which was put into accelerated development in 1964, has a range of 2,500 nautical miles, some 1,000 nautical miles greater than that of the A–2, and more than double that of the A–1. This new weapon not only has a much greater range, but it is extremely accurate and incorporates the latest technological advances to assure that it will be able to penetrate to its target, including those protected by possible ballistic missile defense systems.

[5] Mr. Acheson served as personal envoy of the President to the Geneva conference to mediate the dispute between Greece and Turkey over Cyprus.

"With the A–3, our Polaris submarines will be able to operate over much wider areas. For example, a submarine armed with A–1 missiles for targets 1,000 miles inland has some 700,000 square miles of sea room in which to maneuver. Armed with the A–3, the same targets can be covered and the submarines will have more than 8,000,000 square miles of ocean in which to hide. Operating in the 700,000 square mile area, an A–3 submarine can hit targets nearly 2,500 miles inland."

The statement is more extended. I won't take your time on it, but it will be available for you.[6]

[6] The statement as released by the White House contains the following additional paragraphs:

You will recall that in January 1961 this administration ordered an acceleration of the development of the A–3 missile and a speedup in the construction of Polaris submarines. This resulted in the production of one submarine each month as opposed to one every 2 months under the old schedule. As of this date, 16 Polaris submarines are deployed on station, 8 more than would have been available under the old plans. Under the original schedule the *Daniel Webster* would not have deployed until July of 1965, and with A–2 missiles. The first A–3 would not have been deployed until a year from now.

No land area on this earth is beyond reach of these submerged missile ships of our Navy. They are truly a global deterrent to war.

We have made great strides in developing the Polaris system in a very short time. It was less than 4 years ago, November 1960, when the first Polaris submarine deployed. Now, 16 are on station armed with 256 Polaris missiles.

Eight Polaris submarines have gone to sea for their initial patrols since the beginning of this year. In the next 8 months we expect to deploy 11 more, all but one of which will carry the A–3 missile.

Polaris submarines now operate in the Atlantic and Mediterranean, and before the end of the year will be operational in the Pacific as well.

All 41 Polaris submarines planned as part of our strategic forces will be operational in 1967. Twenty-eight will carry the A–3 missile and 13 will have the 1,500 nautical mile A–2. The A–1 will have been phased out.

The Fleet Ballistic Missile system, highly invulnerable, dependable, and accurate, gives the United States a force which can deliver a crushing and retaliatory blow to an aggressor.

[6.] I am informed by the Atomic Energy Commission and the Secretary of Defense this morning that—[*reading*]— "they are proceeding with the development of a new, high-powered, long-lived reactor which constitutes a major step forward in nuclear technology, and will make nuclear power more attractive in the construction of our aircraft carriers.

"Two of these reactors could power an attack aircraft carrier as compared with eight reactors required for the U.S.S. *Enterprise.* Four are considered for the U.S.S. *John F. Kennedy.* The development program will be under the direction of Vice Admiral Rickover.

"The new two-reactor plants will provide approximately the same total horsepower as that provided by the four and eight reactors. In addition, it will almost double the fuel life. It is important to note that the new two-reactor plant will be less expensive than others, particularly with respect to operating costs. A carrier powered by this new plant will require refueling only once in the life of the ship."

There is some more detail in the statement, but I think it is too long to give to you.[7]

[7.] We have exchanged correspondence between the United States and Brazil, expressions of our solidarity during the Tonkin Gulf incident. Those letters will be made

public to you if you are interested in the exchange.[8]

[8.] Later this month Random House is publishing a book—and it is right here; I am making some editorial changes—in which I will discuss my philosophy of government and my views on the issues. This book is devoted to what I have said and done since becoming President, and what I have believed in all my life.[9] The earnings from the book, if there are any, will be turned over to charity.

I am ready to take any questions now for a few minutes before I take a walk. If any of you want to go with me, you can go with me.

[9.] Q. Mr. President, sir, you said you would withhold a statement on whether you would engage in televised debates until you received the nomination. Will you now engage in debates with Senator Goldwater on a regularly scheduled news program?

THE PRESIDENT. I haven't reached any decision on that. I haven't said I would withhold the statement. I said we would cross the bridge when we got to it. I haven't reached it yet.

[10.] Q. Mr. President, can you give us your reaction to Mr. Nixon's statement that the Democratic Party is now the party of big business?

THE PRESIDENT. No. I haven't heard from Mr. Nixon. I didn't know that he had said anything like that.

Q. He said the Republican Party is now the party of the people. Would you agree with that?

THE PRESIDENT. I think the Democratic Party and the Republican Party both are trying to do what they think is best for all

---

[7] The statement as released by the White House contains the following additional paragraphs:

The Department of Defense and the Atomic Energy Commission are confident that the reactor will be developed in time so that it could be installed in a carrier in the 1968–69 time period.

Development of the two-reactor aircraft carrier propulsion plant is another significant step in the creation of a nuclear powered Navy. It is part of a continuing program to develop reliable, advanced nuclear propulsion plants for both surface and submarine use.

The Department of Defense and the Atomic Energy Commission will have further details.

[8] See Item 561.
[9] Johnson, Lyndon B., "My Hope for America" (New York: Random House, 1964, 127 pp.).

the country, without regard to any specialized segment of the country. I think the whole question is the approach to it, and which course is more likely to attain the best results. I don't think that the Democratic Party wants any business government, any labor government, any big government. It is just interested in the best government for all the people.

I have expressed my philosophy in that field many times. I don't think in order to be for the private enterprise system you have to be against Government; or in order to be for the workingman, to be against business; or in order to be for business, to be against labor.

I think we can all work together. As a matter of fact, I have given a good deal of thought to a big problem that confronts our country. If you will take a little time, I will go over some of my ideas in connection with that very thing.

I think this Nation's most important concern, as far as we can see ahead, is and should be the unity of this country. Never in the history has any people succeeded in building a free society on such a huge scale and with the variety of such different religious denominations, ethnic stocks, and races.

We have witnessed the complete destruction by inner conflict of many nations because they pitted race against race and religion against religion, group against group.

What your question implies or suggests is class against class. That must not happen here in either party. All of us in government, and all of you in the press, and all responsible, constructive citizens everywhere have a responsibility to see that it doesn't.

Against the great odds we build one society from many. There is one good reason for that, because we have been willing to sub-

ordinate our loyalties to any one group to the loyalty to a greater group.

I have expressed that to you many times, and I won't go into a great deal of detail, but probably the most memorable occasion was when I assumed the leadership of the Democratic Party in the Senate in 1952—when we had been routed in the election by a very popular war hero, General Eisenhower—I rejected Mr. Taft's philosophy that it was the duty of the opposition to oppose.

That was his statement: it is the business of the opposition to oppose. I rejected that, and said I think it is the business of the opposition to do what is best for America—that is where our greater loyalty lies, ahead of loyalty to any of these other groups and parties.

We must subordinate our loyalty to any group to a greater loyalty and commitment to the moral principle upon which this Republic was founded, that is, to freedom and to justice and to the brotherhood of man.

We must not lock ourselves in with our prejudices. We must be prepared to learn, to be able to change our minds, to demonstrate compassion and humility toward others of different faiths, different origins, different colors, different sections, different professions.

An underlying theme in the history of the Republic has been the often painful but always successful reconciliation of different people into one national community of Americans.

I think you heard Mrs. Johnson say when she used to address envelopes to send out agricultural bulletins in my district that the thing she thought gave us such great strength was the names indicated they had more than a dozen different nationalities living in that one little central Texas district—a real melting pot in America.

All we have to do to realize the benefits of this principle is to look at the political life today, sitting in the courts, in the executive branch of the Government, the Congress—Protestants, Catholics, Jews, Negroes—many men and women whose fathers came to this country from another land; you heard Senator Pastore say that the other night: that he was the son of an immigrant to this country—men from Japanese-American and Chinese-American minorities, representing both parties and the public interest.

But the point I want to make is not of any special group. We all have a lot to learn about each other and about ourselves, and what is needed most today is, in my judgment, in this country, as I said in the beginning, unity, and, as I say now, understanding. We need a recognition that all Americans of every race, religion, ethnic origin, that all that most Americans want is the right and the opportunity to be treated as Americans, as members of our national community, and to live by the law and under the law.

I want to urge all men and women in this land of ours to resist with all their dedication the spiritual cancer of hate. If we hate others, we not only sin against them in the eyes of the Almighty God, but we undermine and eventually destroy our own integrity. By hating, we indicate and express that poverty of the spirit which is far more dangerous to a nation's future than the economic poverty that we are making war on and that we have announced as our objective to eliminate.

So I want to suggest this morning that we proceed with our adventure in freedom, a part of which is the grand tradition of political campaigns with a firm commitment to law, a just and efficient enforcement of all laws, a faith that a people which has learned to triumph over prejudice will once

more demonstrate the vitality of our most striking ideal: *E Pluribus Unum*—from many, one.

[11.] I expect to be here for the weekend. We have to celebrate Jack Valenti's birthday. He is one year older today, and shows it. He was late to work this morning for the first time. He got in after the sun had been up and had to go pull the curtain, with the sun shining in my eyes. He is usually there early.

[12.] We go out to Detroit for a brief visit Monday. We will be back here. I have a series of meetings coming up the latter part of the week.

That is about all I know to tell you.

[13.] Q. Mr. President, Senator Goldwater today announced a very extensive speaking schedule in the South, Middle West, and East beginning September 15th. Can you give us any clues as to what your campaign schedule will be?

THE PRESIDENT. We will, as I have said before, determine our departures from Washington by the condition of the affairs of the Nation. We have a job to do here, and we are going to try to do that first. When, as, and if we can, we will make as many appearances as we think we can without neglecting the interests of the Nation.

I will try, always, to be accessible to you, available to you. I will meet with you as frequently as is possible, or as often as you may feel the need. But just where I will be at some certain day in October, I can't determine, and I don't want to announce, because then you have me cancelling and adjusting my plans, things of that kind. That makes more of a story than my appearance would make, or maybe what I had to say makes.

I know sometimes you emphasize the change in plans, the details of them, and I don't want to confuse you or frustrate you.

I will announce them just as soon as it is possible for me to announce them.

There will be occasions when even Mrs. Johnson will say to Liz [10] that she hopes to go with me to Detroit and it will be carried as hard news that she is going, even though we have not confirmed it. We talk those things over. But we know reasonably certain we are going to Detroit and this is our plan. But as soon as we did know that, with certainty, we announced it to you.

It still could change, if there was some development in the world that would hold us here. The first consideration is going to be running the country and carrying out the duties of the Presidency.

Q. Mr. President, the Democrats up in Pennsylvania seem to be expecting that you may drop in on them in Harrisburg Thursday night. Can you give us any help on that?

THE PRESIDENT. I answered that question before. As soon as I am able to, I will tell you. It will save all of you a lot of time if you don't speculate. If I had known that I was going to go to the ranch this weekend, I would not hesitate to tell you I would be there. But I have no plans to do it. I can't tell you ahead of time.

I see George's [11] briefings and most of them are taken up in speculation and not a great deal of good comes out of them, because he can't tell you if he does not know and I can't tell you if I don't know.

[14.] Q. You spoke in your statement about pitting group against group, religion against religion, and race against race. In his statement the other day at the opening of his campaign, Senator Goldwater said——

THE PRESIDENT. I don't want to have any

connection with a jab or reference to anybody. You talk to Senator Goldwater about his views. I have expressed mine positively, affirmatively, and completely, without reference to anybody or Senator Goldwater, but just myself. If I say I believe I loved my mother, you would say it is a jab at Senator Goldwater. You just have to be more——

Q. Can I go on with the question? Senator Goldwater said that you are, in a sense, ignoring violence in our streets and he accused you of not providing enough moral leadership. Do you see any contradiction between these persistent remarks of his on violence in the streets and his meeting here in the White House to seek ways to reduce racial tensions in the campaign?

THE PRESIDENT. I think you make your point.

[15.] Q. Mr. President, I read a suggestion that your speech——

THE PRESIDENT. Well, I might say——

Q. Mr. President, I read a suggestion that your speech in Cadillac Square may not be a political speech. That would seem strange to me, but anything can happen. Would you tell us, will it be a nonpolitical or a campaign speech?

THE PRESIDENT. I am still working on it. Is somebody passing out something I am going to say? There are a lot of leaks in this place.

Q. The tone of it. I wasn't there, but I think Mr. Reedy said he was not certain it would be a political speech. Is that true?

THE PRESIDENT. I don't know. I had not seen anything like that. I am going to Detroit to speak to a group of workingmen who invited me 3 or 4 months ago to come out there and make an address to them on Labor Day. I am going to discuss in, I hope, a constructive manner the problems of our country and the times in which we live.[12]

---

[10] Mrs. Elizabeth S. Carpenter, Press Secretary and Staff Director for the First Lady.

[11] George E. Reedy, Press Secretary to the President.

[12] See Item 562.

I don't know, but there may be some of those workingmen that belong to various parties. It is not a party-sponsored affair, except that my expenses will be borne by the party. But that is the only connection that any party has with it. It is not the Democratic Party of Wayne County or Detroit, and so forth.

I have not completed my speech. I am working on it. I believe that it will be acceptable to all Americans. I think it will follow very much my philosophy here that I have outlined to you, as will most of my speeches. I don't want to accept an invitation of a church, or a labor organization, or a group of workingmen or businessmen, or newspapermen, and get into matters that would be offensive to them.

At the same time, I am going to exercise my right of free speech. But I am going to try to do it with judgment, fairness, and a word that I like very much that I reiterated several times, "understanding."

Q. Mr. President, in the past, some other Democratic candidates for President have followed up the Cadillac Square speech with a number of other appearances, going up even to Flint.

THE PRESIDENT. We are not going to plan our activities for the next few weeks based on any traditions or any practices of Presidents who have preceded us. Our first obligation is to do this job that we are doing here, today, and I will be doing it all day today, and I will be doing it all day today and all day tomorrow, right in this house.

But if I can get off a few hours Monday, I am going out there and speak to the folks there at their Labor Day meeting like I would go the Fourth of July. And then I am coming right back here to burn some midnight oil this week, but without regard to who went where, any time.

Q. Mr. President, you are not characterizing this speech, then?

THE PRESIDENT. We never characterize any speech. The President of the United States is not in the business of applying labels and making speculations on matters of this kind. You will have copies of the speech, and if you want to indulge in that, it is all right. You can say it is conservative, progressive, prudent, or radical; it is political or nonpolitical; whatever you want to say about it.

You would get irritated if I commented on your description of it. So you call it what you want to. We don't do it. George has told you many, many times, in repetitions, and you are not going to get him to change his mind. I will not change my mind. We will not say this is going to be a major speech, a minor speech, or a middle-sized speech, or a political speech or nonpolitical, or any of that. Characterize it any way you want to.

[16.] Q. Mr. President, the question of ending the draft was injected into the campaign the other day. Have you seen any early results of a study you requested from the Defense Department on that line?

THE PRESIDENT. As you know, several months ago we told you what we were proceeding to do in that field. We have the best people in the Selective Service and the Department of Defense and the White House examining and evaluating that program, and the whole effect it would have on our mobilization effort, and how many billions extra it would cost if the draft were done away with and how we can maximize the results with a minimum of cost.

One of the distinguished members of the Armed Services Committee of the Congress talked to me the night before last in some detail, or 3 or 4 nights ago, and his estimate was that it would cost us several billions to act precipitously in the matter, compulsively. That is the purpose of this study. We expect probably an interim announcement of some kind in the next few weeks, and probably some definite conclusion early in the spring.

From time to time people are going to read about these things and hear about them and make observations about them. With 190 million people in the country, they are all going to have an interest in this field. But that is the position of the Government.

Governor Stevenson had some thoughts back in the middle fifties sometime about how we could end the draft. I think Senator Goldwater commented on Governor Stevenson's thoughts, but I don't want to advertise either position. If you are interested in making a historical study about it you can see what Stevenson said and what Goldwater said about his action.

You will hear a lot of that in the months to come. But you really would not have a solid, accurate, or substantial conclusion on it, I would think, before early spring, because there are too many bases that have to be touched and too much work has to be done.

Q. Would it be correct to say that you share the view of President Eisenhower in 1956 that, in effect, the draft should not be made a campaign issue, the question of end-ing the draft should not be made a campaign issue?

THE PRESIDENT. Yes, I would agree with General Eisenhower on a good many things, and always have. I don't think that the service of a man to his country ought to be involved in politics. I say that without reference to any individual, General Eisenhower or anybody else. I think we have demonstrated, and I have been on the committee for 24 years up there, and I think the Selective Service System should be free from any politics, Republicans and Democrats and Independent boys wearing the uniform.

Q. Mr. President, sir, I think I understand thoroughly your statement there, but could you explain for us a little more how people who don't want to be in a position of creating disunity, who don't want to hurt the welfare of the country, but who might have honest differences of opinion with, say, the leader of the Government, how would they get their ideas across?

THE PRESIDENT. They don't have any difficulty doing that, I observe.

Alvin A. Spivak, United Press International: Thank you, Mr. President.

NOTE: President Johnson's twenty-ninth news conference was held in his office at the White House at 12:48 p.m. on Saturday, September 5, 1964.

561   Exchange of Messages With the President of Brazil.
September 5, 1964
[Released September 5, 1964.   Dated August 25, 1964]

Dear Mr. President:

I send my very warm thanks for your message of solidarity on the attacks by North Vietnam on United States naval vessels. We found in the Cuban missile crisis in 1962, and again in the Foreign Ministers meeting at Washington in July 1964, that our adversaries take heed when the free world stands solidly together and refuses to be intimidated by wanton aggression or threats of aggression. I especially welcome the renewed strength which Brazil brings to the cause of peace and allied unity. Brazil has a proud tradition of service in two world wars and in its current contributions to the peace efforts of the United Nations in

Gaza and the Congo. Your timely and friendly letter is a reaffirmation of that tradition.

I share your conviction that Brazil and the United States are bound together in a common desire for peace. We want no wider war, as I have said repeatedly. But as you suggest, there comes a point at which countries such as the United States and Brazil, firmly committed to the peaceful solution of problems, must exercise their basic right of self-defense.

The struggle for freedom in South Vietnam is closely related to the struggle for freedom everywhere. We face not only the armed struggle in the rice paddies of South Vietnam, but also—as you say in your recent telegram on the anniversary of Punta del Este—the "struggle of the Peoples" for a future that will enable man "to achieve his just aspirations in a climate of freedom."

We are joined in that struggle in the Alliance for Progress. The Charter of Punta del Este was not only a commitment, but a challenge to achieve that historic mission.

We in the United States have been heartened—and I believe the whole Hemisphere looks to the future with more optimism—because of the vigorous manner in which your government has accepted this challenge. We have followed with great interest the initial efforts of your government to reverse the serious economic deterioration which confronted you when you took office, and to step firmly forward on the road to economic prosperity and well-being. We know that decisive action in the economic life of Brazil can and must come only from the Brazilian government and people. But I want to assure you, as you press forward on constructive programs for the welfare of Brazil, that my country stands ready to give

its sincere support through the Alliance for Progress.

The fraternal commitment which we feel toward Brazil—the sense of responsibility which flows from the policy of the good neighbor—is but a part of the larger common cause which we share with all of the American Republics and with our allies throughout the world. I know, from your speech to the graduates of the Brazilian foreign service academy, that you feel that same commitment. You spoke of Brazil's commitment to the Western democratic system, its support of free enterprise and the orderly encouragement of private capital, its tradition of inter-American solidarity, and of your confidence that our two nations "can join their economic and commercial interests on a plane of honorable policy and friendly reciprocity."

Brazil and the United States, I believe, have entered a new era of understanding and comprehension. The peoples of our two great countries understand that fact; history would not forgive us if we did not understand it and act upon it. In the months and years ahead, I look forward to an ever closer relationship between our countries: to cooperation for the economic and social benefit of our peoples; and to the fulfillment of our solemn commitments to freedom and peace.

Sincerely,

Lyndon B. Johnson

[His Excellency Humberto de Alencar Castelo Branco, President of the Republic of the United States of Brazil]

NOTE: President Branco's letter, dated August 11, 1964, follows:

My dear Mr. President:

I have received from your Ambassador, Your Excellency's message on the armed attacks by North Viet-Nam against warships of the United States on the high seas. Your Excellency is right in believing that I share your deep concern in view of this attack. I consider this resort to force as being contrary to the principles of the United Nations Charter and I deem it to fully justify the exercise of the right of self-defense as was done by the United States of America.

I have instructed the Brazilian representative to the Security Council to act there in accordance with the above indications and to express, furthermore, our hope that the North Viet-Namese authorities will modify their attitude and that all governments will endeavor to prevent the aggravation of tensions in Southeast Asia.

In expressing to Your Excellency my solidarity, I do so with the certainty that Brazil and the United States are bound together in the same desire for peace and in the same feeling of repulsion for violent solutions to international disputes.

With the assurance of my high regard and esteem,

HUMBERTO DE ALENCAR CASTELO BRANCO

562 Remarks in Cadillac Square, Detroit. *September 7, 1964*

Mr. Barbour, Governor and Mrs. Romney, Mayor Cavanagh, Senator Hart, Senator McNamara, Congressman Staebler, Walter Reuther, Governor Swainson, Secretary Williams, my good friends in the Michigan congressional delegation, my fellow countrymen:

This is a great day in a historic place. Here, and today, we begin to move toward new years of achievement for America.

Sixteen years ago an American President came here and he promised that America would "enter a new period of hope." That President was Harry S. Truman.

You gave him support and he gave you that hope. Four years ago another great American stood where I stand today and he said, "Give me your hand . . . and this country can move again." That man was John Fitzgerald Kennedy.

You reached out your hand, and America began to move.

I have come here today to pledge that if all Americans will stand united we will keep moving. This country is not going to turn its back on the future. This country is not going to turn away from the upward course of prosperity or from the urgent hopes of peace.

This country is not going to turn away from the needs of the jobless and the hungry, the poor and the oppressed. This country is not going to turn from unity to hostility, from understanding to hate.

So today I have come here in Cadillac Square to call for national unity. I plead for brotherhood among men and understanding among nations. This is not just a slogan. It is not based on empty hopes or upon remote dreams. It flows from the facts of life in 1964.

I have traveled to every section of this country. I have talked to people in every walk of life. And I have found that most of the American people are united.

There are, of course, issues which stir passion and conflicting interests. But most Americans have the same hopes for themselves and their children. They have the same desires for themselves and their country. They know that, for the most part, we no longer struggle among ourselves for a larger share of limited abundance. We labor, instead, to increase the total abundance of us all.

Responsible business knows that fair wages are essential to its prosperity. Responsible labor knows that fair profits are essential to rising employment. Farmers and city dwellers, bankers and laborers know that by strengthening each group we strengthen the Nation—by pursuing the growth of all, we advance the welfare of each.

And all of us know that we have a mortal stake in the peace of this world. And that the only real test, the only test that really counts, is what is good for America. And what is good for America is good for all of us.

I want to talk briefly today about three of the goals which are good for America, which reflect the common purpose of most Americans, which are the basis of unity in our country. These are the goal of prosperity, the goal of justice, and the goal of peace.

First, the goal of prosperity. This is the 43d month of the greatest peacetime prosperity in the history of all the United States.

The last 4 years, in Michigan alone, unemployment dropped from 10.2 percent to 5.3 percent, the average weekly earnings for manufacturing workers went up 23 percent, a new tax cut will raise personal income by $1½ billion and create 90,000 new jobs.

And what is true for Michigan is true for other parts of America. As long as I am President, I will lead this country toward increased prosperity. We will continue until every man has a job, and until every family has a decent income. And this is what most Americans want.

The second part of our common purpose is justice. Justice is a country where every man has an equal chance to use his talents, to pursue his desires, and to provide for his family.

We seek to give every American, of every race and color, and without regard to how he spells his name, his full constitutional rights under our Constitution and under the law of the land. We seek to conquer the conditions which condemn millions to hopeless poverty.

We seek to find a job for every man who wants to work. We seek to care for the old through medical care under social security, the jobless with increased unemployment compensation, the oppressed with minimum wage protection. And this is what we think most Americans want.

Third among our common goals is peace. Peace is more than the absence of aggression. It is the creation of a world community in which every nation can follow its own course without fear of its neighbors. In that pursuit we have developed a threefold policy.

First, we have built a military strength greater than the world has ever known before.

Second, in Cuba and in the waters around Viet-Nam we proved that we would stand firm in the defense of freedom. And everywhere we have worked to extend the domain of liberty.

Third, we patiently labored to open new avenues to peace.

The result of these efforts since 1961 is our world of 1964. In this world in which we live today, no nation, new or old, has gone Communist since Cuba went in 1959.

In this world the solid unity of communism has begun to crack. We have worked to help the nations of Eastern Europe move toward independence. This is their people's goal and this is our people's continuing resolve.

In this world the influence and the prestige of freedom is on the rise. Hands of friendship have replaced the clenched fists of angry mobs. In this world the strength of freedom is greater and the prospects for peace are brighter.

It is not enough, I think, just to want peace or to talk peace or to hope for peace. We must constantly work for peace. And I want you to know that today your Government is working for peace.

We must heed the command to "follow

after the things that make for peace."

—That is why I, as a Congressman, worked to help pass the Marshall plan.

—That is why, as a Senator during the Eisenhower administration, I went to the United Nations, at President Eisenhower's request, to urge and to invite all nations of the world to join the United States in the peaceful exploration of outer space.

—And that is why, as Vice President of the United States, I worked long and hard for the treaty banning nuclear tests in the atmosphere. We slowed down the deadly poisoning of the air we breathe, and the milk that our children drink. We do not want every mother to live in fear that her baby may be born crippled or deformed.

—And we, too, must remember that we organized the Peace Corps which started the spirit of America and carried it to remote villages on every continent of the world.

—And also that is why, as President, I ordered a cutback of unnecessary nuclear production.

—And that is why I will continue to support every realistic measure that will bring the world closer to peace without increasing the danger to freedom.

Yes, it is men that make peace.

Modern weapons are not like any other. In the first nuclear exchange, 100 million Americans and more than 100 million Russians would all be dead. And when it was over, our great cities would be in ashes, our fields would be barren, our industry would be destroyed, and our American dreams would have vanished.

As long as I am President I will bend every effort to make sure that that day never comes. I am not the first President to speak here in Cadillac Square, and I do not intend to be the last.

Make no mistake. There is no such thing as a conventional nuclear weapon.

For 19 peril-filled years no nation has loosed the atom against another. To do so now is a political decision of the highest order. And it would lead us down an uncertain path of blows and counterblows whose outcome none may know. No President of the United States of America can divest himself of the responsibility for such a decision.

Any man who shares control of such enormous power must remember that "He that is slow to anger is better than the mighty; and he that ruleth his spirit is better than he that taketh a city."

These common purposes—prosperity, justice, and peace—are the foundation of American unity.

Our future is almost upon us. Man has never lived in a more exciting time. The world is changing before our eyes. Either we will move to meet these changes or they will overwhelm us. On the one hand is opportunity of shining promise; on the other is a power to destroy the world. Those nations or individuals who seek today to divide us, who preach strife and dissension, and hate and fear, and smear, strike at our hopes and strike at the hopes of all the people of the world.

When I was young, I often walked out after supper and looked up at the scattered Texas sky. As a boy, on those still nights, I wondered what those heavens had seen, what they would see, and what they might bring to me.

The world has turned many times since then, but still in the evening I sometimes walk out and look across the great Capital City where I live, and I dream the same dreams, and I ask the same questions. Just as you do, I sit and think of today's events and tomorrow's problems. I feel glad in my family and concern for my children.

It is then that I remember the men who

captured my native soil from the wilderness. They endured much so that others might have much. Their dream was for the children; mine, too, is for the child, even now struggling toward birth. What will the observing skies say of the world that we have built for him?

I want all the ages of man to yield him their promise, the child will find all knowledge open to him; the growing boy will shape his spirit in a house of God and his ways in the house of his family. The young man will find reward for his work and feel pride in the product of his skills.

The man will find leisure and occasion for the closeness of family, and an opportunity for the enrichment of life. The citizen will enrich the Nation, sharing its rule, walking its streets, adding his views to its counsel, secure always from the unjust and the arbitrary power of his fellows.

The least among us will find contentment, and the best among us will find greatness, and all of us will respect the dignity of the one and admire the achievements of the other.

At the end of the journey, he will look back and say, "I have done all that a man could do, built all, shared all, experienced all." And then people shall say to people, group to group, man to man, "There on this earth as in the eyes of God walks my brother."

Well, this is my dream. It is not the grand vision of a powerful and feared nation. It concerns the simple wants of people. But this is what America is really all about. All the rest, the power and the wealth, the life of freedom and the hopes for peace, the treasured past and the uncertain future—all of this will stand or fall on this. Reality rarely matches dream, but only dreams give nobility to purpose.

This is the star that I hope to follow. This is the star which I know that most of you at some time have seen, and which I first glimpsed many, many years ago, one night out in the West.

United we stand; divided we fall. So today I say to these thousands assembled here, whose only concern is what is best for their country, let us bring the capitalist, the manager, the worker, and the Government to one table to share in the fruits of all of our dreams and all of our work. And let's leave for our children, as we enjoy for ourselves, the greatest country that any man has ever known.

NOTE: The President spoke just before noon in Cadillac Square in Detroit. In his opening words he referred to Al Barbour, president, Wayne County AFL–CIO, George W. Romney, Governor of Michigan, and Mrs. Romney, J. P. Cavanagh, mayor of Detroit, Philip A. Hart and Pat McNamara, U.S. Senators from Michigan, Neil Staebler, U.S. Representative from Michigan, Walter Reuther, president of the United Auto Workers, John B. Swainson, former Governor of Michigan, and G. Mennen Williams, Assistant Secretary of State for African Affairs.

563   The President's News Conference of September 9, 1964

THE PRESIDENT. I have a few announcements here.

[1.] Here is one we agreed on at a meeting, that I roughed over.

At a regular bipartisan meeting of the congressional leadership called by the President, Ambassador Taylor gave a detailed report of recent political developments in

South Viet-Nam and his assessments of progress toward a more stable government there.

The Ambassador was able to report continued progress in the field in the Vietnamese Army's fight against the Communist Viet Cong, and to answer the leadership's questions about the general situation there. Secretaries Rusk and McNamara and General Wheeler and Mr. McCone also participated in the meeting.

It was a full and frank examination of the whole situation—a discussion of the sort that we have had at least 11 since November and we hope to be able to provide frequently for further meetings of the joint leadership in the future.

You of the press have already received from General Taylor a good account of his report to us. Other meetings were held in November, in December, in January, in February, April, May, and August.

[2.] I am pleased that the Chrysler-United Auto Workers case has been settled peacefully and privately on true good faith and collective bargaining.

I have not seen the actual terms and have no comment on them.

I am gratified, however, by the statements by the parties that this settlement takes full account of both public and private interests, that it will mean more jobs, and that it will be noninflationary.

[3.] On September 16, Canadian Prime Minister Lester B. Pearson and I will join in ceremonies at the International Peace Arch, on the U.S.–Canadian border between British Columbia and the State of Washington, to commemorate the successful conclusion of the Columbia River Treaty.

Prior to the Peace Arch ceremonies, the Prime Minister and I will make an aerial inspection tour of a considerable part of the upper Columbia River Basin, flying over the proposed sites of the dams to be constructed in British Columbia under the treaty, the location of the Libby (Montana) Dam to be constructed by the United States, and some of the existing downstream United States dams concerned.

While in the Pacific Northwest, the Prime Minister and I will consult with regional leaders in our respective countries regarding cooperative steps to be taken on both sides of the border in implementation of the treaty. The Prime Minister and I will also take advantage of this opportunity to discuss current international problems of mutual concern. I have talked to him by telephone earlier today. We will leave here at 6:30 or 6:45, and George [1] will give you the details of the latter, that is on September 16.

[4.] I also talked to three Governors last evening, in regard to the Florida, South Carolina, and Georgia situation and tendered them our assistance and full facilities of the Federal Government in any way we could help.[2]

[5.] I want to announce the formation of a panel of distinguished citizens who will consult with the President during the coming months on major international problems facing the United States. I reviewed this with the leadership earlier today, and I made the statement to them, but this is the first public announcement made. George will have copies of it.

---

[1] George E. Reedy, Press Secretary to the President.

[2] The reference was to the widespread damage from Hurricane Dora which had struck the three States. A White House release, dated September 9, stated that the President had that day declared Florida a "major disaster" area because of the earlier hurricane, Cleo, which had caused extensive damage in nine east coast Florida counties. The release further stated that the President had also made available $300,000 in Federal disaster relief funds for use in the State. Later, on October 31, the White House announced that the President had that day made an additional $2 million available for Hurricane Cleo disaster relief in Florida.

Members of the panel will be consulted in matters where the advice of highly qualified and experienced men in private life may be helpful in finding effective courses of action in the quest for peace and advancement of the national security. They will not act as a committee nor will they hold regular meetings. Instead, they will be asked for advice as individuals, under flexible and informal arrangements suited to the needs of the problem at hand.

Their regular point of contact will be the Special Assistant for National Security Affairs, and their services will be available not only to the President but to the Secretary of State and the Secretary of Defense. I have conferred with both Secretary of State and Secretary of Defense in some detail about the membership on this panel.

All of these distinguished men have served informally in this fashion in the past, but it seems to me useful and important to re-emphasize the role of leading private citizens, without regard to party, as counselors to the President.

The consultants named today have a distinction that is above partisan politics, and their services will be available not only to me this year, but also to the man who is President in 1965. If I am President next year, I expect to use their help.

The members of the panel are: Arthur Dean, John Cowles, Morris Leibman, Gen. Omar Bradley, James Wadsworth, Arthur Larson, James Perkins, Teodoro Moscoso, Robert Lovett, George Kistiakowsky, Roswell Gilpatric, Dean Acheson, Paul Hoffman, Eugene Black, John McCloy, and Mr. Allen W. Dulles.

Q. Who is the chairman?

THE PRESIDENT. They will just have a group, and if they have need of a chairman they will select one, or they will name one.

[6.] Confidence in our economic pros-perity has been growing as indicators continue to point up:

Steel production rose for the fifth consecutive week last week, reaching 37 percent above a year ago; and

New car sales rose to an 8.1 million unit annual rate in August, matching the previous high for this year scored in February.

The Dow-Jones industrial stock average closed at a new high yesterday—851.91—surpassing previous peak reached on July 17th.

With the aid of the tax cut, consumers have been able to score record advances both in their current living standards and their financial savings for the future.

In the first half of this year consumer spending rose $15 billion, the largest peacetime advance in history for a half year period.

New figures which the SEC will release tomorrow show that net financial savings of individuals in the second quarter was $7.7 billion, the highest quarterly total of the postwar period.

The new advance in savings tops a record that was already excellent: In the past 3½ years the net financial saving of American households has totaled $73 billion, or about $1,300 per family. This 3½ year figuree matches the savings of the entire 6 years 1955–60.

As I have stated before, experience in the Department of Defense indicates that every dollar of procurement which can be shifted from sole-source to a competitive basis saves the taxpayer 25 cents. The Department of Defense has steadily raised the rate of its competitive buying since the beginning of this administration. The Secretary of Defense has reported to me that as of the end of the fiscal year, June 30, 1964, the amount of competitive contract awards has risen to a rate of 39.1 percent, the highest level on record.

The fiscal '64 rate represents a conversion of new contract awards totaling some $1.8 billion to a competitive basis for an estimated saving of $450 million. The fiscal '64 rate of 39.1 percent compares with 32.9 percent in fiscal year '61; 35.6 percent in fiscal year '62; and 37.1 percent in fiscal year '63.

Those statements will be made available to you, if I can find someone who will give you copies.

I will be glad to take any questions.

[7.]   Q. Mr. President, as a result of your consultations with Ambassador Taylor, can you tell us, will there be any shifts either in emphasis or in magnitude of our effort in Viet-Nam?

THE PRESIDENT. I think General Taylor's briefing with you this morning pretty well outlines our position, and I would stand on that.

[8.] Q. Mr. President, these civilians you have just listed who you are to consult with on foreign affairs, will you consult with them at a time of crisis, or just any old time?

THE PRESIDENT. Anytime, and whenever we think it is appropriate, on any question on which their particular qualifications may suit them.

[9.]   I have asked—I am going to another subject that I just happened to think of—I am asking the FBI to give me a compilation of their reports on the various problems that we have encountered in cities and in States that could involve a violation of Federal laws, and that do involve disturbances, such as riots and disturbances of the peace. When I get that compilation of the various reports, I will review those and try to compile them if I find any pattern that is common to all of them, and ask that further study be made.

We are informing all of the mayors and all of the Governors, where these problems arise, that we will make available through appropriate channels of their peace officers full information that we may have. We are available for any supplementary work that may be within our authority under existing law. That is true in Mississippi, and Georgia, New Jersey, and New York, and Maryland, and other States that have it.

But out of this compilation of Federal Bureau of Investigation reports we may find some particular pattern that will need to be pointed up, and that may lead us to make further recommendations.

Q. Are you referring specifically to riots such as in Philadelphia and Harlem and so forth?

THE PRESIDENT. I am referring specifically, not exclusively to those, but including all of them, that is, anything that involves a disturbance of the peace where Federal law might be violated or where our jurisdiction and authority might exist.

Q. Mr. President, in connection with this, about 3 weeks or a month ago in Austin, at a news conference, you told us that you were anticipating some break in the Mississippi thing within a short time.[3] Is there any indication?

THE PRESIDENT. No, it is still a short time.

[10.] Q. Senator Goldwater has said that if he is elected he would cut Federal income taxes 25 percent over a 5-year period. I wonder if you can tell us what you think about this, and whether you think that would be feasible without impairing the national security.

THE PRESIDENT. I would say that we made our views on cutting taxes known earlier this year. When we cut the tax rate, that was carefully studied in '63 and '62 by the fiscal agencies of the Government—the Council of Economic Advisers, the Director of the Bureau of the Budget, the Secretary of the Treasury, the Federal Reserve au-

---

[3] See Item 504 [3, 8].

thorities, and all of the fiscal experts. It was carefully worked out and submitted to Congress in '63, after consultation with Mr. Mills and Senator Byrd. It was acted on in the House in '63, and in the Senate early in '64, as I remember it.

That represented our position on the desirability of tax cuts and the extent that they should be made. It involved a very thorough and careful fiscal evaluation, with the advice of the best experts. We have had continuing on since that bill was enacted a study by the same agencies in the executive branch of the Government with the same thoroughness, as well as the Ways and Means Committee of the House of Representatives.

That is a study on the extent of further cuts that would be desirable and effective. In our message to the Congress we will make known our conclusions that these studies justify.

Q. What message would that be?

THE PRESIDENT. When we make our recommendations to the Congress in January, when the new Congress comes in.

[11.] Q. In connection with the FBI reports that you have asked for, you spoke of the possibility that you might find that further recommendations are needed. Do you mean legislative recommendations?

THE PRESIDENT. I wouldn't limit it to legislative recommendations. I would say further recommendations. It is not limited to, but it could include that.

[12.] Q. Mr. President, how disappointed are you, sir, that a Democratic Governor, Johnson of Mississippi, has endorsed Senator Goldwater?

THE PRESIDENT. I think that every person in this country ought to support the candidate of his choice, and the candidate that he feels will best serve.

[13.] Q. Mr. President, is this request

to the FBI predicated on any preliminary information that may already have been gained from the FBI in these terms?

THE PRESIDENT. I think that I understand your question, but I am not sure now. Would you repeat it for me and let me soak it in?

Q. I wondered if there had been some preliminary investigations made by the FBI.

THE PRESIDENT. A good many of them.

Q. Of these disturbances?

THE PRESIDENT. There have been investigations made, and I read about 40 of them every night.

Q. And on the basis of these reports, you are submitting another request?

THE PRESIDENT. I am trying to accumulate them all and put them in one place, and study them as to their effect or such a pattern as may exist in various areas concerning these disturbances, at which time I would have them carefully evaluated and try to make some further recommendations.

Q. Is there any indication, Mr. President, that in this particular pattern which may emerge, is there any indication it may be outside agitators, or politically inspired?

THE PRESIDENT. Well, I think it is pretty well known, if you read the newspapers, that considerable agitation is present in these disturbances.

Q. I have read, too, Mr. President, that I think that they have found known Communists have been among the agitators. Did the FBI reports confirm that?

THE PRESIDENT. I don't want to discuss the content of FBI reports.

[14.] Q. Mr. President, in view of Governor Johnson's announcement on Senator Goldwater, are you hopeful that you might carry Mississippi this November?

THE PRESIDENT. I would like to see every person who felt that our program and our leadership for all America was preferred by them, to vote for us. I would hope that a good many people in all of the States would feel that way. I hope that a majority of them would. But I have no way of telling, at this date, just what the final outcome will be.

[15.] Q. Mr. President, do you favor this resolution that Senator Mansfield put in today to have the Rules Committee investigate the latest charge in the Bobby Baker case?

THE PRESIDENT. I have not seen the resolution, but I have favored a thorough investigation and study of every indication that any Federal law may have been violated. The FBI was ordered to make a thorough and exhaustive investigation. As soon as these facts are brought to my attention, I would be glad to see the Senate take any action it feels is justified.

Q. Do you favor the Rules Committee over the McClellan Committee?

THE PRESIDENT. I think this is a matter for the Senate.

[16.] Q. Mr. President, Senator Kuchel says the President of the United States should make his views known on the apportionment rider that Senator Dirksen is sponsoring. Do you have any comments of the proposal by Senator Dirksen?

THE PRESIDENT. No, sir.

[17.] Q. Mr. President, do you plan any campaign trips this year? If so, when?

THE PRESIDENT. Well, when I do I will tell you. I have one tomorrow that I am going up to Harrisburg on. I am going to make a speech at a dinner. From time to time, when time permits, I will cut you in on them just as soon as I know.

Q. Mr. President, are we going to have the pleasure of another one of those train trips like we had in 1960?

THE PRESIDENT. I think you will have to talk to Mrs. Johnson. I think she has given some consideration to a train trip. I do not have any such plans at the moment. I understand she is giving some consideration to it already. She may have already announced it; I am not sure. If you like to ride the train, get with her; she will be glad to have your company.[4]

Ralph Harris, Reuters-Australian Associated Press: Thank you, Mr. President.

NOTE: President Johnson's thirtieth news conference was held in his office at the White House at 5:05 p.m. on Wednesday, September 9, 1964.

[4] See Item 628.

---

564   Message to the President of Finland on the Death of Ambassador Sakari Tuomioja. *September 9, 1964*

I LEARNED with great sorrow of the death in Helsinki of Sakari Tuomioja. He served your nation well, and served all nations by his work for the United Nations. He died while laboring once again as United Nations mediator in a tangled and dangerous international dispute. Our people join with yours in mourning a servant of peace, and a friend of us all.

NOTE: At the time of his death Sakari Tuomioja, Ambassador to Sweden from Finland, was serving as United Nations mediator in the Greek-Turkish dispute over Cyprus.

565   Statement by the President in Response to Report of the President's Committee for Traffic Safety.   *September 10, 1964*

THE RECORD-BREAKING motor vehicle travel accompanying the Nation's high level of prosperity has increased the need for stepped-up activity to curb traffic accidents.

It is self-evident that we must expand and intensify our efforts to prevent these accidents.

Toward that end, it is indispensable that we initiate greater research into the causes and means of preventing accidents.

We need the active participation of the best minds in the colleges and universities in all of our States. We need to enlist researchers in all of the sciences: medicine, law, engineering, psychology, public information—every field that can help us to learn more about human behavior, and to develop new means of increasing the safety of highways and vehicles.

I am asking the Committee to report back to me as soon as it can as to the current status of traffic safety research in these fields, and what should be done to stimulate broader activity.

This is not to say that our present efforts have been fruitless. With the explosive traffic growth, our plight would be far worse had it not been for diligent safety activities.

Primary responsibility rests in our States, counties, and municipalities; and the Committee's report makes evident that improved performance, overall, has been attained.

The Federal Government and the Congress have cooperated, also, in many ways.

A notable example is the National System of Interstate and Defense Highways, with its many safety features.

The Committee for Traffic Safety has given leadership in stimulating State and community application of the tested and proved accident prevention measures of the action program.

Greater understanding of this program has been developed through national and regional conferences of legislators, public officials, and citizen leaders—both men and women.

The Committee's projects are conducted through its advisory council of national, nonprofit organizations of public officials, and private interests, and Federal agencies.

Nevertheless, our combined efforts clearly fall far short of our requirements. There is urgent need to apply the entire action program more vigorously through day-after-day cooperation of private citizens and public officials. There is need for more technical assistance to these officials from national traffic safety service organizations.

These and many other needs must be met so we may deal more effectively with our critical traffic accident problem. We cannot accept the intolerable drain on our human and economic resources that these accidents are causing.

NOTE: The 34-page summary report, entitled "The Action Program, a Report to the President" and dated September 1964, was made available by the Committee.

566   Remarks in Harrisburg at a Dinner Sponsored by the Pennsylvania State Democratic Committee. *September* 10, 1964

Governor Lawrence, Senator Clark, Miss Blatt, Chairman Morse, Governor Leader, Reverend Clergy, my devoted friends in the Pennsylvania congressional delegation who are doing such a fine job for all of your great State in Washington, my fellow countrymen:

In what I say now, I speak beyond this hall—to all my fellow Americans, regardless of political persuasion or party membership.

One week from tonight we commemorate a proud anniversary, on the 17th of September. It was 177 years ago, here in Pennsylvania, that the Constitution of the United States was born.

Since then the world has been swept by change. Empires have fallen. Thrones have been overturned. Virtually no other country on any other continent is governed now as it was governed then. But the oath that I took last November 22d as the 36th President of the United States was the same oath taken by the first President of the United States, Gen. George Washington.

Our free government and our system stand tonight as the most stable and the most successful in the history of man. This is not a victory of party or of politicians, or even of Presidents. America's great success is the achievement of the American people.

For the American people, this year is a year of great decision. For the 45th time since our great Republic was born, these free people will freely decide the direction that they want America to move. Whatever our allegiance politically, whatever our interests privately, whatever our concerns personally, we must not let our year of decision become our year of division.

The first stated purpose of those who gave the Constitution to us was "to form a more perfect union." That tonight is still our first purpose. If we are to establish justice, to ensure domestic tranquillity, provide for the common defense, promote the general welfare, and secure the blessings of liberty for ourselves and for our posterity, we must labor together to make this Nation whole and this people one.

So long as there has been an America, there have always been white and black, red and brown, Protestant and Catholic, Quaker and Jew, German and Dutch, Italian and Swede, rich and poor, capital and labor. And I would remind you good people tonight that these distinctions have never stood in our way, and they do not stand in our way tonight.

The one division that our forefathers most feared, the division that they warned us against, was the division of extreme factionalism. Jefferson warned against it, Hamilton and Madison warned against it.

In his Farewell Address, the first President, George Washington, warned against it, warned against allowing parties to become "Northern and Southern, Atlantic and Western." He told us to beware of that kind of partisanship which, in his words, "agitates the community with ill-founded jealousies and false alarms, . . . kindles the animosity of one party against another, . . . foments occasionally riot and insurrection."

Well, my fellow countrymen, in this year of 1964, those are words and those are warnings that all responsible Americans must remember. From the election of 1789 to the election of 1960, the choices for the American Presidency have never meant changes in the broad purposes of the American people.

But that is not the choice this year.

There are abroad in this responsible land reckless factions, contemptuous toward the will of majorities; callous toward the plight of minorities; arrogant toward allies; belligerent toward adversaries; careless toward peace. These factions wear many names. They espouse many causes. Standing together they confront the American people and they demand that you make a choice.

They demand that you choose a doctrine that is alien to America—that would lead to a tragic convulsion in our foreign relations; a doctrine that flaunts the unity of our society and searches for scapegoats among our people. It is a doctrine that invites extremism to take over our land. It is a doctrine that plays loosely with human destiny, and this generation of Americans will have no part of it.

I have great faith in the American people. They are neither sick in spirit nor faint in moral courage. They have never been more capable of choosing for themselves what they think is right or wrong. They will reject a spirit of party which Washington once said "agitates the community with ill-founded jealousies and false alarms, or kindles the animosity of one party against another."

Those are the words of the first President. But I believe that spirit must be the spirit of the next President, and every President who follows him.

I know this is the spirit of the men and women of Pennsylvania. It is the spirit of great men of whom we are so proud, like Dave Lawrence of your great State; and my friend Senator Joe Clark, who proudly carries your banner in the Senate of the United States; it is the spirit of great and lovable women like Emma Guffey Miller and Genevieve Blatt. And I am so happy that you are sending her to Washington to work with us next January.

Yes, I am very proud to say tonight that it is the spirit of Bill Scranton and Dwight D. Eisenhower. These Pennsylvanians believe what the majority of Americans believe, that our Nation can only be served by parties which serve all of America, and which serve all Americans in all segments in all sections of the country.

Woodrow Wilson once said that the "success of a Party means little unless it is being used by the Nation for a great purpose." I repeat those words tonight to the members of my own party. But I urge their consideration by those members of the other great party who believe that our highest purpose is still to "form a more perfect union."

Tonight, at this moment of our national history, we stand at the very summit of human success. "A perfect union" is within our reach. We are a people prospering; a Nation progressing. We enjoy freedom; and, thank God, we live in peace. We are prepared, as no other nation has ever been prepared, to defend that freedom and to preserve that peace.

We are realists. We know that if life is good for many, it is not easy for any. Too many men who want jobs still cannot find work. Too many factories stand idle tonight. Too many mines are closed down. Too many families are still poor. But we are resolved to meet these challenges. Our success in the past 4 years points to greater achievements ahead.

For nearly 44 consecutive months now we have had the longest rise in our prosperity in peacetime history, without recession or depression, and with the most stable prices in the Western World.

Our system is functioning as it was meant to function. America is getting answers from this session of Congress. Our people are working together. State governments, local governments, and the Federal Government are working for the people, not against one another.

This is the America that our allies trust and this is the America that our adversaries respect. I say to you tonight that it is a matter of no small significance that no one anywhere is boasting now of burying us. This is America at its best. This is America moving again. This is America as it always ought to be, prosperous and progressive, peaceful and prepared.

The position of your President is clear. The policies of my party are clear.

We intend to keep America prosperous, powerful, and unafraid, unafraid to stand against any enemy in the defense of freedom, and unafraid to sit at any table in pursuit of honorable peace.

We intend to keep America united.

We intend to keep America free and undivided.

We intend to keep America a land of free labor, a land of free enterprise, a land where all free people alike will respect the law and the law respects the people.

We are a nation of lovers and not a nation of haters. We are a land of good homes and good schools, decent wages and decent medical care for the aged. Yes, we want a land of hope and happiness, but never a land of harshness and hate.

Are these your goals? Is this your spirit? Is this the America that you want to produce, and that you want to see, and that you want to fight for?

Then I ask you to join with us tonight in the time ahead. I respect the loyalty of men to the parties of their fathers. But I trust the faithfulness of men and women to the future of our children.

This is, as I said in the beginning, the year of decision. This is the year that you decide not the future of a party or the fate of a man. This is the year that you will be voting on the future of your own prosperity, on your own Nation's progress, and the peace of the world in your time and in times to come.

We do have a choice this year. It is the choice between the mighty voice of the American majority saying "yes" and the fading echo of the few who still say "no."

The majority said "yes" long ago to social security. The echo still says "no."

The majority says "yes" to minimum wage, "yes" to the rights of the workingmen, "yes" to full employment and equal opportunity. The echo still says "no."

The majority says "yes" to responsible relations with our allies, "yes" to the United Nations, "yes" to the opening of the markets of the world to the products of American business and American labor. But the echo still says "no."

The majority says "yes" to better education for our young, "yes" to hospital care for our aged under social security, "yes" to a war on poverty. But the echo still says "no."

The majority says "yes" to equal rights for all, equal hopes for all, equal happiness for all. But the echo still says "no."

This year the mighty voice of the American majority will be heard throughout our land, and it will be heard also around the world. It will be heard saying "yes" to the future, and saying "no" to the echoes of the past.

And how are we going to say it? Well, since the month of May, gains have been recorded in Democratic registrations in nearly every county of this great State of Pennsylvania. And we didn't have to buy a poll to prove that, although we like the polls, too.

In Philadelphia, since the last primary we have registered 100,595 Democrats and 31,049 Republicans, or 74 percent Democrats and 22 percent Republicans. And the edge is the kind of an edge that we like—better than 3 to 1.

In Allegheny County, more new Democrats have registered than in any other presidential year in history, 24,000 new Democrats to 10,000 new Republicans—an edge of better than 2 to 1. In Lancaster County, just next door, new Democrats are outnumbering new Republicans.

I want to conclude by reminding you that you still have 3 more days to register.

Today when great issues of war and peace are before us, the man that I look to and the Nation looks to for help and steady and able guidance is the distinguished Chairman of the House Foreign Affairs Committee, Doc Morgan, from Pennsylvania. Pennsylvania Democrats have a capacity for great-

ness, and we are going to have two great ones leading us in the Senate come next January, Joe Clark and Genevieve Blatt.

So I ask you tonight to join us in this campaign. I ask you to join hands and work with me, to build a greater America for all of our people. You know in your heart that this is right. You know that this is the way that you want to go. So join with me and let us be on our way.

We want to, before we leave, see as many of you as we can and say to all of you and to each of you how grateful we are and how very much we appreciate the sacrifice that you have made for your party and your country. Democrats in Pennsylvania appreciate it and it will help good people everywhere.

Thank you.

NOTE: The President spoke at the Farm Show Arena Building in Harrisburg. In his opening words he referred to David L. Lawrence, former Governor of Pennsylvania, Joseph S. Clark, U.S. Senator from Pennsylvania, Genevieve Blatt, Democratic candidate for the U.S. Senate from Pennsylvania, Otis B. Morse IV, Democratic State Chairman, and George Leader, former Governor of Pennsylvania. He later referred to Emma Guffey Miller, Democratic State Committeewoman, William W. Scranton, Governor of Pennsylvania, and U.S. Representative Thomas E. Morgan of Pennsylvania, chairman of the House Committee on Foreign Affairs.

567 Statement by the President Following Inspection of Hurricane Damage in Florida and Georgia. *September 12, 1964*

ON THE WAY back to Washington last night following our hurricane inspection trip to Florida and Georgia, I had an opportunity to review the damage as I saw it with the Senators of both States and with the Federal officials whose departments can and will contribute to rehabilitation from the storm.

While final damage surveys have not been completed, it is apparent the total dam-

age, public and private, will approximate the $200 million figure estimated by Mr. McDermott, making this one of the most severe storms to hit this area in this century.

I have pledged all possible Federal assistance to the people of Florida and Georgia and we are fulfilling that promise. I have directed Mr. McDermott, head of the Office of Emergency Planning, to augment his staff in both States to insure all possible assistance to State and local authorities. The OEP will coordinate all Federal aid under the Disaster Assistance Act, on my behalf. I have also asked that I be furnished with regular reports of the status of survey efforts in both States.

In addition I have:

—ordered the Corps of Engineers to provide all assistance required to complete damage surveys so that an allocation of Federal assistance funds can be made,

—asked the Small Business Administration to provide adequate staff in the disaster area to expeditiously process applications for loan assistance from eligible property owners,

—directed the U.S. Public Health Service to assist local communities as required to protect the health of citizens in the areas which suffered severe hurricane damage and where water and other utility systems are damaged,

—instructed the Department of Agriculture to continue to provide such surplus foods as are required to evacuated families and to complete its survey of damage to crops and farm properties.

The Bureau of Public Roads is cooperating with State and county highway authorities in a survey of road and bridge damage and has been instructed to proceed immediately with eligible highway system repair.

The Red Cross, which has provided such outstanding help to the people of these States in their time of need, will continue its personnel and services in the affected area.

As soon as accurate damage data has been assembled Mr. McDermott will request a specific allocation of funds from the President's disaster fund. I am prepared to make that allocation promptly and funds for that purpose are available.

I am confident full recovery from the effects of Hurricane Dora will be accomplished, with close cooperation between Federal, State, and local authorities. I was impressed yesterday with the debris clearance and other recovery activities already in progress. I was impressed too with the outstanding leadership demonstrated in this emergency by Governor Bryant and Governor Sanders and I expect to keep in close touch with both of them as recovery work proceeds.

568   Remarks at the Presentation of the 1964 Presidential Medal of Freedom Awards.   *September 14, 1964*

OTHER peoples in other lands have marked their history through the years by moments of glory and war, and moments of greatness in power over empires and dominions.

Our experience in our own history has been quite different. Our glory is peace, not war. Our greatness is in people, not power. Our genius for 188 years has been the excellence of individuals.

The history of America is a history of outstanding achievement by outstanding individuals—inventors and enterprisers, thinkers and doers, creators and constructors.

Our society today is a changing society, changing from rural values to urban values, from manual labor to mental labor, from scarcity to abundance, from provincial horizons to cosmopolitan horizons. Yet, as our society changes, the value of the individual is unchanging. Our trust must and does continue to rest upon the individual who envisions more, aspires to more, and who achieves more for all of us.

What America is to be, America will be,

because of our trust in and of the individual and of his capacity for excellence. Only those who doubt the individual can be dubious of America's survival and success in this century of contest. This belief is mine. It was this conviction that led President Kennedy to the establishment of the Medal of Freedom as our highest civilian honor for outstanding individuals—citizens who share an extra measure of individual excellence in the mainstream of our well-being and our advancement. On the talents of such citizens rests the future of our American civilization, for it is from the genius of the few that we enrich the greatness of the many.

All Americans are proud, as I am proud, to salute today the great Americans here before me. Their lives and their works have made freedom stronger for all of us in our time.

[*The President spoke at the close of the presentation ceremony. Under Secretary of State George W. Ball, Chairman of the Distinguished Civilian Service Awards Board, introduced the recipients, and the President presented the awards and read the citations, as follows:*]

Mr. Ball: Mr. Dean Acheson.

THE PRESIDENT. An architect of the defense and growth of a flourishing Atlantic community, his moral resolve and intellectual grasp have placed all free men in his debt.

Mr. Ball: Dr. Detlev W. Bronk.

THE PRESIDENT. Scientist and leader of scholars, his vision and untiring efforts have advanced science education and helped forge an enduring link between Government and the scientific community.

Mr. Ball: Mr. Aaron Copland.

THE PRESIDENT. Masterful composer and gifted teacher, his music echoes our American experience and speaks expressively to an international audience.

Mr. Ball: Mr. Willem de Kooning.

THE PRESIDENT. Artist and teacher, he has adventured into a new range of artistic vision and opened bold pathways to our experience of the world.

Mr. Ball: Mr. Walter Disney.

THE PRESIDENT. Artist and impresario, in the course of entertaining an age, he has created an American folklore.

Mr. Ball: Prof. J. Frank Dobie.

THE PRESIDENT. Folklorist, teacher, writer, he has recaptured the treasure of our rich regional heritage in the Southwest from the conquistadores to the cowboys.

Mr. Ball: Dr. Lena F. Edwards.

THE PRESIDENT. Physician and humanitarian, she has applied her medical skills and compassionate understanding to the women and children of our migratory work force.

Mr. Ball: Mr. Thomas Stearns Eliot.

THE PRESIDENT. Poet and critic, he has fused intelligence and imagination, tradition and innovation, bringing to the world a new sense of the possibilities for order in a revolutionary time.

Mr. Ball: Dr. John W. Gardner.

THE PRESIDENT. Guardian and critic of American education, he has inspired our schools and colleges toward his own goal of increasing excellence.

Mr. Ball: The Reverend Theodore M. Hesburgh.

THE PRESIDENT. Educator and humanitarian, he has inspired a generation of students and given of his wisdom in the struggle for the rights of man.

Mr. Ball: Mr. Clarence L. Johnson.

THE PRESIDENT. Aeronautical engineer, his genius for conceiving unique airframes and his technical management skills contribute mightily to the Nation's security by creating aircraft of daring design with unmatched rapidity and effectiveness.

Mr. Ball: Mr. Frederick Kappel.

THE PRESIDENT. A creative leader of business, he synthesizes the skills of management with a farsighted appreciation of how technology and communications may better serve our country.

Mr. Ball: Miss Helen Keller.

THE PRESIDENT. An example of courage to all mankind, she has devoted her life to illuminating the dark world of the blind and the handicapped.

Mr. Ball: Mr. John L. Lewis.

THE PRESIDENT. Eloquent spokesman of labor, he has given voice to the aspirations of the industrial workers of the country and led the cause of free trade unions within a healthy system of free enterprise.

Mr. Ball: Mr. Walter Lippmann.

THE PRESIDENT. Profound interpreter of his country and the affairs of the world, he has enlarged the horizons of public thinking for more than five decades through the power of measured reason and detached perspective.

Mr. Ball: Mr. Alfred Lunt and Miss Lynn Fontanne.

THE PRESIDENT. A luminous partnership of artistic talents and personal devotion they have brilliantly enlivened and enriched the American stage.

Mr. Ball: Mr. Ralph McGill.

THE PRESIDENT. Editor and journalist, he has courageously sounded the voice of reason, moderation, and progress during a period of contemporary revolution.

Mr. Ball: Prof. Samuel Eliot Morison.

THE PRESIDENT. Scholar and sailor, this amphibious historian has combined a life of action and literary craftsmanship to lead two generations of Americans on countless voyages of discovery.

Mr. Ball: Mr. Lewis Mumford.

THE PRESIDENT. In the name of sanity, he has constantly worked to rescue and extend the qualities of urban life that will preserve and stimulate the humane spirit of western civilization.

Mr. Ball: Mr. Edward R. Murrow.

THE PRESIDENT. A pioneer in education through mass communication, he has brought to all his endeavors the conviction that truth and personal integrity are the ultimate persuaders of men and nations.

Mr. Ball: Dr. Reinhold Niebuhr.

THE PRESIDENT. Theologian, teacher, social philosopher, he has invoked the ancient insights of Christianity to illuminate the experience and fortify the will of the modern age.

Mr. Ball: Miss Leontyne Price.

THE PRESIDENT. A voice of stirring power and rare beauty, her singing has brought delight to her land and to all those who treasure musical values.

Mr. Ball: Mr. A. Philip Randolph.

THE PRESIDENT. Trade unionist and citizen, through four decades of challenge and achievement he has led his people and his nation in the great forward march of freedom.

Mr. Ball: Mr. Carl Sandburg.

THE PRESIDENT. Son of the prairie, he has helped the Nation and the world to comprehend and share in the great affirmation of American life, asserting always, and in the face of disaster no less than triumph, The People.

Mr. Ball: Mr. John Steinbeck.

THE PRESIDENT. A writer of worldwide influence, he has helped America to understand herself by finding universal themes in the experience of men and women everywhere.

Mr. Ball: Dr. Helen B. Taussig.

THE PRESIDENT. Physician, physiologist, and embryologist, her fundamental concepts have made possible the modern surgery of the heart which enables countless children to lead productive lives.

Mr. Ball: Mr. Carl Vinson.

THE PRESIDENT. Master legislative captain, helmsman, and navigator, his fixed star has always been the national interest.

Mr. Ball: Mr. Thomas J. Watson, Jr.

THE PRESIDENT. A business statesman who combined distinction in private life with a cheerful acceptance of countless public duties placed on him by a grateful government.

Mr. Ball: Dr. Paul Dudley White.

THE PRESIDENT. Physician, humanist, and teacher, he has led the way toward a greater knowledge of heart disease and the promotion of international understanding through scientific medicine.

NOTE: The ceremony was held at noon in the East Room at the White House. The awards presented to Dean Acheson, former Secretary of State, Edward R. Murrow, former Director of the United States Information Agency, and Carl Vinson, U.S. Representative from Georgia, were medals of "special distinction for Government service." Mr. Acheson responded to the President's remarks on behalf of all the recipients.

The Presidential Medal of Freedom, established by Executive Order 11085 (28 F.R. 1759; 3 CFR, 1958–1963 Comp., p. 719) is the highest civil honor conferred by the President for service in peacetime. The names of the 30 winners of the 1964 awards were first made public on July 4 (see Item 447). For the 1963 ceremony see Item 27.

569 Remarks Upon Presenting the Harmon International Aviation Trophies. *September 14, 1964*

Honored guests, ladies and gentlemen:

On this occasion it is my privilege to perform once more a duty that has been performed by six other Presidents in awarding the Harmon International Aviation Trophies.

Since the air age began, our Nation has held a position of leadership in this new horizon of human experience. In this field as in all fields, the accomplishments of our machines are small against the achievements of our men and women themselves. In time to come our machines may perform marvelous feats in the distant realms of space, but I think always their success will rest upon man himself.

This was recognized long ago by Col. Clifford B. Harmon, a pioneer American aviator and balloonist. Colonel Harmon was a man unusually dedicated throughout his life to the promotion of world peace.

Forty years ago he had the vision that the airplane, the airstrip, and the pilots who flew them would some day have a powerful influence in bringing about world peace. It was Colonel Harmon's carefully considered opinion that pilots were better suited than members of any other calling to contribute actively to the prevention of war. It was with these ideas in mind that Colonel Harmon founded in 1926 the Harmon International Aviation Trophies.

Three years later, Colonel Harmon personally proposed to the then existing League of Nations a united air force for peace and defense. His vision was expressed eloquently when he wrote:

"The desire for peace is the finest ideal that the mind of man has ever known. Today as at no other time in the history of the world, we are in urgent need of the realization of that ideal, but we have learned that the desire for peace alone is not enough. That desire must be sustained by power."

Today, Colonel Harmon's native land fully realizes that preparedness is a predicate of peace. Together with free men everywhere, we stand prepared—prepared to defend our freedom, prepared to preserve the peace of all.

So, it gives me a great deal of pleasure—and I am very proud this afternoon—to join in this presentation of these awards of the Harmon Trophy for the most outstanding performances by aviators and aviatrixes in 1962 and 1963.

For 1962 the Aviator Award goes to Maj. Fitzhugh L. Fulton, Jr., of the United States Air Force.

Major Fulton in 1962 piloted a B–58 Hustler bomber beyond its designed performance to set new world altitude and payload records.

For 1963 the Aviatrix Award goes to Mrs. Betty Miller of Santa Monica, Calif. In 1963 she became the first woman in history to fly solo across the Pacific—7,400 miles from Oakland, Calif., to Sydney, Australia.

For 1963 the Aviator Award goes, for the first time, to a member of America's astronaut team, Maj. Leroy Gordon Cooper. Every American knows the story of his flight. We lived it with him as he orbited the earth 22 times, traveling 593,885 miles. As we all remember so well, when the mechanisms failed, it was his pilot's skill that meant so much to the success of that great flight.

So, speaking for all of you here this afternoon, and the millions of other Americans who share the pride that we have, I say to those I have specifically mentioned, heartiest congratulations to all of you from all of us.

NOTE: The President spoke in the late afternoon in the Rose Garden at the White House.

570   Remarks to Representatives of "Rural America for Johnson-Humphrey." *September 14, 1964*

I AM GRATEFUL to you for your presence here today.

I am grateful to you for your confidence in the work we are trying to do here—for all the people.

Our Nation has no more important work to do at home than the work of keeping our historic trust to rural America.

In this country we think of ourselves as a great industrial nation—and we are. Out in the world, however, men in many nations see us in a different view, as the greatest agricultural nation in history. And that we are, too.

Our success in all our endeavors—at home and abroad—is bottomed on our success in the fields and pastures and rural homes of America.

Our great increase in productivity on the farms has released the manpower to operate our industrial complex.

Our great advances in processing and distribution have released more consumer buying power for expenditures other than food than any other nation has ever known.

Our dependable food supply is no small factor in the order and stability of our society—and the success of our political system.

All this underscores how important our agricultural success is to America's total success. It is a source of strength—not to be treated lightly, not to be tinkered with or tampered with carelessly or casually.

Our agricultural policies must never be made blindly. They must never be predicated upon a bias or prejudice against the farmer. Even though his numbers are smaller, the farmer and rancher still ranks as the first citizen of our success.

Successful as our agriculture is, I would be the last to tell you that improvements cannot be made. That is why I welcome your support now—so that we can do together the work that still needs to be done in and for rural America.

Over the last 3½ years we have made progress. For each of the 3 full years of this administration, net farm income has been at least $800 million above 1960. This is not—as some might lead you to believe—due solely to Government payments.

Last year, virtually all the widely-grown cash crops brought in more cash from farm marketings than was the case in 1960. As a result, last year average net income per farm was 18 percent above 1960.

Farm programs enacted since 1961 have reduced our surpluses. Feed grains and wheat in storage are down by 30 million tons. Without the new programs, another 133 million tons of surplus feed grains and another 500 million bushels of surplus wheat would be on our hands by this time.

On all fronts we are striving to meet our responsibilities in rural America. Some 212,000 nonfarm jobs have been created in rural America, another 148,000 jobs have been created indirectly.

We are striving to serve the interest of the farm producer and his family; the rural community and its businessmen and residents; and the consumers throughout our land.

This is a moment of great promise for all America.

The good old days were never like these—and Americans have no desire to turn back to what never was and can never be again.

Our eyes are on the future. With your help, with your support, with your leadership, we will go forward to make the years ahead the best years rural America—and all America—have ever known.

NOTE: The President spoke at 6 p.m. in the Rose Garden at the White House.

As printed, this item follows the prepared text released by the White House.

571 Remarks at the Convention of the International Association of Machinists, Miami Beach, Florida. *September 15, 1964*

President Hayes, Mr. Walker, Governor Bryant, Mayor Burns, my old friends Congressmen Pepper and Fascell, Reverend Parks, officers, executive council members, delegates and guests:

I want to thank you from the bottom of my heart for your warm reception and for the confidence that you have already demonstrated in me.

Seventy-six years ago your union was formed. When your founders met then, they were forced to meet in secrecy and in fear. Labor had no rights, and few rewards. The laboringman and his family sat at the second table in our society. That day is gone, gone forevermore.

The America of 1964 is vastly different from the America of 1888. Sixty-hour weeks are gone. Twenty cents an hour wages are gone. Child labor and sweatshops are gone. You meet as free men ought to meet—out in the open and unafraid, your rights assured, your rewards increased, and your place secure at the first table of our Nation's success.

I am proud for you and for your president, Al Hayes. When he retires in a few months, Al Hayes can know that he spent his life participating in the greatest advance made by labor anywhere in all the history of mankind.

Now, that is the challenge that is before

us. When our work is done, will we know that we, too, have advanced the cause of man? For my part, I am determined that the answer shall be "yes." I am determined that history shall rejoice in memory of our generation.

I am determined that generations to come after us shall shed no tears, or shame, or sorrow when they remember our stewardship as keepers of the flame. And that is why I come today to call you, and to call all Americans, to the works that I believe we must do, that these shall be remembered as America's proudest years.

Our trust today is very great, yours and mine. Our success, the success of all the American people, is running at the flood. In all our years, never have any other Americans known the prosperity that you know today. Old records are being surpassed every month. The August reports have just come in. I read them last night. They show this: More men and women were on nonfarm payrolls last month than ever in American history—59,250,000, up by 1,600,-000 more than a year ago.

Factory employment reached the highest August level in more than 10 years—17,500,-000—300,000 more than a year ago. The factory workweek reached the highest August average since 1950—14 years ago—40.9 hours, and the average premium pay of 3.5 hours was the highest since statistical records began back there in 1956.

Average weekly earnings set a new record for August of $103—$4.50 more than August 1963, and $10 a week more than August 1961. This is what our late, beloved President, John Fitzgerald Kennedy, talked about when he said, "We are going to get America moving again."

In these last 3½ years, 3,743,000 new jobs have been added. We have been adding them at the rate of nearly 90,000 new jobs

per month. In the previous 3½-year period, 1,596,000 jobs were added, a little less than 40,000 jobs per month. We are doing twice as well on new jobs. And on the rise in take-home dollars for the workingman we are doing 7 times better.

In the 42 months before January 1961, workers' average weekly earnings, after taxes, rose only $1.25. But in the next 42 months they rose $8.43—let me repeat, 7 times as much. And that is adjusted to take account of price changes. For all sectors of our economy the story is the same. Whether we look through the eyes of labor or business, white collar or blue collar, farmer or professional, these are years of great success for all Americans. And we appreciate it. That success is our trust, yours and mine.

Entrusted to your care, and mine, is both the greatest success any system has ever achieved and the greatest cause that any people have ever borne. We must not lose that success or fail that cause. And I predict here today that we shall not.

If future generations are to rejoice in their memory of our generation, our great work must be that great word on the banners in this hall—we must work together all the way for "unity" of the American people and the American Nation; all the way this year and every year, because unity is our challenge.

This year, and every year, the prosperity of the many must not be sacrificed to the partisanship of the few. This year, and every year, the progress of all the people must not be victimized by the prejudices of any of the people.

These are first and basic works of unity. What we enjoy today, in our land and in our lives, we are able to enjoy because we in America and the world are at peace. I love peace, and I know you do, too. And I don't intend that it shall be lost—for your children or for mine.

I know the strength of this Nation. I know that we can live as we live now—prosperous, progressive, and unafraid—so long as we live together united, forward-looking, and undivided.

There is far too much work for Americans to do together in the future for Americans to divide today over the past. Too many Americans who want jobs still cannot find jobs. Too many of our families are too poor. Too many of our young people must end their educations too soon. Too many of our older couples must dip too deeply into their lifesavings to pay their hospital bills. And that is why we are working so hard, so long, to try to pass medical care under social security in this session.

And I say to you now, and I say to all Americans everywhere, if you believe in medical care for the aged under social security, now is the time to stand up and be counted.

Yes, we have much work to do in America—in our cities, in our countrysides, and in our classrooms. We are working less hours per day, less days per week, so we have more time to enjoy some of the fruits of American life, and some of the recreation that should be available to every American family. And improving our cities and our classrooms and our countryside is the work that I want you to join us in helping do, so that these years ahead of us will be worthy to be remembered as the proudest years in American history.

There is no problem at home, and there is no provocation in the world, from which we need to turn away. With patience and with perseverance, with faith in our arms and strength in our hands, and peace in our hearts, we can be the masters of our destiny and the captains of our fate.

I believe that you want your leadership and your Government, and your country, to extend their hand, but keep their guard up.

I believe, and I think that you believe, in a test ban treaty that will save us from contaminating the milk of our children.

I believe, and I think you believe, in a policy of the good neighbor that will help those who want freedom help themselves.

I believe, and I think you believe, that one of the proudest moments of our national history was when we wrote a social security bill on the law books of this Nation. And I think that you think the social security law ought to be strengthened and not weakened.

I believe, and I think you believe, that there ought to be a job for every man willing to work.

And there ought to be a classroom and a teacher for every child to get all the education they are capable of taking.

I believe, and I know you believe, because it is your sweat and your toil that has helped to prepare this Nation—I believe that we must always be prepared to defend ourselves from any attack, but also always be prepared to reason out our problems with the nations of the world.

At this time in our Nation's life as we decide our course for the years to come—and this is the year of decision for you—let us all live by the precept of that great American, Thomas Jefferson, who said, "The care of human life and happiness, and not their destruction, is the first and the only legitimate object of good government."

And for however long I may be permitted to lead you and to serve you, the care of human life and happiness will enjoy the highest priority, because I think, as you think, as Jefferson thought, it is the first and the only legitimate object of good government.

Thank you.

NOTE: The President spoke at 10:40 a.m. at the Deauville Hotel in Miami Beach, Fla. In his opening words he referred to Al J. Hayes, president, International Association of Machinists, Elmer E. Walker, general secretary-treasurer of the Association, Farris Bryant, Governor of Florida, Haydon Burns, mayor of Jacksonville, Fla., Claude Pepper and Dante B. Fascell, U.S. Representatives from Florida, and the Reverend A. Gene Parks of the Miami Beach Methodist Church.

572   Remarks After Inspecting Space Facilities at Cape Kennedy. *September 15, 1964*

Mr. Webb, ladies and gentlemen:

Thank you very much for giving me this great privilege to come here and observe the results of your labors. I have had a deep interest in this program for many years. I always get optimistic and ambitious and excited when I am permitted to come here and see the progress that you have made. I feel, as I know you feel, that I want only the best in the world for our great Nation and for our people.

I recognize, as I know you recognize, that we cannot be the leader of the world and the follower in space. For that reason, the taxpayers of our country are making great sacrifices in order that we can get on with the job, get ahead with our research, and come up with the answers.

I am so proud of the team that Mr. Webb has assembled. I am so grateful to each of you who make your own individual contribution to that team.

I came down here today with one of our great young Americans. I awarded him the Harmon Trophy yesterday in the Rose Garden at the White House—Major Cooper. He told me of some of the progress that you were making together as we flew down from Washington this morning on the plane. It gave me great pride to hear what he said, and it gives me great pleasure to see what you have done.

I want to commend each of you. I envy you. You are playing a part in history that your children and your grandchildren will be very proud to point to. I trust when all is said and done, that America will not only be the home of the free and the land of the brave, but will be the nation that is first in space, due primarily to what you people are doing here.

Thank you so much for the good work you are doing.

NOTE: The President spoke at 1:45 p.m. in front of the Spacecraft Checkout Facility at Cape Kennedy, Fla. His opening words referred to James E. Webb, Administrator, National Aeronautics and Space Administration.

573   Remarks Upon Arriving at Malmstrom Air Force Base, Great Falls, Montana. *September 16, 1964*

Mayor Erdmann and my Montana friend:

This is a bountiful and spacious State. But you have known the ravages as well as the rewards of nature. On June 9th I declared a "major disaster" caused by floods in northwestern Montana and allocated $2 million for disaster relief. Today I have approved another $4½ million to finish the job of reconstruction and rebuilding this great State.

We are now on our way to Canada to proclaim a treaty which will make possible the construction of the Libby Dam—bringing jobs and power and recreation to your State. Neither the treaty nor dam would be a reality if it were not for the work of your representatives of both parties in the Congress. I want to congratulate the people of this great section of the United States for the quality of the public servants they select.

I am happy to have been honored at the steps, when I descended from the plane, by many of your great Governors who will be introduced a little later. I came out with some of the leaders of your Nation in the plane—your own beloved Senators Mike Mansfield and Lee Metcalf.

I have come here today to make a report. This has been the greatest conservation Congress in the history of the United States. This has not been a partisan or a sectional work. It has been the achievement of far-sighted men of every party and of every section, and your children will thank you for making that investment in their future.

Your State was once a remote and distant place. Today it is only hours away from Washington. We had breakfast in your Nation's Capital. We will lunch in our neighboring country of Canada.

The resources of Montana underlie the strength of America. The military might of Montana is a bulwark of the defense of freedom, and we must never forget that it is only minutes away from the missiles of our adversaries. Montana, thus, today is a vital link in a united country in a very shrinking world.

Everything we hope for, the greatness of America, the hope for peace, depends upon common partnership in common purpose.

When Captain Lewis first saw the Great Falls of Montana, he reported that in a few days he was attacked by a grizzly bear, a mountain lion, three buffalo bulls, and he woke up the next morning staring at a rattlesnake.

Those were truly impressive dangers, but today the people of Montana and the people of the world face far more towering threats. You live in the midst of the power that could destroy the entire world.

So let us work together so the day need never come when your peaceful soil must send forth instruments of destruction and death to the millions of human beings.

I know that this peace is your dearest wish. We will always keep our hand out and our guard up. As long as I am privileged to be a part of the leadership of this country, I want you to know that peace will be my fixed star. It will be my first objective, as it is your first goal.

Thank you for this warm welcome on this wonderful day under this great sky. May God bless each of you.

NOTE: The President spoke in midmorning at Malmstrom Air Force Base, Great Falls, Mont. His opening words referred to Mayor Marion S. Erdmann of Great Falls.

574   Remarks of Welcome at Malmstrom Air Force Base to Prime Minister Pearson of Canada. *September 16, 1964*

Ladies and gentlemen, distinguished Members of the Congress, distinguished Governors:

Welcome to the United States, Mr. Prime Minister. And welcome to Montana whose majesty and western warmth should remind you of your own great country.

In 1963, Mr. Prime Minister, you said of Canada: "We are so friendly that we feel we can criticize the United States like a Texan does—and in the same idiom." This Texan hopes that you still feel that freedom, for we welcome the comments and the counsel which spring, as yours do, from friendship and understanding. Although I doubt that even with your grasp of languages you will be able to match the Texas idiom.

Twenty-one years ago President Franklin D. Roosevelt and Prime Minister Mackenzie King met in Hyde Park. They agreed to work together to defend this hemisphere and to defend democracy everywhere.

From that day to this we have followed the same path of partnership. Free peoples everywhere are more secure because of our cooperation in NORAD, in NATO, and in the United Nations.

The freedom and richness of our lands, the hopes of the people it serves, depend upon the peace of the world that we live in. It is a symbol of our time that beneath the magnificence of this Montana stand weapons that are powerful enough to devastate much of a continent.

Those of us who seek peace know that only wisdom and patience, and the fortitude of long effort, can bring us near to that goal. But we will always pursue that goal.

You, Mr. Prime Minister, are a symbol of that effort. You have never wavered in the defense of freedom. But you also have given much of your life so that free men might live in peace.

You have done much for your people. You have carried the influence of Canada to the highest councils and to the most hazardous crises of the world.

But we greet you not only as a great Canadian today. We welcome you as a man whose home is found wherever man seeks fulfillment amid the peace that you, Mr. Prime Minister, have labored so long and so hard to build.

NOTE: The President spoke at 10:40 a.m. at Malmstrom Air Force Base, Great Falls, Mont. Prime Minister Lester B. Pearson responded as follows:

Mr. President, distinguished Governors, distinguished Members of Congress, Members of Parliament, ladies and gentlemen:

It gives me a very great pleasure to be on American soil once more and to receive such a kind and generous welcome from you, Mr. President, and from your distinguished colleagues.

This is a very brief visit, but it gives me time and opportunity to bring to you the warm good wishes of the Canadian people toward their American friends. You know, I feel like a neighbor dropping in to make a friendly visit. Indeed, that is what I am doing, because I just dropped in to pick up the President and take him back to Canada.

This is the kind of relationship which exists between our two peoples. It is close, it is informal, it is important, and it is neighborly. Like leaning over a back fence to talk to your neighbor, but a back fence which neither neighbor wishes to pull down and which both are anxious to keep in good repair. Of course, there are differences of opinion and, at times, frustrations between even the best of neighbors, and we have them between our two countries, but they do not prevent a warm underlying friendship and understanding.

Mr. President, you and I will be setting forth today on a fascinating and historic journey to explore from the air—I hope we will be able to see it—the mighty Columbia River and the region of a great cooperative development, a development which agreement between our two governments made possible.

To me the Columbia River project is the kind of enterprise which best demonstrates the partnership between the United States and Canada. This is what our two countries are uniquely fitted to do, to join together in the constructive development of our continent's resources for the benefit of present and future generations, in a world in which I hope we will be at peace.

The Columbia River Treaty is not only an achievement in itself, but an earnest for the future. We must follow it up with other fruitful joint endeavors which will give substance to our friendship which I am so proud to acknowledge this morning, and meaning to our good neighborhood, of which this happy meeting is a witness.

Thank you.

1073

575   The President's Response to Remarks of Welcome by Prime Minister Pearson at Vancouver International Airport, British Columbia.   *September 16, 1964*

Mr. Prime Minister, Premier Bennett, Honorable Ministers and Members of Parliament, citizens of British Columbia, my fellow westerners, ladies and gentlemen:

If you would indulge me just a moment, I should like to introduce to our Canadian friends the distinguished Americans who have come with me today to participate in this most enjoyable occasion, and to commemorate this day.

First of all, I should like to ask the distinguished chairman of our Foreign Relations Committee of the United States Senate, Senator J. William Fulbright, to stand, and his wise and beloved colleague, Senator George Aiken, a great friend of Canada.

From our neighboring State of Montana, we have the great Majority Leader of the United States Senate, Mike Mansfield; his colleague, our friend Senator Lee Metcalf; and Governor Babcock.

From Oregon we have Senator Morse; the distinguished member of the Foreign Relations Committee, Senator Neuberger; the fine young Governor of Florida—of Oregon, Governor Hatfield.

Governor, I hope you will pardon me, because I was in Florida yesterday, and I am going to be in Oregon tomorrow.

From the State of Washington, we have Senator Warren Magnuson, Senator Henry Jackson, and Governor Rosellini.

It is on rare occasions that we have a quorum of the Senate here in the middle of the afternoon!

From the great State of Nevada, we have Senator Alan Bible, Senator Howard Cannon, and Governor Grant Sawyer.

And my own distinguished Secretary of the Interior, Mr. Stewart Udall.

Mr. Prime Minister, Mr. Premier, I want to thank you for your generous welcome. This trip to Vancouver is the first that I have taken outside of my own country since I became President last November.

I think I will be guided by an old Chinese proverb: "When you enter a country, inquire as to what is forbidden; when you cross a boundary, ask about the customs." Well, I have made careful inquiries and I will eat the salmon and praise the B.C. Lions.

It is appropriate that this first trip should be to Canada. Our ties are old and they are strong. We are at once neighbors and friends, and partners and allies, and I am very glad my first stop is Vancouver.

Here is that spirit of adventure and excitement—of building a nation—which is part of the West which is my home also. I won't say that Vancouver reminds me of Texas. I will say, though, when I go home, that Texas reminds me of Vancouver.

Your Prime Minister has said that "the great purpose of international statesmanship today must be to . . . make possible a better life for all." Well, that is the purpose of this visit.

The treaty we proclaim will lay a new foundation of prosperity for Canadians and Americans, for your West and for ours.

We have achieved this partnership because we respect our differences. This continent is a richer and freer place for that respect.

At the same time, we owe much to each other. We can never forget that the rich soil of American freedom has been washed with

Canadian blood, shed in a common effort against foreign enemies.

Nor can we forget that you have an honest interest in our affairs. We will always stand with you in the defense of freedom. But I also tell you that in the years to come my country will spare no effort to achieve a lasting peace for all of us.

I hope to learn more about your country. I hope to encourage my people to discover more of the richness of your culture, the values of your people, and the promise of your destiny.

But this much we already know:

No nation in the world has had greater fortune than mine in sharing a continent with the people and the nation of Canada.

And now, in the midst of a great drought in Texas, we welcome this great rain here.

NOTE: Prime Minister Pearson's remarks of welcome follow:

"Mr. President, Mr. Premier, distinguished guests from the United States, and friends:

"It is a very great pleasure, Mr. President, to welcome you to Canadian soil, as I have been welcoming you to Canadian air space, and especially happy because this is the occasion of the ratification of a treaty which will benefit both our countries and which is the result of friendly cooperation between them.

"It is, I think, appropriate that your first visit, as President, outside the United States should be to Canada, your nearest neighbor, your closest friend, and naturally, therefore, your most candid and constructive critic.

"It is the accepted convention that the first official visit of the head of a State or the head of a Government to another country should be to the capital of that country, but you, Mr. President, are a Texan and, as such, not bound by conventions—at least that kind of convention.

"So your first visit to Canada, and your first visit as President outside the United States, is to British Columbia, to Vancouver, where you are being greeted today by Premier Bennett and other distinguished citizens of this Province.

"It is fitting, I believe, that this should be the case, and it is a recognition of the surge of Canadian development west and north, and of our interest and our destiny across the Pacific. In no part of Canada could your welcome be more sincere than in this great Province.

"But I assure you, Mr. President, that had you landed at our most eastern airport in Newfoundland, 5,000 or more miles away, or at any place between, our welcome to you would have been equally warm both for yourself and as President of the United States of America, the nation which bears today so much of the burden of insuring peace and promoting freedom in the world, the nation which has led the free world through these troubled postwar years, the nation that is our good friend and our good neighbor."

The President spoke at 1 p.m. In his opening words he referred to Prime Minister Lester B. Pearson and to Premier William A. C. Bennett of British Columbia.

576   Remarks With Prime Minister Pearson Upon Proclaiming the Columbia River Treaty.   *September 16, 1964*

THE PRESIDENT. I proclaim this treaty. From this day forth let it be observed in good faith by the Government and by the people of the United States of America.

PRIME MINISTER PEARSON. Mr. President, Premier Bennett, Governor Rosellini, distinguished guests, ladies and gentlemen:

It is raining, and I was going to make a speech, but I think the best thing I can do is to cut my speech short and let you get in out of the rain.

But before I do that, may I say how honored and privileged I am to be here, to participate in this impressive and moving ceremony with the President of the United States of America.

I think the signing of this treaty is an important accomplishment, not only because it will be of great material benefit to our two countries and our two peoples in the development of the resources of this continent, but because it is another illustration of friendship and good neighborhood, and the way two countries can and should work together.

Mr. President, we are grateful to you for coming to this border to make this possible. We are grateful to you for bringing with you distinguished Members of Congress and important men in the political life of your country. We want you to know that you have been very welcome to Canada on this first visit to our country. We would like you to come back.

If you come back you will see, Mr. President, that this treaty has indeed been a constructive one and that it is going to work to the benefit of both of our countries. For that we owe a debt of gratitude not only to the negotiators but to the Premier of this Province who worked with them to bring about this great day in the development of this part of North America and a great day in international cooperation between our two countries.

Thank you very much.

THE PRESIDENT. Mr. Premier, Mr. Prime Minister, distinguished guests on the platform, ladies and gentlemen:

There are many reasons why my first trip abroad as President should be to Canada. In 1839 J. Pinckney Henderson, the Representative of the Republic of Texas to France and to England wrote that Great Britain might delay its recognition of the new republic for fear of the impact in Canada. But Canada remained loyal. Great Britain recognized Texas, and that recognition helped open the door to American union for Texas.

Had that not happened, Mr. Prime Minister, had Texas stayed independent, classical diplomacy suggests that we might very well today be concluding a treaty of mutual defense against the American influence. As a Texan, I can sympathize with the prob-lems of living beside a wealthy and powerful and pervasive neighbor. That is just how the rest of the United States feels about Texas.

More than 3 years ago President Kennedy came to Canada. He told your Parliament his trip was "an act of faith." He said it was faith in our capacity to meet common problems, and in our common cause of freedom.

Well, my trip today is a fulfillment and a renewal of that act of faith. It is both a resolution of a common problem, and a strengthening of freedom's cause.

Lord Durham, in the famous report that laid the foundation for modern Canada, spoke of the possibility of establishing "partners in a new industry, the creation of happy human beings."

That partnership is the purpose of this treaty that we have signed today.

It will supply new electric power to millions of my countrymen. It will supply revenues to Canada, although I was somewhat shocked when I heard you read that cable about receiving $253,999,884, and then to show you what the Canadians really went for, they went for that last 25 cents.

It joins common purpose to common interest in pursuit of the welfare of the free people who share our continent.

My country is grateful for the spacious spirit with which this generous design was conceived and with the way it was carried out, even down to the last quarter. It is another landmark in the history of one of the oldest and one of the most successful associations of sovereign governments anywhere in the world.

What is the secret of this success? It begins with a truth: The only justifiable object of government is the welfare of individual men and women. It is a simple truth. But had others shared it with us, the world would have been spared many dark years.

With this as the animating design, our partnership has been built on four pillars. And the success of that structure might well serve as a model to the world.

The first pillar is peace.

The second pillar is freedom.

The third pillar is respect. One of my predecessors, Woodrow Wilson, said "You cannot be friends upon any other basis than upon terms of equality."

We maintain with each other the relationship that we seek for all the world: cooperation amid diversity.

Pericles said of a state that was much smaller than yours, "We have forced every sea and land to be the highway of our daring."

In the founding of the United Nations, in the Middle East, in the Congo, in southeast Asia, the world has responded to Canadian daring. You have followed not the highway of empire which helped destroy Athens, but you have followed the more difficult path to peace which can save the world.

And you have been a principal architect, Mr. Prime Minister, of that profound achievement.

The fourth pillar is cooperation. This agreement is the latest in an impressive list. We have disarmed our border; we have shared the costs of defense; we have divided power at Niagara; we have built the St. Lawrence Seaway; we have resolved scores of other problems.

Difficulties that divide others have united us. The reason is plain. We share interest and we share purpose. We come to the council table advised by reason, aware of each other's problems, anxious to find final agreement. You told us, Mr. Prime Minister, "As good neighbors we must be able to sit down and discuss problems realiz-ing that solutions will not be found without hard work and without give-and-take on both sides."

We both have problems we must solve within our borders. My country has a war to win on poverty. We must find justice for men of all races. We must crush the forces of division which gnaw at the fabric of our union.

You have your own difficulties. We watch, with friendly confidence in your capacity to merge differences in the grand dream of Canadian design.

But there is also much, Mr. Prime Minister, which we share.

In the world we seek peace, and mounting fulfillment for man. Here we work together, from ocean to ocean, in resources and science, to enrich the life of our two peoples to elevate the quality of our two societies.

Franklin D. Roosevelt once said, "Democracy is the form of government which guarantees to every generation of men the right to imagine and to attempt to bring to pass a better world."

That has been the story of your life, Mr. Prime Minister. It is also the strength of our two countries.

And I believe that future generations will have cause for gratitude that two great democracies—Canada and the United States—shared the most generous continent which God has ever granted to man.

Thank you.

NOTE: The ceremony was held at the International Peace Arch, Blaine, Wash., on the United States-Canadian border. During his remarks the President referred to William A. C. Bennett, Premier of British Columbia.

On the same day the President issued Executive Order 11177 "Providing for certain arrangements under the Columbia River Treaty" (29 F.R. 13097; 3 CFR, 1964 Supp.).

577   Remarks in Seattle on the Control of Nuclear Weapons. September 16, 1964

THANK YOU, Senator Jackson.

My friend Governor Rosellini, my old friend and your great Senator, Warren Magnuson; Senator Aiken, one of the best Republicans I know, and he proved tonight he has good judgment when he told you that he didn't dare come out here and run in Washington. We always want Senator Aiken to remain in the Senate. We want him there from the Northeast—and not the Northwest.

_____

Mayor Braman, Mr. Turner, my friends, my fellow westerners:

Let me begin tonight by thanking my very gracious hosts for their very warm and friendly welcome. I want to especially say thank you to the three great institutions of learning, the Chamber of Commerce, and the other fine organizations that have joined you here tonight in this meeting.

I want to pay my respects to the distinguished leaders in our public life who have come here with us this evening: the distinguished chairman of the Senate Foreign Relations Committee, Senator Fulbright; the distinguished Majority Leader from Montana, Senator Mansfield; the two great Senators from Oregon, Senators Morse and Neuberger; the two distinguished Senators from Nevada, Senator Bible and Senator Cannon; from California, Senator Salinger; and the great Secretary of the Interior, Secretary Udall.

Tonight I want to talk to you about one of the most solemn responsibilities of the President of the United States, and that is the duty to direct and control the nuclear power of the United States.

Nineteen years ago President Truman announced "the force from which the sun draws its power has been loosed." In a single, fiery flash the world as we had known it was forever changed. Into our hands had come much of the responsibility for the life of freedom, for the life of our civilization, and for the life of man on this planet.

And the realities of atomic power placed much of that burden in the hands of the President of the United States.

Let no one think atomic weapons are simply bigger and more destructive than other weapons; that they are just another development like the airplane or the tank. The total number of Americans killed in battle from the Revolution until tonight is a little over 526,000 people. Today a single nuclear weapon can kill more than 526,000.

Our experts tell us as of today that a full-scale nuclear exchange between the East and the West would kill almost 300 million people around the world, and in the midst of that terror and tragedy we could expect that weapon after weapon would soon engulf a portion of mankind. A cloud of deadly radiation would drift and destroy, menacing every living thing on God's earth, and in those unimaginable hours unborn generations would forever be lamed.

Now, in the face of these facts, every American President has drawn the same conclusion:

President Harry Truman said: "Such a war is not a possible policy for rational man."

President Eisenhower said: "In a nuclear war, there can be no victory—only losers."

President Kennedy said: "Total war makes no sense. . . ."

And I say that we must learn to live with each other or we will destroy each other.

Many forces have converged to make the modern world. Atomic power is very high among those forces, but what has the atomic age meant for those of us who have come here to this dinner tonight?

It means, I think, that we have a unique responsibility, unique in history, for the defense of freedom. Our nuclear power alone has deterred Soviet aggression. Under the shadow of our strength, our friends have kept their freedom and have built their nations.

It means that we can no longer wait for the tides of conflict to touch our shores.

It means that great powers can never again delude themselves into thinking that war will be painless or that victory will be easy. Thus, atomic power creates urgent pressure for peaceful settlements, and for the strengthening of the United Nations.

It means a change must come in the life of nations. Man has fought since time began, and now it has become clear that the consequences of conflict are greater than any gain, and man just simply must change if man is to survive.

For Americans, it means that control over nuclear weapons must be centralized in the hands of the highest and the most responsible officer of government—the President of the United States. He, alone, has been chosen by all the people to lead all the Nation. He, alone, is the constitutional Commander in Chief of the Nation. On his prudence and wisdom alone can rest the decision which can alter or destroy the Nation.

The responsibility for the control of U.S. nuclear weapons rests solely with the President, who exercises the control of their use in all foreseeable circumstances. This has been the case since 1945, under four Presidents. It will continue to be the case as long as I am President of the United States.

In this atomic age we have always been required to show restraint as well as strength. At moments of decisive tests, our nuclear power has been essential. But we have never rattled our rockets or come carelessly to the edge of war.

Each of the great conflicts of this century has begun when nations wrongly thought others would shrink before their might. As I and my predecessors have said, we may have to use nuclear weapons to defend American freedom, but I will never let slip the engines of destruction because of a reckless and rash miscalculation about our adversaries.

We have worked consistently to bring nuclear weapons under careful control, and to lessen the danger of nuclear conflict. And this policy has been the policy of the United States of America for more than 19 years now, under both Democratic and Republican administrations.

And this will continue to be the policy of the United States of America.

First, we have worked to avoid war by accident or miscalculation. I believe the American people should know the steps that we have taken to eliminate the danger of accidental attack by our strategic forces, and I am going to talk about that tonight.

The release of nuclear weapons would come by Presidential decision alone. Complex codes and electronic devices prevent any unauthorized action. Every further step along the way—from decision to destruction—is governed by the two-man rule. Two or more men must act independently and must decide the order has been given. They must independently take action.

An elaborate system of checks and counter-checks, procedural and mechanical, guard against any unauthorized nuclear bursts. In addition, since 1961 we have placed permissive action links on several of our weapons.

These are electromechanical locks which must be opened by secret combination before any action at all is possible, and we are extending this system.

The American people and all the world can rest assured that we have taken every step that man can devise to insure that neither a madman nor a malfunction could ever trigger nuclear war.

We have also worked to avoid war by miscalculation.

There may be little time for decision between our first warning and our need to reply. If our weapons could be easily destroyed, we would have to make the final decision in a matter of minutes. By protecting our power against surprise attack, we give ourselves more time to confirm that war has actually begun.

Thus, we have placed missiles in protected, underground sites. We have placed missiles beneath the seas. And we have provided constant and secure communication between strategic forces and the Commander in Chief, the President of the United States.

I do not want us to fight a war that no one ever meant to begin.

We have worked to limit the spread of nuclear weapons. The dignity and the interest of our allies demands that they share nuclear responsibility, and we have proposed such measures.

The secrets of the atom are known to many people. No single nation can forever prevent their use. If effective arms control is not achieved, we may see the day when these frightful, fearful weapons are in the hands of many nations. Their concern and capacity for control may be more limited than our own.

So our work against nuclear spread must go on.

Third, we have developed ways to meet force with appropriate force by expanding and modernizing our conventional forces. We have increased our ground forces. We have increased our tactical air force. We have increased our airlift. We have increased our stock of the most modern weapons.

Thus, we do not need to use nuclear power to solve every problem. We will not let our might make the United States musclebound.

Fourth, we have worked to damp down disputes and to contain conflict. In an atomic world, any spark might ignite the bonfire.

Thus our responses are firm but measured. We saw an example of that in the Tonkin Gulf just a few days ago.

Thus we pursue peaceful settlements in many remote corners of the globe.

Fifth, we constantly work toward arms control. A test ban agreement has ended atmospheric explosions which were poisoning the atmosphere. We have established a "hot line" for instant communication between the United States and Moscow in case of any crisis.

As President, I ordered a cutback of unnecessary nuclear production, and this year we submitted several major new proposals to the disarmament conference in Geneva. I will pursue with vigor all of those proposals.

These are only first steps. But they point the way toward the ultimate elimination of ultimate destruction.

So long as I am your President, I intend to follow that course with all the patience at my command. In these ways, for 19 dangerous years, my 3 predecessors have acted to insure the survival of the Nation, to insure survival of our freedom, and to insure survival of our race. That will always be my policy and this is the wish of the people of the United States.

I want to depart just a moment to say that this next month I will have been in Washington for 33 years, serving as a secretary, as a Congressman, as a Senator, and as Vice President, and now as President. I want to say a genuine thank you to you good, enlightened people from this modern, progressive State for sending to us, through the years, such outstanding, patriotic, competent public servants.

I particularly am grateful to you for having given to all the Nation a man like Warren Magnuson, who has served so well, and no man has done more about the policy that I speak of tonight than "Maggie's" efficient colleague, your junior Senator, and my beloved friend, "Scoop" Jackson.

Now, the thing that concerns us all more than anything else in the world is how we can live in peace, because in the largest sense we will never be safe until the world is at peace and until free men are secure. And that kind of world, my friends, is not going to come to us easily. But it must be the untiring pursuit of every man that is entrusted with the leadership of America. And it is the untiring pursuit of the Washington delegation in the United States Senate, I am proud to say.

Conflict among nations will trouble this planet and will test our patience for a long time to come. And as long as weapons are necessary, wisdom in their control is going to be needed. The man who guides them holds in his hands the hopes of survival for the entire world.

As I exercise my cares every day and every night, I often think of those who have just begun and those who are yet unborn. I want them to have a chance. With all my power, and all the aid the good Lord offers me, I will help give them that chance. And I think so will all of you.

In many ways the world tonight is now in the valley of the shadow. But there is an old poem that ends: "Westward look the land is bright." From this western shore tonight I believe we, too, can see a brightening land. Our country is moving forward. It is carrying with it the advancing ranks of freedom.

Somehow or other, optimist that I am, I just believe that peace is coming nearer. If this is so, we may one day see fulfilled the prophecy of the Bible: "The morning stars sang together, and all the sons of God shouted for joy."

Thank you. Good night.

NOTE: The President spoke at the Olympic Hotel in Seattle, Wash., at a dinner honoring "United States and Canadian Partnership in Progress." In his opening remarks he referred to Henry M. Jackson, Senator from Washington, Albert D. Rosellini, Governor of Washington, Warren G. Magnuson, Senator from Washington, George D. Aiken, Senator from Vermont, J. D. Braman, mayor of Seattle, and J. Douglas Turner, Canadian Counsel General ad interim.

578 Remarks on Conservation at a Breakfast in Portland Saluting the Northwest-Southwest Power Transmission Intertie. *September 17, 1964*

SENATOR MORSE—when you are traveling with Wayne, you are always in for a surprise—I wish he had made speeches that short in the Senate—and I might say that good—thank you very much.

Senator Morse, Senator Neuberger, Congresswoman Green, distinguished Members of the Congress, Mayor, Governor, friends in Portland:

This is a very nice thing for you to do so

early in the morning—on a rainy morning. I know it took a lot of arranging and a great deal of trouble, and very unusual hospitality. I realize that it is your way of showing your respect for the great office I hold, and for the President of this country.

I would like for all the people in the Northwest Public Power Association and the Northwest Electric Light and Power Association to know that I feel a very special debt of gratitude to you for the time you spent, the money you invested, the wonderful public event that you have helped to bring about.

This is a rather discouraging occasion, however. I think of all the effort it took to turn off a few lights in the White House in Washington, and here you all finally settled your differences and you are turning on millions all over the country every day.

In 1844 a fiery young orator warned, "Make way for the young American buffalo. We will give him Oregon for his summer shade and the region of Texas for his winter pasture." Well, it is wonderful to be here in Oregon with you this morning. But I want it distinctly understood I am not ready for any Texas pasture.

Yesterday in a few hours I swept across a continent that it took decades of daring to conquer. It took brave men and strong men to make that crossing. But, most of all, it took men of faith—men of great faith in themselves, in their country, in the future of this land.

So today we inhabit a continent that is made fertile by that act of faith. Napoleon truly said when he sold Louisiana, "This accession of territory consolidates the power of the United States forever."

But it was not territory that made us great. It was men. Our West is not just a place. The West is an idea. The Bible says,

"Speak to the earth and it shall teach thee." And here, in the West, we learned man's possibilities were as spacious as the sky that covered him. We learned that free men could build a civilization as majestic as the mountains and the rivers that nourished him. We learned that with our hands we could create a life that was worthy of the land that was ours.

And that lesson has illuminated the life of all America—east, west, north, and south.

This gathering this morning I think is further proof of that. Your work is a more powerful instrument of freedom than a thousand shouted threats and warnings. In far-off countries, men will look here and learn again that the path of free men is the surest path to progress.

Here, in the Northwest, America is moving again. And all the world knows it. This intertie which is the result of so many brains and so much work, and such great efforts, is the most exciting transmission system in history. It will make us world leaders in direct current transmission. It will carry from the Peace River to the Mexican border enough power for five San Franciscos.

So I come here to tell you, and to tell each of you, that all America is proud of all of you.

I am glad to see this cooperation of private power with public power. The public power yardstick is essential. Private power will always play a substantial and a vital role in the future of this great land. This system is also proof of the power of cooperation and unity. You have proved that if we turn away from division, if we just ignore dissension and distrust, there is no limit to our achievements.

I am going to interpolate for a moment here to tell you of an experience I had as a young man trying to reconcile the views of the leaders of public and private power in my State.

We had the great man who happened to be a spokesman for Electric Bond and Share, who was president of one of our great power companies, and he looked just like a Methodist deacon. He sat back and was dignified, a very attractive man, a very pure individual, very cautious in what he said.

I negotiated with him for 3 days and I never made a dent in his armor. He was looking after those stockholders and he almost looked at me with what I thought was contempt.

Finally I got up in my youthful enthusiasm and some impulsiveness that I am very much against these days, and I said, "So far as I am concerned, you can take a running jump and go straight you know where." The old gentleman didn't get the slightest bit rattled. He just looked back and smiled and said, "I am sorry you feel that way, young man. We have to do these things as we see them. We are men of convictions and we have to carry out our views and the views of our stockholders as we think we ought to." All of my REA and public power people applauded me and said it was a great speech. I started out of the room and they all stood.

As I walked out the door, I saw an old man there that was the general counsel for the water district. He was an ex-Senator. I said, "Senator, how did you like my speech?" He said, "Come by the office and I would like to talk to you about it." I said, "Oh, oh." So I went by and he said, "You are in public life. You are a young man just starting out and I want to see you move along and do well. But," he said, "the first thing you have to learn, son, is to tell a man to go to hell and to make him go are two different propositions."

He said, "Mr. Carpenter doesn't want to go. This is a free country and he is going to stay around here, and he thinks it is pretty hot down there, and he doesn't elect to take your choice." He said, "It took me 2 months to get this group together and you bust it up in 2 minutes. I will have to work now until we can get together again and follow the advice of the prophet Isaiah, 'Come now, let us reason together.' "

Many, many times in the Senate and in the other places of responsibility where I have served I have harkened back to that day in that little courtroom when I expressed my views on the president of the power company. A lot of times I wanted to get up and tell Bob Taft what I thought about his viewpoint and where he ought to go, or Bill Knowland, or Everett Dirksen, or even some of my Democratic friends, from time to time.

But I never could forget what that old, wise general counsel said to me, "Tell them to go and make them go are two different propositions."

I do want you to know, though, that by your reasoning together, by your cooperating together for the benefit of all, I think that is true conservation. This is the kind of conservation action that your Government is going to continue to provide the leadership for.

I grew up on the land. The life of my parents depended entirely upon the bounty of the soil. I devoted much of my public life to protecting for our children the great legacy of our natural abundance.

So I come to report to you that we have not just talked about progress in this field. We have made progress, and we are at the close of the greatest conservation Congress in the history of the United States of America.

The 88th Congress has passed more than 30 important conservation bills.

A new Land and Water Conservation Fund will help the States and the cities set aside spots of beauty for recreation and pleasure.

A Wilderness Act will guarantee all Americans the natural magnificence which has been your heritage.

Water Research and Water Planning bills will speed the development for the soaring water needs of this great, growing Nation.

We established continental America's first new national park in 17 years, 23 new national park areas, 4 new national seashores, and a national riverway.

We began a new Bureau of Outdoor Recreation so that our children will have a place to hunt and to fish, and to glory in nature.

We began the construction of over 200 water resource projects with 70 more scheduled for 1965.

We built or we began more than 5,500 miles of transmission lines in this great land.

Flood control funds were increased by more than 50 percent.

All this we have done, and more. And I pledge you that my administration is going to continue with this progress.

But we must do more than continue. Our problems are changing every day and we must change to meet them.

Three changing forces are bringing a new era to conservation.

The first is growing population. By the year 2000, more than 300 million Americans will need 10 times the power and 2½ times the water that we now consume. Increasing pressures will take our resources, and increasing leisure will tax our recreation.

The second is the triumph of technology. The bright success of science also has had a darker side. The waste products of our progress, from exhaust fumes to radiation, may be one of the deadliest threats to the destruction of nature that we have ever known.

The third force is urbanization. More of our people are crowding into cities and cutting themselves off from nature. Access to beauty is denied and ancient values are destroyed. Conservation must move from nature's wilderness to the manmade wilderness of our cities. All of this requires a new conservation.

We must not only protect from destruction, but we have the job of restoring what has already been destroyed—not only develop old resources, but create new ones—not only save the countryside but, yes, finally salvage the cities.

It is not just the classic conservation of protection and development, but it is a creative conservation of restoration and innovation. Its concern is not with nature alone, but with the total relation between man and the world around him. Its object is not just man's welfare, but the dignity of his spirit.

Above all, we must maintain the chance for contact with beauty. When that chance dies, a light dies in all of us. Thoreau said, "A town is saved not more by the righteous men in it than by the woods—that surround it." And Emerson taught, "There is no police so effective as a good hill and wide pasture." We are the creation of our environment. If it becomes filthy and sordid, then the dignity of the spirit and the deepest of our values immediately are in danger.

In the development of a new conservation I intend to press ahead on five fronts:

First, we seek to guarantee our children a place to walk and play and commune with nature. The demand on our recreational facilities is doubling each decade. We must act boldly or our future will be barren.

We will move vigorously under our recent

laws to acquire and to develop new areas for recreation in this country—emphasizing areas of concentrated population. And we will be ready to expand our programs to meet the developing needs.

A national program of scenic parkways and scenic riverways is on the horizon. I hope, for instance, to make the Potomac a conservation model for our metropolitan areas.

In our cities, open space must be reserved where possible, and created where preservation comes too late.

Second, we must control the waste products of technology. The air we breathe, the water we drink, our soil, our wildlife are all being blighted by the poisons and the chemicals, and all the inevitable waste products of modern life.

The skeleton of discarded cars, old junk yards, litter our countryside—and are driving my wife mad. She thinks that one of the advantages of getting defeated is to give her some time to get out and do something about cleaning up the countryside and these old junkyards along our beautiful driveways.

I intend to work with local government and industry to develop a national policy for the control and disposal of technological and industrial waste. I will work with them to carry out that kind of a policy. Only in this way, I think, can we rescue the oldest of our treasures from the newest of our enemies.

Third, we must increase mastery over our environment through the marvels of new technology. This means rapidly increasing emphasis on comprehensive river basin development. So we plan to cooperate at every level to develop the resources and to preserve the values of entire regions of this land.

It means drawing fresh water from the oceans. Within a few years economic desalinization will be a reality for a large number of Americans.

It means learning to understand the weather and to do something about it. The advance notice that we got on Hurricane Carla saved us thousands of lives and millions of dollars.

It means the use in every field of the newest knowledge to meet the oldest needs. It means encouraging the development of the genius of man in order to unlock the secrets of the earth.

Fourth, we must prevent urbanization and growth from ravaging the land. I will suggest, in cooperation with local government and private industry, policies for such prevention. Their goal will be to insure that suburban building, highway construction, industrial spread, are conducted with reverence and with the proper regard for the values of nature.

Fifth, we must conduct conservation on a global scale. The Antarctic Treaty, weather and fishery agreements, the treaty with Canada that we celebrated yesterday, are all examples of what can be done if nations will devote common effort to common interest.

These are some of the fronts of the new conservation which I will work to carry forward. And I tell you now that this hope will always be among the closest to my heart.

From the beginning we have been a people of open spaces. We have lifted our eyes to the deserts and to the mountains, and now we are lifting them to the stars. But on this earth the ring draws closer around us.

So let us not leave our task with the reproach of our children already ringing in our ears. Far, far too much is at stake. There are the resources on which our future rests.

But there is a good deal more than that. In a thousand unseen ways we have drawn shape and strength from the land. Respect for man and reverence for God have taken root in our spacious soil. In isolation from nature lies the danger of man's isolation from his fellow and from his Creator.

All my life I have drawn sustenance from the rivers and from the hills of my native State. I do not see them so often any more these days, and I am lonesome for them almost constantly. But their message of love and challenge is written in my spirit. I want no less for all the children of America than what I was privileged to have as a boy.

In the book of Matthew, it says "The floods came, and the winds blew, and beat upon that house; and it fell not, for it was founded upon a rock."

The house of America is founded upon our land and if we keep that whole, then the storm can rage, but the house will stand forever.

This morning you have an unusual assemblage in this room. I was escorted to the dais by a progressive young Republican Governor. I was met by a cordial, hospitable mayor. I flew across the continent with a number of outstanding leaders of the Congress, of the House and of the Senate.

You have an unusual quality of leadership in this great Northwest. We celebrated some of the fruits of that planning yesterday in Canada, fruits of the work of men like the two great Senators from Washington, and this wise, veteran legislator from Vermont, George Aiken, who sits on the front row and does me great honor by coming to this area of the Nation with me.

Oregon, Washington, California, and Montana, all the great West, is here this morning, not to just talk about the glories of the past, but to try to pull all the talent of this great region together to undertake an adventure of tomorrow.

I first came to Portland as a youngster fresh out of uniform in the early days of the war to scrap the battleship *Oregon*. I saw then all of the hope and the daring, and the idealism, and the spirit of conservation that I have observed reflected by your spokesmen in the halls of the House of Representatives and in the Senate.

We have come a long way in those 20-odd years, but we have not gone nearly far enough. The eyes of the Nation are looking to you to provide the leadership that will not just make this the best conservation Congress we have ever had, but that will help us to bring our dreams of a more beautiful America, a safer America, a healthier America available to our children as it has been available to us.

Thank you very much for your wonderful hospitality.

NOTE: The President spoke in the ballroom at the Sheraton Hotel in Portland, Oreg. In his opening remarks he referred to Senators Wayne Morse and Maurine B. Neuberger and Representative Edith Green, all of Oregon, Acting Mayor Wayne Bowes of Portland, and Governor Mark O. Hatfield of Oregon.

The cooperation of the Federal Government in the Northwest-Southwest Power Transmission Intertie was announced by the President at his news conference of July 30 (see Item 486 [7]).

579 Remarks in Sacramento on the Steps of the State Capitol. *September 17, 1964*

Governor Brown; I am very pleased to have Mrs. Brown and Kathy here. Reverend Ferguson, Senator Salinger, Speaker Unruh,

Senator Burns, Congressman Moss, my good friends and gracious hosts in Sacramento:

I am very proud to be in the home State of

more Americans than any other. California sets a fine example for the Nation, because here Americans and Texans live together side by side in relative harmony.

Your State was almost my home State, too. When I was a teenager, I heard that California wanted men to match her mountains, so I came out here to apply. But I got a job in the fruit orchards instead and I went back home to the Texas hills.

I am very proud to be here in Sacramento today where everything is done up brown. As the son of a State legislator, I knew the ways and the wisdom of the State House before I ever knew the location of the White House, and my respect for State governments and the people who serve them has never waned.

I might say that Pat Brown knows the way to both the State House and the White House, and the door is open to him in both places. I know that you have no vacancies in the United States Senate, but anything can happen, and so I would like you to meet and to know my Press Secretary, George Reedy. But Pierre was my Press Secretary, too. I always thought he would go a long way, too, but I never dreamed that the day would come when I would be responsible for his public relations.

Four years ago I came to this same scene to ask your votes, to ask your votes for a great and gallant American, John Fitzgerald Kennedy.

On this occasion, at the capital of all the people of this Union's largest State, I come as no partisan. I come as President of all the people of the United States, to speak to all the Nation, and for the Nation, to all the world.

In our history, this is a day of highest honor. On this day 177 years ago our forefathers ordained and established the Constitution of the United States. Over the years our Union has grown—from the Atlantic seaboard to the mid-Pacific, from the Florida Keys to the far north, from 13 States to 50 States, from 3 million citizens to nearly 200 million now.

On that same rock of the Constitution, our Republic still stands. It stands stable, it stands secure, never stronger, never more successful, never so prosperous, never more determined to defend freedom or to preserve peace.

Our system is succeeding as none before—anywhere, at any time—have ever succeeded. Of all the ages that men have lived, this age of America is the best of all. This is the real truth about America now, and you know it.

But others must know this and others must understand it. That is why I have come to California to speak to you as I do today. I want my voice to be heard around the world, for I speak not for myself, but for the people I serve: the strong, the sensible, the moral, the decent, and the peaceful people of the United States.

In this century, time and time again, other men in other lands have misled themselves about what they have heard or what they have read from our land in national election years. From Hitler in 1940 to Castro in 1962, grave miscalculations have been made about America at election time. Our seasons of debate have been miscalculated as seasons of distraction and diversion and division.

There must be no such miscalculation in 1964.

To those who look to us in trust, to all who wish us well, and to any who wish us ill, I say this today: Do not misjudge America's readiness or America's will. Do not miscalculate the unity of all the American people.

Our Nation, conceived in independence

and brought forth in unity, has not now come to a time of disunity, or division, or diversion. Through all our years America's cause has been the cause of all of mankind, and this is our cause still. Our purpose is to live in freedom in a world of peace—and that American purpose will never change.

But this generation of Americans, blooded in battle, matured in peril, living in times when life was never better, but never in graver danger, we know that eternal vigilance is the price of liberty.

We know, as Tom Paine put it, "those who would reap the benefits of liberty must bear like men the hardships of defending it." This we are doing, and this we shall always do.

Here in California I do not need to recite the facts of America's strength and power, for you are the real builders of that strength. We are strong; we are the strongest nation on the earth. Our allies trust that strength. Our adversaries must respect it. Men of all lands can have faith in its wise use.

But the condition of our strength is never static. As dangers change, our strength must change, and we are matching new dangers with sure reply.

Seven years ago America awakened one morning to find a Soviet satellite orbiting the skies. We found that our adversaries had acquired new capabilities for the use, or the misuse, of space.

This administration moved to meet that challenge. We sought and we supported a resolution unanimously approved in the United Nations banning the use of weapons of mass destruction in outer space. We have stated that we have no intention of putting warheads into orbit. We have no reason to believe that any nation now plans to put nuclear warheads into orbit. We have more effective systems today.

At the same time, we recognize the danger that an aggressor might some day use armed satellites to try to terrorize the entire population of the world, and we have acted to meet that threat. To insure that no nation will be tempted to use the reaches of space as a platform for weapons of mass destruction, we began in 1962 and 1963 to develop systems capable of destroying bomb-carrying satellites.

We have now developed and tested two systems with the ability to intercept and destroy armed satellites circling the earth in space. I can tell you today that these systems are in place, that these systems are operationally ready, that these systems are on alert to protect this Nation and to protect the free world.

Our only purpose still is peace, but should another nation employ such weapons in space, the United States will be prepared and will be ready to reply. But this is not the only new development. We are constantly seeking means of protecting this Nation and our allies.

Today I am able to tell you, and I am able to say to the entire world, we have a major increase in our capacity to detect hostile launches against the free world.

Previously, our radar capability had been limited to the detection of objects within the line of sight, but now we have produced, and we are installing, our first facilities for operational "over-the-horizon" radar. This radar will literally look around the curve of the earth, alerting us to aircraft, and especially to missiles, within seconds after they are launched.

This capability will give us earlier warning than ever before of any hostile launches against this country. This means more time to prepare for our retaliatory strike and more time for us to decide, to decide with prudence and reason, the scope and the extent of our retaliatory strike. This is another advance in our vigil of peace to fulfill our responsibility as the sentry of security for all the free world.

Let me also say this for the people of this Nation to all, also, who may listen in the world: Long ago, a great American patriot said to his countrymen, "We have one country, one Constitution, and one destiny." So let all understand that this is America today. We are not a nation divided, or dividing, or divisible. Our will and our work today is that the meaning of our country and our Constitution, and our destiny, shall be the same for all Americans, regardless of their creed or their color or their origins.

What men are in America is not determined by their pedigree or their purse but by their soul and spirit and by their God-given worth. Others have in times past believed that abundance and comfort and contentment would make Americans flabby and soft and weak. I know this generation of Americans is lean and strong and wise.

As we have no delusions about the dangers of the world, we have no illusions about our challenges here at home. We know that we have problems to meet; and we know that we shall meet those challenges.

Our abundance will not produce arrogance, success will not turn us into suspicion of one another, we will never trade the pursuit of happiness for the persecutions of hate. If we have new prosperity in our pockets, we carry priceless values in our hearts.

Our fathers followed the sun westward to open a continent.

Today we guide our course by the star of the Constitution that our forefathers fixed for us as we go forth to open the new age of civilization in America.

Others searched for gold. We search and we seek after far more precious values.

We seek peace and justice and decency for all mankind everywhere.

Our arms shall be always ready, but our hand shall be always extended to those who will join us in a pursuit of peace with honor.

We live in a glorious time in a wonderful land. We have much to be thankful for. We can count our blessings, and they are many. We have much to protect and to preserve and to perpetuate.

You are the leading State in the leading nation in the world. You have produced leaders worthy of your people, and today California stands out in front as no other State in this Nation stands. So let us realize that we are trustees and we are guardians of all that is good, and let us try to be worthy of this land of ours. Let us try to build this State and build this nation as a nation of lovers instead of a nation of haters.

Let us direct and guide our conduct by the Golden Rule of doing unto others as you would have them do unto you.

Let us try to join in a cooperative effort, not a dividing one, to see that our resources are conserved, that we have the water that we need to live in happiness, that we have the roads that we need to travel over, that we have a transportation system that will bring us to work and to our pleasures, that we have a roof over the homes of all of our children, that we have a school for them to attend and a teacher awaiting there to meet them that is competent to lead them.

And then let us see that we not only have this in the great State of California, but we have it in the union of the Nation.

Oh, what you have done to lead the way in the field of education is an inspiration to all of us who come here. So keep up your leadership. Go on your forward march in this great work until the day comes when all have homes, when all children are taught all they can absorb, when we have recreation to take care of our leisure time, and when brother loves brother and neighbor embraces neighbor.

Thank you, goodby, and God bless you.

NOTE: The President spoke at 12:45 p.m. on the steps of the State Capitol in Sacramento. In his opening words he referred to Governor Edmund G. Brown of California and Mrs. Brown and their daughter Kathleen, the Reverend Robert R. Ferguson, Chaplain of the California State Assembly, Pierre Salinger, U.S. Senator from California and former Press Secretary to the President, Jesse M. Unruh, Speaker of the California State Assembly, Hugh M. Burns, California State Senator, and John E. Moss, U.S. Representative from California.

580   Statement by the President on Reviewing California's Plans Under the Economic Opportunity Act.   *September 17, 1964*

I AM PLEASED that the State of California has been so alert to the benefits of this act.

The people of this State and every State can be certain that the Federal Government will do all in its power to erase all blots of poverty from our land.

NOTE: The President's statement was made public as part of a White House release issued at Sacramento following a meeting in Governor Edmund G. Brown's office at which the President was briefed on actions taken by California since the passage of the Economic Opportunity Act.

The release stated that the Governor told the President that the response to the program had been overwhelming. "We have received 100 requests for assistance in qualifying for aid, particularly in community action programs," Governor Brown stated. "Each of these represents a firm intention to follow through. We have received over 1,000 letters and telephone calls from people wanting to volunteer to help in one project or another. We already have more applications than the program will be able to support in its first year. This response has gone far beyond what we expected. It is proof that this program was necessary."

The release further stated that Dr. Paul O'Rourke, coordinator of the State antipoverty task force, reported that interest had not been confined to urban centers, and that many small rural communities in remote parts of the State had also started processing applications.

581   Remarks on Immigration Policy to a Group Interested in the Verrazano-Narrows Bridge Commemorative Stamp.   *September 18, 1964*

YOUR VISIT today reminds me of one of the most memorable and inspiring experiences of my life.

Two years ago this month I visited the city of Naples. There I was privileged to speak to and meet with several hundred families who were leaving their native land to become citizens of our land.

There is no more difficult decision men can make than to leave their homeland and their family ties to begin life anew in another land. In this office I think always of the more than 40 million men and women who since 1820 have made that choice. A President has no greater duty than to use every strength and talent to keep America as a land to which many will want to come—and none will want to leave.

We must have laws regarding immigration. Personally, I believe our laws should not say that the relatives of any Americans are not welcome to become Americans themselves. We are committed to eliminating discrimination in our society. I believe we should also eliminate discrimination in the laws relating to those who would join our society from abroad.

The strength of our Nation has been built

from many groups from many lands.

No group has contributed more—few have contributed so much—as the sons and daughters of Italy.

History sometimes turns on small things. I often think back to the anxious years immediately after World War II—the year of the Italian elections. The whole history of the postwar world—and the struggle between communism and freedom—might have been different if we had not learned to love and trust the Italian people as friends and neighbors in America.

On the cornerstone of that friendship, trust and closeness, America's policy of strength against Communist aggression and subversion was built. Today we rejoice in the freedom, the success, and the high promise of modern Italy.

I am very proud today that Americans who bear fine Italian names play such an important role in our national life and this administration. A good many "firsts" have been established these last 4 years. There is Secretary Celebrezze in the Cabinet. Senator Pastore was keynoter of the Democratic National Convention. Here in the White House, always at my side, is Jack Valenti.

I have learned one thing from my association with them and others. My Italian friends are very persuasive.

You have been very persuasive this afternoon. As far as I am concerned, I believe we should have another first—a stamp commemorating this first great project named after an Italian.

If I have any influence with the Post Office Department, and I think that I may, we will issue the stamp.

NOTE: The President spoke at 12:32 p.m. in the Cabinet Room at the White House to a group of Congressmen and prominent Italian-Americans who had asked him to recommend the issuance of a stamp to commemorate the dedication on November 21 of the Verrazano-Narrows Bridge linking Staten Island and Brooklyn, N.Y. In the course of his remarks the President referred to Anthony J. Celebrezze, Secretary of Health, Education, and Welfare, John O. Pastore, Senator from Rhode Island, and Jack Valenti, Special Consultant to the President.

The stamp was first issued in Staten Island, N.Y., in conjunction with the opening of the bridge.

As printed, this item follows the prepared text released by the White House.

582 Remarks to Members of the NATO Parliamentarians Conference. *September 18, 1964*

IT IS a great pleasure to welcome to the White House this morning the NATO parliamentarians.

They are concerned with a project that is of vital importance to all of the free world in the Atlantic Alliance, and I am pleased that I was able to spend a few moments with them in the Fish Room.

I know, from what Congressman Wayne Hays of Ohio has told me, how much the parliamentarians have done to plan to ensure that this great instrument of the defense of freedom will flourish and continue to keep the peace.

The parliamentarians not only understand the problems of the alliance but they have the capacity and the ability to translate constructive ideas into effective and practical policies. The alliance owes a great deal to the vigorous and constructive leadership that these parliamentarians have provided.

We are proud of NATO's accomplishments. It has been tested many times, and each test has brought new confidence, new strength, and new stature for this great organization.

I participated in its formation, and I have contributed all I could to its support and maintenance.

NATO has done more than provide an effective system of defense. In President Truman's words, it has permitted us ". . . to get on with the real business of government and society, the business of achieving a fuller and happier life for all of our citizens."

I think it would be very dangerous for us to take this alliance for granted. Danger is less apparent now but it certainly has not disappeared. The building of an effective defense system is and must be a continuing task for all of our countries.

There remains a great challenge, of course, to move on to the closest partnership. This requires understanding and cooperation. There will be differences between us at times on tactics and procedures. But over those differences, all of which are a part of the democratic alliance, we really have built a fundamental unity.

We are all determined to preserve our freedom. We are all committed to give further substance and purpose to the alliance. And here the parliamentarians play a very

important role. Their legislative experience and their political role give us a special opportunity to insure that the goals of the alliance are achieved.

The United States has made certain commitments both real and substantial, and we will meet them all. Let no one, ally or adversary, ever doubt America's determination to fulfill its role in the alliance, to live up to its obligations.

We are grateful for your contributions. Your studies and your actions, your recommendations and, most of all, your firm commitment to the purposes of NATO are invaluable as we seek to build a deepening partnership of free nations within the alliance.

I am delighted that you could come here and exchange viewpoints with us. You have my best wishes for your every success.

NOTE: The President spoke at 1:25 p.m. in the West Lobby of the White House. Early in his remarks he referred to Representative Wayne L. Hays of Ohio, United States member and a vice president of the NATO Parliamentarians Conference.

Members of the Conference, an organization consisting of one member from each of the 15 NATO countries, were in the United States to visit various military installations.

583 Remarks to the President's Advisory Council on Federal Reports. *September 18, 1964*

I AM very happy and glad to have the opportunity this morning to meet in the Cabinet Room with the members of the President's Advisory Council on Federal Reports.

We have been talking about the elimination of unnecessary reports to the agencies of the Federal Government.

The question is not whether we should do away with these reports. The question is whether we are getting the right reports from the right sources or whether we are

burdening the American businessman by asking him for reports that we could do without.

There are two ways, we think, to deal with this problem.

The first and the best is to question the need for every new report. Once we cross that bridge and launch a new report, there is not much we can do about it.

Working with the Bureau of the Budget, these men have been able to point out the effects on business and the cost of business that these report requirements make.

We have suggested better and simpler ways of getting the information, and these men have given us very important advice at the right time before it is too late. We are trying to search out and eliminate all reports that the Government requires that may have outlived their usefulness.

Last March I put out a memorandum to every agency of the Government to launch a four-point drive:

First, to simplify all Government reports.

Second, to abolish as many reports as possible.

Third, to save time for the individual businessman as well as the industry he represents.

Fourth, to make better use of the efforts of Government employees.

Through last July 31, we eliminated or simplified 536 reports. This reduced the annual number of responses by almost 3 million. A total of 260 forms involving 2 million responses were completely eliminated and 276 forms eliminating an additional million responses were simplified.

In the same period 146 new reports were started.

So, in the net, we managed to discontinue or simplify 390 reports, and they represented a total net reduction of about 2½ million annual responses.

I think that is a good record, but it is not good enough.

These men have made a tremendous contribution, and I have called upon them not only to give me additional advice on how we can encourage business instead of harassing it, how we can eliminate reports and simplify them, but to give me any other constructive suggestions that would improve the relationship of private enterprise and the United States Government which the enterprise system supports.

We have had a very constructive meeting. I plan to meet with them in the future. And next week I will discuss this matter with the Cabinet as well as the managers of the independent agencies of the Government.

We have made progress but we have much more progress in the offing.

Thank you very much.

NOTE: The President spoke at 1:35 p.m. in the Cabinet Room at the White House.

In the course of his remarks the President referred to his memorandum of March 10, 1964, "Simplification or Elimination of Reports to the Government" (see Bureau of the Budget Bulletin 64–11).

584   Statement by the President on the Death of
Professor J. Frank Dobie. *September* 19, 1964

OUR NATION has lost one of our most gifted, colorful, and constructive citizens with the passing of J. Frank Dobie. His life work of re-creating our rich regional heritage of the conquistadores and cowboys restored for future generations a treasure that might otherwise have been lost.

Mrs. Johnson and I cherished for many years the candor and compassion of Professor Dobie. All of us can be grateful that only 5 days before he died Professor Dobie received the Medal of Freedom, our Nation's highest civil award, in recognition of the contribution he made as a writer and teacher to the enrichment of our American heritage.

NOTE: For Dr. Dobie's citation at the Presidential Medal of Freedom ceremonies, see Item 568.

585 Message to Prime Minister Olivier on the Occasion of the Independence of Malta. *September* 20, 1964

[Released September 20, 1964. Dated September 18, 1964]

Dear Mr. Prime Minister:

Congratulations and best wishes on the occasion of Malta's independence.

The establishment of Malta as an independent state is a tribute to you, the British Government, and the people of Malta. The United States has been deeply impressed by the leadership and courage you have provided in your country's efforts to achieve its independence and secure its freedom.

Malta is well known to us. We have welcomed thousands of Maltese to our shores. Our mariners have been warmly received by your islands since the days of our own independence. In the field of science, the discovery of the undulant fever germ by Sir Themistocles Zammit epitomizes the development of Malta's many skills. Malta's unflinching steadfastness during World War II symbolized the strength of the Maltese throughout an epic history. We in the United States look forward to seeing the friendly ties already established between us grow stronger in the years ahead.

I am happy to have Mr. Richard W. Reuter, the Director of the Food for Peace Program, as my representative and Special Ambassador at the independence ceremonies. He is a distinguished United States public servant who has worked closely with me, and he has a particular sympathy for the great principles of freedom for which you stand. Also representing me will be Mr. Joseph Calleja, the Director of the Maltese Information Center in Detroit, Michigan.

I am confident that Malta's role as an independent member of the community of nations will be bright and constructive. We look forward to working together with you and your government and your people in the great causes of our time—the promotion of peace, freedom, and democracy.

Sincerely,

LYNDON B. JOHNSON

[The Right Honorable Dr. Giorgio Borg Olivier, Prime Minister, Valletta, Malta]

586 Remarks at the Dedication of the Morgantown, W. Va., Airport. *September* 20, 1964

Senator Randolph, Senator Byrd, Governor Barron, my old friend Hulett Smith, Mayor Buehler, my able Administrator, Mr. Halaby, distinguished Members of Congress, Mr. Hechler, Mr. Staggers, my longtime friends and distinguished guests on the platform:

It is a great pleasure to be here with you on this delightful Sunday afternoon. This airport represents the triumph of a dream and a test of the power of unity.

For three decades you have worked to make this modern airport come true. Your faith and energy have surmounted every difficulty. The people of Morgantown can look forward to a brighter and a more hopeful life because of this work that you have done.

This airport was not the work of any single group. It was built by the cooperation of civic groups and local officials, of city, State, and Nation.

It is proof that if we work with each other, instead of fight each other, there is no limit to what we can accomplish. And what is true for Morgantown is true for America.

I want to commend the people of West Virginia for the high quality of public servants that they have selected. I know of no Members of the Senate with whom I have ever served that have been more diligent or more devoted than your able Senators, Jennings Randolph and Bob Byrd. I deeply appreciate the assistance they have given me every time I have called upon them to be of help.

I am grateful for the fine work that your Congressman Hechler and Congressman Staggers and other Members of the West Virginia delegation have given me, and the cooperation they have extended during the time I have been President.

In the years to come, by working together, group with group, section with section, we will defeat the forces of division and we will keep our country moving ahead.

The hills and valleys of this State still echo to the memory of a great American, and a great friend of West Virginia, John Fitzgerald Kennedy.

He often talked to me about this State. He often talked to me about these people. He spoke of your problems, the strength of your people, the courage with which you faced hardship; always the warmth of your hospitality.

He wanted so much to help West Virginia. Not because you helped him, but because he believed the progress of West Virginia was a test of the greatness of all of America.

So I come here this afternoon to tell you that I share his belief, and I will carry on with his work.

West Virginia is making progress.

Unemployment has declined 43 percent.

New food stamp programs are giving strength to the hungry.

Training programs, area redevelopment programs, the Appalachian program, the poverty program, will all give people the skills to find new jobs. They will develop industry to provide those jobs.

West Virginia has known more than its share of poverty and idleness and hunger. But let no one say this was because your people were lazy, or indifferent, or without initiative.

West Virginians opened our earliest frontiers. West Virginians brought forth the resources which made America grow. West Virginians went forth by the tens of thousands to fight for their country. And thousands of West Virginian boys, your boys, now lay beneath foreign soil, a monument to the courage and the patriotism of the people of West Virginia. You have provided heroes in war and you have provided builders in peace.

West Virginia has given much to the land we love, the land of America. America must never forget it, and it will not forget it as long as I am President.

I have traveled through your State and I have talked to your people. I have found strong men and women, willing to help at all times. I have found men who want nothing more than a chance to use their minds and their hands to provide for their families, and to build for their country.

We are going to give them that chance. We are going to do it because it is right; we are going to do it because it is our duty; we are going to do it because America needs a strong and a growing and a prosperous West Virginia.

The problems of West Virginia, your problems, are a consequence of national progress. Industry has moved to new markets. Machines have replaced men. New resources have taken the place of old. These changes were inevitable. They have been part of the growth of a mighty nation. Now the Nation must help those who have been left behind.

From the beginning of our history Government has helped provide opportunity to the people. The canals and the public works of the years before the Civil War were built by Government and private enterprise together. The lands of the West were thrown open to the settlers by the Government. Under Abraham Lincoln the Federal Government stimulated education through the land grant colleges. All of these actions provided new jobs and new chances for business, and new stimulation to growth.

This partnership and this responsibility is the oldest American tradition. It is one that we recognize, and I pledge you it is one that we plan to continue.

Giving a man a chance to work and feed his family and provide for his children does not destroy his initiative. Hunger destroys initiative. Hopelessness destroys initiative. Ignorance destroys initiative. A cold and an indifferent government destroys initiative.

We are going to strike away the conditions which damage a man's dignity and self respect, and capacity for fulfillment. We are going to give every man the chance to build his own place in this abundant land of ours. And by doing this we are going to strengthen the initiative of the individual, strengthen the freedom of the Nation, and bring prosperity to all of our people.

There are some among us who need more skills and a chance to work. There are the hungry still to be fed and the sick to be tended, and the old to be given dignity in the twilight of life. This, too, is part of America's responsibility. God has commanded us, "They shall not harden their hearts to the needy."

The day America hardens its heart, the day the fortunate turn away from the helpless, the day compassion turns to indifference, on that day we will begin to decline from greatness. So let us pray that that day never comes.

Franklin Roosevelt once said, "Too many who prate about saving democracy are really only interested in saving things as they were. Democracy should concern itself also with things as they ought to be."

This ought to be a land, a nation, a country with compassion for the helpless. This ought to be an opportunity for all who seek a better life.

Yes, this is the concern of our democracy. And that is the road that we are going to take as long as I am the leader of this country.

Thank you.

NOTE: The President spoke in the midafternoon. In his opening words he referred to Jennings Randolph and Robert C. Byrd, Senators from West Virginia, William W. Barron, Governor of West Virginia, Hulett C. Smith, Democratic candidate for Governor of West Virginia, Arthur W. Buehler, mayor of Morgantown, W. Va., N. E. Halaby, Administrator, Federal Aviation Agency, and Ken Hechler and Harley O. Staggers, Representatives from West Virginia.

587 The President's News Conference of September 21, 1964

THE PRESIDENT. [1.] I have just put together three appointments for the Comsat Board—Communications Satellite. It is a 12-man board, and 3 appointments by the President. I have appointed Mr. Frederic Donner, who is chairman of the Board of General Motors, and has been since 1958. I delayed you a little bit because I had to have his acceptance. I just received it. I have Mr. George Meany, the president of the AFL–CIO. I will have Mr. Clark Kerr, president of the University of California. Those are the three Presidential appointees.

Q. How is that name spelled?

THE PRESIDENT. D-o-n-n-e-r. This has required a good deal of study and discussion, and I feel very pleased that these men have indicated their willingness to make a sacrifice to lend their peculiar and unusual talents to the direction of this great adventure between Government and free enterprise. Needless to say, all of them have a good many duties at the present time, but because I pointed out the need for their experience and their broad knowledge, they accepted membership.

[2.] That is about all I have to tell you. I will go over some travel plans that I have as nearly as I can make them. I hope you will be understanding with me in case I have to adjust them or modify them in some ways. Sometimes we have to make adjustments from time to time.

On Friday morning I will be in El Paso to meet with President López Mateos.

We will then go to Oklahoma to dedicate the dam 30 miles south of Muskogee. That is a long-standing commitment I made to dedicate this dam, the Eufaula Dam.

I will then go on to Oklahoma City to speak at the Oklahoma State Fair. I had agreed with Congressman Albert, the Majority Leader, and with Mr. Monroney, head of the fair association, some time ago, to be there.

On Monday, September 28th, I hope to visit the New England States. I hold an honorary degree from Brown University, and I have had a very warm feeling for

that institution, and particularly for President Keeney, which I formed through Senator Green, who is a member of the board of trustees there. I hope to be able to call on them. They asked me last spring to come see Senator Green and speak at the university. I agreed to it if the good Lord was willing and the creeks didn't rise. So I am going to be there on the morning of September 28th at the university's bicentennial convocation. It is a long-standing engagement, but unless something intervenes, you can plan to be there with me.

I would like to go on to Hartford, Conn., at noon, and to make stops in Maine, New Hampshire, and Vermont before returning to Washington.

Q. The same day?

THE PRESIDENT. Yes. On Tuesday, September 29th, I will be visiting Mr. Brosio, the Secretary General of NATO. The visit will start here, and where it will end up we are still planning, but it will probably be at one of our interesting installations that command his interest. It will be something that he would like to see. It could be a naval installation, a missile installation, or something else.

On Thursday, October 1st, Dr. Milton Eisenhower, president of Johns Hopkins University, has invited me to speak to the student body and the faculty of that school, and I have accepted.

On Monday and Tuesday, October 5th and 6th, just before you ladies take off on that train with Lady Bird, we will have President Macapagal of the Philippines here for a state visit that has been planned for many months now. I believe that is the time that Lady Bird leaves on her trip.

On Wednesday, it is likely that I will be in the Midwest to make a political speech. I will give you more details as soon as we finish out some of the arrangements that are being made now by the security people and by the advance people.

Q. Of this week?

THE PRESIDENT. No, October 7th.

On Thursday, the 8th, I will be in Cleveland, Ohio, for a Democratic dinner, and there make a Democratic campaign speech.

I have some other plans, but they are tentative and they involve other foreign visitors, and I don't think I had better announce them here until we coordinate with their announcements, so we will not create problems for them, but I will give you them a little later.

[3.] I will answer any questions you have that are important, and then I am going to walk around at least once or twice, around the back here. I am going to take a short walk and a longer swim, but I have some appointments around 12:30. I will be glad to answer any questions you have here. I gave you this before we started the walk because somebody told me Muriel [1] has not permanently fixed the heel on her shoe, and I didn't want her to take notes on the trot.

[4.] Q. Speaking of your travel, do you envision anything beyond the campaign, specifically, trips abroad? Tokyo hears you might go there, and Latin America hears you might go there. Have you thought anything about such trips at all abroad?

[*The question was answered on a "background basis."*]

[5.] Q. Mr. President, sir, do you have any further information on what may have happened in the Gulf of Tonkin and, if so, what do you think were the motives of whatever these ships were that approached the destroyers?

THE PRESIDENT. This is for background.

_____
[1] Muriel Dobbin of the Baltimore Sun.

No, I will let it stand for the record.

I have no further information on the incident other than that given you, other than the information you received Saturday on a background basis. I am unable to speak with any authority on the motives of the persons you referred to.

On Friday morning at around 9 o'clock, which was around 9 o'clock in the evening in the Tonkin Gulf, we received a flash information that has been described to you, namely, that ships were approaching our destroyers. The ships were unidentified; that a warning shot was being fired; and that they would, pursuant to orders, fire additional shots in order to protect and defend themselves.

So I received that information from Secretary McNamara. I asked to be informed immediately upon receipt of any other information. I conferred with the National Security Adviser and asked him to meet with the appropriate officials of State and Defense and keep me informed from time to time.

It was night out there, and it was day here, Friday. I was later informed that the ships or the unidentified vessels continued to approach our two destroyers and they opened fire. The ships disappeared. They would keep us informed. Planes had been launched and were in the air to protect the destroyers and to conduct a search, and to contribute anything they could contribute during the darkness of the night.

As we went into Friday night, which was morning out there, during Friday night the members of our fleet and our planes spent the daylight hours out there, the night hours here, attempting to conduct adequate reconnaissance, locate any hostile vessels that might be in the area.

Saturday morning, which was the end of the day out there, they notified us of their reports through the Commander in Chief of the Pacific, and CINCPAC, both of whom evaluated their reports, which were brought to me here in the Cabinet Room. I spent 2 hours reviewing them with the Secretary of Defense, the Chairman of the Joint Chiefs of Staff, the Secretary of State, and my security people.

At that time I directed Mr. McNamara and the Chairman of the Joint Chiefs to issue an operational statement giving you all the facts that we had been able to confirm from the first daylight hours surveillance we could make, and the first reports we could finalize on that reconnaissance, and to give you specific times and locations and area and types of ships, and all of the details that they could from an operational standpoint, because it has been the custom of the President in my relationship to you to have operational things decided by operational people relayed to you because they have a knowledge of it, and they have a duty and obligation to maintain a relationship with the people in the field.

At the same time I informed them that I would be giving a full background to the people who covered the White House. As soon as they left here, I proceeded to call for you and you were in here shortly thereafter.

[*The remainder of the President's answer was on a "background basis."*]

[6.] Q. Mr. President, the President of Mexico, López Mateos, has already announced detailed plans for the development of the Chamizal Zone on the Mexican side, and the El Paso Times would like to know what you are going to announce for the American side.

THE PRESIDENT. We will see, and I will be in touch with you.

[7.] Q. There is a strike deadline of 6 a.m. tomorrow set by various rail unions.

Do you have any plans to ask for a postponement in that strike deadline?

THE PRESIDENT. I have nothing I would like to say at this point in connection with those negotiations.

[8.] Q. Mr. President, has there been any information at all that would suggest whether these boats in the Tonkin Gulf were torpedo boats like they were before, or larger ones?

THE PRESIDENT. I think you will have to stay with the announcement that Mr. McNamara gave that came from CINCPAC because I think it reflects exactly what happened and is about all of the sure information they have. They saw unidentified vessels on their radar and I don't think I can go beyond that. It is not because I don't want to, but I don't have any additional information.

[9.] Q. On the west coast trip, everyone feels you were way ahead in stating your visit, but they felt this was overconfidence and this was something you were going to have to overcome by shaking up the Democratic organization. Have you talked over that problem of overconfidence yet?

THE PRESIDENT. First, I don't think it exists. I think we all recognize that a very important decision is going to be made in November. I think every patriotic American will want to participate in that decision wherever he is.

My wife is certainly not overconfident, because she is exploring where she is going to vote in absentia. Before a very important election her car was turned over and a reporter asked her, "What was your first thought when you came to?" and she said, "I wished I had voted absentee."

So we don't believe in overconfidence. We think that the people want to hear from us, they want to get our viewpoints on public questions, they want to know how we stand on issues, so we are going to be visiting all over this country. I expect, myself, I will be in many, many States.

I don't have any accurate poll on them, but to just pick a figure out of the air, I would think now, since I have been President, the 10 months and maybe 11 months by election time, that I will be in States that involve a population of 125 million and probably more than 30 States. I know that Luci told me that she was finishing 10 that she had been in. Lynda Bird has been in 8 or 10, and Mrs. Johnson is going to be in some 20-odd.

Luci moved her father's presidential campaign into Indiana yesterday and brought 3,000 Hoosiers screaming to their feet with a plea, "Help me ring the bell for freedom." So I hope she is not criticized now for leaving out the word "freedom" there. At least Luci does her own speeches and she won't take any recommendations from anyone. I found that out the other evening when I tried to make a suggestion to her.

We will all be giving our viewpoints, the family, in places where we can. I will join Mrs. Johnson's train, I hope, someplace for an appearance, and both girls will be with her in and out where the school duties permit, and I will be in as many States as my Presidential duties permit. I would like nothing better, if I could do it, to be in all States. I hope to be in them all while I am President, and I hope I don't have to pick up several between November and January.

We think it is good that people in most of the States indicate their approval of the job that we are doing. We want them to continue to indicate their approval right through November and right through the next 4 years. In order to do that, we are going to look them in the eye like we look you in the eye, and we are going to talk to them and answer their questions and try to be available.

I am glad we came in from Utah the other morning. I got to bed at 5 and I was talking about the Tonkin Gulf the next morning. I was glad it was 9 that morning and not the morning before, because I would have been in Portland, Oreg., then. I could have done everything I did there, but I was just glad from the public standpoint that I was here. So I will be in and out of this office, and this will have first priority. I will be President first, but we will be out campaigning when the opportunity permits, to the extent it permits.

At the same time, we will have to dedicate airports and we will have a dam here and there, and we have visitors from here and there, and we will have interviews and press conferences and we will have all of these other things that are part of the Presidency.

Q. Mr. President, you specifically said that a couple of these appearances are going to be political. Does that rule out politics on the others?

THE PRESIDENT. I am going to make a Democratic fundraising appearance in Cleveland. As I recall, that is the only fundraising I make. I will make Democratic appearances in New England on behalf of the Democratic Party. I don't consider when I meet with you that I am making a Democratic appearance. I consider that I am doing my job as President, and that extends to a lot of places.

I might go to the Hill next week sometime to have a lunch with somebody, and you might consider that. I notice some of you considered the California appearance a political appearance. I don't care what you consider it. You have free speech. I don't want to guide the news. I don't want to try to lead the news. You just consider what you want them to. We had members of the Judiciary, Republican Members of the Senate, Republican Party of California, the Chief Justice of the Supreme Court, and folks of that kind. We were in a defense-interested State. I am sure there were a good many Republicans in the audience. I would think that with a good many people like that, there were some Republicans. In fact, I saw two or three folks that just looked like they were Republicans.

When I go to meetings like that, I try, as I do in my hometown when I invite people to come in, I don't try to be offensive with them. All of you thought my speech in Detroit was a red-hot political speech. I thought I was going out at the invitation of the labor union in Detroit on Labor Day to make a Labor Day speech.

I was very pleased that I had not been partisan in the speech and had not been denouncing any Republicans in the speech when I saw the distinguished Republican Governor had come there to welcome me. I would have felt a little bad to invite him into my home and denounce the Republicans. I would have felt bad to have him invite me on the platform there and then start denouncing him. You can rate or classify that any way you want to.

I know my speech in Cleveland will be about the Democratic Party and will be charged for it, and I know some of my speeches in New England will be at the invitation of Democratic people up there, and so forth. I don't consider reviewing a hurricane as a political thing. It could hurt or help you.

The President has to do that just as I am doing like I am doing now. I will be doing

things like that every day. I don't think you can cut off all announcements and not issue any information and not tell what is happening. You will be seeing from day to day developments in Government between now and November. I am President, and if I tell you about them you will say they are political announcements, and if I don't tell you, you will say we are guiding the press.

Q. Are you going to Atlantic City tomorrow?

THE PRESIDENT. Yes.

Q. Where are you going to be on Election Day?

THE PRESIDENT. I don't know. We have not planned that far ahead.

I am going to make a speech to the Steelworkers.[2] I did last year, and the year before in Miami. I agreed to do this sometime ago, and I will go up and come right back.

Q. Mr. President, the Steelworkers are probably concerned about labor-management. Can you characterize the Chrysler-Ford contract for us?

THE PRESIDENT. No, I don't think I would. I will give some thought this evening to what I say to the Steelworkers and I will try to work out something to them that will be satisfactory.

Q. Might your trip to El Paso include a trip to Los Angeles?

THE PRESIDENT. I don't think so.

Douglas Cornell, Associated Press: Thank you, Mr. President.

NOTE: President Johnson's thirty-first news conference was held in his office at the White House at 12:31 p.m. on Monday, September 21, 1964.

[2] See Item 589.

588 Remarks to a Group of Representatives of Fraternal Organizations. *September* 21, 1964

THIS house is your house, this house is the house of all the people of this land. This office I hold is your office, it is the office of all the people of this country.

In this spirit, I asked you to come here today and I am proud to welcome each and every one of you.

I do not know your politics. I do not care about your partisanship. I do know, and I do care, and I do need your leadership.

If we are to remain a great nation, we must be led by great people. That means leadership at every level, in every section of this great country, in every segment of our great society.

America is not, America must never be, led by one man alone. Leadership is a first duty for all 190 million Americans—whether private citizen or public servant.

Today we are all challenged to stand up and be counted. In our cities and communities, as well as in our country, we are summoned to stand up and be counted as leaders for American unity, and for American understanding. America's progress you have heard reviewed. That progress must be continued.

We are prosperous today—more prosperous than any people have ever been at any time.

We are prepared today—better prepared than ever before in all of our history.

In the last 4 years the American people, through the American Congress made up of both parties, have appropriated from $40 to $50 billion more for defense and space alone than would have been appropriated if we had appropriated for each one of those 4 years the same amount we did in 1960. So we increased the yearly expenditure. For defense and space alone we upped it by $10 billion. Today we have the best preparation that we have ever had and it is a result of the very heavy expenditures that our taxpayers have permitted through their Congress.

We are at peace today—and we are more determined to preserve peace than ever before in our life.

Now I do not need to tell you, but you know, and I know, that we live in a world of peril.

Our success, the strength and unity of our society, are the targets of every tyrant in the world.

If tyrants are to work their will upon the world, the first thing they must do is to spoil America's success; the next thing they must do is to subvert America's strength; and, above all, they must divide us before they conquer us.

That is our challenge. That is yours and mine.

That is why, since I assumed the office of President, I have not indulged in any name calling. And no single statement of mine has been calculated to array class against class or race against race or the rich against the poor or color against color or religion against religion because we need all the strength and all the power that all the diversity of our people will permit.

The great strength of our Nation is that we have been a melting pot. And we have drawn upon the best from many lands and we have brought them here and demonstrated that these men can and do work shoulder to shoulder, side by side for a strong, freedom-loving country.

Abraham Lincoln once said: "If destruction be our lot, we must ourselves be its author and finisher. As a nation of free men, we must live through all time or die by suicide."

I am determined that America shall stand, I am determined that America shall live, through all time.

That is why I have called you here today to ask your help in the work of preserving American unity.

Wherever you live, whatever your station in life, there is much work to do. We must answer the voices of hate with works of love. We must meet the shrill cries of faction with the steady and sober voice of reason.

We must make it clear, to all abroad and to all at home, that America will never permit itself to be divided. Creed will not be set against creed; color will not be set against color; origin will not be set against origin; native born will not be set against foreign born; section will not be set against section.

I know this is the kind of America that our forefathers intended. I know that it is the kind of America that you want, and I believe that it is the kind of America that the members of your organizations want.

This is the spirit that motivates the work of your organizations.

You have ministered to the needy in times of need. You have provided scholarships and educational opportunity for those that are hungering to learn. You have given hospital and medical services to the sick and to the aged. You have brought pleasure and happiness to many Americans who have not always had access to the fullest measure of the blessings of men.

On this principle the great organizations that you represent have grown and prospered in America. Since the first of your organizations were begun a century ago you have now grown to more than two hundred in number that make up the invitation list here today.

Today you insure the lives of more than 10 million people—1 out of every 19 in this country—for almost $12 billion. You invest the assets of more than $3 billion in the economy of this country.

You make America stronger because you care about the lot and the life of the people who live here.

That is the real spirit of our land, and that is the kind of a spirit that we must never lose.

Compassion never corrupts a nation. Compassion has always been, and must always be, a vital part of the strength of America.

We must care about the rights of our fellow man as much as we care about the rights of our own. For none of us is free unless all of us are free; none is strong unless all are strong; none of us can live in dignity unless all of us live in decency.

Our Nation's motto—*E Pluribus Unum*—means "From Many, One." It is in this spirit—this constant striving to build one nation and one people from many nationalities—that has made our land what it is as we leave here this afternoon.

Woodrow Wilson once said: "I hope we shall never forget that we created this nation, not to serve ourselves, but to serve mankind."

And that is what I hope you will take home from this meeting today: that this Nation was not born just to serve ourselves; it was born to serve all mankind.

So today I call upon you to answer your Nation's challenge, to answer it by being leaders for a united America, united and indivisible under God. For he whom the gods would destroy, they first make mad.

And, we might add, they next divide.

It's been wonderful to have you here this afternoon. I hope that you can come into the next room, that I can meet each one of you individually. I would be very happy to have any suggestions that you would care to communicate to me any time.

I believe that you feel as I do that we have a wonderful country, that we cannot just take things for granted and sit in a rocking chair and let the rest of the world go by. We have much to preserve, much to protect—and eternal vigilance is necessary.

NOTE: The President spoke in the late afternoon in the East Room at the White House. Before speaking he introduced Averell Harriman, Under Secretary of State, Douglas Dillon, Secretary of the Treasury, and Kermit Gordon, Director, Bureau of the Budget, each of whom spoke briefly on a phase of Government work in their individual agencies. The President also introduced Luther H. Hodges, Secretary of Commerce, John A. Gronouski, Postmaster General, Anthony J. Celebrezze, Secretary of Health, Education, and Welfare, Raymond F. Farrell, Commissioner of Immigration and Naturalization, LeRoy Collins, Director, Community Relations Service, Department of Commerce, G. Mennen Williams, Assistant Secretary of State for African Affairs, and Michel Cieplinski, Deputy Assistant Secretary of State for Administrative Affairs.

589   Remarks in Atlantic City at the Convention of the United Steelworkers of America.   *September 22, 1964*

President McDonald, delegates of the United Steelworkers:

I had so much fun here the last time that I thought I would come back to Atlantic City.

Were you pleased with the results of the last Atlantic City convention? Well, that is wonderful. I was a little worried at first whether they made the right choice—for Miss America.

I am not here today as a partisan. I am not going to make a political appeal. I think that you should support any candidate of any party who favors strong and progressive labor unions.

In 1937 you won your first contract with United States Steel. And I entered the United States Congress that same year. We have come a long way together since that day, and we are going to keep moving forward together for many years to come.

I remember in 1938 voting for a 25-cent an hour minimum wage bill. They said that would wreck my political career. They said that act would wreck organized labor. But here we are.

There were also those who said that act would doom free enterprise and would destroy American freedom. And they made those same worn out, discredited arguments against every piece of progressive legislation from social security to the war against poverty. They are the same old arguments made in the same old way and written, I suspect, by the same old man. And they are just as wrong in 1964 as they were in 1938.

Neither you nor I, nor the American people have heeded those voices of doom and despair.

The gains of the past 30 years have not been easy gifts. We fought for them through a long and a bitter depression. We maintained them through a hard and a bloody war. We advanced them through an uneasy and a perilous peace. And we are going to keep and strengthen them through the years of challenge and promise which lie ahead.

We will never return to economic stagnation and national drift. We will not return to declining employment at home and declining prestige abroad. We will not neglect our duty toward the helpless or the demands of our oppressed.

We will keep moving toward a nation where every man can find work and a fair reward for his labor, where the old can live in decency and the poor can reach for dignity, where no man suffers from fear or hatred and where every man can seek fulfillment and hope.

That has been the 30-year-old goal of this progressive union. That is the goal of all American labor. That is the goal of most Americans of every section and every interest. And that is the goal toward which I hope to lead all America.

In this pursuit, America needs the vision and the vitality of responsible unions. Under the presidency of Dave McDonald, this union has charted a path of progress and has brought strength to all the American people. Every member of this union, from east or west or north or south, can be proud, as I am proud, of the role that each of you have played.

Your Human Relations Committee has established a fruitful pattern of day in and day out relations between the employer and the union. You have moved steel toward an era of creative, constructive bargaining, recognizing that labor and management have a common stake in each other's welfare, and in the health of the entire economy. You have shown the way to absorb enormous change with enlarged production, and without infringing the interests of your workers.

You have done this because your test is not just what is good for workers or, for that matter, not just what is good for labor. Your test is today, and has been through the years: if this is good for my country, if this is good for America, this is good for me.

And you have been wise enough to know that what is good for America is also good for the American labor movement.

There will still be differences and difficulties. But we approach the future bound together in a common awareness that there is much more to be gained through cooperation than conflict, much more to be gained through greater rewards in harmony than in hostility, a brighter future for all of us in unity instead of unrest.

Recent years have given us proof of this belief. We are today in the 43d month of the longest, strongest unbroken peacetime expansion in American history. This year, for the first time, we have broken the barrier of 70 million jobs, and right now we are creating additional new jobs at the rate of 100,000 every month. Average manufacturing earnings have risen nearly 16 percent, and weekly earnings in the primary metals industry have jumped 23 percent.

The fact is that wages are higher, employment is higher, profits are higher, and the economy is stronger than at any time in American history.

And this is a proud record. But it is characteristic of the American labor movement that we must never be satisfied with past achievement. And I am not satisfied, either. If there are any who think we have hit our peak, that we can just stand pat, or keep cool, or sit back in our rocking chair and enjoy the status quo, that we have finally reached the promised land, they better get out of our way, because I tell you they will be run over by a marching America.

We have a threefold task.

First, we must extend our prosperity to all Americans. Your government is completely committed to full employment and the eradication of poverty in the United States.

Second, we must avoid the pitfalls of recession. A recession today, like those of the 1950's, would mean a loss of $20 billion a year in production, a loss of 1½ million jobs, a 40 percent rise in unemployment. And America just cannot afford a recession like that.

Third, we must harness the forces of enlarging technology and expanding population in order to improve the life of all of our people. By 1970 our labor force will increase at twice the rate that it has in the past decade, the past 10 years. We will need over 70,000 new jobs each week. At the same time, technological change is eliminating unskilled jobs and making old skills obsolete.

That is the challenge of our future. If we master it, we can enter a new era of American greatness. If we run from it, it will overwhelm us. I have no doubt about the choice that America will make. And I have no doubt what the steelworkers will do about it.

Because if you can judge the future by the past, I am here to say to you in the Presidency and the Congress no union in America has gotten up earlier, stayed up later, done more to help this President and help all the people of this country than the United Steelworkers of America. And we have just begun to march.

How do we intend to ensure continued prosperity in the face of these powerful forces?

First, we will continue a fiscal policy which expands purchasing power to meet our power to produce. Our tax cut, which you helped us pass through the Congress, was a part of this policy. And in the months ahead we will not permit Federal revenues to become a drag on our economy. Next year we are going to cut excise taxes.

Second, in every area we will extend the hand of cooperation, not coercion. We will say to business, the employer, and to labor, the employee, "Your Government extends you the hand of encouragement, not the fist of harassment." We will ask both business and labor to join us under the tent that will keep prices in this country stable. That stability is the key to increased purchasing power at home. It is the key to an increased progress in the world market.

Third, we will encourage the expansion and the modernization of American industry through tax incentives and through increased research.

Fourth, we will work to provide our people with the skills and the knowledge that they need to find a place in a changing economy. We have come to understand, in the past few years, that economic growth alone will not solve all of our problems. Men and women without education and without training cannot be absorbed by advancing opportunity.

Fifth, we will extend the helping hand of a just nation to the poor and to the helpless and to the oppressed. We will do this through a program of medical care under social security for all older Americans. We will do this through strengthened unemployment compensation and minimum wages. We will do this through fair and just and equal opportunity for every American of every race, color, religion, and belief.

And we will do all these things because we love people instead of hate them; because we have faith in America, not fear of the future; because you are strong men of vision instead of frightened crybabies; because you know it takes a man who loves his country to build a house instead of a raving, ranting demagog who wants to tear down one.

Well, no one has anything to fear in our beloved land from increasing opportunity for all Americans. History proves and reason confirms, the more Americans who take a productive place in our society the greater the prosperity for all of us. The only real danger to any of us is the failure to use our skills and to use the labor of all.

We need not spend any time looking back. But if we did, we could see what kind of leadership produced the soup lines. And let me say this: If anyone thinks the American people are ever going back to the soup line, they don't know the modern America.

If anyone thinks that the American people are going to shape the future of freedom, the prospect of prosperity, the hope for peace for all of our children—if they think we are going to do that on the basis of fear and prejudice and bigotry, and hatred and division, then I say they just don't know the American people.

Sixth, we will move forward to meet the great public needs of our country, in our exploding cities, in our fading countryside, by beautifying our highways and cleaning out the old second car dumps that blight them; by improving our crowded classrooms, and building new schools with better teachers; and in every other area which has been the victim of neglect or indifference.

This is not an easy job. It will require the work and the sacrifices and the planning of government at every level. It will require the cooperation of labor and of business and of private groups and of private citizens.

But the American labor movement has never hesitated to work toward those goals, and today you are not alone. American business is with you. Most of the American people are with you and the President of the United States is with you.

With these as our policies, we can look to the future with confidence. We must now think not just of next month, not just of next year. But it is your job and it is my job, and it is your responsibility and it is

my responsibility to think and to plan and to work for the next generation.

Many of our children will be working when the year 2000 rolls around. It sounds so exciting I just wish I could buy a little slice of it myself, because by then there will be 330 million Americans living here. We should have more than 120 million jobs, and if we sustain our current progress, our gross national product should be more than $2.4 trillion. And here is something we would all like to have even before the year 2000: an average family income twice what it is today.

Well, that is the goal of your Government's present economic policies.

Our strides toward that future will come from the unity that was forged in the struggles of the past. A united country, a unified America, submerging petty difference in common purpose, will find no limit to its achievement.

We have the knowledge. We have the resources. We have the tools. All we need is the courage and the faith and the vision. And you know in your heart that I am telling you the truth.

There will be voices abroad in the land tomorrow as there were yesterday who constantly tell you that they won't or that they can't. But they did not build this land. And thank God they have not destroyed it. We ask for little, but we will produce much.

A great leader of this great Union many, many years ago inspired me with the simplicity and the eloquence and the depth of his compassion when he, Phil Murray, said "All the working men and women in America want is a rug on the floor, a picture on the wall, and music in the home."

We have the greatest government that human ingenuity ever fashioned. We have the highest standard of living that any people anywhere ever enjoyed. We are prepared to protect and to defend our country as we have never been prepared before.

We are going to seek peace in every capital with every person who will meet us halfway. We know the price of destructive war. We hate it. We love peace. We will always march, though, with our hand out but our guard up. We will never bully or threaten or intimidate or provoke. But we will always stand firm to protect and to preserve the principles of freedom for which our forefathers died.

We love our system of government. It has done too much for us, for us to ever turn our back upon it. But it is a cooperative system that I said earlier was based on encouragement of all segments instead of harassment of any.

If freedom in the world survives, it will be because of the quality of our system. If we permit numbers alone to determine whether freedom or communism prevails, the Communists have more people in the Soviet Union than we have free people in the United States. Their resources are many and are extensive.

But we are relying on our system because the capitalist who can invest his dollar and hope to get back a fair return without it being confiscated, the manager who gets up early and works late to plan that machinery and those men, and working together, hoping some day that he will get a bonus or a profit-sharing plan, the worker who has maximum wages and minimum hours, and other benefits, realizing he has the highest standard of living of any worker in the world—all three of those make up the American system of free enterprise. And don't tell me that they can't produce more,

faster, cheaper than any commissar anywhere can direct.

Yes, we have much to preserve, much to protect. We have a glorious future ahead for ourselves and for our children if we only recognize it, if we only put our shoulder to the wheel, if we only look forward to tomorrow instead of backward to yesterday.

Beware of those who fear and those who doubt, and those who rave and rant about the dangers of progress. Beware of those who say "Don't touch this," "Leave that alone," "Let's wipe this out," "Let's go back to working by yourself against your neighbor."

Embrace those who tell you to follow the Golden Rule, do unto others as you would have them do unto you, and to love thy neighbor as thyself.

So in this hour of our great triumph here, with all the future open to us, let us, in the words of the prophet Isaiah, say to our fellow man, whether it is our worker at the lathe, whether it is our employer in the shop, "Come now, let us understand how much we have to lose by dividing instead of uniting, how much we have to lose by hating instead of loving, how much we have to lose by not having faith in our country," and then ask the butcher, the baker, the candlestick maker to all come under our great family tent and let us reason together to produce the greatest, the richest, the finest, the freest land in all the world for all the people.

NOTE: The President spoke in midmorning at Convention Hall in Atlantic City. His opening words referred to David McDonald, president, United Steelworkers of America.

590   Remarks at the Annual Convention of the International Union of Electrical Workers. *September 23, 1964*

Mr. Carey, my fellow Americans:

I wanted to come here earlier this morning, but Jim Carey is rather conservative and he reminded me that the Bible says, "The sleep of the laboring man is sweet," especially during convention time, so I delayed my arrival because in my heart I knew he was right.

This is the season for new television shows, and I am greatly honored to appear on your six-city network, although I may get some mixed reviews. I am not particularly worried about the Textile Workers in New York, because with a wife and two daughters, I feel like I am helping to maintain full employment in the textile industry.

I am not worried about the Missouri Labor Council in Kansas City because on a lot of things I hear and read these days, I am from Missouri, too. I am not worried about the Tobacco Workers in Miami Beach, or the United Rubber Workers in Chicago, or my friends out there in St. Paul, all of whom I hope are there with us this morning.

I want to salute each of you and thank you for the privilege of visiting with you. Our host here in Washington makes light bulbs, and everybody knows what I do with those.

So I think I should just begin this morning by saying that I hope all of you got enough sleep last night, because from now on you and I, and really all Americans who want to live in a decent, responsible, peaceful land, have much work to do.

President Carey, President Burdon, President Baldanzi, President O'Hare, President Olson, President Rollings, to you and to all of your members all across the land I have come this morning to ask all of you to stand up and be counted. I ask you, I ask businessmen, I ask reasoning and responsible men and women everywhere to stand up and be counted for the character and the conscience of their country.

That is what is under challenge as we meet here. Men may speak of incidents that are far away. They may talk of this headline or that. They may offer slurs today and slanders tomorrow, and more than that in the days to come. But let there be no mistake: It is the heart of our American way of life that is under attack, and those who love it must go forth to save it.

Americans are not presented with a choice of parties. Americans are not presented with a choice of liberalism and conservatism.

Americans are faced with a concerted bid for power by factions which oppose all that both parties have supported. It is a choice between the center and the fringe, between the responsible mainstream of American experience and the reckless and rejected extremes of American life.

If the challenge is loud, the call of duty is clear.

We are called upon to stand up and be counted, for we have a duty, we have a clear and a compelling duty, to make it clear that America has not fallen and will not fall into the hands of extremists of any stripe.

A nation so strong and free as ours can tolerate the widest diversity of opinion and belief, and it actually can be made stronger by full and responsible discussion. But there come times when men must turn and stand against those factions and factions who would lead the people to believe that the road to individual freedom is, in reality, a road to collective serfdom.

This generation of Americans must not be deceived. The success of our system must not be mocked. The factions which bid for power over your lives and the lives of your children, and over the control of your government, bear many names, they wear many masks, they espouse many causes. But they are united today—as they have been united for 30 years—by the determination that your country shall not provide for the general welfare of its citizens.

They may talk of changing the world, but what they mean to change is America first.

Before Viet-Nam was a name, before the Congo was a map, before there was a NATO or a nuclear weapon these factions were working here at home—working against minimum wages, working against the 40-hour week, working against social security, working against labor's rights, working against the TVA and the REA, working against slum clearance and public works, working against the United Nations and the nuclear test ban, working against the Alliance for Progress, working against aid to our neighbors in the world.

Yes, that is where they stood three decades ago, and that is where they stand today. That is where the line is really drawn in America in this election year.

These factions despise the word "democracy," dislike the word "equality," and they distrust the word "peace." They would now reduce the word "compassion" to a whisper, and they would have us mention it only in apology.

Well, on this I refuse to turn and run.

So long as I am President, I intend to honor the mandate of the Constitution that I am sworn to uphold. I intend to see that this Government, as the servant of this great people, "provides for the general welfare."

Welfare is an old and honored work of our system. One of the first acts of the first Congress, under President Washington, was to provide pensions for invalid soldiers. Under John Adams what was to become the Public Health Service was established. President Abraham Lincoln proposed the first assistance for widows and children. President Theodore Roosevelt called the first White House Conference on Care of Dependent Children. It was President William Howard Taft who first established the Children's Bureau.

These were works of compassion, triumphs of justice. But there are factions today which condemn social justice as the work of those that were bent on centralizing power in Washington. They forget their history, and they betray their ignorance of the American people.

For in many works of compassion, States have led the way. In 1898 Utah enacted an 8-hour day. In 1908 Oregon limited the hours of work for women. In 1911 Illinois passed the first statute providing mothers aid, the forerunner of aid to families of dependent children. In 1914 the first old-age pension was established in a State where character has not been collectivized by compassion—the great State of Arizona.

From Plymouth Rock until this day, Americans have been careful about the welfare of their fellow man.

I intend that we shall not be turned from this trait of our American character, or this conviction of our American conscience. I believe that we must, as Teddy Roosevelt once put it, guard "against two besetting sins—hardness of heart and softness of heart."

This generation of Americans rejects the answer of a welfare state for our free society. We reject the regimentation and the stifling of incentive and the limiting of reward. We reject the idea of government decreeing who shall work and where they shall work, or where they and their families shall live.

Here in America we know there is for us a better way. We have fashioned in our years a good society. We shall, in the years to come, dedicate ourselves to making it great. The object of all we do is to give our people a fair start or a new start in the race of life, whatever lot they are born to, whatever fate may befall them.

I believe that I know the American people. I know that they do not intend, on this summit of our success, to forget or to ignore those who need our help to make the climb. We have work to do, not work to quit.

America must keep her trust with her senior citizens. We must let them provide for their hospital care and nursing home care through social security. We must concern ourselves with the level of their income. We must attack the problem of their housing, which is too often inadequate and too often takes more than half of their income.

But America must keep her trust with her children, because in 6 more years there will be 10 million more young Americans—10 million more between the ages of 5 and 17, 5 million more between 18 and 21, and here again we must be concerned with the level of income on which many are supported. We must make sure that they can meet their health needs. We must act in every way to strengthen the life of their families. We must make sure that every boy and girl in America has all the education that they can use.

We must be concerned with the nearly 2 million juveniles who get into trouble each year with the law. We must focus our concern on the causes of their troubles, not only on the youths themselves.

Yes, to you good members of this honorable and responsible union there is work for you to do, for us to do—work to build this good society better, work to make this strong country the foundation of a great and a compassionate civilization.

This is the American way of life, and this is the way that is under attack today from the fringe and from the extremes. I call upon you, here and now, to begin this hour to start fighting in order to save it.

Our directions and our destiny must not be placed in the hands of those who would steer a reckless and a callous course. We must be guided not by those whose compass points backward, but by those whose eyes and hearts are fixed on the stars that lead us forward.

We have no time for arrogance or belligerence. We have no time for callousness or contempt, either in the policies of our Nation or in the hearts of our leaders.

Our duty, our opportunity, is to fulfill the rights of all men all over our land, not only because we shall be judged more by what we do at home than what we preach abroad, but because it is right.

Once a visitor said to President Lincoln, "We trust, sir, that God is on our side." The Great Emancipator turned to him and said quietly, "It is more important to know that we are on God's side."

So we come not with any venom in our blood or any hate in our soul, or any viciousness in our voice this morning. We come and say, let us, then, on this day and in this year, all of us as good Americans who want to do what is best for our country, who want to do what is best for all the people of this great land—let us be sure that the course that we set for our Nation is on God's side.

And what is that course? It is a course of peace, it is a course of understanding, it is a course of living by the Golden Rule, doing unto others as you would have them do unto you. You will be condemned and criticized as Lincoln was. You will be misrepresented and vilified as Roosevelt was. But you must follow in your dealings with your fellow man and with your relations with other nations a course of justice to all, special privilege to none.

You must follow a course of compassion and courage. You must love thy neighbor as thyself, and you must try to point the way, and to lift up the weak so that he, too, may be strong. Yes, you must point a course of courage in these trying times when smear and fear and intolerance are abroad in the land, the same courage that brought this Nation into existence, the same courage that held this Union together.

The same courage that crossed the oceans on two occasions in our lifetime to preserve freedom in the world was never needed more than it is needed today. Unless I miss my guess, it has never been possessed to a greater degree than it is possessed today in the souls of each of you who sit in this room.

Yes, we know not what the future may bring. We know not how we may be led. We know not what may be God's will.

But His course is to do justice, to love mercy, and to walk humbly. I would like to feel, as I leave this room and return to the lonely acres that are surrounded by a big, black, iron fence, that whatever I do, wherever I go, wherever my decisions may lead us, I will have your prayers and your support.

Thank you.

NOTE: The President spoke in midmorning in the Presidential Ballroom at the Statler Hilton Hotel in Washington. His opening words referred to James B. Carey, president of the International Union of Electrical, Radio, and Machine Workers. During the course of his remarks the President referred to George Burdon, president, United Rubber, Cork, Linoleum, and Plastic Workers of America, George Baldanzi, president, United Textile Workers of America, John O'Hare, president, Tobacco Workers International Union, R. A. Olson, president, Minnesota AFL–CIO Federation of Labor, and John I. Rollings, president, Missouri State Labor Council, AFL–CIO.

The President's remarks were carried by closed circuit TV to the international conventions of the United Rubber Workers, in Chicago, the United Textile Workers, in New York City, and the Tobacco Workers, in Miami Beach, and to the State conventions of the Minnesota AFL–CIO, in St. Paul, and the Missouri AFL–CIO, in Kansas City. The remarks were also broadcast by radio to 20 cities throughout the United States.

591   Excerpts From Remarks at a Meeting With the New Panel of Consultants on Peace and National Security.   *September 23, 1964*

I AM delighted to have a chance to meet briefly with you gentlemen and to thank you for undertaking to serve as members of a panel of private citizens to work with us in the quest for peace. You gentlemen symbolize a tradition which goes back for a quarter of a century—the tradition of non-partisan service on matters of war and peace. I see Democrats who have served in Republican administrations, Republicans who have served with Democratic administrations, and a number of men who have held office under both parties. And these party affiliations really don't matter very much compared to the common concern and the great operating principles of our American foreign policy. There are four of these principles, and you gentlemen have worked for all four of them.

The *first* is that the United States must be strong in her arms and strong in her will. When I look at General Bradley and Dr. Kistiakowsky and Mr. Dulles, when I think of Mr. Lovett, who can't be with us today,

I am looking at men who played a great role in building the strength we now have. We have kept on in this same tradition in the last 4 years, and we believe the balanced strength of the United States has never been greater than it is today.

But there is always work to be done to keep our defenses strong and up to date, and we look forward to the advice and counsel which you gentlemen will bring in coming discussions of defense planning for the future.

Second, the United States yields to no one in her loyalty to friends and allies. With us today we have Mr. Acheson, Mr. McCloy, and Mr. Hoffman, architects of the recovery of Europe and the Atlantic Alliance. Western Europe has never been more secure, and the future of Atlantic freedom never more bright that it is today. The leaders of that continent rightly seek a growing role in the common cause of freedom. The differences and difficulties which lie ahead of us are the product of success, not failure. As we go on in this great work, our friends in Europe will be encouraged in the knowledge that we shall have advice like yours to guide us.

I am particularly glad to have the help of such men as Mr. Acheson and Mr. McCloy as our minds turn to the future of central Europe, and as we renew our determination to work for the freedom and reunion of the people of divided Germany. One of the great achievements of the last generation is that we have built mutual trust between democratic Germany and the United States, while never forgetting the proper interests of other allies or even the legitimate concerns of adversaries. In that tradition we shall continue, with your help.

And we shall show equal good faith to other friends and allies in other continents as well. Today this determination finds its hardest test in the difficult and demanding task of helping a young nation to grow and defend itself against Communist terror and domestic disorder—the Republic of Viet-Nam.

We are not discouraged by difficulty, nor will we let ourselves be deflected by partisan critics. In Viet-Nam today, the best of Americans, from private to Ambassador, are making their sacrifice in this hard cause on the spot. They too will be encouraged to know that the Government in Washington can call on men like you for help and counsel as this 10-year-long commitment of three administrations is continued.

Third, the United States has been not merely the strongest of all Nations, and the most reliable of allies, but the leader in proving that we accept the responsibilities of the rich and strong. In the Marshall plan, which Mr. Hoffman ran, and the World Bank, where Mr. Black and Mr. McCloy achieved so much, and later still in the Alliance for Progress, where Mr. Moscoso will always be remembered, we have been willing and ready to help free men to help themselves.

And I agree with what General Eisenhower used to say year after year—that these programs are a great bargain for our own national security. Year after year, as the Democratic Majority Leader, I worked to support the Republican President in defending these programs, which have no constituency of their own. The freedom of Europe, the great hopes of India and Pakistan, the new glow of confidence in South America, are the product of this national, bipartisan effort.

Fourth, and finally, the policy of the United States is not simply peace through strength, but peace through positive, persistent, active effort.

For 20 years, in five administrations, we have been first in our support for the United Nations—and many of you like Mr. Cowles,

Mr. Leibman, Mr. Larson, and Mr. Wadsworth, have been among its most determined friends.

For 20 years, in the age of the atom, we have been first in the search for effective disarmament. Mr. Acheson, Mr. Dean, and Mr. McCloy have played great roles in that continuing effort.

For 20 years, in crisis after crisis, we have sought the way of reason and restraint. No great power in all history has a better record of respect for the rights of others.

So we are strong in our defenses, loyal in our alliances, responsive to the needs of others, and passionate in the positive search for peace. This is the kind of people we are—this is the kind of service you have given. This is the foreign policy which will continue, with your help, in the years ahead.

NOTE: The President spoke shortly before noon in the Cabinet Room at the White House. The formation of the panel including the names of the members was announced by the President at his news conference on September 9 (see Item 563 [5]).

As printed, this item follows the prepared text released by the White House.

592 Message to the Congress Transmitting Eighth Annual Report on the Trade Agreements Program. *September 23, 1964*

To the Congress of the United States:

I hereby transmit the eighth annual report on the operation of the Trade Agreements Program, in accordance with Section 402(a) of the Trade Expansion Act of 1962.

Throughout 1963, intensive preparations went forward for the negotiations made possible by this Act—the sixth round of trade negotiations under the auspices of the General Agreement on Tariffs and Trade. During this same year, U.S. and free world trade continued to set new records, and important steps were taken to expand our exports further.

—U.S. exports reached a new high of $22.3 billion, $5.1 billion more than our imports.

—U.S. farm exports rose to $5.6 billion, an all-time record.

—Free world trade continued to grow, with exports climbing to a record $135 billion.

—Further progress was made in freeing U.S. exports of foreign restrictions.

—Government-industry cooperation in the promotion of our exports was stepped up, notably by the White House Conference on Export Expansion in September, 1963, and the subsequent establishment of the Cabinet Committee on Export Expansion.

—The desire of the less-developed countries to play a greater part in international trade received increasing consideration by GATT and by the United States.

The Trade Expansion Act of 1962 will, I am sure, rank as one of the greatest monuments to President Kennedy's leadership, and I reaffirm the commitment of my Administration to its full and vigorous implementation.

I hope that our friends in other countries will neither underestimate nor undervalue the strength of American support for trade liberalization. We are willing to offer the free nations access to our American markets—but we expect, and we must have, access to theirs as well. That applies to our agricultural as well as our industrial exports.

These are not the kind of negotiations in which some nations need lose because others gain. Their success will be to the advantage of all. They offer the opportunity to build a partnership for progress and prosperity among the industrial nations of the free world, and between them and the developing nations.

At home, we are moving to eliminate poverty among all Americans. We believe that a giant step can be taken against poverty everywhere if the free nations can work together to overcome needless obstacles to the flow of trade among them.

LYNDON B. JOHNSON

NOTE: The "Eighth Annual Report of the President of the United States on the Trade Agreements Program" is printed in House Document 366 (88th Cong., 2d sess.).

593   Remarks Upon Presenting the Collier Trophy in Aeronautics to Clarence L. Johnson. *September 24, 1964*

Mr. Johnson, distinguished guests, ladies and gentlemen:

Through the year we are privileged to welcome here distinguished visitors from many distinguished places. This occasion today, however, is something of a first. I am honored to receive and to welcome the most distinguished citizen of that most unique and distinguished corner of our land, the "Skunk Works."

"Kelly" Johnson and the products of his famous "Skunk Works" epitomize the highest and the finest goal of our society, the goal of excellence. His record of design achievement in aviation is both incomparable and virtually incredible. Any one of his many airplane designs would have honored any individual's career.

Twenty years ago, in 1944, he produced America's first production jet. It was called the P–80, "Shooting Star." This year of 1964 two of our leading breakthroughs in aircraft development have once again borne the "Kelly" Johnson trademark. I suppose I might give a testimonial personally as a satisfied customer. I am very fond of what the newspapermen call "Air Force One-Half," the Jet Star which came from Mr. Johnson's drawing board.

So it is a pleasure and a great privilege to me to personally be able to participate in the presentation of the Robert J. Collier Trophy. This trophy is one of the most honored in aeronautics. It was established in 1912. It is being presented here today for the 49th time.

The Collier Trophy is administered by the National Aeronautics Association. Its annual presentation is sponsored by Look magazine. Last year the Collier Trophy was awarded to the great Mercury team of our astronauts.

There are those who feel that "Kelly" Johnson is a one-man team himself. He works by a rule that is wise for us all: be quick; be quiet; be on time. I have commended that rule, Mr. Johnson, to my staff here at the White House. And I only hope that their products will be comparable to your own.

So on behalf of all the people of the United States, I take great pleasure this morning and great pride in honoring a distinguished American, one who is making a very great contribution to his country and a very great contribution to the cause of freedom for us all in our time.

NOTE: The President spoke at noon in the Rose Garden at the White House. Clarence L. Johnson was serving as vice president for advance development projects at the Lockheed Aircraft Corporation in Burbank, Calif. The "Skunk Works" was his workshop in Burbank where a number of top-secret projects had been developed.

594 Statement by the President Upon Approving Bill Providing for a Site Study for a New Interoceanic Canal. *September 24, 1964*

I HAVE approved a bill to provide for an investigation and study to determine a site for the construction of a sea level canal connecting the Atlantic and Pacific Oceans.

The Panama Canal was a great engineering achievement. It has served world commerce for 50 years. It has been a major source of income for Panama's economic and social development. It has been a key link in our security arrangements. But if we are to meet the challenges of the future, we must begin now to think in terms of the long-range needs of the United States, Latin America, and the rest of the world for a sea level canal across the American Isthmus.

Construction of a sea level canal presents formidable obstacles even after a suitable site is selected. There are enormous technical problems and complex and interrelated political, military, and economic considerations that must be weighed. Under this bill the task will be undertaken by a five-member commission, appointed by the President, with annual reports on the progress of the commission's work submitted to the Congress through the President.

This authorization will permit the study to get underway. Equally important, however, is appropriation of necessary implementing funds. I urge that the Congress act promptly on the supplemental request of $5 million for this purpose for the fiscal year 1965.

NOTE: As enacted, the bill is Public Law 88–609 (78 Stat. 990).

See also Item 809.

595 Letter to the Chief Justice Upon Receipt of the Warren Commission Report. *September 24, 1964*

Dear Mr. Chief Justice:

You have today submitted to me the report of the Commission which I appointed on November 29 last to report on the assassination of President John F. Kennedy. The submission of this report fulfills the assignment which I gave to the Commission, and accordingly I now discharge the Commission with my heartfelt thanks.

In my service as President, nothing has impressed me more than the readiness of outstanding Americans to respond to calls for service to their country. There has been no more striking example of this great American strength than the service of the seven extraordinarily distinguished members of your Commission. I send thanks to you all, as I also send thanks to your General Counsel, Mr. Lee Rankin, and to all those who have assisted in your work.

Your Commission, I know, has been guided throughout by a determination to find and to tell the whole truth of these terrible events. This is our obligation to the good name of the United States of America and to all men everywhere who respect our nation—and above all to the memory of President Kennedy.

I have given instructions for the prompt publication of this report to the American people and to the world. I myself shall give it the most careful study. I commend it to the attention of all Americans and all our friends everywhere.

Let me thank you again for all that you have done. You have earned the gratitude of your countrymen.

Sincerely,   LYNDON B. JOHNSON

[The Honorable Earl Warren, The Chief Justice, United States Supreme Court, Washington, D.C.]

NOTE: The report is entitled "Report of the President's Commission on the Assassination of President John F. Kennedy" (888 pp., Government Printing Office, 1964).

The Commission, of which the Chief Justice of the United States served as Chairman, was appointed by Executive Order 11130 (Item 15, above; see also Item 14).

596 Remarks in El Paso at a Ceremony Marking the Settlement of the Chamizal Dispute. *September 25, 1964*

Mr. President López Mateos, Mrs. Mateos, Governor Connally, Mrs. Connally, Senator Yarborough, Ambassador Carillo Flores, Ambassador Sánchez Gavito, ladies and gentlemen:

These are days when a shaft of light cuts through the darkness and brightens the deepest hopes of man. This is such a day.

Two free and growing nations have resolved an old and divisive grievance.

It is 100 years since the roaring summer floods of the Rio Grande remade this land. Then we were both in the midst of mortal conflict to preserve our nations. We were both dedicated to extending liberty in the face of extreme danger. We were both led by men whose greatness has endured the estimate of history—Abraham Lincoln and Benito Juárez.

Lincoln commanded my nation "to do all which may achieve a just and lasting peace . . . ." Juárez reminded us: "Respect for the rights of others is peace." The goals of these men have guided us to this day.

We approached the council table with respect for each other's rights and determined to achieve a just and lasting settlement. Thus, we triumphed over a problem which has troubled relations for half a century.

In that connection, I want to pay unusual tribute today to our former Ambassador to Mexico, our present Assistant Secretary of State in charge of Latin American Relations, the very able and the very devoted friend of both Mexico and the United States, Mr. Tom Mann.

It is a great thrill to be here on the border of these two countries. It was a great pleasure to see so many of my old friends from both nations. I particularly enjoyed meeting one of the men who has done much to promote the friendship of Mexico and the United States throughout his public life, Judge Ewing Thomason of your own town of El Paso.

So, to Ambassador Flores and Ambassador Mann, and Mr. President López Mateos, let me say: Let Chamizal stand as a symbol to all the world that the most troublesome of problems can yield to the tools of peace. And let us never forget, let us always remember, that another great man whose visionary statesmanship made this settlement possible was John Fitzgerald Kennedy.

Let me take a moment on this occasion to review the progress of freedom and peace, for these are really the twin stars for both of our great nations. I would also like, Mr. President, to talk to my people about the attitudes and policies toward the world, of which this settlement is another shining symbol.

For almost 20 years the world has lived with the ambitions of tyranny and lived with the threat of war, and they are still with us.

But I believe that reasonable men of every party and every nation can agree our world has really become a safer place for freedom.

In Latin America, country after country has chosen the course of democratic development. The followers of communism have made no new conquest, and their numbers have actually dwindled.

Our Alliance for Progress is an effective instrument of social justice, of which you spoke so eloquently, and of economic progress for all the nations of this hemisphere. I know much of its success rests on the fact that it has the same goals as the continuing Mexican revolution which you, Mr. President, have done so much in your term of office to advance.

And it thrills me more, Mr. President, than you know, to realize that here at the end of your term we could meet on an occasion like this, stronger in friendship, happier in achievement, than when we met before you took the oath of office as President of Mexico a few years ago.

Yes, much of the good will and the peace that exists now between our countries and this hemisphere is due to your own understanding and your own efforts in that direction. And here in America we have found peaceful roads to the solutions of differences, from Chamizal to Panama.

In Africa, not one of 20 new nations has chosen communism. Ninety percent of African trade, as we meet here today, is with the West. Ninety percent of its students sent overseas have come to the West. All this, in a continent that many feared a few years ago would fall easy prey to Communist ambitions.

In the Middle East, only a few years ago, it seemed that Communist subversion was nearing success. Today, those nations are stronger in their independence than ever

before. And Israel has grown in freedom.

In Asia the giant of India has endured a powerful assault and a painful transition. Free Japan is flourishing again, and Chinese aggression, by force and by threat, has failed to subdue its neighbors.

In Eastern Europe steadily widening cracks are already appearing in the Communist empire. Nation after nation has sought new ties with the West, and new independence from Moscow. And we will continue to encourage this movement, not through empty slogans or threats, but through patiently building bridges of interest and understanding.

The greatest enemies of freedom in the world are ignorance and disease, and in both Mexico and the United States, we are redoubling our efforts to fight both of these dreadful barnacles. Western Europe today has never been stronger. Its people now reach for new heights of abundance. There are differences, but they come from strength and they come from self-confidence, not from weakness, not from fear. And there is no difference in our resistance to Communist ambition or our devotion to freedom.

The Soviet Union is increasingly absorbed in the disappointments of its economy and disputes with former comrades. Our strength is convincing them that they actually have nothing to gain by war. Increased willingness to reach agreement has brought the test ban treaty in which so many peace-loving nations like your own have joined, one of many first steps toward the day when really the fear of war can finally be banished from this earth.

I do not wish to paint too bright a picture. There is another side of the coin. Every continent carries danger and uncertainty. There are unsolved problems, there are unresolved conflicts, from Cyprus to Viet-Nam, from the Congo to Cuba. Tomorrow's bitter headlines could very well shatter today's bright hopes.

But if we look beyond the problems of the moment, to the larger pattern of events, we see a world where freedom is stronger and where lasting peace is nearer. I believe that we have cause to hope that the great forward movement of history is in step with the deepest hope of man.

This is not the product of a single period, and certainly not the product of a single President. It is the sum of a hundred achievements and acts of courage by every administration, since the first nuclear blast ended one world and started another. Nor is it the product of a single nation. It rests fundamentally on the devotion to freedom of countries which share common hopes around the world.

The foreign policy of the United States has been guided by three cardinal principles, and these are the principles that we intend to continue.

First is determination backed by strength. The United States is the most powerful country in the history of the world. Its might is strong enough to deter any rational aggressor, and is flexible enough to meet any threat from any source.

But I must caution you, and I must remind you, that strength must be matched by courage and wisdom if it is to protect freedom. And where freedom has been under attack, the United States has moved to meet those attacks. We have never rattled our rockets, we have never played the part of a bully, we have never taken reckless risks. We have never pressed our adversaries to the point where nuclear assault was their only alternative. But America has always and will always stand firm.

To our own citizens and to our friends from our neighboring country today I would remind you that this is not an accident of the moment. This was true of President Truman in Greece and Turkey. This was true of President Eisenhower in Lebanon and the Formosa Straits. This was true of President John Kennedy in the Cuban missile crisis. And it was and it is true in the Gulf of Tonkin.

Second is sacrifice of our own resources and our own efforts in order to build the strength of others.

One of the most stimulating and inspiring experiences of my entire public life occurred to me on the streets of Rome just a few months ago when I was Vice President and I was driving down the streets of that beautiful city.

A priest came running from his schoolroom, followed by other teachers, and three or four hundred little boys. He had seen the American flag flying on the Vice President's car.

He threw himself in front of this car and the brakes had to take a screeching halt, and we came to a stop. He dashed up to the door and he said, "I just could not let the American flag go by, because never in the history of all mankind have any people demonstrated so much compassion and so much humaneness. Never have the victors treated the vanquished as the United States has treated us."

And then he turned and looked at the Rome skyline that had been rebuilt since World War II, and he pointed to the magnificent buildings that towered that skyline, and to the smokestacks where industry was thriving, and he said, "There, together, we rebuilt this land. I want you to go back and on behalf of the 400 little children in my school, say thank you to all the people of the United States for the sacrifices they made in order that we could build again."

In my moments of depression, when things seem not to go so well, and some people tell me all the things that are wrong with my country and my beloved land—and few of them ever remind us of the things that are right—I get consolation and comfort from thinking about what the people, the little people, of the other places of the world and the other continents—of the gratitude they feel for the understanding that has been ours.

From the Marshall plan to the Alliance for Progress, the people of the United States have freely given of their abundance to the progress of other nations. We have done this because it is right that the strong and the rich should help the weak and the poor.

And this great leader who honors us with his presence today, President López Mateos, has recognized that principle and put it into effect in America. And as long as I am President of the United States, I am going to recognize it here. He and I both know that the world is safer for others when others have the strength to keep their own freedom.

The NATO Alliance is a tribute to the vision of this policy, and around the world our influence has been on the rise as others have learned we seek not to dominate but to help, we seek not to rule but to cooperate, we seek not to demand their submission but to assist their freedom.

Next Tuesday I am going to welcome to the White House a great leader of the world who is coming there representing NATO. He and I are going to get in my plane, Air Force One, and fly out to the Strategic Air Forces to see General Power so that he can see with his own eyes, and he can tell the people of NATO, that our mission is peace in the world and we have the strength to accomplish that mission.

Third, we have patiently searched for those areas of common interest which might lead to fruitful agreement. A difference in language, a difference in environment, a difference in resources, a difference in people, a difference in customs—all of those are problems that make it difficult sometimes to understand the other fellow. But Americans try to follow the Golden Rule, do unto others as you would have them do unto you. And we have tried to find a basis for reaching agreements that step by step would ultimately lead us to be able to live without fear in this world of our time.

The test ban treaty is a product of this process. The Chamizal settlement is a product of this process. Lasting peace will come from the careful, the patient, and the practical search for these solutions.

It is easy to become impatient and impulsive. It is easy to tell the other fellow, "Here is our ultimatum, and you do as we say—or else." But that will never be the policy of this country under my leadership.

Our Government is not a government of ultimatum. Our Government is a government of respect for the rights of others, and the attempt to understand their problems. We have the strength and we have the self-confidence to be generous toward our friends and to be unafraid of our adversaries. There is no reason why we should tremble in our boots. There is no reason why we should become so frightened that we would frighten others into a nuclear war.

A nation strong in its might, a nation that is secure in its own beliefs, a nation that is steadfast in its own goals, should never be afraid to sit down at the council table with any other nation. That is what the great President of Mexico said to me before he took the oath of office as President. We discussed some of the problems, including the Chamizal. We discussed building dams for the benefit of both of our people. We discussed the problem of health, of education, of transportation, in his country and in mine. We agreed that we could march better shoulder to shoulder, arm in arm, than we could by threatening and intimidating each other.

It is only the weak and the timid that need fear the consequences of communication and discussion. The United States has never been such a nation and we will never be such a nation.

The Presidents of the last 20 years have all been willing to go anywhere, to talk to anyone, to discuss any subject, if their efforts could strengthen freedom and advance the peace of the world. And I pledge you here today I will go to any remote corner of the world to meet anyone, any time, to promote freedom and to promote peace.

President López Mateos, the Chamizal is a very small tract of land. But the principle is a very great one. Let a troubled world take note that here, on this border, between the United States and Mexico, two free nations, unafraid, have resolved their differences with honor, with dignity, and with justice to the people of both nations.

President López Mateos, the statesmanship that you have evidenced in this settlement could well serve as a model for great leaders the world over.

As we meet here, we live in a very complicated world. There are more than a hundred different nations with a hundred different histories, each with its own dreams and each with its own desires. There are rich nations and poor nations. There are strong nations and weak nations. There are white and black, slave and free, friend and enemy.

We cannot abandon all of those who disagree with us. To do so would only leave them at the mercy of communism. We cannot force and bully all others to think and act as we do in the United States. We can recognize their just interests and still protect our own.

We can stand fast in freedom's cause, and that I guarantee you is what we are going to do.

Mr. President, we can and we will welcome the challenge of working toward a peace on a hundred different fronts, in a hundred different ways, for as long as the task may take. In this way, and this way only, we can make steady progress toward freedom and peace, and toward the fulfillment of man.

The struggle for peace is rarely dramatic. There are no marching bands and there are few swift victories. But I believe that this generation has an opportunity for greatness given to no other nation at no other time.

Other great leaders have built victorious empires and they have conquered vast territory. But those achievements have crumbled under the relentless erosion of time and change. So working together with all the free nations in this hemisphere we can help build an order of peace and progress which will endure for generations. No people have ever had a greater challenge.

And, Mr. President, to you and the people of your country, and to my fellow countrymen, I say to you today as prophetic as I know how to be, that I genuinely and earnestly believe that no people in all history have ever been more ready to meet the challenge of peace and more prepared to achieve it.

NOTE: The ceremony was held at the Bowie High School Stadium in El Paso, Tex., where President Johnson and President Adolfo López Mateos of Mexico unveiled a marker indicating the new boundary of the Chamizal tract.

President Johnson's opening words referred, in addition to President and Mrs. López Mateos, to Governor John Connally of Texas and Mrs. Connally, Senator Ralph Yarborough of Texas, Ambassador Antonio Carrillo Flores, Mexican Ambassador to the United States, and Ambassador Vicente Sánchez Gavito, Mexican representative to the Organization of American States. During the course of his remarks the President also referred to Robert Ewing Thomason, U.S. District Judge (retired), Western District of Texas, and former U.S. Representative from Texas.

The convention between the United States and Mexico for the solution of the problem of the Chamizal Border was concluded at Mexico City on August 29, 1963. It was favorably considered by the Senate and after ratification entered into force on January 14, 1964. The text is printed in the United States Treaties and Other International Agreements series (TIAS 5515) and in the Department of State Bulletin (vol. 49, p. 480). For the President's remarks at the ratification ceremony, see Item 58.

597 Remarks in Oklahoma at the Dedication of the Eufaula Dam. *September 25, 1964*

Governor Bellmon, Senator Monroney, Senator Edmondson, Governor Connally of Texas, Congressman Albert, our great Majority Leader, Ed Edmondson, and other distinguished members of the Oklahoma delegation to the Congress, all of whom are making a great contribution to our country:

I want to say on behalf of all the people of this Nation that we, the people of the United States, are deeply in the debt of the people of Oklahoma for the quality of the men that they send to the United States Congress.

I could talk about your Senators, Monroney and Edmondson; I could spend days talking about your House delegation, particularly your Majority Leader; but I want to say that none of the things that we have accomplished this year, and this is one of the finest years, one of the finest hours of the United States Congress, could have happened except under the leadership of the Oklahoma delegation, and particularly that fine, young Majority Leader, Carl Albert.

This is a great day for the Sooners. I thank you for letting a Texan have a little slice of it. But Texans and the people of Oklahoma alike share the memories of the days before dams like this remade the earth.

I grew up on land like this back in Texas. I am going back to it when I finish here this evening. That land is thin soil and scrub oak and blackjack trees. The Pedernales River that runs in front of my little farmhouse was just a trickle in the dry season, but when the rains came down from the hills the Pedernales always drowned all of us.

Many of us remember those days still. We remember the want and the despair, the devastating cycle of flood and drought, the ruined crops and the dust bowl. Worst of all was the great waste, the waste of resources, the waste of crops, the waste of men and women.

I went to Washington then to serve in Congress under a great leader, Franklin Delano Roosevelt. Over the years of progress which he began, we have seen our States change from brown to green, from dry eroded country to grassy land dotted with lakes and pools. We saw a nation afraid become a nation of hope. We saw a people divided become a people united.

And to the memory of that progress, and to the determination that our children will never suffer that neglect, I have come to the great State of Oklahoma today to dedicate this great dam to you great people.

I have devoted much of my 30 years of public career to the conservation of America's natural resources. So have Mike Monroney and Howard Edmondson and Carl Albert and Ed Edmondson. So did our great beloved friend, the giant of them all,

Bob Kerr, who is watching down on us today. This dam was one of his dreams and I only wish that he could be here with us.

You know, in 1940, after I had been in Congress several years, I looked up the number of homes with electric lighting in my State, and we had 59 out of every 100. Today we have 100 percent rural electrification. In Oklahoma they had 55 percent of their homes electrified in 1940, today they have 100. In Louisiana they had 49, today 100. In Arkansas they had 33, today 100. Arkansas had 25 percent of its homes that had runing water in 1940, today it has 72. Louisiana had 44 with running water, today it is 87. Oklahoma had 46, today it is 89. Texas had 56, today it is 91.

The percentage of homes that use wood for cooking: 76 out of every 100 in Arkansas in 1940. Louisiana had 50; today it has 4. Oklahoma had 32—32 homes out of every 100 used wood for cooking; today only 2 out of every 100.

In the number of autos, Oklahoma had 387,000 autos in 1933, today she has 982,000—3 to 1. Arkansas had 155,000, today she has 589,000. Louisiana had 190,000, today she has 1,042,000. Texas had 1,015,000 in 1933, today she has 4,000,011.

The percentage of homes with refrigerators: Texas had 36 in 1940, per hundred, today she has 98. Oklahoma had 31, today she has 98. Louisiana had 24, today she has 98.

The percentage of farmer-owned occupied farms: Arkansas had 37 that had home ownership out of every 100, today she has 76. Louisiana had 33, today she has 75. Oklahoma in 1930 had only 38 out of every 100 farms owned by the man that lived on them—today not 38 in Oklahoma, but 80. And Texas was 38 in 1930, and 78 today.

So you can see the progress that we have made with the help of men that you have sent to Congress in that period of 20 or 30 years in home ownership, in lighting our homes, and in improving our standard of living. And to the memory of that progress and to the determination of the people who led the way, I salute you today.

Our very first President, George Washington, looked at the vast possibilities of harnessing our great rivers and prayed, "Would God that we may have the wisdom and the courage to improve them." Improve these rivers as you have done.

For years we ignored his warning. Reckless exploitation and ruthless plunder lay waste the rich earth. But then some far-sighted men, men of every party and of every section, men like Theodore Roosevelt, men like Franklin Roosevelt, men like John F. Kennedy, men like Robert S. Kerr, men like Mike Monroney and your House delegation, all began to act and to protect and to develop the natural resources, not only of Oklahoma but of all the Nation. And the result has been a fuller and a richer life for all of our people, and a much better life for those children that will grow up.

These men knew that conservation was not a "pork barrel," that it was not "madework," that it was not a "giveaway." It was an investment in the future of America. It was the best kind of economy. In this way we could assure our children the natural resources.

I remember coming to Oklahoma to help dedicate Bob Kerr's book, "Land, Wood and Water," on which the strength of our Nation and the prosperity of our people depended. The Government has a responsibility never to waste taxpayers' money, but the Government also has a responsibility never to waste the Nation's resources. The real wasters, the real spendthrifts, are those who are neglecting the needs of today and destroying the hopes of tomorrow.

Our country just cannot afford this kind of waste.

Only 35 years ago we began to open up the Ohio River Basin. Then men of little vision cried out against this as "pork barrel." They were against this progress. Well, we ignored their warnings. We moved ahead. Since World War II alone, over $21 billion of new industry development has taken place in the counties along the Ohio and its navigable tributaries.

And one of the great statesmen of Ohio is here today. He not only participated in developing the State of Ohio, he has been one of the ringleaders in developing the State of Oklahoma. I want to call his name. His name is the Honorable Mike Kirwan, Congressman from the State of Ohio. Stand up, Mike.

New jobs and new business, and a steadily improving life, have come to all the people of the area. Men like Congressman Kirwan have not been content just to look after their own State or their own section. They have been men with national vision. As a result of their national vision you have the monument here to them today.

Well, that is the story of the development of the United States, and that will be the story of the development of the Arkansas River basin.

The Eufaula Dam is a key part of the development of the Arkansas River. It will provide a new link between the Southwest and our industrial heartland. It will provide relief from devastating floods and give us electricity to homes and businesses. It will mean new industry, new jobs, and new opportunities for the people. It will mean a stronger Oklahoma, a more prosperous Oklahoma, a richer Oklahoma, and a stronger United States.

That development will go ahead, and as President, I am here to promise you that it will go on schedule.

I just had to break my budget one time this year. I had a very prudent budget. I had $1 billion less in the budget this year than we had last year. I was determined to keep it that way until Mike Monroney, Carl Albert, John McClellan, and all this bunch of hijackers from Oklahoma came down there and pounded that Cabinet desk one afternoon and it cost me $14 million. But it got your Arkansas River development back on schedule.

But I would like to look beyond the celebration of today to the challenge of tomorrow, especially to your growing need for water. For this is a land which knows the meaning of water. By the year 2000 more than 300 million Americans will require 888 billion gallons of water a day. This is three times what you are using now. We cannot meet that challenge by looking backward. We cannot meet it by finding things wrong with our Government. We cannot meet it by complaining.

We must meet it by dreaming and executing those dreams. We must meet it by looking forward to the real and to the better tomorrows. We must meet it first by going full speed ahead at every level of government in the comprehensive development of our river basins.

We cannot approach the **problems of water** conservation and flood control and recreation and navigation on a piecemeal and divided basis. We must develop river basins as a whole, to use all of our resources while preserving scenic values.

Second, we must step up our efforts to fight the destructive cycle of flood and drought. We have increased flood control programs by more than 50 percent, but we cannot rest on past achievements if we are to rescue our land from the ravages of nature.

Third, we must develop a national policy to attack the pollution of our water, and the pollution of the air that we breathe. This must require research, this will require increased construction of treatment plants and better methods of control. Polluted water is wasted water, and America cannot afford this waste.

Fourth, we will continue to press ahead with weather satellites, deep sea nuclear weather stations, and other scientific advances so that we can understand the weather and so that we can become its master.

Fifth, I am asking for early passage of the Water Resources Planning Act to help us look ahead to future patterns of water needs, to look ahead to plan our projects so that supply will be ready for demand.

Sixth, we will begin to draw fresh water from the oceans before very long. We already have plants in operation that are converting salt and brackish water into 2½ million gallons of fresh water every day, and within a few years desalted water will be an actual reality for millions of Americans.

Three things—and three things only— sustain life on this planet. They are: a thin layer of soil, a cover of atmosphere, and a little rainfall. This is all that the good Lord has given us. Except one thing: He has given us a choice of what we will do with it. We can waste it. We can pollute it. We can neglect it. Or we can conserve it, and we can protect it, and we can develop it, and we can pass it along to our children, more promising, more abundant than we found it when we discovered America.

I know, I think, what your answer wants to be. I think I know what you want to do about it. I think your answer is here in this great dam that was built because of your confidence, built because of your support, built not only to make life more pleasant and more productive and more prosperous for you, but for your children and for your grandchildren.

The West was not settled by men who looked back. It was not settled by men who called a halt to progress. It is not held by such men today.

Let me say just one thing more.

It was about 10 months ago that we had a great tragedy in Dallas, Tex., and the awesome responsibility of being President of all the people of this country fell into my lap. Although I had spent 33 years in Washington, as a clerk, as a Congressman, as a Senator, as a Minority Leader, as a Majority Leader, as Vice President, I still felt inadequate to the responsibilities of leading 190 million people, and trying to provide hope and leadership for the other free people that live in a world that is made up of 3 billion.

I asked for God's help and for yours. I have done my dead level best. I have worked with everything that God gave me. I have spent all the energy that I had. I have tried to be careful and prudent. I have tried to be fair and judicious. I have tried to be farsighted and foresighted. I have tried to look forward and not backward. I have tried to develop a land that I would be proud of, and my children would enjoy living in. I found that we had much to preserve and much to protect.

We have the greatest system of government in all the world. We have the highest standard of living of any people anywhere. We have a minimum wage that says to our workers they must pay you this minimum and they must work you this maximum, and in just the short period that I have been in Congress we have gone from 25 cents minimum to $1.25 minimum. Just the short time I have been there we are working less hours per day and less days per week, and less weeks per year. We have more time for recreation, more time for the luxuries of life than our fathers and our grandfathers had, to come out to lakes like this and dams like this.

We have a social security system that will give us a modicum of income when we reach our maturity and are no longer able to stay in the labor market. We are proud of the farm programs that we have had that have raised the income of our tenant farmers, that have raised our home ownership, that have brought us rural electrification.

I flew over this afternoon from Muskogee and I looked at all the little ponds that were filled with water that had been built here in just the last few years. I said to Senator Monroney, he must be mighty proud of the efforts that he and other Congressmen from Oklahoma had made because that was a tribute not only to them, but to their people, that they had made this soil better through their own efforts.

Well, there are voices that have questioned me about minimum wage. When I voted for the first bill it was 25 cents an hour, and they told me it would ruin me and they said it would ruin the labor organizations, too. But we are all here, and it looks to me like we are doing better at $1.25 than we were at 25 cents.

I remember before I was elected, when I was just a kid secretary talking to my Congressman about voting for social security, I heard all the scare arguments and all the fright that they tried to put into men. They said it is socialistic, it is compulsory, it is

evil, it will destroy our form of government. I think we are better for it. I think we are stronger for it. I think we are richer for it. I don't think many people would like to do away with either our minimum wage or our social security.

As your President I deal every day with the problems that affect your freedom and affect the peace of the world. Those problems may be remote from this peaceful site out here this afternoon. Not many of you get waked up in the night about Cyprus, or Zanzibar, or Viet-Nam. But I never send a reconnaissance mission out about 11 o'clock in our planes with our boys guiding them to take a look at what is developing, and realize they have to be back at 3:30 in the morning, but what promptly at 3:25 I wake up without an alarm clock, because I want to be sure my boys get back. And sometimes they don't come back.

There are those that say you ought to go north and drop bombs, to try to wipe out the supply lines, and they think that would escalate the war. We don't want our American boys to do the fighting for Asian boys. We don't want to get involved in a nation with 700 million people and get tied down in a land war in Asia.

There are some that say we ought to go south and get out and come home, but we don't like to break our treaties and we don't like to walk off and leave people who are searching for freedom, and suffering to obtain it, and walk out on them. We remember when we wanted our freedom from Great Britain, and we remember the people that helped us with it, and we'll never forget them. So we don't want to run out on them.

So what are we doing? We're staying there and supplying them with some of the things that we have, some of the things that the richest, most powerful nation in the world has developed. We have some tanks, some planes, and some helicopters. We have 20,000 men out there advising and helping them, and we're hoping that some way, somehow, these people that are invading them and trying to envelop them and trying to take their freedom away from them will some day decide that it's not worth the price and they will leave their neighbors alone and we can have peace in the world.

But we are not about to start another war and we're not about to run away from where we are.

Now, our hopes for the future, our hopes for peace, rest on our strength. And I can look you in the eye and I tell you in truth and sincerity today that we are better prepared than we have ever been prepared in our lifetime, and we are prepared because of the strength that you are building here and the qualities that you bring to your work.

I ask each of you to look back to your own lives. Remember not too far back. Just look at the thirties that I was talking about a moment ago, or the early forties, and see if there are any of you, if there's one among you that's not eating better, that's not doing better, that doesn't have better clothes, doesn't make more money, doesn't pay more taxes, and doesn't live in a stronger, a richer, a better, and a finer nation.

Now, what we have in the future and how we rank in the world will depend largely upon you people. If you invited me down here this afternoon and expected me to tell you all that was wrong with your country, and how we have failed, and how everything was in a mess, then you invited the wrong fellow.

Today we have more people working than we've ever had in the history of the United States. They're living in better homes, they're eating better food and more of it. They are wearing better clothes, they are driving better automobiles, they have got more savings, they have got higher wages, they have got better income, their children are better educated, their health is better, their doctors are better, their hospitals are better, they have more of the pleasures of life.

The strength of America today and the strength of America in the years to come will depend upon you and you must build that strength, because it depends upon the vision of the people, and on their willingness to look to the future and not to the past. Here's your look at the future. That's what you dreamed, that's what you saw, that's what you have. Aren't you proud of Oklahoma? I am.

If any of you have martyr complexes, you are going to be disappointed. If any of you are distressed and depressed with yourself and expect me to come down here and feel sorry for you, you are going to be disappointed. I'm proud of you. I recognize what you have done. I recognize what this Government has done with your help, and I want to tell you, we not only have much to preserve and much to protect, but we have much to love.

If we will just go back to the Good Book and practice some of the teachings of the Lord, if we will just follow the Golden Rule and do unto others as we would have them do unto us, if we just engage in a little introspection and look where we were and see where we are, we won't be unhappy very long. We won't feel sorry for ourselves very long.

We have done mighty well. We have a lot to be thankful for, and one of the things that I am thankful for as President is the prayers and the support and the good will and the faith of God-fearing men and women like you, and like this great delegation that you have sent there to help me.

We are not out of the woods. Some of our friends talk about a crisis a week. Well, sometimes I don't think they know much about the Government. We have a crisis a day and a crisis an hour, and we're always having crises. But we're not going to be crybabies. We're going to stand up like men and face them, and we're going to win.

We're going to win because we have faith and because we have the support of the people and because we're builders and because we look forward to leaving this world a better place than we found it.

Thank you for inviting us here. I wish I could stay all day, but I have two other engagements along the road down here in Arkansas and back in Texas tonight. But if you will invite me back sometime, I'll bring my boat and we'll have a good sail together.

Thank you.

NOTE: The President spoke at the site of the Eufaula Dam, Eufaula, Okla. In his opening words he referred to Governor Henry Bellmon, and Senators A. S. Mike Monroney and J. Howard Edmondson, all of Oklahoma, and to Governor John Connally of Texas and Representatives Carl Albert, House majority leader, and Ed Edmondson, both of Oklahoma.

In the course of his remarks the President referred to the late Senator Robert S. Kerr of Oklahoma, Representative Mike Kirwan of Ohio, and Senator John L. McClellan of Arkansas. He also referred to the University of Oklahoma "Sooners" football team, favorites in a game with the University of Southern California which was played the same day the President was in Oklahoma.

598   Remarks in Oklahoma City at the Opening of the State Fair. September 25, 1964

Mr. Gaylord, Senator Monroney, honored members of the Fair Association board of directors, Members of the great Oklahoma delegation in Congress, my fellow Americans:

As Mr. Gaylord was introducing Lady Bird, I was reminded how really old I am, because it was almost two decades ago when we met over in the piney woods of east Texas, and Mr. Gaylord's father came down to Lufkin, Tex., to help us establish our first newsprint mill.

It was an adventure for Texas to try to bring industry from Canada and from other sections of the United States to our own east Texas that bordered Arkansas and Louisiana. It was a great success financially for our public-spirited people in the press, and for that whole area of Texas.

So I am happy to be back here in Oklahoma today, Mr. Gaylord, returning that visit of your father many years ago. He came to our State to help us build industry. I have come to your State to help christen a dam and to watch industry move to Oklahoma.

This morning I stood with the President of Mexico and celebrated the peaceful settlement of a border dispute. Just a week ago I stood on the Canadian soil and, with the Prime Minister of Canada, celebrated an agreement or treaty that we had entered into with our neighbor, the nation of Canada. A few hours ago I dedicated the Eufaula Dam, part of the Arkansas River basin development which will open great opportunities for all the people of this great State of Oklahoma.

Peace between nations, and progress in Oklahoma, may seem like very different things. But they are not. They are both closely connected. You can't have peace in the world unless you have progress, and you can't have progress unless you have peace.

You are lucky enough and you are fortunate enough and you are blessed enough today to live in the most powerful nation in all the world. And it is only a prosperous nation that can maintain the mightiest military on earth, and I saw some of it at Tinker Field when I flew over it today. We are going to keep it there, and we are going to keep it growing and we are going to keep it moving, because it is only a growing America, it is only a thriving America, it is only an enlightened America that can maintain its commitments to other nations of the world.

Only an America which is solving its own problems can convince others that freedom's road, and not the Communist road, is the road to progress. Only an America which is true to its own principles—to justice and to freedom—can help lead other people in the world to follow those same principles.

It is by our deeds and not by our words that we lead the rest of the world in the cause of freedom.

You live in the wealthiest nation on earth. You enjoy the highest standard of living of any people. You eat more, you wear more, you live in the best houses, you have more luxuries than any people anywhere. Nature blessed us with a rich earth, and it blessed us with brave men to work it. But none of us must ever get the idea that success comes from circumstances and good luck.

It came from almost two centuries of partnership, partnership between Government and the people in the cause of a growing America, and, in recent years, as that partnership has become more effective, growth has been more rapid.

This is not a new idea. It is not a radical idea. It is as old as the American Nation. It was Thomas Jefferson who said: "The

freedom and the happiness of man are the sole object of all legitimate government."

Seventy-five years ago, on an April morning, starting guns signaled the opening of this land. No one called it a "giveaway." It proved one of the greatest investments in freedom that we ever made. What came out of it? I will tell you what came out of it. It gave us Oklahoma.

And no one thought it would dull initiative. In fact, it set off one of the greatest demonstrations of individual enterprise in the history of the world. This city was settled between noon and sundown on a single day. This spirit has been sustained to this day.

An Oklahoman, Wiley Post, was the first to solo around the world. An Oklahoman, Gordon Cooper, was the latest American to orbit the globe, and, my, you ought to be proud of him. Jim Webb, whom I drafted from Kerr-McGee, now leads us in the exploration of the planets.

An Oklahoman, Will Rogers, captured the spirit of all America, and all Americans loved Will Rogers. And no man had more vision, more courage, more optimism, more faith, or did more to help build modern America than Robert S. Kerr.

If anyone thinks the partnership of Government and people is eroding our courage or erasing initiative, I say let them come here to the State Fair of Oklahoma and look into these happy faces.

I came here today to talk to happy people. I came here to talk about what is right. I didn't come here to talk about what is wrong. I am proud of America, and I am proud of Oklahoma, and I am proud of you.

For 30 years—step by step and year by year and vote by vote—the men of both parties have worked to build the solid structure of partnership which is the foundation of our present prosperity. There have been deeply felt disagreements on particular programs. We don't always see everything alike. If we did, we would all want the same wife. But there has been broad agreement on the great goals, and there has been broad agreement that it is the duty of the Government to act as an ally of the free enterprise system.

There is one more thing. Once the disagreements were settled, once our course was set, once the structure was built, no leader of any party has tried to tear it down. They knew that far too much depended on it. Those who attack this structure of partnership assault an American tradition as old as this Nation.

And I intend, as long as I am President, to make sure that the American Government is a model of prudence and economy, and that doesn't mean that we are going to neglect the sick or forget the unemployed, repeal social security, or turn our farmers out to the pasture. It means that we are going to have faith in the people, and with the people together work to build a better democracy.

It does not mean that we are going to have a labor Government. It does not mean that we are going to have a business Government. It means that we are going to ask labor and business to join hands and to have a democratic Government. I am determined that Government discharge its solemn duty to cooperate in strengthening our free enterprise system, and to give all the freedom possible to all Americans.

And the fact is that all of the programs of your Government have a single aim: the freedom and the happiness of our people and the vitality of our great free enterprise system which has made America what it is today.

There are two philosophies at each others throat in the world—the Democratic philosophy and the Communist philosophy. If we win, if we survive, if freedom prevails, it is not going to be because we have more people than they do, it is not going to be because we have more acres than they do, because they have several times more tillable acres than we have and they have many millions more people than we have.

It is not going to be because we have more resources than they have. It is going to be because we have a system of government that is better than theirs. It is going to be because our people do not believe in regimentation and centralization and socialization.

Our people believe that a capitalist ought to be able to take his dollar and invest it, that he ought to be allowed a reasonable return on that dollar without fear of having it confiscated; that a manager ought to come along and help invest that dollar in a producing enterprise; and that the manager that gets up at daylight and stays up until midnight and develops stomach ulcers while he is doing it, he is entitled to a 2-week vacation, a bonus once in a while, a little profit-sharing, and social security when he is 65.

With that capitalist who invests his dollar, and with that manager who manages, we have the worker who produces. He gets on the assembly line and every 27 seconds he puts the rivets in the top of a car, and on every one that comes by. And if he doesn't get them all in in 27 seconds, and it takes 28 to put them in, then that car goes out without a rivet. He does that all day long.

But he is the greatest producer in all the world—the American workingman. He doesn't ask much either. He wants a little vacation. He would like to have a little sick leave, he hopes he has a little medical care, he has some things that he wants, he wants a rug on the floor, and a picture on the wall, and a little music in the house. He wants a church that he can worship in according to the dictates of his own conscience. He wants a school that he can send his children to and he hopes they get better education than he got. He doesn't ask for the world with a fence around it. All he wants is to make America a better land.

I am here to tell you that if we all—Democrats, Republicans, and whatnots—do what is best for America, it will be best for us. I want all of you to do everything you can here at home because we have enough to do in Washington without your coming up there and asking our help. I know you don't believe in the Federal Government doing much anyway. But when I come flying into these places, I fly into an airport built with Federal funds, I get on an interstate highway built with Federal funds, and I go downtown and talk States' rights. And I hear about them, too.

We have on the platform today two Governors from our two States, Oklahoma and your neighbor. One of them is a Democrat, John Connally, and the other is a Republican, Governor Bellmon. But we want to work with both of them to make America stronger and better and richer for all of our people. And don't ever get so selfish but what you forget that what is good for your country is good for you.

And let's put aside the slogans and the false warnings. Let's look at the facts. Let's see what your Government actually does.

First, more than half of our national budget, $52.5 billion, is used to defend you. This is the ultimate protector of your freedom. It is what permits you to go to bed at night without fear that somebody will rap on your door at midnight and order you into the hoosegow. I want to tell you as long as I am President, I intend to keep our defenses the best in all the world.

Second, more than 10 percent of our national budget goes directly to help States and communities meet their own problems on the local level. I will talk to you about a few of them, some of your Hill-Burton hospitals, some of your highways, some of your airports, some of your farm programs.

Third, your Government has programs of cooperation and partnership with private enterprise. The Small Business Administration has made more than 20,000 loans to thousands of struggling small businesses. It has created more than 400,000 jobs. The area redevelopment program helped to rebuild stricken parts of our country so that business could come and prosper and men could find new jobs.

The agricultural programs have given our farmers the confidence in the future which lets them invest and modernize. We have not solved all of our farm problems, but we have come a long way from 1933 when they were throwing men out of windows when they tried to foreclose all of our farms.

I don't think anyone seriously believes that we have destroyed the will to work or the will to produce. The truth is that we have the most abundant, free agricultural economy in the history of the world. And I am somewhat proud of the fact that our farmers did such a good job that they had all we needed to feed all the American people, and the Communists had to come over here to buy wheat to make bread for their own people.

Fourth, for our entire history we have worked with local government and private enterprise to develop the power and the water, the roads and the canals which are really the foundation of industry in this country. And as long as I am your President, your Government is going to devote full energy in developing all of these resources, and one of them that we are now developing is the Arkansas River.

Fifth, research and technology have made possible the modern aircraft industry, the atomic power industry, and the nitrates on which agriculture depends.

Sixth, we have an investment partnership in human resources, in education, in skill training, in health. Think about what has been done with polio alone. Think about how every mother in this country dreaded and feared spring and summer to come because they were afraid their children would wind up crippled. And think about how their dreams of some day finding a medicine, a vaccine, that would prevent all of this terrible suffering. And those dreams have now come to pass.

All of these programs are designed to provide America with protection, designed to provide America with the skilled people that it needs, designed to give people a chance to take a productive role in the Nation. And that is why your forefathers set up a system of public education. A great President of the Republic of Texas before we came into the Union once said, "An educated mind is the guardian genius of democracy. It is the only dictator that free men recognize, and it is the only ruler that free men design."

So a system of public education, every dollar invested in education today, brings a return of 10 to 12 percent in national wealth, and that is a pretty good return on a dollar invested—10 to 12 percent.

Seventh, we have a system of Government protection designed to liberate free enterprise for growth. The SEC that was born during the Roosevelt administration has helped make all of us a nation of capitalists. Insurance for your hard-earned savings in your savings and loans, in your banks, has protected the greatest banking system in all the world, and they are not popping like firecrackers as they once were. Antitrust

legislation has made it possible for smaller businesses to survive and for competition to flourish.

The drug laws and the food laws have given the consumer the confidence on which rising sales depend. Other laws, by eliminating abuses, have made it unnecessary to adopt measures which might strangle the workings of our market economy.

Eighth, programs—from the food stamp program to unemployment compensation to social security give people a better chance to stand on their own feet, to help themselves in our own free enterprise tradition.

I remember as a young man standing in the corridors of the Congress back in the early 1930's, when I heard one Congressman that was a friend of mine say that he was seriously considering voting against social security because they used some horrible name about it—they called it socialistic and socialism, and it was changing our form of government. But it is mighty hard to find a man today—you have to travel north, south, east, and west to find one—that would repeal our social security system.

Yes, Americans recognize the duty of a rich and compassionate nation to assist the old, to assist the sick, and to assist the helpless. All of us were taught to follow the Golden Rule of "Do unto others as you would have them do unto you." And that is what your Government is going to do as long as I am your President.

These are the facts and not the slogans.

I just wish that we had as good a chance for rain down home as you have here. We have been caking our old cows all summer, and we are out of pears down there.

But these are the facts and not the slogans. It contributes to the vitality of our free enterprise system and the freedom of the individual.

The fact is that never in our American history has your American business been more alive, been more growing, been filled with greater opportunity than it is now. And I think that you know in your heart that that is right.

And all you have to do is turn on your television, or buy your morning or afternoon paper, or listen to your neighbor down the street, to realize that never in our history have Americans been freer to criticize or to pursue their ambitions, or to live as they want to live, as they are today. And I think that you know in your heart that that is right.

Well, these are the fruits of the partnership that we have built, that your father and mother and your granddaddy helped us build. And this is the partnership we are going to continue between the Government and the people as long as I am your President. And I think you know in your heart that we have so much to be thankful for, so much to protect, so much to preserve.

So let's go home tonight and let's don't weep on our pillow. Let's say our prayers and thank our good Lord Almighty that we are as lucky as we are, and that we enjoy the blessings that are ours.

Goodby and good luck.

NOTE: The President spoke at the Oklahoma State Fairgrounds in Oklahoma City. In his opening words he referred to Edward L. Gaylord, executive vice president and treasurer of the Oklahoma Publishing Company who presided at the ceremony, and Senator A. S. Mike Monroney of Oklahoma.

The text of the remarks of Mrs. Johnson, who spoke briefly, was also released.

599   Remarks in Texarkana at the Dedication of John F. Kennedy Square. *September 25, 1964*

Mr. Russell, Governor and Mrs. Faubus, Governor Connally, Senator Yarborough, Congressman and Mrs. Patman, Congressman and Mrs. Harris, distinguished platform guests, ladies and gentlemen:

First, I want to express my deep regret to all of you and to each of you for our tardiness this evening. It was good of you to want us to come. It was even better of you to be so patient and understanding.

We left Washington early this morning, about 4:30 or 5 o'clock your time, and we have been to El Paso, Eufaula Dam, in Oklahoma, Muskogee, Oklahoma City, and everywhere we have gone we have been meeting and visiting with and talking with, and seeing, good people just like you. So because of the crowds and because of our desire to say hello to each of them, we were delayed tonight. I hope that you are good enough to understand that there wasn't much we could do about it.

We do appreciate your coming here and welcoming us back to our home State. We do appreciate the presence of the two great Governors of Arkansas and Texas, and how they honor us on this platform. We are very pleased that we could have with us our own senior Senator from the State of Texas, Ralph Yarborough; our own Congressman, Jack Brooks.

You know, we in Texas are very proud of our delegation. We have been proud of it for many years in the Congress. When Mr. Garner was Vice President many years ago, and Mr. Rayburn was the Majority Leader getting ready for the Speakership, someone asked him why Texas had such a fine delegation in the Congress. Mr. Rayburn replied, "We pick 'em young, we pick 'em honest, we send them there and we keep them there."

And the reason that Texas and Arkansas both have such a fine delegation in the Congress today is because you pick 'em young, and you pick 'em honest, and you send 'em there and you keep them there.

I think I should say to you people in Texarkana, you are a very fortunate lot. For many years you have had two of the ablest Congressmen in the House of Representatives. You know, there was a time in Texas history when we said we give you two governors for the price of one. Well, in Texarkana you have two Congressmen for the price of one—our own beloved Wright Patman and our own beloved Oren Harris.

Now Texans will understand this because we are quite a modest lot, but while I have a chance to say something to Arkansas, I want to say this: There is no delegation in the United States Congress that has contributed more to the success of that Congress, that has contributed more sound, constructive leadership to the entire Nation, than the great State of Arkansas. There are States in the Union that you can't match in number of tillable acres. There are States in the Union that you can't match in terms of per capita wealth. There are States in the Union that you cannot match in poulation. But I will tell you, the Arkansas delegation is a match for any delegation in either House of the Congress.

John McClellan and Bill Fulbright wear proudly the title of Senator from the great State of Arkansas in the greatest deliberative body in the world. Wilbur Mills, Jim Trimble, Oren Harris, and "Took" Gathings, the other members of the Arkansas delegation in the Congress, are always there and on the job, and all of them have reached positions of seniority where they exercise great influence. I have never seen a single one of them when you called upon them but what they knew what they were talking

about and they had only one criterion, only one yardstick they applied, and that was this: If this is good for America, it is good for Arkansas and it is good for us.

I say to you tonight that the Arkansas delegation in the Congress has made great contributions to the welfare of all of our people. And I honor them and I salute them.

We have come here, though, to commemorate the great life of a great man—John Fitzgerald Kennedy. Ten thousand words would not honor the one thousand days that he served us all. Ten times ten thousand words would not express the sorrow in the hearts of each of us tonight. But John Kennedy would be impatient if we spent even one hundred words eulogizing him or sorrowing over him.

He would want us to honor him as he always honored us: by thinking of tomorrow. By talking of what we must do together to make tomorrow better and brighter and more secure for all men in our land and for all people around the world.

On that September day 4 years ago when John Fitzgerald Kennedy came here to Texarkana and spoke to you, he had this to say:

"Lyndon Johnson and I seek to represent the United States in a very difficult and a very dangerous period. We do not run for the Presidency and the Vice Presidency promising that if we are elected life will be easier.

"But we do promise you that if we are elected this country will begin to move again. This country will move forward. This country will stand strong. This country's brightest days will be ahead."

Tonight you know, and all the world knows, that America is moving forward, America does stand strong, the brightest days that we have ever known are opening before us. And they are opening in every section of the land. I am so proud that we have leadership that is opening those doors to our own beloved section.

But I would not want to mislead you. This is still a dangerous and a difficult time. This generation of Americans wants no promise of a life of ease, for we seek to live the life of the free.

Our concern tonight is for courage enough to win the contest of our times, for we know this: What we have we cannot keep, what we hope to have we cannot reach, unless we hold to our sure and our steadfast course of strength.

America's strength has never been the strength of arms alone. America's missiles are mighty. But the true strength of America lies in the moral might of our cause. It lives in the righteousness of the hearts of the people.

The sons of America are welcome tonight in free lands around the world because all men know that their purpose is peace. And the day must never come when our words or our deeds cause that purpose to be doubted.

Who leads America must speak what is deep in the hearts of Americans, not what comes from the top of the head. And deep in the heart of all America is a love for peace. We so devoutly want peace in the world. We want peace in the lives of all of our people. We want our senior citizens and our young folks, our family farmers and our businessmen, our workingmen and our management people, to live without fear of the future.

In your lifetime and mine, great gains have been made in this land, the greatest gains ever made in any land at any time. And there is no time for us tonight to give those gains away or to allow them to be taken from us. But those gains will go, and they will be taken from us, if ever we allow any people to divide us. Because the ultimate test of moral fitness for men who seek a public trust is their devotion to perfection of our system and their devotion to justice in our society.

All that we are, all that we ever hope to be, is placed in mortal jeopardy by those who would divide us, by those who would set class against class, and creed against creed, and religion against religion, and color against color, and section against section.

Let me remind each of you tonight that here in Texarkana I stand astride the boundary line between the two great States. Only a few miles out yonder and a few miles behind me two other great States join these two. Almost anywhere else in the world these lines would be marked by fences, or barriers, or walls—but not here in America.

As it is among Americans, so it is between us and our neighbors.

Only last week I stood on our border with the Prime Minister of Canada, far away from here. Only today, at noon, I stood on our border with the President of Mexico. On neither border are there fortifications or barbed wire fences or fears. And this is the way that Americans want to live—in the world and at home. And this is another reason why we must guard against those who would erect around our regions or our States prejudice and the barriers of hate or misunderstanding.

My beloved friends, as I stand here before you tonight, looking into your faces and into your eyes, I face to the south. I speak words which were spoken long before when I say, "Abandon all these local animosities and make your sons American." Those are the words of a great son of the South. Those are the words of Robert E. Lee, and they are words by which all of us may wisely live today.

1135

Sixty miles from here my wife was born. In this part of Texas she lived as a young girl and she learned as a young woman. This earth of Texas is part of her, and I am proud to say it is part of me. She has come back home tonight to the soil and to the people that she loves.

One's heart never really leaves home. Although thousands of miles may intrude, and you may walk with kings, queens, prime ministers, and fair ladies, there is forever a part of your birthplace that is bright and that is alive, and that gives you pride.

So tonight I speak to you with a heart full of hope and with a heart full of promise.

But there are voices abroad in the land that have a strange and a brittle tone. They cry out that we are weak, and America is soft and blind. They insist the way to the future is the road back into the past. They demand suspicion as the price of liberty, and belligerence as the alternate for peace. They just can't seem to find anything right with our beloved country and our beloved people. And all they find about us is wrong.

But thank God truth is eternal. Malice may distort it, and ignorance may ignore it, and panic may deride it, but the truth is always there. Truth is the weapon of the people, and truth is their shield against dishonor. Truth will protect them from false prophets and truth will save them from cruel hopes.

The truth is simple and the truth is this: Our beloved Nation was never stronger than it is this hour tonight. And our Nation was never more prosperous than it is this hour tonight. You and all of you know that in your heart I am right, because I know where we have been, so it is easy to measure how far we have come.

Tonight social security is the haven for our elderly citizens, and minimum wages have brought a better life to millions of our little people. The TVA and the REA have banished darkness from the countryside, and some of the voices say that this is all wrong. But the truth says that it is right.

Tonight our free enterprise system was never healthier. Wages were never larger. Profits were never higher, and job opportunities were never brighter, because more than 72 million have jobs tonight. Some of the voices deny this. But you know in your heart that it is right.

Today we have opened the doors to more education for more people. We have widened the horizons of better conservation of all of our natural resources. This afternoon I saw dozens of miles of long lakes where mothers and fathers will take their children for weekends. I saw dams that will save the farmers downstream from floods. I saw homes that will have electricity because of the energy that is created. Yes, the voices say this conservation is wrong. But you know, and I know, in our hearts that it is right.

Tonight we ask for equality under our Constitution and under our Bill of Rights. We ask for equality and justice and fair treatment for all of our citizens under our Constitution, and because of this, some of us are smeared and some of us are told that we should be fearful. But the truth says that it is right.

Today we enjoy more freedom than any American ever enjoyed at any time in our history, and what is important, we have more time to enjoy it because we are working fewer hours per day, fewer days per week, fewer weeks per year. The voices deny this. But the truth says that it is right.

Tonight we have a test ban treaty that keeps the air that we breathe—keeps it clean and free of poison. Some of the voices say that this is a mistake, that this is wrong.

But the mothers of America say this is right, and you know in your own heart that this is right.

Tonight we strive for peace, peace in the world through armed strength and through human understanding, through the United Nations and through God's own rule of doing unto others as you would have them do unto you. The voices say this is wrong. But the truth says this is right.

So my fellow countrymen, I have faith in the truth. The truth made us free. And the truth shall keep us free.

Sometimes in the late of night, when all the Capital City has gone to sleep, I sit by myself behind that big black fence and I read and I think. And oftentimes it is so quiet in the White House that I can almost hear the footsteps of the men who have lived in that house, and the men who have walked its halls and have slept in its rooms, and have stayed awake waiting for the sun to come up—Jefferson, Madison, Jackson, Abraham Lincoln, Theodore Roosevelt, Woodrow Wilson, Franklin D. Roosevelt, Harry Truman, Dwight Eisenhower, and John Fitzgerald Kennedy.

And when the problems and the decisions that are part of every President's life weigh heavily upon me, and my shoulders bend because it just seems that you can't carry any more, I always try to remember that this land was born in struggle and has survived and endured in freedom because truth prevailed and because decency ultimately triumphed.

I also remember that the men who lived in this house before me kept one cause and one aim in their hearts: What is right and what is best for the American people.

Well, here on the platform with my beloved friends Oren Harris and Wright Patman, with my great, able, senior Senator Ralph Yarborough, and with the two distinguished Governors, the chief executives of our States, Orval Faubus and John Connally, I want to say to all of you, with God as my witness, that this is my aim, and this is my purpose: What is right and best for the American people is best for all of us.

And with your help and with God's guidance, with the strength that comes from your prayers, Lady Bird and I will go back and open the gate and get behind the black iron fence on Monday. We pledge to you for as long as we are privileged to be there that we shall do what is right and what is best for all the people of this land.

NOTE: The President spoke at the dedication of the John F. Kennedy Square in Texarkana, Texas-Arkansas. In his opening words he referred to Norman Russell, an officer of the Texarkana John F. Kennedy Memorial Foundation, who presided at the ceremonies, Governor Orval Faubus of Arkansas and Mrs. Faubus, to Governor John Connally, Senator Ralph Yarborough, and Representative Wright Patman and Mrs. Patman, all of Texas, and to Representative Oren Harris of Arkansas and Mrs. Harris. Later he referred to Representative Jack Brooks of Texas and Senators John L. McClellan and J. W. Fulbright and Representatives Wilbur D. Mills, James W. Trimble, and E. C. Gathings, all of Arkansas.

The text of the remarks of Mrs. Johnson, who spoke briefly, was also released.

600   Statement by the President Upon Making Public an FBI Report on the Recent Urban Riots.   *September 26, 1964*

TOGETHER with all Americans, I have been disturbed by the riots which took place this past summer in some of our cities. The

preservation of order in such circumstances is the responsibility of the local communities and the States, but the fact that such riots can occur is a matter of national concern as well as personal concern to me.

I have today asked Mr. J. Edgar Hoover, Director of the Federal Bureau of Investigation, to make public a report summarizing the available facts developed by the Bureau on the causes and development of these riots.

Mr. Hoover's report indicates that:

—No definite pattern was found to exist in connection with the riots from one city to another.

—The riots did not have a single cause and cannot be attributed to any identifiable group of individuals.

—The riots occurred in communities with economic and social problems crying out for solution.

—Local police acted with great restraint in the face of violent abuse.

—The riots, as well as other criminal and juvenile delinquency problems in our cities, are closely connected to school dropouts.

—The mass of people in each community, white and Negro alike, deplored the riots and have cooperated to maintain law and order.

—Each riot began with a single incident and was aggravated by hoodlums and habitual lawbreakers.

—No evidence was found that the riots were organized on a national basis by any single person, group of persons, or organization.

I have taken several steps as a result of this report:

First, I have directed the FBI through its National Academy to make riot training available for all police departments in the United States.

Second, I have instructed the Secretary of Defense to enlarge the program of the United States Army for demonstration techniques of riot control. We will make these tech-

niques a larger part of the training of the National Guard of the various States and we will make them available to local police forces as well.

Third, I have directed Secretary of Health, Education, and Welfare to make a study of the dropout program followed in the District of Columbia—one of the most intensive in the Nation—and other places, and to make recommendations to me as soon as possible on what further steps might be taken by the Federal Government to assist in meeting this important problem.

Fourth, at an appropriate time I intend to call a conference of State and city officials to discuss ways in which the Federal Government can continue to be of assistance in this whole area.

Most Americans have a deep commitment to civil peace. I call upon all our fellow citizens to remember that respect for law and order and regard for each person's rights are the cornerstones of self-government in a democracy.

This administration feels strongly that this must be a society of law and order in which citizens live by recognized rules of conduct. To that end we not only enforce Federal acts but cooperate at all levels of government to assure that civil peace shall be maintained.

Every citizen, regardless of his race, creed, or color, is entitled to equal justice. And every citizen is entitled to be secure in his person on our city streets or in the countryside.

The FBI in the first 8 months of this year has attended 172 police training schools throughout the Nation where the attendance has totaled more than 5,800 law enforcement officers and has offered advice and counsel. In addition, the FBI has sponsored just this summer 228 conferences which were attended by 20,184 people representing 6,406 police agencies on the problems of securing law and justice.

We will continue this kind of coopera-

tion so our citizens may live in dignity and in security.

NOTE: The FBI report (10 pp., processed) is dated September 18, 1964.

The statement was released at Austin, Tex.

601   Remarks in Providence at the 200th Anniversary Convocation of Brown University. *September 28, 1964*

President Keeney, my old and valued friend Senator Pastore and Senator Pell, Congressman Fogarty, Congressman St Germain, Governor Chafee, Governor Gallogly, distinguished scholars, my fellow Americans:

This is a proud day for this university, and for the citizens of this great State. In these times the greatness of States is measured not by their size, but by the worth of their schools. By that measure, no State stands larger than the home State of Brown University.

For 200 years Brown has honored that charter of 1764 by "forming the rising generation" into ". . . a succession of men duly qualified for discharging the offices of life with both usefulness and reputation."

From this campus have come many of the most useful figures of our national life—great educators like Horace Mann; great leaders of business like John D. Rockefeller, Jr., and Tom Watson, Jr.; great public servants like Tom Corcoran, four Secretaries of State, and many distinguished United States Senators.

I speak with personal appreciation today on this subject. In the Senate, I had no more trusted counselors or cherished friends than Theodore Francis Green and John E. Pastore. And your brilliant young Senator Claiborne Pell is taking his place as a leader and a statesman. Today I am proud to have in my administration two men who served

as deans at Brown—Dr. Robert W. Morse and Dr. Donald Hornig.

For all that has gone before, Brown's service to the Nation has never been greater than it is today. On behalf of the Nation I am proud to salute you and all who have made Brown University one of the really great universities in the world.

In other times we might have come to this convocation looking back upon the past—but not today. I know that the face of New England, the face of America, is turned toward the future, and it is of the future that I have come to New England to speak today.

I want to consider with you today the future of an old and fruitful American partnership, the partnership of campus and country. That partnership was formed in 1787 when our forefathers gave us the command, "The means of education shall forever be encouraged."

From that Northwest Ordinance to the Land Grant College Act, from the Smith-Hughes Act to the enactments of this present education Congress, America has kept faith with that command. In all history no other nation has trusted education, invested in it, or relied upon it as a means to national progress so much as we.

A former great President of the Republic of Texas, Lamar, once said that "the educated mind is the guardian genius of democracy. It is the only dictator that free men recognize, and the only ruler that free men desire."

Yes, our partnership has paid us priceless returns. From a backward position, American scholarship has flourished. Today, wherever our country leads, that leadership traces to the contribution of the campus.

Our partnership is challenged now by new dimensions.

From 1776 until the present, our universities have grown—from 9 in the beginning to more than 2,000 today. From the present until 1980, our existing institutions must double in capacity, and 1,000 more must grow with average enrollments of 2,500 each.

But before the total of American scholars has doubled, the sum of human knowledge shall have doubled—or more.

These are challenges that we should welcome, and that we should go out to meet. For the increase in scholarship is not a burden, but a blessing. The growth of knowledge is not a curse, but a cure for the ills of this age.

Our concepts must change in both education and in politics. But our confidence and our courage must grow.

At the desk where I sit in Washington, I have learned one great truth: The answer for all of our national problems, the answer for all the problems of the world, comes down, when you really analyze it, to one single word—education.

Thus, I take a hopeful view, and I call upon you of this campus to join with us who are entrusted with the affairs of a country to help us chart a hopeful course.

President Keeney said last week that knowledge is developing so rapidly that "we can take no comfort in the belief that what appears to be the whole truth today will be the whole truth tomorrow."

I believe that our partnership must be committed, deeply committed, to seeking the truth, for actually it is truth alone that will finally keep us free.

Knowledge is not something which threatens to overwhelm us. Knowledge promises to be our salvation, and we must seek after it, and we must nurture its growth, and we must spread it, spread it among all of our people so each one of them have some of it.

Over the years, leadership of our university system has come from a relatively few great institutions, public and private. Well, I believe that we must regard our existing centers of excellence as natural resources to set standards, to supply teachers, to furnish researchers for the new centers of excellence that we develop.

This is a first responsibility.

A great Nation and a great civilization feeds on the depth of its scholarship as well as the breadth of its educational opportunity.

In the sciences, in the arts, in our understanding of human behavior, all of our tools must be sharpened. Our public policies must encourage further the spread of research and scholarship throughout our system of higher learning. In our graduate schools, your Federal Government—your Federal Government—awards 12,000 fellowships and 35,000 trainees in science and engineering. We spend $850 million—$850 million, almost $1 billion—on the support of research in our universities alone.

The partnership of the Government, your Government—not an enemy way-off-yonder, but something that belongs to you—the partnership of your Government and the universities is closest in the advanced education of postgraduate students. Twenty-nine percent of engineering students, 37 percent of the students in physical science, 46 percent of those in life sciences, and 10 percent of those in humanities are aided.

And there just simply must be no neglect of humanities. The values of our free and compassionate society are as vital to our national success as the skills of our technical and scientific age. And I look with the greatest of favor upon the proposal by your own able President Keeney's Commission for a National Foundation for the Humanities.

We must also make certain that there is no neglect or no compromise of the American devotion to democracy of educational opportunity. Because universal, free, public education is the very foundation upon which our entire society rests today. So our goals must be to open the doors to education beyond the high school to all young Americans, regardless of station or the station of their families.

You and I have an opportunity that is not unlike that of the men and women who first formed these New England States. We have the opportunity to plant the seed corn of a new American greatness and to harvest its yield in every section of this great land.

On the response of our partnership depends the vigor and the quality of our American way of life for many generations yet to come. As a party to that partnership, let me urge you of this campus to admit no compromise in charting our course to excellence. Concern yourselves not with what seems feasible, not with what seems attainable, not with what seems politic, but concern yourselves with only what you know is right.

Your duty is the vision. The duty of the world that I represent is the reality.

There is one thing more that I would like to emphasize.

Three hundred and twenty-eight years ago

Roger Williams founded Providence. He brought into American life a bright flame, which must never be allowed to grow dim. And he said, "I humbly conceive that it is the express and the absolute duty of the civil powers to proclaim an absolute freedom of conscience in all the world."

Our partnership is not as some would have it, a conspiracy against liberty. That partnership exists to reinforce the freedom of higher learning, and it must never be otherwise.

And so long as I hold any public trust, or any private responsibility, I shall devote my every effort to defending against all enemies the freedom of conscience, the freedom of belief, and the spirit of free inquiry on which our American system stands.

The statue atop the State House of Rhode Island is dedicated to the independent man. Man cannot be independent if he or his society are imprisoned in dogma, or bound by bias, or borne down by hate, or fear, or suspicion, or discrimination. At this moment I believe that we have a great opportunity in this country to move forward. As President Keeney has put it, "move forward toward making our society what we know it really should be."

If we turn away from knowledge and truth, we will not succeed. If we believe the worst and suspect the best, we alone will suffer. If we deny our progress, if we are against all of it, if we tear down our accomplishments, we will fill the world with sorrow, and we will blemish our own name with shame.

But if we are courageous and farsighted and farseeing, if we have no fear of the truth, if we seek only after light, then we and our children and our children's children shall know the greatness of this wonderful, beautiful land we call America.

I pray that when historians write the story of this time in our lives, that it may be recorded that this President tried, tried to lead his Nation, tried to lead his Nation with justice and with compassion and with courage—and there was faith and there was firmness in his heart.

May it further be written that the people of the United States cast out their doubts, took great pride in their achievements, and bravely made of this land and this world a brighter, happier place for all mankind.

This is our choice. This is our decision. Let us all be greatly determined that this society shall survive and this society shall succeed. And what it should be will be for all time to come.

As I will return tonight to my large room and my lonely desk in the White House, to cope with the decisions that have come to that desk through the day from all countries of the world, and when I review the problems of our men in uniform and those on strike, when I see the farmer and the laborer seeking justice and believing that his Government will do what is right, my mind will wander back here to the little State of Rhode Island, far away from what was once the largest State in the Nation where I was born. And I will remember back 10 months ago when a terrible tragedy befell the people of this Nation and I was called upon, as best I could, with all of my limitations, to attempt to carry on.

And I will think of the Presidents—Mr. Hoover in New York, Mr. Truman in Independence, Mr. Eisenhower in Gettysburg—all of whom sent me their good wishes and their prayers, who told me that they were at the service of this Nation in this crisis.

And I will remember how the butcher and the baker and the candlestick maker, the little children on the sidewalks, the folks sitting in the old folks home as I drove by— how they all gave me their hopes and their prayers that somehow we might be able to carry on.

But there is nothing I will be more thankful for than the contribution of the people of this State, because in my moment of trial, Congressman St. Germain and Congressman Fogarty, Senators Pell and John Pastore, all walking in the tradition of that great democratic leader Theodore Francis Green, they marched up by my side and said, "You have our talents, our energy, and our prayers."

And however long I may be permitted to continue in my work, I shall always feel deeply in the debt of this great university for the inspiration it has given me through the years, for the honor it has paid me by giving me a degree, and for the little State of Rhode Island, for the quality of the manhood it has produced.

Thank you.

NOTE: The President spoke in Meehan Auditorium on the campus at Brown University, Providence, R.I. In his opening words he referred to Barnaby C. Keeney, president of the university, and to Senators John O. Pastore and Claiborne Pell, Representatives John E. Fogarty and Fernand J. St Germain, Governor John H. Chafee, and Lieutenant Governor Edward P. Gallogly, all of Rhode Island. He later referred to Theodore Francis Green, former Senator from Rhode Island, Robert W. Morse, Assistant Secretary of the Navy for Research and Development, and Donald F. Hornig, Special Assistant to the President.

602   Statement by the President on the Problems of the Textile Industry.   *September* 28, 1964

I KNOW the significant role that textiles have played in the economic life of New England and I know of the difficulties this industry has encountered during the past few years. Fortunately, New England could have no better spokesman in Washington than Senator Pastore (Senator Muskie). He has been untiring in bringing home to all of us the very real problems faced by New England textiles. I can assure you that there is no major official in this administration who has not been made fully aware of the hardships created every time a mill is shut down or forced to operate on part time. We have worked hard at this problem and we will continue to do so.

President Kennedy, as a son of New England, knew these problems well. In May 1961, as you recall, he instituted a seven-point program for the textile industry. Under that program, Government-sponsored research for the industry has been launched. We have provided accelerated tax amortization for the textile industry even ahead of similar benefits for other industries. This year I signed legislation that is greatly helping out cotton textile mills by permitting them to buy cotton at world prices for the first time since 1956.

Among our textile problems has, of course, been the increase of imports. This administration has worked out a solution for the import problems of the cotton textile industry. It developed a long-term cotton textile arrangement. Under the administration of this arrangement, cotton textile imports have been stabilized—and we intend to continue keeping imports from disrupting the market.

All of these measures have contributed to restoring the prosperity of the textile industry, which, as a whole, can look forward to greater prosperity in the future.

I say with a great deal of pride that this administration has done more for the textile industry than any administration in history, and our efforts have not been confined merely to cotton textiles. We have stemmed the tide of foreign wool fabrics coming through the Virgin Islands by administrative action. This alone reduced imports 10 million square yards a year.

We have closed tariff loopholes which permitted some woolen textiles to enter after paying only half the duty they should pay. The Senate Finance Committee has just approved legislation which would close another loophole affecting tariffs on certain types of wool products. We strongly support this legislation.

But the wool textile industry continues to be faced with problems, particularly in New England. In the past 10 years imports have soared from less than 5 percent to 20 percent of American consumption, with particular concentration in worsteds.

The administration has made and will continue to make vigorous efforts to solve this problem. I share with our late, beloved President Kennedy the view that wool textile and apparel imports must be kept at reasonable levels. We have been trying to work out effective arrangements with other wool textile-producing countries. Two missions have been sent abroad for this purpose in recent months. Thus far a multination meeting has not been convened. But we intend to continue our efforts vigorously. I can assure you that we shall work hard at this problem. I consider it essential that the wool textile industry be restored to good health.

NOTE: This is the text of identical statements released in Providence, R.I., and in Portland, Maine. In the statement released in Providence the President referred to John O. Pastore, U.S. Senator from Rhode Island; in the one released in Portland, to Edmund S. Muskie, U.S. Senator from Maine.

For President Kennedy's proposed seven-point program for the textile industry see 1961 volume, this series, Item 161.

603 Remarks in Hartford, Connecticut. *September 28, 1964*

Governor Dempsey; my longtime friend and valued adviser, Tom Dodd; your able and courageous Senator Abe Ribicoff; Congressman Daddario; all Members of the most effective Connecticut delegation to the Congress; my old and trusted and helpful friend who may get us elected, John Bailey; your distinguished Mayor Glynn; my fellow Americans:

I was told before I came here that it was a little bit too early to talk politics in New England. I came on, anyway—because I don't intend to and I guess it is not necessary to talk politics, anyway. I intend to talk today about what I know is on your minds and what I believe is in your hearts—and that is responsibility.

Say what they will, change their stands all they wish, no partisans can conceal the issue before America this year because that issue is responsibility.

This ought not to be the issue. It would not be the issue if the responsible views of the responsible men in the responsible party were represented in this campaign. I say that because I have more respect for the Republican Party than some of those who have taken over its name this year.

Responsibility is the issue.

Responsibility is the choice.

The American people can choose to keep government that is responsible, like the kind of government that you have had 3½ years under Jack Kennedy and 10 months under Lyndon Johnson. Or the American people can choose to change the government to a government that is reckless abroad and reckless at home.

I believe I know what your choice is going to be.

In all this Nation no citizens anywhere value responsibility in government more highly than the great citizens of the great State of Connecticut. You have responsible government at the State level. You have responsible government at the local level. You have gotten good government because you have insisted on it and because you have been active in it.

You people of Connecticut have led the entire Nation since World War II in building highways, in supporting better schools, in rebuilding your cities, in retraining your workers. And the benefits show up in all the faces that I see out there today. They show up in all your lives.

In all this lovable, prosperous, progressive land of the United States, the State of Connecticut is one of the most prosperous States. Your personal income averages $740 more than the average of the rest of the Nation. You have fewer families living in poverty than any other State in the Union, and you ought to be proud of that. In fact, with the help of Congressman Daddario and Abe Ribicoff, Tom Dodd and John Bailey, and Governor Dempsey, if Connecticut holds its progressive course that you are now following, you will be the first State in the Union to win the war on poverty.

I know this is the work that you want to keep on doing. I know this is the work that you want your country to keep on doing.

The character of our country, of all the Nation, was really formed right here in New England. Wherever Americans live, there is a little of New England in them. Our Nation has gotten far more from this New England region than can ever be returned to it. But the greatest of your contributions are two traits that are deep in the American character.

One of those traits is prudence—caution, care, responsibility. The other is progress.

As President Kennedy said, "Keep the country moving." The American people throughout this Nation are a prudent people, and they want and they expect prudence in their Government. But the American people are also a progressive people, and they want to keep on progressing. They want to keep on making progress toward a better land and toward a better life. In short, the American people, from Connecticut to Texas, want to keep moving.

Prudence and progress are the watchwords of this administration that serves you now.

We have increased our Nation's strength until today the United States is the strongest Nation in all the world. We have, at the same time, controlled your Government spending so that the budget that I presented for fiscal 1965 was lower than the budget for 1964.

In relation to gross national product, total Federal spending in 1965—are you listening?—total Federal spending in 1965 will be the lowest in 14 years, and nondefense spending will be lower than it was 30 years ago and lower than in all but 2 postwar years.

We have been frugal without being fatalists and without being fanatical. For we have kept America on the move—we have been meeting our needs, we have been solving our problems, we have been fulfilling the hopes of our people.

This session of the Congress has been the most productive and the most constructive in all American history.

Ten months ago, after that terrible tragedy that thrust upon me, without a moment's notice, the responsibility of the Presidency, I tried to pick up where President Kennedy had left off. I tried to carry forward a program for all of you that he had dreamed of for you.

And when we took the scoreboard, we listed 51 major measures that should be considered. And of those 51 major measures, most of the newspaper people who travel with me today said if we could pass 2 we would have a successful session. If we could pass the tax bill, which was not moving in committee, and the civil rights bill, we would call it a successful session.

I came here to Connecticut today to report to you that we not only passed those 2 bills, and they are already the law of the land, but the United States Senate, of which Abe Ribicoff and Tom Dodd are two of the leaders, has passed each and every single one of the 51 measures. And that is the truth that you can't wash away.

I know that you people out there in that crowd know in your heart that that is good for America.

We have much work yet to do, but we are going to do it. We are not going to turn back the clock. We are going to rebuild our cities as you are rebuilding Hartford.

We are going to meet the people's needs for fast and efficient transportation so they won't lose 2 hours a day trying to get to and from work. We are on the way. We are going to create new jobs and train new people with new skills. Because this is the responsible way and the Democratic

Party is the responsible party, and this is the true American way.

For so long as there has been an America, there have been times when factions have risen up in our land. There have always been people who would divide and conquer. There are people who are trying to divide us now, trying to turn our course off sharply to the left, or trying to turn our course off sharply to the right.

For 175 years, through more than 40 national elections, the American people have said, "No, no, no," to people who would follow this kind of a course. And I think they are going to say "No" this year. Because I think that you know in your heart that we are not going to follow the fringes in November.

I know that we are not going to follow the course of turning class against class, or creed against creed, or color against color, or religion against religion.

No, I am going to ask you folks to leave here today and say to your family and to your friends that we believe that America and the United States should be united; that we want to present a united front, and attack and solve the problems at home and present a united front to all the world abroad.

In the American character there are those qualities of prudence and progress. But there is a deep and abiding commitment to peace, and that commitment to peace and that part of our character that wants peace is going to get peace. We don't have a national police force. We don't have a gestapo that we can send into your town overnight. We have a wonderful Bureau of Investigation that is available to your Governor, to your mayor, and to your local people. We are going to work with them to make our streets and our cities safer, but what we really want to do is to make all the streets

in the world safer for all people.

The first time that I came to Hartford to speak was more than 5 years ago. I came to speak to members of my own party, the Democratic Party. At that moment there was a grim challenge to our country from the Communist forces abroad. The then President of the United States was a member of the Republican Party. I was a leader of the Democratic Party in the Senate.

I told the members of my Democratic Party that night here in Hartford, 5 years ago, as I tell all of you here today, that I was not going to attack that President, the only President we had, even if he were a Republican—I was not going to make his job more difficult. Because I have always, and I will always, put the peace and security of America, the peace and security of my country, ahead of the interests of the Democratic Party.

And I think I know that that is what you, in your hearts, want me to do. I have always believed that if you will do what is best for America, you will do what is best for our party.

And I want to leave another thought with you. I voted for and I supported that Republican President more on his Republican program than some present members of the Republican Party did. And I never at any time called it by another name. At times I differed. On occasions I opposed but I opposed it with dignity and decency. And you never heard from the lips of a single member of the Democratic Party that President Eisenhower's program was just a 10-cent model of the New Deal.

No, I tell you when your country is in trouble, when people are trying to divide, when hate and fear is abroad in the land, it is time for the people of New England to lead the way, to start the march of unity, and to say to the rest of the world that we learned a long time ago, "United we stand; divided we fall."

Now, I know some of you have come out here through courtesy today. Some of you are hospitable. Some of you want to be good to your President. But I do want to ask those of you that are here one little question, because the folks in the United States are listening to you, they are watching you, they will be seeing you on television. I just want to ask you: Are we going to be united in November?

Well, it looks like some of you have heard the echo.

There is a time for party and there is a place for partisanship. But there are times in the history of a Nation when higher values matter more than party, and there are greater issues than partisanship. Your two Senators proved that time and time again. I believe that today is such a time in our national life.

All that America is, and all that you want America to be, is challenged today by those who stand on the fringe. Against such a choice as this, responsible people have only one course of conscience, and that is to choose their country's interests over all other interests. I believe that this is a choice that you will make come this November.

For I pledge you—and hear these words—that the next Johnson administration will follow the course once set by a great President, Abraham Lincoln, who told us: "Beware of rashness, but with energy and sleepless vigilance go forward and give us victories."

NOTE: The President spoke from the portico of the Hartford Times Building in Hartford, Conn. In his opening words he referred to Governor John N. Dempsey, Senators Thomas J. Dodd and Abraham Ribicoff, and Representative Emilio Q. Daddario, all of Connecticut, John M. Bailey, chairman of the Democratic National Committee, and William E. Glynn, mayor of Hartford.

The text of the remarks of Mrs. Johnson, who spoke briefly, was also released.

604   Remarks in Hartford to a Group of Business Leaders.
September 28, 1964

I WANT to first of all say to that policeman up there, if I may have your attention, that any of those nice people that are standing on the steps I believe in them having a little freedom since I have this medal. If they want to, just let them pull up that rope and let them come on down here and talk to us.

I am deeply touched by the thoughtfulness and the generosity that prompted this presentation. All my life I have had great respect for the business leadership of the great State of Connecticut and for that matter, all New England.

I asked when I came here today that I might have an opportunity to meet some of that leadership so I could observe the countenances that had provided the initia-

tive and the adventure and the vision for a substantial part of our free enterprise system in America.

As we meet here, there are two great philosophies that are rivals in the world—and one or the other will ultimately prevail.

One philosophy is the democratic philosophy that has been practiced in this country from the time of our first President, George Washington, up until this moment. Although I have only been your President for 10 months—I was called upon to shoulder awesome responsibilities without a moment's notice—I have had the support and the prayers of the members of this great business fraternity from coast to coast without regard to their business affiliation, their religious affiliation, or their party affiliation.

Because I have had that support as your President, as President of all the people, this whole Nation—Democrats and Republicans and whatnots—enjoys a period of prosperity that has never been equaled before in the annals of the history of this country.

Now while we are enjoying all of that prosperity, we see communism challenging us and challenging freedom on many fronts. I am proud to say to you that we are standing up, we are resisting, and we are trying to halt the envelopment of freedom anywhere in the world. Although there are more than 120 nations in the world, and although there are dozens of nations that have been born in the last decade, we have not lost a single nation to communism since 1959.

Now these two philosophies are in a struggle. They are after each other's jugular, and if we survive it will not be because we have more people than they have, because they outpopulate us. There are many more millions in the Soviet Union than we have in the United States. They have more than 600 million acres of tillable land and we have less than 200 million, so they have a lot more tillable soil. They outnumber us in many of our greatest resources and their potential in other ways far exceeds ours.

So in resources, in human beings, in tillable acres, we are all at a disadvantage. What do we rely on? We rely on the one great advantage that the American people have: that is our system of government.

Now, that system is not built on any one party, or any one people, or any one section, or any one religion, or any one group. That system that we know as the free enterprise system is made up of really four important segments.

The first is the capitalist. Some of you have been known as capitalists in your time and some of you not many years ago were even called royalists—"economic royalists," I believe it was. You have been so referred to from time to time in various campaigns in America because sometimes you asked for it, and sometimes you couldn't avoid it.

But the capitalist is the man that, through prudence, accumulates wealth and takes that money and is willing to invest it. It may be to rebuild a whole new area. It may be to put skyscrapers in the sky. It may be to provide production lines for jobs. It may be to build railroads and dams. It can follow many lines.

But he invests that dollar in America with a reasonable assurance that it will not be confiscated and will not be taken away from him by some government that stages a coup in the midnight hours, and that he will be secure in his possessions without fear that some night at midnight someone will rap on his door and serve him a warrant and lead him off to jail. He hopes that he may get a reasonable return on it. Sometimes he does and sometimes he doesn't. Sometimes he gets it all back plus 5 or 6 percent, sometimes he loses it all.

But anyway, he has hope and he has a chance, he has an opportunity, and he is willing to take care of the rest himself, if you give him that—and he has that in America.

That capitalist is joined by what you call a manager.

That manager is the fellow that gets up at daylight and works to midnight and develops stomach ulcers trying to get a bonus or trying to have a profit-sharing plan, or trying to build a better mousetrap at less cost, trying to compete not only with his fellowman here but with the rest of the world.

He takes his chances where he finds them and if he loses, he fusses with his wife about it, but he takes it in stride. Sometimes he has a good profit. For 43 months now he has had a rather good record, but the next 43 might not be so good, so he has to take it.

But he joins with the capitalist and he manages that dollar, he sees where it is invested and he tries to exercise prudence and yet exercise vision.

Then the third segment there is the worker who gets to work at 8 and works to 5, and he has 27 seconds to put the number of rivets in that car or that plane that he needs to. If he doesn't get them in in the 27 seconds he goes to 28. That car or that plane moves on down the line—and it doesn't have the rivets in it! And you've wound up with a car that is missing a rivet a time or two yourselves. We all do that. But that poor fellow gets a coffee break twice a day. The rest of the time he has 27 seconds to do that job and handle that machine.

He is the worker, and he hopes someday he can have a little hospital care, he can have a little pension, he can have a little social security, he can have a place to take Molly and the babies when he retires. That is his great love. His boys go to war; they fight to preserve this system. He likes his boss and he respects him. He believes in free enterprise, and he does not hate the man who makes a reasonable return.

Now those three—the capitalist, the manager, and the worker—make up free enterprise.

Now, whatever they have after they have produced it, Uncle Sam steps in and takes 52 percent of it. He is the first partner. And every dime you make, I've got a 52 percent interest as President. So I want you to do well. And I think you are doing well, and I am glad that you are.

My 1965 budget—when I came in they anticipated it would be $5 billion more than 1964, because '64 was $5 billion more than '63, '63 was $5 billion more than '62, and '62 was $5 billion more than '61. We have a growing population, we are moving on— we have more schools, more roads, more needs to fill.

But I spent the first 37 days and nights I was in office trying to find some way, somehow, some means to keep that budget under $100 billion, because I thought psychologically it would be a good thing.

I thought if we could not pull down our expenses in a great era of prosperity I did not know when we could pull them down. So instead of a budget of $5 billion more— $103.8 billion—we reduced it. And I had the help of Republicans. President Eisenhower came down and worked with me 2 days. Bob Anderson, the Secretary of the Treasury under President Eisenhower, came down and worked with me almost a month.

I had the budget directors from other administrations come in. I got all of the advice I could get, because nobody needed it any more than I did. We finally developed a budget that was $1 billion less in '65 than it was in '64.

While we were doing that, we passed a tax bill. We put some of the money back for the people to spend instead of letting the Government spend it for them. We put some of the money back for business to invest in new enterprise instead of the Government investing it for them.

So as a result, we have more men working today than we have ever had before. Our profits are higher, our wages are higher, our economics are better, our system is producing.

Don't you tell me for a moment that we can't outproduce and outwork and outfight any communistic system in the world. Because if you try to tell me otherwise, you tell me that slaves can do better than free men, and I don't believe they can. I would rather have an executive vice president, even if he comes from Hartford, Conn., than to have a commissar!

So I say to you men who are the leaders of this community, and through your industries the leaders of the United States, that we are doing reasonably well today but we have got to do better. We have got other fields to conquer. We have other roads to travel. This part of the United States has always led the rest of the Nation and the rest of the world in two fields: prudence and progress.

You have something about you that permits you to keep your eyes on the stars, and still keep your feet on the ground. And if you don't have both of them on the ground all the time you at least have one of them on the ground. So don't ever get both of them off the ground at one time.

Now I am going to conclude by telling you a story. It is one of the real reasons I asked to meet you insurance people up here today.

You remember back in the thirties when we had to have all of the reforms, and we had the problems in the Stock Exchange, and we had men committing suicide and folks jumping out of windows, and banks popping like firecrackers, and all of the economic problems?

Well, during that period Mr. Rayburn had to be the author of the Holding Company Act. He came from a little red, sandy land farm down in Texas, and he was just a farm boy. But he had to author the Stock Exchange Act, and he set up the Securities and Exchange Commission, and he had all of these great economic financial reforms.

Right in the middle of it, Mr. Whitney came in and asked him if he wouldn't come up to speak to the Bond Club in New York City. And he said, "Who is the Bond Club?"

"Well," Mr. Whitney said, "it is a group of people who deal in bonds and investments and who are financial experts. As a prerequisite to membership you have to have a good financial statement—$1 million or more. We would like to hear you and we would like to invite you."

This fellow was testifying before Mr. Rayburn's committee, and he kind of wanted to ingratiate himself anyway. So Mr. Rayburn, very much to his surprise, said yes, he would accept the invitation.

The fellow who extended the invitation was almost sorry that he had ever asked him, because he did not think he would accept. But Mr. Rayburn went up there, and the fellow was a little embarrassed in front of all of these millionaires to introduce this sandy land farmer from Texas who had put all of these reforms through—called it "death sentence," you remember, on holding companies, and they were going to ruin all of the power companies and destroy everything.

So he got up to introduce Mr. Rayburn, and he said, "Fellows, I invited this man to come up here. I don't know why he came. But here he is, Sam Rayburn," and that was the only introduction they gave him.

That is more than you all gave me today. I just had to get up here and talk!

Mr. Rayburn got up and said, "I came up for two reasons. If you don't know why I came, I want to tell you." He said, "All of my life I have been poor. I have just a modicum of wealth, and I have accumulated a little, and I have worked mighty hard for it and have saved it. I haven't married, I've saved every penny I had. I haven't spent it on my family, but I have never yet been able to acquire a million dollars. I wanted to come up and associate with all of you fellows who have been successful, and just hope that a little bit of it would rub off on me.

"So that is the first reason I came."

And he said, "The next reason I came was to show you I ain't scared of you!"

So I really have three reasons for coming up here today. I want to associate with you and learn things from you, and ask you to help your Government and to counsel with us and give us all of the advice you can. Because we need it.

Second, I want to commend you for the contribution you have made to your Government during these 10 months when we have had a real critical period on our hands.

I don't know how much longer I will be there—you may change in November. But I want to ask you to help whoever is President, because it is an awesome responsibility to carry the weight of 190 million people and their future on your shoulders. And no

man ever occupied that office—there have been 35 of them—that didn't do his dead level best. I never have seen a one that I thought ran on a platform of doing what he thought was wrong. They all do what they think is right, but sometimes they make mistakes, and they need your judgment.

Finally, I want to tell you that I appreciate what you have done for me, and with me, and most of all for your Government, for your country, regardless of your religion, or your party, or where you live. And finally, I just wanted all of you to know I wasn't scared of you.

NOTE: The President spoke on the terrace at Constitution Plaza in Hartford, Conn., where a group of business, industrial, and civic leaders were awaiting him following his remarks at the Hartford Times Building (Item 603). He was greeted by J. Doyle DeWitt, president of the Travelers Insurance Companies, and by the insurance firm's vice president, Roger C. Wilkins, who presented him with a Charter Oak Leadership Medal.

605   Remarks at the Airport, Burlington, Vermont. *September 28, 1964*

Governor and Mrs. Hoff, Senator Fayette, Senator O'Shea, Mayor Daley, Mr. O'Brien, Mrs. Schurman, Mr. Ryan, my fellow Americans:

This is my second annual visit to Vermont. I came here last year and, if you extend my welcome, I would like to make it a habit.

We want to thank you, genuinely thank you, for being so patient and understanding about our problems today. This is a wonderful sight to behold from this platform— to see so many friendly, smiling, happy faces from the fire truck over here all the way around. It gives us great joy to know that you would want to come here and say hello to my party.

This is the third appearance I have made

since I left Washington, and every place we have been, we have been met with courtesy and hospitality and enthusiasm. We are very sorry we are late, but we are so happy we finally got here. You know, you can't really object if you are late because you are seeing people. What would really disappoint us would be if we had gotten here ahead of time because there would have been nobody to meet us.

Ten months ago, because of a terrible tragedy, we lost a man we all loved so much as a leader and as a friend, the President of our country. In a matter of moments, I became your President and had to try to pick up where he left off. Since that time we have had the Congress in session and we have been considering the program that President Kennedy had recommended.

We analyzed that program very carefully when we went in, and there were 51 major measures before the Congress that needed attention, and we would hope would be considered. This morning, about 6:45, I talked to Senator Mansfield, the great leader of the Senate, and he reminded me then that all of those 51 measures had passed the Senate as of now.

I want to be fair. Some of them are in conference and will have to be adjusted between the two Houses. Some of them won't be passed by the House of Representatives, I am sure. But I do want to say that we have much to be thankful for, and much to be grateful for.

We want to say to you good people of Vermont that we appreciate the support you have given us, we appreciate the prayers you have said for us, we appreciate the way you have tried to hold up our hand and help us do the very best job that we could do.

Sitting in Washington, surrounded by papers and officials, you sometimes begin to lose track of the real source of the strength of the United States, the real strength of America. That is why it is inspiring for us to come to this State, whose hills and valleys have contributed so much to the leadership of America.

Some of that leadership has come from the ranks of my party. Phil Hoff, your great Governor, has not only given you good government; he has made a national reputation as an outstanding servant of the people, and he is respected throughout the land. I know of no young Governor in any of the 50 States that I have more confidence in, or that I am more anxious to work with.

And when I was here in October, I got to know Fred Fayette. He is proof that you still have more outstanding young men here in Vermont on the way up. I hope that come next January, after we get through with the inauguration, that all of you folks can go from the Capitol Grounds where we begin the parade, up to the Senate Office Building, and see your new Democratic United States Senator, Fred Fayette.

But in Vermont, as in the Nation, leadership dedicated to progress is not confined just to one party. All the patriotism in this country is not in the Democratic Party or in the Republican Party. No party has a monopoly on good judgment, on good service, or on patriotism.

Some of our most distinguished Americans, as well as some of my warmest friends, are Vermont Republicans. There is George Aiken, who has been one of the architects of the bipartisan foreign policy of this country, which has protected freedom through the administrations of four different Presidents.

And it was only last week that I went to see the Prime Minister of Canada. I flew across the Nation. We went there to meet in connection with the treaty between our country and Canada in order to better relations. Senator Aiken was on that trip. He represented not only the Republican Party, but represented all Americans, because he is known as the guiding genius of our relations between Canada and the United States.

Of course, there is the shining memory of Warren Austin, another Republican, who did as much as any man in this century to lead America toward responsible partnership in world affairs.

These men were never divided by narrow partisanship. They were never divided by sectional pride. They asked themselves this question: "What is good for my country? What is good for America?" And they believed that what was good for America was good for them and good for their party.

They drew their strength not from your granite hills, but from Vermont's historic traditions. This is a State which has looked to the future always, which has acted courageously and wisely to meet the challenge of the future:

Vermont's Green Mountain boys, with a little help from New Hampshire and Massachusetts, won the first offensive victory of the Revolution.

Vermont drafted the first State constitution to forbid slavery.

Vermont was the first State admitted to the Union after the original thirteen.

Vermont was the first State to make constitutional provision for a complete State system of education.

Vermont was the first State to set aside land for schools in each township.

Vermonters went West to help build many of the States of the Northeast and the Mississippi Valley.

Half of the able-bodied men of Vermont went to fight in the Civil War.

And in our own time, Vermonters have displayed the same vision and the same leadership on the world scene. From the United Nations to the test ban treaty, Vermonters have been in the forefront for peace and for freedom.

Well, I believe deeply in the Democratic Party. But throughout my career I have worked closely and gained inspiration from Republican colleagues like many of those that you have sent to Washington. I have never put my party ahead of my country; and I never shall.

We had shared a common belief in the future of America and the principles of progress. We believe that this country had a duty to act responsibly and courageously.

And this is not the case this year.

This year our proud tradition of responsible partisanship is endangered. This year the progress won in three decades of patient striving—by Democrats and Republicans alike—is in danger.

At home we have pursued policies that have improved the well-being of all of our people. At home, today, these policies are in danger, and you ought to know they are in danger, and you ought to do something about it. I think you are going to, come next November.

Around the world we have followed the course of using our power with restraint, of helping others achieve freedom and self-government, of learning to live with people who share this planet with us. Well, I tell you today that that course is in danger.

One of our great parties has been captured, captured by a faction of men who stand outside the whole range of common agreement and common principles which have brought us to the summit of success. These men have not just marched out of step with American progress—they have refused and they now refuse to march at all. If they gain control of our Government, they would not change the direction of our march; they would just halt it altogether.

They have already said that their aim is not to pass laws, but to repeal them.

Which laws do they mean?

Do they mean the REA that has brought electricity to all the farm homes of America? Well, they will never repeal that, will they?

They oppose the Minimum Wage Act which gives protection to underpaid Americans, and which has increased the prosperity of all Americans by boosting purchasing power. And I don't believe they are going to repeal the minimum wage, do you?

They oppose legislation to help improve our colleges and our universities. And I don't believe they are going to repeal that law, do you?

They opposed the atomic test ban **treaty** which ended the radioactive poisoning of our atmosphere, and which was supported by Republicans from Vermont. But I don't believe you want to repeal that treaty either, do you?

They opposed the tax cut which means higher incomes and more jobs and expanding business for all of our people, and which will increase income in Vermont by $54 million. Do you want that bill repealed?

Well, most Americans, I think, as I recall back in 1935, when the bill was passed, there were just a handful of votes against it; most Americans, I believe, feel that we should have a social security system which helps old people live in dignity and security. Well, when social security was proposed back there in 1935, I believe, 30 years ago, some of these people called it a "cruel hoax." But most Americans didn't think so, and it was passed. I don't believe they want it voluntary and I don't believe they want it repealed, do you?

When the war on poverty was proposed in January, this faction said it was an attempt to buy votes. But most Americans didn't think so, and they passed the bill in the Senate with the support of some of our friends from Vermont. They passed it in the House. It is now the law of the land and we are going to do something about making taxpayers out of taxeaters. We are going to conduct a war on poverty and try to help the poor find jobs.

Most Americans believe in providing every boy and girl with an education that they can use. Some of this faction has said, "The child has no right to an education."

In the past 4 years dozens of programs and pledges of the 1960 Republican platform have come before the Congress. They have received support from Democrats and Republicans alike. But this faction has opposed most of them.

The philosophy that would tear down these programs, in my judgment, does not represent the people of Vermont and does not even represent the Republican Party of Vermont. They do not represent the Republican Party of America. They do not represent the view of responsible, forward-looking men of any party anywhere.

And they do not look forward to the kind of America which this State for almost two centuries has worked, and fought, and voted to build.

And it is not the kind of America that you are going to vote for, I don't think, next November.

My own party does not believe in partisanship for the sake of partisanship. When I became leader of the Senate, I said I reject the philosophy that it is the duty of the opposition to oppose. I said I think it is my duty as a Democrat to support a Republican President, President Eisenhower, when he is right, and to oppose him when he is wrong. I am here to say to you I kept that pledge and I supported him more and supported the Republican President and the Republican Party and the Republican program more when I was Democrat leader than my opponent in this race supported him then. And he was a Republican!

I intend for the Johnson administration to take account of that principle and to bring into Government men and women of both parties who are pledged to continue the progress of the past 30 years.

When Franklin Roosevelt became President, he selected three Republicans to be in his Cabinet.

When Harry Truman was President, he appointed men like Robert Lovett and John McCloy to high positions.

When John Kennedy became President in 1961, he brought to Washington outstanding Republicans like Henry Cabot Lodge, Robert McNamara, Douglas Dillon, John McCone, Chris Herter, and others.

I believe this is good sense, and I am going to do the same.

I do not believe that the faction that temporarily leads the Republican Party represents all the people. I know it doesn't represent all the Republicans. So, my fellow Americans, let us work together, men of every region, of every religion, of every race, of every party. Let us labor to pass on to our children an America more united, an America more prosperous, an America more progressive, an America more peaceful than ever before in our history.

Let us be faithful to our traditions of the past so that future generations will say of us, as we say of our forefathers, "They guarded and handed on the American dream."

It has been wonderful to be here with you this afternoon. I apologize again for being late. I just want to leave this thought with you: In this country, the people are the bosses. You determine by your vote who you want to lead this Nation. Ten months ago, because of provisions of the Constitution, the Vice President succeeded to the Presidency. I have done, with the ability that I have and such talents as I possess, my dead-level best to lead this country and to do what is right by all of its people.

I have not tried to be a President that believed in a labor government, or a business government, or a farm government, or an extreme government of any kind. I have tried to be a President of all the people. I have made mistakes like other men. I tried to make as few as I could. I have always thought I was doing right. I have done the best I knew how.

You people have given me strength. When I felt depressed, you have inspired me. I have come here today, prior to the time you make a decision. In November you will be called upon to exercise the highest responsibility of an American citizen. You live in the greatest Nation in the world, and how great it is in the future is going to depend upon the wisdom of your decision. In November when you go to that ballot box, you are going to do what you think is best for your country, and that is what I want you to do.

If I were acting for you, I would vote for Congressman O'Shea, and I would vote for Senator Fayette, and I would vote for Phil Hoff, and I won't get personal, but I will tell you somebody else I would vote for!

I am not here to give you a hard sell today. You have the right and you have the privilege, and you have the duty, to make a change and to bring a new government if you think your safety and your security and the future of your children will be best served by that change. If you do, we will have no hard feelings. Actually, I will have more time really to visit Vermont.

But if you decide in your wisdom that you want us to continue, you want us to carry on, we will go back there in January and we will try to pull together the people of this country.

We won't have a government of the north or the south or the east or the west. We will have a government of all sections, of all people, of all regions, of all religions, of all races. We will try to unite instead of divide. We will try to love instead of to hate. We will try to get along in the world instead of abuse our neighbors. We will try to go anywhere, see anyone, do anything that we can do with honor to bring peace to all the people of this world.

We are a very small minority. We have

only 190 million people in a world of over 3 billion. There is ferment, there is unrest, there is division, there is dissension. There are many problems to be solved. I don't know that I am the one to solve them. That is a matter for you to decide.

But I do want you to know this: I don't know how many Presidents are as lucky and as fortunate as I am to get a chance to come here in the autumn season to the lovely little State of Vermont and look you in the face and tell you that I want your help, I want

your hand, I want your prayers. And if you give them to me, I will just do the best I can.

Thank you very much.

NOTE: The President spoke at a rally at the airport in Burlington, Vt. His opening words referred to Governor and Mrs. Philip H. Hoff, State Senator Frederick J. Fayette, Democratic candidate for U.S. Senator, State Senator Bernard O'Shea, Democratic candidate for U.S. Representative, Daniel J. O'Brien, State Democratic Chairman, Mrs. Beatrice Schurman, National Committeewoman, William J. Ryan, National Committeeman, all of Vermont, and Mayor John J. Daley of Rutland.

The text of the remarks of Mrs. Johnson, who spoke briefly, was also released.

606   Remarks in Portland, Maine, on the Steps of the City Hall.   *September 28, 1964*

Mr. Walsh, ladies and gentlemen, boys and girls:

I want to introduce you to my sweetheart—Lady Bird.

[At this point Mrs. Johnson spoke briefly. She commented on the beauty of the fall foliage throughout the New England States, and expressed her pleasure at meeting the people and her appreciation for "this wonderful welcome." The President then resumed speaking.]

Senator and Mrs. Muskie, Governor Reed, Mr. Hathaway, Mr. Curtis, Mr. Dubord, Mrs. Broderick, Miss Mackensen, my fellow Americans:

I want to say this to you tonight: I think this is the most wonderful welcome that May Craig ever received. And I want to tell you something else: She deserves every single bit of it.

When I was sick in 1955 I would wake up in the morning not knowing whether I would wake up that night or not, or whether I would see the sun rise another day. And during that period, Lady Bird was at my bed 24 hours a day.

But every single, solitary day, without ex-

ception, May Craig wrote me a letter and made me want to live and get well. I have wanted to come to Portland, Maine, ever since, and here I am, thanks to all of you.

I have come to the forest city of Portland— in the great State of Maine—to talk to you tonight about your future and about the future of your children, and about the future of your grandchildren, and about the future of America.

First, I pledge responsible government. We believe that it is every American's duty to support his Government, but not necessarily in the style to which it has been accustomed. That is why I have cut the budget by almost a billion dollars. And we have many thousand less people on the Federal payroll today than we did 10 months ago.

The people of Maine work hard for their tax dollars. The Johnson administration is going to make sure that you get full value for every dollar your Government spends.

Second, I pledge a government which will meet the challenges of the future without deserting the traditions of the past. We have built the prosperity of the country on a broad, national agreement about the great goals and the great principles of the great land that we call America.

Forward-looking men and women of every party, from Maine to Texas, from every region of America, have shaped the structure of our modern country. Men like your able, fearless, diligent, courageous, Democratic Senator Ed Muskie; and women like your own great Republican Senator, Margaret Chase Smith, have had a part in shaping the policies in Congress that have built a prosperous America. We are not going to turn it over to extreme and reckless people who would not hesitate to shatter all that has been so carefully built.

Third, I pledge a government devoted to equal opportunity for every section of this Nation. The greatness of this Nation rests on the unity of its people. A beloved New England poet, Longfellow, said:

"All your strength is in Union.

All of your danger is in discord."

So I say to you tonight we do not intend to let the voices of discord and division ever pull this country apart.

But unity does not only mean that every section has a responsibility to the Nation. It means that the Nation has a responsibility to every section.

Tonight we are in the midst of the longest and the largest period of prosperity in American history. We cannot be satisfied until that abundance reaches the life of every State and every citizen.

I say to you tonight that New England has given more than its share to the Nation's past. And I say to you, and I pledge you tonight, that New England will get its share of the Nation's future under the Johnson administration.

As my beloved friend Ed Muskie said to me, "It is now New England's turn at bat."

Three times—three times—Portland was almost burned out, once by the Indians in Colonial days, once by the invading British in 1775, once more in a roaring fire less than a century ago. Each time, through hard work and cooperation, your great city of Portland arose a better place than it had ever been before.

Nature has blessed Maine with a beauty that is unmatched in all the world. And you ought to be proud of it. But the good Lord's greatest gift to Maine is not the beauty of its land. The good Lord's greatest gift to Maine is the quality of its people.

The people of Maine have given America tradition of thrift, of industry, of independence, of courage in the face of every adversity. With these qualities as our foundation, we can work together to create a more abundant future for all the people of this State and this region.

The people of Maine have never been afraid of government—or afraid of anything, for that matter. They have never regarded government as an alien power which threatened their liberty.

More than 75 years ago, Governor Joshua Chamberlain, in his message to the Maine Legislature, said:

"A Government has something more to do than govern and levy taxes to pay the Governors. . . . Government must also encourage good, point out improvements, open roads of prosperity, and infuse life into all the right enterprises."

Well, I tell you tonight that that was the idea of Governor Joshua Chamberlain, and that is the course that Lyndon Johnson plans to follow.

The Johnson administration's program for prosperity will not be giveaways or handouts. No one would dare offer handouts to the people of Maine. But we are working to create new opportunities. We are acting to give people a chance to help themselves, to develop and use their own skills, to provide for their families through their own labor.

I warn you that it is up to you to seize the opportunities that together we help create. Over the past 4 years your Federal Government, working hand in hand with local government and private enterprise, has been creating new opportunity for Maine.

The Area Redevelopment Administration has assisted a new sugar beet industry which will produce 100 million pounds of sugar each year and provide thousands of new jobs. I have instructed the Area Redevelopment Administration to survey other problem areas where plants have shut down through a combination of technological change and competition. I have told them to work with you to get those areas moving again.

In 66 projects across the State, training programs are helping develop new skills for new jobs. We have trained almost a thousand men and more than three-fourths of them are now employed.

We have worked with local officials to establish new industry and services, especially in the fields of conservation and water pollution control and small business loans. And the new Economic Opportunities Act, our poverty program, will give a further boost to the great economy of the great State of Maine.

The first thing I am going to do when I get into Washington tonight is get a good night's sleep and the next thing I am going to do is call up Sargent Shriver and tell him to get in touch with Ed Muskie and the Governor and do something about it right here in Maine.

Our new tax cut will stimulate a $128 million increase in the State of Maine's income, and it will create 9,000 new jobs here in Maine.

President John F. Kennedy loved Maine, and he wanted to do something about it, and he did, during his lifetime. In July 1961 your unemployment rate was 6 percent. This July it was down to 4.1 percent, and that is below the national average. And average weekly earnings in manufacturing have risen 13 percent—up 13 percent.

And we will continue to work until every able-bodied man in the State of Maine who wants a job can find a job. That is our goal; that is our objective. And we will work as hard as we know how in an effort to achieve it.

Every one of these programs, every dollar that we have spent, has one aim and one aim only: to give every American a chance to improve his life through his own work and through his own abilities.

This is in the finest tradition of American Government.

You have heard much through the years about plans to harness the great tides of Passamaquoddy for power. This was a dream 30 years ago of one of our greatest Americans, Franklin Delano Roosevelt. It was the vision and the objective of one of New England's greatest products, John Fitzgerald Kennedy.

And Lyndon Baines Johnson is going to do something about Passamaquoddy, and Hubert Horatio Humphrey is going to help him, and so are these two fine Democratic candidates for Congress, and so is Ed Muskie, and so is Margaret Smith, and so is the Governor of this State. Because we are going to unite and try to get this job done for all you people, whether you are Democrats or Republicans. I will have a report on this project ready for the next session of Congress.

Now my present term runs out on January 20th, but if I am there after the 20th, we will be back here and talk to you again about this proposition. It must meet the standards set by President Kennedy. It must first strengthen the economy of the whole country, and it must enable America to compete better in the markets of the world. I hope and I believe that it will meet that test.

These are some of the fruits of the cooperation of government and people. There are voices which seek to tell us that government is an enemy of the people.

But what is government? Government is the people. Daniel Webster once said, "The people, sir, erected this government." It exists to serve the needs and to advance the dreams of the people.

We used to say down in my country, "As Maine goes, so goes the Nation." Well, when we said that, we were talking about elections.

But in the future, Maine will again be a leader for the Nation, a leader in creating a more abundant America, a leader in building the Great Society, where every man can have a job, where every family can have a roof over their heads, where we will work fewer hours and we will work fewer days, and we will have more recreation for ourselves and our family, where every child will have an adequate schoolroom and will have a competent teacher there to teach him, where the sick can find a hospital bed and have some medical care insurance to help him pay for it, where our countrysides will be improved and we can see the beauty of nature, and we will get rid of all these old cars that are parked out on the sides of the highways.

Yes, Maine will again be a leader, and will serve as a bulwark of freedom and peace in the world. And who knows—I don't guess anybody really knows—who knows;

even in the elections, this year, Maine might resume its tradition of leadership.

I must go to New Hampshire now to conclude a speech that I am 2 hours overdue on, and then I will fly back to Washington. But before I leave here, I want to say to each of you just as simply and as personally as I would if you were sitting in front of the fireplace with me in my home: This has been a delightful day. It has been a stimulating experience for us, to get away from the desks and the papers and the reports, and the crises, and the critical decisions that come to your President, and to come out here and meet the people I work for.

I am the 36th President of this country. While we are one of the youngest countries in the world, we have one of the oldest governments. I have great faith in our system of government. I want to do everything that I can within the limits of my ability to make it work.

I must deal with the leaders of 120 other nations, and I cannot operate a government by ultimatum. They don't want to be shoved around any more than we want to be shoved around. Most of them want to live and let live. Most of them want for their children the same things you want for your children, food for their stomachs, clothes for their backs, a roof over their heads, a school for them to attend, a church where they can go and worship God according to the dictates of their own conscience. They don't ask for much.

I have traveled around the world and I have seen men and women of all colors, of all faiths, of all religions. When I looked into their heart and into their face I see just about what I see out there tonight—good human beings wanting for their children something more than they had for themselves, and willing to work their fingernails off to help them get it.

Now I don't know how long we will be able to live in this world together in harmony. In my lifetime we have had two world wars. I saw men leave, never to return, in order that we could freely assemble out here tonight and have this great privilege.

I hope and pray that I will never see another war. As long as I am your President, I am going to use the 30 years of experience that I have obtained in the House and the Senate and as Vice President, doing everything I can to hold my hand out to other countries, and my guard up.

With your help, with your support, with your prayers, somehow, some way, I think we will come through with flying colors.

Thank you and good night.

NOTE: The President spoke on the steps of City Hall in Portland, Maine. In his opening remarks he referred to Adam Walsh, U.S. Marshal from Portland, Senator Edmund S. Muskie of Maine and Mrs. Muskie, Governor John H. Reed of Maine, William D. Hathaway and Kenneth Curtis, Democratic candidates for U.S. Representative, Richard Dubord, State National Committeeman, Mrs. Faye Broderick, State National Committeewoman, and Judith Mackensen, State Committeewoman for Hancock County, Maine.

The welcome to Mrs. May Craig of the Portland Press-Herald took place at the airport, where the crowd had cheered her as she walked down the steps of the press plane.

The text of the remarks of Mrs. Johnson was also released.

607   Remarks in Manchester to the Members of the New Hampshire Weekly Newspaper Editors Association. *September 28, 1964*

Mr. Piper, my friends, and your extremely valuable Senator, Tom McIntyre; your most distinguished and able Governor, John King; two brilliant young leaders, Ollie Huot and Charles Officer; State Chairman Murray Devine; and my fellow Americans:

First of all, I want to apologize to you, and then I want to say thank you very much. For you to know how I feel, you would have to trade places with me. But I came in the White House late last night from across the Nation, and I left early this morning for this wonderful section called New England. And it was from New England that all of us came. All of us have a little New England in us.

So I wanted to come here and see your people, exchange views with them, tell them what I stood for, and ask them to help me in the job that I am trying so hard to do. And I have one more engagement after this one this evening.

For some reason or other, we have been about 3 hours behind all day. I regret that. I wish there was something I could do about it. I don't want to ask people to wait on me. But I must admit in candor and frankness that I would rather be 3 hours late because people wanted to see me than to be 3 hours early because there was nobody there.

Now that I have told you how sorry we are that we are late, I want to introduce you to my sweetheart—Lady Bird.

[*At this point Mrs. Johnson spoke briefly. The President then resumed speaking.*]

It was 4 years ago that John F. Kennedy came here to Manchester. He answered questions that people from all parts of the Nation had asked him during the campaign.

From Portland, Oreg., he was asked, "How can you be sure that we will have peace?" And he answered, if you will remember, "We have to work at peace . . . the way to maintain peace is to maintain our strength, to speak quietly, to identify ourselves with the cause of other people, to make it very clear to the Communists that we do not want war, that we are going to be firm, that we are building in this country a strong and a vital society."

Well, that policy—strength and firmness matched to restraint and patience—has been the basic foreign policy of every American President, the basic foreign policy of both political parties for the past 20 years. Our hand has always been out, but our guard has always been up.

President Truman said, "Peace requires as much moral stamina as waging a war. . . . It requires undying patience and continuous application."

President Dwight Eisenhower said, "The path for America must be cooperation . . . as together we continue the search for peace, a search in which we shall persevere without tiring or without ceasing, . . ."

Call the roll of Americans who have shaped the world policy of the United States in your lifetime: Truman and Eisenhower and Kennedy, Acheson and John Foster Dulles, Arthur Vandenberg and Walter George, Warren Austin and Henry Cabot Lodge. These were men of every party, and I am proud to say of every section.

Everyone agreed on the great shaping principles of America's foreign policy. Together they offered the Biblical prayer, "Peace be to this house." For them the house of peace was the entire world.

And this is the same course that your Government is following tonight. And, God willing, it is the course that we shall continue to follow as long as I am your President.

Much has happened in the past 20 years. But through change after change, and crisis after crisis, and convulsion after convulsion, we have worked to build the four great pillars of policy on which the house of peace must rest.

First is the effort to persuade our adversaries that any attack upon us would immediately bring their own destruction. For this reason we have built the most powerful military force in the history of the world, and in the last 4 years you have spent $40 billion more than you would have spent had the spending of the last Eisenhower year for military and space continued. In other words, Mr. Kennedy has spent an average of $10 billion a year more on military preparedness and space than we were spending the last year of Mr. Eisenhower's administration, 1960.

Now, what has come from that? Tonight we have more than twice as many bombers that can be put over our adversaries' land than they can put over ours. Tonight we have more than twice as many intercontinental ballistic missiles that we can put over their land than they can put over ours.

We know that nobody can escape a hurricane simply by being in favor of good weather. Our strength is our surest shelter against war.

But don't get the idea that strength alone will deter an aggressor. Our adversaries must also be convinced that we have the will and the determination, and we maintain and intend to at all times in all places defend all American interests. We do not rattle our rockets and we don't throw our bombs around lightly. But we have never given them cause to doubt that America has the will.

In Greece and Turkey, and in Korea, President Truman halted Communist aggression.

In the Formosa straits President Eisenhower halted Communist aggression.

In Cuba—and that was the last country

that has gone Communist—remember, not a single country in the world has gone Communist since 1959—in Cuba, President Kennedy halted the Communist aggression which threatened the mainland of the United States itself.

And in the Gulf of Tonkin, the Johnson administration acted, and will continue to act to halt Communist aggression.

These consistent actions contain two great lessons. We must stand firm when the vital interests of freedom are under attack. And we must use our overwhelming power with calm restraint.

Second, we have worked to strengthen the independence of others. We live in a world with 120-odd nations. We have done this strengthening by helping others resist direct aggression, from Berlin to the island of Formosa. We have done this by working with others to fight indirect aggression—from Viet-Nam to Venezuela.

We are doing this through the Peace Corps every day, through the Alliance for Progress, through foreign assistance, aiding others to build their nations and strengthen their independence, and bring hope to their people and give them education, and keep them from starvation. So we are strengthening the independence of others.

Third, we have worked to establish the rule of peaceful settlement in world affairs. The key to our own success as a Nation is obedience to the rule of law. This is also the hope for peace in the world community. So we will continue to work for this principle and we will continue our wholehearted support of the United Nations.

Fourth, we have worked to lessen the danger that nuclear weapons will destroy all mankind. From the Baruch plan of President Truman to the "open skies" proposal of President Eisenhower, to the test ban treaty and the "hot line," every President has worked to build the structure of agreement on which enduring peace must ultimately rest.

And as long as I am your President, I will propose new initiatives for effective arms control. I will try to reverse the arms race. I will try to lessen the tensions that endanger and imperil the world.

These are the four pillars on which the house of peace must rest.

Today there are some who attack these policies. They assault the steadfast principles of the last 20 years. They seek to substitute a new structure. But I think it is a dangerous, shaky, and unsafe place. For I think it is built on three illusions. These illusions, if believed and followed, would put our freedom and the peace of the world in mortal peril.

Let me, in the words of the prophet Isaiah, "Come now, let us reason together," let me take a moment to discuss these with you.

First is the illusion that force, or the threat of force, can solve all problems. I know you would respect my size and my strength, but I don't think there are many of you in this room who would quake in your boots if I threatened you with using force, and I think what is true of you is true of nations. Ours must never be a government of ultimatum. All people must know that we are slow to start, but hard to stop.

This afternoon I was in Portland, Maine, and I was reminded that the last President to visit Portland, Maine, was Theodore Roosevelt—a great President of another party who visited there in 1902. But what he said back there a half century or more ago is as true tonight as it was then: "Speak softly and carry a big stick."

In my country we are very proud of what we call the Texas Rangers. Sometimes when we have a little row or misunderstanding in our country, they call out a Ranger.

One of our old cow puncher friends took some cattle up to Kansas City to sell, and one of the fellows out in the stockyards said to him, while they were waiting for the bidders to come in, "Please tell me what is really the difference between a Sheriff and a Texas Ranger."

The old man, a Ranger for many years, ran his hand through his hair and deliberated, and he said, "Well, a Ranger is one that when you plug him, when you hit him, he just keeps coming." And we must let the rest of the world know that we speak softly, we carry a big stick, but we have the will and the determination, and if they ever hit us it is not going to stop us—we are just going to keep coming.

Our military strength is vital to our security and it is very important to our influence. But it cannot and it must not be used to compel and to frighten all others into following our command and our every wish. Nor can it build the lasting framework of an enduring peace, because peace does not come from threats or intimidations, or humiliations, or overpowering. The only consequence of such a policy would be constant conflict, rising hostility, and deepening tension.

Force could not rebuild Europe. It took the vision and the statesmanship of the Marshall plan, and the patient molding of the NATO Alliances.

Force will not bring democratic progress to Latin America. It will take many years of the Alliance for Progress to create freedom's answer to false Communist promises. The ancient enemies of mankind thrive in that area of this hemisphere—disease, illiteracy, and ignorance.

Force will not bring an end to the arms race. We cannot coerce others to negotiate. We can't even compel them to be reasonable and wise. It takes skill and it takes patience,

and it takes determination, and it takes a search for areas of common interest.

In the 10 months since that fateful day last November when tragedy cut our President down, and on a moment's notice, I had to step in and pick up and try to carry on for him, first, if you will remember, some of our soldiers were fired upon and killed in Panama, and there were those that shouted "Move in with the paratroopers."

Well, we went over to the Peace Corps and got one of our most skilled diplomats who had lived in Panama for years. We said to them, "We will not negotiate with a gun at our temple. We will not sign a blank check to a treaty, but we will treat you fairly and justly. We are a big Nation and you are a small one, and we are not going to take advantage of you. But you are not going to take advantage of us."

And we were criticized for weeks. But ultimately we reached an agreement on exactly the terms that I proposed the first day by telephone to the President of Panama.

A few days later Mr. Castro decided to cut our water off at our military base at Guantanamo. We were paying him for that water, and we were employing some 3,000 Cubans to do our work there. We were spending about $5 to $6 million a year with them. Suddenly and impetuously and impulsively, and I think irrationally, he cut our water off. The shout went up, "Send in the Marines."

I don't want the newspapermen to think I am quoting anybody now. But we let our coffee cool a little bit and we decided, for better or for worse, that it was wiser to send in one admiral to cut the water off than it was to send in a regiment of Marines to turn it on.

So we told Mr. Castro that we will make this base self-sufficient; we will make our own water. We cut off about $5 million

1163

worth of his exchange. Ever since he has been wanting to have a conference with us.

We had our troubles in Zanzibar. We still have our problems in Viet-Nam. Every day some one jumps up and shouts and says, "Tell us what is happening in Viet-Nam and why are we in Viet-Nam, and how did you get us into Viet-Nam?" Well, I didn't get you into Viet-Nam. You have been in Viet-Nam 10 years.

President Eisenhower wrote President Diem a letter in 1954 when the French pulled out of Viet-Nam, and said, "We want to help you to help your people keep from going Communist, and we will furnish you advice, we will furnish you assistance, and we will furnish you equipment, if you will furnish the men, and if you want to fight for your freedom we will try to help you."

New Englanders haven't forgotten it was less than 200 years ago when we were fighting for our freedom and people helped us. So President Eisenhower wrote that letter and he followed through on it. And President Kennedy followed through. And we have now had four or five governments in the last year. I can't tell you who runs the Government here, much less who runs it in Viet-Nam. As a matter of fact, I suspect some of you are going to have something to do with deciding who runs it here in November.

Now some of our people get awfully worried and talk about we have a crisis a week. Well, I wish we never did have a crisis. I would like to play with my radio or go to a football game, or go out in my speedboat. There are a lot of things I would like to do.

But if you just think we have a crisis a week you are optimistic. We have one a day. And the only thing you can do with them—you can't take an aspirin and get away from them—is you just have to take

the best information you have got, take things as you found them, and make the best judgment you can under the circumstances.

Some of our people—Mr. Nixon, Mr. Rockefeller, Mr. Scranton, and Mr. Goldwater—have all, at some time or other, suggested the possible wisdom of going north in Viet-Nam. Well, now, before you start attacking someone and you launch a big offensive, you better give some consideration to how you are going to protect what you have. And when a brigadier general can walk down the streets of Saigon as they did the other day, and take over the police station, the radio station, and the government without firing a shot, I don't know how much offensive we are prepared to launch.

As far as I am concerned, I want to be very cautious and careful, and use it only as a last resort, when I start dropping bombs around that are likely to involve American boys in a war in Asia with 700 million Chinese.

So just for the moment I have not thought that we were ready for American boys to do the fighting for Asian boys. What I have been trying to do, with the situation that I found, was to get the boys in Viet-Nam to do their own fighting with our advice and with our equipment. That is the course we are following. So we are not going north and drop bombs at this stage of the game, and we are not going south and run out and leave it for the Communists to take over.

Now we have lost 190 American lives, and to each one of those 190 families this is a major war. We lost that many in Texas on the Fourth of July in wrecks. But I often wake up in the night and think about how many I could lose if I made a misstep.

When we retaliated in the Tonkin Gulf, we dropped bombs on their nests where they had their PT boats housed, and we dropped them within 35 miles of the Chinese border. I don't know what you would think if they started dropping them 35 miles from your border, but I think that that is something you have to take into consideration.

So we are not going north and we are not going south; we are going to continue to try to get them to save their own freedom with their own men, with our leadership, and our officer direction, and such equipment as we can furnish them. We think that losing 190 lives in the period that we have been out there is bad. But it is not like 190,000 that we might lose the first month if we escalated that war.

So we are trying somehow to evolve a way, as we have in some other places, where the North Vietnamese and the Chinese Communists will finally, after getting worn down, conclude that they will leave their neighbors alone. And if they do, we will come home tomorrow.

It is not any problem to start a war. That is the easiest thing in the world. I know some folks that I think could start one mighty easy. But it is a pretty difficult problem for all of us to prevent one, and that is what we are trying to do.

The second illusion I want to talk to you about is the illusion that the United States can demand resolution of all the world's problems and mash a button and get the job done.

In this nuclear age we have concern about the affairs of every continent, and that concern on some continents is increasing very much the last few days. That concern does not give us either the right or the responsibility to order the affairs of other nations. For example, two friendly nations, India and Pakistan, have been engaged in a long and often bitter dispute over the area of Kashmir. We are always ready to help. I

have been out there and visited, and I have tried to take this ancient feud and pull these people together.

Most of the problems that we get in are ancient disputes that have been going on not for decades, not for generations, but for centuries among people—the Greeks and the Turks, the Pakistanis and the Indians.

Peaceful solution can mean much to the freedom of Asia, if we could only bring it about. But the responsibility of settlement must remain and should remain with these two nations involved. All we can do about two men that are arguing among themselves is to try to encourage them to settle their argument. We can't run in and get in the middle between a man and his wife because we will wind up getting hit. The same is true in many places throughout the world; independent nations with their own interests, with their own convictions, must work to settle their own problems.

We have willingly accepted the responsibilities of world leadership, and when our own vital interests are challenged we act. But we are not the sole captain of the ship.

Third is the illusion that we could, if only we tried hard enough, put an end to all difficulty and danger, and then retire from the world.

The sound of gunfire in Asia echoes in the homes of Manchester. The speeches of a leader in Moscow or Peiping help shape the life of a subway rider in New York. An angry cry for freedom in Africa requires an understanding act in Washington.

And as long as this Nation endures we are going to be engaged in the affairs of the world.

I welcome this involvement. I believe the American people welcome it. It may bring danger but it brings an added dimension to the prospects of freedom. In this world, as in life itself, there is really no escape from problems. You can't run away from them. No escape from peril.

Each of us in our own family faces continual change. We have our own desires—for a career and for more of the good things of life. These wishes often conflict with each other and with the wishes of others that we love. We must make constant compromise and we must make adjustment.

There are times that come when you have to decide whether the boy or the girl gets the car on Saturday night. There is no end to difficulties. We just can't wish them away or press a button or call on some general to solve everything for us. But we can hope to make progress toward a fuller and a happier life.

You have done that here in Manchester. You have done that in New Hampshire and in New England. You have done it in America.

In our own country, after two centuries—as a united people in an abundant land under a single Constitution—we still face great issues, and we still have difficult challenges. But we have made enormous, unbelievable progress.

How much more uncertain, then, is the life of the world? In six continents live over 100 nations. Some are far more ancient than our own. Others are barely begun. Some pursue hostile ambitions. Others are struggling for their survival. Some are flourishing and abundant; others desperately try to emerge from a poverty that is so bleak that it staggers the imagination.

So let no one tell you in this day and time that the problems of a world will be solved without sacrifice, and will be easily solved without years of effort. Because we just cannot ignore others. We tried to do it and two wars came as a result. Our future is tied to theirs. We can't abandon those who will not do exactly as we wish.

I remember one time when we were fighting an REA project in my State and I negotiated with the president of the power company for 2 days and I didn't make a bit of progress. He just sat there like a Methodist deacon and never gave an inch.

I was somewhat impulsive in my youth, somewhat erratic, and I finally got disgusted, and I said, "As far as I am concerned, you can take a running jump and go you know where." The old man just looked back at me as calm and restrained as he could be, and said, "But I don't want to go there." And all the board of directors came over and congratulated me on the fine speech I made and how courageous I was to tell the president of the power company to go to. . . .

Finally I went to one old lawyer who was wise and who had served me for years. I said, "Senator"—he had been a Senator—"how did you like my speech?" He said, "Well, son, you are young in public life, and I hope you go a long ways. But the first thing you have to learn is telling a man to go to hell and making him go are two different propositions!"

So we cannot abandon those who will not do exactly as we wish. To do this, or to withdraw from the United Nations—and they have prevented almost 20 wars from getting started—to cast aside our commitments, would endanger freedom everywhere. And I think it would end the hope for peace. And it would certainly revive the fast fading Communist hopes for world empire.

I do not think that our future is going to be a simple one. But like all of those who sat in the White House before me, I believe it will be one which free men will welcome.

I expect victory. We are going to have

victory. But it is not going to be a swift victory. It is not going to be the victory of arms, and it is not going to be victory of the grave. Our victory will come over many years as people choose freedom, as nations grow up and become mature, and as they learn independence.

Moreover, as the threat of war fades, that victory, I want to warn you tonight, is going to take great strength and going to take patience. It will take men willing to deal with the real events of a real world and not trapped by the dangerous illusions of fantasy.

But above all, it will mean that we must turn toward the world with the grandeur and the generosity of that American spirit which on this continent has already built an enduring home for freedom.

This has been a delightful day for me in New England. I have come here as your President to counsel with you about your country and your future.

I am the 36th President of this country, but until January 20th I am the only President that you have. If I am weak, you are weak. If I am harassed and harangued, you are harassed and harangued. There is not anything that you can do about it from now until January 20th. But in November you are going to decide what kind of leadership you will have for 4 more years.

I am not here to do like the little boy that left the cotton patch down in my country and went over to hear a Senator speak one afternoon. He came back about dark and the boss said, "Where have you been all afternoon?" He said, "I have been listening to the United States Senator Joseph Weldon Bailey."

"Well," he said, "the Senator didn't speak all afternoon, did he?" He said, "Mighty near." He said, "What did the Senator say?" He said, "Boss, I don't remember. I don't recollect precisely what the Senator said, but the general impression I got was the Senator was recommending himself most highly!"

I believe in prudence and I believe in progress. I cut the budget, after working 37 days and nights, $1 billion instead of increasing it $5 billion as we had been customarily doing on account of the increase in population each year. I had 51 measures that we thought were important to pass in the Congress, and 51 of those measures have already passed the Senate.

I have called the leaders of the workingmen in this country, the labor leaders, to the White House for conference after conference, but this is not going to be any labor government. I have called the businessmen, more than 2,000 of them, from every State in the Union, to the White House to talk to them about their problems, but this is not going to be any business government.

I have called the farmers in to talk about their problems, but this is not going to be any farm government, because if the good Lord lets me live and lets me continue to serve you, I am going to be President of all the people instead of any single group.

But I don't think that we have to have a civil war in order for each person to have his rights. I don't think that labor has to harass business, and I don't think that business has to lock out labor, and I don't think the Government has to harass both of them. I believe if you give them all a fair shake that we can live under one great tent and develop this country, because united we stand; divided we fall.

So if you came out to meet me tonight to hear about my fears, you are going to be disappointed. If you came out to hear me speak like I had a martyr complex and nobody loves me, you are going to be disappointed, because I think that we have the greatest system of government in the world and I am proud of it. If you came out to hear me talk about all the things wrong, you are going home sad, because there are some things wrong, but the things that are right outnumber them a great deal.

I am for things, instead of against them. I know what I am for. I am for uniting my country. I am for a nation of lovers instead of a nation of haters. I am for a nation of trusters instead of a nation of doubters. I am not for arraying class against class, or region against region, or religion against religion, or color against color—because we are all Americans.

I have a dream and I have a hope, and I want to see the day come, and I hope I can speed it, when every home can house a happy family, when every child will have a classroom open to him and a teacher to teach him all he is capable of learning.

I want a nation where the businessman is prosperous and expanding, and taking on new adventures, and where the worker has some leisure time and some social security. I am not going to change my position on that, either. I want a nation of homeowners instead of home renters. I want a prosperous nation, a proud nation, a peaceful nation.

When I drove down the streets of Rome just a few months ago, a priest ran out and threw himself in front of my car. And he had 400 little boys following him. He said, "We want you to thank America—America. It is the only land in the world where the victors would treat the vanquished as you have treated us. You defeated us in war and then you came to help us rebuild. Look at that skyline and look at those people

working, and look at the happiness on these children's faces. That must make you feel mighty good, that you have that much christianity in your country."

It did make me feel good. I don't want to overlook my own people, though. I am going to see that the 43 months of prosperity that we have had in this country is continued. I am going to try to see that the peace that President John Kennedy fought so valiantly to preserve is kept.

You have that great right to change your quarterback. You have had one in now for part of the game. I have been in 10 months. You can change him in November if you want to, and I won't fall out with you if you do.

But I want you to know the kind of man you are going to get for another 4 years if you don't change him. And I want to ask you in advance, because I may just have some kind of illusion and some kind of dream about what is going to happen in November, I want to ask you in advance to give me your hand and give me your help, and give me your counsel and give me your heart, and give me your prayers, because the 37th President of this country is going to need them more than the 36th.

We are still going to have problems to solve, and they must be solved together, not as a divided nation, but as a united people.

Thank you and God bless you.

Before I leave, I want to thank Governor King for his hospitality and for his courtesy. I just left a Republican Governor in an adjoining State that was mighty nice to me. I am glad I walked into the arms of a Democratic Governor. I want to thank your new Congressman, Mr. Huot, and Mr. Officer, who are going to be elected, I think. And I want to thank you for sending to

Washington one of the ablest and most respected Senators that I have seen come in the period of time I have been there, your own Tom McIntyre.

Thank you very much.

NOTE: The President spoke in the Grand Ballroom in the Carpenter Motor Inn in Manchester, N.H.,

at a dinner meeting of the New Hampshire Weekly Newspaper Editors Association. In his opening words he referred to Norman Piper, president of the Association, Thomas J. McIntyre, U.S. Senator from New Hampshire, John W. King, Governor of New Hampshire, J. Oliva Huot and Charles B. Officer, Democratic candidates for U.S. Representative, and J. Murray Devine, New Hampshire State Democratic Chairman.

608   Toasts of the President and the Secretary General of NATO. *September* 29, 1964

Mr. Secretary General, distinguished guests:

I am very pleased today to welcome Secretary General Brosio to this house.

He has come as the chief officer of the NATO Alliance and as the representative of half a billion people united in the defense of freedom under the North Atlantic Treaty.

It gives me pride and a great amount of pleasure to have the opportunity to have assembled in this room some of the chief architects of this great union and some of the men who have played such an important part in its development.

We are particularly honored to have the distinguished ambassadors from the member countries, our own respected General Norstad who served with such distinction, our former distinguished Secretary of State, Mr. Acheson, Mr. Lippmann, and others who have followed the development of this great organization through the years.

General Brosio comes here today as our friend. He has served with great distinction as Ambassador of the Italian Republic to this country. His country's readiness to let such a talented public servant go to work for NATO is real evidence of the deep interest and the very vital role that his country, Italy, plays in this great alliance.

NATO owes much to the distinguished line of men who have served in the high office of Secretary General.

NATO is a vast organization, but it is also a most intimate alliance. In 15 years, it has grown impressively in confidence, in strength, and in character. It is the most successful and the most peaceful alliance in history.

For us in the United States NATO is a tested and a recognized cornerstone of United States foreign policy. It has and it will continue to have the strongest bipartisan support from the leaders of this Government.

After 15 years the Atlantic area is more secure than ever. Aggression and threats to freedom in Europe have been turned back.

All our peoples can take pride in what we have really achieved.

But the real task of defending liberty and freedom is never done. The security of our alliance is only assured so long as we remain determined and strong and insist on protecting our people and their values.

I would have you know again that America's commitment to this alliance is real, firm, and substantial. It was not given lightly.

The considered American decision in 1949 to participate in NATO—and some of the legislators like Senator Anderson are in this room today who participated in its creation—represented a most historic break with isolationism in this country.

Now and in the future this commitment

1169

remains as firm as facts and strength can make it.

Allied defense is indivisible. American security depends on the security of the alliance as a whole, and the alliance in turn depends upon the strategic strength of the United States. We believe that all of our adversaries understand this, and we hope so do the free peoples of the alliance.

As our beloved and distinguished Secretary of State has said so many times, this Nation does not seek to dominate anyone. Within our alliance, there is room for the efforts of us all, and there is room for new patterns of shared responsibility. We are ready and willing and anxious—and eager— to work together with all of our friends to make doubly sure that our strength will be as clear tomorrow as it is today.

America seeks a growing partnership of freedom, a partnership that is based on shared respect of reality and shared responsibility for effective defense.

NATO's strength has increased by virtue of the additional sacrifices that the Congress and our own country has made in the field of building our own strength in the last few years under the unique and highly skilled leadership of our great Secretary of Defense, Mr. McNamara.

Mr. Secretary General, we in the United States, all of us, believe in NATO and that is why we have taken this occasion to come here today and in our own little way honor NATO and honor your presence in this house.

We all know that your's is a vital role in a very vital organization. We are confident that the affairs of this alliance have been placed in good hands, in your hands, and while you are Secretary General and as long as you are, we in America look forward to a period of the closest possible cooperation and support.

So, my distinguished guests, I ask all of you to join me in a toast to Secretary General Brosio who serves a dynamic alliance and through it serves the great cause in which all of us believe so strongly—the cause of peace, the cause of freedom, and the cause of justice for all of the people of the world.

NOTE: The President proposed the toast at a luncheon in the State Dining Room at the White House. Secretary General Manlio Brosio responded as follows:

Mr. President, your Excellencies, the Ambassadors, gentlemen:

I will say only a few words because I am really and deeply moved.

I am moved, Mr. President, by the honor you have done me today in inviting me to this lunch in the company of such a distinguised group of businessmen in the United States and in many allied and friendly countries.

I remember, Mr. President, when I saw you the first time, and then I had the opportunity of meeting you several times at the Senate of the United States. I remember my first meeting with you in your office when I called on you as leader of the majority. I admired you then as I admire you now.

I am moved because I am back here in Washington where I worked over 6 years for my country and for the friendship between the United States and Italy, moved because around here are so many people who cooperated with me then, assisted me with their advice, with their opinions, with their moral support.

Now I come here in a different capacity. I am no more the representative of one ally in the NATO Alliance but I am the servant of the 15 countries of the alliance.

You were so kind, Mr. President, as to use the word leadership. Leadership of the alliance belongs to the countries and especially to the countries who more deserve it by the effort they contribute to its strength and to its moral power. I am only, as I said, a faithful servant, and I hope I will always be.

Certainly I am proud that an Italian has been chosen for this post, and I am glad that a European has been chosen again for this post, as it has been three other times.

I am proud to follow such remarkable men as Lord Ismay, as Paul-Henri Spaak, and as Dirk Stikker.

The North Atlantic Alliance is essentially the mutual defense of Europe and America, and it is good that a European represents the alliance at this post of Secretary General. Because there is great hope for the alliance, Mr. President, in the possibility that Europe through a larger and larger and to a deeper and deeper degree of unity may contribute better with more strength, with more authority to these alliances of ours which should and will remain as the essential pillar of our freedom and of our peace.

I am deeply conscious of this. The only contribution I am sure to bring to the alliance is a part of the little experience, through the confidence of my government, I have gathered in different countries in the last 18 years. The only contribution I am really sure to bring to the alliance is the contribution of a loyalty without reserve, of a conviction without limitations, and with an entire dedication and a will to give all my energies to the consolidation, to the continuation, and to the success of these alliances.

I entirely share your opinion, Mr. President, that the ultimate goal of the alliance, apart from defense, is peace.

I am profoundly convinced that if peace has been preserved with freedom in Europe and in our area, that has been due to the strength and to the unity of the alliance, and as long as the strength and the unity will continue, we will be safe and, today, if something happened in a different direction, we would be in danger.

These are the feelings which move me today and

I owe this visit to your great country which has given such an amazing contribution with such generosity, with such a wisdom to our alliance.

I am glad that I am here and I assure you, Mr. President, that this day has confirmed my conviction that I will always find here full support and full comprehension.

I am not saying just the usual words of compliment if I say that my talks these days with the most responsible people of the United States Government have been extremely frank, extremely useful. And we have tried to get into the main problems of the alliance as deeply as we could, with the sole intent of understanding each other and seeing generally what should be done and in which direction we are going to move in the future.

I believe that this will be the good direction and that with your help, Mr. President, with the help of your country we will succeed. We will succeed in our tasks in defense of peace and in defense of freedom.

May I thank you, Mr. President, and may I thank all of the gentlemen here who have honored me with their presence. May I assure them and assure you, Mr. President, that I will leave this country encouraged and determined even more to fulfill my duties unflinchingly and to be worthy of the great honor which has been done to me and of the great confidence which has been shown for me.

Thank you very much.

---

609   Remarks Upon Arrival at Offutt Air Force Base in Omaha. *September* 29, 1964

[The President was accompanied by Manlio Brosio, Secretary General of NATO]

Secretary General Brosio, Governor Morrison, General Power, my friends of Nebraska and of Offutt Air Force Base:

The Secretary General and I are delighted to be here in Nebraska, and we particularly thank you for this wonderful weather and for this warm welcome.

We came here today in the work of the great alliance for peace which is NATO. The Secretary General has been an old friend of our country and he is a very distinguished servant of his own country—Italy.

Today he comes to us as the civilian spokesman for our alliance as a whole, and it is altogether fitting that we should come to-

gether here in Nebraska.

Mr. Secretary General, you are a son of Italy and your headquarters are now in Paris. More than 150 years ago another son of Italy, with headquarters in Paris, sold this part of the world to the United States of America.

Nebraska has come a long way since Napoleon and Jefferson made that trade. You are now in the center of the part of America which grows food for peace and food for free men. The history of the great State of Nebraska is a history of hard work, a history of steady growth by liberty-loving men that came here from every part of

Europe, and men of Nebraska have gone back to Europe more than once within our lifetime for this same cause of liberty.

As we meet here today, Nebraska is the headquarters of the military strength of freedom, and that is what you and I have come to see together. I have, of course, been here before, and I am confident of what we shall find. So let me say, General, simply,

as we begin our visit, that this enormous strength has only one purpose, and that purpose is to keep the peace for free men everywhere in the world.

Thank you.

NOTE: The President spoke at Offutt Air Force Base, Omaha, Nebr. In his opening words he referred, in addition to Secretary General Brosio, to Frank B. Morrison, Governor of Nebraska, and Gen. Thomas S. Power, Commander in Chief, Strategic Air Command.

610 Remarks Upon Completing an Inspection of SAC Headquarters, Offutt Air Force Base, Omaha. *September 29, 1964*

General Power, General LeMay, ladies and gentlemen:

The Secretary General and I have now completed almost 2 hours of hard work with this brilliant and dedicated staff of the Strategic Air Command. I think that both of us have gained fresh understanding of the intimate relation between the strategic strength of the United States and the defense of the North Atlantic Alliance. We have had presented in some detail the military facts and figures which support the great and simple political reality that is set forth in our treaty, namely that the defense of one is the defense of all.

We have learned again what we already knew, that the strength and the skill of this Command are absolutely vital to the peace of the Atlantic world. We recognize that the mission of this Command is peace. And we had related to us this afternoon the capacity, the numbers, the procedures, the overall plans, and the great amount of thinking that has gone into accomplishing that mission, namely preserving the peace.

This day has thus brought new encouragement to me, and I hope also to my friend, the distinguished Secretary General.

So we are grateful to all of you and to the State of Nebraska for all that we have seen. We also thank you for your distance from Washington. On the plane ride out and back, Mr. Brosio and I are finding a chance for some quiet conversations together concerning the future needs and the future hopes of our great alliance. The success of NATO is evident in every member country, in peace and prosperity, and in confidence in the future. Yet our very success creates new problems for tomorrow.

The work of freedom is really never done, and as we go back to these discussions let me thank all of you again for this very profitable afternoon in Omaha. I have been here several times during the 13 years that General Power has been connected with the Strategic Air Command, and I have had numerous briefings from him and from his staff. I feel as I believe most Americans do, deeply in his debt, and the debt of the dedicated men who serve with him, for their love of country and for their proficiency to accomplish the mission assigned them.

I want to thank the members of the families of the men assigned to this Command. They are called upon to make many sacrifices, and just as their men's mission is peace, I guess they sacrifice with a smile, because wherever I go and I see the Strategic Air Force, I am stimulated and inspired.

Since General LeMay is here with us today, all of you really represent a great monument to his thinking and to his planning. Now that we realize the proof of the pudding is in the eating and you have preserved the peace now for almost 20 years, I think you can return to your homes this evening with a proper and justified "well done" from your Chief.

Incidentally, just to show you that I really mean it, I added a good deal to my budget this year by insisting on a pay raise for all of you.

Perhaps my colleague, Mr. Brosio, would have something that he would like to say to you now.

NOTE: The President spoke following an inspection with Manlio Brosio, Secretary General of NATO, of SAC Headquarters at Offutt Air Force Base, Omaha, Nebr. His opening words referred to Gen. Thomas S. Power, Commander in Chief, Strategic Air Command, and Gen. Curtis E. LeMay, Chief of Staff, Department of the Air Force.

The response of Secretary General Brosio follows:

Thank you, Mr. President; General Power, ladies and gentlemen of Omaha:

I want only to say that I am very happy to be back in Omaha again. I have been here a few years ago, that is in 1957, when General LeMay was still Commander here. I am very glad to be back tonight.

I have seen new, interesting things; I have learned a lot. But I am above all very deeply honored to have had the opportunity of coming tonight on the invitation and in the company of the President of the United States. This is a thing I am not going to forget so easily.

I have seen really the contribution to the defense not only of the United States, but also of Europe by this central base and Command of the Western World which is absolutely indispensable and decisive. That convinces me and convinces all Europeans, I think, of the absolute necessity of continuing the close links which tie us in our essential Atlantic Alliance. I also share entirely what the President of the United States has told you just now, that all this huge preparation which needs an enormous amount of intelligence, of skill, of patience and of courage, is intended only to defend peace, is intended primarily to prevent war. And in these 15 years of life of the Atlantic Alliance, thanks to this preparation, thanks to our unity and solidarity, peace has been preserved. I am sure we will be able to preserve it with the same methods and with the same spirit for the future in the interest of the freedom and the welfare of the people of the United States and Europe.

Thank you, Mr. President.

611   Remarks at a Meeting With Representatives of Veterans Organizations. *September 30, 1964*

Ladies and gentlemen:

This house is your house.

As you entered, no one asked your politics. While you are here, no one will seek your vote. You have been invited, not as voters, nor as veterans, but as Americans. For, whatever the season, the work of our country must go on.

At this moment in your country's life, our success is very great. Our system is strong. Our ramparts are manned. Our people are prospering in lives of peace. The promise for America has never been so bright.

That bright promise must never be dimmed, either from without or from within. And that is your duty, as well as mine.

You have been defenders of America. Today, you are its leaders. Your hands, as well as mine, hold the flame.

Since 1776, 32 million Americans have been called to bear arms. Of every ten who have worn our uniform, seven are living today. Our veterans, and their families, represent 40 percent of our American population now.

Three centuries ago at Plymouth Rock the

Pilgrim Fathers ordained that those disabled in the community's defense should receive the community's care. From that day to this we have kept a special trust with those who have borne the battle, and their widows and their orphans.

This year marks the 20th anniversary of the finest such program of all—the World War II GI bill. Some condemned that bill as the work of a welfare state. But we honor it today as a pride of our free land. The educations that GI bill provided, the homes it built, the new starts it gave have all increased America's strength.

No man could serve here without being grateful to you and your organizations for your constructive support of our veterans programs. I am sure you will agree with me, we can all be grateful together for the service being provided by Administrator Gleason and the Veterans Administration.

But I have not asked you here to discuss these concerns. Our first duty to the 21 million veterans living now, and the 1 million who have died in our wars, is to keep America strong and to keep America at peace.

I am proud to be able to say to you that in all the history of man, no nation has ever been so strong in arms as your Nation today.

The hour of peril for freedom has not passed. It will not pass in your lifetime or mine. In days to come the dangers will be grave, and those dangers may multiply. Our duty is to be prepared—and we are prepared today.

For a world of infinite threats, we are prepared for flexible response.

America has muscle, but we are not muscle-bound.

Your Nation has:

—1,100 long-range bombers, 500 always in the air or on 15-minute alert.

—800 intercontinental missiles, sheltered underground, ready to fire in minutes.

—16 nuclear submarines with 256 Polaris missiles, sheltered underseas, ready to fire in minutes.

—Around the world, we have a variety of tactical nuclear weapons ready, should the Commander in Chief authorize their use.

No other nation has more than a fraction of this force.

Our aim is to defend freedom with the most rational and appropriate force. Let no one doubt that we would use our full force if necessary. But let no one think that this is all the force we have and that we are straitjacketed in it.

Nuclear arms alone are not enough.

The most significant advances of our defense in the past 4 years have been those made to give us selective power to respond to different threats—on land, in the jungles, on the sea, and in the air.

Our Army has grown from 11 divisions to 16.

Special forces to help other nations maintain their freedom have increased by 800 percent.

The Marines are stronger by 15,000 men.

Our tactical air forces have 79 fighter squadrons rather than 55.

Our Navy—already the greatest in the world—has been increased in both strength and readiness.

Our preparedness has only one purpose. That purpose is peace—peace for ourselves, peace for the world. Since last November, I have lived every waking hour mindful that a nuclear war would mean in 1 hour an American death toll equal to 300 World War II's. For your children and mine, too much is at stake for the passions of partisanship to divert America from the pursuit of peace.

We have peace. We must keep it.

But let none misunderstand us or misrepresent us. The American people are in this peace to win it for freedom, for justice, and for the dignity of man.

If victory is to be ours, we shall need more than the strength of arms alone; we shall need the strength of our heads, our hearts, and the finest values of our homes.

What America is to be will not be decided in this house, or on the Hill where Congress meets. America's fate rests with you, and leaders like you, all across this shining land. That is why I ask you here.

Liberty is precious. Peace is our prize. But our unity is priceless beyond compare. America's leaders at every level must work every day to preserve and perfect the unity of our society.

We stand against communism, we stand for freedom, only when we stand together as one nation and one people. America knows no higher patriotism than the works of unity and no more sinister subversion than the works of division.

At this hour, the generation of your brothers and sons walks the ramparts of freedom from the Bering Straits to the Brandenburg Gate. But there are vigils you and I must forever keep in the streets of home.

It is important that men in other lands understand America. It is always of first importance that all in our own land understand America, too. Wherever we live, responsible men and women must go to the heart of the challenge, for there the decision lies.

As individuals and through our organizations, we must work in our streets and in our slums, among our young and among our poor. There is work for us to do in all the places bypassed by our prosperity, in all the corners untouched by our compassion.

Our society was built on respect for law and order and we mean to maintain that. But our society was built also on respect for rights and dignity and we mean to strengthen them.

The kind of nation we are to have tomorrow will be the sum of the kind of communities we build today. The quality of our communities will not be determined by the work of remote governments but by the work of responsible citizens who live there.

This is the challenge to all who are looked to as leaders. This is the duty to which your country calls each of you today.

I know your President will always have your prayers, whoever he may be.

I want you to know that this President wants your help, welcomes your strength, and seeks to work with you in all that will unify this blessed land.

NOTE: The President spoke in the late afternoon in the East Room at the White House.

As printed, this item follows the prepared text released by the White House.

612 Remarks to the Faculty and Students of Johns Hopkins University. *October 1, 1964*

My fellow Americans, Dr. Eisenhower, members of the faculty, student body:

I am delighted to have had this invitation and I am so happy that circumstances allowed me to be here this morning.

I have known your distinguished president for many years, since I was a young man, as he said. I am indebted to him for many things, for this invitation, for his wise counsel through the years, for his willingness to always serve his country and for this laudatory introduction.

I might say it seems to me it is one of the best introductions I ever had, probably the best introduction I ever had except upon one other occasion when I was speaking down in the hills of Tennessee and the Governor was supposed to introduce me. He did not get there and I had to introduce myself.

This is my second visit this week to a great university. Just a few days ago I was up at Brown in Rhode Island.

I regard it as wise for the flame of learning to be applied occasionally to the seats of power.

There is no spirit of partisanship in what I am going to say to you today. Because I have come over here this morning to talk to you about the goals of our country and what Americans should do about them.

Americans today are no longer willing to settle for the average. This generation is committed to strive for the best. On our campuses—and in all our country—there is a determination to seek and to reach for and to obtain the goals of excellence.

As we raise our sights toward the goals of excellence in private affairs, we should and we just simply must do the same in public affairs.

The goals of our public life must be the highest goals of our national life.

We must seek excellence from our Government at every level.

We must demand excellence from our politics.

My life work has been public service. Whatever trust has come to me, I have tried to do my best. For I believe with the ancient Greeks that the end of politics must be the good of man.

If our American politics is to serve the good of man, I believe that the performance of American Government can and must be

improved—and the standards of American politics can and must be raised and elevated.

This age of knowledge deserves, and demands, the politics of understanding.

Instinct and intuition are not enough to rely upon in directing our national destiny. Intellect must be respected—intelligence must be trusted. In public affairs, the average performance and the average performer simply are no longer good enough for our country.

This age of reason deserves, and demands, the politics of restraint.

There are many moments in our national life when the leaders of your country and their followers are given the opportunity to discard prudence and restraint.

I have been in this office only 10 months. Early in my tenure a bearded gentleman, Mr. Castro, cut off our water supply at one of our great defense bases—Guantanamo. There was great provocation and our people were properly and duly alarmed. Cries went up from every corner of the land with many suggested remedies. Some proposed an invasion. Others suggested sending the Marines in. There were some who would have treated it quite lightly.

But after adequate deliberation, after reasoning with all of the trained minds who had been equipped to cope with problems of this kind, we decided that it was the better part of wisdom to send one admiral in to cut the water off rather than to send a battalion of Marines in to turn it on.

We determined to make that base self-sufficient and today we manufacture and furnish our own water there. We released almost 2,000 employees and said to Mr. Castro that "if we cannot depend on our contracts for the water supply, we cannot depend on our contract for the employees, so we will send our own people to man our own base."

The other day our ships were fired upon in the Gulf of Tonkin. Acting upon orders, they defended themselves and destroyed the enemy to the extent that it was possible very promptly.

Forthwith we considered what judgments we should make and what actions should follow. And after due consideration, with full reports from all involved, we selected the nest that harbored these boats, eliminated the areas that involved huge civilian populations, and made prompt and adequate response, destroying substantially that PT fleet and the nest that had harbored them.

So, I use these illustrations to show you that it could have been easy in one wave to wipe out women and children and to drop bombs on North Viet-Nam and on China because these nests were located within 35 miles of the Chinese border.

But government must be restrained in the pursuit as well as the use of power itself. And government must be moderate in the belief of its own infallibility.

This age of hope deserves—and I think demands—the politics of vision.

We are possessed of great power in America—power to destroy all human life or to make human life sublime. Our politics must serve our faith rather than fostering our fears.

We have in our power at this moment the ability to destroy 300 times as many human lives as were lost in the entire many years of World War II.

So the purpose of our politics must be to make man's extinction improbable, and man's fulfillment inevitable.

There are those who talk about the power of the Presidency, and the Presidency has great and awesome responsibilities.

No man can serve in that office or be familiar with its responsibilities without being conscious of his obligation to all humankind.

I sat through 37 conferences involving the Cuban missile crisis—beginning when the sun came up in the morning and frequently lasting into the daylight hours of the next day. While there were frightening and dreadful moments, I think I can truthfully report to you that I was never prouder of the President or the Presidency, because the coolest man at that table was the then Commander in Chief of the American Forces, John Fitzgerald Kennedy.

When I kissed my wife and daughters goodby in the morning I never really knew whether I would see them that night or not.

So I tell you that to point up the fact that this age of peril deserves and demands the politics of unity.

Sitting around that table was a distinguished Secretary of State, a Democrat from Georgia. Across, next to the President on the other side, was a distinguished Secretary of Defense, a Republican from Michigan. At the end of the table was the distinguished Director of the Central Intelligence Agency, Mr. John McCone, a Republican from California.

There were the Chairman of the Joint Chiefs of Staff, the heads of the Army, Navy, and the Air Force of this country, and the long list of dedicated career servants of the State Department and the Defense Department.

You couldn't tell from anyone's comment what their religion was or what their party was, and you could not even observe from their accent where they came from. Because the essence of our American system, the very foundation on which we stand, is unity—not the unity of States alone but the much greater unity of all of our people.

The guiding genius of democracy has

been our great ability in times of crisis and peril for all Americans to unite. Our politics—and our politicians—must constantly seek to widen our common agreement, and not to inflame our mutual mistrusts.

Of course, these goals are high but the attainment of them is not hopeless.

Our modern means of communications have opened up a new era of our democracy. The promise is great and we must fulfill it. Our public affairs must be pursued not as the source of passing public entertainment but as the servant of lasting public enlightenment.

Our politics, and the performance of the public realm, should have, and must have, only one purpose and that purpose is to elevate our national life, not to exhaust it.

I hope you agree with me that Americans' goals of excellence need not, and must not, end at the water's edge. For it is in the realm of our relations with other nations that we have proved already the capacity of our system for excellence.

Over the lifetime of the youngest here today, men and nations of the North Atlantic have done together what none have ever done before.

We have formed together—across the sea—an alliance of purpose between the strongest associations of free men in all the world.

America's part in this achievement has been possible because no mean spirit was ever permitted to override the noble spirit of unity and of united purpose.

President Truman, as Commander in Chief and leader of this Nation, had the strength of a towering Republican Senator standing by his side, Arthur Vandenberg of Michigan.

President Kennedy had the support of Henry Cabot Lodge. When the Nation was led by President Dwight David Eisen-

hower, he had the support—and not the opposition—of the Democratic Party in the Congress of the United States.

I trust I may be pardoned by the president of this great university and the student body for this personal reference, but after the election of 1952, there had been kind of a hurricane across the country—and a great leader and a popular hero had dismantled the Democratic Party. I was selected for some reason or other to try to pick up the pieces and to try to pull together the loyal opposition.

A great party leader who belonged to the other party, the then majority party—and he was then the majority leader—Mr. Taft, had enunciated his viewpoint of the responsibilities of the opposition party, because he had been the leader of the opposition in the Congress for a good many years.

He said, "It is the duty of the opposition to oppose," meaning that it was the responsibility of the loyal opposition to point out the imperfections and the weaknesses and to attempt to prevail over the majority.

When I became leader that morning in the Senate caucus room, I said to my colleagues, "I reject that philosophy and that doctrine in toto. I do not believe it is the duty of the opposition to oppose. I conceive it to be my responsibility as the leader of the loyal opposition to support the President of the United States every single time I can in good conscience—and I am going to resolve any doubts in behalf of the chosen leader of this country."

Well, as an illustration of what happened, I served as Democratic leader for 8 years. I frequently found myself on the front row defending the foreign policy of the President of the United States, and the minority leader on the back row opposing the President of the United States.

As an illustration, during the year 1960,

the Democratic leaders supported the Republican President 96 percent of the time by record roll call. The present Republican leader of the Republican Party supported the President 24 percent of the time.

But I believe that I speak for you when I say that we believe in parties and we have allegiance to them and their principles, but we believe in our country first. As I said one time, in describing my own political philosophy, "I am proud to be a free man first and an American second, a public servant third, and a Democrat fourth, in that order."

I have found that it gives me a clear conscience, it gives me greater satisfaction, and it has met with a reasonable modicum of success to do what you think is best for your country—and your country will do what is best for you.

So the truth is clear. Excellence is far too precious in our society to exclude it from our national endeavors on the basis of party alone.

In the North Atlantic and in Latin America and around the world, our Nation is going to continue to need the excellence that can be contributed by men of talent and patriotism and experience regardless of their political affiliation—men like your own great president, Milton Eisenhower. America must not deny to its armies or its armadas its greatest talents because of their region, their religion, or their party—and they must never be denied service to their country because of the standards of small partisanship.

When we line them up at the reception centers to fit them for their uniforms, we don't say, "What is your church? What is your political affiliation? What section of the country do you live in and who was your grandpa?" We say, "Give him size 42." And as we go on to that battlefield and over the top or onto the cliff or under the sea or

in the air, we judge him only by his capacity and his patriotism and his dedication to his country.

As I speak to you this morning let me say this to you: The day before yesterday I met with the new Secretary General of the North Atlantic Treaty Organization, a great citizen of Italy. We talked about our Atlantic partnership, the 15 great nations that make up that partnership. We talked about its remarkable achievements. We talked about its unlimited promise. We talked about our own preparation and our own strength.

It gave me great pride to fly out to the Strategic Air Command at Omaha, Nebr., and let him see with his own eyes how we, by a pressing of a button—in a flash of a second—could notify our men around the world and could get immediate response.

So we planned parts of the future. We talked about the opportunity to advance and to promote mankind. This is work that just must go on. For our Atlantic partnership is coming to a new and to a much greater time.

We must mobilize the vast strength of our communities to defend freedom, not only in Europe but to defend freedom wherever it is attacked.

We must never forget for a moment that we are one of the youngest nations in all the world with one of the oldest governments in existence. We must never forget how much our ancestors that came ahead of us prized freedom—how much we sought it for ourselves and how much we appreciated those who contributed to our achieving it. Remembering that, we must always be willing to take our position and stand up and be counted when there is a choice between freedom and slavery.

So we must together continue to meet the vast challenge of the underdeveloped world. We are the world's great arsenal of industry and ideas and we just cannot allow a separation between rich nations and poor nations—or white nations and colored nations.

Finally, we must bring the countries of Eastern Europe much closer to the Western Community. This we can do and this we are doing by building bridges to these people—bridges of help, of counsel, of leadership, of trade, of ideas, of visitors, and of humanitarian aid.

Our great American hero, General George Catlett Marshall, recognized—and we firmly believe—that permanent peace requires European civilization to develop within its historic boundaries. This is our aim, and this is the real road to freedom for those who live today behind the Iron Curtain.

In the times ahead, our political community must not merely speak of excellence in other sectors. It must offer examples of excellence from within itself.

I believe that example should begin in our work within the alliance on which the hopes for freedom stand.

You have many hopes. You have many dreams. You have great vision. You have ambitions. But the most important thing in your thoughts today should be the most important subject in the world to all peoples of more than 120 nations.

And what is that most important of all things in this nuclear age? That most important thing is our relations with other nations, our ability to exist and to survive and to get along and reason together. That most important thing, in short, is a 5-letter word—peace—"peace on earth, good will toward men."

Your Nation must always be prepared to have its leader go anywhere, talk to anyone, make any plan that can honorably be made to achieve understanding. The day and the time and the era for government by ultimatum was yesterday and is gone forever.

We cannot pride ourselves on a period when outlaws roam the range and a man's chief claim to fame is his ability to destroy his fellow man and his willingness to follow that pursuit.

No, we had better get back to the Good Book and "love thy neighbor as thyself." We had better go back to the old Golden Rule and "do unto others as you would have them do unto you."

There are moments when we become discouraged, and some become hysterical, and we feel, what is the use? But if we apply a little patience, if we put ourselves in the other fellow's position, if we assume what we would think if we were in his place and if he were in our's, somehow, someway good American judgment will prevail and we may be able to avert and avoid catastrophic consequences.

I was extremely irritated one time by a man who saw things differently and had a different philosophy. After negotiating with him for 3 days, my impulsiveness—that is a word I don't use very often these days—got the best of me and I finally said to him somewhat with anger in my voice, that "so far as I am concerned, I have tried to work out an understanding agreement with you and you won't do anything. You just sit there looking like a Methodist deacon and won't agree to anything. As far as I am concerned you can take a running jump and go to . . . ."

I got great applause from my audience. All approved what I said except one old man who was a general counsel, a lawyer for my group of rural electric cooperatives. I walked over and asked his judgment on how he liked my speech. He said, "Come into my office. I would like to talk to you." I said, "Oh, oh!"

I went in and he said, "You are a young man and you are going to get a good deal more experience as you go through life. But," he said, "you want my judgment and I will give it to you. The first thing you ought to learn is that to tell a man to go to hell and to make him go are two different propositions."

So we just can't mash a button and tell them all to go there, because they don't want to go. It is hot down there. They enjoy it here. They have their own views of religion, region, philosophy, and so forth.

Now, most of the troubles which are on my desk—you hear them referred to as a crisis a week. That is a most generous estimate; it's much worse than that. It's a crisis an hour.

I don't know what has happened since I have been on this platform but I will have more problems when I get back than I had when I left, I can assure you of that. Most of them come as a result of ancient disagreements between lands with which we have had nothing to do. It may be the Greeks and the Turks in Cyprus. It may be some folks on the continent of Africa. It may be many problems out in Asia.

Last night I read a letter written 10 years ago by President Eisenhower to the President of Viet-Nam in which he said, "If you want to help yourself, we will give you advice and support." And we are still giving them advice and support. Sometimes some of our folks think it is not enough, sometimes they think it is not good, sometimes the results are not satisfying. But for 10 long years we have been trying to help those people help themselves, and while we have not achieved total victory, it is pretty difficult to get everything you want when you want it.

We have had laudable purposes. We have had the highest motives. We have done our best and there is not a person in this country of either party who wouldn't like to see a satisfactory solution of that Asian difficulty.

So, we must realize that as leaders of the world, as people who have more to eat and more to wear, better homes to live in, finer cars to drive, more of the luxuries, the highest standard of living of any people in all the world—we make more in a week than most people in other nations make in a year—those responsibilities also carry obligations, because the human beings of the world are not going to always endure the lot that is theirs today.

The ancient enemies of mankind—disease, intolerance, illiteracy, and ignorance—are not always going to prevail. There is going to be a revolution. There is going to be a rising up and a throwing off of these chains and, as a great leader once said, "We must constantly remember that we only have 190 million people of the 3 billion in the world, and half of those people have incomes of less than $20 a month. If a peaceful improvement is not possible, if a peaceful revolution is not possible, a violent adjustment is inevitable."

I talked to a friend of mine the other day. The last country that we lost to communism was Cuba in 1959. Now, for a period of almost 6 years, we have resisted on many fronts with, I think, considerable success. So we do not all need to have a martyr complex and be apologizing for the woes of Uncle Sam and all of his failures.

A friend of mine came in and talked to me about the great ranch that he owned. He is a friend of Dr. Eisenhower's. He is the head of the King Ranch in Texas. His name is Bob Kleberg. His brother brought me to Washington as a congressional secretary in 1931, in Mr. Hoover's administration. He was talking to me about this big ranch that he once owned in Cuba.

You are going to hear a lot of stories of that

kind over the world unless we realize that these ancient enemies of mankind are not going to prevail in the world.

People are going to have food for their children and clothes for their backs, a roof over their heads, and an education for their souls.

We must in someway, somehow lead the way, and with your help we shall.

Now, I did not come here today to ask you your religion, or to ask you how you spell your name, or to ask you what region you live in, or where your ancestors came from. I thought we settled most all of those things in our Bill of Rights.

I did not come to ask your vote—although candor and frankness would compel me to say that I am not totally uninterested in what is going to happen in November.

I came here for one purpose and that was to say to you, come what may, if the good Lord is willing, I am going to be your President until January 20th at least.

I was confronted with a situation 10 months ago in a matter of moments when I had to act and I had to stand up and be counted and go ahead. I couldn't run under the table. I did the very best I could with the talents that the good Lord gave me and with the limited experience and training I had.

I don't believe I have ever met a man in public life that campaigned on a platform of doing what is wrong. They all try to do what is right. Sometimes they don't know what is right and they make mistakes, but I have tried my dead level best, and I think there has never been a period of history in the 200 years of our existence, almost, when the people have done more to try to hold up and prop up and help their President than you have. If I am weak and if I falter, and if I fall and stumble, you are weak and you falter, and America stumbles.

So, from Independence, the next morn-

ing, came Harry Truman. From Gettysburg came Dwight Eisenhower. From New York came Bob Anderson, the former Secretary of the Treasury. From way across the West came leaders of Republican and Democratic administrations.

The president's brother sat down—a General of the Armies—President of the United States—and took a lead pencil and a yellow tablet, without even a stenographer, and wrote for 2 hours on things that I should not do and should do as he had observed it from 8 years of experience and from almost half a century in the public service, not because he wanted to see a great Democrat develop and make a great campaign but because he wanted to see the leader of the Nation succeed.

Eighty-five heads of state came from all over the world.

So, this morning, I came here in that spirit to speak to all of you—Republicans and Democrats, and whatnot—and as I rode over with Senator Brewster, of whom I am very fond and who serves us with great distinction in the United States Senate, I said to him, "It stimulates me to have a chance to go out there and look these young people in the eye and to salute them and to ask them to give me their help, give me their hand, give me their prayers, because I need them so much in the days ahead."

If we were in another setting, on another occasion, I might even ask you to give me something else.

Thank you very much.

NOTE: The President spoke at 11:15 a.m. as a participant in a Johns Hopkins University lecture series. In his opening words he referred to Dr. Milton Eisenhower, president of the University. Later he referred to, among others, Robert A. Taft, former Senator from Ohio, Manlio Brosio of Italy, Secretary General of NATO, Robert J. Kleberg, Jr., president, King Ranch, Inc., Kingsville, Tex., his brother Richard M. Kleberg, former Representative from Texas, and Senator Daniel B. Brewster of Maryland.

613   Remarks at the Swearing In of Philip Nichols, Jr., and Linton M. Collins as Judges.   *October 1, 1964*

Ladies and gentlemen:

I deeply regret that I was detained, but I do not control the other end of all of my telephone conversations—particularly when we have conferees not agreeing with each other up on the Hill.

I am glad to be here on this very happy occasion. The size of this audience compares favorably with New England.

Obviously I ought to have a talk with these gentlemen before they become judges because I need to know how they acquired so many friends on their way up.

Linton Collins is a man of long and wide experience who has won trust and respect throughout his profession, and he has been my friend for several decades.

Phil Nichols is the son of a distinguished Massachusetts family who is held in the highest esteem as a lawyer and as a very able public servant.

I have the highest regard for him except for one thing. Some years ago he took away from me my first secretary by marrying her, and I have just had her on a part-time basis ever since.

The purpose of all we do in this Government is justice. The armies we raise, the fleets we sail, the vigil we keep abroad and at home—all this is done so that every man and woman can stand as equals before the bar of impartial justice. The independence of the judiciary is the cornerstone of our society, and that independence must never be compromised.

Our society is quite complex. The demands upon courts of law are many, and they are varied, but the courts that we create in specialized fields as much as other courts must serve the same end, and that is the good of all men.

We can be grateful in America for the character and quality and the integrity of the men who uphold the tradition of our courts as Federal judges.

I feel positive of one thing this afternoon: these two men that you have come here to honor and to see sworn in will serve with the highest honor to this tradition.

Thank you.

NOTE: The President spoke at 5:56 p.m. in the State Dining Room at the White House at the swearing in of Philip Nichols, Jr., as Judge, U.S. Customs Court, and of Linton M. Collins as Judge, U.S. Court of Claims. Judge Collins and Judge Nichols responded briefly. The text of their remarks was also released.

During his remarks the President referred to Mrs. Dorothy Jackson Nichols, his secretary while in Congress, currently serving as secretary to Horace Busby, Jr., Special Assistant to the President.

614   Letter to the Attorney General Directing Him To Petition for an Injunction in the Maritime Industry Labor Dispute.   *October 1, 1964*

Dear Mr. Katzenbach:

On September 30, 1964, by virtue of the authority vested in me by Section 206 of the Labor Management Relations Act, 1947 (29 U.S.C. 176), I issued Executive Order No. 11181 creating a Board of Inquiry to inquire into issues involved in labor disputes between employers (or associations by which such employers are represented in collective bargaining conferences) who are (1) steamship companies or who are engaged as operators or agents for ships engaged in service from or to Atlantic and Gulf Coast ports from Searsport, Maine, to Brownsville, Texas, or from or to other ports of the United States or its territories or possessions, (2) contracting stevedores, (3) contracting marine carpenters, (4) lighterage operators, or (5) other employers engaged in related or associated pier activities and certain of their employees represented by the International Longshoremen's Association, AFL–CIO.

On October 1, 1964, I received the Board's written report in the matter. A copy of that report is attached hereto.

In my opinion, these unresolved labor disputes have resulted in an actual or threatened strike affecting a substantial part of the maritime industry of the United States, an industry engaged in trade, commerce, transportation, transmission or communication among the several States and with foreign nations, which strike, if permitted to continue, will imperil the national health and safety.

Therefore, in order to remove a peril to the national health and safety and to secure a resumption of trade, commerce, transportation, transmission or communication among the several States and with foreign nations, I direct you, pursuant to the provisions of Section 208 of the Labor Management Relations Act, 1947, to petition in the name of the United States any District Court of the United States having jurisdiction of the parties to enjoin the continuance of such strike and for such other relief as may in your judgment be necessary or appropriate.

Sincerely,

LYNDON B. JOHNSON

[The Honorable Nicholas deB. Katzenbach, Acting Attorney General, Washington, D.C.]

NOTE: On October 1 the Acting Attorney General sought and obtained in the District Court for the Southern District of New York a temporary injunction, to expire on December 20, 1964, against continuation of the strike. On November 30 the Board of Inquiry reported to the President that no agreement had been reached but that the parties had affirmed a willingness to negotiate as extensively as necessary to achieve a settlement before the expiration of the injunction. An agreement was reached on December 16 covering the Port of New York, but it was rejected by the longshoremen. On January 11, 1965, a strike began affecting ports from Maine to Texas.

The Board's reports of October 1 and November 30, 1964, were made available through the Federal Mediation and Conciliation Service.

---

615 Remarks at the Final Meeting of the Alaska Reconstruction Planning Commission. *October 2, 1964*

Senator Anderson, members of the Commission:

As you hold your final meeting at the White House, I want to say: well done.

On March 27 the first reports from Alaska made clear what the subsequent reports confirmed. There was a big job to do—and we would need our best men to help our countrymen in Alaska start forward to get it done. I asked one of the best men I knew—one of the most able and dedicated public servants in America—to lead that effort: Senator Clinton Anderson of New Mexico.

I know how much I was asking of him—and of each of you. But I think I thought more of his personal interests than Clint Anderson did. He responded immediately and enthusiastically—and all of you have worked with this same spirit every step of the way.

On behalf of the Nation, I congratulate you. On behalf of the people of Alaska, I thank you.

When the earthquake struck last spring, all American hearts went out to Alaska. All of us feel a special pride in our largest State. We are proud Alaska's star shines from our flag—and we want very much to see Alaska grow and thrive and increase her strength.

When tragedy befalls strong people, greater strength usually emerges on the other side. I believe this is the case for Alaska. Certainly, the tragedy of the great earthquake has drawn us all closer together—and given to Alaska the new strength of new interest, new confidence, and new understanding from all her sister States.

The work of reconstruction in Alaska is well launched.

Water service has been restored throughout the earthquake region.

The Alaska Railroad is operating normally in most areas. Limited service is available on the balance of the system.

Practically all highways are fully operational—although much work remains to be done.

Design of port facilities has been completed. It will be possible to provide some protection for boats this winter.

The Small Business Administration has approved nearly $50 million in loans to homeowners and businessmen—under very favorable terms.

The Congress has enacted legislation providing grants to offset State and local revenue losses. Other forms of disaster assistance have been provided—much of it entirely without precedent. Any dollars and cents values on Federal assistance would be misleading. The point is that we are determined to do what needs to be done to meet the needs of this great State.

For what has been done thus far, credit is due many. The State of Alaska, the local communities there, Alaska's fine delegation to the Congress—and the people of Alaska themselves—are the heroes of this effort. And I am proud to salute them.

Our next step must be forward—toward a broader and better future for the State. I have taken action today toward that end.

I have signed an Executive order establishing a new Federal Field Committee in Alaska to cooperate with a similar body established by the Governor of Alaska. The purpose is to prepare practical, long-range plans for Alaska's economic development.

The order establishes also a President's Review Committee for Development Planning in Alaska. The Chairman will be the Secretary of Commerce. This committee will provide general direction to the field committee—and will advise me concerning the field committee's recommendations. The Director of the Office of Emergency Planning will have responsibility for coordinating and expediting the reconstruction program.

You of this Commission have no doubts—nor do I—about Alaska's future. Our last great land frontier will grow and prosper far beyond past expectations or present hopes.

You who have served on this Commission will always be able to look to the North and take a measure of personal pride in having been part of this great work.

NOTE: The President spoke at 11:40 a.m. in the Fish Room at the White House. In his opening words he referred to Senator Clinton P. Anderson of New Mexico who served as Chairman of the Federal Reconstruction and Development Planning Commission for Alaska (see Item 241, note).

Earlier in the day the President issued Executive Order 11182 (29 F.R. 13629, 3 CFR, 1964 Supp.) establishing a Federal Field Committee for Development Planning in Alaska and the President's Review Committee for Development Planning in Alaska. The order also abolished the Federal Reconstruction and Development Planning Commission for Alaska established on April 2, 1964.

As printed, this item follows the prepared text released by the White House.

616 Remarks Upon Proclaiming 1965 as International Cooperation Year. *October 2, 1964*

IF YOU have never been late to a meeting you won't understand my position, but I do ask your indulgence and I do thank you very much for what I hope is your understanding.

I have been running late all morning. I didn't know we had as many majority leaders in the Congress as we have. They are all hoping that they can go home this week. I am hoping that they go home, too.

I have just left more ex-presidents of the American Bar Association than I ever realized existed, but since they were "Lawyers for Johnson," I am glad they were there. I had to meet with them, so please forgive me and I promise to try not to be so tardy in my public appointments in the future.

I am very proud to welcome this most distinguished assembly of most distinguished Americans.

I regret that one of the most distinguished of all cannot be with us this morning— Ambassador Adlai Stevenson. He is otherwise engaged in Cleveland and Chicago in a pursuit that I regard as no vice.

You have come here and we are brought together by a very old and a very honored American interest—the interest of fostering international cooperation instead of international conflict. We are here today to proclaim 1965 as International Cooperation Year in the United States of America.

This observance will be commemorated around the world by the members of the United Nations.

For the United States, cooperation with other nations and other peoples is always uppermost in our minds and is the first aim of our policies, the central instrument of our foreign policy, and it is the central goal of administrations of both parties—the great leaders of which many are in the room today.

I know that the American people would not have it otherwise.

The value of international cooperation and understanding is recognized by all of us. The extent of cooperation that is in existence is realized by too few. Today the United States participates in some 80 international organizations. We take part in nearly 600 international conferences, and we faithfully honor 4,300 treaties and agreements that we have made with other nations in the world.

Two points are clear:

First, international cooperation is simply not an idea or an ideal. We think it is a clear necessity to our survival. The greater the nation the greater is its need to work cooperatively with other people, with other countries, other nations.

Second, international cooperation is no longer an academic subject; it is a fact of life, as I have just illustrated. Our challenge is not to debate the theory or the concept, but our challenge is to improve and to perfect and to strengthen the organizations that already exist.

In 1965 it is the hope of your Government that International Cooperation Year may be used for a useful review and purposeful planning. For this end I am appointing a special Cabinet Committee to direct this work and to develop all possible proposals for the future.

It is my thought that we can find many areas to encourage much more progressive and purposeful labor among the nations of the world. This is what we shall be doing. I have asked you here this morning to make a special appeal to you and to request your labors, too.

I hope that each of you will help me and the Secretary of State and others of your Government to carry the story of international cooperation and organization to the American people.

Public understanding, public support, is vital and basic to our success in striving for world understanding and cooperation. You can't be a statesman unless you get elected, and it is pretty difficult for us to be successful in a movement of this kind if we do not have the broad, solid support of the people, because under our system they are the masters.

More than that, I hope that your talents may be turned to systematic study of the next steps that private organizations may take to further this cooperation.

There is more extensive interest in this on the private level than I think there has ever been before. Business organizations, farm organizations, labor unions, universities, church bodies, women's groups, professional societies, are all expanding their interests and their operations abroad and are all concerned with what is happening in the other 120-odd nations in the world to an extent that has never been equaled before, I say pridefully and proudly.

There is much going on in this field in this country and throughout the world. There is much energy and enthusiasm and interest to do even more if we have the right kind of leadership.

So your task is to help bring these together, how to harness these resources and channel them in the proper direction. Those with the experience and background that you have must make known what is going on, what the next steps are, and how those with time and resources can most usefully join these labors.

Because in this day and age man has too many common interests to waste his energies, his talents, and his substance in primitive arrogance or in destructive conflict. In short, you are going to have to be the captains of a movement to lead people to love instead of hate. You are going to have to be the leaders in a movement to guide people in preserving humanity instead of destroying it.

You are going to be the leaders in a crusade to help get rid of the ancient enemies of mankind—ignorance, illiteracy, poverty, and disease—because we know that these things must go, and we also know from our past that if we do not adjust to this change peacefully, we will adjust to it otherwise.

As a great leader said in this room not many years ago, if a peaceful revolution is impossible, a violent revolution is inevitable. So I believe that the true realists in the second half of this 20th century are those who bear the dream of new ways for new cooperation.

You will be frowned upon. Some will call you an idealist. Some will call you a crackpot, and some may even call you worse than that. They may say you are soft or hard or don't understand what it is all about in some of these fields, but what greater ambition could you have and what greater satisfaction could come to you than the knowledge that you had entered a partnership with your Government that had provided the leadership in the world that had preserved humanity instead of destroyed it?

So this year and next year and in the years to come, international cooperation must be an enduring way of life in the community of man.

If I am here—I am speaking now politically and not physically—I don't anticipate any violence, but if I am here, I intend next year to call a White House conference and I want all of you to start thinking about it now. I want you to talk to your friends about it.

I want to call a White House conference to search and explore and canvass and thoroughly discuss every conceivable approach and avenue of cooperation that could lead to peace. That five-letter word is the goal of all of us. It is by far the most important problem we face. It is the assignment of the century for each of you and if we fail in that assignment, everything will come to naught.

If we succeed, think how wonderful the year 2000 will be. And it is already so exciting to me that I am just hoping that my heart and stroke and cancer committee can come up with some good results that will insure that all of us can live beyond 100 so we can participate in that glorious day when all the fruits of our labors and our imaginations today are a reality.

It now gives me a great deal of pleasure to sign the proclamation designating 1965 to be International Cooperation Year in the United States of America. I am very proud this morning that I am a citizen of a country and the leader of a nation that can have voluntarily assembled in the first house of this land the quality and quantity of talent that faces me now. To each of you, for the time you have taken and have waited, for the money you spent in coming here, for the thought that you have given, but more important, for what you are going to do, on behalf of the Nation, I say we are grateful.

Thank you very much.

[At this point the President signed the proclamation, then resumed speaking.]

I suppose that the most indispensable part of every man's life is his family, that they give him comfort, strength, and inspiration when he needs it most. But next to my family, I know of no person that is more beloved or for whom I have greater respect and admiration and genuine confidence than the great and distinguished Secretary of State, Dean Rusk.

NOTE: The President spoke at 12:55 p.m. in the State Dining Room at the White House just prior to signing Proclamation 3620 "International Cooperation Year" (29 F.R. 13627, 3 CFR, 1964 Supp.). Early in his remarks he referred to Ambassador Adlai Stevenson, U.S. Representative to the United Nations.

Among those attending the ceremony were Government officials, congressional leaders, and representatives of some 200 bipartisan groups, including the General Federation of Women's Clubs, Future Farmers of America, National Association of Manufacturers, and the National Conference of Christians and Jews.

Following the President's remarks, Secretary of State Dean Rusk spoke briefly, concluding by reading the proclamation. The text of the Secretary's remarks was also released.

On November 24 the White House announced, in a statement released at Austin, Tex., that the President had named a Cabinet Committee representing 19 agencies to plan and coordinate U.S. participation in International Cooperation Year, 1965. The release listed the names of the members of the Committee, of which Harlan Cleveland, Assistant Secretary of State for International Affairs, was designated Chairman.

617   Special Message to the Congress Transmitting Report on Foreign Assistance Programs.   *October 3, 1964*

To the Congress of the United States:

This report demonstrates the remarkable progress made in strengthening our foreign assistance programs and policies since 1961.

The 1961 Act for International Development called for major changes in the operation and emphasis of these historic programs. For more effective direction, the activities of several agencies were brought together under the Agency for International Development. New guidelines were laid down for our aid programs as part of the bold effort to make the 1960's the Decade of Development.

This report for fiscal 1963 shows clearly the ways in which these new guidelines are being translated into concrete programs. They provide the foundations for the lean, tightly-managed aid program we plan for fiscal 1965. I want to call your attention particularly, therefore, to some significant features of this report which mark our progress during 1963 toward basic and continuing objectives of our foreign assistance policy.

Interest-Bearing Loans Replace Grants

As the 1961 Act directed, interest-bearing loans have replaced grants as the chief mechanism for assistance. Loans represented 57 percent of AID's commitments during fiscal 1963—the highest proportion in the history of the foreign assistance program.

Aid Is More Selective

Our aid became increasingly selective and concentrated in fiscal 1963—a trend that has since been accelerated. Eighty percent of all economic assistance funds authorized that year were for just twenty countries. Sixty percent of total military assistance went to just nine key countries.

Aid to Latin America Increases

To increase the impact of the Alliance for Progress, our aid to Latin America was sharply stepped up in fiscal 1963, reaching 23 percent of world-wide commitments, compared with 18 percent the preceding year and an average of only 2 percent from 1948 to 1960.

New Policies Protect the Dollar

Policies designed to protect our balance of payments produced major results in fiscal 1963—a dramatic jump in the purchases of U.S. products. U.S. producers supplied 78 percent of all AID-financed commodities during the year, compared with 63 percent the preceding year, and less than 50 percent in earlier years.

Increased Participation by U.S. Industry

Under these policies U.S. business and industry exported $855 million in AID-financed goods and equipment to Asia, Africa and Latin America during the year, and American shipping firms were paid about $80 million to carry AID-financed commodities to their destinations in the less-developed countries. These dollars meant more jobs for American workers.

As a result of the same policy, U.S. ships carried more than 80 percent of the total net AID-financed cargo that year, well in excess of the 50 percent required by the Cargo Preference Act.

Private Organizations Play a Larger Role

The 1961 Act also called for greater use of America's vast private resources in the battle against world poverty. During fiscal 1963, about one-fourth of all technical assistance was carried out not by AID personnel, but by American colleges, universities, business, professional firms, and service organizations or contract with AID.

More than 70 of our colleges and universities were at work in 40 countries under AID contracts, helping other people make progress in education, in health, in agriculture, in business and industry.

During the year, there was a four-fold increase in cooperative programs designed to help private citizens organize savings and loan institutions, credit unions, rural electric cooperatives, housing and farm credit co-ops. These programs that go right to the people have continued to grow. To expand this significant work, AID relied heavily on contracts with experienced private groups such as the Credit Union National Association, the National League of Insured Savings Associations, the Cooperative League of America, and the National Rural Electric Cooperative Association.

Increased Emphasis on Private Enterprise

In recognition of the fact that foreign investors helped build our own nation's economy and that private capital must do most of the job for the developing nations, we increased efforts to encourage American investment in the less-developed countries. Twelve countries signed investment guaranty agreements during fiscal 1963, bringing to fifty-five the number of less-developed countries participating in this successful program.

This year, for the first time, AID guaranteed a substantial amount of new U.S. private dollar investment in development banks organized to foster private enterprise in the less-developed countries. U.S. investors applied for guaranty coverage totaling $32 million for new or additional investments in such banks.

Significant Savings by Improved Management

Fiscal 1963 saw the beginning of significant economies in the management of aid programs by the Agency for International Development. Economies made in that year included savings of more than $900,000 by centralized purchase of DDT, $1,200,000 during the first six months of the fiscal year alone through tighter travel policies and regulations, and $34 million saved through an aggressive program to use Government-owned excess property in overseas projects.

Economic Aid to Europe Terminated

Major assistance to Europe under the Marshall Plan had ended by the mid-fifties, but a few smaller supplemental programs continued during the years after. Fiscal 1963 saw the last economic assistance commitment for Europe: a single grant of $125,000 authorized to finance the closing out of prior activities in Yugoslavia.

Finally, let me point out this. It is particularly appropriate that the same year which marked the termination of the historic and successful Marshall Plan for Europe was also the year in which our efforts in the less-developed countries began giving unmistakable evidence of success.

With our help, developed countries like Britain, France and Japan recovered from the war rapidly and were soon in a position to give rather than receive assistance. But when we first extended America's helping hand to the less-developed countries a decade ago, there was no such promise of rapid results. We knew it was right and necessary to help these poorer countries to a better life if we were to preserve our own good life and expand the family of the free. But only recently could we be certain that it was practical and only recently have been able to see with our eyes the proof of our earlier vision. In fiscal 1963, for the first time, it became unmistakably clear that countries like Free China were ending their dependence on AID and that others would follow.

We know today that the progress in con-trolling diseases that have sapped men's strength to build and to work, the steady expansion of educational opportunities, the slow but persistent increase in national income and output in the countries we have aided are leading to further successes. We know that if our goal is still distant, our course is true.

LYNDON B. JOHNSON

NOTE: The report, entitled "The Foreign Assistance Program, Annual Report to the Congress for Fiscal Year 1963," was transmitted to the Congress on October 3, 1964 (Government Printing Office, 88 pp.).

618   Statement by the President on the Effects of Hurricane Hilda.   *October 3, 1964*

I HAVE just been informed by Mr. Ed McDermott, Director of the Office of Emergency Planning, that Governor McKeithen of Louisiana, with whom I talked earlier today, has officially requested a Presidential declaration of "major disaster" as a result of Hurricane Hilda.

Surveys by OEP personnel in the State of Louisiana indicate that the damage to property will be severe. In response to the Governor's request, I have declared those areas of Louisiana adversely affected by the hurricane eligible for Federal disaster assistance. I have also directed Mr. McDermott to take all necessary steps to expedite this assistance. I intend to keep in close touch with the situation as the storm moves through the State of Louisiana toward Mississippi.

I am deeply sorry for the lives that have been lost and the people who are suffering such hardship in this unprecedented storm.

NOTE: See also Item 647.

619   The President's News Conference of *October 3, 1964*

THE PRESIDENT. [1.]   The Federal Government began operations under my first budget on July 1st. The Kennedy year went out June 30th. I spent part of the afternoon with Mr. Gordon yesterday, and we worked on it some more this morning. We now have complete figures for Government operations during the first 2 months of this fiscal year, totaled and complete, July and August. This is what the figures show:

1. Total budget expenditures for this 2 months' period are down $667 million from the same period last year.

2. Civilian employment in the executive

branch in July 1964 was 25,000 below the same month, July, in the previous year. In August of 1964 it was 17,000 down below August of 1963. We expect that the September figures will also be below last year's level. In a few days, when we have our reports calculated from the various agencies, we will give you that information.

Federal nondefense agencies report, in accordance with my reporting requirements, that they took steps to initiate management improvements and cost reductions in July and August which will produce savings of more than $178 million on an annual basis. These savings are in addition to the $100 million reported last April and to the $140 million reported in July. I would caution you that these are figures in nondefense agencies. They are in addition to the $2.5 billion savings actually already realized last year under the Defense Department's cost-reduction program.

The agencies with the largest savings to be realized by actions taken in the first 2 months of our fiscal year, July and August, are as follows:

Atomic Energy Commission, $66 million.
National Aeronautics and Space Administration, $44 million.
Department of Agriculture, $14,600,000.
Post Office Department, $10,500,000.
Agency for International Development, $8,900,000.
Interior Department, $7,400,000.
Veterans Administration, $6,100,000.

These are the largest savings. I will not take time to go into the smaller ones.

These savings were achieved through better procurement methods, tighter controls on employment, elimination of publications which I reported to you, overtime paid, reduction of travel, reduction in communications, greater use of Government surplus facilities and equipment, better organization,

consolidations, cutting out unnecessary layers and eliminating unnecessary functions.

With the adjournment of the Congress we have, last night, totaled up all of the requests for appropriations which I sent to the Congress since I became President, and we have determined that we requested $450 million less than I publicly stated I would request in my budget last January.

The Budget Director informs me that our performance in July and August strengthens his confidence in the 1965 expenditure re-estimate of $97.3 billion which we made to you officially in May. At this level, expenditures will be $600 million below the actual expenditures in fiscal 1964. A copy of that statement will be made available to you, and George [1] will give you a copy.

Federal civilian employment in the executive branch in August was 2,483,559, if you want that figure. Employment in August, last month, was a third consecutive month in which Federal employment was below the figures for the same month in the 2 preceding years.

[2.] I have received today an updated cost-reduction report from the Secretary of Defense. This report contains the final audited savings resulting from the Department of Defense cost reduction program for the year that we ended June 30th. On July 7th Secretary McNamara reported savings of $2,553 million. The figures for the final quarter of the year were estimated, as he so reported. I am happy now to state that the final figures for the year have been audited and the actual savings from the cost reduction program, instead of $2,553 million, as estimated, are $2,831 million, an increase of $278 million over our previous estimates.

On July 30th, I announced that the num-

---

[1] George E. Reedy, Press Secretary to the President.

ber of direct-hire civilian employees in the Department of Defense had been reduced for the first time below one million in many years, to 997,864, the first time since the Korean war buildup that such employment had ever gone under one million.

Secretary McNamara has informed me this morning that his previous direct-hire civilian employment ceiling of 989,920 for the end of the current fiscal year on which I based my 1965 budget estimate that I sent to Congress can now be reduced to 984,553, or a further reduction of 13,311 below the Department of Defense civilian employment level on July 1, 1964, and 5,367 below the previously established ceiling of July 1, 1965.

These reports from Secretary McNamara gave me renewed conviction that I will be able to fulfill my pledge to the taxpayers of America when I assumed this office: to give them a dollar's worth of defense for every dollar spent. The report also makes me confident that the Secretary of Defense will probably exceed his established goal of saving $4.6 billion each year, every year, beginning in fiscal 1968.

[3.]   Six months ago I directed the Secretary of Defense to undertake the most comprehensive study of the draft system ever made in this country, and report that to you through our press and television-radio media. Today Secretary McNamara gave me a progress report on this study.

He is exploring all possible ways of meeting our military manpower needs, including the possibility of not relying on the draft. This study will be completed next April. I am impressed and I am pleased by the very thorough approach which is being given and taken on this very complex and important problem.

The Department of Defense staff is being supported by many other of the civilian agencies and Government departments. I am confident that when the study is completed, it will provide the most extensive information on our military manpower needs and supply that has ever been assembled in this country. Secretary McNamara has undertaken the following:

—A thorough evaluation of the fairness of current and alternative draft selection procedures.

—A series of studies aimed at tracing the influence of the draft on employment, on training, on marriage rates, on education, and so forth.

—Surveys and analyses of the plans and the attitudes of young men of military service age to assist us in designing ways to increase the number of volunteers.

—A review of the potential for extending the use of civilians in place of military personnel in support-type activities.

The Secretary of Defense emphasizes that the current population boom offers an unprecedented challenge to our armed services to try to strengthen their voluntary recruitment program. In this coming year the first wave of the postwar generation will reach military-service age. The number of young men reaching 18 will increase from under 1½ million in the past few years to nearly 2 million during the fiscal year ending June 1965.

While I am encouraged with the progress made thus far in these studies, I must emphasize that it is premature to make responsible forecasts of the outcome at this time. Most Americans would agree that we should minimize the use of compulsion in meeting our military manpower needs, but I believe that few Americans would want us to take risks with our security.

We will consider all of the facts. We will consider all of the reasonable alternatives to the present system. We will weigh them in terms of their effect on the young men of this country and their families, as well as on our military capabilities and national security.

We will receive from the Selective Service, the Joint Chiefs of Staff, and the expert civilians in the Department appropriate recommendations as to their judgment of what is best to be done. We will then offer to the American people that course of action which, after careful and thorough study, we believe to be best calculated to protect our freedom at the least and most equitable burden to our society.

[4.]   I have an economic statement.

This week, as we enter the last quarter of 1964, the 44th month of our economic expansion, we can see the economic record of the year now taking shape. The pace of our advance has quickened.

Unemployment, after remaining stubbornly between 5½ and 6 percent in 1962 and 1963, dropped to 5.3 in the first half of this year, to 5.1 in the first quarter.

Our total national output is growing at a 5 percent rate in real terms.

With the aid of the tax cut, consumers are leading the advance. In the first half of the year, their spending rose by a record $15 billion. Strong gains are now continuing. In July, August, and the first 4 weeks of September, retail sales have been 6 percent or more above this period last year.

Business is investing 13 percent more in plant and equipment this year than last year. Sharply rising profits and depreciation allowances, which as you will recall were running 12 percent above a year earlier during the second quarter, have supplied most of the necessary funds.

Our great gains are not being eroded by inflation. Consumer prices, which dropped a bit in August, rose only 1 percent in the past year, a rise well below the postwar average. Average wholesale prices were

below their levels of a year earlier, and below their level at the time that the tax cut was enacted. Wise and responsible policies by business, by labor, and by Government, working and reasoning together in harmony, can bring us continued solid and sound expansion for a long time to come.

[5.]   Today the first round-the-world cruise of our first nuclear task force will come to an end when the three ships comprising that force return to their home ports in the United States. The carrier *Enterprise* and the cruiser *Long Beach* will put in at Norfolk, and the guided missile frigate *Bainbridge* will arrive in Charleston. I commend this event to your attention as one of great interest. And there is a fuller statement that you can copy.[2]

[6.]   I have a statement prepared on the Congress that will be available to you, but I don't want to take your time from questions to read it. It summarizes the 10 months of hard, painstaking work of the Members and it gives my opinion of the achievements of the Congress.[3]

[7.]   I have a brief announcement on the number of women, since we started our special program to induce the employment and promotion of women, in the Federal service. Since our last report on September 8th, the

_____

[2] The statement as released by the White House included the following additional paragraphs:

These ships have demonstrated a new dimension in our strategic capabilities at sea and they have written a new chapter in the history of our friendly relations with the countries they have visited.

It should be noted by friend and foe alike that these ships in traveling 65 days and more than 30,000 miles did not require a single item of logistic replenishment from any source to complete their mission. They were completely self-sustaining.

The officers and men of these ships are to be congratulated on a job extremely well done, and I have asked both the Secretary of the Navy and the Chief of Naval Operations to go to Norfolk today to convey my personal greetings and congratulations.

[3] Item 620.

departments and selected agencies have reported a total of 88 personnel actions promoting or appointing women in grades GS–12 and above. These additions bring the grand total since January 1964 to 1,542, excluding Presidential appointments. With the Presidential appointments, that brings a total of 1,610. There is more detail on that if you want it.

[8.] There is also a statement here by the Secretary of State and the Director of the Office of Information for providing the United States with a more flexible and effective Foreign Service. I won't read that. If you care to have it, you can get that mimeographed and George will make them available to you.[4]

Now I will be glad to answer any questions.

[9.] Q. Mr. President, can you tell us how many women in GS–12 and above were in Government a year ago?

THE PRESIDENT. No, I can just tell you that we have added that many by promotion and appointment.

Q. Well, this is in addition?

THE PRESIDENT. These are in addition to that. You will remember it was reported—I questioned it at the time—but someone said that we would have at least 50 women in top places in Government. There was considerable splash about it, and stories about the 50, and there has been 1,600-odd.

[10.] Q. Mr. President, can you tell us when you plan to have the President-elect of Mexico and his wife as your guest at the LBJ Ranch, and also your thoughts in making the invitation?

THE PRESIDENT. No.

[11.] Q. Mr. President, in the light of the Warren Commission's report, and the campaign season, there are many stories

about your behavior in crowds and the campaign and your physical well-being. Because of these recommendations in the Warren Commission report, and because of some of these concerns that have been expressed, would this start you to change your style?

THE PRESIDENT. No. I want to be fully responsive to your question, and I have studied the Warren Commission report. I wish you would specify what recommendations you had in mind, because I have been reading some of these articles that are written by people who obviously haven't seen it.

Q. It is not the solid recommendations, but some of the suggestions.

THE PRESIDENT. What specific ones?

Q. Well, that you not go into the thick of a crowd.

THE PRESIDENT. There is no such recommendation.

Q. Well, undue exposure.

THE PRESIDENT. There is no such suggestion. I commend the report to your reading. I have read it and I have the provisions marked, and they point out that the President must have association and contact with them, and they do not recommend that you not do it.

The facts of the case are that when you are visiting with these crowds and shaking hands with people, this is the least dangerous period that the President has. I am just amazed that the press would point up these things as creating a problem.

I would have you know that the director of the Secret Service and all of those associated with him tell me that you frequently quote their opinions and their feeling without authority or without justification, in your stories.

Only yesterday I sent him a story where a usually reliable White House reporter had written about the concern of the Secret Service, and it was not only not a concern, but

---

[4] For the President's statement on announcing a change in the Foreign Service, see Item 621.

they felt that we were following their instructions. I never violate any instructions from them. But the question is whether to follow some reporter who has neither read the Warren report nor who knows anything about security—following his suggestion or following the suggestion of the security man.

Now, this morning I have this note from the Chief of the Service, and this is the feeling of all of the people who have served the President.

Following the assassination, we took a good many precautionary steps. We had the highest people in this Government meet and attempt to work out what additional precautions could be taken. I don't want to go into all of those, because I really think that you all serve no good purpose by playing on these things and inviting the attention of folks who have interests in these fields. But if you want to do it and must do it, I think that you ought to do it with the facts, and not off the top of your head.

The memo from the Chief of the Secret Service this morning says this, which might be helpful to some of you:

"There has been much said concerning the dangerous risk involved when the President personally appears in and mingles with crowds. The Secret Service is quite accustomed to working in crowds, and this responsibility does not make them nervous or jittery or worried. It is the nature of the protective assignment that the Secret Service is always concerned for the safety of the President and the First Family.

"The element of surprise which is gained during impromptu appearances of the President, for example, when he stops his car during a motorcade without notice is often the most important deterrent to risk. The ability to infiltrate any gathered crowd by plainclothesmen and law enforcement officers, both male and female, is another impor-

tant deterrent. The crowd itself also offers some protection by covering the President. It also prevents a potential assassin from performing an act unnoticed and prevents the escape of the individual. When on the same level, only these persons in the front row have fair accessibility to the President."

[*At this point the President spoke off the record. He then resumed speaking on the record.*]

But I would say that we have had the Secret Service meet with the FBI and appropriate people in other investigative agencies and we comply with their requests and with their instructions. I am very pleased with the competence of the Secret Service people that surround me, and with the cooperation that they receive from Mr. Hoover and his group at all times.

We do feel and we have felt all along, that you do need to take advance precautions before you go into a place. We try as best we can to balance their desire that we not overly advertise far ahead of time our exact movement with your desire that you have 2 weeks' notice before we travel, and we try to balance it as best we can.

We think that the Secret Service is not in any way dismayed. They are pleased with the way we are handling ourselves, and I am pleased with them. The only ones I know that are not pleased are some politician that doesn't understand it or some reporter who hasn't read it.

I had the Warren Committee report briefed this morning. Will you get it for me? I think Dick [5] has it here. I had a young lawyer go over it and we are trying to find out all of these recommendations that these folks are writing about, and how we violate it. It just isn't so.

Q. There was an innuendo there about exposure.

----

[5] Richard H. Nelson, Presidential Aide.

THE PRESIDENT. Give me the innuendo. It is just not there. Have you read the Warren Commission report?

Q. Yes, sir.

THE PRESIDENT. What are you referring to?

Q. Well, there were portions in there which said the President should not expose himself unduly.

THE PRESIDENT. There is a matter of degree. No one wants to endanger himself unduly, but the question is this: When you stand in front of a group of 80,000 people for 37 minutes, you are in much greater danger than you are stopping. None of the Secret Service or the FBI are worried about a fellow shaking hands.

Q. Mr. President, I believe one of the recommendations of the Commission was that your personal physician be close to you when you are in public. Dr. Burkley was several cars back in the motorcade when one burst into flame. Will you keep your own doctor closer to you in public?

THE PRESIDENT. No, I think that he is kept as close as is necessary, and as is practicable, and he is really not guarding me. He is a matter of seconds from me. If he happens to be in the second or third car, that is adequate, and they think it is adequate. We try to put first things first, and we believe that we are doing that.

There are some parts of the report that interest me, and I will quote them:

"From George Washington to John F. Kennedy, such journeys have been a normal part of the President's activities."

Another quotation is:

"In all of these roles, the President must go to the people. Exposure of the President to public view through travel among the people of this country is a great and historic tradition of American life. Desired by both the President and the public, it is an indispensable means of communication between the two."

Here is another quotation:

"But his very position as representative of the people prevents him from effectively shielding himself from the people. He cannot and will not take the precautions of a dictator or a sovereign. Under our system, measures must be sought to afford security without impeding the President's performance of his many functions."

This is another quotation:

"An approach to complete security would require the President to operate in a sort of vacuum, isolated from the general public and behind impregnable barriers. His travel would be in secret; his public appearances would be behind bulletproof glass."

Very frankly, they had "behind bulletproof glass" as a recommendation following the Kennedy assassination. On certain occasions, when we go over and under certain dangerous places they have outlined ahead, they try to cover every one of these trips with dozens of men going ahead of us, long before you folks even know what we plan. Sometimes they go and examine places that we don't even go to, because they think that we might go to them.

Quoting further:

"Any travel, any contact with the general public involves a calculated risk on the part of the President and the men responsible for his protection. Some risks can be lessened when the President recognizes the security problem, has confidence in the dedicated Secret Service men who are ready to lay down their lives for him and accepts the necessary security precautions which they recommend. Many Presidents have been understandably impatient with the security precautions which many years of experience dictate because these precautions reduce the President's privacy and the access to him of the people of the country. Nevertheless, the procedures and advice should be accepted if the President wishes to have any security."

We have gone through and analyzed all of the pertinent parts, and I have read the pertinent parts here to you now. Since I became President, we have been following them. It is irritating to go in an old car that sometimes roars and you can't even talk in it, but if they recommend it, that is what we do.

None of you need to be worried about my physical safety between now and November. I am going to follow their recommendations. Of course, no one can tell whether their recommendations are best or not, but I comply with them. I had the same people with me as Vice President when you will remember a good many of you complained in columns and articles and in four speeches about having too much protection.

I remember some Congressmen got up and made speeches about having too much protection, and a waste of money, and so forth. But we follow what these men do. Mr. Rowley [6] is the head of it and Mr. Behn [7] is the head of the White House detail, but the man who has been with me many years, and who travels with me, and really supervises all of the folks with us, is Mr. Rufus Youngblood. He and I never have a difference of opinion or a cross word. We are very congenial and very understanding, and his security recommendations are carried out to the letter.

The memorandum that I read you a moment ago from Mr. Rowley represents the views of the people who really do the actual guarding. It is over his signature, but I have discussed that with him thoroughly because of two or three articles that were written along that line.

---

[6] James J. Rowley, Chief of the U.S. Secret Service.
[7] Gerald A. Behn, head of the White House detail of the Secret Service.

[12.] Q. Mr. President, going back to the budget figures that you read us, have you come to any tentative conclusions as to whether or not next year's budget can be held at this year's budget, or under it?

THE PRESIDENT. We have given to the departments certain guidelines for their exploration in connection with their recommendations to us. We cannot finalize that figure until (1) our task forces have made their reports, which will be the latter part of November, some 15 task forces working on the program which I will recommend to the next Congress; and (2) until the Budget Director and I have a chance to scan their recommendations.

We are anxious to keep the expenditures just as low as we possibly can. We recognize that we have a growing population and we have growing needs, but we are trying, as I have said on other occasions, to take the things that we are now doing, what you call the "haves," if we think they are unnecessary, we reduce them in every way we can in order to give to other new programs for which they now do not have anything—the "have-nots"—and we will take from the ones that can be reduced over to the ones that need to be started.

For instance, we reduced from regular departments throughout the Government—Agriculture, Commerce, Labor, HEW, Defense, and others—more than enough money from what they had to finance our entire poverty program which was a so-called "have-not" at that time. We took from them and put it over here.

I am trying to follow the policy that if I am going to have a new venture, then I have to have some way whereby I can find the money for that, rather than just adding to what we spend. I actually had $1 billion less in our budget this year than last year. I don't know how it will run the coming year. We will have to take a look at it. We are working very hard to keep it as low as possible.

[13.] Q. Mr. President, there has been a good deal of invective—and I use that word—hurled across the landscape lately by some candidates running for high office, words like "lies" and "deceit" and "drift" and "defeat" and words along that line. Aside from what is read into your replies at formal speeches, I wonder if you have anything to say about that kind of campaign?

THE PRESIDENT. No. I would refer you to my previous statements on my belief that the people are not particularly concerned about my opinion of my opponent or his personal opinion of me. Most of them recognize in campaigns that candidates don't spend their time recommending the other fellow.

[14.] Q. Referring to your statement of taking from the Government departments that are involved and giving to those that are "have-nots," in the spirit of the season, it appears there is some material questioning whether you meant to apply this to the executive departments or the country as a whole, and I thought you might want to clarify it. I think we all understand it.

THE PRESIDENT. If there is any confusion, eliminate the words "have" and "have-nots." What I mean to say, by previous appropriation of funds, where a department has those funds and a new program does not have those funds, you have to find places where you can make savings if you are to inaugurate a new program. You have to get the approval of Congress, and I think that is one of the reasons we got our poverty program through, because we had effective savings from those departments that had appropriations. So we have something available to those "have-nots."

[15.] Q. Mr. President, could you tell us, sir, what the status and the meaning are of this nuclear treaty that Sir Alec Douglas-Home and Senator Douglas,[8] among others, talked of in the past few days?

THE PRESIDENT. There is no secret of any kind. It seems to me that the question raised by one of the candidates yesterday—my opponent—on a train, was somewhat impulsive. Most of you have had these news briefings and will recall that back in January I made a public announcement on the television and radio networks of this country, and have said several times at press conferences, that we propose new agreements to stop the spread of nuclear weapons to nations not now possessing them. We put forward that proposal publicly and officially in Geneva. All of you know it has been under constant discussion ever since.

I am convinced, as I said in Seattle, that the spread of nuclear weapons is one of the great dangers to peace, and as long as I am President, I shall continue to work as hard as I know how to work to seek agreements that will stop that spread.

Unfortunately, as you know, and as the public record clearly shows, the Soviet Union so far has refused to support our proposal and, as all the world knows, the Chinese Communists have violently opposed any nuclear agreement of any kind.

So there is no secret here. It is simply some more evidence that impulsive people should probably get themselves properly briefed.

[*At this point the President again spoke off the record.*]

[16.] Q. Mr. President, would you comment on the failure to get the medicare bill, and particularly whether it was satisfactory

---

[8] Sir Alec Douglas-Home, Prime Minister of Great Britain, and Senator Paul H. Douglas of Illinois.

to you that we also failed to get the social security benefits increased?

THE PRESIDENT. We regret that we could never get Congressman Mills, the chairman of the committee, and Congressman Byrnes, the chairman of the Republican Policy Committee, and Congressman Curtis to yield or to moderate their views.[9]

The Members reported to me that there was an impasse and they just would not have any part of a Senate proposal this year. I did everything that I could to get it accepted in the Senate and the House. I had many, many conferences with many, many people. But they felt that they couldn't get agreement and they had several meetings and several votes, and like many conferences they just couldn't agree.

I think Senator Gore very properly presented the situation when he said that it is now a matter that the people of this country can pass judgment on. I hope that we get a mandate in November. There are about 19,700,000, about one out of every 10 people, who are on social security, and we think that one of the most important domestic problems is to provide some hospital and medical care for them. It does not in any way involve doctors, and we think it is better for the individual and his employer to provide that by contributing to a fund than to shovel it out of State funds, as you do in other programs.

The Senate agrees with us, but as is often the case, you have difficulty getting both Houses to agree on the same thing at the same time. However, we confidently feel that we will find a way to get agreement in the next session.

We are just sorry that one of our Democrats agreed with two Republicans. I know

he was sincere and I know he thought he was doing the right thing, and men do have different opinions.

[17.] Q. Sir, do you think any good can ever come from a situation in which testimony given to the Warren Commission is released to the public by someone other than the Warren Commission?

THE PRESIDENT. I would think any matter involving the testimony of the Warren Commission at this stage of the game is a proper inquiry for the Warren Commission.

[18.] Q. Mr. President, can you give us your view on the suggestion that your administration is soft on communism?

THE PRESIDENT. I don't know that I want to reply in kind to the charge of that nature. I see in the papers—that is the only information that I have—the new and frightening voice of the Republican Party is merely trying out this charge at the moment to see if it works. On that basis, my own advice would be to drop it.

I also saw it reported that he was advised along these lines by Mr. Hoover and Mr. Nixon, former President Hoover, but both President Hoover and Vice President Nixon are men I have known for many years and have worked with them, and I doubt very much that either of them would make such a suggestion about me or about my Cabinet or this administration.

My own belief is that this sort of nonsense was the product of some third-string speech writer and accidentally got into the public print without prudent or careful screening. As far as I am concerned, I intend to ignore it. I think when the Republican candidate really has a chance to think about it and study it, he will stop it.

William Eaton, United Press International: Thank you, Mr. President.

Q. Mr. President, we all have more questions.

---

[9] The President referred to Representatives Wilbur D. Mills of Arkansas, John W. Byrnes of Wisconsin, and Thomas B. Curtis of Missouri.

THE PRESIDENT. I am sure that would be true if I stayed here all day.

NOTE: President Johnson's thirty-second news conference was held in his office at the White House at 3:05 p.m. on Saturday, October 3, 1964.

620   Statement by the President Reviewing the Work of the 88th Congress.   *October* 3, 1964

TODAY the 88th Congress of the United States had its final session.

After almost 10 months of hard, painstaking work its members are going home. Some will campaign for reelection. Others will talk with the people they serve—learning about their problems and telling about the work of this Congress.

They have a wonderful story to tell.

I spent 30 years in the United States Congress. I know of no Congress that has done more for the Nation.

The majority of its members have spent long days and many hours considering the most important needs of America. They have put aside private interest and sectional interest to meet the urgent needs of the entire Nation.

On many important matters, leaders have worked together, submerging partisan difference in the cause of building America and keeping the peace.

Most Congresses deserve praise if they pass a handful of major bills. This Congress has passed more than 50.

Most Congresses would find a place in history if they made an important contribution to a single major area of American life. This Congress has moved far ahead in half a dozen areas.

As bill after bill has come to my desk for signature, I often remarked that this Congress would be known for that particular piece of landmark legislation.

I said it would be known as the "Education Congress," as the "Health Congress," as the "Conservation Congress," and then as the "Full Prosperity Congress."

But its accomplishments are limited by none of these.

This is simply the Congress that has done more for America. Its achievements reach into every city and every home of our Nation. It has broadened the horizons and improved the life of every citizen. And they have made the future brighter for every family in this land.

They have done this because they worked at it—because they were not afraid to tackle difficult problems—because they hammered out differences with careful debate—and because most of its members always put America first.

As a result they have:

—improved the Nation's economy and the Nation's security.

—improved the Nation's use of its resources.

—improved the Nation's education.

—improved the National health and well-being.

—improved the Nation's capacity to provide equal opportunity for all its people.

There are very few bills which can truly be called milestones in the history of public policy. There are not many pieces of legislation which impart new direction and force to American progress. Often many years and many Congresses go by between such acts.

This Congress has passed three bills of such shaping importance.

One was the tax cut. That bill will ultimately produce $11 billion of increased purchasing power—putting it into the hands of American consumers to buy more of the things they need. It will help create more than 2 million jobs. And it has already given the economy a substantial upward lift. It represents almost the first successful effort to use fiscal policy to prevent a recession before it started, and to make a growing economy grow even faster.

A second was the poverty bill—the Economic Opportunity Act of 1964. This was our country's declaration of war on poverty. It expressed our national determination to eliminate poverty for the first time in the history of any nation. It does this, not through charity or handouts, but by attacking the poor health, the poor education, the poor homes which are the cause of poverty. Its aim is to help people lift themselves from the ranks of the poor.

A third was our civil rights bill. This bill was supported by the leaders of both parties in both houses of Congress, and by the majority of Members from each party. It represents a fundamental American commitment to ensure all our people their full constitutional rights, and equal opportunity to share in the blessing of American life.

These bills alone would make this a Congress to be long remembered.

But this Congress also took enormous strides forward in several areas of urgent concern to all Americans.

The first was education. It enacted five major pieces of education legislation. A Higher Education Facilities Act will help our colleges construct the facilities they need to meet a growing demand for knowledge. The expansion of the National Defense Education Act will allow more of our young people—through fellowships, grants, and loans—to go to college on the basis of ability rather than income. Other legislation will train more workers in new skills, more doctors for growing population, more expert teachers for our young.

The second area was the protection and development of our natural resources. This Congress passed more than 30 measures to preserve the natural abundance which God has granted this Nation.

Among the highlights was the wilderness bill to set aside threatened areas of natural beauty so that our children might enjoy them as we have.

—a Land and Water Conservation Fund Act—to help cities and towns create areas for recreation and the enjoyment of nature.

—dozens of new national park areas, four national seashores, a bill providing for research into ways to meet our exploding need for water.

The third area was the health and well-being of our people.

One bill attacks the growing pollution of the air we breathe. Another makes our first large scale effort to help parents prevent mental retardation, or care for children already retarded.

We have provided for the training of nurses and doctors, increased construction of hospitals, new research into basic diseases and afflictions—such as heart and cancer—which menace the well-being of all our people.

These are some of the major areas. But hardly any important aspect of American life has been left untouched.

In our cities new legislation attacks the problems of mass transportation and the need for better housing.

Among the underprivileged a new food stamp program helps ensure that none go hungry in a land bulging with food surpluses.

Among our farmers new feed grain and

commodity programs help ensure that those who feed the Nation will get a fair reward for their labor.

Among those who serve the Nation a military and civilian pay bill has helped soldiers and Government employees keep pace with the rising cost of living—and made it more possible to attract the best talent to the affairs of the Nation.

These are some of the highlights of one of the most productive Congresses in American history.

But no story of this Congress would be complete without praise for a monumental product of bipartisan statesmanship—the treaty banning nuclear tests in the atmos-phere. This single act virtually ended the radioactive poisoning of the atmosphere—a threat to the health of every child on earth—and brought the world one step closer to lasting peace.

The majority of the members of the 88th Congress have supported much of this progressive legislation. They have acted wisely and after careful consideration. They have been selfless and untiring—compassionate and constructive—resolute and unafraid—alert to the needs of all the people.

They have served their Nation well.

And a grateful Nation is proud of what they have done.

621   Statement by the President Announcing a Change in the Foreign Service.   *October* 3, 1964

I AM PLEASED to announce an action taken by the Secretary of State and the Director of the United States Information Agency which will do much to provide the United States with a more flexible and effective Foreign Service.

Under the new arrangement, the vast majority of USIA career Foreign Service officers will become an integral part of the Foreign Service. Affected will be almost 900 officers now working for the Information Agency. The arrangement will:

1. Provide a single pool of carefully selected, highly trained talent from which both agencies may draw to fill key posts.

2. Increase substantially the efficiency and the flexibility of those personnel available to represent the United States abroad.

3. Permit a greater exchange of personnel between State and USIA, thus insuring that our officers acquire the wide range of experi-ence and contacts so vitally necessary to the effective conduct of foreign policy.

4. Meet recommendations of the Herter Committee, the Advisory Commission on Information, and various other study groups that USIA career officers be given the same rights and perquisites and be subjected to the same stringent judgment of performance as personnel already in the Foreign Service.

5. Increase greatly the already high level of cooperation and joint planning between State and USIA.

In my opinion, this action, which I wholeheartedly endorse, is a major step forward in our constant efforts to improve the efficiency of the Foreign Service of the United States—a Service that is vitally necessary in an era when the burdens of world leadership are heavy upon us.

622 Remarks to a Group of College Student Leaders. *October 3, 1964*

I DIDN'T realize until I heard your applause what a wonderful speaker Bill Wirtz was.

My older daughter who came in with us, who is really my "college authority in residence," gave me a good many instructions about what to say to you today. She said, "Now Daddy, don't give them your usual stuff. Don't tell them how well the economy is doing because after this trip to Washington they are all going to be broke, anyway. And don't talk about the beauties of frugality because those of us living on college allowances already know all about frugality."

She did say that I could leave the lights on until it gets dark tonight.

I am sure that you have been told already that this is a nonpolitical meeting. I can't tell you to cast your first vote for the Democrats, and I absolutely refuse to misguide you in any other direction.

I try to be nonpartisan; as evidence of it my Secretary of State is a Democrat, my Secretary of Defense is a Republican, or was, and it may be weighed a little bit, one way or the other. Secretary Wirtz is a Democrat, too.

I want to welcome you warmly to the White House this afternoon.

Our country very much needs the influence of this young generation. I have read the tags often applied to your age group, the "quiet generation," the "apathetic generation," the "cool cookies," the "security chasers, interested only in sports cars, a split-level, and an annuity."

But I am not really impressed by those statements because I just don't believe in labels.

I know too many young people dedicated to goals beyond the pursuit of mere self-interest. I have met hundreds of them throughout the world that are now giving dedicated service in the Peace Corps. Thousands more have written to me since I have been President saying that they intend to volunteer for the war on poverty, or volunteer in dozens of other ways to help our country and our Government, and to help make our communities more humane centers of living.

As a matter of fact, I believe that it would be appropriate to say that yours is the "volunteer generation." You seem ready and eager to take on the tasks which call for a real personal sacrifice.

This country needs those virtues. We need your boundless energy. We need your curiosity—your inquisitive minds about every aspect of our living. We need your belief that the impossible is only a little more difficult to do; your sophistication which tells us to be hardheaded and your generous instincts which tell us that mere sophistication is not enough.

You were born to the hangover of a depression and a World War. If you think your elders did not do so well themselves you certainly have reasons for it. And your time to do something about it is on its way, it's coming.

As you know so well, freedom is never a static doctrine. Freedom is an active, dynamic, rolling credo.

The basic meaning of freedom remains the same but the specific techniques to protect it and to advance it vary with the needs of a changing America and a changing world.

Thoughtful Americans—Republicans and

Democrats—years ago came to substantial agreement on the demands of freedom in that day.

We followed their prescription and we built a mighty Nation—it is bursting with opportunity.

History hurried on. We became a highly industrialized, highly urbanized society. Then, that new society was swept into a world that was tossed by revolutionary forces and operating under the awesome fact of nuclear power.

Once again thoughtful men, without regard to any political party, came to substantial agreement on the needs of freedom.

Able leaders, whether the Republican, Theodore Roosevelt, or the Democrat, Woodrow Wilson, pointed to the bedrock fact: In an increasingly complex Nation, greater activity of Government and more social-minded attitudes of all private institutions were needed to protect the genuine freedom of the individual.

In foreign affairs able leaders—whether the Democrats, Franklin Delano Roosevelt, Harry Truman, or John Kennedy—whether the Republicans, Arthur Vandenberg, Wendell Willkie, or Dwight Eisenhower—pointed to a similar bedrock fact: In a nuclear world the security of freedom requires great and infinite patience—patience with the stubborn realities of the pursuit of peace and requires great caution to avoid even the appearance of a foreign policy of bluster.

These changing techniques in American freedom, conceived and executed by so broad a consensus of our national leadership, have been remarkably effective.

At home and abroad we have not only protected freedom, we have steadily expanded it. I genuinely believe that rather than giving up freedom we are acquiring more of it, both in the world and at home.

I believe there is more freedom in the other nations today than there was when I was your age, for the individual citizens of those nations.

I sincerely and genuinely believe that I have more freedom today than I had when I was your age.

A genuinely free society cannot be a spectator society. And this is my real message to you.

Freedom, in its deepest sense, requires participation. It requires full and zestful, knowledgeable participation.

Toward that end, I have today established a new program entitled "The White House Fellows."

The purpose of the program is to give the Fellows first-hand, high-level experience with the workings of the Federal Government and to increase their sense of participation in our national affairs.

The Fellows will be younger men and women, aged 23 to 35, chosen from business and law, journalism, the universities, architecture, and other occupations. Each will have demonstrated high moral character, exceptional ability, marked leadership qualities, and unusual promise of future development.

There will be 15 White House Fellows and they will serve for 15 months. One Fellow will be assigned to the office of the Vice President; one to each Cabinet officer; and four as members of the White House staff. In addition to their daily work, the Fellows will take part in seminars and other activities that are especially planned to advance the purposes of this program.

The Fellows will be named by the President on the recommendation of a distinguished Commission on White House Fellows that will be headed by Mr. David Rockefeller.

Some of the members of the Commission, I am very happy to say, are here with us, and if I could, I would like to take a moment to present them if they have not left:

Mr. James Carey, president of the Electrical, Radio and Machine Workers.

Dr. William Friday, president of the University of North Carolina. He is not only going to do this job for us, but I have a little secret in store for him. We are getting ready to borrow one of his best men for our poverty program.[1]

Mr. John Gardner, president of the Carnegie Foundation.

Mr. Francis Keppel, United States Commissioner of Education.

Mr. John Macy, Chairman of the United States Civil Service Commission.

Dr. Harry Ransom, chancellor of the University of Texas.

Other eminent Americans who will serve on the Commission but who cannot be present tonight are:

Dr. Ernest C. Arbuckle, dean of the Graduate School of Business at Stanford University.

Judge William Hastie of the Third U.S. Circuit Court of Appeals.

Mr. John Oakes, editor of the New York Times.

Senator Margaret Chase Smith of Maine.

Dr. O. Meredith Wilson, president of the University of Minnesota.

The program of the White House Fellows is being financially supported by the Carnegie Foundation headed by Mr. John Gardner.

I hope that I will be seeing some of you again when you come here as White House Fellows. I am not recommending anyone

specifically, but I do hope the judges will take judicial notice of my observation.[2]

One of the most satisfying jobs of my life was when I was at the age of 27, when President Roosevelt asked me to head the National Youth Administration in Texas. The job was so satisfying because I and the other young people working with me—and the 30,000 young people we were trying to work with and help—knew that we were part of what FDR and his associates were doing in Washington.

A hundred years from now when historians look back on the Johnson administration, I hope very much that they will be able to say: There, once again, was an era when the young men and the young women of America and their Government really belonged to each other—belonged to each other in fact and belonged to each other in spirit.

We are so happy to welcome you here today. We hope this has been an eventful experience for you. We look forward to having you back sometime.

Thank you.

NOTE: The President spoke at 6:05 p.m. in the East Room at the White House to some 230 college

---

[1] On October 22 the White House announced that the President had named Dr. Otis A. Singletary, chancellor of the University of North Carolina, at Greensboro, as Director of the Job Corps in the Office of Economic Opportunity.

[2] On November 25 the President announced an intensive, nationwide search for the 15 ablest young men and women with a talent for leadership. The White House release containing the President's announcement stated that more than 3,000 applications under the White House Fellows Program had already been received. The release further stated that the President expected civic, professional, academic, and business leaders would make further nominations, so that the Rockefeller Commission would have before it the names of the most promising young leaders in the Nation.

The release added that the Fellows selected would participate in an intensive orientation program conducted by the Brookings Institution, and that seminars and discussions with leaders in Government, business, labor, and the professions would allow them to explore in depth the major policy problems and public issues which affect the National Government.

students from across the country. In his opening remarks he referred to Secretary of Labor W. Willard Wirtz. Later he referred to, among others, David Rockefeller, president of the Chase Manhattan Bank in New York.

During the political campaign a Student Body President's National Advisory Committee was formed to work for the President's election at colleges throughout the Nation. On November 1 a White House release stated that the President welcomed the support of this group and that he had been particularly pleased with the enthusiasm of young people for his program. The release listed the names of the 91 members of the Committee, some of them "former Republicans," and stated that they had worked to keep the President as well as State and National Democratic Party officials abreast of political sentiment on college campuses throughout the Nation.

623   Remarks of Welcome at the White House to President Macapagal of the Philippines.   *October 5, 1964*

Mr. President:

For the American people and for myself, may I say welcome to this land and to this city.

Our country is honored for you because you come representing a people that Americans honor greatly.

The United States enjoys friendship with many nations, but with your nation, Mr. President, there is and there always will be a special friendship, a special quality of understanding between us.

Our nations grew up together. We fought together for common beliefs. We work together today for common goals. Our eyes are on the future but our hearts will never forget the past.

A part of the soul of America remains forever on Bataan and Corregidor. Our sons and your sons died together there so that we might stand together here in independence and in freedom.

We have peace and we prize it, but we prize freedom and honor more. If any break the peace and attack freedom, we are prepared and ready to give firm and appropriate reply.

We shall remember always the price that free men once paid in the Pacific for doing too little too late. We are determined that those words shall never be heard from free men again.

Ten years ago in Manila, the Southeast Asia Treaty Organization was formed. On that cornerstone the cause of freedom stands in southeast Asia and the United States stands steadfastly in its support.

Mr. President, the success of your dynamic democracy shows to all that freedom is the wave of the future for Asia and for all the nations that rim the vast Pacific.

The honor is ours today to have you here with us.

In this house and wherever you go in this land, you will find the affection and the warmth of a nation that regards with great warmth and deep affection your nation and all of your people.

Thank you.

NOTE: The President spoke at 11:49 a.m. on the South Lawn at the White House where President Diosdado P. Macapagal was given a formal welcome with full military honors. President Macapagal responded as follows:

Mr. President:

From the bottom of my heart, I thank you for the warmth and graciousness of your welcome and for the generous words that you have uttered about my country and the relations between us.

I am certain that the sentiments that you have expressed are fully appreciated and reciprocated by our people.

I come to the United States of America as President of the Philippines in response to an invitation extended to me by the President of the United States, His Excellency Lyndon Johnson.

I am profoundly aware of the honor of the invitation, and I am here to renew the friendship between my country and the United States. That friendship has a long history.

As the representative of the Filipino people, I am proud to reaffirm the honorable auspices of that amity. It is based on a common commitment to ideals that have been sustained and mutually affirmed by our two peoples in the ordeal of crucial struggles to maintain peace and to uphold freedom.

This common commitment, Mr. President, we have reaffirmed in war. I consider it my distinct privilege in behalf of my people now to reassure its continuity in peace.

Mr. President, as I present the greetings of the Filipino people to you who symbolizes the authority of the American people, I also wish in my people's name to pay homage of respect to the obelisk we see from this impressive White House Lawn because, to us in the Philippines, George Washington epitomizes the idea of freedom that is the rampart of this great democratic country and the guiding inspiration of our history as a people.

Thank you.

624 Statement by the President on the New Labor Contracts in the Automobile Industry. *October 5, 1964*

I AM PLEASED that the General Motors strike is settled and the Big Three of the auto industry and the United Auto Workers have now reached agreement.

I am also pleased with the announcements that the 1965 models will sell at the same prices as this year's. Stable automobile prices have helped auto sales reach their present record levels and have helped the country achieve its fine record of price stability.

1. While the auto settlement was a generous one, it must be judged in the context of the auto industry's very high profits arising from higher sales, lower costs and taxes, and very high productivity combined with maintained prices.

2. Both labor and management realize the unique nature of the auto settlement. I expect that other industries with profits below the high level in autos will not use the auto settlement as a pattern.

3. In recent years the United States has had the best record of price and cost stability of any industrial country in the world.

4. Business, labor, and Government have shown more awareness of the importance of price stability—in keeping America competitive and sustaining our record-breaking economic expansion.

5. The price-wage guideposts have contributed to this awareness, by providing a standard for judging whether price and wage decisions are in the public interest. Responsible business and labor leaders want to consider the public interest in making their own decisions.

6. The guideposts continue to represent a sound standard for noninflationary wage and price decisions.

7. We expect that the record for all wage settlements for 1964 will show an average reasonably close to the guidepost levels.

8. We know that a new round of inflation could erode our export surplus and undermine our great expansion. All of us have a vital interest in maintaining price-wage stability.

625   Message to the Second Conference of Nonaligned Nations Meeting in Cairo.   *October 5, 1964*

PEACE in our troubled world is the hope of all men of good will. All governments that would faithfully serve their people, that would strive to realize their dreams, must have the unwavering quest of peace as a primary concern. So the delegations gathered in Cairo have an opportunity in their deliberations to help advance this great common cause of mankind.

You have recognized this opportunity— and this challenge—by making the safeguarding and the strengthening of world peace your first order of business. Every positive step taken to settle international disputes peacefully—or to eliminate their causes before they reach crisis proportions— brings us all closer to the goal we share.

As you all know, the United States has been in the forefront of those seeking to strengthen world peace through sensible and safeguarded measures of disarmament. We pledge ourselves anew to this great task.

The United States enjoys friendly relations with nearly all nations represented at your conference. The United States shares with all your peoples the same basic values and aspirations—for human rights and the dignity of the individual, for freedom from all forms of exploitation or domination by outside forces, for the right of each nation, in every area of the world, to develop political and economic systems of its own choosing, and to realize its own dreams in its own way.

Unfortunately, these legitimate national aspirations are still denied to many peoples. Unfortunately, aggression often masks itself in new forms of imperialism while attacking the imperialism of the past. Unfortunately, the centuries-old problems of poverty, illness,

and illiteracy continue to afflict a high percentage of the human race.

The United States has joined with most of you in the past in trying to deal with these difficult and complicated problems by peaceful means. We hope to continue and expand this cooperation.

A year ago this week, one of our most important accomplishments—the Nuclear Test Ban Treaty—went into effect. We Americans are proud of the role that President Kennedy and the United States Government played in obtaining that treaty. It was a great step forward—but it was not enough. We will not be satisfied until the awesome power of the atom is harnessed for peace alone, and men can live out their lives with assurance that they will not be suddenly obliterated in the night.

John F. Kennedy is no longer with us. We mourn his loss, and work to make real his dreams for a better world. Another great peacemaker, Jawaharlal Nehru, has also been taken from us, but his visions for a better world were never more alive.

We Americans live in a diversified society. We are a nation of many minority groups— from almost every land. For this reason, we cherish as a guiding principle the right of men and of groups to hold diverse views so long, of course, as the expression of those views does not interfere with the security or the welfare of others.

We defend that principle among ourselves. We support and respect its application in our relations with all responsible governments.

Finally, we greet you as fellow members of the United Nations, which has done so much to guard the peace and to point the way to a better world order. There we join together in a parliament in which the strong and the weak, the rich and the less prosperous, the old and the new nations share the floor, the platform, and the responsibility in common cause. These are rights to be cherished by us all as we sustain and strengthen our organization to better serve us all this year, next year, and into our common future.

626 Toasts of the President and President Macapagal. *October 5, 1964*

Mr. President, Mrs. Macapagal, distinguished guests:

This house of the American people is honored tonight by the presence of the President and the First Lady of a land that Americans love—the Republic of the Philippines.

Ten months ago, Mr. President, you came on a mission of sorrow to the funeral of our beloved President John F. Kennedy. All Americans are grateful to you for that moving gesture.

We are proud that you have returned tonight under happier circumstances on a mission of friendship.

When we first met in Manila, our guest and I were both Vice Presidents. He has since succeeded in being elected President and, needless to say, I find that example commendable tonight.

As we all know, our guest's election to his nation's highest office has opened a new era in the Philippines. To his people's courage and devotion to freedom, the President is adding a new dimension of responsible statesmanship. He has been unremitting in his efforts to bring about Asian solutions to problems that threaten conflict among Asian nations.

In your land and in mine, Mr. President, new generations are at the helm. In all free nations, new generations are on the threshold of leadership. These new generations must test the ties among free allies and must judge for themselves their value and their strength, but I have no doubt what that decision will be.

Those ideals which inspired so many people to reach for independence are not Western values or Asian values. They are abiding human values.

The worth of those values is eternal.

Our mutual devotion to them will be everlasting.

If freedom is to stand strong, free men must be devoted to strength, must be devoted to social justice, to the dignity of the individual, and to the love of peace.

On these principles the Philippines have risen from the ruins of war to build an economy offering the people one of the highest standards of living in all Asia. That economy is built on the foundation of free enterprise and on the foundation of private initiative.

The example of the Philippines shines to all nations seeking economic and social progress with freedom for the individual.

Mr. President, the Philippines have also been in the forefront of the fight against external challenge to the freedom that we so cherish.

You have met and you have defeated Communist subversion in the Philippines itself.

You were founder members of the SEATO alliance. You have extended a helping hand to Laos and Viet-Nam as they resist the common peril.

Tonight, the independence of free men is nowhere more threatened than in southeast Asia. So, I was greatly heartened when you told me personally this afternoon of your purpose to do all that you can to help meet this challenge.

In turn, I pledge again the full and continuing support of the United States to the Philippine Republic and to other like-minded and true friends.

None can know just how long the fight for freedom in southeast Asia will take, but we of the United States are resolved not to falter or to grow weary in the struggle.

Our constant and continuing hope is that around the realm of the great ocean named for peace there will grow a great community of peace. Our effort is directed toward building such a community where free men can trade together, where free men can work together and prosper together in freedom, in peace, without war.

In the creation of such a community, the Philippines serve as a valuable bridge of understanding between the East and the West.

We are so happy to have the distinguished Ambassador from your country in our house tonight. We honor him and have deep affection for him.

We are also delighted to have our own Ambassador, Ambassador Blair, return here with you. We think highly of him, and we hope that he enjoys his visit in your country.

So, Mr. President, we receive you in this country as the representative of an old and very valued ally.

But we welcome you even more as the leader of the new Philippines and as a new leader for freedom's cause everywhere.

So, I ask all of you here tonight to join me in a toast to His Excellency, the President of the Republic of the Philippines, to the continued friendship between the peoples of his Republic and ours and to the success throughout the world of freedom's cause.

NOTE: The President proposed the toast at a dinner in the State Dining Room and the Blue Room at the White House. President Macapagal responded as follows:

"Mr. President, Mrs. Johnson:

"Mr. President, you and I are in a very peculiar situation at this moment. We are separated by a room and walls but still we can hear each other, and we are friends.

"Our two countries are just like we are at this moment. They are in different places, separated by the vast Pacific Ocean, but they can hear each other's voice, and they are friends.

"There is really some similarity between the career of President Johnson and myself. Both of us were, first, Vice Presidents and then we became President. Now he is running for President. Next year, I am running also for President, so I am very anxious about this election here because I confess I am very superstitious about similarities.

"It is a great honor for my people and myself that you, Mr. President, have invited me to make this state visit to the United States.

"We regard this visit as a kind of family reunion. We share to the full the feeling of indestructible friendship and the sense of common purpose between our two peoples which this reunion serves to confirm.

"We are deeply moved by the kind words which you, Mr. President, have uttered. Permit me to say that your generous references to me and my people are warmly reciprocated. They have struck in our hearts the deepest chords of respect, admiration, and affection.

"The ties that bind the American people and the Filipino people are the ties and ideas and ideals—democracy, freedom, love for peace, and the rule of law—long shared in common. The strength of these bonds has in the past been subjected to the terrible ordeal of battle, and their durability to the strenuous task of peace.

"Let my presence here attest to the resolve of the Filipino people that these bonds of mutual dedication shall withstand any trials which the future may bring.

"It should be of interest to you and to the whole American people what the attitude of the Filipino people is towards the United States and the American people and how the Philippines has been faring 18 years after the severance of our political ties.

"The Philippine attitude toward the United States during the last decade is premised on the basic heritage that you bequeathed to us.

"From Spain, which ruled over the Philippines for 377 years, we inherited, firstly, the Christian religion so that 95 percent of our people are Christians, and, secondly, a true appreciation of Western culture.

"From the United States, which ruled over us for 48 years, we in turn inherited the processes of democracy and a system of mass public education which is unparalleled in colonial history. These are legacies which have become the cornerstone of our vigor and future as a nation considering that the success of democracy depends upon the level of enlightenment and education of the people.

"To carry out its unprecedented policy of mass education, America sent hundreds of American schoolteachers to the remotest hinterlands and to the hills to educate our children, with the result that the Philippines today enjoys the second highest level of literacy in Asia and the desire for education has become a passion among our people.

"I myself am a product of the American public school system in the Philippines. Coming from one of the humblest families, my only opportunity to acquire an education was the American-established public schools.

"I have had the privilege and distinction of having been tutored by many American teachers during my school days. The fact that one who comes from among the poorest families could go through the public school system established in the Philippines to become President of the Philippine Republic by virtue of a free and democratic election, is concrete proof that democracy, based on a system of mass education implanted by the United States in the Philippines, possesses the efficacy to improve the lot of the common man in freedom. Thus, to us Filipinos, democracy and not communism is the system that can elevate the masses of Asia from poverty to a better life.

"Because of this basic American heritage of the processes of democracy and mass public education, the attachment and affection of the Filipino people today for the American people are as strong as ever, and, I dare say, these will continue to be as strong in the future.

"Our affinity and common ideals of democracy, freedom, love of peace, and the rule of law should render it relatively easier to thresh out problems pending between our two countries in a just and honorable manner and on the basis of sovereign equality and mutual respect.

"Indeed, we appreciate the blessings of democracy so deeply that we are prepared to share in the responsibility of upholding, defending, and preserving freedom in our part of the world. This is the basis of the active participation of the Philippines in Afro-Asian affairs, particularly our endeavor to bring about a peaceful settlement of the Malaysian-Indonesian dispute. This is the basis of the Philippine support for American policy in southeast Asia, particularly in Viet-Nam.

"The retaliatory action ordered by you, Mr. President, in the Tonkin incident heartened the free nations of Asia because the struggle of the people of South Viet-Nam is essentially one that involves the right to govern themselves.

"The fall of Viet-Nam to communism would endanger the security of its southeast Asian neighbors, and your endeavor for freedom in that part of the world merits the support of the other free nations of Asia. We believe that these nations should be disposed under proper legal framework and within their capabilities to participate in the struggle to sustain the democratic cause in Viet-Nam.

"As to how the Philippines has been faring since its independence, I must say in all humility that in our administration we have arrested and greatly reduced the rampant graft and corruption that have plagued our government since the end of the war.

"We have successfully restored free enterprise after 12 years of economic controls. We have finally succeeded in initiating a land reform program which abolishes the centuries old tenancy system which enslaved our farmers in poverty and prevented our agro-industrial progress.

"To fight poverty, we have launched a long-range 5-year socio-economic program calculated to offer greater opportunities to our people for an improvement in their lives.

"We have done all these and we are ready to do more to prove the vitality of democracy as a way of life. We believe that should democracy fail in the Philippines—the only Asian country which was formerly a colony of the United States—American leadership in Asia and elsewhere in the world for the cause of democracy and freedom will be less convincing and be weakened. On the other hand, the success of our efforts to improve the livelihood of our masses under freedom will enhance the cause of freedom and help lighten the enormous load of the United States in leading the free world.

"In your hands, Mr. President, as head of the American Nation and leader of the free world, rests a heavy responsibility. That responsibility is to insure the survival of man in a world of freedom. In your hands, too, lies the power, moral as well as material, to discharge this responsibility with patience and wisdom where required, with strength and resolution when necessary.

"We who love freedom stand beside you. We who long for security pray for you. May the Almighty steady your hand and steer your heart as you guide America and lead the legions of free men everywhere.

"In this spirit, may I ask all to join with me in a toast to the health and success of the President of the United States, His Excellency Lyndon B. Johnson, and to the enduring partnership for freedom of our two peoples."

During President Johnson's remarks he referred to the Philippine Ambassador Oscar Ledesma and the U.S. Ambassador to the Philippines William McC. Blair.

627   Joint Statement Following Discussions With the President of the Philippines. *October 6,* 1964

THE PRESIDENT of the United States and the President of the Philippines today concluded the fruitful discussions they have held over the past days. These talks dealt with Philippine-American relations and matters of international significance to both countries. They were the latest in the long history of exchanges between Presidents of the two countries and reflected the spirit of special friendship and cooperation which has existed between the Philippines and the United States over the years. The two Presidents expressed their confidence that the American and Philippine peoples would continue to benefit from this close association in the future.

The two Presidents exchanged views on the situation in southeast Asia and pledged themselves to maintain the unity of commitment and purpose between their countries in defense of the right of the free nations of southeast Asia to determine their own future.

President Johnson noted with deep appreciation the response by the Philippines to the requests of the Government of Viet-Nam for aid in its defense against communist subversion and aggression. The two Presidents agreed that it is of the utmost importance to free men throughout the world that communist force not be permitted to dictate their future. Noting the struggle of the people of South Viet-Nam against communist aggression and its implication for all free people, the two Presidents reaffirmed their intention to stand by the peo-

ple of South Viet-Nam and reiterated their commitment to the defense of southeast Asia under the SEATO Treaty.

President Macapagal noted that prompt and decisive action by the United States in the Gulf of Tonkin had once again confirmed American readiness and determination to resist aggression in southeast Asia to help assure its progress under freedom.

President Johnson expressed his appreciation to President Macapagal for the latter's efforts to bring about a peaceful settlement of the dispute between Indonesia and Malaysia. Both Presidents agreed that it is vitally important that this dispute, which now threatens the peace and stability of the Southwest Pacific area, be resolved.

The two Presidents recognized that the aggressive intentions and activities of Communist China continue to present an imminent threat in the Far East and in southeast Asia. They reviewed, in this connection, the importance of the Mutual Defense Treaty between the Philippines and the United States in maintaining the security of both countries, and reaffirmed their commitment to meet any threat that might arise against their security. President Johnson made it clear that, in accordance with these existing alliances and the deployment and dispositions thereunder, any armed attack against the Philippines would be regarded as an attack against United States forces stationed there and against the United States and would instantly be repelled.

The United States and the Philippines agreed to study their mutual requirements for security, to review existing programs, and to consider changes needed to achieve increased capability and flexibility in the Philippine response to aggression and threats of aggression.

The two Presidents agreed that the relationship between their respective countries was a dynamic and flexible association with a history of past achievement and a heavy stake in a common future. In the spirit of this alliance, the two Presidents agreed that any matter of interest to either party related thereto should be the subject of friendly and frank discussion, and each President invited the views of the other in this regard.

The two Presidents likewise took cognizance of matters pertaining to Philippine veterans of World War II and agreed on the establishment of a joint commission to study this subject further.

President Macapagal reviewed the economic progress made by the Philippines in recent years. President Johnson commended the land reform program, initiated by President Macapagal this year, as holding out renewed hope to the Philippine people for the solution of the land tenure problems which, for decades, had beset a major sector of its economy. President Johnson noted past United States support for Philippine agrarian reform and expressed his hope that American assistance could continue in the future, particularly in the realization of the land reform objectives of the Philippines.

Both Presidents discussed the disposition of the Special Fund for education, provided for in the Philippine War Damage legislation. They agreed to consider plans including the possible formation of a joint committee which would ensure use of this fund to further educational programs to the mutual advantage of the Philippines and the United States, among which educational programs pertaining to land reform would be eligible.

President Macapagal explained the goals of his Socio-Economic Program and its objective of alleviating the plight of the common man in the Philippines. President Johnson reiterated his belief that it was the responsibility of this generation everywhere to join the campaign against poverty and the ills associated with it and pledged American support for worthy projects contributing to the economic development of the Philippines. The two Presidents noted that one area of particular interest which could bring great benefit to the Philippine people was rural electrification. President Macapagal said that Philippine Government plans envisage the establishment of generating and distribution electric systems in 607 towns and 400 selected barrios. President Johnson observed that a team of American experts has arrived in the Philippines and, working with private and public Philippine energy experts, would cooperate in developing plans for this nationwide system of expanding power generation and distribution with its special attention to rural areas.

The two Presidents looked to developments in the trade between their respective countries and in the world trading community that could assure expanding markets for the leading exports of the Philippines, including sugar, coconut products, abaca, lumber, minerals and others. The Philippines expressed their readiness and willingness to supply additional sugar to the American market.

In response to President Macapagal's report of the damage inflicted in the Philippines by recent typhoons, President Johnson indicated his Government's intention to donate 25,000 tons of grain available under the Food for Peace Program. In addition, he pledged United States readiness to make available for purchase 100,000 tons of rice deliverable in 1965 to the Philippine Government under Public Law 480, Title I.

President Johnson and President Macapagal agreed that representatives of the two governments would meet at a mutually agreeable date for negotiations leading to the solution of the current aviation problems.

The two Presidents noted the major contribution made by foreign private investment to the development and continued strength of their countries. President Johnson pointed out in this regard that United States economic relations with the Philippines would be seriously impaired if an enforcement of the Philippine Retail Trade Nationalization Law were to prejudice the position of long-established American firms. He observed that the Government of the Philippines had committed itself that the United States firms would not be affected by the Retail Trade Nationalization Law. He expressed confidence that the Government of the Philippines would uphold its long-standing commitments contained, *inter alia,* in a note of the Department of Foreign Affairs of August 4, 1954.

The visit of President Macapagal was also the occasion for the signing of a treaty for the avoidance of double taxation and prevention of tax evasion. The two Presidents agreed that the treaty reaffirmed the historic ties between their countries and strengthened the revenue administration of their respective governments.

The Presidents agreed that their Governments should continue their studies of matters relative to the United States-Philippine Trade Agreement.

President Johnson and President Macapagal concluded that the understandings reached, as well as the personal relationship established during this visit, will contribute greatly to the good will and friendship which traditionally support Philippine-American relations and to the mutual effort of the two countries to uphold, defend and preserve the common ideals of democracy, freedom and the rule of law which their peoples share.

628   Remarks at the Station in Alexandria, Va., at the Start of Mrs. Johnson's Trip Through the South.   *October 6, 1964*

Governor, Mr. Chairman, ladies and gentlemen, boys and girls:

Alexandria has been chosen as the first stop for one of the greatest campaigners in America, and I am very proud to announce that I am her husband.

Tonight I am going to catch up with her in Raleigh, N.C., although I know I will never really overtake her. I plan to use the jet Air Force One tomorrow to try to meet her in New Orleans, but Lady Bird on her train will probably beat me there. She always does. Since I don't dare try to compete with her too much, we are going separate ways tomorrow.

Tomorrow I am going out to the Midwest heartland of America. I am going to report to the American people. I am going to talk about the proud record of our administration, the Kennedy-Johnson administration of the last 4 years.

I am going to present the overwhelming and the urgent issues of this campaign, and I am not going to tear down any person or any group in doing that.

Never before within the memory of any

person here have the American people been asked to make a basic and radical departure from the beliefs and values which are the source of our economic health and our hopes for peace. I do not believe they are going to make that choice. They are going to choose to keep and build on the careful work of the men of both parties, the hard, patient work that has been going on for more than 30 years now.

They are going to choose to look ahead to the new problems which are rushing in upon us, our overcrowded cities, our inadequate schools, the growing mastery of the machine, the need to use our leisure time wisely and creatively. They are going to choose to, I think, continue the search, the quest, for peace, with reason and restraint—and, I hope, with constructive imagination.

From now until election day we are going to talk about the problems of the future, for this should be a campaign in which we explore the different ways to meet the new challenges of America in the turbulent sixties. Instead, the gauntlet has been thrown down, not to the future, but to the proved and tested values and solutions of the past. This is far less related to the real needs of our present day world. But it is a more fundamental challenge. We have no choice but to meet it, to crush it, to discard it, and then to get on with the tangible and difficult work of this fast-moving decade that we live in.

I want to ask each of you to pledge yourselves this morning to go out for the next 4 weeks, for the next 30 days, and contribute your time and your talents and your energy to your country by supporting Gus Johnson for Congress and Lyndon Johnson and Hubert Humphrey for the Presidency and the Vice Presidency.

This is a wonderful crowd. We thank you so much for coming out. I now want to introduce to you my daughter, Lynda Bird.

NOTE: The President spoke at about 8:30 a.m. at Union Station, Alexandria, Va., at the beginning of Mrs. Johnson's tour of the South aboard the "Lady Bird Special."

Mrs. Johnson addressed the crowd just before the President spoke. The text of her remarks follows:

"Friends:

"Sunshine and lots of friends—what could be a better way to start the whistlestop? Right here in Alexandria, in view of the monument to one of your first and foremost citizens, George Washington, I am delighted to be on this platform with several Johnsons, two of whom are candidates for office.

"This is a campaign trip, and I would like to ask you for your vote for both Johnsons. And because this is the beginning of a 4-day trip that will take us down the railroad track 1,682 miles to New Orleans, I would like to tell you some of the reasons I am going.

"For me, this trip has been a source of both anxiety and anticipation—anxiety because I am not used to whistle stopping without my husband; anticipation because I feel that I am returning to familiar territory and heading into a region that I call home.

"I wanted to make this trip because I am proud of the South and I am proud that I am part of the South. I love the South. I am fond of the old customs, of keeping up with your kinfolks, all your uncles, your cousins, and your aunts, right down to the fifth cousin; of long Sunday dinners after church; of a special brand of gentility and courtesy.

"I am even more proud of the new South, the glistening new skylines of the cities, the spirit of growth, the signs of prosperity, both in the factory and on the farm. There are so many advances in the South, in its economy, in its interest in the arts, in its progress and education.

"I am proud of what the South has contributed to our national life. I am proud of the valor with which southerners have served their country in every war in which we have been engaged. Even before we were a nation, southerners were supplying learning and leadership to the task of building our great country.

"We can all recite the record of our Southern statesmen through the many years of our Nation's trials and triumphs—12 Presidents, 15 signers of the Constitution, 15 Secretaries of State, from Thomas Jefferson to Dean Rusk. Yet in recent times we recognize the strain in the South from the national life as a whole. I have shared with many of you the concern that has come with this strain. I share the irritation when unthinking people make snide jokes about the South as if the history and tradition of our region could be dismissed with ridicule.

"None of this is right. None of this is good for the future of our country. We must search for the ties that bind us together, not settle for the tensions that divide us. A great southerner, Robert E. Lee, said it best when he advised his fellow southerners, 'Abandon all these local animosities and make your sons Americans.'

"So these are the main reasons I wanted to make this trip. I wanted to tell you from Alexandria to New Orleans that to this President and his wife the South is a respected and valued and beloved part of this country.

"We are a Nation of laws, not men. And our greatness is our ability to adjust to the national consensus.

"The law to assure equal rights passed by Congress last July with three-fourths of the Republicans joining two-thirds of the Democrats has been received by the South for the most part in a way that is a great credit to local leadership, to mayors and ministers, to white citizens and Negro leaders, to all the Mr. and Mrs. John Citizens who live in our communities. This convinces me of something I have always believed, that there is in the Southland more love than hate.

"I have, as you have, I am sure, thrilled to see Southern legislatures put education as their top priority; to watch city councils make headway with community conflict. Certainly there are problems ahead, but my husband has always felt that problems are there to be solved, not just deplored. I think we all understand that the hard duty of assuring equal rights and constitutional rights to all Americans falls not only on the President of the United States, but upon all who love this land. I am sure we will rise to that duty.

"I asked for this assignment for many reasons. This trip takes me not only to the queenlike cities of the South, but to the small towns and rural areas. I was born in such an area and I am at home there. I believe it is well for the people of the crossroads and the back country, in the timberlands and the mountain coves, and the sand hills where the pavement runs out and the city people don't often go, to have a personal part in this election. They all have an equal share in the Government.

"To me, as to you, the South is not a place of geography, but a place of the heart. And so it is with great joy that I undertake what is for me in every sense a journey of the heart.

"And now I yield to the speaker in my family, my husband, and the President of the United States."

During their remarks both the President and Mrs. Johnson referred to Augustus C. Johnson, Democratic candidate for U.S. Representative from Virginia's 10th District.

The text of the remarks of the President's daughter Lynda Bird, who spoke briefly, was also released.

629 Remarks at a Meeting of "Scientists and Engineers for Johnson-Humphrey." *October 6, 1964*

THIS HOUSE is honored by the presence of such talent and I am deeply grateful for the purpose which brings you here.

In this age, no President can make the vital decisions facing him without utilizing the best of the Nation's scientific and technical advice. Each day I rely more and more on your colleague, Dr. Donald Hornig—not only as my Science Adviser but as counselor on many other subjects.

But I am glad that I have come to this office with long and wide acquaintance in the scientific community—including many of you.

Over the years it has been my privilege and good fortune to be closely involved with many of those issues where science and politics have met—atomic energy, space, national defense, medical research, and others.

The political community is not always receptive to new ideas. I have taken the brunt of much abuse at various times for my own support. But I have guided my course by a view I once read from an early American journal. Written back in 1786, those words were:

"It is the part of every patriot philosopher to pursue every hint—to cultivate every enquiry, which may eventually tend to the security and welfare of his fellow citizens, the extension of their commerce and the improvement of those arts which adorn and embellish life."

For myself, I regard it as the mandate of all our experience that we insure the flourishing of science and technology in America—as nowhere else on earth.

Science and technology have served us faithfully in our national defense. But there is a purpose so much larger, and more noble. I believe the American people and people everywhere want human intelligence to be employed for human advancement—to enrich and elevate our way of life.

That is your challenge and mine in these times.

Your Government has given its support to scientific research—and to the education of bright young minds—on a scale without parallel in history. Dollar and cents figures have little meaning because the investment has paid for itself many times over. American science, medicine, and engineering is second to none—and we intend to keep it that way.

For all we have done, I am constantly aware of how much more there is which we have scarcely begun. New horizons beckon to us within our own planet, beneath the sea and out in space. But the most exciting horizons are in the life of man himself— and what we can do to improve it. We can eliminate poverty. We can cure man's ills, extend man's life, and raise man's hopes.

This is the call we must answer.

In all that we do, we must strive to channel science and technology and all of human wisdom towards human betterment and away from human catastrophe.

I hope we may build a Nation which encourages men to learn and honors men of learning.

Science transcends partisanship. Many of you have served both Democratic and Republican administrations—and I hope your talents will be always welcome, always respected.

Science transcends national boundaries— and this, too, must always be so.

America owes an immeasurable debt to scientists, engineers, and scholars from many nations around the world. But we owe a special debt to those who have chosen the United States in search of freedom from persecution for their beliefs.

Our Nation must always respect knowledge and the pursuit of knowledge. For along the road to learning lies our hope for peace among men and nations and that is the goal we seek.

NOTE: The President spoke at noon in the Cabinet Room at the White House to a group of 38 leading scientists, engineers, and physicians who had called at the White House to pledge support for the Johnson-Humphrey ticket. The delegation, including 10 Nobel Prize winners, 2 university presidents, and several well-known industrial executives, was reported in the press as representing "Scientists and Engineers for Johnson-Humphrey" with a claimed membership of more than 50,000.

As printed, this item follows the prepared text released by the White House.

630   Remarks at a White House Luncheon for Businessmen. *October 6, 1964*

MY BUSINESS is your business—the Government of the United States of America belongs to all the people.

I want to talk to you about the business

of government.

In trying to keep unnecessary expenditures down I believe the President ought to be as unsatisfied as a little boy's appetite.

This is what I have tried to do.

—My first budget called for a reduction in the level of expenditures—an event which happened only once before in the last 9 years.

—I have asked Congress for $450 million less in appropriations than I said I would when I submitted the Budget in January.

—The latest figures show that actual expenditures so far in this fiscal year were $676 million below the same period last year.

—The latest figures on Government employment show that there are 17,000 fewer Government workers than there were a year ago and 16,800 fewer than 2 years ago.

In fact:

—Federal spending this year will be lower in relation to gross national product than at any time since 1951.

—Federal employment will be lower in relation to population than at any time since 1950.

—The Federal debt will be lower in relation to gross national product than at any time since 1941.

You have all been following Secretary McNamara's cost-cutting program which last year produced identified savings of $2.5 billion. Similar programs are going forward in other branches of the Government.

—So far this year nondefense agencies have reported to me management improvement actions which will save over $400 million on an annual basis.

—Our drive to cut out unnecessary Government publications has resulted in the elimination of 240 existing publications, the cancellation of 130 proposed publications, and the consolidation of 50.

—In our drive to reduce the burden on the public of Government reports and questionnaires, we have dropped or simplified 320 reports, representing a net reduction in annual responses from the public of 2,536,000.

But fiscal responsibility does not mean the lowest possible Federal budget, obtained by ruthlessly slashing existing Federal programs and never proposing new ones.

Our expenditures safeguard the strength of our Nation and of our people, at home and abroad. We must not evade our responsibilities for the defense of the free world and the security and economic progress of free peoples who need our help to remain free.

At home, we have to meet the needs of a society rapidly growing in population, in wealth, and in complexity.

—We have to improve our programs in education, in vocational training and retraining, and in health.

—We have to help our States and cities to fight urban decay, crime, and delinquency— and help them provide adequate transportation systems.

—And in a society with our high and rising living standards, we have to look with compassion on needs of our aged and disabled, and meet the minimum needs of all our people.

I believe we can make great achievements without great increases in Federal spending:

—by cutting back on obsolete programs, and

—by applying the same careful efficiency to Government as a prudent businessman or householder applies to his own affairs.

But a responsible fiscal policy does not end with better programs and their frugal administration.

An ever-broadening consensus—conservative and liberal, labor and business, Republican and Democratic—now recognizes the further responsibility of the Federal Government to take account of the impact of its total spending and its taxing on our economic life—on markets, on jobs, on wages and prices.

That consensus recognizes that true fiscal responsibility will achieve a balanced budget out of the rising revenues of a healthy and prosperous economy—not by reckless cutbacks of expenditures to fit the shriveling tax revenues of a sick economy.

Reflecting that consensus, 70 percent of all Republican Senators and 84 percent of all Democratic Senators joined forces to cut taxes by $11½ billion this year. The results of that prudent action—carefully tailored to our present economic situation—are seen everywhere in rising sales, expanding payrolls, shrinking unemployment—and without a sign of the inflation that some critics feared would inevitably result.

We are proud:

—of the new vigor in our long-lived expansion;

—of the Nation's output now rising at an annual rate of 5 percent;

—of the 1.2 million jobs added thus far in 1964;

—of the unparalleled advances in consumer spending and living standards; and

—of the stability of average wholesale prices, today lower than they were at the start of the expansion and at the time the tax cut was enacted.

These are just the first steps to an expanding economy that will be limited only by our vision and our will.

We will take other steps. I have already appointed a task force of prominent Americans to study ways of improving the competitive effectiveness of American business.

Many of our most important national objectives depend upon how effectively American business competes in world markets. Our capacity for meeting the Nation's worldwide commitments and our success in strengthening the dollar as the world's principal reserve currency depend heavily on the foreign exchange earnings of American business.

On the domestic front, the maintenance of economic prosperity, high levels of employment, and rapid economic growth are closely related to a vigorous growth in American exports.

I have asked this task force to examine the current practices of the Government and the business community to determine whether any of them hinder competitive effectiveness of American industry. I have also asked its members to explore new avenues by which the Government and business community can contribute toward a more vigorous American participation in world markets. This task force will report to me by November 15.

This is what it means to Americans today to have responsible and responsive fiscal and monetary policies. And these are the policies that I shall continue—with your help.

NOTE: The President spoke in the State Dining Room at the White House.

As printed, this item follows the prepared text released by the White House.

631 Remarks in Raleigh at North Carolina State College. *October 6, 1964*

Governor Sanford, my fellow countrymen:

I cannot tell the good people of this great city and this wonderful State how deeply I feel in your debt for the very warm hospitality and the wonderful greeting that you have given to me and my family today.

I have much to be thankful for, and if I attempted to enumerate all those things this evening, I would ask your indulgence longer than I wish to, but I do want to say that for many years I have had a great admiration for the leadership of the State of North Carolina.

I am glad to be back here tonight in the home of my ancestors. My great grandfather, George Washington Baines, was born near Raleigh on December 29, 1809. He had the good sense to marry a beautiful Southern belle from North Carolina, Melissa Ann Butler, and for the life of me I have never been able to understand why he left North Carolina.

But I guess he just got so much religion here in the land of Billy Graham that he became a Baptist preacher in a land of Baptist preachers, and he decided to spread the good word from Alabama to Louisiana, to Arkansas, and he even went into Texas. Some say that he crossed the Jordan to get there, but one side of the family claims that he left the Promised Land to do it.

This is the first Tuesday after the first Monday in October, and it is a great Democratic night in Raleigh. Four weeks from tonight will be the first Tuesday after the first Monday in November—and that is going to be a great Democratic night in America!

I came here tonight for two reasons: First, I knew that Mrs. Johnson was going to have a pretty full day with 14 speeches, and I wanted to be here to join you in giving her a warm, Southern welcome.

The other reason is that I am starting out on a 4-day trip through America's heartland tomorrow morning on some political business, and Raleigh is as friendly a place as I know to get started.

I remember a candidate for the Presidency coming here when the going was so hard and not many people thought much of the Democratic prospects. He disagreed, and so did you, and you and he were right. That was 1948, and his name was Harry S.

Truman. I talked to him last night and he asked to be remembered to every Democrat here.

When I say the business of this trip is politics, we all know what we mean.

We don't mean tearing down anybody or anything. We don't mean mudslinging or speaking unkindly of our fellow man.

Politics is the people's business, and that means it has to be the politics of responsibility. This country must have responsible government, and it is going to get a responsible campaign from Hubert Humphrey and from me.

Some of my newspaper friends have been waiting for me to label some of my adventures across the country political. Well, I am saying tonight that this campaign trip will be a report on how we have been building a better and a stronger America, and it will make clear the basic choices that all Americans are going to have to make come November.

Most important of all, this trip is going to be a report on where we go from here, on which way is up.

Let's get right to business. Let's get down, as we would say, to brass tacks here in North Carolina.

This Fourth Congressional District is one of the great agricultural areas of the entire United States. North Carolina is one of our most important farming States in the Union.

On April 11th of this year, I signed the Wheat-Cotton Act of 1964. I worked hard on that bill. I knew it was needed to help our textile mills meet foreign competition and to make cotton competitive with synthetic fibers. I know it was needed to reduce the cost to the consumers of America.

The Wheat-Cotton Act of 1964 is only one part of a program of progress during these past years that has paid off in real human dividends.

1221

There is much more to be done, and the choice, of course, must be clear to us.

One course is offered by those who have called for "prompt and final termination of the farm subsidy program."

Do you know, have you ever thought, what it would mean to the good people of North Carolina to completely terminate the farm program?

For the Nation it would mean that our $12 billion net farm income would be reduced in half. It would drop—drop—drop by $6 billion.

One out of every five farmers would be completely bankrupt.

Cotton would sell for under 21 cents a pound, tobacco for less than 45 cents a pound.

Corn would go below 80 cents a bushel, soybeans below $2, and cattle would go to less than $17 a hundredweight.

Farmers all over the country would lose 50 cents of every dollar that they presently clear. In this great State of North Carolina this decrease would mean a loss in net income of $1,450—$1,450—for each and every farm in the great State of North Carolina. North Carolina alone would lose at least a third of a billion dollars a year, more than $333 million.

Can anyone present tonight suggest one single good reason why our tobacco program should be "promptly and finally terminated"?

Well, this is the issue, and I believe and I know that North Carolina is not going to choose to go down that path of bankruptcy. We've been there before.

The way to raise farm income is not to launch a farm depression. As long as I am your President, we are not going to plow under the family farm in this country, and we are not going to sit back in our rocking chairs, whittling, and see our small towns wither and waste away.

I am going to talk tomorrow, in Iowa and Des Moines, about a broader farm program for the future. That program will recognize the special needs in connection with certain special commodities and crops such as poultry, peanuts, feed grains, cotton, and tobacco.

All I have to say is "1939" and you will know exactly what I mean. In 1939, the year that we had no tobacco program, the people of North Carolina received 15 cents a pound for your flue-cured tobacco and 17 cents for your burley, and your total receipts from tobacco that year were only $125 million.

The tobacco program has been one of the most effective farm programs ever written for this Nation, and over and over and over again the tobacco growers of this Nation have approved it by referendum margins of 97 and 98 percent.

I realize that tobacco has some special problems, but the way to solve them is not to destroy the program. Only 2 months ago I approved an increase of $2 million for a crash program of tobacco research in the United States. Research is a way, I think, to solve these problems.

America's farm program will be only part of a whole new program of keeping the American economy at top efficiency.

The tax cut we made this year, reducing the taxes of the people of this country and the corporations of this country by $12 billion, is a part of our Democratic program. Our opponent voted "no"—"no" on that tax cut. But Congress passed it by an overwhelming majority, notwithstanding, and the results of the tax cut are already evident.

What has it given us? Again, let us get down to brass tacks.

That tax cut means that our people have $11½ billion more in their pockets to buy goods with. In North Carolina alone this tax cut will mean:

—an increase of over half a billion dollars in total income, an average of over $300 for a family of four.

—37,000 new jobs will be provided in North Carolina.

—increased State and local revenues in North Carolina will amount to $52 million.

—$140 million less will be deducted for income tax payments from North Carolina's paychecks.

—an average of about $120 for a family of four. A family of four will pay $10 a month less in taxes.

Well, now, there are other issues that are important to you people.

The production of electrical energy has risen in this progressive State from 10 million kilowatt hours in 1950 to 24 million in 1963.

The rural electrification program has been an important part of this development. And I pledge you not to repeal the REA but to continue to support the REA.

You can be proud of the level of education in North Carolina. It has risen steadily since 1940. There are tonight twice as many students in your colleges and universities as there were in the colleges and universities of North Carolina only 15 years ago.

I believe that every boy and girl in this great State and in this great country has a right to all the education they can use, and as long as I am your President, I intend to work with your State and local governments to make this right a reality.

Now, most of all, our prayers and our plans are for peace on earth. We move nearer to it with each year and each month. It is a painfully slow progress. It takes courage to climb the long hill to peace. But we have that courage.

Yes, that 5-letter word—p-e-a-c-e—is the most important word in the English lan-

guage. It is the most important objective of the American people.

When, in a moment of tragedy 10 months ago, I was asked to assume the terrifying responsibilities of the Presidency, I called upon men of good will in this land and in all lands to help me in that task.

For a period there was uncertainty in our land and around the world, but because I pled for peace and spoke in the name of peace, I brought to the council and Cabinet tables in the White House, men of government, men of business, men of labor, men of agriculture, men of the ministry, and, in the words of the prophet Isaiah, we reasoned together.

We talked about the awesome responsibilities in this era of nuclear power.

We reflected over the confrontation that our Nation had with the Soviet Union just a few months before in the Cuba missile crisis.

We realized that by one impulsive act you could press a button and wipe out the lives of 300 million people before the sun went down, and once done, you can never recover from it.

Could there be any greater objective for Christian people anywhere than peace or earth, good will toward men?

In those 10 months that I have been your leader I have had your hopes and your prayers, and I have called to the Capital of our Nation the heads of state from 85 countries in the world. We have exchanged viewpoints about our problems and their problems, our people and their people, our children and their children. We don't see everything alike, even in North Carolina, because if we did, we would all want the same wife. We don't see everything alike in America, as you can see from the divergent viewpoints that are being expressed between now and election day in November.

We don't see everything alike in the world, but we know that communism is on the march and freedom is on the march, and these two philosophies are at each other's throats.

I am proud to report to you tonight that I get great strength when I review the record of freedom in the world, because freedom has not lost a single nation to communism since we lost Cuba in 1959.

Oh, I hear those that are distressed and despaired. I hear those who are frantic and who sometimes are hysterical. But every day, as I go abroad in this land, I see by the hundreds of thousands, men, women, and children who love freedom and know they have it, and appreciate it, and are going to preserve it and protect it.

And don't let anyone tell you that there is not more freedom in all the countries of the world tonight than there has been in any time in your lifetime. More nations are being born. The yoke of colonialism is being torn away from more necks. More peoples are becoming independent and going on their own. And yet we hear the voice of doom and men of little faith say, "We have lost our freedom."

Well, I haven't lost my freedom, not a bit of it. I am freer tonight than I was a year ago because of the test ban treaty, because the air I breathe tonight is not as polluted as it was a year ago. I am freer tonight than I was when I was that boy's age, because we didn't have groceries on the table and we were chasing rabbits for food for our children. I haven't forgotten the restrictions of freedom that we had when we had our soup lines and 5-cent cotton, and we burned our corn and we killed our old cows and burned them.

No, this year we have the highest standard of living of any people on the face of the earth. We have more of our heads of families working than at any time in our history, 72 million profitably employed, making more than $60 billion more after taxes than they made only 4 years ago.

When you add $60 billion to your income after taxes, that doesn't sound like you have lost any freedom; it sounds like you have gained $60 billion worth. Corporation profits, after taxes, have increased 60 percent in the last 4 years, and one company alone made over $2 billion this year, or 25 percent on equity capital.

I don't say this in criticism, because if our system survives, and if freedom in the world prevails, it is going to be because our forefathers, many from the South who helped to draft that Constitution, prepared for us a better system of government than human ingenuity has ever devised.

And don't tell me that the capitalist puts his dollar out there and invests it in hope of getting a fair return, and the manager who manages that dollar and gets up at daylight and works until midnight and develops stomach ulcers running that plant, and the worker that gets in a trot and works all day long trying to produce the goods in that factory, when they all slice that pie and all get the incentive that comes from those profits—don't tell me that free men can't produce more than slaves directed by any commissar anywhere in the world.

Men of little faith, reckless people, dangerous people, would try to make you believe that America is losing, that your country no longer leads the world. Well, let me, as your Commander in Chief, say to you tonight as straight as I know how to put it on the line, America is the strongest nation in all the world, and stronger than all the rest put together.

This year we have tried in our 10 months to have a prudent Government and a progressive Government. For the first time in

9 years I reduced the annual budget by over $1 billion.

In the month of July there were 25,000 less men working for the Federal Government than were working last July. My budget went into effect June 30th of this year, and during the months of July and August—we don't have the figures yet on September—but during the months of July and August—are you listening?—we in the Federal Government spent $678 million less than we told you we would spend and less than you appropriated to us. And as long as I am your President you are going to get a dollar's worth of value for every dollar we spend.

It is getting late, you are tired, and you have been here a long time. There are a good many points I want to cover.

But first of all, I want to tell you that this is just about the most beautiful hall I have ever seen. I like the decorations and I like the Democratic enthusiasm.

And I like the kind of people that send to Washington men like Sam Ervin and Everett Jordan. And the kind of folks that select, and have selected throughout my years in Washington, one of the finest congressional House delegations of any State in the Union.

Don't let folks mislead you and tell you that you ought to change horses in the middle of a stream.

Someone asked Mr. Rayburn one time why it was that Texas had a Vice President, and Texas had a majority leader of the House, and Texas had seven chairmen of committees. They said, "How do you have that rank among your congressional delegations?"—and one time we had the chairman of the Agriculture Committee that Harold Cooley now has for North Carolina.

Mr. Rayburn answered him in a minute. He said, "I will tell you how we got there.

We pick them young, and we pick them honest, and we send them there, and we keep them there."

I have enjoyed working with your dynamic, young, progressive Governor Terry Sanford through the years. And after you go to the polls in November and vote the Democratic ticket from the courthouse to the White House, I am going to enjoy working with your own great Governor Dan Moore.

We have a job to do. We must build a land in which all men can worship God and live in peace with one another. We must all learn somehow to submerge our individual differences to the common good. There are so many more things that unite us than divide us. There are so many more people in this world that love instead of hate. And we ought to be a nation of lovers, not of haters.

Yes, we have the faith of our fathers. We believe in the Golden Rule of doing unto others as you would have them do unto you.

I don't know when I am going to get invited back here to North Carolina, but if I am your President again, and if I get invited, I am going to take a great deal of pride in coming here with our yardstick and pointing out to you where we were in the year of our Lord 1964, and where we are when I come back—because this State is going to move forward, as all America is going to move forward.

I had so much to say to you and so much to thank you for that I forgot a part of my speech. And if some of you have never forgotten a part of your speech, you're entitled to criticize me. But all of you that have forgotten it some time or other, you sympathize with me.

One of the best friends I have in the world and one of the men in whom I have the most confidence is Luther Hodges from North

Carolina. And he sits in my Cabinet—a reasoned voice, a wise judgment, the man of seasoned intellect. And he helps me get over some of the rough spots that face me every day. And I thank you from the bottom of my heart for sending us a man like Luther Hodges and a good lady like his wife.

NOTE: The President spoke at 9:45 p.m. at the Reynolds Coliseum of the North Carolina State College, University of North Carolina, Raleigh, N.C. His opening words referred to Governor Terry

Sanford of North Carolina. Later he referred to the Rev. William F. (Billy) Graham, Senators Sam J. Ervin, Jr., and B. Everett Jordan, and Representative Harold D. Cooley, all of North Carolina, Dan K. Moore, Democratic candidate for Governor of North Carolina, and Luther Hodges, Secretary of Commerce, and Mrs. Hodges.

Mrs. Johnson and Lynda Bird both spoke before the President's remarks. In brief words of welcome Mrs. Johnson told the audience that after making 14 stops and 14 speeches that day she was "mighty glad" to yield her time to the real speaker of the family.

632 Recorded Statement Marking the Inauguration of Television by Communication Satellite Between the United States and Japan. *October 7, 1964*

THIS BROADCAST which carries my voice and my image to your television sets in Japan and in the United States has been made possible by our new communication satellite Syncom III.

This amazing satellite and the facilities in Japan and in the United States which make its operation possible are the product of the vision and inventiveness of our scientific communities—both private and Government.

I welcome the opportunity to applaud this latest triumph in the application of science to the field of communications. It opens for us new vistas of friendship and understanding in the fields of education, cultural exchange, business, and entertainment.

I think it most fitting that this system could come into operation as the 18th Olympic Games take place in Tokyo.

The youth of the world will be assembled there to engage in sports. Some of these events had their beginnings in ancient Greece, others started in ancient Asia. For a few days Tokyo will be the scene of a quest for excellence among all the young

people of the world. Upon them all of our hopes must rest.

It is heartening that the Olympic Games— a symbol of peaceful competition among nations—can now be seen simultaneously by those actually present and by peoples throughout the entire world.

The United States and Japan can be deeply gratified, I believe, to have shared this dramatic expression of partnership that binds them in many fields.

I now look forward to seeing satellite communication systems extend throughout the world. It can be a great contribution to our international understanding—really a vital steppingstone toward helping us achieve lasting peace among peoples of the world.

NOTE: The message was filmed and taped in the Fish Room at the White House on October 3 for later release via the satellite Syncom III in connection with the opening of the Olympic Games in Tokyo. Secretary of State Dean Rusk and Japan's Foreign Minister Etsusaburo Shiina also relayed messages, the text of which was made public.

An earlier White House release, dated July 22, announced completion of plans with Japan for bringing television coverage of the 1964 Olympic

Games, to be held October 10–24, across the Pacific for viewing in the United States, Canada, and Europe, pending the successful launching of the satellite Syncom III. The satellite was launched at Cape Kennedy on August 19 as part of the National Aeronautics and Space Administration's regular experimental satellite program.

633   Statement by the President at the Beginning of a Campaign Trip.   *October 7, 1964*

THE OFFICE of President is the office of all the people. As have the other 35 men who have held this trust, I am leaving today to report to the people in person on the stewardship of their office.

I look forward to this experience with zest and enthusiasm. There is nowhere I would rather be than out with the American people.

I believe there is a strong tide running in America today. It is a tide of support for responsibility—and that tide is gathering strength.

Our long and patient efforts under administrations of both Democratic and Republican Parties are bearing fruit at home and in the world.

This administration is the first in history not to experience a recession or depression.

This administration is the first since World War II under which no nation has fallen to the control of communism.

Our efforts toward a better life at home—and for support of freedom in the world—are succeeding. Our gains are much too great to gamble on partisanship for partisanship's sake alone. Our progressiveness and prudence have brought us to this summit of success and the American people have no desire to turn from the path of prudent progress this year.

It is my hope that the campaign will be kept on a plane worthy of the Presidency. What two men say about each other matters very little when the freedom, prosperity, and peace of 190 million people are at stake.

634   Remarks at the State Capitol in Des Moines.   *October 7, 1964*

My friend and your fighting Governor Harold Hughes, lovely Mrs. Hughes, Mayor Iles and the gracious Mrs. Iles, my longtime friend, your able fighting Congressman Neal Smith, the other congressional candidates, and my fellow Americans:

I am happy to be here in the State that has such an able chief executive as Governor Hughes. I commend you on your choice. Neal Smith is one of the most effective Congressmen in Washington, but he needs some more Democrats down there to help him.

I think the people of Iowa know what the issue is in this campaign. The basic issue is responsibility versus irresponsibility. And for my part, this is going to be a responsible campaign.

I am here to talk about the politics of responsibility this morning. This campaign is going to give the people of America a clear mandate for a farm policy that will restore full parity of income and opportunity to all of the American farmers who live on American farms!

My roots are deeper in the soil than most

Presidents' have been. I am proud to be the son of a tenant farmer; I am proud of land of my own. I love that land.

I think I know what farmers want and what they need.

They don't want political flattery; they want understanding of their problems.

Farmers don't want promises; they want policies that work.

Farmers don't want Government handouts; they want real, effective bargaining power in the marketplace.

Farmers don't want Government storage bins; they want new and expanding markets for their efficient production.

Farmers want freedom to grow, to prosper, freedom to operate competitively and profitably in our present economic system.

Farmers are farmers in the first place because they have the deep-seated instinct to raise crops, not to cut them back, not to leave the land unproductive.

America's farmers want, America's farmers need, and America's farmers deserve not promises but more income and more opportunity.

The Democratic answers to these needs include three sets of programs, which I shall enumerate:

—We intend to continue but to improve commodity programs. We intend to strengthen farm income.

—We intend to assure rural Americans full partnership in the building of our Great Society.

—We intend to increase, wherever we can, the consumer demand for our agricultural products.

I want to emphasize particularly the importance of the choice that farmers have in regard to the commodity program.

You can choose our proposal to continue but to improve commodity programs, or you can choose the contrary proposal to wipe those programs out altogether.

The opposition has already spoken plainly. The opposition has called—and I am quoting verbatim for you to hear and for you to remember—the opposition has said "prompt and final termination of the farm subsidy program." And it has said, and again I am quoting verbatim, "there can be no equivocation here."

In North Dakota, at the plowing contest, an attempt was made to soften these words. Our farmers were told, and again I quote, "Nothing would be done to bring disaster upon you suddenly."

Well, I guess they think disaster is better if it comes by degrees! Or I guess they think they could get by with it easier if they gave it to you in small doses.

Disaster is exactly what their position would bring to the farmers of Iowa.

The most careful and responsible studies, some of them by your own widely respected authorities at Iowa State University, have shown what would happen if we terminated farm price supports. And here is what your own experts say:

First, net farm income throughout the Nation would be cut in half, or $6 billion. Do you want that to happen?

Second, one out of five farmers would be bankrupted. Do you want that to happen?

Third, corn would sell for less than 80 cents a bushel, wheat for less than $1, and soybeans would sell for less than $2 a bushel. It would mean 17-cent cattle and 13-cent hogs. Do you want that to happen?

Well, that's not all.

—Here in Iowa, the land with the richest soil in the Union, net farm income would fall by more than $422 million. Every person in the great State of Iowa, whether he lives on a farm or not, would suffer. And all of you better remember that.

—Net farm income in the corn belt would

drop by $1.8 billion—$1.8 billion—a devastating blow to the heart of America's economy.

To such a disastrous policy, I believe, and I think you believe, and I think all America believes, that the answer ought to be no!

We know from bitter experiences that depressions are farm-led and they are farm-fed, and I say to you that the Democratic Party under my leadership, as long as I am President, is not going to repeat that experience.

We propose, instead, to find in our present feed grain program, our wheat program, our programs for other commodities, those elements which need to be strengthened, and then to improve them. Under these programs, gross farm income has averaged $4 billion a year since 1960. Net income has averaged $900 million a year higher, or $600 more per farm family.

But all of us wish we had done better. And we will do better.

The Democratic goal is parity of income for the farmer. We are making progress toward it. We will make more progress by going forward, learning as we go, building on what we have already done.

But parity of income is not enough. Our goal is more than that. It is parity of opportunity for rural America in the broadest meaning of the term.

In the past, our farm programs have been designed to protect against disaster. Now we must aim at preserving and strengthening the structure of the whole rural society, based on the family farm, based on the rural communities that have contributed so much to the American tradition. This is the kind of a life that I grew up in. I know its values. I know its worth.

We must make it possible for young people to spend their lives in the rural communities where they grew up if they choose to do so, instead of being forced by economic ne-

cessity to tear up their roots and to move away to distant cities.

We will work together to make more effective use of our food abundance. There is no justification for any person in this country going hungry in the midst of plenty.

The food stamp program has worked well. The Democratic Party under my administration proposes to expand the food stamp program.

The Food for Peace program has worked well. It is good international policy. It is good economic policy. People who are hungry are weak allies of freedom. We broadened that program this year, and we will make it still better as we go along.

One out of every six dollars earned by farmers today comes from export markets, things we sell abroad, and one out of every four acres harvested today produces for markets overseas. Our agricultural exports for dollars climbed last year to $4½ billion, up 20 percent in one year, 35 percent greater than in 1960.

And there is another exciting prospect for our agricultural markets. Our studies show that if about 80 of the newly-developed countries increased their per capita income by just $100 a year, we can double America's export market for food that we produce in Iowa and the other farm States. I intend to continue to improve and build America's export market for the family farm, and I pledge you that we will get that job done if you will return the Democrats to office on November 3d.

I look forward to the day when we can rely less on cutbacks and more on programs to sell abroad all that we produce.

I look forward to the day when our great cooperatives and other private enterprise institutions can perform most of the marketing functions with a minimum of Government involved.

Rural America must take a leading role in building the Great Society here and in the world. And rural America, led by the greatest State in the farm belt—Iowa— must take the lead of all on November 3d in electing a Democratic President and a Democratic Congress.

It was the initiative, it was the vision, it was the enterprise of America's farmers, Iowa farmers, that developed our great land frontiers. The same initiative, the same vision, the same enterprise must help now in building a better, a more prosperous America for every boy and girl born in the United States.

So let's join together to get the job done, not just as Democrats, not just as Republicans, but Americans first.

Before I leave I want to tell each of you how proud the rest of the Nation is of the great State of Iowa for the responsible State Government that Harold Hughes has given this State. We are proud of his education program. We are proud of his State responsibilities. We are proud of his State's rights. He is a living and walking example of what bipartisanship can mean and that kind of cooperation we intend to put into effect in Washington on the national level, and your President and your Governor are going to walk shoulder to shoulder to get the job done.

Yes, we pledge you people today on our word of honor that we will give you an administration that is representative of all the people and all the parties, and all the States of this Union.

Peace, a five-letter word—p-e-a-c-e—peace is our first priority. America is the most powerful Nation in all the world, but we must use our power and our responsibility carefully and with restraint—not injudiciously, never recklessly.

Some of you may remember a few months after that terrible tragedy when we lost our great President, John Fitzgerald Kennedy, we had a problem at Guantanamo. Mr. Castro notified us that he was cutting off the water that our boys stationed at Guantanamo had to drink. There were immediate shouts from all over the land. They gave us various forms of advice. Some of that advice said, "Send in the Marines."

Well, we didn't act hastily. We acted cautiously and carefully and deliberately, because some of those Marines come from Iowa and Texas and the rest of the States of this Union, and every one of those Marines means something to his home and something to his President. So what did we do? Instead of sending the Marines in to turn the water on, we sent in one admiral to cut it off!

Recently near Viet-Nam, in the Gulf of Tonkin, when they fired on our flag, we retaliated in kind. We not only sank the boats that fired upon it, but we immediately moved to destroy the nests that housed those boats. But we didn't drop a bunch of bombs on civilian women and children in an act of desperation or in a thoughtless moment.

We used our power with judgment and with restraint, and I want you to know that if I am continued as your Commander in Chief, I am willing to go anywhere, I am willing to talk to anyone, I am anxious to sit down and get the advice of men in both parties.

You will remember it was Arthur Vandenberg that advised with Harry Truman. You will remember I was the Democratic leader of the Senate when President Eisenhower was the Republican President. It is now your own Bourke Hickenlooper who sits on the Foreign Relations Committee and comes in and advises with us. In matters of foreign policy, it is not Democratic, it is not Republican. It is what is best for your country.

We have more freedom today than we have had at any time in our lifetime. We have more prosperity today than we have had at any time in our lifetime.

But that doesn't mean we shouldn't cut the budget. That doesn't mean we shouldn't cut waste. That doesn't mean we shouldn't cut taxes. And this year, under the Democratic leadership and in a Democratic Congress, with the Republican opposition opposing that bill, the Republican leader in this campaign voted "no," and we reduced your taxes $12 billion.

We reduced your budget $1 billion, and I say to you that if you will give us some more Democratic Congressmen from Iowa to join Neal Smith, if you will support the strong right arm of Governor Hughes, if you will return to Washington a Democratic administration, we will work and fight and give you prosperity and peace for the people of this country.

I wish I could stay here and visit with each of you. But we must cover several more places today. We must be on our way and all I can say is thank you from the bottom of my heart.

Good luck and God bless you. I hope that each and every one of you can come to the inauguration. Wouldn't that be a wonderful sight in Washington in January?

NOTE: The President spoke at 12:05 p.m. at the Iowa State Capitol. In his opening words he referred to Governor and Mrs. Harold E. Hughes of Iowa, Mayor and Mrs. Charles S. Iles of Des Moines, and Representative Neal Smith of Iowa. Later he referred to Arthur H. Vandenberg, U.S. Senator from Michigan during the Truman administration, and Senator Bourke B. Hickenlooper of Iowa.

635   Remarks in Springfield, Ill., at the Sangamon County Courthouse. *October 7, 1964*

THANK YOU for this wonderful weather. Thank you for your smiling, happy faces. Thank you for the great State of Illinois, the CWA, the Letter Carriers Local 477, and all you good Democrats that have come out here to help us to victory.

My good friend Governor Otto Kerner, we are going to reelect you Governor by one of the largest majorities any Governor has been elected by in any State in this Union. I am happy to be here on the platform with one of the greatest United States Senators this Nation has ever produced in all of its history—my friend Paul Douglas of Illinois.

And now I have some work for you to do. I just left Des Moines, a great city in the great State of Iowa. They told me we had 200,000 to 225,000 people out there, and they promised me that they were going to send us at least three additional Democratic Congressmen come November.

Now, you have some Democratic congressional candidates here in Illinois, and they ought to cease being candidates and start being Congressmen come next January, so put this down and don't forget it: Let's get out and work and vote and help and pray for Lester Collins to go to Congress—and John Desmond and Bernard Hughes.

Mr. Attorney General Clark, State Auditor Howlett, Miss Dorothy O'Brien, who rode out here on the plane with me, State Chair-

man Jim Ronan, my old beloved friend Scott Lucas, the former majority leader of the Senate, ladies and gentlemen, fellow Democrats:

It is much warmer here in Springfield today than the welcome that Springfield gave its most distinguished citizen when he arrived here 127 years ago. Shortly after that arrival, Abraham Lincoln wrote a letter to a friend, and he said in that letter, and I quote him, "I have been spoken to by but one woman since I have been here, and should not have been by her if she could have avoided it."

I guess Mr. Lincoln didn't realize that all Springfield women are naturally shy, although if those I see here reflect their grandmothers' beauty, I can see why Mr. Lincoln was disappointed.

I have come here today as Lincoln did, on political business. I have come to the American heartland to set the issues of this campaign before the American people, so let us get on our way right now.

Do the American people want to continue the programs that have brought us unprecedented national prosperity? Do you want to continue the policies that have kept the peace through the most dangerous 20 years in human history?

Well, let me discuss prosperity first.

I began my public life in Washington 32 years ago. In those days we set out to save and to strengthen our economy. Our economy was on the brink of total bankruptcy. In the fire of that crisis we forged a policy for economic strength that has become the bulwark of American prosperity ever since.

For 30 years, five Presidents, from both political parties, have supported that policy. And so do I.

No part of that policy has meant more to the good people of America than social security, and we are not about to destroy it, either, by making it voluntary.

For 30 years every President, Republican and Democrat alike, has supported social security and strengthened it. And so do I.

We built into our economy a system of safeguards to protect the farmer and the workingman, the small businessman and the investor, from forces that were beyond their control.

Leaders of both parties supported these safeguards and supported these programs. And so do I.

When we started those programs, we could only dream that they would lead us to prosperity.

Today the dream has become a reality. Today the American people are prosperous as never before. Today, for the first time in history, over 70 million Americans have jobs. Personal income after taxes has risen by $80 billion since 1961. Corporate profits after taxes have increased over 12 billion since 1961.

The stock market has reached an alltime high, and the people who own the stocks on the exchanges know that the value of those stocks today is more than 100 billion in excess of what it was last November when I took office as President.

We are in a great agricultural State. We produce food for Illinois, the United States, and the world. Our total farm exports have increased 70 percent.

Today Illinois is in the vanguard. Illinois is on the move. And Governor Kerner and Paul Douglas and I intend to keep it on the move. We have one of the greatest public servants ever selected in America running on the ticket for Vice President— Hubert Humphrey—and he is going to help us.

Right here in Illinois today, more people are at work earning more money, living better, than at any time in American history.

The unemployment rate in Illinois has been reduced by more than one-third in the last 3 years. It has come from 6.4 in July of 1961 to 4.1 in July of 1964.

Well, that didn't just happen by chance. This happened because the economic policies that we have followed for 30 years under five Presidents, of both parties, those policies represented the consensus of the American people.

But let me tell you today: Those policies are in jeopardy and are in danger.

You have made a clear choice, and you are going to have a chance to go to the ballot box and exercise that choice November 3d. What will that choice be? Are you going to abandon and forget the tested policies that have worked for the last 20 years to go to dangerous, uncertain policies that you know not of? Or will you hold steadfast on the highway to prosperity set by the leaders of both parties over the last 30 years?

But prosperity is worthless unless we keep the peace. The most important thing in the world to every mother, to every boy, to every American citizen, is peace in the world.

And don't you forget it when you get in the polling booth and vote November 3d. You vote for the man or woman, the candidate that in your judgment is most likely to promote the cause of peace in this land and in this world. You vote for yourself. You have judgment. You have conscience. You have knowledge. You can look into their faces. You can hear their voices.

So you go and vote for Molly and the babies; you vote for peace in the United States between labor and business and Government; you vote for peace in the world among all people.

America's policy for peace rests on two foundations: strength and reason.

We are today, as we meet here, the greatest military power on this earth.

We possess 1,100 long-range bombers, nearly half of them on 15-minute alert. And the only nation that contests with us for superiority has only a small fraction of that number.

We have more than 800 intercontinental ballistic missiles with nuclear warheads. That is four times as many as the other fellow has.

We have 256 Polaris missiles on 16 nuclear-powered submarines—far more than the Communists have.

And so long as I am your President we shall never use this awesome strength to start a war. Because we have it, we may never need it.

But the second foundation of peace is reason—willingness to use our minds and our hearts as well as our muscles and our strength. This has been the policy of all the Presidents of your time and my time in both parties.

These Presidents of both parties have used our strength with resolution, but never recklessly. They have never been afraid to stand up for freedom, and they have never been afraid to sit down at the council table to seek an agreement. They have been resolute, but they haven't been reckless. They have been courageous, but they have never been careless. True, they have not built a perfect world, but I can tell you this: They have achieved a safer world.

Today we celebrate the first anniversary of the signing of the limited nuclear test ban treaty. Next week I will report by nationwide television so that every home and every mother and every child and every son in this country can hear that report. I am going to tell you what has happened in the first year of the nuclear test ban treaty, and how successful that treaty has been.

A year ago, when Senator Douglas and other great men ratified that treaty, our beloved President John Fitzgerald Kennedy said, "In its first two decades, the age of nuclear energy has been full of fear, yet never empty of hope." Today the fear is a little less, and the hope is a little greater.

Well, so long as Lyndon Johnson is your President, I will continue to nurture and to strengthen that hope.

I can tell you that the air you breathe is not as polluted, the milk that you drink is not as dangerous, and the unborn babies do not have the problems that they would have had except for the nuclear test ban treaty. And I hope that every mother in this crowd, every citizen of America, every student here today will listen in on the television next week when I talk to you on the accomplishments of the first year of the nuclear test ban treaty.

Those policies of power plus reason are wise. They are strong. They are tested. And they have worked.

I don't believe that you want to give up those tested policies. Do you?

I don't believe that you want to start off on a dangerous, uncharted course where you don't know where you are going. Do you?

I believe that you want to continue to guard freedom's gate with strength, and to guard it also with good judgment and good sense.

Well, that is the choice in this election.

I don't want just 95.9 percent of the labor force of Illinois at work, as it is today. The Democratic administration wants every man and every woman that is willing to work to have a job.

We don't want prosperity for just 85 percent of Illinois families who enjoy it today. We want to wipe out poverty along the line so that the 15 percent of Illinois families that live below the poverty line can have a better standard of living.

We are already on our way to greater pros-

perity. The tax cut, enacted by this session of Congress, will, when effective, put over $500 million into Illinois wage-earners' pockets. It will create 130,000 new jobs in Illinois. It will generate an increase in total income of almost $2 billion. It will boost State and local revenues by over $160 million.

Next year, with your help, I am going to ask the Congress to cut our excise taxes. I am going to ask the Congress to improve and to extend our social security. And depending on how successful we are in this election November 3d, we may ask the Congress to act on social security earlier than you think.

Four years ago we promised to get America moving again. We have honored that promise: America is moving.

Your vote in this election November 3d will decide whether to keep the engines of progress roaring forward or whether to throw them into reverse and turn sharply from the course they now follow.

I have faith in the American people. I believe that 3½ weeks from now you will keep America steady, you will keep America safe, you will keep America on the high road to peace and increasing prosperity for all of our people.

We live in a world with more than 120 other nations. We live in a Nation with 50 States. We have our differences and we have our problems, and we never settle those differences or those problems with ultimatums. We don't intend to bury anyone in the world, but we don't intend to be buried, either.

We have stood firm with the Communists in the Tonkin Gulf and at Guantanamo. You will remember not many months after I took office when I was trying to unite the American people and asked them to come and help me carry on the job that President

Kennedy had left. I was trying to bring neighbor and neighbor and brother and brother together, and Mr. Castro went out and cut off the water to our Guantanamo base. I got emotional appeals from all over the Nation. I got this wire from this section and this wire from this section, and people advocated moving immediately. One man even said, "Send in the Marines."

Well, I know a lot about the Marines. There is one of the greatest ones in the world right there on the platform—Paul Douglas. But we tried to evaluate the situation and carefully consider it, and we finally concluded that it would be wiser to send in one admiral to cut the water off instead of a bunch of Marines to turn it on.

We believe that communism is the wave of the past, and freedom is the wave of the future.

In Latin America communism has been on the run—in Chile, in Brazil. And the rest of the hemisphere has isolated Castro in Cuba, and more than 350,000 of his people have fled their homeland.

No, we must have peace and prosperity in this country. Arthur Vandenberg worked with President Truman for a two-party foreign policy and a bipartisan foreign policy. Lyndon Johnson, as Democratic leader, worked with Dwight Eisenhower, a Republican President, to present a united front before the world. Bourke Hickenlooper worked with John Kennedy to try to make our foreign policy nonpartisan.

And I ask all of you, Democrats and Republicans, and whatnots—and, if you please, good Americans first of all—to realize that we are living in a critical era, in a difficult period, which will test our patience and our judgment. And we must keep our guard up, but we must keep our hand out. We must be strong enough to defend America and that flag wherever it may be challenged, but we must not go around over the world rattling our rockets and threatening our bombs.

So realize that you have one of the most priceless privileges that human beings anywhere have. You have the right to vote. Now go exercise it November 3d. Go vote for peace and prosperity.

I could spend all afternoon recommending myself, but I am not going to do that. I am going to recommend this to you: You study this matter, you look at the record, you listen to the statements, and then you go and do not what is best for the Democrats, not what is best for the Republicans, but you go and do what you know in your heart is best for America.

This has been a delightful afternoon. I want to thank all of you for your wonderful courtesy. I want to ask you to give me your help, give me your hand, give me your prayers in the job that I am trying so hard to do. If you will do that, we will have the greatest victory for good government and for all the American people on November 3d that you ever read about in all American history.

NOTE: The President spoke at 3:16 p.m. at the Courthouse in Springfield. In the opening words to his formal remarks the President referred to Illinois Attorney General William G. Clark, State Auditor Michael J. Howlett, National Democratic Committeewoman Dorothy O'Brien, Democratic State Central Committee Chairman James A. Ronan, and former Senator Scott Lucas of Illinois.

636   Remarks on the Courthouse Steps in Peoria. October 7, 1964

Governor Kerner, my friend and your wonderful Governor, Otto Kerner:

Illinois is going to give you the greatest majority come November that any Democratic Governor in this Nation received.

I want to pay tribute to your fighting Senator, the representative of all the people, all the time, Paul Douglas.

I have enjoyed traveling through Illinois this afternoon with Lieutenant Governor Samuel Shapiro, Attorney General William Clark, State Auditor Michael Howlett, your candidate for secretary of state, Paul Powell, your National committeewoman, Dorothy O'Brien, your congressional candidate, Mr. Cole Baker, your State chairman, Jim Ronan.

Now, my fellow Americans, we have come to the end of a long and busy and thrilling and inspiring day. Everywhere we have gone, from the time we left early this morning until late this evening, we have seen young Democrats, middle-aged Democrats, senior Democrats, Independents, Republicans who want to vote for a President in November that will represent all the people.

I think I can tell you that the ticket of Johnson and Humphrey is going to lead this Nation to a great victory come November.

Four weeks from today the American people will have made their choice. I have come here tonight to set that choice before the people.

This is a great day in America's heartland. America today is the richest nation and the most prosperous nation and the most powerful nation on earth, and as long as I am your President I intend to keep it that way.

Illinois is today the powerhouse of America, and Governor Kerner and I intend to keep it that way. Let me be specific:

Today, for the first time in history, over 70 million Americans have jobs. Personal income after taxes has risen by $80 billion in 3 years and corporate profits after taxes have increased over $12 billion. The stock market has reached an alltime high. The value of the stocks on the New York Stock Exchange are worth $100 billion more than they were when I took office last November. Total farm exports have increased 25 percent.

And in this great surge, Illinois has been one of the leading States of the Nation.

Illinois is today one of the top States in the Union, as Governor Kerner said, in exports to foreign nations—both industrial and agricultural exports.

Illinois today has one of the lowest unemployment rates of any industrial State in the Union, and I'll tell you who has been fighting to bring that about—your own great Senator Paul Douglas.

Illinois was the only industrial State that was able to reduce its public aid under Federal programs last year.

Illinois today has more men and women learning more new skills under the Manpower Development and Training Act than any other State in the entire Union.

In 1961 the unemployment rate in Illinois was 6.4 percent. In July of this year that rate had been slashed more than 33 percent. Since August of 1961, more than a dozen labor areas of Illinois have been taken off the list of "areas of substantial unemployment"—including your own great city of Peoria.

I understand that a man who works in the Unemployment Compensation Service is afraid if things keep on going this way, he will be out of a job pretty soon.

Yes, you are rebuilding Peoria. You have

a positive program. You stand for something. You believe in moving forward. You believe in going ahead. You are not just a bunch of negative "aginers." The excitement of rebirth is everywhere in this city. You can see it. You can feel it. It is in the air. We are moving on. You have new office buildings, you have new civic buildings, you have new highways, you have new motels.

Yes, this is a proud, new city of the future in the 20th century, and you are entitled to 20th century leadership, and you are going to get it November 3d.

One of your great industrial companies expects its first billion-dollar-year this year. All the signs read "Help Wanted," "Men at Work."

And we intend to keep it that way.

None of this has happened by accident. It has happened because you had the vision to rebuild your city. It happened because your State and National Governments have pursued policies that made progress possible, policies that insured economic growth. Let me give you just one example.

The biggest tax cut in American history, recommended by our late beloved, martyred President John Fitzgerald Kennedy, and supported by most of the men in the House of Representatives and in the United States Senate, was enacted by the Congress.

In that tax bill we reduced the tax bill of the average taxpayer by 20 percent. We created 130,000 new jobs in Illinois. We generated an increase in total Illinois income of $2 billion. We boosted State and local tax revenues by $160 million. We cut Illinois withholding tax payments by $500 million.

Four years ago the mighty industrial and agricultural center of Illinois was stalled on dead center.

Today, Illinois is on the move, and we intend to keep Illinois moving forward.

There are those who say "no." There are those who say "stand still." There are those who say "hold back." There are those who say "retreat." There are those who say "repeal the bills that have made America great."

We say, "Let us keep moving. Let us continue," and that is the choice before the American people this November.

You have a clear, unmistakable choice between continuing those policies that have brought us to a peak of prosperity, or turning to policies that will wreck our progress.

Let me give you one example: The social security system has made it possible for 19,-700,000, almost 20 million Americans—one out of every 10 persons in this country—to live under that social security system and they are permitted to live their later years in dignity, with security.

Now there are those in this land who believe that our social security system should be changed. They say it ought to be voluntary. Even members of their own party say a voluntary plan would wreck social security, it would bankrupt the system.

Let me make this clear this afternoon, here in Peoria: This is one of the most important issues in this campaign. Americans are not going to gamble on social security. They are not going to risk destroying a program that has proved the bedrock of security for our older citizens.

And the position of Johnson and Humphrey is clear: We are going to fight for and strengthen and defend and protect social security, and we are going to extend it when the Congress meets again! The Illinois AFL–CIO State convention meeting here in Peoria has fought for social security. Reuben Soderstrom and his colleagues have worked to make America a stronger Nation, they have worked to make it a better place to live.

So has another great American, Paul

Douglas. He was one of the architects of the Social Security Act of 1935, and through the years he has been its staunchest friend.

This is the choice the American people have to make in November: Do you want to go back to the 1930's when all the doors were closed, when all the signs read "No help wanted"? Or do you want to move forward to the wide open vistas of the 1960's?

For 30 years, under 5 different Presidents, we have followed a course to a stable, prosperous, and good society, where child labor is outlawed, where minimum wages are guaranteed, where the elderly receive social security and the young find opportunity; where labor and industry bargain freely; where our Nation is safe with a defense system stronger than those of all the other nations on earth combined.

We are not about to give any of those rights up. Working together, Republicans and Independents and Democrats alike, we shall go forward to the greatest goal: Peace on earth, good will toward men.

The road to peace is not an easy one. It is fraught with many perils. It has many side turns. There are no short cuts. But we move along it and we must move calmly. We must move patiently. We must move confidently. We must move with resolution, and above all, as good Americans, we must move carefully and responsibly at all times.

President Woodrow Wilson, one of our great Presidents, traveling through the United States, once said in the great city of St. Louis: "Things get very lonely in Washington sometimes. The real voice of the great people of America sometimes sounds faint, and sometimes sounds distant."

Well, we have to get away from Washington once in a while to come out and see the young Democrats and the great citizens of this land. And I think if Woodrow Wilson were here in Peoria this afternoon, he would not think that your voices sounded faint or distant, because he would know that we are here in the heartland of America, and that you are going to lead us to victory in November.

Yes, all day I have seen your smiling faces. All day I have looked into your happy countenances. All day I have seen the family life, the mothers and the children of America here in the heartland of the great State of Illinois. And those voices sound powerful to me. They sound clear. They sound free.

And when I return to the White House, and the policemen turn the keys on those locks on those big black gates, and I get to those few acres that are back of our house, it is going to be folks like you that sustain me in my labors and in my thoughts. It is going to be prayers like yours that give us inspiration and hope and leadership and make it possible for us some way, somehow, to achieve peace on earth.

And I want each of you to know that you have a part to play in American history, that you have a responsibility as citizens of the most powerful nation in the world, that you have an obligation as Americans— whether you are Democrats or whether you are Republicans, or whether you are Independents—and that obligation is to go out and work and fight and give the best talents you have to make democracy live.

Ten months ago, in a tragic moment, I was called upon to assume the awesome responsibilities of President of this country. And I told you that afternoon, after I took the oath of office in Air Force One, that I wanted you to give me your help and give me your hand, and give me your prayers; that all I could tell you was I would do the best I could.

We had a difficult transition period because all the world was looking at us. Our great, young leader had fallen. And our own people and the other peoples of the world were watching what course America would take. You sustained me with your strength. You helped me with your prayers.

America united—the businessman, the labor man, the farmer, the Congress—all put their shoulders to the wheel, and America became a united nation instead of a divided nation. America became a nation of lovers instead of a nation of haters. America became a nation of people who have faith instead of people who have doubt.

As I leave you this afternoon, I want you to know that I have faith in you, I trust you, I know what you are going to do: You are going to do what is best for your country. You are going to do what is best for America. You are going to the polls on November 3d and give us the greatest victory that any party ever had.

NOTE: The President spoke at 6:05 p.m. on the Courthouse steps in Peoria, Ill. In his opening words he referred to Governor Otto Kerner of Illinois. Later he referred to Senator Paul H. Douglas, Lieutenant Governor Samuel Shapiro, State Attorney General William G. Clark, State Auditor Michael J. Howlett, Paul Powell, Democratic candidate for secretary of state, Dorothy O'Brien, Democratic national committeewoman, Cole Baker, Democratic candidate for Representative, James A. Ronan, chairman of the Democratic State Central Committee, all of Illinois, and Reuben Soderstrom, president of the Illinois State Federation of Labor-Congress of Industrial Organizations.

637   Remarks in Peoria at the Convention of the Illinois State Federation of Labor.   *October 7, 1964*

Mr. Soderstrom, Governor Kerner, Senator Douglas, Governor Shapiro, Attorney General Clark, State Auditor Howlett, Mr. Paul Powell, secretary of state, my friends:

You and I have a job to do on November 3d, and we are going to do that job, and we are going to take one thing at a time. But the first job is to get out of convention, get back home, quit our big talk and our bragging, and get down to work and get our friends and our uncles, and our cousins and our aunts to the polls, and elect Lyndon Johnson and Hubert Humphrey by the greatest landslide.

Then we are not going to repeal these laws that we have been passing ever since the days of Franklin D. Roosevelt. We are going to keep them. I wish I had all night to talk to you about them, there are so many of them. But together we have come a long way in 30 years, and there is not a single man or woman in this room that would go back where we came from or would want their children to go back where we came from.

We have abolished child labor and the sweatshops, and we don't want to go back to it. We rejected the arguments of those who fought our social security program and said it ought to be voluntary, and we are not about to go back to it. We have made collective bargaining the law of the land and we are going to keep it that way. We have said that we believed a laborer was worthy of his hire, and we have passed minimum wage laws and maximum hours laws, and we are not about to turn our back on them.

Today we have 20 million people living in decency and dignity off their social security checks. And we are going to make the system sounder and more sensible, and improve it and extend it, and not destroy it. We are not going to sit idly by and let a few men defeat us in our attempt to give this Nation a sensible, sane, wise medical care plan under social security.

We believe that every boy and girl in this land ought to be entitled to all the education that he can profitably take, and it doesn't make any difference how long we have to work, or how many speeches we have to make, or how many States we have to cover—we are going to build those schoolhouses and put a teacher in every schoolroom until that job is done.

We believe in equal rights for all Americans and special privileges for none, and we are going to solve our problems just like you workingmen solve them around the council table when you have a difference. We are going to reason them out. In the words of the prophet Isaiah, we are going to come now and let us reason together. We are not going to allow anyone to tear this Nation to pieces.

We don't hate, we don't fear, we don't doubt. We have faith, and we love our country and love its people and each other.

For 56 years I have been listening to these voices of doom. I heard them first talk about Franklin D. Roosevelt being a dictator, and when that old dog wouldn't hunt any more, they talked about poor little Fala. I heard them abuse Harry S. Truman from every stump in the land, and I was one that saw that great big banner headline on that unreliable Chicago Tribune that said, "Dewey sweeps to victory."

I saw them when they tried to control a Republican President, President Eisenhower, and he wanted to do something to bring peace to the world, and some of them would go back on the back row and fight him. I looked up my record the other day on foreign policy matters, and I had voted with President Eisenhower three times as much as the Republican leader had voted with him.

Well, are we going to get the job done and are we going to do it up brown? Well, now, Dewey thought he was going to do it up brown. The polls had him ahead, too, you know. We have to go out here to the heartland of America and we have to carry the message to the people. They have to know that all these things that they believe in, all these things they have fought for, all these things that they treasure and that they want to pass on to their children so their little ones can have a better life than they have had—they have to know that they can all go down the drain on November 3d if you just sit in your rocking chair at home and don't vote.

I left Washington early this morning. I have been going all day long. I am going to continue to go until November 3d.

On election night I am going to be at my little ranch home on the banks of the Pedernales, down the road from where my mother, my father, my grandfather, my grandmother, my great-grandfather and great-grandmother are buried, and I am going to be waiting until we hear from the great State of Illinois. I think I know what I am going to hear, if you don't let me down.

I think that Senator Humphrey and I are going to be proud of what you do between now and November 3d, and we are going to be proud of what you do that day, but more important, I think you are going to be prouder yourself.

If you will give us the mandate, if you, by your vote, will give us your approval, we will go back to that Capital City on the Potomac and we will take the programs that were started by Franklin Delano Roosevelt and carried on by Harry S. Truman, and advanced by John Fitzgerald Kennedy, and we will build a greater America.

During our 4 years it may not be possible for us to enact a program that will make every man a king, but it will be possible to preserve what we have, and to add to it, and to make this land a better place for all of us to live in.

So remember all the things that are at stake. Remember that you have much to preserve and much to protect.

Now, go and do your duty.

NOTE: The President spoke at 6:40 p.m. in the Armory in Peoria. His opening words referred to Reuben Soderstrom, president, Illinois State Federation of Labor-Congress of Industrial Organizations, Governor Otto Kerner, Senator Paul H. Douglas, and Lieutenant Governor Samuel Shapiro, all of Illinois, State Attorney General William G. Clark, State Auditor Michael J. Howlett, and Democratic candidate for Illinois secretary of state, Paul Powell.

638   Television Address to the American People. *October 7, 1964*

My fellow Americans:

I have been in this office for almost a year—ever since that black and unforgettable day when America lost one of its greatest leaders—cut down in the fullness of his manhood and promise.

I have drawn much of my strength in this task from loyal and dedicated public servants. Most of all I have drawn strength from the warm support and understanding of the American people.

I will always be grateful to you for that.

I am now on a tour that will take me to every section of the country—to discuss with you the important issues of this campaign.

Few presidential elections in our entire history have presented—as this one does— a basic choice that involves the fundamental principles of American life.

We must decide whether we will move ahead by building on the solid structure created by forward-looking men of both parties over the past 30 years. Or whether we will begin to tear down this structure and move in a radically different, and—I believe—a deeply dangerous direction.

Most of you listening to me have felt the steady progress of American prosperity in your own life and the life of your family. Most of you, more than ever before, can look forward, with confidence, to a steadily improving life for your children.

Our prosperity is not just good luck. It rests on basic beliefs which a generation of leaders has carefully woven into the fabric of American life.

Our prosperity rests on the basic belief that the work of free individuals makes a nation—and it is the job of Government to help them do the best they can.

Our prosperity rests on the basic belief that our greatest resource is the health and skills and knowledge of our people. We have backed up this belief with public and private investment in education and training, and many other programs.

Our prosperity rests on the basic belief that older Americans—those who have fought our wars and built our Nation—are entitled to live out their lives in dignity. We have backed up this belief, for over 30 years, with the social security system—supported by every President of both parties.

Our prosperity rests on the basic belief that individual farmers and individual workers have a right to some protection against those forces which might deprive them of a decent income from the fruits of their labor. We have backed up this belief with a system of fair collective bargaining. We have backed it with agricultural programs which have kept the farmer from suffering the neglect and despair of only a few decades ago.

Today our whole approach to these problems is under attack.

We are now told that we the people acting through Government should withdraw from education, from public power, from agriculture, from urban renewal, and from a host of other vital programs.

We are now told that we should end social security as we know it, sell TVA, strip labor unions of many of their gains, and terminate all farm subsidies.

We are told that the object of leadership is not to pass laws but to repeal them.

And these views have been supported by a consistent record of opposition in the Congress to every progressive proposal of both parties—Democratic and Republican.

This is a radical departure from the historic and basic current of American thought and action. It would shatter the foundation on which our hopes for the future rest.

Too many have worked too hard and too long to let this happen now.

I propose to build on the basic beliefs of the past, to innovate where necessary, to work to bring us closer to a growing abundance in which all Americans can seek to share.

The choice is yours.

For 20 years our country has been the guardian at the gate of freedom. Our cause has been the cause of all mankind.

The strength of that leadership has come from the fact that every President, and the leaders of both parties, have followed the same basic principles of foreign policy. They have built our strength—so that today America is the greatest military power on earth.

They have moved with courage and firmness to the defense of freedom. President Truman met Communist aggression in Greece and Turkey. President Eisenhower met Communist aggression in the Formosa Strait. President Kennedy met Communist aggression in Cuba.

And, when our destroyers were attacked, we met Communist aggression in the waters around Viet-Nam.

But each of these Presidents has known that guns and rockets alone do not bring peace. Only men can bring peace.

They have used our great power with restraint—never once taking a reckless risk which might plunge us into large-scale war.

They have patiently tried to build bridges of understanding between people and nations. They have used all their efforts to settle disputes peacefully—working with the United Nations. They have never been afraid to sit down at the council table to work out agreements which might lessen the danger of war without increasing the danger to freedom.

But today these established policies are under the severest attack.

We are told we should consider using atomic weapons in Viet-Nam, even in Eastern Europe should there be an uprising.

We are told we should break off relations with Russia—and with it any hope of lasting agreement. We are urged to withdraw from the United Nations and stop our help to other countries.

We have heard the test ban treaty denounced. This is the treaty that has halted the radioactive poisoning of the air we breathe.

We are urged to threaten others with force if they don't do as we say.

We are told, in effect, to withdraw into an armed camp—with a few carefully selected friends—and try to intimidate our adversaries into submission.

This kind of attack contradicts the entire course of America in the postwar period.

If we should follow this course—if we should discard the tested policies of the last 20 years—the peace of the world will be in grave danger.

I will not discard them. I will continue them. I will match firmness to strength. And I will continue, with all the skill at my command, the patient search for lasting peace.

Here, again, the choice is yours.

I will discuss these issues in the next few weeks. They are among the most important questions ever presented to the American people.

It is you who will decide these questions. And you will decide them on November 3 in polling booths across the Nation. No person can afford to sit comfortably at home, confident that others will take care of the job. You must work, and register, and vote.

For this is a turning point in the history of our Nation. At stake is all that we have so carefully built, and all the hopes that rest upon it.

I will do all I can.

I need your help.

Then we can turn to our work. Together we will build the Great Society—a place where every one of us has the chance to seek happiness and fulfillment to the limit of his abilities.

And we will work together to make the world a place where free men can live in peace.

NOTE: The President's remarks, filmed and taped at the White House on October 6, were telecast nationwide by the Columbia Broadcasting Company at 9:30 p.m. on October 7.

639   Remarks at Washington High School, Lake County, Indiana.   *October 8, 1964*

Governor Welsh, Indiana's two fighting Senators, Vance Hartke and Birch Bayh, the next Governor of this great State, that great American Roger Branigin, Congressman Ray Madden:

I want to thank you for that wonderful introduction. I think it was the best introduction I have ever had in my political life, except one. One time down in Texas the fellow that was supposed to show up didn't get there and I had to introduce myself— *Mayor Katz, Mayor Dowling, Mayor John Nicosia, my fellow Americans:*

Our business here this morning is politics, so let us get right down to business. I understand that there have been some other political speeches around here recently. Well, this one is going to be different. I am not going to tear down anybody or anything.

I am proud that you have a responsible government in Washington and in Indianapolis. I think the best way to keep it there is to make this a good, responsible campaign.

We are going to be responsible. This goes for your great fighting Senator, the next senior Senator from Indiana, Vance Hartke. This goes for that great statesman on the Rules Committee of the House of Representatives, Ray Madden. This goes for your next Governor, Roger Branigin. This goes for that brilliant, new, young star, Birch Bayh, and you better keep your eyes on him because he is going places in this Nation.

If we are honest with ourselves, and we have to be, political issues affect us all personally. It does not degrade our hopes for peace in the world that we want most of all to be alive, and to be sure that our sons and our daughters have the right to live. It does not degrade our hopes for prosperity.

I believe in full employment. I believe that every man and woman who is willing to work should have a job and have a chance to work. The recession of 1957–58 hit hard here. Unemployment was above 8 percent.

Six years ago, Vance Hartke ran for United States Senator. This industrial area was in trouble. I came here to work for Vance Hartke and I am mighty proud I did, because he has delivered and has made a good Senator.

Many steelworkers at that time were on a 4-day week. Four years ago things were not much better. We were in another recession. We met that challenge. Today East Chicago and Hammond and Gary are boomtowns. Unemployment is down. Profits and production are up.

From the beginning our business system has been developed by wise public policy. For the first time in history more than 70 million good Americans are working. For the first time in history the profits are higher than ever before.

And I say to anyone who thinks that we are going to stop here, even to rest, you better move over or you are going to get run over!

First, I think we must start with our children. They are the future. I believe that every American boy or girl is entitled to all the education that he can master.

Second, we must build an economy in which every man or woman who is willing and able to work will have a job and a fair wage for doing it. Our tax cut was designed to move us in that direction. That tax cut is generating three-quarters of a billion dollars in income for your individuals and for your businesses.

Third, we must build a society in which the advancing years of life bring rewards for work well done.

There is no limit to what America can do. And that is why, as I come here to this wonderful industrial area this morning, this city where my Press Secretary, George Reedy, one of the best human beings I ever knew, was born—and I want to salute George here this morning—that is why I say that our program must be peace for all of our people, jobs for all of our people, education for all of our children, and prosperity for all families in America.

We must do something about our immigration laws. Two-thirds of the total immigration quota goes under that law, to people who never use all their quota.

President Roosevelt, with a good Dutch name, proposed the immigration law be changed.

President Truman, with a good English name, proposed the law be changed.

President Eisenhower, with a good German name, proposed the law be changed.

President Kennedy, with a good Irish name, proposed that the law be changed. And now a President, Lyndon Johnson, with an English name, and with an Irish name, and with German and Scottish and French forebears, proposes this law be changed.

We want to abolish those discriminatory quotas gradually over a 5-year period and raise the overall limit by 9,000, or 1/80th of 1 percent of our work force. This would permit families to unite which have too long been broken.

We stand for a compassionate nation, not a callous nation. Will you stand up with us and help us in that fight? We stand for uniting our country instead of dividing it. Will you stand up with us in that fight?

We are a nation of lovers instead of

haters, and we are proud of it. Aren't you? We are all Americans. We are one nation—one people. There is room for all of us in this great land, so let's get on with the job. There is just one thing that really amounts in your life that is the most important thing to you, and that is whether we have peace in the world or not.

We have more power than any nation in all the world. But we must not be rash and we must not be reckless and we must not be careless. We must use that power with good judgment and we must use it with restraint.

Not long ago, a dictator, Mr. Castro, cut our water off at our base at Guantanamo, and there were voices in the land that immediately rose up and said, "Let's send in the Marines." Well, we considered it carefully and we decided it would be a lot wiser to send in one admiral to turn the water off than to send a bunch of Marines in to turn the water on.

Now, we are concerned with peace in Washington. We are going to keep our strength. We are going to keep our guard up, but we are going to keep our hand out. We will go anywhere, any time, to talk to anyone, if we can promote peace in the world. We do not want war, we do not believe in rattling our rockets or talking about dropping our bombs. We have been through two World Wars, and we know the price we paid for them. So that is why we are going to keep strong. That is why we are going to keep sensible.

The next thing that is important is to stay prosperous, to try to see that every child has a schoolroom to attend, and a teacher to teach him. Try to see that every father has a job to send that kid to school. Try to see that he is paid decent wages. In this election, all of those things are at stake.

We fought for social security 30 years ago.

Twenty million Americans today draw social security. We don't want it to go down the drain. That is why you better go vote on November 3d if you don't want social security to become voluntary.

We believe in equal rights for all Americans, and special privileges for none. But that is why you better go vote on November 3d, and you better vote Democratic. We believe in strong unions. We believe in collective bargaining. We have fought for that right and we want to preserve it and protect it, and that is why you better go vote on November 3d.

I remember a great labor leader one time said that the working people don't have much and they don't ask much. They are not a selfish group. They get up early in the morning, they wash the kids, they dress them and send them to school, and they are on their way to work. They work hard all day long, and they come home in the evening for that family meal, say their prayers and go to bed reasonably early. That was before the days of television, I guess. But we are still mighty proud of that family unit.

And this great leader of the Steelworkers of America, Phil Murray, said:

"We don't ask for much. We want the right of collective bargaining. We want a shorter workweek. We want better pay for what we produce. We want a share of the profits. But we haven't asked for too much for our labors. We would like to have a home, a roof over our heads, some food for our bodies, some clothes to cover our forms. We would like to have a home with a rug on the floor, with a picture on the wall, and with music in the living room."

All of those things are at stake in this election. You have a choice. You have a privilege. You have a right to exercise. You have an obligation to your family.

I haven't come out here to sling mud and say ugly things. You use your own judgment. But you use it; don't sit by and neglect it. Don't talk about how proud you are to be an American and how you want your boy to avoid war, and then sit home and not vote. You go and vote, and you vote for the man in your judgment, and the ticket in your judgment, that is most likely to protect your job, your prosperity, and your home and your children.

You go vote for the man and the ticket that in your judgment is most likely to preserve peace in the world.

If you do that, if you vote for peace and prosperity for yourselves, according to the dictates of your own conscience, Lyndon Johnson and Hubert Humphrey will be mighty happy.

NOTE: The President spoke at 9:23 a.m. in the athletic field at the George Washington High School in East Chicago, Ind. In his opening remarks he referred to Governor Matthew E. Welsh, Senators Vance Hartke and Birch Bayh, Roger D. Branigin, Democratic candidate for Governor, and Representative Ray J. Madden, all of Indiana, Mayor A. Martin Katz of Gary, Mayor Edward Dowling of Hammond, and Mayor John Nicosia of East Chicago. Later he referred to Philip Murray, president of the United Steelworkers of America, 1942–1952.

640 Remarks in Indianapolis at Soldiers and Sailors Square. *October 8, 1964*

Governor Welsh, Senator Hartke, distinguished guests on the speaker's rostrum, ladies and gentlemen:

I came out here to beautiful Indiana today to tell you that we need your help in sending two good men to Washington—Vance Hartke and Andy Jacobs. Vance Hartke has served with great distinction in the United States Senate, and Martha has helped him along every step of the way. We need him back. Won't you help us?

And you ought to be represented in a Democratic administration, in a Democratic year, by Democratic Congressman Andy Jacobs.

I want to also tell you what a grand young pair of people you sent us 2 years ago, Birch and Marvella Bayh. They have brought great pride to this State and great pride to my administration. I am so happy they are there, and I am so glad they are my friends.

Indiana on other occasions has voted for another party, but I know that you want to consider this very carefully this time. In the first place, I am not just sure whether there

is a real Republican candidate to vote for this year.

Then, I think probably you will want to think back to when Indiana did vote for a Democratic President. That was back in 1936. The choice that year was something like the choice this year—between the past and the future.

Indiana in 1936 voted for the future, and Indiana in 1964 is going to vote for the future again.

The Bible tells us "Every man's work shall be made manifest." This is true, too, of our Government.

Seldom has an administration's work been made manifest more abundantly than this one. We promised 4 years ago, under the leadership of that beloved, great champion of this country, John Fitzgerald Kennedy, that we would get the country moving again. Well, it is moving.

In the 44th month of unbroken advance, the record of the Kennedy administration speaks not just for itself, but it speaks for all of you—you, the American people.

Americans today are earning $89 billion more than they were earning 4 years ago.

Your stocks on the Exchange are worth $100 billion more than they were worth 10 months ago.

Manufacturers are pouring out 29 percent more goods.

Four million additional jobs have been created since 1961.

Our economy is producing one-fifth more goods and services than 4 years ago.

Prices have been kept stable. Wholesale prices are actually down 1 percent from last year.

Our economic growth is now 5 percent annually. In the 4 years of the present administration, our growth is greater than in the entire 8 years of the previous administration.

And thanks to the foresight and the vision and the courage and the love of humanity of John Fitzgerald Kennedy, his administration was unblemished by the scars of depression or recession. And we have carried on for him.

I want to thank the people of the good State of Indiana, the Democrats, the Republicans, the whatnots—but first of all, all Americans—I want to thank you for the share that you have played and that you have contributed to this tremendous prosperity. The record bears it out. Let me cite that record.

In the last 3 years the unemployment rate in Indiana has dropped from 8.4 percent to 3.4 percent. In 1960 Indiana's per capita personal income was below the national average. By 1963 it was far above the national average.

And this is only the beginning. When the tax cut becomes fully effective, here is what it is going to do for your State of Indiana:

—It will increase your total income by over three quarters of a billion dollars. It will increase your income by an average of $350 for every single family of four.

—It will create 50,000 new jobs in your great State.

—It will boost State and local revenues by more than $64 million.

—It will cut the taxes, the withholding payments that you now pay, by $210 million a year, and that is an average saving in withholding payments of $125 per year for a family of four.

They all said it could not be done in Indiana or anywhere else, but it has been done. We have the job done.

I said again and again and again for the first 37 days that I worked on my budget, that as a Democrat I believed in a responsible fiscal and monetary policy. And the proof that I believe in fiscal and monetary responsibility is in this administration's record.

As a percentage of our gross national product, Federal spending in this fiscal year will be the lowest in 14 years. The budget I presented for fiscal 1965 was almost $1 billion lower than the budget in 1964, and that is only the third such decrease in 10 years. For the months of July and August this year, the first 2 months of the Johnson budget, the fiscal year ended June 30th, our Government spent $676 million less, in July and August this year, than it did last year. In July this year your Federal Government had 25,000 less employees than they had in July last year.

That is a demonstration of a responsible fiscal policy.

Our prosperity is the basis for our strength.

In 4 years we have built a military might that is first among all nations, and I promise you that we are going to keep it first. We will use our strength with restraint. We will use firmness always, prudence always, because these are the twin pillars of our national policy.

That was Harry Truman's policy.

That was Dwight Eisenhower's policy.

That was John Fitzgerald Kennedy's policy.

And that will be Lyndon Baines Johnson's policy.

Now, let there be no mistake. The experience of 20 years in a nuclear age tells us that our foreign policy must not be conducted by men that are "carried about with every wind of doctrine." Only those should lead us who, in the words of the scripture, are "swift to hear, slow to speak, slow to wrath."

As long as I am your President, that will be my policy.

Ten months ago, in a moment of tragedy, I was called upon to assume the awesome responsibilities of the Presidency. Our great leader had fallen, and the rest of the world and the rest of this country looked to America during that transition period. I told you then that I would do my best to embrace his program and lead America forward as best I could. I could promise you only that I would do my dead level best. I have done that.

On that day, the 22d of November, our beloved President, John Fitzgerald Kennedy, had 51 major recommendations pending before the Congress of the United States. Last weekend I sat in the White House and looked down that list, and observed that we had passed every single one of those 51 measures through the Senate of the United States.

And the three or four that didn't pass through the House of Representatives are going to pass through the House of Representatives when we get this election behind us.

The senior citizens of this country are not going to allow any two or three men to keep them from having medical care.

I am proud to be standing here only a few blocks from the War Memorial Plaza which honors men who sacrificed for freedom.

I am happy to be here in this great city where the American Legion has its headquarters. I know what the Legion has done to maintain our vigilance in the struggle against communism.

The men of the Legion know war. They love peace. They want peace, and so do I, and so do we all. But we must know in order to have peace we must have strength, and we must always be willing to keep our guard up, but our hand out.

We do not get peace by bluff, or bluster, or ultimatum. We do not get peace with the other 120 nations in the world by rattling our rockets or threatening with our bombs.

I say here on this peaceful, beautiful day, in this peaceful State of Indiana, that I need your help. I want your hand. I ask for your prayers.

I am willing to go anywhere, I am willing to talk to anyone, I am willing to do anything that I can with honor to bring peace to the world. It will not be an easy achievement. It will not be one that can be reached by pushing a button. It will take patience. It will take understanding. It will take people who will follow the Golden Rule of "Do unto others as you would have them do unto you."

Freedom is marching in the world. We have an adversary in communism. The Communists thrive on the ancient enemies of mankind: disease, illiteracy, ignorance. But I would have you know that freedom is marching, too. The last nation the Communists took over was Cuba in 1959, and of all the new nations that have been born, not a single one of them has joined the Communist orbit.

Because the other peoples of the world want for their children what you want and what you have for yours—a school with a schoolroom, with a teacher, a home, a church where they can go and worship their God, freedom to think and to speak, they want what democracy gives.

And it is our responsibility as leaders of the world to follow the Golden Rule with all the peoples of the world just as we do with ourselves: "Do unto others as you would have them do unto you."

I have faith in people. I have hope for the future. I have no doubt that freedom is going to survive and democracy is going to win. But we are not going to win by talking about each other, and using a lot of ugly names, and slinging a lot of mud, and chewing on each other. America cannot win by dividing brother against brother, sister against sister; we must have a united America—united we stand; divided we fall.

It makes you feel so much better to have faith than to have doubt. You are a lot happier if you love than if you hate. So let's look to the future with hope and faith and courage. Let's extend a helping hand to those that have not been quite as fortunate as we have been here at home and abroad. Let's try to find the areas which can unite America instead of the few, petty things that divide America.

Let's teach our children to love thy neighbor instead of hate each other, and let's say to those men of little faith, let's say to those doubters and those critics and those who are distressed and those who are frustrated, and those who are bitter, let's turn the other cheek. Let's look up there and say, "God, forgive them, for they know not what they do."

Let all the good people of Indiana, of all religions, of all colors, of all faiths, of all parties—let us all as good Americans do not what is good for the Democratic Party or what is good for ourselves, or what is good for the Republican Party. Let us, on November 3d, go and do what is best for our country.

If I had some time I would go into some detail on telling you what my personal opinion is about what is good for our country. But I have enough confidence in your good judgment and the good judgment of the people of Indiana to just leave it with you.

Thank you and goodby.

NOTE: The President spoke at 12:12 p.m. at Soldiers and Sailors Square in Indianapolis, Ind. In his opening words he referred to Governor Matthew E. Welsh and Senator Vance Hartke, of Indiana. Later he referred to Andrew Jacobs, Jr., Democratic candidate for Representative, Senator Hartke's wife, Martha, and Senator Birch Bayh and his wife, Marvella, all of Indiana.

---

641   Statement by the President Upon Signing Bill Extending the Agricultural Trade and Assistance Act.   *October* 8, 1964

I AM very happy to sign this bill. It will extend for 2 years legislation of enormous importance both to the United States and to the rest of the free world. It authorizes continuation of the Food for Peace program. This program makes possible the sharing of our abundance on a scale unparalleled in

the history of the world. It stands as a monument to the miracle wrought by the American farmer and to the generosity and practical wisdom of the American people.

The Food for Peace program authorized by this law will permit us to use our agricultural abundance to combat malnutrition and hunger in the less developed countries and to promote their economic growth. At the same time, this program will help us to attain vitally important economic and foreign policy objectives. It benefits all of the people, directly or indirectly.

During the past 10 years we have shipped $12.2 billion in food to needy people, under Public Law 480. Our food has gone to over 100 countries. It has relieved the hunger of many millions of men, women, and children.

Most of us, in this rich land of ours, find it difficult to imagine what food assistance really means to the half of the people in the world who have too little to eat. This kind of assistance means a noon meal for 40 million foreign schoolchildren. It means emergency supplies when catastrophe strikes—drought, floods, hurricanes, earthquakes. To millions of people it means the difference between an inadequate and barely adequate diet.

Our food also promotes economic growth in the less developed countries. It helps control inflation. It generates local currencies, which the United States can grant to less developed countries, to help them build their industry, their agriculture, their communications, their schools, and their hospitals.

The United States is also a prime beneficiary of the program.

The Food for Peace program authorized by Public Law 480 makes constructive use of the abundant production of our farmers and ranchers, thereby increasing their incomes. It stimulates business for American industry and creates jobs for American workers. It builds, through market promotion and economic development, the basis for expanded cash sales of American farm products.

The Food for Peace program furthers our foreign policy objectives. It helps strengthen many other countries of the free world—which is certainly in our mutual interest. It creates good will for the United States. It gives all countries a chance to see how remarkably efficient our free agricultural system really is—especially when compared with the regimented and depressed farming of the Communist world.

This bill, however, contains several features which concern me. Of these, two provisions are particularly undesirable. One seeks to give either the House Committee on Agriculture or the Senate Committee on Agriculture and Forestry a veto power over certain proposed dispositions of foreign currencies accruing from sales under Public Law 480. The other seeks to prevent the President from making certain loans at interest rates below a specified level unless he has concurrence of an advisory committee composed in part of Members of Congress and in part of his own executive appointees.

In recent years four Attorneys General of the United States have held that legislative provisions vesting in congressional committees the power to approve or disapprove actions of the executive branch are unconstitutional. The Acting Attorney General now advises me that a provision vesting such power in a committee made up in part of Members of Congress stands on no better footing. Both such provisions represent a clear violation of the constitutional principle of separation of powers. This is the position taken in similar cases by President Eisenhower, President Kennedy, and by myself.

However, I appreciate the desire of the Congress to be informed and to be consulted on the operation of all aspects of the Public Law 480 program, and I am directing that executive officials see that this is done.

Two other provisions of the bill are disturbing. The first, by preventing any foreign currency sales to any Communist countries, inhibits our ability to deal selectively with countries that may demonstrate a tendency toward political and economic independence from communism. I note, however, that the effect of this restriction is somewhat offset by the authorization to make dollar sales on credit to such countries. The second, by requiring that our surplus inventories of extra-long staple cotton be offered for sale at world prices, could create serious problems in our foreign relations. I am directing that this provision be administered with great care so as to minimize any harmful effects on the economies of the free world countries which are the principal exporters of this commodity.

But the overriding fact is that the bill I have just approved will permit the Food for Peace program to continue uninterrupted for another 2 years. Both in its tangible and intangible benefits, this vital program deserves and, I believe, enjoys the overwhelming support of the American people. It has and will continue to receive the wholehearted support of this administration. If the past is any guide to the future, I am confident that Food for Peace will represent a growing force in our efforts to advance the cause of freedom throughout the world.

NOTE: As enacted, the bill (S. 2687) is Public Law 88–638 (78 Stat. 1035).

The statement was released at Indianapolis, Ind.

642   Remarks at a "Salute to President Johnson" Dinner in Cleveland.   *October 8, 1964*

Mayor Locher, and your courageous and fighting United States Senator Young, whom the people of Ohio are going to return to the United States Senate not only to serve Ohio but to serve all the Nation and all the free world:

I am going to take a moment here before I start talking other matters to you to tell you that I first went to Washington in Mr. Hoover's administration. I have been there since 1931. I have worked with and for five different Presidents. I have served with more than 3,000 different men.

I cannot truthfully say tonight that I ever served with any man, Democrat or Republican or whatnot, that I thought went to Washington on a platform of doing what was wrong. They all thought they were doing the right thing. They all wanted to do the right thing. Their wives wanted them to do the right thing. Their families wanted them to do the right thing. But they didn't all see

things alike.

Now, I don't know that my judgment is any better than the average fellow, but I do want you to have it and consider it, and reject it if you choose, or evaluate it if you will. It would please me a lot and would help me a great deal in my awesome responsibilities I bear.

I don't know of any man that I ever served with in the House or the Senate—and I have served 12 years in each body, and I was leader 2 years when Bob Taft was the Republican leader, I was his opposite; I was leader 8 years when President Eisenhower was the Republican President; I was the majority leader 6 years—but I don't think I ever served with any man in either House or Senate that in my heart I believed worked for the people, the average people of this country, more than Steve Young.

I am willing to recognize tradition and good families and good names, and I have great respect for the memory of the late Senator Taft, for his family. But if I have anything to say about it, I wish they would nominate those people for President or Vice President, or something else, but please don't let Ohio step in and take one of my trained, trusted helpers that is working with me every day.

I want to thank you people for lending to me Secretary and Mrs. Celebrezze. He carries a very heavy load with a smile, with intelligence, with loyalty, and is always there when you need him. You never have any doubt about his compassion for his fellow human beings.

I am glad that I am here with Congressman Mike Feighan. Mike and I have been friends for a long time. I want to put him on notice now, though, that Bill Miller and I have different views on immigration.

I realize that this is a melting pot, America is, and I never spend a lot of time checking up on how a man spells his name, because when I looked into my family tree I found out I had some Irish, some Scotch, some English, a little French, a good deal of German, and sometimes they get down in certain countries and they think "Yonnie Yohnson" has a little Swede in him.

Most of the people that have come here from all the various countries of the land have come here to help us build America. I want to see my administration and my Democratic Congress pass an immigration bill that will permit families to reunite and will give us an opportunity for some of the people to come in who can be taken in and meet with their families.

I made my recommendations to the Congress this year and the Congress didn't act on them. The first message that I send to the Congress next year, if I am President, is going to be that message, and in every message after that I am going to refer to it

when I talk to the American people because I think we are entitled to have a decent and a fair immigration policy and at least have some action on it.

I am happy to be here with my old friend Charles Vanik, with whom I have worked closely in the Congress. It is good to be here with Bert Porter, State chairman, and I enjoyed seeing my longtime friend Bill Coleman again tonight. I have spent many pleasant years working with and for and under Mike DiSalle. And I salute Frank Celeste and all of my fellow Americans who are here.

I think it is important that the Democrats of Ohio get out and get to work. And every time they get ready to say something uncomplimentary about some other Democrat, remember what Mr. Rayburn said about the three most important words in the English language: "Just a minute." Just stop there and see if you hadn't just as soon fuss at a Republican as a Democrat.

Let's try to pull the Democratic Party in Ohio together. Let's get the maximum strength for all the people, because there are a lot of human beings in this State and in this Nation that are looking to us to be united.

If we are united, no force in the world can defeat Democrats in Ohio. But when we get divided and we get lazy, they come in. We all have to give a little bit, moderate our views some, temper our convictions, but we have two really important jobs to do between now and the next 25 days.

I would say first and foremost of that job is to reelect Steve Young as United States Senator. My friend, Congressman Ludd Ashley, is here, and I want to say a word about Congressmen in referring to Ludd. I think all of us ought to give him a hand, though.

The greatest service that Ohio voters can

perform this year is to elect and to send to Washington the full ticket of Democratic congressional candidates. So let's work and pray and give and fight to make democracy live.

I have heard it said that the issues in this campaign were not emerging clearly. Well, they are now. The issue of our foreign affairs, of war and peace, is one issue, and it has to be bluntly stated, and I am going to be blunt: it is responsibility versus irresponsibility.

The issue of our domestic affairs is whether the whole course of American development up to this time is right or wrong. That is blunt, but it is responsibility versus irresponsibility in foreign affairs.

In domestic affairs it is whether we have been right or whether we have been wrong.

I am just going to visit with you like you were home folks and I am going to talk with you a few minutes about this domestic issue.

I don't know anyone who thinks that every decision we have made in the past years, all that time that I told you I had been in Washington, that we made as a people, I don't know anyone that thinks we have been right every time.

But I think I do know this: We have shared experiences together. We have shaped together in the past 30 years the firmest and the soundest and the most constructive program that the American people have ever formulated in all their history.

So the domestic issue is whether we are going to wipe out and throw away that program of 30 years under five Presidents. The argument to go back, to repeal the present and to veto the future—and you will remember that there is a voice in the land who says "I intend to repeal laws and not pass them"—well, I have been listening to these people talking about repealing laws,

and all the bad laws we have passed. I have been listening to them for 30 years. But I haven't seen them repeal one single law in the 8 years Republicans had control under President Eisenhower.

But they tell us that that is their object, and what do they say they are against?

—They would abolish the graduated income tax.

—They would destroy the whole basis for social security by making it voluntary. At least that is what they would have done in New Hampshire. I don't know how many times it has been changed since then.

—They would sell the TVA. That may have been modified down to the TVA fertilizer now. They are dealing in fertilizer, but originally it was TVA.

—They would end all farm commodity programs.

—They would withdraw from our responsibilities in the United Nations.

—They would oppose the agreement of 105 nations to stop nuclear bomb tests.

Those are some of the things that they are against, that they want to do away with.

On the test ban treaty, I just want to say this: I doubt that there is anything that has happened during your lifetime that is as important to you and your children as the test ban treaty. We were poisoning the air that we breathe, and the milk that we drank, and we were affecting the lives of men who lived in the future, and we could have serious effect on babies that were yet unborn.

But we got 108 nations together, and we entered into a treaty, and most of the members of the United States Senate supported that treaty, men of both parties. All of them didn't. I am not going to call any names, because I said in the beginning of this campaign I am not going to advertise. But I am going to tell you tonight that within the next few days I am going to go on television and tell the American people what has happened in the last year.

The anniversary of that treaty is Saturday, the first anniversary. Every person in this room ought to go home tonight and thank the good Lord that John Fitzgerald Kennedy gave us the leadership that made that treaty possible. I think we must understand clearly what it is in terms of accomplishments and results that these individuals want to repeal. They have said their purpose is not to pass laws but to repeal them.

The proof of the policies they oppose has been in the living.

Let's see where we were a generation ago, the 30 years ago that I mentioned a moment ago, and let's see where we are tonight. Then let us decide whether we want to repeal what this generation has accomplished.

The average weekly pay of a factory worker 30 years ago was $20, $20 a week, and one out of every four workers had no job at all; 25 percent unemployment. Today that weekly average pay is $103.07. Money values have changed. The broader comparison is that the purchasing power of a week's labor of an American factory worker has more than doubled in this generation of democracy. In plain terms, we are living more than twice as well as we were living 30 years ago.

The net financial wealth of all Americans was about $150 billion 30 years ago, $150 billion. This year it is crossing the trillion dollar mark—not $150 billion, but $1,000 billion!

The percentage of people who own their own homes has increased during this period from 48 percent to 62 percent, and before you vote in November, you ought to satisfy your own heart that every man that you send to that Congress is the kind of man that would work and fight and vote for policies to make every family a homeowner in this country.

Thirty years ago 3½ million American workers belonged to labor unions, 3½ million 30 years ago. Tonight the number is 16½ million.

There were 2.7 million small businesses then, and now there are 4.6 million.

A child born tonight can expect a life that is 9 years longer than a child born in 1934.

Now, aren't you proud of those things?

I am not trying to wave the flag and I am not trying to stir you up, and I am not trying to take all night to say these things, but I want to reason them out with you. These things just didn't happen. All of you worked together to bring them about, and we are not going to let anyone get them undone.

I am not responsible for these things, but I am proud to say that I have lived in this period and I have lived this history—along with many of you. It wasn't easy. The going was all uphill. And every argument made tonight to go back was made along the way on each of these measures.

When I first went to Congress in 1937, we had a measure that provided a minimum wage of 25 cents an hour, and they said it was socialism, statism, communism, would wreck my political career, and would wreck labor unions. And I was one of three Congressmen from my section of the country that signed a petition to pass a 25-cent an hour minimum wage bill. I am not an old man now. And it didn't destroy me, and it didn't destroy the labor unions either, this wage and hour provision of the Fair Labor Standards Act.

One of the Members, I remember, got up on the floor of the House and called it "the road to economic hell." But when the motion was put, America voted aye. And the ayes still have it and are going to keep it.

Women in my State, mothers of children, were then working for 7 cents an hour in the pecan shelling plants, and they said we would wreck the economy if we made those employers pay them 25 cents an hour.

When we proposed legislation to help the farmers, one member of the opposition said, and I am going to quote him, "This is the beginning of the end of our kind of government." But when the motion was put, America voted aye. And the ayes still have it and are going to keep it.

When the Federal Deposit Insurance Corporation was proposed, you remember how we found things in this country. Banks were closing, they were just popping like firecrackers, like popcorn, all over the country. You couldn't drive down the street without seeing people lined up trying to get there before they closed.

When we came in and said we were going to have a Federal Deposit Insurance Corporation, one member of the opposition got up and he sounded like some voices I hear today. I heard one of them on television talking about me before I came over here tonight. And he said it would "completely destroy the entire banking system of this Nation." But when the motion was put, America voted aye. And the ayes still have it, and we are going to keep it.

When we proposed the Social Security Act, one member of the opposition called it a "cruel hoax." Tonight, 20 million people, 1 out of every 10, live in decency and dignity with their monthly social security check. And we are not about to make it voluntary and abolish it. And when that social security bill came up for a vote, when the motion was put, America voted aye. And the ayes still have it, and the ayes are going to keep it.

Then there was the Wagner Act, estab-

lishing man's right, woman's right, to collective bargaining. We had the Supreme Court about to hold it unconstitutional. We had every charge that could be made made about it. But when the motion was put, the ayes voted and the ayes had it. And we got it and we are going to keep it.

And then there is the Tennessee Valley Authority, and the Securities and Exchange Commission, and the United States Housing Authority. Each time there were cries from the small band of nay-sayers, the status quo fellows, the fearful, the doubters. But when the motions were put, America voted aye, And the ayes still have it, and we are going to keep it.

I was in Congress in 1944 when education was made available to 9 million veterans through the GI bill of rights. And I thought when I voted for that bill what a wise founder of the Republic of Texas back before we were a State had to say about education, and every time I get an audience where they can't get out the door I repeat that statement. I want you to listen to it. This is what that wise man said, and it is just as true tonight as it was then:

"Education is the guardian genius of democracy. It is the only dictator that free men recognize, and the only ruler that free men desire."

And when the vote was put on educating 9 million veterans, the motion was put and the ayes had it. And we are going to keep it.

I was there when the Employment Act of 1946 was passed, the Full Employment Act, and I know the protests, for I heard them all. But America voted aye. The ayes still have it, and we are going to keep it, because we believe that every man and woman that is willing to work, who wants to work, has a right to work in America, and ought to have a job.

Then came these past 3½ years. They started from another period of stagnation. During the year before you voted John F. Kennedy into office, the year before, a million workers had lost their jobs, had to give them up. Real earnings had leveled out, so that in 4 years earnings for a manufacturing worker with a family of four had increased by less than $1 a week.

Well, I am proud to have been a part of a team, the Kennedy-Johnson team, that reawakened the American people in the passage of more legislation to help more people than had been passed in three decades.

I can't go into all of them. But after that tragic day when we lost our President, and a cruel assassin took him away from us, on a moment's notice I had to assume the awesome responsibilities of the Presidency and carry on as best I could. And I called on God and I called on you to help me.

I looked to see where we were in order to see where we could go. And I knew the eyes of the world were looking on America to see how our system would function and how the transition would take place, if at all. I knew the uncertainty that was in the hearts of 190 million people here who had seen their leader taken from them, and had seen what had happened in other countries with takeovers under such circumstances.

And when I returned to my little office in the Executive Office Building that night, and sent my wife home to our daughters, I evaluated the problems I had. And within the week 85 leaders from 85 countries—85 out of the total of 120 in the world—came to see me and to talk to me; and the leaders of business, the captains of industry, like one that I see out here tonight; the leaders of labor, the leaders of the farmers, the teachers, the preachers of all faiths.

President Truman packed up his little valise and started out from Independence, and President Eisenhower came down from Gettysburg, all to try to help in that transition period, to steady things. The stock market was fluttering. People were hesitant. They were unsure.

I looked at the legislation that we had pending. For almost a year we had a tax bill that hadn't been acted on. For almost 9 months we had a civil rights bill that hadn't been acted upon. We had three education bills that hadn't been accepted by both Houses. We had a mass transit bill that hadn't been acted upon. We had 51 major measures for your benefit, to serve you, that you need, programs that are good for America.

And they were there with President Kennedy's recommendations, but President Kennedy was gone.

The other night, I sat in the White House and about midnight I looked over the list of those 51 bills that had been pending there on that November night when I took over. I am proud to tell you that your Senators and your Congressmen and other Senators and other Congressmen that went along with me—we passed all 51 of them in the Senate. And we passed most of them in the House.

But Appalachia—we got the money for the commission when we got the enabling legislation, so we made some progress. And medical care went to conference, the Senate voted it in, and two Republicans and one Democrat were on the conference from the House and those three men would not agree to take the social security increase with medical care. So the Senate and the House would not agree. The Senate wouldn't give up medical, and the two Republicans, the Chairman of the Republican Policy Committee and another fellow named Curtis from out in St. Louis, and the Chairman of the Committee, the Honorable Wilbur Mills, from Arkansas—those three said, "We won't allow medical care." So we came to an impasse. But we are going to pass medical care.

We passed the Area Redevelopment Act, the Manpower Act, the Trade Expansion Act, new housing legislation, three education bills, and don't forget this, the Nuclear Test Ban Treaty.

I remember some newspaper reporters said, "If you just pass two bills, if you can just get a bill where we can take all these fights out of the streets and put them in the courts, the civil rights bill," and you will remember we had the Birmingham episodes and all the serious problems, "if you can just take it out of the streets and put it in the courts." And it is now in the Supreme Court and we have had lots of difficulty with it, but we have tried to be patient and we have tried to be understanding. And we have had a good deal of integration of schools this year in some of the most difficult places in the United States—the State of Mississippi, and they have integrated their schools.

We have talked to the Governor day after day, and we have talked to their leaders there and they have handled the situation where the situation didn't get as bad as it did back in some of the earlier days before the passage of the act. But they said, "If you can pass the tax bill"—it had been tied up for a year—"and the civil rights bill," that would be enough, that would be a very successful Congress.

Well, we passed them and all these others that I have talked about. We passed the poverty bill, the Economic Opportunity Act. We closed down enough obsolete bases, and we saved enough in efficient, competitive bidding in the Defense Department to give us a billion dollars to put on our Economic Opportunity Act, our poverty act, so we can take the people that are at the bottom of the heap, the families that earn less than $3,000, and do something about the poverty situation.

President Roosevelt came in and he talked about the one-third that were ill clad, ill housed, and ill fed—and that was 30 years ago. President Johnson came in and he talked about the one-fifth that were ill clad, ill fed, and ill housed. But think, I am not thrilled but I am pleased that we have cut it from one-third to one-fifth; that we have reduced it from 33 to 20. What I am going to be so proud about is when we wipe out that 20 percent that are poverty stricken altogether. That is a long list, but this is a critical point.

Almost every one of these programs that I have had to list for you in this time tonight is under attack today and tonight and tomorrow in this 1964 election.

Our whole way of doing things is at issue.

I told you the foreign policy: responsibility versus irresponsibility. I told you the domestic issue: whether you want to do what we have been doing for 30 years or whether you want to wipe it out.

We have been driving uphill for 30 years, and now we are told not to just turn back but to drive over the precipice. America's answer is not just no to that opposition. It has just got to keep on driving ahead, for we have a lot further to go, and we are going under Democratic leadership.

I don't resent the ugly things that have been said or the personal things, or the mudslinging, or the name-calling, or the epithets that have been applied to me. Most people understand that when folks get desperate they are not always careful, cautious, prudent, and wise, and they do waste everybody's time by talking about these matters. But they are not going to—they may enjoy it and get their own blood pressure up and feel a peculiar sensation, but if they can just keep on talking, maybe we won't have to keep on traveling so much.

I am going to try to look at it as objectively as I can. I am going to try to really do what the Good Book advocates, "God, forgive them for they really know not what they do." I do get a little disappointed.

I was reading some of the columns that some of the candidates in this election had written after I took over as President. They were rather complimentary about me. They recommended me most highly, and just a few weeks later, after they got the smell of the election this year, and we got within 8 or 9 months of the election, they had a 180-degree turn toward me.

It isn't even the attempt to strip our gears that is so bad. What I don't like is that they want to shift into reverse. It is dangerous business to throw her into reverse when this country is going faster than we have ever been going before.

I am not asking you to put your finger on the trigger; I am not asking you to put your thumb on the button. I am going to ask you one simple thing for your own good, and this decision you make in November ought to be in your interest and nobody else's.

Don't you vote for grandpa or brother-in-law or anything else. You vote for yourself. And you vote for the man and the program that you think is best for your country. I will follow that criterion, and I will abide by that judgment.

But I just want to ask you here, while we are visiting with each other and save me taking a poll, is there anyone here tonight that came out because their wife made them or their brother-in-law brought them, or something? Is there anybody here that really wants to throw things in reverse?

I regret one thing deeply, and that is this senseless argument about what has already been decided defeats what ought to be the purpose of this campaign. This campaign's purpose is to decide what our course is for the future.

The argument shouldn't be between the present and the past. The argument ought to be about the present and the future. This has been a generation of democracy. We look ahead, and we are looking ahead to a generation of greatness.

A great historian, Walter Prescott Webb, who lived in my hometown, was a philosopher of the frontier. In most countries, he said, they think of the frontier as the edge, as the place where there are fences with gates to keep people out, or to keep them in.

Well, America's frontier is different. It lies inside our country, not at the edge. It lies inside each of us.

Each of us, in our own way, is the product of a frontier, and the builder of a frontier in their time. Our children will find frontiers of their own, and so will their children, if you don't close the gate on them. America, our beautiful America, is the land of the perpetual frontier.

Today's frontier is not new land, challenging man's endurance, challenging his plow. America's frontier is the vast, barely charted sea of knowledge. And as we cross it we will multiply our abundance and we will brighten our aspirations.

We must carry with us the old virtues that we have needed on every frontier: courage, faith in God, honesty, eagerness to work hard. But we must add a new indispensable: the ability to perceive, the ability to apply thought, to put in order what we have learned, to give wings to our hopes.

I have in mind for this country a Great Society, where every boy and girl has a right to all the education they can take; where every man and his wife have a right to hope for and an expectancy to get a home that they can call their own; where every man and woman who is willing to work can work; where we work fewer hours per day and fewer days per week; and we have a beautiful countryside—someday I hope to get rid of all these old secondhand autos out on the highway—to have a beautiful countryside with seashores and parks where the kiddies can go and play and enjoy the land of their fathers.

Oh, what I perceive for this Nation in the year 2000 is so exciting to me that I just hope the doctors hurry up and get busy and let me live that long.

I think I know something about the people of Ohio. I think they are good, patriotic Americans. Some of them are Republicans and some of them are Democrats and some of them are Independents. Nearly all of them are pretty independent. But I believe when the chips are down, whether it is when the draft calls them or Uncle Sam summons them, I believe that most of them do what they think is best for their country, regardless of their party, and that is what I want you to do.

I think most of you are Democrats here tonight, but I don't want you, as a Democrat, to ever oppose a Republican President just for the sake of opposition.

When I became Democratic leader, I said, "I reject Senator Taft's philosophy." He had said it was the duty of the opposition to oppose. I said, "I don't believe that a minute. I think it is the duty of the opposition to do what is right. And every single time President Eisenhower is right, a Republican President, I will look at his proposal, and if I can in good conscience support it, I will grab his flag and hold it up, and I will support him because he is the only President I have. And if he is wrong, and I can't in good conscience go with him, I am going to tell him so, in a low voice, quietly, and I am going to oppose him with decency and dignity. And he is going to know he has had a fight. But I am going to do it on principle without regard to personality. And he never need fear that I will criticize his wife or his children or his dog."

It is late and I must be on my way. I have to go to Louisville tonight. I have enjoyed visiting with you.

I just want to say this before we leave: We spent $10,000 the other day of money that we didn't have in the Democratic Party, and you people in Ohio don't send us as much as you ought to. But I know how you feel about sending money to Washington.

A little boy wrote a letter to the Postmaster General and said his daddy was dead and his momma had a house full of orphan children. He wrote the letter to God.

He said: "Dear God: Please send us some money. Send us a hundred dollars, God."

The Postmaster General didn't know what to do with the letter when it wound up on his desk. He felt sorry. He had been working for Prudential Life Insurance and had a little money he had saved, so he sat down and put a $20 bill in there and sent it back to the little boy.

In about 2 weeks he got a letter back from the little boy and it said: "Dear God: I appreciate your prompt reply to my letter, and it helped. But I need another $100." And he said, "Dear Lord, this time please don't route it through Washington because I had an 80 percent deduct."

We took a poll out here and that poll

shows that as of now, last week, if the people here were voting, 65 percent of them would vote the Democratic Presidential-Vice Presidential ticket, 35 percent voting the Republican Presidential-Vice Presidential ticket. All that means is this: If they get their 35 percent to the polls, and most of them are going with blood in their eyes, because a good many of them, I have found, are pretty excitable people that feel pretty tense on some of these things, and we only get 34 percent of ours to the polls—and we will be awfully lucky if we get 70 percent of the people to the polls—then we have had it, and you have had it, too, and everything you have done for 30 years.

The eyes of the world are upon America because we are the leader of the world, and the most important thing in the world is not this election; the most important thing in the world is peace and good will toward men—that little five letter word, p-e-a-c-e.

You don't get peace by rattling your rockets. You don't get peace by threatening to drop your bombs. You must have strength, and you must always keep your guard up, but you must always have your hand out and be willing to go anywhere, talk to anybody, listen to anything they have to say, do anything that is honorable, in order to avoid pulling that trigger, mashing that button that will blow up the world.

You would expect my opponent to think well of himself, and I think well of him. You would expect me to think well of myself, and I don't think that you ought to be guided or guarded by what we say. I think what you have to decide in your own heart, in your own conscience, in your own home with your own prayers is—in this perilous hour in which we live, with these critical uncertainties confronting us, when we have a test ban treaty and we have a "hot line"—when you hear that phone ring, who do you want to answer it?

When they cut off our water in Guantanamo—a little bearded dictator called Castro impulsively and emotionally cut our water off—I got a lot of advice. I had just been in office a few days. I remember one of the advisers said, "Send in the Marines."

Well, we considered it carefully and we finally concluded that the incident was such that we ought to preserve that base, where it would be sufficient in its own strength, and we oughtn't have to depend on anybody, so I called up an admiral and told him to go down there and turn that water off. Instead of sending the Marines in, I sent one little admiral to turn it off, and things have been going reasonably well at Guantanamo ever since.

You are going to have to decide who you want to have the civilian responsibility over the admirals and the generals, and the captains and the corporals in the world. You are going to have to decide which man's thumb you want there next to that button.

I sat for 37 days and nights with a man much younger than I was, and I thought much less experienced than I was. But he was my Commander in Chief during the Cuban missile crisis. I left home many mornings not knowing whether I would ever see my wife and my daughters that night again. I didn't know whether I would be back or whether they would be there, or whether any of us would be there. I am proud to say to you that the coolest man in town those 37 days was John Fitzgerald Kennedy.

It is with some sadness that I observed some criticism when he wasn't here to defend himself of his conduct in that crisis. Because after those 37 days Mr. Khrushchev had to take his missiles and put them on his ships and put his tarpaulins over them and take them back home.

But both Mr. Kennedy and Mr. Khrushchev had been there eyeball to eyeball with their thumbs close to the button, and both of them had realized that if either touched that button, 300 million lives would be snuffed out in a matter of minutes. It was an experience for a man.

I was happy when I reduced some of our nuclear production that we have in great surplus, and I said, "I am not going to operate a nuclear WPA." When I reduced it, after I came in, I notified Mr. Khrushchev I was going to do it, and I gave him the hour and the day, and I said, "Here is what we are going to do because of these reasons. But if you really want peace in the world, you can do likewise and make some move along the same direction."

As I was rising from my chair to be introduced at the Associated Press in New York, at 2 o'clock, they brought a little yellow ticker paper that said Mr. Khrushchev was making a simultaneous announcement that he was reducing also.

Freedom is on the march in the world, and I don't think communism is ever going to defeat freedom. As I said earlier, I am going to keep all the strength that this Nation needs, and we have more than any nation in all the world, and more than all of them put together. I am going to keep it. But I am not going to destroy the world by

throwing my weight around without achieving something for it. I am going to try to do as the Good Book says, the prophet Isaiah. I am going to say to all the leaders of the world, "Come now, let us reason together."

So that is the decision that you are going to have to make, whose hand do you want on the throttle, whom do you want to answer the phone? I am not going to recommend to you. I am just going to tell you my hopes. I need you. I have a lonely, frightening job, and I am doing my dead level best to do it right.

So I want to ask you for your hopes and for your help, and for your hand, and for your prayers, because I don't know a man in the world that needs them more than I do.

Thank you.

NOTE: The President spoke at 9:37 p.m. at Convention Center in Cleveland, Ohio. In his opening words he referred to Mayor Ralph S. Locher of Cleveland and to Senator Stephen M. Young of Ohio. Later he referred to, among others, Secretary of Health, Education, and Welfare Anthony J. Celebrezze and Mrs. Celebrezze and Representative Michael A. Feighan, of Ohio, Representative William E. Miller of New York, Republican candidate for Vice President, Representative Charles A. Vanik of Ohio, Albert Porter, chairman of the Cuyahoga County Democratic Executive Committee, William L. Coleman, chairman of the Ohio State Democratic Executive Committee, Michael V. DiSalle, former Governor of Ohio, Frank Celeste, former Mayor of Lakewood, Ohio, and Representative Thomas L. Ashley of Ohio, Representative Thomas B. Curtis of Missouri, Senator Bourke B. Hickenlooper of Iowa, chairman of the Republican Policy Committee, and Representative Wilbur D. Mills of Arkansas.

643   Remarks in Louisville, Ky., at a Breakfast for Indiana and Kentucky State Party Leaders.   *October 9, 1964*

Mr. Chairman; Governor Breathitt; my old friends and great Kentucky patriots, Happy Chandler and Bert Combs, Keen Johnson, Governor Wetherby, Lawrence Wetherby, Earle Clements; my old friend the coura-

geous Governor of North Carolina, who happens to be over here doing some missionary work, Terry Sanford; one of Kentucky's ablest Congressmen, to whom I am deeply indebted, Bill Natcher; Congressman Stub-

blefield; Congressman Watts; Congressman Perkins; Congressman Chelf; and the man and woman that Kentuckians are going to send to Congress, Charles Farnsley and Mrs. Frances Mills; my friend Congressman Denton of Indiana; and all of you, my fellow Americans, who have done so much for so long in order that the Democratic Party could have an opportunity to lead this State and lead this Nation:

In less than 4 weeks we will be at the end of another campaign. How well we do between now and then will largely depend upon you, your experience, your know-how, your heart, your energy, your willingness to neglect your own private affairs and to give up part of your family obligations and go out and work for your party.

I believe that you will do for me and the Democratic Party between now and November what Kentucky has done for the Democratic Party in this State for many years.

I don't want this to be a long, rambling, political speech this morning because you are professionals, and you have listened to them through the years. That is one of the things that has earned for you that medal of honor that you are entitled to wear. But we do have a very simple situation before us this November.

There are only two men running for President—Lyndon Johnson and the Republican nominee.

We only have two men running for Vice President—Hubert Humphrey and the Republican nominee.

We have very definite, clear-cut issues and we could spell them out at great length, but you know them perhaps better than you need to know them. In short, there are two policies that are to be decided: One is our foreign policy, our relation with other nations. What will it be the next 4 years?

Who will direct it? Who will be the spokesman for this country? If that telephone rings, who answers it? If that conference comes, who attends it? If that treaty is indicated to be desirable, who submits it and who advocates it?

In short, do we continue the bipartisan efforts that we have made over the last 20 years since World War II, to try to preserve peace in the world, or do we junk it and start off on a new direction and what I think is a dangerously deep departure from what we have known since World War II?

It isn't easy to get Republicans and Democrats to agree, but most of the time when their country is at stake and they think the danger is big enough, they always submerge their party differences and try to pull together.

Since that tragic day in November, I have done my best to unite the people of this country—business, labor, farmers, the Government—and I have not tried to harass them or humiliate them. I have tried to pull them together and get them to see that if they all did well, each of them would do well, and that we ought to spend more of our time trying to unite our people than to divide them.

I have tried to do the same thing on the world front. I have seen the leaders of 85 of the 120 nations, and I am very stimulated and pleased at the treatment that has been accorded me by most of the leaders of the world. I think at this time the respect for our country and the affection for our country is one that we can take pride in.

President Truman met the forces of communism in Greece and Turkey, and Arthur Vandenberg, a great Republican, reversed a lifetime record of isolationism and joined with him, and they successfully stopped communism in Greece and Turkey.

President Eisenhower came along, and during the period he was President I was Democratic leader. I looked at the record the other day, the last year of our service. I supported the Republican President more than 90 percent of the time in the field of foreign policy, and that was about four times as much as the Republican leader supported him. He supported him about 25 percent of the time.

Then after President Eisenhower came President Kennedy, and we had the Cuban missile crisis, and men like Senator Hickenlooper and others stood up with a Democratic President and they presented a united front. Khrushchev had to take his missiles and load them on his boats and take them out of the country, very much to his humiliation.

I am very sorry and I am saddened at what has been said about that in recent days. I sat in every one of those meetings on the Cuban missile crisis, 37. I never left home in the morning that I was sure I would see my wife and babies when I got back that evening. It was as tense a situation as I have ever been in—I have been scared a lot of times, from the time they took me snipe hunting on down.

But through all that rather terrifying experience, the coolest man that sat at either end of that table was our late beloved President John Fitzgerald Kennedy. And now when he is not here to answer for himself, and he can't speak up as he did so effectively in every State of the Union when he was here, to have it said of him, your President and your leader, that he manufactured all this for political purposes, is sufficient indictment of the author of that statement to let everyone know who they ought to vote for for President.

I have been in office a little less than 11

months. We have had several test tubes run on us. They have put a thermometer in my mouth several times.

One of the first experiences was that they shot four of our men, our soldiers, in Panama, and they demanded we negotiate an agreement and sign a blank check. Well, we didn't do it. We said we would make no precommitments; we would sit down and do what was right and just. In a period of 2 months, they finally agreed to the terms we submitted the first day of the meeting.

We had a little flare-up at Guantanamo, at our base in Cuba. The bearded dictator went out one day and decided to cut the water off for that base. I got a lot of advice, free advice, from specialized quarters, and some of them said, "Rush in the Marines. Send in the Marines." It is mighty easy to start a fight, get into a war mighty quick.

We got the recommendation of the Marines, the Army, Navy, and the Air Force, the Secretary of Defense and the Secretary of State, and we unanimously concluded that instead of acting impulsively and sending in the Marines to turn the water on, it would be wiser to send in one little admiral to turn it off, and to tell them we were going to make that base self-sufficient where we wouldn't have to depend on them any more, that we would make our own water.

A lot of new nations have been born in this world. There are more than 120 of them now, and a lot of them are going through a perilous period. They are like children learning to walk.

Some of the nations, Khrushchev says, have grown up like children and now they are too big to spank. So he has a lot of problems with some of his satellites.

But we have a varying situation all over the world. During this period we have done our best to advance the cause of freedom and to make free men a little bit stronger. We have had to help some of them, we have had to prop them up, we have had to lift them up, we have had to put them in a toddler to teach them to walk, teach them to govern.

They have changed overnight and they have had this explosion and that one, but the last nation that we lost to communism, to the Communist cause, was Cuba in 1959. President Kennedy was rather proud, and I am rather proud, and I think the American Nation can be proud, not of Democrats, not of Republicans, but of Americans, that the cause of freedom in the world is not a backward cause and it is not one that is receding, and it is not one that is diminishing.

The Communists, with their problems between Russia and China now—if you think we have some headaches just think about their problems among themselves. So the big question you have to decide, then, is: do you want to try to hold the country together and provide a bipartisan, nonpartisan foreign policy that will face up to these problems as Americans and not as party people, or do you want to change and go off in this new direction?

You will have to be the judges of that, and your people will have to be the judges of it. That is the first big issue, though, whether you are going to have responsibility in the conduct of your foreign affairs, or whether you are going to have irresponsibility.

The second thing is your domestic affairs. We could spend all day talking about that. But we have 72½ million people working this morning. That is more than ever worked anywhere. They are making $60 billion more after taxes than they were making 4 years ago. The corporations of this country are making the highest profits in their history. They made $12 billion

more after taxes than they did 4 years ago. Our farm income is up. We have farm programs and we are trying to improve them.

We are told that we ought to turn all of these things back to the States, we ought to sell the TVA, we ought to take no more interest in these various programs that we allocate for the States, whether it is health, schools, highways, or the other things; that we have too much government in Washington, and you ought to do away with all of that. Well, you can do away with it.

You can do away with our farm programs and the first thing you do away with is you reduce the farm income to the farmers of this country from $12 billion to $6 billion. If you want to do away with it, you can do it and you can outvote the farmers because they are in the minority, but I don't think the people of Kentucky are ever going to do that, because we have memories and we know that depressions are farm-led and farm-fed, and if you neglect the farmer, you neglect yourself.

On social security, when that was first passed, some of the Republicans said it was a "cruel hoax." That is their language. Today we have 20 million people on social security, one out of every 10 in this country. All through New England my Republican opponent campaigned on making it voluntary. He has moderated and modified some since then.

My judgment is as time goes along he is going to adjust himself to the needs of the occasion, but if you make a program like that voluntary, you kill it.

Now, if you want to kill social security, you can do it, if you have a majority. But I don't think they will ever get a majority of people in Kentucky to make social security voluntary. You have unemployment insurance, you have collective bargaining, you have minimum wages.

When I was a youngster and went to Washington, Happy Chandler served in Congress in those days, Senator Barkley was there, a good many of the folks in this room remember that period. They submitted a minimum wage law. Women in my district, mothers of children, who lost their husbands, were down at work every morning at daylight and worked until dark and made 7 cents an hour.

That is in my lifetime, and I am not an old man. I am getting a little thin on top, but I am not eligible for a pension yet.

But they recommended a 25-cent-an-hour minimum wage, and they called it socialism. They said it would ruin this country, that it was socialistic.

I was one of three from the southern part of the country that signed a petition forcing a caucus to act on minimum wages. They said it was governmental interference, and it was. It interfered with that fellow that was running that pecan shelling plant. It told him he couldn't pay that little widow 7 cents any more, that he would have to pay her a quarter.

It was governmental interference. They said it would ruin my political career if I voted for it. Well, they are going to have a chance to ruin it November 3d. It hasn't ruined it up to now, anyway.

If you want to, do away with these gains that you have made, this progress that we have made, over 30 years.

In this country I believe in full employment. I think that every man and woman who wants to work and is willing to work ought to have a chance to work. I believe in full education.

I think that when our working people can make $60 billion more after taxes, and our corporations can make $12 billion more after taxes, and our auto manufacturers can make over 20 percent on their equity—I think that every boy and girl who is delivered into this world ought to have the right to get all the education they can take, because in this technological age, in this space age, they are going to need something besides reading, writing, and arithmetic.

I am not one that thinks that you can just ignore this general subject of education, or that you can ignore this general subject of poverty and just say, "Well, if they are poor, they ought to have done better for themselves."

A lot of people would do better for themselves if they could, and if they knew how. Nobody really wants to be poor. But a lot of them have problems trying to meet these things.

I want the Government to be a compassionate government and an understanding government, and a government that wants to do something about them.

The hardhearted and the heavyhanded and the ruthless dynasties that have led some of the States in this Union have never led the people of Kentucky. You have had differences of opinion in the party, and you have had some good, real, knockdown dragouts. I have looked down here a time or two since I have been talking just to be sure I wasn't standing in any blood.

But there is not anything that has happened to me in this campaign that makes me quite as proud of the patriotism and the Americanism and the love of country as these distinguished former Governors and former Lieutenant Governors that put on the Democratic uniform and marched in there.

When this terrible tragedy occurred, I didn't have any chance to consult any books in the library. I had to get down in the back seat of a Ford police car and rush to an airplane so I could get it in the air as soon as I could, because they didn't know how deep the conspiracy was, and whether it was to wipe out all the Government or not.

I didn't have any long speech for the people of this country. I just as humbly as I knew how said that I was going to pick up and try to carry on for our fallen leader:

"I don't know how well I will do; we will have to let time decide that. But the eyes of the world are on the United States right this moment and they don't know which way we are going to go. They have seen governments fall before and they have seen leaders change before, and I want to try to give the people of this country some confidence and I want the people of the world to settle down just a little bit and not get too excited.

"I want to have a transition period where we can show that our system can carry on— it is not the man, but it is the system in this country. So all I can say to you is, I will just do the very best with what the good Lord gave me.

"I have been in Washington since Mr. Hoover's days, 1931, and I have had a lot of association and experience in that period of time that my people have been good enough to give me. I will take that experience and I will use it to the best I can with it. With God's help and with your help, we will see how we come out."

President Truman got on the train in Kansas City and he came to Washington to tell me what he would like to do to help. President Eisenhower got in a helicopter and he came down from Gettysburg. President Hoover called up from the Waldorf-Astoria and said that he would like to give me his ideas and he would help.

And people from all over the country came in to try—even my opponent wrote some very friendly columns and said the way

we were picking up and carrying on was very good. So the people did their best to help hold me up, prop me up, and go along.

I looked at that program that was left to me. The tax bill hadn't moved in a year. It was in committee and Senator Byrd hadn't reported it out. He was one of the first visitors that I had.

Men who served with him like Happy and Earle know that Senator Byrd is not a man to change his mind easily. He never changed it. He voted against the bill. But I let him take a peep at my budget and instead of increasing the budget $5 billion, I reduced it $1 billion. He allowed me to report my tax bill and we passed it.

That tax bill put $12 billion back in the people's pockets and in the companies' pockets that we have used to provide extra jobs and expenditures.

But there were 50 other bills besides the tax bill on President Kennedy's list. Of those 51 bills—last Friday night I sat there in the White House and looked at them— we passed every single one of the 51 in the Senate of the United States. We passed most of them in the House of Representatives, all but 2 or 3.

We appreciate the Congress and the people working with us.

We had our problems in Cyprus and we still have them.

We had our problems in Viet-Nam and we still have them. I didn't get us into Viet-Nam. I didn't ring up out there and say, "I want some trouble." I was out there in '61, one of the first things that I did. President Kennedy sent me out there when we were worried about the stability of the government there. We can't pick other people's governments. We have enough trouble picking our own.

If I had my way, I would just tell you all how to select this Government here without even asking you to ratify it. But it looks like 50 States are going to tell me what to do November 3d, instead of me telling them. That is the way it is out there. We just can't tell every country or mash a button. It is not that simple.

These folks who think you can have government by ultimatum are wrong. You better get a little closer to prophet Isaiah and the Good Book and "Come now, let us reason together," because there is not an ultimatum that any President can issue that could have produced one of these former Governors on this platform, not a single ultimatum. You could take all the tanks in our combat divisions and all the planes in the sky, and all the Polaris missiles, and you couldn't have made a one of them come up here. But you can reason with them.

So that is our problem right out there in Viet-Nam. Mr. Eisenhower sat down and wrote the President of Viet-Nam after they were divided, after the agreements in 1954, and said to them, "We want to help you help yourselves, and we will provide you advice and military assistance to preserve your country and keep the Communists from enveloping it if you will help yourselves."

For 10 years we have been doing that, and sometimes it goes from bad to worse, and they have changed governments three or four times in the last few months. You know what a problem we have had here at home just changing it once and getting adjusted.

We are trying as best we can not to enlarge that war, not to get the United States tied down in a land war in Asia, and not for American boys starting to do the fighting that Asian boys ought to be doing to protect themselves. We don't want to pull out and come home and say, "We will turn it all over to you."

So if you don't want to enlarge it and you seek no larger war, and you don't want to pull out and run home, the only thing you can do is what we are doing. We let them know that when they shoot at us as they did in the Tonkin Gulf, we will make prompt, adequate, and sufficient reply.

So as we go into campaign now, we have those two big issues:

Do we undo everything we have done in the field of foreign affairs for 20 years in a bipartisan way? There are some that want to do it. Some are just frothing at the mouth to do it.

Do we want to junk all of the advances we have made in 30 years in social security, minimum wages, collective bargaining, education, roads, all these programs where we have worked together? If you do, you can. But you will have to answer that on November 3d.

This State has always had a peculiar spot in my affection. Kentucky has done more for me than any State in the Union, I think, except Texas, and sometimes more than Texas. Even if at some time every Democrat in the State wasn't for me, I don't know any of them that really did anything against me or hated me. Most of them were for me.

I never forget your loyalty through the years in the House and Senate to Mr. Rayburn, when Fred Vinson was there.

When Fred Vinson put me on the Naval Affairs Committee against California, against Oregon, and against Washington, all of them that had a coastline, I wasn't within 400 miles of water. But if you had a Kentuckian running the Ways and Means Committee, you didn't have to have merit on your side. So that is where I got interested in military affairs.

I just want to say this to you: You are mighty good to come up here to breakfast and to be so attentive.

Mr. Rayburn went back home one time

after he had been in the Congress 50 years. He went to the little place where he had taught school, where no one would take him in, board him. The banker, the preacher, and the rest of them didn't have room. But the old blacksmith gave him a place to board.

They all came around this night—when he was Speaker—and said they wanted him to go home and stay all night. "No," he said, "I'll stay with the blacksmith, if he invites me—old man James."

So, sure enough, old man James came up—with his blue overalls on—and asked him to stay all night with him and Mr. Rayburn said, "Yes."

They went out and he said they talked until 2 o'clock; about 1 o'clock the wife and daughter went on to bed. Finally, Mr. Rayburn said, "James, I have to make seven speeches tomorrow. I'm in a campaign. I'm going to have to go to bed."

Old man James said, "Well, Sammy, if that's the way you feel about it I guess you'll just have to do it. But I'd like to stay here and talk to you 'til daylight.

"Because," he said, "Sammy, if the momma and the girls and me ain't your friends, it's just because we ain't got sense enough!"

That is the way I feel about all the people of Kentucky, regardless of any differences any of us may have ever had about anything: I would just like to stay here and talk to you 'til daylight, because if I am not your friend, it's just because I haven't got sense enough!

NOTE: The President spoke at 9:07 a.m. in the Grand Ballroom at the Sheraton Seelbach Hotel in Louisville, Ky. In his opening words he referred to the Chairman of the Kentucky State Democratic Committee, Frank Paxton, who acted as chairman of the breakfast, Governor Edward T. Breathitt, Jr., of Kentucky, former Kentucky Governors A. B. (Happy) Chandler, Bert T. Combs, Keen Johnson, Lawrence W. Wetherby, and Earle Clements, Governor Terry Sanford of North Carolina, Representatives William H. Natcher, Frank A. Stubblefield, John C. Watts, Carl D. Perkins, and Frank Chelf, and Charles P. Farnsley and Mrs. Frances J. Mills, Democratic candidates for U.S. Representative, all of Kentucky, and Representative Winfield K. Denton of Indiana. Later he referred to, among others, Arthur H. Vandenberg, U.S. Senator from Michigan during the Truman administration, Senator Bourke B. Hickenlooper of Iowa, and Senator Harry F. Byrd of Virginia.

644 Remarks at the Courthouse in Louisville. October 9, 1964

Governor Breathitt—Kentucky's young, fighting Governor Ned Breathitt; my old friends and great Kentucky patriots, Governor Happy Chandler, Governor Bert Combs, Governor Keen Johnson, Governor Lawrence Wetherby, Senator Earle Clements; the fighting, courageous Governor of North Carolina, Terry Sanford; Congressman Bill Natcher; Congressman Stubblefield; Congressman Chelf; Congressman Watts; Congressman Perkins—all great and powerful Members of the Kentucky delega- *tion in Congress:*

And I want to say just a special word for the man and woman that Kentuckians are going to send to Congress—Charles Farnsley—stand up, Charles. We need this man in Washington. You need this man in Washington. The world needs this man in Washington. Now don't forget; go and vote and get your uncles and your cousins and your aunts and your mommas and your poppas to vote for Charles Farnsley.

We have a shortage of good Democrats.

We need good Democrats in Washington. Kentucky has one of the finest Democratic delegations, but we want to make it finer, and we want you to go and vote for Mrs. Frances Mills for Congress. Please stand up.

So many of my ancestors come from Kentucky that I can sing "My Old Kentucky Home" with almost as much feeling as you. My daddy's mother was born in Russellville in 1849. I have some real Kentucky blood in my veins. My great-great-grandmother, Phoebe Ann Desha, was the sister of Joseph Desha, a former Governor of the great State of Kentucky, and she also had a brother who was a Congressman from Kentucky at the same time, and also a brother who was a Congressman from the State of Tennessee.

My great-great-grandfather, John Huffman, farmed in central Kentucky until 1851. He was the first man to breed shorthorn cattle in Texas, and he introduced the Sir Archer breed of horses to the great State of Kentucky.

This is a great day for Louisville. We are honored by the presence of your fighting young, progressive Governor, who is in the spotlight of all the Nation. We are honored by the presence of five former Governors of Kentucky. Let me just tell you this: Any time you can get all five of them in one place at one time on the same platform for the same man, it is a great day for Kentucky. I want all five of them to know now, before they fall out, that I will remember each one of them as long as I live for coming here today and standing up and being counted.

Stand up there, fellows.

We are honored by the presence of the distinguished mayors of many of the great cities of Latin America. I understand that some of these gentlemen are going to visit TVA tomorrow. Well, you will have a great experience awaiting you.

We Americans feel that TVA is a symbol of the genius and the greatness of the democratic system. And Kentucky is not going to turn away from the upward course of American abundance. And we are not about to sell the TVA.

Kentucky is not going to abandon the policies which have given a decent living to the American farmer. We are not about to have 10-cent tobacco.

Kentucky is not going to be afraid of the difficult, patient task of bringing peace to the world. And neither am I.

The names of Kentucky live in American folklore. There is Daniel Boone, Casey Jones, and old Zachary Taylor. All of them drew courage from your soil. All of them were ready to seek the new horizons.

And this is the heritage of the great State of Kentucky that will not listen to those who want to tear down instead of build; listen to those who want to run from the future instead of face up to it; listen to those who retire behind old frontiers instead of being willing to open new ones.

I have come here this morning to the great city of Louisville to put that issue before the American people. The issue of this campaign is whether the American people are going to continue to move forward or whether they are going to stand still.

I want to talk to you a moment about your future, about the future of the Upper South, about the future of America.

The billions of dollars worth of new industry that TVA has already brought to the Upper South is nothing compared to the development that lies ahead. The Upper South is fast becoming one of the most exciting new industrial frontiers anywhere in America.

In 1929 personal income from agriculture was twice as important in Kentucky as manufacturing. But by 1960 manufacturing was three times as important as agriculture.

Between 1960 and 1963 the average personal income in Kentucky jumped 17 percent, and that is one-third faster than the rate for the other States in the Nation.

The unemployment rate here in Louisville has been cut in half since 1961. But this is not good enough, and it is only half the story.

Over 38 percent of all the families in Kentucky live today with an income of less than $3,000, and I tell you that if I am elected President of the United States, and I have a chance to serve this country for 4 more years, I am going to serve the 38 percent of Kentucky families that are in the poverty group.

One of the first things that we did after I became President was to get the Congress to pass the tax cut bill. That tax cut bill restored $12 billion in purchasing power to the American people. It created 24,000 new jobs for Kentucky. It generated an increase in total income in this State alone of $360 million. It boosted the State and local revenues by $29 million. It put $88 million extra into the wage earners' pockets that had been withheld.

And this is a powerful boost to the State of Kentucky. But it is not enough.

The poverty program will attack poverty on a scale that no government has ever attempted in all history. We are going forward to develop this Upper South in the years of opportunity that lie ahead.

First, we want maximum development of the entire Ohio River valley. This development will mean more industry. More industry will mean more jobs. More jobs will mean more income for the good families that live in this State.

Second, we are going to wipe out poverty in this region, in the rural mining areas as well as in the cities of Kentucky. When Franklin Roosevelt spoke to the people of this Nation, he said one-third of our people are ill clad and ill housed and ill fed—that was in the 1930's.

Well, I say to you today that we are very proud that we have moved that one-third down to one-fifth, but we have just begun to fight, and this Government, under my leadership, will never rest secure and will be as unsatisfied as a little boy's appetite as long as there is any poverty in our land.

Third, we want full development of all of our natural resources, development of our land, development of our water, development of our underground to improve the economy and the way of life.

Fourth, we want to continue the tobacco program, and by other measures insure small farmers a fair share of our Nation's general prosperity. We never want to go back to the farm-led and farm-fed depression days. We are never going back under my administration to any 10-cent tobacco.

We want to push forward our national economic programs that will continue our upward trend. We want every child born in this region to have a chance at the best education he can absorb. We want to improve and extend the social security system, and we are not going to make it voluntary, either.

We want to continue to help the people of the Upper South lift themselves by their own bootstraps. We want to help you realize the promise of this great region. We want to help contribute to the strength of the entire Nation. And until want, and misery, and despair are banished from every American home, I, as your leader and as your President, will not be satisfied.

Now, when we passed social security some people told us it was a "cruel hoax." When we passed minimum wages they said, "It will wreck your political career." When we passed our farm programs they said it was socialism. When we provided jobs for our men who were hungry to work, they said that was statism.

Well, those same old voices that said those same old things are now writing these same old speeches. Today they say "halt" and "fall back" and "slow down" and "status quo." The Democrats say, "Put your hand on the throttle and full speed ahead." Some of them say "empty dreams." We reply, "Franklin Roosevelt and George Norris dreamed dreams and we built the TVA."

Franklin Roosevelt was a Democrat. He came from New York. George Norris was a Republican. He was from Nebraska. But they worked together and they laid the groundwork for an industrial revolution in the Upper South. I am from Texas, and I am a Democrat. But I am first the President of all the people.

So here, today, in the great city of Louisville, in the happy State of Kentucky, I ask you to send us two more Democratic Congressmen to help us in the House, and I appeal to your two Republican Senators in the Senate to help us save the social security system, to keep us from selling TVA, to keep us from letting go down the drain all the accomplishments of the last 30 years.

No, we are not going to sit back in our rocking chairs and take it easy. We are going to continue, in the words of John Fitzgerald Kennedy, "to move."

I want to thank you for being so warm in your welcome. You know, the one thing that makes me so proud of my party, the one thing that makes me so proud of my friends, the one thing that makes me so proud of the people that wear these little LBJ hats and the red, white, and blue caps, is this: They are people of faith. They are happy people. They enjoy life. They like the South. They are good folks. They are not saying evil things about anybody. They

are not slinging mud. They are not talking about their neighbors. They are not doubting the future. They are not worrying that socialism is taking over the country because we extend the hand of compassion to an elderly lady who has a social security check. They love people.

Yes, what makes our group so wonderful is that America is really, with a few exceptions—some people have had disappointments, some have had frustrations, some have gotten a little mixed up as they went along, but most of the people of America are people of great faith, with great religion, who love people instead of hating people. Most of your neighbors, most of your friends, most of the folks that you like the best are the folks that follow the Golden Rule, "Do unto others as you would have them do unto you."

So when you hear these bombshells and these explosions, and all these ugly things that you hear the last few weeks of a campaign, when you hear all these things I want you to keep your smile on your face. I want you to keep your blood pressure down. I want you to stay happy. I want you to turn the other cheek and look at the fellow that is desperate and is losing and is falling, and is upset about it, and just say——

I have to move along now. If there are any of you folks from over across the river, you have a mighty wonderful Congressman and I sure want you to give a great mandate and give him a wonderful reelection vote— Winfield Denton. Stand up, Winfield.

Now we have to move up in Old Hickory's territory, up in Nashville, because we want to see those good folks up there, and we want to tell them that we are going to help them save the TVA.

But before I leave, I want to especially thank you folks here in Louisville for the way you treated Lynda Bird when she was down here. She just loves Kentucky. I want to tell you that Lady Bird and Luci and I just listened to her stories about Kentucky for day after day. And now when I go back she is going to have to listen to me day after day.

We are proud of this State. Fred Vinson and Alben Barkley and Henry Clay, and all these great men here on the platform—they have all done what they thought was best for America all the time. And I don't have the slightest doubt but what Louisville and Ken-

tucky are going to do what is best for their country on November 3d.

Thank you.

NOTE: The President spoke at 10:55 a.m. at the Courthouse in Louisville, Ky. In his opening words he referred to Governor Edward T. Breathitt, Jr., of Kentucky, former Kentucky Governors A. B. (Happy) Chandler, Bert T. Combs, Keen Johnson, Lawrence W. Wetherby, and Earle Clements, Governor Terry Sanford of North Carolina, Representatives William H. Natcher, Frank A. Stubblefield, Frank Chelf, John C. Watts, and Carl D. Perkins, all of Kentucky. Later he referred to Charles P. Farnsley and Mrs. Frances J. Mills, Democratic candidates for Representative from Kentucky, and Representative Winfield K. Denton of Indiana.

645 Remarks at the War Memorial Building in Nashville. *October 9, 1964*

Governor Clement:

I hardly know how to tell you people of Tennessee how good you make me feel by the warmth of your welcome, and the wonderful Southern hospitality that you have extended to me and my party ever since we came into your State.

I think that Governor Clement, who is known far and wide in this country as one of the most eloquent speakers that we have ever produced, really outdid himself in his introduction. I honestly believe that is the second best introduction I ever had in my life. The best one was when the Governor was supposed to introduce me one time at Memphis and his legislature was in session and he didn't get to come, and I had to introduce myself.

The Governor told you that there wouldn't have been a Texas if there hadn't been a Tennessee. I agree to that, and I am proud of that. It just goes to show how much vision and foresight the people of Tennessee have always had, because Texas is back here today to tell you that we are not going to sell Tennessee, not for a dollar, not for a

dime, not for anything. And if there are any would-be purchasers lurking around the corners over there four or five blocks away, I want them to know that the Johnson administration is not going to sell any other rivers in this country.

I want to thank my old friends Governor Cooper, Governor Browning, and Governor McCord for honoring us with their presence. They have all had distinguished careers in this State. They have come over here to appear at this meeting today. I was thrilled beyond compare when I spoke in Louisville and five former Governors of the great State of Kentucky united and came there and held up my hand. The reason there were more in Kentucky than there are in Tennessee is that Kentucky changes her Governors oftener. But I am grateful to these men for coming here to help me today.

I want to salute my old friend, one of the most courageous and one of the ablest Members of the United States Senate, Albert Gore. His voice is heard from one end of this Nation to the other, with respect, and with influence, and the only one that I know that fights harder and may have better judgment than Albert is his gracious wife Pauline.

I want to thank the people of Tennessee in advance for producing that fighting young man that you are going to send to the United States Senate, Congressman Ross Bass. Senator Herb Walters has filled that seat with distinction, and he has always had a warm place in my heart and always will.

I want to thank my friend Joe Evins for coming here and leading me through these crowds today and pointing the way. I want to reiterate what my daughter Luci says, that there is no Congressman in the country that can make a better speech than Dick Fulton, and I am happy that he is here. Luci said, "Daddy, if you would just keep this fellow Fulton in some other States like you did in Minnesota and Michigan, I think we would carry all of them." And we are giving consideration to asking him to go into all of them.

I want to thank "Fats" Everett for coming here and helping me. I know that his district is going to give us a great majority, and I appreciate his service and help in Washington, as well as my old friend, Congressman Cliff Davis.

A group of outstanding young men who proudly represent Tennessee in the Congress I have referred to, but there are some more that we need to join them in January because we are going to need a good, solid, working majority in the next Congress, and we are going into 30 or 40 States this year and asking the people to give us support and give us a hand, and give us a mandate so that we can keep this Government for the people and continue to develop the program that John Fitzgerald Kennedy began.

So we hope that you will do your bit and put in a good word and help George Grider, Capt. William Anderson, Willard Yarbrough, Robert Summitt, and Arthur Bright.

If you do that, and they can all come in, my, what a wonderful day that would be for the Nation!

I want to thank State Chairman Jim Peeler and National Committeewoman Mrs. Ruth Russell, and all the good Democrats that helped make this meeting possible. I don't think I have ever attended a better Democratic meeting in all my political life. This is not my first trip to Nashville, and I promise you now it is not going to be my last.

The ties between Tennessee and Texas are pretty close. Some of my ancestors lived up here in Sumner County, your neighbor to the north. Sam Houston studied law in Nashville and served as Governor of Tennessee, and really bloomed out in Texas. David Crockett was born on a mountain top in Tennessee, but won his final glory at the Alamo in Texas. One son of Tennessee, one Texan that we never forget, was the closest friend that I ever had in Congress—Sam Rayburn of Rowan County, Tenn.

Another great man of Tennessee from Nashville did not go to Texas, but he did go up in the world and he became President of the United States. He was "Old Hickory" Andrew Jackson. I have heard it said that on the day he died, the family pastor was talking with one of the President's closest friends. "Do you think that the General will go to Heaven?" the pastor asked. The old man thought a moment and replied, "Well, if he wants to go, who is going to stop him?"

Well, it is men like that that have led Tennessee through all the years, and it is men like that that are going to lead and speak the voice of Tennessee in the future.

We are told in the scriptures that there is a time to every purpose under the Heaven—"a time to break down, and a time to build up."

Well, I believe that this is a time to build

up. And that is really the main issue in this campaign.

The issue is whether the American people want to continue to build our Nation on those policies and principles that have guided us for generations to new heights of greatness, or whether they want to tear down all that we have worked to achieve.

I came to Nashville today to talk to you about this. I think I know what the answer is going to be in Tennessee. But I will tell you now what my answer is going to be.

I am not going to do away with any of this forward program, and I am not going to sell the TVA. No matter how much they offer and no matter how much they want for it, and no matter what names they call it, I am not even going to sell the fertilizer part of it that they need. And I will tell you, I have a good reason.

In the first place, it doesn't belong to me. It belongs to the people of the Upper South. It really belongs to all the people of America. It is part of the blood and the bone of Tennessee. It is part of the greatness of America, and it is not for sale.

Some day, and you mark my prediction—I don't take pride in being a prophet—the time will come in your lifetime when these men of little faith and great fear who are marching around under another banner not of their forefathers, but another banner today, the blush of shame will come to their cheeks and they will hang their heads when they are told by their children that they supported a party that wanted to sell the TVA.

One of the first official acts of President Franklin D. Roosevelt was to send a message to Congress requesting legislation to create the TVA. Franklin Roosevelt did not do this because he was a Democrat. He did it because he was an American.

His strongest ally in the Congress was a Republican, Senator George Norris. Together they worked to give new life to the Upper South, and in those days, 30 years ago, we could only dream that TVA would some day come true, and that TVA would some day make this region bloom and hold its head high again.

Well, today that dream is a reality. A billion dollar industry has grown up along one short stretch of the Tennessee River—more than 30 new lakes with 10,000 miles of shoreline, with 320,000 acres being developed into parks and recreation areas, beautiful countryside, where the hornyhanded sons of toil at the end of the week's labor can take their Molly and the babies and let them have a little recreation and a little vacation of their own.

Yes, TVA is the great pioneer of the 20th century. It has shown what the Government and the people, working together, shoulder to shoulder, can do to conquer hostile nature and create a blessed home for the human spirit.

On November 3d the people of this Nation, I believe led by the people of Tennessee, are going to say, "We are not about to tear all this down."

The investment that we made in this valley has been repaid manyfold: low-cost water transportation has brought new industry; power has brought new industry; flood control has provided flood-free industrial sites.

In the last 4 years you have taken great strides, leaps, forward—faster, far faster, than the national average, and twice as fast as you did from 1956 to 1960.

The number of employed workers in Tennessee has increased almost twice what it did from the last Republican administration of 1956 to 1960. In Nashville, employment has risen by 24,000, from 1960 to 1963, more than three times the increase of the preceding

4 years.

Those steps forward didn't just happen. They weren't accidents. Our prosperity is not an accident. It is not a gift. We worked for it. We built it. We have earned it.

It is the work of the men of both parties, working together, faithful to free enterprise, resolving their differences, fixed on the common goal of American prosperity.

But today those principles are under attack, and I think that attack endangers you, because the same leader, the same voice, that talks about selling TVA, or parts of TVA, also says that we should withdraw from education at a time when the number of students in higher education in Tennessee has doubled since 1950.

That same voice says we should eliminate our farm program, and that would cut farm income from $12 billion to $6 billion. You folks that do business here in Nashville, and don't get out on any of these dirt roads, you wait until you cut that farm income from $12 billion to $6 billion, and you will see the biggest depression that is farm-led and farm-fed you ever heard of.

And they are going to bring it and put it right on your doorstep if you permit it to happen.

John Fitzgerald Kennedy said in the 1960 campaign that it is time to get America moving again. Since that campaign the profits of American corporations after taxes have increased more than $12 billion per year. Since that campaign we have reached the astronomical number of having 72½ million people working on good payrolls. Those people are drawing today $60 billion more after taxes than they drew when John Kennedy made that statement.

America is moving again, and I resent those people who attack him, when he is not here to answer, and say they are going to do away with that program.

Eleven months ago, after that great tragedy, I was called to pick up on most short notice and carry on as best I could. I told the people of my country and the people of the world that I promised them that with God's help and theirs I would do the best I could, and I have done the best I could. Uncertainty was in the air. Divisions had occurred.

The world was frightened and concerned, and we did not know what the next moment held for us. But we tried to look calm and to proceed with caution and with care, and to appeal to the Americanism in every person in this land, and we asked them for their prayers, and for their help, and for their support.

We told them what they had heard at their mother's knee, that united we stand, divided we fall. They rallied around their President in those dark hours and we showed all the world and all our adversaries that we had a system that would carry on, regardless of the individual, regardless of the man.

When I came back to the White House and sat there with that grieved Cabinet, 85 leaders of the world came to attend the funeral. I set aside a portion of my days and nights for many days and nights to talk to each of them about the problems of the world.

Their number one problem in every country is the same number one problem that we have in this country, and that is their relations with other nations: How can we live in the world without destroying each other? How can we achieve peace?

Well, I will tell you one way we can't achieve it: by rattling our rockets, or talking about throwing our bombs around and defoliating areas. We can do it by building the strongest nation in the world with all the power that we will ever need to defend it under any conceivable circumstance, and I am here to tell you as your Commander in Chief today that we have that power. We are the strongest nation in the world; we are stronger than all of them put together. But that doesn't mean that we ever want to use that power. Just because we have a button here that will put off a blast over yonder is no reason you want to put that thumb on that button.

Here in Tennessee you conceived and you produced and you developed the most awesome and the most frightening and the most mighty power that was ever known to humankind anywhere in the world. By mashing that button you can destroy and wipe out the lives of 300 million human beings in a moment.

You have a responsibility, and you have an obligation, and you have a guardianship and a trusteeship, and the good Lord is watching you right this minute to see how you are handling that thumb on that button. You have that strength in order that you will never have to use it.

I sat in 37 meetings of the National Security Council, with the Chairman of the Joint Chiefs and the Joint Chiefs in their gold uniforms, and the Secretary of State and the Secretary of Defense, and the Chairman of the CIA and all of the great minds of this Government—37 long meetings during the Cuban missile crisis.

I never left home in the morning knowing whether I would see my wife and babies when I got back that night. You have read of it. But I don't know whether you have ever felt those chill bumps come up on you or not, but I am not one that can't say I have never been scared. I have been scared most of my life, ever since they took me snipe hunting when I was a kid and they left me out in the dark.

I was scared every moment that the Rus-

sians had their missiles there pointed toward this country. But I am proud to tell you that the coolest head in Washington during all that period was a man that is not here to answer the attacks on him today.

The coolest man in Washington was President John Fitzgerald Kennedy. And because of his caution and because of his care, and because of the steel in his spine and the brain in his head, the American leader and the Russian leader were there eyeball to eyeball, and after that confrontation over a very tense period, when the chips were down and the thumb moved toward the button, both leaders decided that they could never in the eyes of God justify wiping out humanity.

And Mr. Khrushchev picked up his missiles and put them on the decks of his ships, and with our helicopters whirling overhead with their photographic machinery, he took them back home.

But ever since then the leaders of their country and the leaders of our country have thanked the good Lord that nothing worse happened, because what might have been would be too horrible to think of.

You are going to make the decision on who sits in those conferences that try to find a way and a means to peace in the world. You are not ever going to have a more important decision to make for yourself, for your wife, for your children, or for your uncles, or your cousins, or your aunts. You have a little over 3 weeks to make up your mind and to help your neighbors make up their minds. I am not an objective person to make a recommendation.

I am not going to be like the old Senator down in my country was, after the little boy picking cotton went off and stayed all afternoon. And he came back and the boss said, "Where have you been?" He said, "I've been over listening to United States Senator

Joseph Weldon Bailey make a speech."

He said, "The Senator didn't speak all afternoon, did he?" And the little boy said, "Mighty near, mighty near."

"Well," he said, "what did the Senator speak about all afternoon?" The boy said, "Well, boss, I don't recollect precisely everything the Senator said, but the general impression I got from most of his remarks was, the Senator recommended himself most highly."

You don't need any recommendation from me to know that the most important subject in the world is peace, and to know what you can do about it.

You don't need any recommendation from me to know what kind of a program we have been building together in foreign policy for 30 years, from the day that Harry S. Truman joined up with Arthur Vandenberg, a Republican, and gave you bipartisan foreign policy; from the day that Dwight Eisenhower took the Democratic Senate, led by Lyndon Johnson, and we cooperated for 8 years, when he met the Communist threat in the Strait of Formosa.

I am proud to say that even though I was criticized by some people in the country when I was Democratic leader, that I said, "I am proud first I am a free man, second that I am an American, and third that I am a United States Senator, and fourth that I am a Democrat—and in that order.

"When the best interests of my country are at stake, if the President is right, even if he is a Republican President, I am going to hold his hand high and support him, because I think if you do what is best for your country, your country will do what is best for you."

So during that period—I looked at the record the other day—in 1960, I voted with President Eisenhower, as the Democratic leader, 95 percent of the time on his foreign

policy issues. And the leader of the Republican Party that year voted with him 25 percent of the time, and I think referred to his administration as a "Dime Store New Deal."

So I say to you that the one decision you have to make is what is best for you and your family. Can we meet the Communists, as President Truman did, with the support of both parties, in Greece and Turkey? As President Eisenhower did in the Formosa Strait? As President Kennedy did in the Cuban missile crisis? Or do we want to adopt some new, radically different departure and start off in another direction?

Well, I had a little trouble down in Guantanamo. A bearded dictator went in one day and said he was going to cut our water off at our base there. The first thing I heard was all these folks on the Hill started making recommendations, and one of them jumped up and said, "Send in the Marines." I was new in office and doing the best I could, and I wanted to consider what people had to say.

I called in the admirals, the generals, the Secretary of State and the Secretary of Defense, and we all talked it over. And we finally concluded that it would be a lot wiser if we sent in one little admiral to turn the water off rather than send in all the Marines to turn it on.

Now, you are going to be called upon to make some of those decisions in the month ahead. All I ask you to do is to remember that we have two big issues—peace and prosperity.

President Kennedy had a prosperity program going, and he left us with 51 bills to carry it out, and they hadn't passed the Congress. In 10 months that we went to work on them—I looked at them last Friday night and we had passed every one of the 51 bills in the Senate and all but 4 of them in the House.

I not only don't think you can have government by ultimatum abroad—I believe in trying to get along with the rest of the world—but I want our people to get along here at home.

I want business and labor to get along together. We have had less manhours lost by strike than any comparable period in our history except during World War II. We have lost only 14/100ths of 1 percent of the number of hours worked due to strike. So we have business and labor, and the farmers and the Government all working together.

I want these businessmen and these labor men to get along together, because every time they make a dollar, I get 52 cents of it. And the more they make, and the more prosperous they are, the better off we are.

So we not only want peace in the world, we want peace at home.

When you go to the polls on November 3d, you vote for the man and for the party and for the principles that in your judgment will be most likely to bring to your family the peace that you have prayed for and the prosperity that you have worked for.

Thank you.

NOTE: The President spoke at 11:55 a.m. at the War Memorial Building in Nashville, Tenn. His opening words referred to Governor Frank G. Clement of Tennessee. Later he referred to Tennessee's former Governors Prentice Cooper, Gordon Browning, and James N. McCord, Senator and Mrs. Albert Gore, Senator Herbert S. Walters, and Representatives Ross Bass, Joe L. Evins, Richard H. Fulton, Robert A. Everett, and Clifford Davis. He also referred to George W. Grider, William R. Anderson, Willard V. Yarbrough, Robert M. Summitt, and Arthur Bright, Democratic candidates for Representative, Jimmy Peeler, chairman of the State Democratic Executive Committee, and Mrs. Ruth Russell, national Democratic committeewoman, all of Tennessee.

646 Remarks Upon Arrival of the "Lady Bird Special" at Union Station in New Orleans. *October 9, 1964*

Senator Ellender, Senator Long, Members of the congressional delegation, Governor McKeithen, my beloved friend Hale Boggs, who has spent the last 4 days coming through our Southland carrying the message to our own people:

You have heard from the stars and the sensations of this special train, but I want all of you to know that I think so much of the South that gave me birth that I have given the South the best I had for the last 4 days.

Eleven months ago on that tragic day when I became your President and returned to the White House that night, I said to the people of this country and the people of the world that with God's help and your prayers, I would do my best to be President of

all the people.

That was a difficult period of transition. A good and wise and courageous leader had started moving this country again, and he had been President of all the people. And he had given all that he had to give—his life—in the service of it. I promised my Maker and I promised my family if I were spared that as long as I occupied the position that he had left vacant I would carry on for him and for you, in his program and in your program, of peace and prosperity for all the people of all the world.

For 20 years we have had a bipartisan foreign policy and President Truman, with the help of Arthur Vandenberg, met the Communists at Greece and Turkey, and stood up and was counted, and we won. President Eisenhower, with the help of a Democratic Congress, and with the support of the then Democratic leader, Lyndon Johnson, stood up in the Strait of Formosa, and let the world know that freedom was on the march.

John F. Kennedy, with the support of the leaders of both parties, stood up in the Cuban missile crisis, and Mr. Khrushchev packed up his missiles and put them on his boat and took them home. And when they fired upon our destroyers in the Gulf of Tonkin, we made prompt, appropriate reply.

Now, I do not think that we can lead the world, as Luci says, I do not think we can unite other peoples, if we are divided ourselves. And I have done everything I know how to do to treat all Americans equally and alike and fair.

I have invited the leaders of both parties to give me their counsel and their wisdom and their support. I have invited all the States of the Union to share in the fruits of our efforts and to contribute everything they could to help us achieve peace in the world.

We are going through a critical time, and there are those who would conquer us by dividing us. But I am proud to say that they were in the minority in America during the first 11 months of my term as President, and they are going to be very much in the minority on November 3d.

We are going to continue to be the strongest nation in the world. We are going to keep our guard up, but our hand out. We are willing to go anywhere, any time, to talk to anyone, to do anything with honor to get peace in the world, and we are going to have prosperity at home. We are going to educate our children. We are going to have jobs for the people who want to work. We are going to improve our countryside. We are going to protect our farmers.

I may cut out the lights of the chandeliers in the White House, but we are not going to turn out REA in Louisiana!

I am going to repeat here in Louisiana what I have said in every State that I have appeared in, and what I said the night that I walked to the White House to take over the awesome responsibilities that were mine: As long as I am your President, I am going to be President of all the people.

We are not going to have any business government, we are not going to have any labor government, we are not going to have any farm government. We are going to have a government of all the people, and your President is going to protect the constitutional rights of every American.

Those that want to be fair and those that want to be just, and those that want to follow the Golden Rule of doing unto others as you would have them do unto you, we invite them to come and join us. Those that have other views are welcome to them, and this is a free country. They can express them as strongly as they want to with such vehemence as they may choose and we will listen, but we will not follow. Because this democratic land of ours is going to be a united land.

In the words of Robert E. Lee, I am going to say tonight, let's try to get our people to forget their old animosities and let us all be Americans.

It is wonderful to be back in New Orleans where I was in 1960. I thank you for your hospitality, for your understanding. I will appreciate your support and your help, and I will try to be worthy of your confidence.

Thank you.

NOTE: The President spoke shortly after 8 p.m. at the Union Station in New Orleans where Mrs. Johnson concluded her tour of the South begun at Alexandria, Va., on October 6 (see Item 628). In the course of her 4-day tour Mrs. Johnson visited 8 States, made 47 speeches, and covered more than 1600 miles.

In his opening words the President referred to Senators Allen J. Ellender and Russell B. Long, Governor John J. McKeithen, and Representative Hale Boggs, all of Louisiana.

The text of Mrs. Johnson's remarks, together with brief remarks by her daughter Luci who had joined the party in Charleston, S.C., was also released.

647   Further Statement by the President on Hurricane Hilda.   *October 9, 1964*

IF A STATE could be awarded a medal for coolness under fire, I would be here today to give one to Louisiana.

The evacuation of over 100,000 persons from the coastal areas in the 96-hour warning period before Hurricane Hilda struck was a miracle of organization. It was a tribute to the qualities of your State and community leaders, from Governor McKeithen on down. It was a great display of the courage of the people of the State of Louisiana.

Hilda was probably the best tracked and most accurately predicted hurricane in history. We had 4 full days' notice, which is enough time to prepare for the worst, and thereby to avoid much of the disastrous death toll of Hurricane Audrey in 1957, when 534 lives were lost.

This is an example of the way in which your Government makes the fullest use of modern technology in the interests of our people. Hurricane Hilda was under surveillance by four different land-based weather radars. The Tiros weather satellite provided valuable observation of the storm. Most important of all, Hurricane Hilda was traced by reconnaissance planes of the United States Air Force and the United States Weather Bureau. Those civilian employees of the United States Government were willing to risk their lives to probe the severe interior of the storm. They, too, deserve our praise.

From the moment the storm was dis-covered a wide range of Federal activities were begun. Even before the storm hit the coast, Federal disaster experts from the Office of Emergency Planning were dispatched to Louisiana from around the Nation.

During this preparatory period, and ever since, cooperation among Federal, State, and local officials was of the highest order.

As you know all too well, the property damage and the loss of life, while less than it might have been, was nonetheless a tragic loss.

Immediately upon receipt of Governor McKeithen's request for aid last Saturday afternoon, I declared a "major disaster." Within minutes of my declaration $1 million in Federal disaster relief funds was flowing to Louisiana. Long-term, low-interest loans under the Small Business Administration are available to individual victims of the hurricane, and teams from the Department of Agriculture and the United States Public Health Service have been on the scene to help you.

The American National Red Cross, through the efforts of dedicated volunteers, had provided shelter and sustenance to thousands of displaced persons.

You will not bear this tragedy alone. We will work together to restore your highways, repair your public facilities, and protect the health of your citizens.

We must continue to work to improve our weather warning services so that these devastating storms can be tracked and predicted even more accurately. The time has also come to find out whether there is any-

thing that can be done to diminish the destructive force of the storm itself.

NOTE: For the President's earlier statement on the effects of the hurricane, see Item 618.

648   Remarks at a Fundraising Dinner in New Orleans. *October 9, 1964*

Mr. Chairman; Governor McKeithen; your great senior Senator Allen Ellender, my old friend; your fine mayor, Mayor Schiro; Mrs. Long; my longtime and my valued friend and colleague, one of the most promising young men in this Nation, Russell Long; Congressman Willis, Congressman Morrison, Congressman Thompson, Congressman Gillis Long—all of whom serve this Nation and this State with great distinction and with credit to Louisiana and the Congress; Mr. Marshall Brown; Mr. Donelon—all my friends in Louisiana:

You have touched me with your generosity and your cordiality. I deeply appreciate the very fine welcome that you gave Lady Bird and Luci when they came in this evening. Every 4 years we seem to have a habit of coming home to New Orleans, and ending our trip on a whistlestop in this lovely, enterprising city. I, through the years, have always felt close to the people of Louisiana because I was born and reared in an adjoining State, in a neighboring State.

I have, as Russell said, spent some time in the Congress, and through those almost 30 years there the Louisiana representatives have always been fair, and just, and effective. I would much rather have them with me than against me, and I have had them both ways.

Finally—after having opposed Russell on two or three items, on various amendments, on my bill, just before they got ready to

pass them, he would get up and offer an amendment and take that left hand and talk Senators into voting for it—I finally just told the Secretary of the Senate that I was going to start voting for Russell's amendments—it was easier to join him than to fight him. And I have been doing that through the years now, and I have been signing his bills.

Senator Ellender gets me to do nearly everything he wants me to without any pilon or lagniappe. But when the going gets tough and he just really has to move heaven and earth, he will put on one of those good feeds of his and he will bring up some of this New Orleans candy that he makes, that we call pralines.

I thought he just reserved it for myself until the other day when I went over to have lunch at the White House and the table was empty, with just one plate there. I said, "Where in the world is Mrs. Johnson?" And they said, "She is up eating with Senator Ellender."

I said, "How long has she been gone?" And they said, "About 15 minutes."

So I put on my hat and invited myself. I went up there and I was the only man there except Allen, and he had all the pretty women in Washington up there in the room eating with him!

So this Louisiana delegation is something that I am very proud of, something that I have enjoyed working with. And I want to remind the people in New Orleans and all Louisiana what Mr. Rayburn said one time when they asked him why Texas had such a good, effective delegation in the Congress. He said, "Well, we pick them young, and we pick them honest. We send them there, and we keep them there."

The last 4 days I have followed that train trip through every yard of the South, and I have called three or four times a day myself just to see how everything was getting along. I don't need to tell you what great pride I have had in my wife and in my daughters and, most of all, in their affection for the people of their homeland and their willingness to come out and stand up on their tiptoes and look them straight in the eyes and tell them what they thought of them and how much we cared and how much we needed them. And I particularly appreciate the way you have reciprocated here in Louisiana.

Now, on this occasion, at the close of this week of our campaign, there ought to be grateful pride in the heart of every American. On the main streets of America, history is being made. From Maine to California, from the Midwest to the Deep South, the people of America are coming out. And they are coming out to stand up and be counted for their country.

On the streets of all sections we are seeing the largest crowds that we have ever seen in any election period. You know, and I think I know, what this means, and if you don't know what it means, I am going to tell you what it means.

Our cause is no longer the cause of a party alone. Our cause is the cause of a great Nation. Our cause is the cause of the country that you love. Our cause is the country that you would die for, and the people are laying down their partisanship.

They are asking us to take up their trust.

They are asking us to keep this Nation prosperous. They are asking us to keep this Nation progressive. They are asking us to keep this country, and all the world, at peace.

The party of the people will not fail the trust of the people. And our first trust is victory, itself, on November 3d, and that is what we are going to have.

Too much that is precious, too much that we prize, too much that is part of America itself is at stake for any Democrat, anyone who takes pride in being a Democrat, to rest these next 24 days.

This year, as in no year before, you work not as partisans for party, but you work as Americans for America. If victory is our first trust, no less a trust is the margin by which that victory is won.

If our position in the world is not to be weakened, if we are to spare ourselves wasteful years of antagonism and division, and animosity here at home, the American people on November 3d must give a decisive reply that will be understood and heard throughout the world. And make no mistake about it, the spotlight of the world is on you November 3d.

When victory is ours—for our country, not for ourselves—I want it to mean a mandate for beginning a new era in American affairs, an era of courage, an era of commonsense, and an era of American confidence.

When the next President takes the oath of office next year, it will be 20 years since the end of World War II. When that war ended, you remember and I have not forgotten what we were told.

Voices at home, and voices abroad, predicted:

—That depression would be inevitable.

—That communism would be irresistible.

—That war would be unavoidable.

And the American people listened and heard, but refused to accept those doctrines.

In hope, in faith, in confidence, we took our stand.

In the Full Employment Act of 1946 America made a commitment against depression—and made a commitment for prosperity—here at home.

In the Truman doctrine and the Marshall plan of 1948 we made our commitment against the spread of communism and for the strength of freedom throughout the world.

In all that we did, we honored our oldest commitment as a Nation and as a people, against war and for peace.

The years have been long. The trials have been many.

The burdens have been great. But the times are beginning to respond to America's steadfast purpose.

This administration is the first in a century not to experience a recession or a depression. This administration is the first since midcentury under which no Nation in the world has fallen to communism. This administration is the first of the postwar age to offer a record not only of peace preserved but of peace courageously and effectively pursued.

What the American people set out to do is coming true.

Others would have you believe that prosperity is false. Well, ask yourselves or your wife when you go home tonight if that is true. You know it is real.

Others would have you believe that freedom is faltering, but you know that you are freer now than you were when you were 21. And the yoke of dictatorship and the yoke of colonialism is being thrown off of nations all around the world, and new nations are being born, and independence and freedom are on the march.

Others would have you believe that the pursuit of peace is unworthy work, but you know it is the most noble work that any nation can do.

The point that I am making is simply this: The meaning of our victory in November will be just this—to assure this confident people of leadership with confidence to match their own. There is work to do, and we can either do it together, united, or we can do it divided, eating on each other.

The platform on which I stand says: "The Federal Government exists not to grow larger, but to enlarge the individual potential and achievement of the people. The Federal Government exists not to subordinate the States, but to support them."

I quote the words, but I might offer them as my own, for those words I wrote into the platform. Those words are my beliefs and they have been my beliefs all my life. For so long as I serve in the White House, your Government will be dedicated not to encroaching upon the rights of the States, but to helping the States meet their responsibilities to their own people.

Let me be specific.

If we are to heal our history and make this Nation whole, prosperity must know no Mason-Dixon line and opportunity must know no color line. Robert E. Lee, a great son of the South, a great leader of the South—and I assume no modern day leader would question him or challenge him— Robert E. Lee counseled us well when he told us to cast off our animosities, and raise our sons to be Americans.

From the tip of Texas to the tip of Florida, this crescent of the Gulf offers one of the great opportunities of the Western World. I want to see that opportunity fulfilled.

I want us to wipe poverty off the face of the South—and off the conscience of the Nation.

I want us to assure our young the best of

education at every level, and the expectation of a good job in their home State when their school years are through.

I want us to assure our aged that when they need hospital care they will have it, and they will have paid for it in advance, by themselves, and with the help of their employers, under social security.

I may turn out the lights in the White House chandeliers but I am determined that no one will turn out the lights of the REA in the farmhouses of Louisiana.

I so much want us to maintain a prosperous, free enterprise economy, so your Governor can continue bringing in new plants and new payrolls and new jobs in the north and in the south of your State.

Yes, I see a day, and I know that you see it, too, when New Orleans will stand as a Queen City on this crescent.

—A center of trade with the world.

—A center of culture for the Nation.

—A terminal for waterways reaching the heart of America.

—A port for the spaceships that are returning from outer space.

—A good and gracious city for your families to call their home.

We are not going to lose that tomorrow in divisions over things of the past. For all America, that will be the meaning of the victory that we seek November 3d.

We are going to show the courage to unite America, the commonsense to keep America strong and prepared, and the confidence to seek after peace for the lives of our own people and the lives of all mankind.

Courage, commonsense, and confidence— those are the qualities that will serve our country's cause, and in this election our country's cause is the cause that we are determined to carry to victory.

When I became Democratic leader after General Eisenhower had sent the party of which I was a member to a terrible defeat in 1952, I told the Members of the Senate who were in the Democratic caucus that I was a free man first, an American second, a Senator third, and a Democrat fourth, in that order; that when my President was right and when he spoke for all America and when he sought to unite us against a common enemy, he would have my support.

When I thought he was wrong, I would oppose him with decency and dignity, and I would give him my reasons for it, and I would try to suggest an alternative. But I would never personally attack him or assassinate him or talk about his wife or his children or his dogs.

I kept that pledge, and for 8 years I served as leader of the Senate during a period that we had a Republican President and a Democratic Congress. And every election, every 2 years, they rewarded us by increasing my majority. The people of America want public servants in America to do what is best for their country first, and if they do what is best for their country, they will do what is best for themselves.

When I was called upon in a matter of moments to assume the awesome responsibilities of the Presidency following that tragic day in Dallas, I said to the people of this Nation and the world that with God's help and with your prayers I will do my dead-level best. I have done that.

I have spent long hours, I have worked hard, I have worked with a clear conscience, I have done everything that I could with the talents that the good Lord gave me to try to unite this country and to try to have peace in the world.

We had a crisis in Panama a few days after I went in and they shot our soldiers. We had a crisis in Guantanamo, and some of our people in the country hollered, "Let's send the Marines in," and I said, "No, we will send the admiral in to cut the water off instead of a Marine in to turn it on."

We had our ships fired on in the Tonkin Gulf, and we made a prompt reply, an appropriate reply. But we have never lost our heart and I hope we will never lose our head. We are going to keep our eyes in the stars, but we are going to keep our feet on the ground.

I think it is a wonderful thing for Louisiana to do, to give us this dinner tonight. I am proud of your delegation. I am especially grateful to Hale and Lindy Boggs and Tommy for all the hard work and days that they spent with Lady Bird, Luci, and Lynda, helping them through these States that we love.

I don't want to conclude this talk, though, without telling you that some of my political philosophy was born in this State. As a young secretary, I came to New Orleans before I ever went to Washington. I saw something about the political history of Louisiana. And I saw a man who was frequently praised, and a man who was frequently harassed and criticized, and I became an admirer of his because I thought he had a heart for the people.

When I went to Washington in the dark days of the depression as a young country kid from the poor hills of Texas, I had a standing rule with the page office that every time Senator Long took the floor, he would call me on the phone and I would go over there and perch in the Gallery and listen to every word he said. And I heard them all.

I heard a lot about the history of this State. I heard a lot of names in this State. But I never heard him make a speech that I didn't think was calculated to do some good for some people who needed some speeches made for them and couldn't make them for themselves.

The things that I am talking about from coast to coast—I talked to six New England States last week and I am going to speak in six western States next week—the things I am talking about from coast to coast tonight and tomorrow and next week are the things that he talked about 30 years ago.

He thought that every man had a right to a job, and that was long before the Full Employment Act.

He thought that every boy and girl ought to have a chance for all the education they could take, and that is before the GI bill of rights.

He thought that the old folks ought to have social security and old age pensions, and I remember when he just scared the dickens out of Mr. Roosevelt and went on a nationwide radio hookup talking for old folks' pensions. And out of this probably came our social security system.

He believed in medical care for those so that they could live in decency and dignity in their declining years, without their children having to come and move them into their house with them. He was against poverty and hated it with all his soul and spoke until his voice was hoarse.

Well, like Jack Kennedy, he believed in those same things. But their voices are still tonight, but they have left some to carry on. And as long as the good Lord permits me, I am going to carry on.

Now, the people that would use us and destroy us first divide us. There is not any combination in the country that can take on Russell Long, Allen Ellender, Lyndon Johnson, and a few others if we are together. But if they divide us, they can make some hay. And all these years they have kept their foot on our necks by appealing to our animosities, and dividing us.

Whatever your views are, we have a Constitution and we have a Bill of Rights, and we have the law of the land, and two-thirds of the Democrats in the Senate voted for it and three-fourths of the Republicans. I signed it, and I am going to enforce it, and I am going to observe it, and I think any man that is worthy of the high office of President is going to do the same thing.

But I am not going to let them build up the hate and try to buy my people by appealing to their prejudice. I heard a great son of Texas who came from an adjoining State, whose name I won't call, but he was expelled from the university over there and he started West, and he got to Texas as a boy and stopped to see a schoolmate of his.

He liked things so well in Texas that he just decided to make it his permanent address. In 4 years he went to the Congress. After he had been in the House 2 years, he became the Democratic leader, and he served a few years as Democratic leader. And he went to the Senate and he served in the Senate 4 years and he became the Democratic leader in the Senate. He served the district that Mr. Rayburn later served.

When Mr. Rayburn came up as a young boy of the House, he went over to see the old Senator, the leader, one evening, who had come from this Southern State, and he was talking about economic problems. He was talking about how we had been at the mercy of certain economic interests, and how they had exploited us. They had worked our women for 5 cents an hour, they had worked our men for a dollar a day, they had exploited our soil, they had let our resources go to waste, they had taken everything out of the ground they could, and they had shipped it to other sections.

He was talking about the economy and what a great future we could have in the South, if we could just meet our economic problems, if we could just take a look at the resources of the South and develop them. And he said, "Sammy, I wish I felt a little better. I would like to go back to old"— and I won't call the name of the State; it wasn't Louisiana and it wasn't Texas—"I would like to go back down there and make them one more Democratic speech. I just feel like I have one in me. The poor old State, they haven't heard a Democratic speech in 30 years. All they ever hear at election time is Negro, Negro, Negro!"

So we have the law of the land, and we are going to appeal to all Americans that fight in uniform and work in factory and on the farm to try to conduct themselves as Americans. Equal opportunity for all, special privileges for none, because there is only one real big problem that faces you. It is not even the economic problem and it is not the Negro problem.

The only problem that faces you is whether you are going to live or die, and whether your family is going to live or die.

I sat through 37 meetings of the National Security Council during the Cuban crisis. I never left home in the morning but what I realized I might not ever see her again that day. She might not be there or I might not be there. I sat at that table with the most trained generals and admirals we had, with four and five stars, and their war maps were out, and they took us from this stage to that stage, and we had our fleet moving, and we had our planes in the sky, and we had them loaded with our bombs. And we knew they had their missiles pointing at us.

And the coolest man in that room, whose thumb was sitting there that could be put on the button, was the Commander in Chief, John Fitzgerald Kennedy, who had been abused all over that country.

He is not here to defend himself, but I say shame on you that in his absence would attribute to him unworthy motives.

At Oak Ridge we have developed the mightiest, most awesome power that human ingenuity could contemplate or conceive. By a thumb on a button you can wipe out 300 million lives in a matter of moments. And this is no time and no hour and no day to be rattling your rockets around. Or clicking your heels like a storm trooper.

I say that because this is a moment when all nations must look all ways to try to find some ways and means to learn to live together without destroying each other. I have no reference to any nation, any country, or any individual. I just say that when you look at history, and you see what has happened to us in our lifetime, we have gone through two wars, and then you see what the next war could bring us, it is no time to preach division or hate.

If there ever was a time for us to try to unite and find areas of agreement, it is now. We are the mightiest nation in all the world, but that power must be used to prevent a war, instead of starting one.

I don't want to imply that there is any man in my party that wants to start one or anyone in any other party that wants to start one. I think the Republicans are just as patriotic as the Democrats. And I haven't met any man that I know that I think wants to involve this country in any danger that he can avoid.

I just say it is time for all of us to put on our thinking caps. It is time for all of us to follow the Golden Rule. It is time for all of us to have a little trust and a little faith in each other, and to try to find some areas that we can agree on so we can have a united program.

I told you about the support that Vandenberg gave Truman in Greece and Turkey, about the support that I gave Eisenhower, Republican and Democrat, about the support that President Kennedy received in the Cuban missile crisis. And this is an hour when we must not become so bitter or so divided or hate each other so much in an election period that we will let the other nations think we are divided.

The Kaiser thought we were divided and wouldn't go to war and he sank the Lusitania and we became involved. Hitler thought we were divided because a few Senators were preaching isolationism and talking about munitions makers and he thought that he could take a part of the world and we would sit there in our rocking chairs and do nothing about it. And he got fooled.

Let no would-be conqueror ever mistake Uncle Sam. We do not seek any wars. But we are prepared and ready and willing to defend our freedom. And we are not about to yield it or sacrifice it or whittle it away to anybody.

The election is coming up November the 3d. You have your choice. You have two parties. You have two tickets. You have men on both tickets who are experienced in the Congress, who served there many years. You don't have to have anybody come down here and tell you what is right. You don't have to have anybody come down here and tell you what you ought to do. You know what is best for you, and you go do it. And I am not even going to make a recommendation to you.

If you think in your own heart that the course of wisdom for your country is this course, then you follow whatever you think it is. Because I believe that every other man is actuated by the same motives that I think I am actuated by. He wants to do what is right.

I have never seen a man in Congress that I thought went there on a platform of doing what is wrong. He wants to do what is right. And I know the people of Louisiana want to do what is right.

And I hope if you do what you think is

right, that somehow or other it is the same thing that I think is right. But if it is not, I won't question your patriotism, I won't question your Americanism, I won't question your ancestry. I may quietly in the sanctity of our bedroom whisper to Lady Bird my own personal opinion about your judgment.

NOTE: The President spoke at 9:40 p.m. in the Grand Ballroom at the Jung Hotel in New Orleans. In his opening remarks he referred to the chairman of the dinner, Ray Morvant, State Director, U.S. Savings Bond Division, Department of the Treasury, Governor John J. McKeithen of Louisiana, Senator Allen J. Ellender of Louisiana, Mayor Victor H. Schiro of New Orleans, Senator and Mrs. Russell B. Long and Representatives Edwin E. Willis, James H. Morrison, T. A. Thompson, and Gillis W. Long, all of Louisiana, Marshall Brown, Louisiana State Democratic committeeman, and Thomas F. Donelon, president of Jefferson Parish, Louisiana. Later he referred to Representative Hale Boggs of Louisiana and Mrs. Boggs, and their son Tommy. He also referred to Huey P. Long, U.S. Senator from Louisiana from 1932 to 1935 and father of Senator Russell B. Long.

649 Remarks Upon Arrival at the Phoenix Airport. *October 11, 1964*

Ladies and gentlemen, boys and girls:

I want to say a deep thank you from the bottom of my heart for your warm welcome to this wonderful State of sunshine here in Arizona.

This is not a day for politics. This is a day for God, and since this is God's day I will leave very shortly and go with my old and longtime friend, Roy Elson, down to hear his preacher. He recommends him pretty highly, and I want to see if he is as good as the preacher I would have heard at Johnson City had I gone to church at home this morning.

The reason I didn't go to church at home this morning was because that beloved and venerable and wonderful man, than whom there is no other like him in all the world, Carl Hayden, the Chairman of the Appropriations Committee, said to me, "I think if you are going from your ranch in Texas to the sidewalks of San Francisco, you better not do it without stopping in Arizona."

And when the Chairman of the powerful Appropriations Committee makes a slight suggestion to the President, I hope the President is smart enough, and I know he loves Carl Hayden enough, that his suggestion is my command. So here I am.

I want to thank Governor Fannin and Governor McFarland, my old boss that taught me so much and I love so much, and Edna, for coming out here to meet me.

I want to tell you how grateful I am that Arizona furnishes one of our Cabinet members, Stewart Udall, and his lovely wife, and I am very proud of him. He is doing a wonderful job. We have done the best work on water and on power and on conservation that has been done any years since I have been in Washington. This has really been the conservation Congress.

I want to thank Congressman Udall and Congressman Senner for coming here and welcoming me this morning. I am going to leave with Roy now in just a moment and I won't be seeing you any more, but I am coming back to these wonderful, happy, smiling faces, and this dry air and this fine sunshine because it is good and it invigorates you. It makes you count all your blessings and think about really how fortunate we are to be Americans.

Now, all of you people out here have faith

and have hope and have vision or you wouldn't be in this "Promised Land of Arizona." If you were afraid, and if you were doubters, and if you didn't have vision, you would be in some ghost town somewhere instead of a State like Arizona and a city like Phoenix that is a "Go-Go State" and a "Go-Go City." Do you know that by the year 2000—and we are really closer to the year 2000 now than we are to the year 1918 when we had our "last" war, even when I was born, 1908, we are pretty close to the year 2000—in the year 2000 Arizona's growth will be twice what it is in the rest of the Nation, the Nation's average. I don't want that to be repeated out where it gets back and drifts back over into Texas because some of my opponents over there will be saying I said Arizona is twice as good as Texas, and I don't want to say that.

But I do say that your resources, your people, your management, your faith, your vision, your 20th century methods, your modern ideas, your great electronic industry and other industries that are coming to Arizona—that you will be growing twice as fast as the rest of the Nation in the year 2000.

You have one problem, and it is a mighty big problem. [*Laughter*] No, no, now. I told you this wasn't going to be a political day and it is not. You get the wrong impression. Now wait a minute.

You have one big problem, and that problem is—water.

I never go down a corridor of the Capitol that Roy Elson doesn't catch me by my coattail and say, "Can't you help us with the problem of water in Arizona?" I never went into the Appropriations Committee but what Carl Hayden didn't catch me by the lapels of my coat.

I am not that intimate with your other Senator, and I didn't come out here to advertise

him. But I do want to be fair and frank. He has talked to me a good many times about your water problem, and he wants to help on it. And he has wired me, urging me to take certain action in connection with water for Arizona. So it is not a partisan thing between Democrats and Republicans and Independents. We all have to find an answer to this water problem because that is going to be the answer to the 20th century.

I will tell you what I am going to do about it. We are going to continue under the program that Stewart Udall has working now, and we are making progress on it every day. In your child's lifetime, if not in yours, and I think in yours, but in your child's lifetime we are going to be using the water from the sea to make the deserts bloom.

Just think about what a wonderful land this will be when all the people are smiling and happy, when all the grass is green and we have nothing but a beautiful vista on the mountainside, where our cattle and our sheep can graze and our children can play.

Now, that is the kind of a world that we want.

I want to leave you with just one little thought for today. I am not your preacher, and I hope you all go on from here to church. But I want to just leave this thought with you: A great man named Abraham Lincoln, of another party, said, "I trust, sir"—when someone said to him, "I trust, sir"—meaning President Lincoln, "that God is on our side," in a very hectic period in our national life, Lincoln replied, "Well, let us hope that we are on God's side."

What I want to say to you this morning is that all of you made great sacrifices to come out here and be courteous to me and be kind to me. I don't interpret it any other way. I think that you are really warm, and I hope not only that God is on our side, but I do hope that all of you are on God's side.

Thank you very much.

NOTE: The President spoke at 9 a.m. at the airport in Phoenix, Ariz. During the course of his remarks he referred to Roy L. Elson, Administrative Assistant to Senator Carl Hayden of Arizona and Democratic candidate for Senator, the Reverend Dr.

Charles R. Ehrhardt, pastor of the First Presbyterian Church of Phoenix, and Senator Carl Hayden. He also referred to Governor Paul Fannin, former Governor Ernest W. McFarland, who served as Senate majority leader during the 82d Congress, and his wife, Edna, Secretary of the Interior and Mrs. Stewart L. Udall and Representatives Morris K. Udall and George F. Senner, Jr., all of Arizona.

650   Remarks at the Municipal Park, South Gate, California.   *October 11, 1964*

Mr. Chairman, Governor Brown, Senator Salinger, Congressman Van Petten, Congressman Holifield, and other Members of the California delegation on the platform, my fellow Democrats, my beloved Americans, ladies and gentlemen:

Oh, what a wonderful morning! My what a wonderful day!

Back in my boyhood, we had breakfast at home on Sunday morning, then we went down the road to church, then we had dinner-on-the-ground in front of the Pedernales River.

This morning we had breakfast at home in Texas, we flew out by jet and went to church in Arizona, and now we have come all the way out to the shores of the Pacific to have dinner-on-the-ground. And it is a late dinner, too, I will tell you that.

I am sorry, but when people are good enough and kind enough and friendly enough to leave their homes on the Sabbath Day and come out to wave a welcome to you, you just can't drive by them in a big car and not see them and not shake hands with them and not thank them. And I have been doing that. I know you understand it. I hope you will accept my apology.

When I finished high school back in 1924, I came out to California looking for a job. I am happy to say to you now that I am employed full time right now. I have the

best employers in the world, and when my contract is up for renewal I hope you will be satisfied with my performance.

But I didn't ride all the way to California to talk about today. I have come out here to talk to you about the future. Because the future must be the first concern of all Americans in all of our States, just as the future has been your concern in the greatest State and the largest State in the Union, the State of California.

Most of you remember learning long ago that great parable about those who used the talents given to them and were called wise, and those who only hoarded their talents and did not use them were called foolish.

This generation of Americans is talented. As free men and women, enjoying the blessings of peace—and you ought to be thankful that you have peace—enjoying the blessings of prosperity, and there has been a day when we didn't have these prosperous conditions, I believe that each of us bears a deep moral obligation to make use of our talents and to prepare our country for the future and prepare our children for the future.

When the next President of the United States takes the oath of office next January, the year 2000 will be closer to us than the year 1929.

In the years between now and then, our

population will have grown by 140 million people.

Americans will be living longer than they ever lived before. I shook hands with a lady in Gary, Ind., the other day who is 116 years old, and she is voting for the first time this year. She is a Negro lady that lived in a State that had not been allowed to vote, but she is voting this year.

Most of the killing diseases that we know now, like cancer, heart condition, and strokes, that have gone on before us, will be unknown. Men and women are going to be living to be 90 or 100 years old, and they will be able to work all those years.

Long before then, America is going to be a land of young people. In only a few short years, half of our population in the United States is going to be under 25.

So if America is to mean for those who come after us what it means to you, you have a lot of work to do.

Now, what do you have to do? You have schools to build; you have teachers to hire; you have cities to improve; you have resources to develop; you have rivers to harness; you have new fields to plow; you have new horizons up there to explore.

Over the next three decades, the next 30 years, one horizon beckoning to us will be the sea around us. To a far greater extent than you realize, the sea, s-e-a, will be a center of most intensive exploration. We shall learn to travel across it at speeds of 100 miles per hour or more. We shall learn to carry larger quantities of goods beneath it in efficient cargo submarines. We shall learn to make much more extensive and profitable use of the products of the sea. We shall learn how to farm the beds of the sea, to feed two mouths around the world where now we feed only one mouth.

We have a moral obligation to begin meeting that now.

Out here in the West, other generations learned the hard lesson of squandering our resources. So we must conserve our resources. We must conserve our wealth. We must conserve our values and our heritage.

We must keep America strong militarily, and we shall. We must keep American momentum strong and keep it going, and we shall.

We shall permit no godless "ism" to bury America by force. And neither shall we permit any system that is alien to individual freedom to overtake us by greater dedication or zeal, or purpose, or extremism.

We must use our heads to guide us in doing the work that our heart tells us has to be done. We must keep our eyes in the stars but keep our feet on the ground.

These works can be done only if we live together, if we work together, if we move forward together as one Nation and as one people. "United we stand, divided we will fall."

The time has come in our national life for us to be together, not apart. It is time to bind our wounds and heal our history and make this Nation one nation, indivisible.

America cannot stand strong at home or in the world if her people struggle against one another on the quicksand of suspicion or cynicism or hate. We must do away with our fears and our doubts, and we must embrace our vision and our hopes. We must be a nation of lovers, not a nation of haters. We must be a nation of builders, not a nation of destroyers. We must be a nation where all men have equal opportunity and none have special privilege.

America cannot stand strong at home, and America cannot stand strong in the world if her people fight each other, if we struggle against each other, because if we are to be the peacemakers, and if we are to lead the world, we must strive to keep the peace of our own lives, of our own people here at home. We cannot be the peacemakers of the world if business is fighting labor, if labor is fighting the farmer, if the Government is fighting all three.

So I have tried, as your President, since that tragic day when our beloved President was taken from us, I have tried as best I could, with the talents that the good Lord gave me. I have done everything I knew how to heal this Nation. I have never preached hate, I have never preached doubt, I have never preached fear, I have never preached division, I have never tried to array class against class, group against group, race against race, or religion against religion, and I never will.

If we are to be the champions of freedom for individual man everywhere or anywhere, we must be champions for freedom at home. We must be champions among the poor and among the rich. We must be just as willing to protect the constitutional rights of a poor man as we are willing to protect the private rights of a rich man.

So among the poor and the rich alike, among the weak and the strong alike, among the silent citizens as well as among those who raise their voices the loudest, I want each and every American of whatever faith, of whatever color, of whatever religion, of whatever party, to know as long as I am carrying on for John Fitzgerald Kennedy, as long as I am President of the United States, I am going to be the President of all the people.

But I want you to know this: that no one person, not even with Lady Bird and Lynda Bird and Luci Baines to help him, can lead this Nation by himself. That night I returned to that empty White House, that room that was vacant because our leader had fallen, I said to the American people on the television that with God's help and with your prayers, I would do my best. I have done my best.

Our beloved President had a program for all the people of America. It included mass transportation, it included reduction of taxes, it included economy in Government, it included a farm bill, it included equal employment, it included poverty, it included civil rights, it included space, it included technology, it included science, it included the heart disease, the cancer program, the libraries, and education of our children.

I counted those bills. President Kennedy, when he was taken from us, had 51 major measures for the people, p-e-e-p-l-e, p-e-e-p-u-l. I mean the great mass of human nature that make up 190 million, and they have one leader. They just have one President. I am the only President you have.

But he had 51 bills there and we picked up on a moment's notice. We couldn't go to the library and look anything up. We couldn't debate and decide whether we wanted to or not. We had to take part in that transition. The world was watching us to see what would happen to this country when it had lost its leader. We had to make decisions and we had to move. And we did move, and we have moved.

Last Friday night, sitting there in the White House about midnight, I looked over that list of 51 major measures. The Congress had come; the Congress had gone. The tax bill had been passed and the citizens had been given back $12 billion. We had more people working than ever before in history—72 million. The businessman made $12 billion more this year after taxes than he made when Mr. Kennedy took over. The laborers, the workingmen, made $60 billion more after taxes than they did when Mr. Kennedy took over. More people were working than ever worked before. We had the greatest prosperity in history.

I looked at those 51 bills, and so help me, we had passed each and every one of the 51 through the United States Senate. They have said some ugly things about us on the way, and they had not given me too good recommendations, some of the members of the other party. But I want to tell you this: I came out here today to thank you people of California for giving me Pat Brown to help me. He has, as your Governor, and I am grateful.

I want to tell you something else: I told you I couldn't do this by myself. And right in a pinch, when we needed him, when we lost one of the best friends I ever had, Clair Engle, he gave me Pierre Salinger, who has been my strong right arm. This is something I want you to put down in your noggin. I want you to put it in your notebook and I don't want you to forget it. If you are going to forget it—some of you are forgetful people, I know that—but if you are going to forget it, don't forget it before November 3d.

I want you to send Pierre Salinger back to the United States Senate, because California, the coming State, the State that is on the move, the modern State, the 20th century State, California needs Pierre Salinger. But the President needs him, too. And you can't do any good just passing them in one House. You have to pass them not only in the Senate but in the House, too, and Van is the man. Come up here, Van. All the way with Van the man.

On this day I have much to be thankful for. I saw my old friend Chet Holifield. He nominated me for Vice President here in California. I came out here to seek my fortune. I never could find it. I worked out here 2 years, 1924, and I went back to Texas. That was your gain, I guess, and Texas' loss. But anyway, I am coming back here again after November, if you invite me.

If you don't invite me, I am going to be like the little boy down in my country that didn't get the invitation to the ball. I am just going to sit down and write myself one.

On this day, though, let us remember that the happiest days of the week are the Sundays, the days when families can be together, the days when we can be home with our loved ones, the days when we can be out in the park enjoying the rest and recreation, because we are working fewer hours per day and fewer days per week.

The happiest years of our lives that are ahead of us will be those years when we at last are together, together as one Nation, together as one people. We cannot have peace in this world if we are divided. We cannot unite other peoples until we unite ourselves.

Do you know that the Commander in Chief of this country and the leader of the Soviet Union hold the mightiest, the most awesome, the most frightening power at their thumb tips that any person could imagine?

I sat in 37 meetings in the National Security Council with President Kennedy during the Cuban missile crisis. I saw the men come in with the stars and the admirals come in with their braid and I saw them make their recommendations. And I saw a solemn Secretary of State, a wise and good man, and he said, "We are eyeball to eyeball." There were Mr. Khrushchev and his missiles in Cuba, 90 miles away, pointed at us. Our planes were ordered off the ground with their bomb bays loaded. Our whole military force was shifted in this country, moved in one direction. And every morning when I left home I didn't know if I would see my wife again that night.

But I am proud to say to you, because he can't be here to defend himself, that the wisest and the coolest man that sat at that table was the President of the United States, John Fitzgerald Kennedy.

It adds no luster to a man's statesmanship, and it is no tribute to a man's character, to refuse to give John Fitzgerald Kennedy the credit that he is justly entitled to, when he is not here to claim it for himself.

So I am not trying to improve my character; I am trying to be just and fair and honest, and say to you this: In the 11 months that I have had this awesome responsibility, I have had forces shooting our soldiers in Panama, I have had them cutting off our water in Guantanamo, and some men getting excited and saying, "Send in the Marines." I have seen our men die in Viet-Nam and I have seen our destroyers fired upon in the Tonkin Gulf.

I have been required to make the firm decision that when those destroyers were fired upon for us to destroy them and make appropriate reply. And we did. But the only thing that is really important to you good people in this park today is your families, your future, your prosperity, your job, your loved ones. But all of that goes down the drain, all of that goes poof, up in one blow.

The only thing that counts is peace in the world—peace, peace, peace, and you better work at it, and you better help others work at it, and you better support it.

You are not going to get peace in the world by rattling your rockets. You can't have government by ultimatum. I remember when I was a young fellow and pretty impulsive—I don't like to use that word because some people think I am taking a jab at somebody else, but I am not. Young men, most of them, are impulsive. I said one time when I got in a fight with a head of a power company that wouldn't let me build a little REA line in my country district in Texas, I said, "As far as I am concerned, you

can take a running jump and go straight to—" and everybody applauded me, and the board of directors thought I was brave and great. One old man, though, the general counsel, who had been a lawyer a long time, and mighty wise, and had been in a lot of fights, he didn't applaud. He just looked serious. He was an ex-Senator.

I said, "Senator, what did you think of my speech?" He said, "Come by my office, and I will tell you."

I went by his office and I said, "Senator, what did you think of my speech?" He said, "Young man, you are just in public life, you are just starting. I hope you are in it a long time. I hope you go a long way. I am going to try to help you, but the first thing you have to learn is this: telling a man to go to hell and then making him go are two different propositions."

He said, "First of all, it is hot down there and the average fellow doesn't want to go, and when you tell him he has to go, he just bristles up, and he is a lot less likely to go than if you hadn't told him anything. What you better do is get out the Good Book that your mama used to read to you and go back to the prophet Isaiah and read what he said. He said, 'Come now, let us reason together.'"

I don't know how many old soldiers I am looking at, and I don't know how many boys out there are going to be taken away from their mothers and called into uniform. But so far as I am concerned, I am one President that had rather reason and talk than fight. Fight I will, if fight I must, or if fight I need to, but I just won't do it as a Sunday afternoon exercise just to entertain somebody. We live in a world with 120 nations, and each one of those nations has its own idea about what is best for its own people.

There are men of different colors, men of

different languages, men of different religions. Some of them are short men, some are tall men, some are fat men, some are slender men. I am trying to learn how to live with them without putting my finger on a button that would destroy humanity.

Do you know what the might that came out of Oak Ridge is? Do you know what that is? Do you know that in a matter of moments we can destroy the lives of 300 million people? Do you know in a matter of hours 100 million people, more than half of the United States, would be wiped out?

Do you know that yesterday was the first anniversary of the test ban treaty that President Kennedy got 108 nations to sign?

I am going to talk about that treaty next Thursday night. I want every one of you to listen, because it is pretty important to you mothers, because the danger that you faced of your unborn children has passed on. The danger you faced with your children drinking that milk has been lessened. The danger in the air you breathe and the food you eat, the radioactive particles in the atmosphere have been lessened, because of the wisdom and the patience of John Fitzgerald Kennedy and the other men who supported him.

We are the strongest, the mightiest Nation in all the world, and we are going to continue to be. We seek no large war, we covet no one's land. We seek only freedom in the world. We remind you that of all the new nations that have been born, of all the countries that have thrown off colonialism, of all the nations that have their new independence—and they add up into the dozens—not a single one of these new ones has embraced communism.

I would remind you of something else when you want to feel sorry for yourself and get to be a martyr and think about how bad America is. Ask yourself what other country you think is better. I just tell you. I don't know what plane you want to take or what continent you want to go to, but I will tell you this: I have been to all of them, and wherever your plane lands when you leave here, you can fill it up with local folks on a return flight if they can get into America. The last nation to embrace communism was Cuba in 1959.

We have a bipartisan foreign policy and it has been working reasonably well for 20 years and we want to improve it and strengthen it. We want men of good will of both parties to help with it.

We have a prosperous community, we have a prosperous Nation, more people working, better jobs, more pay. We have a frugal, economical Government. I cut a billion dollars this year under last year's budget, and I took the Kennedy budget that I inherited and I cut it $1 billion 100 million before I wrote my own budget and cut it. We have 25,000 less people working for the Federal Government on the Federal payroll today, this July, than we had last July a year ago. We have cut our taxes $12 billion and returned it to our taxpayers.

We are taking our poverty program, because of installations that were obsolete, that we didn't need, that we closed up, and we took the money for poverty and we are going to make taxpayers out of these young men that have been taxeaters on our daddy's relief rolls.

We have the finest, the mightiest, the happiest nation in all the world, and we ought to be ashamed of ourselves when we hear these crybabies coming around talking about what is wrong.

You have a water problem that we have to solve. You have some other problems— to get jobs for people in California, because every day that that calendar ticks, you have to find thousands of more jobs for your increasing population. The first thing you know you are going to be twice as large as you are. In the year 2000 the average family income in the State of California is going to be $15,000 a year.

I remember the first President I ever saw, and the greatest President I ever knew. I saw him stand up one day in his braces, with pain in his legs, and anguish in his face, but vision in his head and hope in his eyes. I saw him talk to almost this many people, maybe more. It was a rainy, cold day in March 1933. The banks were popping in the country just like popcorn, just like firecrackers going off at Christmastime. They were closing.

The railroad men had come running down to Washington and the insurance companies and all these captains of finance, all these smart conservatives, and the roof had caved in. People were burning their corn. Cotton was selling for 5 cents. You couldn't find a job and relief lines were longer than from here to that airport I landed at, and that is 15 miles away.

But this man stood up in that time when things weren't near as good as they are today, with the braces on his legs, out of his wheelchair, and he grabbed that microphone, and he stuck his chin up, and his jaw out, and he said, "The only thing we have to fear is fear itself," and he electrified a nation, and he saved a republic.

I say to you today, in the presence of his wonderful son Jimmy Roosevelt, who sits on this platform, that we must cast away the shadows of doubt and these harassing fears that frustrate some of our citizens. We must ask them to take them back down to the basement and we will put them on sale next month when business is not so good.

The only thing that America has to fear is fear itself. And if I know anything about America, and I have traveled in 33 States, Americans are unafraid.

Goodby, goodby. God bless all of you.

NOTE: The President spoke at 2:50 p.m. at a rally in South Gate Municipal Park, South Gate, Calif. In his opening words he referred to Richard English, Los Angeles attorney who served as chairman of the rally program, Governor Edmund G. Brown, Senator Pierre E. G. Salinger, Harry O. Van Petten, Democratic candidate for Representative, and Representative Chet Holifield, all of California. Later he referred to Representative James Roosevelt and the late Senator Clair Engle, of California.

651 Remarks in Washington Square, San Francisco. *October 11, 1964*

Mr. Chairman, Governor Brown, Mr. Ambassador, Senator Salinger, Congressman Burton, Mayor Shelley, ladies and gentlemen:

I have just taken the most memorable Sunday afternoon drive of my whole life.

There are very few cities in the United States where so many citizens come out and wave and shout when their mayor goes by. But the same thing seems to happen every time I ride with Mayor Shelley.

I want to make one thing clear, on behalf of Governor Brown, Senator Salinger, Congressman Burton, and myself: We don't usually enjoy bringing up the rear as much as we did bringing it up today.

This great and gracious city has much of which it can be proud. But the real glory of this city of the Golden Gate is the strength and the unity that is forged here from such rich diversity among your people.

Together we honor a very proud day for America and around the world. All the world could well pause to honor Columbus

Day. He found the first real home for the human spirit.

For five centuries the world has been responding to the opportunity opened by the voyage of that honored son of Italy. The pace has not always been swift. The course of human progress has not always been sure. But since the opportunity of this new world became known to man, he has lifted himself up to stand a little taller each year, to walk a little prouder generation by generation. He has become the master and not the slave of his environment.

Because there was a land of opportunity, man has moved bodily, boldly, and confidently toward freedom. Man has moved toward justice, and he has moved toward lasting peace.

Today the great opportunity is peace. This moment began to form 20 years ago here in San Francisco. For so long as there is human life, your city will be remembered and your city will be revered as the birthplace of the United Nations.

This moment found substance 1 year ago yesterday when nations first agreed to limit the testing of nuclear weapons in the earth's atmosphere. The air that we breathe here, the air that free men and their loved ones breathe in other lands, is cleaner, human life is safer, because of the test ban treaty that was proposed and passed by a great leader and accepted by 108 other nations, and that great leader was John Fitzgerald Kennedy.

Today, we and all the world are beginning to sail on high seas of new discovery. Man has the capacity to end human life or to end human want. Whether we reach these new shores of promise and opportunity, or whether we turn back and lose this great moment rests upon our unity of purpose, our unity of principle within our own society. We just must now draw ourselves

together so that none can pull us apart. The will to heal must always overcome the willingness to hate. In the veins of America there flows the blood of many lands. We should cherish that diversity with pride, but we should jealously guard that diversity against any who seek to exploit it as the basis for our division.

The meaning of America for us all is opportunity. When divisions arise, when suspicions flourish, when hatred flowers, opportunity perishes and passes away. On this day, when we honor our heritage as free men and a peaceful nation, I ask of you, I ask all of you as Americans, that we pledge ourselves to stand up and to be counted for the best in America, because when you do what is best for America, you do what is best for yourselves.

So I hope you will always remember, I pray that you will never forget, that we should stand together for an America that knows no hate, that condones no division, that remembers no north or no south, or no east or no west, but steers its course only by the fixed stars of peace, of freedom, and of justice to all people. A great son of Italy made it possible for us to know about this continent and for us to meet here this afternoon in freedom. We are a nation of almost 200 million people in a world of over 3 billion people, so in the world we are outnumbered 15 to 1. If we choose to demand a decision based on language, we are outvoted; on population, we are a minority; on color we are just a small segment; but we prefer to be judged by one standard, and that is our love of freedom for all people. Congressman Rodino, Congressman Burton, Senator Salinger, and all the others here who serve with me in the Congress know that we are working together so that we can unite families, so that we can make it possible for some of our kinfolks to come here as our forefathers came here, so that we can continue not only to unite families but to unite countries.

Not long ago I was driving down the streets of Naples, and a young priest dashed and threw himself in front of my car. He had 400 young boys in his school. He said: "Please, Mr. Vice President, can I give you a message for America? Please tell the American people that never in all the history of the world has the victor treated the vanquished as America treated Italy. You extended the hand of friendship and helped to rebuild our cities. You look at that beautiful skyline of buildings," and he pointed to buildings like these. "You helped rebuild those buildings. Today our people are a prosperous people, and we honor and we revere and we love America."

Can you think of anything that you would rather hear about your country? Can you think of anything that you would rather have someone say about your land than to say, "We love your people"?

So let's always try to remember, and particularly on the Sabbath Day, that we have much to be thankful for, that we are a blessed people, that we have much to preserve and much to protect; that we have a great obligation, a moral obligation, not just to our 200 million people, but to the 3 billion people of the world, all of which can be met if we only follow the Golden Rule: Do unto others as you would have them do unto you.

You have a wonderful celebration here today. I am happy to see your smiling faces. Never in my life have I seen more people in one day more happy than I have seen in California, and if this were a government day or a political day, I would say I just hope I am as happy November 3d as you are now.

But we have a job to do. We have schools to build, we have our health to improve. We have more teachers to select. We have our poverty people among us. We have our working conditions to improve. We have our standard of living to raise. We have a lot of things to do for our country.

But the first thing we have to do is learn to "love thy neighbor as thyself," and to live in the world with other people.

For 11 months I have tried to help us have peace in the world, and if I can have your help, if I can have your hand, if I can have your heart, if I can have your prayers, if the good Lord is willing, I will continue to try to lead this Nation and this world to peace.

NOTE: The President spoke at 5:35 p.m. in Washington Square in San Francisco. His opening words referred to John A. Ertola, a San Francisco attorney who served as chairman of the event, Governor Edmund G. Brown of California, Ambassador Sergio Fenoaltea of Italy, Senator Pierre E. G. Salinger and Representative Phillip Burton, both of California, Mayor John F. Shelley of San Francisco, and Representative Peter W. Rodino, Jr., of New Jersey.

652   Remarks at the Convention Center in Las Vegas. *October 11, 1964*

Mr. Chairman, distinguished guests, ladies and gentlemen:

When I was a boy, we used to get up in the morning and go down the road to church, and then when the services were over we would have dinner-on-the-ground

on the river bank and have a real reunion with our neighbors.

This morning, this Sunday morning, we got up early, we got in a jet plane to have our breakfast over Texas, we went to church in Phoenix, Ariz., we had dinner-on-the-ground over in Long Beach, Calif., and here I am in Grant Sawyer, Alan Bible, and Howard Cannon country for supper!

I am so sorry I am late. I apologize for being late. I frankly must tell you I usually am late. I spend most of my life trying not to be. Today I meant to just do some quiet Sunday visiting among some old and good friends, and I guess I did do that. But the number of my friends who turned out was just, to put it mildly, larger than I anticipated.

From Portland, Maine, to Portland, Oregon, from the Great Lakes to the Gulf, everywhere we have been in this country we have been seeing good Americans, smiling, happy people—and the reception has been the same.

The American people this year are standing up and being counted as they have never been counted before. And I have never seen them stronger for their Government or their country, or for peace or prosperity, than they are now. The people are being counted for unity. The people are being counted for strength. The people are being counted for prosperity. The people are being counted for peace. And, above all else, the people are being counted for the kind of America that they know and they trust, and they want their children to enjoy.

I hope to set before the Congress early next year a broad program of important legislation. I came out here tonight to do two things: first, to thank each of you, and all the other good people of Nevada, for being one of the two States in the West that went Democratic and voted for John Fitzgerald Kennedy and Lyndon Johnson in 1960.

The second thing I wanted to thank you for, and talk to you about, is this: I need your help because I need Howard Cannon there in the Senate next year to help me with my program. One time someone called me the third Senator from Nevada.

I just want to say this for Nevada: Nevada knows how to vote, Nevada does vote, Nevada votes right. It supported Senator Kennedy and me in 1960. It sent us two strong Democratic Senators.

Alan Bible is one of the ablest and one of the strongest men in the Senate. He serves on the Appropriations Committee, and this year we appropriated for expenditures $1 billion less than we did the preceding year, and that is only the second time in 10 years that we have cut back from the year before. He is a member of the Small Business Committee that has helped the small businessman and provided jobs all over this Nation. He is a member of the Interior Committee that this year produced more conservation legislation than any Congress in 30 years that I have served in Washington—so much legislation for the good of the people, for the recreation of the people, for the good of their children, that we call it the conservation Congress.

We owe no one a greater debt than that honored statesman that sits here, Alan Bible.

Yes, we have much to do in this country, and Nevada has been helping us to do it.

You do have two Democratic Senators there to help me. When President Kennedy was taken from us, on that tragic day in November, on a moment's notice I had to become President, and I took his program and said to the people, "With God's help and with your help and your prayers, I will do my best." Now, I have done that. I have done the very best I knew how.

You are going to have a chance to either approve what I have done, or to turn me out after 11 months next month, 3 weeks from today. You will make that decision, but last Friday night I sat in the White House and I looked at the program that was pending in the Congress when I became President that tragic day. There were 51 major pieces of legislation that the Congress had yet to dispose of.

Last Friday night, the Congress had come and gone, and they had passed every single one of those 51 bills in the Senate of the United States, and all but three or four of them in the House of Representatives.

Nevada had a lot to do with passing that program, and except for these two strong men, there were times when some of those bills would have failed. A number of times we just won by 1, 2, or 3 votes, and Texas couldn't even help me as much as Nevada, and Texas, you know, used to be the largest State in the Union. It is still the largest State in the Union south of the North Pole. But Texas can only give me 1 Democratic vote.

We went off and wandered around and they elected a Republican Senator down there. So the smallest State in the Union can give the President 2 votes to help him keep the peace in the world and keep prosperity at home. And the biggest State in the Union can only give him 1 vote, because the other Senator is just against anything or everything.

Your Governor has been mighty helpful to me and I am grateful to Grant Sawyer. He has been head of the Governors' Conference. He has been cooperative. He has been a great leader. He has worked with the administration. He has worked with the President. For those of you who made that possible, again I thank the people of Nevada.

We have much to do in this country. I do not intend to meet the problems of our growing population with inaction or with a policy of standing pat, or looking the other direction, or turning back on reality, because if we do not act now, our children are going to be neglected and they will not get the best education in the world. If we do not

act now our highways will become clogged with traffic. Our cities will decay. Our streams will be poisoned. Our dwindling natural resources will be wasted. The consequences of apathy and indifference will be severe. We would face mounting unemployment, a faltering economy, and growing tension between our people.

I have been in 33 States in the Union, and I can honestly and genuinely tell you that I believe the American people want their Government to be prudent and careful, but progressive. And I know they want action.

We also have challenges abroad that must be met by action that seeks to end the cold war and reduce international conflicts; and to create the conditions of peace and freedom and justice. I believe that you want your Government to pursue peace with every possible means at our command.

The issues are clear: Are we going to work together to resolve the problems that we face at home? Are we going to close our eyes and just hope they go away? Are we going to keep on seeking ways of easing world tensions and thereby reducing the dangers of nuclear war? Or are we going to repudiate those policies and walk an unknown, an uncertain and dangerous path down through the edge of darkness?

Well, you are going to have to decide whether you support the foreign policy that has maintained freedom since World War II, when Harry Truman worked with the Republicans led by Arthur Vandenberg; when Dwight Eisenhower worked with the Democrats led by Lyndon Johnson in the Senate; when John Fitzgerald Kennedy worked with the Republicans led by Everett Dirksen.

We have had a bipartisan foreign policy. We have taken the position that what was good for America was good for us. And you are going to have to decide whether you want to junk that long, successful program and chart an unknown course that leads you to you know not where.

Well, I have been out traveling in the country. We have had a great trip across this lovely land in the past week. We started in the Midwest last Wednesday. Then we spent Saturday at the ranch. Today we started in Phoenix, and then we went to Long Beach, and San Francisco, and now we are here in Nevada. Tomorrow we are going to criss-cross the great West—Nevada, Reno; Montana, Butte; Wyoming, Casper; Colorado, Denver; Idaho, Boise.

We are going to demonstrate tomorrow how the great West can be won. And we hope to be back in Washington tomorrow night, back at work again. And we will return there with a sense of renewal that always comes from the sun and wind of the West.

I can tell you this, and it is no secret, and it is not off the record: The West is on the move. The West is the "Go-Go" section of America.

In my grandfather's time, and my father's time, the West was an isolated, neglected region of this Nation. Tonight the windows of the West are open to the world. Tonight this region is pushing forward to realize its real greatness. And I came out here to Nevada to thank you for '60, to ask you to send me Howard Cannon, and to promise you that the region is pushing forward and that we are going to keep it that way in Washington.

I know some people don't like what Washington does. As a matter of fact, when things don't go to suit me, I don't like it myself, sometimes. But your National Government that leads you in fighting our wars and preserving our peace is your friend. Your two great Senators are part of it, a big part of it. It is your friend; it is not your enemy.

When I came into this great State tonight, I landed on a beautiful airstrip that was built by the Federal Government, that brings a lot of people to Nevada. They land there. I came down a beautiful highway that the Federal Government helped to construct. I came here to a beautiful city made up of fine, progressive people, and I was just thinking when Howard Cannon sat back there on the Space Committee with me, and we worked and planned and thought and deliberated and tried to help with the Nevada test site.

And I think my service as chairman of that committee, and Howard's service on that committee with me, had some little something to do, with Alan's help and others, with employing 9,500 people in this State.

Now, I wouldn't talk about a mean old man that provided that many jobs. In the first place, you are not mean people; you are happy people. You are hopeful people. You are pioneers. You have faith. You look to the future. You are not looking back to the last century. You are looking forward to the next one. Your grandpa wasn't a cry baby and your daddy wasn't either, or they wouldn't be out here in the land of the West.

Some people get upset and frustrated, and when they go to talking about the other party, and they want to get the ins out and they want to get a man's job, like Howard, and have them take their place, well, they find a lot of things that are wrong, and they have a lot of ugly things to say about it. But I hope you all won't hold that against them too much or pay too much attention to it. You learn to expect that.

When a man is challenging your Senator, you don't expect him to recommend him very highly. He has to try to find something wrong.

You know, I remember back when I was a boy in the early 1930's, when we had a lot of relief kitchens and a lot of soup lines, and a lot of CCC camps, and our people didn't have any jobs. They worked for a dollar a day. We had to give our wool away, and our cotton sold for 5 cents a pound. We had some things to say about the Government then, too. But it was a different kind of government then. And if it ever gets back in that shape again, I am going to have something to say about it.

But from what I read in the papers about what some of these fellows say about the Presidency, it looks like they are running against it instead of running for it.

I think what you ought to do with Howard is what we did down in my country one time. A little boy was picking cotton and he left in the middle of the day and he didn't show up until weighing-in time late that evening. The boss said to him when he came back, "Where in the dickens have you been all afternoon?" And he said, "Well, I have been over to the Old Settlers Reunion." The boss said, "What were you doing over there?" He said, "I was listening to United States Senator Joseph Weldon Bailey make a speech."

The boss said, "The Senator didn't speak all afternoon, did he?" The boy said, "No, but mighty near, mighty near all afternoon."

The boss said, "Well, what did the Senator speak about all afternoon?" The little boy scratched his head and said, "Well, boss, I can't recall precisely everything the Senator said, but the general tenor of his remarks and the general impression that I got from what he said was that the Senator was recommending himself most highly."

Now, I want to recommend Senator Cannon most highly, and if you will just allow me, I would like to put in a little recom-

mendation for myself as I go along.

You really have just two things you have to decide, but you are the boss and you are going to decide. I am not going to tell you how to decide them. I could, if I wanted to, but I don't want to. I am going to tell you the two big issues, though.

The biggest issue in your life is peace, whether we are able to live with the other people in the world. You are either going to have a responsible foreign policy or an irresponsible one. Since I have been President just 10 months, they have killed our soldiers in Panama.

We have had an incident at Guantanamo where they took our base and turned our water off so our boys couldn't get any water. You will remember I got a lot of advice on how to handle the situation. Some of them jumped up and hollered, mighty upset and frustrated, and said, "Send in the Marines."

Well, I talked to the Marines, and I talked to the Joint Chiefs of Staff, and all the smart men we had around Washington, and they deliberated, and we carefully looked at the problem we had. We finally decided that it would be a lot wiser and more prudent to tell one little admiral to go over there and cut that water off than to send in all the Marines. And that is what we did.

And we told Mr. Castro we were going to make that base self-sufficient. We brought in our own machinery and now we make our own water and we don't have to depend on him for the water, and we don't have to depend on the Marines either to go down there and turn it on or off.

We have some problems out in Viet-Nam. We have had them for 10 years out there. We are doing the best we can with them. We are trying to help those people save their freedom.

And freedom is on the march. We have a bunch of new nations that have their independence that have thrown off colonialism. And not one single new nation has embraced communism, not one. And the last nation to go Communist was Cuba in 1959.

As long as I am head of your Government, we are going to press forward to build a better life for all of our people. We are going to keep our Nation standing strong and steadfast at the gate of freedom. We are the mightiest nation in all the world, and we are going to stay there. But we are going to keep our guard up, but our hand out. We are willing to go anywhere, anytime, talk to anyone, to try to reason together for peace. We would rather talk than fight.

To do these things, I can't do them alone. No one man can lead all this Nation. All I can do is the best I can. I need you. I need your help. I need your hand. I need your heart. I need your prayers. Because we are living with 120 other nations, different colors, different religions, different customs, different habits, different incomes.

Do you know half of the nations in the world have an income of less than $8 a month, and the ancient enemies of mankind have their hands around their necks—disease, illiteracy, ignorance, impoverishment.

We have to do something to try to lead the rest of the world because if a peaceful revolution is impossible, a violent revolution is inevitable. And that is what we are trying to do, because we are the most powerful nation in the world. We have the moral obligation to do unto others as we would have them do unto us.

It is mighty easy to issue an ultimatum and tell them to do this or else. You can rattle your rockets. We have more than anyone—twice as many. You can talk about your bombers, with the nuclear weapon on them. We have more than twice as many as anyone.

But rattling your rockets and boasting about your bombers and issuing ultimatums is not going to really scare anybody or threaten anybody, or really bring peace to the world. I sat there in the National Security Council's 37 meetings when Mr. Khrushchev had his missiles in Cuba, and I never left my home in the morning knowing whether I would see my wife and daughters when I got back that night, or whether I would get back or not.

But I am proud to tell you that during that period we were cautious and we were careful, and we were firm, and we were mighty, and we had our men on guard and our planes in the air and our bombs loaded and our ships at sea going in the right direction. And the coolest man at that Cabinet table in Washington was John Fitzgerald Kennedy, the President of the United States.

You know what happened there. I don't know what tomorrow offers, or the next week, or the next month. I wish I could give you assurance for the days ahead. I do know that we have much to preserve and much to protect and much to be thankful for, that we are a blessed people, and we ought to get down on our knees and thank the good Lord for the opportunity that we have here in America and the freedom that we have here in America.

I sometimes wonder about all these folks that talk so much about how terrible things are in America—where it is they would rather live than here. I like people that have faith instead of fear. I like people that love instead of hate. I like people that can find something good about their country instead of always talking about things that are bad about their country. I guess that is why I like Nevada, and I hope that is why Nevada likes me.

In 3 weeks you have to determine whether you follow a policy of bipartisanship that has worked for 20 years and has saved Western Europe, that has maintained our position in Asia, that has helped the African Continent, that has made us the leader of the world, or whether you will abandon it and go to evils that you know not of.

You will determine policy, whether you will follow the policy that has 72.5 million men working, the largest number in the history of the world, at the highest wages they have ever been paid; that has 20 million drawing social security in this country and living in decency and dignity; that has corporations that are making $12 billion more after taxes this year than when you Nevadans elected John Kennedy; paying $60 billion more to workers in this country after taxes than they were paying when you elected John Kennedy.

You have to determine whether you want the government that saved $676 million in the month of July and the month of August under what we spent last July and August a year ago; a government that had 25,000 less Federal employees this July than we had last July a year ago.

You have to decide whether you want to keep that kind of management or whether you want to turn them out. That is your decision. Whatever your decision is, I know it will be the right one, and I know it will be according to your heart, what is best for your country.

Thank you.

NOTE: The President spoke at 8:50 p.m. at Convention Center in Las Vegas, Nev. His opening words "Mr. Chairman" referred to State Senator D. Mahlon Brown, chairman of the State "Citizens for Johnson" Committee. Later he referred to Governor Grant Sawyer and Senators Alan Bible and Howard W. Cannon, all of Nevada.

653 Statement by the President on the Anniversary of the Nuclear Test Ban Treaty. *October* 11, 1964

ONE YEAR AGO today, the Limited Nuclear Test Ban Treaty came into force. Upon deposit of separate instruments of ratification, the United Kingdom, the Soviet Union, and the United States consummated a solemn pledge not to test nuclear weapons in the atmosphere, in outer space, and in the oceans. The world embarked on the first step to remove the threat of oblivion that for two decades has stalked the earth.

More than 100 nations have now signed the test ban treaty. The air is cleaner, the world is safer, and the hopes for peace are a little brighter because of this act of commonsense. Next week, I will report to the Nation on our progress under the test ban treaty.

This weekend, in our homes and houses of worship throughout the land, I think it appropriate that all Americans pause to mark in gratitude, in pride, and in prayer the historic anniversary we now observe.

NOTE: On October 15, the day before the detonation of the first Chinese nuclear device (see Item 675), the White House made public the 6th report by the Federal Radiation Council giving up-to-date information relating to fallout. The report confirmed earlier predictions of fallout levels and concluded that health risks from radioactivity in food for the next several years would be too small to justify protective actions to limit the intake of radionuclides through the diet. The report indicated the following changes in the fallout situation since 1963:

1. Short-lived radionuclides produced by nuclear testing, iodine 131 and strontium-89, had disappeared from the environment.

2. The inventory of the long-lived nuclides strontium-90 and cesium-137 in the atmosphere by mid-1964 had been reduced to one-half that in January 1963, at the end of the last test series.

3. Long-lived nuclides had reached a delayed peak in the diet during 1964 and would decrease in future years.

The Council, under the chairmanship of Secretary of Health, Education, and Welfare Anthony J. Celebrezze, was established by Executive Order 10831

of August 14, 1959 (24 F.R. 6669, 3 CFR, 1959–1963 Comp., p. 365), to advise the President with respect to radiation matters directly or indirectly affecting health.

The President's statement of October 11 was released at Austin, Tex.

654   Memorandum Outlining Some of the Major Issues of the Campaign.   *October* 11, 1964

1. LAST WEEK in my television address to the country I said I would discuss the issues that are important in this campaign. In the Midwest and the South I put particular emphasis on social security, the policies that make for prosperity, TVA, and the fundamental unity of the country.

Tomorrow I intend to talk a lot about my view that government can be both progressive and compassionate on the one hand and prudent on the other.

2. The reasons:

(1) People want a frugal government.

(2) To be responsible in fulfilling unmet public needs, government does not need to be a reckless spender.

(3) It is a myth that the Democratic Party wants to spend for the sake of spending.

3. Some facts:

(1) My first full budget—fiscal 1965—lowers instead of increases expenditures—only the second budget in 10 years to do so.

—Reduces instead of increases the number of government employees—the first budget to do so in 8 years.

(2) Budget expenditures for the first 2 months of this fiscal year are over ½ billion dollars below the same period last year.

(3) The number of employees in July 1964 was 25,000 below the same month in the previous year.

(4) I have asked nondefense agencies to wage a war against waste, like Secretary McNamara has done in the Department of Defense. We expect to save hundreds of millions annually.

(5) We now estimate that we will be able to reduce budget expenditures in fiscal 1965 some $676 million below our original January budget estimate. And this follows upon our accomplishment in the fiscal year just ended during which we reduced expenditures $1.1 billion below the original budget submission.

4. I don't believe any administration in modern times has been as successful as we have been in reducing costs.

(1) Secretary McNamara predicted he could save $1.5 billion—he actually saved $2.8 billion. At the same time we were greatly improving our military strength. (Fiscal Year 1964)

(2) Jim Webb tells me he believes NASA will save $128 million in his cost reduction program—almost $50 million more than he expected to be able to save.

(3) John Gronouski is handling more mail with fewer employees—and doing it at less cost. If output per postal worker today were the same as in 1961, the cost of operating the Post Office would be $140 million more than it is.

(4) John Gleason has revitalized the VA insurance program and has increased the productivity of its employees by 24 percent.

5. The crucial fact is this: a "cut cost" policy does not mean a "do-nothing" policy. Government's challenge is to reduce costs,

curtail less urgent activities, and find other savings which will permit us to expand essential services or start important new services.

(1) For the last 3 years over 70 percent of the increase in Federal spending went for 3 purposes: (a) a stronger defense, (b) space exploration, (c) uncontrollable interest charges.

(2) Our 1965 austerity program permitted us to take several steps to improve the Nation's well-being, promote better education, and develop our natural resources:
—the war on poverty
—urban mass transportation
—Housing Act of 1964
—major education bills
—Land and Water Conservation Fund Act
—and other programs designed to meet definite needs and improve the lives of our people.

Within an austere total budget, therefore, we have been able by practicing rigorous economy to undertake more forward looking programs for the American people than at any time in recent decades.

6. Summary

This is one of the most important issues of the campaign—whether the Government is going to turn its back on the mounting needs of a growing country under the pretense of a "conservative fiscal philosophy"—or whether the Government is going to serve the interests of our national strength, economic progress, and human compassion.

The first is a radical philosophy. The second is a responsible philosophy.

Efficiency in government should be not the cause of stagnation but the companion of progress.

And that is why I intend to make this a major theme tomorrow.

NOTE: The memorandum was released at Long Beach, Calif.

---

655 Remarks at the State Building in Reno. *October 12, 1964*

Governor Sawyer, Mrs. Sawyer, Senator Bible, Senator Cannon, Congressman Baring, distinguished guests on the platform, my fellow Americans:

I want to thank you so very much for coming out here in Reno today and extending the warm hand of welcome to your friend and your neighbor who has come to see you at this time of the year. I came out here because the two Senators from Nevada have done much to help me in the 11 months that I have been President to pass a program for the benefit of all Americans.

Alan Bible, serving on Appropriations and the Interior and Small Business Committees, has helped us to have one of the most eco-nomical sessions of Congress, one of the most progressive sessions of Congress, and one of the most conservation-minded Congresses in the history of the Republic.

Howard Cannon, serving on the Space Committee, has been of great value to me in connection with the Nevada test site, which is the largest employer in the State of Nevada, and I feel that in the next administration—that is going to be a Democratic House, and 60-odd Democratic Senators—that the State of Nevada will want Howard Cannon to continue his Democratic service. Nevada needs Howard Cannon; the U.S.A. needs Howard Cannon; and LBJ needs Howard Cannon.

I hope the people of Nevada will also return to the Congress Congressman Baring, who has had a distinguished record there, and who sits on the platform with us this morning as the Democratic nominee in this State.

Grant Sawyer has been the chairman of the Governors' Conference and has been very helpful to your President. I want to express to him and to all of you my deep gratitude for his service not only to Nevada but his service to the entire Nation.

Here on the frontier of the West, the watchword has always been freedom. But you and I know that in the building of the West, we boasted about our rights—but we banked on our responsibility.

We know how the West was won. It wasn't won by men on horses who tried to settle every argument with a quick draw and a shot from the hip. We here in the West aren't about to turn in our sterling silver American heritage for a plastic credit card that reads, "Shoot now; pay later."

This land was settled and made to prosper by sober and responsible men and women who built the homes, tilled the soil, and looked after the stock and raised their families, and let the drifters be the ones to whoop it up on Saturday night.

The frontier's story, like America's, is that people aren't free for very long unless they are also responsible.

We didn't build this Nation by everyone scratching and clawing for himself. We built it, like we built the West, by pitching in together and by always acting responsibly.

So we must go on building today. There are some of those among us who say that "we, the people" should get out of business, as a people, acting through the Government.

Well, I say, and so do you, that "we, the people" are going to stay in business and "we, the Government" are going to do together the things that we can't do alone.

One candidate is roaming around the country saying what a terrible thing the Government is. He seems to be running against the Office of President instead of for the Office of President.

Somebody better tell him that most Americans are not ready to trade the American eagle in for a plucked banty rooster.

He better know that most people just don't believe the United States Government is a foreign power or an enemy.

You feel that government must act with restraint, and so do I. You feel that government must be responsible, and so do I.

We have a Bill of Rights. We are also developing a Bill of Responsibilities, and that will be the guidepost of my administration.

Article I of the Bill of Responsibilities is that government must be prudent. I am in favor of government that doesn't take in a cent it doesn't need and doesn't spend a cent it doesn't have to. Instead of increasing Government expenditures, my first budget, the first Johnson budget to the Congress, calls for lower expenditures—$1 billion lower—and it is only the second budget in 10 years to be lower. Instead of increasing the number of Government employees, the Johnson budget calls for a reduction, and it is the first budget to reduce Government employees in 8 years.

This is a fact that I would like for each of you to remember: During the first 2 months of my first fiscal year, July and August just passed, the Johnson administration spent $676 million less than we spent last July and August. And this July, in the Johnson administration, had 25,000 less Federal employees on the payroll than we had in July of last year, 1 year ago. I intend to pursue the same course of efficiency in meeting the needs of this Nation.

Article II of the Bill of Responsibilities is that government—local, State, and Federal—where necessary, must keep the domestic peace. There is no place and there must be no place in this country for violence or for civil disobedience.

Article III is that the Government must keep peace in the world. Peace is the most important subject to you today. We are proud that history has thrust upon us the responsibilities of leadership for the free world. And the United States, under my leadership, does not intend to retreat from those responsibilities.

Article IV is that the Government of the United States must discharge the responsibilities of leadership throughout the free world which history has thrust upon us.

Article V of the Bill of Responsibilities says that we must encourage and permit the American economy to make full use of our farmlands and our ranchlands, and full use of our plant capacity, and to reach full employment. I am glad to say that per capita-wise, the Federal Government has more people working for it in Nevada than any other State in the Union, and I hope that you like your employer.

Article VI says that we are responsible for seeing to it that our children, all of our children, of all races, of all colors, of all religions, from all families, get all the education they can use.

Article VII says that we will, as stewards—and Theodore Roosevelt said it is the duty of the President of the United States to be the steward of all the people—we will, as stewards, preserve and develop our natural resources. America the beautiful is our inheritance. We want projects like Lake Tahoe. It is also our responsibility to develop them.

Article VIII of the Bill of Responsibilities is that we will see to it that every person who

lives a productive, useful working life enjoys a secure and a meaningful older age. And that means that the 20 million now on social security are going to be protected, and we are going to make the system stronger, not weaker, and we are not about to make it voluntary, either.

Article IX is that we will draw no false lines through our society, on the basis of race, religion, national origin, sex, or age.

Finally, it is our responsibility to be sure the channels of democratic action are kept clear and clean so that Government is the people's servant, not the people's master.

By working together, by acting responsibly, we know we can do the things we cannot do alone. We have learned that by working together, by acting responsibly, we can make the Bill of Rights come to life and come true. And that is what a Bill of Responsibilities can mean—not less personal freedom, but more personal freedom.

Do you know that more people have more freedom in the world today than they have ever had before? Do you know that Americans have more freedom today than they have ever had before? We were not very free in 1932 when the Hoover administration had us burning our old cows and giving our wool away, and selling our cotton for 5 cents, and we had soup lines all over the country.

We are much freer today with 72 million people working at high wages, getting $60 billion more after taxes for their work, and the corporations making $12 billion more after taxes than they did in 1960.

That gives you an economic freedom that means a lot to your personal life. And that is what our free enterprise system of government gives us, and that is why I am so glad that in all the nations that have thrown off colonialism, not one single nation has joined communism. The last nation that was lost to the Communists was lost in Cuba in 1959.

So that is what our American form of government is all about, that is the kind of responsible government that we have had, when we made the greatest advances for personal freedom and prosperity in this country. And that is the kind of responsible government that I am going to continue if I am selected as your President. Working together with the people of Nevada, that great democratic State leading the way, we will continue it.

We have about six States to go into today, and we must run along. But I do want to tell you that it means a lot to me to see this many people this early in the morning, in this small State, out to see their President. It is not a tribute to the President; it is a tribute to the people of Reno, Nev.

I don't know who your chief of police is, and I want to stay in good with him—at least until I get out of his jurisdiction—but I do want him to come up here and take off those Goldwater glasses and take another look at this crowd, because I look through those glasses sometimes myself. But it looks like to me that I see here the largest 15,000 crowd that I have ever seen in all of my campaigning. And I know I never saw a friendlier crowd. I hope I am right in assuming that it is a Democratic crowd.

It is less than 3 weeks until the election, and you can do something these last 20 days, and we want you to do it. We think that the time to show America and show the world dramatically, effectively, and overwhelmingly that the American people believe in a responsible, bipartisan foreign policy, and responsible leadership and prosperity in this country is in the next 20 days. Won't you join me?

Well, anyway, I just want you to know, whatever your crowd is—maybe I am looking through Goldwater glasses—I will tell you this: I thought the crowd last night was just the most wonderful crowd I had ever seen in Nevada, but the crowd this morning is a lot larger, or something has happened to me overnight.

Flash—Flash—Flash—Correction: They just brought me a message and said the chief of police said 50,000, not 15,000.

Well, I want to apologize. It is not the chief of police that has on Goldwater glasses; it is Howard Cannon that needs a hearing aid. Didn't you say 15,000, Howard? Well, he said it was a slip of the tongue.

Anyway, folks, I don't need to tell you how much I think of your people. I came out here many years ago to ask you to elect Alan Bible. He is one of the great men of the Senate. I came out here to ask you to help elect Howard Cannon. No two men from any State in the Union have worked more for the people, have been more bipartisan, have tried to do what is best for America more than these two stalwart sons of this small State.

I hate to say it, but Texas used to be the largest State in the Union, but we can produce only one Democratic Senator while the smallest State in the Union produces two big ones. I hope you will send them back to help me with my program. I hope you will send Walt Baring back there to help me with my program.

In the meantime, I must run along, but I do want to tell you, thank you very much.

Good luck, goodbye, God bless you all.

NOTE: The President spoke at 9:57 a.m. at the State Building in Reno, Nev. In his opening words he referred to Governor and Mrs. Grant Sawyer, Senators Alan Bible and Howard W. Cannon, and Representative Walter S. Baring, all of Nevada.

656   Remarks at the Civic Center in Butte.
October 12, 1964

Mr. Chairman, Senator Mansfield, Mrs. Mansfield, Senator Metcalf, Congressman Olsen, the next Governor of Montana, Roland Renne, ladies and gentlemen, boys and girls:

I haven't been here very long, but I don't have to be here very long now to see how the West is going to be won.

It's great to be in Montana again. My grandfather once drove cattle up here from Texas, but he went back home. He said it was too cold for him up here.

Well, there is nothing cold about your welcome here today—and I thank each of you from the bottom of a grateful heart.

I am very proud to be in Maureen Mansfield's home town, and it is nice to see her husband, too.

Mike Mansfield, the pride of Montana and the Nation, was the leader of the Senate during its most productive session in this century. He possesses those two qualities that especially belong to a leader—reason and calm judgment. And I know that you are going to let us have him back in Washington where all the Nation needs him.

It would be such a wonderful thing for you to do, such a kind and deserving thing to do, if you would send Mike Mansfield back to the Senate by the largest majority per capita of any Senator elected this year. That would show that you home folks approve of the leadership of your home boy, and that would be a signal to the rest of the Nation to get behind that leadership.

I have come to Butte today to set the issues of this campaign before the American people. I have come here this morning to talk to you about responsible government.

Four years ago June, the unemployment rate in this area was almost 14 percent.

Since John Fitzgerald Kennedy was sworn in as President, that rate has been cut in half. It has been cut because of the economic policies for all the people that have kept this country moving ahead.

And I intend to keep this country moving ahead.

Our fathers and our grandfathers came out here to build the West. They built an empire, but it was an isolated empire, and it faced the hardships of economic isolation.

Today the westerner is linked to all the world. Our State and national and local governments, working together, have tamed our rivers, have provided cheap barge transportation, and we send the products of the West around the globe. They have built an unmatched highway system, a concrete tie-in between the West and the rest of the Nation. And I call this responsible government.

Your Yellowtail Dam is near completion. Recently, Prime Minister Pearson of Canada and I signed the Columbia River Treaty. Under that treaty we will build the Libby Dam. Those two dams together with two more—Hungry Horse and the Fort Peck Dam—will give this region the water and the power that it needs to create new industries, and that means new jobs for the people.

But we are not satisfied. We don't want 97 percent of Montana's labor force employed. We want all of Montana's men working. We will not be satisfied with just 80 percent of Montana's families living well. We want all of Montana's families living well.

This administration stands ready to meet its responsibilities to the people of Montana and to the people of the Nation. That means creating new jobs. That means providing tax cuts as we did this year, and as we will next year.

The National Government, however, cannot, and it should not, do it all.

Your local governments and your State governments must work together with us, and they will work together with us under the leadership of your next Governor, Roland Renne.

And I want to thank you for sending Congressman Olsen to Washington because he has been a good team player and he has helped us build the Nation. Thank you very much.

It is very unusual for any State, much less a small State, to supply the two Senators that are in the Senate most of the time, but Lee Metcalf presides over the Senate more than I did when I was Vice President. And he is doing a wonderful job and making a fine record.

These men work with each other and love each other, and they don't hate each other and they don't spend any time fighting each other. They are not men of little purpose. They are not men that fear, men that doubt, men that hate. They are men of faith. They are men of hope. They are men that love. And isn't it better to be a nation of lovers than a nation of haters?

You don't know how much better it makes me feel to look into the faces of people that look like they just stuck in their thumb and pulled out a plum, instead of looking at someone that looks like he had a teaspoon full of vinegar.

You know, we have a wonderful group of people in America. We have good Democrats, we have good Republicans, we have good Independents, we have good whatnots, but in this campaign, I found yesterday how to pick a fellow that was really opposing me.

We drove 15 miles from the airport to where I was speaking. The police estimated that we saw between a million and

a million and a half people. That is why I ran 2 hours late all day long. But about every mile and a half I would see three or four or five that I knew weren't going to vote for me. And I'll bet you you don't know how I knew they weren't—because they just looked—[*the President grimaced*].

They were unhappy at home, and you could see it in their countenances. They were unhappy in California, and you could see it written all over their faces.

They were unhappy with their country. You would think they were running against the Presidency instead of for it. They are unhappy with the world, and they are going to be unhappy on November 3.

But I like happy people. I like smiling faces. I like people who love their country and who believe in it, and who look forward to living in the year 2000, when the average income of a family will be $15,000 a year; when we will cross the oceans on top of the water and under the water with our cargo, when we will have a new world opening up to us in the space field.

Oh, it is such a wonderful, hopeful prospect that now I am trying to get the doctors to find out how they can control heart disease, and cancer, and stroke, and all the things that kill men early. I want to be around in the year 2000 to enjoy it, and I know I am going to enjoy it if I am here.

And I sure want to be happy when I enjoy it because it must not be very pleasant to have to take these dyspeptic pills. And you don't take them if you really look and see what America has done during your lifetime and mine.

The world is growing smaller, though. You live out here in the wide open spaces. But spacecraft girdle the globe. And in this nuclear age the fate of all mankind is linked together.

But America is going to meet her responsibilities to mankind. We met them last year with the nuclear test ban treaty, the first glimmer of light at the end of a black tunnel.

President Eisenhower worked for that treaty.

President Kennedy negotiated it and ratified it. And responsible leaders of both political parties approved it in the United States Senate.

Senator Mike Mansfield and Lee Metcalf are Democrats and they come from Montana. Senator Everett Dirksen is a Republican and he comes from Illinois. But these Senators, these men who put their country first, worked together for all mankind and they got that treaty approved by an overwhelming vote.

Not far from where we are meeting stands a 150-unit Minuteman missile complex that is soon to be expanded, and it is a symbol of our determination to pursue peace through strength. Peace is the most important subject to every man, woman, and child in this hall.

But you will meet your responsibilities to mankind best in the 3 weeks that are remaining between now and November 3d, and in the years ahead, by conducting yourselves as responsible leaders of the world, of the free, that we are.

Because good politics is good government. If you will do what is best for America, you will do what is best for your party and for yourself.

I haven't come out here to reflect on your intelligence with a lot of name-calling or mudslinging, or muckraking. On November 3d you are going to decide between two parties, you are going to decide between two leaders, you are going to decide whether you want our foreign policy, which has been bipartisan since World War II, to continue.

It was Arthur Vandenberg that worked as a Republican with Harry Truman, a Democrat.

It was Lyndon Johnson and Mike Mansfield, as leaders of the Senate, Democrats, that worked with Dwight David Eisenhower, as a Republican.

It was Everett Dirksen that worked with John Fitzgerald Kennedy.

But we, both Democrats and Republicans, have worked together to make America responsible and to make America united.

If I am elected, I shall continue that policy. I will try to unite our people; I will never try to divide them. I will try to bring our people together; I will never separate them. I will try to get our people to love thy neighbor as thyself, instead of hate thy neighbor and distrust everybody.

And I predict if I am elected, that the extreme groups that have infected this country, the spotlight of publicity will be put on them. And the Klan and the Birch Society and those others who preach hate will have their robes pulled open where the American people can see them.

Because a long time ago it was said, "United we stand, divided we fall." That statement was true then and it's truer today.

I have tried to set before the American people the basic issues of this campaign—leadership, responsibility, unity, peace, prosperity. And on November 3d I think that you are going to choose an administration that you believe is responsible.

Do you know, I have been President only 10 months. I had to assume this office on a moment's notice. I didn't have any chance to reflect and retrace my steps, and make additional preparation, and go to the library. I had to act, and act immediately. And I said to you then and I repeat today, with God's help, with your prayers, with the unity of all of our people, I will do the best

I can. I have done the best I could for all Americans.

Montana is a peaceful State. Since I was a little boy, I have seen Montana Senators stand up and try to fight to lead the Nation— Tom Walsh, Burt Wheeler, Mike Mansfield, Lee Metcalf.

But a few months ago, I sat in the National Security Council when Mr. Khrushchev had his missiles in Cuba, and I never left home a single morning to attend 37 meetings of that Council that I knew I would ever see my wife and daughters again that night.

I saw strong men sit around the table and debate about what course we should pursue. I heard men say, "Let's move," and we put our bombers in the skies, loaded with their bombs. We put our ships on the sea, and our submarines under the water, and we moved in the directions where we thought they might be needed.

But that order that would take us into war and would destroy and snuff out 300 million lives was not given, because the coolest man in Washington sat at the head of that Cabinet table, and his name was John Fitzgerald Kennedy.

He remembered, and I have not forgotten, that you expected him to be a man of care and caution; that you expected him to be a man of patience who wanted to preserve the world; that you had selected him with his thumb to be in the vicinity of that button; and when he mashed that button, you knew that he would know that there was nothing left to do but do it.

But he never got that thumb on that button because he was calm, because he was patient, because he was reasonable, because he analyzed the other man until the point was reached that these two leaders, as Secretary Rusk said, stood there eyeball to eyeball, until they both realized that there was nothing to gain for anybody by killing 300

million human beings.

So you have 3 weeks now to decide. You will decide which thumb you expect to be in the vicinity of that button. You will decide which voice you want to pick up that "hot line" if Moscow calls. You will decide who you want to lead this Nation in its relations with other nations. You will decide what you want to do about the prosperity and the programs we have now.

I don't know what you will decide. I am not even going to recommend.

But I am going to tell you a story of an old boy that works in a store down in my country where we go to buy our groceries. He said the salesmen come through every day and say, "Are you for Johnson or that other fellow that is running against him?"

He said he finally got so tired of answering so many questions that he went out to the little local bank and bought him 15 Kennedy half dollars, and he put them in his pocket. He said, "Now when the salesman comes in and says, 'How is this country going? Is this Johnson country or what kind of country is it?'" he said, "I don't even answer him. I just rattle those 15 half dollars and say, 'I like it pretty well as it is.'"

So you will decide whether we will move forward, whether we will face up to our responsibilities both at home and abroad, whether we will build a better life for our families and our children, whether we will build a safer world for all human beings, whether we will build a peaceful world for all mankind.

That will be your decision. The American people don't ask much. They ask their leaders to keep their guard up but their hand out. They ask their leaders to be firm, but to be understanding and to be patient, and not to be hotheaded. They ask their leaders to try to make it possible for every child to get the education he can take, every family to have a roof over their heads, everybody to have clothes to cover him and food to sustain him.

And as the great labor leader, Phil Murray, one time said, "The American people don't ask for much—a school for their children, a church for them to worship in according to the dictates of their own conscience, a picture on the wall, and a rug on the floor and a little music in the house."

I believe that this is Democratic country. Am I right?

Well, I have four more appearances in four more States today, and I will be getting on my way. But you have your job to do in the next 3 weeks, so let's get on and get going, and get doing it.

NOTE: The President spoke at 12:45 p.m. at the Civic Center in Butte, Mont. In his opening words he referred to Joseph Shea, chairman of the State Democratic Committee, Senator and Mrs. Mike Mansfield, Senator Lee Metcalf, Representative Arnold Olsen, and Roland Renne, Democratic candidate for Governor, all of Montana. Later he referred to Prime Minister Lester B. Pearson of Canada, Senator Everett McKinley Dirksen of Illinois, former Senators Thomas J. Walsh and Burton K. Wheeler of Montana, Secretary of State Dean Rusk, and Philip Murray, president of the Congress of Industrial Organizations, 1940–1952.

657   Remarks at the Natrona County Courthouse, Casper, Wyoming.   *October 12, 1964*

Senator McGee; Teno Roncalio; my old friend, former Senator Joe Hickey; my close and able assistant, Mike Manatos, from Rock Springs; ladies and gentlemen; boys and girls:

This looks to me like it is Democratic country. I know now how we are going to win the West—right here.

I have come out here today to discuss our economy and to satisfy my wife.

She came out here last month—and she hasn't stopped talking about it ever since.

But Wyoming is familiar territory. As Gale told you, I visited here 6 years ago. I asked you to give us your help, give us your hand, give us your heart, send a young man to Washington that was young enough to do the job and able enough to get it done. You did it. I want you to send him back.

Today Gale McGee holds 6 years' seniority on the most powerful committee in the Congress, the Appropriations Committee. And I don't believe you people want to change horses after you have one that is reliable, you have one that gets the job done, you have one that loves your State, and you have one that your President needs to help him keep peace in the world.

Today Gale McGee holds a place as my trusted friend and confidant.

Today Gale McGee is one of the most able Senators in Washington.

When beef prices went into a slump, we had a drought all over the country, our cattle prices started going down, Gale McGee went into action. Instead of just beefing about it, and being a crybaby, he did something for beef.

He started the biggest promotion of beef ever done in this country, and he has not only done it in this country, he has done it all over the world where we are now shipping some of our cattle. Yes, he pushed beef exports. He got us to buy more beef for our soldiers, more for our schools and more for our people in need.

He started to work reducing imports. We set up a Presidential commission to study the marketing practices of food chains, and he is a member of that commission and a very able one.

Today, for the first time in 2 years, imports are down and prices of fat beef are going up. This rising trend will reach the feeder cattle people and we do not intend to stop until it does. I am proud of what Gale McGee has done to help the cowmen of America.

This is the kind of responsible government your President believes in.

Responsible government means prudent government. And that is why, as your President, I have waged an all-out attack against waste in government. That is why the first day I went in as your President, I said I will say to the taxpayers of this country I am going to give you a dollar's value for every dollar spent. That means spending your tax dollars only where they need to be spent.

Some people laughed when I started saving on light bulbs around the White House and turning out a few lights and chandeliers. But they quit laughing at me when the Defense Department savings reached $2,800 million. They didn't laugh at me.

They quit laughing when other departments managed to save more than $400 million this year, and the year is not over yet. They didn't laugh so hard when we cut this year's budget nearly $1 billion under last year's budget.

They didn't laugh so much when this July we had 25,000 fewer employees working for the Federal Government than we had July a year ago.

So prudent government, careful government, businessman government has tightened its belt. We have streamlined its operations. We have begun to do a better job for less money.

But responsibility means more than that. And that is why Gale McGee and I have been working to build Wyoming's prosperity.

We passed the wilderness bill to help preserve nature's wealth in Wyoming and the West.

You know how Gale McGee voted, and you know how my opponent voted. My opponent voted "no."

We passed the biggest tax cut, a $12 billion tax cut, in the history of the Nation.

You know how Gale McGee voted, and you know how my opponent voted. He voted "no."

We passed a bill for higher education to help meet the needs of our children, needs which have doubled in the last 10 years.

You know how Gale McGee voted. You know how my opponent voted. Well, I guess you guessed it—he voted "no."

I believe this kind of spending that we have done has been responsible spending.

I think it was prudent when we spent $11 million during the last 3½ years to help Wyoming's small businessmen, when we spent $975,000 to develop Jackson Hole as a great recreation center; when we spent $80 million, this past year alone, to help build Wyoming's highways.

And there is a final responsibility.

The war on waste has a third front. For the world's greatest waste would be the waste of human lives in a nuclear holocaust. I think that you know that as one of the products of Oak Ridge today we hold in our hand the most awesome, the mightiest, the most frightening power that was ever held in the hand of man.

I think that you know just a few months back when President Kennedy sat with his Security Council for 37 meetings when Mr. Khrushchev had brought his missiles into Cuba, I think you knew that your Commander in Chief, day and night, got the best advice that he could get in this Nation, and you had selected his thumb to be the thumb that went on the button if it had to go there.

But his caution and his care and his good judgment resulted in these two men looking at each other, eyeball to eyeball, and both of them deciding that it was not wise, that it was not just, that it was not right to put their thumb on that button and automatically wipe out the lives of 300 million people.

You have 3 weeks to make your choice of what thumb you want controlling that button. You will select one of two parties. You will select one of two persons. You will select one of two leaders to conduct the relations of America with other nations.

The most important single thing in your life is peace, peace at home, peace in the world. In the 10 months since I have been President, I have conferred with 85 of the world's leaders. I have tried to reason with them. I have tried to plan with them. I have tried to submit to them proposals for consideration that would bring about disarmament.

As long as I am your President, I am not going to rattle our rockets, I am not going to bluff with our bombs. I am going to keep our guard up at all times and our hand out.

But I am going to be willing to go anywhere, see anyone, talk any time to try to bring peace to this world so these mothers will not have to give up their boys and have them wiped out in a nuclear holocaust.

We are the mightiest nation in the world. We have more bombers, we have more missiles, we have well trained men. But if we do not have peace in the world, everything else fades into insignificance.

So I hope that you people will realize that in the next 3 weeks you are going to make a choice. You are going to make a selection, you are going to determine who you want to represent you in the next 4 years. You are going to determine what kind of an economic policy this country has, whether we go back-

wards or whether we go forward.

Today, wholesale prices are 1 percent down from what they were a year ago. Today 72 million men are working. Today corporations are making $12 billion more after taxes than they made 4 years ago when Mr. Kennedy came in. Today the workers of America are getting $60 billion more after taxes than they got in 1961. Today our farm income is $12 billion, and you pull down all of our programs and all of our plans and you will cut that income overnight the first year to $6 billion.

Well, you want to think that over. A fellow down in my country the other day said the traveling salesmen kept bothering him, coming in wanting to know who he would vote for, for President. He said he finally went out and got 15 Kennedy half dollars and put them in his britches pocket. He said every time one of them came in and asked him, he started rattling those half dollars and said, "This sounds pretty good to me. I like it the way it is."

The future of this Nation lies here in the West, but you must have leadership. You must have vision. You must have progressive men to carry forward your plans. You have that in Teno, if you send him to Congress; you have that in Gale, already with 6 years' experience in the United States Senate. I need them both. I plead with you to go out, in the next 3 weeks, and help elect them as representatives of the State of Wyoming.

I have been to Wyoming a number of times. I like your white-faced Herefords. I like your cowmen. I know your oilmen. I know something about the economy of this State and the problems of this State. I think I have been your friend and I just want to repeat to you today what I said that awesome afternoon when tragedy befell us and our great President was taken from us, and on a moment's notice I had to assume the awe-some responsibilities of the Presidency.

I said then with God's help and with your help, and with your prayers, I would do the best I could. I have done the best I could. I have represented all the people of this Nation. I have been President of all the States.

If you think I should be turned out after 11 months, you have that privilege and that right, and that is your duty to do it November 3d.

But if you think we should go forward with a program of peace in the world, of trying to love thy neighbor as thyself, trying to live with other nations instead of destroying them, if you think we should continue to move this Nation forward, that we should have vision, we should have plans, we should have programs, we should have education for our children, we should have highways to transport our people, we should have a good, sound agricultural program, we should have business and labor trying to work together, instead of spending all their time

fighting—in short, we ought to have peace in the world and peace at home—if you think that, I will appreciate your voting the Democratic ticket November 3d.

This has been a delightful day. We visited many States. We yet have to go to Denver and then to Boise, Idaho, and then into Washington tonight.

I want to thank all of you. Wyoming is one of the smaller States in the country. This is one of the largest crowds I have seen. I expect per capita-wise you have just about bested all the other States, and I want to tell you that I consider it a great tribute to your people. I am deeply thankful to you for coming out.

Goodby and God bless you.

NOTE: The President spoke at 3:30 p.m. at the Natrona County Courthouse in Casper, Wyo. In his opening words he referred to Senator Gale W. McGee, Teno Roncalio, U.S. Chairman of the International Joint Commission-United States and Canada and Democratic candidate for Representative, and former Senator J. J. Hickey, all of Wyoming, and Mike N. Manatos, Administrative Assistant to the President.

658   Remarks at the Coliseum in Denver.
October 12, 1964

My longtime friend, Governor McNichols; Congressman Aspinall; Congressman Byron Rogers; Senator Roy McVicker; Representative Frank Evans; my beloved old-time friend from the Senate, Ed Johnson; my friend and my former colleague in both the House and the Senate, former Senator John Carroll; ladies and gentlemen; boys and girls:

If I had all night, and I don't have but 20 minutes or I will be late to Boise, Idaho, and we are late enough anyway—we won't get to Washington until 5 o'clock tomorrow morning—but if I had all night, I couldn't

tell you how much you have touched me, how deeply grateful I am for your generous welcome to us in this great outpost of the West.

We left home yesterday morning and went out to the great State of Arizona. We got a wonderful welcome—not as big a welcome as this one, but Arizona is not as big a State as this one is. But everywhere we have gone in the West, in California, Nevada, here in Colorado, Wyoming, Montana—I've been in all of those places today—and every place we have gone, every person we have seen, makes us believe that the people of this country believe in this country.

I don't know how to really judge this crowd tonight, but the way you sound, that must have been the echo they have been talking about around here.

Seriously, I want to speak to you very briefly about a subject that is very close to all of us, and may well determine what kind of a world we live in. That subject is education. I believe that it is a bedrock issue in this campaign. I think that you do have a clear choice.

Our opponent has said: "The child has no right to an education. In most cases, the children will get along very well without it."

And we say, and I say, and the leadership of your country says, that every child has the right to as much education as he or she has the ability to take.

I want this for our children's sake, but I also want it for our Nation's sake, because nothing can mean more to the future of America. A great President of the Republic of Texas once said: "Education is the guardian genius of democracy. It is the only dictator that free men recognize, and it is the only ruler that free men desire."

Our great former President and Vice President Thomas Jefferson said, "If we expect a Nation to be ignorant and free, we expect what never was and what never will be."

Our school system was founded on that truth. We have come a long way, but I am here to tell you tonight, and to ask your help: we still have a long way to go.

Tonight, 40 million students are enrolled in our public schools in America; 5 million more students will enter by the end of this decade. And we must be ready for them.

Unless we act now, 1 out of every 3 students now in the fifth grade will drop out before they finish high school—1 out of 3. And 4 out of 5 juvenile delinquents between 15 and 18 years old—4 out of 5—are school dropouts.

So let those take note who preach against crime on the one hand, and on the other deny our children the right to have an education: It doesn't do you any good to just go around the country talking against crime. You have to vote against crime, and when the roll is called on measures in the Congress that will control crime, that will drive away the ancient enemies of mankind—disease, illiteracy, poverty, and ignorance—you must answer those rollcalls. One reason that we are in the shape we are in is, too many have been answering those rollcalls with a loud "no."

It is getting harder and harder to get a job if you don't have a high school diploma. Twenty percent of our 18 to 24 year olds with less than an eighth grade education are unemployed. That is four times the national average, and then when you try to do something about taking these taxeaters that are eating off the relief rolls off the front porch and putting them to work, and giving them some training in the poverty program so they will become taxpayers instead of taxeaters, you hear these people that talk about crime vote "no" on poverty.

This crime business is just not an autumn fever. It is just not something you talk about in September and October every fourth year at election time. It is something you vote against, it is something you fight against, it is something you work against, it is something that you do in the Congress to provide education, employment, and training for people so they can be constructive citizens instead of destructive citizens.

During the last 10 years, jobs filled by high school graduates increased 30 percent. Jobs for those without high school diplomas dropped 25 percent.

I had some experience in this field back

in 1924. I graduated from the Johnson City High School in a class of six. For some time I had felt that my father was not really as smart as I thought he ought to be, and I thought that I could improve on a good many of my mother's approaches to life. So when I got my high school diploma I decided to follow the old philosopher Horace Greeley's advice and "Go West, young man," and seek my fortune.

With $26 in my pocket and a T-model Ford automobile, five of my schoolmates and I started out early one Saturday morning on our way to the Golden West, the great State of California. We got there in due time, minus most of my $26, and I got a very well paying job of $90 a month running an elevator. But I found at the end of the month, after I paid for three meals and paid for my room and my laundry that I was probably better off back there eating mama's food than I was in California.

So I went back to Texas and I got a job with the Highway Department. We didn't have to get to work until sunup, we got to quit every night at sundown. We did have to go to work on our own time. We had to be at work at sunup, and that was usually 20 or 30 miles down the road, and we had to ride home on our own time after sundown. I got the magnificent salary of a dollar a day.

After a little over a year of that, I began to think that my father's advice that I should go and take some more training and not be a school dropout—maybe he was wiser than I had thought a year before. In other words, he became a lot smarter while I was gone to California. And with the help of the good Lord, and with a mother persistently urging me to go back to school and get some training, I hitchhiked 50 miles to get back into the classroom where I spent 4 years. And I have been reasonably well employed

ever since. I now have a contract that runs until January 20, 1965.

So I have come out here to the West to tell you about my work and some of the problems I have, and what my job consists of, and perhaps to make an application with you to renew that contract after January the 20th.

But I have also come here to make this pledge to you and to the people of America. I make it to the parents, and I make it to all of their children: I intend to put education at the top of America's agenda. And if you do not quite understand the details of what I mean by the top of America's agenda, I will say this: that regardless of family financial status, education should be open to every boy and girl born in America up to the highest level they can take.

I guess you see from that that we really have a choice, we really have an honest difference of opinion, because I do not believe that in most cases the children will get along very well without it. I don't think they will get along very well at all without it.

Our job is cut out for us. First, we need 660,000—660,000; more than a half million—new classrooms, and 200,000 new teachers in the next 4 years just to keep up.

Second, we must make an all-out effort to improve schools in city slums and in poor rural areas.

Third, we must expand and enrich our colleges. Our college population will double—double—in the next 10 years.

Fourth, we must encourage our adults to go back and get the schooling they need to keep up with technology so they can continue to be taxpayers and not go on relief and be taxeaters.

And finally, we must keep control of our schools where it belongs—with the people. I believe that you should run your own schools, and you will do that as long as I am

President.

You are going to provide an answer on November 3d to those who distrust education. I believe that you are going to veto the philosophy of the candidate who says your children don't have a right to education. Am I wrong?

It was a little over 10 months ago, following a terrible tragedy on November 22d, that in a matter of moments I assumed the awesome responsibilities of the most powerful position in the world, the Presidency of the United States. I said when I went to the White House from my plane that evening, that with God's help and your help, I would do my best. I would do the best I could do.

Our beloved President had formulated a program that met with the approval of a good many of the leaders of the Congress, men of both parties. Patriotism is not limited to one party, but there was pending 51 major measures in the Congress on that night of November 22d, when the first inventory was made. Last Friday night when I left my office in the White House, the Congress had come and gone in these 11 months, and I had done the best I could. And thanks to the Congress and men like Congressman Rogers and Congressman Aspinall, and other patriots of both parties in the Congress, the United States Senate had passed every single one of those 51 bills, and all but three or four of them had passed the House of Representatives.

There are two real issues that stand out in this campaign. One is peace in the world. You can't get peace by rattling your rockets. You can't get peace by bluffing with your bombs. You must get peace by reasoning with men, and trying to find agreement with men, as President Kennedy did with 108 nations with the test ban treaty.

We have had a very successful postwar relation with other nations, and our foreign policy, I think, has generally been effective.

Harry Truman stopped the Communists in Greece and Turkey with the help of that great Republican Arthur Vandenberg, who brought the men from both parties together to support a united country.

Dwight Eisenhower stopped them in the Formosa Strait with the help of Lyndon Johnson and Mike Mansfield, the Democratic leaders of the Congress.

President Kennedy negotiated the test ban treaty with the help of the distinguished Republican leader, Mr. Everett Dirksen of Illinois, who said, "I don't want it written on my tombstone that I had a chance to do something about taking radioactive poison out of the air we breathe and the milk we drink, and that I had failed and refused to do it." But those two men, working together, passed the treaty in the Senate. And now 108 other nations have agreed upon it.

I believe in continuing that kind of bipartisan foreign policy. And I do not believe in going off on a tangent in a dangerous course, leading to evils that we know not of. I believe the leadership of this country should try to unite America instead of divide Americans.

I believe the President of this country ought to encourage neighbor to love neighbor instead of neighbor to hate neighbor. I believe the President of this great Republic and the leader of the world must have faith and must have hope and must have a desire to improve the lot of humanity here and throughout the world.

That is one of the questions that you are going to have to decide on November 3d: which party, which leader, which man you want to sit there with his thumb that may have to decide whether to push that button. You have to decide which man you want to sit there to pick up that "hot line" telephone when it rings and Moscow is calling.

You have judgment, you have training, you have experience, you know your needs and you know your wants. I don't think there is anything that I can add to them. But this is going to be as serious a decision as you ever made, and you ought to make it based on what you think is best for America.

Tonight, more Americans are working than ever before in the history of our country—72.5 million. They are drawing higher wages than they have ever drawn before. They drew $60 billion more after taxes this year than they did when John Kennedy took office. Business is doing better than ever before. They made $12 billion more after taxes this year than they did when John Kennedy took office.

The farmer has an income of $12 billion, but if you, overnight, pull all the programs away from him, that income will drop from $12 billion to $6 billion.

I am here to say to you that I want to unite business and labor and the farmer, and not only have peace in the world, but have peace and prosperity here among our own people. I love our country. I have faith in our people. I think we have the best system of government that human in-

genuity ever devised. If you want a leader that believes those things, then go vote Democratic on November 3d.

I believe in the responsibility of the President of this country. I think he has a duty and an obligation to lead this country, and if I am chosen to perform that obligation, I will lead it prudently and carefully and cautiously, progressively, with our eyes on the stars but our feet always on the ground. But I will not try to divide brother and brother. I will not array class against class, or race against race, or region against region, because I think that America needs to be united now more than ever in its history.

And if I am your President I am not only going to preach the Golden Rule throughout the world and throughout this land, of do unto others as you would have them do unto you, but I am going to practice it.

NOTE: The President spoke at 6:35 p.m. at the Coliseum in Denver, Colo. In his opening words he referred to former Governor Stephen L. R. Mc-Nichols, U.S. Representatives Wayne N. Aspinall and Byron G. Rogers, State Senator Roy H. Mc-Vicker and State Representative Frank E. Evans, Democratic candidates for U.S. Representative, and former Senators Edwin C. Johnson and John A. Carroll, all of Colorado. Later he referred to Arthur H. Vandenberg, Senator from Michigan during the Truman administration, and Senators Mike Mansfield of Montana and Everett McKinley Dirksen of Illinois.

---

659   Remarks Upon Arrival at the Airport in Boise.
October 12, 1964

Mr. Chairman, Reverend Clergy, Mr. Mayor, Senator Church, Congressman Harding, Congressman White, ladies and gentlemen, boys and girls:

One morning earlier this year Mrs. Johnson kissed me goodby and said, "I am going West, young man," and she did come out here to see the land and to see the people. The girls and I made out as best we could

because we wanted her to have a good rest for a long time.

When Mrs. Johnson returned from the Western trip, she came in to me and said, "I have just enjoyed the happiest trip anybody ever had anywhere."

Yesterday morning I kissed Lady Bird goodby and this time I headed West. Since then we have gone to Arizona, California,

Nevada, Montana, Wyoming, Colorado, and now tonight I am here with my old friend Tom Boise in Idaho.

Every mile of the way, every block of the way, we have seen the people of the West. The friendly, happy, confident people of the West have turned out as they seem to have never turned out before. The officials estimate that we have seen more than 1½ million people in the West since I ate breakfast yesterday morning.

So tomorrow morning when I get back to the White House about 5:30, I am going in and wake up my Lady Bird, and I am going to say to her, "Now I have enjoyed the happiest trip anybody ever had anywhere."

I am happy not for myself, but for my country. I am happy because when I see Americans coming together in their cities, coming out to line the streets to stand and be counted for the same cause, I know that this Nation is united, and this Nation is not going to be divided.

What we have seen in the West we have been seeing all across this land, in New England, in the Midwest, in the South. Everywhere the crowds are the largest that have been seen in years, and in many places they are the largest that have been seen at any time.

What does this mean? I believe that we are finding out whose country this is. This is the country of responsible Americans, that is who. The men and women of this Nation are thinking of what they have and what they want their children to have after them. So without regard to party, responsible Americans—Democrats, Republicans, Independents, and whatnots—are uniting this year because they do not intend to turn their heritage or their hopes over to factions and fractions which stand against all that both parties have ever stood for in America. The people want responsibility in Washing-

ton. The people want performances in the Presidency, not promises.

The people of the United States know, the people of the world know, that in these perilous, critical times the President of the United States has to be right the first time, and if he is not right the first time, there may be no second time for him to change his views or explain them or correct them, or there may be no time for the Nation to change its choice.

Out here in the West the people of your State and the people of all of these fine, progressive, prudent Western States want our country to pull together. They want a unified America. We do not have a Continental Divide on our opportunity, or on our progress, or on our unity. We want the young people of the West to have as much opportunity all their lives as young people of every other region have. We don't want them to have to leave home to find it.

We want the West to make progress as the whole Nation makes progress. We want life in America to mean the same on both sides of the Continental Divide, and that is our goal and that is our purpose.

These years ahead of us, the years between now and the end of this century, can be the best years of our national life. We can do the things that we have so long needed to do. We can bind up our wounds and heal our history, and we can make this great Nation of ours whole again. We can work to give States like your wonderful Idaho a full share in the strength and the future and the prosperity of our times.

Idaho's potatoes are wonderful, but Idaho can produce greater treasures for America in the lives and in the minds of Idaho's sons and daughters.

Here in Idaho and all across the West there are rivers and resources to develop. There is work to do. There are new jobs to create.

There are better opportunities to provide for all the people.

The standard of opportunity must continue to rise for all Americans, whether they live in the large cities or the small towns; whether they live on the little farms or whether they live in the large States.

And our purposes can be accomplished if—if—we unite our country, if we stay strong to keep this Nation and keep the world at peace, if we do the works for our people which our hearts and our conscience have always told us were right, and if we do those works with prudence, with care, with caution, with an honest regard for the taxpayer, and with a full respect for our American heritage of thrift and frugality.

This year, for the first year in many years, I reduced the Federal budget $1 billion under last year. I did not do that alone. I did it with the help of President Truman and President Eisenhower, who came down from Gettysburg and spent several conferences with me shortly after I took office; with Secretary Anderson, a former Republican Secretary of the Treasury; with the Director of the Budget; with Mr. McNamara, the Republican Secretary of Defense; with Mr. Dillon, a Republican who is Secretary of the Treasury.

Together, we all felt that we must have prudent, progressive government. We must keep our eyes in the stars and have a vision of tomorrow—but we must keep our feet on the ground today.

My first budget went into effect July 1st of this year. The Congress just finished appropriating for it. The fiscal year starts July 1st. During the month of July, and during the month of August, we have just totaled the expenditures of the Government. During those 2 months we spent $676 million less than we spent last July and last August, a year ago. This July we reduced the Federal employees to the point where we had 25,000 less people working for the Government in July 1964 than we had in July 1963.

Idaho's role in this effort will be greater, and it will be more effective if you have as your voice in the House of Representatives the youth and the experience and the strength of this young man, Ralph Harding, who sits on this platform with us tonight. Comp White has done a wonderful job for this State, and I have no doubt but what you will want to return him to the Congress where he can work for you another 2 years.

They asked Mr. Rayburn, who became Speaker of the House, and who served in the House 50 years, and who both parties recognized as probably the most popular and most effective Congressman in that body—they asked him one time why it was that Texas had the standing in the Congress that it had. It had 8 chairmen of committees out of 15. It had the Speaker and the Vice President. It had the leadership of the majority party of that Congress.

Mr. Rayburn in his quiet, simple way, said: "We have a little formula down home that we follow for our Congressmen. We pick them young, we pick them honest, we send them there, and then we keep them there. They grow in experience and they grow in seniority, and they grow in stature and they grow in understanding. As a result, they achieve the leadership that comes that way."

That is happening to Idaho. That is happening to Idaho in the form of your eloquent and able young Senator and his charming wife who helps Frank do such a good job. I have always agreed with the people of Idaho on your choice of Churches. There is no Senator that Washington respects more, and none that the Nation needs more, and none that your President values more, than

Frank Church.

On November 3d you have one of the most exacting obligations of citizenship. You have one of the greatest responsibilities that will ever come to you. It is just as important for you to live up to that responsibility as it is for your son to put on his uniform and fight to protect that flag when need be.

On November 3d, 70 million to 80 million people in this country, in accordance with Thomas Jefferson's view that the collective judgment of the many is much to be preferred to the individual decisions of the few, the collective judgment of 75 million people will be recorded that night by the computers of the Nation. And you 75 million will determine the type of leadership that you want to guide the destiny of this Nation for the next 4 years.

That day you will determine the man that you want to entrust the responsibility of our awesome military posture to. That day you will determine the man that you want to be your Commander in Chief, the man whose thumb will rest close to that button if it ever has to be touched; the man whose hand will have to lift up that "hot line" from Moscow if that phone rings and hear the voice on the other end.

You have an obligation to yourself and your children to select the person that you know is the most experienced, and the most capable of handling the future of your country and its citizens.

I did not come here tonight to tell you who that man is. You have intelligence enough to know in your conscience what you ought to do. I did come here to tell you that you must do your duty. Once you see it, you must get that job done, because the eyes of the world are on America.

The leadership of the world is in the hands of America. We are the richest, we are the freest, we are the most powerful nation in all the world, and the other 3 billion people look to us for example, and they follow it, so they know that the number one problem in the world is how do we live with other nations without destroying each other?

After Oak Ridge, we came into possession of the mightiest power ever known to the human race, and we are the steward and the guardian of that power.

President Kennedy sat at the head of the Cabinet table for 37 meetings during the Cuban missile crisis and, as Secretary Rusk said, Mr. Khrushchev and Mr. Kennedy sat there eyeball to eyeball. Mr. Khrushchev had his missiles in Cuba, 90 miles away. But both men, after counseling for days with the ablest minds in their respective countries, concluded that it would be too horrible to contemplate to put your thumb on that button and wipe out 300 million lives in a matter of a few moments. So Mr. Khrushchev loaded his missiles on his ships and took them back home, and we breathed easier for a while.

Your Nation will face other crises in the days ahead, and in the time when it does, I know that you will do for whoever is your President at that time what you did for President Kennedy: give him your confidence, give him your strength, give him your prayers. I am proud to say to you tonight that I sat in all but one of those 37 meetings, and the coolest man in that room all the time was the man that you people had selected to lead you, John Fitzgerald Kennedy.

So when you go to make your choice, you will choose a Commander in Chief, you will choose a man that will try to find peace in the world, but will also try to find peace at home—peace between the farmer and the consumer, peace between the businessman and the laborer, peace between the manufacturer and the trade union. Because little good does it do us to become a mighty industrial nation if we waste all of our talents chewing on each other.

I am happy that we settled the railroad strike that had gone for 4½ years without a resolution.

I am happy that we today have the lowest number of lost man-hours due to strikes that we have ever had in the history of the United States, and that is because the businessman and the laboringman and the farmer are working together. That is because America has hope, America has faith, America does not live in fear and doubt. And that is why we have that good domestic record in this country.

So you will select the leader to find peace in the world, and the leader to find peace at home, and the leader to develop a program that will bring prosperity to our people. Today we have 72 million people working, more than ever before in our history, drawing higher wages than ever before in our history. Corporations made $12 billion more after taxes. Workers made $60 billion more after taxes.

So times are good, but we can't just sit back in our rocking chair and expect them to be good. You have to work to make them good. You have to plan to make them good. You have to be equitable and just

and fair to make them good. And we are now doing our best on that job.

The day that I returned to the White House after that tragedy, I said to the American people, with God's help, with your prayers, I will do the best I can. I have done the best I could.

I have tried to be the President of all the people, of all the States in this country, and I hope that the good people of Idaho will join all the other States in the West and I hope a good many States in every section of the country, because I really want to know no North, no South, no East, or no West. I just want to know the United States of America.

I hope that on November 3d you will go and send us some good, experienced Congressmen back to Washington like Ralph Harding and Compton White; that you will vote the Democratic ticket for President and Vice President. And if you do, I give you my pledge that we will do our dead level best to preserve peace in the world, peace at home, and prosperity throughout this Nation.

Thank you and good night.

NOTE: The President spoke at 9:10 p.m. at an airport rally in Boise, Idaho. His opening words referred to Lloyd Walker, chairman of the Idaho State Democratic Committee, John L. Clarke, president of Ricks College in Rexburg, Mayor Eugene Shellworth of Boise, and Senator Frank Church and Representatives Ralph R. Harding and Compton I. White, all of Idaho.

660   Remarks at the Mall Shopping Center, Bergen, New Jersey. *October* 14, 1964

Governor Hughes, Senator Williams, Daniel Amster, ladies and gentlemen, and distinguished guests:

In the past week I have visited 15 States. I have seen more than 2 million people. In

New England and the West, in the Midwest and the South, the story has been the same all across this land.

The American people are coming out of their living rooms, they are leaving their offices. They are turning away from work and play. They are coming together to stand together, side by side, as Americans have seldom done in our times. They are coming out as never before because they want the world to know that this is a nation united, one nation indivisible, under God.

For 11 months I have guided my every act by this one belief, that any man who serves as President must serve as President of all the people. Americans do not want the White House to be a house where some citizens are privileged to enter and others are turned away at the door because they were born "wrong," because they believe "wrong," or even because they voted "wrong."

I have found that the vast majority of Americans want to help their President, not hurt him. I have had greater strength than my own on which to call, from business and from labor, from west and from east, from the conservatives, from the liberals, from the Republicans, and from the Democrats.

From that I learned much about the American people.

I believe they are weary of those who preach that America is failing in the world and faltering at home. The people are tired of being told that their character is in question, that their moral fiber is riddled with "rot and decay."

The American people want leadership which believes in them, not leadership which berates them.

This year, good Americans of both parties are determined to put their country first. They intend to vote to preserve the traditions of our country.

But other traditions are at stake, too—a two-party system, for example. That system is not in danger when the leaders of both parties represent those common principles and those broad agreements that have developed down through our history.

The two-party system dangles by a slim thread when the faction that controls one party wants to repudiate the policies that have built our progress step by step over 30 years.

I do not believe that responsible Republicans are going to let control of their party rest for very long with men who want to repeal the present and veto the future. History tells us that once such a faction seals its control of a major party, the fate of that party is also sealed.

The Republican Party today, now, is in temporary receivership. Responsible Republicans can't do anything about it.

But they will have a chance on November 3d to do something about it, and they are going to do it November 3d. And I am here this morning after traveling all over the United States to tell you that all the American people are going to do something about it.

I want to thank the people of this area for the support they have given me in sending that wonderful Senator to Washington— Pete Williams. I hope that you can send us Eddie Ihnen and Henry Helstoski to Congress to help him out.

Come next January, we are going to meet in the Capital and have a program for all the people of this Nation, not just Democrats, not just Republicans, not just Independents, but a program of peace and prosperity for all Americans in all regions of all this great land of ours.

We have the most wonderful country in all the world. We want to protect it. We want to preserve it. The way to do it is to go to the polls November 3d and give us a Democratic victory.

NOTE: The President spoke at 10:30 a.m. at the Mall Shopping Center in Bergen, N.J. His opening words referred to Governor Richard J. Hughes and Senator Harrison A. (Pete) Williams, Jr., of New Jersey, and Daniel Amster, chairman of the Bergen County Democratic Committee. Later he referred to Edward H. Ihnen and Henry Helstoski, Democratic candidates for Representative.

661   Remarks at a Rally at the Wilkes-Barre–Scranton, Pa., Airport.   *October 14, 1964*

Chairman Mellody, Senator Clark, Senator Blatt, Governor Lawrence, Congressman Flood, next Congressman Jim Haggerty, ladies and gentlemen, boys and girls:

Within the past week I have talked to people in 15 States. I have seen more than 2 million Americans. I came to this clear conclusion: Americans are more excited about their future than they have ever been before.

They are willing to work hard to build America's greatness.

They are proud. They are not ashamed of their country. They know that we have problems to solve, but they are eager to solve them.

And they believe that their Government is a partner in the enterprise of liberty and not a predatory enemy trying to devour their rights.

After traveling 10,000 miles across this great land in 1 week, I know some of the things that Americans don't want. I have talked to them about these issues, and I can still hear their response ringing in my ears.

They don't want to gamble with the future of social security by making it voluntary.

They don't want to dash the hopes of the farmers by the prompt and the final termination of our farm program.

They don't want to weaken collective bargaining and threaten the rights of our workingmen and our workingwomen.

They don't want their Government to turn its back on our children's rights to an education.

They don't want to tread an uncertain and an untried path in the pursuit of peace. They don't want a government that threatens other nations with "do-it-our-way-or-else" ultimatums.

I think I know some of the things that the Americans do want. They want their President to be a source of leadership and responsibility. They know that a President who strides forward to do the people's business is a bulwark against the decline and chaos in this country. They know that a President who is willing to move ahead, whose means are just, whose ends are democratic, can be the difference between national stagnation and national progress.

And the people want progress. They want to keep moving.

Americans know that the Presidency belongs to all the people. And they want the President to act and be President of all the people.

Something else is very clear. The source of the President's authority is the people. A President who refuses to go out among the people, who refuses to be judged by the people, who is unwilling to lay his case before the people, can never be President of all the people.

The people want to see their President in person. They want to hear first-hand what he believes. They want to decide if he can act for them.

And unless the President goes to the people, unless he visits and talks with them, unless he senses how they respond as he discusses issues with them, he cannot do the

President's job. The voice of the people will be lost among the clamor of divisions and diversities, and the Presidency will not become a clear beacon of national purpose.

As long as I hold it, I will keep the office of President always close to all the people. I think I know what it is the people want, and I make that as a solemn pledge.

It is wonderful to be here in Pennsylvania with you today. I have had a delightful trip to all places in the country, but I came down here to talk to you folks and tell you I need your help. When I became your President almost 11 months ago, I told you that with God's help and with your prayers I would do the best I could. I have done that.

Never before in the history of our country have so many people worked so hard to help their President make a success. Business and labor, farmers and women's groups, young people throughout the land, the high schools and the colleges, have all come into the White House and have tried to help their President give this country good government. No one man can lead alone. He must have other people to help him.

Pennsylvania is a great State. You have a great senior Senator there—Joe Clark. He needs a junior Senator, Genevieve Blatt, to come and help him in the Senate. And when Genevieve Blatt becomes your junior Senator, with Joe Clark your senior Senator, this great State will have two good Senators working with their President for all the people of this State.

We need Jim Haggerty in the House, and I hope you people will help us send him there. I spent the morning with Jim. We have been flying all morning. We had a wonderful rally in New Jersey, and we have been talking about some of the problems of this district and this State.

I just want to say this to you people: If you will get out and do your duty the next 3 weeks of this campaign, if you will talk to your neighbor and kinfolks, your uncles and your cousins and your aunts, if you will get them to go to the polls on November 3d—that's 3 weeks from yesterday—and reelect your good Congressman Dan Flood, elect Jim Haggerty, and give us a new Senator in Genevieve Blatt, we will have good government for all of Pennsylvania.

We are operating a prudent government. In the first 2 months of this fiscal year, we spent $676 million less than we did in July and August of last year. We had 25,000 less people working for the Federal Government in July of this year than we had in July of last year. We reduced our deficit in half. We cut the budget over a billion dollars.

We have saved on the things that we did not need to have so we would have the things that we needed to buy. We have a good poverty program. We have a good health program. We have a good education program. We have a good highway program.

We are moving America forward. We need Pennsylvania's help. We need Genevieve Blatt. We need Jim Haggerty. We need Dan Flood. And Hubert Humphrey and I need you November 3d.

NOTE: The President spoke at 12:25 p.m. at the Wilkes-Barre–Scranton Airport, Avoca, Pa. In his opening words he referred to Patrick J. Mellody, chairman of the Lackawanna County Democratic Committee, Senator Joseph S. Clark of Pennsylvania, Genevieve Blatt, Secretary of Internal Affairs for Pennsylvania and Democratic candidate for Senator, former Governor David L. Lawrence of Pennsylvania, Representative Daniel J. Flood of Pennsylvania, and James J. Haggerty, Democratic candidate for Representative.

662   Remarks in New York City at the Annual Dinner of the Alfred E. Smith Memorial Foundation.   *October* 14, 1964

Your Eminence, distinguished guests at the head table, ladies and gentlemen:

It is a source of great pride to be invited by His Eminence Francis Cardinal Spellman to participate in this dinner in honor of one of America's greatest men—Alfred E. Smith.

I am particularly proud to say that in 1928, although I was not old enough to vote, I campaigned for his election to the Presidency of the United States. And it is with the deepest pride that I participated in helping our late beloved President, John Fitzgerald Kennedy, prove to the world that there are no religious bars to the highest office in our land. And what I say to you tonight represents what I believe Al Smith would have endorsed had he been here tonight, because he was a man of true compassion.

I have prepared a statement somewhat more lengthy than I think would be appropriate to give at this late hour, but I shall try to hit the high points, and I stand upon everything in the somewhat fuller exposition.

I was delighted to be welcomed back to the great State of New York by my old friend, the affable Governor of this State. I gather that he does not share some of his colleagues' views on immigration, or perhaps we are still free at least to emigrate between the States!

In any event, I always find it a source of strength to come to this, the leading city in America, this, the melting pot of our country. Here I get inspiration and stimulation.

America's policies toward the world have been carefully built through the years by the leaders of both parties. We will continue to follow this course because it has brought us a hopeful world.

We are, and we will remain, the strongest nation on earth. We are, and we will always be, ready to defend freedom anywhere.

Strength and courage are essential, but they are like the fuel in an airplane. You can't go without it. But neither will it take you where you want to go. For that you need a sense of direction, caution in the cockpit, and an experienced pilot.

But strength is not enough. Other nations feared the might of Hitler, but they would not follow him. They will not associate themselves with us just because of our bombs or our missiles or our factories. We have learned that to deal with the world it must be seen in all of its fantastic complexities.

Almost all general statements about the world are wrong. They are not necessarily false; they seem to me just to be inadequate.

It is true, for example, that communism is a deadly danger, but Russia is a different kind of danger from Yugoslavia. A small Communist Party in Africa is a different danger from the Government of Red China. These different dangers require different policies and different actions, and different replies.

As President, I have no special gift or prophecy. But I do have a special perspective, and a very special responsibility to anticipate the dangers and the opportunities of the future.

Tonight I would like to look forward to this future in three fields:

First, we will work to make the greatness of our institutions match the grandeur of our intentions. I intend to do even more to attract the best minds and the most brilliant talents to our foreign operations, regardless of background or race or party.

I want, also, to bring more young people to the conduct of foreign policy. This is the first generation to come of age in an outward looking America. It is a concerned generation. Its members are our greatest asset. We intend to encourage them and to give them early responsibility. This will be the first order of our business. Beyond the association of the West is the association of the world. I do not intend to withdraw from the United Nations. I do not intend to weaken it. I intend to do everything I can to strengthen it.

A second field of danger and opportunity is in our confrontation with Russia and Communist China.

Today there is no longer one cold war; there are many. They differ in temperature, intensity, and danger.

Our relations with the Soviet Union have come a long way since shoes were banged on desks here in New York and a summit meeting collapsed in Paris.

In Asia there is a different prospect. The final outcome will depend on the will of the Asian people. But as long as they turn to us for help, we will be there. We will not and we must not permit the great civilizations of the East—almost half of the people of all the world—to be swallowed up in Communist conquest.

In Viet-Nam we believe that, with our help, the people of South Viet-Nam can defeat Communist aggression. We will continue to act on this belief without recklessness and without retreat.

A third field of opportunity and danger is our relation to the developing world. I do not believe that our island of abundance will be finally secure in a sea of despair and unrest or in a world where even the oppressed may one day have access to the engines of modern destruction.

Moreover, there is a great moral principle

at stake. It is not right in a world of such infinite possibilities that children should die of hunger, that young people should live in ignorance, that men should be crippled by disease, that families should live in misery, shrouded in despair. I will propose steps to use the food and agricultural skills of the entire West in a joint effort to eliminate hunger and starvation.

We will seek ways to stabilize the prices of the tropical commodities which are the life blood of many economies. I will press for prompt execution of the worldwide coffee agreement, and seek action for other products.

We will give our support most of all to those governments whose efforts are directed toward the welfare of all their people and not just a privileged few.

We will always give first attention to our close friendship with the people of Latin America.

You and every citizen of this land can be proud of the role that we have played over the past 20 years. None has ever given of itself so freely to the needs and the protection of others as the United States of America.

Of course, we acted out of enlightened self-interest. We are a nation responsible to our people. But the pages of history can be searched in vain for another power whose pursuit of that self-interest was so infused with grandeur of spirit and morality of purpose.

We have done this because this is the kind of people we are, and this is the kind of a country that we have built.

We have done this because we have never believed the complexity of human experience could be bound in an iron cloak of dogma.

We have deep beliefs. But we have followed where reason and experience led, never sacrificing man to the abstract arrogance of ideology.

There were those who thought this was a flaw in freedom, this was an advantage to the Communists. Well, they were wrong. Unquestioned obedience to an unyielding system will not satisfy the needs of man. And time is slowly unfolding this truth to all the world and to the Communists themselves.

All of us who live today are also a race to be envied. These next decades can set the course of the world for a thousand years or more. There is much danger. But there is also the joy of great expectations. We are not in the grip of history. We are the makers of history. We have the power and the faith to forge on the anvil of the world an age tempered to the hopes of man.

How fortunate we are to live at such a time, with such a belief, in such a young and resistless land.

So come with me into that uncertain day already touched with dawn.

Thank you.

NOTE: The President spoke at 11:20 p.m. at the Waldorf-Astoria Hotel in New York City. In his opening words he referred to His Eminence Francis Cardinal Spellman, Archbishop of New York, founder of the Alfred E. Smith Memorial Foundation. Later he referred to Governor Nelson A. Rockefeller of New York.

The complete text of the President's prepared statement (see reference in the third paragraph of the foregoing remarks) is printed below as released by the White House.

STATEMENT BY THE PRESIDENT

America's policies toward the world have been carefully built by leaders of both parties over a generation. We have followed a steady course, not as the result of a conspiracy, and not because we have stifled debate. We have followed it because these policies are the only way to defend freedom and keep the peace.

We will continue to follow this course.

It has brought a more hopeful world.

Let me be clear about the foundation of our policies. We are, and we will remain, the strongest nation on earth. We are and we always will be ready to defend freedom.

Strength and courage are essential. But they are like the fuel in an airplane. You can't go without it. But neither will it take you where you want to go. For that you need a sense of direction, caution in the cockpit, and an experienced pilot.

On these qualities we have built our leadership in the cause of freedom.

To lead, we must be respected. Strength is not enough. Other nations feared the might of Hitler, but they would not follow him. They will not associate themselves with us just because of our bombs or our missiles or our factories.

There must be identification with our ideals and our intentions—confidence in our wisdom and restraint—faith in our vision and our purpose.

We have not been blinded by the illusion that all the world is divided into satellites or enemies.

We have not been blinded by the illusion of placing all our trust in bombs and armies.

We have not been blinded by the illusion that we could have our way through threat and ultimatum.

Because we have been firm as well as patient, we have the trust of our allies.

Because we have proved our passion for peace, we have been supported in time of danger.

Because we have turned our support to the forces of progress, the forces of progress have begun to turn to us.

Because we have been responsible in control of our power, we have won the confidence of all who know the terrors of the atom.

Let us be clear.

If this country is ever guided by policies which do not command this kind of respect, no force in all the world will keep the grand alliance of freedom from being scattered like sand before the wind.

We have learned that to deal with the world it must be seen in all its fantastic complexities.

Almost all general statements about the world are wrong. They are not necessarily false. They are just inadequate.

It is true, for example, that communism is a danger. But Russia is a different kind of danger from Yugoslavia. A small Communist Party in Africa is a different danger from the Government of Red China.

These different dangers require different policies, different actions, and different replies.

Beware of those who come to you with simple slogans. Theirs is the path of peril and not of peace.

As President I have no special gift of prophecy. But I do have a special perspective, and a special responsibility to anticipate the dangers and opportunities of the future.

Tonight I would like to look toward this future in three fields.

First, we will work to make the greatness of our institutions match the grandeur of our intentions.

Foreign policy does not work in the abstract. It is conducted by men working within institutions. Its effectiveness depends upon the talent of the men and the toughness of the institutions.

You are already served with devotion and love of country by thousands of outstanding men and women you do not know, in places you cannot name. I am proud of them.

I intend to do even more to attract the best minds and most brilliant talents to our foreign operations—regardless of background, or race, or party.

I want, also, to bring more young people to the conduct of foreign policy. This is the first generation to come of age in an outward looking America. It is a concerned generation. Its members are our greatest asset. We intend to encourage them and give them early responsibility. This will be a first order of business.

We will strengthen not only our own institutions but those which we share with others.

We will continue to work toward European unity and Atlantic partnership, knowing that progress will require initiative and sacrifice from us as well as from Europe—that success will come from years of patient effort and not a single dramatic move—that the steps ahead may be more difficult than the ones behind.

Beyond the association of the West is the association of the world.

I do not intend to withdraw from the United Nations. I do not intend to weaken it. I intend to strengthen it.

The United Nations has flaws and it has had failures. It now faces a major constitutional crisis. That crisis must be resolved so that every nation bears its full share of the costs and burdens.

Let no one think this position is shaped by the pressures of an election. This principle is vital if the United States is to command the respect and confidence which its great purpose requires.

With all its defects, the United Nations has been a source of innumerable achievements for peace and for the dignity of man.

And wherever it has gone—from the Congo to the Gaza strip—the Communists have not conquered. This is not because it is our ally in the cold war. But it is on the side of the independence of nations. And that is the side we are on.

Twenty years after World War I the League of Nations was dying and war was near. Twenty years after World War II the United Nations is stronger than ever and peace is nearer.

A second field of danger and opportunity is in our confrontation with Russia and Communist China.

There is no longer one cold war. There are many. They differ in temperature, intensity, and danger.

Our relations with the Soviet Union have come a long way since shoes were banged on desks here in New York and a summit meeting collapsed in Paris.

The test ban treaty and the "hot line" would not have been possible 10 years ago. Conditions did not permit such acts of reason.

When this is so men must work to change these conditions. This we did, from the Marshall plan to the Cuban crisis.

And men must also have the vision to seize the day of opportunity when it comes. This too we have done.

I believe we may be nearing a time for further and more lasting steps toward decreasing tensions and a diminishing arms race. I will try to take those steps—always in consultation with our friends.

I will expect respect for our courage and our convictions. I will offer understanding for the concerns and interests of others.

I will work for the growth of freedom and the survival of man.

In Asia there is a different prospect. On that strife-streaked continent an ambitious and aggressive power menaces weak and poor nations.

Here—as we have done in Europe—we must help create the conditions which can make peace possible. The task is different and more difficult. It is not less important.

We will assist against attack. We will strengthen our commitments of alliance. We will work with the nations of Asia to build the hope and self-confidence on which their independence must rest.

The final outcome will depend on the will of the Asian people. But as long as they turn to us for help we will be there. We will not permit the great civilizations of the East—almost half the people of the world—to be swallowed up in Communist conquest.

Let no one be foolhardy enough to doubt the strength of that unyielding American commitment.

In Viet-Nam we believe that, with our help, the people of South Viet-Nam can defeat Communist aggression. We will continue to act on this belief without recklessness and without retreat.

A third field of opportunity and danger is our relation to the developing world.

Here, there is a lesson from our own history—one that I know so well. America still bears many scars because our South lagged behind while the North leaped forward. That gap contributed to a civil war and a great depression.

Today Rio and New Delhi are close to New York; closer than Atlanta or Johnson City once were.

I do not believe that our island of abundance will be finally secure in a sea of despair and unrest, or in a world where even the oppressed may one day have access to the engines of modern destruction.

Moreover, there is a great moral principle at stake. It is not right—in a world of such infinite possibilities—that children should die of hunger, that young people should live in ignorance, that men should be crippled by disease, that families should live in misery, shrouded in despair.

If we truly mean our commitment to freedom, we must help strike at the conditions which make a mockery of that hope.

Since President Truman announced the point 4 program we have extended the hand of compassion toward the world's oppressed. We will continue this help. But it is now clear that the tools we have developed will not do the job alone.

I will propose steps to use the food and agricultural skills of the entire West in a joint effort to eliminate hunger and starvation.

We will seek ways to stabilize the prices of the tropical commodities which are the life blood of many economies. I will press for prompt execution of the worldwide coffee agreement, and seek action for other products.

We will give our support most of all to those governments whose efforts are directed toward the welfare of all their people and not a privileged few.

And we will always give first attention to our close friendship with the people of Latin America. Those who share the views and values of our civilization, who share our convictions in the council chambers, must also share the dividends of progress and the dignity of freedom.

We have the skills and resources to improve the life of man. I do not believe we lack the imagination to find ways to shatter the barrier between man's capacity and man's needs.

These are some of the difficulties through which we will move in years to come. There are many others.

For 20 years, under four Presidents, we have kept faith with the same broad principles in pursuit of the same basic goals.

You, and every citizen of this land, can be proud of the role that we have played.

No great power has ever acted with a more abundant spirit or spacious vision than the United States of America.

None has ever given of itself so freely to the needs and protection of others, as the United States of America.

None has ever walked the stage of the world so exempt of ambition for conquest or domination as the United States of America.

Of course, we acted out of enlightened self-interest. We are a nation responsible to our people. But the pages of history can be searched in vain for another power whose pursuit of that self-interest was so infused with grandeur of spirit and morality of purpose.

We have done this because this is the kind of people we are, and this is the kind of country we have built.

We have done this because we have never believed the complexity of human experience could be bound in an iron cloak of dogma.

We have deep beliefs. But we have followed where reason and experience led, never sacrificing man to the abstract arrogance of ideology.

There were those who thought this was a flaw in freedom—an advantage to the Communists.

They were wrong. Unquestioning obedience to an unyielding system will not satisfy the needs of man.

And time is slowly unfolding this truth to the world, and to the Communists themselves.

In 1776 John Adams wrote to a friend: "You and I . . . have been sent into life at a time when the greatest law givers of antiquity would have wished to live. How few of the human race have ever enjoyed (such) an opportunity . . ."

All of us who live today are also a race to be envied. These next decades can set the course of the world for a thousand years. There is much danger. But there is also the joy of great expectations. We are not in the grip of history. We are the makers. We have the power and the faith to forge on the anvil of the world an age tempered to the hopes of man.

How fortunate we are to live at such a time, with such a belief, in such a young and resistless land.

Come with me into that uncertain day already touched with dawn.

NOTE: This is the text of a White House release entitled "Statement by the President at the Al Smith Dinner, Waldorf-Astoria Hotel, New York City." See also note, page 1331, following the President's remarks at the dinner.

663 Statement by the President Upon Approving a Veterans' Life Insurance and Pension Bill.   *October* 14, 1964

I HAVE approved H.R. 1927, a bill relating to veterans' life insurance and pension programs.

This bill will immediately increase pensions for over 1 million needy veterans, widows, and children. It will also reopen National Service Life Insurance for approximately 4 million veterans with service-incurred disabilities and for those veterans who are so seriously disabled they are no longer commercially insurable. I urge all eligible veterans to explore this opportunity to help provide financial security for their families.

This legislation also increases the options of those veterans who now carry National Service Life Insurance policies so that they can, if they so desire, convert their policies to plans providing for level premium payments during the rest of their lifetime. Many can avoid premium increases every 5 years, which grow progressively higher as they grow older, often becoming an intolerable burden in their old age when their financial resources tend to be substantially reduced.

Finally, the legislation will make im-

portant improvements in the veterans' pension program, while adhering to the principle that veterans' pensions are based on need as determined by graduated income scales and tests of disability and unemployability. Over 1 million pensioners will receive at least a cost-of-living increase of about 7 percent, and those with the lowest incomes, who are in the greatest need, will receive increases of 15 to 17 percent.

Of particular significance is the change in the pension provisions dealing with recoupment. Until now, in determining eligibility for pensions, veterans were permitted to exclude from income the lump sum value of any contributions they may have made to social security or other retirement systems. Now, H.R. 1927 substitutes a new provision spreading recoupment over the life expectancy of the individual, allowing a deduction of 10 percent annually of the benefits received by the veteran under his social security, annuity, or other retirement systems.

This legislation will substantially strengthen our services to our veterans.

NOTE: As enacted, H.R. 1927, approved October 13, is Public Law 88–664 (78 Stat. 1094).

664 Statement by the President Upon Approving Bill Authorizing a Retirement System for Certain Employees of the Central Intelligence Agency. *October 14, 1964*

I HAVE signed H.R. 8427, a bill which would authorize a special retirement and disability system for a limited number of employees of the Central Intelligence Agency, whose work is of a demanding or specialized nature. This legislation is fundamentally meritorious.

However, I must express objection to a provision in this bill which would require that the rules and regulations prescribed by the Director of Central Intelligence for the establishment and maintenance of the retirement system not take effect until approved by the chairmen and ranking minority members of the Armed Services Committees of the House and Senate.

Four Attorneys General of the United States have held that legislative provisions vesting in congressional committees the power to approve or disapprove actions of the executive branch are unconstitutional. This conclusion is equally applicable to the provision in H.R. 8427 which vests such power in particular members of congressional committees. Such a provision attempts to confer executive powers on the members of the legislative branch, in violation of the constitutional principle of separation of powers.

However, I recognize that the adoption of this objectionable provision is due in large part to the fact that the anticipated coverage of the retirement system, which was explained to the committees, cannot for security reasons be set forth in the bill. Accordingly, I shall treat this provision as a request for consultation with the named committee members, and shall ask the Director to comply with it on that basis.

NOTE: As enacted, H.R. 8427, approved October 13, is Public Law 88–643 (78 Stat. 1043).

665 Statement by the President Upon Approving the Reserve Officers' Training Corps Vitalization Act. *October 14, 1964*

I HAVE approved H.R. 9124, the "Reserve Officers' Training Corps Vitalization Act of 1964."

The roots of the ROTC program reach back more than a century to 1862 when the Morrill Act required the land grant colleges to offer courses in military training. The program as we know it today is founded on the National Defense Act of 1916.

Under the authority so wisely provided, the ROTC has become familiar to all and has trained many, many thousands of our young men in the leadership so necessary in the three major conflicts in which we have been engaged during this century. Today,

this vital program constitutes the largest single source of trained officers not just for the Reserves, but for the Regular forces as well.

I am convinced that the bill I have approved today will bring about a marked improvement in the ROTC programs being conducted in our colleges and universities, and I congratulate the Congress for the changes it has made to this end.

The bill permits the establishment of new 2-year ROTC programs, in addition to continuing the traditional 4-year programs authorized by previous legislation. This will open the ROTC to many young men who have been unable to qualify before, either because they were transferees from a junior college or because the heavy academic load of freshman and sophomore years has prevented them from participating.

The bill also permits the Army and the Air Force to award scholarships comparable to those which have been authorized for the Navy since 1947 under the so-called Holloway plan. While these scholarships should help to strengthen the 4-year ROTC programs for which they have been provided, I earnestly hope that the Congress will later see fit to make them available to participants in the new 2-year program as well.

The bill, however, contains one feature which concerns me. This involves provisions which specify that junior ROTC units in secondary institutions must be established within prescribed numerical limits if the institutions meet certain standards and

criteria. The bill further provides that the President shall promulgate, by January 1, 1966, the regulations prescribing such standards and criteria.

I am aware of the fact that the junior ROTC program has been the subject of some controversy over the years. Even though the program fulfills no direct military requirement, it continues to occupy the full time of several hundred members of our active military personnel. Before I promulgate any regulations relating to the expansion of the program, I have asked the Secretary of Defense to conduct a thorough study of it and to ascertain whether it can be made responsive to the needs of our national defense and yet be conducted at the lowest possible cost.

NOTE: As enacted, H.R. 9124, approved October 13, is Public Law 88–647 (78 Stat. 1063).

666   Remarks at a Rally at the Rochester, N.Y., Airport. *October 15, 1964*

THANK YOU, Bob Kennedy. I treasure those statements. I consider them as among my most prized possessions. I know of no one who is in a better position to know my relationship and my work with our late, beloved President than you, and you make me feel very humble and very proud and very obligated to, as I said before, continue with the ideals that he enunciated and which he was in the process of carrying out.

Mayor Lamb, Mayor Wagner, Governor Harriman, my friend State Chairman McKeon, Secretary Folsom, our two wonderful congressional candidates, John Williams of Rochester in the 36th District, and Neil Bubel in the 37th District, Chairman Bob O'Brien, ladies and gentlemen, boys and

girls:

I feel so good about having a chance to come back here and be with you. I was here a good deal of my time in 1960 and never have I been any place where I found more interested people in the affairs of their country, more genuine friends, and more happy and progressive citizens. So I like Upstate New York, and I am so happy when you ask me to come back here again.

I have told Bob Kennedy that after we get this election behind us in November, and the things that flow with it, and we get the votes in the box, and the results are announced, that one of the things I want to do is to come with your new Senator to Upstate New York and evaluate and study your problems, and try to be of such help as I can, not only to putting him to work for New York, but putting his great abilities and talents to work for the entire Nation and the entire world.

Now, this country needs its most able, most talented, most progressive men that are available in the service of their country. The country needs Robert Kennedy in Washington. New York needs Robert Kennedy in the United States Senate. There is really no conceivable way that the Senate can keep from being Democratic.

It now has 67 Democratic Senators. The best estimates are that we will increase that number by several. The worst estimates are that we would lose two or three. But we are going to have a majority, or more than 50. So the chairmen and the majorities and the important assignments are going to be made by the majority party. And New York ought to have its Senator participating in those majority decisions, and I think you will have Bob Kennedy doing that after November 3d.

Bob Kennedy has a reputation that is known throughout the world. He has a name that is beloved in every household. But that, in itself, is not reason alone to select him as a public servant.

I think the thing that each of you should weigh in your mind in selecting your officials is the same thing that you consider in selecting someone to work with or that works for you.

Robert Kennedy has experience. He has training. He has demonstrated ability. His experience in fighting crime, his great knowledge in the field of education and training of our children, his understanding and participation in our housing problems, his expertness in the field of defense and his intimate association with the Joint Chiefs of Staff and the Secretary of Defense, his contributions in the all-important—the number

one important—problem in the world, the area of peace, make him a most unusual and a most valuable and a most needed public servant.

The greatest aid that New York citizens can give to their country now is to make certain that Robert Kennedy and Democratic New York Congressmen are sent to Washington to work for a program for the people next January.

And you don't just send Bob Kennedy to Washington when you elect him Senator. He, like the rest of us, outmarried himself and you send one of the most effective, intelligent, and gracious persons that I have ever known—Ethel Kennedy. I think so much of her that when we had great problems in my State and we were evenly divided, the first person I asked to come to Texas, even before I asked the Democratic presidential candidate, was Ethel Kennedy. She visited practically every major city in that State, and everywhere she went she left indelibly imprinted on their minds an impression of a competent, dedicated person.

I will also appreciate your help in sending John Williams, of Rochester, because we need his effective services in the House of Representatives, and you need him as your Congressman. Young, energetic, talented, and able—he can do things for New York, and you want things done for New York.

And we all need to have Neil Bubel join him from the 37th District, because we can work there as a team, a team to bring peace to the world and prosperity to all of our people.

So I hope that you will concentrate the next 3 weeks on helping Bob Kennedy, and helping John Williams, and helping Neil Bubel. And if you have any time left over, help Hubert Humphrey and me.

I think here in this great city of Rochester you know something about the meaning of responsibility. This is the hometown of one of the most responsible Americans who ever lived in our country, a crusader for equality and human rights—Susan B. Anthony.

Here in Rochester, great corporations have flourished, and you have fostered a long and proud tradition of healthy trade unions. You have made Rochester a byword for invention and for technological innovation. And you have used the fruits of your economic foresight and enterprise to enrich your lives. This is the spirit of responsibility that has built this great city.

I believe the American people want a responsible government. And that means a government that works actively to promote the prosperity of all Americans.

This has been the goal of the Kennedy-Johnson administration. Here in the State of New York, responsible policies are paying off, responsible Government decisions.

Employment in Rochester has increased by 16,000 jobs. Our goal, our objective, is the day when every man and woman who wants to work in Rochester will be able to work in a decent job.

A responsible government will not turn its back on workers whose jobs have been taken over by machines. You know, last year we trained nearly 9,000 men and women in new skills in New York. I intend to speed up that training and that transition of workers into new industries.

A responsible government will not gaze into the sky while millions of Americans live in poverty. Fourteen percent—14 percent—of your New York families live in poverty, below the poverty line. Now, we are not going to abandon them and we are not going to forget them, and we are going to do something about them.

We abolished slavery in this country 100 years ago, and beginning this year we are going to abolish poverty in this country, because a responsible government is going to put education on the top of the list of our unfinished work. In the next 10 years, 30 million boys and girls—30 million—will be ready to work. We intend to do something about these needs.

The Johnson administration, aided by your two Congressmen that you are going to select, and Senator Kennedy, will be guided by the principle that regardless of family financial status, education should be open to every boy and girl in America up to the highest level that he can possibly take.

A responsible government will do something about the conditions which foster crime. It's not enough just to talk about crime in September and October of every fourth year. Crime is something you just don't talk against. Crime is something you must work against. Crime is something you must fight against. Crime is something you must vote against.

In Congress you vote and you work to provide employment, education, and training for people to become constructive citizens. And I intend in the next 4 years, if you are willing, to continue and to improve those programs which take our young people off the streets and to give them a decent break in life, and equal opportunity.

Responsible government means a government that works actively to build our strength and to maintain the peace.

I am very proud to be able to say to you that in all the recorded history of man, no nation has ever been so strong in arms as your Nation is today. With the Presidents before him, but particularly with President John Fitzgerald Kennedy, he developed that strength for one overriding purpose: because he had a passion for peace, and we have an obligation to him to keep the peace.

In 37 meetings of the Security Council

during the frightening days of the Cuban missile crisis, surrounded by the most expert military geniuses that West Point and Annapolis could produce, the coolest man in that room, the man with the most cautious and careful judgment, I am proud to say, was the man that you had selected as your Commander in Chief—John Fitzgerald Kennedy. And sitting there with him through the days and the nights that followed was his loyal and dedicated brother who gave him excellent and helpful assistance.

Now, we know that we will not keep peace by bluff, by bluster, or by ultimatum. Patience and strength are the road to peace. Understanding of why people do certain things and what our reaction must quickly be, are important considerations. These courses must be walked with vigilance.

I have no doubt that freedom is going to survive in this troubled world. I have no doubt that democracy is ultimately going to win. But we are not going to win it by quarreling with each other, by questioning each other's patriotism, or by mudslinging, muckraking, or getting personal with the men who are doing their dead level best in the interest of their country. We are not going to do it by questioning or tearing down our cherished institutions.

We have in Washington dedicated Republicans that President Kennedy brought there—the Secretary of the Treasury, the Secretary of Defense, the Chairman of the Central Intelligence Agency, and others too numerous to mention. And all of these men want to do what is best for their country. None of them went there on a platform of doing what is wrong. They are trying so hard to protect our institutions, and this is no time for us to try to win by dividing brothers against brothers.

I know I feel, and I hope that all the other members of my party feel, as good Republicans on this platform this morning feel, that what is good for your country is good for your party and yourself. And that ought to be our sole criterion.

How can we unite the world and lead it if we divide among ourselves? How can we be the example for the rest of the world if part of us go in one direction and part in the other, if some of us preach love and faith, and the others preach doubt and hate?

So let us all, as good Christians, focus on those values that can unite America, and try to overlook the petty things that divide America. There are so many more things that unite us than divide us.

Let's try to lead our country and our friends. Let's try to teach our children to love and to respect their neighbors instead of hating and suspecting them. Let's say to those that join these secret societies and march in the night with masks on their heads, that this is not really the thing that built America. Let us all come out in the open and unite behind one program, and that is, preserving our country first.

Let's say to these men of little faith, the doubters and the critics, who sometimes become frustrated, and other times become bitter—let's say, "Let's turn the other cheek," and say, "God forgive them, for they really know not what they do."

Here in New York, the leading State in the Union, let all the people of all religions, of all ancestries, regardless of how they spell their name, of all colors, of all faiths—yes, of all parties—let us, as good Americans first, do not what is just good for the Democratic Party, or the Republican Party. Let us on November 3d go and do what each of us in our own conscience tells us is best for our beloved America.

Thank you.

NOTE: The President spoke at 10:59 a.m. at a Democratic rally at the airport in Rochester, N.Y. In the opening words of his formal remarks he referred to Mayor Frank Lamb of Rochester, Mayor Robert F. Wagner of New York City, W. Averell Harriman, Under Secretary of State for Political Affairs and former Governor of New York, William H. McKeon, chairman of the New York State Democratic Committee, Marion B. Folsom, former Secretary of Health, Education, and Welfare, John C. Williams and Neil F. Bubel, Democratic candidates for Representative, and Robert O'Brien, chairman of the Monroe County Democratic Committee.

667   Remarks at the City Hall in Buffalo.
October 15, 1964

General Kennedy—thank you, Bob Kennedy, Mrs. Kennedy, Congressman Dulski, Mayor Kowal, my beloved friend Bob Wagner, whose father I knew and whose father was one of the greatest Americans we ever produced that represented this State of New York in the Senate of the United States for many years, Governor Harriman, who now serves with such distinction, my old friend Chairman McKeon of the State Committee, Peter Crotty, your very able leader in Erie County:

We need some help down in Washington in the Congress. We have a Democratic Congress, but sometimes we win President Kennedy's program and my program by just two or three votes.

So we want to ask you between now and November 3d to talk to your friends and your neighbors, and ask them if they won't replace this fellow Bill Miller with Wesley Hilts. He could join the majority party instead of having a man representing the minority.

He could join the majority party and he and Richard (Max) McCarthy, working close together with the other members of the Democratic majority in the House—and the Senate is made up of about two-thirds Democratic Senators, so it is going to be a Democratic Senate even if you should have a Republican President—and I can't imagine the intelligent people of Buffalo wanting to send a Republican down to work with a bunch of Democrats that are in control of the Congress.

So let's do our job; let's take Wesley Hilts, Max McCarthy, and Bob Kennedy and send a real fighting team.

There are a good many reasons why this is important and I will touch on them very briefly because I know you don't want a long speech.

But New York State, the leading State in the Union, needs a Democratic Senator to work with the leading Senators in the Senate. You don't often, when you go out to select an employee, find one with the experience and with the training and with the knowledge and with the associations and with the understanding not only in Washington with the Cabinet, with the Senate, with the House, but throughout the world—you don't very often find a person that has the understanding and the ability and the heart, the compassion, that Bob Kennedy has.

He has been leading the fight in the United States on fighting crime. He has been an authority in the field of education. He has worked closely with the late President and all of us on developing new housing programs.

He has associated with the Joint Chiefs of Staff and the Secretary of Defense in planning the strongest defense any nation ever had, and in the all-important—and, really, this is the most important, the only thing that

1341

is really important—in the all-important field of peace in the world. He has traveled around the world and he knows the leaders, and he is in a position to help us obtain peace in the world. And that is the most important job we have for you.

It doesn't do you any good to come when they are taking your boys away from you or they are marching away to war and say, "I am for peace." The time to do something about peace is right now, and you ought not to do it just in the world. You ought to have peace at home. You ought to try to have peace among the races.

One of the proudest things in my life was when President Kennedy paid me the compliment of permitting me to join with him to prove not just to the United States, but all the world, that we had no religious bigotry, and he could be elected President of the United States.

We have had problems in our constitutional rights field because of our educational problems, because of our poverty problems, because of our dropout problems, because of our not treating Americans equally.

We had these problems in the streets. We have tried, because we are a nation of laws, to bring these problems from the streets into the courts where they could be adjusted and all Americans could be treated equally. And we are making progress in that field.

I was talking to some folks coming up on the plane this morning and Bob Kennedy said this to me: "We have international conferences. The United Nations has averted a number of wars because men sat down and reasoned together." He said, "Somehow or other I don't believe that our people talk enough with each other about their own problems. So why, if we can take the people from the Asian Continent and from the African Continent and from the European Continent, and from the

Western Hemisphere and bring them all together, a hundred-odd in the United Nations, why shouldn't we try to obtain peace at home between business, the men who employ our people, the capitalists who make the investments, the workers who produce the goods, the Government who has a 52 percent take in everything that they make?

"Why couldn't we have a meeting of all those people, area by area, and try to find out what it is that we can do—for instance, to keep New York the outstanding State in the Union and to keep all of her people employed—to make plans to expand business instead of contracting it and closing it, to make plans for extra jobs instead of trying to find some unemployment insurance program to take care of them after they have lost their job, to make plans to retrain them so they will have skills in the space age, to find ways and means that the Government and the employers, and the labor unions and the schools, and the Republicans and the Independents and the Democrats can all work together to have peace at home and to have prosperity at home, so that every man that wants to work can have a job?"

After Bob Kennedy made that suggestion, I talked to Congressman Dulski. And if you will send me these other two Democratic Congressmen, when we get this little detail of the election behind us, we will start out here on this eastern seaboard—we are not going to cut it off and throw it out in the Atlantic, either; we don't believe in that—we will start out here and we will go all across this Nation by areas.

We will take the best economists, we will take the best business leaders, we will take the best labor leaders, we will take the best Government leaders, we will take the best educators, and we will say, "What is it that we can do for America so that everyone can have a job, every kid can have an education, we can get these folks off the streets, we can put an end to this crime, and, in time, we can have the Great Society that we are all entitled to?"

A hundred years ago there were a good many ugly things being said about another President. His name was Abraham Lincoln. I was reading what he said the other day about when he went back to Illinois. He said he went down the street and no one would speak to him except one woman, and she wouldn't have if she could have avoided it.

In this day and time, instead of us talking about each other, why don't we look back to Lincoln's day and see the real mistakes we made and the problems he had, and let's try to profit from it.

Abraham Lincoln had a slavery problem. A good many of the citizens of this land were in bondage and were slaves, and he abolished slavery.

Franklin Roosevelt came along. And you people in New York that gave us Al Smith and gave us Bob Wagner, gave us Franklin Roosevelt. You sent him to the Presidency in a day when the Republic was wavering. We didn't know whether we could sustain our society or not. He stood there in his inaugural address and he said to the people, "The only thing we have to fear is fear itself." And that is as true today as it was then. We must not be afraid.

So if Lincoln could abolish slavery and if Roosevelt could take the one-third that were ill clad and the one-third that were ill housed and the one-third that were ill fed and move them from 33 percent down to 20 percent, where it is one-fifth now, why can't you and Bob Kennedy and Congressman Dulski and the Democratic leadership in this country ask the Republican leadership to join us, because they are patriots, too? And if Lincoln abolished slavery, let us abolish poverty.

There will be some ugly things said about us. They will say that we are do-gooders, and that we ought to let everybody root for himself, and all this kind of stuff—that they don't need any education anyway. But that doesn't bother us. The things that I am proudest of in my life are the things that were the most difficult to do and the things that they quarreled with me most about doing when I did them.

Four years ago, you folks here in Erie County gave John F. Kennedy a record-breaking plurality of 72,000 votes. Up to his last moment he was always so proud of that, and proud of you. That was the greatest increase in the Democratic vote in any single county of the more than 3,000 in the United States. Aren't you proud of that?

I didn't just come up here to brag on you; I came up here to ask you to do that again.

This campaign has really become a crusade, not against anyone, because I am not going to get down to personalities or mudslinging, or muckraking, or questioning people's patriotism.

I think that most of the men, and this includes my opponents, most of the men that I have served in Congress with for 30 years love their country just as much as I do. We have different ideas about how to go about saving it. Some of them want to do something and some want to do nothing.

We had that problem when President Roosevelt came in. That was one of our problems. We had been doing nothing. So we had great relief lines, people were hungry. In our country they were burning cotton, and the calves were dying. They were giving the hogs away. The corn wouldn't sell for anything. You couldn't get a job. If you got one, it just paid a dollar a day.

The law we passed on civil rights is in

effect in practically all the States of the Union except 19. We just said that if a man is working, we want him treated right, and we don't want him displaced. We think everybody ought to be employed on merit. Merit ought to be the test. If you are there and you have seniority and you have your job, it ought to be preserved. We ought not to hire people on any other basis than merit.

But a friend of mine told me on a trip that I made last week, when Lady Bird wanted to go back home and tell her people what she thought about conditions in the world, and ask their help—I went down to meet her.

One of the men came in that I had known a long time that was a laboringman. You know, they have a lot of time to think when they are fixing their rivets or using their saw, or taking up their steel rods. He said, "Lyndon, we got a serious problem here on this so-called civil rights thing, and our people don't understand it. They think some way or other that it is going to take a job away from one man and give it to the other. I know it isn't at all, because it really helps the man who has a job to preserve it.

"But," he said, "I want you to know this: I am not as upset as some of them. What I want is all Americans to have a chance to eat, and sleep, and worship their God, because they will be more peaceful and it will be a stronger Nation. They all fight for it." He said, "I had much rather stand by the side of a good American Negro in a plant working where he earns money for his children than stand behind him in a soup line where the Government handout has to feed us all."

That is what we have to plan to do something about. When President Kennedy was up here in 1960, he said that America was tired and worn out, according to what his opposition was saying, and that we were

doing all we could. He said that some of them thought we had lost our vitality, and that the economy had reached its peak. Well, they said that, the opponents, but *not* John Fitzgerald Kennedy.

There are people today that are crying out against these programs of getting our country moving. There are people who want to arrest our progress. There are people who want to turn back the gains. There are people that say, "You are doing enough, and let's have the status quo." But one of them is not your President, Lyndon Johnson.

With the help of the men you give me, with the help of the leaders of both parties, I intend to press forward the attack on all these problems, the enemies of idleness, of health, of ignorance, and the infirmities of old age.

First, I will not be satisfied until every American who wants to work can find a decent job. We have 72 million working today, and for the first time in history the workers in manufacturing average $104 a week.

The second enemy that we have is ignorance. And the crisis of our schools is appalling. Beginning in 1960, and between 1960 and 1970, there will be 5 million more children in elementary school—5 million more youngsters in high school; 3 million more in college; 13 million more in elementary, high school, and college. And unless we act, our educational system is going to be deficient, and it will really crack under the pressure.

Every community has the right to run its schools as the people see fit, and my administration will not interfere with the operation. But we must intend to see that every child born in this world, boy or girl, poor or rich, has a right to all the education he can take in this space age.

The third enemy we face is infirmity of

the aged.

Half of the aged couples in this country have incomes of less than $200 a month. Half of those living alone have incomes of less than $80 a month.

The old get sick more often and the old stay in hospitals twice as long. When sickness strikes, it wipes out their savings that they have carefully put away for a lifetime. It is gone overnight.

What can we say to these people? Can we say, "Yes, you have given a lifetime of toil for your country; you have produced the boys that have fought and carried that flag around the world and brought it back without a stain on it; you have helped us become great, but we no longer need you, and your troubles are not our concern; go see your kinfolks"?

Well, that is not what I think you ought to do about it, and that is not what the Johnson administration is going to do about it.

When Congress is back in session again, I am going to ask them to do what the Senate did this year—fight for medical care for the aged—as long as I have energy at my command. And if you will give me Wesley Hilts, Max McCarthy, and Bob Kennedy, we will put up a fight, and we will fulfill our obligations to the most noble of our duties—the care of the sick and the helpless.

I think this is what you want.

Am I wrong?

These are just the first steps toward a Great Society where everyone worships as they please; where every child has a classroom and every classroom has a teacher; where we have a countryside to spend our recreation; where we have abolished the things that bring us to death early, like heart disease, cancer, polio, and all those things; where we have a healthy nation; where we have peace in the world; where

we have our businessmen making good profits, dividing those profits with the laboringmen who do good production; the farmer coming in and producing at fair prices the food we need to eat and the fiber we need to wear; and the Government reaching in and getting its slice of the pie, because the bigger that pie is, the better off it is for everybody.

What can you do about this?

Well, one thing you can do about it, and this is what has encouraged me all over this Nation—the biggest crowds that ever came out in the history of a presidential campaign are coming out this year. They are eager, they want to learn, they want to make up their minds, they want to see what they can do about it. You just have 2½ weeks now.

In that 2½ weeks you cannot only come to these meetings, you not only can help Bill, Max, and Bob, and if you are really generous you can help Hubert and me a little bit as we go along—but you can talk to your neighbor. You can say, "You have a big decision to make."

You can put a bumper sticker on your car. I will bet you there are cars here today, and I will bet you Peter Crotty could get you a sticker some way to put on your car to let the people know that you are good Americans and you are really going to stand up and be counted November 3d. You would do it if we called you to war, so why don't you do it in peace?

Eleven months ago, in the greatest tragedy in my lifetime, in a matter of moments, without any chance to talk to anybody or get any information, or go to a library, I had to become President, to carry on for the man who had faith in me and trust in me. I said to all of you that night on television that with God's help, and with your prayers, and support, I would just do my best. I have done my best.

President Kennedy left 51 programs for all Americans. This Congress had the biggest ever in any history—the test ban treaty, all those important bills, the tax bill, the civil rights bill, the works bill, education bills, the conservation bill, all for the good of each one of you. He had 51 pending. Last Friday night I looked over that list and somehow or other I thought he was looking over my shoulder wondering if I had done my job and if the Congress had done their job. We had passed every one of those 51 bills through the Senate, and all but four or five through the House.

Our friends in the other party wanted to go home and campaign and they wouldn't help me pass them through the House. But we are going to pass them when we get back there; that is, if you will help me, and give me men that will help me pass them.

A few months ago, about 2 years ago, we all met at the White House and looked at the pictures, and saw the Russian missiles in Cuba 90 miles from our shore. We had a lot of advice about bombs and invasions and sending in the Marines.

The President called every person that he could, including Republicans and Democrats from the Congress, Republican Director of the CIA, the Republican Secretary of Defense. They are all patriotic without regard to party. He tried to determine what he could do. He knew that he could mash a button and wipe out 100 million Russians in a matter of moments, and when he did that, they could mash a button and wipe out 100 million Americans. No sane man would want to mash that button and start that kind of an operation, but what else could you do? You couldn't sit there until the missiles were turned on us.

So we had 37 meetings, and I was present at 36 of them. Bob was present at all of them.

He and I sat on an Executive Committee of seven members, with a Republican CIA Director, Mr. McCone, with a Republican Secretary of the Treasury, Mr. Dillon, with a Republican Secretary of Defense, Mr. McNamara, President Kennedy, Robert Kennedy, and Lyndon Johnson. And we considered everything, because they weren't just going to kill Democrats or Republicans.

This was America, and I am proud to testify to you today that it was one of the greatest things in my life.

Some people wondered why I ran for Vice President and quit the powerful majority leadership to help President Kennedy win over Mr. Nixon. I will tell you. I had all the satisfaction I ever needed when I sat in those meetings, because the coolest man at that table, the wisest man at that table, was John Fitzgerald Kennedy.

We had trouble getting adequate communications, adequate information, adequate knowledge. A man's knowledge and a man's judgment are no better than the information he has. But out of those meetings, both leaders decided that it would be foolhardy, when they were eyeball to eyeball, to put their finger on that button.

So Mr. Khrushchev pulled his missiles out of Cuba and took them back home, and he agreed to a test ban treaty. We celebrated the anniversary of it last Saturday.

I am talking on the television about it tonight. The milk that your babies drink is no longer as dangerous as it was before. The chance of having a deformed baby is no longer as dangerous as it was before. The food that you eat from our soil that was contaminated is no longer as dangerous as it was before. The danger of men becoming sterile has been removed.

The results are truly marvelous because we agreed not to test in the atmosphere, and 108 other nations agreed not to test, too.

So I am going to tell you about the results tonight in that.

Out of that came the "hot line" where we can call Moscow and they can call us. And we can say, "This is what we are disturbed about and you must not do that," and they can say it back to us.

You are going to decide which man, in your judgment, which party, you would rather have close to that button. You are going to decide which man you want to pick up that telephone when Moscow rings. You will never make a more important decision. It ought not to be based on how I look or where I come from, or how I spell my name or my ancestry. It ought to be based on what is best for your country and you and your children. I don't want it based on anything else.

So you go home today and you think about it, the alternatives that are open to you, and then you do what is good for your country. And you will do what is good for your party and what is good for yourself.

Thank you.

NOTE: The President spoke at 12:55 p.m. at City Hall in Niagara Square in Buffalo, N.Y. In his opening remarks he referred to Robert F. Kennedy, Democratic candidate for Senator from New York and former U.S. Attorney General, and Mrs. Kennedy, Representative Thaddeus J. Dulski of New York, Mayor Chester Kowal of Buffalo, Mayor Robert F. Wagner of New York City, W. Averell Harriman, Under Secretary of State for Political Affairs and former Governor of New York, William H. McKeon, chairman of the New York State Democratic Committee, and Peter Crotty, chairman of the Erie County Democratic Committee. Later he referred to Wesley J. Hilts and Richard D. (Max) McCarthy, Democratic candidates for Representative, and Representative William E. Miller, Republican candidate for Vice President.

668   Remarks in Albee Square, Brooklyn.
October 15, 1964

Ladies and gentlemen, boys and girls:

I want to show you one of the reasons for Bob Kennedy's success and one of the reasons he is going to be the next Senator from New York.

Stand up, Ethel.

———

Senator Kennedy, Governor Harriman, Congressman Murphy, Congresswoman Kelly, Congressman Keogh, Congressman Multer, Congressman Carey, my old and longtime friend John Rooney, Abe Stark, Abe Beame, State Chairman McKeon, my fellow Americans:

I want to thank you for this, the largest crowd that I have seen in all my travels from Maine to California, and I want to thank you in advance for the greatest majority you are going to give us on November

3d of any area in the United States.

Mr. Rayburn said about our Congressmen from Texas one time—after they had most of the chairmanships in the House and a lot of the influence, and they asked, "How do you do it?"—he said, "We pick them young, we pick them honest, we send them there, and we keep them there." That is what I want you to do with your Congressmen.

The United States needs a young, dynamic, compassionate, fighting liberal representing New York in the United States Senate—Bob Kennedy. His knowledge of housing, his knowledge of slum clearance, his knowledge in fighting crime, his knowledge in education, his knowledge in bringing peace to the world is what Brooklyn needs voting in the United States Senate.

[*At this point someone in the crowd asked, "How about the Navy yard?"*]

That's another reason you need him. He has already been down there talking about this Navy yard so much that I am going to have to get an earphone.

We have peace in the world and we must keep it. We need the unity of our people. We stand against communism. We stand for freedom. We must work in our streets and our slums, among our young people and among our poor people. There is work for us to do on all corners. It is untouched by our compassion.

Our society was built on respect for law and order and we mean to maintain it. This is a challenge to all of us to look for real leaders. You have real leaders in the House of Representatives. Now send us a real leader for the United States Senate.

I want to tell you this has been a long and exciting day. November 3d we are going to have a great Democratic victory if all of you will go to work, put your shoulder to the wheel, and do what is best for your country. If you do that, I promise you we will do what is best for you.

Thank you and goodby.

NOTE: The President spoke at 7 p.m. at Albee Square in Brooklyn, N.Y. In his opening remarks he referred to Robert F. Kennedy, Democratic candidate for U.S. Senator from New York, and Mrs. Kennedy, W. Averell Harriman, Under Secretary of State for Political Affairs and former Governor of New York, Representatives John M. Murphy, Edna F. Kelly, Eugene J. Keogh, Abraham J. Multer, Hugh L. Carey, and John J. Rooney, all of New York, Abe Stark, Borough President of Brooklyn, Abraham D. Beame, Comptroller of New York City, and William H. McKeon, chairman of the New York State Democratic Committee.

669 Remarks in Madison Square Garden at a Rally of the Liberal Party of New York. *October 15, 1964*

Mr. Chairman, Governor Stevenson, General Kennedy, George Meany, Mayor Wagner, Phillip Randolph, Reverend Harrington, Dr. Costello, my fellow Americans:

I am proud to come once again before the Liberal Party of New York. In 1960 you received me with warmth and friendship. Your loyalty and your support since that hour have never wavered.

I am happy to say to you tonight that this President counts as his great friends Tim Costello, David Dubinsky, Alex Rose, and every patriotic member of the Liberal Party. I am glad, too, to be here tonight with my old friend Bob Kennedy by my side.

I have said everywhere I have spoken in New York, yesterday and today, that the need in Washington is great for more Democratic Congressmen and a Democratic Senator from the State of New York.

Bob Kennedy's wide experience in fight-

ing crime, his demonstrated knowledge in the field of education, housing and slum clearance, national defense, will make him one of the most valuable members of the entire Senate, and the people of New York and the Nation will be the gainers. So let the Liberal Party and the Democratic Party join hands and hearts in sending to our Nation's Capital men of vision and compassion, fighting liberals who care about people.

There are those who say that the old battles are over, that the old causes are won, that the old issues are dead. They say that we no longer need the American who cares. Well, don't you believe them. The American people don't believe them and the President of the United States doesn't believe them, either.

We are still carrying on the fight to assure every American of every race and belief equal opportunity in our abundant land. And that battle isn't over yet, but together we will win it.

A hundred years ago, Abraham Lincoln led the movement in this country to abolish slavery. A hundred years ago he signed the Emancipation Proclamation—and emancipation was a proclamation. But it is not a fact and there is still much work for us to do.

As the then President led the movement to abolish slavery, the present President, with your hands and with your hearts and with your support, is going to lead the movement to abolish poverty in this country.

We are still trying to live up to the duty of a just and compassionate country, to assure a decent life for its elderly, to hold out a helping hand to the sick and the hungry, the depressed and the unemployed. And that battle isn't over yet, either, but we will win it.

I have some information for you if you are listening and interested. We are not going to kill social security or we are not going to make it voluntary. We are not going to sell TVA. We are not going to sell any other river in America. In fact, we are not even going to turn over the White House to them.

Tonight America has to face a whole new set of problems. I have summed up this challenge in my call for the Great Society.

The Great Society is not a slogan. It is an idea.

The Great Society is not something brand new. It is a dream as old as our civilization. The difference is, for the first time in man's history we really have the resources to make it possible, to make the Great Society a reality.

The Great Society is not some vague, dreamlike Utopia. The Great Society is a very clear and very definite objective, a very definite goal. It will be met by specific programs, directed at concrete problems, carried out by dedicated and determined men.

We recognize that our abundance must be extended to all of our people. But that is not the Great Society. That is simply the base on which we will build it.

We build our strength and we keep the peace. But that is not the Great Society. It is the shield behind which we build.

We did not establish freedom and we did not work for two centuries simply to pile up more money in our bank accounts, more goods in our homes, and more power in our arsenals.

We built this Nation for the people of this Nation and we will not now permit our people to be overwhelmed by our growth and our progress, walled in by our cities and our signs.

Our brave men did not die in battle—our pioneers did not risk their lives and fortunes—so that their descendants could sit in expensive apartments with washing machines and television sets without a place to walk and touch nature, breathing poisoned air beside polluted rivers, unable to send their children to a decent school or even to a decent playground.

We cannot, we must not, and we will not sacrifice natural beauty and the sense of community, the creations of art and the joy of thought, in the rush to become bigger and stronger and more wealthy.

We will not permit ourselves to be mastered and stifled by machines and buildings and highways.

We want to grow and build and invent, but we want progress to be the servant of man and not have man become the victim of progress.

Well, that is the Great Society—concern for the quality of the life of each person in America.

Nowhere is that concern more urgent

than in the American city. By 1975 we will have to shelter and sustain a new urban population equal to the entire 1960 metropolitan population of New York, Chicago, Los Angeles, Philadelphia, Detroit, Boston, Baltimore, and Johnson City, Tex.

We will have to build at least 2 million new homes a year compared with the current rate of just a little over a million. We will have to rebuild the 7 million homes that tonight do not have running water or even decent plumbing.

We will need schools for 60 million children. We will need welfare and health facilities for 27 million people over the age of 60. We will need transportation facilities for the daily movement of 200 million people in 80 million or 90 million cars.

We will have to improve the health and the beauty of our cities. Our air and our water are being contaminated. Open spaces and parks are disappearing. Careless highways and unplanned buildings are destroying the trees and the fields which are part of our American heritage. You can't drive out of the city limits without being confronted on both sides of the road with a bunch of old, ugly, junked automobiles. And if you take away the gift of nature, you erode the finest values of the heart and mind.

More important, we want to create a sense of community, a sense of closeness to our neighbors. It is isolation and ruthlessness which help create anxiety and unrest.

We will have to help our new urban immigrants, those coming from rural America. We will have to help them adjust to the strains of urban life. By 1980 three-fourths of all Americans will be urban people. The newcomers need to learn social skills as well as trade skills.

We need to develop the regional cooperation which can give the maximum of local choice. We do not want our cities to settle into a drab uniformity, directed from a single center. Each area must be free to choose its own path of development, whether it is to join cities together or to build entire new metropolitan areas. This means experimentation with new forms of regional direction. It means developing a new set of relationships between the Federal Government and the American city.

I intend to work with your local officials and to present a series of proposals designed to help meet the challenge of urban America. These proposals will discard a piecemeal approach to individual problems and deal with the total needs of a metropolitan area.

These proposals will build on the cooperation of Government with industry, the same sort of cooperation that has built our national defense, the same sort of cooperation that has allowed us to explore the stars.

These proposals will call for design and form as well as size and numbers. They will preserve nature and they will create open spaces.

These proposals will look forward to the development of our human resources among our young and our old, our women and our suburban young people. In this way we can strike at the roots of aimlessness and of lost purpose.

The proposal will look to science and technology to help us master our problems. For housing to have a research program equal to that of most growth industries, it would have to expand its research 10 times. Yet housing is one of our most pressing needs.

These proposals will not involve the Federal Government alone. The work of our cities will require the cooperation of the State and the city, and of business and of labor, and of private institutions and of private individuals.

We must not only seek peace in the world. In order to have peace in the world, we must have peace at home, and we must try to get these groups working together.

The Federalism of the future, creative Federalism, is not just the relationship between States and Washington, but among all the institutions and Government units whose influence and problems cut across traditional jurisdictions.

The work of the American city is a challenge that is worthy of the finest traditions of American liberalism. We are never going back in the direction of the past. We are going to go, go forward. We are going to make our cities a place where men cannot only live, but where they can live the good life. We have so much to be thankful for. We have so much yet to achieve.

This has been a stimulating and exciting experience for me to be here in the great State of New York. In Buffalo and in Rochester, and all through Brooklyn, until the moon came up this evening, we saw smiling people, we saw happy faces, we saw people dedicated to democracy and the American way of life. Now and then we saw a sourpuss with a sign with a picture on it that we recognized, and I think that they were in the proper proportion all day long.

Tonight we have over 72 million people employed. Tonight they are working in manufacturing industries at an average weekly wage of about $104.

We are taking from the obsolete, archaic operations of the Federal Government funds and personnel, and closing down installations that are not usable, and we are not operating the Defense Department as another WPA. And we are taking those funds and putting them in health, education and retraining, and our poverty program.

In the month of July we had 25,000 less employees working for the Federal Government than we had July a year ago. We spent $676 million less in July and August of this year than we estimated to the Congress we would spend. We are going to get a dollar's worth of value for every dollar we spend.

We do not believe that because you are prudent you can't be progressive. We do believe definitely that we should take the leadership in health research so the days of strokes and cancer and heart disease will be like polio, a thing of the past.

We do think that we ought to strengthen and improve our social security system, and we do think that we ought to have medical care under social security, and we are going to have it.

We think that every boy and girl born under that flag has a right to all the education that he or she can take. And it will be our goal to see that there is a classroom there waiting for them with a competent, well-paid teacher to man it.

We believe in the protection and the development of our countryside, and opening of new national parks and recreation areas, because we are going to work less hours per day and less days per week.

We believe in fair and generous profits to the investor of his capital. We believe in due recompense, even a good bonus, to the manager of that capital.

We believe in collective bargaining and a fair wage for the man that produces this wealth and utilizes these resources. I want them all to do well, because, as the President of the biggest company in this country, I get 52 percent of what is left of all they make, so we believe in encouraging people and not harassing them. We believe in incentive.

We believe that in this struggle between communism and democracy, it is not their superior numbers that will dominate the world; it is not even their superior resources

in many fields. If it were, we would be
fighting a losing battle. But the thing that
is going to save us is our system of government, because free men can out-think and
free men can out-work, and free men can
out-produce slaves.

But peace at home will be of little value
if an impulsive thumb moves up toward
the button that can destroy 300 million people in a matter of moments. Peace at home
and prosperity among our people will get
us nowhere if we have a government by
ultimatum, and we bluff about our bombs,
and we rattle our rockets around until we
get into a destructive war.

I sat with President Kennedy in the Security Council along with his distinguished
brother, here this evening, and the wise and
beloved Ambassador to the United Nations,
Mr. Stevenson. And we discussed with the
admirals and their braid and the generals
with their stars, and the diplomats with their
great foreign service experience, what we
could do about those missiles that were almost operational 90 miles from our shores.

I never knew any morning when I left
my wife and daughters whether I would see
them that night again or not. But I am
proud to say to you that you helped America
to select a man who presided over those
meetings, and during all that frightening
crisis he had the steadiest thumb—the steadiest thumb—the greatest heart and the coolest
mind in that room.

You will see from your morning paper,
or you will learn from your evening radio,
that changes and uncertainties in this big
world in which we live give great weight
to our own need for a stable and sure and
steady course, on the basis of a tested bipartisan policy.

President Truman had Arthur Vandenberg by his side when he stopped the Communists in Greece and Turkey.

I supported President Eisenhower in a
bipartisan foreign policy in the Formosa
Strait.

Everett Dirksen stood up and supported
President Kennedy in our test ban treaty.

You can abandon this bipartisan foreign
policy and let it go down the drain, and
follow a dangerous adventure that leads to
evils we know not of if you want to, but I
don't think you are going to.

There is a seething in Africa and Asia
tonight. Where our friends are strongest in
Western Europe we are happy, but today
there is an indication that there is a change
in the Soviet Union.

The announcement that Chairman Khrushchev has been replaced may or may not be
a sign of deeper turmoil or may be a sign of
changes in policies to come. But for ourselves, the need is clear: that we should keep
steady on our goals—that peace is the mission of the American people, and we are not
about to be deterred. We will be firm, but
we will be restrained. We can meet any
test, but our quest is always for peace.

Our purposes and our principles are the
purposes and principles of peace and freedom, as I set them forth at length only last
night.[1] The text appeared in the Times this
morning and I hope that each of you could
read it.

The turmoil around the world will only increase the steadfastness of the American people. We must keep our eyes and our vision
on the stars, but our feet—both of them—on
the ground. We do not want to bury anyone anywhere, and we do not intend to be
buried ourselves.

We do not know how many wars the
United Nations has helped us avert, but
you can't count them on both hands. We do
know that the trials and tribulations and the
patience that is required is much easier to

---
[1] Item 662.

give than to expend human lives. We do not intend to abolish the United Nations. Peace is our purpose; prosperity is our goal.

I said 11 months ago, after that tragic day when our beloved leader had fallen and had been taken from us that I had no time to prepare or to deliberate. In a moment I had to assume terrifying responsibilities and awesome responsibilities. I said with God's help and your prayers, I would do the best I could.

I have tried to appeal to all Americans, not on the basis of their race or their religion or how they spell their name, or what region they lived in, or whether they were capitalists, businessmen, managers, or laborers, but most of them have come and tried to unite our Nation in this trying hour.

In the last few weeks there has been a little unsettlement here and there. Some people have gotten a little upset about some things. I read in the paper from day to day where I am called everything but a good milk cow. But I get some comfort out of looking back and seeing what they said about the Father of our Country and what they said about Jackson, Jefferson, Lincoln, Wilson, Franklin D. Roosevelt, and John Fitzgerald Kennedy.

But last Friday night I looked—in my office behind those black gates that had the keys turned in them where no one can enter—I looked at a long list that President Kennedy had left me, 51 major measures: the civil rights bill, the tax bill, the library bill, three education bills, the farm bill, the wilderness bill—bills too numerous to mention. And of those 51 that he in his vision felt were essential to good government and to the people of this country, we had passed all 51 of them through the United States Senate.

Now, we didn't get Appalachia through the House. We got it through the com-

mittee and on the calendar, but some of our Republican friends got in a hurry and just wanted to go home and we couldn't get the bill up. We didn't get medical care past the House, but for the first time in history we passed it through the Senate and we are going to pass it in the House.

You people of the Liberal Party are people of vision and faith and hope. You are not people of fear or people of doubt. You have something that we need. We need your support, we need your dreams, we need your hand, we need your help, we need your heart to help us send more progressive Congressmen and Senators like Bob Kennedy to Washington.

With equal opportunity to all, with special privilege to none—with equal opportunity to all and special privilege to none—we will get this program passed if God is willing and you will help.

There is not even 3 weeks left. You wouldn't hesitate to give your life to defend your country. Yet your country is never going to need you more than on the November election day.

So please—please take the time from now until then to talk to your friends and talk to your neighbors and to try to excite and arouse their interest to the point where they will help you do what is best for your country.

You go and vote and select the men that in your judgment are best calculated to help you do what ought to be done for America. And if you do your duty as citizens and you do what is best for America, you will do what is best for yourselves.

Thank you and good night.

NOTE: The President spoke at 8:25 p.m. in Madison Square Garden in New York City. In his opening words he referred to William H. McKeon, chairman of the New York State Democratic Committee, Adlai E. Stevenson, U.S. Representative to the United Nations and former Governor of Illinois,

Robert F. Kennedy, Democratic candidate for U.S. Senator from New York and former U.S. Attorney General, George Meany, president, AFL–CIO, Robert F. Wagner, mayor of New York City, Phillip Randolph, president, Brotherhood of Sleeping Car Porters, the Rev. Donald Harrington of the Community Church, an officer of the Liberal Party of New York State, and Dr. Timothy W. Costello, professor of psychology at New York University and chairman of the Liberal Party. Later he referred to David Dubinsky, president, International Ladies Garment Workers Union, Alex Rose, president, United Hatters, Cap and Millinery Workers International Union, Arthur H. Vandenberg, U.S. Senator from Michigan during the Truman administration, and Everett McKinley Dirksen, U.S. Senator from Illinois.

670 Remarks to a Group Outside Madison Square Garden. *October 15, 1964*

BEFORE I get going on my long, hour speech, I want to introduce to you two of my favorite women—my wife and the wife of the next Democratic Senator from New York, Ethel Kennedy.

We have had a little session inside, and I don't know whether you heard us or not, but there is not much that I can add to what I said except this: that I think we are both down here at this late hour tonight for the same reason. I know why I am here, and I am going to be presumptuous enough to imagine why you are here.

I am here because I care about people and I think that is why you are here, too. You believe in peace in the world. You would rather talk than fight, and so would I.

You believe in prosperity at home, you believe that every man and woman that wants a job and who is willing to work ought to have a job, and so do I.

You believe in social security, and so do I.

You believe in collective bargaining, and so do I. You fought to help abolish the sweatshop, and so did I.

You believe that peace should be our mission and prosperity should be our program, and so do I.

As we look back at Lincoln, Wilson, Roosevelt, and Kennedy, and Lehman and Al Smith and the great leaders of this State, we see what we can do if we will only unite together. Now, come November 3d, you are going to have a chance to help us unite. You can't do it by sitting home in your rocking chair. You have to get up early that morning and work until late that night and send down to Washington a man who will support the programs of Roosevelt, Kennedy, and Johnson—Bob Kennedy. You have to send some Democratic Congressmen to help him.

After you get through, if you are not too tired, you can put in a lick or two for Hubert Humphrey and me.

NOTE: The President spoke at 9:13 p.m. outside Madison Square Garden in New York City. In his opening remarks he referred to Mrs. Robert F. Kennedy, wife of the Democratic candidate for U.S. Senator from New York.

671 Statement by the President on Walter Jenkins. *October 15, 1964*

WALTER JENKINS has worked with me faithfully for 25 years. No man I know has given more personal dedication, devotion, and tireless labor.

Until late yesterday, no information or report of any kind to me had ever raised a question with respect to his personal conduct. Mr. Jenkins is now in the care of his physician and his many friends will join in praying for his early recovery. For myself and Mrs. Johnson, I want to say that our hearts go out with the deepest compassion for him and for his wife and six children—and they have our love and prayers.

On this case as on any such case, the public interest comes before all personal feelings.

I have requested and received Mr. Jenkins' resignation.

Within moments after being notified last night, I ordered Director J. Edgar Hoover of the FBI to make an immediate and comprehensive inquiry and report promptly to me and the American people.

NOTE: On October 22 Mr. Hoover reported that an investigation of the case had revealed no evidence that Mr. Jenkins had compromised the security or interests of the United States in any manner.

---

672   Statement by the President Announcing a Joint U.S.–Israeli Water Desalting Study.   *October 15, 1964*

I AM PLEASED to announce that the Governments of the United States and Israel have agreed to a second step toward the solution of Israel's critical water needs.

The first step was taken last June when Prime Minister Eshkol and I established a joint United States-Israeli study team to conduct technical surveys. These have already been completed.

Now we have agreed that our governments will share equally in the cost of a detailed engineering study for a large water desalting

project to meet Israel's pressing demands for more fresh water.

Both governments will promptly issue invitations to American engineering consulting firms to participate in the second step. A joint board, with each government equally represented, will assist in making the selection, and will oversee the effort.

NOTE: For the establishment of the U.S.-Israeli Joint Team of experts see Item 380. See also Item 480. On October 26 the White House released a statement briefly summarizing the joint team's report.

---

673   Remarks at a Tree-Planting Ceremony at the White House.   *October 16, 1964*

I HAD hardly anticipated that you would expect a speech from me this morning, unaccustomed as I am to public speaking. And after having read about the 49 or 50 speeches that Mrs. Johnson made last week, I thought she would have taken care of this tree ceremony. But I am happy that I have a moment to come here and participate with you.

We are keeping the custom that has been kept by nearly all who have ever lived or served in the White House. The planting of

trees on the White House grounds is especially fitting as a symbol of the Presidency itself. As has been said, "A man does not plant a tree for himself. He plants it for posterity." And the real work of any President is not for his own time but times to come.

Today, as never before, Americans must be conscious of the times to come. Before these two trees mature there will be two Americans or more for every American that is living today. America's challenges will be many. But one of the most important will be the challenge of conserving the beauty of nature that is so much a part of our heritage in this land.

It is Mrs. Johnson's wish, as it is my own, that the planting of these trees may be the occasion for us all to dedicate our efforts anew to preserving our heritage of "America the Beautiful."

When America is more crowded the children must know more than just the concrete under their feet. They must see more than the smokestacks and the skyscrapers in the sky. The shade of a tree and the beauty of its branches must be always within the reach of our people, young and old, wherever they live.

The trees, therefore, that we are planting today, are a laurel oak and a willow oak. These are trees native both to the Atlantic seaboard—and it's still there, it is not floating out in the ocean yet—and the region and State which Mrs. Johnson and I know as home. They grow strong enough to stand in any wind. They grow tall enough to be seen from nearly any view.

We hope that the many who see these trees through years to come, will know that there lived here those who loved this land. And I am delighted that you would observe with us this very special historic moment. It is more historic today than you think. We have a change of leadership in the Soviet Union and we have an announcement that the Chinese have detonated their bomb, and we have a lot of things that we are dealing with. But it's nice that we could take a moment to come here in the quietness of this garden and make plans, preparations for our posterity.

Thank you very much.

There is no significance to the returning to the endeavors of my childhood. I spent 2 years of my life doing nothing but this, getting up at daylight in the morning and working until sundown in the evening, putting my foot on a shovel like this. My mother finally convinced me that I would enjoy life more if I would use my head instead of my foot!

NOTE: The President spoke at 11:20 a.m. on the South Lawn at the White House. The commemorative trees—a willow oak and a Darlington oak—were planted outside the President's office on each side of the flagstone walk leading to the roadway.

674 Statement by the President Following a Meeting With the Russian Ambassador. *October 16, 1964*

THIS MORNING I received Ambassador Dobrynin and talked with him for 45 minutes. The Ambassador brought me a first message from the new Soviet Government. The message stated the desire of the Soviet Government to continue in seeking for steps toward a more solid peace.

I told the Ambassador that I welcomed this assurance and that the Soviet Government and all governments could rely on the determination of the United States to persevere steadfastly in its own proven determination to serve the cause of peace and international understanding.

I reviewed the developments which have occurred in relations between the Soviet Government and the West in recent years and expressed the purpose of the United States to continue in the quest for peace.

NOTE: The President read the statement to members of the press at 1:20 p.m. in the Fish Room at the White House.

675   Statement by the President on the First Chinese Nuclear Device.   *October* 16, 1964

THE CHINESE Communists have announced that they conducted their first nuclear test today. By our own detection system we have confirmed that a low yield test actually took place in Western China at about 3 a.m. Eastern daylight time.

As Secretary Rusk noted on September 29, we have known for some time that the Chinese Communists had a nuclear development program which was approaching the point of a first detonation of a test device.

This explosion comes as no surprise to the United States Government. It has been fully taken into account in planning our own defense program and our own nuclear capability. Its military significance should not be overestimated. Many years and great efforts separate the testing of a first nuclear device from having a stockpile of reliable weapons with effective delivery systems.

Still more basic is the fact that if and when the Chinese Communists develop nuclear weapons systems, the free world nuclear strength will continue, of course, to be enormously greater.

The United States reaffirms its defense commitments in Asia. Even if Communist China should eventually develop an effective nuclear capability, that capability would have no effect upon the readiness of the United States to respond to requests from Asian nations for help in dealing with Communist Chinese aggression. The United States will also not be diverted from its efforts to help the nations of Asia to defend themselves and to advance the welfare of their people.

The Chinese Communist nuclear weapons program is a tragedy for the Chinese people who have suffered so much under the Communist regime. Scarce economic resources which could have been used to improve the well-being of the Chinese people have been used to produce a crude nuclear device which can only increase the sense of insecurity of the Chinese people.

Other Asian nations have wisely chosen, instead, to work for the well-being of their people through economic development and through the peaceful use of the atom. In this way, they have made a great contribution to the peace and to the security of the world.

The Chinese Communist nuclear detonation is a reflection of policies which do not serve the cause of peace. But there is no reason to fear that it will lead to immediate dangers of war. The nations of the free world recognize its limited significance and will persevere in their determination to preserve their independence.

We join all humanity in regretting the contamination of the atmosphere caused by the Chinese Communist test. We will continue in our own efforts to keep the atmosphere clean. We will pursue with dedication and determination our purpose of achieving concrete, practical steps on the roads that lead away from nuclear armaments and war, and toward a world of cooperation and development and peace.

I reviewed with the executive head of the National Security Council, Secretary of State, Secretary of Defense, Director of the CIA, and other appropriate officials this morning these developments. I plan to have another meeting with them on Saturday.

NOTE: This statement was read by the President to members of the press immediately following the reading of Item 674 at 1:20 p.m. in the Fish Room at the White House.

On the preceding day the White House released a report by the Federal Radiation Council outlining the changes in fallout levels since the cessation of nuclear weapons testing by the United States and Russia (see note to Item 653).

In view of the nuclear weapon detonation by Communist China, Secretary Celebrezze, Chairman of the Radiation Council, later reported to the President that the Division of Radiological Health of the Public Health Service had taken action to supplement the normal surveillance program, by making daily evaluations of radioactivity levels in the atmosphere on a nationwide basis, and by making weekly analyses of radionuclides in milk. He added that the Radiation Surveillance Center would maintain a daily assessment of the situation as it developed.

The Secretary's report, in the form of a memorandum dated October 19, was released by the White House on October 26.

676 Remarks Upon Signing Bill Amending the National Defense Education Act. *October 16, 1964*

Ladies and gentlemen, friends, and fathers and mothers of education:

I want to welcome you to the East Room and tell you how good it makes me feel to know of your interest in this most vital of all subjects, and to have you here to participate with us in this historic occasion.

The 88th Congress is gone but its good works continue. The measure before me is one of the finest works of this very fine year.

For reasons personal, as well as Presidential, I am pleased and I am proud to be able to sign this measure into law today.

In 1958 I was privileged to be one of the authors of the National Defense Education Act which this legislation extends and expands. If it will not be construed as an intrusion on the bipartisan nature of this ceremony, I might mention that the other author was the Senator from Minnesota, Mr. Hubert Humphrey.

So 6 years ago our Nation was sorely concerned about the future. We were concerned about how our system was faring in the contest of this century. There were voices of despair and there were cries of doom. But we turned back to the vital source of our Great Society's strength and our people's capacity for renewal. We turned back to the wellspring of education.

We committed ourselves to do many of the works in education which had long been neglected and which had been left undone.

When this original legislation was enacted, I said—and I hope you will pardon me if I repeat it today: "History may well record that we saved liberty and saved freedom when we undertook a crash program in the field of education.

"We have not gone far enough fast enough. There must be an awakening not only here in the Congress but throughout this great country of ours. And first things must come first."

Today under your leadership, because of your courage and your counsel, there has been an awakening. We face the challenges and the contests of the world with much greater certainty and sureness than we did 6 years ago. Our effort in education is succeeding and is moving forward. More than 3,100 young men and women have been trained for college teaching. Five thousand more are already enrolled. Over 600,000 students have been helped to secure a college education under the NDEA student loan programs. Much has been done.

But as I said in '58 to the Congress, first things must still come first. In our colleges today the student enrollment is about 6.3 million. In only 6 more years the enrollment will be over 7 million. Already the American families must expect to spend from $4,000 to $5,000 for the college education of each of their children. These costs may be expected to increase by nearly half again in the next 10 years.

We are now losing more than 100,000 high school graduates of the highest ability who cannot afford to go to college.

Now, ladies and gentlemen, this just must not continue. The challenge is obvious and we must meet it. Higher costs must not put higher education out of reach.

The Continental Congress was the first to pledge "that the means of education shall forever be encouraged." Now it's up to us to keep that pledge in our time.

That is the purpose of this legislation that I sign today. Under this program we will increase our training of teachers fivefold. We will, under this program, extend guidance and counseling to almost 45 million elementary school pupils.

Under this legislation we will establish 10 new graduate and 60 undergraduate language centers. And we will do much more than a growing America requires us to do.

The 88th Congress represents a turning point for education. There is a consensus. There is a commitment to unite and to move ahead in education. And I, with the forces that I see here, the leaders in this Congress, we are just going to do that.

I said the other night in Denver, Colo., to the largest facility they had for seating people—and every seat was full and there were almost an additional 15,000 or 20,000 outside—that we must say as a matter of national policy in the United States of America that every boy and girl born in this country under that flag has a right to all the education that he or she can take.

Now these Powell-Morse amendments represent a long step forward. And special thanks are due for the fine work of all the Members of the House and the Senate Education Committee, especially Senator Morse; and my own beloved Senator, Senator Yarborough; and Congressman Powell; Con-

gressman Perkins; and Mrs. Green; and others who I will not take the time to enumerate because I have talked about those of you that have talked to me so often and so much on this subject. But I know you would yield to all the others in their dedication to this great program.

I have just been in a meeting with the Ambassador from the Soviet Union. They have a new government in the Soviet Union. And new governments bring new problems. We spent 45 minutes—he, assuring me that he was directed, on behalf of the new government, to tell our people that they wanted to continue to explore with us every possible means of achieving better understanding and relieving the tensions in the world.

We have just confirmed the detonation by the Chinese of a nuclear bomb. It is a rather crude weapon, but it is the beginning of a series of steps that I anticipate will be harmful and injurious, and require great sacrifices on the part of the Chinese people.

Now living in this kind of a world—even our good friends, the British, have a new Prime Minister that I must talk to this afternoon, if I can—we just can't rely on dropouts, on fourth-grade intellects, and on any people that have not acquired all the training and all the education that they are capable of acquiring. That is the investment that would pay us the greatest dividends of any investment we can possibly make.

A great President of the Republic of Texas once said, and I have repeated it so much that I hope my colleagues in the Senate will indulge me, "that the educated mind is the guardian genius of democratic government, of democracy." The educated mind—it is the only dictator that free men will ever recognize. And it is the only ruler that free men desire.

So as we sign this bill this afternoon, let's let this be another step along the road that we have taken and when we come back here, whenever that may be, let's be prepared to go all the way.

NOTE: The President spoke at 1:45 p.m. in the East Room at the White House. During the course of his remarks he referred to Senator Wayne Morse of Oregon, Senator Ralph Yarborough of Texas, Repre-

sentative Adam C. Powell of New York, Representative Carl D. Perkins of Kentucky, and Representative Edith Green of Oregon.

Among those attending the ceremony were members and officials of the National Education Association.

As enacted, the bill (S. 3060) is Public Law 88–665 (78 Stat. 1100).

677   Remarks at the Swearing In of Sargent Shriver as Director, Office of Economic Opportunity.   *October 16, 1964*

I AM HAPPY that those of you that were present for the signing of the NDEA bill could stay here. And I want to particularly and enthusiastically welcome to this house the associates of Sargent Shriver and his friends who have done so much to make this event possible and to launch in this country a coordinated and comprehensive war on poverty.

One hundred years ago Mr. Lincoln abolished slavery in this country. And we have a modern day Lincoln from the State of Illinois whose objective is to abolish poverty in this country. Mr. Roosevelt rolled up his sleeves a few years ago and pointed out to the Nation that he needed their support for the one-third that were ill clad, ill housed, and ill fed.

Mr. Shriver is here this morning to assume the awesome and exacting responsibilities of directing the administration of a program that will serve not the one-third, because since Mr. Roosevelt's day we have reduced it from 33⅓ percent to 20 percent. He's here to ask your help in abolishing poverty among the one-fifth that are ill clad, ill fed, and ill housed.

In the measure that I just signed and the oath administered here that I will administer in a few moments, there is one common objective: that is to increase opportunity for all Americans.

We believe in equal opportunity for all, special privilege for none. And there is no work that is more prudent or more progressive or more genuinely American than this work.

For as long as there has been an America, much of our progress has been the product of good laws and good men to administer them and assure their success.

The Economic Opportunity Act of 1964 is a good law. In my judgment, it is one of the best laws. The reason it's a good law and the reason it is one of the best is because this good, competent man poured his very soul into it for days and weeks and months.

This measure rejects the approach that America has outgrown. It rejects handouts, it rejects the dole. It rejects complacency. It rejects growing relief rolls. Instead, this measure keeps faith with and puts faith in the dignity and the capacity of the individual to grow, to bloom through education.

The concept represents modern America at her best. The need is obvious for leadership which represents modern America at her best. And for that leadership, in my judgment, I have selected the best equipped by personality, by training, by head and heart and heels. I have selected the best personality in this country for that job. He was not an applicant for it. He urged me to take many more good men and he would have said "no" to anyone except his President.

But he is the kind of a person that goes where his President leads him because he loves his country that much. And our Nation is indebted to him already for the great feats of leadership that he has performed in this country.

His work was brilliant in the '60 political arena when John Fitzgerald Kennedy was selected to lead us. His performance and the contributions that he made in helping to man this Government with men of high character, deep conviction, great purpose, is almost unbelievable. And I am so proud that those men are staying to help me.

His work in the Peace Corps has helped an entire generation of most able, most dedicated, and most enlightened young Americans to fulfill the vision of their minds and the hunger of their hearts.

In this new and added capacity, Sargent Shriver will have a part in helping the less fortunate young Americans. These are rare opportunities for any man. But we have a rare man in Sargent Shriver.

Americans today enjoy a good life but we know that we can never expect a free life to be an easy life. If we want to live in peace and prosperity at home, we must commit ourselves to doing the works in the world which are not easy and not comfortable and not pleasant.

There is no doubt that young Americans are willing to undertake such works and they need only the opportunity to accept the challenge. Out in the world, here at home, in remote nations, in next door neighborhoods, there are difficult and demanding tasks waiting for Americans. So we must take up those challenges and we must mark our lives by commitment rather than contentment.

The allies of freedom's enemies have always been poverty, illiteracy, and disease. These are the curses that we can and we must conquer. If peace is to have purpose, if peace is to be our mission, we must use it to destroy those ancient enemies of mankind rather than allow them to lead us toward man's own destruction and war against himself.

So it's a very high privilege for me to be here on this occasion to observe the swearing in of the man who will start this year not to abolish slavery in this country, but a most noble calling to abolish poverty in this country.

Mr. Shriver.

NOTE: The President spoke at 2:20 p.m. in the East Room at the White House shortly after signing the National Defense Education Act Amendments (Item 676).

For the President's remarks upon signing the Economic Opportunity Act of 1964, see Item 528.

678   Remarks Upon Arrival at the Greater Cincinnati Airport. *October 16, 1964*

Governor Breathitt, Senator Young, Congressman Chelf, my old friend Brent Spence, Chairman Paxton, my good friends of Kentucky and Ohio:

If I can just make a few more visits to this State this year, I am going to be eligible to call Kentucky my home. It is wonderful to be with you. Sometime when I can stay longer, I am going to write myself an invitation and come back and spend an afternoon here in Covington.

Today we are mixing bluegrass and buckeyes. I hope the results will be a winner on November 3d for the Democratic ticket. Of course, I wouldn't want to make any recommendations, but I will offer this impartial, objective statement: that the people of this district could not make a wiser choice than to keep in the Congress my good friend Frank Chelf, and keep in the Senate my good friend Steve Young.

You have a tradition of sending some of your finest citizens to Washington to serve the Nation. I have known and served with many of them, but none have ever stood higher in my estimation than Brent Spence.

If your neighboring State of Ohio is the mother of Presidents, Kentucky is the father of great Governors. We had many of them together a week ago, and they demonstrated a great trait of Kentucky Democrats—the ability to unite. But one of the finest Governors of the land is your Governor now, my friend Ed Breathitt.

These are sobering hours in the history of the world. But there is no business anywhere that is more serious than the election of the leadership of the strongest nation on earth.

I had not intended to speak very long. At these airports you usually have a problem of people standing, the problem of planes flying, and the problem of not talking too often, too much, or if you do, you won't be able to talk at all. But I think I will tell you of a somewhat exciting day that I had this morning.

I was up at 6:30 and I read about 15 newspapers and all the reports that had come in overnight, and the morning cables. Then I went to my office, and we planted two trees on the White House lawn. It is customary for Presidents to plant trees when they live there, and we planted two trees that are oaks, that are grown both in the Atlantic seaboard and in my own section of the country. They grow tall and they grow straight, and they provide a good shade.

Then I visited for about an hour with the Soviet Ambassador, and he told me of the problems that exist in their country today, and the new government that has just taken over from Premier Khrushchev. One man runs the government and one runs the party. He assured me of the friendship of their people for our people and he wanted to make it clear that he was instructed by the new government to inform our Government that there had been and there would be no change in their foreign policy and their attitude toward us and their hope that we could, together, find some way to peace in the world, some way to reduce our armaments, and some way to relieve the tensions.

When I finished talking with the Soviet Ambassador, I met with the Secretary of State, the Secretary of Defense, the Chairman of the Central Intelligence Agency, the Executive Secretary of the National Security Council, and the Under Secretary of State, and we talked about the problems in southeast Asia, and our forces in Viet-Nam. We talked about the implications of the new government in the Soviet Union and why they had decided to change. We took all of the reports we had received and evaluated them. The Secretary of Defense and the Secretary of State stayed on later, and the Security Council will meet tomorrow to further go into those problems.

We received complete confirmation that the Chinese had detonated a nuclear weapon today—at 3 a.m. our time this morning. It is a crude weapon, but it means another nation can contaminate the atmosphere, and it means in due time that they no doubt will have other weapons and will probably develop the capacity to deliver them. It is really a sad day for the Chinese people, because with all their hunger and their many unfilled needs, they have to take their resources and put them into nuclear weapons.

I then went over and met with the leading educators from all over the country, and we signed one of the most comprehensive education bills in the history of this country. We talked about the great increased need of educated minds in our country, and how many people were unemployed because they had no specific training, and how in this space age, when the Soviet Union was sending three men into space, and when the Chinese nation has developed the nuclear bomb, how important it is for every child in this land to have all the education that he is capable of taking.

We finished with that meeting and I made a statement to a group of civic leaders of the Nation, and swore in Mr. Sargent Shriver, who is inaugurating a billion dollar program to drive out poverty in our land. The people that oppose it say it is not enough to do any good. The people that oppose it say it is too much to spend on people. So either way you go, you get criticized.

But as I was standing there getting ready to swear in Mr. Shriver, I thought of my experience as a young Congressman. We had women working in my district that made 7 cents an hour—in 1937. They tried to support their family on 56 cents a day. We introduced, in accordance with the President's recommendation, a minimum wage-maximum hour law. That law provided that the minimum pay per hour would be 25 cents an hour. It would be unlawful to pay anyone less than a quarter an hour.

There were only three men from my section of the country that signed a petition to force that caucus, and all three of us were told that we were ruining our political careers. That was in 1938—25 cents an hour. We were told that we would hurt labor, and we would hurt ourselves. The other two men that signed that petition with me and brought that question to a vote were defeated in the next July primary because they had sought to vote for a bill that paid 25 cents an hour. Now, think how far we have come since 1938.

It was about that same period that our great leader, President Roosevelt, who bore awesome responsibilities, concluded that we ought to try to do something about the poor people. He said a third of our Nation, one out of every three, was ill clad, ill fed, and ill housed. He looked forward to the day when he could reduce that percentage, and he did reduce it. That was 30 years ago.

In 30 years we have reduced it from one-third to one-fifth, from 33 percent to 20 percent. But there is still 20 percent of our people, 1 out of every 5 families, that live below the poverty line. Children born into those families grow up, become adults, unable to find a job, ill equipped, ill trained, and they become taxeaters instead of taxpayers. So we decided if President Roosevelt and his successors could reduce it from one-third to one-fifth, that maybe we could reduce it to one-tenth.

One hundred years ago, Abraham Lincoln abolished slavery in this country. It is almost unbelievable that we held people in bondage and we had our fellow human beings as slaves. But we did, 100 years ago.

And 100 years from now, I think your children are going to look back on the day when I swore in Sargent Shriver and say, "It is almost unbelievable that 20 percent of our people lived in poverty." Because just as Abraham Lincoln abolished slavery, we are going to abolish poverty in this country.

We want peace in our world. That is our number one objective. We want to learn to live with other nations. We want to be able to exist in a land where we don't have to worry about a nervous thumb moving up toward pushing that button that will wipe out 300 million lives. We don't want to sit there and listen to that "hot line" ring and the call coming from Moscow, and what they are going to say on the other end of the line.

We went through the terrifying and frightening experience of the Cuban missile crisis, when two men looked at each other eyeball to eyeball and finally Mr. Khrushchev had to pick up his missiles and take them home.

We want responsibility in foreign affairs like we have had for 20 years since World War II. Our friends in Western Europe have largely recovered. We are standing by our friends in Asia. We are making great progress in the Western Hemisphere.

Many nations have thrown off the yoke of colonialism and there is more freedom in the world today than there was 20 years ago. In all the new nations that have been born, I know you must take great pride in the fact that not one single one of them has embraced communism. The last nation that we lost to communism was Cuba in 1959.

We had a change of governments today in Great Britain. It fell my lot and my duty to call the Prime Minister of Great Britain and to welcome him for a visit and to talk to him about the problems that he will encounter and that will mutually confront our allies. So that is something about my day. The Prime Minister, I guess, went out to take his siesta and have his tea, and I came to Covington and Cincinnati and Dayton.

In addition to peace in the world, we very much hope for prosperity among our people. In the last week, I have seen more than 2 million people. Almost that many have scratched my hand. But it is a real invigorating experience, and it is a wonderful sight to look into the eyes of your bosses, the people that employ you, the folks you work for, the men and women who trust you, the ones who have faith in you and have faith in their country and have hopes for their future and their posterity. It is an exciting experience to be a leader in a democratic land. You want your people to be happy.

I have seen so many smiling, happy faces that the most dreadful thing that could happen to me would be to see a war come on or to see a depression come on. So today I gave instructions to my economic advisers to make a new study of how we could keep this prosperity going after next spring.

I may not need that study myself, as somebody else may be using it, but I think you have to think ahead, and I think you have to be optimistic for the future. I think you have to plan. I don't think you can just sit back and take things for granted.

I want to see the day when every man and woman who wants to work will have a job. I want to see the day when heart disease, cancer, and strokes will be banished and everyone can live to the ripe, old age of 100, and we are going in that direction.

I want to see the day when there will be a classroom for every child and there will be a qualified, well-paid teacher to man that classroom in this country.

The average manufacturing wage now is $104 a week, and we have 72½ million people working. There are less people that have lost time through strikes this year than at any time in our postwar history.

We had problems with the railroad strike for 4½ years, we had those differences. But with the help of the good Lord, the leaders of both the railroads and the workers, we settled it. We had problems with the auto strike, but we have gotten most of those working out all right. We are losing only fourteen one-hundredths of 1 percent of the hours at work. Not 1 percent, not a half of 1 percent, but fourteen one-hundredths of 1 percent.

So we are proud of what has developed

along that line. We have given back our taxpayers $12 billion that would have otherwise gone into the Treasury, so they could make new capital investments to provide more jobs, so they could have more take-home money. And, generally speaking, I think our folks on the average are doing well. We want to keep it that way. We think that the man that you select to lead this country and the kind of government you select will have something to do with not only peace in the world, but prosperity at home.

I have not come here today to say anything about any other choices or about my opponents. I have never felt that the voter cared very much about what one man thought about the fellow that was trying to get his job.

I have been in this business for a long time. My first campaign was for Al Smith when I was 20 years old. I am considerably older now, but for more than 30 years I have been going among the people and I have often observed that mudslinging and muckraking, and personal denunciations lost candidates more votes than it gained them.

So I have not come here for the purpose of telling you that Senator Humphrey and myself are the only two men in this country that are capable of leading these people. You people would do all right with just almost anybody leading you, because we have good citizens, and we have a good Nation, and we can weather these storms.

Look at what happened when our leader was stricken and fell, on the tragic day in November. Our people united. They pulled together—business, labor, women, farmers, groups all over the country—and we presented a united front to the world. We have gone forward. He left 51 bills behind him, and last Friday night I sat at my desk and I looked at the inventory and we had passed every one of those 51 bills in the United States Senate.

If you feel that we are worthy of it, if you think that we have the experience, if you think we have the head and the heart and the heels that these responsibilities require, we most earnestly solicit your support on November 3d.

NOTE: The President spoke at 4:47 p.m. at the Greater Cincinnati Airport in Covington, Ky. In his opening words he referred to Governor Edward T. Breathitt, Jr., of Kentucky, Senator Stephen M. Young of Ohio, Representative Frank Chelf of Kentucky, former Representative Brent Spence of Kentucky, and Frank Paxton, chairman of the Kentucky State Democratic Committee.

679 Remarks at Government Square in Cincinnati. *October 16, 1964*

Mr. Chairman, Senator Young, ladies and gentlemen, boys and girls:

I brought Steve Young out here to Ohio with me today, and I am expecting you to send him back to Washington. We need him in Washington and we would like for Ohio to send with him Bob Sweeney, Jack Gilligan, and Harry Sand to give us a good Democratic delegation.

I am glad to see here your county chairman, Vincent Beckman. I would say from what I hear about his service as county commissioner, one good turn deserves another.

I am glad to see my old friend Mike DiSalle on the platform. I am especially honored today by the presence here of one of America's most distinguished and most useful citizens, Dr. Sabin. I am so deeply proud that Dr. Sabin and Mr. Fee have announced their support today for the Johnson-Humphrey ticket. That is Hubert Humphrey I am speaking of.

Over the last 24 hours, the meaning of this election has become clear. It is clear, as it should be clear always, that the destiny of a great nation is not to be determined by partisan consideration.

This generation of Americans stands face to face with the reality of our age. The world will not respond to the promises of politicians. It will not respond to the peeves of partisans. In an age of peril, when danger lurks across the land, the world respects and the world responds to performance, the effective performance, of a bipartisan system in the American way.

Strength we have, and strength we must have, and strength we will keep, and strength we will increase. But the strength of arms alone is not enough. We must show stability to match our strength. We must show steadiness to match our purpose. Only by strength and stability and steadiness can we lead the cause of freedom in the world.

This is the meaning of the last 24 hours. In that short span of time, the world has changed. In our oldest ally in the free world, the government has changed. I talked to the new Prime Minister of Great Britain on the telephone just before I left Washington.

In the strongest nation in the Communist world, the government changed yesterday.

In the most anti-American capital of the Communist world, the Communist rulers of the Chinese mainland have come into possession of their first nuclear device.

We cannot know the road ahead. We know there is peril, as there has been peril all of our lives. We know there are trials, as there have been trials all of our lives.

But we must understand and we must not forget that the meaning of the future will be influenced by the choice you make on November 3d. That is the reality of our age.

The course to be chosen in Moscow, the course to be taken in Peiping, the course to be pursued in the capitals of the free men around the world will be guided by the decisions that the Americans make on November 3, 1964, so be sure of what you do and be sure you know you are right.

In this year, as in all years, others will be reading our election returns. What they conclude from what they read may well decide the destiny of this decade, and the longer course of this century. There just simply must be no miscalculation. There simply must be no room for misinterpretation. The world must know on election night that America will not turn from the course we pursued.

Harry Truman faced the Communists in Greece and Turkey, and with the bipartisan support of Arthur Vandenberg, we won. Dwight David Eisenhower faced the crisis in the Formosa Strait, and with the support of Lyndon Johnson and Mike Mansfield, we won. Jack Kennedy faced the Cuban missile crisis, and with the support of Everett Dirksen, we won.

You will not be electing a President alone on November 3d; you will be electing the kind of life that you want to lead and the kind of world you want your children to grow up in. The vote you cast will count as much as the vote you do not cast, for if you fail to vote, your future will be chosen for you.

This is the season of decision for free men. Men who cherish their freedom and who cherish peace for their children and who hope for prosperous and peaceful tomorrows will not allow that decision to be reached by default. More Americans than ever stand firmly in the center. Our course is guided by the wisdom of experience and the goal of common purpose. We do not want to open that American center to attack or to division or to disruption from extreme factions on the fringe.

On November 3d, the choice of the American people can be a choice of promises or it can be a choice of performance. It can be a choice made in prudence or it can be a choice made in passion. I have no doubt what the American people want that choice to be.

The office of the American Presidency is a great and honorable office, created by a great people. Over the last 175 years, only 35 other Americans have held the trust that I hold today. One out of five of those men— one out of five of those 35—have been sons of your State of Ohio. If they could all stand here beside me now, I believe all who have served before would agree with me on these facts:

—The President cannot make the world sure for Americans, but he can and he must make the world sure of America.

—The President cannot wipe away the burdens of freedom, but he can and he must work to control and to eliminate the waste of freedom's resources.

—The President cannot talk a budget down with words, but he can and he must bring the budget down by hard and understanding work.

—The President cannot give the people freedom, he cannot grant the people rights, for their freedom and their rights are no man's to give or no man's to withhold. But the President can and the President must be willing to give all that is his to protect freedom and to preserve those rights of our fellow Americans.

On this quiet side of election day, when a man sits alone in the office where I serve now,

promises of political campaigns mean little. Performance means everything. Since that tragic day last November when this office was thrust upon me, I have tried my best to keep the pledge I made to you, to do the best I could with your prayers and with the help of God above.

I am proud and I am grateful that in these 10 months that I have served you, our prosperity has continued to run unbroken. I am grateful that in these months our preparedness and our peace has grown without interruption. I am grateful that we still have and the world still has peace to enjoy.

I cannot promise, and no man can pretend to promise, all that lies ahead. We cannot know tomorrow or next week or even next year.

I can promise, and I do promise, that whatever may arise, your country—America— will be the strongest nation in all the world and will be prepared.

I can promise and I do promise that if we are called to great challenges, your Government will be ready to perform.

I can promise, and I do promise, that the time to come will be used to unite America, and I will never do anything to divide your country. I love the people of this land; I do not hate them. I have faith in them; I do not have fear of them.

I can promise and I do promise that I will give you all the strength that is mine to bind our wounds, to heal our history, and to make this Nation whole for the trials and for the tests that are ahead.

Some people say we are wild spenders, but in their hearts they know they are wrong. In my first 10 months in office, I cut the deficit in half. In my first 10 months in office, we reduced the budget under the last Kennedy budget by $1 billion. This July and August just passed, under this administration, the Government spent $676 million less than it spent in July and August of last year. We have cut the Federal work force of employees. Today there are 21,000 fewer Federal employees working for the Federal Government than there were the day I became President.

We are encouraging business and we are not harassing it. We know that the more prosperous business becomes, the more jobs are created, the higher wages can be paid to the workers. We have determined that this Government shall be solvent, this Government shall be secure, and this Government shall always be strong.

To do this, we must be fiscally responsible. We must watch every dollar so that we can get back a dollar's value for each dollar we spend. These are the facts, and the facts tell us that for the first time in many years, the budget, the deficit, the Federal work force, are all going down together. And profits—$12 billion more after taxes. Work-

ers—$60 billion more after taxes. Wages, income, private employment up 5 million people in the last 4 years.

The opposition knows this, for the truth and the facts tell them that they are wrong, and a prosperous, free America knows we are right. And we are going to tell them in language that they will all understand on November 3d.

Thank you.

NOTE: The President spoke at 5:34 p.m. at a rally in Government Square, Cincinnati, Ohio. His opening words referred to Vincent Beckman, chairman of the Democratic Central Committee of Hamilton County, and Senator Stephen M. Young of Ohio. Later he referred to, among others, Robert E. Sweeney, John J. Gilligan, and Harry Sand, Democratic candidates for Representative, former Governor Michael V. DiSalle of Ohio, Dr. Albert B. Sabin of the Children's Hospital Research Foundation, George Fee, Cincinnati attorney, Arthur H. Vandenberg, U.S. Senator from Michigan during the Truman administration, Senator Mike Mansfield of Montana, and Senator Everett McKinley Dirksen of Illinois.

680   Remarks on the City Hall Steps, Dayton, Ohio. *October 16, 1964*

Judge Love, Senator Young, Chairman Bill Coleman, Chairman Horstman, my fellow Americans:

I almost feel like saying my fellow Ohioans. I always feel at home in your great State.

I especially like it here in this fine city of Dayton. I don't know why Orville and Wilbur Wright wanted to fly when they could have kept their feet on the ground in a hometown like this!

Dayton is the birthplace of the air age, but Dayton's best years, and Ohio's best years, are still ahead. Thirty years from now, Ohio will have a population of 20 million people. There will be as many people living in your cities alone as live now in

your entire State.

You have work to do for the future, as all America does, and you need forward-looking men in the Ohio tradition to serve you, and none have more vision and none have more confidence, and none is a better friend of mine or a more trusted friend of mine than your own good Senator Steve Young.

I brought Senator Young out here this afternoon on Air Force One, and I am counting on you to send him back to Washington with a prepaid ticket on November 3d. When Steve Young flies back there as the winner, I want him to arrive with some new Congressmen at his side—Judge Rodney Love, Robert Mihlbaugh, and Jerry Graham.

This is going to be a Democratic year, and I suspect that it is going to be the biggest and the best Democratic year of all here in Ohio.

I want to thank you for these wonderful signs. I want to express my appreciation for your warm welcome. I want to tell you how good it makes me feel to see your happy, smiling faces. I am proud to be here in this city, so close to the Democratic Party, through James M. Cox, the father who ran for President with FDR at his side, and the son whose fine newspapers stand with the Democrats in this great campaign.

There is a special reason why I feel so much at home here in Ohio. You may not want to take the blame for it, but if it hadn't been for the people of Ohio, there wouldn't have been a Texas today.

One hundred and twenty years ago, Texans declared their independence. Their ranks were thin. Their arms were few. But they believed their cause was right, so they took their stand and they made their fight. At the hour when all was blackest, help arrived. The army of the Republic of Texas received their first and their only artillery as a gift from the people of Ohio.

If you have forgotten this history, no Texan ever forgets, because every schoolboy in my State learns that Ohio made our independence possible. And you are going to make our election possible.

We had a very exacting and exciting day in Washington. I came in late last night after having visited the great State of New York. This morning at 6:30 I was up reading reports from the Congo, Viet-Nam, Cyprus, and places all over the world where there are problems that we are concerned with.

Then I went down and planted two trees. It is traditional with Presidents to plant trees on the White House grounds. We planted two oaks, oaks that stand tall and oaks that give a good shade, and oaks that stand straight.

Then I went in and met with the National Security Council, Secretary of State Rusk, Under Secretary Ball, Secretary of Defense McNamara, the head of the Central Intelligence Agency, Mr. John McCone, and we reviewed all of the intelligence from all over the world. We talked about the change in government in the largest Communist country in the world, the things that are taking place that replaced Mr. Khrushchev last night, and how it would affect their foreign policy and how it would affect our foreign policy, and how it would affect the world in which we live.

Then we talked about the elections yesterday in Great Britain, and the selection of a new Prime Minister in Great Britain. Then we decided that we would meet a little later and review some more problems and have another meeting of the Security Council tomorrow.

I then received the Russian Ambassador, Mr. Dobrynin. He came in and for almost an hour he gave me a message from the new rulers in the Kremlin. He told me that it was the hope of the people in the Soviet Union that they could continue their search for peace with us, that somehow, some way, we must find a way to live in the world together, without wiping each other out with nuclear bombs.

I told him that our policy would not change, that we were the strongest and the mightiest nation in the world, but that strength would be used for deterrents, that we did not rattle our rockets and we did not bluff with our bombs; that our guard was always up, but our hand was always out. I told him we preferred to judge men by their acts instead of their words.

But as your President, the only President that you have, as the trustee for the American people—as Theodore Roosevelt once said the President is really the guardian, the President has a very special obligation as the steward of all the people—I said I will go anywhere, I will talk to anybody, I will go to any lengths that an honorable man can go to try to seek peace in the world.

More than 20 years ago I was in the war, and for more than 20 years I have been in the cold war. I saw Harry Truman, with the help of Republican Arthur Vandenberg, meet the Communist guerrillas in Greece and Turkey and win. I saw Dwight David Eisenhower, with the help of Lyndon Johnson as the Democratic leader, meet them in the Formosa Strait and win. I saw Everett Dirksen, the Republican leader, give us support. And I saw John Fitzgerald Kennedy win in the Cuban missile crisis.

We seek no wider war, but we are prepared and we intend to preserve and to protect and to defend the United States of America.

On this trip around the country in the last few days I have seen more than 2 million people. I believe at least 2 million and 1 have grabbed my sore hand. But the trip has been a great thing for your President.

I don't believe that any candidates in the history of the United States have ever been received by so many people and given such a warm welcome as Hubert Humphrey and I have been given by the American people.

I am not sure that the people realize that this is going to be their only chance in 4 years for the real decision-makers in this country to make the most important decisions that they will ever be called upon to make.

And I am not going to insult your intelligence with trivia. I am going to talk about the issues, and the only issue is responsibility versus irresponsibility. Peace or war, prosperity or recession? You hold that deci-

sion in your own hands.

One important question, and there has been a good deal of attention to this one, is whose hand and whose thumb is going to be trusted by the American people with control of the most awesome power, the mightiest power, the world has ever known? When you get ready to push that button, whose thumb do you want on that button?

But even more important right now is whose hands are going to mark the ballots and pull the levers in America's voting booths on November 3d? I hope they are Democratic hands. I think, very frankly, that too many people in this country are taking too much for granted in this campaign. I think that every person here better decide for himself or herself in the next 3 weeks what they are going to do for their country. And then November 3d they better go vote for what is best for America.

The polls show, and some people think, that the country will not take seriously the opposition candidates who are disavowed by their own party, who propose to undo everything that we have done in 30 years, who propose to sell the TVA and make social security voluntary, and wipe out our farm programs, and undermine collective bargaining, and get out of the United Nations, and break the nuclear test ban treaty, and play with atomic bombs when the stakes of life are high.

I don't believe it either, but I am not going to gamble with it.

I haven't come out here to indulge in any smears or muckraking or mudslinging. They are always the weapons of desperation and fearful, frightened men. You can usually judge them by their words, if not their signs.

I propose to use this campaign for the broad purposes that a campaign is meant for: a campaign to educate, educate the

American people and the candidates themselves.

A campaign can tear open old wounds and it can pour salt on fresh wounds. It can divide America instead of uniting it. You do not serve the best interests of your country when you divide your country. You must unite your country if you want to have an effective America. A small faction can seek to rally votes by raising the specter of fear. A faction can appeal to what is worst in a few Americans instead of appealing to what is best in most Americans. We must all learn together.

If this generation is blinded by hate and fear, America will perish. If this generation allows prejudice to blot out justice, America will perish. What about this generation?

I remind you of matters that we often forget. From 1790 until 1900, 21 million people settled west of the Mississippi. That was the greatest frontier. We think of it as one of history's most massive and significant migrations. This generation has lived through a change more massive and more significant.

From 1930 to 1963 the population of our urban centers increased by 56 million people. The migration to the cities in the past 30 years was 2½ times as great as the westward migration that lasted over 100 years.

Today, 70 percent of us live in metropolitan areas. The percentage is surprisingly consistent everywhere. My own State of Texas likes to say, "Don't fence me in."

But 75 percent of our people are urban. One American in five moves each year. Today, young people are most likely to get hurt by pressure of a changing society.

Each year, between 1½ million and 2 million children get in trouble with the law. More than a million are arrested. More than half a million end up in court.

Ninety-five percent of the 17-year-old delinquents are school dropouts. Eighty-five percent of the 16-year-old delinquents are school dropouts. Children without roots, children without education, children who face discrimination—they all tend to become delinquent children.

The war on poverty, which I started by swearing Sargent Shriver in today at the White House, is a war against crime and a war against disorder. The continuing effort to increase educational opportunity is part of stamping out juvenile delinquency.

There is something mighty wrong when a candidate for the highest public office bemoans violence in the streets but votes against the war on poverty, votes against the Civil Rights Act, and votes against major educational bills that have come before him as a legislator. The thing to do is not to talk about crime; the thing to do is to fight and work and vote against crime. You can't deal with the crime problem and you cannot solve the crime problem in this country by making a political speech on a Fourth of July every fourth year about crime.

You must educate your children. You must take care of the delinquent. You must get out and work and vote and fight and give and do something about it.

So what do I say? What do the Democrats say? What does our platform say? We say that every American child has the right to an education and we are going to see that that right is honored.

We have made great progress, but I see ahead today, closer than ever before, the kind of a nation that I want to see, the kind of a country that I will take pride in, the kind of people I love.

I see a day ahead with a united nation, divided neither by class nor by section nor by color, knowing no South or North, no East or West, but just one great America, free of malice and free of hate, and loving thy neighbor as thyself.

I see America as a family. It may have its arguments as families do, but it respects each member's dignity and freedom and his right to be different from the others; and it takes care of all of its members in time of adversity.

I see America as a land where the poorest among us will have as fair a chance to fulfill himself in life as the richest among us.

I see our Nation as a free and gracious land with its people bound together by common ties of confidence and affection, and common aspirations toward purpose and duty.

I see our Nation as a magnanimous land, strong and compassionate and just and fair, and ready to help other peoples throughout the world to save their freedom and to help their children not to starve.

I see America as a democratic republic which has woven the strands of diversity into an enduring fabric of opportunity and liberty of faith and hope.

So in this spirit, let us work together to construct an even more spacious future for all of our people, and, more important, for all the people of the world.

I feel a great obligation to you men and women, to you boys and girls. Almost 11 months ago, after that tragic day in Dallas, on a moment's notice I had to assume the awesome responsibilities of the Presidency.

I said to you that night that I had no time to confer and make plans; I couldn't even go to a library to read up. I had to effect the transition. I had to show the world that America could stand and that we were a government of laws that could carry on even if we had lost our great leader.

I said to you that with God's help, with your hands and your heart and your prayers, that I would do my best for this country. I

have done that. I have kept that pledge.

And I pledge to you that if God is willing, and you vote right on November the 3d, I will lead this country to a greater society where every man and woman who wants a job can work and find a job, where every child that wants an education will have a right to an education, where our collective bargaining will be protected and our minimum wage and maximum hours will be improved, where our social security system will not be thrown down the drain by making it voluntary, but we will strengthen it by giving medical care to the aged.

A great American President led this Union in a war against slavery 100 years ago. Lincoln abolished slavery in the United States. Today we are starting another war to abolish poverty in the United States among our people.

So you have a duty and you have an obligation to yourself and to your children. You have an obligation to your country. You have the precious, the priceless right of suffrage, the right that no one can take away from you.

So on November 3d, you must go down to that ballot box and you must cast your vote, and who should you vote for?

[*Audience response: "LBJ!"*]

I would hope that that would be your ultimate decision. But I would hope that you would engage in a little introspection, and ask yourself whether you are a Democrat, a Republican, or Independent; say to yourself that the spotlight of the world is on America, the people are watching what you do and what we do. They want to follow us, they want to emulate our example.

I would say this: that you ought to ask yourself, "What is best for my country?" And then you ought to vote for what you think is best for America, the judgment that is best for America, the experience that is best for America, the character that is best for America, the platform that is best for America.

If you believe in a bipartisan foreign policy, if you believe in a United Nations, then I want to lead you. If you want to chart a new course and throw away the program we have followed for 20 years successfully, then you want another leader.

If you believe in social security, if you believe in medical care, if you believe in collective bargaining, if you believe in equal opportunity for all Americans, if you believe in prudence and economy and progressiveness, then I want your vote. If you don't believe in it, you ought to go you know where.

We have so much to be thankful for. We must recognize it before it is too late. We have so much to preserve and so much to protect.

I believe, like you, that we want to see a land that is better for our children and one for ourselves. We want to see a beautiful countryside where they can spend some of their recreational hours. We want to work less hours per day and less days per week. We want to see a laborer worthy of his hire. We want to see the businessman successful, too, because the more both of them make, the better off the whole country is.

We are proud that 72 million Americans are working today at the highest wages in their history. We are proud that 5 million more people are working today than there were 4 years ago. We are proud that John Fitzgerald Kennedy said, "We are going to get America moving," and she is on her way.

In the quietness of our polling booth, let's say to these apostles of fear and these apostles of smear and these apostles of doubt that "there may be a time for you, but it is not in Ohio, and it is not in the 20th century."

Now I must go back to the White House. I must spend my day tomorrow with our Security Council, trying to work on the plans that we have for the new governments and the new problems that confront us. I am going to leave here with the great inspiration that comes from looking at this mass of faces. I know the people are good people. I know they want to do what is right. I have not the slightest doubt what you are going to do.

A great friend of mine told me before I left Washington, from Ohio, this afternoon, "You don't need to go to Ohio, because we are going to carry Ohio for prudent, progressive, forward-looking, peaceful government by 300,000." I said, "Well, wouldn't it look better if I went ahead and kept those engagements that I have in Covington, Ky., Cincinnati, and Dayton?"

Luci told me, "There is no use of your going out there, I have already been to Dayton." But I said, "Wouldn't it really be better for us, wouldn't it be better for the Soviet Union, wouldn't it be better for Great Britain, wouldn't it be better for Germany, wouldn't it be better for all the people of the world who are looking to us for leadership if we carried Ohio by 400,000 instead of 300,000?"

You folks get out here and make it as big as you can. You go and go to work, and you talk to your uncles and your cousins and aunts. You are going to run into a few people that won't agree with you, but go and see at the hardware store if you can't get them a coal oil lantern and let them play fireman for a while.

Goodby and good luck.

NOTE: The President spoke at 7:53 p.m. at a rally on the City Hall steps in Dayton, Ohio. His opening words referred to Rodney M. Love, Democratic candidate for Representative and former probate judge in Dayton, Senator Stephen M. Young of Ohio, William L. Coleman, chairman of the State Democratic Executive Committee, and Robert

Horstman, chairman of the Democratic Executive Committee for Montgomery County. Later he referred to, among others, Robert H. Mihlbaugh and Jerry Graham, Democratic candidates for Representative, James M. Cox, publisher of the Cox newspapers, Dean Rusk, Secretary of State, George W. Ball, Under Secretary of State, Robert S. McNamara, Secretary of Defense, John A. McCone, Director of the Central Intelligence Agency, Anatoly F. Dobrynin, Russian Ambassador to the United States, Arthur H. Vandenberg, U.S. Senator from Michigan during the Truman administration, Senator Everett McKinley Dirksen of Illinois, Sargent Shriver, Director of the Office of Economic Opportunity, and Luci Baines Johnson, the President's daughter.

681 Message of Congratulation to the Right Honorable Harold Wilson. *October 16, 1964*

Dear Mr. Prime Minister:

My warmest congratulations on your election victory. As you enter the great office of Prime Minister, I want to extend my very best wishes for success for you and your government and the people of the United Kingdom. I look forward to the continuation of the close and friendly cooperation, based on mutual confidence and respect, which has bound our countries so closely for so long.

With warmest personal regards.

Sincerely,

LYNDON B. JOHNSON

[The Right Honorable Harold Wilson, O.B.E., M.P., Prime Minister of the United Kingdom]

682 Message to President de Valera on the Occasion of His 82d Birthday. *October 16, 1964*

Dear Mr. President:

Mrs. Johnson joins me in sending our heartiest congratulations on your eighty-second birthday. We wish you many more years in which you can lead and inspire the great Irish nation and lend your wise counsel to us all.

Sincerely,

LYNDON B. JOHNSON

[His Excellency Eamon de Valera, President of Ireland, Dublin]

683 Statement by the President Upon Signing Executive Order "To Facilitate Coordination of Federal Education Programs." *October 16, 1964*

THERE is nothing Americans care about more deeply than the education of their children. The Federal Government is spending large sums to help States, local communities, and institutions strengthen their educational programs. A number of Federal agencies have programs which aid education. We want to be certain that every dollar is spent in such a way as to strengthen our schools, preserve local initiative, and contribute to better opportunities for the boys and girls

and young men and women of this Nation.

NOTE: The statement was released with the text of Executive Order 11185 (29 F.R. 14399, 3 CFR, 1964 Supp.).

684   Statement by the President Upon Signing Bill Relating to Claims of U.S. Nationals Against the Government of Cuba. *October* 17, 1964

I HAVE signed into law H.R. 12259. The basic purpose of this bill is to authorize the Foreign Claims Settlement Commission to determine the amount and validity of claims of United States nationals against the Government of Cuba.

The Castro regime has expropriated over $1 billion worth of property of United States nationals in total disregard for their rights. These unlawful seizures violated every standard by which the nations of the free world conduct their affairs.

I am confident that the Cuban people will not always be compelled to suffer under Communist rule—that one day they will achieve freedom and democracy. I am also confident that it will be possible to settle the claims of American nationals whose property has been wrongfully taken from them.

This bill will provide for the adjudication of these claims of American nationals. I have signed it because of the importance of making such a permanent record while evidence and witnesses are still available.

There is, however, another provision of this bill that requires further study. This provision vests in the Federal Government ownership of certain assets of the Cuban Government now held in the United States. These assets are already blocked and are thus of no further use to the Cuban Government. The proceeds from the sale of the vested

assets will not be available to American nationals whose properties were expropriated, but will be used to pay for the expenses of administering the bill.

The United States strongly adheres to the sanctity of property. The vesting of the property of foreign governments or nationals is not a step that we should undertake without careful consideration.

I am, therefore, requesting the Secretary of State to make a full study to determine the effect of the vesting provision on American interests abroad and its implications for the conduct of our foreign relations.

I am also requesting an opinion by the Attorney General concerning the precise scope and application of the vesting provision. The language of this provision is ambiguous concerning its possible application in various circumstances. It is unclear, for example, whether the provision applies to the property of American nationals that was unlawfully expropriated by the Castro regime. Similarly, there is doubt whether it applies to certain properties in which other countries have substantial interests.

In the light of these studies, I may find it necessary to propose amendatory legislation with regard to the vesting provision. The present bill provides for a 6-month waiting period before the vesting provision becomes operative. If I conclude that the amendatory legislation is required, I will propose it early next year so that it can become effective before the end of the 6-month period.

NOTE: As enacted, H.R. 12259, approved by the President on October 16, is Public Law 88–666 (78 Stat. 1110).

685   Exchange of Messages With the Secretary General of the North Atlantic Treaty Organization.   *October 17, 1964*

[Released October 17, 1964. Dated October 1, 1964]

Dear Mr. Secretary General:

As you leave the United States, I want to tell you again how pleased we were to have you here as our guest and for the opportunity for extended discussions.

I found our talks on the state of the North Atlantic Alliance and its future needs and hopes useful and rewarding. I was particularly pleased that you were able to join me in visiting the Strategic Air Command in Omaha for I think it gave both of us another opportunity to see how closely the strategic strength of the United States and the effectiveness of the Alliance are tied together.

As I have emphasized several times, the United States is dedicated to NATO. The American commitment to the Alliance is firm and real. We in the United States remain ready, as I know you do, to work with all our allies to insure that ours is a growing partnership of freedom based on shared responsibility for the most effective defense of our people and our freedom.

More personally, I would like you to know that your visit here gave us a new sense of confidence in your leadership and your dedication to a most challenging task. You have my assurance that this Government will give you the closest possible cooperation as you carry on at the helm of the North Atlantic Treaty Organization.

Good luck, and very best wishes.

Sincerely,

LYNDON B. JOHNSON

NOTE: Secretary General Manlio Brosio's message, dated October 6 and released with the President's message, follows:

Dear Mr. President:

Upon my return to Paris, I would like you to know of my profound gratitude for the very warm welcome you gave me and for the highly useful and satisfactory discussions which took place during my visit to the United States. As a result, I am even more deeply convinced than before that there is no substitute for personal meetings in order to find a complete understanding.

I am particularly grateful that you, at a time of heavy personal engagement in domestic affairs, were able to give me so much of your precious time. It was a great honor for me to be your guest at the White House in the midst of such distinguished company, and in your remarks that day I found the most unequivocal assurances of American dedication not only to the ideal but also to the concepts of our alliance. I need not emphasize the satisfaction with which I listened to your statements.

The visit to the Strategic Air Command headquarters demonstrated in a most concrete manner the substance of the American commitment to the defense of our freedom. It is an impressive experience to see directly the proof of American concern over the security not only of your country and people, but of the other NATO members as well. At this point I would like to pay tribute to the evident superior qualities of the men at Omaha who are entrusted with these grave responsibilities.

In closing, Mr. President, I want to thank you both for your boundless hospitality and for the assurances of support in my tasks, a support which I consider absolutely essential to the success of my mission.

With warm regards,

Sincerely,

MANLIO BROSIO

686   Radio and Television Report to the American People on Recent Events in Russia, China, and Great Britain.   *October* 18, 1964

[Broadcast from the President's office at 8:30 p.m.]

My fellow Americans:

On Thursday of last week, from the Kremlin in Moscow, the Soviet Government announced a change in its leadership.

On Friday of last week, Communist China exploded a nuclear device on an isolated test site in Sinkiang.

Both of these important events make it right that your President report to you as fully and as clearly and as promptly as he can. That is what I mean to do this evening.

Now, let me begin with events in Moscow. We do not know exactly what happened to Nikita Khrushchev last Thursday. We do know that he has been forced out of power by his former friends and colleagues. Five days ago he had only praise in Moscow. Today we learn only of his faults.

Yet the men at the top today are the same men that he picked for leadership. These men carried on the administration of the Soviet Government when he was absent from the Soviet capital, and that was nearly half of the time that he was in power.

Mr. Khrushchev was clearly the dominant figure in making Soviet policy. After Lenin and Stalin, he is only the third man in history to have made himself the undisputed master of Communist Russia.

There were times when he was guilty of dangerous adventure. It required great American firmness and good sense—first in Berlin and later in the Cuban missile crisis—to turn back his threats and actions without war.

Yet he learned from his mistakes and he was not blind to realities. In the last 2 years,

his government had shown itself aware of the need for sanity in the nuclear age.

He joined in the nuclear test ban treaty. He joined in the "hot line" which can help prevent a war by accident. He agreed that space should be kept free of nuclear weapons. In these actions he demonstrated good sense and sober judgment. We do not think it was these actions that led to his removal.

We cannot know for sure just what did lead to this secret decision. Our intelligence estimate is that Khrushchev learned of the decision only when for him it was too late.

There has been discontent and strain and failure—both within the Soviet Union and within the Communist bloc as a whole. All of this has been evident for all to see. These troubles are not the creation of one man. They will not end with his removal.

When Lenin died in 1924, Stalin took 4 years to consolidate his power. When Stalin died in 1953, it was not Mr. Khrushchev who first emerged.

But two men now share top responsibility in the Soviet Union, and their exact relation to each other and to their colleagues is not yet very clear. They are experienced, but younger men, and perhaps less rooted in the past. They are said to be realistic. We can hope that they will share with us our great objective—the prevention of nuclear war.

But what does all this mean for us in America? It means at least four things:

First, we must never forget that the men in the Kremlin remain dedicated, dangerous Communists. A time of trouble among Communists requires steady vigilance among free men—and most of all among Americans. For it is the strength of the United States that holds the balance firm against danger.

Second, there will be turmoil in the Communist world. It is likely that the men in the Kremlin will be concerned primarily with problems of communism. This would not be all good, because there are problems and issues that need attention between our world and theirs. But it is not all bad, because men who are busy with internal problems may not be tempted to reckless external acts.

Third, this great change will not stop the forces in Eastern Europe that are working for greater independence. Those forces will continue to have our sympathy. We will not give up our hope of building new bridges to these peoples.

Fourth, our own course must continue to prove that we on our side are ready to get on with the work of peace.

The new Soviet Government has officially informed me, through Ambassador Dobrynin, day before yesterday, that it plans no change in basic foreign policy. I spoke frankly, as always, to the Soviet Ambassador. I told him that the quest for peace in America had never been more determined than it is now. I told him that we intend to bury no one, and we do not intend to be buried. I reminded the Ambassador of the danger that we all faced 2 years ago in Cuba. I told him that any Soviet Government which is ready to work for peace will find us ready in America. I said to the Ambassador that I would be ready to talk to anyone, when it would help the cause of peace.

I believe that this was a good beginning, on both sides.

That same day the Chinese nuclear device was exploded at a test site near a lake called Lop Nor, in the Takla Makan desert of the remote Central Asian province of Sinkiang.

The building of this test site had been known to our American intelligence for several years. In recent weeks the rapid pace of work there gave us a quite clear signal that the long and bitter efforts of this regime were leading at last to a nuclear test.

At first, in the 1950's, Russia helped the Chinese. This assistance in the spread of nuclear weapons may now be regarded with some dismay in Moscow. We believe that this help was ended in 1960 as the quarrel among the Communists grew sharper. Soviet technicians left suddenly, with their blueprints under their arms. And the unfinished facilities were just left there standing, and the expected supplies were cut off.

But the Red Chinese kept to their chosen purpose, even as their economic plans collapsed and the suffering of their people increased.

Our own distinguished Secretary of State, Mr. Rusk, gave timely warning as the preparations at Lop Nor advanced. And when the test occurred, I at once told the world that this explosion will not turn Americans and other free peoples from their steady purpose.

No American should treat this matter lightly. Until this week, only four powers had entered the dangerous world of nuclear explosions. Whatever their differences, all four are sober and serious states, with long experience as major powers in the modern world.

Communist China has no such experience. Its nuclear pretensions are both expensive and cruel to its people. It fools no one when it offers to trade away its first small accumulation of nuclear power against the mighty arsenals of those who limit Communist Chinese ambitions. It shocks us by its readiness to pollute the atmosphere with fallout.

But this explosion remains a fact, sad and serious. We must not, we have not, and we will not ignore it.

I discussed the limited meaning of this event in a statement on last Friday. The world already knows

—that we were not surprised,

—that our defense plans take full account of this development,

—that we reaffirm our defense commitments in Asia,

—that it is a long, hard road from a first nuclear device to an effective weapons system, and

—that our strength is overwhelming now and will be kept that way.

But what I have in my mind tonight is a different part of the meaning of this explosion at Lop Nor.

Communist China's expensive and demanding effort tempts other states to equal folly. Nuclear spread is dangerous to all mankind.

What if there should come to be 10 nuclear powers, or maybe 20 nuclear powers?

What if we must learn to look everywhere for the restraint which our own example now sets for a few?

Will the human race be safe in such a day?

The lesson of Lop Nor is that we are right to recognize the danger of nuclear spread; that we must continue to work against it, and we will.

First, we will continue to support the limited test ban treaty, which has made the air cleaner. We call on the world—especially Red China—to join the nations which have signed that treaty.

Second, we will continue to work for an ending of all nuclear tests of every kind, by solid and verified agreement.

Third, we continue to believe that the struggle against nuclear spread is as much in the Soviet interest as in our own. We will be ready to join with them and all the world—in working to avoid it.

Fourth, the nations that do not seek national nuclear weapons can be sure that if they need our strong support against some threat of nuclear blackmail, then they will have it.

The two events I have discussed are large and full of meaning, and I will discuss them at some length tomorrow with the legislative leaders of both parties. They are coming here to the White House for a full and complete briefing tomorrow afternoon. Yet they do not change our basic policy. They just reinforce it.

Now let me take a minute to say that the same thing is true about another important event this week. It is the victory of another party with another leader in Great Britain.

The British Labor Party is the same party that held power when the Atlantic Alliance was founded; when British and American pilots flew the Berlin Airlift together; when Englishmen joined us in Korea.

It is a party of freedom, of democracy, and of good faith. Today it has the confidence of the British people. It also has ours.

They are our friends—as the Conservatives before them are our friends—and as governments of both parties have been friends for generations.

We congratulate the winners. We send warm regards to the losers. The friendship of our two nations goes on. This is our way with all our trusted allies.

This has been an eventful week in the affairs of the world. It is not the first such week, nor will it be the last. For the world has changed many times in the last 20 years. Great leaders have come and gone. Old enemies have become new friends. Danger has taken the place of danger.

Through this period we have steadily moved toward a more hopeful world. We have moved toward widening freedom and toward securing a more lasting peace.

We will continue in this direction.

What happens in other countries is important.

But the key to peace is to be found in the strength and the good sense of the United States of America. Tonight we are the strongest nation in all the world, and the world knows it. We love freedom and we will protect it and we will preserve it. Tonight, as always, America's purpose is peace for all men.

Almost 11 months ago, at a still more fateful hour, just after I had assumed the Presidency, I spoke to all of the Congress and to our people of the purpose of America. Let me close tonight by repeating what I said then:

"We must be ready to defend the national interest and to negotiate the common interest. This is the path that we shall continue to pursue. Those who test our courage will find it strong, and those who seek our friendship will find it honorable. We will demonstrate anew that the strong can be just in the use of strength; and the just can be strong in the defense of justice."

Thank you—and good night to all of you.

687   Statement by the President on the Strike at General Motors.   *October* 19, 1964

THE General Motors strike is now in its fourth week and is beginning to have an impact upon production and employment in other industries.

Our economy is now in its 44th month of continuous advance.

Failure of the General Motors Corporation and the United Automobile Workers to settle their differences at the local plant level will jeopardize the continuous upward thrust of our economy.

On October 5 I said I was pleased that the General Motors Corporation and the Auto Workers had reached an agreement at the national level. In the past 2 weeks significant but slow progress has been made in settling the 130 local plant disputes. The remaining disputes are unquestionably important to the individual workers and the local plant managers, but I sincerely hope that a speedy solution to them is possible.

I urge the officers of the General Motors Corporation and of the Auto Workers Union at the national and local level to reason together, to unite in purpose so that the presently prolonged auto strike can be brought to an end. Such a settlement will be in the best interest of the parties, of the economy, and of the general public.

NOTE: For the President's statement of October 5, see Item 624.

688   The President's News Conference of *October* 19, 1964

THE PRESIDENT. [1.] Today the President held his 12th meeting with the Members of the leadership of both parties in the Congress and related his observations resulting from his personal conversation with British Prime Minister Wilson, Soviet Ambassador Dobrynin, and other Government leaders.

The President presented to the leadership

a highly classified briefing on recent events in the Soviet Union and Communist China.

Director McCone and Chairman Seaborg presented details on the development of the Chinese nuclear effort.[1] Mr. McCone reviewed in detail the evidence which supports the conclusions the President announced in recent days.

Secretary McNamara reported in detail on the U.S. defense plans and deployments which take full account of the Chinese effort now and for the future. He emphasized as well the enormous cost to all mankind of any nuclear holocaust, and he showed how the heavy strategic superiority of the United States deters, and will continue to deter, all possible opponents.

Ambassador Thompson[2] discussed the probable causes and estimated meaning of the removal of Chairman Khrushchev and reviewed the evidence with which political developments in the Soviet Union are observed, assessed, and analyzed by U.S. experts.

The Secretary of State reviewed the political meaning of these important events and explained the political and diplomatic steps which the United States is taking in support of the basic positions set forth by the President last night. The Secretary also reported that the President had talked with Prime Minister Wilson and now intends to have a preliminary discussion of international problems early next week with the new British Foreign Secretary, Patrick Gordon Walker.

The President invited the Members of the leadership to offer their own evaluations and to pursue any questions of interest to them,

and a thorough discussion followed. The President expressed his pleasure at the cooperation of the leadership of the Congress in all matters affecting our country's foreign policy. The President reaffirmed his conviction that while these new developments require a careful watch by the United States, they only reinforce the need for continuation of our basic bipartisan foreign policy.

I will give that to the radio and television people as soon as they can have it.

[2.] In addition to that, I made brief statements concerning the civilian employment of the Government and the expenditures for the first few months of this fiscal year.

[3.] I also pointed out that I would try to meet in the next few days with the group that I set up to counsel with me on international matters, made up of General Bradley, Mr. John Coles, Arthur Dean, Allen Dulles, Roswell Gilpatric, George Kistiakowsky, Bob Lovett, John McCloy, and Honorable James Perkins and James Wadsworth. And I expect to try to meet with them Wednesday before we go out to have some visits with people.[3]

[4.] I pointed out that the Federal civilian employment in September was 2,449,327. At this level, it was 14,000 under the preceding month, down 14,000, down 21,000 from the beginning of the Johnson administration, the lowest level in 2½ years.

I pointed out that we spent $676 million less in July and August than last July and August. The figure for September looks like we spent $635 million more. We have a net difference of probably $41 million less expenditure for the 3 months than last year's 3 months. In other words, our expenditures for the first quarter, fiscal quarter of the Johnson administration, is $41 million less than the 3 months for the other administra-

---

[1] John A. McCone, Director of the Central Intelligence Agency, and Glenn T. Seaborg, Chairman of the Atomic Energy Commission.

[2] Llewellyn E. Thompson, Ambassador at Large for the Department of State and former Ambassador to the Soviet Union.

[3] See Items 591, 696.

tion. It would have been $250 million or $300 million more except we borrowed $134 million for FNMA, and Civil Service made a big lump contribution that was not spread out over the years for the Government Employees' Trust Fund.

The important thing is we have 21,000 less people working now than we had when we took over. We had 25,000 less in July and 17,000 in August and 14,000 less in September, but the net is as of October 14th through the month of September we had 21,000 less working, which is the lowest level in 2 years, and for the quarter we spent $41 million less. I reviewed that with them.

[5.] I also told them about the Hoover report involving Mr. Jenkins,[4] that we would get those facts and what the indications were at this time. I made available to them a copy of Mr. Dillon's [5] letter to the Attorney General where he says he was not checked further with District of Columbia authorities, the Secret Service, nor were any other high officials informed of the report, speaking of the '59 incident. It was not specifically brought to the attention of any member of the White House staff, the Kennedy staff, in 1961 and 1962, the then Vice President, or any member of his staff. That is the result of the study by the man in charge of the Secret Service.

[6.] I reviewed with them some of the efforts that I am making in the budget field to try to keep our employment down and our expenditures down, notwithstanding the new programs and the first quarter spending below last year, notwithstanding a major civilian pay increase in July, notwithstanding two military pay increases effective October 1, 1963, and September 1964. So notwithstanding those three increases we are

still, for the quarter, under it. That will fluctuate, but we are trying to make rather material reductions under what we had last year, and we think we will be able to.

I also expressed appreciation for their consideration of my budget. It was cut about 3 percent, a little over 3, the lowest budget cut in years.

I think that is about all.

[7.] Q. Mr. President, when you referred to going back to visiting people, did you mean on Wednesday?

THE PRESIDENT. I hope to. I don't have any definite plans at the moment, but I will check as soon as I get out. I have not had my lunch. You worry about my health, and I want to get my lunch. I was never in better health. I never felt better, notwithstanding some of the rather heavy problems that have come across my desk this week.

[8.] I have had a heavy schedule of meetings with my advisers in USIA, Defense and Treasury, Secret Service, with Mr. Hoover, and other people. And I would hope that I can get this group in here Wednesday—Mr. McCloy and company, Arthur Dean, Bob Lovett—and review with them this world picture.

I have been with Mr. Erhard twice, and there is the situation in Germany; with a new government in Britain; Mr. de Gaulle just made his trip to the Latin American countries; we have had very interesting developments in Brazil—and Chile has given us some concern, and Panama and Cuba, since we have been here; but we think the OAS meeting with 19 out of 20 passed a resolution which is very good.

We are trying to keep abreast and be very prompt in our actions on this hemisphere. We are happy for the work Tom Mann [6] has

---

[4] Walter Jenkins, former Special Assistant to the President (see Item 671).

[5] Secretary of the Treasury Douglas Dillon.

[6] Thomas C. Mann, Secretary of State for Inter-American Affairs, U.S. Coordinator, Alliance for Progress, and Special Assistant to the President for Latin America.

done. He has brought us where we can act quickly and cut the red tape over there, and he has funds obligated which were not piled up. I talked with the businessmen's committee, headed by David Rockefeller.[7] I want to get their ideas.

We have a new government in India. We have a new government in Russia. And I want to draw upon their wide experience on a bipartisan basis, from Lovett and McCloy and Dean and Kistiakowsky, Dean Acheson, all of whom I have had individual talks with in the last few days, but I want to have their collective thinking.

I also asked these people to give me any suggestions they could. I will be glad to have any criticism they have to offer or any corrections that they would like to suggest.

[*At this point the President spoke off the record. He then resumed speaking on the record.*]

I pointed out to them that we now have over 11 countries that have moved into Viet-Nam. We now have something over 1,000 people that those countries are contributing. It is now exceeding the 1,000 mark and General Taylor[8] has just told us and we are very appreciative of the efforts of various countries—Australia and others. I think that is about all we said.

They didn't ask any questions. I don't want to imply that their silence approved what we said or did anything, although I asked for corrections and suggestions as falling within that area. Some questions were asked to develop information on what is happening in this area of the world or that one.

Ambassador Thompson gave a very excellent review, as did Secretary Rusk and Secretary McNamara who went into everything from warheads to airplanes and all those things.

That is it now.

NOTE: President Johnson's thirty-third news conference was held in the Cabinet Room at the White House at 4:03 p.m. on Monday, October 19, 1964.

[7] Business Group for Latin America (see Item 169).

[8] Gen. Maxwell D. Taylor, Ambassador to Viet-Nam.

---

689 Remarks to Members of the Press Following a Meeting of the Cabinet. *October* 20, 1964

WE HAVE just completed a 2-hour Cabinet meeting and I will summarize briefly statements made at that meeting.

Since the significant developments in the world last week, responsible officials of your Government have carefully evaluated their meaning for our country.

Out of our discussions and deliberations, certain conclusions have been reached for the present:

First, the changes in the Communist world and in the free world do not at this time indicate sharp or sudden changes in the policies of the United States.

Second, it is of the utmost importance that there be continuity and stability in United States policies and purposes during this period of international change.

Third, we shall pursue a course of reasonable and responsible watchfulness. We are able to do so, because we are confident of our strength militarily, we are confident of our stability economically, and we are confident of the all-important unity of our society on which our strength stands at home and abroad.

Fourth, we do recognize that it is very important for the United States to continue to be prepared for the long pull. Our responsibilities in this regard are clear:

First, we must continue to maintain, to increase, and to strengthen our preparedness. No one must doubt our capacity for appropriate response to any challenge presented to freedom anywhere in the world.

Second, in actions as well as in words we must assure our allies and adversaries alike that we seek only peace in a world of honor and justice and individual dignity.

Third, we must pursue those policies at home which will continue our domestic growth, our expansion, and our prosperity without recession, depression, or inflation. Whatever the future may hold, we can take special satisfaction from the strength afforded by the success of America's economy today.

The picture of the economy in the third quarter is now nearly complete. We reviewed it in some detail in the Cabinet today. The great gains of the first half of the year have been extended. Compared to the third quarter a year ago, here are some of the key gains outlined at the Cabinet meeting.

Our gross national product is up $40 billion. The income of consumers, after taxes, is up $138 per capita. Total nonfarm employment is up 1.6 million. Total retail sales are up 7.2 percent. Business plant and equipment expenditures are up 11.4 percent. By preliminary estimate, corporate profits after taxes are up 21.7 percent. Wholesale prices are up only one tenth of 1 percent.

Fourth, considering the demands the future may impose upon us, it is more important than ever that in our governmental planning and programs we be relentless in our war on waste. I have asked each Cabinet officer to review his program and policies and see that we eliminate all waste possible and to report back to me. Progress must continue to overcome the deficits of the past and meet the challenges of the future, but that progress must go hand in hand with the self-discipline of fiscal prudence.

Fifth, we must continue in every way open to us to perfect the unity of our people. Divisions and suspicions among our people will only open doors for those adversaries who seek to divide us and to weaken our leadership. There must be no misunderstanding of America's purpose and there must be no miscalculation of America's will.

In direct communications to new governments and in public statements here at home, we have sought to make clear that the objectives of United States policy are unchanging. Our first purpose is peace. We are prepared to defend peace and freedom and do it promptly against any act of hostility or aggression anywhere.

We face the future hopefully in the confidence of the strength that we have all built together. But we face the future with a full sense of responsibility for the trust that we are privileged to bear for the cause of humanity and the cause of freedom everywhere.

NOTE: The President spoke at 3:55 p.m. in the new television studio located in the Theater at the White House.

690   Statement by the President on the Establishment of Permanent Task Forces To Assist Communities Faced With Plant Closings.   *October 20, 1964*

ALTHOUGH rapid economic growth during the past several years has sharply lowered the level of unemployment, and reduced the incidence of plant closings, individual cases of large-scale layoffs will undoubtedly continue to occur in a dynamic economy. The Federal Government must be prepared to move quickly to the assistance of communities affected by such layoffs.

NOTE: The statement is part of a White House release announcing that the President had taken steps to establish a permanent task force to assist the economic recovery of communities faced with defense plant closings. The task force, working in cooperation with State and local officials, would, as outlined in the release:

1. Draw up emergency and long-range programs to open job opportunities through the creation of new industries and the expansion of existing ones.

2. Conduct an industrial procurement conference to be attended by officers of local firms and representatives of Federal procurement agencies, so that all firms in the area would be fully informed on the possibilities of and requirements for Government contracting.

3. Arrange for training programs under the Manpower Development and Training Act.

4. Expand the surplus food disposal program of the Department of Agriculture.

5. With the Federal Housing Administration and the Veterans Administration, arrange for the approval of mortgage forbearance agreements.

6. Determine the possibility of establishing special programs for the employment of older workers.

691   Proclamation 3625 Announcing the Death of Herbert Hoover.   *October 20, 1964*

By the President of the United States of America

A PROCLAMATION

To the People of the United States:

It becomes my sad duty to announce officially the death of Herbert Hoover, the thirty-first President of the United States, on the twentieth day of October, nineteen hundred and sixty-four, at 11:35 o'clock in the morning.

Mr. Hoover's service to our country, spanning a period of nearly a half century, was marked by a signal honesty of purpose, a devotion to fundamental principles of ethical conduct, and a deep concern for the welfare of all of his fellow men. Among the rich products of his efforts have been the advancement of the cause of peace, the strengthening of our bonds with other na-

tions, the enrichment of the lives of millions of human beings around the world, and a vital improvement of the operation of this Government. His patriotism knew no partisanship.

A gentle and tolerant man, Mr. Hoover will be long remembered for his humanitarianism, his genuine humility coupled with a determined courage, and the strength of the faith which motivated his actions. He has earned the abiding respect and affection of the people of this Nation and of other nations throughout the world.

We in this country will be joined by his many friends abroad in mourning the death of this truly dedicated American. But we can take comfort in the inspiring legacy of ideals and example of devotion which he has bequeathed to us all.

Now, THEREFORE, I, LYNDON B. JOHNSON,

President of the United States of America, in honor and tribute to the memory of this great and good man, and as an expression of the public sorrow, do hereby direct that the flag of the United States be displayed at half-staff at the White House and on all buildings, grounds, and naval vessels of the United States for a period of thirty days. I also direct that for the same length of time the representatives of the United States in foreign countries shall make similar arrangements for the display of the flag at half-staff over their embassies, legations, and other facilities abroad, including all military facilities and stations.

I hereby order that suitable honors be rendered by units of the armed forces under orders of the Secretary of Defense on the day of the funeral.

IN WITNESS WHEREOF, I have hereunto set my hand and caused the Seal of the United States of America to be affixed.

DONE at the City of Washington this twentieth day of October in the [SEAL] year of our Lord nineteen hundred and sixty-four, and of the Independence of the United States of America the one hundred and eighty-ninth.

LYNDON B. JOHNSON

By the President:
DEAN RUSK
Secretary of State

NOTE: On August 6 the President issued a proclamation in honor of President Hoover's 90th birthday anniversary (August 10), urging the people of the United States to reflect upon his many accomplishments on behalf of humanity, and especially urging the youth of America to emulate the patriotism, integrity, and high ideals that had marked his career (Proc. 3604, 29 F.R. 11489; 3 CFR, 1964 Supp.).

692 Statement by the President on the Death of President Hoover. *October 20, 1964*

MRS. JOHNSON and I want to extend our deep personal sympathy to Herbert Hoover's sons and the other members of his family.

We have lost a wise American, and the world has lost a humanitarian citizen of all mankind. His steadfast leadership served us undaunted through good times and bad— as businessman, provider for the poor and hungry, President, and elder statesman.

He combined the best of our national heritage with broad-gauged understanding of the tumultuous times in which he lived. A man of character and conviction, he was both profound and practical in meeting the many tasks he undertook for his fellow men.

He lived a full and useful life, and we are all deeply in his debt.

We shall miss his thoughtful counsel and kindly spirit. But his unquenchable sense of public responsibility for both our Nation and a troubled world stand as an example that will endure.

NOTE: The statement was also read by the President to the members of the press in the Theater at the White House. The text of the final paragraph, as read by the President, follows:

"I shall miss his thoughtful counsel and his kindly spirit. Shortly after I assumed the Presidency, after that tragic day in November, he was among the first to volunteer his services and his advice. And they gave me strength and comfort during those trying days. His unquenchable sense of public responsibility for both our Nation and our troubled world will stand as an example that will long endure."

693   Remarks in Memorial Hall, Akron University.
       October 21, 1964

Dr. Auburn, Mayor and Mrs. Erickson, my longtime, faithful friend Steve Young, Miss McGovern, candidate for Congress, Mr. Sweeney, candidate for Congressman at Large, Mr. Leonard, ladies and gentlemen, boys and girls:

I almost said fellow Ohioans. This is my third visit to Ohio in the last 2 weeks, and they seem to be getting better every time I come. It is a little chilly outside in that 42 degree temperature, but I am getting a mighty warm feeling inside my heart for Akron.

I said to my friend here representing the Rubber Workers how beautiful I thought those balloons were with the union label on each one of them, and he said, "Well, we just wanted you to feel like you felt back in Atlantic City a few weeks ago, and it is going to be almost as good a vote here as it was there."

I want to thank all of you nice people for being so good to Mrs. Johnson when she was here in Akron. After meeting her, I guess you know why I think the country needs more women in public affairs. There is something that you can do about that.

I don't know how much time you have, but there are just a few days left. You have a highly intelligent, gracious, charming, effective lady that would be delighted to come down to Washington and competently help your President with a program for all the people of this country. Her name is Fran McGovern.

Now, Fran McGovern has been working with us on the Employment Security Council. We need her down there to work with us on our program. She will listen to the testimony, she will analyze the bills, and she will vote for all the people. She won't just vote "no" automatically when the roll is called.

One good turn deserves another. She has been a former member of your Ohio Legislature. She is experienced with your Public Utilities Commission. And you need her in Washington. Go and do something about it, won't you, please?

I am counting on you, too, to get out there and work and send my colleague and my old friend in the House of Representatives, and in the Senate for many years, a most effective public servant, a most conscientious one, one of the great men I know—Steve Young. We need in the Congress, too, as your Congressman at Large, and I hope you won't forget this, Mr. Robert Sweeney. So go and give him a good vote.

We have some other interests in common. I understand that unemployment in Akron was something over 6 percent 3 years ago. Now we have it down to under 3 percent. I want to find out how you have done it, because we are going to get full employment—and I mean full employment—in the entire country.

The tax cut bill that we passed earlier in the year is going to help some. It means another $651 million for your own use here in Ohio. It means $37 million in the Akron area alone. It means more jobs.

And I have also been looking into some of these Federal-local partnership projects before I came out here. We have been working together now for 3½ years. You have three new urban renewal programs. You have two college housing act loans to the University of Akron, one of the finest institutions I know anywhere in the country.

It produced your great mayor and it produced your next Congressman, and we are all thankful for that.

We have 421 beds in the City Hospital, St. Thomas Hospital, St. Edwards Nursing Home, under the Federal legislation, the Hill-Burton Act. We are learning how to make this system of ours work a little better.

A great former Senator of yours is the author of that legislation, along with Senator Hill. We have gotten a good many things done in the last 3 years.

You remember President Kennedy told you when he visited Ohio so many times in 1960, "Come, lend me your heart, lend me your hand, give me your support and we will get this country moving again." And this country is moving again.

But our job is never done. There is no rest for the weary. There is a lot left to do. I hope that you are going to agree with me to do it on November the 3d.

I am not going to say anything ugly about my opponent. I don't believe in muckraking or slanderous comment, or mudslinging. I have rarely found it necessary to mention my opponent or to mention his name, or to get personal with him in the House or the Senate, or when I was Vice President.

In the 30 years I have been in public life, I never have been quite desperate. I have never been so far behind that I had to cling to a sinking raft.

But somehow or other I believe that the people are wise enough, are intelligent enough, to look and see and listen and judge for themselves, and judge what they hear and what they see. I want to appeal to your intelligence and not to your emotion.

I must say a time or two when I have turned on a television spot or have turned on my car radio, I have heard some rather uncomplimentary comments about the President, and for a moment it distressed me some.

But when I got back home and I looked back over what they had said about Washington, Jefferson, Jackson, Abraham Lincoln— Abraham Lincoln said he went back to his hometown and no one there spoke to him except one woman and she seemed to wish she could have avoided it. I remember what they said about Wilson, Roosevelt, Eisenhower, and Kennedy.

So I think the best thing we can all do is try to look at our problems, analyze them, see how we can try to solve them together, and hope that our people will stand together and unite during a period when we need the best that is in all of us. The eyes of the world are on America.

The German people have a new government—following Mr. Adenauer's long period of service—in their Chancellor, Mr. Erhard. He has been here twice to see me since I have been President. We are working very well together. Their nation has made a wonderful comeback.

The British just made a decision a day or two ago and they have a new government. I have talked to their Prime Minister. Their Foreign Minister will be in Washington to see us next week.

I visited with General de Gaulle when he was in Washington. He has just made a trip of this hemisphere, in Latin America. I didn't get to see him then, but he has shown his interest in the problems of this hemisphere.

The Italians have had some changes in their government since I was there and since they have been here. It is a new government that we need to work with very closely.

The Indians lost their great leader Mr. Nehru, and they now have Mr. Shastri, and he is in charge. He is very concerned today about the problems of the world and the developments in the recent days.

The Soviet Union has decided to select

others to lead their people. So now in the next 2 weeks you Americans are going to be watched and looked upon for your decision.

I think our country is going to have a great opportunity to stand up and speak with the rest of the leaders of the world, and to try to find some area of agreement on the most important problem in the heart of every person, every race, every color, of every country in the world. And that is, how can we live together, how can nations live with each other, without a nuclear holocaust, without destroying hundreds of millions of lives.

So on November the 3d, this election of ours will come at a time of great events in our world. Those events I think have made it clear to the American people what their choice will be.

I know they have made it clear to me, what course the American people want me to follow. Let me tell you how I know.

Last week the Communist Chinese exploded an atomic bomb, and they added to the poisoning of the air we breathe.

Last week, the Soviet Union threw out its old leadership and put new men at the top.

Last week the British Labor Party took over the government of Great Britain.

Last Saturday I met with the National Security Council of our country. On Monday I summoned to the White House the congressional leaders from both the Republican Party and the Democratic Party to meet with our leading diplomatic and military men. Yesterday I met for almost 3 hours with the members of my Cabinet.

I can say this to you, you Americans for whom we all work: I can say this with great pride—you have every right to be proud of the kind of leadership that your country has produced.

All of those men that I met with, men from both the Republican and Democratic Parties, were in agreement on the broad course of American foreign policy. No one advised me to break the nuclear test ban treaty. Instead, we discussed ways of making it apply to other nations.

No one advised me to break off relations with the Soviet Union. Instead, we discussed ways to make our relations with the new Soviet leadership more productive.

No one advised me to withdraw from the United Nations. Instead, we talked about the need to strengthen it.

No one advised me to make threats or issue ultimatums, or to talk about lobbing one into the men's room in the Kremlin. Instead, we talked about how we could avoid expanding conflicts, instead we discussed ways to reduce tensions, instead we sought means of trying to reason together and resolve any differences that exist between nations.

All of those who met with me and all of those who contributed counsel, agreed that our country should continue on the path of strength and restraint, which we have followed under all administrations for the last 20 years, since World War II.

You will remember that it was Arthur Vandenberg, a great Republican Senator, who joined President Truman in a bipartisan policy of stopping the Communists in Greece and Turkey.

You will remember that I, as Democratic leader of the Senate, joined President Eisenhower in his crisis in the Formosa Strait and the other critical decisions that he had to make in foreign policy.

You will remember that it was Senator Dirksen, the Republican leader from Illinois, that supported President Kennedy on the nuclear test ban.

And it has been Senator Hickenlooper, Republican Senator from Iowa, who has worked closely with us on our foreign policy so we could present a united front to the world.

But there are those who would not follow this responsible bipartisan course. There are those that have placed under attack all the policies which have brought us through these years of the cold war closer to peace. They stand in opposition to the collective wisdom of the leaders of both parties, experienced in foreign affairs.

I think I know that the American people are not going to follow that course of obstruction. I think I know the American people are not going to junk the bipartisan course of 20 years and fly to evils that they know not of on a dangerous adventure that they know not where it leads.

Sunday night I talked about the problems of the world on television. More than 63 million Americans listened to that discussion. The great majority of them are, I think, united behind the responsible foreign policies of this country that have kept peace for us. I believe that they are going to choose those policies on November the 3d.

What is the real foreign policy issue of this campaign?

The issue is whether we will use our great power with judgment and restraint.

The issue is whether we will continue the long, the hard, the patient search for a lasting peace.

I intend as your leader and as your President to work to strengthen the United Nations, because I think they have prevented a number of wars already, and I think they can help us on the road to peace in the days ahead.

The United Nations, with all of its defects, has been a source of many achievements for peace and for the dignity of man.

I will continue to work to find areas of common interest with the Soviet Union. We do not know what course the new Russian leaders will follow. But if they are willing to seek peace, if they sincerely and genuinely want peace, then I can say to them and I can say to you they will find the United States ready.

Our scientists are working with their scientists, and their scientists were here a few days ago and I sent them by plane to some of our great desalinization plants which offer one of the really great hopes for all the people of the world, when we can take the water from the sea and convert it, take the salt out of it, and we can use the oceans to make the deserts bloom.

It is not really important how a man spells his name if we can find the right answer to it. We have these brilliant scientific geniuses from several countries working with us to find that answer. We have already gotten it down where we can produce it for less than $1 a thousand, but if we can get it down to where we can produce it for 25 percent of that amount it will be a great victory for humanity all through the 3 billion people in the world.

I intend to pursue goals of this kind. I intend to submit new proposals in Geneva to slow down the arms race, and to lessen the tensions and lessen the danger of war. And I hope that we can get agreements from other nations to do the same thing. We are going to keep on trying.

I can assure you that your country is the mightiest nation in all the world. But we do not intend to use that might to bury anyone. And we want all to know and read us loud and clear: we do not intend to be buried, either.

In Asia we face an ambitious and aggressive China, but we have the will and we have the strength to help our Asian friends resist that ambition. Sometimes our folks get a little impatient. Sometimes they rattle their rockets some, and they bluff about their bombs. But we are not about to send American boys 9 or 10,000 miles away from home to do what Asian boys ought to be doing for themselves.

President Eisenhower said in 1954 to the Government of Viet-Nam, "President Diem, we want to help you help yourselves. We will give you advice, we will provide leadership, we will help you with material things, with your weapons and the things that you do not have, to protect your independence because we are so proud of our independence we would like for you to have independence, too, and not be swallowed up by the Communists."

We have been doing that for 10 long years under three Presidents. We have now some 18,000 men in Viet-Nam, officers and men, advising, counseling, leading them. We have a good deal of material that we have sent there, very costly to our taxpayers each month. The reports that come in are gloomy from day to day.

But we have a choice. We can seek a wider war. China is there on the border with 700 million men, with over 200 million in their army. And we could get tied down in a land war in Asia very quickly if we sought to throw our weight around. Or we could retreat and pull out and say "Goodby" to the rest of the world, that we are going to live on our own shores, and we would let Asia go to other people. But we don't seem to think that either of those alternatives is the wise decision.

We are going to continue to try to make these people more effective and more efficient, and do our best to resolve that situation where the aggressors will leave their neighbors alone, and they will finally learn to live together in peace as they have in other parts of the world.

So we are going to assist them against attack as we have. We will work to help

them achieve progress and self-confidence. We will not permit the independent nations of the East to be swallowed up by Communist conquest.

In the developing world, the great continents, other continents, that we are interested in—Latin America, Africa—we have only a single goal. What is that goal? America does not seek slaves or satellites. We do not seek domination or dominion. We only want those countries to live in freedom and independence. We want them to be strong enough to resist the aggressions of others. We want to help them meet the needs of their people for food and shelter and education.

These are some of the policies that we have followed. They are the policies we are going to continue to follow.

The White House has a very special atmosphere when great events are happening, as they happened all last week. As I sit in my office late in the evening, at night, I am very deeply conscious of the immense powers that this Nation commands.

So this great power cannot be put into the hands of those who would use it either impulsively or carelessly. We must constantly be deliberate, prudent, and restrained. Before we shoot from the hip, as Mr. Rayburn, the great political leader, used to say, the three most important words in the English language for everyone are, "Just a minute."

So let's say to the rest of the world that the world's hope for peace cannot be left with those who really have no faith in the possibility of a lasting agreement, and who really predict war. The future of man should not be entrusted to those who would tear down the institutions and policies which a threatened world has carefully built for its own protection.

That is our central concern. It is also the concern, I think, of a watching and worried

3 billion people in other parts of the world.

But we will not have peace just because we desire it, not just because we want it. There is only one road to peace, and that is to work at it, patiently, deliberately, wisely, step by step, year by year, never to become reckless, never to become weary of the journey and irritated with folks who may not agree with you the first time you talk to them. That is the course, I think, that we should follow, the course of the prophet Isaiah, "Come now, let us reason together."

Here are two great powers. When they put their thumb on the button, they can kill 100 million Americans in a matter of hours. When we move our thumb up on that button and sound the alarm, and the bell rings, we can kill 100 million Russians in a few hours. A total of 300 million people could be wiped out from daylight to dark.

But that is not the kind of world that you want to live in. So the prophet Isaiah says, "Come now, let us reason together."

And I say to all the world that we are a mighty power, but we don't brag about it and we don't throw our weight around. We have more strength and we are going to maintain it, at great sacrifice from our taxpayers. We have more strength than any other nation, more strength than all nations put together, and we are going to keep it. Our guard is always going to be up, but our hand is always going to be out.

The leadership, the responsible leadership, of both parties in this country—and I believe in the two party system. And that is why I so earnestly want every person to go and vote his convictions so all can see that there are not many people who approve the temporary captivity leadership of the present Republican Party of extremes. And we will be voting for a strong two party system on November the 3d.

When they pass on these extremists, the men who booed others at San Francisco, the men that are intolerant of others' opinions, the men who speak off the cuff—when they act decisively on their judgment, then there will be a new group of moderate leaders come in and build a stronger and a more effective Republican Party.

But we will always maintain our bipartisan cooperation, and together we will do what is best for America, because when you do what is best for your country, you do what is best for your party and for yourself.

So the hour is here, the clock is ticking, the calendar is moving. You have a privilege that millions in other countries are denied. You have a right, an obligation, and a duty to see that you and yours go to the polls November the 3d and select the leadership that in your judgment most nearly represents the best interest of this country.

I am not going to discuss individuals in this matter. That is a decision you can make for yourselves by listening to the radio, seeing the television, reading the morning newspapers.

I am very happy that the college permitted me to come here today and have free speech. This is a great university and I treasure this invitation.

I am also mighty grateful to the Akron paper for their endorsement yesterday. I must run along because I can just intuitively feel Mrs. Johnson getting ready to send another note up here. But I can't leave until and unless I tell you that they say that it has been more than 100 years since some of these papers have endorsed a member of my party.

But I want to tell you about my party. I said my philosophy many years ago: I am a free man first, I am an American second, I am a public servant third, and a Democrat fourth—in that order.

We must not be complacent about what is happening in the world. We must not be complacent about what is happening at home. You have a duty to do, so go do it in accordance with the dictates of your own conscience.

I saw a poll coming down here this morning. It showed that I had most of the Democrats and had 30 percent of the Republicans. But that distressed me, that I only had 30 percent of the Republicans. Those are good people if they get the truth and if they get the facts, and we have to improve that situation between now and November the 3d.

So let's all put our shoulders to the wheel and unite instead of divide, and again in the words of the prophet, let's go out and reason together.

Thank you.

NOTE: The President spoke at 12:33 p.m. at Memorial Hall at the University of Akron, Akron, Ohio. In his opening words he referred to Dr. Norman P. Auburn, president of the University, Mayor and Mrs. Edward Erickson of Akron, Senator Stephen M. Young of Ohio, Frances McGovern and Robert E. Sweeney, Democratic candidates for Representative from Ohio, and Ernest Leonard, chairman of the Democratic Executive Committee for Summit County. Later in his remarks he referred to former Senator Harold H. Burton of Ohio, Senator Lister Hill of Alabama, Arthur H. Vandenberg, U.S. Senator from Michigan during the Truman administration, Senator Everett McKinley Dirksen of Illinois, and Senator Bourke B. Hickenlooper of Iowa.

Mrs. Johnson also spoke briefly. The text of her remarks was released.

694   Remarks in Belleville, Illinois. *October 21, 1964*

Governor Kerner, my old and dear friend Paul Douglas, one of the Nation's most effective Congressmen, Mel Price, Governor Shapiro, Mayor Fields, Paul Powell, Jim Ronan, and my good friends of Illinois:

It is good to be in Illinois and with your neighbors and my friends, Senator Symington, Senator Long, Mayor Gunn of St. Louis, Congresswoman Sullivan, Congressman Frank Karsten. You know, somehow or other I have a feeling in my bones this afternoon that this is going to be a great Democratic year for Otto Kerner, one of the great Governors in this Nation; Stu Symington, one of the great Senators in the Nation; Sam Shapiro; Leonor Sullivan; Frank Karsten; Mel Price; and, I would hope, Lyndon Johnson and Hubert Humphrey.

Standing here by this plaque dedicated to our late beloved President, John Fitzgerald Kennedy, I am aware again of the sense of high purpose that he brought to the Presidency of the United States.

He had a vision of a world at peace. "We will not reach that goal today," President Kennedy said, "or tomorrow. We may not reach it in our own lifetime. But the quest is the greatest adventure of our century."

President Kennedy is gone today, but the vision remains and the great quest for peace stretches before us. Peace is the most important issue of this campaign, for one simple reason: without it, we will never have the chance to do something about the other issues that concern us.

The question is not who wants peace. I think everybody wants peace. The real question is what is the best way to achieve peace, what is the best way for us Americans to keep the peace.

I think you have a clear choice. On the one hand is the choice of a government which believes that the best way to keep peace is to be prepared to use power with restraint and to always be firm but always be fair. And this is the policy that I follow.

I believe we must turn back Communist aggression wherever it threatens. But at the same time, I believe that we must work patiently and calmly to ease the tensions in the world just as we tried to ease the tensions and the differences in our own communities.

I believe that we can never turn our back on the Communists or relax our guard. But I believe that we can, and I believe that we must, try to convince them that peace is just as much in the interest of their people as it is in the interest of our people.

I believe that we can put twice as many intercontinental ballistic missiles over the Soviet Union as they can put over America. But I also know that the Russians have the power to kill millions of my people. There would not be "total" victory, but there would be "total" devastation, and the survivors would be jealous of the dead.

In such a world as this, a nuclear world, there is no room to rattle our rockets, or to bluster and bluff and be belligerent. There is room only for courage and intelligence and reason. There are some people who may believe differently.

There are some people that talk about nuclear war as if it were inevitable, and of nuclear bombs as if they were "merely another weapon."

They sound as if force or the threat of force can solve our problems. This is dangerous talk. Our military strength is vital to our security. And throughout my entire public career of more than 25 years in the Congress, I have constantly voted to increase our military strength when some people have voted to reduce it.

But I would counsel my fellow Americans today in this friendly, happy crowd, in this beautiful city of Belleville, where Americans love their country and they are out here to demonstrate it—I would say to you that we cannot and we must not use this strength to try to compel, to try to frighten others into following our every command. That course can only lead to constant conflict.

These people also believe that the United States can demand quick resolution to all the problems of the world. From the way some of them talk, all that we need to do is to snap our fingers and ancient disputes that have gone on for centuries will be instantly settled.

Well, I wish there was some giant economy size aspirin tablet that would work on international headaches. But there just isn't. The only cure is patience and strength, with reason mixed in.

Some people seem to believe that we can put an end to all difficulty and danger, and then we can retire from the world.

Well, that is just not so. In this world, as in life, itself, there is no escape from problems, there is no escape from peril. The sound of gunfire in Asia echoes in the homes of Illinois and Missouri. An angry cry for freedom in Africa requires patience and human understanding in Washington.

To abandon our commitments, to withdraw from our responsibilities, would endanger free men and free women everywhere, and would bring the hope for peace to an end. I don't believe that you want to do that.

I believe in victory, the victory of love over hate, the victory of man's hopes over man's fears, the victory of peace over war, and the victory of freedom over tyranny. And I believe you believe in that, too.

In the shadow of this afternoon as the sun is about to set, we stand here by a memorial to a great President. John Fitzgerald Kennedy also believed in that victory. He is gone and so is another wonderful man who loved peace and who longed for the day when our swords would become plowshares—President Herbert Hoover, who passed away yesterday. On his 90th birthday this year, President Herbert Hoover spoke words that have a very special meaning here today. President Hoover was a Republican. I am a Democrat. But his hopes for America and my hopes for America, his hopes for humanity and my hopes for humanity are not partisan.

And so I would like to close my little talk with you today by quoting my friend's words, by quoting President Hoover who was my counselor when I assumed the responsibilities of the President. He was one of the first to call and extend his aid. Here are the words that he used, and I quote, and I hope you will listen carefully:

"Our American form of civilization has been deluged with rising criticism from both home and abroad. . . . So perhaps the time has come for Americans to take stock and to think something good about themselves. . . .

"On the moral and spiritual side we could suggest that . . . (we) fought for free men in two world wars and asked no indemnities, no acquisition of territory, no domination over other peoples. We could point to a spirit of Christian compassion such as the world has never seen, and prove it by the tons of food and clothing and billions of dollars we have provided as gifts in saving hundreds of millions of people overseas from famine, and many governments from collapse. . . .

"We could point out that our American system has achieved the greatest productivity, the highest standard of living of any nation on earth. True, we have large natural resources—but other nations also have such resources. What, then, has brought us such abundance?

"We have freedom of choice. And the produce of our freedom is the stimulation of our energies, initiative, ingenuity, and creative faculties. Freedom is the open

window through which pours the sunlight of the human spirit and of human dignity."

Thus said a great President who has passed on.

Now, in this campaign, you will have a decision to make. Two weeks from yesterday you will go and select your leaders for this country and the leaders for the free world for the next 4 years.

You have two issues that stand out: Shall we continue the foreign policy of bipartisanship, where Senator Arthur Vandenberg, a Republican, worked with President Truman, a Democrat, to stop the Communists in Greece and Turkey?

Shall we follow the bipartisan policy of President Dwight D. Eisenhower, who worked with Lyndon Johnson, a Democratic leader of the Senate, in the crisis in the Strait of Formosa, when our country was united and we put our country ahead of our party?

Shall we follow the policies of Senator Dirksen and Senator Hickenlooper, who worked with John Fitzgerald Kennedy in the Cuban missile crisis and in the test ban treaty?

Or shall we go off on another adventure to fly to evils that we know not of on a very dangerous course?

You will decide that course.

In our domestic policy, unemployment in this State is at an alltime low. Income is at an alltime high. Corporation profits after taxes this year are up $12 billion. Workers income after taxes this year is up $60 billion.

Yes, in the words of our great President, this country is moving again. That is what John Fitzgerald Kennedy predicted and that is what we are doing.

So now I must run along. I leave that choice up to you. I hope that you will be understanding. I hope that you will do your duty. I hope you will realize your obligation. The spotlight of the world is on America on November 3d. They are going to look to us for leadership.

We have new governments in Germany, England, in the Soviet Union, Italy, and other places. They have seen the transition that has taken place since President Kennedy was taken from us. They are looking to see what kind of leadership you are going to select.

Well, I will tell you what kind you are going to select. You are going to search your conscience and regardless of what party you belong to, you are going to do what your conscience tells you is best for your country, and whatever your decision is it will be satisfactory to Hubert Humphrey and to me.

Thank you very much.

NOTE: The President spoke at 5:40 p.m. in the Public Square at Belleville, Ill. His opening words referred to Governor Otto Kerner, Senator Paul H. Douglas, Representative Melvin Price, and Lieutenant Governor Samuel Shapiro, all of Illinois, Mayor Alvin G. Fields of East St. Louis, Ill., Paul Powell, Democratic candidate for Secretary of State for Illinois, and James A. Ronan, chairman, Democratic State Central Committee. Later in his remarks he referred to, among others, Senators Stuart Symington and Edward V. Long of Missouri, Donald Gunn, acting Mayor of St. Louis, Representatives Leonor K. Sullivan and Frank M. Karsten of Missouri, Arthur H. Vandenberg, U.S. Senator from Michigan during the Truman administration, Senator Everett McKinley Dirksen of Illinois, and Senator Bourke B. Hickenlooper of Iowa.

695 Remarks in St. Louis, Missouri.
October 21, 1964

Mr. Chairman, Governor Dalton:

I'm with good neighbors and good friends whenever I'm in the State of Missouri!

Mrs. Johnson and I feel at home with Stu Symington, one of the great and wise men of the United States Senate, and one you are going to return with a landslide majority November 3d.

We are extremely fond of your junior Senator, Ed Long, who serves Missouri with such distinction in the Senate. We are happy to see Leonor Sullivan and Frank Karsten, who help make the Missouri delegation one of the finest in Congress. I appreciate the welcome of acting Mayor Gunn.

I am glad to see some of my old friends from Missouri on the platform. There are too many of them to mention them all, but I particularly was happy to see Mrs. Freeman, Stan "The Man" Musial, my old friend Tony Buford, and I hope that Morris Shenker is right, that we are really going to get going out here by November 3d.

The events of the past week have made clear the one central issue in this election. That issue is how America is to discharge its responsibilities as the leader of the free world.

These events have brought to the front the underlying crisis of our period of history: the struggle between those who wish to be free and those who want to enslave mankind through a Communist world revolution.

One proposal is to resolve this problem by smashing the Communists once and for all through military means. The trouble with this solution is that we live in a nuclear age. A full nuclear exchange would so devastate the Northern Hemisphere that there would be no victory for anyone.

Hundreds of millions of people would be dead, and the survivors would be organized on a totalitarian basis.

The other course is the one that has commended itself to the great majority of Americans of both parties for more than a half century.

It offers no simple, it offers no easy, solution. It marks out rather the Ten Forces of Freedom that we must draw upon to fight and to defeat communism.

First, we fight communism through a defense——

[*At this point there was a general disturbance in the audience.*]

Now you folks come on and be happy, come on and be happy. You will find a few like this in nearly any big crowd. But they are getting fewer and fewer as the days go on.

You know, I visited downstate Illinois for a while this afternoon, and we never saw such large crowds. But a good Republican came up to me and said, "I remember when you were Democratic leader and you were serving under a Republican administration, and a Republican President, President Eisenhower.

"And I always believed that you put your country first, that you did what was best for America because you thought that was what was best for all the people, and if it was good for America it was good for you."

He said, "I have noticed in the last 48 hours a trend of Republicans away from the leadership, the temporary leadership, of their own party."

He said, "It is not backlash; that is gone. It is not frontlash. It is the smear lash. Because when some people get desperate they get dangerous, and when they get dangerous they are not cautious. And when they get to fearing and doubting and smearing— why, even some of their own people don't want to go along with them!"

So I want to say to all of you good people, whether you are Democrats, Republicans, or Independents, we want to welcome you to a program that puts your country first regardless of your party.

We have no unkind words to say about anyone. We don't indulge in any muckraking or any mudslinging, because we don't think that is what the American people will listen to. We think they want to have the issues discussed. They want to have their leaders tell them what their problems are, and they don't want to deal in personalities.

I was talking to you about the hundreds of millions of people in the world that would be dead and the survivors would be organized on a totalitarian basis. The other course that we can follow, that has commended itself to the great majority of Americans of both parties, is that we mark out Ten Forces of Freedom that we draw upon to fight and defeat communism—Ten Forces.

Now, what are those ten? I want to outline them briefly and hurriedly, because I am grateful for this wonderful, large, inspiring audience and I don't want to keep you too long.

First, we fight communism through a defense establishment that your own man Stuart Symington has had a great deal to do with building, that is powerful enough to make it completely clear that if the Communists themselves resort to war it will lead to their own complete destruction.

Second, we fight communism by strengthening the defense capacity of other nations and other people, who want to be free and who do not want to be enslaved by the Communists.

Third, we fight communism by maintaining superiority in every field of science and technology which does or can affect the security of our Nation.

This applies to the exploration of outer space. We dare not leave this area of our universe to become a monopoly in the hands of those who would destroy freedom. We must therefore obtain and maintain a leadership for the free world in outer space and we are trying to do that.

Fourth, we fight communism by giving our support to the concepts of liberty upon which our Republic was founded. And this means very especially the determination to be fair, to be just, to ensure that all of our citizens, regardless of creed, religion, national origin, or color enjoy the liberties which are inherent in the notion of freedom.

Fifth, we fight communism by building a Great Society here at home. We must show the world that the processes of freedom can contribute more to human dignity and human well-being than can the Communist totalitarianism. The Great Society is a powerful weapon against man's enslavement.

Sixth, we fight communism by uniting nations and uniting people in their determination to be free. You do not divide your forces. People who would defeat us want to divide us, and conquer us. They want us to hate each other instead of love each other. They want one group going one direction and one group going the other direction. Now is the time for all good Americans to come to the aid of their country, and unite behind their country.

In this hemisphere we had a vote the other day in the Organization of American States, and 19 out of the 20 countries in this hemisphere voted together. This means in the Western Hemisphere that we must have support for our Alliance for Progress. The alliance represents a commitment to help the people of this hemisphere achieve economic and social development.

Seventh, we fight communism by supporting the Peace Corps. The young men and women that I see out there in that audience, the young men and women that I have seen all around the world, have put on their hats and rolled up their sleeves and gone out into the world to show them what American life is like.

They are tonight, as we meet here, demonstrating in the villages and in the countrysides of dozens and dozens of countries what we in America as a people are all about. They are stimulating the young people of other lands to commit themselves to public service in the interest of their own freedom. And we need more young men and young women in the service of this country.

And when I am elected your President November 3d, I am going to send out special talent teams to bring young men and women into the service of their country.

Eighth, we fight communism by expanding world trade. The free world has demonstrated its capacity to perform economically far beyond the capabilities of the muscle-bound Communist economies.

The bonds of trade can tie free men together and give them a community of interest. Do you know, I looked at the figures yesterday, and since this administration came into power, our exports to foreign countries have increased by more than 25 percent.

So what we want to do is not only have peace in the world, and avoid a nuclear holocaust that would wipe out 300 million men and women overnight, but we want to have peace at home.

We want the capitalist who invests his dollar to know that it is not going to be confiscated and that he has a right to expect a reasonable and fair return.

We want the manager that manages that dollar and that worker who gets up at daylight and outlines his plans, and sometimes works until midnight and develops stomach ulcers—we want him to have a good bonus at the end of the year so that he has an incentive and something to work for.

And to the worker who stands there putting those rivets in the cars as they come down the assembly line every 27 seconds, he has to have his job done; to the workers of

America—and we want them to have their social security program, and not a voluntary one, either—we want them to work fewer hours per day and fewer days per week. We want them to have more leisure and more recreation for themselves.

We now have the average manufacturing pay in this country up to $104 a week, the highest in the history of any nation in the world. We tonight have 72.5 million people employed. We have today the businessmen of this country earning $12 billion this year, the year I have been President, $12 billion more than they did last year after taxes.

We have the stocks on the exchanges today worth $100-odd billion more than they were worth last November 22d, when we took over. We have the workers of America tonight, this year, drawing $60 billion more after taxes than they did last year.

That is the kind of country we want. We want peace between the capitalists, we want peace between the management, we want peace between the workers.

Do you know that we have lost this year less time due to strikes than we have lost in any year in our national history, except during the war years when they had no strikes? We haven't lost 1 percent of the hours worked because of strikes, not one-half, not one-quarter—fourteen one-hundredths of 1 percent of our time has been lost.

So, ladies and gentlemen, we have the capitalist, we have the manager, we have the worker, and we have the Government—all working shoulder to shoulder, not fearing, not doubting, not hating, but hoping and believing and producing and leading the rest of the world. We are going to fight communism by building a family of free men through the widest opportunity for international exchanges, in the fields of all human activities.

We have our scientists on their way to the Soviet Union this month to sit down and talk to them and try to evolve ways and means to convert the sea water of the oceans and take the salt out of it so we can make the deserts of this country bloom. We are trying to understand mankind instead of destroy mankind.

We are the mightiest nation in all the world. We have more power than any other nation in the world to destroy. But we don't want to destroy. We have more power than all the nations put together. But we don't intend to bury anyone. We just don't intend to be buried.

We are not going to rattle our rockets and bluff with our bombs. We are going to always be alert, and cautious, and careful, and realize that we are dealing with the lives of 3 billion people that live in the world and that we are a small minority of 190 million. We are going to keep our guard up, but our hand out.

We are willing to go anywhere and talk to anybody that offers us any hope of promoting better relations between nations. We would rather talk than fight.

We will not withdraw from the United Nations. We will strengthen it. We will make firm the Atlantic partnership, and we will build new bridges from it to the other nations of the free world, and we won't do it through a task force; we will do it through the official channels of our Government.

This course has been charted over a half century by the Presidents of both parties. President Woodrow Wilson saw it, but he died a martyr to his frustrations. A few men doubted and feared and hated, and they blocked his plans for a successful League of Nations.

President Herbert Hoover, whose passing sobers us tonight, pushed that course forward. So did the four great Presidents who followed him, Democrat and Republican alike.   And this is the course which we must follow if the fight for freedom is to be won without the destruction of the civilized world.

This is the course that I propose to follow as your leader with the help of your Congressmen, with the help of your two great Senators, with the help of your Governor, and all of those who treasure peace in the world.

I hope that you folks will try to help us, try to remember that one of the best ways that you can help us is to send Sid McClanahan, the Democratic candidate, to Congress to help us in the next session.

It was about 11 months ago when we had a terrible tragedy and in the matter of moments I had to assume the responsibilities of the Presidency.   I said that night—when I walked into the White House—to the people of this Nation and to the people of the world that with God's help and your prayers I would do my dead level best.

Our beloved President, John Fitzgerald Kennedy, had sent to the Congress 51 major recommendations that were pending on November 22d.   Many of them he had worked on—long and hard.   Many of them had proceeded through this committee or that.   But there were 51 there that needed acting upon.   I talked to your Senators, they talked to their colleagues, I talked to your Congressmen and they talked to their colleagues, sometimes men of both parties.

The other night when the Congress was leaving, I sat there late in the White House waiting to receive the call, and I looked over that list of 51 unfinished matters that were left to my stewardship, and left to the Congress.   Together we had passed every one of the 51 through the United States Senate. We didn't get the Appalachia bill, we didn't get the coffee agreement bill, and we didn't get medical care through the House.   But we are going to do that when we get back to Washington next year.

No one man can lead this country.   No dozen men can lead it.   We have 50 states with 50 different populations, with almost that many religions, with men of many colors, of different atmospheres, of different environments, of different training, of different education.

Theodore Roosevelt, the great Republican President, once said, "The President of the United States is the steward of all the Nation."   And I want so much to be the President of all the people.

I want a government that will encourage business instead of harass it, but I don't want a business government.

I want a government that will lend a helping, encouraging hand to labor and the workingman, who never has too much, but I don't want a labor government.

I want a government that is fair and just and equitable with the farmer, but I don't want a government that is run by the farm bloc.

I want a government of business, and labor, and farmer, all of them working shoulder to shoulder, doing what is best for their country, because when you do what is best for America, you do what is best for yourselves.

November the 3d you are going to have to do your duty.   You are going to have to stand up there as good American men and women should and walk in that polling place and make that decision for your Nation.

The rest of the world is looking at the kind of government that you are going to provide, the kind of leadership that you are going to select.

I didn't come out here to tell you what you ought to do or what you would do.   I have too much confidence in your intelligence to have any doubt about what you are going to do.

But I do want you to know since I was a little boy that went to the post office, in the general store, the first time and put on my first pair of Buster Brown shoes that were made here in St. Louis, I have always had great faith in the people of Missouri.

I know they are going to do their duty, and I know when they do their duty on November the 3d that I am going to get a telephone call down at my little ranch on the banks of the Pedernales saying, "Every-thing went all right in St. Louis and Missouri today."

NOTE: The President spoke at 6:46 p.m. from a platform erected at Eighth and Locust Streets in St. Louis, Mo. His opening words referred to John J. Dwyer, chairman of the St. Louis City Democratic Committee, and Governor John M. Dalton of Missouri. Later he referred to Senators Stuart Symington and Edward V. Long, and Representatives Leonor K. Sullivan and Frank M. Karsten, all of Missouri, Donald Gunn, acting Mayor of St. Louis, Mrs. Frankie Freeman, Stan Musial, Special Consultant to the President on Physical Fitness, Anthony Buford, St. Louis attorney, Morris Shenker, St. Louis attorney and coordinator of the Johnson campaign, and Sidney B. McClanahan, Democratic candidate for Representative.

696   Statement by the President Following a Meeting With the Panel of Consultants on Foreign Affairs.   *October* 21, 1964

I HAD my second meeting this morning with some of the most distinguished men in this country—members of my panel of consultants on foreign affairs. Many of these men—like General Bradley, Mr. Dulles, Mr. McCloy, Mr. Lovett, Mr. Hoffman, and Mr. Acheson—have played great parts in our bipartisan foreign policy over the last 20 years, and I value these opportunities to meet and talk with them frankly.

Part of our business was to discuss the events abroad which have occurred in the last week, but my main purpose was to ask their help in thinking ahead to the great problems which this country will have to face after the coming election, whoever is chosen to go on.

I asked these men to give me their counsel on three important matters:

First: Our relations with Communist countries. We must both defend freedom and advance the prospects of peace.

Second: The affairs of the great Atlantic Community. We intend to move on to greater achievement in a partnership which has gained so much in strength over the last 15 years.

Third: The struggle to limit the spread of nuclear weapons.

I expressed to the panel my own strong sense of urgent purpose in all three of these areas, and I have asked them to continue in working session with Secretary Rusk, Secretary McNamara, and others of my senior advisers within the Government.

I expect to meet again in the weeks ahead with the members of this panel, and I want to take this occasion to express my gratitude for their willingness to serve their country in this way.

NOTE: For the President's first meeting with the members of the panel see Item 591. The panel was first announced by the President at his news conference of September 9. For a list of the members see Item 563 [5].

The statement was read by the President to members of the press in the White House Theater.

697   Statement by the President Upon Making Public a Tabulation
of Major Industry Gains, 1961–64.   *October 22, 1964*

THESE impressive gains made by our major industries show clearly what has been accomplished through the cooperative efforts of business, labor, and Government in the past 3½ years. They reflect the sustained prosperity which our economy has enjoyed.

They are the product of our private enterprise system, operating in a favorable climate created by the Revenue Acts of 1962 and 1964 and other measures sponsored by this administration.

PROGRESS IN 12 MAJOR INDUSTRIES, 1961–1964

Industry and item	Unit	Beginning of Kennedy–Johnson Administration—1961	Latest available figures—1964	Percent increase
Iron and steel:				
Industrial production............	Index 1957–59=100 (seas. adj.).	76 (Jan.)......	134 (Sept.)........	76. 3
Exports......................	$ Million [1]........	110 (2d Q)....	166 (2d Q)........	50. 9
New plant and equipment expenditures.	$ Million (seas. adj., annual rate).	1,350 (1st Q)..	1,600 (4th Q, est.).	18. 5
After tax profits................	$ Million [1]........	229 (2d Q)....	325 (2d Q)........	41. 9
Nonferrous metals:				
Industrial production............	Index 1957–59=100 (seas. adj.).	100.0 (Jan.)...	133.2 (Aug.)......	33. 2
Exports......................	$ Million [1]........	100 (2d Q)....	117 (2d Q)........	17. 0
New plant and equipment expenditures.	$ Million (seas. adj., annual rate).	300 (1st Q)....	500 (4th Q, est.)...	66. 7
After tax profits................	$ Million [1]........	137 (2d Q)....	200 (2d Q)........	46. 0
Food and beverage:				
Industrial production............	Index 1957–59=100 (seas. adj.).	108.3 (Jan.)...	120.1 (Aug.)......	10. 9
Exports......................	$ Million [1]........	705 (2d Q)....	1,003 (2d Q).......	42. 3
New plant and equipment expenditures.	$ Million (seas. adj., annual rate).	950 (1st Q)....	950 (4th Q, est.)...	....
After tax profits................	$ Million [1]........	340 (2d Q)....	400 (2d Q)........	17. 6
Petroleum products:				
Industrial production............	Index 1957–59=100 (seas. adj.).	106.2 (Jan.)...	121.7 (Aug.)......	14. 6
Exports......................	$ Million [1]........	101 (2d Q)....	105 (2d Q)........	4. 0
New plant and equipment expenditures.	$ Million (seas. adj., annual rate).	2,700 (1st Q)..	3,550 (4th Q, est.).	31. 5
After tax profits................	$ Million [1]........	712 (2d Q)....	960 (2d Q)........	34. 8
Paper and paper products:				
Industrial production............	Index 1957–59=100 (seas. adj.).	107.2 (Jan.)...	132.4 (Aug.)......	23. 5
Exports......................	$ Million [1]........	68 (2d Q).....	94 (2d Q)........	38. 2

See footnote at end of table.

PROGRESS IN 12 MAJOR INDUSTRIES, 1961–1964—continued

Industry and item	Unit	Beginning of Kennedy–Johnson Administration—1961	Latest available figures—1964	Percent increase
Paper and paper products—Con.				
New plant and equipment expenditures.	$ Million (seas. adj., annual rate).	750 (1st Q)....	1,000 (4th Q., est.).	33.3
After tax profits...............	$ Million [1].......	151 (2d Q)....	194 (2d Q)........	28.5
Chemicals:				
Industrial production...........	Index 1957–59=100 (seas. adj.).	115.3 (Jan.)...	161.1 (Aug.)......	39.7
Exports.....................	$ Million [1].......	448 (2d Q)....	547 (2d Q)........	22.1
New plant and equipment expenditures.	$ Million (seas. adj., annual rate).	1,500 (1st Q)..	2,050 (4th Q, est.)..	36.7
After tax profits...............	$ Million [1].......	566 (2d Q)....	765 (2d Q)........	35.2
Textile:				
Industrial production...........	Index 1957–59=100 (seas. adj.).	96.2 (Jan.)......	123.9 (Aug.)......	28.8
Exports.....................	$ Million [1].......	114 (2d Q)....	153 (2d Q)........	34.2
New plant and equipment expenditures.	$ Million (seas. adj., annual rate).	500 (1st Q)....	900 (4th Q., est.)..	80.0
After tax profits...............	$ Million [1].......	60 (2d Q).....	108 (2d Q)........	80.0
Nonelectrical machinery:				
Industrial production...........	Index 1957–59=100 (seas. adj.).	102 (Jan.).....	146 (Sept.)........	43.1
Exports.....................	$ Million [1].......	899 (2d Q)....	1,208 (2d Q)......	34.4
New plant and equipment expenditures.	$ Million (seas. adj., annual rate).	1,150 (1st Q)..	1,600 (4th Q, est.).	39.1
After tax profits...............	$ Million [1].......	309 (2d Q)....	553 (2d Q)........	79.0
Motor vehicles and parts:				
Industrial production...........	Index 1957–59=100 (seas. adj.).	98 (Jan.)......	152 (Sept.)........	55.1
Exports.....................	$ Million [1].......	270 (2d Q)....	398 (2d Q)........	47.4
New plant and equipment expenditures.	$ Million (seas. adj., annual rate).	700 (1st Q)....	1,500 (4th Q., est.).	114.3
After tax profits...............	$ Million [1].......	429 (2d Q)....	945 (2d Q)........	120.3
Transportation equipment (except motor vehicles):				
Industrial production...........	Index 1957–59=100 (seas. adj.).	94 (Jan.)......	110 (Sept.)........	17.0
Exports.....................	$ Million [1].......	190 (2d Q)....	126 (2d Q)........	−33.7
New plant and equipment expenditures.	$ Million (seas. adj., annual rate).	400 (1st Q)....	500 (4th Q, est.)...	25.0
After tax profits...............	$ Million [1].......	79 (2d Q).....	150 (2d Q)........	89.9
Mining:				
Production....................	Index 1957–59=100 (seas. adj.).	102.4 (Jan.)...	113.0 (Sept.)......	10.4
New plant and equipment expenditures.	$ Million (seas. adj., annual rate).	950 (1st Q)....	1,100 (4th Q, est.).	15.8
After tax profits...............	....	n.a...........	n.a..............	n.a.

See footnote at end of table.

PROGRESS IN 12 MAJOR INDUSTRIES, 1961–1964—continued

Industry and item	Unit	Beginning of Kennedy–Johnson Administration—1961	Latest available figures—1964	Percent increase
Electrical utilities:				
Industrial production	Index 1957–59=100 (seas. adj.).	116.8 (Jan.)...	152.0 (Sept.)......	30.1
New plant and equipment expenditures.	$ Million (seas. adj., annual rate).	5,350 (1st Q)..	6,000 (4th Q, est.).	12.1
After tax profits (large corporations only).	$ Million........	447 (2d Q)[1]....	542 (2d Q)[1].......	21.3

[1] Since seasonally adjusted data are not available, the second quarter figures are used in both years for purposes of comparison.

698 Recorded Remarks on the 19th Anniversary of the United Nations. *October 23, 1964*

TOMORROW we celebrate the 19th birthday of the United Nations. All over America and in 112 other countries, thoughtful people will salute the U.N.'s work of peace.

In these 19 years the United Nations has done well. Nineteen years after the League of Nations was founded, in 1938 the world's hopes for peace were dying in the shame of Munich. Today the United Nations is strong. Our hopes for peace are high.

For 19 years, in every corner of the world, U.N. missions have helped to keep the peace. At the same time, U.N. agencies have been at war with the enemies of man that pay no attention to national frontiers—hunger, and sickness, and ignorance.

The victories of the United Nations do not always make headlines, but they do make history. The United Nations is teaching all of us to work with other peoples as a good and necessary part of our own national life. The United Nations is not perfect at all. This year, in fact, it faces a real crisis unless all of its members can agree to bear their fair share of its costs. But we will not tremble

before every passing threat and we will not give up our glowing hope for the U.N.'s future.

More than 85 percent of Americans are in favor of the United Nations, and so am I. We will never withdraw from the United Nations and we will never do anything to weaken it. Instead, we will try to be the very first among those who work to make it grow in strength and in service to peace.

As we celebrate the U.N.'s birthday, we should all take a moment to pay tribute to four great men who helped make it strong. Two have been in the doctors' hands lately, Dwight Eisenhower and Harry Truman. Fortunately, both of them are on the mend. Two are gone—Franklin Roosevelt and John Kennedy.

So let us give special thanks today for President Roosevelt, who created the United Nations, and for President Kennedy, who loved it so well.

For myself, I can only repeat what I said to Secretary General U Thant at a dark hour last November: It will be hard to be a more vigorous and effective supporter of the

United Nations than President Kennedy was, but if I can manage it, that is what I will be.

NOTE: The President's remarks were video-taped in the Theater at the White House.

699   Recorded Remarks Congratulating the U.S. Olympic Team and the Members of the U.S. Olympic Committee.   *October 23, 1964*

I WANT to extend the congratulations of all your fellow Americans for the championship performance and the sportsmanlike spirit of our U.S. competitors at the 1964 Olympics.

We are all proud of the record that you have made and the way in which you have served as ambassadors of good will for our country. You have made clear the vigor and the fair play that best represent our own national character. You and the athletes from other nations have provided heartening testimony that common ground can be found among the people of this earth, and that genuine fellowship is attainable.

Healthy competition can be a spur to bring out the best in all of us, and international understanding that leads to peace is possible even in the presently troubled world.

We are proud of you, and gratified for the example that you have set. As soon as the team members return, I will invite all of the winners of medals in this year's games to join me here for lunch at the White House in the Capital City so that I can personally express to them the happiness of a proud and grateful nation.

NOTE: The President's remarks were video-taped in the Theater at the White House. For his remarks at the luncheon for the medal winners see Item 782.

700   Recorded Remarks After Further Study of the Report of the Council on Pennsylvania Avenue.   *October 23, 1964*

LAST June, shortly after I received the report of the Council on Pennsylvania Avenue, I stated that I would welcome widespread reaction to the Council's proposals. There has been reaction, almost all of it favorable, from many quarters.

During these past months, I have also been able to give the Council's report some further study. Although I recognize that details may require modification, and that any plan such as this must remain flexible, I believe that it should be accepted as a worthy and challenging goal for our Nation's most important street, our Nation's ceremonial drive.

The new building for the Federal Bureau

of Investigation is already being designed in accordance with the plan. Private development, which has already begun, should also have the plan as a guide. Every Government agency and department which received and reported on the Council's plan has approved it, some with suggestions for improvement or for further study.

I was particularly impressed by the approval of the National Capital Planning Commission, which really has the major responsibility for the development of the city; by the Commission of Fine Arts; and by the District of Columbia Board of Commissioners. I have likewise been heartened by the enthusiastic response to the plan from so many national and local organizations concerned with the development of our Nation's Capital.

Congress must, of course, be consulted, and must approve the concept of the plan. Meanwhile, however, I believe that we should undertake an immediate study of the best arrangements for implementing the plan and making whatever adjustments and modifications may be necessary.

NOTE: The President's remarks were video-taped in the Theater at the White House. For his earlier remarks after receiving the Council's report in June, see Item 379 [12].

701   Remarks on the River Front in Memphis.
October 24, 1964

Mr. Chairman, Governor Clement:

It is good to see so many old and true friends here in Memphis today. I am deeply touched by that most eloquent introduction by that man who has been such a faithful Democrat, your great Governor, and my old-time friend, Frank Clement.

I always want to come to Tennessee because I get to see one of my most reliable allies and your able former Governor, my beloved friend, Buford Ellington.

My good friend with whom I served in the Congress and who was once your distinguished mayor gave me a good welcome today, my old friend Walter Chandler. And throughout the years your Congressman and his beloved and most capable wife have been some of the best friends Lady Bird and I have, Cliff and Carrie Davis.

It is good, too, to be here on the platform with a man who takes such good care of the Eighth District up there, Congressman Robert Everett. I am sorry that Bill Ingram is ill today, and I join all of you in wishing him a speedy recovery, but I will tell you, he had the best representative he could select to come out and welcome me, that beautiful wife of his.

I am happy that my old friend and a great Tennessee patriot came here to be with me and give me comfort, your great Senator,

Herb Walters. It is good to see my other friends, Paul Rand Dixon, Chairman of the Federal Trade Commission; Congressman E. C. (Tuck) Gathings from Arkansas; and my friend Douglas Wynn from Mississippi.

You know, it is not every election that the people of a State have a chance to send two good men to the United States Senate at the same time. Tennessee has an enviable reputation of electing truly outstanding men to the United States Senate, men who represent not only their own State, but who represent the interests of all America. Such a man is your most able and distinguished public servant, my longtime friend and co-worker in the House and Senate, Albert Gore, and I want to say this to you: Tennessee needs him in the Senate and the Nation needs him in the Senate.

I know that you will want to keep Tennessee with a good working team in the Senate and I don't think there is any doubt but what you are going to elect that great progressive, that Member of Congress, the new member of the team, the Democratic nominee, Ross Bass.

You here in Memphis are going to have a highly effective team in Washington when you send that great Democrat, George Grider, to the Congress. That effective Tennessee team is dependent upon the reelection in the House of Representatives of Robert A. Everett from Union City; Dick Fulton from Nashville; Tom Murray, my old colleague in the House, from Jackson; my great friend Joe Evins from Smithville, who has been doing such a splendid job in managing this unified campaign. And today I would like to say: "Happy birthday, Joe Evins. We hope that you enjoy today as much as we are going to enjoy November 3d."

I know that you are going to keep that Sixth District in sound Democratic hands when you elect Capt. Bill Anderson. I think in these days when a steady hand and a cool head are so important, it is highly appropriate that you people here in Tennessee will be sending two former submarine commanders to Washington, Captain Anderson and George Grider.

The people all over Tennessee are concerned this year about keeping their National Government in responsible hands. I would not be surprised to see the folks in east Tennessee send three men to Congress this year—Bob Summitt from Chattanooga, Willard Yarbrough from the Second District, and Arthur Bright up in the First District. This will be a team that will reflect credit on Tennessee. This will be a team that your President can work with, and I can assure you this will be a team that will work with and for you.

One week from Tuesday the American people will go to the polls. For the 45th time in our history, the people will choose their national leadership and decide their national directions. There will be two names at the top of the ballot, but there will be only one choice and only one decision that matters to the future.

History will not count Democratic votes or Republican votes. History will not count Southern votes or Northern votes. History will not count white votes or Negro votes. All that really counts is whether or not Americans are willing to stand up and be counted for responsibility.

Responsibility was the issue when this campaign began. Irresponsible campaigning cannot change that issue. Whatever your party, whatever your philosophy, when you go to cast your vote, the decision of this decade and the outcome of this century is going to be resting in your hands.

For 155 years or more, men and women in Memphis and the great Midsouth have been building this mighty city, and have been developing this great, growing region. There have been many trials and tests that we have gone through together.

One hundred years ago this region was the richest in the Nation. Nine out of the Nation's 13 wealthiest States were in those days in the South. But when war came, and when death and devastation came, this region, our own beloved region of the South, was left as the Nation's poorest region.

But today the Nation sees a new day dawning in this Midsouth and in all of our beloved Dixie.

These are the stakes in this election, for you and for all Americans. Now, let me be more specific.

We live no more in the age of the cavalry charge. If nuclear war should ever come, the casualties of the first exchange would leave dead in the United States and Russia 400 times more men, women, and children than the entire population of Memphis today. So if peace is to be preserved, American voters, like American leaders, must be right the first time, for there will be no second time.

We must be responsible to the peace of all mankind. We must also be responsible to the progress of all Americans.

Before another 35 years have passed, the

population of America will have grown the equal of about 300 new cities the size of Memphis.

So all through this land we just must be preparing for that new tomorrow, and, my friends, this is no time to be thinking or talking of selling the TVA.

You must realize that you have a great obligation and a great duty to do, and this is just no time to be thinking or talking of turning out the lights of the REA. This is just no time to be thinking and talking of making social security voluntary and getting rid of it as we know it.

Those of you that have worked so faithfully and dreamed so dramatically through the years, and whose fathers and mothers and grandfathers and grandmothers pioneered ahead of you, don't be coming back and talking and saying, "If I had just known what would happen after November 3d!" Now is the time to think and talk and work and do something about it.

If you want to maintain your social security system and strengthen it, and make it sound to serve each of you the day you need it, you can't do it by making it voluntary.

If you want to improve your REA and electrify every farm home in the land, and reduce your rates, you can't do it by a philosophy that doesn't believe in it.

If you want to preserve the TVA as an example for all the Nation and all the foreign nations to look at with pride, you can't do it by even starting off to selling its fertilizer plants.

If you in Memphis, the hub city, the center, the capital of the Midsouth, and Arkansas, and Mississippi, if you want agriculture to blossom and bloom, if you want to keep the boys on the farm, if you want to encourage the tiller of the soil, you can't go back to the days of 1932 when cotton was selling for 5 cents a pound, when we were burning our corn, when our cattle would bring us nothing, when the produce from our agriculture lands was rotting in the fields.

We just must not abandon the programs of agriculture and we are not going to under a Democratic administration.

The settled issues of the 1930's are not the issues of the 1960's, and that is really the choice you have to make. Do you want to go back to the thirties or do you want to go forward with the sixties? The American people are not sick in their soul or in their spirit.

Most of the Americans that I have seen— and there are very few crowds that I have ever seen that go down in this direction for more than 100 yards, that dot the hills, that go back as far as they can go to that building over there, that dot the hills, that go all the way here and in back of us—those people are proud, those people are confident, those people are unafraid, and if you will just look out there, with a rare exception now and then that come here to advertise themselves—I don't see any of them here today, but just nearly everybody, even people that are not happy, they like to be in a good crowd, with good people, once in a while.

I am so indebted to you for coming to this meeting, confident, unafraid, with hope, with faith, and with love, and happy and ready to go out and meet the challenges that face us all tomorrow.

If I take my compass or my ruler and take a direct line down the center of this crowd and divide you, we can do little; but united, as we are, there is little that we cannot do. And you know one of the things that I think we ought to do, and I say this as a man that has spent all of his life and cast his every vote in Texas, and as the grandson of two Confederate veterans, I think one of the things that we are going to have to do is wipe away the Mason-Dixon line across our politics.

And because we are good people and because we are fair people, and because we are just people, and because we believe in the Good Book, we are going to have to follow the Golden Rule, "Do unto others as you would have them do unto you," and when we do that, we are going to wipe away the color line across our opportunity.

The mandate of this election is going to be a mandate to unite this Nation. It is going to be a mandate to bind up our wounds and to heal our history, and to make this Nation whole as one nation, as one people, indivisible, under God.

Let me remind you that you are the mightiest, most advanced nation in the world. Here in Tennessee, you developed the awesome and mighty power that makes us the undisputed strongest nation in all the world.

Let me remind you that by two men exercising their bad judgment and putting their thumb on the button, that you can, in a matter of moments, wipe out the lives of 300 millions of people as a result of your mighty discoveries at Oak Ridge.

Let me remind you that on this election day of November 3, less than 2 weeks from now, all the world of 120 nations and 3 billion people, of which we are just one-fifteenth, are going to be watching you as Americans and watching your vote. The election returns will be read in the capitals of the world—the free world and the Communist world.

I want the mandate of this election to be written loud and strong, and clear, so that none, anywhere, will mistake the meaning. We have Chancellor Erhard in Germany. We have a new British labor government just selected this week. We have General de Gaulle in France. We have Mr. Shastri in India, who succeeded Mr. Nehru. We have the new rulers in the Kremlin.

I want them and all the world to know what campaigns of hate, campaigns of fear, and campaigns of smear—I want them to know that we Americans are proud that we have faith and hope, we have love in our hearts, and a campaign of smear cannot succeed among the American people.

I want them to know that when they deal with Americans, they deal on the basis of reason and judgment and not on the basis of hate or emotion.

I want those who wish us well to know that America stands strong and stands steady, and stands firm, using its great power with great restraint; always ready to meet any aggressor, but always ready to search for an honorable peace.

I want them to know that the mightiest nation in the world, supported by the strongest, most patriotic loving people, always have their guard up to protect themselves, but always have their hand out to find a workable peace.

I want the mothers who must supply the boys, and I want the boys who must die in the wars, to know that no impulsive act of mine, no heat of emotion, is ever going to cause me to do a rash, dangerous, adventurous thing that might wipe out 300 million Americans.

I want any who may wish us ill to take notice this morning to understand that our beloved America cannot be divided by region, by religion, or by race.

And I want the country to know and the world to know that we are going to preserve law and order in the streets of America, and we are going to preserve reason and responsibility in the policies of the Government of America.

In our land and around the world, America is going to stand proudly and confidently for the pursuit of peace and progress, freedom and justice for all mankind.

That is your duty, that is your obligation, that is the price you must pay for the privilege of being Americans. Don't wait until the bell rings, don't wait until the bulletins flash over your television sets, don't wait until you hear the newsboys screaming the emergency headlines. Act now. Work now. Exercise your citizenship now, because it is your boys, it is your lives, it is your families that you must have led, and you must select the leader for them November the 3d. That will be the mandate, and that will be the meaning of this election.

Now I am going along. I am going to Chattanooga, and I am going to Baltimore, and I am going back into Washington tonight, and to Florida and Georgia tomorrow, and all across this land all next week.

I am not going to talk hate. I am not going to preach doubt. I am going to try to appeal to the best that is in us all, because I think men, regardless of their religion, their politics, their race, or their region or their party—I believe they want to do what is best for America. And that is all I am going to ask any American to do.

Eleven months ago, on a tragic day, a moment that I will never forget, without notice or warning, my constitutional responsibilities required me to assume the awesome responsibility of being your leader, and to try to effect a transition between a dear, beloved leader who had fallen, and to demonstrate to the world that was watching that it was our system that would function, that we were a nation of laws and not just a nation of men.

So that night when I walked into the White House, as Governor Clement said to you, I said to the American people, "With God's help, with your prayers, I will do the best I can."

Under our democratic system, in less than 1 year from that day, you must decide whether I should step aside and whether I should move over, and whether you should have another leader.

That is your right and that is your privilege and that is your duty, to decide. All I can say to you is this: Whatever your decision is, I want it to be based on no emotion, no flattery, no religion, no race, no region of the country. I want it to be based on qualifications and experience and merit.

But really, what it all adds up to is I want it to be based on your conscience, whatever your heart tells you is right. You don't develop character, integrity, and leadership by bragging about it and pointing to it. You don't develop and do what is right by saying so on a billboard. A great man said one time in a great public speech that men don't talk about their integrity and women don't talk about their virtue, if they have it.

So in this hour of trial, ask yourselves what is best for free men, what is best for Americans, what is best for Memphis, and Tennessee, and Mississippi, and Arkansas. And then ask yourself, "What is really best for me on the only two things that are really important, survival and prosperity, peace in the world and peace at home?" Ask yourself that question. Free men, Americans, Tennesseans, and then yourselves, in that order.

And whether you are Democrats or Republicans, you go in that polling booth and do what you know is right in your heart.

NOTE: The President spoke at 11:45 a.m. from a platform erected at Court Street and Riverside Drive in Memphis, Tenn. His opening words referred to James E. Irwin, chairman of the Shelby County Democratic Committee, and Governor Frank G. Clement of Tennessee. Later he referred to, among others, Buford Ellington, former Governor of Tennessee, Walter Chandler, former Mayor of Memphis, Representative and Mrs. Clifford Davis and Representative Robert A. Everett of Tennessee, W. B. Ingram, Jr., Mayor of Memphis, Senator Herbert S. Walters of Tennessee, Paul Rand Dixon, Chairman of the Federal Trade Commission, Representative E. C. (Tuck) Gathings of Arkansas, Douglas C. Wynn, Mississippi State chairman of the Democratic campaign, Senator Albert Gore of Tennessee, Repre-sentative Ross Bass, Democratic candidate for Senator from Tennessee, George W. Grider, Democratic candidate for Representative, Representatives Richard Fulton, Tom Murray, and Joe L. Evins of Tennessee, and William R. Anderson, Robert M. Summitt, Willard V. Yarbrough, and Arthur Bright, Democratic candidates for Representative.

702   Remarks at an Airport Rally in Chattanooga. October 24, 1964

Governor Clement, ladies and gentlemen, boys and girls:

I am very happy to see so many proud and happy and smiling faces here in this great section of the United States. My grandfather was born just across the line in Georgia—and Georgia has never gone Republican, I remind you, and is not going this year—and my wife came from Alabama, and I am just about to claim Tennessee.

I appreciate that fine introduction that Governor Clement gave me. It is the second best introduction I ever had in my life. The other one was when he was supposed to introduce me once before and he didn't get there, and I had to introduce myself.

This new terminal has a special meaning today, as I know it does to you, because it is dedicated to the memory of Estes Kefauver, the great Senator from Lookout Mountain who died just a year ago. In Washington we miss Estes Kefauver. We miss his humanity and his dedication to the cause of equal opportunity for all of our citizens.

You have an outstanding opportunity here in this State this year to elect not one great Senator, but two great Democratic Senators: Albert Gore is one of the real leaders of the Congress, and you have another man here who will be a source of pride to this State in the Senate. I have served with Albert in both the House and the Senate, and I look forward to having him help me put my pro-gram through the next Congress. Stand up, Albert.

Ross Bass has made one of the most distinguished records in the Congress, and he is going to make it more distinguished after you elect him in November. We want to hear his voice in the United States Senate for the next 6 years, and many more. Stand up, Ross.

Senator Walters has done an able job in filling Estes Kefauver's old seat in the Senate and he is one of my dear friends. Stand up, Herb.

These men are carrying on a great tradition. They tell me—I asked Nancy Gore this afternoon—someone told me that I was running about 55–45 down here in Tennessee.

I said, "How is Albert running?" And they said, "He is running 85–15."

I said, "Who is helping him get that 85?" And they said, "Nancy is his campaign manager."

Stand up, Nancy, I want them to meet you. I hope after that kind of bragging and introduction, I hope she will be mine the last week of the campaign.

The Volunteer State of Tennessee has given this Nation three Presidents, and some of the most distinguished leaders in our history. Tennessee sent Sam Houston to build Texas. Tennessee sent David Crockett to give his life at the Alamo. And this is still frontier country with a great frontier spirit that I believe believes in the New Frontier, and I think will vote Democratic come November 3d.

I am very pleased to see that you people here in Chattanooga have bright, young, able public servants, like Bob Summitt, and I hope you send him to Congress from this District. Stand up, Bob.

We really have two big problems confronting us, and your President needs a Congress to help him. One is to continue the bipartisan foreign policy that we have had for 20 years. Republican Arthur Vandenberg helped Democrat Harry Truman stop the Communists in Greece and Turkey. Democrat Lyndon Johnson helped Dwight Eisenhower, when I was Democratic leader, on his problems in the Suez and the Formosa Strait, and politics stopped at the waterline. Everett Dirksen, the Republican leader, helped John F. Kennedy on the test ban treaty when we all needed to pass that treaty so we could stop the pollution of the air and the food we eat and the milk we drink. All bipartisans, working together for a foreign policy. I want to continue that foreign policy.

My opponent has different ideas about it. I don't want to see the bipartisan foreign policy of this country go down the drain. For that reason, I need men like Bob Summitt up there to help me.

No man has served his Nation, his State, with more patriotism than my old friend Congressman Joe Evins. Today is his birthday. I hope he is as happy on November 3d as campaign manager in this State as he is today by seeing this large crowd. Stand up, Joe.

I am glad to see Mayor Kelley. I am grateful to him for this warm turnout of hospitality, and I appreciate more than you know all these happy, smiling faces that are here today.

Here in Tennessee you are fortunate in having Frank Clement as your Governor, fortunate for many reasons. I am particularly fortunate because he gave me two of the best introductions I have ever had today. He has given this State strong and vigorous and able leadership, and this State deserves it.

Frank Clement understands the meaning of the partnership between the Federal Government and the State Government. I am happy to say that over the last 4 years, we have gone far in this partnership. Per capita income in the State of Tennessee rose over 4 percent every year, almost twice as much as the national average in other States. That growth rate in income is twice as fast as it was between 1956 and 1960.

There were 74,000 new nonfarm jobs in this State between 1960 and 1963, and that is almost twice the increase of jobs from 1956 to 1960. Just last week, the number of nonfarm jobs in the Chattanooga area passed the 100,000 mark for the first time in this city's history, and I know you are proud of that.

Before I pass along, I want you to know how grateful I am, not only for how wonderful you make me feel and for all of you coming out here and saying hello, but I particularly want to thank the Chattanooga Times, a good newspaper, for helping me in my campaign. It has helped this city and it has helped this State move ahead, and we want you to keep moving ahead as fast as that famous old Tennessee cavalryman Nathan Bedford Forrest, who used to say that his only problem was to "git thar fustest with the mostest."

There is a candidate who called the Tennessee Valley Authority "an unfortunate socialistic venture," and "a Federal white elephant." In one of his more inspired moments, he referred to your TVA as a "socialistic octopus."

Well, this city of Chattanooga is in the heart of the TVA, and I think everybody in this city, and in this State, knows what this "socialistic octopus" has done for Tennessee and has done for the Nation, and I think I know what you are going to do to him November 3d. This great institution of TVA, which is the marvel of the entire world—hardly any foreign leader comes to Washington but what he wants to see the TVA—has transformed a whole region and made it better.

And I don't, as long as I am President, intend to give it up, or give it away. I think it can build this region even more. I think it is up to us to build on this foundation and not to tear it down. I want to strengthen TVA, not call it into question.

The first thing that we must do for our future, and for the world's future, is to keep the peace, and that is what I have really come here to Chattanooga to talk to you about today.

There are two central questions in this campaign.

First, will we preserve and strengthen the programs for justice and progress that have brought a better life to our people? I think I know what your decision will be. I think it will be to stand fast for justice and to stand fast for progress, and more of it.

Second, will we carry on the bipartisan foreign policy that has guided this Nation safely through 20 perilous years? Again, I know what your decision will be. I think you will stand fast for peace.

For the last 20 years the architecture of our foreign policy has been a policy of unity, and now that unity of national purpose is called into question for the first time. It is challenged by men who represent not the majority of their own party, not the majority of Americans, but a fringe that wants to repeal the present and a fringe that wants to veto the future.

Four years ago we faced a united world Communist movement. Nikita Khrushchev was boasting about his Sputniks and threatening open war over Berlin, and telling us that he was going to bury us. He had smashed the summit conference.

All over Europe the Communist satellites were following Moscow's command. They saw no other choice.

In Asia the Communists also moved as one bloc. They were on the march in Latin America. The new countries of Africa were weak targets of Communist ambitions.

Well, in 1961, when John F. Kennedy took office, and when this administration came to office, we set out firmly and patiently to frustrate communism's ambitions and to help build allies and help them build their own security.

First, we strengthened our ties with NATO. Peace Corps volunteers went forth to show the world that our interest in peace was more than a good intention. Then we launched the Alliance for Progress in Latin America. At home we set out to build our own strength as the free world's guarantee of survival.

Well, what has happened in 4 years?

The Communists are still here, although Mr. Khrushchev has not buried us and it looks like he is not in control anymore. The Communists are still dedicated. The Communists are still dangerous. But in Eastern Europe the Communist bloc no longer wears just one face. Mr. Khrushchev said some of those countries are like children that have grown too big to spank.

In Asia, in Africa, in Latin America the

tide of communism is running out. In the Kremlin Mr. Khrushchev's successors know that the United States of America intends to bury no one, but they also know that we will not be buried.

But a foreign policy of resistance to aggression would be only half a policy. We here in America have combined it with an unceasing fight for peace, and I think that we are winning that fight. There is no easy way to world peace and security. They are not achieved by the jiffy solution or the reckless threat.

The Bible admonishes us to "run with patience the race that is set before us."

Run with patience, and that is what I intend to do. We have grown strong in the last 4 years, and we must continue to increase that strength. We must hold firmly to these four principles of peace:

One, we must continue to resist Communist aggression.

Two, we must support the United Nations, and advance the unity of our NATO allies, and of the entire Atlantic community.

Three, we must assist the developing nations to become stable members of the free world community.

Four, we must enlarge the ban on nuclear tests, and we must keep the ultimate purpose always before us of a world that is free of the threat of nuclear destruction.

The foreign policy of this Nation is as strong as the resolve and the concern of the individual Americans who constitute this Nation.

Each one of you is an architect of that foreign policy.

Each one of you on November 3d will cast your vote for or against the policy of peace and responsibility that we have been building for 20 years.

I count on your judgment to sustain that policy. I don't think that in your lifetime you have ever faced a more important decision. I don't think that you have ever been called upon to live up to a more important responsibility or to discharge a more important obligation.

Eleven months ago, on that tragic day when we lost our President, our fallen leader had gone, I had, on a moment's notice, to assume the responsibilities of the Presidency.

I had sat with John F. Kennedy through many perilous moments. I sat in 37 meetings of the National Security Council with him when Mr. Khrushchev had brought his missiles into Cuba, 90 miles from the United States, and they were pointed toward our people.

I saw our leader meet there day after day with the Joint Chiefs of Staff, with our leading naval authorities, our leading military men, our leading aviators.

I heard the Secretary of State and the Secretary of Defense and the Chairman of the CIA all give their judgments.

I am proud to say that the coolest man in that room was our own Commander in Chief, the President of the United States, John Fitzgerald Kennedy. He was firm and steady. He was not frightened, but he was not provocative.

He did not rattle his rockets, and he did not bluff with his bombs, although he ordered our planes off the ground, fully loaded, fully prepared for any emergency. But he showed great patience and great judgment, and as a consequence we avoided a nuclear holocaust that would have wiped out 100 million Americans, over half of our population, in one day's time, and would have killed 100 million Russians in the same period of time.

On November 3d you are going to select the man whose thumb will have to touch that button if it is ever touched. You are going to select the man that has to pick up that "hot line" telephone when Moscow is calling. It is up to you to determine what man you want to do that job.

For 11 months I have done the best job I could for you. I told you that night, when I took over, that with God's help and with your prayers that I would do the best I could. And I have done that.

No one man can lead this Nation alone. It requires the help of all of you, and if you want me to lead it, I will tell you today, as I told you then, with God's help and with your prayers, I will do my best.

But I think you are going to have to make up your mind in the next 10 days what you are going to do about it, and then you are going to have to talk to your kinfolks and your uncles and your cousins and your aunts. And you are going to have to see on that morning of November 3d not that you take your boy down to the draft station, not that you are willing to go and volunteer yourself, but that you exercise the priceless privilege that is your heritage, to go into that polling booth and cast a secret ballot. And that ballot ought to be based on what you know in your conscience is good for your country, what you know in your heart is right.

I haven't come down here to try to mislead you or persuade you, or to convince you. I think that is a reflection on your intelligence. I came here to meet you, to look at you, to speak with you, to discuss some of our problems. And I have confidence in your decision on those problems.

I think that you know what is best for your country, and whether you are a Republican or whether you are a Democrat, or whether you are Independent, I think that you are going, on November 3d, and vote for what is best for America.

I will tell you this: If you will do what is best for America, you will do what is best for you.

Thank you and goodby.

NOTE: The President spoke at 3:22 p.m. at a rally at Lovell Field in Chattanooga, Tenn. His opening words referred to Governor Frank G. Clement of Tennessee. Later in his remarks he referred to Estes Kefauver, U.S. Senator from Tennessee during the fifties and early sixties, Senator and Mrs. Albert Gore, Representative Ross Bass, Democratic candidate for U.S. Senator, Senator Herbert S. Walters, Representative Joe L. Evins, and Robert M. Summitt, Democratic candidate for Representative, all of Tennessee, and Mayor Ralph H. Kelley of Chattanooga.

703   Remarks Before Two Groups at the Fifth Regiment Armory in Baltimore. *October 24, 1964*

Senator Brewster, Mayor McKeldin:

I am going to take a little longer than I think you would like for me to take, and I am going to speak a little more than I normally do because I am so touched by the depth of your hospitality and the warmth of your reception, and the good hand of fellowship that you have extended that I just can't go back home without letting you know how I feel.

So many of my good friends through the

years have been residents of the great Free State of Maryland, so many men that I have served with in the House and in the Senate and in public life have been chosen by you to represent them. When I saw young Tommy D'Alesandro out at the airport tonight, I thought of the years of service I had had with his father in the House. When I saw Herbert O'Connor up here a few moments ago stepping into the footsteps of his father, I thought of the kind and good man that had worked with me in the Senate so long.

When I first went to the Senate as a youngster back in 1949, one of the great men of the Senate was the chairman of the Armed Services Committee, and I was assigned to that committee the first day I went there. He came from the great Free State of Maryland, and his name was Millard Tydings. One of the great regrets of my life is that in a moment of temporary misunderstanding, he was confronted with some of the same forces that confront me today. I am so happy that you people that are proud to wear the label of the Democratic Party in this State are going to send Joe Tydings up there to take his place.

Mayor McKeldin, you did a very unusual thing when you, as mayor of this great city, came out to the airport tonight to welcome me. I will always remember it. I think you came perhaps for two reasons:

One, you are a courteous and hospitable man who speaks for all the people of this city, and when the President of this country visits this city, you want him to be welcome, regardless of what party he comes from.

But secondly, I think you came because you genuinely believe that the present President of this country is trying his dead level best to do what is best for this country, regardless of party.

Mayor McKeldin, I want to make a personal pledge to you tonight. It is a pledge that I made to myself some time ago. That pledge is this: that if the good Lord will give me the sight to see the right, I will do the right, and do what is best for my country, regardless of my party.

So I am deeply grateful for your welcome to Baltimore. I take new strength and inspiration and courage from those warm words, Mayor, that you uttered, and I am profoundly thankful for that tribute to me and to those ideals that we both hold as Americans.

The Old Testament tells us to be strong and of good courage; fear not nor be dismayed. And with God as my judge and as my guide, each day I try with all that is within me to do what is right and do what is just for my country and for all the people of America. For, Mr. Mayor, I think I know, as you know, that if we are to survive as a free nation, if we are to prosper as a happy people, it will be because we have held our courage and we are not afraid.

One of the most important national resources that we have in America is responsible leadership. We have it in the White House, in the Congress, and in many of our State capitals and cities. And here in Maryland you have given your State and you have given your country outstanding leadership throughout the years.

Joe Tydings, your next Democratic Senator, is young and he is aggressive, and we need his ability and his vigor in Washington. And when the going was tough, and when the campaign was rough, Maryland produced a courageous and a valiant Senator to uphold my hand, and he stood in for me when I couldn't be here—my old and good and trusted and beloved friend, your great Senator Danny Brewster. And Carlton Sickles, who is here on the platform with me tonight, has served you well as Congressman at Large.

I want each of you to remember that it takes as many votes to send Carlton back to the House as it does to elect Joe to the Senate. I know that you are going out there and see that he gets those votes November 3d.

For many years, one of my best friends and one of the great leaders of the House of Representatives, one of Mr. Rayburn's old friends from the Fourth District, who is now in line for the powerful chairmanship of the House Public Works Committee—an important job—and I don't think that you are going to let the dean of your delegation down. I think you are going to give George Fallon the greatest majority he ever had.

I would like to run like this fellow is running in the Third District. He won his reelection by his able service. He has no opposition tonight. He deserves to have none. I know he is going to be elected—my friend, Ed Garmatz.

And Sam Friedel has served the Seventh District since it was created in 1952, and he has been my good friend ever since he came to Congress. You just can't afford to lose his seniority or his experience. I know that you will send Clarence Long from the Second District back because we need him there to work with us. Harry Hughes and Hervey Machen are campaigning hard. They are working from daylight to dark. You are going to have to get out there and help them because we must elect these promising men. They are in the First and Fifth Districts. Don't forget to put in a good word for them.

It has been a pleasure to have a chance to renew my friendship and pleasant association with Governor Tawes, your great Governor; your Attorney General, my old friend Tom Finan; and Comptroller Louis Goldstein, who always gives me a warm welcome when I come to Maryland. Governor Tawes is an able national committeeman. Dr. Mildred Otenasek is every bit his equal as national committeewoman. And Herbert O'Connor, Jr., and Francis Keller are the kind of State campaign cochairmen who win elections, and Philip Goodman and Thomas D'Alesandro III are doing a fine job as Maryland's city campaign chairmen, and I hope it shows up on Tuesday, November 3d.

It is a great honor to me to have my old friend Senator Radcliffe of many years

standing come here and join us on the platform tonight. I am honored by it. I thank you for it, Senator.

One of the good things about a political year is that it makes us pause for a moment and take stock. Tonight I think is a time for all Americans to ask themselves: What do we want, where are we going? What does it mean to be an American, what does America mean? What does America stand for in the world?

Well, I have been all around the world. I have been to more than 40 countries in the world, and I think I can tell you tonight what America stands for. It stands for hope, because America is the hope of the world; because today we Americans are responsible not only for our own security, but we Americans are responsible for the security of all the free nations in the world.

Let there be no mistake. I want all of you to know, and I want all the free nations of the world to know, that tonight America is prepared to meet every challenge.

In every area of military might, in every area, we are stronger tonight than we have ever been before in all our history. We are stronger, in fact, than the combined might of all the other nations in the history of the world.

Recently we have heard——

[*Demonstration from the floor*]

I am so glad that you good people welcomed our friends. In most States of the Union we have from 30 to some places 35—up in Pennsylvania we have 37—percent of the Republicans, and as I have observed the last few days, we occasionally have visitors that come to our meetings because they like to associate with good people, and they like to attract attention.

After all, we need everyone we can get, and we want to welcome them all to our fold. I will bet you that some of those people that came in here unexpected and kind of delayed us for a moment, kind of—you know—I will bet you that they are going to join with us and elect that good Democrat Royce Hanson. I believe some of them have already dropped their original signs that they brought in and now they have Royce Hanson signs over here.

That is something I don't want any of you to forget. You can get two for the price of one here. You can get rid of a Republican Congressman and you can get a Democratic Congressman.

I guess I can have a little fun on Saturday night, can't I? One of these nice fellows from Maryland that always has a good joke stood up here just now and said, "Do you know what those signs are? Now don't get upset about them."

And I said, "No, what?"

He said, "Don't you see them back there?"

I could see them, but I don't have good eyesight for a long distance. I said, "No, what do they say?"

And he said, "They say 'Gold for the rich, water for the poor, and Johnson for President.'"

Really, I don't want you to get angry with them. Let's be charitable with everybody. Let's turn the other cheek and be nice.

We want to get down to some serious business now and talk to issues. It is getting late, so let's go.

Recently we have heard some very reckless and heedless talk and accusations about our country's military power. There are some people who have said our defenses are weakening, that America is falling behind.

I think it is fortunate that these reckless voices are not believed by our friends in the world or by our adversaries, and I might add that they are not believed by the American people.

Your Government must keep the record straight, because we will not let anyone, anywhere, be fooled by these reckless and false charges. Why?

We know from tragic experience what can happen when the enemies of freedom deceive themselves about America's strength. How do we know that?

The Kaiser listened to some voices in America and deceived himself and sunk the *Lusitania* because he didn't think we would fight or were prepared to fight, and he brought on World War I.

Hitler deceived himself and listened to some voices here at home that were reckless, and he brought on World War II, because he didn't think we could get ready or we were ready or we would do anything about it.

Red China deceived itself and brought on an expanded war in Korea.

This is pretty important business to you people that are furnishing the boys that must die in these wars. These lessons of history must not be lost.

The first act of this administration, after President Kennedy met Premier Khrushchev in Vienna, was to come back home and re-examine and strengthen America's military power. And we have vastly increased that power.

When people talk to you about peace through preparedness, you tell them that since President Kennedy became President, the 4 years of this administration, we have spent $30 billion more on defense and $10 billion more on space, a total of $40 billion more, $40 billion in addition to what we would have spent if we had spent at the last rate of the last year of the administration before President Kennedy. He raised expenditures $30 billion in defense and $10 billion in space, or a total of $40 billion over 4 years.

And what did we get for that $40 billion? We increased our nuclear power that was on the alert, ready to go, 2½ times, and our nuclear superiority is continuing to grow every day.

We have now, tonight, more than 1,000 fully armed intercontinental ballistic missiles and Polaris missiles ready for retaliation against any attack on America.

We have more than 1,100 strategic bombers tonight, more than twice as many as our adversary could put over this country.

We have vastly increased our forces to fight conventional war.

We have raised the number of Army combat-ready divisions by 45 percent.

Tonight we and our NATO allies have more than 5 million men in uniform under arms.

Our adversaries attempt today to subvert our freedom—and the freedom of our allies—by terror and by subversion, and by guerrilla warfare.

But since January 1961, we have trained more than 100,000 officers in antiguerrilla warfare alone.

We have heard others claim recently that they have a patent on preparedness. Well, few Americans will be deceived by such claims. But it is important that our adversaries abroad never be deceived by this misleading talk, because it is dangerous talk, and it is deceptive talk, and it is talk that brought us into two conflicts.

We just must not in this nuclear age lead ourselves innocently into another one. When we Americans debate the whole world listens. Our friends and our enemies alike seek clues to what the next President will be like.

They are debating all around the world tonight—3 billion people—what kind of a President will America have for the next 4 years. We must, therefore, deal in facts and

not fantasies.

My record is clear. So is our opponent's.

The record shows—and Al Smith used to say, "Let's look at the record"—the record shows that in 1953 our opponent voted—this Air Force general, now—voted not to give the Air Force $400 million more for aircraft purchases. I voted for that increase for the Air Force of $400 million.

In 1954 our opponent voted not to spend $350 million more for Army personnel and maintenance. I voted for that increase.

In 1955—let's just come right on up to date—our opponent voted not to invest $46 million more for our Marine Corps. I voted for that $46 million.

In 1955 our opponent voted against a $420 million increase in appropriations for military assistance to our allies abroad. I voted for that increase.

In 1956 our opponent voted not to increase Air Force procurement funds by $800 million. I voted for that increase.

In the last Congress before this administration took office our opponent voted against an increase of $233.9 million for the Army to procure missiles and equipment. I voted for that increase.

Our friends and allies alike, my fellow Americans, are going to judge for themselves which of the two candidates for President has truly, through the years, not just at election time, through the years, truly supported military preparedness.

Our friends and allies alike can judge for themselves whether we will maintain military preparedness in the years to come.

Now, you must also make a decision. Your decision is the choice between words and deeds, between strong words or strong action, between the strength we have and the strength we will keep, and the strength that we will increase. And in Berlin, in Cuba, in Viet-Nam, and in the Tonkin Gulf we have shown that our will matches our might.

I think you want, and I know your President will speak softly and act with prudence because we are firm in the knowledge of our strength. We know that bravado is not bravery, and we know that loud voices frighten only the weak, or those who are deceived.

We know that we gain very little by trying to threaten and scare other nations. This business of rattling your rockets and bluffing with bombs is not the road to peace.

Our adversaries are not weak. They are strong, but I can assure you faithfully tonight that America is stronger. And I want to announce to them and I want to announce to you that they should have no doubts or illusions about America's strength.

In the words of the Bible, "When the strong man armed keepeth his palace, his goods are in peace."

We have strength in our country tonight, and you young men that must patrol our borders and wear those uniforms must maintain that strength.

We have peace in the world tonight, and you mothers that produce those sons and raise them to maturity must help us keep both the strength and the peace.

Eleven months ago and 2 days, all America awakened to a great tragedy. Our leader had fallen. On a moment's notice, I had to assume the awesome responsibilities of the office I now hold.

Our Constitution provided that I would have to accept those responsibilities. I didn't have time to call in a group of wise men. I didn't have time to search through the shelves of the libraries. I had to stand up and take that oath while jet planes were roaring in the background.

But I said that day to you people and to all the people of the world, that with God's help and your prayers I would do my best. And

I tell you tonight from an honest heart I have done my best.

Now the buck passes back to you. Now the decision is yours. You are the masters, not the servants. We are the servants. You have the high privilege that not all the people of the world have, of deciding whom you want to have his thumb next to that button.

You have the great duty and obligation to that flag and to that seal to select the man that you want to pick up that receiver at the end of the "hot line" when they say, "Moscow is calling."

You have nearly 2 weeks to decide what you want to do about it, and I haven't come over here to stampede you or to try to influence you, or to say any ugly things about any other men. I don't believe in indulging in personalities. I am a man that loves and not hates.

I am a man that has faith and not doubt. I am a man that has hope, not fear. I know what I stand for and I have told you. I stand for a policy of strength, backed and supported by firm restraint. I follow the Golden Rule as President with my own people and with the people of all nations, "Do unto others as you would have them do unto you."

I stand for a policy of peace in the world and peace at home, where the businessman can get along with the laboringman, and where both of them can have a bigger pie to slice between each other instead of fighting all the time.

I am proud that fewer men are idle tonight than at any time except in wartime in the history of America. We have lost only fourteen one-hundredths of 1 percent—not 1 percent, not a half of 1 percent, not a quarter of 1 percent, but fourteen one-hundredths of 1 percent of the hours we have worked we have lost by strike, which means that we have actually lost very little, if anything. I am glad that our employers and our employees have their shoulder to the wheel and the average weekly wage in manufacturing industry tonight is $104.

I remember when I first went to Congress I voted for a 25-cent minimum wage, and they told me it would defeat me because I was from the South. They told me it would ruin the labor organization. But I don't think it has ruined either one of us. Do you? So I stand for a peaceful nation and I stand for a prosperous nation. I stand for a policy where every man and woman who wants to work can have a job, where every boy and girl of whatever religion, of whatever region, whatever section, whatever race, whatever color, that is born under the American flag has the right to all the education he can take.

I stand for a Government that has as its basic national policy the best social security system in all the world, and under the Johnson administration I tell you now it is not going to be voluntary.

I am not going to muckrake and I am not going to mudsling, and I am not going to say anything ugly about what anybody else stands for. That is their business. "By their acts ye shall know them; by their words ye shall judge them."

But don't expect your boy to be willing to go and die in the trenches for you, don't be willing to expect the leader of this country to exercise prudence and caution and judgment and experience for you if you sit back there in your rocking chair on November 3d and don't even go and exercise your great heritage, your great privilege of voting.

So as I leave to go back to that locked gate behind those big black bars, where the White House sits, and I will meet in the morning and get some spiritual strength

from one of the great men of this United States—as I go back there tonight, I am not even going to ask you to vote for Lyndon Johnson.

I am going to ask you to vote for the person that your own conscience tells you is best for your country, not your party, not yourself, but best for your country, because when you vote for what is best for your country, you will vote for what is best for yourself.

Let's preserve this Nation as our forefathers intended it should be—a nation of peace with honor; a nation of prosperity for all; a nation where all men are treated equally and where there is special privilege for none.

Thank you.

NOTE: The President spoke at 10:10 p.m. in the Fifth Regiment Armory in Baltimore. His opening words referred to Senator Daniel B. Brewster of Maryland and Mayor T. R. McKeldin of Baltimore. During the course of his remarks he referred to, among others, Thomas D'Alesandro III, Maryland's city campaign chairman, Herbert R. O'Connor, Jr., State campaign cochairman, Millard E. Tydings, U.S. Senator from Maryland for many years, and his son Joseph D. Tydings, Democratic candidate for Senator, Representatives Carlton R. Sickles, George H. Fallon, Edward A. Garmatz, Samuel N. Friedel, and Clarence D. Long, of Maryland, Harry R. Hughes and Hervey G. Machen, Democratic candidates for Representative, Governor J. Millard Tawes of Maryland, Maryland's Attorney General Thomas B. Finan and Comptroller Louis L. Goldstein, Dr. Mildred Otenasek, Democratic national committeewoman, Francis Keller, State campaign cochairman, Philip Goodman, Maryland's city campaign chairman, former Senator George L. Radcliffe of Maryland, and Royce Hanson, Democratic candidate for Representative.

———————

[*Earlier, at 9:27 p.m., the President spoke informally in Auxiliary Hall at the Armory. The text of his remarks follows.*]

Ladies and gentlemen, boys and girls:

Your hospitality touches me deeply. I am so grateful that my schedule was such that I could come back here to the great city of

Baltimore. I have so many fond memories of this city and of this great State and their loyalty to me through the years.

I saw Tom D'Alesandro out there tonight and I served with his father in the House. I saw Herbert O'Connor out there tonight and I served with his father in the Senate. I saw Joe Tydings out there tonight, and I served with his father in the Senate, and I am going to have him over there next year.

This is Saturday night, and after next Saturday night there will just be 3 more days before you make one of the most important decisions that you ever made in your life. I don't know whether this is true or not, but I want each of you to seriously consider what all you can do for your country, for yourself, for the city of Baltimore, and for the Free State of Maryland.

On November 3d, next Tuesday a week, you are going to select the leader of your country with all the nations of the world.

You are going to approve of our bipartisan foreign policy, where Senator Arthur Vandenberg worked with President Truman to stop the Communists in Greece and Turkey, where Lyndon Johnson, as Democratic leader, worked with President Eisenhower in the Formosa Strait, where Senator Dirksen worked with President John F. Kennedy on the test ban treaty.

Are you going to throw all that bipartisan foreign policy out the window and let it go down the drain, and follow a new and dangerous course that leads to evils we know not of?

Tonight in America we have 72.5 million people working. Tonight in America we have 20 million people drawing social security. Tonight in America the average wage for manufacturing employees is $104 a week. Tonight in America we have minimum wages that protect our poor.

We have collective bargaining that gives our workingman an equal chance. We have equality for all Americans, and special privilege for none.

We have some of the best education bills any Congress has ever passed. We have some of the best health care bills any Congress ever passed, and we are going to pass medical care when the Congress gets back there, under social security.

We have workmen's compensation, we have unemployment compensation, we have the best social security system in all the world, and we are not about to let it go down the drain by making it voluntary.

So what can you do about it? You can continue a bipartisan foreign policy that has kept us at peace for 20 years, where the leaders of both parties work together. You can continue on a domestic policy that believes in prosperity for all the people. Or you can vote Republican.

I am not here to tell you how to vote or for whom to vote. I am just here tonight to tell you how I stand and what I believe in, and what I work for, and I hope that you good people will exercise your obligation. I hope you will live up to your responsibility.

I know if your boy had to leave and go to war you would go to the station with him. I know if there were an emergency where your country needed your help you would give your last drop of blood.

But I want to tell you that November 3d is going to be a red letter day, and you are either going to do your duty and exercise your priceless heritage, or you are going to be sorry. So please go to the polls and vote for what your conscience tells you in your heart is right.

I hope that you will give me a young, intelligent, dedicated, United States Senator to work with me, and we need Joe Tydings. One of the best helpers that I have in the United States Senate is my beloved friend

Danny Brewster, a great Democrat, and there has been no better friend of mine and no greater leader of the Democratic Party than His Excellency, your great Governor, Millard Tawes.

You don't know how proud it made me feel, and how wonderful I think it was of Baltimore that when your President came over to visit you tonight that your own mayor, Mayor McKeldin, was out there to greet him, and I want to thank you for it.

Eleven months and 2 days ago we had a terrible tragedy in America, and on a moment's notice I had to assume the Presidency. I didn't have time to make a study in a library. I didn't have time to go out and get a lot of advice from wise men. But I said to you people of America that night that with God's help and with your prayers, I would do the best I could, and I have done that for 11 months.

If you want a foreign policy that is prudent, that is careful, that is cautious, that is fair, if you want peace in the world, then I will give you the best efforts I know how.

If you believe that every man and woman who wants a job ought to have one, and that every boy and girl born in the United States has a right to an education, and that all men and women ought to have equal opportunity, and special privilege for none, then I will give you that under the Johnson administration.

So let's just don't talk, and let's just don't yell and let's just don't brag. Let's talk to our kinfolks and our uncles and our cousins and our aunts, and let's go do our duty November 3d and vote Democratic.

NOTE: See note on page 1421.

704   Letter to the President, Board of Commissioners, on Crime in the District of Columbia.   *October 25, 1964*

[Released October 25, 1964. Dated October 20, 1964]

Dear Mr. Tobriner:

Thank you for your letter discussing both the problem of crime in the District of Columbia and the various programs in operation to combat crime in the District. As your letter makes clear, crime within our cities is basically a responsibility for local authorities, but one in which the Federal Government must be helpful and cooperative. I am glad that in the District there has been such cooperation and that officials and citizens are working together to solve the District's crime problems.

I am particularly pleased that the District's major effort to reduce juvenile delinquency is now underway. Early this year in recommending the District budget to the Congress, I stated that the District—and the Nation—faced no more important social challenge than the increase in juvenile crime. I pledged my support then to the most comprehensive attack on this evil that could be devised.

You may be assured that this Administration will continue to stimulate, aid and encourage the District efforts in every way. This Nation deserves and must have a capital city which is in the very front rank in respect for law by its citizens, and in safety for its residents and visitors.

Sincerely,

LYNDON B. JOHNSON

[Honorable Walter N. Tobriner, Commissioner, District of Columbia Government, Washington, D.C.]

1423

NOTE: In his letter, dated October 19 and released with the President's reply, Mr. Tobriner pointed out that juvenile offenders were largely responsible for the increased crime rate in the District of Columbia, and that a major effort was under way to reduce juvenile delinquency. He stated that with financial and other assistance from the President's Committee on Juvenile Delinquency and Youth Crime, officials and citizens were cooperating in a comprehensive and coordinated attack, and that "adult as well as juvenile crime will decrease as we improve employment opportunities, remedy the inadequacies in education and training, provide more decent homes and better home environments, improve recreation and health facilities." Programs being developed under the Economic Opportunity Act of 1964, he said, would also provide vital assistance in reducing the District's crime rate.

The Board of Commissioners, he added, had sought and secured appropriations to enlarge the effective force of the Police Department and to institute a police cadet program to increase the supply of qualified police officers. He said that the Commissioners and the Police Department "are diligently seeking to increase the respect for and appreciation of the Department by citizens and citizen groups," and that a Community Relations Unit had recently been created to work with local citizens on programs to ameliorate conditions which lead to crime.

Mr. Tobriner expressed appreciation for the support of the administration, particularly the summer job programs for disadvantaged youth and efforts to reduce school dropouts. He concluded by stating that with the "continuation of your support and that of so many members of your administration, we are confident that Washington can and will become a pacesetter for the Nation."

705   Statement by the President on the Agreement With the Soviet Union for the Exchange of Weather Information. *October 25, 1964*

I AM HAPPY to be able to announce that we have reached an agreement with the Soviet Union for the exchange of weather information between Washington and Moscow.

This is a good step forward in building the World Weather System to which I repledged American cooperation last June at Holy Cross College.

This cooperative effort has grown out of the beginning made by President Kennedy in his speech to the United Nations on September 25, 1961. He said then that our country ". . . would propose cooperative efforts between all nations in weather predictions and eventually in weather control. . . ."

In 1961 and 1962, the United Nations called upon the World Meteorological Organization to develop a program of cooperation that would strengthen weather service and research. The Organization responded with a concept of a world weather system and has designated Moscow and Washington as two world weather centers.

The United States and the Soviet Union have been working out an agreement to exchange weather information over a direct communications link between the two capitals. The agreement we have now reached provides for the exchange on a reciprocal basis of weather information gathered by satellites. For a short initial period conventional data will be exchanged. We hope that other member nations of the World Meteorological Organization may eventually participate in the exchange of data over this weather link.

We expect that the formal terms of this new agreement will be released next week at a meeting in New York of the United Nations Committee on Peaceful Uses of Outer Space.

In addition, I expect to be able in the near future to announce the opening of the world weather center in Washington. We have already been exchanging test transmissions on an experimental basis. We know that the new link, when in operation, will be a substantial step forward in speeding the transmission of valuable weather data in both directions. The American weatherman and the American public will immediately benefit from these improvements.

I take this opportunity to release a letter that I have sent to Secretary Hodges. This letter emphasizes my continuing support for international cooperation in weather matters, and my desire to ensure that all departments and agencies of the United States Government do their full part in support of international weather activities.

October 23, 1964

Dear Mr. Secretary:

As you are fully aware, we have over the past few years witnessed a substantial increase in international cooperation in weather matters. The nations of the world are exchanging meteorological data and pooling their activities to a greater extent than ever before to provide early warnings of severe storms and other calamities of nature, to further the safety and efficiency of air and sea travel, and to promote industry, commerce, and agriculture within their own borders. The most recent significant event in international weather cooperation has been the agreement among the member nations of the World Meteorological Organization to accelerate the development of a World Weather System. When the System is brought into full operation, it will bring substantial benefits both to our own coun-

try and to the less developed nations of the world. I have pledged the cooperation of the United States in the development of the System because of its importance to us and to the world at large.

A number of Federal departments and agencies are presently involved in international activities in meteorology and have a concern with one aspect or another of United States international meteorological policies. With the growth of international cooperation in weather matters, and particularly with the quickening of international efforts to develop a World Weather System, there must be even more continuing consultation among them and effective coordination of their activities than has been necessary up to now.

I therefore direct that you take such action as you may deem necessary to bring the interested Federal departments and agencies into closer consultation and coordination with regard to international activities in meteorology and the formulation of United States international meteorological policies and programs to ensure that the United States will continue to make a significant contribution to international meteorological activities.

Sincerely,

LYNDON B. JOHNSON

[The Honorable Luther H. Hodges, Secretary of Commerce, Washington, D.C.]

NOTE: The text of the Memorandum of Understanding and the accompanying Protocol is published in the Department of State Bulletin (vol. 51, p. 792).

706 Statement by the President: National First Voters Week. *October 25, 1964*

I HAVE designated the week of October 25, 1964, as National First Voters Week. The purpose is to bring to public attention both the promises and the problems of our youngest generation of voters.

Nearly 10 million new voters are eligible to vote in the forthcoming national elections for the first time. These young citizens form the most energetic, enthusiastic, and forward-looking group of all our people.

Our forefathers won for us—and preserved for us—the precious right to a voice in the selection of those who will guide the destinies of our land. It is heartening that this heritage is being honored by the millions of today's young Americans who are participating so actively, so intelligently, and with so great a sense of responsibility in the campaigns and elections this year.

Our hope for a better America lies today, as always, with the talents, wisdom, and will of young Americans. They embody the ideals and devotion, the strength and courage which we shall need in the years ahead to combat and overcome poverty, disease, ignorance, and division in our own land—and to meet the stern tests of this century's contests between freedom and totalitarianism. By encouraging these young men and women to exercise their precious heritage of the franchise, and especially by encouraging those eligible for the first time to do so, we hope to lay the firmest possible foundation for America's future safety and security.

The strength and character of America's youth have been misjudged in many generations past, but let none miscalculate or misrepresent the fiber of this generation for they are a solid rock on which America's future rests firmly. We pray for them that the course of their Nation will permit their generation to serve freedom only in the battles of peace and never in the battles of war.

NOTE: The period October 25–October 31, 1964, was designated National First Voters Week by Proclamation 3624 (29 F.R. 14471; 3 CFR, 1964 Supp.).

707 Statement by the President Announcing a Series of Statements on Economic Issues. *October 25, 1964*

GREAT ISSUES lie before the country for decision. The supreme issues of life and death are in the field of foreign policy—as Red China's bomb and the changes in Moscow so forcibly remind us.

But the strength that underlies our world leadership is anchored in the prosperity and stability of the American economy. Our 4-year record of strong and balanced economic advance knows no parallel in this or any other country. Maintaining this great prosperity is a vital task that challenges our free society.

So the American people have every right to do more than just "look at the record." They have every right to ask where I stand on the key economic issues that will determine the health and growth of our economy.

In a series of brief White House statements over the next few days, I will outline my position on some of the most important economic issues before the country today. I

shall deal with the following topics:
1. Maintaining Prosperity
2. Monetary Policy for Stability and Growth
3. Strengthening Our Balance of Payments
4. Responsible and Effective Fiscal Policy
5. Further Tax Reduction
6. Strengthening State-Local Government
7. Improving the Tax System
8. Expanding World Trade
9. Promoting Responsible Price-Wage Decisions
10. Achieving Full Employment

NOTE: For the individual statements on the 10 topics, see Items 708, 714, 722–724, 730, 731, 739, 740, and 743.

708   Presidential Statement No. 1 on Economic Issues: Maintaining Prosperity.   *October 25, 1964*

1. OUR PROSPECTS for maintaining prosperity start from the solid base of a 44-month expansion that shows no signs of faltering:

—Nearly 5 million new nonfarm jobs have been created since early 1961.

—Our total production is now expanding at a 5 percent annual rate.

—Profits after taxes are up more than 65 percent since early 1961.

—Wages and salaries after taxes are up nearly $60 billion.

2. Excesses and speculation have been avoided:

—Prices and costs have been more stable than in any other industrial country in the world.

—Inventories have been rising very modestly, far less rapidly than sales.

—Credit expansion has been moderate, and the money supply has risen less than the Nation's output.

—Expansion of plant capacity has been closely geared to developing markets.

3. This unprecedented period of peacetime prosperity has broken the historical rhythm of recessions after every 2 or 3 years of expansion. It stands in sharp contrast to the recent history of recessions in 1953–54, 1957–58, and 1960.

4. It would be wrong to say that recessions are a relic of the past. But we are convinced that recessions are not inevitable, and sustained prosperity is our realistic objective. Many of the free economies of Western Europe have gone more than a decade without a business decline.

5. The best way to avoid recessions is to maintain strong and steady forward momentum. A continued partnership of Government and private enterprise can supply that momentum:

—by continued restraint in costs and prices, combined with steady progress in modernization, improved management, and cost-cutting investments;

—by further tax reduction, with excises first in line, carefully timed and tailored to maintain continued growth and to head off recession;

—by monetary policies to provide adequate credit for steady expansion without inflation;

—and, finally, by a spirit of constructive cooperation, not angry antagonism, between Government and private enterprise.

6. A good offense—a vigorous program for sustaining prosperity—is our best defense against recession. But *if* recession were to threaten, a well-timed tax cut would be one

of our most effective measures. And within the bounds of efficient Government expenditures, a speedup of public works and other Federal outlays could also take up economic slack.

NOTE: For a statement by the President announcing a series of statements on economic issues, see Item 707.

709 Remarks in Boca Raton at the Dedication of Florida Atlantic University. *October* 25, 1964

President Williams:

There is something about this Florida air, clean and alive, that reminds me of Texas. There is much similarity between Texas and Florida that has nothing to do with oranges and grapefruit, but it has to do with people and climate. The sun is warm, the people are friendly, and the tomorrows are always bright with hope.

Thank you, President Williams, for your gracious welcome. Thank you, too, Dean Pilcher and Dean Miller. It is good for me to be with two of the great Senators of our time, your own senior Senator and my longtime friend Spessard Holland. Florida citizens have shown good sense and sound judgment in keeping this good man in the United States Senate where he can serve his State and his Nation. And I am so glad today to see my old colleague and my loyal friend for many years, your brilliant, young Senator George Smathers. He has distinguished Florida by his record and his ability in the United States Senate.

Thanks, Governor Bryant, for your being here with me, too. I am so proud to call you my friend, and I want to say here in Florida how much all the people of the Nation regard you as a good American.

There are few congressional delegations that have more competent representation than Florida's. My friends Paul Rogers and Dante Fascell, and Claude Pepper, are in the forefront of all that is valuable for your State and your country. I was happy to have welcome me outstanding citizens of this great State, like Warren Goodrich, Tom Fleming, and Mrs. Annette Baker.

I would like to pay tribute to the consistent leadership of the Florida State cabinet. I commend the people of Florida for men like Tom Adams, Ed Larson, Ray Green, Jim Kynes, Tom Bailey, and Doyle Conner.

This is a proud occasion, President Williams, for you and for your colleagues, for this community, and for Florida, and for me. It is always exciting to dedicate a new university.

The Good Book tells us that "one generation passeth away and another generation cometh," and if I speak with special feeling about this, it is partly because I was a teacher once. I like to think sometimes that I still am. This feeling also goes back 30 years to my work with the National Youth Administration. My job was to see that thousands of boys and girls were not denied an education because of the financial hardship of their families.

As a tenant farmer's son, I almost didn't get any college education, and I know how much difference a full education makes. For me, it was a passport out of poverty.

Not long after I became President, I was having dinner one night with the Canadian Prime Minister and Secretary Rusk, Dean Bundy and a number of other people. They were talking about their college days. Finally, I had to give the toast of the evening, and I said, "It is such a privilege to be here this evening, with three graduates of Harvard, two of Yale, four from Princeton, five Rhodes scholars, and one graduate of the San Marcos State Teachers College."

So it means a great deal to me, President Williams, that you would ask me to come here today, and give me this honor. Your plans for Florida Atlantic University are drawn from the experience of the past, and they meet the specifications of the future. You reflect in these plans what I see of the new future for education in America, and particularly in our part of America.

There are three elements in it.

First, it must be a new future of full equity in educational opportunity for all Americans.

Second, it must be a future of new learning to meet new demands.

Third, it must be a future of new methods which are necessary to teach much more to many more.

I wish that as we meet here on this Sabbath Day, in all the freedom, luxury, and prosperity that is ours, that we could count the blessings that are ours and somehow bring it home to each of us that we are no stronger than the weakest among us.

The great privilege and the responsibility of your next President of the United States, whoever he may be, will be to participate in two great new prospects, and I would hope that the modern, intelligent, imaginative, patriotic Floridian would furnish great leadership in these prospects.

The first prospect is the conquest of outer space. I would remind you that we cannot be first on earth and second in space.

The second prospect is the development of the inner man. I believe, I genuinely and sincerely believe, that every American boy and girl born under this flag has an un-

qualified right to all the education that he or she can make good use of, and a responsibility to get it. Now, if in our local communities we can make adequate provision for all the classrooms we need, and we can man all those classrooms with adequately trained and properly paid teachers, well and good, because the best government is the government that is closest to the people.

But if we find somehow in our economic operations that it is necessary to have some State support, then before we turn our back on realizing the ultimate potential of each individual, we must have the State join with us.

And rather than to sit idly by and do a mediocre job, or only do part of a job, and ultimately wind up, in the classification of 120 nations, way down that list, then it is necessary to draw upon the National Government to support and to supplement, and to do whatever may be required to see that every Florida, every Mississippi, every Alabama, every Texas, every New York boy and girl has all the training up here in this technological age that he can properly take, because the competition in this century is great and is dangerous.

Now, so far we have not recognized in this country either this right of every boy and girl, all the little ones sitting at that fence, to all the education they can take, nor have we recognized this responsibility.

Almost a million boys and girls drop out of school each year, or they are pushed out by forces beyond their control. They face a jobless future. Every year more than 100,-000 school graduates with proven ability drop out and do not even go on to college for one reason: because they cannot afford it.

How many world leaders, how many great admirals, how many imaginative generals, how many Presidents and Senators and Congressmen and educators and presidents of great universities we lose we do not know.

But we do know that more than 21 million youngsters now in grade school—21 million—1 out of every 9—will end their education short of college in a technological age when all the skill that they can acquire is not necessary just for them, but is essential to our survival. We do know that 1 out of 9 is going down the drain unless you do something about it.

Science and technology have moved so swiftly that advanced education is no longer a luxury just to be enjoyed by the child of the banker, or by the children of fortunate families. In this afternoon of our life, as you sit here, I say to you that it is a necessity for every American boy, and I repeat and try to drum it into all of our heads that it is the right of every American boy and girl.

To deny it to the children of poverty not only denies the most elementary democratic equality, it perpetuates poverty as a national weakness. And it denies our democracy and our great free enterprise system of government. It denies them the educated citizens that we must have if we are to lead and stay in the forefront of the other 120 nations in the world.

So, what of it? We must, therefore, prepare the next generation for the great decisions that it will have to make.

When I was a boy—my grandfather moved away, 50 years before I discovered America, from the prairies of Texas to the hills in order that he could enjoy more freedom. He wanted to get away from the trains that passed through every night and disturbed him. He went out into a new, uncharted wilderness, and he chose well, because he settled Johnson City almost 100 years ago and there hasn't a train come through there since.

But in the day and age now in which we live, it is not the question that the oldtimers

said when they did bring the first train to the prairie where they were, "They will never get it started, and if they get it started, they will never get it stopped."

Here in the State where we will send our first American to the moon, we must think in terms of the 21st century and the 22d century, and not the 18th century and the 19th century.

And ask yourself tonight whether you want your grade school Florida boys, and you want your high school Florida girls competing with the ruthless Communists who have Ph. D.'s, and expect them to outproduce them, to outthink them, and to outlead them.

In the last century we decided in this country, in a very forward step, on a certain amount of free education for all children. Well, that decision, that decision more than any other, put America in the forefront of civilization's advance in the world.

So I think it is time now, I think it is past time, for a new, adventurous, imaginative, courageous breakthrough, for a new revolution in education in America.

I am old enough to remember some of the voices of gloom and doom that opposed universal free education. I remember some of my State legislators talking about the loss of their freedoms when we passed a compulsory attendance law in our State.

But I would remind you that the freedom that we lost by educating our children is nothing to compare to the freedom we would lose if we didn't educate them.

Universal free education through high school—that was the decision of a century ago. But it no longer meets the test of the current times. The high school boys are not going to keep the Cape Canaverals functioning in the year 2000. So our goal must be to open the doors of higher education to all who can possible meet that standard and qualify.

The proud achievement of the GI bill—and it doesn't seem to me that you ought to have to go into uniform and go to boot camp, and spend 2 or 3 years in the service in order for your Government to have an interest in your education. And yet there is not a Member of Congress today that would look back on that GI bill and say, "We made a mistake in making that great adventure and that great decision."

The GI bill challenges us to programs of loans and scholarships enabling every young man and woman who has the ability to move beyond the high school level. So I think we just must not rest until each child—GI or no GI, boy or girl, rich or poor—has the opportunity to get the kind of education that he needs and that his country needs for him to have in order to defend it.

And I think it is a little wiser policy to do a little better planning, to take the boy out of the cotton field and train him in his normal high school years and his college years to develop himself, rather than to issue an emergency order and jerk him off overnight and send him on a train to a boot camp and then try to teach him how to fire a missile or handle a B–52 over Moscow without much notice.

So there is no real disagreement, I think, in this country about what I am talking about. We all want very much to do these things. But we are not doing them. We have stumbled in our efforts. Why? Because of various differences, because of lack of initiative, because of budget problems, because of the differences that we have had regarding segregation, because of the difficulties we have had about the relationship of public and private schools, because of the concern that I referred to a little earlier about local responsibility, and State responsibility, and Federal relationships.

These have been difficult problems. They are still difficult. But if we are going to be the leader of the world, and if we are going to survive in this world, they must be worked out. And we can, and we will, and we must find ways of working cooperatively together to achieve our common purpose.

Now, finally, we must turn the genius of science and technology to the service of education as we have to the service of medicine and other disciplines. The planners of the Florida Atlantic University have placed very special emphasis on bringing significant innovations to the methods of education. You are moving far toward making the partnership between campus and country stronger, so that the harvest of the future will be more fruitful for all of our people.

President Williams, a great challenge awaits you and this faculty. You are starting here today new, which I think gives you infinite opportunity. The road ahead is, as I must have implied, not easy for a new university. But I urge you to remember the admonition: "Let us not be weary in well doing; for in due season we shall reap." The past is your teacher, but it holds you in no bondage.

So I join you this evening in dedicating Florida Atlantic University to the responsibility of preparing the sons and daughters of Florida to meet the future, to meet it on its own terms, and on yours.

A great son of Georgia came to Texas to become one of the early Presidents of the Republic of Texas. He said in words that I shall always remember, and that I would hope you would not forget: "Education is the guardian genius of democracy. Education is the only dictator that free men recognize. And education is the only ruler that free men desire."

Now I must go along. I want to tell you what a pleasure it has been to be here with you. You are one of the modern States of America. The rest of the country looks to you folks who have come here from all the States of the Union, and those of you that were born here to lead us into a fuller and better life.

And your sons that represent you in the temples of justice and who are your spokesmen in the legislative chambers of the Nation, are among the most dependable and most enlightened. I know that you would want to be able to say that about your grandsons and about your grandchildren's children, too.

So I implore you to recognize before it is too late that while the Soviet Union can put up Sputnik I, and while we are debating about it, Sputnik II is saying "Beep, beep, beep" in the sky, that we are sometimes mighty slow to start, but mighty hard to stop. We don't need argumentation about the desirability of preparing our children to think and to act with judgment.

But remember, whether it is the man that picks up the telephone on the end of the "hot line" that is calling from Moscow, or whether it is the man that sits there with the responsibility of his thumb close to that button, who must act on a moment's notice, that no man's judgment on any given question is any better than the information he has on that question. And he can't get all the information he needs in this space age hunting and fishing. He can't get all that he needs on the football field or the baseball diamond. He has to get it in grade school, high school, in college, in graduate work, because Americans must never be second to anyone.

NOTE: The President spoke at 5:27 p.m. at the Florida Atlantic University at Boca Raton after being awarded an honorary degree of doctor of humane letters. His opening words referred to Kenneth R. Williams, president of the University. Later he referred to Palmer C. Pilcher, dean of Academic Affairs, and Roger Miller, dean of Administrative Affairs, of the University, and Senators Spessard L. Holland and George A. Smathers, Governor Farris Bryant, and Representatives Paul Rogers, Dante Fascell, and Claude Pepper, all of Florida, Warren Goodrich, chairman of the Florida State Democratic Executive Committee, Thomas F. Fleming, State Democratic campaign coordinator, Mrs. Annette Baker, State Democratic committeewoman, and the following members of the Florida State cabinet: Tom Adams, Secretary of State, J. Edwin Larson, Treasurer, Ray E. Green, Comptroller, James Kynes, Executive Assistant to the Governor, Thomas D. Bailey, Superintendent of Public Instruction, and Doyle E. Conner, Commissioner of Agriculture.

---

710 Remarks in Miami Upon Receiving a Book Relating to the Interama Cultural and Trade Center. *October 25, 1964*

Governor, Senator Smathers, Senator Holland, Congressman Fascell:

I think this is a generous thing for you to do, and very thoughtful. I know the deep interest that each of you have taken. I know how you feel about it, Governor.

I am happy that it seems to be on the way to a favorable solution. Claude Pepper talks to me about it every day, and I am going to have a little more time now to do something else. Senator Holland and Senator Smathers have given it top priority on their list.

At the White House the other day we talked to them and asked them to reexplore it. I think this is not only going to be a wonderful thing for the United States Government, and all the Western Hemisphere, but I think it will be a great thing for the progressive and forward-looking State of Florida. For some of you, it is a dream that has come true.

As long as I am in a position to do so, I will try to contribute what I can to what all of you have envisioned as a most worthwhile and public project.

Thank you for this. I will treasure it.

NOTE: The President spoke at 7:40 p.m. in the Terrace Room at the Dupont Plaza Hotel in Miami,

Fla. His opening words referred to Governor Farris Bryant, Senators George A. Smathers and Spessard L. Holland, and Representative Dante B. Fascell, all of Florida.

The book presented to the President contained an illustrated description of "Interama," a cultural and trade center for Latin American countries, under construction in Miami.

711   Executive Order 11186 Establishing the Federal Development Planning Committee for Appalachia.   *October* 25, 1964

WHEREAS representatives of the Federal Government and of the Governors of the States in the Appalachian region have been cooperating in the preparation of plans and programs for the long-range development of Appalachia; and

WHEREAS such plans have provided for coordinated action by Federal, State, and local agencies in carrying out programs to further the development of Appalachia and to facilitate and encourage private investment in that area; and

WHEREAS the Governors of various States of the Appalachian region have requested that such cooperation be continued; and

WHEREAS the proper discharge by the Federal Government of its responsibilities to the people of the Appalachian region requires that such cooperation be continued and that related planning activities of the Federal Government be effectively coordinated:

Now, THEREFORE, by virtue of the authority vested in me as President of the United States, it is ordered as follows:

SECTION 1. Establishment of Committee. (a) There is hereby established the Federal Development Planning Committee for Appalachia (hereinafter referred to as the "Committee").

(b) The Committee shall be composed of the following: (1) a Chairman, who shall be appointed by the President, (2) members,

one of whom shall be designated by and represent each of the following-named officers, respectively: the Secretary of the Interior, the Secretary of Agriculture, the Secretary of Commerce, the Secretary of Labor, the Secretary of Health, Education, and Welfare, the Secretary of the Army, the Housing and Home Finance Administrator, and the Director of the Office of Economic Opportunity, and (3) a member who shall represent the Tennessee Valley Authority and shall be designated by the board of directors of the Authority.

(c) The Chairman may request any Federal agency head not referred to in subsection (b), above, to designate a representative to participate in meetings of the Committee concerned with matters of substantial interest to such agency head.

SEC. 2. Functions of the Chairman. (a) The Chairman shall cooperate with representatives designated by the Governors of States in the Appalachian region in:

(1) Fostering surveys and studies to provide data required for the preparation of plans and programs for the development of Appalachia;

(2) Preparing coordinated plans for the development of Appalachia deemed appropriate to carry out existing statutory responsibilities of Federal, State, or local agencies. Such plans shall be designed to promote

1433

optimum benefits from the expenditure of Federal, State, and local funds and to facilitate and promote private investment in the development of Appalachia; and

(3) Preparing legislative and other recommendations with respect to both short-range and long-range programs and projects for Federal, State, or local agencies.

(b) With the approval of the agency head concerned the Chairman may arrange for recommended surveys and studies to be made by any Federal agency with respect to matters falling within the existing statutory authorities and responsibilities of that agency.

SEC. 3. Functions of the Committee. The Committee shall:

(a) Advise the Chairman with respect to (1) surveys and studies needed for the preparation of development plans, (2) the concrete proposals for surveys and studies developed by the Chairman in cooperation with the representatives of the Governors, and (3) desirable development objectives and programs for the Appalachian region.

(b) Receive, review, and comment on all tentative development plans or other tentative recommendations developed by the Chairman in cooperation with the representatives of the Governors; and

(c) Receive and consider final plans and recommendations and transmit them, with its own comments, to the President and the heads of interested Federal agencies.

SEC. 4. Administrative arrangements. (a) If the Chairman of the Committee does not concurrently hold other compensated office or employment under the United States, he shall receive such compensation under this order as shall be fixed in accordance with the standards and procedures of the Classification Act of 1949, as amended.

(b) The Department of Commerce is hereby designated as the agency which shall provide administrative services for the Committee and for the Chairman.

(c) Each Federal agency the head of which is referred to in Section 1(b) of this order shall, as may be necessary, furnish assistance to the Committee in accordance with the provisions of Section 214 of the Act of May 3, 1945 (59 Stat. 134; 31 U.S.C. 691).

(d) Each Federal agency shall, consonant with law and within the limits of available funds, cooperate with the Committee and with the Chairman in carrying out their functions under this order. Such cooperation shall include, as may be appropriate, (1) furnishing relevant available information, (2) making studies and preparing reports pursuant to requests of the Chairman, (3) in connection with the development of programs and priorities of the agency, giving full consideration to any plans and recommendations for the development of Appalachia, including recommendations made by the Committee, and (4) advising on the work of the Committee as the Chairman may from time to time request.

SEC. 5. Construction. Nothing in this order shall be construed as subjecting any Federal agency, or any function vested by law in, or assigned pursuant to law to, any Federal agency, to the authority of the Committee or the Chairman, or as abrogating or restricting any such function in any manner.

LYNDON B. JOHNSON

The White House,
    October 23, 1964

NOTE: On the same day the White House, in announcing the establishment of the Federal Development Planning Committee for Appalachia, made public a portion of the President's letter to John Sweeney, Special Assistant to Under Secretary of Commerce Franklin D. Roosevelt, Jr., appointing him Chairman of the Committee. In his letter the President said: "From your previous work in connection with the problems of Appalachia, you are familiar with the tasks confronting the Committee. Also, you are aware of my concern for the people of Appalachia and of my deep and continuing inter-est in the economic development of the Appalachian region."

712   Remarks in Orlando, Florida.
October 26, 1964

Governor Bryant, Mayor Carr, my old friend Martin Andersen, my fellow Americans:

I would like for the record to show this morning, plainly and clearly, and I want to say it loud and clear: I like Orlando! After that warm and friendly welcome last night, and your wonderful hospitality this morning, I am quite ready to accept Orlando citizenship.

It is good to have your next Governor on this platform with me, Haydon Burns, an able, energetic public servant, who can do what Florida needs to have done for the future of this great State.

I am deeply indebted to my old and true friend, Governor Farris Bryant, for his gracious and wonderful introduction, and for his friendship through the years. My long-time friend, George Smathers, has been so kind to me on this trip that I am glad that Florida has the good judgment to send him to the United States Senate and to keep him there. Spessard Holland, your senior Senator, has been my friend ever since I went to Congress, and there is no more dedicated, no more honest, or no more effective public servant in Washington than Spessard Holland.

I am so pleased and proud to receive the full endorsement of the great Florida State cabinet—Tom Adams, Ed Larson, Ray Green, Jim Kynes, Tom Bailey, and Doyle Conner. And I am mighty pleased to have welcome me outstanding citizens of Florida like Warren Goodrich, Tom Fleming, and Mrs. Annette Baker.

I am glad to be here in Orlando. I can now understand why Martin Andersen says it is a privilege to live in central Florida. And it is also a privilege to visit with you as your President, and with your help November 3d I will visit with you again someday.

When I come back, I will still be with Senator Spessard Holland, because I know you are going to keep him up there, that fine Florida habit of sending back Senator Holland to Washington where he does so much for the people of all of this State.

I understand that another colleague of mine, Syd Herlong, will also be back. We need and we hope that you will send Tom Kenney to represent you in Washington. You need him in Washington and the free world needs him in Washington.

You have far too much at stake not to send the strongest possible team to your Nation's Capital.

In the last 4 years, per capita income in Florida has gone up twice as fast as the previous 4 years, and unemployment has been cut almost in half. Our new tax cut will increase family income in Florida by an average of $374 and add $79 million to local revenues, and create 52,000 new jobs for this progressive State. But this abundance is not an end in itself.

The real test of America is the larger purpose to which we turn our prosperity. We must, in the words of the Bible, "Learn to do well; seek judgment, relieve the oppressed, judge the fatherless, plead for the widow."

In that pursuit, we will give special attention to the problems of the older Americans in our country. Today there are 18 million

Americans over the age of 64. By 1980 there will be 25 million. We must make sure that these older Americans can spend their later years in security and dignity, and not deprivation and fear.

That is one of the major choices in this election. The issue was clearly drawn in this State. Programs to protect older people against the crushing cost of illness were attacked. The entire social security system supported by every President of both parties has been threatened. To strike at the hopes of older Americans is not courage, and when you make social security voluntary, you do strike at the social security system. It is callousness; it is not conservative. It is a radical departure from the whole course of American policy.

A voluntary plan would destroy social security as we know it. The payment of benefits to older Americans depends on receiving premiums from working Americans. So a voluntary program would drastically cut these premiums. The entire system would soon be on the edge of bankruptcy. The protection you have counted on over the years would be menaced.

I intend as your President to follow a different course.

I offer a new charter of opportunity for older Americans. We will make constructive use of the wisdom and the energies of older Americans as volunteers in the Peace Corps and our war on poverty.

We will end discrimination against older Americans in Federal employment.

We will increase benefits under social security to the 20 million now receiving benefits, and to the 2 million receiving old-age assistance.

We will expand our housing programs for the 50 percent of our people 65 and over that are living in substandard homes or housing unsuited to their needs.

We will provide medical care through social security to help 17 million Americans meet the crushing cost of hospitalization.

With this charter of opportunity, we can move toward the day when advancing years will bring a renewal of hope and personal happiness.

These programs are not charity and they are not handouts, and they are not undeserved blessings.

They are insurance programs, paid for over years of labor. They are a recognition of the fact that a prosperous Nation has an obligation to those who have fought its wars, to those who have built its industry, to those who have developed its country, and to those who have fed its people.

And they will help all America by giving older citizens a chance to keep contributing to the life of the Nation.

This is your choice, a choice between steady progress, building on the gains and the programs of the past, or tearing down all that we have done, leaving our citizens to face a retirement of fear and hopelessness and poverty.

I have no doubt which course the Florida people will take. One week from tomorrow you, the masters—not the servants—will go to the polls and select the leadership for this country and for the free world for the next 4 years.

I think you want responsible leadership. I think you want experienced leadership. I think you want prudent leadership.

I think you want a bipartisan foreign policy, where the Democrats and the Republicans can work together, as Senator Arthur Vandenberg worked with Harry Truman, as Lyndon Johnson worked with Dwight Eisenhower, as Bourke Hickenlooper and Senator Dirksen worked with John Fitzgerald Kennedy.

I think that you want a Nation of peace,

and I think you must understand that in order to have peace, we must be prepared. We cannot be second in space and first in the world, and this is the first space State in the entire Nation. Florida leads all the way.

There are some in the past who have laughed at our space effort. They have talked about basketballs "Beep, beep, beep" in the air. But I say to you that the work that you people in Florida are doing, the work that our Nation is doing, is absolutely essential to our survival. And I think you are going to lead the way, and I think you are going to support the effort on November 3d.

Today your State is prosperous. Today 72 million men and women work in this country. Today the average weekly wage is $104.

Today our farmers have an income that far exceeds what it was when President Kennedy took office.

So I say to you the businessman who last year received $12 billion more after taxes than the year before, the workers who received $60 billion more after taxes than they did the year before, I say it is your duty, it is your obligation, you do it for yourself, when you go to the polls November 3d and vote for peace, vote for space, vote for prosperity, vote for Florida to continue to be one of the fastest growing States in all the Nation, in all the world.

When you select the man as your President to lead you, you want to select the person who loves peace and has the knowledge, has the experience, and has the desire to try to achieve it.

When you select your next President, the man who must sit there with his thumb close to that button, the man who must reach over and answer that telephone, that "hot line," when Moscow is calling, you want to select the person that, in your conscience, you know has the experience, has the judgment, and that you know will do what is best for his country.

We are fortunate in this country to have two great parties. You have a nominee from each party to choose from. You have the intelligence to weigh the experience, to look at the training, to determine in your own mind and in your own heart what is best for your country.

If you will go and vote next Tuesday week for what is best for your country, you will vote for what is best for yourself.

Thank you. Goodby and good luck.

NOTE: The President spoke at 9:45 a.m. at the Colonial Plaza Shopping Center in Orlando. In his opening words he referred to Governor Farris Bryant of Florida, Mayor Robert S. Carr of Orlando, and Martin Andersen, publisher of Orlando daily newspapers. Later he referred to Mayor Haydon Burns of Jacksonville, Democratic candidate for Governor of Florida; Senators George A. Smathers and Spessard L. Holland of Florida; the following members of the Florida State cabinet: Tom Adams, Secretary of State, J. Edwin Larson, Treasurer, Ray E. Green, Comptroller, James Kynes, Executive Assistant to the Governor, Thomas D. Bailey, Superintendent of Public Instruction, and Doyle E. Conner, Commissioner of Agriculture; Warren Goodrich, chairman of the Florida State Democratic Executive Committee, Thomas F. Fleming, State campaign coordinator, Mrs. Annette Baker, State Democratic committeewoman, Representative A. Sydney Herlong, Jr., of Florida, Thomas S. Kenney, Democratic candidate for Representative, Arthur H. Vandenberg, U.S. Senator from Michigan during the Truman administration, Senator Bourke B. Hickenlooper of Iowa, and Senator Everett McK. Dirksen of Illinois.

713 Remarks at a Rally in Hemming Park, Jacksonville, Fla. *October 26, 1964*

Senator Holland:

It is good to be in Jacksonville, the Gateway City. Your welcome is as warm and wonderful as the sun in the sky, and I am grateful for both.

This Gateway City is a vigorous and a growing community. You are adding much to the wealth and the wisdom of Florida, and, indeed, to the whole country. I am very proud to be on this platform with some of the great men that Florida has produced.

Spessard Holland, the senior Senator from Florida, is a wise man and a good man whose life has been dedicated to the service of the people of Florida and the Nation. And I know that Florida's citizens will keep him in the United States Senate where he will continue to serve all Americans.

George Smathers, my old friend, an able Member of the leadership of the Senate, your young and effective Senator. His star is rising in the Nation's Capital. He is distinguishing you by his valuable contributions to our Nation. He is one of the outstanding authorities on this hemisphere, and he does much to promote the relations between the nations in this hemisphere.

Farris Bryant, your Governor, whose record of accomplishment is well known to the whole country, has been my friend, and I have been his admirer, for many years.

Haydon Burns, your own mayor and the next Governor of Florida, has great plans, has told me of his great plans, for the continuing growth of this great State of which he will be the chief executive. So let him help you make this a greater State.

Congressman Billy Matthews and Congressman Charles Bennett are the kind of men who have helped make the Florida congressional delegation one of the most respected of all the States in the Union. Congressman Billy Matthews and Congressman Charles Bennett—Congressman Bennett has earned the gratitude of Jacksonville and his Florida neighbors especially for his work in making the cross-Florida barge canal come closer to reality.

I am glad that one of the first acts of my Presidency was to include in a budget an item to begin the cross-Florida barge canal which someday will mean so much to all the people of this great State. Charlie Bennett has been my good friend and my helpmate. And all the Members of your delegation have always been reasonable and fair in dealing with us.

The members of your State cabinet have earned my gratitude by their endorsement: Tom Adams and Ed Larson, Tom Bailey and Doyle Conner, Ray Green and Jim Kynes. And I want to say this to you: that I earnestly believe that a week from tomorrow, when the polls from all the Nation come in, and we call the roll of States, I believe the progressive and the proud and the thinking people of Florida are going to put Florida in the Democratic column with Johnson and Humphrey.

In the audience today are many municipal leaders from all over Florida. I am mighty pleased to see them. The source of America's strength emerges from the kind of leadership that we have in our cities and in our towns. Nowhere, I think, is this stronger than it is in the State of Florida.

I was thrilled to hear of the good women of this community coming out to the coffee this morning and joining with the lovely Miss Ann Sheridan, who came here, and I am happy that she is here with us today. She is visible evidence of the beauty and the charm of Texas women. I would like the press to note that at this point in my speech I also said that Texas and Florida women are among the Nation's fairest!

I take pride in welcoming to this platform Mrs. Annette Baker and Tom Fleming, and Warren Goodrich and Lacy Mahon. But most of all, I say I am glad to be here with all of you good people, my friends and my fellow Americans.

Four years ago, John Fitzgerald Kennedy came here and said in Jacksonville, "I ask you to join us in starting again to move America forward."

That promise that John Fitzgerald Kennedy made in Jacksonville has been kept by the Kennedy-Johnson administration.

I have come back here today to ask you again, 4 years later, to join with the rest of America to keep the United States on the march.

Will you be at my side in that great cause? Do you want to work with your President to keep our prosperity rising in this country? Shall we work together to advance the cause of freedom and to bring the world closer to a lasting peace?

Well, now, these are the choices that the American people will make next week. I think that all of you should try to understand that in this year 1964 there is just one real issue before you, and you must make your decision Tuesday, a week from now.

I have not come here today to talk about personalities. I have not come here to muckrake, or to mudsling, because when you have no issues to talk, you can always resort to that.

But in this campaign, you have only one big issue, and that issue is this: Whom do you want to lead America? What party and what person do you think gives you the best

opportunity and is likely to give you peace in the world?

To understand what this election means for our future, let's just look for a moment at our past.

This country is less than 200 years old. That is a very short time in the life of nations. In that moment of time, America has created the greatest success story in the history of the world.

Our wonderful democracy has spread to dozens of other countries. Everywhere men hope for freedom. The words "Give me liberty or give me death," the words "All men are created equal," are on their lips and are in their hearts.

And this success rests on many pillars. And none more important than the fact that our great political parties have always represented varied interests and the broad, common judgment of the American people.

I have been in political life for 35 years and I have observed that neither of our parties have spent much of their time preaching hate and preaching division. They have not stood for extreme views or narrow opinions. They have never asked us to tear down the institutions and the achievements of the past.

I remember, as you must remember, the campaign of Wilson, the campaign of Harding, the campaign in more recent years of Roosevelt, and Truman, and Dewey, and Kennedy, and Nixon. But none of these men tried to split our country wide open. None of these men preached hate. None of these men preached division.

Today, for the first time since the Civil War, there is some division in our land, there is some hate in our land. For the first time, the next chapter of the American success story is in question.

For under the wild charges and the impulsive statements of the opposition is hidden a deadly intention that would initiate policies which I think would radically change the American way of life.

Our peace is at stake. Our prosperity is at stake.

In the past 4 years the income of the people of Florida has grown at twice the previous rate. You have built roads that increase tourism and commerce, and this cost $100 million last year. We helped small businessmen keep alive and thriving, and this cost $10 million last year. We made social security payments—they weren't voluntary, either—to some 600,000 older citizens of Florida, and this cost a half billion dollars last year. We helped to provide lunch and milk for a half million schoolchildren, and this cost us $10 million in Florida last year.

The story is the same for schools and hospitals and training programs. Our tax cut will boost your economy. Our fiscal policies have cut unemployment and raised production.

And today we are told that Government must abandon many of these programs and turn them out and back to the States. We are told that we must abandon education; we must make social security voluntary; we should sell the TVA and get rid of public power; we should forget our farm programs.

Well, these are the most radical proposals that have ever been made to the American people. They would destroy the foundation of Florida prosperity. They would destroy the hopes for the future growth of this State.

But even more is at stake. The peace of the world and the survival of your sons and this Nation is really what you are going to decide Tuesday week.

Our strength is not the issue. We are the mightiest, we are the strongest nation on earth.

Our determination is not the issue. We are ready to defend freedom whatever the risk.

Patriotism is not the issue. The true patriotism is that of men who work to preserve and strengthen the Nation, not those who call for reckless acts which would weaken it.

Courage does not consist in threats and bluster. Courage does not consist in rattling your rockets and bluffing with your bombs. Courage does not consist in refusing to try to lessen the danger of war, in withdrawing from all contact with those who don't agree with us. In that way lies disaster.

True courage in this nuclear age lies in the steadfast pursuit of peace, whatever the setbacks, whatever the difficulties, however long the journey.

Here again, if we throw away the tested policies of the past, the bipartisan foreign policy that Arthur Vandenberg helped Harry Truman fashion to stop the Communists in Greece and Turkey, the bipartisan foreign policy that Lyndon Johnson worked with Dwight David Eisenhower in the Strait of Formosa, the test ban treaty that Everett Dirksen worked with John Fitzgerald Kennedy to pass through the Senate—if we throw away these tested policies of the past, we place in danger your lives, the peace of the world, and the future of this Nation.

These are some of the stakes in this election. They, in my judgment, are the highest stakes ever presented to any generation of Americans.

A great American party has fallen into the hands of a narrow and an extreme group. They ask you to tear down the past. They ask you to take unnecessary risks with your future.

There is now, in my judgment, only one course: We must Tuesday week go to the polls and crush this threat to American life. We must restore the health of our two-party system. We must get on with the work of building peace in the world and peace at home.

We must stop this business of talking about each other and quarreling with each other. We must love thy neighbor as thyself. We must preach love and not hate. We must preach unity and not division. We must preach equal opportunity for all Americans and special privilege for no Americans.

We are already the mightiest nation in the world. We have a foreign policy that is tested, that has brought together most of the leaders of both parties. We have a fine space program in which Florida is leading the rest of the Nation. You have a great cross-Florida canal that we are just starting. We have much work that is yet to be done.

Today we have more people working than we have ever had before. They are drawing better wages than they have ever drawn before. Seventy-two million people are working; $104 a week. The businessman and the laboringman are not fighting each other. They are not hating each other. They are working together.

This year we lost less time by strikes than any year in our history except in the middle of a war. We didn't even lose 1 percent of the hours worked in strike, or a half percent, or a quarter percent. We lost fourteen one-hundredths of 1 percent.

I am so glad that I sent a message just 2 or 3 days ago and General Motors and UAW have finally settled their differences and they will all be back to work soon. What does this do when we reason together, as the Good Book says, instead of divide? The corporations of the country this year made $12 billion more after taxes than they did last year. The people who worked for those companies made $60 billion more after taxes than they made last year.

So why do we want to endanger the system that has taken us 30 years to build, with unemployment compensation, with social security, with the development of our resources, with our fine space program, and let it all go down the drain in a moment of an election year? I don't think you are going to do it.

I repeat: There are just two issues—and only one real, important one, and that is peace in the world, because if we get wiped out with an atomic holocaust there won't be anybody here to have any prosperity. So what you must decide between now and next Tuesday is whose thumb do you want to be close to that nuclear button; whose hand do you want to reach over and pick up that "hot line" telephone when they say, "Moscow calling"?

When you decide those questions, based on your judgment of what is best for you, then our country will move forward and lead the rest of the world to enjoy the peace and prosperity that is so abundant here.

I am told that this is somewhat an unusual assembly for Jacksonville. Jacksonville is the great Gateway City. It is made up of people of all political philosophies, of all religions, that belong to many churches, people of different races.

But we are all equal on election day and we are all proud we are Americans.

And when the bugle blows and when the bell rings and when you mash the button, it doesn't make any difference what church you belong to, it doesn't make any difference what section of town you live in, it doesn't make any difference how you spell your name or the color of your skin. You go out and you enlist to defend that flag and to protect that flag.

Twice in my lifetime we have taken it around the world and brought it back without a stain on it and we are going to keep the defense that will assure we can do it again.

Before I close, I want to thank and welcome some of these folks over here of another philosophy. You know, at nearly every meeting we have they send some of their children over to visit with us, and we like for them to be here where they can see happy, smiling people. We like for them to know that we have no fear in our hearts and no hate in our souls.

I am really hoping that come election day a good many of these people that have exposed themselves to happy Americans with hope and faith and trust in their country— that they will get rid of their bad feelings and come and join us because the wonderful thing about this question of peace is it doesn't make any difference whether you are Democrat or Republican, if you have a nuclear holocaust, you are gone.

And in this campaign from Maine to California, I have found 30 and 40 percent of the Republicans have come over and joined us in a program for all the people regardless of party.

I think you ought to know here, in closing, that most Americans think more of their country than they think of their party.

So I will leave you now. I haven't said anything unpleasant or critical about any

personality. I want to leave you with this thought: You go to the polls November the 3d and do what you think is best for your country.

I think the people from Maine to California are going to do the same thing. I predict that there will be more votes polled in this election, I predict there will be more votes cast in this election, than any national election we have ever had.

And I also predict that we are going to need every single one of you, because we want all the world to know, we want all America to know, that we want to do what is best for our country. So you go do it.

NOTE: The President spoke at 12:07 p.m. at Hemming Park in Jacksonville, Fla. His opening words referred to Senator Spessard L. Holland of Florida. Later he referred to Senator George A. Smathers and Governor Farris Bryant of Florida; Mayor Haydon Burns of Jacksonville; Representatives D. R. (Billy) Matthews and Charles E. Bennett of Florida; the following members of the Florida State cabinet: Tom Adams, Secretary of State, J. Edwin Larson, Treasurer, Thomas D. Bailey, Superintendent of Public Instruction, Doyle E. Conner, Commissioner of Agriculture, Ray E. Green, Comptroller, and James Kynes, Executive Assistant to the Governor; Mrs. Annette Baker, State Democratic committeewoman; Thomas F. Fleming, State campaign coordinator; Warren Goodrich, chairman of the State Democratic Executive Committee; and Lacy Mahon, Jr., Jacksonville. He also referred to Ann Sheridan, actress, of Denton, Tex.

714 Presidential Statement No. 2 on Economic Issues: Monetary Policy for Stability and Growth. *October 26, 1964*

1. MONETARY policy is one of our crucially important tools for maintaining a healthy and noninflationary economy. The job is never easy. But the results over the past 4 years have been remarkable:

—Ample but not excessive credit has been available to businesses, homebuyers, and State and local governments.

—At the same time, short-term interest rates have been pushed up to reduce capital

outflows and help correct our balance of payments deficit.

—Yet long-term interest rates, which are so important to domestic borrowers, have remained moderate—in fact, home mortgage rates and the rates paid by State and local governments are lower today than in early 1961.

2. All this has been made possible by close ties between our monetary and our fiscal

and debt management policies, and close harmony among the men responsible for these policies:

—We have maintained the Federal Reserve's traditional independence within the Government.

—Yet the Federal Reserve and the administration agree entirely on the practical need for informal coordination among the various economic programs of the Government.

—The President meets periodically with a group consisting of Secretary Dillon, Chairman Martin of the Federal Reserve Board, Budget Director Gordon, and Chairman Heller of the Council of Economic Advisers, and they in turn are in close and continuous contact.

—These efforts have resulted in govern-ment by consensus, not by conflict, in economic policy.

3. In the future as in the past, our monetary system must remain flexible, and not be bound by any rigid, mechanical rules:

—In an atmosphere of private and public moderation, monetary policy has been steadily expansionary for 4 years.

—With continued moderation, there can be the continued monetary expansion essential to economic growth.

—But if inflation develops, or if excessive outflows of funds occur, the Federal Reserve System is in a position to do what is necessary.

NOTE: For a statement by the President announcing a series of statements on economic issues, see Item 707.

---

715   Statement by the President Upon Making Public a Report on the Desalting of Sea Water.   *October 26, 1964*

I AM PLEASED to release the report of the Secretary of the Interior and the Chairman of the Atomic Energy Commission, made at my request, on a proposed program for developing the technology to desalt sea water economically.

The demand for water is increasing steadily throughout the world. Water shortages in some sections of this country threaten to restrict further economic development. This problem is even more acute in many arid, developing countries where future economic growth is absolutely dependent upon finding new sources of fresh water. Within the next decade desalted water will be the cheapest—in some cases the only—way to obtain new water supplies in many areas.

The record shows that the United States stands ready to share its technology in this field with other nations. We have already begun cooperative studies with Israel, Mex-ico, and the Soviet Union, and have actively participated on the Panel on the Use of Nuclear Energy for Desalination of Seawater of the International Atomic Energy Agency. As President Kennedy stated over 2 years ago: "There is no scientific breakthrough, including the trip to the moon, that will mean more to the country which first is able to bring fresh water from salt water at a competitive rate. And all those people who live in deserts around the oceans of the world will look to the nation which first makes this significant breakthrough. . . ." [1]

We have a lot of work to do to bring this technology to a useful stage, as this report shows. We have had a good program in the past, but we are going to ask the Congress for some more money so that we can learn how to produce desalted water more eco-

---

[1] "Public Papers of the Presidents, John F. Kennedy 1962," Item 337.

nomically. This report will serve as a useful guide.

NOTE: The report, transmitted September 22, is printed in two parts, separately paginated, but under a single cover and with the overall title "Report to the President: Program for Advancing Desalting Technology" (Government Printing Office). The same heading appears on the title page of the Interior Department's part of the report (35 pp.). The remainder of the pamphlet, containing the Atomic Energy Commission's report, is entitled "Reactor Development Program for Large-Scale Desalting Plants" (20 pp.). The Interior Department report is also published as a separate pamphlet (35 pp., Government Printing Office).

See also Items 480, 672.

716 Remarks at City Hall, Macon, Georgia. *October 26, 1964*

Governor Sanders, distinguished platform guests, ladies and gentlemen:

My heart is happy today. I am back in Georgia where I feel at home. There is much in Georgia to remind me of Texas—the people are loyal, the people are hospitable, and the people are kind. Your future is bright because you look to the future and because you want Macon and all of Georgia to be more prosperous tomorrow than it is today.

I am sorry that my longtime and my dear friend Senator Dick Russell could not be here with us today. For 8 years I served in the leadership of the Senate, and every time my name was put before a Democratic caucus, he nominated me for that leadership.

Nothing could please me more than to have by my side my old friend, your able Senator, my loyal colleague, one of the promising young men of this Nation, Herman Talmadge. He is diligent, he looks after the people's business, he is a wise and able young man, and you are mighty fortunate to have him in the Senate. I am mighty proud to count him my friend.

Here in Georgia you have another very valuable possession, one of the most promising, one of the most respected, one of the ablest Governors in the United States—Carl Sanders. He is a man of the people. He is honest, he is energetic, and he is not afraid to stand up and be counted. He works day and night for the future of Georgia, and I am going to work arm in arm, shoulder to shoulder, with him to make Georgia a more prosperous State.

I am touched this afternoon to be here with one of my wisest counselors, one of my best friends, our beloved Carl Vinson. How I wish he were going to be in the next Congress so I could rely on him for advice and wise counsel in Washington. But I am going to rely on him for advice and wise counsel in Milledgeville just the same. I know he is going to be back home in Georgia, the place that he loves most, and I know Uncle Carl won't mind too much if I keep that telephone line busy talking to him occasionally.

The Georgia delegation to the Congress of the United States has always been one of the most effective and one of the most respected. This delegation ranks with the finest: Congressman Phil Landrum, who led the fight to wipe poverty off the face of this land, and who will be remembered in history for this victorious beginning of a great crusade in a modern 20th century; and your diligent and your able and your farsighted Congressman Jack Flynt, who has worked so hard, so long, to lead the way for programs and plans that will make this a wiser and a stronger Nation and a better State, and now he is going to help Macon make her contribution to this Nation. So keep him in the Congress and let him serve you and all the country.

I am glad to see Congressman Bob Stephens; my old friends Russell Tuten and J. L. Pilcher, Charles Weltner and John Davis. All of these men are patriots and they all deserve the applause of a courteous and a grateful people.

I want to thank Mayor Merritt for his hospitality and for the courtesy of this great city. One of my oldtime friends lives here. I have known him since I was a young man. It was worth coming to Macon if I didn't get to see anybody but Peyton Anderson.

There is no finer State Democratic chairman anywhere in the country than J. B. Fuqua, and I am pleased to have him on the platform with us this afternoon. I might add, while Peyton is here, and I want to be sure that he doesn't go back on his commitment, that I am not the least unhappy about the position that his newspaper is taking in this campaign.

I have just come from Warner Robins Air Force Base. When I was in Congress, I was one of those who helped to bring this base to Macon. I was proud of that achievement then; I am prouder of it now. Moreover, I want all of you to know that as long as Lyndon Johnson is President of the United States, the manned aircraft program, to which Warner Robins contributes so much, and the Warner Robins Base will continue to be a part of our defense system in this country.

I don't think there is but one real issue in this campaign. Who do you think is best able to secure peace in the world?

[*Audience response:* "LBJ!"]

As much as I enjoy hearing you express your approval, and as much as I recognize the few visitors who have come over here from the opposition camp to get in good company this afternoon, I think that you would like to know that in this world in which we live the most vital decision that you are going to be called upon to make is the man and the party that you select to lead you in the next 4 years.

You are going to have an overwhelming Democratic Senate, made up of overwhelming Democratic Members. You are going to have a large majority of the Members of the House of Representatives who are Democrats. I think, I hope, and I believe that you are going to have a Democratic President to work with them.

Some people like to talk about personalities. Some people like to write signs about individuals. And I guess I would do that, too, if I didn't have any issues to talk about. But we have issues, and we are going to spend a few minutes' time that we have before we go to Augusta and to Columbia exercising our right of free speech in a free country to talk about those issues.

Here in this town, where Warner Robins means so much, I think I will just read the record. Al Smith used to say, "Let's look at the record." There is a lot of "fear talk" in this campaign, and there is some "smear talk" in this campaign.

But when my opponent was down here visiting you good people the other day, he neglected to mention, when he was here in Georgia, that in 1953 when they called the roll on adding $400 million to the Strategic Air Force for aircraft purchases, Goldwater voted "no" and I voted "aye."

And to those people that are interested in the defense of our country, and in this popular phrase that has been developed, "Peace through preparedness," let's go up to 1954, when we voted on adding $350 million for our Army personnel and to strengthen the maintenance of our Army. Goldwater voted "no"; I voted "aye."

In 1955 when we had the roll called on adding $46 million to strengthen the United States Marine Corps, Goldwater voted "no"; I voted "aye."

In 1955 when they called the roll on adding $420 million for military assistance abroad, Goldwater voted "no"; I voted "aye." In 1956 when they called the roll on adding $800 million for Air Force procurement, Goldwater voted "no"; I voted "aye."

In the last Congress before the Kennedy administration, when they called the roll on Army missile procurement, Goldwater voted "no" on the $233 million item; I voted "aye."

I could go on reciting these votes all afternoon, but the record speaks for itself. You must judge a man and rate him by his deeds in off-election years instead of his words in election years. And besides, as all of you have observed, some people get confused anyway.

I am glad to be back here in Macon. When I was Vice President, I spoke at Mercer University at the Walter F. George Law School. This was a sentimental journey for me, for Walter George was my counselor and was my guide. He was one of the great Georgians of our time. How often I wished that he could be here to counsel me today. I am happy that his son, Heard George, is here with us.

Now, I want the good people of middle Georgia to know that I am familiar with your great program of river development in this State, that I am interested in your Flint River basin and the Altamaha River basin, and I supported the development of our rivers when I was in Congress. And I will continue to support the development of these resources in Georgia when I am your President.

It was 78 years ago when a great young son of Georgia journeyed to New York to speak of the new South. I remember he said one time that fields that ran red with human blood in September were green with harvest in June.

But when Henry Grady went to New York, he told his fellow countrymen, "We have wiped out the place where Mason and Dixon's line used to be."

Henry Grady spoke in the spirit of Robert E. Lee, and he spoke in the spirit of Lincoln, too.

That was 78 years ago. It has taken that vision a long, long time to come true, but there are still those who want to divide our country. There are still those who are trying in this election to play the politics of diversity, of division, and of difference.

I say when you divide your country, that is wrong.

The new South is here in America.

What Americans want today is a new politics, a politics of national unity, a politics concerned with progress and peace for the Nation, a politics of honor, and a politics for decency for all.

And when the returns come in 1 week from tomorrow, America will know, and the world will know, that in this land of the free there is no North, no South, no East, no West. We are one Nation, united, indivisible.

It is the sons of Georgia that have carried that flag to every corner of this globe, and they have brought her back without a tarnish on it. They know there is only one Nation, one people, one flag, one Constitution, united and indivisible under God.

I think most of you people that are not emotional realize how far Georgia has come in the last 30 years. The per capita income in Georgia in 1932 when I went to Washington—the per capita income was $175 per year. There are some people on this platform that remember that. One hundred and seventy-five dollars a year, a little less than $15 a month per person. Well, today the per capita income in Georgia, thank God, is more than 10 times that much.

Ninety-eight percent of the farms in Georgia in 1932 used coal oil lamps and lanterns. They were without any electricity. Today, with REA, 98 percent of all the homes have electricity.

Two million people in the South suffered from malaria in 1932. In 1964 that disease has been completely eradicated from our section, and we look ahead. We look ahead not as any region, but we look ahead as a united Nation, and when the voters come in on November 3d, we are going to have a mandate from every region for America to continue to move forward.

Never before anywhere have any others had so many things as we have now. Never before anywhere have any others had the opportunity that we enjoy to enrich our lives with nobler things of the spirit.

The great State of Georgia has a motto that all Americans can and should understand. That motto is "Wisdom, justice, moderation." Wisdom, justice, moderation—these are qualities of the spirit.

These are the qualities that have helped to make America the strongest, the mightiest, the most respected, the most trusted nation in the history of man, and Georgia's sons have contributed to it all.

I have come here to Macon this afternoon to declare and to predict that we are not going to exchange these qualities for cynicism, for extremism, for impulse, at home or in the world.

We will keep America strong against any danger. We will keep America strong against every threat. We will keep America strong against all perils.

We will keep America on the tried and the tested and the trusted course of responsi-bility, and in this nuclear age, neither we nor the world can afford even a moment of reck-lessness, not even a breath of bluff or bluster. All that we have, and all that free men have, could be wiped out in the first hour of a nuclear war.

On November 3d, the people of every region will vote for a new politics of responsi-bility to get on with the building of a new America, an America of peace, an America of progress, an America of growing pros-perity for growing numbers of people who love instead of hate, of people who have faith instead of doubt, of people who don't know what it is to fear or smear, but for people who love thy neighbor as thyself.

One hundred years is long enough to bur-den down our future with the divisions of the past. The time has come—the time is now—to bind up our wounds, to heal our history, and to make our beloved America whole again.

The entire world watches our decision tomorrow week. The entire world knows that there is just one issue in this campaign, and that is peace in the world. The entire world is watching to see whose thumb you will put close to that nuclear button, whose hand you want to reach over and pick up that "hot line" when Moscow is calling, and answer that phone.

You people of Georgia don't need any ad-vice on how to mark your ballot. You have been marking it all through the years of this Republic, and you have never had the blush of shame come to your cheek because of the question of your decisions.

So I did not come here today to talk to you about personalities, or to speak illy of my colleagues, or to criticize my opponents. I came here to give you the record and to sub-mit to you that you must next Tuesday week do what in your conscience you know is best for America.

You must next Tuesday week go with your uncles and your cousins and your aunts, because we need every single one of you. You must go and do what you know in your heart is right for your country.

Thank you and goodby.

NOTE: The President spoke at 3:19 p.m. at City Hall in Macon, Ga. In his opening words he referred to Governor Carl E. Sanders of Georgia. Later he referred to, among others, Senators Richard B. Russell and Herman E. Talmadge, and Representatives Carl Vinson, Phil M. Landrum, John J. Flynt, Jr., Robert G. Stephens, Jr., J. Russell Tuten, J. L. Pilcher, Charles L. Weltner, and John W. Davis, all of Georgia, Mayor B. F. Merritt, Jr., of Macon, Peyton T. Anderson, Jr., publisher of the Macon Telegraph and News, J. B. Fuqua, chairman of the Florida State Democratic Committee, and Walter F. George, Senator from Georgia from 1926 to 1956, and his son Heard.

717   Statement by the President on the Textile Industry. *October 26, 1964*

THE TEXTILE industry plays a vital role in the health of the American economy.

Almost 2¼ million Americans—one out of every eight industrial employees—work in the textile and apparel industries. Hundreds of thousands more are employed in producing materials, machinery, other services and supplies for this enormous industrial complex.

No region of the country contributes more to the health and prosperity of textiles than the American Southeast.

When this administration took office serious difficulties confronted this industry.

Between 1950 and 1960 approximately 275 mills closed, and 341,000 textile mill-product employees lost their jobs. Profits were down. Growth capital for research and expansion and improvement was in short supply. The result was not only a stricken industry, but damage to the economic health of the entire Nation.

When this administration took office it recognized the importance of the textile industry and the special nature of its problems. It was determined to find answers.

We worked hand in hand with Congress to develop a seven-point program for textiles. This program would not have been possible without the farsighted leadership of Carl Vinson. He served as the congressional spokesman of textile matters and worked closely with the administration.

The result is a classic example of the benefits of constructive cooperation between Government and business.

A number of bilateral and multilateral trade arrangements have been negotiated and implemented to bring about more orderly world trade in cotton textile products. New tax depreciation schedules have encouraged plant expansion and improvement. This year a new law made it possible to buy American cotton at the same price it is sold abroad for the first time since 1956. Even in the difficult area of wool products, so vital to Georgia, we have taken significant steps to stem the tide of certain imports which have entered this country through unintended loopholes in our tariff laws.

The result has been increasing confidence and well-being for the industry and its workers. Wages have been increased—twice within the past year. The Department of Commerce estimates a 1 billion bale increase in domestic cotton consumption this year. The demand for textile products is good. The industry is planning recordbreaking investments in plant and equipment. Annual capital expenditures averaged $414 million in the 1950–1960 period. They are expected to approach $800 million in 1964. This is a rate of increase not surpassed by any other major American industry. Textile machinery sales are up. Thousands of new jobs are being created.

These are impressive accomplishments. We know the job can be done. We must now focus on the remaining weak spots, and implement the rest of our program.

We must move ahead with a permanent one-price system.

We intend to keep cotton textile imports from disrupting the market.

Wool product imports must be kept at reasonable levels. For it is essential that the wool textile industry be restored to good health.

I am convinced that our program for textiles is in the best interests of all America. I intend to pursue it to a successful conclusion.

NOTE: The statement was issued at Macon, Ga. For an earlier statement by the President on the textile industry, see Item 602.

Representative Carl Vinson of Georgia served as chairman of a special group in the House of Representatives which had studied the textile program.

For the seven-point program for the textile industry see "Public Papers of the Presidents, John F. Kennedy 1961," Item 161.

718   Remarks at a Rally in Augusta, Georgia.
October 26, 1964

Governor Sanders, ladies and gentlemen, boys and girls:

When I come to Georgia, it is like coming home. My roots are deep in Georgia. Georgia has given me much to be proud of. Georgia has given much to this Nation's progress, and there is a great deal more yet to be done.

I have been welcomed warmly first in Macon and now in Augusta, this lovely, gracious city. One of Augusta's greatest prides, and justifiably so, is the fact that it is the hometown of one of the ablest and the brightest young men in the United States, your own Governor, Carl Sanders. He is not afraid to stand up and be counted for what is right, for you and for our country, and I am proud of him and I know you are proud of him, too.

It is good to have by my side my longtime friend and loyal colleague, the great Senator from Georgia, Herman Talmadge. He is one of the great Senators of our country and he bears a name that stands for service and duty to the people in Georgia.

You are wise to have chosen as your Congressman my friend Bob Stephens. No man works harder in the Congress to advance the cause of Augusta and the cause of Georgia than does Bob Stephens, and I salute him and congratulate him here today.

I am glad that Jack Flynt is here, too. He has been my friend and he is one of Georgia's ablest Congressmen.

I wish that my dearest friend and one of my wisest counselors, Senator Dick Russell, were here. In my days in the Senate, no man was kinder to me or gave me more help than this great Senator.

I am glad that J. B. Fuqua, your State chairman, is here. I know he is a competent chairman, and I also know from the weekend that he spent at my ranch that he is a good hunter.

Augusta is moving forward. Just last week we broke ground on a new permanent Signal School at Fort Gordon. In the last year we have put $30 million in new construction into Fort Gordon. So I am proud of the way that the Democratic administration has demonstrated its faith in the future of Fort Gordon.

This, I might add, is in sharp contrast to the way the previous administration treated Augusta, when it closed the Augusta Arsenal and put 500 Augusta families out of work.

Today I understand that you have a 4-year college on this same ground, and you know how I feel about education. I know that you know how the opposition feels about education.

We are all proud of the Savannah River plant. We welcome here this evening the great and learned and distinguished Governor, Donald Russell, of the State of South Carolina. We are proud to have my old ally and my loyal friend, the senior Senator from South Carolina, Olin Johnston, here with us tonight.

So far as the Savannah River plant is concerned, we are working now to help you convert this installation and all of its facilities into peaceful purposes so that this installation will continue to serve the United States in any crisis.

The great Clarks Hill Reservoir was built in a Democratic administration. It established flood control. It stabilized the Savannah River flow so that now you have an inland port. And the Corps of Engineers is now working on a 9-foot channel all the way from Augusta to the Atlantic Ocean. The reservoir has played an important role in bringing new industry, in bringing new jobs, in bringing more income into every home in Augusta.

The Democrats try to create jobs. The Democrats try to build business. The Democrats try not to turn back the clock to lower wages and fewer jobs.

In Augusta in the past 12 months, $100 million of new industry has been announced.

This is progress. This is the positive, forward motion of a people on the move. Augusta and the great State of Georgia are sharing in the greatest and the longest span of prosperity in all the peacetime history of the United States.

For 44 months this prosperity has gone unbroken. Moreover, it was the Democratic tax cut of $12 billion that is helping fuel this business expansion, a tax cut that my opponent voted against, but thank God Democrats and Republicans alike joined to vote for the tax cut and pass it in the Congress.

Augusta has a right to be proud of its great medical school, named after the father of the great Senator from Georgia, Herman Talmadge.

One hundred years ago there lived in this city of Augusta a small boy who saw with his own eyes and felt in his own soul the awful price of the war that divided this Nation. When he was grown, he once said, "The only place in the world where nothing has to be explained to me is the South."

That small boy was the last President of the United States that was born and raised in the South—Woodrow Wilson.

So I say to all of you this evening, and I say to all of the South—and I want to say to all of the Nation—what Woodrow Wilson said then: "The only place in the world where nothing has to be explained to me is the South."

I know the burdens that the South has borne. I know the troubles that the South has seen. I know the ordeals that have tried the South through all of these years. And I want to see those burdens lifted off the South. I want the ordeals to end and the South to stand where it should stand as the full and honored part of a proud and united land.

There are 190 million people in the United States, but there are in this world more than 3 billion. So if freedom is to stand, if our hopes are to survive, if our dreams are to be fulfilled, your President, the President of all the people of the United States, must be able to win and to hold the trust and to have the respect of not only those millions here at home, but those billions around the globe. He must be able to say what the American people want the world to understand about America. The free capitals of the world must understand. The friendly capitals of this hemisphere must understand, and Moscow must understand and Peking must understand.

In our nuclear world tonight, there can be no misunderstanding of America's purposes or America's policies, or America's Presidents. Such understanding begins at home.

The American people want to make this a better land with a better life for better people, and any man who leads America must understand that Americans do not want to turn back to the past. They do not want to spend their years undoing what generations before them have done so well. They do not want to give their time to reopening old wounds or recalling the pains of old history.

Americans today want to bind up those wounds. They want to heal that history. They want to make this Nation whole, and in the months that have been mine, this is the work that I have tried to do, and this is the work that I pledge to continue if this trust is vested in me on November 3d.

The people of America do not want a President to waste these years in stalemate with the States or with a deadlock with the Congress. I think that the people of America want, and I think the people of America expect, that the White House and the State House should work together, as your good Governor Carl Sanders and I have worked together these past 11 months.

The people of America want and expect the executive branch and the legislative branch to work together, as we have done with the help of men like your Senator Dick Russell and Herman Talmadge and Carl Vinson, and your own good Congressman Bob Stephens, and others.

The people of America want their President to work for peace. They want him to work through preparedness.

Now, this I have done, and this I will continue to do. The people of America want their President to keep his head without losing his heart. They want him to be frugal with the public funds, but they want him to be faithful to the public needs of the young and the old. They want him to be concerned with the poor and they want him to be just to the well-to-do, the workingman, and the businessman, and the farm family, and the city family alike. This I have done, and this I will continue to do.

Your support, your great sense of patriotism, has been strength for me throughout the time that I have served as your President. In this election, I do not call for a victory of party, I do not call for a victory of region. I call for a victory of all the people, a victory for all America.

In my heart I think, as I believe you think, that our country is stronger if we reason out our differences together. I think it is better to use the head and the heart than to use the tongue and the voice.

I know when you see people, as you have seen them at some conventions when they don't want other people to talk, when the Governor of a great State is not even permitted to speak to his own convention because of others who would interfere, or when the President of your own country would be stopped and interrupted while he was trying to talk to you in your own land—can you imagine what kind of leadership that would do for the world if that were practiced on other people?

Now, might does not make right, and I would imagine I would know where the might is here if we needed to do it. But I was always taught as a little boy when people didn't know any better, and when they made mistakes, and when they were rude, and when they didn't show good manners, to turn your other cheek and say, "Dear Lord, please forgive them, for they know not what they do."

And I think that is the way that the people of the 50 States are feeling. We don't feel hurt, and we don't feel angry. We just feel sorry. And I think that on November 3d they are going to feel sorry, too.

I think that—I know in my heart that this is how Georgia will vote. I was in an election campaign 4 years ago and I returned to my home State in the last days of that campaign. We went to the hotel to wash up before we went to a luncheon meeting, but the entrance was blocked and the hecklers were there. They harassed us and they hounded us and they knocked my wife's hat off. They spit on us, they called us traitors, and they called us treason artists. And they had ugly signs and they dealt not in a single issue that we were debating. They had only to talk about personalities and little petty things because they were little, petty people.

As we walked from one hotel to the other in a free American city that had never known anything but democratic leadership and democratic ways and democratic freedoms, it took us more than an hour to walk across the block because of the chants and the saliva that was running out of their mouths, and, really, some of them were diseased; they were just really upset.

The next morning I talked to a great public servant of Georgia; he called me on the phone. I believe it was about Wednes-

day of the week before the election on Tuesday. He said:

"I want to know where I can join your plane tomorrow, because in the State of Georgia we don't spit on people we disagree with. We don't knock the hats off of their ladies, and we do permit them to move down the street from one hotel to the other without danger. I would like to come and say to the people of America that these tactics that we have read about and that we have seen don't represent a majority of Americans. They represent a minority of poor, unfortunate souls that ought to be pitied instead of criticized."

So I think here tonight in Georgia, I think in my own heart, and I think in your heart, that all of you know how the South is going to vote. In my heart and in your heart, I think you know that this is how the Americans of all regions, of all religions, of all races, will vote on November 3d.

I want to especially thank you good people who came to listen and to learn and to try to find out about the issues. I want to tell you that 11 months ago when I took over the Presidency, I didn't have any time to go to the library or to bring in a council of advisers. In that tragic moment after Dallas, I suddenly had this awesome responsibility thrust upon me. I said with the good Lord's help and with your prayers, I would try to do my dead level best. And I have done that.

Now, under our constitutional system, next Tuesday week you will be called upon to turn me out or to select me for 4 more years, and I think I know that in your heart you know what is right.

There is only one real issue in this campaign, and it is a very important issue, and it is probably the most important issue that you will ever decide in your lifetime. That issue is peace or war. That issue is whether you have nuclear holocaust or whether you have peace.

If you move a thumb up to a button that launches a nuclear holocaust, in a matter of moments you can snuff out the existence of 300 million men and women and children. One hundred million alone, more than half the people in America, would be wiped out in a matter of moments. That is so much more important than anything else that an intelligent man can think of that that is what should occupy our time, and I think that is what will occupy your time.

You have to sit down in the quiet sanctity of your home, and with your wife and with your family, determine what leadership you think is best equipped, is best experienced, has the prudence, has the understanding, and has the training to try to pull together the people of the world instead of dividing them, to try to heal the differences that divide us and make them unite us.

There are so many more things that we agree upon than we disagree upon, but we must have a leader who loves instead of a leader who hates. We must have a leader who has faith in our country instead of a leader who has doubt in our country. We must have a leader who really is running for the Presidency instead of a leader who is running against the Presidency all the time.

We have got to have someone who believes in the capacity of this country, the future of this country, and the potential of this country, instead of having someone who is frightened, fearful, doubtful, and constantly concerned about us going to hell in a hat.

Well, I am not going to tell you how to classify these individuals. You can do that in your own home, in your own way, and then you can go and express yourself. The only one thing I want to tell you is this: There is danger abroad in the world. We are living in a critical period. Your patriotism was never needed more.

There are parents in this crowd that took their son down to the depot to say goodby to him in World War I and World War II, and I pray they will never have to do that again. But I do hope that you take that son and go down to the polling place. I am not saying that you go there and vote for this party or vote for this man. I am saying you go there and do your duty and do your obligation, and live up to your responsibilities of citizenship just like you do when this Nation is confronted with danger in wartime. You go there and do what you think is best.

President Eisenhower was a Republican President. I voted for him in 1960 in his foreign policy and his relations with other nations 95 percent of the time. My opponent, who belongs to, or is supposed to belong to, the same party voted for him 25 percent of the time. I want to continue a bipartisan foreign policy, where the leaders of both parties will let politics stop at the water's edge.

I said when I was elected leader of the Democrats in the Senate, after Dick Russell nominated me and I was elected unanimously, when President Eisenhower was taking over the Presidency and had a majority of the Senate—the Democrats had been defeated and had been routed—I said, "Here is going to be my policy: When the Republican President, Mr. Eisenhower, is right, I am going to stand up and proudly support him, and ask my Democrats to follow me. When he is wrong, I am going to oppose him, in decency and dignity, on the basis of the issue and without regard to personality or his children or his dogs," because I believe it is every American's duty if he wants to be a good citizen, when he casts his vote either in Augusta or in the United States Senate, to vote for what he thinks is best for his country, regardless of his party.

So when they asked me what my political philosophy was, I said, "I am a free man first, I am an American second, I am a public servant third, and I am a Democrat fourth, in that order."

So if in your judgment and your wisdom you decide that after the 11 months that I have tried to do the best I could and pick up where our beloved President John Fitzgerald Kennedy left off and carry on—if you don't join the few voices that would turn me out, and you ask me to stay there for another 4

years, I pledge you that I will give you all that is within me to try to unite the world instead of divide the world, to try to have peace instead of have war, to try to have prosperity instead of have depression, to try to help lead and build a new South, but most of all, a new America that knows no North, no South, no East, no West.

NOTE: The President spoke at 5:38 p.m. at the Richmond-Augusta County-Municipal Building in Augusta, Ga. In his opening words he referred to Governor Carl E. Sanders of Georgia. Later he referred to Senators Herman E. Talmadge and Richard B. Russell, and Representatives Carl Vinson, Robert G. Stephens, Jr., and John J. Flynt, Jr., all of Georgia, J. B. Fuqua, chairman of the Georgia State Democratic Committee, and Governor Donald S. Russell and Senator Olin D. Johnston of South Carolina.

719 Remarks on the Steps of the State Capitol, Columbia, South Carolina. *October 26, 1964*

Senator Johnston, Governor Russell, distinguished guests on the platform, ladies and gentlemen:

Today I have been visiting the part of America that we love, the South. Today I have been in Orlando and Jacksonville, Fla., in Macon and Augusta, Ga. And now the climax of the day, and the night here in this great, historic, and beautiful city of Columbia. And by my side have been the great men of the South: Senator Smathers and Senator Holland and Governor Bryant of Florida; Senators Herman Talmadge and Dick Russell and Congressman Carl Vinson and Governor Carl Sanders of Georgia.

And here tonight I am so proud to be with my lifelong friend, my loyal ally and my great colleague in the Senate of the United States, your own good and great Senator Olin D. Johnston. No man ever came from any people or from any State who has fought harder for justice and peace and honor and prosperity than this outstanding southerner

of our times—Olin Johnston.

I am proud to be here with a man of dignity and courage and valor, your Governor Donald Russell. He has set a model for the Nation. He has given a demonstration of leadership and statesmanship that is respected from Maine to California. He is a wise man, a temperate man, one who has advanced the cause of progress in the United States of America, but particularly the cause of progress in South Carolina, and we are so grateful in the White House to Mrs. Russell for coming there and for standing by Lady Bird's side on her wonderful train trip all through the sunny southland.

Now I would like to say a word about the great South Carolina congressional delegation. It is respected and it is effective. It is a delegation with men like John McMillan, with whom I have served for many years, dean of the South Carolina delegation, with Bob Ashmore, with William Jennings Bryan Dorn.

Also on this platform is a very intelligent and energetic man who should be called to duty by the people of South Carolina, Tom Gettys. Send this man to Congress where we need him, where South Carolina needs him, and where the whole Nation needs him. I thank you for the kind of men that you have sent to Washington.

Mayor Bates, Governor Ransome Williams, Governor George Bell Timmerman, I thank you for being here tonight, and thanks, also, to my old friend Senator Edgar Brown, Governor McNair, Yancey McLeod, Attorney General Dan McLeod, and the other distinguished South Carolinians who have come here to stand up and be counted with us.

I see every day in one of the rooms of the White House the portrait of a man whose boyhood home stands here in Columbia, S.C. It is a sobering portrait of a heartbroken man. Woodrow Wilson wanted one thing—peace in the world in his time, not for himself, but for all mankind.

That great yearning for peace may have been bred in this house on Hampton Street. His father, who taught at the old Columbia Theological Seminary, may have nourished that dream when he talked at the supper table with his high-school-age son who was later to become the great President of the United States. Woodrow Wilson came close, mighty close, to making that dream come true, but he could not finish his work. But you and I can—and you and I will.

Lasting peace between peoples in the world is tonight within our sight and within our grasp. It will be within our children's reach. The great Savannah River nuclear production plant marks the new, more perilous, yet more promising path to peace.

There is just one important, just one overriding issue in this election this year, and that is why I am not going to indulge in any muckraking or any mudslinging or even discussing personalities, because candidates never discuss personalities if they have issues to discuss. When you hear a fellow talking about his neighbor, or his friend, or his opponent—and remember that the man is not supposed to recommend his opponent very highly—when you hear him talking about that, you know that he doesn't want to talk about the things that count, the issues in your life.

The big issue that we want to talk about tonight is whether we will stay on this path of peace. The President that you will select and elect a week from tomorrow has to assure full responsibility for the stewardship of your survival if a time should come for a nuclear decision.

Your President will have in his hand, inescapably, the power of life and death for hundreds of millions of people on this planet. Your President will have to make for America and for a large part of the world important, key decisions which may determine whether the air we breathe is to be free from fallout, or full of it; whether the milk that we give our little children is to have any poison which stunts their growth, or be free from it.

You know the policies of one man who seeks your trust. That man offers a policy of brinkmanship with nuclear power. He urges that we consider using atomic weapons in Viet-Nam, even in Eastern Europe, if there should be an uprising. He voted to cut back our efforts to try to control the arms race. He voted against the agreement—one of just a dozen—to stop the nuclear tests which poison the air that you breathe. That is a policy of gambling with your destiny.

I offer you instead this policy: First, our nuclear power must be great enough that any potential enemy understands and knows that a nuclear attack would be suicide if he tried it.

Second, we must exercise great care against any use of this power to destroy the world, to poison the world's atmosphere, or to cripple any single human being.

Third, we must speed the development of nuclear energy for peacetime purposes.

Nuclear energy is being used tonight
—to power the U.S.S. *Savannah,*
—to power isolated lighthouses and communications equipment for our satellites,
—to process chemicals and plastics,
—to sterilize medical supplies,
—to preserve food in America.

We are studying ways to use nuclear energy to excavate canals and mines, and to desalinate ocean waters, to take the waters from the oceans and remove the salt so that we can make the deserts of the world bloom again.

The future defies imagination. But we must be eternally vigilant to make certain that this is a future of peace; that this is a future of security; that this is a future of progress. And that is what I intend to do as your President. We are not children playing with sticks and stones. We are nations with the power to destroy millions of human beings in a matter of minutes.

So peace in the world demands from America today a foreign policy which
—assures our allies of our support,
—which assures our adversaries of our strength and our determination,
—and which assures the whole world of America's steadfast search for honorable peace for honorable men.

Our great President Woodrow Wilson said, "There is such a thing as a nation being so right that it does not need to convince others *by force* that it is right." And I say to you good people here in Columbia, S.C.,

tonight your United States *is* right. And if you will give us your help, and if you will lend us your hand, and if you will help us unite this Nation, and if you will give us your prayers we will patiently convince other nations that the United States is right.

With patience and good sense, and the help of God, we will not have to use what we have created to defend ourselves.

Remaining always prepared we can devote ourselves to building a Great Society for all of our people where every man and woman who wants to work has a job and can work; where we have minimum wages and collective bargaining, and we respect the man who works with his hands; where every boy and every girl born under that flag has a right to all the education they can take; where, in the twilight of our life, and in the sundown of our career, we have a strong, solid social security system that is not voluntary, but one that will meet our needs; where our farmers are treated with dignity and with decency and with equity at the market place, and they receive true value for what they produce; where we conserve our great natural resources, our rivers, and our forests and our countrysides; where in time to come we can labor less hours per day, less days per week, less weeks per month, and less months per year, so that we can have the time to enjoy the benefits of education and the leisure time that would mean so much to the human being.

Yes, we want an America where every man, woman, and child born under that flag, regardless of his religion, regardless of his region, regardless of his race, has equal opportunity for all and special privilege for none.

Yes, there is much work to do, but 11 months ago when I tried to pick up where my fallen leader had left off, in that tragic day in Dallas when, on a moment's notice, I was called to assume the awesome responsibilities of the Presidency of the United States, the 36th man that has ever held that office, I had no time to call in my counselors of wisdom, I had no time to go to the stacks in the library. I had to stand up then in that airplane with roaring jet motors behind me, take that oath of office, and say, "Let's get back to the Capital and effect this transition."

I told you then as I tell you now that with God's help, with your prayers, I will do the best I can. That was 11 months and 3 days ago, and I tell you tonight I have done the best I could.

This is an election year, and you have the priceless heritage and privilege as a free American to go to the ballot box and in the secrecy of that booth select the man that you want to lead this Nation for the next 4 years. You ought to select the man that you think is best for America. You ought to select the man that you think is best for the free world. You ought to select the man that you think is best for South Carolina. And if you do that, you will select the man that is best for you.

And so I say here tonight to you that the next man that sits there as the President may be called upon to move his thumb up toward that nuclear button that could wipe out 300 million people in a short time; that that next President may hear that phone ring that is there by his bed and by his desk, that "hot line" from Moscow, and you have to select the man that you want to answer it.

That is your decision; that is not mine. I will have a very small part in it. But that is the decision that you ought to think something about before you make it, and that is the decision that you ought to talk to your friends about, and your family about,

and you ought to be sure that you are doing what is best for your country.

There is not a boy in that crowd that wouldn't gallantly march down to that railroad station and put on that khaki uniform if he thought this flag was in danger tomorrow. The blood of the sons of South Carolina is strewn through many nations because they have carried that flag many places in the world and they have brought it back without a stain on it.

But your job Tuesday week is how to avoid war, not how to provoke war. Your job Tuesday week is to try to select a man that can unite this country instead of a man that can divide this country. Your job Tuesday week is to select a leader that has faith and hope and love instead of a leader who has fear and doubt and hate. And you will know in your own heart what is right. All the slander, all the smear, all the television, and all the propaganda somehow or other will go by the wayside Tuesday week. They will just be a mass of old banners, old pictures, and old television films, if they haven't been canceled between now and next Tuesday.

And you have only yourself to answer for. I haven't come down here to presume on your prerogatives, and to try to dictate to you what you ought to do. It is naturally to be assumed that I would recommend myself most highly. But I am not going to take my time to do that.

Well, I will tell you a little story before I go home. This happened down in my country. We lived out on a cotton farm when I was a boy, and we had a little boy there that left a little after lunch one day and went over to the Old Settlers' Reunion, the Old Confederate Reunion, and he didn't come back until dark that night—just about weighing-in time—just about the time we were unloading our sacks and weighing in.

And the boss said, "Where in the world have you been all afternoon?"

He said, "I have been over to the Old Confederate Reunion."

The boss said, "What did you do all afternoon at the Confederate Reunion?"

The boy said, "Well, I listened to a United States Senator make a speech."

The boss said, "Well, the Senator didn't speak all evening, did he?"

The boy said, "Mighty near, mighty near."

The boss said, "Who was the Senator and what did he speak about?"

"Well," the boy said, "Boss, his name was Senator Joseph Weldon Bailey, from Texas, and I don't recall precisely all the Senator talked about, but the general impression I got all afternoon was that he was recommending himself most highly."

So I hope that you will think of your country and your obligation, and not treat it lightly on November 3d, tomorrow week. I hope you will go select the man that you want to lead you, that in your conscience you believe is the best man to preserve peace, to preserve peace in the world and prosperity at home.

Tonight we have 72.5 million people working. Tonight we have an average wage in the manufacturing industries of $104 a week. Tonight we have 5 million more heads of families working than we had 4 years ago. Tonight our banks are full of money. We seldom hear any more of failures.

Tonight our farm income is up. Tonight our textile employment is increased, and we passed the cotton bill this year after great efforts of the Democratic administration to try to help the people of Georgia, South Carolina, and North Carolina.

Tonight we want to try to carry on, not to be satisfied with the status quo, but to move ahead in a spirit of tolerance and understanding, in a spirit of the Golden Rule, "Do unto others as you would have them do unto you;" in the spirit of the Good Book, "Love thy neighbor as thyself."

We think that we can do more united than we can divided. We think we can do more with love than we can with hate. We must always be prepared and have the arms and the strength to defend America. We must always keep our guard up, but always keep our hand out.

I, as your President, am willing to go anywhere to talk to anyone at any time that I think I can reason with him and bring peace in the world.

But just because we are mighty, and just because at Savannah and Oak Ridge you have created mighty, awesome powers that can destroy entire civilizations is no reason for me, as your President—and I will never be guilty of it—rattling our rockets and bluffing with our bombs.

Government of the people must not be government by ultimatum. Other people have other views, just as we do. You know, we don't see everything alike because if we did we would all want the same wife. We have different approaches, so we must try in the good words of the Good Book, we must try to reason together, and that is what we are trying.

If you down here in South Carolina will take your duty on election day as close to your heart as you do your duty when we have a declaration of war or your duty on Armistice Day, I have not the slightest doubt what your decision will be. But you must go vote. You must get your neighbor to vote. Every single individual is equal on election day, and we need every vote in that ballot box we can get, because we want to show the people of the other 120 nations of the world—we want to show the people of the other 49 States in the Union, that the people of South Carolina are good, Christian, peace-loving people who want prosperity for their folks, education for their children, and a bigger and brighter day for all America.

NOTE: The President spoke at 8:18 p.m. at the State Capitol Building in Columbia, S.C. In his opening words he referred to Senator Olin D. Johnston and Governor Donald S. Russell of South Carolina. Later he referred to Senators George A. Smathers and Spessard L. Holland, and Governor Farris Bryant, of Florida, and to Senators Herman E. Talmadge and Richard B. Russell, Representative Carl Vinson, and Governor Carl E. Sanders, of Georgia, and Mrs. Donald S. Russell. He also referred to the following, all of South Carolina: Representatives John L. McMillan, Robert T. Ashmore, and W. J. Bryan Dorn, Tom S. Gettys, Democratic candidate for Representative, Mayor Lester L. Bates of Columbia, former Governors Ransome J. Williams and George Bell Timmerman, State Senator Edgar A. Brown, Lieutenant Governor Robert E. McNair, Yancey A. McLeod, chairman of the State Democratic Party, and State Attorney General Daniel R. McLeod.

720 Statement by the President on the Occasion of a Ceremony at the Statue of Ukrainian Poet Taras Shevchenko. *October 26, 1964*

IT IS most fitting that those who love and admire Taras Shevchenko should meet to seal and place in the crypt of his statue certain documents which will be of interest to American citizens in years to come.

The love for the Ukrainian poet laureate is fully understandable and pride in his accomplishments wholly justifiable.

It is most appropriate that here in the Capital City of this great and free Republic a statue of Shevchenko should have been erected to serve as a reminder to all the living, and those who follow us, of his greatness.

Shevchenko well deserves the honors paid him. He was more than a Ukrainian—he was a statesman and citizen of the world. He was more than a poet—he was a valiant crusader for the rights and freedom of men. He used verse to carry on a determined fight for freedom. His poetry was of and for the people. It gave hope to those in despair and stirred to action those who might otherwise have been resigned to enslavement.

So widespread was his audience and so great his influence that his words were read and loved far beyond the frontiers of his own land. So valued were the copies of his poems that families struggled to own two books—the Bible and Shevchenko.

As a Member of the United States Senate back in 1960, I sent a message to your organizations saying, "I would like to congratulate you for reasserting the spirit of freedom and liberty held by Ukrainians everywhere. I am convinced that the Democratic Party best serves the cause of Ukrainians everywhere in the world."

This is also my message to you in 1964. As President of the United States I renew my congratulations for your accomplishments and assure you that this Nation and this Government earnestly desire the return of freedom to all peoples from whom it is even now denied. And Shevchenko's poetry will serve as a constant reminder of this most important task.

721 Message to President Kaunda on the Occasion of the Independence of Zambia. *October 26, 1964*

Dear Mr. President:

I extend to you and, through you, to the people and Government of Zambia the sincere best wishes of the American people and Government. We rejoice that Zambia has become free and now joins the other independent states of Africa in seeking a better life for its people.

During the past ten years the United States has warmly and sincerely welcomed many African states into the community of nations. As we welcome Zambia to this community and extend our congratulations to the people of Zambia, we wish to express our personal admiration to you, Mr. President, for the vital role you played during the recent years of preparation for this joyous occasion.

We especially admire your success in achieving mutual cooperation and understanding among the different racial elements in Zambia. We sincerely hope that this achievement will be taken as a lesson and example by the entire world. Our interest in your example is greatly heightened by our own efforts to eliminate racial discrimination in the United States.

The American nation seeks constantly to foster the development of free nations cooperating for their mutual benefit. We encourage the building of world and regional institutions for joint action and cooperation. We seek the elimination of violence and aggression of any sort in relations among na-

tions, and we support the economic and social development of each nation in the interest of the development of all nations. We believe that this community of free nations can fully achieve the universal goals expressed in the United Nations Charter only when all governments are based on the consent of the governed. We know that Zambia shares these objectives with us. We look forward to close cooperation with you and your Government in pursuing these mutual objectives in the councils of the world and in our relations with each other.

Zambia's independence will permit us to strengthen the ties of friendship and cooperation which have been built up between Zambians and Americans over many years.

With every possible good wish for the future success and well-being of Zambia and its people, I extend personally to you and to your Government my warmest congratulations for all that you have accomplished thus far. I pledge my friendship and that of my people and country in the years ahead.

Sincerely,

LYNDON B. JOHNSON

[His Excellency Kenneth D. Kaunda, President of the Republic of Zambia, Lusaka]

NOTE: The message was delivered to President Kaunda, whose country became independent on October 24, by Charles W. Engelhard, Personal Representative of the President with the rank of Special Ambassador.

722 Presidential Statement No. 3 on Economic Issues: Strengthening Our Balance of Payments. *October 26, 1964*

1. WE HAVE made much progress over the past 4 years in strengthening our balance of payments.

—Our surplus of merchandise exports over imports is 40 percent above 1960.

—Our balance of payments deficit (on

regular transactions) has been cut by more than half—from an average level of $3.9 billion in 1958–60 to $1.7 billion during the last fiscal year.

—Confidence in the dollar has been restored.

—As a result, the gold outflow—which averaged an alarming $1.7 billion a year from 1958 through 1960—was cut in half in 1961 and 1962, and has ceased entirely over the past 12 months.

2. This progress has not come at the expense of our other vital responsibilities

—for maintaining and improving our defenses abroad,

—for providing needed assistance to developing nations, and

—for sustained and rapid growth at home.

3. Moreover, we have refused to seek "easy" and fast solutions to our balance of payments problem through damaging controls and restrictions that would have curbed economic freedom, hurt our domestic prosperity, or damaged other countries' trade.

4. Instead, we have chosen the slower but surer path of progress through a more competitive, efficient, and prosperous domestic economy—an economy fully equipped to maintain and expand its share of rapidly growing world markets.

5. To assist American business in tapping the great potential of these world markets, this administration has pursued a vigorous program of export promotion and expansion. Five permanent American trade centers have been established abroad since 1961; 19 commercial exhibits at foreign trade fairs have been sponsored by the Department of Commerce in the past 2 years. With the assistance of the export expansion program, about 4,000 U.S. firms have made export sales for the first time since 1960.

6. During the past year we have cut back hard on the U.S. Government flow of dollars abroad; we have passed the interest equalization tax and raised short-term interest rates at home to cut off an excessive flow of capital abroad. Moreover, our policies have helped to maintain the price stability that has advanced our trade and we have made investment at home more attractive by stimulating healthy economic growth.

7. The task of restoring balance in our external payments has not been completed. We will maintain our forward momentum and capitalize on the very real gains of the past 4 years through further efforts to expand our exports, create conditions that will attract more of our capital into domestic investment, and pursue responsible fiscal and monetary policies that will retain the world's confidence in the American economy and the American dollar.

NOTE: For a statement by the President announcing a series of statements on economic issues, see Item 707.

---

723   Presidential Statement No. 4 on Economic Issues: Responsible and Effective Fiscal Policy.   *October 27, 1964*

1. RESPONSIBLE and effective fiscal management is a key obligation of the Federal Government. It requires:

—Comprehensive control of expenditures to insure maximum efficiency in operations, to cut back low priority and outmoded programs, to get a full dollar of value for every dollar spent.

—Strong and innovating Government programs that meet fully and efficiently our responsibilities at home and abroad.

—A tax system which distributes the

burdens and raises revenue equitably without blunting the incentive and efficiency of the private economy.

—Clear recognition of the budget's impact on our economic performance. Federal expenditure and tax programs are inevitably powerful influences on jobs, profits, and production in our private economy. The influences can be good or bad, depending on our wisdom in selecting and timing fiscal actions. By remaining alert to the economic effects of the budget, we can manage our fiscal affairs to create jobs and promote stable prices.

—Pursuit of the goal of a balanced budget in an economy balanced at its full potential.

As history demonstrates, when men and machines are idle, the low incomes of an unbalanced economy hold down Federal revenues and create deficits. In such a situation, we must take steps to stimulate production and create jobs, to restore the health of the economy—even though these measures may temporarily add to the deficit.

In other instances, when total demand would otherwise outrun our capacity to produce, we must diligently insist on budgetary surpluses and debt retirement.

In short, we must continuously pursue policies to promote steady and sustained prosperity without inflation—not merely to counter recessions and unsustainable booms after they begin.

2. We have put these principles into operation in 1964:

—by effecting substantial economies and cost reductions through close scrutiny of every expenditure program. As a result of careful management we are able to decrease both expenditures and Government civilian employment in the 1965 budget—for only the second time in 9 years.

—by using the fruits of frugality to contribute to human compassion and national progress. We have launched new programs to attack poverty, support urban mass transportation, improve housing, promote better education and training, and make more effective use of our natural resources.

—by providing the largest peacetime fiscal stimulus in history through the Revenue Act of 1964, thereby strengthening and broadening our prosperity.

3. And we will continue to follow these principles in the years ahead.

As long as the economy remains prosperous, rising incomes will increase the revenues of the Federal Government by roughly $6 billion a year at current tax rates. Unless a major increase in defense was required by unanticipated international developments, revenues would therefore tend to rise relative to expenditures. Economic conditions in a particular year might make this a desirable outcome. But fiscal policy must be constantly alert to the danger that a steady growth in revenues relative to expenditures could choke off our economic expansion, as it did in the late 1950's.

There are many ways by which this "fiscal drag" can be countered. The possibilities include: further tax reductions, increases for top-priority Federal programs, and an increased flow of funds to State and local authorities.

The size of these adjustments and the choice among them at any given time must and will depend on the changing needs of our people, state of our economy, and demands of national security—not on some rigid mechanical formula fixed for years in advance.

NOTE: For a statement by the President announcing a series of statements on economic issues, see Item 707.

724 Presidential Statement No. 5 on Economic Issues: Further Tax Reduction. *October 27, 1964*

1. TO SUSTAIN the prosperity of the economy, this administration has enacted the most far-reaching tax reductions in our history. We have already cut both individual and corporate income tax liabilities by nearly one-fifth. We have pledged excise tax cuts in 1965, and we anticipate further income tax cuts in the years ahead as part of our program for a prospering, peacetime economy.

2. In 1962, important measures were taken to help industry modernize its facilities.

—The revision of the depreciation guidelines added $1½ billion a year to corporate cash flow.

—The investment credit lowered business tax liabilities by more than $1 billion a year.

3. The Revenue Act of 1964 cut personal and corporate income tax rates, raising private after-tax incomes directly by $11½ billion. This reduction has given a great boost to the economy, as our advances in the past year—3d quarter 1964 over 3d quarter 1963—plainly show (annual rates):

—The gross national product is up $40 billion, or 4.6 percent in stable dollars.

—Corporate profits are up 22 percent (preliminary estimates).

—Business investment in plant and equipment is up 11.4 percent.

—Consumer income, after taxes, is up $32 billion—and consumer buying is up $27 billion, the greatest such increase in our peacetime history.

4. The size and timing of further tax reduction must be tailored most carefully to fit

—the developing budget program as a whole;

—changing business conditions, so that tax cuts serve to sustain prosperity without inflationary excesses.

5. Currently, the Treasury Department is intensively studying each of the 75 excise taxes to design a rational program of excise tax removal and reduction. Later, we will again focus on income taxation—both personal and corporate—as the major areas for anticipated future tax cuts.

NOTE: For a statement by the President announcing a series of statements on economic issues, see Item 707.

725 Remarks at the Presentation of a Commission to Lt. Col. John H. Glenn, Jr. *October 27, 1964*

Colonel Glenn, Secretary Nitze, ladies and gentlemen:

This is a very unusual and very peculiar pleasure for me this morning to have with us one of our most distinguished Americans and his family. I would not have this privilege if we had followed Colonel Glenn's wishes, because he felt an unselfishness that is all too rare among all of us and particu-larly among people in the Federal Government.

Colonel Glenn felt that his promotion would take from another worthy American a reward that he did not want to see him deprived of. And rather than do that, he would be willing to forego it himself. There are few people who reason that way.

I first got to know Colonel Glenn real

well when I met him early one morning at the culmination of a very exciting adventure at the Grand Turk Island. As you know, he was the first American in outer space. The thing that impressed me deeply was that Colonel Glenn did not just see the potentialities of space. He did not just see outer space. Colonel Glenn had a very penetrating look into the future. And in seeing space, he was seeing the future of all mankind.

Another thing that impressed me greatly was that each of the astronauts was given the reward, I guess I should say the privilege, of naming his own ship. Characteristically of his patriotism, his vision, and his love of his fellow man, Colonel Glenn named his capsule "Friendship."

So this morning I insisted that he come here to the first house of the land to receive from his Commander in Chief an honor that he did not seek and one that he did not desire—a promotion in rank. Now I went to the Congress with this matter. It was individual. And we were all unanimous that it was wonderful for him to feel that he should not take this promotion from another man, but that by adding one he would not do it, and we should not be

deprived of doing what we knew was right.

And so I have just signed his commission as a full colonel in one of the greatest organizations ever known to man, and I have proudly done so. But even the President promoting Colonel Glenn does not equal the high rank that he has already received from all the American people.

He is the kind of man that you would want your boy to be. He is the kind of man that we want all Americans to emulate. And he is the kind of fellow that I like to call my friend.

NOTE: The ceremony was held at 1:20 p.m. in the Rose Garden at the White House. The President's opening words referred to Lt. Col. John H. Glenn, Jr., and Secretary of the Navy Paul H. Nitze.

A White House statement released September 29 announced the President's nomination of Colonel Glenn for promotion to the grade of full colonel. The release stated that Colonel Glenn had not been chosen for promotion by the annual selection board because he had written to the Commandant of the Marine Corps requesting that his name not be considered in order that another officer might be selected. In his letter he stated that it was his intention to retire from the Corps as soon as his health would permit. At that time Colonel Glenn was recuperating from a head injury he had received in a fall in his home.

The President's reference to the Grand Turk Island meeting with Colonel Glenn was to the trip he made as Vice President in order to accompany Colonel Glenn back to the United States after his orbital flight.

---

726   Remarks to the Members of the Inter-American Committee on the Alliance for Progress.   *October 27, 1964*

Ladies and gentlemen:

We have just had a meeting with the membership of the CIAP group and discussed the relations in this hemisphere and we have found the developments to be quite encouraging. Harmony exists. There is a feeling of friendship between the neighbors in the Western Hemisphere. We regularly have these meetings.

The CIAP group has just completed a country-by-country review of the social and economic progress that the various individual nations have made. Eleven months ago, the first week that I was in office, I took somewhat far-reaching steps to overhaul the machinery and to strengthen the personnel in the agencies that dealt with our neighbors in this hemisphere.

At the end of the fiscal year, all the money that had been appropriated had been allocated. Red tape had been cut. Decisions were no longer being delayed. The watchword of the Administrator, Mr. Mann, who had the authority of the White House and the State Department and the Alliance for Progress all wrapped up under one hat, was such that he could make a decision, and did.

So we got out our allocations and made our decisions. We proceeded on the premise that we could not really have a successful relationship that we could take great pride in, unless we successfully attacked the ancient enemies of mankind in this hemisphere— poverty, disease, ignorance, illiteracy, ill health, and so forth; that we must have land reform; that we must have fiscal reform; we must have tax reform; we must have budget reform.

We have watched with great interest the improvement that has been made in these various fields. But I also concluded—and my view, I think, was shared by Secretary Rusk and Mr. Mann—that you could take all the gold in Fort Knox and it would just go down the drain in Latin America, unless the private investor, upon which our whole system is based, free enterprise, could have some confidence that he could make his investment and it would not be confiscated and that he would have an opportunity to make a fair and a reasonable return.

So we worked very closely with a number of leading businessmen and we worked very closely with some of the great thinkers, some of whom are represented here this morning, in trying to make it possible to make private investment increase and also make it safer. In 1963 we made investments of around $60 million in other countries. In 1964, at the rate we are going, it will be over $100 million, almost twice as much. So, progress is being made.

We have had a good many momentary difficulties. We had our water cut off at Guantanamo, but we solved that without a major debacle. We had some difficulties in Panama, but with patience and judgment we solved that without a major catastrophe. We had problems in Brazil and now we are working very closely with them to give them major assists. We had an election in Chile and that has been decided. Nowhere, really, have the Communists taken over any governments, or have any governments gone communistic since Cuba in 1959.

In retrospect, as we look over the 12 months of our relations with our neighbors in this hemisphere, we can look at them with confidence, with respect, and with pride. And now I am going to ask Mr. Mann to make a full and detailed report on these developments to me quickly, shortly.

I am going to ask Dr. Sanz here with CIAP to realize that we maintain an open door policy and that that door there to the President's office is always open to him and to his group for suggestions, for criticisms, for ideas. Because we do have a very genuine respect not only for the independence of our fellow men in this hemisphere but for their lofty and worthy desires to achieve for their people a better standard of living and a better way of life.

And because so many people helped us develop our economy and to become a strong and mighty nation politically and economically and educationally, we feel a debt of gratitude and we want to, in part, repay it by working with our other neighbors. Because the stronger they are, the stronger America is.

Thank you very much.

NOTE: The President spoke about 2:15 p.m. in the Rose Garden at the White House. During his remarks he referred to Thomas C. Mann, Assistant Secretary of State for Inter-American Affairs, United States Coordinator for the Alliance for Progress, and

Special Assistant to the President for Latin America, to Dean Rusk, Secretary of State, and to Carlos Sanz de Santamaría, chairman, Inter-American Committee on the Alliance for Progress (CIAP).

The text of Mr. Mann's report, dated October 30, 1964, is printed in the Department of State Bulletin (vol. 51, p. 706).

727 Remarks in Boston at Post Office Square. October 27, 1964

Mr. Speaker, Monsignor Griffin, my dearest friend and my staunchest ally, the great Speaker of the House of Representatives John McCormack, your vigorous next Governor of the State of Massachusetts, Frank Bellotti—this young man has great promise, great ability, and great honor. Massachusetts can perform a useful public service by electing Frank Bellotti overwhelmingly as your Governor. And I just hope that you vote the ticket straight, the Democratic ticket, all the way from the courthouse to the White House.

My beautiful and gracious friend Joan Kennedy. What pride all of you must have in this lady of great grace and dignity. I think that Ted Kennedy ought to be enshrined among the successful men of our time if for one reason alone: he had the good fortune to marry Joan.

Mayor Collins, my friend of long standing Governor Peabody, my loyal allies who for many years have been Members of one of the most effective and one of the most respected congressional delegations in all this Nation: Congressman Tip O'Neill, Congressman Phil Philbin, Congressman Torbert Macdonald, Congressman Jim Burke, and I haven't seen Eddie Boland here tonight, but if he is not here, I will tell you where he is: he is out in Ohio getting votes for the Johnson-Humphrey ticket, working until midnight to help us carry that State— and my friend Harold Donohue, my fellow Americans:

Thank you for your wonderful welcome.

It wasn't entirely unexpected. My friend and associate Dave Powers told me on the way up here about one of the five O'Sullivan brothers. He had just had a terrible quarrel at home and he walked to the corner and met a friend, and he said to him, "I am so angry I am going to go out and disgrace the entire family. I am going to register Republican!"

Four years ago I came to the great Boston area and we formed the pact of "Austin to Boston." And I am back here tonight to tell you that when the people from Austin make a pact with the people of Boston, Mr. Speaker, that is a contract as long as I have breath in my body. They tell me that Boston used to be known as the home of the bean and the cod, and I hope after next Tuesday that it will be known as the home of the Kennedys and the Johnsons.

This city and this State are among the leaders of this Nation. Your industry from shoes to electronics enriches America. In fact, I have more men from Massachusetts in the White House than from all the other States put together, and I will be just as proud to say that in Texas as I am proud to say it in Boston. Larry O'Brien, Kenny O'Donnell, Dick Goodwin, and other loyal allies of John Fitzgerald Kennedy have helped to make this administration what it is tonight.

But this modern city of today is also a memorable city of the past. Your streets are rich in American memories. Here have come the scholars and the soldiers and the statesmen and the diplomats to guide the destiny of the great Republic.

But no memory is more fresh and none is so bright, and none so mingles pain and gratitude as the memory of John Fitzgerald Kennedy of Massachusetts. He led an entire Nation and he found his way to the secret hopes of man. But he was Irish, he was Massachusetts born, and he was Boston bred.

He belongs to the world. But a part of him belongs especially to you, and you are richer for it. When he died the sound of mourning was heard in every street of the earth. But tears came more plentifully to Boston eyes, and grief more painfully to Boston hearts.

His qualities were many, but two especially explain his hold on men. He made them believe that they were better than they had thought they were; that perhaps, on earth, God's work could truly be their own.

And he could absorb in his imagination the dreams and the longings, the fears and the ambitions of others, whether they lived in mud huts in Africa or whether they lived in the palaces of kings. Somehow they understood that this was so.

But when he said "the torch has been passed," he was not speaking of himself, or of any individual, or of any group. It was the light of an idea about this country. It illuminated what we were and what we could be.

That idea was not struck down by a murderer's bullet. That idea is not ready to be carved on marble monuments. That idea will not be put away on the dusty shelves of memorial libraries. That idea is living tonight. It is breathing, it is growing every hour. And we will carry it forward until it swells to burst the bonds which limit men to less than they can be.

Before his inauguration, he spoke to the Massachusetts Legislature. He said the future would ask four questions of his administration and our Nation. These same questions will also be our standard.

First, he said, were we truly men of courage? Today we know the answer is yes. We saw an example of that courage in Cuba when determination brought a Communist withdrawal, a memorable victory for the cause of freedom, and a turning point in the cold war.

We will continue on the path of courage and bravery in time of crisis, firmness in the face of threats, and the undramatic but the ultimate courage to pursue our goals despite frustration and setback, and regardless of the length of the journey.

Second, he said, were we truly men of judgment? The answer to this question is also yes. We saw that judgment after Cuba. We did not press our victory or try to humiliate the Soviet Union. Instead, he seized the chance to move toward meaningful and lasting settlements which might lessen the danger of war. One of the results was the test ban treaty.

We will continue to apply judgment, not impulse; to apply restraint, not recklessness; apply wisdom, not uncontrolled emotion. Yes, we will apply these to the great problems of the world. We will ask respect for our interests. We will offer understanding for the honest fears of others. In this way, we can carry on the work of building a lasting peace.

Third, he asked, were we truly men of principle? The answer, again, is yes. Nowhere did this integrity shine more brightly than in his fight to secure equal rights to all Americans. Neither the political cost, and it was high, nor the pain of controversy, and it was great, caused a single deviation from the pursuit of full equality for men, special privilege for none.

Democratic politics requires accommodation and adjustment to the views of others. But where great principles are at stake, compromise must not obscure the demands of justice. The fulfillment of the promise of our Constitution, and an end to American poverty, are among such principles.

Just as Abraham Lincoln abolished slavery 100 years ago, it is the dedicated purpose and objective of the Democratic Party in our time to abolish poverty in the United States of America. And when John Fitzgerald Kennedy was taken from us, he had this program on the drawing board. And thanks to the leadership of the Massachusetts delegation and that towering giant, the Speaker, that program was passed in less than 12 months from the time John Kennedy planned it.

Fourth, he asked, were we truly men of dedication? The answer, again, is yes. In every area, dedication to the public good came first. That dedication remains our own:

—that the life of each citizen shall improve as the Nation improves and grows

—that the hungry shall be fed, that the old shall be protected, that the ignorant shall find learning

—that business and labor and farmer and consumer will move forward to the benefit of each and at the expense of none

—that America will be strong enough to resist any enemy and generous enough to help any friend

—that neither personal pride nor political gains will stand in the way of the pursuit of peace.

John Kennedy said the high court of history would measure our success by these answers. For him, judgment is now in. He has been placed among those who, in the words of the Bible, "were honored in their generations and were the glory of their times."

But for the rest of us—for you and for me—judgment still waits.

In that speech President Kennedy told us that John Winthrop, setting out for America, said to his shipmates, "We must always consider that we shall be as a city upon a hill—the eyes of all people are upon us."

Well, America tonight is a city upon a hill, and those who watch us look not to our tall buildings or our prosperous streets, or to our mighty arms. They look uncertainly, and hopefully, to see burning in the midst of the city a light of freedom, a flame of the spirit, the brightness of the nobility which is in man, and the arms of the Statue of Liberty awaiting them.

This is at once our bequest, our burden, and our brightest expectation.

Eleven months and three days ago, without notice, on that tragic day November 22d, amid the roar of the jet airplanes in the background, without opportunity to counsel and without being able to go to the libraries, I attempted to pick up where my beloved benefactor and friend had left off. And that evening I said to the people of this great land that with God's help and your prayers, I will do my best. I came back to the White House and got behind that lonely, black, iron fence, and the Secret Service turned the gate lock on me, and there I have been most of the time for 11 months and 3 days.

I looked over the inventory of his plans that he had left, and they constituted one of the greatest and most advanced social programs in the history of man. Fifty-one measures, spelled out in detail, that had meant the burning of a lot of midnight oil, had gone to the Congress.

A few days ago I sat in that same office

after the hour of midnight looking over many measures that had to be signed to become law. The Congress had come and the Congress had gone, and of those 51 major measures on the program of John Fitzgerald Kennedy, every single one of them had passed the Senate of the United States, and all but three or four had passed the House and were in conference. And they are going to be passed, God willing, come next year.

I have carried on as best I could. I have done what I told you I would. I have done the best I can. I came back here tonight to Boston because this is where I started 4 years ago, and the hand of fellowship and the hand of friendship and the hand of comradeship of my fallen leader—his friends came out and welcomed me to their homes and to their flats. I came back tonight not because I have the slightest doubt about Boston or Massachusetts, because I don't, but I came back because I never wanted them to have the slightest doubt about me.

I am sorry I was so late the other evening, but I seem to always run an hour late and a dollar short. But one of the most remarkable men that has ever been born in this country in my judgment is out in your hospital, God spared his life—Teddy Kennedy. He knew what was best. In due time—I am not a prophet but in due time he will lead a lot more people than those of Massachusetts.

He sits in the Senate as a symbol of all that is good and all that represents duty, and all that represents understanding and patience. He had to be patient the other night because I didn't get here until after midnight, but I hope that you will just do an especially good job for him come November 3d because he is not here tonight to do it for himself.

I thought maybe by coming up here I might just stimulate two or three or four or just a few dozen extra ones to go there and give Teddy and your new Governor that extra majority that they want that will make the Nation stand up and salute and take pride in Boston.

Now I am due in Pittsburgh—a few minutes ago—and then I am going to Evansville, Ind., to join my wife, who is working the other side of the street, the other section of the country. And then we will go to bed sometime in the evening in Albuquerque, N. Mex.

But we do want to carry on the spirit, the ideals and the program that was begun by that son of Boston, John Fitzgerald Kennedy. He went from one State in this Union to almost every State in the Union, and to many I went with him, and he said, "Give me your help, give me your heart, give me your hand and we will get America moving again." And America tonight is moving again.

I saw him come back from Vienna after his meeting with Khrushchev. He called the leadership in. In somber tones he told us the danger that our Nation faced. And then he began to build the mightiest military machine that man has ever known. We have more might tonight than any nation in the world, and more might than all of them put together because of John Fitzgerald Kennedy. He added $40 billion in 4 years to the military expenditures and to space expenditures, because he had a vision. His eyes were in the stars and his feet were on the ground, and he knew we could never be first on the earth and second in space.

And then came the Cuban missile crisis that men sometimes talk about now when he is not here to defend himself. I can't tell you, I just can't tell you, how sad it makes me feel to think that any worthy public servant would reflect on his conduct or his motives in that period. I don't want to even discuss it because I just think they must not know what they do. But I sat at that table in 37 meetings of the 38 that were held of the executive committee, and at the end he sent us a little silver calendar with each date of that month circled from the day we learned they were there until the day we learned they were gone.

I saw the generals with all their stars, and the admirals with all their braid, and the Secretary of State with a long record of great diplomatic performance behind him, distinguished service; and the Secretary of Defense, the former manager of the Ford Motor Co., at a salary of more than half a million a year that he gave up to serve his country. But the coolest man in that room always was the man that sat at the head of the table, John Fitzgerald Kennedy.

I never left my wife and daughters in the morning knowing whether I would see them that night, because those missiles were about to become operational. But I saw those two men, the spokesman for the Soviet Union and the spokesman for the free world, and there they stood while we went through 38 meetings, eyeball to eyeball, with their knife right on each other's ribs and never quivering or never moving until Mr. Khrushchev picked up his missiles and put them on his ships and took them back home.

We have much to remember, much to be thankful for, and all of our lives will be better because he passed our way.

Thank you.

NOTE: The President spoke at 5:50 p.m. in Post Office Square, Boston, Mass. In his opening remarks he referred to John Forbes Thompson, Speaker of the Massachusetts House of Representatives, the Right Reverend Monsignor Christopher P. Griffin, chaplain of the Massachusetts Senate, Representative John W. McCormack, Speaker of the U.S. House of Representatives, Francis X. Bellotti, Democratic candidate for Governor, and Senator and Mrs. Edward M. Kennedy, Mayor John F. Collins of Boston, Governor Endicott Peabody and Representatives Thomas P. O'Neill, Jr., Philip J. Philbin, Torbert H. Macdonald, James A. Burke, Edward P. Boland, and Harold D. Donohue, all of Massachusetts, David F. Powers, Special Assistant in the White House Office, Lawrence F. O'Brien and P. Kenneth O'Donnell, Special Assistants to the President, and Richard N. Goodwin, Assistant Special Counsel to the President.

728 Remarks at the Civic Center Arena in Pittsburgh. *October 27, 1964*

Ladies and gentlemen, boys and girls:

This is a great Democratic Tuesday in Pittsburgh, and a week from tonight it is going to be a great Democratic Tuesday.

When I was a little boy, living in a small house, in a small town, in the backwoods of my State, I remember hearing a political leader say at the Fourth of July picnic that he loved freedom so much that he just wished all the people had a little bit of it. And as I came into this magnificent building tonight, and I saw the new Pittsburgh, and I saw all of these happy, smiling faces, I just wished that everybody in our country could be here, because I think it would be contagious.

What a wonderful land it would be if all of our people were as happy tonight as you are. I even wish that some members—some temporary members—of another party could be here tonight so a little bit of this happiness would rub off on them.

It would be such a nice thing if these prophets of doom and gloom, and these apostles of fear and doubt, and these voices of smear and hate, and these suspicious persons who deal in petty things could just come here and see the heart of America, see them with faith and with hope, and with vision and with happiness, and with belief in the future of our land.

You people of Pittsburgh have a "can do" mayor, a man who looks ahead, who doesn't spend his time talking about the past, who has kept this city growing, who has kept it prospering. He is a great mayor and he is my friend and your friend—Joe Barr.

Before I get into my main speech, and it is not going to take over an hour or so, I want to ask you to do a few things for me if you can and if you can find the time, and I will get along with them just as soon as I can, because I have to meet Lady Bird in Evansville, Ind., for another speech. And then she and I are going to have a little anniversary, kind of a little 30-year honeymoon over in Albuquerque tonight.

You know, that poor girl has been traveling since daylight this morning and she has been through Texas, Arkansas, Oklahoma, and she is winding up in Evansville tonight, and I'll bet I have seen more people in this hall than she has seen all day. But I wouldn't be a bit surprised that she convinced a lot more of them than I have.

Here is what I want you to do for me. Here in the 14th Congressional District, you will be sending back to Congress to help me and to help the Nation, and to help Pennsylvania, a straight-thinking, a straight-talking friend of yours and of mine for many years. I want you to get out there tomorrow and start to work for him. Be sure that you give him a majority that he can brag about. That is Bill Moorhead.

From the 20th District you have a fellow who has fought awfully hard for me, and he has fought long and he has fought effectively. He is down at the White House getting a pen for some law that he has passed nearly every few weeks. He is the Congressman from the 20th District. He has been very

helpful, and I hope you will give Elmer J. Holland a good majority.

Then there is Westmoreland County, that "Get it done, and get it done now" Congressman, John Dent.

I don't know of a single man in America, and I don't make any exceptions, who is more valuable to this Republic, or who has done more for it in his own quiet way, always amenable, always reasonable, always enlightened. But he has done more to improve our relations with other nations and to bring peace in the world, and to keep your boys out of another war, than most any other man in either House.

He is a quiet, unassuming man. He never goes around slapping backs, talking big, smoking cigars, and telling you how he did it, but he is the kind of man that every district needs in Congress, and that every mother wants there to represent her in dealing with other nations. His name is Doc Morgan, and he is Chairman of the Foreign Affairs Committee.

He takes bills and he holds them in his committee and he has hearings for weeks on them. He has the best witnesses and the experts from all over the Nation. Then he reports them out with almost a solid vote from his party. He brings them to the House of Representatives. He passes them as they should have been passed, and he never even tells you about it. You have to call him up and it takes you a day or two sometimes for him to even answer the phone, and he says, "Thank you very much."

I want you to know, Doc, that we want you to have a great majority when you come back there.

Pennsylvania needs John Young and Frank Reed in the Congress. In fact, from the courthouse to the White House, we are going to need some more Democrats to help us keep this country moving. And you want to keep moving, don't you?

Next Tuesday will show that in this Keystone State of democracy, you agree with me that the Government of this country needs more women in general and it needs in particular your lovely and remarkable Genevieve Blatt.

I heard that someone intimated the other day that I had been strong for bringing women in Government, but they wanted to kind of imply that the President might perhaps not be too unhappy if another man was elected to the Senate, and came back there and Genevieve was defeated. Well, now, that is just one man's viewpoint. If he is quoted correctly, it is only his viewpoint.

Someone said to me the other day that Genevieve was one of the most competent women in this country. I am somewhat reluctant to tell you I disagreed. I think Genevieve is one of the most competent people in this country, man or woman, and if you want Pennsylvania to rebuild, if you want Pennsylvania to move again, if you want the voices of Pennsylvania to dominate the greatest deliberative body in the world, with their eloquence, with their respect, and with their influence, you give us two Democratic Senators from that State to work together like a team and we will give Pennsylvania some real results.

I don't think your State can do any greater service than to send this able and dedicated woman to the Senate. Pennsylvania needs her there. The Nation needs her there, and the President wants and needs her there, and hopes you will help him.

She could serve alongside of that fighting patriot who never turns away from what he believes to be right and just for all the people. He doesn't even turn away from giving me a lick now and then when he thinks I am wrong. But he is an independent, able, and courageous fighter for the people all the time, and for the right as he sees it all the time, Senator Joe Clark.

Now, those are a lot of recommendations to make, but when you have taken good Democratic care of your interests, and you have taken care of these people in the House, and you have taken care of these people in the Senate, I have another little cowcatcher suggestion that I want to make to you, and that is, I hope you will take care of Hubert Humphrey and Lyndon Johnson. These are all Democratic requests, but we are all Americans first and we are members of a political party second. This is especially important this year.

I know your Governor well. I have always had respect for his judgment, and I thought that he really made some good bipartisan points last July out at San Francisco. Bill Scranton seemed to me to be saying what deep in his heart he knew was right. So let's make next Tuesday not just a great day for Democrats, but let's make it a great day for Americans, because the last poll that we concluded in Pennsylvania last week showed that nearly 40 percent of the Republicans of this State are going to vote Democratic.

If a neighbor comes into your house, even if he is not your kinfolk, you bring out the welcome mat and you are cordial and you make him feel at home. If 40 percent of the Republicans are willing to come in and help us with good government, let's welcome them in under the tent.

There is another thing I want to thank you good folks for, and that is a man that you knew as mayor and that you knew as Governor. He is a man that I have known as a long personal friend since I was a young boy. He is a counselor and servant of Presidents, of the people, and of the Democratic Party, a man the Democrats know as one of the alltime great political leaders that either party has produced in this Nation.

I had an old friend of mine come up and he was talking about the young people that were taking the leadership. There was a young Governor, I believe from Oregon, who had some part on the program out in San Francisco. He said, "Who selected Dave Lawrence to be chairman of this extremely important committee?"

I said, with a great deal of pride, "I did."

He said, "I thought the Governor had retired and had gotten out of politics. With all of these young people that are full of ambition and vinegar and everything, and just like to keep moving ahead, why did you pick Dave Lawrence?"

I said, "Well, let's talk about that a little later."

We went ahead and we kept on the television. In a few minutes, Dave Lawrence came in with a steady nerve and with a solid step and with good countenance and with a strong voice, and he read a report. He said, "Mr. Chairman, I move the adoption of that report."

The chairman hit his gavel and said, "Without objection, the report is adopted unanimously."

I turned around to my friend and said, *"That* is why I selected Dave Lawrence."

I am happy tonight. I feel very cheered to see my old and my loyal friend Dave McDonald here. Dave is always there when you need him, and his heart is always on the side of the people. And I believe he has more Steelworkers here tonight than he had at the convention in Atlantic City.

I just couldn't be more pleased at the unity that you people have shown to your President. There are so many more areas of agreement, there are so many more things that unify us than divide us. Any one of you can find something to disagree and fight about. Every man and his wife have

differences. None of us see everything alike; if we did see everything alike we would all want the same wife. But when your President comes here, I like to see people stand united.

I just couldn't be happier tonight, and I have to say so publicly, than to see and visit with my longtime friend, a counselor of mine, one who has acted as my legal counselor in the Senate and times when I called him from Pennsylvania to come down and help me on certain legislation. That is Justice Mike Musmanno. His kind of loyalty and his kind of steadfastness is what I think is going to make the Democratic Party an enduring and effective instrument for progress and prosperity.

If Bill Scranton, after all the letters he wrote, and all the statements that he made, and all the things that he thought, can go out here in Pennsylvania and introduce Goldwater, I am happy that Mike Musmanno can come up here and sit on a platform with Genevieve Blatt and Lyndon Johnson.

Mrs. Emma Guffey Miller, I want to thank you from the bottom of my heart for your being here tonight. You have been one of my favorite girls for a good many years. I am not going to say how many. But I appreciate your coming over here and I am proud to be with you and my other fellow Democrats.

There are two great plans for progress in America today, and Pittsburgh is a blueprint for both of them. Lincoln abolished slavery 100 years ago, and we are going to abolish poverty under Democratic Party leadership in this country. There is no real reason for Americans to be prisoners of the nagging fear of unemployment or of destitution or of despair.

We have a gross national product of over $600 billion, and we don't make money just to make money. We make money for the betterment of man and for the fuller and richer life for human beings, And we are going to do that when we build the Great Society. This is what you in this city have meant by the Pittsburgh renaissance.

Not many years ago Pittsburgh was a worn-out, old city, known more for its waste than for its wealth, known more for its slums than its skyscrapers, known more for its polluted rivers than its precious resources. Its skies were blackened with smoke. When you saw the blue, it just meant the mills were down and the people were hungry. Then you got to work. You started doing something about it.

Today Pittsburgh is a city of clear skies, it is a city of clean buildings, it is a city of uncluttered streets. It has lovely parks and beautiful homes. I always like to come and stay at this hotel and get up and look out my window and see what used to be and what is. And your world famous, and now world conquering, Pittsburgh Symphony Orchestra—those are things you people ought to take a lot of pride in.

To these people who talk about raw, naked power, and these people that talk about Government centralization, these people that talk in these glittering generalities, covering everything and touching nothing, to those who want to repeal the progress of our times, I say, then, let them come here and take a look at Pittsburgh.

Four years ago a beloved American, John Fitzgerald Kennedy, came here and he looked at you as I am looking at you tonight, and he talked about a "new partnership." He believed and I believed—and you have shown—that progress has to be a partnership affair. To those who want to repeal the whole idea of people working together through Government where necessary, I say

to them, then, come here and look at Pittsburgh!

I believe deeply that Government must not be bigger by a single bureau or a single employee or a single dollar than it has to be. And I would have you know that I reduced the deficit from nearly $9 billion to $5 billion this year. I would have you know that during July and August we spent $676 million less than we spent last July and August. I would have you know that we had 25,000 less Federal employees on the Federal payroll this July 1964, than we had July 1963.

But honest government is government that doesn't waste a cent of money, or a minute of time, and the people's business has to be carried on, and a lot of what we want to do has to be done together—the city, the county, the State, the Federal Government—and this is a key issue in this election.

The opposition candidate has voted to cut out or cut down every program of common responsibility for anything, from national defense to education, social security. When he says make social security voluntary, our answer is that old age and the sickness that comes with it is not voluntary, and we believe in more insurance in old age and not less. While he is talking about Bobby Baker, Walter Jenkins, and Billie Sol Estes, we want to talk about urban renewal, we are going to talk about low-income housing, we are going to talk about area redevelopment, we are going to talk about his vote against aid to education.

All of these things he opposed. All of these things he voted no, no, no on. We have unfortunate things happen to us and we have disappointments; and 3 million men working for the Government, they make mistakes. The only thing we can do with them, when we find out about the mistakes, is to take their job away from them, ask for their resignation, and turn it over to a non-partisan agency to investigate to see if they have violated any laws. That is what we have done. Some in the other party get promoted.

There are a lot of things that have helped rebuild Pittsburgh, and on all of these things that have, he voted against them.

I think these things that I just listed will help build the Great Society and I think you are for them.

Our opponent voted against the Manpower Development and Retraining Act that Congressman Holland and Joe Clark had so much to do with. They got it passed. He opposed it. If he had had his way, it would be dead. This act has already helped 5,400 Pennsylvania workers win their fight against machines, and get retrained, and we are for that and he is against it.

And when we say as a Nation "In God We Trust," this doesn't mean everybody for himself and the devil takes the hindmost. Government is not the end of people. Government, prudent government, responsible government, is the people, and that is what this election is all about, the responsibility of people, acting together, to keep prosperity here at home, to keep peace here at home, to keep peace between business and labor and Government, and to keep peace in the world.

The opposition candidate voted against this year's tax cut. We Democrats believe in making the economy stronger. He voted against the nuclear bomb test agreement. We believe in making the world safer, and our milk cleaner. Our opposition protests that the issues are not being drawn in this campaign. Well, me thinketh he protesteth too much.

What are the issues in this election? Well, I will tell you what they are. The issues in this election are our votes, the Democratic votes, for and his votes against the Civil Rights Act, his votes against the Trade Expansion Act, his votes against the Mass Transit Act, his votes against the Wilderness Act, his votes even against the war on poverty. These are all issues in this campaign, and we are wrapping them right around his neck.

These are not issues that necessarily divide Democrats and Republicans, because the opposition candidate in this campaign voted 25 times in the past 4 years against major proposals which were in the 1960 Republican platform and were supported by a majority of Republican Senators. That is almost unbelievable, isn't it, that the Republican nominee voted 25 times on 25 separate roll calls against provisions in the Republican platform that were supported by a majority of Republican Senators!

I looked up the record the other day when he was talking about sending General Eisenhower to Viet-Nam. I don't think he took the time to talk to General Eisenhower about it. But it did make a headline momentarily.

I just wondered. He said he was going to follow everything on foreign policy. I remembered he said that the Eisenhower administration was just another dime-store New Deal. So I went back and looked at the record. I found out that in the year 1960, the last year President Eisenhower was there, I voted for President Eisenhower's foreign policy 95 percent of the time, and the Republican nominee voted for it 25 percent of the time.

When President Eisenhower became President, he really wrecked a lot of Democrats, and he broke a lot of dishes on the table, and a lot of them went home and were defeated. There weren't many people there

1475

to take the leadership. They elected me as the Democratic leader.

The first thing I said to my caucus was, "I want you to know when I think the President is right I am going to raise his hand high and I am going to support him. When I think he is wrong, I am going to oppose him, but I am going to do it with decency and dignity and without regard to personalities and I will never talk about his boy or his dogs or things of that kind."

I remember that it was a great Republican Senator, Arthur Vandenberg, that stood shoulder to shoulder with Harry Truman and stopped the Communists in Greece and Turkey. I remember that Lyndon Johnson stood right by the side of Eisenhower in the Suez and in the Strait of Formosa. I remember in his tax bill that I stood there in 1954 and supported it when a substantial number of my own party wouldn't go along with me.

So I don't think there is going to be a Republican peace or a Democratic peace, but I think there is going to be a peace only for all Americans and for all the world. When they lead your boy down to that railroad station to send him into boot camp and put a khaki uniform on him to send him some place where he may never return, they don't ask you whether you are a Republican or Democrat. They send you there to defend that flag, and you go.

So there is no Republican peace or no Democratic peace, and there can't be prosperity for Democrats or prosperity for Republicans. But there can and will be, as long as I am President, peace for all Americans and prosperity for all Americans.

Some people say that we passed an act up there that is going to take a lot of jobs away from folks. I want to meet that one head-on. That is pure dirty racism and propaganda that is being passed around.

There is not any bill that Congress ever passed that takes any job away from anybody. It gives a lot of people jobs, it provides extra jobs, it provides retraining for jobs that our Republican opponent voted against every time he had a chance. But they put out a lot of words to try to smear and fear and scare people who are working, by saying that some other man is going to get his job. Well, I want to answer that with a little story Lady Bird told me.

A man came up to her in Alabama on her train trip, where she had gone to school in the summer, where she went to the University of Alabama when she was a young girl. He said, "Lady Bird, I have been thinking about this problem a lot and they have put out a lot of stories down here about what has happened. But I believe that I would rather have a Negro stand beside me on an assembly line than to stand behind me in a soup line!"

Men who have jobs and who have seniority are going to be employed on the basis of their merit. And every State except 19 States, most of them in the South, already have laws stronger than we have passed.

We all know that it was 100 years ago that a great President, a man that we all revere—there is not a man, woman, or child in this house that would get up tonight and even whisper a word about him, although he said when he returned to his hometown in Illinois he went down the street and not one human would speak to him except one woman, and she wouldn't have if she could have gotten out of it. That is what Abraham Lincoln said. That is what they said about him during his turbulent career.

But we know that he signed the Emancipation Proclamation 100 years ago. We have had some deliberate speed for 100 years. Emancipation was a proclamation but it was not a fact.

We are not going to say that the good Lord intended that the tall men should be treated different than the short men, or that the white men should be treated differently from the black men or the brown men, because if we do, we are outnumbered in this country 15 or 20 to 1 throughout the world. We live in a world of 3 billion people, and you better not ever choose to fight it out on the basis of color. If you do, the white folks are in trouble, I will tell you that.

So we are not going to make any special appeals to any special groups. I think I demonstrated in 1960, after John Fitzgerald Kennedy had defeated me overwhelmingly and humiliatingly. He came to my room the next morning and asked me to go on the ticket with him as Vice President.

I had never thought that I would ever do anything like that. I thought for 7 or 8 hours and it finally boiled down to two things.

I just knew in my heart that it was not right for Dick Nixon to ever be President of this country.

And I also knew that one morning at an Air Force site in Europe the boys had completed their 50 missions and were ready to come home to see their wives, sweethearts, and mothers when a commanding officer walked in and said, "We have a most dangerous mission that must be performed today, and we want volunteers. All of you have already finished your missions, but we need some volunteers."

The first two men that stood up were Joe Kennedy, Jr., from Boston, a Catholic, and a young blond from Texas, from Fort Worth, Tex., with a wife and two babies, who walked up and stood by his side. He was a Baptist. And they took off in that plane and they never came back. But there is no one who dared ask them that morning what church they went to.

I thought I would just like to take a little slice of the proposition of proving to all the world that we elected our Presidents and Vice Presidents, and we treated our citizens of all races and religions and color alike, and that we could elect a President of this country who was a Catholic, and we could elect a Vice President of this country who was a southerner. And that is what we did.

Eleven months and three days ago, that tragic day of November 22d, our leader fell. And without benefit of council and without time to go to the library stacks, without a moment to call in anyone to consult, with the Secret Service men on top of me stretched out in a little Ford police car, I got in a jet plane with the motors roaring in the background and took the oath of office as President.

I swore to uphold the Constitution, and I swore to myself that I would carry on, I would continue for my partner who had gone down ahead of me.

The transition period was a difficult period. The heads of 85 nations came here. We talked over problems and agreements that had never been reached and we made decisions that had to be made, and the budget had to be formulated, $100 billion in 30 days. And we kept that light burning in the White House—notwithstanding what they tell you about my cutting them off—we kept them burning there until 2 or 3 o'clock many mornings.

But we looked down the inventory that he had left on his desk. He had 51 major bills, the greatest agenda of bills that I guess any President had ever sent a Congress in modern times: the tax bill, the civil rights bill, the mass transit bill, the housing bill, three education bills, the farm bill, the wilderness bill. I could name them all night, 51 of them.

I went back to that room the other night,

when the Secret Service turned the key on the black steel gate we entered, and they said, "Do you want to get off at the house or do you want to go to the office?" I said, "I will go back to the office."

About 1 o'clock I took those bills and I started looking down that list that he had left me. The Congress had come and the Congress had gone away. But on that list every single one of those 51 bills had passed the United States Senate, and all but 4 or 5 of them had passed the House. They were in conference—medical care, the coffee agreement, Appalachia. But I put it into effect by an Executive order [1] and we are going to put it into effect by legislation as soon as Joe and Genevieve get back up there and start voting as a team.

And we have some more things that we have to do for America. I said let us continue. But I also said at the convention I want a mandate, I want a mandate not just to let us continue but I want a mandate to begin.

I want a program for all the people of this country, equal opportunity for all and special privilege for none. I want every man and woman that wants a job to have a job. There are 5 million more working now than there were when Jack Kennedy took the oath of office. We have done something about it but not enough.

Corporations made $12 billion more after taxes this last year than they did the year before. So business is doing reasonably well. The workingman made $60 billion more after taxes than he did the year before, so he is doing reasonably well.

The farmer's income is up $12 billion this year, and if you would follow my opponent's

_____
[1] Executive Order 11186 "Establishing the Federal Development Planning Committee for Appalachia," issued October 23, 1964 (see Item 711).

advice and cut out all of these programs it would drop in half, to $6 billion, and we would be back where we were in 1932.

And don't you think it can't happen here, because it has happened here. It happened here before some of you were born or some of you are willing to admit that you were born. I think that is why next Tuesday will be not just an all-Democratic day. I think it is going to be an all-American day.

So we must get on with our work because there is so much to do. No city or country is ever all that that city or country ought to be. A nation, deeply understood, is an opportunity for service, a dedication to an unfinished dream.

The Great Society is when America's promise and her practice come together. The Great Society just isn't a dream of mine. It is as real as tomorrow, and it is yours for the working at it.

And here is how we do it: We care about every single man, woman, and boy in this country. Not just about some of them. Not just about most of them.

The Great Society under a Democratic President cares for all of them. And then we set our sights high, higher than we expect to get, at least higher than we expect to get right away, for we know that all we need to do in this country is to decide to do it.

We're as big as our ideas. We're as strong as our purposes. So here is the Great Society.

It's the time—and it's going to be soon—when nobody in this country is poor. Do you know that in the year 2000 the average annual income in this country is going to be $15,000 per family?

It's the time—and there's no point in waiting—when every boy and girl in this country, every boy and girl that is born under that flag, has the right to all the education that he can absorb.

It's going to be the time when every older man and woman has not just full social security, but it has meaning and it has purpose, and it has pleasure.

It's going to be the time, as I said, when we have a job for everyone who is willing to work, and he is going to be paid a decent wage.

It's the time when every false distinction—of what your race is, or your creed is, or your sex, or how you spell your name, or where your folks came from, or how you pray—it's going to be a time when none of that makes any difference.

Yes, under the Great Society, they want me to spell it out so I am just going to give you a little preview of it tonight.

It's the time when every slum is gone from every city in America, and America is beautiful.

It's the time when man gains full dominion under God over his own destiny.

It's the time of peace on earth and good will among men.

The place is here and the time is now.

Eleven months and three days ago my mind went back to that terrible tragic period during the Cuban crisis, when I saw the generals with all their stars and the admirals with all their braid, and the Secretary of State with all of his diplomatic background, and the Secretary of Defense with his great industrial experience march into a room to try to decide what to do about the Russian missiles that were located 90 miles from our shore, that were pointed at us and might be operational any moment.

I never left home a single day during those 38 sessions that I knew for sure I would see my wife and daughters again that night.

And there amidst the best brains and the greatest advice that a President could collect, a young, fearless man sat at the head of the table as Commander in Chief. I am proud to tell you that John F. Kennedy was the coolest man in that room.

As he and the leader of the Soviet Union came eyeball to eyeball, and their thumbs started inching up—that was the day before the "hot line" when you could pick up the phone and Moscow would be calling—their thumbs started getting closer to that nuclear button, their knives were in each other's ribs almost, literally speaking, and neither of them was flinching or quivering. About that moment, Mr. Khrushchev in his wisdom decided that he would wrap up his missiles and take them home.

Our bombers were in the skies and our bomb bays were ready to be opened. They were loaded. Our ships were in their proper places. Our men had their proper instructions. But when the time finally came, the good Lord somehow or other decreed that there would not be a nuclear holocaust that would wipe out the lives of 300 million people, 100 million right here in our own land.

And now, to have someone speak ill and critically of that crisis and of President Kennedy's conduct is too sad to even justify a response, because he is not here to answer it himself.

But we are going to answer it for him on November 3d. We are going to say to the world that our policy is strength through restraint. We are going to keep our guard up at all times, alert, but we are going to have our hand out. We are willing to talk to anyone, any time, who offers any hope of an honorable peace.

We are not going to bury anybody, but nobody is going to bury us.

We are not going to rattle our rockets or bluff about our bombs. But we are going to continue to be the mightiest nation in the world. We are going to speak softly and we are going to act prudently, and if you will just send me these two Democratic Senators, Joe Clark and Genevieve Blatt, if you will send me these Congressmen I have talked to you about, and my old friend Congressman Frank Clark—I want to put in a word for him.

I want you folks to know that this is about as important a decision as you will ever make when you decide what man's thumb, which man's thumb, you want to be close to that button, what man you want to reach over and pick up that receiver on that "hot line" when they say "Moscow is calling."

That is your decision. That is your judgment. You have to make it with your God and your own conscience.

I haven't come here to say anything personal or bad or ill-willed, or sling any mud, or have any muckraking. I have come here to tell you the problems and the issues that exist. You have to do something about it. Every single vote is going to count. Every single Congressman is going to help. Every single Senator is going to be needed.

Now, don't sit around here and wait until they start playing a patriotic song and you go to packing up your boy's suitcase. Step in here. Don't wait like they did with Woodrow Wilson. He envisioned a peace and he almost was in reach of it. Then he lost it and we went to World War II. Then Franklin Roosevelt came along with the United Nations, and they have saved a dozen wars.

But now here, with two great powers arrayed, let's continue this bipartisan policy, let's bring the Republicans in with the Democrats, let's reason together, let's be patient, let's be firm, let's be restrained, let's don't issue ultimatums, let's don't shoot from the hip. Let's don't use our tongue more than our head.

That is your job—to pick the person that you want to lead you. You won't have another chance after next Tuesday. It will be 4 long years and there are a lot of things that are going to happen in the next 4 years.

I am going to be down on the banks of the Pedernales in a little village in Texas, and I am going to be waiting for Joe Barr to call me. I am going to be wondering how well you do your job.

Thank you—and good night.

NOTE: The President spoke at 9 p.m. at the Civic Center Arena in Pittsburgh, Pa. During the course of his remarks he referred to Joseph M. Barr, mayor of Pittsburgh, William S. Moorhead, Elmer J. Holland, John H. Dent, and Thomas E. Morgan, U.S. Representatives, John Young and Frank J. Reed, Democratic candidates for Representative, Genevieve Blatt, Democratic candidate for Senator, Joseph S. Clark, U.S. Senator, William W. Scranton, Governor, and David L. Lawrence, former Governor, all of Pennsylvania, David J. McDonald, president of the United Steelworkers of America, Michael A. Musmanno, judge of the Pennsylvania Supreme Court, and Mrs. Emma Guffey Miller, Democratic national committeewoman, and Frank M. Clark, U.S. Representative, both of Pennsylvania.

729 Remarks at an Airport Rally in Evansville, Indiana. *October 27, 1964*

Senator Hartke, my dear friend Senator Hartke, Senator Bayh, Mayor McDonald, Governor Welsh, Governor Branigin, Governor Breathitt, Congressman Denton, my fellow Americans:

I really came here to Evansville tonight to meet Lady Bird. I wanted to check up on how many votes she had gained this week. But I guess as long as I am here, we might as well talk a little politics.

I never saw a Hoosier, or a Texan, who minded talking politics. I didn't come out here to say anything bad about anybody. I am not mad at anybody.

I don't want to fight anybody. I want to unite. I want to unite this Nation.

We do have a story to tell in Evansville, in Indiana, and in the country. It is a story of the greatest peacetime prosperity in the history of any land. It is the story of peace, and I think you are going to keep it that way—by your votes next Tuesday.

I worked in the office until 4 o'clock this afternoon and then I went up to Boston and had tea. After we saw our first half million, we decided we better leave town before sundown and we went over to Pittsburgh and had dinner. I guess we will just have a nightcap here in Evansville and go to sleep in Albuquerque.

But I have traveled across the Nation this fall. When I get to Albuquerque tonight I will have been in 43 States since Labor Day, and everywhere I have gone, everywhere I have been, everything I have seen, the signs all read the same: "Men at work." That looks good to me. I know that you, too, here in Evansville, have had more than your share of hard times, but you didn't surrender. You shouldered primary responsibility for helping yourselves, and this administration, with its manpower retraining program, with its area redevelopment programs, tried to come in and help. And we stand ready to continue to do that.

I think you can see the results all around this Nation. New industry is under construction, men are back at work. There are more than 5 million more at work than there were when President Kennedy took the oath of office, and an unemployment rate that has been cut almost in half in the last 3 years.

This prosperity just didn't happen. It came about because of the tax cut, a $12 billion tax cut, and other economic policies of this administration; because this administra-

tion cooperated with State and local governments; because this administration helped responsible business and responsible labor work together; because this administration helped responsible private citizens do their part; and because the responsible leaders of both political parties in the Congress voted together, not for their parties but for their country.

And that's the way it ought to be.

Two of the most responsible men in the United States Senate today are your own Senators, Vance Hartke and Birch Bayh. I came to Indiana in 1958 to try to help Vance Hartke come to the Senate. I got here about this time of night and I met Vance and we went to the hotel to unpack my suitcase. I told him that I would speak for him the next day. I would speak either for him or against him, whichever he thought would help him the most, and Vance outlined how he wanted me to recommend him and what he wanted me to say about him, and just where to say it and when to say it, and how to say it.

I spent a very pleasant day in the Hoosier State asking you people to give him a chance and let him come to the Senate and make his mark. Evansville can be proud of Vance and Martha Hartke, and we hope so much that all of you in Evansville, all of you in Indiana, will send them back to Washington to help us out and help you out, and help the world out.

I have two young daughters, one is 20 and one is 17, and I just see them as they flit down the hall going out on a trip or coming back from one. Luci told me this morning that she had been in 19 States, and she said, "What do you think about a young lady of 17 that hasn't had a free weekend since May?"

Well, I didn't think very long, but I guess the reason she hasn't is because Birch Bayh took the Young Democrats and he has perfected them with Marvella's help into one of the finest organizations in this entire campaign. I want to publicly thank them both for their great contribution to the Democratic Party.

Your responsible and experienced Congressman, Winnie Denton, is playing an increasingly important role in the Congress. He has fought consistently for better flood control programs for the Ohio valley, and he has gotten those programs. As a key member of the powerful Appropriations Committee, he is one of the few men who lead the Congress. Seven good terms, I think, deserve another.

They asked our beloved Speaker Sam Rayburn one time why it was that Texas had a Speaker, a Vice President, a majority leader, and 8 of the 15 chairmanships in the House of Representatives. And he said, "Because Texas people have the good judgment," speaking of picking their Congressmen and their Senators, "to pick them young, to pick them honest, to send them there, and to keep them there."

I know you have picked them young and I know you have picked them honest. I know you have sent them there. Now, let's finish up the job and let's keep them there!

You need responsibility here in Indiana, and I hope you won't mind if I commend to you a man with a brilliant future who is going to make a great chief executive, your next Governor, Roger Branigin. He has a program for a new Indiana, and if you will just give it that little extra "umph," that little extra push that he needs between now and next Tuesday, he will put Indiana on the map. Roger has worked with business and industry in this State. He has worked for the Federal Government. He knows from his long experience what Indiana needs, and if Roger is Governor of this State and if I

am President of this country, this State and this Nation will work arm in arm, shoulder to shoulder, to get the job done for the people of Indiana.

We have a lot of work ahead of us. We want to expand our social security program. We don't want to destroy it, either, by making it voluntary.

We want to improve, not shrink, our children's education. We think that it ought to be the right of every American boy and girl that is born under that flag to have all the education that he or she can take. To do that job, we need to unite our people instead of divide them, and we need to have national unity and for all of us to work together. To do it, we must have aggressive, prudent, responsible leadership.

If we want to go on to the Great Society where there is full employment for our workers, where there is maximum development for our industry, where there is full education for our children, where there is adequate protection for our parents, and where there is full opportunity and equal opportunity for all of our citizens, then we are going to have to unite and start working with each other instead of fighting each other, start loving each other instead of hating each other, start uniting with each other instead of dividing with each other.

I have talked to you about some of the lesser issues in this campaign. I talked to you about conservation and social security, full employment, area redevelopment, flood control. But beyond all of this, and far above all of this, lies the greatest single issue in all of our lives. That issue is peace.

How do you attain peace in a dangerous world? In a matter of minutes—well, in a matter of moments on that tragic day November 22d, before I had a chance to consult any adviser, before I could even walk in a library and get back into the stacks, before I could even think what I should really do, I found myself on the bottom of a Ford police car with a Secret Service man on top of me, racing to an airport, and in the back end of Air Force One, with one hand on the Bible and the other raised to my side, taking the oath of office of President of the United States, with the most awesome responsibilities that go with it. I said then to the people of this country and to the people of the world, that with God's help, with your prayers, I would do the best I could.

We went through the transition period. We visited with the leaders of 85 nations. We submitted the Federal budget. We took up President Kennedy's unfinished program that he had worked out in great detail with all of his leaders and the leaders of his Cabinet, and one of the most constructive and comprehensive programs ever submitted by any President to any Congress, and we started to work to do the best we could.

There were 51 major measures in that legislative program, and your two Senators and your Congressmen have worked their hearts out trying to help me do the best I could. The other evening I came home from another trip out to see the people and I went to my desk that was piled high with reports and papers, and one of them was a comprehensive report on the Congress. The Congress had come since November 22d, and the Congress had gone away.

I looked down that list of 51 major bills and every single one of those 51 bills had passed the United States Senate, and all but three or four had also passed the House of Representatives. And if God is willing and the creeks don't rise, they are going to pass the House of Representatives next year.

But in a matter of minutes that catastrophe happened to America, and in a matter of

minutes a nuclear catastrophe could overwhelm us all.

Next Tuesday, the 3 billion people of the world are going to be looking at you in Indiana and 49 other States to see which man, to see what man, to see the kind of man and type of man, and what experience he has, and what his temperament is, and what his judgment is—what kind of man you are going to select to have his thumb near that button, what kind of man you are going to select when that telephone rings on that "hot line" from Moscow, who you want to answer that phone, and what you want him to say.

That is your decision, and now, as never before in man's history, you are going to be called upon to exercise your priceless privilege of citizenship. You are going to need all the responsibility that you can summon. The stakes are much too high to be negligent. And the cause is much too great to be reckless. The finger on the nuclear button can trigger hundreds of millions of deaths.

As your Commander in Chief, I tell you tonight that we are the mightiest and we are the strongest nation on earth. Our military might is greater than that of all the other nations in the world combined. But we must be wise as well as strong. We must be reasonable and never be rash. We must always be intelligent and never impulsive. We must be resolute, but never reckless. We must always be alert and keep our guard up but our hand out. We don't want to bury anyone, but we don't intend to be buried, either.

I didn't stop by here tonight to talk about petty little things or little men. I didn't come here tonight to talk about personalities. I came here to talk to you about the issues of peace in the world and prosperity at home. I think you will have a lot to do with what happens. I think your decision may make the difference. I think every single person is equal on election day. And I think every single ballot is going to be needed.

And if the bell should ring, if the call should come, if the summons should arrive, I have not the slightest doubt that every man and woman here would take their son to the railroad station tonight to see him go away to boot camp and put on the khaki uniform, maybe never to return again, just as they did in World War I and World War II.

But for 20 years now we have had a bipartisan foreign policy. Senator Arthur Vandenberg, a great Republican Senator from Michigan, joined President Harry Truman, a Democratic President, and together they stopped the Communists in Greece and Turkey. Lyndon Johnson joined with Dwight Eisenhower in the Formosa Strait. In the last year of his administration in 1960, Lyndon Johnson, the Democratic leader, voted with Dwight David Eisenhower, the Republican President, 95 percent of the time on his foreign policy, while the present leader of the Republican Party voted with him only 25 percent of the time.

When the test ban treaty was before the Senate, which prevents our air from being polluted, which prevents your children from drinking milk with radioactive poison in it, that prohibits your mothers from giving birth to babies that are deformed—when that test ban treaty was before the Senate, it was Everett Dirksen from the State of Illinois, a Republican Senator, that stood there with John Fitzgerald Kennedy and helped that treaty become a reality, and it has now been affirmed by 105 other nations, while the present leader of the Republican Party was one of 12 Senators to oppose it.

If you want to junk all we have done for 20 years trying to preserve the peace of the world, if you want to see bipartisanship go down the drain and flush out of existence, then you ignore my warning. But if you want to continue to put your country ahead of your party, and if you want peace in the world more than you want anything else, then you appeal to the good men of both parties to join together and let politics stop at the water's edge; and let them come with the leaders of other nations and not rattle their rockets and not bluff with their bombs. But in the words of the prophet Isaiah, come and reason together.

Now we are going on to Albuquerque and we won't see you for a long time. I have told you what we think about the wonderful people you have sent us to help us. I hope that each one of you will go home tonight and feel like there is just some little extra something you can do between now and next Tuesday. I hope you realize that we know how important you are or we wouldn't be out here this time of night talking to you. We need your help. We want your support.

We ask you to give us your hand, to give us your heart, to give us your prayers, because this is a mighty nation of patriotic people whose ancestors came from many shores and spelled their names in many ways. They are made up of many colors, many religions. But there is one thing about them, they are Americans first, and they put their country ahead of their party. And if next Tuesday you will go early and cast your ballot and do what you know in your heart is right, we will be happy.

NOTE: The President spoke at 11 p.m. at a rally at the Evansville Airport, Evansville, Ind. His opening words referred to Senators Vance Hartke and Birch Bayh of Indiana, Mayor Frank McDonald of Evansville, Governor Matthew E. Welsh of Indiana,

Roger D. Branigin, Democratic candidate for Governor of Indiana, Governor Edward T. Breathitt, Jr., of Kentucky, and Representative Winfield K. (Win-

nie) Denton of Indiana. Later he referred to Senator Hartke's wife, Martha, and Senator Bayh's wife, Marvella.

730   Presidential Statement No. 6 on Economic Issues: Strengthening State-Local Government.   *October 28, 1964*

1. IN LINE with the Democratic platform, this administration is moving ahead on the "development of fiscal policies which would provide revenue sources to hard-pressed State and local governments to assist them with their responsibilities."

2. At the State and local level we see responsibilities rising faster than revenues, while at the Federal level an average annual revenue growth of some $6 billion provides a comfortable margin for Federal tax reduction, Federal programs, and more generous help to State and local units.

3. The National Government, as a constructive partner in a creative federalism, should help restore fiscal balance and strengthen State and local governments by

making available for their use some part of our great and growing Federal tax revenues—over and above existing aids.

4. It should also strengthen existing programs of Federal-State-local cooperation in such vital areas as public assistance, public health, urban renewal, highways, recreation, and education.

5. Intensive study is now being given to methods of channeling Federal revenue to States and localities which will reinforce their independence while enlarging their capacity to serve their citizens.

NOTE: For a statement by the President announcing a series of statements on economic issues, see Item 707.

731   Presidential Statement No. 7 on Economic Issues: Improving the Tax System.   *October 28, 1964*

1. THIS administration carried through the most extensive overhaul of our tax system since the war. The improvements have made our tax systems fairer, and have strengthened the economy.

2. The administration did not get everything it initially proposed to the Congress in the area of income tax reform; but many significant reforms were enacted.

3. Within the framework of major net tax reduction, the Revenue Acts of 1962 and 1964 enacted $1.7 billion of revenue-increasing reforms:

—$855 million in the Revenue Act of 1962

—$835 million in the Revenue Act of 1964

—three times more than all of the revenue-increasing reforms enacted during the previous 20 years.

4. Important and much needed reforms involving revenue losses were also enacted. The major reforms of this nature included:

—the minimum standard deduction—which eliminated over 1.2 million low-income taxpayers from any tax liability;

—the introduction of a moving expense deduction;

—a badly needed averaging device providing tax relief for individuals with widely fluctuating incomes.

5. The income tax rate structure was sharply improved.

—Prior to the 1964 Revenue Act there were extreme differences in the way the tax system treated different kinds of income: personal income was taxed as high as 91 percent, corporate income at 52 percent, capital gains at 25 percent, and dividend income enjoyed a preferential treatment through the dividend credit. These wide discrepancies created enormous incentives for people to alter their business operations in order to minimize tax liabilities.

—This differential treatment has now been markedly reduced: starting in 1965 personal income will be taxed at a top rate of 70 percent, corporate income at 48 percent, capital gains still at 25 percent, and the dividend credit will be eliminated. These reduced disparities are in themselves a major reform.

6. This administration intends to seek further tax reform. A better excise tax system is next on our agenda. After that, we will turn again to the income tax.

NOTE: For a statement by the President announcing a series of statements on economic issues, see Item 707.

732 Remarks in Albuquerque at the University of New Mexico. *October 28, 1964*

Governor Campbell, Senator Anderson, Senator Montoya, Congressman Morris, ladies and gentlemen, señores, señoras:

Buenos días, mis amigos. ¿Cómo le va? Usted tiene muy buena ciudad aquí. Yo tengo muchos amigos aquí.

I came to New Mexico because I want my friends in this great and this growing State to understand the real, difficult decision that your President has in the real, difficult problem that confronts him. Eleven months ago I became your President, and since that time I have tried to pass programs for your people. But here in New Mexico you can help me. I flew a long way from Boston to Albuquerque after 5 o'clock yesterday to ask you to help me. Of course, I want you to vote for me next Tuesday. Of course, I expect New Mexico to be in the Democratic column. But more than that—and I think really more important than your being in the Democratic column—is for those of you who are building and planning and working for a wiser and a stronger New Mexico and a

better America, I think that it is very essential that each of you go to the polls and vote for Joe Montoya so we will have two Democratic Senators to help us with our program.

You have a future in space, you have a future in atomic energy, you have a great agricultural future, you have minerals galore in this State, you have wonderful climate. The only real thing that you need is water, and Clint Anderson and I worked together many years ago on starting a program that will someday convert the oceans into ample water supplies for us all. We will make the deserts bloom. But the next Senate is going to have 65 to 70 Democrats out of 100, and they are going to sit over on the majority aisle.

I picked up your morning paper this morning and I saw where they had a rally out here yesterday for a Republican Senator. That is fine. I wouldn't say anything ugly about him at all. But it just seems to me that if I lived in a State that I wanted to move ahead, and I wanted my family to move ahead, and if I had a chance to get a person that had experience and had training, and could work with Clint Anderson, it just seems to me that you would be better off to have two men standing up in the Senate and fighting for your progress, coming down to the White House and uniting behind your State, than to have one man coming there and the other one standing up and fighting the President all the time. So I want you to know that I think this State needs Joe Montoya. I think this Nation needs Joe Montoya. I think I need Joe Montoya.

Mr. Rayburn used to say the reason Texas had a good delegation was, "We pick them young, we pick them honest, we send them there, and we keep them there." You picked Clint Anderson and sent him to the House. He did a wonderful job. You promoted him to the Senate. He became one of the great statesmen of the world. He is chairman of the Space Committee of the United States Senate now. Many years ago he saw space, but that wasn't too important, although it was very important. What was important, he saw the future.

You sent Dennis Chavez, as a young Congressman, when I went to Washington after the Hoover days. He came there and represented you with increased effectiveness in the House. Then you had him trained and you moved him over to the Senate. And until the day of his death he was always working for the people of New Mexico.

Now you have Joe Montoya. You have an investment in him. You brought him in, you have told him how to punch the time clock, you have shown him where his job is, you have told him what to do, he has the experience, he has been there working. You ought to take advantage of that experience and of that training and of that ability to work with Senator Anderson, and most important, to work with the majority of the Senate. The minority party—what good will 30 votes do New Mexico in the Senate? It takes 50 to pass anything. So I think that you can see through that, and I hope you realize that this is the only time you will get to make this decision for 6 years. What you do will vitally affect your future, and I think that most of you out there in the audience know that in your heart it is right to send Joe Montoya to the Senate.

I don't think Tom Morris has any problem. Tom Morris has problems in Washington, but he always comes down and all of us like to solve them for him because he is always loyal, he is always devoted, he is always diligent. I know you are going to send him back where he can continue to serve you.

I hope you elect Johnny Walker, who will be a worthy successor to Joe Montoya, and we will have those men working for New Mexico in the Senate.

One week from today the shouting and the talking is going to be over. I hope most of the counting will be done. We think we know what the counting is going to show. We think that it will show that this beloved country of ours believes in itself, believes in its strength, and its goodness, and believes in all that we have been doing together these past 4 years.

We think that it will show that the overwhelming majority of Americans want to keep on the present path to peace. The only real issue in this campaign is peace, how to preserve it, how to acquire it, how to maintain it.

We want to continue prosperity that today is in its 44th month, almost 4 years, the longest period of time in the history of America that we haven't had a recession.

We want to fight an all-out war against poverty. We don't like to see poor people.

We don't like to see unemployed people. We don't like to see hungry people.

We want to build the Great Society of our dreams. Abraham Lincoln abolished slavery and we can abolish poverty. So let's get on and do something about it and give me the men to help me do something about it.

We think that that counting that will take place a week from today will show that the vast majority of voters in America believe that in this election those who speak for the Democratic Party speak for America.

But I say this: Anybody who counts on those votes before they are in the ballot box is gambling with his life and with the future of his Nation. The risk is too great, and that is why I have gone to 43 States in this Union since Labor Day, and those that I have missed Lady Bird and Lynda Bird and Luci Baines have picked up.

I met Luci coming out of the elevator when I was on my way to Boston, and I said, "Well, where have you been, young lady?" She said, "I have covered the Dakotas, I have made speeches there, and in Nebraska, and it is pretty difficult country, but I think we are going to carry it, and I will be so happy because I haven't had a weekend of my own since last May." Seventeen-year-old girls don't really approve of that.

I hope nobody here this morning and nobody in this country wakes up next Wednesday morning and looks over at their wife or their kinfolks around the breakfast table and says, "Gee, I just wish I had tried a little harder. I wish I had worked a little longer."

You know, down in Texas in 1941 President Roosevelt was very popular and he asked me to run for the Senate, because he said he needed me to help him, he needed another Senator to work for his program. And I went down there and we worked awfully hard. The morning after the election

we led by 5,000 votes; and 3 days later we lost by 1,311, out of a million and a half. We lost by 1,311.

Then we waited 7 years, to 1948, when we ran again.

The night before the election I met Lady Bird—she had been campaigning in one part of the State and I had been campaigning in the other; we had been trying to cover every city—and I said, "Come on, honey, we are going home and spend the night at the ranch."

She said, "Oh, no, we are not. I am going back to Austin and I am going to get your mother, your sisters, your aunts, and your uncles, your friends, and your cousins, and I am going to take the telephone book and I am going to assign one of them all the A's, one of them all the B's, one of them all the C's, one of them all the D's, right through the Z's, and we're going to call and say, 'Won't you please go to the polls and vote for my husband?' 'Won't you please go to the polls and vote for my son?' 'Won't you please go to the polls and vote for my brother?'—or 'my cousin?'" And she did that. She went through that telephone book—and we had another million and a half votes.

We had the highest percentage of votes in Austin in that area we have ever had before, because so many people said, "Gee, I forgot to go vote. I have been busy. I thought I would vote and I would go to the grocery store, but I got busy washing the dishes and I haven't gone yet. Yes, I will go vote."

We got out the highest percentage we had ever gotten out. I won the nickname of "Landslide Lyndon" because I won by the magnificent total, out of a million and a half, of 87 votes! And the Republicans have been talking about it ever since.

I have been thinking about it ever since, because if it hadn't been for that extra work that she and my mother and my sisters and my cousins put in that day, Texas would have lost a good Senator.

There is a lot at stake in this election. There are special concerns. People have different interests and there are special interests in various parts of the country. I know, as just one example of the special problem that you have here in New Mexico, because we have it down in Texas—we just don't get enough water. And we have a drought-stricken livestock industry. We know that New Mexico's cattlemen are facing a lot of trouble because I am facing it myself on my own ranch.

I buy my cattle out here in New Mexico, the best breeds, and ship them down to Texas, and then talk about what fine cattle we raise down there. I just have to make a confession. I buy them from a fellow whose judgment about cattle is a lot better than his judgment about politics. He is Albert Mitchell, who used to be Republican national committeeman. But he sure does have fine cattle.

I know the problem we all have with them, and we know the problem of breaking up the breeding herds because of no grass, because of no winter wheat, because of the cattle and feed prices. We have tried to do something about this. We have tried to do it in the Congress, we have tried to do it in the administration. We have allowed grazing on 180,000 acres of the cropland reserves. We have moved 120,000 hundredweights of grain sorghum, 34,000 bushels of corn. We have brought them in here at reduced prices with the freight paid.

We have worked out voluntary agreements with countries like Australia, New Zealand, and Mexico, which have been sending beef here. We have asked them to hold their beef and keep it off our market. We passed a bill on imports that brings us 25 percent

below the 1963 level.

In August Congress passed, and I signed, a law to cover this situation that I just referred to in reducing the amount of meat we bring in. We have purchased over 300 million pounds of beef, more than $150 million worth, for the school lunch and needy families so we could try to hold up the price of cattle.

We have entered into agreements to sell 40 million pounds of beef abroad under the Food for Peace program. We have had our Secretary of Defense quit buying beef for our soldiers overseas, but to ship it from here over there, even though the cost may be a little more.

If more has to be done, we are going to do it, because I think that we know something about the cattle business in New Mexico and in Texas.

The business of the Government I think is the people's business. We are not going to turn our backs on trouble anywhere in this country. I think poverty in the midst of today's prosperity is a disgrace, and I think we ought to do something about it.

I think the denial of a complete education to any young man who can use it, or any young woman, is wrong, and we are going to do something about it. I think every boy and girl born in this country, regardless of his religion, regardless of his race, regardless of his region, has a right to all the education that he can take.

And Clint Anderson next year, like this year, is going to lead us up to the Promised Land where we have a medical care program for our elder citizens, and we are going to pass it through the Congress under social security.

There are 8,500 more jobs, 8,500 more, in New Mexico today than there were when our beloved President took office, the late John Fitzgerald Kennedy. Unemployment has been reduced and reduced and reduced down to where it is just a little over 3 percent. But this is still too much, and we are going to get the full employment that we have been talking about.

The tax cut bill will mean an additional $42 million of expendable funds in New Mexico, and an additional $14 million here in Albuquerque that we were taking in taxes that we are now sending back here. But if additional tax changes are necessary to get our economy moving faster, and our country moving faster, and getting us to produce more jobs, then we will consider making those changes in the next Congress.

We are going to make this system of ours work better and better and better. Part of the responsibility of Government is to see to it that it doesn't get in the way, and that it doesn't waste a cent of money or it doesn't waste a minute of time. But when there are things that we have to do together, we will work together, and that is what I am doing with your great Governor, Jack Campbell.

Government is not an enemy of the people. Government is the people themselves.

The greatest prospects, the greatest risks, that we will vote on next Tuesday, involve the future—the future of your children, the future of the peace of the world.

Only a year ago your children were drinking radioactive milk. The test ban treaty was passed through the Congress. Only 12 men voted against it. Our opponent did. But President Kennedy had the support of the Republican leadership and men like Senator Anderson and others, and they passed it, and now 105 nations have adopted it. The air we breathe and the milk we drink and the food that comes from our soil is all cleaner because of it.

So the stakes in this election are high. They are success, but more important than

success they are survival, survival for you and your children. The issue really is, if you want to boil it down, recklessness against responsibility.

We cannot and we will not abandon the bipartisan foreign policy that the Republicans and the Democrats have hammered out together in this country over the past 20 years. The risk is too great.

We cannot and we will not abandon the test ban treaty to which I just referred, which is the world's insurance policy against polluting the air we breathe and the milk we give our children.

Already that policy has paid off more than you will ever know, and since this agreement was signed and the tests stopped, the dread strontium-89 and iodine 131 have disappeared from the environment. The amount of strontium-90 and cesium-137 has already been, in 1 year, cut in half. This is technical language, but what it means is that we can breathe safely again.

And one thing I want to thank you especially for is that wonderful sign of the scientists and engineers of New Mexico. You have some of the best in the world located here, and about the best supporters I have in the United States are the scientists and the engineers.

They work with their test tubes, they work in their laboratories, they are not political speakers, although I wish some of them would get on the television out here and tell you people the facts of life, because they know what is happening in the world; they have created these things; they have brought them into existence. They know the dangers. They know the only thing really important is survival.

I don't think we will listen to those who voted against that treaty. I don't think we will let them lead this Nation. I don't think we will give them that trust. Why? Because the risk to you and your children is too great.

We cannot and we will not play the war game of bluff and bluster. We want to speak softly and act prudently. We want to be prepared, the mightiest nation in the world, with all the bombers we need and all the rockets that are necessary.

But we don't think that we ought to rear back and throw out our chest and shoot from the hip and say, "We are going to rattle our rockets and we are going to bluff you with our bombs, and we are going to issue ultimatums to all the other 120 nations that 'You do it like we do or else,'" because we don't think that will keep peace in the world.

So what we are going to do is to keep the strength that makes our adversaries sure that America can defend herself and will. We will keep the steadiness of purpose that makes our allies—and I saw the Foreign Secretary of Great Britain only yesterday morning—sure that we are going to be responsible. We will keep the course that makes our adversaries and our allies alike sure that the number one thing that we are dedicated to in America is peace on earth, good will toward men. We will keep the peace.

Now that, most of all, is what this election is all about, keeping the peace.

Which man do you think can keep the peace?

Which man do you want to have his thumb close to that atomic button?

Which man do you want to reach over when that line rings, when that phone jingles, and it is the "hot line" and it is Moscow calling? Who do you want to have pick up and answer it and speak for you?

You have to decide that. I haven't come out here to tell you. That is a matter for your judgment. That is a matter for your conscience.

No mother will ever make a more important decision. No young man or woman between 21 and 29 will ever make a more important decision because it may involve their life, it may involve their home, their future. It involves everything.

I think it would be presumptuous for me to indicate that I have any special powers or that I am any more patriotic, or any more concerned with the welfare of people than men in the other party, because that is not true, but you have to make a decision which of the two you want.

I think that I know enough about the people of the United States because I have been from Maine to California, I think I know that they know in their hearts what is right and they are going to do it November 3d.

Now, folks, I want to tell you good luck, goodby. I have to get away from here because Clint Anderson, Tom Morris, and Joe Montoya have already talked to me about two new projects for New Mexico, and they will have my coat and my shirt if I don't go on to California.

Thank you and goodby.

NOTE: The President spoke at 9:15 a.m. in Johnson Gymnasium at the University of New Mexico in Albuquerque. In his opening words he referred to Governor Jack M. Campbell, Senator Clinton P. Anderson, Representative Joseph M. Montoya, Democratic candidate for Senator, and Representative Thomas G. Morris, all of New Mexico. During the course of his remarks he referred to, among others, E. S. (Johnny) Walker, Democratic candidate for Representative at Large from New Mexico, and Albert K. Mitchell, former Republican national committeeman.

The text of the remarks of Mrs. Johnson, who spoke briefly, was also released.

733   Remarks at City Hall in Los Angeles. October 28, 1964

WHICH Johnson do you want? Lady Bird? All right.

[At this point Mrs. Johnson spoke briefly. She said, "It is a thrilling thing to look at the faces of so many of the people for whom my husband tries very hard to do a good job. Thank you for coming out to welcome us to your beautiful State." The President then resumed speaking.]

All right, now, I guess it is all right for me to go ahead.

———

My fellow Americans:

It is great to be back in the biggest city in America, to see the biggest crowds of all time, and to have you tell me that you are going to the polls next Tuesday and give the Democrats the biggest election victory in the history of California.

Ever since the war California has been the biggest in everything. Coming from Texas, where I do, that is really saying something. California has the biggest growth of any State in the Union. California has the biggest problems of any State in the Union.

Your great Republican Governor, Earl Warren, saw those problems coming and he made long-range plans to solve them. Your beloved and great Democratic Governor Pat Brown reworked those plans and has carried on and has worked out new programs to solve those problems to the point that today California is the number one State in the Union. And your brand new Senator, Pierre Salinger, is going to come down to Washington, and with Senator Kuchel, and with your good delegation in the House, and with what I hope will be a Democratic President, we are going to continue to keep California moving.

You need Pierre Salinger in the Senate. I need him in Washington. The Nation needs him, because this forward-looking State must have a forward-looking Senator, not a turnback one. California must have a Senator who says, "I believe we can do it, I am a 'can-do man'" instead of one who says, "It is socialism. I doubt it. We have failed. Let's go back to the status quo."

You need, and the Nation needs, Ed Roybal back in the House, where he can continue to fight the people's battles for the people's good. He has stood by my side when I was Vice President, when I was President, and helped me represent all the people of this Nation, the richest and the poorest, the wisest and the ones that were dropouts. But he has stood up there fighting every inch of the way that we have equal opportunity for every American, regardless of how he spells his name, regardless of what church he goes to, regardless of his color—equal opportunity for all, special privilege for none.

Chet Holifield nominated me for Vice President. Jimmy Roosevelt brought me to Washington and helped me when I was a secretary there. I would like to tell you all about this wonderful California delegation, but my wife has already told me that I speak too long and we have five more speeches today, so all I want to do is to thank you for the good Democrats like Chet Holifield, Cecil King, Jimmy Roosevelt, and the dozens of others that you send to Washington, and that includes all the Democratic Members of your delegation. I commend you for it, because no State in the Union can boast of a harder working, a more effective group of Congressmen than the State of California.

Now, I want to get down to a little business with you. This session of Congress that has just ended accomplished so much for just one reason: The responsible leaders of both political parties worked together for the good of the country. That is the way I think it ought to be. Pat Brown is a great Democrat, but he has carried on in the great tradition of a Republican Governor, Earl Warren. And that is the way it ought to be.

In the White House for the last 20 years, five Presidents from both parties have adopted a bipartisan foreign policy. That bipartisan foreign policy has kept us out of war and has kept us at peace, and has left your boy at home. And that is the way it ought to be, and that is the way it is going to be after November 3d.

As we meet here today, the United States is in the 44th month, almost 4 years, of unprecedented national prosperity. We have 72.5 million men and women working. They are drawing an average weekly wage of $104, the highest in the history. They are working fewer hours per day, fewer days per week, fewer weeks per month, fewer months per year. The corporations of this country that employed them in the last 12 months made $12 billion more after taxes than they did the year before, and I am glad they did, because the laborers that work for them made $60 billion more after taxes than they did the year before.

So we have peace in the world and we have peace between the employer and the employee.

We had a little argument up at General Motors, but it didn't last very long. We didn't get very tough. We didn't issue any ultimatums. We didn't put any pistols on our hip. And we didn't shoot from our hip, either.

But we talked to both Mr. Reuther of the UAW and we talked to Mr. Donner of General Motors, and we said, "Both of you are responsible, both of you are smart, both of you are intelligent"—General Motors is the biggest corporation in this country, they spent $16 billion last year; Mr. Reuther is the head of one of the strongest unions—"Now, you sit there across that table and in the words of the Bible, the prophet Isaiah, you reason together and you find some solution. And if you don't do it, when it gets to hurting America, I am going to come up there and pull my chair up to that table and talk to you!"

Do you know that since November 22d, when I became President, we have not lost even 1 percent of the number of hours that we have worked because of strikes, not even one-half of 1 percent, not even one-quarter of 1 percent. We have lost fourteen one-hundredths of 1 percent of the hours we have worked—that is almost too small to calculate—and we did that accidentally.

So I think it is good when business is doing well, when labor is doing well, because if they have a great big pie that they can divide when they get through paying their expenses and their wages do you know what happens? I come in representing all the people, Uncle Sam, and I take my butcher knife and I slice out 52 percent of it for the Government. So the better business is, the better wages are, the better times are, the better off it is for the Government.

I don't believe in harassing people; I believe in encouraging them. I don't believe in hating people; I believe in loving them. I am not filled with fear; I am filled with faith. I am not going around grouchy always doubting that it will work.

I remember we had an old man in my town in Texas. We lived way out in the country. Finally we got a little railroad 30 miles from where I lived. When it got there, the old man said it would never work, and so forth. Finally the day came and we had the queen cut the ribbon and the train started off for San Antonio. The old man said, "Well, I have been saying now for 3 months they would never get her started and

I don't think they will ever get her stopped."

Now, that kind of faith in the future is not what built California. That kind of faith in the future is not what made this the greatest educational State in the Union. That kind of faith in the future is not what made this the greatest space and the greatest aeronautical and the greatest missile, the greatest technological State in the Union. That kind of faith is not what has given you your great University of California and all your fine institutions of higher learning.

But we are not satisfied. We are going ahead full speed. We are going forward to a future of horizons that are unlimited.

The first horizon that we seek is unlimited opportunity for every citizen, regardless of where his poppa came from, regardless of the color of his skin, regardless of the church that he goes to, regardless of the region where he lives. We are all Americans.

The second horizon that we seek is the best educational opportunity that every child can get, and we want every boy and girl born under that flag, when he or she discovers America and comes in squealing, we want him to know that he has the right to all the education that he can absorb. Because I will tell you, these dropouts and these folks that finish grade school in the year 2000, when we have an average income predicted of $15,000 per family per year, it is going to be pretty hard for them to compete in this technological age, so we ought to prepare them for what they face up to. Twenty-one million dropped out of high school and didn't go on to college.

If we are going to compete with the Soviet Union, we are not only going to have to have the best heels and the best hearts that we can, but we are going to have to have the best heads. You don't want some boy that went to a red schoolhouse and dropped

out in the third grade and went off as a road-hand like I did when I ran off to California when I finished school, you don't want him to be in your spaceship with John Glenn orbiting the earth. You want somebody that knows where the buttons are and how to mash them and touch them.

The third horizon that we seek is the horizon of personal security. We are not going to make our social security system voluntary. That is just another way of saying, "Well, let her go."

I don't know how much you have—you may have some debts, and you may have a husband at home, and you may have some grandchildren—but the thing that is really important to every person out there in that audience today is that social security card, because that is going to permit you to live out the twilight of your career in decency and dignity without going to the poorhouse or without having to have your kids come and take care of you.

I was so glad to see some of the leaders that had been active here in California in promoting the cause of our elder citizens. I was so happy to see them standing out there today—Mr. McLain and others—on the sidewalks waving as we went by.

I came here to tell you direct, not through any interpreter or third person, that if you will send Ed Roybal back there and these Democratic Congressmen to help me, and give me Pierre Salinger, to represent the State of California and stand up on that floor and fight like a tiger, we are going to expand that social security system and we are going to strengthen it. We are going to make it stronger and better, and we are going to add medical care under social security.

They say I have talked 20 minutes. I have five more speeches today. They don't want me to run down before next Tuesday.

[*At this point there was a disturbance in the crowd.*]

Don't you Johnson people do that. Let's always be nice. When your neighbor comes over to your house, and he has been living there alone for a long time and he gets lonesome, and he comes to visit you, even if he does kind of start doing all the talking, you be nice to him and courteous, because everybody is entitled to associate with good company every once in a while.

A fellow told me yesterday, I guess it was in Boston, they actually found an adult up there with one of those signs. We had about a 33-mile caravan and they looked it all over very carefully, but they finally found one adult that had one of those signs. I asked him what was on it, and he said, "Well, we thought it was an ugly sign until we got up close to where we could read. It was a home-made sign and it said, 'Gold for the rich, and water for the poor, and Johnson for President.'"

Let's let them come in here and talk about socialism. When I went to Washington under President Roosevelt in 1933, when he was talking about keeping the banks from being closed, and he was trying to reopen them again, when he had the soup lines, when he had the CCC, when he was trying to do things where people didn't starve to death, they just talked about socialism, socialism. And finally one old boy said, "You can't eat socialism."

It is that same old crowd. I remember when we had the minimum wage up. We had a minimum wage in 1938 for 25 cents an hour. My daddy was on this death bed and he died that night, and I was sitting there listening to the radio with him when President Roosevelt went on the radio and appealed to us to come back to Congress so that widow women wouldn't have to work in pecan-shelling plants for 7 cents an hour,

56 cents a day, trying to feed their families. He said, "Let's come back and have a minimum wage of 25 cents an hour." They all said, "socialism." And the same old crowd is saying the same old lines, and I think they are written by the same old man.

But it takes all kinds of people to make a world. We don't all see everything alike. If we did, we would all want the same wife.

Things are getting better, things are getting better every day. All we need to do now is to go around and talk about positive things, about the issues, about peace, about prosperity, about social security, about jobs, about medical care. We talk issues; we don't talk personalities. And listen, let them talk about anything they want to, because if they get happy and enjoy it, and they get a great thrill out of hollering "socialism," let them be happy.

That is one thing that worries me about seeing some of these folks that oppose us, because I like the lot of them. But if you look at them with these signs, you rarely ever see a fellow that has one who is smiling. I asked a little boy the other day, and they just paid him 50 cents an hour to carry them. And the minimum wage is $1.25!

But let me talk about the horizons now. I got interrupted. I want to talk about the horizons.

The fourth horizon—some of these people don't understand horizons because they look backward, they don't look forward— the fourth horizon is the horizon of discovery. We face the unknown challenge of outer space. When the Russians sent up Sputnik I, anybody that could read and write in this country got frightened.

I immediately went to Washington and called an investigation, and we had the best military experts in the world come there and testify. While they were testifying, the Russians sent up Sputnik II, "Beep, beep, beep," around in the air.

They called for some comments from some leaders. I said we better get going, we better step up our effort. My opponent said, and this is approximately what he said, about what he said, "I am not worried about somebody putting a basketball in the air that says, 'Beep, beep, beep.' I would rather lob one into the men's room in the Kremlin."

That is a problem for us. You cannot be first on earth and second in space. That is just impossible. If you want to lead the world, you have to lead it. The British had the greatest navy in all the world and she dominated the seas and she led the world for centuries. We came along with the airplane, an industry that was begun here in California, and because we had the greatest air power in the world we have led the world and we have preserved peace for 20 years. We won World War II with the airplane.

Now what we do in space is going to determine how we live. Tiros IV told us 48 hours in advance that we were going to have Hurricane Carla, and we moved all the people from Galveston, Tex., up to our capital, 200 miles, bumper to bumper, and we never lost a life because we had that notice. In 1905 we had the same kind of a hurricane and we lost 100 or 200 lives.

So that is what space is doing for us. That is what your technicians are doing. That is what your scientists are doing. We face tremendous revolutions in science and technology.

John Glenn came in yesterday and I promoted him to full colonel. I had a little fun out of him. I said a fellow that can orbit the earth and didn't know how to stand up in a bathtub—there is something wrong with him.

But we must act now to control and to apply what we learn to improve our daily lives.

First, we have to learn to discover the cause of disease, heart attacks, high blood pressure, strokes, cancer. I have a committee working on that now and they are eagerly searching, trying to find that answer.

Second, we are going to have to rebuild our cities. They have filled up with slums and we see kids out there playing in the streets when the cars are trying to drive by. It is a terrible disgrace. We are going to have to reshape our mass transit facilities because some men spend 3 hours going to and from work every day—3 hours wasted. They ought to go in 20 minutes. We can't go in a horse and buggy any more. We have to improve our mass transit. If John Glenn can go around the world, we have to find some way to get from a suburb to our plant.

We have to purify our air and we have to desalt our oceans. Now just put your head to working just a minute. Think about when we are able to go out in the Atlantic and the Pacific and the other great bodies of water in the world and take all the salt out of it and make pure water. We are going to make all the deserts bloom.

This little problem that you have with my friend, who has temporarily captured the Republican Party, about water in Arizona; I want all these folks that are asking me what about this other fellow—I don't want to call his name—I want to ask what is Arizona really going to do to California in this water situation?

I want each of you to give a little thought to it and ask yourself that question. But our program has to be to desalt the seas and rebloom the deserts. There are a hundred other ways that we can make our world a better place to live. So why do we want to go around being grouchy?

Fifth, we must pursue with patience and

perseverance, with strength and with sanity, the unlimited horizon of universal peace.

When I was a young man first entering politics, I had an argument about an REA project and I got very irritated after 2 or 3 days because the old president of the power company wouldn't give in at all. I finally got up one day and made a little speech before the board of directors, and I said, "You can take a running jump, as far as I am concerned, and go straight to you know where," and everybody applauded me. I was mighty brave. I was bravado. I talked big, and I told the president of the biggest power company in the State of Texas to go straight to—and they all applauded me except one old man who was general counsel, a lawyer. I went by, and he was my friend, and I said, "How did you like my speech?" I could tell from the way he looked how he liked my speech. He said, "Come by the office, son, when this is over. I want to talk to you." I went by, and he said, "You are young, and I worked up this meeting and got the board of directors of the REA and the power company together. It took me 2 months to get the meeting together, and you busted it up in 2 minutes." He said, "Any jackass can kick a barn down. It takes a carpenter to build one."

He said, "Let's analyze what you said. You said that this fellow could go straight to hell. In the first place, he doesn't want to go, and you have no power to make him go." He said, "It is hot down there, and from what he has heard about it, it is not a very desirable place to live. And if you can't get him to enter into this agreement on REA, you can't get him to agree with you to go straight to——"

He said, "The first thing I think you ought to learn, because I hope that you go somewhere in public life—you are a young Congressman, you have great chances, President

Roosevelt has tried to help you—the first thing that you ought to get in your noggin is telling a man to go to hell and making him go are two different propositions."

I thought about that when Bob Taft was the Republican leader of the Senate and I was Democratic. A lot of times I felt like getting up and saying, "You go straight to——" When Bill Knowland from your great State of California, when he was the leader, I had on occasions some indications that I might want to express very freely, but I kept thinking about what that old man told me. When Senator Dirksen came along and we disagreed, I thought the same thing.

So now that we live in a world with 120 other nations and 112 of them are in the United Nations, you can't have government by ultimatum. Just because we are powerful, we can't just mash a button and tell an independent country to go to—because they don't want to go to—and we don't get very far rattling our rockets or lobbing them into the men's rooms, or bluffing with our bombs.

I saw President Kennedy in the Cuban crisis in 38 different meetings, and we got up to the last hours. Khrushchev had his missiles trained on this country that would completely wipe out San Francisco and Los Angeles. There would be no life left.

Those men stood there, one speaking for the United States and the free world, and the other speaking for the Communist world. They got eyeball to eyeball, and I saw the generals with their stars come into the room and the admirals with their braid, and the Secretary of State with all of his diplomatic experience. I listened to every word.

I never left home a single morning that I knew I would get back that night to see Lady Bird and those daughters.

So as a little boy in my country used to say, we were doing some pretty heavy thinking, because we were right up to the gun.

But Mr. Kennedy put his knife right there in his ribs and he held it, Khrushchev put his there and he held it, and neither one of them shook or trembled or developed palsy; neither one of them wobbled. Our planes were in the air. They had their bombs in them. Our Navy was on the seas; they were ready.

But Mr. Khrushchev finally decided rather than to see 300 million people killed and the Soviet Union wiped out—and they could wipe out America, too—that humiliating as it was, it might be a little wiser to wrap up his missiles in those tarpaulins and put them on those ships and take them back home, and that is what he did.

We are going to educate our people, we are going to give them jobs, we are going to provide social security, we are going to give them more leisure time, we are going to improve the countryside, we are going to have more recreational areas, we are going to treat all Americans equally and then there won't be a single one that will want communism.

But in that time when we sat in that room trying to decide what was best to do, and even after it was over we didn't brag about it, we didn't say much about what had happened because we didn't want to provoke anybody and make it more embarrassing— we worked out the test ban treaty a little later, we worked out the "hot line" a little later, we worked out the agreement not to use armament in space a little later, we worked out the desalinization agreement a little later—what I want to say to you is during that period I sat across on one side of the table as Vice President and the President of this country sat across on the other, and I am proud to tell you that the coolest head in that room was John Fitzgerald Kennedy.

There are some voices going around talking about how he framed it all up, and they are making charges they didn't make in his lifetime. They are making accusations that he is not here to answer. But I think you are going to give them an answer loud and clear next Tuesday.

Economic and social progress are only a part of a President's job. Far above them and far above everything else is the President's inescapable and awesome responsibility that I just talked about in the Cuban missile crisis. His first responsibility, the only real issue in this campaign, the only thing that you ought to be concerned about at all, is who can best keep the peace?

There are great and troubled changes going on in the world as we meet here. I heard about some of them in the trailer when I talked to Washington a moment ago, and when they break upon the world, the Government of the United States must act.

Mr. McNamara called me and told me that our destroyers had been fired upon, our flag had been shot at, and we had to act, and we did act in the Tonkin Gulf, but we had to think before we acted. In the nuclear age, the President doesn't get a second chance to make a second guess. If he mashes that button, that is it. So we cannot make a foreign policy, we cannot keep the peace by bluff and bluster and by threats and ultimatums.

We can keep the peace and we can only keep the peace by two methods: first, with a strong defense, and we are today, I tell you as your Commander in Chief, the mightiest nation in all the world; and second, we can keep the peace in the words of the prophet Isaiah, by reasoning together, by responsibility, by negotiation.

Strong defense comes first. As your Commander in Chief I have told you of how we stand with the other nations on this earth, stronger than all of them. And you helped make it that way.

President Kennedy spent $40 billion more

on defense and space in 4 years than was being spent when he went in. That is why we are strong, and that is why we are going to continue to be strong, and that is why I am going to keep it that way.

But it is not enough to be strong. You must also be prudent, and you must also be wise, and you must also be firm, and you must also be reasonable. We must be brave. I admire a brave man. But there are some people that have more guts than brains, and we must be, above all, responsible. The stakes are too high to be reckless; you have too much to lose to be reckless.

Now, more than ever before in history, now in the nuclear age, now with the world-shaking changes, now that the Communists have the bomb, that is another nation that has it. We just can't afford to take reckless or needless chances. Somebody said the other day after the Chinese got the bomb that it would really be bad if both of them got it at the same time.

We must dedicate ourselves with all of our heart and all of our strength and with all of our intelligence, all our wisdom, all of our patience, to the greatest undertaking in the world. And what is that? Bringing the peoples of the earth together in enduring peace. "Love thy neighbor as thyself," "Do unto others as you would have them do unto you." No matter how long it may take, no matter how difficult it is, this above all else is the great horizon toward which we march united. I say united, Republicans and Democrats alike.

Do you know that Senator Arthur Vandenberg changed his isolationist record after he had been in the Senate many years and he went in to help President Truman stop the Communists in Greece and Turkey? Lyndon Johnson, as Democratic leader, went in and supported President Eisenhower in the Suez and in the Formosa Strait. I voted for his foreign policy 95 percent of the time in 1960, and the present Republican nominee voted for it only 25 percent of the time.

We must keep both parties trying to let politics stop at the water's edge. I have been in office 11 months. You make a decision next week whether you want me to have my first elected term, or whether you want me to go back to the ranch in Texas. I have read in the paper where some people do, but I just sure hope that they don't live in Los Angeles.

So let's keep a smile on our face, let's keep faith in our heart, let's keep hope in our vision, let's move on to conquer unknown frontiers. And let's leave this land a lot better for our grandchildren than we found it for ourselves.

NOTE: The President spoke at 1:23 p.m. at City Hall in Los Angeles, Calif. During the course of his remarks he referred to, among others, Chief Justice Earl Warren, former Governor of California, Governor Edmund G. Brown, Senators Pierre E. G. Salinger and Thomas H. Kuchel, and Representatives Edward R. Roybal, Chet Holifield, James Roosevelt, and Cecil R. King, all of California, Walter Reuther, president of the United Automobile Workers, AFL–CIO, Frederic G. Donner, chairman of the board of directors, General Motors Corp., and George McLain, chairman of the board of trustees of the California League of Senior Citizens.

734   Remarks at the Riverside, California, County Courthouse. *October 28*, 1964

Ladies and gentlemen, boys and girls:

This is a great day in Riverside, and I hope you will make it an even greater day

next Tuesday in the entire Nation. I want to see this city and this county stand up and be counted on the side of responsible government for this Nation and for peace in the world.

You already have responsible government in this State under Governor Pat Brown. Another vote for responsibility in government is a vote for Senator Pierre Salinger. Pierre knows this State and he knows the great policy questions that we have to decide in the Nation and the world, and California needs a spokesman like Pierre Salinger in the United States Senate.

John Tunney is one of the finest young congressional candidates that I have ever seen in America. He came out to March Field while he was in the Air Force and he got so enthusiastic about Riverside he just decided to stay. But you need him and we need him, his drive, his intelligence, and his enthusiasm, in Congress. We need him to punch hard for programs for Riverside and California.

These next 4 years will be decisive for this country, and I think they will be decisive for the world. These 4 years may well decide our destiny and may well decide the world's destiny for the next 40 years.

To make the right decisions, we must move ahead on two broad fronts: Here at home we must strengthen our economy and we must bring dignity and opportunity to the lives of all Americans. Abroad we must constantly work for peace. We must work for peace every day and every hour, with every ounce of strength and patience that we can muster.

At home we are going to continue the unprecedented prosperity of the last 45 months of the John F. Kennedy-Lyndon Johnson administration. Since John Fitzgerald Kennedy took the oath of office, we have added 5 million new jobs to our economy, and of these 5 million, 500,000 of these jobs came to the State of California. Wages and salaries after taxes are up nearly $60 bil-

lion, and the Nation's total production is expanding at the rate of 5 percent a year. This is progress without precedent.

But we are not satisfied. We are going to press forward with broad-gauge social security, opening up new jobs, keeping our economy strong, and we are going to fight an all-out war on poverty.

While we make ourselves strong at home, we must keep our guard up abroad. We must remain strong. Responsible America is the world's best guarantee of a just and continuing peace. But I want to say to you now that all our strength at home and abroad is of no use if we do not use that strength wisely and we do not use it prudently, and we do not use it with restraint and good judgment.

There is no room in America for trigger-happy threats in a world that is made dark by the shadow of nuclear catastrophe.

I understand that the last President to visit Riverside was William Howard Taft 55 years ago. President Taft began his inaugural address that I went back and read the other day when I decided to come here, and he started that address by saying, "Anyone who has taken the oath that I have just taken must feel a heavy weight of responsibility."

That responsibility in the nuclear age is frightening and is awesome indeed. And it is inescapable. It cannot be delegated.

For the last 20 years 5 Presidents of both political parties, working with the responsible leaders in Congress of both political parties, have forged a bipartisan foreign policy. And I do not think that America is going to change that responsible, bipartisan foreign policy next Tuesday.

It used to be said that the hand that rocks the cradle is the hand that rules the world. Today the hand that pushes the button is the hand that could destroy the world.

The Communists know that America is

strong. They know because we turned them back at Berlin and Cuba and in the waters around Viet-Nam.

But I pledge you that we shall be responsible always, as well as strong. We will use our minds as well as our muscle, and we will let others use their vocal cords and their tongues and America will win the peace.

You have been called upon several times in your life to make important decisions, but in this world, with 119 other nations, with all the feuds and differences that have gone on for centuries between those nations, you will likely never be called upon to make a more important decision than to select the leadership for the free world next Tuesday. You will select that leadership based on information, based on knowledge, based on judgment; not based on fanaticism or emotion.

The kind of leadership you want is the kind of leadership that your heart tells you is right for your country and for your family.

California is the number one State in the Union. California is the leader of the rest of the States. California has a peculiar obligation to be prudent and be careful and be cautious and be responsible. We have had enough of reckless talk. We have had enough of impulsive action.

It is mighty easy to talk like a bravado when you are talking about someone else's sons, but when you get up where your thumb has the responsibility for touching that button, and you get to thinking about the consequences of that act that will kill 300 million people, it is a time for prayer, it is a time for sober reflections, and the hotheads ought to go back to the bench in the hothouse.

I am not going to tell you that one party has all the mortgage on the patriotism of this country. Men in all parties love this country and are patriotic believers in our system of government.

The Democrats have no mortgage on patriotism because it was Senator Arthur Vandenberg, a Republican Senator, who joined with President Harry Truman to stop the Communists in Greece and Turkey. It was Senator Lyndon Johnson who joined with President Dwight Eisenhower in the Suez crisis and in the Formosa Strait. It was Senator Everett Dirksen, a Republican from Illinois, that joined with John Fitzgerald Kennedy, our beloved President, when other men were harassing him, when other men were opposing him, when other men were voting against his test ban treaty.

So for 20 years we have maintained the peace through strength, but through the cooperation of good Republicans and good Democrats who thought more of their country than they did of their party.

I was in Pennsylvania last night. I looked at a poll that they brought me in Pittsburgh. In that poll I found that 37 percent, almost half, of the Republicans that had made up their minds were going to vote for responsibility, were going to vote for the present President of the United States on November 3d. They are not voting for him because he is a Democrat. They are not voting for him because he is a Republican. They are voting for him because they want to see this country united. They want us to be able to come here and meet in the square in freedom, not as Hitler's groups used to meet, not as they meet in the Communist squares under the commissars, but to meet here with freedom of speech, where every man has a right to his say, and you can listen to their voices, and by their acts ye shall know them.

We have a new government in Germany, Chancellor Erhard. We have a labor government in Great Britain that has only a majority of four votes. We have a new government in Italy. Only last week we found that Mr. Khrushchev was dispossessed and deposed and we have two men running the Soviet Union. The big question you have to decide is how can the United States formulate a policy and prepare a program that can get these people to learn to live in a world together without using our rockets and without dropping our bombs, and without killing humanity.

The Golden Rule says, "Do unto others as you would have them do unto you." The Good Book says, the prophet Isaiah, "Come now, let us reason together." I am happy that most of you people have come out here this evening not to see a show and not to participate in a vaudeville, and not to try to attract any attention for yourselves. But you have come out here to look at your President, to listen to your President, to hear him talk about the issues, not the personalities, because it is petty men that deal in personalities.

The American people really don't give a tinker—don't care about what I think about my opponent, and I doubt that they have much doubt about what he thinks about me. What they do want to know is how do we feel about the bread and butter issues that feed their families; how do we feel about every man and woman having a job; how do they feel about the right of every child to have an education; how do we feel about the United Nations, which has prevented a dozen wars; how do we feel about trade with the world; how do we feel about space; how do we feel about technology and the leadership that California is showing to the rest of the world in all of her missile development and her space technology; and how do we feel about that most important thing: peace in the world.

I came here in 1924 to seek my fortune. I got off a T-model Ford over here at San Bernardino, and I stayed around there almost

2 years. I finally decided I had a better chance to get a fortune where I had come from than where I had gone, so I went back to my mother and my father.

I came back out here to seek your support for Vice President, and for 3½ years I have served you as Vice President. The most memorable experience of that period was the Cuban missile crisis.

Our photographs showed us that the Soviet Union had brought within 90 miles of our shores enough missiles to seriously handicap and destroy large portions of this country. There were some people that said, "Send in the Marines." There were some people that said, "Push the button; drop the bombs." There were some people who said, "Put your planes in the air and load them and tell them to put up or shut up."

And for 38 meetings we met there in the Cabinet Room, morning, afternoon, past midnight many nights. Pierre Salinger sat in those meetings. The men with the stars on their shoulders who represent our Chiefs of Staff sat in those meetings. The admirals with the braid on their arms, they came, they learned, they saw, and they recommended. The Secretary of State with all his diplomatic experience, a Rhodes scholar, sat there with furrows in his forehead and tried to decide what course we could follow.

I never left home a single morning but what I thought I might not see my wife and daughters again that night, because we did not know when those missiles would become operational.

But during that whole period, the man that we have heard heckled and harassed, the man that we have heard in the last few days criticized when he is not here to answer himself, the man that was your President, your Commander in Chief, was the coolest man in that room, and his name was John Fitzgerald Kennedy.

He didn't shoot from the hip. He didn't talk first and think afterwards. He didn't get confused. He listened and he learned, and finally on the last hour as the clock was ticking and we were within moments of action, Mr. Khrushchev came in with a letter and he wrapped up his missiles in his tarpaulin canvases, he put them on his boats, while our helicopters flew over their decks, and we watched them take them out one by one by one. A war was prevented, a Republic was saved.

But what is more important, 300 million people live today that would not have lived had we not had the cool, calm, wise leadership of that man who watches over us in heaven this afternoon, John Fitzgerald Kennedy. He gave his life for his country, and there is not a man out there that wouldn't give his if he thought he could save his country by doing so.

But you are not called on to do that today. You are called on next Tuesday to go down as a free American, without restraint, without influence, without pressure, and act upon the basis of your judgment on what is best for your country. I came to California to ask you to do that.

I leave what is best to do for your country to your own decision in the full knowledge that I know that you will know in your heart what is right.

NOTE: The President spoke at 4:27 p.m. at the Riverside County Courthouse, Riverside, Calif. During the course of his remarks he referred to Governor Edmund G. Brown, Senator Pierre E. G. Salinger, and John V. Tunney, Democratic candidate for Representative, all of California.

735   Remarks at a Rally in San Bernardino. *October 28, 1964*

Governor Brown, my friends in San Bernardino:

I am glad to be back home tonight. I enjoyed riding that elevator tonight more than I have ever enjoyed it before. The last time I was here was 40 years ago. I came in a T-model Ford. The only reception committee that greeted me was the boy that ran the elevator, and I am happy that my friends have increased and we have got a larger reception committee out here tonight.

This is a sentimental visit for me, and I am not going to talk long, and I am not going to talk too political. I want to first of all thank you people of San Bernardino for sending to Congress a most competent and able colleague of mine and my friend for many years, Harry Sheppard. Harry is a very young man and was probably playing marbles when I was here but I remember Phil Swing used to represent this district. Do any of you remember that?

The last Congress was one of the most productive in history, and I think this was because the responsible leaders of both parties worked together. The next Congress that starts in January is going to be productive, too. We are all going forward together, Republicans and Democrats alike, because all good Americans want to do what is best for their country before they do what is best for their party.

We are going to build a bigger and a better America. We are going to build it in the broad and vital center of the American political landscape, and we are not going to build it on the shaky, quaking fringes.

California and San Bernardino are a growing State and a growing city—and a growing population needs a growing economy. That is exactly what we have in the United States today. For the first time in all of our history, 72 million Americans have jobs, 5 million more than had jobs when President Kennedy took the oath of office 4 years ago. Personal income has risen by $80 billion after taxes, and corporate profits after taxes have already increased over $12 billion.

In the stock market today, the value of stocks on the exchange is worth more than $100 billion more than they were worth when I took office November 22d, 11 months ago. And in this great surge forward, California has led the way. Right here in the San Bernardino-Riverside-Ontario area, the number of jobs increased by 27,000 between 1960 and 1964. And I am here tonight to pledge you that we are going to keep on increasing them, we are going to keep on moving ahead.

You and I believe in thinking ahead about our country's future. We believe that social security benefits should be extended. I was just talking to my friend Mrs. Platt, of the Platt Building, down there before I came up here, and I told her that I believe that our elder citizens have a right to decent medical care under social security after long lives of service to this country.

We believe that every child has a right to the best education he can use.

I am told that this is the largest county in the United States. I have a little special favor I would like to ask of you, and if you have already made up your mind and you can't do what I want you to do, I won't get mad at you, I will forget it, but if you can, I will appreciate it.

I would like to see the biggest county in the United States deliver the biggest plurality for economic and social progress in the election next Tuesday. I would like to see the biggest county give the biggest vote to

Pierre Salinger for United States Senator. I would like to see the biggest county give the biggest vote to Ken Dyal for Congressman to succeed Harry Sheppard.

And if you haven't worn out your lead pencil, or if the voting machine lever is still there and you are still in a good humor, I would like for you to vote for Lyndon Johnson and Hubert Humphrey, too.

Economic and social progress are only a part of a President's job, because more important than anything else is the President's inescapable and awesome responsibility to keep peace in the world. Every mother here is more concerned with peace and keeping her boys from going to war than she is with her own life.

There are great and there are troubling changes that are going on in the world today. In the space of 24 hours, Mr. Khrushchev has toppled in the Soviet Union. In a space of 24 hours, 700 million Chinese, more than 3½ times our population, have exploded a new nuclear bomb, and the government in Great Britain has a sudden change and only has a majority of four. When such changes come upon the world, then that is the time for the United States to be prudent, to be stable, to be sound, to be sure, and to act. But before we act we must think. We just can't guess.

In the nuclear age, the President does not get a chance to make a second guess. We cannot make a foreign policy, we cannot keep the peace by ultimatum, by rattling our rockets, or by bluffing with our bombs.

We can keep the peace, and we can only keep the peace, by two methods: first, by a strong defense; and second, by reason and responsibility and negotiation.

Strong defense comes first. As your Commander in Chief—and Harry Sheppard had a lot to do with this—I can tell you tonight that the United States is the strongest and the mightiest nation in the world—the United States is stronger than all the other nations of the world combined.

You good Americans out there in that audience that are interested in your Government by coming down here after dark, you helped us to make it this way. And I am here as your President to tell you that I intend to keep it that way.

In World War II California was the first State in the Union in aircraft production and in shipbuilding. And tonight, California is responsible for 23.1 percent of our defense effort in the United States, more than twice as much as any other State in the Union. Fifty percent of our entire space effort is carried out in the great State of California, and this is up from 40 percent when President Kennedy took office in 1961.

This growth has come because America needs what California has to offer. It has come here strictly on merit. And so long as I am your President, it will continue to come here strictly on merit, and so long as I am your President, the Department of Defense stands ready to help any community, any industry, any individual that may suffer temporary dislocation because of changes in technology.

You can count on that. And I think that I know that you are patriotic enough that I can count on you to help me keep America strong and mighty.

But it is not enough to be powerful. Power alone is not enough. America must also be wise. We must be strong, but we must be sensible. We must be resolute, but we must be responsible. The stakes in the 20th century are too high to be reckless.

It is not easy to keep the peace in the world, but for 20 years we have kept the peace. We have turned back Communist aggression more than once. We will continue to stand guard at freedom's gate. This Nation is respected because we use our strength with restraint, and we use our responsibility with judgment.

So tonight I come here to ask you to affirm our dedication to responsibility and restraint on November 3d by voting for the only old San Bernardino resident on the national ticket this year.

We must run along now. People are waiting for us in San Diego, and then we have to go to Salt Lake City tonight. But before I leave, let me ask you, you just have 1 week: Talk to your kinfolks, talk to your neighbors, talk to your church workers, talk to them about peace in the world and prosperity at home, and tell them that you want the biggest county in the United States to give the biggest majority to the biggest effort that will ever be made to keep peace in the world and prosperity at home on November 3d.

Now I want to tell you how good it is to come back here and to have you be so warm and kind and generous. I want to tell you how good your Governor and his lovely wife have been to me. I want to tell you how nice your new Congressman, Ken Dyal, has been, and how wonderful Harry Sheppard has been through the years. I want to tell you that Pierre Salinger is doing a bangup job in Washington. Now I want to introduce you to the President's boss.

[*At this point Mrs. Johnson spoke briefly. She said that she had been hearing about the President's "adventures in California and in San Bernardino for just about all of the 30 years that we have been married. . . . When he came out here on that adventure, age 15 and just right out of a little, small-town high school, nothing like this loomed before him. It was the farthest thing from his thoughts or from any of those who knew him. One of the things that made the difference," she said, "was the fact that he finally went back home and went to college and got a good education." The President then resumed speaking.*]

Lady Bird is wrong about one thing, and

I want to clear up the record before we leave. I got plenty of vocational education in there on that elevator!

NOTE: The President spoke at 5:50 p.m. in the Platt Building in San Bernardino, Calif. His opening words "Governor Brown" referred to Governor Edmund G. Brown of California. Later in his remarks he referred to, among others, Representative Harry R. Sheppard, former Representative Philip D. Swing, Senator Pierre E. G. Salinger, and Ken W.

Dyal, Democratic candidate for Representative, all of California.

In 1964 a bronze plaque was placed in the lobby of the Platt Building to commemorate the President's brief residence in San Bernardino in 1925. Following is the legend which appears on the plaque:

PRESIDENT LYNDON B. JOHNSON
As a youth he ran this elevator in 1925.
As an attorney's clerk he began the study of law in this building the same year.
(Placed by readers of The Sun-Telegram in 1964.)

736   Remarks at Lindbergh Field, San Diego.
October 28, 1964

THANK YOU very much. I appreciate your welcome and your generosity, and I just wish I could spend all evening with you, but we must fly to Salt Lake City tonight and our time here will be limited.

I am so happy and I am so proud tonight— happy that I could be here with you happy people in San Diego, proud that I could sit there on the front row and observe this virile, patriotic, intelligent, modern young Senator introducing me to the people of San Diego.

I have seen this son of California work under great stress and strain for two Presidents. I have seen him work in the greatest deliberative body in the world, the United States Senate, but I was never prouder of him than when he was saying those nice things about me tonight.

I hope that you people will remember that we just have a few days between now and next Tuesday, and that it is going to take the best effort of all of us to elect Pierre Salinger as Senator, Lionel Van Deerlin back to the House where we need him greatly, and Quintin Whelan there to join all of us to pass a good Democratic program for all the people of this Nation.

Mr. Carpenter and Mayor Kern, I have been traveling all day with Governor Brown and his gracious wife. Governor Brown is

one of the outstanding public servants in this Nation. He is the spokesman for the largest State in the Union, the fastest growing State in the Union, the most progressive State in the Union, the State in the Union that has the best educational facilities, the State in the Union that is constantly working with us on international relations. I want to thank you people of California for electing a man like that Governor of your State.

This day is an anniversary. It is an anniversary that all free people should remember. Two years ago, on October 28, 1962, the United States of America achieved the greatest success of the nuclear age. After weeks of fright and danger and tension, after America's firmness and coolness and unity were proved, it was on that date that Chairman Khrushchev announced that he would get his missiles out of Cuba.

In all the history of man, there has perhaps never been a moment of greater peril than the Cuban confrontation. I attended 38 meetings with the President and his Security Council; the generals and their stars; the admirals and their braid; the Secretary of State, a Rhodes scholar, with his great diplomatic experience; the Secretary of Defense, the former president of Ford Motor Co. at $550,000 a year. And the President went around the table and got the suggestions from all those present, including the Vice President.

There were moments when I guess some men were a little more hotheaded than others. There were moments when some were a little more impulsive than others. There were moments of distress and indecision while we were looking at all the facts, because no man's judgment on any question is any better than his information on that question.

And yet, when all is said and done, it gave me a great deal of satisfaction that you people out there, just you lay people of the United States, had selected the Commander in Chief by your votes, and the coolest man in that room during all those 38 meetings was John Fitzgerald Kennedy.

During that time, that was the moment when human understanding caught up with nuclear knowledge, and reason regained its rule over force. That moment proved a truth that some had doubted, that the power of American arms is the guarantee of the world's peace and that America's might is the necessary instrument of right.

You no doubt remember, and I shall never forget, the brave and good and careful President who steered us surely and safely through those weeks of trial. I saw him do it. I never left my wife and daughters a single morning that I was sure I could see them again. But I know how calm and how wise John Kennedy was.

We may hope when this campaign is over that one unthinking, unthinkable charge will be removed from this political record: that what happened 2 years ago today, some said, was an election trick—by a martyred President—who is not now here tonight to defend himself.

In a sense, that is what this campaign

and this election is all about. The one overriding issue is our handling of the fact of our infinite power. The one overriding issue is our sense of responsibility and its use. The one overriding issue is our respect for the elementary right to live.

I state my position about this squarely, and I believe and I hope, and I think next Tuesday will prove, that it is your position, too, that it is America's position.

First may I deviate just a moment to say that I was in Boston last night and I am across the Nation tonight. But in neither place did I go to speak about personalities or to muckrake or to mudsling, or to deal with individuals. I want to talk about the big things.

I think you would have your President deal with problems and principles instead of petty personalities. I don't think you care what I think about my opponent. And I don't think you really care what he thinks about me.

I think what you do care about is what each one of us thinks about you and your future, and whether we respect your intelligence or whether we try to appeal to your emotions.

So I am here tonight to talk to you about the principal issues in this campaign.

First, we must treat our nuclear weapons—and they are awesome and they are mighty, and by moving your thumb over on a button like that, you can wipe out 300 million people in a matter of moments—we must treat our nuclear weapons with the greatest care. We know we need them, and we know we have plenty of them. We know they are dangerous, and we know they can bring death to us all, and we know that just testing them in the atmosphere has poisoned the air that we breathe and the milk that our children drink, and it endangered unborn children. So we must be careful about them.

The one who must be most careful for all of you, the most prudent, cautious person in the United States, ought to be your President of the United States.

I know that duty, as other Presidents have known it before me. I know that the responsibility for exercising that duty is the President's, and it is his alone, and he is alone a great deal of the time. He is lonely most of the time. But I am solemnly pledged with whatever ability the good Lord gave me, whatever energy and talents I possess, to do my dead level best to keep our world at peace—and with all that is in me I am determined to keep that vow to you.

Second, we must push the search for peace. It isn't automatic. It just doesn't come accidentally. It won't take care of itself alone. We know that we have to work at it—and we do work at it every day.

We reject the view that there is only one enemy in the world—the Communists; only one weapon—the nuclear bomb; only one policy—the policy of bluff and ultimatum.

We know that peace demands hard, steady work on many fronts: first, arms control, trying to get an agreement—one of the first things I did was submit to the Geneva conference a proposal on what we would do if they would do likewise; second, the banning of nuclear tests in the atmosphere, and all but 12 United States Senators went along with President Kennedy, and 105 nations out of the 112 that belong to the United Nations, 105 of them joined with us, and all the 100 Senators joined with us except 12, and one of their names I am not going to mention; and third, we must search for foreign trade.

We must trade with the rest of the world, because people that you meet and you work with and that you talk with and you trade with you get along better with. We have increased our foreign trade since President Kennedy took office by 25 percent. It is up now to $24 billion and that means extra jobs for your men. That means extra profits for your industry, and that means extra taxes for Uncle Sam.

And then the Peace Corps, these young men and women from good, wonderful, wholesome families, fresh out of college maybe, some of them perhaps almost ready to retire, they wanted to go to all the corners of the world to try to help others help themselves. There has never been another success story like it, and I am so proud of it.

We must try to be responsible for the help for other nations, because our per capita income is more than $200 a month per person. Yet half of the world lives off of a per capita income of less than $8 a month. And the ancient enemies of human beings are not just each other; the ancient enemies are ignorance and poverty and disease and illiteracy, malaria, tapeworm, leprosy, and all those things. Those are the ancient enemies of mankind.

We, with all of our power and all of our resources, and all of our blessings, are doing something to reach down and extend a helping hand to our neighbor, and to love thy neighbor as thyself.

There is another viewpoint. And other candidates have it. They can tell you about how everybody has robbed us, and how terrible we have been. And they can tell you about all the socialism that is taking place, and they can tell you about how much freedom we have lost.

I came out here to California in 1924, and the depression came along a few years later and I wasn't very free. I wasn't free to buy a good meal. I just didn't have the dough to do it; I wasn't free to sleep in a good bed because I just didn't have the money to pay for it. I wasn't free to have a good job because there just weren't any.

One fellow said to Lady Bird the other day when she put on her high heels and just decided she would go through the South because she didn't want them to feel that they were not wanted in the Union, and she got on a train and went through all the Southern States, went through Alabama where they won't even let our name go on the ticket. One of the fellows that had done a lot of thinking came up and said,

"You know, it looks to me like we are getting along better than some folks said we would after we passed the equal rights bill. I have just about figured out that I had rather have a Negro stand beside me on the assembly line than to have him stand behind me in the soup line."

Mr. Rayburn was my teacher. He was the Speaker of the House. He served for over 50 years. He came from a poor little sandy land farm. But he told me one time that we had corporals and sergeants, and second looies and first looies, and captains and majors, and colonels and generals, and if they didn't know more about how to fight a war than he did, we had wasted a lot of money on West Point all these years.

But I am not talking to you tonight about how to fight a war, so I am not going to pay much attention to these generals, whether it is General Thurmond, General Wedemeyer, General Doolittle, or a good many other generals. I have great respect for them, but what we are trying to do now is to figure out not how to fight or when to fight, but how we can learn to live without fighting, particularly when we have a nuclear weapon that will destroy civilization. That is our big problem.

A great son of the South that was raised in South Carolina where I spoke the night before last, at Columbia, Woodrow Wilson, had a dream of peace for all the people of the world. It was wrapped up in the League of Nations. He saw five willful men in the Senate destroy that dream. Then another man came along after another great war—Franklin Delano Roosevelt came along after World War II—and in San Francisco, in the great State of California, the United Nations was born, and all the leaders of the world came to this State to help give it birth.

What I am thinking about and what I hope you are thinking about, and what we all ought to be thinking about, is this assembly that has the spokesmen for each of the 112 nations. We ought to be trying to figure out—we know they have avoided a dozen or so wars already, minor ones, moderate ones, and some major ones. They have talked instead of fought. And what we ought to be trying to figure out is how can we strengthen the United Nations.

Harry Truman had a problem with the Communists taking over Greece and Turkey and he drew the line, the Truman doctrine, because he felt if they took Greece and Turkey they would sweep all Western Europe right after World War II. And the man that stood up by his side and did the most to help him was a Republican, Senator Arthur Vandenberg, of Michigan. He put his country ahead of his party. He put our foreign policy ahead of his politics. And we drew that line and they never crossed it.

When General Eisenhower was elected President, I was elected Democratic leader of the Senate, and the first thing I told my colleagues was, "When he is right I am going to vote with him, I am going to support him. When he is wrong I am going to oppose him, but I am going to do it with decency, and with dignity, and without any character assassination. I am not even going to say a word about his boy or his dogs or even his golf."

And when he had the crisis in Suez, and when he had the crisis in the Formosa Strait, the Democratic leader Lyndon Johnson stood up on the Senate floor and held his arm high because he wanted to present to our enemies and our adversaries in the world "United we stand, divided we fall" and "you can't divide and conquer us."

And when President John Kennedy decided that your children were drinking milk that they shouldn't be drinking, and you faced problems that we shouldn't face, and we were breathing air that was polluted, it was Everett Dirksen, the Republican Senator from the State of Illinois, the leader of the Republicans, that came to the White House and sat there with us and agreed that he would pick up that Kennedy treaty proposal and he would carry it on his broad shoulders right through that Senate.

That is the bipartisan foreign policy that is an issue in this campaign. Are we going to junk it? We have had it for 20 years. Are we going to flush it down the drain and let us go to evils we know not of? Well, we are not, if you elect me.

They asked me at the University of Texas in 1957 what my political philosophy was, and I said I am a free man first, I am an American second, I am a United States Senator third, and I am a Democrat fourth—in that order.

So the point I want to leave with you good people, Republicans and Democrats, and Independents, and folks who do your own thinking, the thing I want to leave with you before I go to that tabernacle in Salt Lake City and meet that wonderful man, President McKay, who has given me great spiritual strength and given great leadership, I want to leave this with you: We work for peace not as Democrats, not as Republicans, but as Americans.

I have told you how I feel, and it is about time for me to get on my way. But just in case the other side doesn't have equal time and they can't come back here to San Diego, I think the record ought to show—because you know a great man once said, his name was Al Smith, "Let's look at the record"—

There is one candidate in this race for the Presidency who voted against the test ban treaty.

There is one candidate who voted against our new disarmament agency.

There is one candidate that voted against the Trade Expansion Act.

There is one candidate that voted against the United Nations bond issue.

And on all of these votes, every single one of them, he voted against the overwhelming majority of the Senators of both parties. Everybody seems to be out of step but him.

I am proud to be a Democrat, and I want to make that clear. But I am humble, I am humble in the belief that on the issue of war, when you take your boy down to the depot to say goodby, maybe never to see him again, on the issue of war and peace I share the view of the Presidents of both parties who have preceded me, and I share the view of what I think is the overwhelming majority of Americans today.

We believe that the courage of the age is demonstrated only by handling carefully—and never carelessly—any test which may arise. There are many of them, and there is no way to prevent them. We must be ready to handle them when they come. We must do it with care and with coolness and with courage. This we have done.

We were tested in Berlin. President Kennedy sent me there and he sent troops in marching down the streets to let them know that we were there and we planned to stay.

We were tested in Cuba and a thumb on a button could have caused a nuclear holocaust. And hotheads all over the country were hollering and rattling the rockets and shouting and saying we ought to do it. But it took patience, judgment, and restraint. And we stood firm.

We were tested at Guantanamo, right after I went into office, and in Panama. They took a thermometer and put it in my mouth and took my temperature. They knew we had lost our President. They wanted to see what kind of a transition we could have.

Castro went out and turned off the water at our Guantanamo base. Immediately one of the candidates for President shouted, "Send in the Marines." I considered sending in the Marines. I think the Marines would have been willing to go if I just mashed that button and said, "Gentlemen, that is your duty." But I never saw a Marine that just went out and invited holocaust and disaster and suicide.

So we thought about it a few minutes before we sent in the Marines. And we finally decided after we talked to the best advisers we could get that it was a lot wiser to send one little admiral down there to cut that water off than to send in all those Marines to turn it on. And then we borrowed one of your desalinization plants here in San Diego, and we took it out there. Now we make our own water and we fired 2,000 Cubans and told them, "We are not going to give you any money any more and you go back and tell Castro he cost you your job."

The Marines were ready and the Marines were willing. But some nights I have to give an order to send planes out at 11 o'clock on very important missions, in various parts of the world. And generally those boys—one of them is right here, from San Diego—generally they come back about 3:30 our time.

I have learned somehow or other to read my reports for an hour or two and then doze off to sleep. But at 3:25—I don't need an alarm clock—I immediately wake up to see if my boys got back home.

And I call the Situation Room and I say, "Have they gotten back yet?" And two or three nights I called and they said, "No, Lieutenant Klusmann didn't get back. Another one is on a hill and the helicopter was hovering over him but they started shooting at the helicopter and they couldn't pick him up and he was captured. But he finally escaped on his own."

That makes the goosepimples come up on you when you mash that button and tell them to go out and they don't come back at 3:30, because you know they are some mother's son, and except for the grace of God it might be my mother's son. I try to keep that in my mind.

So when we were tested in the Gulf of Tonkin, when they shot at our destroyers, we answered appropriately and promptly. We located their nests where they had these little PT boats, and we saw a city there that had a lot of women and children in it that was on the Chinese border where there are 700 million people, but we didn't see any reason that we should take that target and kill a lot of innocent people, women and children. What we wanted was where those PT boats were nesting. We wanted to get the old hen's nest.

So we looked at the targets and we picked this one and we picked this one and we picked this one and this one, and then your heart kind of comes up in your throat a minute, but you say, "Go on in, men," give them the order, and the answer is to go ahead. The order goes out, and those boys get their planes off the deck and they went in and they destroyed their nests, and nearly all of them came back.

So the world knows, all the world knows, what you know tonight, that America says what it means and means what it says about keeping the peace against aggressors.

And fourth and finally, all Americans know in this world of danger that we must be calm and we must be clear.

Just in these last 2 weeks the world has been stirred by two great events among the Communists, the change of leadership in the Kremlin and the explosion of a nuclear device on a Chinese desert.

The eyes of the free world turned to Washington and it became the duty of your President, the only President you have, to speak up for your country. This is what I did 10 days ago, and the response that we received from all around the world shows that our strength and our fairness and our firmness are understood. The world knows that our course is steady and our purpose of peace is unchanged.

For a long time now, for many years, the world has had its spotlight on America. They have looked to America for power and for leadership. For many years now, under many Presidents, from both parties, America has proved worthy of that confidence. America's strength is respected. We are just 190 million out of 3 billion. We are outnumbered 15 to 1 in population. But our strength is respected and our purpose is honored, and our word is trusted.

There have been dark days and there have been great dangers in the past. Who knows, tomorrow morning may bring new challenges.

There is danger and there is difficulty tonight in parts of the world, particularly in Southeast Asia, and there is work undone, work undone for freedom in every continent of the world. I can tell you that freedom is stronger tonight than it has been in any time in 20 years. I can tell you this: that the foes of freedom, the enemies of freedom, are more divided than they have been in 20 years.

You heard the Hitler objective of divide and conquer. There are some who do it deliberately and there are some who do it maliciously, and there are some who do it because they don't know any better, but it is not to your interest to hate your neighbor. It is not to your child's good to fear your friend.

This preaching of hate and fear, and doubt and division, and distrust and doubt about your Government—that is what destroys governments, but we have so many things to be thankful for. We have so much to protect, so much to preserve, and besides you are just so much happier when you love than when you hate.

So let's look back and see what our grandpa and our grandma and those that came here in '49 and those who came and started to establish a government in '76, let's look back and see how far they have come from their covered wagons to our Air Force One, our 707's, to our supersonic planes that are now on the drawing boards, that will go over 2,000 miles an hour.

Let's just see if we can't find something good about America, and let's see if we can't take a little pride in that flag, and let's see if we can't have a little feeling well up in us and see if we can't get down on our knees sometime during the night and thank God that I am an American.

I have traveled around the world and I have been in many countries, and I have seen the glories of art and architecture. I have seen the sun rise on Mont Blanc. But the most beautiful vision that these eyes ever beheld was that American flag in a foreign land.

And I think I tell you the truth when I say that my 707 has never touched down in any country on any continent where we were met by any person that wouldn't like to trade places with us.

So let's get rid of our martyr complexes and our psychotic tendencies, and let's try to get back to work to unite America, just like we were in other dangerous periods that we all went and bought our liberty bonds, and let's try to put in our nickel's worth and make our suggestions. But let's don't be mean and vicious and dirty about it. Let's try to heal the wounds.

As I said last night, Lincoln abolished slavery 100 years ago. Now let us have a worthy objective. Even though some of us have money in our pockets, clothes on our backs, and food in our stomachs, let's dedicate ourselves in the next few years not to abolish slavery but to go out and abolish poverty among all people.

You are inspiring just to look at and I would like to talk all night, but they keep walking up in front of me and telling me that the plane is ready to go.

On next Tuesday I am going to be at my little library room down at the Pedernales where my grandfather and grandmother and mother and father and uncles and cousins and aunts are all buried on the banks of that little river, and I am going to pick up the telephone now and then and talk to some neighbors across the country.

I just hope that by your decision, by your following your conscience and doing in your heart what you know is right, I just hope that Pat Brown or Pierre Salinger or whoever can call without calling me collect—maybe Lionel Van Deerlin, Quintin Whelan or Mayor Kern—I hope some of you will call me and say, "California, here I come."

NOTE: The President spoke at 7:30 p.m. at Lindbergh Field, San Diego, Calif. During the course of his remarks he referred to Senator Pierre E. G. Salinger, Representative Lionel Van Deerlin, and Quintin Whelan, and Paul B. Carpenter, Democratic candidates for Representative, all of California, Mayor Frank Kern of San Diego, Governor Edmund G. Brown of California and Mrs. Brown, and David O. McKay, president of the Church of Jesus Christ of Latter-day Saints, Salt Lake City, Utah.

The text of the remarks of Mrs. Johnson, who spoke briefly, was also released.

737   Remarks in Salt Lake City at the Mormon Tabernacle. *October 29, 1964*

President Brown, thank you for that inspiring invocation, President Tanner, my fellow Americans:

I am honored to be in this famous tabernacle this morning. I am proud to be on this platform with President Brown. It also makes me glad to be here with four patriotic Utah citizens whose hopes and lives are dedicated to their State and to their country.

Senator Frank Moss, who introduced me, known as Ted Moss, is my friend of many years. He has worked closely with me in trying to make our country greater, stronger, and wiser, and the growth of our Nation and how it fulfills its responsibilities of the future depend in large measure on men of this type, men like Ted Moss.

Calvin Rampton, a distinguished Salt Lake City lawyer; David King, who worked so effectively for Utah in the Congress; and Bill Bruhn, an able and energetic citizen of Ogden, these are the kind of men that I think make this country great and help it to endure all the trials and tribulations that we face in these perilous times.

For me, this occasion this morning is deeply moving and very meaningful.

Only a year ago last month, there stood here—where I stand now—the President of the United States. None could know when he spoke here how tragically short was the time that remained for his life and his leadership among us. But all who knew him know that you gave to him a gratifying moment which brightened his life to the very end.

President Kennedy returned from Salt Lake City knowing, as he had not known before, that the people of America supported his efforts to make this world safer for all mankind. For that gratification that you gave to him, by your affirmation of America's devotion to peace, I would like this morning to express to you my deeply felt appreciation.

Over these last 11 months, all of us have had occasion to reflect—reflect as seldom before—upon what it means to bear the burdens of responsibility that are borne by our particular generation of Americans. In that one awful and incredible instant last November, we looked deeply into the chasm of change. If what we saw together made us more humble, I believe it also served to make us more hopeful.

Men and nations learn from revelations. In that moment, it was revealed to us how much America means to mankind, and really, how much we mean to each other. In all of our purposes and pursuits since then, it seems to me there has been a growing will among the people to heal their wounds, to come a little closer together, rather than to risk having our society divided and coming apart.

This is the truth about America. This is the truth that each of us must never forget. In your lifetime and mine, there has never been a moment when America more needed its unity, or the world more needed a united America, than today.

Over these last 11 months, and particularly over these last 2 weeks, the world about us has had sweeping changes.

In the dark corridors of the Kremlin, new leaders have moved to power.

In Communist China, nuclear bombs have been unleashed.

In England, our great ally, the people have chosen a labor government.

In Japan, the Prime Minister has resigned and a new government is now being formed.

In India, the great leader Nehru has passed on and Shastri has taken his place.

In capitals of the free world, in capitals of the Communist world, and in capitals of the emerging world there has come—and continues to come—change of a magnitude and moment that are seldom known to man.

I believe that we are entering a new era in the affairs of man. I am certain that we and the world really have two directions that we can go.

We can, in the words of one of your old hymns, commit our efforts to moving "on to eternal perfection." Or we can, in folly and foolhardiness, allow the world to move recklessly toward eternal damnation.

For whatever may unfold, you and I are cast in very decisive roles. This generation of Americans, more than any other, will decide by our example and our enterprise whether change shall serve creative or destructive purposes for humankind.

So in today's changing world, and in today's turbulent sea, all mankind seeks a rock to cling to. America must stand as that rock. It will be that rock if we follow our fixed star—the ideals of a free society that have guided our Nation through its gravest dangers and shaped our country through its finest hours.

First, we must meet our moral responsibility to the resources with which God endowed our land.

Waste is wrong, wherever we permit it, and the first thing I did as President was to put all the resources of the Government to work immediately stopping waste. We just must not permit the waste of what God gave us all. We must conserve and we must develop the earth, the air, and the water on which all life depends and, really, all success rests.

Second, we must meet our moral responsibility to our own people, to the young, to the aged, to the laborer, the manager, and the producer of our food and fiber and our minerals, to those in urban areas and rural areas alike, encouraging independence and always encouraging self-reliance and individual initiative.

We must provide for our children an opportunity for the best education that he or she can absorb, because in this technological age they are going to be at a great disadvantage if they have not accumulated all the information and knowledge available to them.

We must provide for every person of advancing age the dignity and the care that honorable years deserve.

For every man who labors, there must be respect for his rights and opportunity for his advancement in a growing America.

For every man who ventures in business with his capital, there must be the opportunity to compete fairly and to profit fairly in proportion to his initiative and his abilities.

For this richest and strongest and most successful society in the history of mankind, there just must be a moral commitment to wipe away the causes of poverty and ignorance and disease.

We are all God's children, and the true morality of private life is the true morality of a free society: the Golden Rule, do unto others as you would have others do unto you.

Third, we must, as a moral people, meet our moral opportunities to other peoples as well as our own. For those who aspire to be free, we here in America must keep aflame the torch of liberty, by being strong ourselves, and being steadfast and sure in all that we do.

Around the world more millions are enslaved by hunger than by tyrants. All the world's religions call on man to give to the poor, and as a nation we have done so.

We have not done this merely to halt communism. Our generosity flows from deeper springs of human compassion, and we just must never allow those springs to dry up in our private life or in our public policies.

If we do in the world what is right and just and good, if we keep our moral responsibilities and if we meet our opportunities, our purpose and our conduct can change the entire world.

Fourth, we must learn to live in the closer family of man here at home and in the world. At home we must ever strive to be a more tolerant people, not because laws require it but because our conscience commands it.

Whatever destiny determines that we must do, we can do it only as a nation united. This morning as we meet here, as never before in all of our lives, we very much need a tolerant condition of our national mind, to assure the unity of our people in all our purposes and all of our pursuits.

Finally, in the world of our times, in a world of great change, it must be America's unchanging purpose to lead in the quest for peace. Our task, our urgent and our ever present task, is to change civilization's careening course and change it away from the ultimate folly—change it toward the ultimate fruitfulness of a world that knows no war.

America has great strength. The world trusts both our will to use it and our will will always be to use it with appropriate restraint. Neither the world's trust, nor our own restraint, must ever be lost or must ever be left in doubt. In what we do, America must be guided by self-confidence, and not by self-doubt.

All political systems change. They are forced to by historic circumstance. And it would be dangerously foolish to believe that Soviet Russia or Communist China will soon become open societies. But it would be equally foolish to think that they will never change. Inside Russia, the Soviet Union, today a powerful force for change is already at work. Education, the bedrock of democracy, the enemy of dictatorship, is plowing its way.

Inside the Communist bloc, powerful currents are surging against the dam. Premier Khrushchev a short time before he was deposed, speaking of some of the satellite countries, said, "Like children, they have grown up and now are too large to spank."

So we cannot sit idly by—we must work to guide the inevitable changes that lie ahead. This has been—and this will continue to be—my course and my leadership.

When the Soviet Government changed governments last week, I sent word to Moscow that America's basic policy remained unchanged. This week I received an answer from Mr. Kosygin. He is the new head of the Soviet Government. In his response he said that the Soviet Union would maintain its present policies and would seek better relations and maintain its own search for peace with the West. He said that the Soviet Union would continue its communication with the United States.

The Ambassador of the Soviet Union came to spend an hour with me. He said that the Soviet Union would continue to explore areas of mutual interest.

Well, this is a heartening response. We must never underestimate the danger of communism, but neither should we underestimate the danger to all of us and to all of the world if nuclear bombs are unleashed and in a moment of anger we should wipe out the lives of millions that we can never restore if we do not constantly, uppermost, as our first priority, seek and search and plead and pray that we may find a way toward peace.

As your President, the only President you have, as the leader of the mightiest nation in all the world, I can assure you that we intend to preserve that might as a deterrent to others and as a requirement to defend ourselves.

But, on the other hand, while we will always keep our guard up and we will always keep alert, we will always have our hand out. We intend to bury no one, but we don't intend to be buried, either.

We will constantly try to be vigilant and prudent. We will constantly try to be strong and cautious. We will try to be careful and restrained, and never careless or bombastic.

There is nothing to be gained from rattling our rockets or bluffing with our bombs, because we know, and our adversaries know, that we have the might. We will expect respect for America's interest, but we will continue with every resource at my command to work for a lasting and a just and an honorable peace among men.

We want our children to survive. We want our children to say, that was the generation that split the atom, and that was the generation that united all mankind.

NOTE: The President spoke at 9:03 a.m. at the Mormon Tabernacle in Salt Lake City, Utah. In his opening words he referred to Hugh B. Brown and N. Eldon Tanner, counselors to David O. McKay, president of the Church of Jesus Christ of Latter-day Saints. Later he referred to Senator Frank E. Moss, Calvin Rampton, Democratic candidate for Governor, and David S. King and William G. Bruhn, Democratic candidates for Representative, all of Utah. He also referred to Aleksei N. Kosygin, chairman of the Council of Ministers, U.S.S.R., and Anatoly F. Dobrynin, Ambassador to the United States from the Soviet Union. The text of the messages of the President and Mr. Kosygin was not released.

738   Remarks Recorded for the Dedication of the Graduate Research Center of the Southwest. *October* 29, 1964

Governor Connally, Mayor Jonsson, Mayor Ryan, Dr. Berkner, my fellow Americans:

I am particularly proud to take these moments this afternoon to join with you in marking this milestone of progress for the Graduate Research Center of the Southwest.

In our land, our future is influenced by the choices of our elections.

But, in a much more important way, the fate of our freedom rests upon the faithfulness with which we honor and keep our society's oldest commitment—the commitment to education.

We have learned in America that the surest safeguard against centralization of political power is the diffusion of human knowledge. As Mirabeau Lamar once said—and as I like to repeat in every State—"The educated mind is the guardian genius of democracy."

The more strong centers of learning and research that are built across our Nation, the stronger becomes the fabric of our freedom and the fiber of our Great Society.

The Graduate Research Center of the Southwest, under the leadership of Dr. Berkner, helps to fill a vital need for the vigorous future of Texas and the Southwest. It has long had my admiration and my support.

Too often too many Americans conclude that our country has completed its course. Actually, America is still only a very new land—a young land, still putting in place the foundation for the greatness of a growing society. We have one of the oldest governments but one of the youngest countries.

Among our regions, few have so much promise and potential as the southwest part of our country. Where we have seen dramatic change over the past two decades in the Southwest, the remaining decades of this century will bring far more profound changes—in the growth of our population, our cities, our economy, our horizons.

If those Americans who come after us are to know and are to enjoy a life of the first class as free and responsible citizens, then we must keep faith with that early Texas commitment to education of the first class.

It is important to that future that we employ human knowledge to better and to improve human life.

It is important to the security and well-being of our country that we continue to exercise leadership in all aspects of human knowledge.

It is important to the moral and political values of our society—and to their preservation—that we set for ourselves goals of excellence as the only goals acceptable for this free and responsible people.

Our tasks ahead will not be easy tasks.

None of the tasks facing Americans today can honestly be described as easy or simple or uncomplicated. In States such as Texas—and in regions such as the Southwest—the future before us is complex and challenging and demanding. But our region, like all our Nation, is blessed with many resources, the greatest of which are our human resources.

I am confident that the Graduate Research Center of the Southwest will, through the years to come, play an invaluable role in helping us to fulfill the potential of the human resources of a great region.

That is why I am so especially proud to participate this afternoon in these ceremonies. They are symbolic of the awakening which is running throughout our Nation. It is an awakening that will find its reward in the greater strength we of this generation contribute to the generations to come after us.

On the strength we build today rests the outcome of the contests of this century between the way of freedom and the ways of darkness. A strong nation, a united nation, a nation committed to the education, the enlightenment and the advancement of its people is the nation that will succeed in the struggle to win those contests between a world of war or a world of peace.

NOTE: The President's remarks were video-taped in the Fish Room at the White House on October 27 for release at the dedication on October 29 of the Graduate Research Center of the Southwest, located near Dallas, Tex. His opening words referred to John B. Connally, Governor of Texas, Erik Jonsson, mayor of Dallas, Herbert Ryan, mayor of Richardson, Tex., and Dr. Lloyd V. Berkner, president of the Center.

739 Presidential Statement No. 8 on Economic Issues: Expanding World Trade. *October 29, 1964*

1. THE POLICY of trade liberalization—pursued ever since the Trade Agreements Act of 1934, by both Democratic and Republican administrations—has served this country well. Our foreign trade, which amounted to only $3.8 billion in 1934, is now running at an annual rate of $42½ billion—$24½ billion in exports and $18 billion in imports.

2. Our exports provide jobs for about 3.6 million American workers and outlets for the crops of one out of every four acres of our farms. Our imports provide essential raw materials for our industries, maintain a healthy pressure on our own producers and workers to step up their efficiency, offer our consumers a wider choice of goods at competitive prices, and counteract domestic pressures for price increases.

3. On the basis of the Trade Expansion Act of 1962, we are currently able to engage in the sixth round of international negotiations under the auspices of the General Agreement on Tariffs and Trade (GATT). The Trade Expansion Act is one of the great legislative monuments to President Kennedy's leadership, and this administration is fully committed to its vigorous implementation.

4. The current negotiations will not impose burdens on some nations to provide gains for others. They are being conducted on a basis of reciprocity, and their success will be advantageous to all participating nations. The negotiations may be lengthy, complex, and at times difficult, but we are prudently confident of fruitful results.

5. Special import difficulties confronting particular sections of our economy may at times require remedial action. This administration has taken action to meet the problems of meat producers and of cotton textile and apparel manufacturers. We are also seeking to work out arrangements among the woolen textile-producing nations which would be in the mutual interests of all.

6. However necessary, such remedial actions are the exception rather than the rule. The main thrust of this administration—as of Democratic and Republican administra-

tions for the past 30 years—will be toward trade liberalization.

NOTE: For a statement by the President announcing a series of statements on economic issues, see Item 707.

740   Presidential Statement No. 9 on Economic Issues: Promoting Price-Wage Decisions.   *October* 29, 1964

1. THE PRICE-WAGE guideposts were developed under President Kennedy and reaffirmed by this administration to facilitate decisions by business and labor that help us preserve price stability.

2. The guideposts provide the public with a means of judging whether the price and wage decisions made by business and labor are noninflationary and therefore consistent with the public interest.

3. They reflect the fact that overall stability of prices can be assured if wage increases do not exceed the economywide rate of gain in productivity and if industries with exceptionally high productivity gains reduce their prices.

4. With some exceptions, price and wage decisions have been within the framework of the guideposts in the 1961–64 period:

—Price increases in industries with below-average productivity gains have been offset by price decreases elsewhere.

—Average wage and benefit increases have not exceeded the long-run rise in the productivity of our workers, so that labor cost per unit of output has not risen since the beginning of 1961. In fact, it has fallen by 3.4 percent in manufacturing.

5. Our remarkable record of price stability has (a) protected consumers at home by maintaining the purchasing power of the dollar and (b) enabled us to strengthen the competitive position of our goods abroad

and improve our balance of payments:

—Wholesale prices are, on the average, 0.1 percent below 5 years ago, and down 0.3 percent since the beginning of this year.

—Industrial wholesale prices have fallen 0.3 percent over the past 5 years.

—Since 1961 the wholesale price record in the United States is the best of any major country in the world. For example, while wholesale prices here were falling a bit, they rose in all the major European countries, from about 3 percent for Germany to 11½ percent for Italy.

—Consumer prices have also been more stable than in any other major country in the world. As compared to our consumer price increase of slightly less than 4 percent since the 1st quarter of 1961, major European countries experienced increases of 10 percent to 19 percent.

6. The guideposts are not compulsory and do not fix prices or wages. In our economy, those are matters properly left to free markets and free collective bargaining. The term "guideposts" conveys exactly what was intended—not hard and fast prescriptions for every wage settlement or price decision—but criteria for responsible action by both labor and business.

7. The guideposts are a sound basis for continued price stability and are increasingly important as our economy rises closer and closer to its full potential. They have made

all of us—in business, in labor, and in Government—more keenly aware of the importance of our own actions for price stability and sustained prosperity. This increased understanding and sense of re-

sponsibility can strengthen our economy in the years ahead.

NOTE: For a statement by the President announcing a series of statements on economic issues, see Item 707.

741 Remarks at an Airport Rally in Wichita.
October 29, 1964

Mr. Chairman, distinguished platform guests, my neighbors here in the great State of Kansas:

One great resource that you have in Kansas is able, dedicated men—men like Harry Wiles who is going to be your next Governor. Harry is an action man. He is determined to make Kansas a more prosperous and a stronger State. Kansas citizens can perform no more beneficial service for themselves and their families than to make sure next Tuesday that Harry Wiles is their leader and is elected.

You have a good many good men running for Congress. I urge you to work for them, to support them, to vote for them, men like Bill Bork from the First Congressional District; John Montgomery from the Second Congressional District; Clayton Dial from the Third Congressional District Jack Glaves from the Fourth District, here in Wichita.

In the days ahead you are going to need these men in Washington. I need them in Washington. So please send them there next Tuesday.

I am glad to see my old friend Frank Theis and Mrs. Marie Vickers, and my old friend Mrs. Georgia Gray, and Mrs. Olive Ann Beech.

My friends, I have been in Wichita before. You are a very hospitable people. I shall never forget the visits that I have had with some of your leading citizens with regard to your reservoir here when I was majority

leader of the Senate. But the yellow rose of Texas has turned into a sunflower today.

We are so hopeful about Kansas, and we think so much of Kansas, that both Hubert Humphrey, the next Vice President, and I are both Jayhawkers this afternoon. Actually, we almost met here in Wichita this afternoon, but Hubert told me that he thought it really wasn't necessary to meet in Wichita because we ought to be seeing a lot of each other after next Tuesday at the White House.

These are good times in our country. These are good times in Kansas. For almost 45 months, that is nearly 4 years, we have had the longest and the strongest peacetime expansion in the history of our Nation, and we have maintained the most stable prices of any nation in the Western World.

The old rhythm of recessions and depressions seems to have been broken. This administration is the first in more than a century not to have either a recession or a depression, or even a downturn in our prosperity. This record is not the record of Washington alone. This record is the work of a united and a happy and a responsible people working together to assure the success of our system in every section.

We are going to keep right on that course of responsibility. And let's give a little thought at this serious meeting this afternoon on what this responsibility has meant to the good people who live in Kansas, the people who have put their faith in America's private enterprise economy by cutting taxes this year.

This tax cut that I put into effect when I signed the bill this year giving back $12 billion to American taxpayers—this tax cut put money into Kansas pocketbooks, $22 million more in Wichita alone, $80 million more in the State of Kansas alone. That tax cut is helping to create more jobs. It is helping to put more Americans to work.

Here in Wichita where we meet today, there are 13,000 more jobs than there were 3 years ago. The unemployment rate was 4.6 percent 3 years ago. Today it is down to 3 percent, well below the national average for the other States. When the tax cut is fully effective it will mean 22,000 more jobs for Kansas workers. Yes, responsibility is serving America, and I think and I hope, and I believe, that you people in Kansas want it to continue next Tuesday.

Americans are proud that their country stands as the strong and the stable and the steady center of a changing world, and we are determined this will not change. You here in Wichita know that America is strong because you are helping to build the strength that makes this Nation second to none. We are the strongest, we are the mightiest nation in all the world today.

We are proud of the contribution that Kansas has made to the cause of preserving peace and that contribution is great. Kansas ranks in the 50 States 31st in the Nation in total manufacturing, but Kansas ranks in the 50 States 20th in the Nation in defense contracts.

There is talent here, there is ability here, there is capital here, there is management here. There are workers here. And we put them together in Kansas and they build America's strength. I pledge you that we plan to continue to build that strength, for so long as there has been an America, our

people and their Presidents have worked for peace. That is not going to change.

We have a moral responsibility to lead all the nations toward the goal of a peaceful world, toward the goal of a just world and a free world, and we are not going to shirk that duty, and we are not going to fail that responsibility.

When the people of America go to the polls next Tuesday in all our 50 States, I believe that they are going to vote their pride and not their partisanship, and certainly not their prejudices.

We want to be citizens of a country that all the world respects, not a country that all the world fears. We want to be a part of the building of a better world. We don't want to be part of tearing down what men have labored so long and so patiently and so hopefully to raise up.

We know that in this nuclear age there is always a choice, a choice of wiping out human life or wiping away human want and human suffering.

Eleven months and three days ago, when I assumed the awesome responsibilities of the Presidency, after that tragic day when we lost our fallen leader, I told you people then that with God's help and with your prayers, I would do the best I could. The next week the transition began to take place. Eighty-five leaders from the world came to the White House to talk about their relations with America, to talk about their problems with each other. Since that time we have continued to try to build a program for all the people.

I do not want a business government; I do not want a labor government; I do not want a government that is fighting with either business or labor. I want a government of all the people, and I want to be President of all the people. I want to be progressive and still be prudent. I want to be conservative without being reactionary. I want to put a stop to all the waste that I can find, and I want to put a start to using all the resources we have.

I think I know something about your State. I have plowed the fields in a neighboring one. I have roamed the hills and herded the cattle and spent my lifetime in the pursuit of vocations that a lot of Kansans enjoy. I think that your people are a people with vision and a people with foresight, and a people with patriotism who are always ready to defend themselves but never want to provoke anyone else into an unnecessary fight. We do not seek any land that belongs to anyone else, or any additional power in the world. We do not intend to bury anyone, and we do not intend to be buried.

We believe in the Golden Rule of doing unto others as you would have them do unto you, and we love thy neighbor as thyself.

We do not preach hate. We do not preach division. We preach faith and hope and love. And in this critical time, when a nuclear holocaust can cost you 300 million lives, it is a time for us to walk and work in the search for some way, somehow, for a plan that will bring peace to the world and permit man to live with man without dropping bombs and destroying him.

My political philosophy is that I am a free man first, and that I am an American second, that I am a public servant third, and a Democrat fourth—and in that order. I always put my country before my party.

So I appeal to the people in Wichita, in this progressive city that turns out so many products that make our Nation strong and great—I appeal to the people of this city to take the leadership that is theirs now, to get out between now and next Tuesday and talk to your neighbors and your kinfolks and your friends. And let's try to unite this country because we need to be united as never before.

Divide and conquer—that is the slogan of one of our adversaries of a few years ago. We have new governments taking over in different places. This is a time for Americans to stand up and be counted, be counted in the American way with peace as our objective, with prosperity as our desire, and with the hope that all Americans can love each other instead of hate each other.

And finally, next Tuesday, you, the masters and not the servants, you the masters will select the servants. It will be one of the most responsible decisions that you ever made in your life.

I sat in the Cabinet Room for 37 meetings during the Cuban missile crisis. I saw Mr. Khrushchev bring his missiles into Cuba, 90 miles from our shores, and point them in our direction. I saw Mr. Kennedy bring in all the men with the stars on their shoulders and the gold braid on their uniforms. I saw the great diplomat, the Secretary of State, the Rhodes scholar, come in and make his recommendations.

I never knew a single morning when I left home that I would see my wife and daughters again that night. It looked like that it was just about the time, the clock was ticking. But I am proud to tell you after we were careful and cautious, and deliberate and sober, and sound, the coolest man in that room was John Fitzgerald Kennedy, your President.

We do not know what the future holds. Anyone can start a war, but no one can ever recoup the damage it has done in the first few hours when 300 million lives are wiped out.

The kind of leadership America has in this period is a matter for you to decide. I haven't come to say anything ugly about anybody. I spent 12 years in the House of Representatives; I spent 12 years in the Senate; I spent almost 3½ years as Vice President; I have spent almost a year as President. If God is willing and you approve, next Tuesday I will tell you what I told you that terrible night when I walked into the White House and that office was bare and our leader was gone: With God's help, with your prayers, I will do my dead level best to make this country safe and secure and prosperous. I believe in a nation where we have equal opportunity for all and special privilege for none.

You owe me nothing; you have already given me much. Next Tuesday you owe a lot to yourselves and to your family. I am not here today to do your thinking for you, because when we all think alike it means that one man is doing all the thinking.

So I just want to leave this thought with you: Between now and Tuesday—and I will be waiting Tuesday night to hear from

Wichita—you ask yourself what in your heart is right for you and your family. You ask yourself what course, what leadership, you think would be safer and saner for your Nation. And then, by all means you and your family go and register your vote, that priceless privilege that is not enjoyed in many lands today, and you select the kind of leadership that you think will weather the storm and that will carry us forward to peace abroad and to prosperity at home. And whatever your judgment, whatever your decision, it will be all right with me.

I will be waiting to hear from you. Thank you and good night.

NOTE: The President spoke at 12:35 p.m. at a rally at the Wichita Municipal Airport, Wichita, Kans. His opening words "Mr. Chairman" referred to Frank Tice, Democratic State committeeman. During the course of his remarks he referred to, among others, Harry Wiles, Democratic candidate for Governor, and Bill Bork, John Montgomery, A. Clayton Dial, and Jack Glaves, Democratic candidates for Representative, all of Kansas.

The text of remarks of Mrs. Johnson, who spoke briefly, was also released.

742   Remarks in Convention Hall, Philadelphia.
October 29, 1964

Chairman Smith, Governor Lawrence, Mayor Tate, Senator Genevieve Blatt, my old friends Congressman Barrett, Congressman Nix, Congressman Byrne, Congressman Toll, and Congressman Bill Green, my old friends Mike Musmanno and Richard Dilworth:

A little while ago we arrived at the hotel after one of the largest and the warmest welcomes of this campaign. I went into my room and Frank Smith was with me. When I sat down in a chair there by the window, Frank looked over to me and said, "Mr. President, 1 year ago tonight at this

very same hour, in that very same chair that you are now sitting in, sat John Fitzgerald Kennedy."

If I may, I want to say a word to you tonight and to all Americans about the role that fate has entrusted to me this year.

For 11 months and 1 week now, I have borne the torch that passed from the hands of that great and good and gallant President on that tragic November day in 1963. I have traveled more than 100,000 miles into 44 States of this land, and every mile of the way that I have walked, I have walked the path that was opened for us and the path that was pioneered for us by John Fitzgerald Kennedy.

In your great city and in every city I have seen millions of Americans. I have seen a proud and a prospering and a peaceful people, and I have known that that pride and that prosperity and, above all, that peace is what John Fitzgerald Kennedy left to them.

Of all that I have done in my life, nothing has given such great pride and satisfaction to me as to stand as I did in the campaign of 1960 by the side of John F. Kennedy. I am proud and I am grateful to have been a part of the campaign which proved forever that in America no man shall be denied the opportunity to serve his countrymen because of the region in which he lives or the religion which he has.

Tonight, America is a better and a stronger nation for all of us because of that campaign that we waged in '60. Philadelphia is a city of homes and families, just as all of America is a nation of homes and families, and in the life of such a city and in the life of such a nation, religion has always, and religion must always, play a part in all that we do or all that we hope to do.

I hope that the day will never come when any man, for any cause, will try to keep religion out of our national decisions on who shall lead us or the direction we shall go.

Thank God that Americans welcome into their homes and into the lives of their families the preachers and the priests and the rabbis who serve us all so faithfully and so unselfishly.

The men of the pulpit have a place in the leadership of our people and they have a place in our public affairs. We should be grateful for their concern over the well being of this land, for that is what America is all about, and that is what brought men to these shores, and particularly to this great State of Pennsylvania.

I do not condemn our churches or our clergymen for being concerned that America meet her moral responsibilities for peace, for preserving human freedom, and human life, and for doing what a rich nation can and should do to wipe poverty from our land. I not only don't condemn them, I thank God for their courage.

As I go on tonight to carry on the works of John Kennedy and the program that he began, I want your help, I want your hand, I want your prayers, I want your support to see that we get that job well done.

I want your help and I want you to know just how you can help me. And you can also help yourself when you are helping me. You can also help America when you are helping me. You can send Genevieve Blatt to the United States Senate. There on this program where we will have equal opportunities for all Americans and special privileges for none, Genevieve Blatt will join Joe Clark—and Pennsylvania will have two votes for all the people all the time.

I want to acknowledge and thank you for the presence tonight of one of my old colleagues who was in Congress when I first went there, Mike Bradley from Pennsylvania. He and Frank Myers and so many other men from this State have done so much to help me in the rough spots along the road that we have traveled. And Dave Lawrence just tied the blue ribbon on the package up at the Atlantic City convention, and I want to acknowledge that.

Several years ago when I was majority leader of the Senate, late in the evening, we had a crisis develop. I called upon a very fine and able citizen that night to come from Pennsylvania to help me, to give me legal advice that I needed, and he gave me that help. I have never forgotten what that help meant. It came from my friend Mike Musmanno. And I do so hope that on next

Tuesday Judge Musmanno and every single friend that he has in Pennsylvania will come to my help again by sending Genevieve Blatt to the Senate of the United States.

When Genevieve comes there and joins her able colleague, I believe that with their support and with the support of the Democrats and Republicans across the land, we will keep the flame, we will keep America moving, we will keep this Nation—and I pray the world—on the path to peace and progress, and to a better life for all mankind.

I want to thank each of you that paid to come to this dinner tonight, and the sacrifice that you made, that your families made, in order that you could come here to help your party help your country. Lady Bird and I are both grateful for it and we won't forget it.

I am so proud to be back here in Philadelphia. I am proud that I can come here—to the cradle of American liberty—and express to you a sure and strong and solid pride in this generation of Americans.

When this campaign began, that most of you wish had been over a long time ago, there were those who predicted that the people of America could be persuaded to vote their divisions and to fill the ballot boxes with their frustrations and dissatisfactions.

Tonight, as this campaign nears its close, I know, and I think you know, that that is not the case. There is one crack in the Liberty Bell, but come next Tuesday there won't be another.

Like the patriots of Independence Hall nearly 200 years ago, this generation of Americans stands for a united America, for an America that is devoted to peace, for an America that is dedicated to human progress and human prosperity, to an America that is unafraid of the challenges of the future at home or anywhere in the world. And

above all else, this generation of Americans stands proudly for responsibility. And that is just what the vote is going to show next Tuesday.

Since Sunday evening I have been in New England and in the new South, from Boston to Los Angeles, from Philadelphia to Miami. I have been in the Far West and the Midwest, and tonight I am here in one of the really great metropolitan cities of the world.

I am confident tonight of one thing: In their hearts, the people of America know what is right. The people of America know that it is right that America should continue to stand as the strong and the steady and the stable center of the cause of all free men.

The people of America know that it is right that America should continue to work with compassion and courage and confidence to make life better for all of man. For so long as there has been an American nation, the American people have been devoted to the principles of prudence, to the practice of frugality and thrift, and to the purposes of conservation and renewal.

We have made this Nation strong by warring on waste. Today, at the summit of our success, we want to change the waste that we see throughout too much of our national life.

Abraham Lincoln wiped slavery from this land 100 years ago and we here in the Brotherhood City tonight pledge that we will wipe the waste of human poverty from this land in our lifetime.

We want to wipe out the waste of idle men and idle machines.

We want to wipe out the waste of decaying cities and dying towns, and I take such pride in the great work that you have done in Philadelphia and Pittsburgh in this respect.

We want to wipe out the waste of untrained youth, unemployed fathers, and uncared-for grandparents.

We know that the happiness and the health of our people is not served by government which is indifferent to the burdens that are imposed upon them. We want compassionate government. We want concerned government, but we want government that is not careless or wasteful with the taxpayers' dollar.

There are changes that we want to make and that we must make, prudent changes, responsible changes, changes I think for the better. But we never want to change the character or the conscience of our American system.

And that is what you are going to prove in this election next Tuesday. The vote that you cast, and the vote that every American casts on next Tuesday will be heard around the world. America today is living in a goldfish bowl. The spotlight of 3 billion human beings is looking to us for leadership, and waiting and watching to know and to learn what kind of leadership you are going to offer yourselves and the world.

In the capitals of the free world—and in the capitals of the Communist countries—new men in new positions, some that they just took over last week, are there waiting for Philadelphia's election returns to come in. They are waiting to learn whether we of this strongest and this most successful nation on earth—whether we intend to lay down the burdens of responsibility, and whether we intend to lay down the opportunities of leadership, and whether we intend to abandon all the gains of 30 years and, in the words of some, turn it back to the States.

Well, I know, and I think you know, that the returns that they read will serve notice that this generation of Americans intends to hold the course of peace, of patience, of perseverance, of prudence, of progress, and of complete and absolute preparedness.

When this election is over, when the votes are counted and when the returns are in, the free world and the Communist world will know that the alliances of free men are going to stand in greater unity. They are going to stand with greater purpose, and they are going to stand with greater confidence for whatever we have to face.

The meaning of this election will be clear to all: that a united America is going to lead the world in uniting free men to win the contests of this century for freedom, for justice, and for decency on earth for our fellow man.

We have in this land tonight the strongest and the freest and the most successful system of government—we have the richest and the most prosperous society that has ever been known anywhere, by any people, at any time.

And your vote on next Tuesday is a vote to decide whether we can and whether we will keep what we have and what has been wrought for us by all who have given their lives and their labors in the years before.

And if ever there has been an election when matters of party and partisanship mattered for little, then it is this election this year.

You will not be voting for party. You will not be voting for personality. The outcome of this election will not be a mandate for one man. It must be and it will be a mandate for one nation and one people, with one purpose, under one great Constitution, with one meaning for all Americans.

For too long, much too long, this Nation, born here in the city of Brotherly Love, has been a nation with its strength divided. For too long we have been a nation of North and South, and East and West, a nation divided by region, by race, and by religion. And I believe that there is a will among the people tonight for all of us Americans to come together instead of coming apart.

And on Tuesday next the vote of the people I think will prove to all in this land and in every land that there is not going to be another crack in that Liberty Bell.

When William Penn founded this city almost 300 years ago, he wrote out a prayer for Philadelphia. And in that prayer, as most of you, I know, remember, there are these words:

"What love, what care, what service, what travail has there been to bring thee forth and preserve thee from such as would abuse and defile thee. . . . My soul prays to God for thee that thou may stand in the day of trial, that thy children may be blessed of the Lord, and thy people may be saved by His power."

Those words express the prayer in my heart tonight for the people of Philadelphia and for the people of America. So many have given so much to win for us what we have tonight—together. We must not and we shall not lose all of this in one moment of passion or frustration or recklessness with the peace, or a moment of irresponsibility with our unity.

Thirty-five men before me have held the office that is entrusted to me tonight. All of those men, from George Washington to John Kennedy, have worked and prayed and hoped for peace, for unity, for progress and prosperity for their people. And so long as the trust of this office is mine to uphold that will be my work, that will be my prayer, that will be my hope for all Americans.

NOTE: The President spoke at 8:31 p.m. in Convention Hall in Philadelphia, Pa. His opening words referred to Francis R. Smith, chairman of the Philadelphia County Democratic Executive Committee, David L. Lawrence, former Governor of Pennsylvania, James H. J. Tate, mayor of Philadelphia, Genevieve Blatt, Democratic candidate for Senator from Pennsylvania, William A. Barrett, Robert N. C. Nix, James A. Byrne, Herman Toll, and William J. Green, U.S. Representatives from Pennsylvania, Michael Musmanno, judge of the Pennsylvania Supreme Court, and Richardson Dilworth, former mayor of Philadelphia. Later in his remarks he referred to Senator Joseph S. Clark, Michael J. Bradley, former U.S. Representative, and Francis J. Myers, who served in the Congress from 1939-1951, all of Pennsylvania.

743   Presidential Statement No. 10 on Economic Issues: Achieving Full Employment. *October 30, 1964*

1. UNDER the mandate of the Employment Act of 1946, we are striving for "maximum employment." Our objective must be to provide job opportunities for all individuals willing and able to work.

2. We have already made considerable progress: unemployment *fell* from over 6½ percent in January 1961 to about 5 percent today. In the previous 4-year period—1957–1960—unemployment *rose* from 4 percent to over 6½ percent. The continued expansion in the economy for the past 44 months has expanded job opportunities while two economic recessions during the period 1957–1960 destroyed jobs.

3. About 1,500,000 new jobs a year have been created in nonfarm employment during the past 3½ years. This triples the gain of about 500,000 jobs a year in the previous 4 years—1957–1960.

4. In 9 months of 1964 alone:

—Unemployment has fallen from about 5½ percent to about 5 percent.

—The number of civilian jobs has risen 1.1 million.

—The unemployment rate for married men has fallen below 3 percent.

—The rate for all men over 20 years of

age has fallen below 4 percent.

5. But the task is far from complete. Despite recent gains, jobless rates for the unskilled, the young, the Negro worker are far too high.

6. We are now beginning to feel the impact of the postwar baby boom in the labor market. There are now 1 million more 17 year olds than 18 year olds. The labor force is expected to rise by about 1½ million next year. These young people, on balance, are better trained than new entrants to the labor force have been in the past and they afford a reservoir of talent for the continuing improvement of our standard of living. To use this talent effectively we must accelerate the growth of new jobs.

7. New programs are being developed to extend the economic advances of the past 4 years. We must promote continued expansion of total demand, and, at the same time, devise special measures to deal with youth, the long-term unemployed and the disadvantaged groups in our population. Our ultimate employment goal—job opportunities for all persons willing and able to work—can and will be achieved in the years to come.

NOTE: On the same day the White House released an accompanying statement, entitled "Gains From Effective Policies for an Expanding Economy." Included as part of the statement were figures comparing actual economic activity with what it would have been if economic growth in the last 4 years had continued at the same pace as during the period 1953–60. The comparison shows, the statement pointed out, "exactly how much difference it has made to have healthy expansion instead of increasing slack." The difference was summarized as follows:

$35 billion more gross national product annually
1.7 million more nonfarm jobs
$111 more annual income per person
$7 billion more in investment
wholesale prices stable, instead of 6 percent higher.

For a statement by the President announcing the series of statements on economic issues, see Item 707.

---

744 Statement by the President on the Results of a Survey of Compliance With the Civil Rights Act. *October* 30, 1964

GOVERNOR LeRoy Collins, Director of the Community Relations Service, has today informed me of the results of a survey the service has just conducted on compliance with the new Civil Rights Law. These are the first hard facts on compliance we have had since the law was enacted on the 2d of July—and I know the whole Nation will be proud of what they show.

This survey shows widespread compliance. What is most important, it shows the law is being obeyed in those areas where some had predicted there would be massive disobedience.

The survey covered 53 cities of over 50,000 population in the 19 States which do not have their own public accommodations laws.

—In 51 of these cities more than two-thirds of the hotels are desegregated.

—In 46 of these cities more than two-thirds of the motels are desegregated.

—In 50 of these cities more than two-thirds of the chain restaurants are desegregated.

—In 49 of these cities more than two-thirds of the theaters are desegregated.

—In 48 of these cities more than two-thirds of the sports facilities are desegregated.

—In 50 of these cities more than two-thirds of the public parks are desegregated.

—In 52 of these cities more than two-thirds of the libraries are desegregated.

Governor Collins tells me that there is still considerable work to be done. The exceptions only serve to point up the basic fact that the general rule is compliance.

This encouraging report vindicates the confidence and trust in our citizens which led to the overwhelming majorities which supported the civil rights bill in both Houses of Congress and in both political parties.

Equally encouraging are the facts regarding the continuing advance in the educational sector:

This fall nearly 100 school districts were desegregated. For the first time in our history there are desegregated institutions of higher education and desegregated public schools at the lower levels in every State of the Union.

The most important factor, however, is that this year for the first time this desegregation was accomplished without violence, without injury, and almost without notice.

There are sections of our country where these changes represent the reversal of generations of customs and practice. But adjustment to the law of the land is being accomplished. And recognition is due those who have provided the leadership that has produced these encouraging developments— public officials, clergymen, educators, businessmen, labor leaders, and other community leaders and countless private citizens have made the difference. Deserving of special note are those Members of Congress who opposed the civil rights bill with all their strength and eloquence while it was being debated and who, once the bill was enacted, urged their constituents and followers to comply with the "law of the land."

As Governor Collins has said, much remains to be done. But I find great encouragement in the results of the first 4 months of operation of the Civil Rights Act. At long last, we as a Nation have faced up to the most persistent and difficult problem this country has known and the prospects for solving it have never been brighter. With conscientious effort, patience, and understanding we will move steadily towards that day when all men are judged by their character and their performance, not by their color, religion, or how they spell their name.

NOTE: The Civil Rights Act was approved by the President on July 2, 1964 (78 Stat. 241). For the President's remarks upon signing the bill, see Item 446.

745 Remarks at an Airport Rally in Detroit.
October 30, 1964

Governor Williams, Senator Hart, Governor Staebler, Members of Congress, ladies and gentlemen, my old friend Pat McNamara:

I am so happy to be back here in Detroit again. I want to thank all of you for coming out here this morning. You have made this a great Democratic rally for Detroit, and we are going to make next Tuesday a great Democratic day for Michigan.

Four years ago a young man stood on Michigan soil and asked for a chance to get this country moving again. His name was John Fitzgerald Kennedy. You gave him that chance and he got this country moving again, and if you will vote the Democratic ticket next Tuesday, we will keep this country moving again.

We have a lot of work to do, and I ask your help in doing it. I know you will send back to the Senate a man that we know, a man that we can always count on, a man that will work with his colleague, one of the great Senators in the Senate, Pat McNamara.

I want all of you to go to the polls early, stay late, and vote for Phil Hart all day long.

We have a House of Representatives. We have close votes. We have votes between the interests and between the people, and we need people who will come there and vote for the people. So I hope you will send back to the House of Representatives men and women who always have a record for voting for the folks. That is John Dingell, that is Martha Griffiths, that is Charlie Diggs, that is Lucien Nedzi.

But they are not enough. We need some more Democratic Congressmen from Michigan, and there is not a reason in the world why you can't send Weston Vivian and Billie Farnum and John Conyers and Frank Sierawski and Bill Ford.

I don't know whether you know it or not, but if you don't, you ought to: The whole United States is watching and waiting for you to elect a new Governor in Michigan, Neil Staebler. Neil and I don't mind working together, don't mind having our picture made together, don't mind standing for the same things.

I have known him for many years, in and out of Government. I knew him as a veteran of the last war. I know him as a dedicated leader of our party and this great State. I know him as an able, hard-working, responsible Member of the Congress, and I don't think that he is ashamed to stand up on the same platform with his nominee for President.

So if you will give us a Democratic delegation in Washington, and a Democratic Governor in Michigan, we will keep these people working and we will keep Michigan moving forward.

It is mighty nice to be welcomed by these candidates on this platform. I don't have the slightest bit of hesitancy about endorsing any of them, and I don't detect any hesitance on their part to come out here and be seen with me.

They tell me that the time is past in this campaign to talk facts and figures, and they say it is not good to talk facts and figures at an airport rally, anyway, but this wasn't a scheduled rally. You know, I got my arm twisted on this one. I am due in Milwaukee right now, but ever since this campaign began, I have had so many friends that made me do so many things that I have always run an hour late and a dollar short.

I received last night some figures that say a lot about one thing that I really think this election is all about. First of all, prices—prices of the things you buy—are up only one-fifth of 1 percent over August. This puts them only 1.2 percent above September, 1 long year ago. We wish that they weren't up at all, but what this record says is that we have the most stable price level of any single industrial nation in all the world.

This is going to be the first airport rally arithmetic lesson in the history of all of American politics. I suspect that some of you folks out there listening to me—and any of you that may watch the television that is recording it—are interested in wages and earnings last month. These figures are about prices and wages and earnings.

Weekly wages in September averaged $103.94. And that is the highest level in the history of the United States of America. I think I will interpolate a little bit here and say I think that wages like that are good for the workers, and I think what is good for the workers of this country is good for the United States of America.

But there is more. This September figure is $14.86 higher than it was the day our late, beloved President John F. Kennedy took the oath of office. That was some 44 months earlier.

But here is another comparison. If you take an average worker with three dependents and you calculate his weekly earnings and his taxes and the change in the cost of living, he and his family are $9.84 a week better off than they were in January 1961 when John F. Kennedy became President.

What does that mean? That is an 11.8 percent increase, really 12 percent increase, in these last 44 months. And then if you look at what happened to that same average worker during the preceding 44 months, he had a gain during that period of $1.31, or only 1.7 percent compared to 12 percent. You know which administration is best for you—1.7, less than 2 percent, compared to 12 percent, 6 to 1. So the improvement in that family situation during these 44 months is exactly a little over 6 times what it was during the preceding 44 months.

All right. That is the prosperity story, and I have tried to tell it in a nutshell where each one of you can figure it out in your own pocketbook. This is the pledge that I want to make to you: We are not going to repeal that prosperity and that progress next Tuesday. We are going to renew and extend that prosperity and that progress next Tuesday. And after that, we will talk about it again.

It was 35 years ago yesterday, on October 29, 1929, that the New York stock market crashed and brought the American economy crashing with it.

We have learned in these 35 years that the price of prosperity is not repeated depressions. The price of prosperity is only responsibility.

The prosperity of the past 44 months didn't just happen. It is the result of re-

sponsible management and responsible labor leadership. It is the result of responsible restraint about wages and prices.

It is the result of responsible Government policy, and as long as I am your President, I am going to spend my time trying to have peace in the world and peace at home. I am going to try to encourage business and encourage labor to work out their problems between themselves as they have here in Detroit, instead of having a Government harass them and put them in a straitjacket.

Then there was the Area Redevelopment Act that I think ought to interest you. I intend to ask the Congress to extend it and strengthen it next year, because no wise and no humane nation can ignore the depressed communities where their distress is caused by the reduction of job opportunities in privately-owned plants, the closing of public facilities, or other factors.

The partnership of the Federal Government with State and local governments and with private business is essential to lift up these communities and to help get their citizens off relief rolls and back on payrolls. This act will help us to make taxpayers out of taxeaters.

Again, there was the Accelerated Public Works Act that Pat McNamara has had so much to do with.

There is the Manpower Development and Training Act that has meant retraining projects for over 11,000 Michigan workers.

Then there is the increase in the amount of minimum wage, and its extension to over 3 million additional employees.

This year's Federal tax cut has already had a substantial effect, and the leaders in the State of Michigan had as much to do with helping us get that tax cut as the leadership in any State in the Union, and I want to thank them for it. That doesn't mean just political leaders. That means labor leaders, and that means business leaders.

Henry Ford and Walter Reuther smiled at each other and Pat McNamara and Phil Hart looked at that smile and decided they both better vote with me and pass that tax cut, and they did. It has made jobs and it has fed hungry mouths, and it has brought prosperity to every State in this Union.

When it is fully effective, here is what it will mean in Michigan: an increase in total income of over $1.3 billion a year, 89,000 new jobs, an increase in average family income of $476 per family.

Well, it just didn't happen. We planned it that way. We worked long and hard to get it done that way. We did it even though my opponent opposed it every step of the way. So we are prosperous in the United States today because we have been responsible in the United States.

That is really the basic issue in this campaign: responsibility for prosperity at home; responsibility for peace in the world.

I want to tell you about a new step forward that we are taking with the Peace Corps, which is another form of responsibility.

The AFL–CIO and 20 leading industrial concerns, some of them located here in this industrial State of Michigan, are working together with the Peace Corps to put into effect a program to use skilled American workers all over the world.

The Peace Corps is going all out to recruit the blue-collar worker to fill the needs for skilled workers in the developing nations. Ford Motor Co., General Motors, Chrysler, International Harvester, Mack Truck, John Deere, and other major United States industries, have instituted leaves of absence, policies that guarantee reemployment, seniority, pension rights to workers that volunteer for Peace Corps service.

These men will be invaluable to these new, developing nations.

And I will tell you, no one has done a better job with the new, developing nations than your own Michigan Governor—Soapy Williams. He and I have at least some things in common. We both outmarried ourselves and his wife has been helping him.

These new nations need people who can do things, who can roof houses, who can build buildings, who can fix automobiles, teach wood and metal working.

This program opens up a whole new field for the Peace Corps, and although the Peace Corps never was intended only for college graduates, many people thought it was. Sargent Shriver told me this morning that he plans to have at least 2,000 skilled workers in the Peace Corps before Christmas of 1965.

George Meany has appointed AFL–CIO Vice President Joseph Beirne to head the committee that will work with the Peace Corps.

Let me say just this much about the overriding issue of peace and war. For 20 years now a mushroom cloud has shadowed our lives. For 20 years every American President has worked to reduce that danger. Today we must work more urgently than ever before.

Harry Truman worked with the Republican Senator Arthur Vandenberg. Lyndon Johnson worked with the Republican President Dwight Eisenhower in the Formosa Strait and in the Suez crisis, just as Vandenberg worked in Greece and Turkey. Everett Dirksen worked with the Democratic President on the test ban treaty, John Fitzgerald Kennedy.

If you want to junk this bipartisan foreign policy and flush it down the drain, then you don't go vote next Tuesday or you go vote Republican, because we are not going to junk it if we have Democratic leadership. We are going to preserve peace in the world.

We have a problem not of creating tensions, but reducing tensions among nations. We don't believe the United Nations ought to be abolished. We believe that it has prevented many wars.

So today we must work ever more urgently and more earnestly to try to stop the spread of nuclear weapons. The peace depends upon our strength. As your Commander in Chief, I report to you today that the military might of the United States of America is greater than that of all the other nations in the world put together, but might doesn't make right. Peace also depends not just upon might, but upon responsibility in using it, and upon reason.

We, of course, must be strong, but we must not be reckless. We, of course, must be firm, but we must not be foolish. One miscalculated, impulsive, reckless move of a single finger could incinerate our civilization and wipe out the lives of 300 million men before you could say "scat."

That is what it means to be President of the United States in this nuclear age, and, really, that is what is at stake in this election.

Jobs are important, schools are important, medicare is important—all these things are important. But they fade into insignificance compared to the one overriding important issue, and that is peace in the world.

Yes, we are a mighty nation. We know it and they know it. We covet no one's territory. We seek to dominate no people. We know it and they know it. That is why you gain nothing from bravado; that is why you gain nothing from rattling your rockets and bluffing with your bombs. That is why you get nowhere by saying you'll lob one into the men's room in the Kremlin.

That is why I say to you most earnestly

today that the United States of America loves peace and hates war, and we do not intend to bury anyone, nor do we intend to be buried.

If your life was at stake, if your country faced a crisis, every man and woman out there would take their boy to the railroad station to see him go away to boot camp to put on that khaki uniform as they did in World War I and as they did in World War II. You are not being asked to do that today. But you are being asked to go not to the railroad station, but go to the polling booth and vote for what in your heart you know is right. The vote you cast will be your own, and the world that you save will be your own.

These rallies are nice. They give you a chance to see the people that you work for.

We have a wonderful setup in this country. Jefferson once said that the collective judgment of the many is much to be preferred to the individual decision of the few, and somehow or other, the people, the collective masses, know how to select their leaders.

Everyone running for office wants peace. Lyndon Johnson has no mortgage on peace. Everyone running for office, I think, is patriotic. I have no mortgage or monopoly on patriotism.

But the question you have to decide is which man's thumb you want close to that button. The thing you have to decide is when that telephone starts jingling and you hear the ring on the "hot line" and they say, "Moscow is calling," you have to decide which man you want to lift up that receiver and what you want him to say.

[*At this point there was a demonstration in the crowd.*]

Wait a minute. They have already told me I have talked too long and I have got to finish. I want to tell you one more story.

That is not going to be any monkey business. That is going to be serious business. I will tell you why it is serious business. I don't know whether you had a newspaper strike out here 2 years ago or not. I hope you will get this one settled that you have had all these months.

I do want to commend the responsible leadership of the automobile companies and the responsible leadership of the unions for doing what is best for their country in working out their agreement. I appreciate the fact that we don't have a lot of men unemployed all over the country today.

They asked me what I was going to do about it, and I said, "Well, I think that General Motors, Ford, Chrysler, and American Motors have some fellows that are experienced and know how to negotiate, and I know from some of my own experiences in this office that Walter Reuther knows how to negotiate, and I am just going to let them handle it between themselves, because we believe in collective bargaining."

We are not going to repeal it and go back to the 19th century, either, and we are not going to make social security voluntary, either, and we are not going to be satisfied the rest of our lives with Kerr-Mills, either.

But 2 years ago, I guess, yesterday, we were meeting in the White House, and they were coming in the back gate, the Army and Air Force men; the generals with the stars on their shoulders; and the Navy men with the gold braid on their arms; and the distinguished Secretary of State, with all of his diplomatic experience, a Rhodes scholar; the distinguished Secretary of Defense that used to make a half-million a year as President of Ford—all of them with their briefcases bulging.

They were sitting there realizing that 90 miles from the United States we had mis-

siles that were almost operational, and in a matter of hours and days could be touched off to destroy the industrial might of America. The question was what do you do about it? Well, there were some of them that were saying, "Send in the Marines." There were some of them saying, "Drop your bombs." There were some of them that said, "Cut loose and let go."

But for 38 long meetings we met there every day, and I never left home in the morning when I was sure I would see my wife again that night. That is how serious I knew it was.

The coolest man at that table was the man that the collective masses of this country had selected to be their Commander in Chief, and his name was John Fitzgerald Kennedy. Mr. Khrushchev with those missiles already moved in and located and set up, and we had pictures of them, literally held a knife in Mr. Kennedy's ribs, and it wasn't held by a hand with palsy. It was held pretty firm and pretty straight, and it protruded enough that you could feel it.

Mr. Kennedy had a knife in his stomach, and he kept it there. And hour after hour and day after day those two leaders of millions of people, affecting billions of people, were eyeball to eyeball, and every mother, every child, and every human being that had any sense was living in great doubt about tomorrow.

Because of that leadership and because of that judgment, and because of that experience, our Commander in Chief used power with restraint. He had his airplanes in the air and he had them loaded with bombs, and he had men that knew how to open that bomb bay. He had his carriers located at their proper places, and he had his Marines ready to jump out of those planes.

But he was cool and he was calm, and finally the break came. Mr. Khrushchev picked up his missiles, put them on the decks of his ships, covered them with tarpaulins while our helicopters flew overhead counting them.

That must have been a humiliating experience for him, but it was a great source of pleasure and joy and relief not only for our people but for his people, because millions of lives were saved because of good leadership and good judgment.

We all pray that we will never have to move that thumb toward that button again. We all pray that we will somehow, some way, learn how to live in the world with other people. But we do know that we have a new government in Russia in the last few days, and we do know that Mr. Khrushchev is no longer the leader of that country. We do know that the Chinese have developed a nuclear bomb, and that they have 700 million people to develop more of them.

So we do know that we are going to require leadership and we are going to require experience, and we are going to require

judgment. Well, I am not here to say that I am the only man that has those qualities. I am here to appeal to you and ask you to appeal to your neighbor and your friends and your kinfolks and your uncles and your cousins and your aunts to be patriotic enough next Tuesday to go down there and search your conscience and exercise your judgment and vote for the man that in your heart you know is the leader of this country.

Thank you and goodby.

NOTE: The President spoke at 11:48 a.m. at a rally at the airport, Detroit, Mich. In his opening words he referred to G. Mennen Williams, Assistant Secretary of State for African Affairs and former Governor of Michigan, Senator Philip A. Hart, Representative Neil Staebler, Democratic candidate for Governor, and Senator Pat McNamara, all of Michigan. Later in his remarks he referred to, among others, John D. Dingell, Mrs. Martha W. Griffiths, and Charles C. Diggs, Jr., U.S. Representatives, and to Lucien N. Nedzi, Weston E. Vivian, Billie S. Farnum, John Conyers, Jr., Frank J. Sierawski, and William D. Ford, Democratic candidates for Representative, all of Michigan.

The text of remarks of Mrs. Johnson, who spoke briefly, was also released.

746   Remarks in Kosciusko Park, Milwaukee. *October 30, 1964*

Governor, Mayor, Senators, members of the delegation, ladies and gentlemen:

I am proud to be here today in the city of Milwaukee, and in your famous 14th Ward. This is good Democratic territory. You gave Franklin D. Roosevelt some of the greatest pluralities in history. You voted resoundingly for Harry Truman. You gave a tremendous vote of confidence to John Fitzgerald Kennedy. So why don't we get together and set some new records next Tuesday?

They say that you can tell a man by the company he keeps, and this is great company that you and I are in today. The American

Mayors Association knew that when they elected as their new president your own outstanding Mayor Henry Maier. The people of Wisconsin knew that when they elected as their Governor a man whose judgment I have come to respect and whose friendship I value greatly, Governor John Reynolds.

Please be sure that we get the chance to keep on working together, and please keep Wisconsin's representation in the Senate just exactly the way it is. Any State is lucky, and the country is lucky, when it has Senators like Bill Proxmire and Gaylord Nelson.

Bill has the independence that Wisconsin

is famous for. So when we agree, I always know I am right, and when we disagree, I always take another look. We were colleagues in the Senate, and you and I both need Bill's help greatly in helping us to pass a program for all the people in the years ahead. I hope you will give him one of the greatest majorities in the Nation come next Tuesday.

I just can't begin to tell you how much I depend in the House of Representatives on your own grand Congressman Clem Zablocki. Clem is my strong right arm. He is always there to be helpful. He is always constructive. He always does what he thinks is best for his country, and that goes, too, for Henry Reuss, a member of the Joint Economic Committee. Clem, you know, is on the House Foreign Affairs Committee, and that is quite some distinction for this city and for this State. I hope, I believe, and I know that the people of Milwaukee will send them back to Washington next Tuesday with a great majority in back of them.

And I hope, too, that you will send Jim Buckley from the Ninth Congressional District. We need his voice, we need his vote, we need his constructive support behind our new Democratic program. We also want you to send Lynn Stalbaum from the First District to sit beside them and to vote beside them in the next Congress. We need new, good, able men like Lynn, and please help us send him there.

The whole country knows about the remarkable resurgence of the Democratic Party in Wisconsin in recent years, so keep it up. Keep it moving. Keep it going, with people like Pat Lucey and Bronson La-Follette.

I know the history of this park and how much it has had to say in this election. It is almost 60 years now since you dedicated it.

Many of the people who lived here 60 years ago had come from the old world, escaping from oppression, looking for freedom and for opportunity. They found it here—and gave in return as much as they got.

What they sought the most was opportunity itself—opportunity for every man to do the best he can for himself and his family; freedom for each; justice for all. We are going to keep open those doors of opportunity and freedom and justice. We are going to keep them open for all people.

We have had 44 months of uninterrupted, steady, healthy prosperity in these United States under the Kennedy-Johnson administration. And we are not going to throw this progress away next Tuesday. We are going to keep moving steadily forward.

This year the annual personal income of Wisconsin citizens——

[*At this point there were disturbances in the crowd.*]

I appreciate your wanting me, but don't mind what happened because we all live and learn, and you are just getting an example of what kind of government you would get. That doesn't just apply to Democrats.

You remember that those people were—well, I want to be generous—they felt so strongly that they wouldn't even let their Republican Governor Rockefeller speak at the convention. They booed him down. They talk about the Constitution and free speech, and freedom to assemble, and then they come to our meetings and don't want us to talk.

Now, we have a speech in Rockford and then we are due in Chicago at 3:30. We are going to run a little late. But there are some things that are more important than what I have to say.

If you don't mind, let's just silently, quietly, calmly, take a look around there and see what condition they are already in. Look.

Don't get upset and don't get angry, because if they are bruised up that much today, think what is going to happen to them next Tuesday.

Actually, though, I have been in 44 States, and I have watched these boys. Most of them they don't pay but 50 cents an hour. But I did find one the other day in one of the big metropolitan areas that was an adult—and old enough to vote.

This year the annual personal income of Wisconsin citizens reached $10 billion—$10 billion. That is a new record high in the United States. The unemployment rate for this city of Milwaukee, and the unemployment rate for the entire State is down to a record of 2.5 percent—only 2.5 percent—97½ men out of every 100 are working. That is less than half what it was when you elected John Fitzgerald Kennedy.

Business has prospered this year. Corporation profits in Wisconsin went over $1 billion for the first time in history. Prosperity and progress were not just accidental. They are both the rewards of hard work.

They are the rewards of responsible leadership. This year alone, under your great Governor Reynolds' leadership, Wisconsin brought 147 new industries into this great State of Wisconsin. And here in Milwaukee, you and Mayor Maier are changing the skyline of a great city with a great new rebuilding program.

Prosperity and progress are the rewards of a partnership, a partnership between responsible government and responsible business and responsible labor.

We are still going forward, shoulder to shoulder, as friends, as partners; not as haters, not as dividers, but, rather, as uniters.

This year's tax cut alone will, when fully effective, create 42,000 new jobs in Wisconsin. But we aren't satisfied. We still believe in new opportunity. We believe in men's opportunity to enlarge and enrich their lives as well as their pocketbooks.

We believe in

—The right of every American child that is born under that flag, boy or girl, to have all the education that they can take, and we are going to try to put that program into effect.

—The right of our fathers and mothers, our grandfathers and grandmothers, to social security, to decent medical care.

—The right of every American family to live in a decent house, in a clean, beautiful city.

—The right of every American to enjoy the great outdoors and the countryside that God gave to all of us.

—The right of every American to expect of his Government a strong national defense and a responsible foreign policy, free from waste.

These are some of the things that we mean when we speak of the Great Society that we are going to put on the statute books.

[At this point there was a further demonstration by members of the audience.]

You have some nice, courteous, hospitable people out there, I see.

Governor Reynolds, working with local leaders like Mayor Maier, with your Senators and Congressmen in Washington, has already laid the cornerstones of that Great Society right here in beautiful Wisconsin.

He started the greatest college and university building program in Wisconsin's history. He moved this State forward in aid to local schools, in help for the elderly, in care for the sick, in conservation programs.

I have come here to Milwaukee today to tell you that under a Democratic administration in Washington, we will keep it moving.

The Great Society must be built on individual communities. No massive programs directed from Washington can do this job, nor should any Federal aid program ever be forced upon any State or local community. Local government can act more effectively in partnership with the private community through its responsibilities to overall need.

The Great Society is much more than mortar and bricks. It must be built in the architecture of our ideals.

It is a part, therefore, of the plan of the Great Society that the immigration laws be changed. Two-thirds of the total immigration quota now, under the present law, goes to people who never use all the quota they already have.

We want to abolish those discriminatory quotas gradually over a 5-year period, and we want to raise the overall limit by 2,000, or one-eightieth of 1 percent of our work force. This would permit the reuniting of families that have too long been broken up, we are all Americans. We are one nation, one people.

We live in an age of great opportunity and great danger, and rapid change. The other day a crack appeared in the Kremlin wall. It spread to the Iron Curtain. We cannot know what the future will bring, but we do know now that there are vast changes going on in the Communist camp.

Red China has challenged the Soviet Union for leadership of the Communist camp, and the restless stirrings in Europe suggest that Moscow can no longer impose its will on the tragic captive countries of Eastern Europe. Mr. Khrushchev is reputed to have said not long ago that the satellite countries had already grown up— like children, they were too big to spank any more.

So the task for the United States is to keep our policies flexible, to keep them responsible, and to search for new opportunities to favor freedom in a rapidly changing world.

Above all, we must stay strong, but we must stay responsible. We must stand resolute; we must never be discourteous or reckless. In the nuclear age the stakes are too high to gamble with the pushbutton of destruction.

And so long as I am your President, I will keep that trust.

Twenty years ago Franklin D. Roosevelt told us, "The only limit to our realization of tomorrow will be our doubts of today." You know what the promise of tomorrow means. You are working for that promise right now for yourselves and for your children and for your country. And I want you to vote for that promise at the polls next Tuesday.

It was a little more than 11 months ago when a great tragedy made me your President. When I assumed the oath of office, I said to the American people and to the world that with God's help and with your prayers, I would do the best I could.

It was a little over 2 years ago when we had the Cuban missile crisis. I was a member of the National Security Council as Vice President of the United States. For 38 meetings we sat with all the generals and their stars and the admirals with their braid, and the great Secretary of State, the Rhodes scholar, the Secretary of Defense, the former president of the Ford Motor Co., that made a half-million a year, but came into the Government to help us build a strong defense. And at the head of that table sat the man that you had selected as Commander in Chief.

I never left home a single morning that I was sure that I would see my wife and daughters again that night.

Mr. Khrushchev had his missiles 90 miles

from our shore and they were pointed in our direction. Our Commander in Chief had put our bombers in the air, loaded with their bombs. Our carriers were on the sea in the strategic places. There these two great leaders of these two great world powers stood eyeball to eyeball, taking each other's temperature.

And as I sat in that room and the President went around the table, it was so serious, so critical, so dangerous, and so important that I hoped that he would ask somebody else before he got to me so I would just have a little more time to think. But one thing impressed me. I remembered what Thomas Jefferson had said.

Thomas Jefferson said that the judgment of the many is much to be preferred to the decision of the few, and the great mass of the American people, beginning here in the wonderful, beautiful State of Wisconsin, and throughout the other 49 States later, had selected a leader, had selected our Commander in Chief.

The coolest man that sat in that room during those 38 meetings was our President, your Commander in Chief, John Fitzgerald Kennedy.

On next Tuesday you will have to go and in your own best judgment and in your own conscience select a new President. For 11 months I have picked up where he left off and I have done the best I could. And if I am selected for another 4 years I will give the job all the limited ability and all the talent I have, and I will try to search for peace in the world. I will try to maintain our strength and keep our guard up, but our hand out. I will be willing to go anywhere, to talk to anyone, to try to seek an honorable peace.

We want to bury no one, but we don't intend to be buried, either. We believe in unemployment compensation, and we believe

in social security, and we don't think it ought to be voluntary, either. We believe in medical care. We believe in adequate income for the farmers. We believe in collective bargaining. We believe in the right of every man and woman who wants to work to have a job. We believe in the right of every boy and girl born in this country to have an education.

We remember that it was 100 years ago that Abraham Lincoln abolished slavery. And it is now our lot and our time, and our opportunity, to abolish poverty from the United States of America.

So if you want us to continue, you will have to search your hearts and your conscience, and make that decision.

You are the masters. This will be as important a decision as you have ever been called upon to make, because we have a new leader in the Soviet Union, you have 700 million people in China that have the nuclear bomb, you have a new British labor government, you have a new government in Germany, a new government in Italy. You have all these problems of the world, and we have Viet-Nam, we have Cyprus, we have Laos. We have 120 nations and we are trying our best to lead them in the direction of peace.

So if you want peace and if you want prosperity, then I ask you to lend me your help, lend me your hand, give me your heart, give me your support. And if you do that on Tuesday next, we will have one of the greatest majorities that any President ever had.

And when we do that, there will be such a minority in the other party that the good, moderate men who have built that party, the party of Abraham Lincoln, will go back and stand for the fine principles that it advocated through the years. We will have a bipartisan foreign policy again. We will have Republicans and Democrats sitting

1539

in our Cabinet. We will have men working together. We will have politics stopping at the water's edge.

So I hope that you will seriously consider that this is one of the great decisions you will be called upon to make, and that you will go and vote Democratic next Tuesday.

NOTE: The President spoke at 1:40 p.m. in Kos-ciusko Park in Milwaukee, Wis. In his opening words he referred to Governor John W. Reynolds, Mayor Henry W. Maier of Milwaukee, Senators William Proxmire and Gaylord Nelson, and Representatives Clement J. Zablocki and Henry S. Reuss. During the course of his remarks he referred to James P. Buckley and Lynn E. Stalbaum, Democratic candidates for Representative, Patrick J. Lucey, Democratic candidate for Lieutenant Governor, and Bronson LaFollette, Democratic candidate for State Attorney General, all of Wisconsin.

747   Remarks at an Airport Rally in Rockford, Illinois. *October 30, 1964*

Governor Kerner, Governor Shapiro, Senator Douglas, Postmaster General Gronouski, Attorney General Clark, State Auditor Howlett, my old friend Paul Powell, Jim Ronan, Mayor Schleicher, Robert Brinkmeier, Miss Dorothy O'Brien, my fellow Americans:

If my history is correct, this is the first time that a Democratic President has visited the city of Rockford. But I am telling you now that it is not going to be the last time.

I have come here in excellent company. Otto Kerner has been a distinguished Governor of the State of Illinois. He has been one of the great Governors of the United States of America. Governor Kerner knows the problems of this State and he knows how to solve those problems. For 4 years he has worked quietly and capably, patiently and effectively for you down at Springfield. And I hope that next Tuesday you will give him a resounding mandate for his next term.

Bob Brinkmeier, your Democratic candidate for Congress, is a very able man, a teacher from Forreston. I was a teacher myself once, and I think we should use more schoolteachers in government by electing Bob Brinkmeier.

The last time this district sent a Democrat to Congress was in 1852. As a strong supporter of the two-party system, I think it is time for a change!

On this occasion I am grateful for the reception I have received here in a city and in a district with such long and such strong and such loyal devotion to the Republican Party.

I am proud to be a Democrat. I am proud to be a member of the party of Jefferson and Jackson and Cleveland and Wilson, Franklin D. Roosevelt, Harry S. Truman. I am especially proud to be a member of the party of that great and that gallant American, John Fitzgerald Kennedy.

But I am prouder that over a career of more than 30 years in public life, I have always been the kind of Democrat who could and would work together with my fellow Americans of the party of Lincoln and McKinley, Herbert Hoover and Dwight Eisenhower, Robert Taft, Arthur Vandenberg, and Everett Dirksen.

Whatever our traditions, whatever our affiliations, whatever our partisan beliefs, we all know that America will stand strong and secure only when we faithfully put our country ahead of our party in every cause.

On this bright autumn afternoon, I remember—and I know you have not forgotten—another day such as this 11 months and

1 week ago. On that day, November 22d, we were happy and smiling and all seemed secure.

Then in one terrible, incredible instant our world and our times changed. A vicious bullet from an assassin had felled a noble man.

Wherever we were, whatever we were doing, Americans laid down their own interests and had only one thought: their Nation's interest. All across this land no man or woman that day had any thought of party. All Americans were thinking only of preserving our system and saving our country, and saving all that we cherish in our life.

When night had fallen I returned to Washington, bearing on these shoulders the burdens and the trust of every home and every family and every free man.

I said to the Nation and to all the people what was in my heart that night. I had taken the oath of the highest office in the land in an airplane compartment with the jet motors roaring behind me in the background. And I told my people when I walked into that lonely White House that evening with God's help and yours I would do the best I could.

In all our history only 35 other men have borne these burdens and have known these tasks. But I know what each of them must have known.

This is an office that makes men humble. This is an office that sends men to their knees to pray for wisdom and help and not for power.

Presidents are not infallible, and I hope there is never one who thinks otherwise. A man cannot serve in this office 1 hour or 1 day without knowing how much he needs all the help that he can get, from all the people that are willing to help their country.

In those moments last November I turned to the most experienced and to the best men that I could find in America. We were in a goldfish bowl. The spotlight was on the United States. Eighty-five rulers and leaders of countries of the world had come to Washington to pay their last respects to President Kennedy and to size up President Johnson.

When I turned to these experienced men, all of them that I could find, I did not ask their party, I did not know their party, I did not care about their party. All that mattered to me in those critical moments was the survival of the United States and whether these men wanted to do and help me do what was necessary for us to survive, and what was necessary for the best of our country.

I was proud that the first citizen who called upon me to offer his strength and his support was General Dwight David Eisenhower. He spent more than 2 hours in my office with a lead pencil and a yellow tablet, writing his suggestions.

And then from Independence came that happy warrior, President Harry Truman.

I was grateful—and I am more grateful now—that among those who have been my closest advisers from November until now were some men who were Republicans by party but patriots by conviction—men like the Secretary of Defense, Robert McNamara; men like the Secretary of the Treasury, Douglas Dillon; men like the Director of the Central Intelligence Agency, John McCone; men like John McCloy and Robert Lovett; men like Arthur Dean and Arthur Larson.

The man who sees me most often each day, sometimes before I get up in the morning, frequently after I have retired for the evening, is the man in charge of the National Security Council's executive operation, a Republican named McGeorge Bundy, the former Dean of Harvard University.

On matters of fiscal policy and foreign policy, and our pursuit of peace, men upon whom your President leans are good Republicans, such as President Eisenhower's former Secretary of the Treasury, Robert Anderson. He spent 2 days with me giving me his judgment on our last budget. Men like President Eisenhower's former Secretary of State, Christian Herter, who now serves as my spokesman in the Kennedy Round in connection with all of our trade relations. The man who served Republican administrators in negotiations with the Communist bloc in the test ban treaty, Mr. Arthur Dean, one of the great lawyers of the Nation.

These men, and many more, are all Republicans, good men, patriots, and good Republicans. But first of all they are good and great Americans.

I am very grateful and very humble that in this critical hour of this campaign I have the voluntary support of at least four members of President Eisenhower's Cabinet. I am very grateful that in the Senate, as in the Presidency, I have had the friendship and the trust of men who sat across the aisle as Republican leaders when I was Democratic leader, men like Bob Taft, Bill Knowland, and Everett Dirksen.

Today I speak as I do only because I deeply believe that the ultimate success of our democratic system and our survival and the preservation of peace in the world lies largely in the strength of bipartisan government in our land.

Twenty years ago, a former isolationist, a great Republican Senator named Arthur Vandenberg, from the State of Michigan, stepped up and joined Harry S. Truman, the President of the United States, and together they laid down the Truman doctrine and united the country, Republicans and Democrats, and stopped the Communists in their

tracks in Greece and Turkey.

A little later, the Republicans swept the country and General Eisenhower became President, but Lyndon Johnson became Democratic leader, and for 8 years President Eisenhower dealt with the Democratic leader.

Six of those years the Democrats had the majority, but I looked up the record the other day and the Democratic leader supported President Eisenhower's foreign policies 95 percent of the time in that year 1960, when the present Republican candidate supported it only 25 percent of the time.

Everett Dirksen supported the test ban treaty in a critical hour in the Senate when without his support it may not have become law, when the present Republican candidate was fighting it. Together, Everett Dirksen and John F. Kennedy passed that treaty that 105 nations ratified that makes the air that you breathe safer and the milk that you drink cleaner.

This spirit of bipartisanship between the two parties must never be lost.

America today cannot be served by the politics of patronage and privilege. America can only be served by the politics of responsibility. That is the only kind of politics I know and the only kind I want America to know. I have always tried to find the basis for consensus, to take the other man's viewpoint into consideration—in the words of the prophet Isaiah, to reason together, and to work with him for the good of our country and the success of our land.

In these dark days, in these hours of danger, when the Soviet Government changed their rulers only last week, America cannot march under a Republican flag or a Democratic flag. America can and America must march only under one flag of one nation, of one people.

Republicans and Democrats have walked side by side in uniform. They have died side by side in the trenches. They have fought side by side in battles, and no one even asked them what party they belonged to. And there is no reason why they cannot work side by side in the task of preventing a nuclear war and preserving peace and defending freedom, and keeping America moving and keeping America prosperous.

The course that America takes the next 4 years will be the course that the people choose themselves, and you will do that in the privacy of the polls next Tuesday. You are the masters. You select the director. You name the President. You appoint the Commander in Chief.

I want every good Republican in this Nation and every good Independent in this Nation who yearns for peace, who believes in prosperity—I want every businessman who believes in profits and prudence, every labor man who wants adequate wages and reasonable working conditions, to get out and do some heavy thinking now. You have a week to do it, and to exercise your own precious and personal right of choice.

I do not know what that choice will be— the farmer in Illinois, the worker in Detroit, the businessman on Wall Street, but I do believe that good Americans, good patriots, good Republicans, will consider seriously and soberly what is best for their country, and I do believe they will vote on no other basis.

I do believe that good Republicans want for their party understanding, tolerance, judicious leadership in the tradition of Abraham Lincoln, humane leadership in the tradition of Herbert Hoover, experienced leadership in the tradition of Dwight Eisenhower. And in the days to come, I believe

that it is this responsible heritage of the Republican Party that will emerge after this election to regroup, reform, strengthen, and return to the principles of high patriotic responsibility that marks the Republican Party's history.

So today I want to tell you, and through you I want to tell the Nation, that I want them to know and to understand that so long as Lyndon Johnson may serve as your President, I will share with them the opportunity as well as the obligation of saving America and saving our system of free enterprise.

I will share with them the opportunity and the obligation of bettering our working conditions, employing all of our people, raising our standards of living, increasing our strength, encouraging our growth. And remembering that it was this great State that gave to the Nation the man that abolished slavery 100 years ago, in these next few months I will give them the opportunity and the obligation to join me in helping to abolish poverty among humans.

Yes, it is not just the Democrat or the Republican or the Independent. It is all Americans that must pursue the search for peace in this unsettled world.

I have not forgotten that in one of our country's darkest hours, President Roosevelt called two great Republicans forward, and they stepped up to cast aside partisanship amidst great criticism, and serve in that war period as patriots. Those men were Henry Stimson, Secretary of War, and Illinois' own Frank Knox, under whom I served when he was Secretary of the Navy.

The dangers to freedom then were no greater than the dangers we face today.

On November the 3d, next Tuesday, I believe that this generation of responsible Americans, I believe that every mother in her kitchen, and every husband at his vocation, will remember that the free world and the Communist world are looking at us through a goldfish bowl. The spotlight of 3 billion people is turned toward what America does and who leads the world.

I think they will be reading our election returns, and I believe that Americans will, by their votes, say to the new leaders in the Kremlin and in Great Britain and in Italy and in Germany, and in India since Nehru is gone and Mr. Shastri has replaced him, and in Japan, where Mr. Ikeda has resigned—I believe they will say that America is going to have a foreign policy that unites all of our people instead of divides them, a policy that preaches love instead of hate, a policy that preaches faith instead of doubt, a policy that preaches hope instead of despair. I believe they will say that you can depend on America to stand solid and safe and united and steady on her course.

That will be the mandate—the only mandate—of this election. There will be no mandate for a man or for a party. There will be a mandate for progress. There will be a mandate for social consciousness, there will be a mandate for strength and responsibility in the policies and the purposes of the world's strongest and the world's most responsible nation.

Finally, it was just 2 years ago that I sat around the Cabinet table in the Cuban missile crisis. On one side of the President sat a Rhodes scholar, a great diplomat, who is Secretary of State. On the other side sat the former president of the Ford Motor Co., who left a half-million-dollar-a-year job to run the Defense Department, a Republican. Across the table sat Secretary Dillon, a Republican Secretary of the Treasury.

In that room we knew no parties. We knew we were only Americans. And Mr.

Khrushchev and Mr. Kennedy stood there eyeball to eyeball, each with a knife in the other one's ribs, and neither quivering or quaking. There was no palsy in their hands.

I never left my home a single morning when I knew that I would be back that night, or whether there would even be a Capitol or a White House.

There were those that said, "Send in the Marines," and there is a gallant Marine that wears the scars of battle, Paul Douglas, who did go in.

There were those who said, "Defoliate and drop our bombs." There were a lot of hotheads all around the place. But as those generals came in with the stars on their shoulders, and the admirals walked down the corridors with the gold on their braid, I am proud to tell you that the coolest customer, the wisest man in that room, was the man that you, in your wisdom, the masses of the people, had selected to be your Commander in Chief, John Fitzgerald Kennedy.

I proudly served with him and beside him for 3½ years.

I know not what the future holds. I can tell you only today, as I move on to Chicago, where I was due 30 minutes ago, that I believe you Republicans, Democrats, Independents, and whatnots realize that we are living in a critical period of history, and that you have a critical and important decision to make—not for me, because it doesn't make much difference to me.

You have given me everything a person could have. I was an NYA administrator. We worked with boys and girls. I was a Congressman for 12 years. I was a Senator for 12 years. I was leader of my party for 8 years. I was Vice President for over 3 years, as President Kennedy's assistant and his helper, and now I have been President for almost a year. But you will go and vote not for Lyndon Johnson and not for the Democratic Party. You will go vote for yourself and your family.

I know when I am sitting down there on the banks of the river in my little house near where I was born on the Pedernales River in Texas, and Governor Kerner or Paul Douglas calls me Tuesday night—I know that they will tell me that you voted for what you knew in your heart was right.

NOTE: The President spoke at 3:07 p.m. at a rally at the airport at Rockford, Ill. His opening words referred to Governor Otto Kerner, Lieutenant Governor Samuel H. Shapiro, Senator Paul H. Douglas, United States Postmaster General John A. Gronouski, State Attorney General William G. Clark, State Auditor Michael J. Howlett, State Representative Paul Powell, Democratic candidate for Illinois Secretary of State, Daniel J. (Jim) Ronan, Democratic candidate for U.S. Representative, Mayor Benjamin T. Schleicher of Rockford, Robert E. Brinkmeier, Democratic candidate for U.S. Representative, and Dorothy G. O'Brien, Democratic national committeewoman, all of Illinois.

748 Remarks at the Chicago Stadium. October 30, 1964

Governor Kerner, Mayor Daley, Senator Douglas, ladies and gentlemen:

Nobody in this world can put on a political parade and a political rally like that great executive Dick Daley of Chicago. He makes it so much fun being a Democrat that you don't see how anybody could be anything else. I think he is one of the greatest political leaders in all the world.

I have a few favors to ask of you tonight. A President works closely whenever he can with the State Governors, so please be sure that here in Illinois it is Otto Kerner. And no one helps me more to fight for the people of Illinois, the people of the United States, and all the people of the world, than your Senator, Paul Douglas, and Emily Douglas.

Please send us every single Democratic Congressman that you can. It will take a strong Democratic Congress to keep this country moving ahead.

When I say that I think, and so do you—and it makes us proud, but it makes us humble—of the man that we wish most of all were here with us tonight, that gallant leader, John Fitzgerald Kennedy.

We are proud tonight to be Democrats.

We are even prouder to be Americans.

And I want to talk tonight as an American to Americans, for that is the way the people will be voting next Tuesday.

The plain fact is that this election won't have settled all the things that it should have settled. This country will decide not to go back, but there will be differences left about how to go forward.

We will win this election. But we will know that the voters of this country have not written a blank check; that there are differences which remain, and those differences must be honored. And they will be honored.

But these things have been made clear: We have been settling for too little in this country. We are going to raise our sights. We are going to see that every American child has an equal chance at the fullest education that child can use. We have been educating most of our children. Now we are going to educate those who need it most.

We have declared war on poverty, and we mean all-out war. Abraham Lincoln, a product of Illinois, abolished slavery 100 years ago. And now the Democratic Party adopts as its program the abolishment of poverty in this land. Prosperity for four out of five is not enough.

Older age doesn't have to be a time of fear and want. Its difficulties are not voluntary, and we are not about to make the social security system voluntary. We will increase social security benefits. We will add hospital and nursing home care, Medicare, to its protection. We are going to make sense out of life's pattern, instead of letting age defeat so many of us.

We will mean what we say from here on about full employment. We will have a government that doesn't waste a penny doing what is foolish, but doesn't waste a minute doing what is wise.

The thing that all of us want most of all is a united policy for peace for all peoples. Republicans and Democrats are partisans at home—and better for it. But we are partners before the world, because our life depends upon it.

The one overriding obligation of a leader of this democracy is to find or to forge a united policy for peace. I mean that tonight, and I will mean it tomorrow just as I meant it in 1960.

There was a Republican President, Dwight Eisenhower, then, and I was the Democratic leader in the Senate. On foreign policy matters I voted with that Republican President 96 percent of the time. And in this campaign now, we are against another man who was in that same Senate and who voted on those same issues against that same Republican President 76 percent of the time. So the Democrat voted with the President 96 percent of the time and the present Republican nominee voted against him 76 percent of the time.

I am proud to ask my Nation's trust in the continued building of its bipartisan foreign policy. But even here there must be no blank check. So I state my understanding: It is

that Americans, almost as one, agree that to keep the peace we must be so strong of arm and arms that none anywhere can doubt that strength.

As your Commander in Chief I tell you tonight that our military might is greater than that of all the other nations of the world put together. You want it kept that way and so do I.

But you count strength alone not enough. And so do I. World peace depends upon reason, on restraint, on negotiation, and on responsibility.

We must move forward on many fronts.

We must continue to strengthen the United Nations.

We must strengthen and expand the Peace Corps.

We must build new bridges, new bridges to the friendly peoples of Eastern Europe.

We must, most of all, take this world out from under the shadow of a poisonous toadstool cloud.

We want our children to say that this was the generation that split the atom, and this was the generation that united all men in peace.

We are a powerful nation, but we are humble before our God. We believe that man has made his own problems, but that man can solve them.

The road to peace is long and hard, but the road to war is short and deadly. We choose the road to peace.

So we tonight, assembled here, pledge ourselves to democracy's greatest tradition, the New Freedom of Wilson, the New Deal of Roosevelt, the Fair Deal of Harry S. Truman, the New America and the New Frontier of John Fitzgerald Kennedy, and after Tuesday, November 3d, the Great Society of Lyndon Johnson and Hubert Humphrey.

These are not campaign slogans. These are the beating pulse of the greatest political party in this country. They are the heart-beat of a Nation that is looking up at the stars and eager for tomorrow's dawn.

NOTE: The President spoke at 8:37 p.m. at the Chicago Stadium in Chicago, Ill. In his opening words he referred to Governor Otto Kerner of Illinois, Mayor Richard J. Daley of Chicago, and Senator Paul H. Douglas of Illinois. Later he also referred to Mrs. Douglas.

The text of remarks of Mrs. Johnson, who spoke briefly, was also released.

749   Remarks at the Old State House, Dover, Delaware. *October 31, 1964*

Governor Carvel, Chief Justice Terry, Congressman McDowell, distinguished guests on the platform, ladies and gentlemen, boys and girls:

I feel so good this morning and you have a lot to do with it. This little State of Delaware all through the years has had a very special spot in my heart, because the people that I have known that have lived here are very much like my people. They stand for the same things that we stand for. They try to raise their children the same way we raise ours. They come to the Congress and they try to work for their country and do what is best for their Nation.

I was going to the largest State in the Union today. I am going to tour Nassau County this afternoon, and we are going to close out the campaign in New York at Madison Square Garden tonight. I was asked to stop by here, so I got up a little earlier and finished some of my work at the White House a little quicker, and decided that I would drop by at Dover and Wilmington, and primarily say "hello" and thank each and every one of you for how good you have been. You have been good, you have been friendly, you have been kind, and you have been very helpful to me in the 11 months that I have been President.

First of all, Harris McDowell over here, your Congressman, is one of the few Congressmen in the Nation that has stood there and helped me pass a program for all the people, a program that in my judgment will help us to avert war, and a program that in my judgment will help us to maintain prosperity. So first of all, I want to thank you for sending Harris McDowell to the House of Representatives, and I hope you will send him back with a wonderful majority.

I have known Bert Carvel for a good many years. He is as solid as the granite that comes in our country. He is as friendly as any man can be. He believes in your State and he works hard for it. He has come to Washington several times on behalf of the people of Delaware. We need him in the Senate. We need him to help with our Democratic program of peace in the world and prosperity for all the people here at home. We hope that you will send Bert Carvel to Washington to help us as a Democratic Senator.

Judge Terry is your candidate for Governor. You have a Democratic Governor. A majority of the States have Democratic Governors. We are going to have, I think, more than 70 Democratic Senators in the next Senate. We are going to have a large majority in the House of Representatives. We are going to have a large majority of Governors in the States. So with the Governors working with the Congress, working with the President, we can make a real team to move this country forward. And I think Delaware wants to move with the country.

We all have our private catalog of grudges.

Right at the top of my list is waste, w-a-s-t-e. More and more I think we will get the right answers to most of the questions that we face in this country if we in Government will declare a war on waste. I mean waste in all of its forms, and I am going to discuss them briefly for you because mine is not a campaign of personalities, mine is not a campaign of mudslinging, mine is not a campaign of charging my opponent with anything. I am not going to do any muckraking and name-calling.

We should deal with waste in all of its forms. A depression—and there are some of you out there that are old enough to remember the last one—brings tragic waste, economic and human waste.

The great depression 30 years ago cost this country, it is estimated, $600 billion. The three recessions that we had in the 1950's cost this country $70 billion, and 10 billion man-hours of productive labor. I think that is why we should keep our economy from going into periodic booms and busts and that is a major campaign front, the war on waste.

For Presidents and governments, as for all others, economy should begin at home. As a child, when I was growing up in a land where almost everything seemed to be in short supply, I learned some habits of thrift that are deeply imbedded in me. One of my first actions as President was to personally review the 1965 budget that was going to Congress. The result was that this budget became the second in 9 years that called for a reduction instead of an increase in Federal expenditures.

I need some help on that work. I need a good Congressman like Harris McDowell. I need a good, solid, economy-minded Senator like Bert Carvel. I hope that you will help me send them there.

In these past 11 months, since President Kennedy was assassinated, and since I assumed the office of President, we have made economy the first order of business in every department of the Government. We can't earn a penny in the Government, but we can save billions of dollars. And we have.

Last year, Secretary McNamara's cost reduction program in the Defense Department alone saved the taxpayer $2,800 million, and some of it was saved right out here at your Dover Air Force Base. I know you are interested in that base, but I know you are also interested in saving all the money that you can.

The Government owes the people the very best management of the people's business. I am proud to be able to tell you that the money that you are giving us to pay for our national defense is being spent wisely and is being spent prudently. I have insisted that all Government agencies step up their efforts to increase efficiency and reduce both employment and cost.

For instance, this last July we had 25,000 less Federal employees on the Federal payroll than we did July a year ago. We had reduced the amount by 25,000. Don't you think that is a good start? In another instance, I urged all agencies to cut out all unnecessary publications. First we eliminated 521 publications right off the bat. Then we canceled 133 that were proposed to be published. We effected, in addition, over 50 consolidations. We saved $2,796,640 by that act alone.

Management improvements and cost reductions in the nondefense agencies have yielded savings on an annual basis that amount to over $400 million per year. My special task force made up of able men that I called in and set up for this particular purpose has now recommended that we now put into effect an organized, formal cost-reduction program on a long-range basis in every single department and agency in the Government. And I am going to take their recommendations and we are going to do it. If you will help me, we will get results.

This means that each department and agency will adopt the same kind of program that the Department of Defense has adopted. I have called upon every Federal employee at every level, and particularly on their supervisors, to make cost reduction a personal goal, and to redouble their efforts to identify and to achieve savings through more efficient conduct of Government activities.

Spending by the Federal Government in and of itself is neither bad nor good. It can be bad when it involves overstaffing or duplication, or poor management, or the Government getting into areas where it doesn't belong. It can be good when it is put to work efficiently in the interest of our national strength and our economic progress, and our human compassion.

When budgetary restraint leads the Government to turn its back on new needs and new problems, economy becomes but another word for stagnation. But when vigorous pruning of old programs and procedures releases the funds so that we can have new opportunities, economy becomes the companion of progress.

I want to say this finally: The most awful waste of all waste is war. We believe in economy, but the falsest economy would be military weakness. I would not approve or I would not permit a cut in our defense budget of a single dollar or a billion dollars if it meant increasing the risk to one single boy's life. We will not be pennywise and peace foolish.

I pledge a war on waste—waste. And I ask you to help me to fight that war.

My higher pledge is to exercise the highest responsibility a President bears to do all within my power to prevent the inconceivable, the unmeasurable, the inhuman waste of war.

It was just a little over 11 months ago, 11 months and 1 week ago, when we had that terrible tragedy that took our President from us and I was called upon to assume the awesome responsibilities that I now bear. When I walked into that airplane with the jet motors roaring in the background, and took my oath of office, I said to you people that with God's help and your help, and your prayers, I would do my best.

Since that time, values on the stock market are up over $100 billion.

Since that time, more than a million extra people are at work.

Since that time, the corporations are making $12 billion more after taxes.

Since that time, the workers are making $60 billion a year more after taxes.

Since that time, we have had problems in Panama and problems in Guantanamo, problems in Brazil and Chile, problems in Turkey and Viet-Nam.

And we have tried to stand up with firmness and with prudence, with strength and with restraint. And with your help, I think the United States has made good progress.

It was just 2 years ago this month that we were confronted with another serious crisis. It is just going to be a few days until you are confronted with the most critical decision that you may ever be called on to make. Two years ago Mr. Khrushchev moved his missiles into Cuba.

President Kennedy called the Security Council, of which I was a member, as Vice President, together. He called in all the generals with the stars on their shoulders, the experts that had graduated at West Point with honors, and the ablest men we had.

He called in the Navy men with the gold on their sleeves, the Chief of Naval Operations, the Secretary, the ablest men we had. To his right sat the Rhodes scholar, the great Secretary of State. To his left sat the Secretary of Defense, who had left the Ford Motor Co. at a half million a year to take a $25,000 job to try to help his country.

We had 38 meetings. During all that time there were clamor, editorials, arguments, cool heads, hot heads, and some were saying, "Send in the Marines," and some were saying, "Drop the bomb," and all kinds of advice that was free was being received.

President Kennedy began his preparation. He put his planes in the air loaded with their bombs. He had strategic movements of the entire Naval fleet. He put everybody in the Nation on an alert. But he was cautious and he was careful and he was never reckless.

The coolest man that I saw in that room during those 38 meetings was John Fitzgerald Kennedy, your President of the United States.

Mr. Khrushchev and Mr. Kennedy came eyeball to eyeball. Each had a knife in each other's ribs. Neither quivered. But neither rattled their rockets or bluffed with their bombs, or shot from the hip, because if they had, we could have wiped out 300 million in a matter of moments.

I never left Lady Bird a single morning when I knew whether I would be back home that night or not, or whether she would be there to greet me.

That is the kind of a world that we are living in. You don't create those conditions, but under our democratic system, Thomas Jefferson said that the judgment of the many is to be preferred to the decision of the few. You must be the judge and you must select the man whose thumb you want to press that atomic button. You must select the

man next Tuesday that you want when that "hot line" rings and that telephone jingles, and they say, "Moscow is calling," you want to select the man that you want to answer that phone.

So you are going to have to do some pretty heavy thinking between now and next Tuesday. I am not up here to say anything about my opponent or to say anything about his party, or to say anything about any of the people in his party. I primarily stopped off here on my way to New York to say "howdy," to say thank you to you good people that have been my friends ever since I went to the Senate.

I have been here in Dover before. I have heard from a good many of you by letter. I know you have one of our great defense installations out here that I am interested in. But I do ask you, as I would ask you if we were at war and you had to carry your boy down to the railroad station to see him put a khaki uniform on to go to boot camp, I ask you to spend a lot of time thinking between now and next Tuesday.

The first thing you do Tuesday morning is get up and go and exercise the privilege that so many people in the world don't have—a private, a secret ballot. The citizens all over America will be doing the same thing. There will be 75 million of them.

I believe that it will be true, what Jefferson said, that the judgment of the many is better than the decision of the few. We saw the mistake that Hitler made when he was the only one to make the decisions. We saw the mistakes that Khrushchev made when he was the only one to make the decision. You must make the decision on who you want to lead you.

If you want me to lead you, I will do what I told you when I took this oath 11 months ago. I don't want to lead you because you owe me something. You have done everything for me that people can do. I served 12 years in the House, 12 years in the Senate, 8 years as leader, Democratic minority leader, Democratic majority leader with President Eisenhower, and Vice President for 3½ years, and now President for 11 months.

So that is not the question. You are not going to vote for that next Tuesday. You are going to vote for your family, for your wife, for your children, for your sons.

You are going to have to vote for what kind of an economy you have, whether you have a booming economy, prosperity, with people at work; whether you continue your social security and don't make it voluntary; whether you try to have some of the good things of life that you are having now; or whether you want to turn around and go backwards; whether you continue to have a bipartisan foreign policy, like Arthur Vandenberg, the Republican, worked out with President Truman, to stop the Communists in Greece and Turkey; like I worked out with President Eisenhower and followed him in the Formosa Strait and the Suez crisis; like Senator Dirksen worked out with President Kennedy in the test ban treaty.

That is what you have to decide. I am not going to try to tell you what your decision must be. But I am going to say this: if you want me to have that responsibility, you can say so. If you want to turn me out and not give me a first term, and just let me serve out the 11 months, that is your privilege.

But if you do want me to continue, then send me people who will work with me and who will help me, and who will join me and put our shoulders to the wheel.

Let's don't divide this country. Let's unite this country. Let's you all get behind us and let's try to find some way besides threaten-ing people. Let's try to love instead of hate. Let's try to have faith instead of fear.

Let's don't try to threaten people by ultimatum and tell them what we will do with our bombs. Let's try to reason out with them some way to avoid war, like the "hot line," like the agreement in space, like the nuclear test ban treaty that President Kennedy worked out. All of these are small steps, but they are steps that can save you and make it possible for us to survive.

So when you go into that ballot box, take that lever and pull it all the way down and vote the Democratic ticket straight. Don't go in there and start messing here and here and here, and get your ballot all mixed up, where you don't know yourself how you voted and they can't count and they throw it out. Just go in there and say, "We are going to do what we think is best for our country."

If you think it is best for your country to vote for the other nominee, Mr. Goldwater, then pick that ballot and the people running with him and vote that ticket so he will have support and men that will try to help him in running the Government.

But if you want your President to continue as he told you 11 months ago, with your prayers, with your help, to do the very best he can do, then take that lever and pull her straight.

And I want to tell you this: I am going to be down home at my little farm waiting to hear from this little State, and I hope that somebody calls me and tells me that all these thousands of people that I saw out here in this beautiful sunshine on Saturday morning, that I dropped by to see on my way to New York, that they kept the faith, that they cast their vote, and Delaware went Democratic.

Thank you.

NOTE: The President spoke at noon on the steps of the Old State House in Dover, Del. In his opening words he referred to Governor Elbert N. Carvel, Democratic candidate for Senator, Charles L. Terry, Jr., Democratic candidate for Governor and former State Chief Justice, and Representative Harris B. McDowell, Jr., all of Delaware.

The text of remarks of Mrs. Johnson, who spoke briefly, was also released.

750 Remarks at an Airport Rally in Wilmington, Delaware. *October 31, 1964*

I HOPE you want me that much next Tuesday morning!

We are going up to New York and New Jersey, and we are going to record a program with some of the outstanding women in the United States, Mrs. Oveta Culp Hobby, who was Secretary of Health, Education, and Welfare in Mr. Eisenhower's Cabinet; Mrs. Patricia Harris; Mrs. Clark Kerr, the wife of the president of the University of California, and other very talented ladies. We will spend most of our afternoon working there and then this evening we will have a big rally at Madison Square Garden.

But I didn't want to pass over the State of Delaware and, just because they had always been so good to me and to my family, let them think that in the closing days of the campaign that I had been in 43 States and I was just going to take them for granted, because I don't know whether you are going to vote for me or not—but I sure hope you do.

I think the American people are taking this election very seriously, and you boys and girls, I have a little special message for you, and I am going to put you to work before this day is over with.

The American people have, this year, registered in record numbers, and in the States that I have been in, and this is 44 of them, I have never seen as many people come and make a sacrifice to leave their work or their home to listen eagerly and earnestly to a candidate talk and try to make up their minds what was right and what they ought to do.

The people are listening closely, and they are listening critically. They are doing this, I think, because they are deeply concerned with the leadership of their country, and they are deeply concerned with the outcome of November 3d.

They are right to be deeply concerned because many elections have come and gone without raising any question about the basic structure of American life. But this year, this time, you face a very fundamental decision. For the last 30 years practically all of us, Democrats and Republicans alike, have gotten together and agreed on the general direction in which we wanted our country to go, and we have agreed on the policies of strength and peace, prosperity. And some of the leaders in the peace movement are leading Republicans, men like Senator Arthur Vandenberg, men like my old friend Doc Eaton, over in the House of Representatives; men like Jim Wadsworth, a great Republican who did more to make this Nation strong than almost any Democrat; men like Senator Hickenlooper now; men like Senator Everett Dirksen.

I have worked—I saw Senator Vandenberg. I served on the same committee with him, the Atomic Energy Committee, and I saw him work every day and you couldn't tell whether he was a Democrat or a Republican. He was an American first and he did what was best for his country.

Then when President Eisenhower came in, he was a Republican President for 8 years, but the Democrats controlled the Senate 6 of those 8 years, and I worked with him in the Strait of Formosa and in the Suez crisis, and in Dien Bien Phu and other places, and we tried to put our country first and our party second.

But today, now, this year, a very small group of men declare that these policies are wrong, this bipartisan foreign policy we have been following ought to go out the window. They want to veto the programs that we have worked out together. They want to turn and change course and go in another direction. They want to do it in foreign policy and they want to do it in domestic policy.

I think their meaning is clear. I don't criticize them for it. You can't find one ugly word that I am going to say here in this State today about anybody, whether he agrees with me or disagrees with me. I am going to try to talk about the issues, not the personalities. But I do think these people want to turn back, they want to return to what they believe were "the good old days."

But those days, as I remember them, were not very good. I grew up in the middle of some of them, in the thirties, and I think some of you did.

America is just not going to repeal all that we have done under the administrations of Franklin Roosevelt, Harry Truman, Dwight Eisenhower, and John Fitzgerald Kennedy.

Let's just visit here a little bit on this Saturday afternoon. We are not in any hurry. Let's go back for a minute to October 1929. That was 35 years ago last Thursday, October 29, 1929, 35 years ago last Thursday.

At the New York Stock Exchange, scrambling and yelling traders radically dumped 16,410,000 shares of stock. Shortly after that, unemployment started rocketing toward the 13 million mark and the price of corn started sinking toward 30 cents.

Two years later, a Chicago newspaper reported "men, women, and children are digging in the garbage dump. They are grabbing bits of food and vegetables."

I personally, in 1935, saw little Mexican children go into the garbage cans in San Antonio, Tex., in the back of cafeterias, and take grapefruit rinds that had been discarded from the tables at breakfast that morning and take those grapefruit rinds out and hull them with their teeth to get something to eat. The poor were everywhere.

That is what they talk about as "the good old days."

The Americans of 30 years ago were just as able as we are, and I think they were just as hardworking and just as honest as we are. They loved their country just as much as you do, but they had not yet learned that the 20th century requires a partnership of business and labor and farmers and consumers and Government.

Now, we want peace in the world, we want nations to get along with each other. We don't want to be dropping atomic bombs around and killing people. But we ought to also want peace at home. It is not necessary, to have good times for yourself, for the corporations you work for to have bad times. The bigger the profits and the better the company that you work for does, the more they can do for you; and the better that you do and the stronger you are, the better you feel and the healthier you are, the more likely you are to get into a trot, the better you can do for them.

If you can get the businessman, the big company, the big corporation, and the people that work for them, if you can get them to understand that what is good for one of them is good for the other, and we can have understanding instead of harassment—and I am just foolish enough to think that somehow or other we can do that, and I have been promoting it for 11 months, I have been bringing them in and talking to them.

If business puts everything that it has and all it can muster into the pot, and you put, as workers, everything you have into that pot, and then you take a spoon and scoop it up and make a big pie out of it, the bigger that pie is the more you will get and the more they get if we divide it reasonably equitably.

I will tell you something else that is important: After business gets a return on their investment and their machinery and their management, and the worker gets a return on his sweat and what he did all day long, then Uncle Sam, the Government, I come in and I take my knife, and the bigger that pie is the more I get for the Government because I get 52 percent of all that is left.

So it just seems to me that it is good sense for all of us to try to have peace at home and try to get along. That is why you don't hear me talking about economic royalists, big business, big labor, racketeers, profit-makers, and things like that.

We have laws that determine what is equitable and what is just, and we follow those laws. The laws will be just. There are some people who don't want to follow the laws, but the laws, in the end, will be just. If we will follow those, and try to all work together, in the end we will have peace at home.

Now, that is what we are trying to do in the world, too. We had a little problem right after I came in down at Guantanamo. Mr. Castro—that bearded fellow—came out there one morning and decided to cut our water off, and wouldn't let our servicemen have water at the base. We were contracting with him to buy water. And then everything went up. We have hotheads everywhere, you know, and smart alecks, and folks that have ideas. So they immediately started giving suggestions, and we got a lot of them. But we decided that we ought to move one of our plants from California and make our own water and quit paying Mr. Castro for it, let him take his outfit and go on home.

We have had a good many illustrations like that, and that is the partnership, I think, that has created our great system of Government. We have, by our economic system, dispelled fear of disasters like the depression of 1929. For 44 months now, we have had prosperity. The profits of that partnership that I talked to you about are written in the record.

Do you know that this year the companies are making $12 billion more after taxes than they did last year? Do you know the workers are making $60 billion more after taxes than they did last year?

In the 1920's only four families in ten had incomes that were sufficient to cover the real necessities. Now we have that figure up to eight out of ten, from four out of ten to eight out of ten. That is real progress.

What I want to ask you to do—and that is one reason I stopped off here in Wilmington—is we have it from four out of ten families having enough to have all the necessities—and that was a few years ago—and now we have it to eight out of ten. We have improved it—and you will admit that things have improved the last few years. Now what we want is not eight out of ten, but we want it to be ten out of ten.

The average fellow that works, his real wage in terms of what it will buy has more than doubled. There were about 2½ million small businesses then. Today there are 4½ million. That is almost twice as many, large or small. They were failing then at about twice their present rate. I don't think we ought to turn that back.

We don't all agree about the details of

how we should go forward. We know we have some differences among ourselves on how to work them out. We recognize the duty, when this election is over, to take a count of the honorable differences of reasonable men and call them in and try to get an agreement. But this election will have settled this, and this is one thing I want you to help me settle in this election. I am going to wait and hear what you do in Wilmington next Tuesday.

I want you to say loud and clear that Wilmington is not in favor of turning back. I want you to say in language that even a fellow with an earphone can understand: America doesn't want to run in reverse. More than that, we have found a new sense of what we can do, and that we can do more than we ever realized we could do. We see more clearly now. We look ahead further.

We can see an abundant America where science and technology have been fully harnessed to the needs of all our people. We see a skilled America in which every child knows the richness of learning and is prepared to the limit of his capacity. We can see over there an America where our cities are not a problem, but a glory, and where from sea to shining sea the works of man blend with the beauties of nature.

We can see a compassionate America, where no one is ill without hospital care, medicare, and no one is in trouble without help. We can see a lively America where the lamps of variety are lit in every home and that knows all the wondrous world of good books and the arts.

We see these things not a hundred years away, but we see them within our reach, in this period of the American breakthrough. So let the old days lie dead and buried. We are ready to move on to that America that we can vision and that we can see. We must keep our eyes in the stars and our feet on the

ground. We must be progressive, but we must be prudent. We must be conservative and careful and cautious and not reckless, but we don't have to be right-wing reactionaries.

So I think that is the kind of an America you want. Isn't it?

The Soviet Union last week changed its leaders. We don't know what that means for America. Mr. Khrushchev is no longer in charge. We don't know what it means. But Mr. Khrushchev sat there 2 years ago with Mr. Kennedy, our President, and they were eyeball to eyeball, and I sat in those meetings, 38 meetings, when the National Security Council met and those missiles were pointed towards us, 90 miles off our shores in Cuba.

I never left home a single morning when I knew I was coming back that night. I didn't know what would happen that day.

I saw the Army generals come in with all their stars and the Navy men with all their braid, and the Secretary of State, a great Rhodes scholar, the Secretary of Defense— the president of Ford Motor Co. at a half-million a year—all the men with the big brains, and they all tried to figure out what to do. Any fool could have put his thumb on the button and turned on the atomic bomb. Anyone could have started a war right quick.

We have an old saying in Texas—you may not have ever heard it: "Any jackass can kick a barn down, but it takes a good carpenter to build one." So we want to be careful and not kick anything down. We want to be careful not to start anything that would wipe out a hundred million Americans, and wipe out a hundred million Soviets. So we considered and we thought and we deliberated. I sat there as Vice President, I am proud to tell you.

As Thomas Jefferson said a long time ago, your third President and former Vice President, one of the greatest men we have produced—he said that the decision of the many is much to be preferred to the judgment of the few. Hitler found out that when he could mash a button and make a decision, it wasn't always a wise one. We found out that the decision of the many, those in Dover, those in Wilmington, those in New York, and those in Johnson City, Tex., every 4 years they have to make this decision, and now you are going to have to make it. You made it in 1960, and the man that you sent into that room, that sat at the head of that table, that watched those movements over 38 long meetings of the Security Council, he was the calmest and the coolest and the wisest man in that room—John Fitzgerald Kennedy.

So you are going to have to select the man whose thumb will be close to that button. You are going to have to select the man who will answer that telephone, that "hot line" from Moscow, when that bell starts jingling, ting-a-ling-a-ling, and they say, "Moscow is calling." You are going to have to select the President, and you have only one President.

You are going to decide that next Tuesday, and you are going to decide it not on what is best for me, because you have done everything in the world anybody can do for me. You gave me a place as a congressional secretary, and an NYA administrator, in 1931, Mr. Hoover's administration; you made me a Congressman for 12 years; you made me a Senator for 12 years, and you made me a leader, a Democratic leader, minority leader and majority leader of the United States Senate, the greatest deliberative body in the world for 8 years; and then you made me Vice President by the votes of all the people.

For almost a year I have been your President. You can turn me out next Tuesday,

or you can—well, what you ought to do is search your own conscience and summon all the sincerity and intelligence at your command and in your family, and you ought to do what is best for your country.

I would hope that after you have thought it over and after you have considered both sides, and after you have looked at what is happening, after you see the experience record of both men, and after you have heard them all, I would hope that you would reach up there and take that Democratic lever and pull it down all the way.

Someone down there in the ranch country started a slogan back in 1960, and wonderful little Delaware stayed with me all along. They were my friends. But they had a slogan, "All the way with LBJ."

We are going to have a Democratic Senate. It is going to be made up, in my judgment, of about 70 men and women. It is going to be predominantly Democratic. Out of the 100, I think we will have 70. I think in the House of Representatives we will have a majority. I think you want to send a Democrat to work with a Democrat, and I need some help.

I hope that when you give consideration to everything that you will look at the fine, solid record that your good Governor has made and send him down there to help me. Delaware needs Bert Carvel in the Senate. He can work with the other Democratic Senators and with the President, and with the Democrats in the Cabinet, and he can do more for Delaware than anyone I know. I think the Nation needs him in the United States Senate.

You have a wonderful Congressman, and you don't know how much Harris McDowell has helped me, all through the year when we had difficult bills and we wanted to do something. We just didn't want to talk, talk, talk; we wanted to get some action. We passed education bills, we passed other good measures, we passed a tax bill that turned back $12 billion in taxes. We cut our budget $1 billion.

In every one of those votes, Harris McDowell was over in the House of Representatives, and there are not many Congressmen from Delaware—just Harris McDowell. But I will tell you, so far as your President was concerned, I went home many nights after midnight, tired and distressed and depressed, but never on account of him, because Delaware was always 100 percent with me.

They say there is a lot of moral decay in the country and they say we can't trust our young people anymore, and we do have a disturbance here and there and a riot here and there, and we all deplore them. A lot of it is on account of the families and a lot of it is because of the schools, and a lot of it is on account of poverty, and a lot of it is because the kids play in the streets. But in my judgment, the children of today are morally all right and they are stronger and better. I have two daughters, one of them is 17 and one of them is 20, and I think they are both better at their age than I was, and I know they are smarter than I was.

So I have faith in you. We have to work at this problem and we have to improve on the situation we have. We have to have not just some of you educated; we have to have all of you educated. First we have to have a job for every man and woman that wants to work in this country. That just has to be the rule.

Second, every boy and girl born has to have the right to have an education to all he or she can take, even if they are from poor families they have that right, and we have to do something about it.

Third, we have to improve our social security system and we have to strengthen it, and we have to make it better. As the cost of living goes up, we have to increase it. We have to have medical care so that when they get sick and go in the hospital they don't have to send for their daughter, their brother-in-law, their son-in-law, or somebody to haul them over to their house to try to take care of them. We have to have medical care for them so they can live their lives in decency and dignity. And we are not about to, under the Johnson administration, if I have anything to do with it, and you will decide that next Tuesday, we are not about to make social security voluntary and kill it that way.

What can you do about it? You have Lyndon Johnson and you have Hubert Humphrey, Bert Carvel and Harris McDowell, and you have your candidate for Governor, all of these Democrats. Don't go to messing around there and looking here, there, and over yonder, trying to pick over everything and nibble here and nibble there. The best thing to do is to just walk in with your chin in and chest out and say, "I believe in peace and prosperity."

I asked an old boy the other day, I said, "What do they ask you down here about the election?" He said, "Well, all the salesmen come in so often and ask me about the election that I just went out and got 15 of these Kennedy half-dollars. I put them in my pocket and every time a fellow asks me, I just rattle them and say, 'I like her pretty well as she is.'"

So what you do is just reach up there and get that lever and just say, "All the way with LBJ."

Your mamas and your papas and your grandpas, some of them are going to forget this. But I am depending on you young folks who are going to have to fight our wars, and who are going to have to defend this country, and who are going to get blown up if we have a nuclear holocaust—I am depending on you to have enough interest in your future and what is ahead of you to get up and prod mama and papa and make them get up early and go vote.

NOTE: The President spoke at a rally at the airport at Wilmington, Del. During his remarks he referred to, among others, Mrs. Oveta Culp Hobby, Secretary of Health, Education, and Welfare in President Eisenhower's Cabinet and Director of the Women's Army Auxiliary Corps during World War II, Mrs. Patricia Roberts Harris, of Washington, D.C., member, United States-Puerto Rico Commission on the Status of Puerto Rico, Mrs. Clark Kerr, wife of the president of the University of California, and Governor Elbert N. Carvel, Democratic candidate for Senator, and Representative Harris B. McDowell, Jr., both of Delaware.

751 Remarks in Madison Square Garden. *October 31, 1964*

Mayor Wagner and my fellow countrymen:

I heard about your little party and I just thought I would drop by. Your welcome has been affectionate and warm and generous, and Lady Bird and Lynda and Luci and I just can't thank you enough.

I guess about all we can say is that we are very grateful and may God grant that I never disappoint the great and gallant man who selected me as Vice President, John Fitzgerald Kennedy, and that I never disappoint you or fail you.

To those talented people who produced and created this great show tonight, I send my personal gratitude. I want to especially thank Jerry Finkelstein, Eddie Weisl, Jr., Martin Davis and his staff, Hy Brown and his staff, and Kirk Douglas and my very dear friend Gregory Peck, and Mitch Miller, Tony Bennett, Diahann Carroll, Bob Merrill, Connie Francis, Jill St. John, and all of the many others who had such a part in making this such a delightful evening. Thank you from the bottom of our hearts.

I have come to New York in the final hours of this campaign. I come to say to you once again that your President will need your prayers and your President will need your support, and your President will also need Democratic Congressmen in the House and Bob Kennedy in the Senate.

I don't have to tell you of Bob Kennedy's talents or his energy or his great patriotism. He has demonstrated this in ways and actions that are far beyond my inadequate description, but it seems to me—it seems to me that this great State, symbolizing America and its ancestors, ought to have, and deserves to have, at least one Democratic Senator.

So help your country, help your President, help your State. Work hard, vote early, and send to Washington a full delegation of Democratic Congressmen and send Bob Kennedy to the Senate where he can continue to work with Hubert Humphrey and work with me for the people of New York.

This is the last chapter in a great tradition. This is the last presidential campaign to reach its climax in this arena. But it is the continuation of another tradition, for here we end a campaign which will see the American people choose the leadership of the Democratic Party. And won't that be a wonderful day for all the country?

Four years ago I came here one night with John Fitzgerald Kennedy, and he promised you that we would get America moving again. We have fulfilled that pledge. In fact, this administration has passed more legislation, has made more progress, has fulfilled more promises than any administration since the New Deal of Franklin Delano Roosevelt.

I came up here to New York tonight to tell you that we have just begun. We are going to keep moving forward. We are going to keep moving forward with the leadership and the support of the great State of New York.

The leaders of New York have always believed in the future. When I first came into the White House, I moved a desk into my office which had been used by one of the towering figures of American history, Franklin D. Roosevelt of the State of New York. I was so happy to greet his great manager, that ever youthful Jim Farley, who came up on the platform a few minutes ago.

And now whenever I feel that I have done a good day's work, whenever I feel that I have really accomplished something, I look at that desk and then I go back to work because I know I have only begun.

Franklin Roosevelt once said, "Too many who prate about saving democracy are really only interested in saving things as they were. Democracy should concern itself also with things as they should be."

So in this campaign we face those who are interested in destroying things as they are. These fellows are not conservatives in the American tradition. They are just interested in tearing down institutions, not in preserving them. They are dedicated to extreme ideas, not to old values. They advocate aggressive interference with other nations, not increased reliance on others to order their own affairs.

This is not a conservative philosophy. This is not even a Republican philosophy. This is not a philosophy ever embraced by any major American leader. "Conserva-tive" may be written on their banner and in their books, but "radical" is in their hearts.

We were promised this time that the American people would be offered a choice and not an echo. This was to be a debate about basic principles.

And here, tonight, we are in the closing days of this campaign, and what do we hear? We hear not philosophy, but mud-slinging; not ideas, but smears and scandal; not programs, but the old worn-out slogans of an old worn-out effort, written by the same old worn-out man trying to frighten the American people.

Well, I don't think you are going to let it work. Are you?

I think I can tell you why they are doing it. They found out that the American people would overwhelmingly reject their ideas, would reject their programs. They found out that the great silent vote was a myth. They discovered that the revolution of the extremist was a dying ember.

They ran smack into the solid, good sense of the American people. They discovered, as far as the American people are concerned: extremism in the pursuit of the Presidency is an unpardonable vice, and moderation in the affairs of the Nation is the highest virtue.

They are going to learn their final lesson on next Tuesday night.

New York has had many great leaders. One of them has an important meaning for this campaign—that great American Al Smith. When he received the presidential nomination, he said he would follow the principles of Woodrow Wilson: "First, the people as the source, and their interests and desires, as the text, of law and government. Second, individual liberty as the objective of all law."

Well, today there are those who call upon

us to abandon our historic principles under the pretense of pursuing that individual liberty which Al Smith prized so highly. And yet, time and time again, they themselves have struck at the foundation of our American freedom.

They call for freedom and then they attack the courts which protect that freedom.

They call for freedom and they would strip away the rights of those accused of crime, rights developed over centuries to protect against arbitrary power.

They call for freedom and yet accuse their opponents of being soft on communism or even worse, branding as heretics or traitors all those who ever disagree with them.

They call for freedom and they attack our religious leaders for trying to exercise their ancient responsibility—as clergymen and citizens—to guide people in the course of life.

But worst of all, they call for freedom and yet they help create the atmosphere of hate and fear and suspicion in which individual liberty faces its maximum danger.

Well, the American people prize their liberty too dearly. They have fought for it too hard to yield it now to these attacks. And somehow I think that you are going to help me make that plain in a few days.

We are going to take another course. We are going to work to enlarge the freedom of the American people, and we have the capacity to do that on a scale that is greater than ever before in the history of man.

Our first task is to complete the work of the last 30 years. So we will work to give every citizen an equal chance to hold a job, to vote, to educate his children, to enjoy all the blessings of liberty, whatever his color, his religion, or his race.

Will you stand with me on that?

We will work to eliminate the conditions which chain men to hopeless poverty, and in this way to eliminate poverty in America.

One hundred years ago Abraham Lincoln abolished slavery. Tonight, the Democratic Party pledges itself to abolish poverty in this land. We will work to protect the old and feed the hungry, and care for the helpless.

Will you stand with me on that?

But this is just the beginning. We are rich and we are powerful, but that is not enough. We must turn our wealth and our power to a larger purpose. Even the greatest of past civilizations existed on the exploitation of the many. This Nation, this people, this generation, has man's first opportunity to create the Great Society.

It can be a society of success without squalor, beauty without barrenness, works of genius without the wretchedness of poverty. We can open the doors of learning, of fruitful labor and rewarding leisure, not just to the privileged few, but we can open them to everyone.

These goals cannot be measured by the size of our bank balance. They can only be measured in the quality of the lives that our people lead.

Millions of Americans have achieved prosperity, and they have found prosperity alone is just not enough. They need a chance to seek knowledge and to touch beauty, to rejoice in achievement and in the closeness of family and community.

And this is not an easy goal.

It means ensuring the beauty of our fields and our streams and the air that we breathe.

It means the education of the highest quality for every child in the land.

It means making sure that machines liberate men instead of replacing them.

It means reshaping and rebuilding our cities to make them safe and make them a decent place to live.

Yes, it means all these things and more, much more.

I have already assembled more than a

dozen groups, the best minds of America, the greatest talent that I could find, to help get the answers to these problems that I have talked to you about tonight. For the first time in man's weary journey on this planet, an entire people has greatness almost within its grasp.

This is the goal within our sight. This is your goal. This is America's goal. This is the goal to which I pledge that I will try to lead all of you.

I have taken a long journey from a tenant farm in West Texas to this platform in Madison Square Garden. I have seen the barren fields of my youth bloom with harvest. I have seen despairing men made whole with enriching toil. I have seen America, my America, grow and change, and I have seen it become a leader among the nations of the world.

In our early days, some thought that the Mississippi would be our final boundary. But farseeing Thomas Jefferson sent his ex-plorers across the continent and the American tide rolled after them.

We, too, stand at the margin of decision. Ahead is the prospect of a shining nation of towering promise. Behind is a threatening tide of change and growth, of expanding population and exploding science. And there is only one way to go.

The only way to preserve the values of the past is to meet the future. The path to progress stretches in front of us, not back along the way we came. And with the help of that Almighty God who has guided us whenever we have been true to Him, that is the way that we are going.

NOTE: The President spoke at 10:45 p.m. in Madison Square Garden in New York City. His opening words referred to Mayor Robert F. Wagner of New York City. Later in his remarks he referred to, among others, Robert F. Kennedy, Democratic candidate for Senator from New York, and James A. Farley, chairman of the Democratic National Committee, 1932–1940, and Postmaster General during the first two terms of President Franklin D. Roosevelt's administration.

752   Letter to the Attorney General in Response to a Report on Crime and Law Enforcement. *November* 1, 1964

[Released November 1, 1964. Dated October 31, 1964]

Dear Mr. Attorney General:

I am sure that every American shares my deep satisfaction with the effective and expanding federal effort against crime described in your encouraging report on the subject. Under the program begun by Attorney General Kennedy and continued under your direction, federal law enforcement agencies have pursued, exposed, and prosecuted racketeers as never before.

This record results from exceptional efforts by many individuals—your attorneys in the Criminal Division of the Department of Justice, the able agents of the FBI, the Internal Revenue Service, the Bureau of Nar-cotics, the Secret Service, the Bureau of Customs, and other federal law enforcement agencies. Their work is important and demanding—days and weeks spent away from home, long hours, and physical danger. They deserve the Nation's gratitude.

Success in combating and conquering crime depends upon cooperation among all levels of government and most significantly on public understanding, support and cooperation. The results set out in your report demonstrate how much more effective the federal government's efforts in this area have been as a result of the new attitude and strengthened coordination. I hope you will maintain and even strengthen this trend. In addition, I urge that the Department develop any additional legislative suggestions that will enable the federal government and other levels of government to meet our responsibilities in eliminating crime. The war against crime must be waged with all the vigor and strength we possess.

Sincerely,

LYNDON B. JOHNSON

[Honorable Nicholas deB. Katzenbach, Acting Attorney General, Washington, D.C.]

NOTE: The Acting Attorney General's report, in the form of a letter dated October 30, 1964, pointed out that indictments of racketeers had increased from 49 in 1960 to 615 in 1963 (541 to date in 1964). Convictions had increased from 45 in 1960 to 288 in 1963 and 466 in 1964. The report attributed these gains to three factors:

(1) New legislation—such as the statutes for-

bidding interstate transmission of gambling information, machines, and paraphernalia—which had given the Federal Government new or increased authority to deal with racketeering.

(2) New interagency coordination. Before 1961 the Department of Justice had received only limited information about racketeers, and then only from the FBI. Today, the report stated, all 26 Federal investigative agencies were pooling their information daily. This coordination had made possible joint action against individuals whom a single agency was previously unable to prosecute.

(3) New enforcement energy had been demonstrated by the Department of Justice and by the other agencies. The number of attorneys had been more than tripled. Permanent field units had been established in four cities and special units had operated in a number of others.

While emphasizing the successes in the fight against racketeering the report also pointed out that the Federal Government does not have—and should not have—"authority to act in the place of local police against most types of crime."

753   Statement by the President Making Public a Report on the Balance of Payments Position.   *November 1, 1964*

I AM HAPPY to be able to make public a report from Secretary Dillon which shows that for the first time in 7 years we have been able to increase our total gold holdings. This is the result of outstanding work by American exporters and full cooperation by all agencies of the Government.

We have not yet finished the job of closing our dollar gap, but we have taken a long step forward. With the continued effort of both business and Government we can reach our goal.

NOTE: Secretary of the Treasury Douglas Dillon's report, in the form of a letter dated October 30, 1964, stated that the payments deficit for 1964 had been running at an annual rate of about $2 billion, as against $3.9 billion in 1960 and $3.3 billion in 1963.

The improvement was due in part to the fact that

exports were 12 percent above 1963 and 27 percent above the 1960 level. "Much of this improvement reflects the stable price level we have achieved domestically over these years, making our goods increasingly competitive in markets abroad," Secretary Dillon pointed out.

He also stated that a significant part of the improved balance of payments position was the result of actions taken to stem the outflow of dollars for Government spending abroad. "In that regard," he added, "we are well on our way toward reaching the target of a $1 billion reduction in Government spending from 1962 levels which was set in President Kennedy's Balance of Payments Message of July 18, 1963."

Secretary Dillon's report further stated that the improvement in our balance of payments had been the key factor inspiring new confidence in the dollar in markets throughout the world. "This improvement has been crucial in bringing our gold losses to a halt," the report concluded. "Indeed, our total gold holdings so far this year have shown an increase for the first time in seven years. . . ."

754   Presidential Policy Paper No. 1: Education.
November 1, 1964

I BELIEVE that every child has the right to as much education as he has the ability to receive. I believe that this right does not end in the lower schools, but goes on through technical and higher education—if the child wants it and can use it.

I want this not only for his sake, but also for our Nation's sake. America badly needs educated men and women. And America needs not just more education, but better education.

Nothing matters more to the future of our country. Not our military preparedness—for armed power is worthless if we lack the brainpower to build a world of peace. Not our productive economy—for we cannot sustain growth without trained manpower. Not our democratic system of government—for freedom is fragile if citizens are ignorant.

Thomas Jefferson once said, "If we expect a nation to be ignorant and free, we expect what never was and never will be." Our Nation's school systems were founded on that proposition.

Today, 41 million students are enrolled in our public schools. Four million more will enter by the end of this decade. But that is not enough. One student out of every three now in the fifth grade will drop out before finishing high school—if we let him. Almost a million young people will quit school each year—if we let them. And over 100,000 of our smartest high school graduates each year will not go to college—if we do nothing.

This cannot continue. It costs too much: we cannot afford it. The whole Nation suffers when our youth is neglected.

Twenty percent of our 18- to 24-year-olds with an eighth-grade education are unemployed—four times the national average—while jobs in America are hunting for trained men and women. Jobs filled by high school graduates rose by 40 percent in the last 10 years. Jobs for those with less schooling decreased by nearly 10 percent.

In the next 10 years, 30 million boys and girls are going to enter our job force. Unless we act now, 2½ million of them will not see the inside of a high school; 8 million will not finish high school; and too many of our schools and colleges will be jammed like city buses at rush hour. Our youth will suffer a handicap that no amount of time—no amount of money—can remove.

We must act. I pledge now to put education at the head of our work agenda. First, we must broaden and improve the quality of our school base. We will need a minimum of nearly 400,000 new classrooms in our public schools during the next 5 years to eliminate overcrowding and replace unsatisfactory facilities. We will need over 800,000 new public school teachers in the next 5 years to keep up with expanding enrollments and to replace those teachers who retire or resign—and we need to increase incentives so that our best people will be attracted to the teaching profession. But most of all we must provide a good education for every boy and girl—no matter where he lives.

Second, we must concentrate our teaching resources in the urban slums and the poor rural areas. Our war on poverty can be won *only* if those who are poverty's prisoners can break the chains of ignorance. This means that we must give our best a chance to do their best.

Third, we must expand and enrich our

colleges. Our college enrollment is due to double within this decade. It will reach almost 9 million by 1975, and will probably expand to four or six times its present size before this century ends.

Fourth, we must recognize that education is a lifelong process. In today's world, we cannot neglect the adult's need for schooling to keep up with technology.

Fifth, we must strengthen our State and community education systems. We do not intend to forsake our tradition that schools and colleges should be controlled at the local level.

This is neither new nor radical. The late Senator Taft declared, "Education is primarily a State function—but in the field of education, as in the fields of health, relief, and medical care, the Federal Government has a secondary obligation to see that there is a basic floor under those essential services for all adults and children in the United States."

Every President from Franklin Delano Roosevelt to John Fitzgerald Kennedy worked to build that floor. I plan to get on with the task.

NOTE: The White House release of which the policy paper on education was a part also included policy statements on health, conservation of natural resources, and farm policy (see Items 755–757). The release stated that other policy papers would be issued from time to time.

755 Presidential Policy Paper No. 2: The Nation's Problems of Health. *November 1, 1964*

AMONG the ancient foes of man, disease still ranks as public enemy number one.

Our scientists and doctors have made great strides. With ever increasing inventiveness they have found ways to cure our afflictions and to stretch our life expectancy.

In 1900 the average American citizen could look forward to reaching the age of 47. Today he can look forward to 70 years.

The miracle of medicine has not reached its limits. But neither has the misery of disease.

Today more than 74 million Americans are afflicted with chronic disease.

Mental illness—in all its forms—casts a shadow on 18 million of our people. The mentally ill fill half of our hospital beds.

Heart disease cripples 12 million.

Arthritis and rheumatism, 12 million.

Diabetes, 3 million—and half of them don't know they have it.

The catalog is long and large.

In our war on disease we have won great successes. Twenty years ago fewer than one out of every five cancer patients could hope to survive. Today the ratio is one out of every three. Experts tell us that, if we continue the fight, one in two can be saved.

But success in fighting disease means more doctors, more nurses, longer hospital care, better clinical facilities.

With the help of wise Federal programs we have begun to meet the need.

We have added more than 5,000 hospitals and nursing homes.

We have supported more than 150 projects to meet problems of the aged and the chronically ill.

We have increased support for medical research—18 fold in the last 16 years.

We are supplying construction aid to schools of medicine and dentistry, as well as loans for students entering these professions.

Less than a month before his tragic death

President Kennedy signed into law a comprehensive program for mental health and mental retardation.

Our war on disease is well begun. But the needs are staggering.

Three thousand communities in America exist without a doctor.

Big city hospitals are chronically overcrowded. A survey in one city showed that one out of every two pregnant women had not seen a doctor before delivery.

Our goals are not high enough.

We need 50 percent more young men and women training to be doctors and dentists just to keep the present ratio with our growing population.

We need 60 percent more nurses by 1970.

Last year State and local health departments had only 51 percent of their staff adequately trained, and more than 5,000 positions vacant. We need at least 17,000 more public health workers by 1970.

There are areas in which we have hardly begun to meet our responsibilities.

First, we must provide adequate hospital and nursing home care for our senior citizens by a sound program financed through contributory social insurance. I pledge that the legislation to accomplish this will head my program next year.

Second, we must step up the fight on mental health and mental retardation. I intend to ask for increased funds for research centers, for special teacher training, and for helping coordinated state and local programs.

Third, we must expand our program to help train the doctors, dentists, and technicians this Nation desperately needs. Right now the statistics show that we are importing interns and resident physicians from other countries which can ill afford to lose them.

Fourth, we must enlarge programs to help disabled citizens rehabilitate themselves for useful employment.

Fifth, we must increase existing programs of medical assistance to children of low-income families.

Sixth, we must work to correct the deficiencies of young men who are rejected for military service because of health.

Seventh, we must move ahead in the effort to protect the purity of the water we drink and the air we breathe. Air pollution, according to one estimate, causes $11 billion damage each year to property alone. No one can measure the damage to our children's lungs.

The Great Society which we mean to build in America must be a healthy society. I pledge my wholehearted energies to make it that way.

756 Presidential Policy Paper No. 3: Conservation of Natural Resources. *November 1, 1964*

WHEN America began there seemed no limit to the riches of the earth. Then came a time of reckless exploitation and ruthless plunder. Greed and ignorance combined to lay waste our resources and threaten our domain with destruction. Farsighted and courageous men—men like Theodore Roosevelt, Franklin Roosevelt, and John Kennedy—acted to halt decay, preserve our splendor, and develop our resources. That battle still goes on. We intend to win it.

But three changing forces are bringing a new era to conservation.

The first is growing population. By the year 2000 more than 300 million Americans will need 10 times the power and 2½ times the water we now consume. Increasing pressure will take our resources and increasing leisure will tax our recreation.

The second is the triumph of technology. The bright success of science also has a dark side. The poisons and chemicals, the junked automobiles, and the waste products of progress are threatening the destruction of nature.

The third is urbanization. More of our people are crowding into cities and cutting themselves off from nature. Access to beauty is denied and ancient values are destroyed. Conservation must move from nature's wilderness to the man-made wilderness of our cities.

All of this requires a new conservation.

We must not only protect from destruction but restore what has been destroyed—not only develop old resources but create new ones—not only save the countryside but salvage the cities.

It is not just the classic conservation of protection and development, but a creative conservation of restoration and innovation.

Its concern is not with nature alone, but with the total relation between man and the world around him. Its object is not just man's welfare but the dignity of his spirit.

Above all, we must maintain the chance for contact with beauty. When that chance dies a light dies in all of us. We are the creation of our environment. If it becomes filthy and sordid, then the dignity of the spirit and the deepest of our values are in danger.

And once nature is destroyed or beauty blighted it can rarely be restored. It is gone forever. It is our children who will bear the burden of our neglect. We owe it to them to keep that from happening.

We have made progress. The 88th Congress—the greatest conservation Congress in our entire history—passed more than 30 important conservation bills.

A new land and water conservation fund will help States and cities set aside spots of beauty for recreation and pleasure.

A Wilderness Act will guarantee all Americans the natural magnificence which has been your heritage.

A Water Research Act will speed development for the soaring water needs of a growing nation.

We established continental America's first new national park in 17 years—23 new national park areas—and 4 new national seashores—and a national riverway.

We began a new Bureau of Outdoor Recreation so that our children will have a place to hunt and fish and glory in nature.

We began construction of over 200 water resource projects with about 70 more scheduled for 1965.

We built or began more than 5,500 miles of transmission lines.

Flood control funds were increased by more than 50 percent.

We have explored the wonders of modern science pressing ahead with research into every area of resource development—using the atom for power—sending satellites to predict weather—moving toward the day when we can make fresh water from the oceans, oil from shale, and harvest the riches of the sea. All this we have done, and more.

I pledge my administration to continue this progress.

But we must do more than continue. Our problems are changing, and we must change to meet them.

In the development of a new conservation I intend to press ahead on five fronts.

First, we seek to guarantee our children a place to walk and play and commune with nature. The demand on our recreational facilities is doubling each decade. We must act boldly or our future will be barren. We will move vigorously under our recent laws to acquire and develop new areas for recreation—emphasizing areas of concentrated population. We will expand our programs to meet developing needs.

A national program of scenic parkways and riverways is on the horizon.

I hope to make the Potomac a conservation model for our metropolitan areas.

In our cities open space must be reserved where possible, and created where preservation comes too late.

Second, we must control the waste products of technology. The same society which receives the rewards of technology must, as a cooperating whole, take responsibility for control. I intend to work with local government and industry to develop a national policy for control and disposal of technological and industrial waste. In this way we can rescue the oldest of our treasures from the newest of its enemies.

Third, we must increase mastery over our environment through the marvels of new technology. This means rapidly increasing emphasis on comprehensive river basin development. We will cooperate with government at every level to develop all the resources while preserving all the scenic promise of an entire region. The scale of our programs must match the scope of our problems.

It means drawing fresh water from the oceans. Within a few years, economic desalination will be a reality for large numbers of Americans.

It means learning to understand the weather and become its master. Weather satellites, deep sea nuclear weather stations, are part of a developing technology which will ultimately make it possible not only to talk about the weather, but do something about it.

It means the use in every field of the newest knowledge to meet the oldest needs. And it means encouraging the development of the genius of man in order to unlock the secrets of the earth.

Fourth, we must prevent urbanization and growth from ravishing the land. At this moment a working group is studying ways to protect the integrity of nature in cities and suburbs. The nation is growing. We want that growth to be a blessing and not a blight.

I will propose—in cooperation with local government and private industry—policies to help ensure that suburban building, highway construction, and industrial spread are conducted with reverence and regard for the values of nature.

Fifth, we must conduct conservation on a global scale.

The oceans and atmosphere are the property of all people. Scientific discoveries in one land can benefit all nations. There are no political boundaries in man's ancient and continuing struggle for mastery over nature.

The Antarctic Treaty, weather and fishery agreements, and the Columbia River treaty with Canada are examples of what can be done if nations will devote common effort to common interest.

These are some of the fronts of the new conservation which I will work to carry forward.

It is often difficult to invest, when results may be a generation or more away. So many immediate needs crowd around us. But our history is witness to the wisdom of investment in our natural resources. It has returned its cost many times. And it has preserved the patrimony of America. I deeply believe in economy and prudence in government—we must be mindful of the financial debt we leave to our children. But

I do not want to leave them the tragic and irretrievable debt of a devastated land and dwindling resources.

From the beginning we have been a people of open spaces. We have lifted our eyes to the deserts and mountains, and now to the stars. But on this earth the ring draws closer around us. Let us have space and resources, here in America, to fit our children's hopes.

757 Presidential Policy Paper No. 4: Farm Policy. *November 1, 1964*

AMERICA'S farmers want and need and deserve—not promises—but more income and more opportunity.

The Democratic answers to these needs include three sets of programs:

—We intend to continue and to improve commodity programs, and to strengthen farm income.

—We intend to assure rural Americans full partnership in the building of the Great Society.

—We intend to increase, wherever we can, the consumer demand for our agricultural products.

We emphasize particularly the importance of the choice farmers have in regard to the commodity program. Farmers can choose our proposal to continue—and to improve— commodity programs, or they can choose to wipe those programs out altogether.

The most careful and responsible studies have shown what would happen if we terminated farm price supports.

First, net farm income throughout the Nation would be cut in half, or by about $6 billion a year. Net farm income in the corn belt alone would drop by $1.8 billion— a devastating blow to the heart of the American economy.

Second, one out of five farmers would be bankrupted.

Third, corn would sell for less than 80 cents a bushel, and wheat for less than a dollar. Soybeans would sell for less than $2 a bushel. It would mean cattle at 17 cents a pound and hogs at 13 cents a pound.

We know from bitter experience that depressions are farm-led and farm-fed. And we are not going to repeat that experience. We propose instead to find in our present feed grains program, our wheat program, and our programs for other commodities those elements which need to be strengthened and improved.

Under these programs:

Gross farm income has averaged $4 billion a year more since 1960 than in the 4 years before 1960.

Net income has averaged $900 million a year higher, or $600 per farm.

But we are openminded: we want to make these programs work even better.

Our goal is parity of income for the farmer. We are making progress toward it, and we will make more progress by going forward, learning as we go, building on what we have done already.

But parity of income is not enough. Our goal is more than that—it is parity of *opportunity* for rural America in the broadest meaning of the term.

In the past our farm programs have been designed to improve the economic position of the farmer and to protect against disaster— sudden or otherwise. Now we must aim at preserving and strengthening the structure of the whole rural society, based on the family farm and the rural community that have contributed so much to the American tradition. We must make it possible for young people to spend their lives in the rural communities where they grew up—if they choose to do so—instead of being forced by economic necessity to tear up their roots and go to distant cities.

The development of these community programs must be a partnership enterprise. The rural community itself will provide the leadership. The States have a role to play. And the Federal Government will do its part.

We will work together to make more effective use of our food abundance.

There is no justification for any person in this country going hungry in the midst of plenty. As we win our war against poverty it will mean more customers for America's farm produce.

The food stamp program has worked well. We propose to extend it.

The Food for Peace program is good international policy and it is good economic policy. People who are hungry are weak allies of freedom. We are learning to use food more effectively to promote economic growth. We will broaden this program still further.

One out of every $6 earned by farmers today comes from export markets, and 1 out of 4 acres harvested today produces for markets overseas. Our agricultural exports for dollars climbed last year to $4½ billion—up 20 percent in 1 year—35 percent greater than in 1960, providing critically needed foreign exchange and contributing significantly to national economic progress.

We must continue to improve and build the export market for the family farm. This will take patient negotiation, hard determination, and calm reason in the critical GATT negotiations now underway.

And there is another exciting prospect for agricultural markets that is seldom recognized. Our studies show that if about 80 of the newly developed countries increase their per capita income by just $100 a year— we can double our export market for food.

We look forward to the day when we can rely less on cutbacks, and more on programs to sell abroad all we produce above our own needs. We look forward to the day when our great cooperatives and other private enterprise institutions can perform most of the marketing functions with a minimum of Government involvement.

We all know the difficulties there are in shrinking supply to fit demand. We must get on with the job of stimulating worldwide demand to use our tremendous God-given production.

We are working now, tirelessly and with success, to keep the trade channels to the Common Market and other parts of the world open—and to open new markets.

Rural America must take a leading role in building the Great Society—here and in the world. It was the initiative, the vision, the enterprise of America's farmers that developed our great land frontiers. The same initiative and vision and enterprise will help now in building a better, a more prosperous America.

758   Statement by the President Announcing an Expanded Program To Control Cotton Insect Pests.   *November 2, 1964*

AT THE present time, between 10 and 20 percent of the cost of producing cotton is spent on insect control mainly through the use of chemical pesticides.

Despite the progress that has been achieved in insect control, several problems have emerged that require immediate attention to achieve effective control of these cotton pests.

Many of the most important insect pests have become partially or completely resistant to some pesticide chemicals. A concerted effort is being made to find alternate means of effective pest control including those which do not require the use of chemicals. I have proposed and Congress has approved funds to support this effort.

In addition, long-range measures that need to be taken include greatly increased attention to biological methods of control. To this end, increased support must be provided for fundamental research on insect biology, and for the training of insect biologists, both within the Government and in our colleges and universities.

Such research will seek ways to use native and foreign parasites and predators of cotton insects.

We need more information on infectious agents that specifically harm cotton insects and can be used to control them. Prompt field testing is an important part of this research.

Increased plant breeding research may lead to new varieties of cotton, resistant to insect pests.

Eight and one-half million of our citizens depend on cotton production and processing for at least part of their livelihood. Another 3 to 4 million people service the industry and sell its products.

As research progresses, the threat of decreasing yield and increasing costs of cotton production can be averted, and indeed it can be anticipated that more effective insect control can be achieved at less cost.

Our need for pesticide chemicals will not disappear. On the contrary, we must push the search for new, more specifically acting and less persistent chemicals.

759   Statement by the President on the Fourth Anniversary of the Peace Corps.   *November 2, 1964*

FOUR years ago today John Kennedy proposed the Peace Corps. Then it was a promise. Now it is a reality.

To the 10,000 volunteers serving in 46 countries—to the 110,000 Americans who have applied to become volunteers—go the thanks of this Nation. Through their hard work and devoted service the pioneering tradition of America has been renewed, and our name is honored anew among the develop-

ing nations of Africa, Asia, and Latin America.

But this is no time to rest on the achievements of the last 4 years. This is the time to go forward.

In the next 4 years we must double the size and still further raise the quality of the Peace Corps. Nearly every country where volunteers are now serving has asked for more—often two, three, or four times more. Many countries are on the "waiting list." We must not lose this practical opportunity to assist friendly nations in their self-help efforts in peaceful development.

For the next stage of the Peace Corps, we need applications to serve from about 10 percent of the graduating class of our colleges and universities, we need more applications from skilled workers in our factories and on our farms, we need more experienced teachers, more doctors, more nurses, more senior citizens.

And as 5 to 10,000 volunteers return from 2 years of overseas service we must see that their first-hand experience is put to good use, in our schools and universities, in American private enterprise, in our city and State governments, in our war on poverty, and in all our Federal services, including the Foreign Service.

NOTE: For President Kennedy's proposal of November 2, 1960, see "The Speeches of Senator John F. Kennedy, Presidential Campaign of 1960," p. 1260 (Government Printing Office, 1961).

760 Remarks at a Rally in Houston.
November 2, 1964

Mayor Welch; my friend Senator Ralph Yarborough; one of the wisest and most effective Congressmen in the entire Nation, a man who really knows how to introduce Presidents, Albert Thomas; my good friends, the outstanding Congressmen in the Texas delegation, Congressman Bob Casey, Congressman Jack Brooks, Congressman Clark Thompson; my fellow Texans:

Your warm and generous welcome makes Lady Bird and Lynda and Luci and me know that we are home again among our home folks, our neighbors, and our loyal supporters.

I came back here today to ask again for your help. I hope that the people of Houston will send back to the House of Representatives that able, hardworking Congressman who represents the views of his constituents, Bob Casey. I need Albert Thomas and you need him in the House of Representatives. His advice and his counsel are valuable to both of us.

And in the Senate, no Member of the Senate that I have known since I have been in Washington has more loyally or capably

supported a Democratic program, his own President's program, the program of the President, the first President from Texas, than has Ralph Yarborough. When there is a contest you can be sure that you will find Ralph Yarborough fighting for the folks and for what he thinks is right, working for what he believes is just, voting for what he feels is best.

So I will deeply appreciate your voting for these men and putting in a good vote for your able, effective, efficient Congressman at Large, Joe Pool.

These are the final hours of the campaign. Tomorrow, all across our land, the people of America will make their choice for leadership. In an hour or so I will be going to the hill country where I was born to await the people's decision—your decision.

Three hundred and forty-five days ago a senseless tragedy in this State thrust me into this office. In every one of those days I have tried with all that God has given me to do my dead level best, to do what I thought was right.

A President understands that no man is

infallible. He learns that people are his cause and their freedom his trust. He learns to believe in their wisdom. Most of all, he prays for the guidance of God as he works for peace in the world.

Thirty-four years ago when I was a very young man I lived in this great city. I taught at the old Sam Houston High School, no more than a dozen blocks from where I stand tonight.

One of the most valuable Americans I know, one of the most competent, capable, dedicated, patriotic persons I have ever met, is a graduate of Sam Houston High School, the University of Houston, and Harvard Business School, my trusted and loyal aide—Jack Valenti of Houston.

But since Jack and I were at Sam Houston High School, the world has changed in these years. But the change has not been all bad or all good.

For Houston, it has been good. You have grown and you have prospered. You have not been afraid to venture or to build. You have built on the banks of these bayous one of the great cities of America.

You have accepted change and you have made it work for you. You have had the leadership of progressive and prudent newspapers, like the Post and the Chronicle.

This is the work that we are trying to do in the family of nations, like you have been doing here in Houston in the community of the Nation; like our very able and effective Governor has been trying to do in the great State of Texas. And there is no finer Governor in the Nation than John Connally.

And this is the work in the Nation that your President has before him, and this is the meaning of this election.

I have said, as plainly as I know how, what I hope for America, what I hope for you and your family and for generations yet unborn.

And now on this night among friends, so many of them who I see here, who have stood by me, by my side, all through the years, I want to tell you again my hope for America. I want to tell you again my pledge for the Nation.

First, I pledge my total commitment to try to preserve peace while protecting freedom. I want to reduce the threat of nuclear war; to maintain Presidential control over all of our nuclear weapons; to strengthen in every way we can our alliances with other nations; and to advance the cause of freedom all around the world.

Second, I pledge you that we will continue to be the mightiest nation in all the world, stronger in military might than all the nations of all the world combined. But we will always use our power responsibly.

Third, I pledge to work to keep our Nation's prosperity growing and to build the strength of our free enterprise system.

Fourth, I pledge a war on waste in Government—wherever it exists.

Fifth, I pledge to keep your Government frugal and prudent with the people's money. We will get a dollar's value for every dollar spent.

Sixth, I pledge a compassionate Government, one that seeks to abolish poverty, that fights disease and ignorance, and brings to older citizens new hope and increased dignity.

Seventh, I pledge that the constitutional rights of every citizen will be protected, and law and order will be maintained.

Eighth, I pledge to do all in my power to meet our Nation's growing education needs so that every boy and girl in America can receive all the education that they can use.

Ninth, I pledge to conserve our resources, to protect the air and the water from pollution, to make sure that our children and their children will not be robbed of nature's beauty and nature's bounty.

And finally, and the thing I would like to see happen so much here in Texas, and it can happen here, and I believe it will happen here, and I pray that it does happen here, I pledge to work as President of all the people in a land that knows no South, no North, no East, and no West. I hope that somehow we can learn to love thy neighbor as thyself. I hope that somehow we can refrain from speaking badly of our fellow men.

Our work after this election is going to be to heal the wounds of the campaign, and to try to rebuild the unity of all the people of America. We cannot endure in bitterness. The greatness of this great country rests on our being a united people—the United States of America.

With trust in God, let this Nation take fresh strength in renewed hope—and let this land and all who love it move forward, move forward as you have moved in Houston— one people, one Nation, with liberty and justice for all.

Thank you.

NOTE: The President spoke at 5:30 p.m. in the parking lot of Musical Hall in Houston, Tex. In his opening words he referred to Mayor Louis Welch of Houston and Senator Ralph Yarborough and Representatives Albert Thomas, Bob Casey, Jack Brooks, and Clark W. Thompson, all of Texas. Later he referred to Representative Joe R. Pool of Texas.

The text of remarks of Mrs. Johnson and daughters Lynda and Luci, who spoke briefly, was also released.

761   Remarks in Houston at Sam Houston Senior High School. *November 2, 1964*

Mr. Chairman, my friend Ed Ball; Reverend Clergy; our beloved Congressman, your own Albert Thomas; my warm friend, your great Senator, Ralph Yarborough; my friend, the able Congressman from the other district, our friend Bob Casey; ladies and gentlemen, boys and girls:

Eleven months and eleven days ago a tragedy happened here in Texas, and I had to assume the duties of the Presidency and take the oath of office in an airplane with the jet motors roaring in a Dallas airport.

That day, when I took the oath and became the 36th President of this country, I said with God's help and with your prayers, I would do the best I could. I have done that every day I have been your President.

Thirty-four years ago, before most of you were born, late one afternoon I left Sam Houston High School to go to Washington, and I remember the school paper said, "We predict that we will hear some more about Mr. Johnson." I guess that somehow or other they anticipated that I might be coming back here to see you tonight.

I have been all over this Nation. I have been in 49 States, and I have landed in 44 of them. I have flown over the others. But Mrs. Johnson went to Alabama and Mississippi that I didn't get to stop in. I flew over them. And Luci went to North Dakota and South Dakota. I didn't get to land in them. I flew over them. And Lynda went to Hawaii.

With the help of my loving family we have been in 49 of the 50 States and we have tried so hard to be President of all the people, for all the people.

We have tried to reason with the leaders of the world, and I saw 85 from 120 countries.

We have tried to bring peace and brotherhood among our fellow men.

We have tried to find jobs for every man

and woman that wanted to work, and 5 million more people are working today than were working when Jack Kennedy and I took the oath of office 4 years ago.

We have tried to improve the working conditions and the standard of living for all of our people. And the working people of this country in the last 11 months that I have been President drew $60 billion more in wages than they did the 11 months before, after taxes. We are working fewer hours per day and fewer days per week, and we have more leisure time. The average manufacturing wage is $104 per week, which is the highest in the history of the United States for our working people.

We have tried to improve the education of our children. We have in our platform and we have in our program that we believe and we hope and we will work toward an education for every boy and girl in this country to the extent that he can use it. All that he can take is his right when he is born in America.

We believe that our elder citizens should be able to live their life in decency and dignity, and we are preparing a program for medical care for our elder citizens. We propose to improve and to strengthen the social security system that a Democratic President first gave America, and we don't intend to make it voluntary and ruin it, either.

So we came home tonight to tell you just some of the things that we have been telling the people from Maine to Oregon, from New Orleans, La., to Massachusetts. I am particularly happy to be here on the North Side because you have one of the ablest and one of the most powerful and one of the most effective Congressmen in all the United States, and one of my best friends, Albert Thomas.

I am happy to have my friend Bob Casey

on the platform with me tonight. He is a hard working, able Congressman who tries to serve his constituents and their views at all times, and I am happy that he honored me by coming here with me.

Then I want to ask you and tell you something else about Texas. Texas is a great State. It is a growing State. It is a growing State and Houston is leading the way for all the rest of the country.

When President Kennedy was assassinated, he left 51 bills that represented major improvements, and practically every one of those bills was for the average citizen or to improve the lot of the working people, or to help make America better. And the other night when the Congress had come and gone, it was almost midnight, I was sitting there in the White House and I was looking over that list of 51 bills that he left me to carry on for him. And we had passed every one of those 51 bills that he left through the United States Senate, and there is no Senator from any State of the Union at any time that ever gave a President's program more loyal support than your able and your eloquent and your good and your hard working Senator Ralph Yarborough.

Many of those bills improve working conditions for working people. Many of those bills improve education for our children. Many of those bills aided veterans who had carried our flag around the world in two world wars, and who now look to their Government for recognition and for assistance. I am proud to say that on every one of those bills, when they called the roll, Ralph Yarborough was standing up fighting and voting for the people.

I don't know what is going to happen tomorrow, but I know what I am going to do. I am going to get up early, and I am going down to that Johnson City, Tex., courthouse and I am going to put a vote in for Ralph

Yarborough, and I am not going to do it just because I like him or because he is a friend. I am going to do it because I think that he has loyally and effectively worked for the Democratic program for all the people, and I want to be President of all the people.

You have a precious privilege that many people in many countries don't have. Some of them are fighting for it and many of them would die for it, and a good many have died in order that you might have it. That is the right to go and cast a secret vote. There are great interests at work in the world that would take from you some of the things that you now enjoy. They talk about making your social security voluntary. They talk about collective bargaining. They talk about repealing a lot of laws that have been passed for labor. They talk about throwing away the TVA.

Tomorrow you are going to decide the kind of leadership that you want for this country. I don't know what you are going to decide, but I hope you will go early, I hope you will see that your neighbors go, I hope you will vote for Albert Thomas, Ralph Yarborough, Governor Connally, and those of you from Bob Casey's district, for Bob Casey, and if you are feeling good and don't forget it, I sure know Hubert Humphrey and I would appreciate it if you would throw one in for us.

NOTE: The President spoke at Sam Houston Senior High School in Houston, Tex. In his opening words he referred to Edgar L. Ball, Monsignor Paul Pieri, pastor of the St. Rose of Lima Church in Houston, and Representative Albert Thomas, Senator Ralph Yarborough and Representative Bob Casey, all of Texas. Later he referred to Governor John B. Connally of Texas.

Early in his remarks the President referred to the time, December 1931, when he left Sam Houston High School, where he was a teacher of speech and debate coach, to go to Washington to work as secretary to Representative Richard M. Kleberg of Texas.

762   Remarks at a Rally in Pasadena, Texas. *November 2, 1964*

Congressman Casey, Congressman Thomas, Senator Yarborough, Mrs. Yarborough, Mrs. Thomas:

I have been coming to Pasadena for a long time, and Albert Thomas used to tell me every time I came to Houston I had to come to Pasadena. I came here and led your parade. Now Bob Casey is telling me to come here—and Ralph Yarborough—my good friends, tonight.

We all decided before we left Houston and got away from all the skyscrapers and went up to the capital of Texas to close the campaign—the campaign that has taken my family into 49 States, where I visited 44 States myself since Labor Day—that we would come out here to Pasadena and say

"hello" and thank you all, because we know you are going to vote Democratic tomorrow.

I haven't come here tonight to say anything ugly about my opponent, sling any mud, do any muckraking, talk about anybody. I don't hate anyone. I try to love everybody. I "love thy neighbor as thyself," and I hope you do, too.

We are trying to live in a world with 120 other nations and they have their plans and their programs and their ideas. They are different colors, they have different religions, they have different atmospheres, they have different temperatures. Most of them are hungry, most of them have illiteracy, poverty, and disease. They have old feuds that involve us, that are never our troubles, but they have had trouble getting along with themselves.

But we have learned this: that when war breaks out anyplace in the world, it usually involves us. We are the strongest and the most powerful nation in the world. So for 20 years, since World War II, we have done our best to find a way to live with other people.

Arthur Vandenberg was a great Republican Senator, and he worked with President Harry Truman, a Democratic President, to have a foreign policy, a bipartisan policy. They stopped the Communists in Greece and Turkey.

Then President Eisenhower came along as a Republican President. I was Democratic leader of the Senate. I worked with President Eisenhower in the Suez crisis and the U-2 incident, in the Strait of Formosa.

Some of them said to me, "Why don't you take advantage of the mistakes that have been made? Why don't you get up and criticize and point out all the errors?"

I said, "Because I don't think that we ought to use foreign policy as an issue, that we ought to try to capitalize on anything that might be misunderstood by foreign countries. He is the only President we have, and I am going to support that President, because if I make him weaker I make America weaker."

So the Democratic leadership, I, supported President Eisenhower 95 percent of the time in the year 1960 when my opponent in this race, a Republican, supported his own President only 25 percent of the time.

But we let politics stop at the water's edge, and we tried to unite our country. That is what I have tried to do in this campaign. I have tried to say to our people that I think our President ought to keep control of nuclear weapons instead of turning them over to various commanders throughout the world.

I have said that I thought our people ought to be united instead of divided, and I have tried to preach love instead of preach hate. I have tried to preach faith instead of preach doubt. I have tried to bring our people together and heal our wounds instead of make them angry and fighting each other. I think that we do have a more united people as a result of what I have done in this campaign and I think tomorrow night you will hear something about that unity in America when you hear the returns come in.

I hope that Pasadena will set the example for the rest of the Nation. I hope you will do it by voting for your Democratic Congressman Bob Casey, who works for this district. I hope you will do it by going early and voting for your able, strong, United States Senator Ralph Yarborough. And if any of you happen to be over in Albert Thomas' district, drop in and vote for him.

We have a Democratic team and I hope that you will realize that the Democratic Party is the party of the people. It is the best party for the people. It is the party that recognizes that the people of this country have interest and have concern and have a partnership with Government, and we ought to vote the Democratic ticket from the courthouse to the White House—and I hope you do tomorrow.

The Democratic Party believes in the working people. It is the party that has declared it a part of its policy that every man and woman in this country who wants a job ought to have a job and ought to be able to work. It is the party that has improved our living conditions, improved our higher standards of living. It brought us the minimum wage. It brought us the maximum hours.

Today we have an average manufacturing wage in this country of $104 a week, the highest in the history of the Nation, and we put 5 million extra people to work since John F. Kennedy took the oath of office as President and I took the oath of office as Vice President in 1961.

You will make a decision tomorrow as to the kind of leadership that you want for this country. It was 11 months and 11 days ago as a result of a terrible tragedy that I became your President. I had served for over 3 years by President Kennedy's side as his Vice President, the second Vice President from Texas. I am the first President that Texas has ever had.

You will determine tomorrow whether after 11 months and 11 days I shall continue for another 4 years in the White House or whether I shall leave. I leave that decision to you.

I have tried as best I could to lead this country to peace and lead this country to prosperity. I have tried to be President of all the people. I have tried to treat every man equally. I have tried to protect his constitutional rights.

I sat with President Kennedy during some very dark days of this Republic. It was only 2 years ago this month when we had the Cuba missile crisis. I attended 38 meetings of the National Security Council.

The Soviet Union had moved their missiles into Cuba, 90 miles from the United States. They had them trained on this country. Mr. Khrushchev and Mr. Kennedy, both leaders of great powers, were there eyeball to eyeball looking at each other, almost with a knife at each other's ribs, just holding it steady and not showing any weakness, either one.

The Army came in with all the generals and the Air Force with all their stars, and the Navy with their gold braid, and the best minds that we had in America tried to advise us what to do. Some men were saying, "Send in the Marines." Some men were saying, "Let's load our bombs and get going." Some said, "Let's have an invasion before it is too late."

Thirty-eight times we met in serious meetings of that Security Council in the Cabinet Room. I never left home a single morning when I knew whether I would see my wife and daughters again that night. But that was an experience that I will never forget, and I think most of you remember.

I am mighty happy that during that period when the hotheads were around and when people were yelling all kinds of advice, that the coolest, the calmest, the ablest man in that room was the man that you had selected as Commander in Chief, your President, John Fitzgerald Kennedy. He tried his best to serve you, but he was given only 3 years, and he was taken from us.

I had no time to go to the library and no time to call in any advisers. I had to pick up on a moment's notice. Albert Thomas just happened to be standing there with me. He was in the Air Force One when I took the oath of office, and the jet motors were roaring in the background and we had to take off in the plane, get it off the ground.

I have done the best I could to serve this Nation and serve the world. If you want me to continue, then I pledge you that I will continue to be President of all the people, and work for your welfare, work for the peace of your families, work for the prosperity of all of my people.

I am glad to be back in Pasadena tonight. I love the people of Texas. I love you people. I thank you for coming and honoring me. I hope that you will go to the polls tomorrow. I hope you will go early, I hope you will stay long.

I hope you will see that all your neighbors and your uncles and your cousins and your aunts will vote, and I hope you will give us the greatest Democratic victory that Texas has ever had!

Thank you, and don't forget Senator Yarborough, Congressman Casey, Congressman Thomas, and if you can, you put in a vote for Hubert Humphrey and Lyndon Johnson, too.

NOTE: The President spoke on the grounds of the First Pasadena State Bank in Pasadena, Tex. His opening words referred to Representative Bob Casey, Representative and Mrs. Albert Thomas, and Senator and Mrs. Ralph Yarborough, all of Texas.

The text of remarks of Mrs. Johnson and daughter Luci, both of whom spoke briefly, was also released.

763 Remarks at the State Capitol in Austin, Texas. *November 2, 1964*

Governor Connally, Congressman Pickle, my old friend and your able Congressman who is making such an effective imprint in Washington:

Jake Pickle has again put me in his debt tonight by the wonderful leadership that he has given to this meeting. I want to tell you how proud all of us in Washington who love Texas are of Jake and Beryl for the fine contribution they are making in the Nation's Capital.

I can never repay, but I can always be grateful, for that dear friend, that loyal ally, through thick and thin, through right and wrong, for more than 25 years, the beloved and the able and great Governor of this State, John Connally.

I am proud that I can say to the people of my home State tonight that the senior Senator from Texas has been an unwavering supporter and a dedicated fighter for the President's program in the United States Senate from top to bottom.

I am grateful to the able Lieutenant Governor of this State for honoring me by his presence on this platform, and I appreciate his dedicated service to the people of the Lone Star State.

For many years I have enjoyed a warm personal friendship with your brilliant young Attorney General, and I thank him for coming here tonight with his charming wife to welcome us.

Mayor Palmer, I think you started something when you made this Lyndon Johnson Day in Austin and John extended it to Texas. If it is without objection from the crowd, I will just make it Lyndon Johnson Day in the entire Nation tomorrow.

One thing that distinguishes the Democratic Party, or at least did until recently, from the other party, is that we didn't always see everything alike within our party, and we reserved the right to be independent. There is no more independent delegation in the country than the Texas delegation. But when the chips are down and when you need them, and the going gets rough, and the enemy gets tough, the first ones I look to are these boys from Texas.

Old Tom O'Brien, the dean of the Chicago delegation, came over to the Senate one time and said, "I have to get a little private bill passed." And I told him how difficult it would be to pass it.

He said, "Let me tell you something. I have been in the House for 30 years. Mr. Rayburn has been sitting up there as Speaker and just when the roll call gets tight he motions that little finger and says, 'Tom, come up here to the desk.' And he leans over and whispers, 'Tom, get those Chicago fellows in line.' And I always got Chicago in line. Now, I want Texas to get in line and help us."

Well, now, once in a while I have to say to these Congressmen from Texas, "Fellows, please help us get in line here. There is a little heavy lifting to do."

I want to express publicly my deep appreciation for their devoted service to this State. Even though sometimes they have disagreed with me, they have always tried to be helpful and have been responsible largely for such success as I have enjoyed in the 11 months and 11 days I have been President. That is Congressman George Mahon, who has come all the way from Lubbock, the Chairman of the House Appropriations Committee; my friends Bob Poage and "Tiger" Teague and John Young; and my dear daddy's friend Wright Patman, and my friend for many years.

My father told me when I went to Washington 27 years ago and caught that train down at the station, and I got up on it, the last thing he told me was, "Son, when you get ready to vote and you are in doubt, and there will be times when you are in doubt and you don't know whether to say yes or no, and they start calling the roll, just pass and wait until Wright Patman votes and then vote like he does, because I was his deskmate in the House of Representatives and he always voted for the people."

I want to particularly thank my friend Hunter McLean, who has been a devoted friend for many years and made many sacrifices for me. He used to limit himself to the Fort Worth district, but now the assignment is getting a little more difficult and he has had to take in all Texas. I don't know, if things don't go as well as we expect them to tomorrow, we may have to ask him to help us in the Nation.

I appreciate all the wives of the officials here tonight, particularly Nellie coming and lending charm and grace to this platform, and bringing back memories of many years, and the presence of Mrs. Yarborough, Mrs. Connally, Mrs. Pickle, and the others.

I came home to this city tonight. It is the city I love, and I wanted to be with the people I love on the night before. As I came up to the stage tonight, I saw a good many people that came out to my house one Sunday afternoon and asked me to run for Congress. One of them is Miller Ainsworth, from Luling, just standing here at the edge of the platform.

You are among my oldest and closest friends. I cannot say, but I think you will know, what is in my heart tonight. Whatever I am, whatever I have to offer my country, you are a part of it.

I don't think you will want and I don't think you would expect a campaign speech tonight, for the campaign is really over. I have been in 44 States, and Lady Bird, Lynda, and Luci have been in 49. Tonight I can look back with you and I hope look ahead.

If it is America's decision tomorrow that I maintain her trust, the days ahead will go forward as they have ever since I came to Austin 30 years ago.

All of these years have been in preparation for this responsibility.

It was here in Austin that I first learned that America is many people, from many countries, speaking many languages, many colors, with many different ideas, but moving always closer and closer together. And ever since, I have built my public life on the conviction that progress depends heavily on the narrowing of differences.

I do not accept Government as just the "art of the practicable." It is the business of deciding what is right and then finding the way to do it.

Usually the way is to get rid of the underbrush of misunderstanding, because most people want the same things and dream the same dreams. More and more as I have traveled in the world and as I have traveled around this land I am sure that this is as true around the globe as it was 30 years ago here in Austin. We will have peace when we can get the world's nations to understand each other as well as the people in those nations do.

It was here that I first learned with you in the days of the depression that failure is man's fault—and that he can repair that failure.

It was here, as a barefoot boy around my daddy's desk in that great hall of the House of Representatives where he served for six terms and where my grandfather served ahead of him, that I first learned that government is not an enemy of the people. It is the people.

The only attacks that I have resented in this campaign are the charges which are based on the idea that the Presidency is something apart from the people, opposed to them, against them.

I learned here, when I was the NYA administrator, that poverty and ignorance are the only basic weaknesses of a free society, and that both of them are only bad habits and can be stopped.

I learned here that the only honest government is a frugal government, and that a public servant can be both thrifty and progressive.

It is not a matter of reducing public service. It is a matter of reducing public waste.

I did not mean to speak so personally.

A very different part of history is heavy on my mind tonight. I want to complete here tonight a journey that was cut short 11

months and 11 days ago. On that tragic morning when John Kennedy was coming to Austin, he carried with him a speech that he intended to deliver here that night.

He would have said then, and so I am going to say it for him now:

"This country is moving and it must not stop. It cannot stop. For this is a time of courage and a time for challenge. Neither conformity nor complacency will do. Neither the fanatics nor the faint-hearted are needed. And our duty as a party is not to our party alone, but to the Nation, and, indeed to all mankind. Our duty is not merely the preservation of political power but the preservation of peace and freedom.

"So let us not be petty when our cause is so great. . . . Let us stand together with renewed confidence in our cause—united in our heritage of the past and our hopes for the future—and determined that this land we love shall lead all mankind on to the frontiers of peace and abundance."

Those words were President Kennedy's words and they are etched on our minds and in our history by the acid of tragedy, and the ideals that they set forth will be that much stronger for it.

And now we look ahead. For those who look backward to the past will surely lose their future.

Tomorrow is a fateful day for our Nation and for the world.

Its prize will not be the Presidency. It will be progress for America, and it will be peace for the world.

Around the world tonight, millions watch and wait. A stillness is on the earth tonight, in London and in Moscow, in Peking and in Cuba, in humble huts and in mighty palaces around the world. Yes, millions enslaved and millions free await to hear your decision tomorrow. On that decision rests our future, and largely theirs, and the future of our children, and largely theirs.

And if it is my lot to serve my Nation further, I will say simply, as I did when I took that oath in Dallas 11 months and 11 days ago: "With God's help and yours, I will just do the best I can."

Beyond that, I want to add only that it seems to me tonight here in Austin, the great capital of this great State, that I have spent my life getting ready for this moment.

So have we all.

The rest is only dedication.

But before I say good night, and go up to the little place where I was born on the banks of the Pedernales, I want to tell you that I am thinking of many who are here tonight and thinking how rich I am in your friendship. I am thinking of many who are not here, like Governor Allred who used to be over there, Mayor Miller that used to be down there, Mr. Perry that used to be out here, Dr. Givens who used to be over there—I could spend all night reminiscing, but I won't.

But I do have the good fortune to have been blessed with the greatest family that any man could have. And I want each one of them, in case something ever happens to me, to have the friendship that I have had, because there is nothing that is as rewarding, there is nothing that is as enriching, there is nothing that gives man's life the fulfillment as the bonds of understanding that exist between you and me.

Lady Bird started out with me here in Austin 30 years ago, and 10 years later Lynda came along, and then in 3 or 4 years, Luci.

Against my advice, Lady Bird got on the train and went all through the South and made 49 speeches in 8 or 10 Southern States. She came to see the people that she was raised with, and saw the people that she loved, and she also saw some ugly signs along the route and she heard some ugly things. But she went direct to them, face to face.

Little Luci has been in 22 States and she came back the other day and said, "Daddy, I have been in the Dakotas and Nebraska this weekend and I haven't had a single free weekend since last May. Do you think that is right for a 17-year-old?" Well, she is going to have a free weekend, thank the Lord, if the good Lord is willing and the creeks don't rise, this weekend.

And Lynda has been all the way from Hawaii to New York City, and everywhere she has gone she has carried the story of Texas. She has left your footprints somewhere around the line.

So if you will just indulge us 3 or 4 more minutes, I want them to say hello to you. I will start out with Lady Bird and let her introduce the others. In the meantime, I won't be back, but God bless you and I love you all.

[*At this point Mrs. Johnson spoke. "November and Austin have been for the Johnsons inseparable through the years," she said, "so there was no question in our mind when we planned where we would be spending election eve. It was sure to be right here with you." There were many there, she felt sure, who would remember "27 years ago when Lyndon's name first appeared on the ballot in Texas." She concluded by expressing appreciation for the faith and support of their friends over the years. Following Mrs. Johnson's remarks, daughters Lynda and Luci spoke briefly. The President then resumed speaking.*]

Now let's go home and have a good night's sleep and pray for each other and get up and go vote early in the morning the Democratic ticket from the courthouse to the White House.

Thank you.

NOTE: The President spoke at 10 p.m. in front of the State Capitol Building in Austin, Tex. In his opening words he referred to Governor John B. Connally and Representative J. J. Pickle, of Texas. Later he referred to Mrs. J. J. (Beryl) Pickle, Senator Ralph Yarborough, senior U.S. Senator from Texas,

Lieutenant Governor Preston Smith, Attorney General Waggoner Carr, Mayor Lester A. Palmer of Austin, all of Texas, and former Representative Thomas J. O'Brien of Illinois. He also referred to, among others, Representatives George H. Mahon, W. R. Poage, Olin E. Teague, John Young, and Wright Patman, of Texas, Hunter McLean, Texas State coordinator for the Johnson-Humphrey campaign, Mrs. John B. (Nellie) Connally, Mrs. Ralph Yarborough, Miller Ainsworth of Luling, Tex., James V. Allred, Governor of Texas, 1935–1939, Tom Miller, former mayor of Austin, Edgar H. Perry, and Dr. Everett Givens of Austin.

764 Radio and Television Address to the American People on Election Eve. *November 2, 1964*

My fellow Americans:

I am here in the White House with Mrs. Johnson and Lynda and Luci.

In a little while Mrs. Johnson and I will go to Texas to vote and to await the election returns. It is appropriate that the White House should be empty tomorrow, for you will be selecting the man who will live here for the next 4 years. Whatever your decision, I want to thank all of you for the support that you have given me.

Eleven months and eleven days ago I came to you and asked your help. You gave me your wisdom and your strength and together we made this a year of memorable achievements. I would like to think that John Kennedy tonight knows how hard we have tried to measure up to his expectations.

But tonight I come to you on a different basis. I ask the renewal of your trust, not in a dark hour of tragedy, but on your confidence in my ability to be an instrument of America's purpose.

I have campaigned across this country—in 44 States—discussing the issues, learning from your views. Lady Bird has been my closest and most valuable campaigner. And I want her to tell you something of her impressions of the last few weeks.

[*At this point Mrs. Johnson spoke briefly. The President then resumed speaking.*]

My fellow Americans, election day is both a time of renewal and a time of decision. You will renew the most solemn sacrament of democracy—the consent of the governed from which the just powers of government derive.

You will choose the President of the United States.

We take for granted this right of ours. But what a really remarkable thing it is!

Our forefathers established the great experiment of democracy in a world where government by the governed had been extinguished for 2,000 years. Few thought that we could succeed. But we did succeed. And the light of that success now illuminates much of the world.

Your privilege of self-government has been granted to only the tiniest fraction of all those who have ever lived on earth. Your vote is a victory and a vindication for all those in every age who suffered for the ideal of democracy. Treasure it. Take pride in it, and use it.

For more than a generation this Nation has held a steady and consistent course.

I remember when I first came to Washington 32 years ago. The people who sent me to Congress were poor people. Many were hungry. But I soon saw they were only a few of the victims of a stricken land. Their recovery would only come as the entire Nation recovered and grew strong.

I watched, and sometimes I helped a little,

as America forged, in the bitterness of common disaster, a new partnership between Government and business and farmers and workers.

And I watched, and sometimes helped, as a compassionate Nation built new protection for the helpless and the needy.

Those measures have endured these 30 years. Most of all the principles have endured. Each part of our society—Government and private—has accepted its responsibility to work within the framework of the common welfare. In this way we have increased the abundance of all.

Over the years we have built on these principles. No President of either party has ever renounced them or called for their destruction. They are the basis of our present prosperity, they are our hope for future abundance.

I ask each of you to pause for a moment tonight in your homes, with your families by your side, and ask yourself if these principles have not enlarged your freedom, enriched your life, and strengthened your confidence in your children's future. It is hard to believe that we should now be asked to throw them all away.

Yet today, these principles are all under attack. We are now told that every responsible leader of both parties has been wrong, and that the American people have been wrong to support them.

We are asked to dissolve the partnership between Government and people. We are asked to cut away the protections for the old and the helpless.

We are told to end social security as we have known it and as every President has supported it. Time and time and time again they have called for a voluntary program. But payments out to older Americans depend on premiums coming in from working Americans. A voluntary program would drastically reduce such payments since workers would no longer have to pay. The system, I think, would soon be on the edge of bankruptcy. And such a program is simply, I believe, an indirect way to destroy our whole social security system.

And almost every other program, from TVA to education to REA, is embraced in this unprecedented and wholesale assault.

Let us be clear. This is not a return to the past. It is not an effort to even preserve the status quo. It is an intention to shatter the tested foundation of our economy. And it will bring disaster.

Nor does this attack on our continuing traditions stop at the water's edge.

For much of our history the office of President has been the center of the Nation. Twenty years ago it became the center of the world. In these two decades since, four Presidents—of each party—have woven the common fabric of American world responsibility.

We are now told that in foreign affairs, as well, the responsible leaders of the past have been wrong. The American people have been wrong to support them. And the free world has been wrong to welcome our leadership.

We are told to regard as fruitless the search for lasting agreements, such as the test ban treaty.

We are attacked for our restraint in the use of our mighty power.

We are told to ignore or discard the great dream of the United Nations.

We are told that tactical nuclear weapons are simply a new kind of conventional explosive.

If these views prevail, if we abandon the proven principles of both parties, I have no doubt that our hopes for peace and the cause of freedom will be in serious peril.

Let there be no mistake. There is no check or protection against error or foolhardiness by the President of the United States. He, alone, makes basic decisions which can lead us toward peace or toward mounting danger. In his hands is the power which can lay waste in hours a civilization that it took a thousand years to build.

In your hands is the decision to choose the man that you will entrust with this responsibility for your survival.

These are some of the elements of the basic choice that you must make tomorrow.

Shall we move forward, innovating where necessary, but building on the programs and the policies that are nourished by progressive men of both parties?

Or shall we strip the house to the foundation, throw aside the work of decades, discard the wisdom of a generation of trusted leaders, and strike off in an uncertain and, I believe, a deeply dangerous direction?

Your vote will make that choice.

But if you fail to vote, you will also make a choice. If you and your neighbor disagree and if he votes while you stay home, you have increased the importance of his vote. You will influence the election but in a way that is opposite to your own beliefs.

I believe in the importance of a healthy two-party system. But that will be best restored by an overwhelming repudiation of the small minority which has seized the Republican Party and is already planning to keep it. Only a massive defeat can drive them from their places of present power.

I wish with all my heart that this had been another kind of campaign. I wish it had been possible to debate the path to our future rather than the wisdom of our past.

That future has many challenges.

We must work to extend increasing abundance to all our people.

But we have also learned that man does not live by bread alone. The satisfactions of life cannot be measured just by the size of a salary check. Jefferson did not dream, or Lincoln suffer, or Roosevelt toil so that future Americans would live in overcrowded cities—without a decent school for his children—afraid to walk his streets—shut off from trees and grass—breathing poisoned air by the side of polluted rivers—fearful that a machine might destroy his security.

We have the resources and the knowledge to move away from these dim threatening valleys into the broad, sunlit uplands of a nation which is fulfilling the values of its past through a search for greatness in its future.

Let us, tomorrow, rise up by the million and the tens of millions. Let us cast out those views that are so dangerously removed from the real concerns and passions of this exciting time in which we live.

Then we can bind up the Nation's wounds, draw together men of good will, unite those of every pursuit and party. Then we can do battle with the huge army of the world's desires. Then we can go together into that uncertain day already touched with dawn.

This will be our choice, in our election, in our country. But in Moscow and Paris, in New Delhi and Rio, men will also wait tomorrow. Whether they wish us well or ill, they know that the peace of the world and the freedom of man will rest, in large measure, on our leadership.

What Longfellow once wrote is as meaningful for us today, I think, as it was then. I hope you will carry it in your memory tomorrow.

"Sail on, O ship of State!
Sail on, O Union, strong and great!
Humanity with all its fears,
With all the hopes of future years,
Is hanging—breathless—on thy fate!"

Thank you, my fellow countrymen, good night, and God bless you.

NOTE: The President's remarks were video-taped in the Diplomatic Reception Room at the White House at 1:45 p.m. on November 2 for broadcast at 10 o'clock that evening.

765   Radio and Television Remarks to the American People at the Close of Election Day.   *November 4, 1964*

My fellow countrymen:

No words are adequate to really express the feeling of this occasion. Most of all, I wish to be equal to your confidence, and to the hopes of all of the people of America. We have voted as many, but tonight we must face the world as one.

To our great Governor, my friend of a quarter of a century, to my loyal wife and two daughters who have stood by me so steadfastly through all of these trials of many weeks, to every worker in every block in the land, to the people of both parties, and especially to you good people here in my home who have been so patient and understanding all the years, and who made it possible to have the decision that was made today, I say thank you.

I know that I was only one of many, because we had a group of outstanding candidates throughout the Nation, and we had men of independent views and men and women of both parties who put their country before their party. Now, tonight, our purpose must be to bind up our wounds, to heal our history, and to make this Nation whole.

I know that this is more than a victory of party or person.

It is a tribute to the program that was begun by our beloved President John F. Kennedy—a program that he carried on until he was taken from us.

It is visible evidence of the work of a devoted and unselfish Cabinet, men like Dean Rusk, Bob McNamara, and Douglas Dillon, and all of the other members of the Cabinet and the independent agencies whose service has not been partisan, but has always been in the national interest.

It is a tribute to the men and women of all parties in the Congress and the Nation.

It reaffirms the achievements and the policies which have emerged over generations from common American principles.

It is a mandate for unity, for a government that serves no special interest, no business government, no labor government, no farm government, no one faction, no one group, but a government that is the servant of all the people.

It will be a government that provides equal opportunity for all and special privilege for none. It is a command to build on those principles and to move forward toward peace and a better life for all of our people.

So from this night forward, this is to be our work, and in these pursuits I promise the best that is in me for as long as I am permitted to serve. I ask all those who supported me and all those that opposed me to forget our differences, because there are many more things in America that unite us than divide us, and these are times when our Nation should forget our petty differences and stand united before all the world.

I would like to leave you tonight with the words of Abraham Lincoln, as a century ago he left his friends and neighbors to become President of the United States. He said, "Without the assistance of that Divine Being who ever attended him, I cannot succeed. With that assistance I cannot fail. . . . To His care commending you, as I hope in your prayers you will commend me, I bid you an affectionate farewell."

I do not know what happened in every hamlet or voting box in America today, but I think I discerned what happened in all America today. I doubt that there has ever been so many people seeing so many things alike on "decision" day. And with that understanding and with the help of all of them, we will be on our way to try to achieve peace in our time for our people and to try to keep our people prosperous.

So to all of you that have gone this long road with me, particularly to the press and television people who have worked 18-hour days for many weeks now, I say I hope you have a good rest tomorrow.

Good night to all of you, and thanks to all America.

[At this point Mrs. Johnson and daughters Lynda and Luci spoke briefly. The President then resumed speaking.]

And now I want to tell you that we have **a great event in store** for all of you: The happy warrior, the eloquent spokesman for the Democratic Party, the new Vice President of the United States, is arriving tomorrow at noon, and in his honor and in the honor of the men and women who traveled with us in this campaign, we are going to have a barbecue out on the banks of the Pedernales.

I knew in Atlantic City that I had made the right recommendation to that convention so far as the Vice President was concerned, because I had observed him very closely ever since I became a Member of the Senate, but in the weeks that have followed that convention, I know even more that in my heart I was right.

Hubert Humphrey left that convention with no orders and no instructions, and he traveled to 40 States and made no mistakes. Everywhere he went the people received him warmly and applauded his pronouncements. I predict that he, aided by his charming wife, Muriel, and their lovely family, will make one of the greatest Vice Presidents that this Nation has ever known.

Thank you very much.

NOTE: The President spoke at 1:40 a.m. in the Municipal Auditorium in Austin, Tex. The text of the remarks of Mrs. Johnson, Lynda, and Luci was also released.

766   Remarks by Telephone for Ceremonies Marking the 50th Anniversary of the Port of Houston.   *November 10, 1964*

Ladies and gentlemen:

I am very proud to participate in these ceremonies in this way, both as President of the United States and as a former resident and a longtime admirer of the city of Houston.

Back in the early 1930's when Houston was my home, I remember there were those

who were skeptical of the value of the ship channel. Today we know that the vision was not too great as some said then, but was, if anything, too small. Many factors have contributed to Houston's growth and the growth of our great gulf coast. No one factor can be singled out for individual credit, but we all know that the reality and the symbolism of the ship channel project had much to do with moving the entire area forward.

There is another factor worthy of mention. In Houston and all along the coast, the industrial growth evident day to day has come almost entirely from products and processes that were unknown even 30 years ago. Our times are marked by the most rapid expansion and explosion of human knowledge ever known. We cannot know what the future will bring, but we do know that we can and that we must put in place the foundation on which that growth can rise in orderly fashion.

Houston, I am proud to say, is still looking ahead and planning ahead, and so is your country. It is my hope that throughout America we can get down to the business of building for a stronger and a more prosperous future by doing the work that will un-

lock opportunity for all regions of our Nation.

We have great challenges ahead, abroad and at home. I discussed some of them this morning with the Secretary of State and the Secretary of Defense. There is no question of our ability to meet them if we will work to keep the peace and if we will work to pave the way for progress of all our people in all sections of the Nation.

On the 50 years past, you have my congratulations; on the 50 years ahead, you have the Nation's confidence. Houston's destiny and America's destiny is greatness, and that greatness will be fulfilled by the faith we place in our responsible vision.

Now I am happy to press this button to start the construction of Houston's new horizon of expansion in enterprise and progress.

NOTE: The President spoke by telephone from the LBJ Ranch, Johnson City, Tex.

767   Remarks of Welcome at the LBJ Ranch to the President-Elect of Mexico. *November 12, 1964*

Señor and Señora Diaz Ordaz, Governor and Mrs. Connally, Governor and Mrs. Brown, distinguished guests, my friends:

I should like to, before I make a few very brief observations, introduce some of our most honored guests who thrill us by their presence here today.

First of all, I want to introduce the distinguished Ambassador from Mexico, Ambassador Carrillo Flores; and our distinguished Ambassador to Mexico, Ambassador Freeman; one of the truly great American public servants, our own Tom Mann, Assistant Secretary of State from Laredo, Tex.

It gives me a great deal of pleasure to introduce to you one of the men who served Texas probably longer than any other Gov-

ernor, the Honorable Allan Shivers, Governor of Texas; and the Honorable John Burroughs, former Governor of New Mexico; and Judge Reynaldo Garza, from Brownsville; our distinguished Secretary of Agriculture, Mr. John White; our own able and popular Congressman, Henry B. Gonzalez.

And this is one fellow that we really wanted to see come in, Congressman and soon-to-be-Senator Joe Montoya—and maybe already Senator; I am not sure. A longtime friend, Congressman Kika de la Garza.

We welcome here today to this peaceful Texas hill country President-elect Diaz Ordaz and his lovely, gracious wife.

Mr. President, I have not discussed this matter with you, but as one who has just finished a campaign, and will be installed formally in my office 1 month and 20 days after your inauguration, I can only say that it is much more cheering here after a campaign than before one.

Mr. President, I am pleased to tell you that I received no support from anyone that was greater, or perhaps more unanimous, with warmth, than that given me by the many thousands of Americans of Mexican ancestry who live in the United States of America.

And so today, at the end of the long, long trail, after more than 44 States, Mr. President, I speak the beautiful sound of the words I heard so often throughout America, "Mr. President, viva México."

It is part of the feeling of kinship between the great Republic of Mexico and the United States that the two Presidents should meet and should talk and should counsel and should be friends. Our border is long and it is friendly. We have no armed men on either side patrolling the river. So it is our tradition to be neighbors.

Mr. President, you and I share common purposes and similar objectives for both of our countries. Our countries are enjoying today very prosperous times. We want them to keep that way.

Both our countries look to the other country for tourists and for travel, and we want to keep it that way.

Trade between our two countries is at an alltime high level, more than $1½ billion in 1963. But you and I are meeting here to discuss ways and means to increase that trade, and we have already begun the explorations this morning.

But you and I are never going to be satisfied with the course of either of our countries as long as there is a single man who wants to work and cannot find work; so long as there is a single child without a school or a teacher; and so long as there is a single family without a home.

So we are meeting here to talk together and to work together, and to take up arms together against the ancient enemies of mankind—disease and poverty and hunger and ignorance. So, Mr. President, in all that you do and in all that I do we try to preserve the freedom of our people, to protect the treasures of our society, and to always enhance the dignity of our people.

In both of our countries we seek to give everyone an opportunity to achieve his highest aspirations. We have found in your country and in mine that if we give our people the incentive to invest their energy and their income, we can achieve much higher rates of economic growth.

Mr. President, we both know that it is not our vast resources or even our geography, or even our arms that have made our nations great. The thing that has made them great has been the genius of our people and the political and most importantly the economic systems that our people have created.

Americans have invested in Mexico, and we think we have contributed greatly to Mexico's growth.

Many billions have been invested in this country, the United States, by wise and by good and by thrifty and honorable people from many other nations in this world in which we live, and both of our countries have been the beneficiaries.

As Mexico becomes stronger and wealthier, Mexico will be able to help others just as Mexico is helping others today in Central America. For, Mr. President, the alliance is not just governments; it is the will and the desire and the noble ambition of people— people who give opportunity and incentive, and they can make this Western Hemisphere and, indeed, they can make the entire world, a better, a healthier, a more peaceful, and a much safer place to live in.

We have problems. We are here to discuss them. And in the days ahead we will resolve them in peace, with reason, with justice to each other.

So, Mr. President, it gives me and Mrs. Johnson the greatest of pleasure to welcome you here today and to welcome your lovely, gracious wife. You make us very proud to be in our home and on our land and to have you in our presence. As they say it so beautifully in your land, your country, where 30 years ago my lady and I spent our honeymoon, we say to you today, *mi casa es su casa*.

Ladies and gentlemen, the President-elect of Mexico, Diaz Ordaz.

[*At this point President-elect Diaz Ordaz spoke. The President then resumed speaking.*]

Eighty percent of the Americans of Mexican ancestry that live in the United States of America live in the largest State in the Union from the standpoint of population—California—and the once largest State in the Union from the standpoint of area—Texas. We are highly honored today to have the two great leaders of those two great States come here and lend dignity by their presence.

I want to remind all of you that a few weeks ago we started out a long campaign in Atlantic City, and these two great Governors started with me and finished with me. It is my great honor to present the Chief Executive of the great State of California, Pat Brown, and his lovely wife, Bernice Brown.

And I know that all Texans share with me the pride and affection that we all feel for our own beloved and able and honored Governor, John Connally and his darling wife Nellie. John said he is just glad that the election is behind him. All he wants to say is thanks to everybody, and so do we. Thank you all for coming.

NOTE: The President spoke at 3:25 p.m. at a barbecue at the LBJ Ranch at Johnson City, Tex. In his opening words he referred to President-elect and Señora Gustavo Diaz Ordaz of Mexico, Governor and Mrs. John B. Connally of Texas, and Governor and Mrs. Edmund G. Brown of California. Later in his remarks he referred to Antonio Carrillo Flores, Ambassador to the United States from Mexico, Fulton Freeman, Ambassador to Mexico from the United States, and Thomas C. Mann, Assistant Secretary of State for Inter-American Affairs, United States Coordinator for the Alliance for Progress, and Special Assistant to the President for Inter-American Affairs. He also referred to former Governor Allan Shivers, Reynaldo G. Garza, U.S. district judge of the Southern District, State Secretary of Agriculture John C. White, U.S. Representative Henry B. Gonzalez, and U.S. Representative-elect Eligio (Kika) de la Garza, of Texas, and to former Governor John Burroughs and U.S. Representative Joseph M. Montoya, of New Mexico.

The text of the remarks of President-elect Diaz Ordaz follows:

Mr. President, Mrs. Johnson, officials and friends:

First of all, I want to express to you my deep satisfaction in being able to visit you as a representative of my people and receive the overwhelming hospitality that has been given to me by the Johnson family.

I am very happy to be here and spend these hours with you in this beautiful place, and I am especially grateful to President Johnson and the distinguished First Lady because they did not issue to me a cordial invitation to visit them in their official residence, but rather, were good enough to invite me so that we could be together in the sweet intimacy of their home, the place where they come to rest.

This I want you to know is a tremendous honor both for Mrs. Diaz Ordaz and myself, and something for which I am profoundly grateful. This visit of mine to you has a specific purpose which is to establish a personal knowledge between President Johnson and myself. We are two men who have the greatest responsibilities entrusted to us by our respective people.

It is vitally important that President Johnson and I, as heads of our two respective Governments, be able to know each other personally so we can work together in the future to solve any existing problems and any possible problem that might arise in the relations between our two countries.

So I am here to seal a friendship with a warm handshake with President Johnson from me and the Mexican people, and to him and through him to the American people. I hope and I know that we will be able to work together with reciprocal respect and joint cooperation to maintain the principles that have inspired our two peoples.

Our own history is not a brilliant one in that we have obtained spectacular victories, but it is a history that we cherish because throughout the years, at the cost of great sacrifice and great effort, we have won our independence, we have won the freedom of our people, and we are working to increase the prosperity of the people of Mexico. I can assure you that in the future, all the men and women of Mexico are going to redouble their efforts to maintain our freedoms, to maintain our independence, and to increase the well-being of all of our citizens.

It is a pleasure for me to come here to restate and reiterate the bonds of friendship that unite our great people. It is sometimes easy to be friends from a distance, but it is also very difficult, sometimes, to be friends with your neighbors, and this is a friendship that we have achieved.

We have a long border, a very long border, which does not divide us but, rather, brings us together, and we have come here today, crossing this border, in order to study some of the problems that have come up and to be able to work them out together.

Mexico and the United States have given an example in just the past few weeks of how one of the most powerful nations in the history of the world has yielded to justice with a country which economically and militarily is very weak by solving this very old problem on the basis of fairness and reason and justice. This could well be a lesson that we could give to people throughout the world who want to be friends, one with another. This is what we have come here to reinforce and to strengthen, the example that we have given in the solution of this problem.

Our relationships have been friendly and warm for many years and have grown to this state in spite of the adverse conditions that have existed at one time or another. But we have now found bonds of friendship and of closeness that unite us and have become very great friends and neighbors with the people of the United States.

As I was saying, we have shown to people throughout the world how differences can be eliminated through mutual respect, through the sharing of common ideals, through good faith, and with a spirit of justice. I say to you, Mr. President, and through you to the people of the United States, that I come extending the hand of friendship from the Mexican people that I am honored to represent during the next presidential period.

I want to come to you and speak to you with the same frankness and fairness and nobility of spirit that has always characterized the exchanges between our two peoples, and I know as you said a while ago that neither you nor I nor our people will rest as long as there is a family in this hemisphere that does not have a roof over its head or bread to eat, as long as there are any children that have no schools to attend, as long as there are any ill people that have no medical attention to take care of their ills.

We will continue to work together on the basis of this personal contact we are making here in these hours that we will be together, on the basis of reciprocal respect, one for another, to fight very strongly and energetically together to keep the peace of the world, to fight with equal energy and strength to maintain all of the freedoms of our respective peoples. That relationship is going to be based on democracy which, in turn, is going to be based on all of our freedoms.

Thank you very much for your kindness.

768 The President's Toast to Gustavo Diaz Ordaz, President-Elect of Mexico. *November 12, 1964*

Mr. President-elect, Señora:

Mrs. Johnson and I want you to know how proud and how happy we are to have you in our home.

Mexico and the United States share more than a common frontier. We share a set of ideals and a sense of the future. I pray that the mutual respect and friendship which is rooted deep in the conscience of both our countries will grow and endure.

We are friends. We must remain friends.

We honor each other's hopes, and we seek honorable agreements between our nations.

On December 1, Mr. President-elect, you will assume the heavy duties and responsibilities as the leader of your country. I propose a simple toast: to the President-elect of Mexico and his charming wife—may Mexico prosper in peace under your leadership.

NOTE: The President proposed the toast at a dinner at the LBJ Ranch at Johnson City, Tex.

769   Statement by the President in Response to Report of the
      Inter-American Committee on the Alliance for Progress.
      November 13, 1964

THE Inter-American Committee on the Alliance for Progress—called CIAP from the Spanish initials—has completed the first cycle of its work. In the year since it was created it has reviewed the development efforts of each of the countries of Latin America under the alliance. Its report measures both the internal resources and efforts and the foreign assistance which, together, must support these development efforts.

This report will be forwarded to the Lima meeting of the Inter-American Economic and Social Council which begins on November 30. CIAP's report, and the meetings of the experts and ministerial representatives of all the nations of the Inter-American system at Lima, suggest an appropriate opportunity for me to renew our support of the Alliance for Progress.

Firm and continued support for the principles of the Charter of Punta del Este is the central theme of all we do in the hemisphere. The United States considers itself a partner with the peoples of Latin America. Theirs is a struggle to create a new future, a better way of life, in which each human being of the hemisphere may reach his own full potential. We are proud to say that we will continue to play our part by support and participation in the work of the CIAP.

We are encouraged in this by developments in the hemisphere during the last year.

All the problems of the Alliance for Progress have not of course been solved in the rapid unfolding of events in 1964. Obstacles are still before us—obstacles which all nations of the hemisphere must bend their efforts to overcome.

There must be peaceful changes in the countryside, in order to bring full social justice to the poor who work the lands, to increase the production of food and fiber to feed the rapidly growing population of Latin America and expand markets for the burgeoning industries of the hemisphere.

There must be improved revenue systems in the administration of taxes. Nations afflicted by the disease of inflation must carry forward their programs to bring stability to their currencies.

We must continue and improve planning efforts so that scarce public resources available for investment and development can be directed to the needs of highest priority and in order that the changes of national policy essential to growth be identified and instituted. The efforts and will of all the peoples of America in these and other fields—labor, health, housing and urban planning, cooperatives, community development, national budgeting, water and sewerage, education, transportation, public administration—can build the new hemisphere toward which we all aspire.

We must release the energies and resources of the private sector for growth through cooperatives, through democratic, free trade unions, through community organizations and citizen groups and private business and industry. Development and growth are not a matter solely of governments. The energies of all the people must contribute.

There must be a full effort to expand the range of economic opportunities within Latin America, by creating and strengthening national markets in each nation and by further progress under the Central America Common Market and the Latin America Free Trade Area. At the same time, all the nations of the free world trading community—including the United States—must make special efforts to improve the conditions of international trade.

There is a quickened interest by the nations of Europe, by Japan and by Canada, in Latin America. We look forward to a greater and more closely coordinated participation by all members of the industrialized free world in the economic, social, and political development efforts of Latin America.

I congratulate the efforts of Dr. Carlos Sanz de Santamaría and the members of CIAP. I have on a number of occasions met with him, and from time to time, with the ambassadors of our alliance partner nations and the members of CIAP. As all officials of our Government know, and as I have said often in the past, I regard the work of the CIAP as deserving of our sincere support.

NOTE: The "Report of the Inter-American Committee on the Alliance for Progress (CIAP) Presented to the Third Annual Meetings of the Inter-American Economic and Social Council" is dated November 14, 1964 (Pan American Union, General Secretariat of the Organization of American States, Washington, D.C., processed, 179 pp., CIES/621).

For remarks of the President to the members of the Inter-American Committee, which met in Washington October 26–31, see Item 726.

The statement was released at Austin, Tex.

770 Proclamation 3627: Thanksgiving Day. *November 13, 1964*

By the President of the United States of America a Proclamation:

As the harvest season draws to a close and our storehouses bulge with the bounty of the land, it is our desire to observe, in the custom and tradition of our forebears, a special day dedicated to giving thanks to God—a day on which to lay aside our daily tasks and cares and pay joyous homage to Him. We are impelled to raise our voices in His praise and to proclaim our heartfelt gratitude for another year in which we have been blessed with a bountiful harvest, with intellectual, humanitarian, economic, scientific, and technical advances and achievements, and with other gains too numerous to mention.

Although we have been blessed with unsurpassed prosperity, we recognize that poverty and want exist throughout the world—even among us—and we pledge ourselves to the eradication of those evils.

We know, too, that the foundation for a peaceful world is still to be built and that even now armed strife exists in parts of the world. We are saddened that gallant men of our Armed Services have fallen in the eternal quest for peace with freedom, dignity, and justice for all. We share with their bereaved families and friends a sense of tragic loss. In the words of Abraham Lincoln, we resolve "that these honored dead shall not have died in vain," and vow that their loss will spur us ever onward until man's great dream of universal peace is realized.

Yet we are filled with an instinctive impulse to give thanks for

—our free society of free men, free institutions, and free elections;

—our freedom of speech, our freedom of the press, and our freedom to worship as our conscience dictates;

—our emphasis upon the dignity, equality, and worth of man;

—our humanitarian instincts;

—our unalienable right to life, liberty, and the pursuit of happiness;

—our confidence in our ability to meet the challenges of today and of the future.

For these are the things that set us apart as a Nation—that made our Nation great—that will keep our Nation great.

So as our forefathers in Virginia, in New England, and throughout this land have done for more than three and one-half centuries, let us appoint a special day on which all of us, in keeping with the dictates of our own conscience, will give thanks to the Lord for His manifold blessings. And on that day, let us rededicate ourselves to meeting the challenges of the present with the fortitude and faith with which our forefathers met the challenges of the past.

Now, THEREFORE, I, LYNDON B. JOHNSON, President of the United States of America, in consonance with the joint resolution of the Congress approved December 26, 1941, 55 Stat. 862 (5 U.S.C. 87b), designating the fourth Thursday of November in each year as Thanksgiving Day, do hereby proclaim Thursday, November 26, 1964, as a day of national thanksgiving.

On that day, let us gather in our homes and in our places of worship and in other suitable places to give thanks to God for His graciousness and His generosity to us—to pledge to Him our everlasting devotion—to beseech His divine guidance and the wisdom and strength to recognize and follow that guidance—and to pray to Him that the forces of evil, violence, indifference, intolerance, and inhumanity may soon vanish from the face of the earth and that peace, reason, understanding, and goodwill may reign supreme throughout the world.

IN WITNESS WHEREOF, I have hereunto set my hand and caused the Seal of the United States of America to be affixed.

DONE at the City of Washington this thirteenth day of November in the year of our Lord nineteen hundred and [SEAL]   sixty-four, and of the Independence of the United States of America the one hundred and eighty-ninth.

LYNDON B. JOHNSON

By the President:
DEAN RUSK
Secretary of State

---

771   Remarks at the Swearing In of Gardner Ackley as Chairman and Arthur Okun as Member of the Council of Economic Advisers. *November 16, 1964*

IT IS a little unusual, Walter, for you to be so much in the background this morning. I want to apologize to you and the Secretary of the Treasury, Gardner, and others for detaining you and your distinguished guests. This is the first morning I have been back in town since my extended vacation. I was delayed by the Secretary of Defense and others who had some problems which needed attention for a moment and I couldn't get away.

I want to thank all of you for coming here. I hardly know whether to scowl or to smile. I can't be happy over Walter Heller's departure from Washington, leaving the Council, and at the same time I am very happy and, of course, couldn't be unhappy over the strength that he has left behind on this Council.

For nearly a year Walter has been consulting with me and a subject at all of those conversations either at the beginning or the end was about his desire to leave public service. I did everything I know that I could do to dissuade him. I didn't want him to pass out of here and go back to his work. I thought if we could get the pay bill through that might stop him, and I did something unusual after the House turned me down the first time—I tried, and tried, and tried again and finally got it through. But it was not the pay that he was really interested in; it was Minnesota. His persistence in getting out of here has caused me to reflect a little the past week about the real condition of our economy.

But for every conversation that Walter and I have had about his leaving, we have had two or three about what he is leaving behind and the quality and the caliber and the character of the men who would constitute the Council of Economic Advisers.

So, the chairmanship of the Council passes today to one of the Nation's most respected economists, one of my most trusted counselors, a man in whom I think the Nation will have the fullest confidence and the man for whom I have great respect and affection, Gardner Ackley.

Coming on to the Council after most distinguished service as a senior member of the Council staff is another outstanding member of the profession, Dr. Arthur Okun. If we can do as well by the Nation as I believe we are doing by the Council, the country is in for the best times that we have ever had over the next several years.

What has been the progress these past 4 years toward fulfillment of the meaning of the act of 1964 which created the Council, I think, is quite important. Over these years, economics has come of age in policy-making in this Government. The American people, I think, have begun to appreciate the need for their Government to manage its budget so that it will work to assure balanced and sustained expansion and not retard our progress.

I think nothing has done more for public understanding than the great tax cut of 1964. In that connection I want to pay tribute to the Council, and I particularly want to pay tribute to that man who has sacrificed so much of his private life for public service, the able and beloved Secretary of the Treasury, Mr. Dillon, who honors us with his presence this morning.

Today, 8 months later, the benefits are clear, and I think they are clearly enormous. Consumers are earning more and they are spending more. Businesses are receiving record profits. Sights have been raised on investments. Unemployment has declined, yet our price stability is intact and our Federal revenues are rising.

Our gains have been many, but we are not about to become satisfied with ourselves.

Unemployment is still far too high. More young people than ever are looking for their first jobs. We have 3,200,000 18-year-olds who want to go to school or want to find a job this year. Educational opportunities, therefore, must be increased.

Our citizens must be enabled to meet more fully their needs. We can do what America needs done only if we can continue with this prosperous economy, and we just cannot have it continued by wanting it to continue. We have got to work at it.

In that connection, there is no one in this Government who is going to carry any heavier responsibility than Gardner Ackley and the Council that he leads and over which he presides. I am going to continue to expect from him what I got from the Council of which he was a member. So I want to assure you that I look to the Council with confidence, knowing the caliber of the leadership of those who have been serving as the leaders and the members. I am particularly going to rely on the fine qualities and discernment of its new and able chairman and its new and able member.

This is a somewhat sad moment for me to see a man leave the White House and go back to his own backyard, but I guess you have to expect those things. The time is here, and I guess the appropriate way to end this up, Walter and Gardner, would be:

"Sunset and evening star,
  And one clear call for me!
And may there be no moaning of the bar,
  When I put out to sea."

NOTE: The President spoke at 12:25 p.m. in the Cabinet Room at the White House. In his opening remarks he referred to Walter W. Heller, outgoing Chairman of the Council of Economic Advisers, who had resigned to return to a professorship at the University of Minnesota, and Douglas Dillon, Secretary of the Treasury.

The text of the remarks of Mr. Ackley, Mr. Heller, and Mr. Okun, each of whom spoke briefly, was also released.

772   Remarks at the Presentation of the White House Thanksgiving Turkey.   *November 17, 1964*

FIRST of all, I want to thank you very much for your thoughtfulness in coming here to the White House today and bringing me a turkey to eat on Thanksgiving. I hadn't been quite sure what I was going to eat Thanksgiving, but I am glad I can eat turkey instead of crow.

You know, Ben Franklin wanted the turkey to be the national symbol. He thought it was much more respectful than the eagle, but we do have the eagle to symbolize our preparedness, our desire for peace in the world, and we do have a lot to be thankful for.

I hope that every family in this land will be able not only to enjoy a bountiful Thanksgiving, because we have so much to be thankful for, but that they will be able to enjoy—with their prayers that I am sure all of them will have for their families, their future, and this country and the freedom that is ours—some good turkey.

We look to the turkey to participate in this great Thanksgiving Day that is a national holiday, when all of us should take time out to thank our Maker and our country for our lands and our families, the bounties and the blessings that are ours.

One thing that I think we must constantly be aware of is that no people anywhere during any period of history have ever had so much to be thankful for as we Americans. Those of you who were thoughtful enough to bring me a turkey to be thankful for, I will tell you I will use that turkey in my Thanksgiving Day participation. All of you good folks—even some of you columnists that get things mixed up sometimes—I am going to use in my prayers.

NOTE: The President spoke at 1:10 p.m. in the Rose Garden at the White House. The traditional presentation of the Thanksgiving Day turkey was made by members of the Poultry and Egg National Board and the National Turkey Federation.

773   Remarks in the Cabinet Room at the Unveiling of a Bust of John F. Kennedy.   *November 19, 1964*

Mrs. Shriver, ladies and gentlemen:

All of us who knew him, loved him, and worked with him here in this historic room are grateful today for the opportunity to display this magnificent bust of President Kennedy. In his thousand days of our leadership, President Kennedy made decisions which will be remembered and respected for a thousand years. Certainly so long as men are free, and so long as they inhabit this planet in peace and in courage and in calmness, October 1962 will be honored.

Through many of those anxious hours when life on this earth was in the balance, John Fitzgerald Kennedy's finest moments were spent here in this room at that table.

I am personally grateful, and I know the Nation will be grateful, to Mrs. Kennedy for giving us the privilege of placing this bust here until it is moved to the John F. Kennedy Memorial Library at Cambridge.

This fine work done by Mr. de Weldon was commissioned by President Kennedy's three military aides, General Clifton, Captain

Shepard, and General McHugh. Fortunately a bronze replica is being shown publicly in the Kennedy Library Exhibit, which is traveling across the Nation, and many Americans will have the opportunity to see this work in that form.

For all of us, the tragic anniversary of this weekend makes this a very sad and sober time. We can here reflect upon the irony that President Kennedy himself had placed in this room a bust of another martyred President, Abraham Lincoln.

As was said of the Great Emancipator, we can say of our friend and our brother and our great leader: He belongs to the ages.

NOTE: The President spoke at 12:10 p.m. in the Cabinet Room at the White House. His opening words referred to Mrs. Sargent Shriver, sister of President Kennedy, who represented the Kennedy family at the unveiling. Following his formal remarks the President read the text of a proclamation "John F. Kennedy, a Rededication," issued on the same day (see Item 774).

The bust, the work of Felix de Weldon of Washington, was commissioned by Maj. Gen. Chester V. Clifton, USA, Capt. Tazewell T. Shepard, Jr., USN, and Brig. Gen. Godfrey T. McHugh, USAF, Aides to President Kennedy, as a gift to Mrs. Kennedy.

774   Proclamation 3629: John F. Kennedy, A Rededication.   *November 19, 1964*

By the President of the United States of America a Proclamation:

In John Kennedy's life he drew guidance from history. In death he has entered and enriched it.

For history is more than the record of man's conflict with nature and himself. It is the knowledge which gives dimension to the present, direction to the future, and humility to the leaders of men. A nation, like a person, not conscious of its own past

is adrift without purpose or protection against the contending forces of dissolution.

Thus America will draw continual strength and direction from his story. And the intensity and love with which we celebrate his greatness will be a measure of our own.

He had one quality which we must now strive to share. He saw the world and its problems in all their fantastic complexity. A thousand blending shades of interest and outlook made up a challenge where difficulty was piled upon difficulty and danger upon danger.

Yet he was unshaken in his faith that man's problems could be solved by man, and in his determination to make the effort.

We too must have the courage to confront complexity, never permitting it to sever the nerve of action or dull the edge of faith.

He had qualities of greatness. But it is among the hazards of fortune whether character will join with circumstances to produce great deeds.

It can be said of him, as Thomas Jefferson said of George Washington: "Never did nature and fortune combine more perfectly to make a man great, and to place him in everlasting remembrance."

Now, THEREFORE, I, LYNDON B. JOHNSON, President of the United States of America, do proclaim Sunday, November twenty-second, 1964, a day of national rededication.

On that day, let the word go forth, to friend and foe alike, that the vision of John F. Kennedy still guides the Nation which was the source and the object of his greatness.

In churches and homes everywhere, on November twenty-second, let us rededicate ourselves to the pursuit of those ideals of human dignity in which he believed and whose course he so brilliantly illuminated.

IN WITNESS WHEREOF, I have hereunto set my hand and caused the Seal of the United States of America to be affixed.

DONE at the City of Washington this nineteenth day of November in the year of our Lord nineteen hundred and [SEAL] sixty-four, and of the Independence of the United States of America the one hundred and eighty-ninth.

LYNDON B. JOHNSON

By the President:
DEAN RUSK
Secretary of State

---

775   Remarks at a Luncheon of the Committee for Economic Development. *November* 19, 1964

Mr. Wilde, my fellow Americans:

Unaccustomed as I have become to public speaking over the past 15 days, I particularly welcome this opportunity to come to talk with you today.

For more than 20 years the Committee for Economic Development has contributed much to enlighten the discussion of America's most difficult economic problems. Individually and together you have made a most valuable and quite unique contribution to responsible public policy. In the years ahead I hope your example will not be so unique but I hope it will be much more universal.

The great opportunity—and greater obli-gation—of this moment in our national life is the opportunity and the obligation for all segments of our society to try to be constructive.

Together we have achieved a rather broad and deep consensus.

It is not a consensus on personality. It is not a consensus on party.

It is a consensus on national purpose and national policy.

We know now—as we could not know in the years before—that we are a people who are more united than divided on America's goals.

Out of the events of the past 364 days we have emerged as a more mature, a more reflective, a more discerning and determined people.

We know—better, I believe, than any other generation of this century—what kind of country we want America to be. We know what we want to preserve, what we want to pursue at home and in the world.

For any nation, such a moment, I think, is rare.

For our Nation, such a moment is too rare to lose.

So, this moment of consensus must last and live and grow into a long age of constructiveness—an age in which all sections, all segments, and all sectors contribute their best to building strong foundations for greatness that we hope is still to come.

I said during the recent campaign that I believe we are entering a new era in the affairs of the world. All around the globe new leadership is at the helm of nations which are old and young, that are free and that are communistic. Within both the free world and the Communist world new forces and new factors are at work.

None of us can know the full meaning of these changes that are taking place, but we can realistically, I think, recognize that the era ahead will be more challenging, will be more competitive, will be more exacting and, yes, it is going to be more demanding.

Old precepts, old premises, and old patterns may be less and less pertinent to the realities of the new era, and we must be the first and not the last to recognize reality.

But the change of our times is not confined to the world that is beyond these shores. In all the world, I think there is no nation that is changing more dynamically than our own.

I mention only one measure of such change.

Since this administration began, the population of the United States has increased by more than 10 million, and that is equal to half the population of Canada. Since the tragic day that I came to the Presidency a year ago, there are now about 2½ million more Americans.

Here at home—as in the world—a new era is beginning. If we are to put in place sure and solid foundations for our future, I believe we must test the realism of the precepts, premises, and patterns of many of our public policies and attitudes.

The temptation is great today to talk in terms of programs.

There is a time and a place for that, too, but I would rather, with this audience, speak in terms of principles which must and principles which will guide us on our programs.

Specifically, I want to speak in terms of principles relating to the fiscal policies of the Federal Government.

For much too long, the constructiveness and the creativity of the American people have been dissipated by divisions over our Federal budget.

I just left a long discussion with my Cabinet where that was a priority subject. As my Director of the Budget, Kermit Gordon, has emphasized to you, our very definitions of conservatism and liberalism have come to mean attitudes toward budget size.

For myself, I believe that the budget of our Government should be an area of broadest consensus—not an arena of the most partisan contention.

I might say that we did not get an exact consensus on the last budget I submitted, but it wasn't because I didn't try. I had 37 days and nights that I worked over it, and for the first time in many years, we changed the direction of it. We actually submitted less to the Congress than we had spent the year before. The first man to see that budget was Harry Byrd who did not agree with all of it, and John Williams, the ranking Republican on the Finance Committee.

To specify, I want to say I believe that:

1. Barring massive changes in defense spending, your Federal Government does not have to grow in size relative to the size of the economy.

2. With the continuing drive for economy and efficiency which we are waging relentlessly—and if you read the morning papers you will see where Mr. McNamara has put some substance to my promise and it is not just a coincidence that he announced the closing of these defense installations to the Congressmen this afternoon and I announced my departure for Texas simultaneously—we can keep Government budgets under control so that they grow no more rapidly, and I would hope may grow less rapidly, than our economy grows.

3. By the same approach, we can have fewer Federal workers per thousand of the total population. I might add that in September you had fewer Federal workers than at any time in the last 2½ years. I hope to have a reduction in October although I have some doubts.

4. Programs that no longer serve a vital purpose can and must be pruned away and all programs must be administered with the same careful efficiency as a prudent householder or a prudent businessman applies.

5. A frugal budget need not and should not be a stagnant budget. It must have room for new programs to meet the aspirations of the American people and to help us meet unfilled needs. At the same time new programs should be undertaken only when they offer a higher value to the Nation than we would get if the taxpayers spent the money themselves.

6. The Federal Government must take into account the impact of its total spending and its taxing on our economic life, on markets, on jobs, on wages, on prices, on capital investments.

The Committee for Economic Development recognized this principle long ago. An ever-broadening consensus—conservative and liberal, labor and business, Republican and Democrat—now accepts it. That consensus recognizes that true fiscal responsibility will achieve a balanced budget out of the rising revenues of the healthy and prosperous economy. Budgetary balance will not be achieved by reckless cutbacks of expenditures to fit the tax revenues of a sick economy.

But can these principles be applied? I think the answer is definitely yes, because this is what we are doing.

Let me give you these examples:

1. To meet the demands of a society that is rapidly growing in population, wealth, and complexity, we are spending more for education, vocational training, and retraining. A child with a grammar school education will earn during his lifetime an average of $152,000. A child who goes through high school earns not $150,000 but $272,000. A child who will go through college and beyond in his lifetime will average $452,000.

So, in plain, hard figures, it means that a college trained person earns $300,000 more than one who has not had elementary, secondary, or college education. When Uncle Sam will get, say, 52 percent of that extra $300,000, we get a pretty good return on the investment we made in training that person.

So, I submit, to increase the earnings of every American child, it is not only bankable but it is a prime investment. If private financing lends a man $20,000 over 25 years to build a house which does not grow and make a profit, it is my position that the same homeowner can be loaned the money to build his son into an educated man whose income will grow $300,000 on a mere $20,000 loan.

We must build more hospitals. We must have more money for medical research and public health. You take the great loss that this Nation suffers—resources—every year by the millions who are stricken down with strokes, with cancer, and with heart attacks. It makes it absolutely essential that we pursue with vigor and a sense of urgency a means for finding the answers to those man-killers.

We must have a fight on poverty and we must make it stronger than it has ever been before in our history.

Total Federal spending in 1965 will be the lowest in 14 years in terms of our gross national product.

Nondefense spending will be lower than it was 30 years ago in terms of our gross national product.

2. There are fewer Federal employees now than there were a year ago when I took office. That is unusual with a growing population. It is unusual with so many of our unfilled needs that we have actually cut not only Federal expenditures but we have cut Federal employees. Federal workers now are 3.9 percent of total nonfarm employment.

In 1953 they were 4.6 percent. You see the reduction in the percentage that has been made.

Eliminating the employees of the Defense Department, Post Office Department, and Veterans Administration—the three big, substantial employers—your Federal Government now operates with fewer civilian employees than the Nation's telephone industry.

3. What about the prospects in regard to defense?

Well, for the past 4 years, military spending has risen by almost 25 percent—defense expenditures up 25 percent the last 4 years. We have spent roughly $30 billion more on defense than we were spending in 1960 in these 4 years.

After President Kennedy came back from Geneva, we felt that we had better increase our preparedness efforts. We have spent about $10 billion more on space than at the rate we were spending in 1960—from $41 billion in fiscal 1960 for defense to nearly $50 billion in fiscal 1964. Today, for fiscal 1965 and beyond, the level of defense spending is going to remain constant or we will make a slight reduction if there is no significant change in the threats that we face. I emphasize *if* there are no significant changes.

There were significant changes that faced President Kennedy after the conference that he held with Premier Khrushchev.

There are two reasons. First, we have achieved many of the needed changes and increases in our military force structure as a result of this heavy expenditure and, second, we have begun to benefit from the rigorous 5-year cost-reduction program which last year alone saved $2.8 billion in unnecessary expenditures and in operating costs.

I have pledged that we will remain first in the use of science and technology for the protection of our people. I do not think that we as a Nation can be first in the world and second in space.

We are now spending more than $6 billion per year for military research and development, and research costs will probably increase in future years.

But the budgetary impact of increased military strength will be more than offset by savings from Mr. McNamara's cost-reduction program. That program should by fiscal 1968 be saving us $4.6 billion each year—$4 billion a year.

My point then is simply this: in the new era beginning for our country, we are challenged to do more than we have ever done to preserve peace, to defend freedom, to assure freedom's full meaning for all Americans. But we need not and we must not restrict our response to these challenges by being either parsimonious or prodigal with our public moneys.

The kind of constructive and creative spirit that CED has fostered can help us, I think, find new guides, better ways, more satisfactory answers—just as the $14 billion tax cut is doing.

Many of you had much to do with making the tax cut possible.

Benefits are evident everywhere in rising sales, in expanding payrolls, all without the inflation many feared.

When you encourage men to go out and make capital investments and you give them the hope—we hope it is a prudent hope, too—that they can recover a reasonable return on that investment and not have it confiscated, you do many things. First and foremost, you increase payrolls. Second, you increase price stability because the more competition you have and the more productive capacity you have, the more likely you are to have stable prices and not have shortages.

We are maintaining, I think, the best record of overall price stability of any industrial country in the world, and we are doing it without the iron hand of price or wage controls. We are doing it with a free spirited competition, and we are doing it by going out and making new capital investments and by creating additional productivity with a sense of restraint and responsibility, and that is not a one-way street either.

We must have responsible businessmen and responsible labor leaders, and they must put their country ahead of themselves.

Wholesale prices are no higher than they were last January, and they are the same as the 1959 average. Prices that consumers pay have inched up since 1961 at half the rate of the preceding 4 years.

Our economy is expanding without excesses and without distortions and without the tightening of credit and without the boosting of interest that can so easily turn expansion into a recession. We so very much hope that we will not have these boosts and that we will not have this recession.

I know that there are some advocates in some quarters of the business community, and there may be some necessary actions that have to be taken, but we are very proud of the fact that we have now gone 45 months without any dip, without any recession. That is the longest in the history of this country and we are fighting to extend that record.

This price stability has enabled us to cut our international payments deficits in half. Our balance of payments, I believe, was 3.3 last year and will perhaps be 2 this year and stop the outflow of our gold.

The price level in a free economy can remain stable only if wage advances generally stay within the bounds of the economic gains in productivity—and if industries which enjoy very high productivity gains share their gains with consumers in lower prices to offset the rising prices of services where productivity often lags.

This, then, is our basic guidepost. There is no "big stick" policy to enforce such a policy—only the force of good business judgment, only the force of responsible union policy, only the force of an informed public opinion.

But I believe, as I said earlier, that there

is a strong consensus of responsibility, prudence, and understanding in America. There is a will to be constructive, there is a will to be progressive and to be prudent.

What the new eras abroad and at home may hold, none can know, but with this spirit here I think we can embark upon the new age with confidence in our country and strength in its successes.

The next 4 years we are going to try to have progressive and prudent government leadership. This is going to be no business government. This is going to be no labor government. We are not trying to apply any special label and we are not trying to court any specific segment of our population.

I want very much to be President of all of the people, and I want every businessman in this land and every workingman to know that it is my purpose and my goal to give equality of treatment and to give the kind of leadership that is dependable and that is calculated to earn the confidence of all of the citizens.

I do not interpret the selection as a mandate to any reckless, novel, dangerous, or unique course. Our emphasis is going to be this next 4 years just as it was when the Republic of Texas was founded.

The President of the Republic of Texas said, "Education is the guardian genius of democracy. It is the only ruler that free men recognize and the only dictator that free men desire."

So, our budget is going to emphasize reform in cutting out any unnecessary expenditures that we can cut out, and we are going to place a very special emphasis on teaching people and preparing people and qualifying people and trying to make taxpayers out of taxeaters.

I have gone into the unemployment pockets of this country. I have seen the hope in the eyes of the people that a better

day would come notwithstanding what you might hear, see, or believe.

Most every citizen in this land wants a job and would like to work. The only way that I know that we can realize—in fact, we will never realize full employment but we want full employment opportunity. We may not have all of our people fully educated but we want full educational opportunity.

I do not want to see several generations come and go, never having known private employment.

We have 3,200,000 18-year-olds that are coming into that age group this year. We came back from the war and we started adding to our families, and now there are 3,200,000 coming in that group. There will be more than half a million of those who will find the college door closed to them—you can't enter because we have no room for you—and they will find no jobs available at the doors on which they knock. We have to do something with them. We can let them become a nuisance, a delinquent, or we can prepare them to be qualified to do what needs to be done.

I was in one State and they told me that they had unemployment of 138,000 but they had 93,000 vacancies that they could not get filled because the men were not equipped to fill the jobs and they were not equipped or skilled to perform the work.

I particularly need good men in the Federal Government. I have spent my nights ever since the election—I am the only man in town, I think, who has not had a vacation. When they have been feeding me Cabinet officers at the rate of two or three a day with their budgets, they call it a working vacation—whatever that is. I guess it is because I breathe fresh, unpolluted air down on the Pedernales—that's what you call it.

We need topflight men, and those of you

who find time to criticize the mistakes we make can spare us some of those mistakes and some of that foolishness if you will just look into your own organizations and find a man or two who needs some Washington training and experience in administration—that we need.

There are some men who have stayed here as long as they can afford to stay. They are out of money and the bankers are calling their loans. I lost an Under Secretary of the Treasury, a real financial genius, because a banker would not extend his loan and Congress would not pass the pay bill.

In the days ahead, I would be very grateful if you would let the Chairman of the Civil Service Commission, Mr. John Macy, know of any competent executive leaders whom you think might be persuaded to come here and help us do the most important job in the world—trying to preserve it and trying to lead it, trying to keep our eyes on the stars and our feet on the ground. I never want to keep both of them there all the time, but I want to take one step and, when I do, be sure the other one is holding steady. I don't want to get both of them off the ground at the same time, as some people do.

So, we do need good, trained leaders in Government because the rest of the world looks to us to set an example, and I look to you to help me.

The doors of the White House are open to you. I cannot see each of you every time that you may have a problem that you want to discuss but I do want you to know that I feel your problems are mine. I do want to see you prosper and make profits.

Profits after taxes this year are up 20 percent. Labor's wages after taxes are up some 6 or 7 percent. We are doing well, we want to continue to do well, but we can do better.

I am distressed sometimes when I see the divisions in the country that you should not think that that should concern a man who got the support of the people that I did in such overwhelming numbers. I do not expect unanimity in our ranks. I do know we will have differences of opinion, but I said when I became Democratic leader, and Mr. Eisenhower was a Republican President, that I would support the President when he was right, and I would hold his hand high, and if he were wrong, in my judgment, I would try to submit an alternative to his program and let the people choose between the two, let the Senators choose. If I disagreed with him, I would say so courteously, candidly. I would not discuss personalities or indulge in them, and I would not talk about his family or his dogs.

The people did not let me stay in the minority but 2 years, and they selected a Democratic majority to work with a Republican President the remaining 6 years—because I think they approved of the responsibility.

I am pleased to say without getting political that a good many members, a good many voters in this country, a good many citizens of this country still feel the same way. They think a man's first duty is to his country and that is my philosophy.

When asked to explain whether I was a liberal or conservative, or rancher or banker, or businessman or public servant, I said I am all of them. I do not go by any label. First, I am proud I am a free man. Second, I am proud I am an American. Third, I am proud I am a public servant. This may be a little dangerous to say to some of you, but, fourth, I am proud to be a Democrat. But in that order.

We do not have any corner on patriotism. People who differ with us on party principles love their country just as much as we do and have fought for it just as much as we have and have bled for it just as much as we have. So let's try to avoid these deep divisions that personalities create.

Let's try to keep our eye on the big thing. We are the greatest Nation in the world, and we have so much to preserve and so much to protect. We are going to preserve it and we are going to protect it. We are going to develop it, and we are going to utilize it.

We are going to leave this place a better place than we found it.

Thank you very much.

NOTE: The President spoke at 2:55 p.m. at a luncheon in the State Room at the Mayflower Hotel in Washington. His opening words referred to Frazar B. Wilde, Chairman of the Board of Trustees, Committee for Economic Development. During his remarks he referred to Kermit Gordon, Director, Bureau of the Budget, Senator Harry Flood Byrd of Virginia, Chairman of the Senate Finance Committee, Senator John J. Williams of Delaware, member of the Finance Committee, and Robert S. McNamara, Secretary of Defense.

776 Statement by the President at a Cabinet Meeting: The Great Society. *November 19, 1964*

1. BUILDING the Great Society will require a major effort on the part of every Federal agency in two directions:

—First, formulating imaginative new ideas and programs; and

—Second, carrying out hard-hitting, tough-minded reforms in existing programs.

2. All of you, I am sure, are convinced of the need of new ideas. I have been impressed with the imagination and vision you have shown in this area. But I want to impress on you the equally essential need to be bold in reforming existing programs.

3. The Great Society will require a substantial investment. This means:

—That as a Nation we cannot afford to waste a single dollar of our resources on outmoded programs, which once may have been essential, but which time and events have overtaken.

—That as a Government we must get the most out of every dollar of scarce budget resources, reforming old programs and using the savings for the new programs of the Great Society. The Congress and the

American people will provide the budgetary means to build the Great Society only if we take positive steps to show that we are spending only where we legitimately need to spend. Only if we are imaginative in reform will we be allowed to be imaginative in new programs.

4. Reform comes in two packages:

First, we simply cannot afford to keep on doing the same thing year after year merely because that's the way we did it in the past. In particular, we cannot afford to spend scarce budget dollars

—to meet needs that no longer exist;

—to alleviate hardships that have long since been overcome; or

—to subsidize services that can be provided adequately at full cost.

Second, in what we do undertake, we must get the maximum value per dollar spent. I will continue to insist, as I have in the past, on increased productivity and greater efficiency.

5. Each of you must take a cold, hard look at your existing programs. I expect each of you to be as bold and as imaginative in

reforming ongoing programs as in proposing new ones.

6. I think there are many cases where boldness in reform will pay off.

To be sure, every program needing reform has a pressure group which will fight reform. But I want to make the decisions as to those fights which it will be worthwhile to take on and those which it won't. I want you to give me plenty of such decisions to make.

If we are going to make an impact—and history will find no excuse for us if we don't—there will be no better time than this coming session of Congress.

7. I need your help in this. I depend upon your sharpness of vision, and your knowledge of the programs in your department to identify the reforms needed.

The speed with which we can move ahead to the Great Society will depend upon how well you do this job

—now,

—in this budget, and

—in this legislative program.

I think it is also very important that each of you get to know personally the new Members of Congress, Republicans as well as Democrats.

We are planning a reception here from 6 to 8 p.m., on December 9, for the new Democratic Members of the House and Senate, and I want each of you to attend. This will not suffice, of course, for personal efforts on your part to get to know these men and women. In the long and short runs, I believe this personal relationship between senior members of the administration and new Members of Congress will return handsome dividends.

---

777   Statement by the President at a Cabinet Meeting: Personnel Appointments. *November* 19, 1964

I AM SURE each of you shares my conviction that the character and effectiveness of our administration will largely be determined by the quality of men and women appointed to leadership positions.

This means our presidential appointees must be men and women of character, ability, and devotion.

I want to conduct a continuing talent search, in all professions and in all parts of the country, to discover these people.

The White House will play a leading part in this search and work closely with you in selecting presidential appointees who meet these high quality standards and who will be strong and responsive representatives of the administration's programs.

Since the men and women selected will directly assist you in carrying out your policy and management responsibilities, they must meet your standards but they must also pass muster as members of the Johnson administration.

I will establish a single office within the White House to work with you and me in meeting these vitally important staffing goals.

For the period between now and the inauguration, I have asked John Macy to assist me and the White House staff in working with you on this important task. He will be talking with you about the pending vacancies and how we can better meet the staffing needs of the administration.

I want to be especially sure that each of you selects a top man to serve as your legislative liaison. Next to the Cabinet officer himself, I consider this the most important position in the department. If we are to get our legislative program through, you must have heavyweights in these jobs— people with political sensitivity and substantive knowledge of your programs. I expect them to keep you thoroughly informed of the situation affecting your programs on the Hill, and in turn, I expect you to keep me informed *at all times*. You will personally be responsible for your legislation, so I know you will want a congressional liaison office of the first order.

778 Remarks at Southwest Texas State College, San Marcos. *November 20, 1964*

Dr. Flowers, Dr. McCrocklin, my fellow Americans:

If I were to get sentimental, you would miss your dinner this evening, so I hope you will forgive me for not reminiscing this morning, and understand that you are the winner. I am so happy to be back home and to see so many friends, some of whom I knew when I first came here 40 years ago, and some whom I welcome as the new leaders of this great institution.

I was just telling Dr. McCrocklin that shortly after I became President, the Prime Minister of one of our neighboring countries paid his first visit to Washington and the scholarly Secretary of State, Mr. Dean Rusk, had him to a very small dinner party that evening.

After they had all toasted each other at some length, I had to give the toast of the evening. I looked around just to see what kind of company I was keeping. I saw the distinguished former dean of faculty of Harvard there, I saw one of the leading members of the faculty of Princeton there, I saw three of Harvard's outstanding graduates there, and there was Senator Fulbright, Secretary of State Rusk, and at least two more Rhodes scholars.

So I concluded my toast by welcoming to the dining room that evening four Rhodes scholars, three Harvard graduates, two from

Yale, one from Princeton, and one from San Marcos State College!

So I am truly glad to be back home again. I am very happy to be at the inauguration of your new president. In fact, I think I like it so much I believe I will very soon just have one of my own.

I have taken great pride in the leadership of Dr. Flowers, Dr. Evans, and many memorable faculty members of this institution. I having been a former janitor and worked out on the rocks on the campus, and part-time secretary with Tom Nichols in the president's office, I am very deeply impressed with the importance of the head of this institution.

When we thought we might be able to come today, I asked my assistant, Jack Valenti, to call Dr. McCrocklin's office and ask him does the President speak first or last. The answer came back, "The president speaks last and Mr. Johnson speaks first."

I have traveled a long way from this college to the office that I now occupy. In few times, yes, in very few nations, in man's journey has it been possible for any man to travel such a road.

In Washington I am surrounded by men who have come from every walk of life to the most responsible posts of government. For that is what your government really is. It is not a strange and alien power in a remote and menacing city. It is a banker from New York and a druggist from Minnesota, the son of a tenant farmer from Texas. Some day it may very well be some of you.

America has succeeded more than any other nation in the world in making it possible for a man to achieve whatever his ability would allow. The idea that man's only limitation would be his talent and intelligence, and his willingness to work, has been at the heart of the American dream, and for some of us it has come true.

Yet this pursuit is never a finished task. Each generation is charged anew with extending opportunity to more of our people and elevating the horizons of all of our people.

Today we are at the edge of a new era of progress toward the American dream. It is an opportunity as large and as exciting as that granted to those who settled this continent.

Our basic goal has not been changed, but the growth of our Nation, the progress of science and knowledge, the change in our way of life, makes it necessary to shape new tools to reach old goals. And by moving ahead only can we hope to preserve the values of the past.

First, we must strike down the barriers which limit the hopes and the achievements of some of our people. No person should be stifled and restricted because of his race, or the circumstances of his birth, or the lack of an adequate education, or because he comes from a poor home. Through our pursuit of equal opportunity, the war against poverty, we are going to change things in this country.

Your own very able and popular Congressman is leading the way in that effort. The people of this area of Texas know the taste of poverty. For generations the adobe-caliche soil has yielded forth a harsh living to those who worked it in this area.

We have come a long way since those days when I lived in the school garage here on the campus. Incidentally, I lived there 3 years before the business manager knew about it. And I don't think he ever would have if the coach hadn't told him that I was bathing in the gymnasium. But in that period, want and hunger were no strangers to San Marcos.

The energy and the will of the people of this area have created a city of hope and fulfillment for many. But now we have an opportunity to unite in will and heart and spirit to bring a final end to poverty.

Along with Congressman Pickle, Senator Yarborough, and your distinguished Governor Connally, we propose that San Marcos be the first city in the entire Southwest to organize and to begin to fight the war against poverty.

I would like to establish here where Dr. Evans and Dr. Flowers served so long, this institution that graduated Jesse Kellam, Bill Deason, and a good many others that I see here this morning, and sent them forth to lead their fellow men—I would like to establish a job corps camp to train between 1,000 and 2,000 young men in the skills which will make it possible for them to find rewarding work and to contribute to the prosperity of this community and to ultimately become leaders of their fellow men.

If this idea is to become a reality, then your officials and civic leaders and educational leaders must meet and organize and prepare this community to share in a cooperative effort with your Government. I have asked the very able, talented, and attractive director of the war against poverty, who sits with me in my Cabinet, Mr. Sargent Shriver, to come to Texas next Wednesday. And if you are ready, and if you have done your work by then, he will come to San Marcos and he will meet you here, and we will begin. So you are privileged to be among the first in this Nation to attack and to end the curse of poverty. Because so much of it began here.

There is the challenge. We are ready. The rest is up to you.

The expansion of education is going to receive special emphasis in the budget that I am now preparing. We have one of our Cabinet officers, Secretary Udall, who wonders how much education is going to take from the resources that he is interested in, the conservation effort. But I am going to take him down here when we get through here this morning and do something that I had really never anticipated doing before: walk him from the campus to Riverside along the same route that I used to walk with a lovely blond, through the fish hatchery. I hope it will be as attractive to him as it was to me.

Next we must move to enlarge the horizons of all Americans, and this effort is what we will pursue in the Great Society. It is founded upon the idea that the ultimate test of any society is really the quality of the men and women that it produces, and the quality of the life that they are permitted to lead.

These goals can never be measured in guns or statistics. They do not flow automatically from wealth or power. They must be made a careful, conscious objective, and they must be pursued with dedication and labor.

And that we intend to do.

Even the greatest of past societies were founded upon the exploitation and the misery of many. So we in beautiful America can be the first to enrich the quality of the life of all of our people.

We do not make money just to build factories. Yes, we have the tools to do such a job. We make money to make it possible to enrich the lives of human beings. We are the richest and we are the most powerful nation on earth. Our knowledge and our insight into our own problems are growing daily. And now I believe today we can see our real goal.

That goal is not an idle dream. And it is not a vague Utopia. It has concrete goals and it requires specific programs.

Even as we meet here today, some of those programs are being prepared for my review. The one I just announced I reviewed on the helicopter coming down here this morning.

These programs will attack the problems of making our cities a decent place to live in. They will seek to preserve the beauty of our land. They will strive to make it possible for every child born in this country to receive an education of the highest quality, to the full limit of his ability, no matter how poor he is, no matter where he lives, no matter which side of the tracks he was born on.

It will do all these things and more, much more. It will not be a program for a hundred days or even a program for the next 4 years. It will point toward the year 2000. But it will provide the base on which America moves forward and builds.

Let there be no mistake. The objectives we seek will not be handed to you by a beneficent government. The work of a few men in Washington will not make life easier. No one man can lead this Nation, and you cannot sit idly by, quietly waiting for the day when someone else will make everything better for you.

These goals are going to demand your effort and your work and your sacrifice, and the best from every American. It will mean that each of you must participate in the affairs of your community and your State and your Nation. It will require the help of government at every level, of labor and of business, of farmers and consumers.

A President can lead and teach, and explore, and set goals. He can have his eyes in the stars, with a vision that will flow therefrom, and he can have his feet on the ground, with a solid foundation that we need.

But no leader can make a people more than they are, or make them more than they really want to be. My success and America's success will depend on you.

It was a hundred years ago, in 1864, that Abraham Lincoln abolished slavery in this country. A hundred years later, here in the hills of home, we are inaugurating a movement to abolish poverty in this country.

I rode on the train to Washington from where I opened my campaign here in San Marcos in 1937. A great President, a fearless leader, a man who preserved our Republic in its most challenging period, talked to me about the third of our land that were ill fed, ill clad, and ill housed, and he sought to do something about it.

I had seen him stand in front of that Capitol only a few years before, when the banks were popping like firecrackers, when the farmers were burning their produce because they had no market to sell it in, and when soup lines were stretched around the corners of city blocks.

But I saw him bring hope to a great Nation. He said, "The only thing we have to fear is fear itself."

During his leadership and the leadership that followed under President Truman, President Eisenhower, and President Kennedy, we have reduced that one-third that were ill fed, ill clad, and ill housed, to one-fifth

today. So we put on our robes and march forth to abolish that one-fifth who live on incomes of less than $3,000 a year.

I know that those of you who have enjoyed the fruits of your own labors, and have been the beneficiaries of the leadership and the planning of others, like Dr. Evans and Dr. Flowers, are willing to reciprocate by helping those less fortunate.

So I call upon every student of this institution and every graduate of this college, every faculty member, to pledge himself not to the Emancipation Proclamation that Lincoln signed a hundred years ago, or not to freeing the slaves, but, instead, to declaring a war and abolishing poverty in this land.

What a great example that would be for the rest of the world. They look to us. We are the one of 120 nations that sits there in a goldfish bowl for all to observe and for all to judge.

You can look around and see some of the boys that came to this school, and what you did for them in moving them out of that one-third group. You can look not far away to the University of Texas and see some of its products, like Mr. Pickle, who was a poor boy and came there, and he, too, worked for the NYA.

The great leadership that is being given this State now by your Governor, one of the ablest chief executives and one of the soundest leaders that we have known, was made possible because when he came from Floresville without a dollar in his pocket, he got an NYA job at 17 cents an hour—and he is now the chief executive of what was once the largest State in the Union.

So the opportunity is here if you have the will and the leadership and the determination. I could think of no better epithet, I could think of no greater sense of satisfaction or achievement that could come to anyone than to have it said of him that he led this way in this noble undertaking. I believe and I know that you and all of my fellow Americans will be equal to this task. So let's be on our way.

NOTE: The President spoke at 10:45 a.m. in the gymnasium at the Southwest Texas State College, San Marcos, at the inauguration of Dr. James H. McCrocklin, as president of the college. His opening words referred to Dr. J. G. Flowers, the college's outgoing president. During his remarks he referred to, among others, Dr. C. E. Evans, former president of the college, Jack Valenti, Special Consultant to President Johnson, and Representative J. J. Pickle, Senator Ralph Yarborough, and Governor John B. Connally, all of Texas. He also referred to R. Sargent Shriver, Director of the Office of Economic Opportunity, and Stewart L. Udall, Secretary of the Interior.

779 Thanksgiving Day Message to Members of the Armed Forces. *November 25, 1964*

TODAY all Americans thank the blessings of the Lord for the bounty of their land. In homes at peace, in houses of worship that are untouched by rancor or anger, families are gathered in gratitude for all that God has given them and for the blessings that He has rained upon our Nation.

Many of you will not be with your families today. Nearly all of you will be far from your homes and your friends and the land that you now defend. But all of us here at home remember you with gratitude. We owe much to those who over centuries have stood the long, hazardous, and often lonely vigil of freedom around the world. Our twin blessings of peace and abundance have always rested on those who were willing to risk, whatever the danger, and to sacrifice, whatever the cost, for the freedom of America.

Those same blessings depend upon you today. The first Thanksgiving was celebrated by a small group of valiant pioneers. They were beset by the harshness of nature and the hazards of enemies. Behind them lay a year of heavy toil. Ahead lay the uncertainties of the New England winter. Yet, they thanked in sincere joy the God who had permitted them to survive the year and reap the harvest, and brought them to a place where a man could hope to be free.

Today we are prosperous and mighty beyond the farthest imagining of those men and women. Yet, we mark the same glad and humbling ritual. It reminds us that freedom is always in the midst of peril, that democracy is a goal and not an achievement. Peace comes only to those who work for it and are ready to defend it, and the rewards of the world are at the mercy of that just Providence who has thus far seen fit to bless this land.

For that we give thanks and pray that we may continue to deserve His blessings.

NOTE: The message was taped at 2:35 p.m. in the President's office at the LBJ Ranch, Johnson City, Tex. It was relayed to the U.S. armed forces overseas via Syncom and Relay communications satellites.

780   The President's News Conference at the LBJ Ranch.
November 28, 1964

THE PRESIDENT. [1.]   The present discussion of the Atlantic Alliance that we see in the press and by the commentators, on television and radio, is, I think, partially the result of a neglect of first principles that are worth some new attention this morning.

The ultimate essentials of the defense of the Atlantic community are the firmness and the mutual trust of the United States and Europe. The United States position I should make abundantly clear. The safety of the United States depends upon the freedom of Europe, and the freedom of Europe depends upon the strength and the will of the United States. That strength and that will have never been clearer, have never been more necessary than today.

The United States is committed to the increasing strength and the cooperation of the Atlantic community in every field of action—economic, commercial, and monetary. There are no problems which we cannot solve together, and there are very few which any of us can settle by himself.

The United States sees no safe future for ourselves and none for any other Atlantic nation in a policy of narrow national self-interest. One of the great aspirations within the Atlantic community is the aspiration toward growing unity among the free peoples of Europe. No nation on either side of the Atlantic has done more to support this purpose than the United States. This support will continue.

Since 1945 the United States has borne a special responsibility for the nuclear defense of the free world. The costs and the complexities of modern nuclear weapons make it inevitable that this American responsibility will continue far into the future. While we cannot divest ourselves of this awesome obligation, we can and we will work earnestly with all of our friends to find new and better ways by which all interested members of the alliance can increase their own sense of safety by sharing responsibility in the unified defense of the alliance as a whole. This is the meaning of our present interest in the multilateral forces. This is the meaning of our continued readiness to discuss these problems with every interested ally.

I believe that the Atlantic Alliance is only at the beginning of its time of greatest achievement. Its success has been proved in 15 years of Atlantic peace. Its differences are differences among peoples who have learned in the torment of war that the freedom of each requires the freedom of all. I look forward with confidence to the resolution of present differences and the reassertion of the unity which is so deeply in the common interest of us all.

[2.]   Let me add here this statement voluntarily before I submit for questions, a word about the Congo and about Africa, which has engaged our very special attention, as you know, this week. This terrible experience, this reign of terror and disorder, these innocent lives sacrificed in political reprisals, constitute a tragedy for Africa and for the Congo as well as for the rest of the world.

What has happened in Stanleyville has happened far too often to Congolese and foreigners alike on both sides in various conflicts in the Congo in recent years. The Congo has suffered through more than 4 years of violence and bloodshed and disunity. It has been an arena of power struggles and ideological wars. I hope now that it can have at last a chance for peace and order, and economic recovery, so that the ordinary people of the Congo can hope for improvement in their lot and for protection against the daily threat of violent death.

I have wired the relatives of our citizens who lost their lives there my feelings and expressed my great sympathy for them in this hour. We lost three Americans.[1] Undoubtedly we would have lost dozens more had we not acted promptly and decisively in cooperation with the Belgian paratroopers. As you know, more than 4,000 Congolese themselves, most of whom were people with education, more than 4,000 Congolese in recent months have lost their lives because of these disorders.

I would like to stress to those of you here at the ranch this morning that the United States has no political goals to impose upon the Congo. We have no narrow interest. We have no economic gain to be served in the Congo. We seek to impose no political solution, neither our own nor that of some other outsider.

We have tried only to meet our obligations to the legitimate government, and to its efforts to achieve unity and stability and reconciliation in the Congo.

So we hope now that everyone who has had a part in this 4-year agony of the Congo will bury past differences and try to work together in a spirit of compassion, to help reach these goals of unity and stability and reconciliation. If this could happen, perhaps the hundreds of innocent lives, Congolese and foreign, that have been sacrificed will not have been sacrificed in vain.

We were necessarily a party to the decisions, and I assume full responsibility for those made for our planes to carry the para-

troopers in there, in this humanitarian venture. We had to act and act promptly in order to keep hundreds and even thousands of people from being massacred. And we did act in time.

The paratroop force that we moved in there will be moved out tonight, and it will be moved out of the Congo to Ascension Island in the South Atlantic Ocean.

[3.] Another matter which we have spent some time on in the last few days is the monetary situation.

This week we witnessed a rather remarkable demonstration of the strength of international monetary cooperation. Eleven nations, including the United States, and the Bank of International Settlement, arranged with the United Kingdom to provide credit facilities totaling about $3 billion to defend the pound sterling against speculative pressure.

We are gratified that these arrangements were worked out so speedily and with such widespread international participation. This action should give the United Kingdom the breathing space needed to carry out an effective program for improving its balance-of-payments position.

Of course, none of us was pleased that the Federal Reserve was obligated to raise our discount rate as a precautionary move in response to international developments. However, as Chairman Martin has clearly stated, this move is not, repeat *not,* intended to restrict the availability of credit to the domestic economy and does not lead us to expect any significant increase in the cost of domestic long-term credit, either from the banks or in the capital market.

We can count on monetary policies that continue to meet the credit needs of a non-inflationary expansion. This expansion, as you know, is about to enter its 46th consecutive month, an unprecedented record of

---

[1] Dr. Paul Carlson of California, Phyllis Rine of Mount Vernon, Ohio, and Joseph Tucker of Lamar, Ark., all missionaries.

peacetime prosperity.

Although strikes in the automobile industry dampened our economic performance in October and early November, there is encouraging evidence that the underlying economic forces remain strong. I presume it has almost become traditional for me to discuss economics, and I will certainly do so as long as you will follow me and it is desirable, at least.

But I would like to point out that our housing starts showed a welcomed 9 percent rise in October. Our new orders received by manufacturers continued to exceed shipments, which would indicate further strength in manufacturing production in the coming months.

Outside of durable goods manufacturing, which showed the effects of the strike, nonfarm payroll employment scored a good gain, 180,000 persons in October. Excluding sales by auto dealers, retail sales were 6.5 percent above last year for the 4 weeks that ended November 21st.

Now that the auto strikes are behind us, this underlying strength should again become fully apparent. The coming holiday season will find our economy setting new records for production, employment, income, and sales.

I think I should add that I have been kept in close touch with the auto people. I communicated with Mr. Reuther when he was abroad, and he came back and I have talked to him since we have been here. I am very happy that the employment situation in the auto industry as a result of the agreements between the management and labor has been worked out, and we can look forward to full production and more complete employment.

[4.] As you know, I will complete today a rather thorough review with each Cabinet officer of items that we will put in the budget

for fiscal year 1966. Mr. Katzenbach [2] and some of his associates will arrive shortly and will spend part of the day with me. Later in the day I will have the Chairman, the distinguished Chairman, of the Appropriations Committee of the House of Representatives, Mr. Mahon, flying in to give him an up-to-date review of what the agencies are asking, and to invite the suggestions of the Congress and certainly his committee on any suggestions they might have.

I must tell you that in candor and frankness no one can tell what this budget figure will be. What we have done is, we have had each department present to the Budget and to the President what they feel are their minimum demands for this year.

The Budget Director has not scrutinized each of those demands nor has the President. We will do that during the next 30 days.

This is the first preliminary presentation and there will no doubt be some increases to what they have asked at this time, depending on developments abroad and here, and there must be a good many reductions.

The figure that they are asking is in the neighborhood of $108 billion, between 108 and 109. As I say, there will be some additions to that and there will be some reductions. But that process is now underway.

I have a perspective on the budget expenditure and the employment trends in relation to other trends in our great and growing economy.

It has been a rather interesting study that must continue until early January. I asked the Budget Director when he was here the other day to present two charts which would show how the Federal budget expenditure and Federal employment have behaved over the past decade. All of our people are interested in this, but they have to support

---

[2] Nicholas deB. Katzenbach, Acting Attorney General.

other divisions of Government, and I wanted to see how our expenditures compared with our gross national product and how our employment compared with our population.

We all realize that we have new people, 3 or 4 million, coming into our population each year. There will be additional needs for them, and so forth. The Federal expenditures shown on this chart show what they would have been had they kept their '55 relationship to State-local government spending and to the gross national product.

You will see we started out at $64.4 billion in our 1955 expenditure, and if we had gone and spent the same amount as the State-local governments did, we would have a budget this year of $143 billion. If we had spent only the same percentage to our gross national product as we did in 1955, we would be spending $109.8 billion.

I think that that is what the managers of our departments feel would be a—felt last year and feel this year—would be the desirable and almost necessary level.

You will recall the 37 days and nights that we worked. We anticipate this year an expenditure of somewhere in the neighborhood of $97.2, about $700 million under what I had estimated at the beginning of the year. That may come up some the next few months, depending on any needs that we have. But if we had spent like the States and local people spent, it would be $143 billion. If we had spent in accordance with the increase in our productivity, our gross national product, it would be $109 billion. It actually is between 97 and 98. They are asking for 108 next year. These charts show our general relation to the gross national product and State and local government expenditures.

We have here an employment chart that tells somewhat the similar story. We had 2,371,000 in '55. If we had added the same

number of employees that the State and local governments have added according to their relationship, we would have 3,886,000. If we added only in accordance with our population needs, it would be 2,783,000. As you can see, during this period, it held about the same, or actually it has declined a few thousand since we went in.

That will necessarily increase some because we have an increasing population, we have a steadily growing economy, we have expenditures in employment in Federal programs that are new, that are just coming up. At the same time, I think it is imperative that we do our best to increase efficiency and productivity in Government programs and reform existing programs to meet the needs of today and tomorrow.

These charts show that both Federal spending and Federal employment are under tight and effective controls and I plan to keep it that way. So we are putting together a budget which will continue these favorable trends but we are trying to find substantial places where we can eliminate programs and where we can make reforms that will give us some leeway to institute new measures.

[5.] The United Steel Workers officials are meeting Wednesday to draw up their wage demands. I know you must have observed that, and I think that every person in this country has a very vital interest in the outcome of these negotiations.

I am very pleased with the current prosperity of the steel industry. Production this year will reach an alltime peak. Steel profits are up 26 percent over last year. Employment is up 80,000 since last December. Steel prices have been essentially stable since October 1963, and I hope and I expect that they can remain that way.

As the period of bargaining approaches, I am anxious to preserve stability in this great industry. I know I can count on both sides to do their utmost to resolve the important local and national issues before them, again avoiding the dislocations of a strike.

I also look forward to a responsible settlement which preserves stable labor cost per unit and thus contributes to continued stability in steel prices. I am sure that the parties have the wisdom to reach a new agreement without a strike and without labor cost or price increase. We can then look forward to continued balanced expansion with our record of cost-price stability remaining intact.

Now, if you would like, I will take questions. I know that you don't want to be kept too long. But you can extend your period of questioning a little bit if you want to because we have some people from our State that may want to add to your usual time. It may be that you will want to eliminate some of these volunteers that don't interest you. I just wanted to review with you what we have done here in the last week.

We will be returning tomorrow afternoon, sometime between 1 and 3. I have spent the morning talking to Secretary Dillon, Secretary Rusk, Secretary McNamara, Mr. Bundy, and the Budget Director [3] in the usual routine conferences we have by telephone instead of in person, when we are here. Now, if you care, you can take the next 20 minutes so you don't get deprived of any of your opportunity to ask questions.

[6.] Q. Mr. President, is expansion of the Viet-Nam war into Laos or North Viet-Nam a live possibility at this point?

THE PRESIDENT. I think Mr. Kilduff [4] reviewed with you yesterday the feeling of this administration. I don't want to give you any particular guideposts as to your conduct

in the matter. But when you crawl out on a limb, you always have to find another one to crawl back on.

I have just been sitting here in this serene atmosphere of the Pedernales for the last few days reading about the wars that you have involved us in and the additional undertakings that I have made decisions on or that General Taylor [5] has recommended or that Mr. McNamara plans or Secretary Rusk envisages. I would say, generally speaking, that some people are speculating and taking positions that I would think are somewhat premature.

We have had many conferences in the last year in connection with the South Viet-Nam situation. It has been a serious problem for many years. Secretary McNamara has made several trips out there. Secretary Rusk has made two trips out there since I became President. The first meetings I had as President were with Ambassador Lodge [6] who was called in. I have had other meetings with General Taylor and other conferences. We have scheduled them in Honolulu.

In retrospect, as you look back over your writings during all of that period, they are somewhat similar to what they are today. I don't know whether you have a black sheet that you take out every time we have a meeting on it and rewrite it, but in Honolulu we had these dire predictions and we served notice on the world that we were about to launch a big new effort.

I would say the situation is always serious. It is quite a problem. Periodically we will have meetings with our top people. Every few weeks we will have General Taylor or Mr. Johnson or General Westmoreland [7] or

---

[3] McGeorge Bundy, Special Assistant to the President, and Kermit Gordon, Director, Bureau of the Budget.

[4] Malcolm M. Kilduff, Assistant Press Secretary.

[5] Gen. Maxwell D. Taylor, U.S. Ambassador to Viet-Nam.

[6] Henry Cabot Lodge, former U.S. Ambassador to Viet-Nam.

[7] U. Alexis Johnson, Deputy U.S. Ambassador to Viet-Nam and Gen. William Westmoreland, Commander, U.S. Forces in Viet-Nam.

some other people from out there in here. We will evaluate the situation. We will do everything we can to make it more effective and more efficient. The only thing we need to do to end our real problem in that area is for some folks out there to leave their neighbors alone. We hope in due time that that can be brought about.

At the moment, General Taylor will report to us on developments. We will carefully consider those reports. He is meeting with Secretary McNamara and Secretary Rusk, Mr. Bundy and Mr. Harriman, I believe, today and tomorrow. I will meet with him in the early part of the week.[8] I anticipate that there will be no dramatic announcement to come out of these meetings except in the form of your speculation.

[7.] Q. Mr. President, have you given any thought to a meeting with the new leaders of the Soviet, and do you think such a meeting could serve a useful purpose in the next few months?

THE PRESIDENT. We have no plans for such a meeting.

[8.] Q. Mr. President, in connection with your statement on Western Europe, there have been questions about your own personal commitment to the multilateral force. Do you strongly believe in it as the main essential in your program for Western Europe at this time?

THE PRESIDENT. I touched on that in the statement a moment ago. We are now preparing ourselves for a conference with the Prime Minister of Great Britain who will be here in a few days.[9] We have just concluded meetings between Mr. Rusk and Mr. Schröder.[10] I think the general feeling of the President and this Government is outlined in the statement I just gave you. We do realize that for many years to come we will have great responsibility in this general area.

We want to work out with all of the nations, the free nations, the best solution possible. We are not going to be adamant in our attitudes. We are going to try to be cooperative and helpful, and we hope that we can obtain a meeting of the minds of all of our allies.

[9.] Q. Mr. President, do you foresee the meeting with Wilson as the beginning of a round of bilateral talks with allied leaders, and including one with De Gaulle?

THE PRESIDENT. No, I wouldn't say it is a beginning. I would say it is natural and

---

[8] On December 1 the White House announced that the President had reviewed the situation in South Viet-Nam with Ambassador Taylor, Secretary of State Dean Rusk, Secretary of Defense Robert S. McNamara, Central Intelligence Agency Director John A. McCone, and Gen. Earle G. Wheeler, Chairman of the Joint Chiefs of Staff.

The release stated that Ambassador Taylor reported that the political situation in Saigon was still difficult, but that the new government under Prime Minister Tran Van Huong was making a determined effort to strengthen national unity, to maintain law and order, and to press forward with the security program. Over the past few months, he said, security problems had increased in the northern provinces of South Viet-Nam, with uneven progress elsewhere; however the strength of the government's armed forces was being increased by improved recruiting and conscription, and by an increase of nearly 100 percent in the combat strength of the Vietnamese Air Force. Ambassador Taylor also reported that increased interdiction of communication routes by the Viet Cong was interfering to some extent with commerce within the country.

The meeting, the release noted, also reviewed the accumulating evidence of continuing and increased North Vietnamese support of the Viet Cong and of North Vietnamese forces in, and passing through, the territory of Laos in violation of the Geneva Accords of 1962.

The release concluded by stating that the President had "reaffirmed the basic U.S. policy of providing all possible and useful assistance to the South Vietnamese people and government in their struggle to defeat the externally supported insurgency and aggression being conducted against them."

[9] See Items 795–797.
[10] Gerhard Schröder, German Foreign Minister, who was in Washington November 22–26.

normal for the allies to confer and exchange viewpoints. We are very happy that the Prime Minister is coming, and we look forward to a very productive visit. We will be very glad from time to time to meet with the other leaders. As you know, Secretary Ball [11] and Secretary Rusk both have trips to Europe planned this year, and there will be other exchanges. I wouldn't say that the meeting with Wilson is necessarily the beginning. I would say it is a normal routine, and we will carry on with them and explore every possible matter of mutual interest.

Q. Do you foresee one soon with De Gaulle?

THE PRESIDENT. We don't have any scheduled at the present time.

[10.] Q. Mr. President, sir, do you plan any sort of reprisals against the rebels in the Congo to hold them responsible for killing the Americans?

THE PRESIDENT. I think that the Secretary has stated our position, that we feel outraged by the actions that were taken, not only against some of our people but against the Congolese themselves, that resulted in thousands losing their lives, and we certainly hope that the perpetrators of these outrages are brought to justice.

[11.] Q. Mr. President, do you feel that J. Edgar Hoover's usefulness has been impaired because of the controversial statements he has made about Martin Luther King, the Warren Commission, and the Supreme Court?

THE PRESIDENT. We have individuals from time to time that give their views in various situations. Both persons that you mentioned have exercised their freedom of speech on occasions. My problem is to try to prevent the strong divisions that could come to pass from time to time, instead of

[11] George W. Ball, Under Secretary of State.

provoke them. We are very anxious that each person receive the protections of the law in this country and be adequately protected in their constitutional rights.

Mr. Hoover has been called upon by the President and by others on many occasions to do work in the examination and in the study and investigation in this field, particularly the field of civil rights. He has been diligent and rather effective, and I would hope that in the months ahead we would have further evidence of the outstanding capacity of his people, and that this would not degenerate into a battle of personalities.

As you know, in the campaign I did all I could to keep that from happening, and I will continue to.

[12.] Q. Mr. President, is it the estimate of our Government today that an increase or an expansion of the war in Viet-Nam would probably lead to Chinese Communist retaliation?

THE PRESIDENT. I think that we will evaluate the entire situation out there with General Taylor in the coming week and take whatever action we think is in the national interest.

[13.] Q. Mr. President, do you intend to name——

THE PRESIDENT. I am not hearing you, and I am having a little static over here.

Q. Do you intend to name a new Attorney General anytime soon, Mr. President?

THE PRESIDENT. I have named Mr. Katzenbach to direct the activities of the Justice Department. When and if I have any changes in that situation, I will be glad to promptly announce them.

Q. Mr. President, do you anticipate any other Cabinet changes?

THE PRESIDENT. Yes, I think from time to time there will be changes in the departments. A good many men who came there expecting to stay 2 or 3 or 4 years—their time has already run out. I have one that I can announce to you this morning.

The Under Secretary of the Treasury, Mr. Roosa, had agreed to stay on 3 years when he came to Washington, and because of the situation in our Government following the loss of President Kennedy, we asked him to stay on. He agreed to help us through this year. He is resigning to go into private business, and he has written me a letter of resignation. I have responded.

If Mr. Reedy will have those letters mimeographed, they will be available to you and you can release them in the morning.

But there will be changes in the administration from time to time because of the long period that some men have served, because of financial demands, because of family problems. I don't anticipate that I will have the degree of changes that you would have in a change of administration. I hope that we will have reasonable continuity, and I think we have had. It is rather unusual. I am deeply indebted to the men and women who have made sacrifices to continue in public service.

[14.] Q. Mr. President, to get back to J. Edgar Hoover for 1 minute, have you given him assurances that he can remain as Director of the FBI as long as you are President?

THE PRESIDENT. We had a public ceremony regarding Mr. Hoover, and I will ask Mr. Reedy to give you a full transcript so you can have exactly what happened and what was said.[12]

[15.] Q. Mr. President, do you have an agreement with Vice President-elect Humphrey as to what would happen if you suffered some disability as other Presidents have had?

THE PRESIDENT. No, I don't.

---

[12] See Item 333.

Q. Do you plan something like that?

THE PRESIDENT. I do—when he is Vice President.

[16.] Q. Mr. President, a number of African nationalists have charged that our intervention in Stanleyville was an act of imperialism. What answer do you have for those?

THE PRESIDENT. I think I have told you what actuated us and what motivated us. We went in solely for humanitarian reasons. We were asked by the Belgian Government to assist with transportation in order to prevent massacre of our citizens and of other citizens of the world, including citizens of the Congo.

We gave great consideration to that and we saw there was no responsible government that had been able to give us any assurances that the lives of our people would not be taken and the lives of other nationals would not be taken. And we had seen that thousands of Congolese had lost their lives.

So we felt that our concern for humanity, our own national interest, dictated that we comply with the request to furnish transportation. We made that decision. We acted. We carried out our part of the bargain and we think we saved hundreds and thousands of lives, not only of Americans but others. And I thought we had no alternatives.

[17.] Q. Mr. President, are you going to give Mr. Marvin Watson a post in your administration?

THE PRESIDENT. I would like to, but I have no plans whatever to. He has other problems, other duties now, and there is not anything in the offing. I see a good deal in the press about it. But if they had taken the same caution you do, they wouldn't have misled their readers.

[18.] Q. Mr. President, have you made any decision on the vacancy on the Federal Power Commission?

THE PRESIDENT. No, I haven't. When I have any appointments to make, we won't keep those secret. We will make a public announcement of them. In cases of all commissions, we will submit their names to the Congress for confirmation where they will be carefully considered and perhaps debated.

[19.] Q. Mr. President, could you tell us anything about your personal contact with General de Gaulle?

THE PRESIDENT. Yes, we have had contacts from time to time when I was Vice President, and since I have become President, personal, official, orally, and in writing. No doubt we will have others from time to time.

[20.] Q. Mr. President, there have been reports, including one in a speech by Senator Humphrey, that you plan to submit a very extensive Federal aid program for elementary and high schools. Can you tell us a little bit about that?

THE PRESIDENT. No. We have reached no agreement about that.

[21.] Q. Mr. President, do you still hope to keep your budget below $100 billion?

THE PRESIDENT. I would always hope to keep it as low as possible. I have told you about what I know, and I think that it would be pure speculation to say—well, I have said many times that I like to keep the budget as low as possible. I hope it could be $100 billion. But I have given you the facts as I see them, and maybe your speculation on that is as good as mine. It is very difficult to know now whether you can reduce these requests to that area or not. I would rather doubt it at the moment.

[22.] Q. Mr. President, before the convention, we understood that you expected to expand the duties of the Vice President. Have you talked to Senator Humphrey about this and could you give us something more specific about the tasks you expect him to do?

THE PRESIDENT. Yes, I have talked to him about it, and I will be talking to him about it from time to time, and will be asking him to assume additional responsibilities as the need for them arises. I expect to engage his counsel and his years of experience in connection with the budget before it goes to Congress so he will be generally familiar with the operations of each department.

I would hope that because of his long association in the Senate and his familiarity with the legislative program that he would not only as presiding officer of that body under the Constitution but as a former Member of it he would be of great service to the country, acting with the Legislative and the Executive in trying to help formulate our program for the year.

I know he has demonstrated an intense interest in our space activities, and under the Space Act he will be the new Chairman of the Space Council, which is composed of the Secretary of State, the Secretary of Defense, the Chairman of the Atomic Energy Commission, and the Space Administrator. Because of his activity and his interest in the constitutional rights field, I know that he will give us his counsel and leadership in connection with equal employment and preventing discrimination against any of our citizens because of race or religion or region.

From time to time there will be particular assignments that I will want him to undertake because, as I told you before, I have an extremely high regard for his capacity, and he has a rich background. I want to call upon him every place I think he can make a contribution.

He has already been here, as you know. He was the first to come. We talked at some length about what he would do. Some of that was on the record, such as I have just repeated to you. Unfortunately, the horse got in the way and took the headlines. But he will be very busily engaged.

[23.] Q. Mr. President, you may remember that during the campaign you had to cancel a dinner engagement in Dallas. Do you expect to be able to keep that engagement before the end of the year?

THE PRESIDENT. No. I never had an engagement in Dallas, and I did not cancel any engagements. There was some tentative planning that included a number of visits in Texas. We did not confirm those and we were unable to continue with our planning in that regard because of developments regarding the Chinese nuclear situation and the change of government in Russia.

I welcome every opportunity to come to Texas, and I will no doubt be visiting you perhaps more frequently than you would like because I know it is a long way out here on a slow bus, and part of your responsibility is to look after, look over, and look out for the President, and keep in touch with his activities. But I will be back, in and out from time to time, and I would like very much to visit other parts of the State.

[24.] Q. Mr. President, can you give us any sort of a preview of the program you will place before the new Congress, at least the items to which you will give top priority?

THE PRESIDENT. Yes. I don't think the Cabinet and the President, and my staff people, have closed it up yet, but we have been working day and night since the election in thinking, researching, studying, and inviting the counsel of business people, medical leaders, educational leaders, and Government experts, and we are trying to assemble these ideas and suggestions for my considera-

tion and for the Cabinet's study, and for the Budget Director's attention.

We feel very strongly that the parts of the program that were not enacted in the last session should be acted upon at an early date. Those include medical care, Appalachia, ARA, the immigration bill. All of those are a part of what the Johnson administration feels is of immediate interest and need to the American people.

In addition we are now evaluating very carefully the requirements of the three educational bills that I signed into law, the hospital and library bills that I have signed into law, the poverty program which we have inaugurated, which they received their money for in October. They are very carefully trying to wisely apportion that over the country. We want to see what expansions we can make in that field.

We will have a very heavy emphasis, as I indicated in the campaign, on natural beauty, on conservation, on education, on health, on economy, and we will continue with our scientific studies and try to advance and accelerate improvements in the Defense Department, our weapons systems, and our space effort. All of those will be submitted to the Congress from time to time.

We will have some general observations to make early in the year, but I have already reviewed with the leadership what I would like for them to act on in the way of medical care, excise taxes, unemployment compensation modernization, and the detailed provisions on health, education, conservation, agriculture, natural beauty, will come along from time to time.

Reporter: Thank you, Mr. President.

NOTE: President Johnson's thirty-fourth news conference was held on the front lawn at the LBJ Ranch, Johnson City, Tex., at 10:45 a.m. on Saturday, November 28, 1964.

781   Message Greeting Sir Winston Churchill on the Occasion of His 90th Birthday.   *November 30, 1964*

I KNOW I speak for all Americans, your fellow citizens, in extending warmest congratulations and affectionate best wishes on your 90th birthday. As you celebrate this milestone in a full and eventful life we remember with gratitude, and future generations will continue to do so, your magnificent eloquence, your unfailing courage and your great service to the cause of freedom and human dignity.

LYNDON B. JOHNSON

NOTE: The text of Sir Winston's reply follows:

I am most grateful to you, Mr. President, for your heartwarming message. As an honorary citizen of the United States, I send my compatriots my thanks and my true good wishes.

WINSTON S. CHURCHILL

782   Remarks at a Luncheon for the U.S. Olympic Medal Winners.   *December 1, 1964*

I HOPE you are understanding people. I appreciate your patience and ask for your forgiveness. I would like to introduce to you a few of our distinguished guests today.

There is a saying among some people to never spend your time on a colonel if there is a general in the vicinity. And my beloved friend and distinguished Vice President-elect, Senator Hubert Humphrey, I observe has a rule, "Never sit by a man, if there is a lady in the room." Stand up, Hubert. I want to introduce you.

And that may account for the unusually high percentage of female voters that were recorded in November.

I would also like to present Mr. Kenneth L. Wilson, the president of the United States Olympic Committee which did such a superb job of administering affairs for our team and three other high officials of our Government who made their own sparkling place in the record book of sports. If you will, hold your applause until I introduce the other three distinguished guests today.

My good friend and very great public servant, Mr. Justice Byron R. White, presently a member of the Supreme Court, the fabled "Whizzer" White, everybody's All-American when he played football at the University of Colorado.

My Secretary of the Interior, the imaginative and man of vision, Mr. Stewart L. Udall, who was a star guard on the 1946 championship basketball team of the University of Arizona and is presently a star guard in the Cabinet of the United States.

Finally, my old friend, Stan Musial, "Stan, the Man," who I am privileged to have serving with me as my Special Consultant for Physical Fitness, and, so far as I know, anticipates no senatorial aspirations.

This is an especially happy occasion for Mrs. Johnson and me. Like most Americans, the Johnson family followed the 1964 Olympics with avid interest and a very warm sense of satisfaction.

In all the long and exciting tradition of these international games, I doubt if there has ever been a finer representation of the essential Olympic spirit. Some 6500 young men and women from some 94 nations presented a memorable demonstration of winning without strutting and losing without whimpering. Certainly the 1964 competition notably advanced the Olympic ideal of promoting respect between the peoples of the world.

The Japanese are artists in hospitality and on this occasion they outdid even their reputation. They left nothing to chance—nothing at all, not even overlooking the 36 extra dogcatchers along the route of the marathon to protect those celebrated shins of yours.

And the athletic records came tumbling down, as all good records should. Of course, I will say nothing about the brilliant run of medals that were won by the American team. But perhaps you will forgive me if I note that the "Star Spangled Banner" was played so often that people in Tokyo went around humming it like the number one hit tune of the day.

Mrs. Johnson and I are very happy to welcome you medal winners of the American team and you United States officials of the Olympic Committee. We wish there had been room here in this White House to invite all of those who represented America so superbly. But we are delighted today to greet you as the representatives of all of the athletes and the officials.

The American people are very proud of their 1964 Olympic team. They are proud of what you have accomplished and, what is more important, they are proud of what you are.

You young athletes chose a difficult and a demanding endeavor. You represent excellence finely honed to the keenest possibilities.

You exemplify the ideal of our Nation for all phases of our national life. In every occupation, in every endeavor, public and private, let us go at the task fullheartedly and let us demand results that meet the most severe and the most exciting standards.

Our poets have told us, America is promises. America is fulfillment, fulfillment in the richest and the most zestful sense of that word.

Years ago the founder of the modern Olympics declared: "The important thing in the Olympic games is taking part. The essential thing in the Olympic games is fighting well."

You have symbolized for all of us Americans what taking part—a genuine, dedicated, all-out taking part—can produce, and we salute you with a pride that carries the fullest measure of American gratitude for all the people who are privileged to be citizens of the same country that you claim.

It is such a privilege to have you here in the first house of the land. It is equally satisfying to have in this house some of the first of the land.

Thank you very much.

NOTE: The President spoke at 2:45 p.m. at a luncheon in the East Room at the White House. Attending were about 100 of the U.S. Olympic medal winners.

A White House release of November 30, announcing the luncheon, stated that immediately after the close of the games, held in Tokyo October 10–24, the President cabled the following message to Kenneth L. Wilson, president of the U.S. Olympic Committee:

"The Nation is proud of its Olympic representatives and their accomplishments. Please give my warm congratulations to the committee and the whole team. Would like to greet all of you personally at the White House. Since that is impractical please invite on my behalf as representatives of the whole group the four officers of the committee and the winners of medals to lunch with me."

Because many of the athletes had previous commitments in other countries, the release further stated, the luncheon was delayed until December 1.

783   Remarks Upon Presenting the Distinguished Service Medal to Gen. Thomas S. Power.   *December 1, 1964*

Distinguished fellow Americans:

We have come this afternoon to honor an outstanding officer and to express this Nation's gratitude for his long and his faithful service to his country.

When General Power was born, Orville and Wilbur Wright were still trying to sell the Army Signal Corps, over at Fort Myer, our first military airplane. He has lived to see the United States Air Force become the greatest air arm that any nation ever possessed.

By his dedication and his great personal effort, often at sacrifice, he has helped to make that Air Force a bulwark of peace around the globe. Not only was he one of the distinguished air strategists of World War II, leading and directing the first large-scale raid on Tokyo, which hastened the end of that bloody and that costly conflict, but in his role as Commander of the Air Force Research and Development Command, General Power has contributed vitally to the scientific and the technical development of the foremost space-age air force in all the world.

For the past 7 years he has directed our Strategic Air Command, that airborne armada on which free nations rely for continued peace and for their security. No matter how impressive our aircraft, no matter how ingenious our weapons, they would all be worthless without the skill and the lifelong dedication to duty of the men who man them.

General Power has displayed such skill and such devotion, steadfastly and unstintingly all through his career.

So, as we tardily meet here this afternoon, in the presence of his friends and his associates, on behalf of a most grateful Nation I am privileged and I am proud to present General Power with another addition to his long list of honors, his second Distinguished Service Medal.

Secretary Zuckert will now read the citation.

[*Secretary of the Air Force Eugene M. Zuckert read the citation, the text of which follows.*]

CITATION TO ACCOMPANY THE AWARD OF
THE DISTINGUISHED SERVICE MEDAL
(FIRST OAK LEAF CLUSTER)
TO
THOMAS S. POWER

General Thomas S. Power distinguished himself by exceptionally meritorious service to the United States in a position of great responsibility as Commander in Chief, Strategic Air Command, from 1 July 1957 to 30 November 1964. During these years General Power's outstanding command ability and professional knowledge have contributed significantly to developing and maintaining our nation's deterrent forces. In a time of revolutionary change in military weapons systems, he directed the introduction of operational missiles into the Strategic Air Command weapons inventory and brought the missiles to a high state of readiness despite stringent schedules, thereby providing a significant addition to our deterrent force. His inspiring leadership, resoluteness and exceptional managerial ability in building and maintaining a superb world-wide strategic organization have contributed immeasurably toward promoting the security and prestige of the United States. The singularly distinctive accomplishments of General Power culminate a long and distinguished career in the service of his country, and reflect the highest credit upon himself and the United States Air Force.

LYNDON B. JOHNSON

NOTE: The presentation ceremony was held at 5:30 p.m. in the East Room at the White House.

784 Remarks at the Ground-Breaking Ceremony for the John F. Kennedy Center for the Performing Arts. *December 2, 1964*

Bishop Hannan, Mr. Justice White, General Kennedy, Mr. Stephens, trustees of the Kennedy Center, my fellow Americans, distinguished members of the diplomatic corps, ladies and gentlemen:

John Kennedy once said, "I look forward to an America which will steadily raise the standards of artistic accomplishment and which will steadily enlarge cultural opportunities for all of our citizens."

As I sat here on the platform this morning, I reviewed some of the efforts that were made as a result of his inspiring leadership to make possible the ground breaking that will take place here today.

I recalled that we all met in the White House under the leadership of his mother-in-law, and we used the first house of this land one of the first times to raise funds to make this event possible.

I remember going to Mrs. Post's home and meeting with patriotic and dedicated citizens who in their generosity were willing to come there and spend the evening to try to add their bit to this great effort.

I recall the contribution of the Members of the Congress, and, through them, all the people of the United States who took the funds from the farmer and the laborer, the banker and the artist, to appropriate them so that we might be here today and participate as we are.

We are taking a very important step to-ward that dream that President and Mrs. Kennedy had, and to which most of you have contributed your bit. This center will brighten the life of Washington, but it is not, as I have said, just a Washington project. It is a national project and a national possession, and it became a reality, as General Kennedy has observed, because of the willingness of all the representatives of all the people to make it possible. It is dedicated to the common awareness of all men. It was conceived under the administration of President Eisenhower. It was inspired and encouraged and led by the imagination and the purpose of President Kennedy. And after his death, the Congress, realizing that, named it in his memory and generously, and I think wisely, provided the matching funds so that we could get on our way.

If it fulfills our hopes, this center will be, at once, a symbol and a reflection and a hope. It will symbolize our belief that the world of creation and thought are at the core of all civilization. Only recently in the White House we helped commemorate the 400th anniversary of Shakespeare. The political conflicts and ambitions of his England are known to the scholar and to the specialist. But his plays will forever move men in every corner of the world.

The leaders that he wrote about live far more vividly in his words than in the almost forgotten facts of their own rule.

Our civilization, too, will largely survive in the works of our creation. There is a quality in art which speaks across the gulf dividing man from man and nation from nation, and century from century. That quality confirms the faith that our common hopes may be more enduring than our conflicting hostilities. Even now men of affairs are struggling to catch up with the insights of great art. The stakes may well be the survival of civilization. The personal preferences of men in government are not important—except to themselves.

However, it is important to know that the opportunity we give to the arts is a measure of the quality of our civilization. It is important to be aware that artistic activity can enrich the life of our people, which really is the central object of Government. It is important that our material prosperity liberate and not confine the creative spirit.

The role of Government must be a small one. No act of Congress or Executive order can call a great musician or poet into existence. But we can stand on the sidelines and cheer. We can maintain and strengthen an atmosphere to permit the arts to flourish, and those who have talent to use it. And we can seek to enlarge the access of all of our people to artistic creation.

As a veteran of 24 years in the Congress, I am not a prophet but I do want to suggest to my friend, the new Senator from New York, he is in for listening to more poetry than he would surmise in some of the morning sessions of the Senate.

Last September, I signed a bill establishing the National Council on the Arts. Versions of this proposal had been under consideration since 1877. I intend to consider other ways in which Government can appropriately encourage the arts. I want to, as the leader of this country, express my personal gratitude to the persons on the platform with me, and particularly to the persons like Mrs. Auchincloss and others that I see in the audience, for the sacrifices in time and effort they have made to encourage, lead, and direct this effort.

This center will reflect the finest artistic achievements of our time. It is our hope that it will house the leading artists and performers. Almost every industrialized nation in the world, on both sides of the Iron Curtain, has one or more national centers for the arts. Washington has lagged behind. Far too often, American actors and singers and musicians must travel to foreign countries to even be heard. Now, because of President Kennedy's leadership and your efforts, they will have a stage here in the Capital of their own country.

I expect this center to be a living force for the encouragement of art. Washington needs new theaters and new concert halls. But if that is all that we are building, we will have fallen far short of today's expectation and promise.

This center will have a unique opportunity to bring together worlds of poetry and power—and bring it to the benefit of each of us. It must give special attention to the young; to increasing their interest and stimulating their creativity. It can serve as a model and instructor to other cultural centers around our Nation. It should open up new opportunities to be heard to young singers and filmmakers and playwrights. It must take the lead in bringing the best in the performing arts to every part of our beloved and rich country; so that theater and opera are not the privilege of the lucky citizens of just a few metropolitan centers.

Yes, this is our ambitious program. But so was the vision of the man in whose memory this center is today named.

Pericles said, "If Athens shall appear great to you, consider then that her glories were purchased by valiant men, and by men who learned their duty."

As this center comes to reflect and advance the greatness of America, consider then those glories were purchased by a valiant leader who never swerved from duty—John Kennedy. And in his name I dedicate this site.

NOTE: The President spoke at 12:20 p.m. at the site of the John F. Kennedy Center for the Performing Arts on the banks of the Potomac River in Washington. In his opening words he referred to the Most Reverend Philip M. Hannan, auxiliary bishop of Washington, Byron R. White, Associate Justice of the Supreme Court, Senator-elect Robert F. Kennedy of New York, former Attorney General, and Roger F. Stephens, chairman of the Board of Trustees of the John F. Kennedy Center for the Performing Arts.

Early in his remarks the President referred to the meeting of the trustees and Advisory Commit-

tee of the National Cultural Center held at the White House November 14, 1961 (see "Public Papers of the President, John F. Kennedy 1961," Item 467). He also referred to President Kennedy's mother-in-law, Mrs. Hugh D. Auchincloss, chairman of the Greater Washington Area Committee for the Center, and Mrs. Merriweather Post, who gave a reception at her home in the fall of 1962 to publicize a closed-circuit TV fundraising program for the center, broadcast in November 1962.

The National Cultural Center was established by the National Cultural Center Act, approved September 2, 1958, by President Eisenhower (72 Stat. 1698). It was renamed the John F. Kennedy Center for the Performing Arts, as a memorial to President Kennedy, by act of Congress, approved January 23, 1964 (78 Stat. 4; see also Item 142 above).

The National Council on the Arts was established by the National Arts and Cultural Development Act of 1964, approved September 3, 1964 (78 Stat. 905).

785   Remarks at a Luncheon for Supporters of Radio Free Europe.   *December 2, 1964*

Mr. Greenewalt, gentlemen:

I want to thank you for coming to the White House today. In the last year I have had the pleasure of welcoming many of you on other occasions here. Some of you have come as valued advisers on matters of general policy. Others have come as representatives of the great American business community. A few of you have even come to help in a political election. But you are all welcome today, without regard to what you may have said or thought or done in the months before November 3. Our business today is the business of freedom, and that is a subject on which Americans are always united.

I have been a supporter of Radio Free Europe since its earliest years. I have watched it grow and become a major link between the world of freedom and the brave peoples of Eastern Europe. Radio Free Europe has helped to keep alive their longing for freedom. In their own languages,

in voices of their own countrymen, it tells the truth. It tells what is happening in Europe and America and Asia and Africa. It even tells them what is really happening inside the Communist world.

As President, I am proud that our people, through their contributions to RFE, help to support direct communication with the people of Eastern Europe.

Radio Free Europe is now more significant than ever. History is again on the march in Eastern Europe, and on the march toward increased freedom. These people—and some of their rulers—long for deeper, steadier, and more natural relations with the West. We understand this longing and we intend to respond to it in every way open to us.

We will welcome evidence of genuine willingness on the part of East European governments to cooperate with the United States Government in joint endeavors. We will reject no such overtures out of hand. We will judge them in terms of the true interests of our own people and the people of these countries. We wish to build new bridges to Eastern Europe—bridges of ideas, education, culture, trade, technical cooperation, and mutual understanding for world peace and prosperity. In this process there is no greater instrument than truth. And truth is the daily business of Radio Free Europe.

When the peoples of Eastern Europe are again able to enjoy radio broadcasting from their own capitals which tells them as much as Radio Free Europe does, then Radio Free Europe will have finished its job. Until then, RFE has work ahead of it, day in day out, year in year out.

I urge you all to continue to support Radio Free Europe vigorously. I ask you to tell your friends and associates, your neighbors and colleagues how much I care about Radio Free Europe, how proud I am of the strong backing given to it by the American people; above all, how vital I believe it is that this strong voice of truth and freedom have the means to keep up its good work on behalf of the people of Eastern Europe.

So I thank you again for coming, and now I would like to turn this meeting over to a man who has been doing a magnificent job of leadership in this great work, Mr. Crawford Greenewalt.

NOTE: The President spoke in the State Dining Room at the White House. His opening words referred to Crawford H. Greenewalt, head of the group of about 80 business and industrial leaders from throughout the United States, supporters of Radio Free Europe, who attended the luncheon.

786 Remarks Recorded for the Commissioning of the U.S.S. *Sam Rayburn*. *December 2, 1964*

My fellow Americans:

Today we are commissioning our 28th nuclear-powered Polaris submarine. This submarine will be named for a great American—the late Speaker of the House of Representatives, Sam Rayburn.

Polaris submarines are named for great patriots who have rendered distinguished service to the cause of freedom.

Nothing could be more appropriate than to honor in this fashion Sam Rayburn.

In our times, no man pursued that cause with greater fervor, nor with greater distinction, than did this great representative of the people.

He served in the Congress for nearly half a century. He held the high office of Speaker longer than any other American. His achievements and his example will endure so long as this Republic stands.

Mr. Rayburn was a man of peace—but he was also a man of firmness and courage. He knew that peace and freedom could be preserved only if we, as a nation, held steadfast to a course of firmness and courage. Many of the victories won on fields far away began in the leadership of Mr. Rayburn— and others like him—in the halls of our Congress.

When Mr. Rayburn died in 1961, only two Polaris submarines had been deployed. Soon there will be 41 on patrol beneath the seas of the world, virtually invulnerable to surprise attack by any enemy.

Yet the purpose of this new submarine— like those which came before—is not war, but peace. While such power exists, no potential enemy can hope to profit from an unprovoked, surprise attack on the United States.

Our Polaris missiles, together with our strategic bombers and our long-range missiles ashore, guarantee any adversary that retaliation for a nuclear attack on this country would be inevitable and devastating.

Because the world knows this, the chances of war are lessened—and the chance of lasting peace is greater.

As we put this fine ship into commission, let us reaffirm our dedication to the cause of peace, and the pursuit of justice among men around the world.

We of this generation share responsibility not only for our own security, but for the security of the entire free world.

In facing these responsibilities, we pursue not our own interests, but the interests of all mankind. It was by this standard that Sam Rayburn served his country and it is by this standard that we live and labor today.

Our great strength exists not to destroy, but to save—not to put an end to life as we know it, but to put an end to conflict and war as man has known it since time began.

With God's help, that is what we shall do.

NOTE: The President's remarks were taped earlier at the White House for use at the commissioning ceremony held at Newport News, Va., at 2 p.m. on December 2.

787 Remarks to the Members of the Business Council. *December 2, 1964*

ONE HUNDRED years ago, at the midpoint of the decade of the 1860's, this Nation emerged from a paralyzing period of division, bitterness, and strife.

A spirit of new unity and confidence appeared. As a result, America entered the most expansive decades of the last century. Our Nation grew. Our economy grew. The hopes and horizons of our people began to grow—as never before.

From Maine to California, the foundation was put in place for the great thrust forward which has brought us the system and society we know today.

I believe there is a parallel with our own times now.

In this year of 1964, the people have expressed their will that the division, bitterness, and contention of our times be laid aside.

A fresh spirit of unity and confidence is strong—in all sections and among all segments. As a result, we are approaching the midpoint of this decade of the 1960's ready—as never before—for America's greatest expansion, growth, and success.

We of this generation have the opportunity—and we have the obligation—to put in place the foundation for the America of the 21st century.

This challenge is our chief concern in Washington.

I know it is your chief concern in your businesses, also.

That is why I would like to speak to the Business Council tonight about the contributions both Government and business have to make in the years immediately ahead.

Over the past 12 months I have said many times that it is my hope—and purpose—that Government and business should operate in partnership, not as antagonists.

That will always be my goal.

Government cannot maintain a healthy, prosperous economy by its own efforts. But neither is it fair nor possible to demand that business solve our economic problems alone.

We must work together—and we shall.

Times are good—we hope and expect them to continue.

But if we made a list of the foremost economic problems confronting us today, that list would include these four:

1. Maintaining and, if possible, accelerating our rate of economic expansion to continue whittling away at unemployment and unused capacity.

2. Maintaining our excellent record of price stability.

3. Continuing to strengthen our balance of payments.

4. Finding ways to reduce the tragically high rate of unemployment among teenagers, and assuring adequate economic opportunities for all our people not now in the mainstream of American prosperity.

In each of these four areas, Government has an important role—and so does business. I want to spell out my views in this regard—and assure you that your views are welcome by this administration whether in agreement or disagreement.

First, there is the problem of sustaining prosperity.

I believe the Federal Government's role is to create a climate conducive to prosperity. To do this, there are six primary obligations.

1. A tax system that does not overburden businessmen or consumers—and maintains the incentives for productive effort.

2. Expenditure programs that promote development of human and natural resources and make the social investments needed to support private activity.

3. Keeping a clear field for private initiative in the wide range of activities where competitive enterprise is the most efficient way of getting things done.

4. An overall budget policy that promotes balance between purchasing power and productive capacity.

5. Monetary and credit policies that provide funds to nourish an expanding economy without overfeeding it.

6. Finally, there must be an alertness and a willingness to act promptly and decisively when the Nation is threatened by either recession or inflation.

These are obligations this administration has been willing to assume. And we have met them through such measures as last year's tax cut, our frugal but forward-looking budgets, and the policies of the Federal Reserve and the Treasury.

But if prosperity is to be realized, obligations must be met by business and labor and consumers, too. We look to business to contribute through these means:

1. The production of high-quality goods and new and improved items that merit the consumer's dollar.

2. Initiative in cost reduction.

3. Selling efforts that realize the full potential of domestic and international markets.

4. Employment policies that offer job security and incentives to able workers.

5. Investment policies that contribute to smooth expansion.

6. Careful, efficient management to avoid the inventory problems which have so often been a source of economic instability in the past.

I believe it is especially important for business to recognize prudently that we live in a growing economy—and an increasingly stable economy. Demand is growing 50 percent in a decade. To share in that growth, firms must expand both capacity—and employment.

The task of sustaining our domestic prosperity in the year ahead faces a new handicap not of our own making.

Events overseas have compelled the Federal Reserve to raise our discount rate. At the same time, the Federal Reserve and the FDIC have lifted the ceiling on the interest rates banks may pay on certain types of deposits—with primary emphasis on short-term deposits. Increases in these short-term rates were necessary at this time to guard against the possibility of an outflow of funds from this country.

We had to do this to protect the dollar abroad. And we will keep short-term rates at these levels as long as the international monetary situation requires it.

These actions demonstrate once again that we will do whatever is required to safeguard the strength of our dollar.

But Chairman Martin—both by his words and by the actions of the Federal Reserve—has shown his determination to assure the continued ample availability of reserves to banks and therefore of credit to business. He does not believe—nor do I—that the discount rate action will either lead to any appreciable rise in market yields on long-term bonds—or justify any general increase in the rates which banks charge their customers.

What troubles me is the risk that a general upward movement of bank lending rates might slow down our economic advance.

The first casualty of such a slowdown will be the support I need for my determined effort to control Government expenditures in order to get back to the balanced budget we must have—a balanced budget in a prosperous economy.

If our Federal revenues slip off because the economy is running slower, the Federal deficit will surely grow. But pressure will also converge on the Congress and the President to keep Federal expenditures up in every section of the country.

I am confident that American bankers will consider the long-term interest of the Nation in sustaining a healthy and vigorous rate of economic growth. I am sure they know that their own long-term interest is inseparable from the prosperity of the Nation.

The second concern facing us on both sides of the desk is whether we can achieve rapid economic growth without sacrificing reasonable price stability. We can if both Government and business make the contributions they should.

For its part, Government must avoid overheating the economy, encourage cost-reducing investment in the private sector, support steady and sustained growth of markets, and plan now for future public and private needs to help lessen bottlenecks to expansion in the future.

I believe, also, that through wage-price guideposts Government can offer leadership on the kind of voluntary private wage and price policies that are consistent with achieving sustained prosperity, full employment, and price stability.

Business—for its part—can contribute to price stability by supporting and practicing active competition in free markets and by looking beyond short-term economic conditions. It is imperative that business policies provide a steady flow of new low-cost capacity to meet our growing demands, assure the training of the kinds of workers our economy will need before bottlenecks arise, seek profits from market expansion rather than exploitation of short-run opportunities, and pass on high-productivity gains through lower prices.

The third concern is with our balance of payments.

On this, Government's responsibility is major—and we take this responsibility most seriously. That is the reason for our strong commitment to cost and price stability, and to reducing the flow of short-term funds abroad.

Government payments abroad have been cut back—from more than $3.8 billion in 1960 to $2.7 billion this year, a cut of nearly one-third. Further cuts in overseas costs are due next year—without cutting our effectiveness.

We are trying in every way to help American exporters find and develop profitable markets abroad. We are seeking continually to remove foreign barriers to American goods—and the trade negotiations now starting in Geneva will be conducted on a truly reciprocal basis.

I remind you, Government cannot sell American goods abroad. Business itself must do that—and I urge every American businessman to make sure no profitable export possibilities are being neglected.

Fourth—and finally—we face the problems of teenage unemployment and economic opportunities for our minorities.

Overall, our unemployment rate is 5 percent. That is too high. But the teenage unemployment rate is almost three times higher—at 14.5 percent. And among the nonwhite teenagers in our labor force, the rate is an almost unbelievable 30 percent.

I have said before—and I say again: we cannot solve the social problems of our society at the end of a billy club. If we are to assure ourselves of law and order, if we are to reduce crime and delinquency, if we are to enjoy together the life of one nation and one people, we must make sure that opportunity is equal for all our people—of all ages, all races, all religions, all regions.

Discrimination in all its forms—including the lack of comparable education oppor-

tunities—is costing us nearly $20 billion a year. That is more than 3 percent of our GNP. It is a cost the public and private sectors together must labor constantly to reduce and remove.

As a Nation we have made great headway on these problems this year—in national legislation, in local community programs, in attitudes of employers and workers.

We must not allow that progress to be slowed now.

Our young people must be better trained for productive roles in our economy—and there must be assurance of jobs for them once they are trained, regardless of their race.

For all the challenges before us, the answer cannot come from Government alone—nor from the man who occupies the Presidency alone. The quality of America's future depends upon the quality of America's leadership—at every level.

I welcome and am grateful for the effective role of the Business Council. I hope that through your example a closer partnership may come between business and Government. On that partnership—and partnership with all segments—we can build more wisely and successfully for America's greatest years. For that is our opportunity and obligation now at this turning-point time in the decade of the 1960's.

NOTE: The President spoke at 9:30 p.m. at the Mayflower Hotel in Washington at a closed session of the Business Council. During his remarks he referred to William McC. Martin, Jr., Chairman of the Board of Governors of the Federal Reserve System. As printed, this item follows the prepared text released by the White House.

788   Remarks at the 175th Anniversary Convocation of
Georgetown University. *December 3, 1964*

Most Reverend Apostolic Delegate, Most Reverend Archbishop O'Boyle, Very Reverend Father Bunn, Very Reverend Father Campbell, my distinguished friends:

Robert Frost once said the greatest test of a college student's chances is when we know the sort of activity for which he will neglect his studies.

And so I hope that the presence of all of you here today is a very promising sign.

When it was proposed that a telegraph be set up between Texas and Maine, Thoreau commented: We are in a great rush to establish instant communication between Texas and Maine. But how do we know that Texas and Maine have anything to communicate?

I might add that last November, Texas and Maine were in close communication.

This is also a central problem of today's world. For almost the first time, the interdependence of nations is not a remote goal or a ringing slogan. It is a fact which we neglect at our own peril.

Communication satellites, atomic rockets, jet transports have made distant capitals into close neighbors. Our challenge is to transform this reality into an instrument for the freedom of man.

Today the cost of failure to communicate is not silence or serenity, but destruction and disillusion. Nowhere is this more true than in our relations with the nations of Western Europe.

Since World War II, we have sought a Europe growing in intimacy and unity with America. If we look beyond the clamor of daily reports and the voluble doubts of skeptics, we can see that this effort has been the greatest success story in the history of the West.

From desolation has come abundance. From division has come a degree of unity not achieved in a thousand years or more. From weakness and vulnerability have come stability within and increased security from without. From the ashes of holocaust has emerged the second strongest industrial civilization in the history of the world.

This is the triumph of the people of Europe and it is a tribute to the generosity of America. But most of all it stems from those men of vision who saw that the interests of their own people lay in increased unity and in partnership with the United States of America.

It was perhaps fortunate that the greatest threat came when the memory of past failures was still fresh. Out of the common experience of disaster and the onrush of new danger came the course that we have charted.

We must not now let success and prosperity strengthen the forces of inertia or dull the sense of urgency. Our very success opens the door to the revival of the ancient rivalries which have so often torn the fabric of our society.

We are not joined together by experience or convenience in pursuit of temporary goals. European unity and Atlantic partnership are based on deeply shared values and dangers, and interests, and the wise pursuit of the interest of each will strengthen the connection among all our nations.

The United States has no policy for the people of Europe, but we do have a policy toward the people of Europe. And we do have common hopes and common objectives shared with most of the people of Europe.

Answers to our common problems must emerge from the consent of free countries, and that consent, in turn, will be based on discussion and debate and respect for the ideas and the proposals of all. But there must be progress.

A Chinese proverb says there are many paths up the mountain, but the view from the top is always the same. We are always ready to look for a better or easier path, but we intend to climb to the summit.

First, we must all seek to assist in increasing the unity of Europe as a key to Western strength and a barrier to resurgent and erosive nationalism.

Second, we must all work to multiply in number and intimacy the ties between North America and Europe. For we shape an Atlantic civilization with an Atlantic destiny.

Third, we must all make sure that the Federal Republic of Germany is always treated as an honorable partner in the affairs of the West. Germany has labored to build a stable and a free society in complete loyalty to European unity and to Atlantic partnership. And the people and the leaders of Germany have bound themselves to peace and reconciliation with their European neighbors, and especially with France. They have rejected all separate adventures, especially, and I think most wisely, in the field of nuclear weapons.

In particular, our friends and comrades throughout Germany deserve assurance from their allies that there shall be no acceptance of the lasting threat to peace which is the forced division of Germany. No one seeks to end this grim and dangerous injustice by force. But there can be no stable peace in Europe while one part of Germany is denied

the basic right to choose freely its own destiny and to choose, without threat to anyone, reunion with the Germans in the Federal Republic.

Fourth, those of us who are ready to proceed in common ventures must decide to go forward together, always with due deliberation, with due respect for the interests of others, and with an open door for those who may join later. We shall always seek agreement. We shall never insist on unanimity. This is the course which has brought fruitful results and almost every major advance in the 20 years since World War II.

The Atlantic Alliance is not in the midst of crisis, as some alarm mongers would have you believe. But it is in the midst of change.

Every important period of progress has been marked by the same kind of discussion and debate that is now in progress.

The Coal and Steel Community, the integration of Germany into NATO, the Common Market, itself—raise some blood pressures among excitable people, arouse question and concern and warning. And we were told that such steps might be against the interests of America. We were told that it might become harder to deal with the Soviet Union. We were told that we might encourage German militarism. We were told that we might divide Europe or arouse hostilities.

To change patterns of thought or the shape of institutions is never very easy. Today's discussion and debate, the flow of ideas and proposals, is proof of coming change and a spur to continuing action.

The agenda for future progress does not consist of an isolated or a single dramatic step. It is made up of action—action across the whole range of common interest, which is the bedrock of our alliance.

We have a common interest in the defense

of the West. For 20 years the atomic might of the United States has been the decisive guard of freedom. Ours remains the largest strength and ours a most awesome obligation. But we recognize the reasonable interest and concerns of other allies, those who have nuclear weapons of their own and those who do not. We seek ways to bind the alliance even more strongly together by sharing the tasks of defense through collective action, and meeting the honorable concerns of all.

This is the meaning of the proposals that we have made. This is the meaning of the discussions that we expect and that we welcome, with all interested allies. We come to reason, not to dominate. We do not seek to have our way, but to find a common way.

Any new plans for the handling of weapons so powerful we think deserve most careful discussion and deliberation. No solution will be perfect in the eyes of everyone. But we all know that the problem is there. It must be solved. And we will continue to work for its solution.

We have a common interest in a rising standard of living for humanity. This will require a continuing effort to lower industrial tariffs in the Kennedy Round, and a joint study of the political and human problems of agriculture.

We have a common interest in assisting the freedom and the growth of the developing world, and none of us will be finally secure in a world that is divided into hostile camps of rich and poor, or black and white.

We must also seek progress towards stable prices and nondiscriminatory trade for our basic commodities.

We have a common interest in building bridges of trade and ideas, of understanding and humanitarian aid to the countries of Eastern Europe. These countries are increasingly asserting their own independence and we will work together to demonstrate that their prospects for progress lie in greater ties with the West.

We have a common interest in increasing political consultation among the nations of the alliance. This may well require more frequent meetings among all the ministers or deputy ministers of the NATO Alliance. It clearly demands that all of us be ready for those patient and determined efforts to meet each other halfway, without which no real agreement is ever possible among strong and honorable states.

Most of all, the Atlantic nations have a common interest in the peace of the world. In the past 4 years, we have taken several steps toward lessening the danger of war. The United States is prepared in full consultation with its allies to discuss any proposal with the Soviet Union which might increase the chances of a lasting peace.

These are some of the areas in which we must work together. At every turning point for 20 years we have risen above national concerns to the more spacious vision of European unity and Atlantic partnership. This, too, must be such a time.

So let no one mistake a brief calm for the end of the storm. The world is still full of peril for those who prize and cherish freedom. Across the earth from Asia to the heart of Africa forces are loosed whose direction is uncertain and whose portent is full with challenge.

All day yesterday the workers and the thinkers and the doers of your Government were occupied with the future of Africa. All day into the early hours of the morning the day before, the thinkers and the planners and the doers, if not the talkers or writers, were evaluating and searching for a solution to some of the problems of Asia. The unknown tide of future change is already beating about the rock of the West.

These fruitful lands washed by the Atlantic, this half-billion people unmatched in arms and industry, this measureless storehouse of wisdom and genius, can be a fortress against any foe, a force that will enrich the life of an entire planet.

It is not a question of arms or wealth alone. It is a question of moving ahead with the times, and it is a question of vision and persistence, and the willingness to surmount the barriers of national rivalry against which our ancestors have always collided.

There are so many things, so many more things in the world, that unite us than that divide us. And in this hour of trial, now is the time to come to the aid of your world by trying to be a force for unity instead of a voice for division.

Only yesterday, one of the notable men of this generation called to talk to me, and I had to postpone his call. I said to my assistant, "We can wait for him until tomorrow because he is a force for division."

So if we have the qualities of which I have spoken, then the first age with the power to destroy—destroy the world—can be the first, also, to put an end to that destruction. No one person, no individual, regardless of his heritage or his training, can alone lead us to the summit of the good things that are ahead. But I do in my own humble way appeal to each of you to forget the emotionalism that would bring hate to our hearts, and try to remember the sentiment that would make us all brothers in a world of great opportunity, in a time of great need.

Thank you.

NOTE: The President spoke at 11:30 a.m. in McDonough Gymnasium at Georgetown University in Washington, D.C., after being awarded an honorary doctor of laws degree. In his opening words he referred to the Most Reverend Egidio Vagnozzi, Apostolic Delegate to the United States, the Most Reverend Patrick A. O'Boyle, archbishop of Washington, the Very Reverend Edward B. Bunn, chancellor of the university and retiring president, and the Very Reverend Gerard J. Campbell, the university's newly inaugurated president.

789   Statement by the President on the Supersonic Transport Program.   *December 3, 1964*

THE development of a commercially profitable supersonic transport is a very difficult and complex undertaking. I believe that this country must take, in the words of Senator Monroney, "time for deliberate, proven development" and time to make certain that this will be the best supersonic in the world's airways.

NOTE: The statement was made public as part of a White House release which noted that the President had that day directed the Administrator of the Federal Aviation Agency to extend the current contracts of the engine and airframe manufacturers so that they could continue to study the problems associated with a commercial supersonic transport. The release also noted that the President's Advisory Committee on Supersonic Transport was expected to make recommendations early in 1965, following completion of economic studies by the Department of Commerce and of studies on sonic boom phenomena by the National Academy of Sciences.

See also Items 294 [5] and 355.

790 Remarks at a Ceremony Marking the 10th Anniversary of the Government Employees' Incentive Awards Act. *December 4, 1964*

Director Gordon, Chairman Macy, members of the Cabinet, ladies and gentlemen:

This is an opportunity that I welcome. A President's day is never long enough for all the things that he might like to do. I would like to get out and meet with the people who work with me. I would like to see more of the men and women who are in charge of the bureaus. I would like to just sit and talk with them, listen to their ideas, perhaps get them to listen to some of mine. I should like to meet with employees, to discuss ways to keep Government service alert and proud.

I so much want our Government service to be strong. I want it to have those qualities that make this a great and a decent country. I want it to be compassionate. I want it to be human, yet free of venality. I want it never to take itself for granted because that is the mark of a bad servant. An unmistakable sign of integrity in government is a sense of responsibility to the taxpayers.

I have said I believe in the tight fist and the open mind—a tight fist with money and an open mind to the needs of America. I want us to keep up with the times, but keep our feet on the ground. I want that same state of mind to prevail in every department and in every bureau of this Government.

I expect to find it at every level of responsibility, from Cabinet members down to the newest and the youngest recruit.

I want every supervisor to remember that your example is really what determines the attitudes of the men and the women who work with you. You are the officers of the line who lead the way and bear the burden and the responsibility.

A man will sometimes think that because his rank is modest he is insignificant in the great scheme of things. But I have read of what Nehru said as he worked with his colleagues and the British Ambassador on plans for a free India: "You know, we are small men and unimportant. But the cause in which we work is great—and some of that greatness touches each of us." That is the whole spirit of the public service with which I have been so proud to have been associated all of my adult life.

When I became your President 1 year ago, I assigned top priority to efficiency and economy in Government. I pledged that we would root out waste and inefficiency wherever we found it.

I believe we have made good on that pledge. I believe we have the people's confidence in our sincerity. But we must continue to earn that confidence. Controlling waste is somewhat like bailing a boat—you have to keep at it.

I have no intention of easing up on my insistence on getting a dollar of value for each dollar we spend. Economy "once in a while" is just not enough.

We have our work cut out for us in the years ahead.

I have asked all Americans to join in creating the Great Society. The abundance of this great land must be put to work for the benefit of all of our people. We must eliminate poverty. We must wipe out discrimination. We must provide education and employment opportunities. We must help to create great cities. We must conserve the land and the open spaces, and we must serve all of our people all the time.

I do not think that any of this is beyond the reach of a purposeful and resourceful people.

Theodore Roosevelt said that the President must be steward of all the people. So Government will play its proper part in this important work, and we cannot advance if our way is blocked with the debris of inefficiency or obsolescence, or downright waste.

We can afford only the essential. Whatever fails to meet that test must be put aside.

This is why we are closing defense installations that we no longer need.

This is why I have ordered every department to install a cost-reduction program patterned after the biggest department in terms of employees—the Defense Department—and in terms of budget.

This is why I am prepared to do whatever is necessary to stop spending scarce dollars on programs and services which have outlived their day.

We are going to put "thrift" back in the dictionary. As President, I can and I will make the major decisions on holding total spending to the rock bottom.

But most of the opportunities to increase efficiency and to find less costly ways to do business occur in the work that you do every day. And here is where I just must look to you and rely on you, because no one person can do this.

I want your help. I want every supervisor, I want every employee, to continually ask themselves two questions: What is it costing to do this work? Is there a way to do it as well or better that would cost less?

I want you to think of your bureau or your unit as though it were your own little private business. Would you have as many employees on your personal payroll? Would you be willing to write them checks every 2 weeks, the same amount that you are writing them with Uncle Sam's name signed? If they were working for you, would they be producing more? Could you make a profit with the practices that you are following? Where would you start to cut expenses if you didn't?

After all, really this is your business. You are the ones that are supporting it with your "deducts," with your taxes, and you ought to be concerned with it.

This is what a manager is there to do, and it is why I like to see tough-minded but fair people come into Government, with business experience. They are accustomed to market competition where quality and low unit costs make the difference between swimming and sinking. They can bring that state of mind to the management of the public's business. Where they do, everybody benefits.

But I am convinced that we have career managers in Government who are just as good as any managers in private business. I see evidence of this every day as our cost-reduction program produces improvements and savings.

And what I want you to understand this morning is that these talents must now be put to work at full capacity.

I am asking for your help.

I am asking for your cooperation.

I am asking for your very best effort.

And you will have the gratitude of your country and the gratitude of your President.

Today we observe the 10th year of the incentive awards program. We honor the Government employees who have been diligent in seeking ways to reduce costs, and diligent in increasing efficiency.

This program has already achieved much.

In a single year it produced 118,500 employee suggestions which were adopted. Its potential is vast.

Now I want to see another new record set in the coming 12 months. I have faith in you and I trust you, and I believe in you. Therefore, I just know you will do it.

Thank you very much.

NOTE: The President spoke at 11:52 a.m. in Constitution Hall. In his opening words he referred to Kermit Gordon, Director of the Bureau of the Budget, and John W. Macy, Jr., Chairman of the U.S. Civil Service Commission.

A White House release of December 2, announcing the awards ceremony, listed the 30 award winners and summaries of their special achievements. The release stated that the winners, chosen from more than 150 nominees, were selected for three types of contributions: cost-reduction achievements by employees, successful encouragement of employee economy contributions by supervisors, and cost-improvement action by program management officers.

The incentive awards program was established by the Government Employees' Incentive Awards Act, approved September 1, 1954 (68 Stat. 1112).

---

791 Statement by the President on the November Employment Report. *December 4, 1964*

THE November employment report is both encouraging and sobering.

The overall 5 percent figure for general unemployment conceals both a major breakthrough and a continuing crisis.

The unemployment rate for married men is down now to 2½ percent—its lowest point in 7 years.

We have reduced unemployment among this group by a third in the past 12 months.

There are a million and a half more people at work in this country today than there were a year ago.

The November figures also point out sharply where the worst problem remains: the unemployment rate for boys and girls under 20 is almost 15 percent—six times as high as the rate for married men.

There are gains on this front, too. Three hundred and thirty thousand more teenagers are at work than there were a year ago.

But they are pouring into the work force at an unprecedented rate. There will be a greater increase in the number of 18- and 19-year-old boys and girls in the work force in the next 12 months than during the entire period between 1950 and 1960.

We have got to get these boys and girls into jobs, or training programs, or back into school. We can't afford the price of turning down one out of every seven young Americans who apply for admission to responsible citizenship.

---

792 Statement by the President Upon Approving Civil Rights Regulations Covering the Programs of Federal Departments and Agencies. *December 4, 1964*

THIS NATION'S commitment to the principle of equality of treatment and opportunity for all Americans will be well served by the new regulations assuring that Federal programs are available to all citizens without regard to their race, color, or national origin. All key Federal officials have been instructed to cooperate with State and local governments and with private organizations and individuals participating in Federal programs to ensure that there is complete understanding of the regulations and compliance with the congressional mandate. Just and reasonable procedures have been prescribed to insure that disputes or failure to comply with the principle of nondiscrimination in administering Federal programs will be promptly and justly decided.

The broad and encouraging compliance with the Public Accommodations Title of the Civil Rights Act has demonstrated the overwhelming desire of the people of this Nation to accept and to comply with the law of the land. I am confident that the provisions of the Civil Rights Act to be implemented by these regulations will be received in the same spirit of acceptance and cooperation.

NOTE: The statement was part of a White House release which noted that the President had approved the regulations on December 3 and that similar regulations covering other agencies would be issued "in a few weeks." The regulations approved December 3 were those for the Departments of Interior, Agriculture, Labor, and Health, Education, and Welfare, together with those for the General Services Administration, Housing and Home Finance Agency, and the National Science Foundation. They are published in the Federal Register of December 4, 1964 (29 F.R. 16273).

793   Remarks at the Presentation of the Medal of Honor to Capt. Roger H. C. Donlon, USA.   *December 5, 1964*

Mrs. Donlon, Senator Hayden, Senator Keating, Senator-elect Kennedy, Secretary McNamara, ladies and gentlemen:

This is a proud moment for all Americans. We are here today to present this Nation's highest honor to Captain Roger H. C. Donlon, United States Army.

On July 6th of this year, Captain Donlon was the Commanding Officer of the United States Army Special Forces Team A-726, at Camp Nam Dong in the Republic of Viet-Nam.

Under cover of night, a reinforced Viet Cong battalion launched a full-scale attack on the camp. A violent battle took place lasting 5 hours. The Viet Cong enemy used mortars, grenades, and very heavy gunfire.

Captain Donlon was wounded four times—in the stomach, in the leg, in the shoulder, and in the face. Wounded though he was, Captain Donlon directed a successful defense of the camp. He moved from post to post and man to man within the camp perimeter. Despite his multiple wounds, Captain Donlon, with great courage and coolness, inspired the American personnel and the friendly Vietnamese troops to a successful defense of their camp.

No one who has seen military service will fail to appreciate and understand the magnitude of Captain Donlon's heroic performance under enemy fire in the darkness.

This Medal of Honor awarded in the name of the Congress is the first such honor to be bestowed upon an American military man for conspicuous gallantry above and beyond the call of duty in our present efforts in the Republic of Viet-Nam.

Individual bravery among the members of our forces there is much more the rule than the exception. I think it detracts nothing from the honor that a grateful Nation pays today to Captain Donlon to say, as I am sure he would say, that we proudly salute all the men of all the services who are participating so valiantly in that effort.

I had a full and complete report from General Taylor which gave me great pride in all the men in that area. And it is not given to all of us here at home to be called upon to make the choice of sacrifice and risk that Captain Donlon made at Nam Dong this summer. But it is given to us to draw new strength and inspiration from the gallantry and the unhesitating bravery of this man's action under hostile fire.

The Vietnamese are seeking to triumph over communism manifested by insurgency, terrorism, and aggression. Because we recognize the justice of their cause and its importance to all free men, we are there to provide them with support and assistance.

Now let any who suggest that we cannot honor our commitment in Viet-Nam find new strength and new resolution in the actions of this brave man and his comrades in arms far away from us today.

To you, Captain Donlon, may I personally express the gratitude and the respect of all your fellow countrymen. The example that you have set shall not be lost. As we pray for peace in the world, as we maintain the strength that supports our resolve to uphold freedom and the cause of justice around the world, we shall always be grateful for the inspiration that you have given to us in these times.

This ceremony should remind us all of the times in which we live and the values that make living really worthwhile. In this age, the whole of our society, the whole of our Government, is committed in the struggles between peace and war, between freedom and tyranny, between justice and cynicism. For each of us, whatever our station in life, this means that we as individuals must give of ourselves as dedicated, committed Americans.

We have much, we have vastly more than any other peoples in history. We greatly value what we have. We want other peoples to enjoy the same for themselves. But we cannot keep what we have and we cannot preserve the brightening flame of hope for others unless we are all—repeat *all*—committed; all—repeat *all*—willing to sacrifice and to serve wherever we can, whether it be in Viet-Nam, whether it be at home, whether it be far away.

In the early hours of this morning, I awoke and I read again the account by my bedside of Captain Donlon's heroic feat. I wondered how many of us could stand in his presence today and say confidently that we, too, have done all that we could to support and to serve the cause of our country and mankind.

There are some men in Washington and some men throughout the Nation, and women, too, who resist the glamor of gold and come here at great sacrifice to do for freedom in the capital of the free world what Captain Donlon did for freedom in Viet-Nam. So very often 9 to 5 hours, Saturday at the country club, profit sharing and pension trusts all mean so much that the call of country is sometimes answered with a "no."

But I was thinking this morning about that old World War I recruiting poster, with Uncle Sam pointing his finger and saying, "Your country needs you."

Well, your country does need you today in these times. And the finger points at every American, of every age and of every station. We need women and we need men for service in the cause of freedom, in the cause of this great Government, this noble cause—men and women from industry, from business, from labor, from banks, from campuses, and from farms.

1640

America needs from civilian life as we have, I am proud to say, in our military forces, the very best talents and minds of these times.

And standing to my right as a civilian is one of the great examples of which I speak, the Secretary of Defense, Mr. McNamara. He represents to me in our civilian life what Captain Donlon represents in military life, the very best of America. And this Government must have the very best.

So, I hope your example, Captain Donlon, will help to inspire others to step forward and to answer "yes" when their country calls.

Captain Donlon, as President of the United States, it is now my very high privilege to decorate you with the Medal of Honor, awarded to you in the name of the Congress of the United States.

The distinguished Secretary of Defense, Mr. McNamara, will now read the citation.

[*Secretary McNamara read the citation, the text of which follows.*]

The President of the United States of America, authorized by Act of Congress, March 3, 1863, has awarded in the name of The Congress the Medal of Honor to

CAPTAIN ROGER H. C. DONLON
UNITED STATES ARMY

for conspicuous gallantry and intrepidity in action at the risk of his life above and beyond the call of duty:

Captain Roger H. C. Donlon, Infantry, distinguished himself by conspicuous gallantry and intrepidity at the risk of his own life above and beyond the call of duty while defending a United States military installation against a fierce attack by hostile forces on 6 July 1964, near Nam Dong, Republic of Vietnam. Captain Donlon was serving as the Commanding Officer of the United States Army Special Forces Detachment A–726 at Camp Nam Dong when a reinforced Viet Cong Battalion suddenly launched a full-scale, predawn attack on the Camp. During the violent battle that ensued, lasting five hours and resulting in heavy casualties on both sides, Captain Donlon directed the defense operations in the midst of an enemy barrage of mortar shells, falling grenades, and extremely heavy gun fire. Upon the initial onslaught, he swiftly marshaled his forces and ordered the removal of the needed ammunition from a blazing building. He then dashed through a hail of small arms and exploding hand grenades to abort a breach of the main gate. Enroute to this position he detected an enemy demolition team of three in the proximity of the main gate and quickly annihilated them. Although exposed to the intense grenade attack, he then succeeded in reaching a 60mm mortar position despite sustaining a severe stomach wound as he was within five yards of the gun pit. When he discovered that most of the men in this gun pit were also wounded, he completely disregarded his own injury, directed their withdrawal to a location thirty meters away, and again risked his own life by remaining behind and covering the movement with the utmost effectiveness. Noticing that his team sergeant was unable to evacuate the gun pit, he crawled toward him and, while dragging the fallen soldier out of the gun pit, an enemy mortar exploded and inflicted a wound in Captain Donlon's left shoulder. Although suffering from multiple wounds, he carried the abandoned 60mm mortar weapon to a new location thirty meters away where he found three wounded defenders. After administering first aid and encouragement to these men, he left the weapon with them, headed toward another position, and retrieved a 57mm recoilless rifle. Then with great courage and coolness under fire, he returned to the abandoned gun pit, evacuated ammunition for the two weapons and, while crawling and dragging the urgently needed ammunition, received a third wound on his leg by an enemy hand grenade. Despite his critical physical condition, he again crawled one hundred and seventy five meters to an 81mm mortar position and directed firing operations which protected the seriously threatened east sector of the Camp. He then moved to an eastern 60mm mortar position and upon determining that the vicious enemy assault had weakened, crawled back to the gun pit with the 60mm mortar, set it up for defensive operations, and turned it over to two defenders with minor wounds. Without hesitation, he left this sheltered position and moved from position to position around the beleaguered perimeter while hurling hand grenades at the enemy and inspiring his men to superhuman effort. As he bravely continued to move around the perimeter, a mortar shell exploded, wounding him in the face and body. As the long awaited daylight brought defeat to the enemy forces and their retreat back to the jungle leaving behind fifty-four of their dead, many weapons, and grenades, Captain Donlon immediately reorganized his defenses and administered first aid to the wounded. His dynamic leadership, fortitude, and valiant efforts inspired not only the American personnel but the friendly Vietnamese defenders as well and resulted in the successful defense of the Camp. Captain Donlon's conspicuous gallantry, extraordinary heroism, and intrepidity at the risk of his own life above and beyond the call of duty are in the highest traditions of the United States Army and reflect great credit upon himself and the Armed Forces of his country.

LYNDON B. JOHNSON

NOTE: The presentation ceremony was held at 12:10 p.m. in the East Room at the White House. The President's opening words referred to Mrs. Marion H. Donlon, mother of Captain Donlon, Senator Carl Hayden of Arizona, Senator Kenneth B. Keating and Senator-elect Robert F. Kennedy, both of New York, and Secretary of Defense Robert S. McNamara.

794 Message to President Segni of Italy. *December 7, 1964*

[Released December 7, 1964. Dated December 6, 1964]

Dear Mr. President:

I learned with deep regret of your resignation, although I appreciate the reasons for your decision. We Americans have come to know and admire you as a good friend and trusted ally. Your devotion to the principles of peace and social justice and your gallant struggle with affliction will remain an inspiration to us all.

Mrs. Johnson joins me in hoping that you will enjoy a quick and complete recovery.

Sincerely,

LYNDON B. JOHNSON

[His Excellency Antonio Segni, Rome, Italy]

NOTE: The message was read by the Press Secretary to the President, George E. Reedy, at his news conference held at the White House at 11:55 a.m. on December 7, 1964.

795 Remarks of Welcome at the White House to the New Prime Minister of Great Britain. *December 7, 1964*

Mr. Prime Minister, Mr. Secretary of State, distinguished guests:

Mr. Prime Minister, it is a pleasure to welcome you here today both to this country and to this house. For you and for me as individuals, positions and responsibilities have changed somewhat since last you were a visitor in this city.

But the relations between our countries and the common purposes of our peoples remain unchanged.

Your visit underscores the certainty that there will be no change.

Under Democratic and Republican administrations in this country, and under Labor and Conservative governments in your country, the collaboration between Great Britain and the United States has meant much of enduring value to all mankind, not only to our two peoples but also to our friends and our allies everywhere in the world.

Today we realize as surely all other nations must realize that the world has come to a beginning of a new era of change. It is opportune that at this formative period, early in each of our respective administrations, that we meet together to seek the basis of continuing responsible undertakings.

The problems of our Nation, the problems of all nations are many today. Yet, we can and we do justifiably believe that this is a hopeful time for man—the most hopeful since time began.

In all of history never has man had so great a capacity for ending war and assuring peace and bringing it to the world; overcoming poverty and laboring to that end; providing plenty; mastering the causes of human misery and enjoying the fullness of human happiness.

In confidence that our countries and our peoples with our allies have great contributions to make and great gains to realize, the progress of the years ahead, we meet now for a series of working sessions where we can begin together to explore the complex and the important problems that are facing us and our allies.

As we welcome you to our country, we welcome you and your countrymen to the continuation of this great work. May our labors help to strengthen the hope for peace and the cause of freedom as have the labors of our predecessors on both sides of the Atlantic.

As we stand here this morning in this beautiful sunshine in Washington, I trust that this is only the first of many meetings that will bring men who love peace and who hate war together in the hope that we can make a contribution to peace and freedom throughout the world.

NOTE: The President spoke at 11:25 a.m. on the South Lawn at the White House where Prime Minister Harold Wilson was given a formal welcome with full military honors. The Prime Minister responded as follows:

"Mr. President, Mr. Secretary of State, and members of both administrations:

"First, sir, may I on behalf of my colleagues and myself thank you for your warm and hospitable welcome to the United States.

"We are all of us happy to be back in Washington. None of us are strangers here. All of us have many friends, many personal friends of a quarter of a century standing here in Washington and in your administration.

"The talks on which we shall be engaged will be frank and straight to the point as befits talks between friends and as befits the size and the scale of the problems that we are facing.

"This is a first get-together in what I hope will be a series of discussions at all levels in our respective administrations, of discussions with our NATO allies and more widely, and covering as the talks now and later proceed a growing range of topics.

"We do not expect this week to solve the problems which the Western alliance, the free world, and the world communities are facing. Rather, we would hope to set the guidelines for our future joint attack on these problems.

"There could be no more challenging or exciting time for us to be meeting. We face urgent problems within our own alliance. For 2 years there have been growing stresses and strains which we cannot suffer to continue, much less to grow.

"We come here, Mr. President, to express the firm determination of Her Majesty's Government to do all in our power to strengthen our alliance and to make it more effective.

"We shall throw our proposals into the common pool of Western thought and we shall be prepared to make our full contributions in hard, real terms; in particular, in a shrinking world where traditional categories of thought and approach, whether in defense or in relations between peoples, are being daily rendered more obsolete through the central fact of thermonuclear power.

"We recognize the need by thought and by deeds to centralize and collectivize our common responsibility and concern in matters of nuclear strength.

"But I am sure that in a wider sense our discussions will transcend even the challenging situation within the alliance.

"We shall be seeking together all possible means to strengthen the work of the United Nations on which are centered our common hopes for the future of mankind; in particular, our joint contribution to its authority, to its peacekeeping role and to its role in the only war we seek—the war against poverty and squalor, illiteracy and disease.

"We shall be seeking now the means through agreed initiatives based on our common interests whenever the prospect presents itself or can be created for measures to reduce tensions between East and West and, in particular, to move decisively in the world of effective disarmament and measures to prevent the spread of nuclear weapons.

"Mr. President, we look forward to friendly and fruitful talks. We come here not in the posture of asking anything for ourselves; rather, that in asking what between us we can do to speed our common purpose.

"We in Great Britain know that our influence in the world depends on what we can contribute to that common purpose. We have on tap reserves of skill and craftsmanship of science and technology, of talent for design and production which, when encouraged to put forth their full power, as they will be encouraged, will delight our friends and surprise the world.

"As partners with the United States in war and in the task of building a new world out of the ruins of the war, we come here inspired with the experience of working with you.

"In the changed circumstances of the sixties, we seek still a closer relationship based on common purposes and common aims, on consideration for the interest of Great Britain's partners within the Commonwealth and of our allies in Europe and elsewhere.

"The theme of these talks, as I conceive them, Mr. President, whether for the strength of our alliance or for our wider approach to the fight for a constructive peace is expressed in the one word 'interdependence'—truly as among men so among nations we are all members one of another, and this, Mr. President, is how we approach these meetings. This, I believe, is the way in which the world would have us approach them for what is at stake here goes far beyond the interests of our two countries. What is at stake is the contribution that we can make to security and to peace for mankind."

In his opening words the President referred to Secretary of State Dean Rusk.

796   Toasts of the President and Prime Minister Harold Wilson.   *December 7, 1964*

Mr. Prime Minister and distinguished guests:

Unaccustomed as I am to public speaking, since November 3, I want to ask your indulgence this evening in order that I may present to all of you some of the individuals that I want you to know and whom some of you may already know but all of whom have played or are playing a very vital part in the life of our two countries.

First of all, I want to present the Foreign Secretary, Mr. Patrick Gordon Walker.

The Defence Secretary, Sir Denis Healey.

An old friend, Lord Mountbatten.

Our own beloved Chief Justice Warren.

The Vice President-elect, Mr. Humphrey.

The next Chairman of the Committee on Foreign Relations of the Senate—if the Republicans come to power—Mr. Hickenlooper.

Our own Secretary of State, Dean Rusk.

Our Secretary of Defense, Bob McNamara.

Our Secretary of the Treasury, Mr. Douglas Dillon.

One of the great leaders of our time, the former Secretary of State, Mr. Dean Acheson.

We are very honored and very privileged that we could have in this house this evening three men who over a long period of time have represented with great distinction our country in the United Kingdom.

First, I want to present Mr. Lewis Douglas, former Ambassador to Great Britain.

Now, Lew, you stand up a little longer. There are some girls down here who didn't get to see you.

The former distinguished Ambassador, and my friend, Mr. Jock Whitney of New York.

The present great Ambassador, Mr. David Bruce.

One of the bright lights of the ambassadorial corps and one of our great friends, Lord Harlech.

So, this house is honored tonight by the presence of a most welcome and a most distinguished visitor and his party.

This is one of many talks that we have had and are going to have in the future, and I trust just one of many visits.

Mr. Prime Minister, I want you to know that I am really enjoying them, although sometimes diplomatic negotiations recall Mark Twain's story of his visit to a friend up in New Hampshire.

Mark Twain was walking along the road and he asked a farmer, "How far is it to Henderson's place?"

"About a mile and a half," the farmer answered.

He walked awhile longer and he met another farmer and he asked the same question, "How far is it to Henderson's place?" The farmer answered, "About a mile and a half."

Mark Twain walked a little farther and he met a third farmer and he again asked, "How far is it to Henderson's place?" "About a mile and a half," the farmer answered.

"Well," said Twain, "Thank God I am holding my own."

For the information of my own constituency, I would like to observe tonight that I am not sure that I am holding my own—after today's discussions.

We have many difficult problems. I am sure the traditional British ability to find reasoned solution will ultimately prevail.

During World War II the British Minister in Algeria was called upon to mediate a dispute between British and American officers. The American officers wanted drinks served before their meals. The British wanted their drinks served after their meals. He came up with this answer: "In deference to the British," he said, "we will all drink after meals and in deference to the Americans, we will all drink before the meal."

This kind of British genius has solved a great many problems.

I had some very special advice, Mr. Prime Minister, just a few minutes before you arrived. My wife whispered in my ear as we were coming out to greet you this morning. She said, "Dear, this is Judgment Day and be sure you use plenty of it!"

I have tried to follow her advice. As I sat in these meetings throughout the day, I heard in my mind the sound of an ageless phrase: "There will always be an England."

As I listened to the distinguished Prime Minister and the Foreign Secretary and the Defense Secretary, I think I heard, also, the voices of the British people—those few, those happy few, that band of brothers who won freedom for that island, were also the architects of a way of life that today is measured in freedom and in hope and in light.

Scattered out among 3 billion persons in the world, the British love liberty and they embrace freedom and they despise bondage. Those who would destroy freedom in the world will always find the British people undaunted and unafraid and undismayed and ready to defend that freedom, whatever the cost or whatever the burden.

All of us can remember early in World War II, when the light of freedom flickered and for a time almost lost its flame. Britain stood there at the bridge like Horatio of old, and held slavery at bay until the world beyond the ocean's sea could awaken and could arm and could join them in the fight.

So, on this night of the anniversary of Pearl Harbor, I believe that whenever liberty is threatened, whenever the choice is between freedom and slavery, the voice of Parliament will be heard and the support of the British will be ready, ready again to preserve and to protect the way of life that they love and they have taught all of us to love.

So, when the role of honor is called and the stewards of freedom are acclaimed, no people will have a contribution as large or as strong or as persistent as this Island of Great Britain.

It gives us much pleasure and great happiness to have the distinguished Prime Minister and his party here with us this evening. And I now should like for all of my special friends to join me in raising our glasses to Her Majesty, the Queen.

NOTE: The President proposed the toast at a dinner in the State Dining Room at the White House. Prime Minister Wilson responded as follows:

"*Mr. President, Mrs. Johnson, Mr. Vice President-elect, Your Excellencies, Mr. Chief Justice, my Lord, ladies and gentlemen:*

"First, Mr. President, may I on behalf of all my colleagues here tonight and all your English guests express our very warm thanks for your kind hospitality to us not only tonight but throughout the day.

"I feel that tonight's dinner here in your home is a memory we shall treasure for the rest of our lives. If I could mention just one thing which I think all of us will remember, it was the pleasure of something I have not met before, anyway not outside of Vienna, and that was the singing violins we had in these last few minutes.

"I don't say that we can produce anything in Britain to compare with this though when, as I hope you will, Mr. President, come to Buckingham Palace to visit London. I think we can promise you that as you dine there you will suddenly be surprised by the arrival of some of Denis Healey's and Lord Mountbatten's Scots Guards or it might be the Watch or it might be the Gordon Islanders if they have not amalgamated themselves out of existence now—suddenly parading around and playing the bagpipes in your ears as you try to eat. And you thought you had the great deterrent.

"Mr. President, when we come to Washington especially, we all know we are among friends. All of my colleagues have been here many, many times before. I think this is my 15th visit. My first visit was during the war, in 1943. When I managed to get in—it was a little difficult to travel in those days—by posing as a member of the staff of Averell Harriman, he signed a certificate saying I was a member of his staff. I was at that time secretary of one of the combined boards, Combined Resources Board and Combined Raw Materials Board, and my joint secretary at that time was one of your Ambassadors, Sam Berger, now back in this country. I remember my luggage on that occasion was consigned in care of Mr. David Dubinsky.

"When we came to Washington—I spent some 4 months living here once on an AFL mission—we never thought we would get that report out, but we did anyhow. When we come here, of course, we meet so many old friends.

"In the talks to which you have referred, Mr. President, we have observed the proper protocol and courtesies and address one another by our proper names. It is like when you form a new government, which we just had to do. In our cabinet procedure, we never refer to anyone by their name. It is always the First Secretary of State, the Secretary for Defense, and with other new boys we keep slipping, calling one another Jim, Patrick, Denis, and the rest, and I must say we have had the same difficulties today. How often have we had to call ourselves to order and talk about the Secretary of State and the Secretary for Defense when really we have been biting our tongues off to say Dean and Bob and Doug, and all our other friends.

"Tonight, also, it has been a great pleasure for us all to see former Ambassadors to the United Kingdom whom we have come to know so well, and if you can quote Isaiah, Mr. President, we can quote a well-known hymn, 'Those angel faces smile whom we have loved and long since lost,' and it is nice to see them around the board tonight.

"I suppose I can claim to be the first Prime Minister of Great Britain to have two ex-members of your Government. I will not give their names. I don't want them to become the target of any more problems."

[Interposing, the President said, "Only two?"]

"Only two, Mr. President, and suddenly tonight in looking at the Secretary of State I realized with horror I did not make it plain that we formed our government in somewhat of a hurry and forgot to count in a number of directions, and it was only tonight that I realized that we have more Gaelic men in our administration than you have.

"We have no Texans, Mr. President—not yet. But in trying to assimilate our problems and our achievements, I suppose really to have a Yorkshire Prime Minister and a Yorkshire Secretary for Defense is the next best thing.

"May I say we are the largest state in our Union and we have no Alaska.

"Mr. President, it is very difficult to define a Yorkshireman, but if you think of a Texan, you understand about what we have in Yorkshire.

"One thing you and I have in common, and Vice President-elect Humphrey, we have all recently been through the furnace of a democratic election. We hope your hand will soon be better.

"It may be, if we took the elections as seriously as you, we would have had a majority like yourself. All I can say is if the British people were free to express their votes in your election, your majority would have been even better than it was.

"I don't think it is appropriate for any of us to try and rationalize the decision and the decisiveness of the decision that the American people have reached, because we have a tradition of not interfering in one another's elections. We are always neutral. It doesn't mean that we think neutrally on all occasions, but it would be wrong for me to express any views on the issues of policy, whether at home or abroad, which form the warp and woof

of this great election in your country.

"But there is no doubt as far as we are concerned that this great victory of yours, apart from those policy issues, was attributed first to the quality of leadership that your people saw in you, Mr. President, and one thing I can say even if it involves an element of policy—because on this issue it involved more than just American significance—it had a world significance.

"Your victory was the tribute of the United States people to great and unrivaled political courage, not only in the United States. Even in Great Britain now we are finding the ugliness and evil of this problem of race relations. Our Foreign Secretary who went through the fire on this knows what I mean. The world has watched anxiously how the United States, faced with this age-old problem within its borders, would react when this became an issue, as it inevitably did, in a democratic election.

"All of your friends, Mr. President, all friends of the United States, are proud of the firm, uncompromising, and courageous way in which this issue was tackled over these past few years by your predecessor and by yourself.

"All of us feel that in the great fight that you led, Mr. President, and in which the Vice President-elect played so distinguished a part, to promote this legislation on civil rights—and I am not saying this in any spirit of trying to interfere with your domestic politics because you were not there fighting only a domestic battle; you were fighting a world battle— you gave heart, you gave courage, and you gave encouragement to all of us who wanted to see our friends give a lead to the world in an issue which, in the next 30 or 40 years, in the remaining years of this century, mean more to more people than any of the issues, even of the nuclear weapon or anything of that kind.

"If there are millions whose lives are dominated by the thought of nuclear weapons, even of war and peace itself, there are still more millions to whom the question of race and of color are significant and more significant in their lives than perhaps any of the issues that we in our little northern world think is so important. That is why, Mr. President, all of us owe this deep debt of tribute to you and your colleagues for the leadership you have shown in this great issue.

"You referred to our discussions. I think all of us approach these problems that we are discussing today in a spirit of partnership, of interdependence, a phrase which you and President Kennedy, Mr. President, have said represent the answer to the problems that we are facing.

"Sometimes our partnership is too easily taken for granted. We regard it as so automatic that sometimes there are others who feel that it means less to us than we know in our hearts that it does

1647

mean to us. That partnership was created by our common heritage. In the presence of the Chief Justice whom we look forward to welcoming to Great Britain next year—it is a matter of equal excitement for you as well as for us that we shall be celebrating next year the 750th anniversary of the Magna Carta, and the Chief Justice is coming to make one of the major speeches on that occasion.

"We shall also be celebrating the 700th anniversary of Simon de Montfort's parliament. Wrapped a little bit in security, I think he was a rebel against the throne when he actually called that parliament, but we have had more respectable ones since that time.

"But our close relationship has developed over the years, in this room presided over by the portrait of Abraham Lincoln. It is no secret that Carl Sandburg's 'Life of Lincoln' is my favorite reading, and I have read it more times than I would like to recall.

"I think the links between our countries were closer and perhaps more expressive than at any time before when the working people of Lancashire, facing starvation, facing misery, hunger, and poverty as a result of the denial to them of raw cotton, which was the basis of their livelihood—what we now call the fashionable establishment in London, including the Times and including a lot of other people who should have been ashamed of themselves, were working hard in support of the southern cause—when the working people of Lancashire passed a resolution supporting Abraham Lincoln and all he stood for even though they looked like they were starving. And the message he sent to the working people of Manchester on that occasion is one of the most moving messages in our joint venture and joint history.

"Our partnership was forged further in war.

"Last Monday I had the pleasure of going to visit Winston Churchill on his 90th birthday. As long as Winston's memory and Winston's writings, whether 'War Memoirs' or his great 'History of the English-Speaking Peoples,' because he never asked, in his sense of history, disentanglement of your tradition from ours—as long as these survive, our partnership will be maintained.

"The problems we face, Mr. President, in these discussions—and we have all said this is the beginning of a series of discussions—are problems that we know we are going to be able to solve because of our common purpose in solving them.

"We have our differences. There are always differences between friends. We are good enough friends to speak frankly to one another, but there will never be anything peevish or spiteful. If we ever have differences, we will look you straight in the eye—and we will expect you to look us straight in the eye—and say what you would expect we can do as friends and only what we can do as friends.

"We hear arguments. I have heard this often enough about whether there is a special relationship between the United States and Great Britain. Some of those who talk of the special relationship, I think, are looking backwards and not looking forward. They talk about the nostalgia of our imperial age. We regard our relation with you not as a special relationship but as a close relationship, governed by the only things that matter and that is a unity of purpose and that is the unity of objective. We don't come to you at any time on the basis of our past grandeur or of any faded thoughts of what that grandeur was. I think it was Charles Lamb, whom you, Mr. President, quoted in a different context today, who once said, 'There is nothing so irrelevant in nature as a poor relation.'

"We have, and we always shall have, a close relationship, because we agree about the same things and we are going to work together with our own distinctive and unique contributions to achieve those things.

"In that spirit, Mr. President, may I ask all my fellow guests of yours to rise and drink to the health of the President of the United States and Mrs. Johnson."

Early in his remarks the President referred to Secretary of State for Foreign Affairs Patrick Gordon Walker, Secretary of State for Defence Sir Denis Healey, Admiral of the Fleet the Lord Mountbatten, all of Great Britain, Chief Justice of the United States Earl Warren, Vice President-elect Hubert H. Humphrey, Senator Bourke B. Hickenlooper of Iowa, Secretary of State Dean Rusk, Secretary of Defense Robert S. McNamara, and Secretary of the Treasury C. Douglas Dillon. He also referred to Dean Acheson, former Secretary of State, Lewis W. Douglas and John Hay (Jock) Whitney, both former United States Ambassadors to Great Britain, David K. E. Bruce, United States Ambassador to Great Britain, and Lord Harlech, Ambassador to the United States from Great Britain.

797   Joint Statement Following Discussions With the Prime Minister of Great Britain.   *December* 8, 1964

THE PRESIDENT of the United States and the Prime Minister of the United Kingdom met in Washington 7th December to 9th December. They were assisted by Secretary of State Rusk, Secretary of Defense McNamara and Under Secretary of State Ball and by the Foreign Secretary, Mr. Gordon Walker and the Secretary of State for Defence, Mr. Healey.

In the course of a wide ranging exchange of views, the President and the Prime Minister reviewed the current international situation in light of the responsibilities which their countries carry for maintaining, together with their allies and friends, peace and stability throughout the world. They reaffirmed their determination to support the peacekeeping operations of the United Nations and to do all in their power to strengthen the systems of regional alliance in Europe, the Middle East and the Far East to which they both contribute.

They recognized the importance of strengthening the unity of the Atlantic Alliance in its strategic nuclear defense. They discussed existing proposals for this purpose and an outline of some new proposals presented by the British Government. They agreed that the objective in this field is to cooperate in finding the arrangements which best meet the legitimate interests of all members of the Alliance, while maintaining existing safeguards on the use of nuclear weapons, and preventing their further proliferation. A number of elements of this problem were considered during this initial exchange of views as a preliminary to further discussions among interested members of the Alliance.

They also agreed on the urgency of a world-wide effort to promote the non-dissemination and non-acquisition of nuclear weapons, and of continuing Western initiatives towards arms control and disarmament. They recognized the increasing need for initiatives of this kind in light of the recent detonation of a Chinese nuclear device.

The President and the Prime Minister reaffirmed their determination to continue to contribute to the maintenance of peace and stability in the Middle East and the Far East. In this connection they recognized the particular importance of the military effort which both their countries are making in support of legitimate Governments in South East Asia, particularly in Malaysia and South Vietnam, which seek to maintain their independence and to resist subversion.

They recognized also that a nation's defense policy must be based on a sound economy. The President and the Prime Minister, while determined that their countries should continue to play their full parts in the world-wide peacekeeping effort, affirmed their conviction that the burden of defense should be shared more equitably among the countries of the free world.

They agreed also on the need for improvement in the balance of payments and in the productivity and competitive position of both their economies in order to ensure the underlying economic strength which is essential for fulfilling their heavy international responsibilities. In this connection they arranged to explore in detail the possibilities of closer cooperation between their two countries in defense research and development and in weapons production.

The President and the Prime Minister reaffirmed their belief in the importance of close allied cooperation in international affairs. They agreed that this meeting was only the first stage in their consultation in which the matters that they had discussed would need to be examined in greater detail. They looked forward, too, to continuing discussions at all levels both within the Alliance and in wider international negotiations in pursuit of nuclear and conventional disarmament and all measures to reduce world tension.

798 Remarks Upon Receiving Report of the President's Commission on Heart Disease, Cancer and Stroke. *December 9, 1964*

Dr. DeBakey, ladies and gentlemen:

A day here in the White House can take on many different tones. Today is a day of electric possibilities.

Year after year the health of the American people is threatened by three relentless enemies: heart disease, cancer, and stroke. Together, these three diseases are responsible for seven in every ten deaths.

Nine months ago your President named this Commission on Heart Disease, Cancer and Stroke. The instructions to this Commission were quite demanding: find out, with rigorous precision, just what the situation is. Tell us, with candor and imagination, just what we can do to improve it and to improve it rapidly.

Today, it is a very high honor and great privilege to receive the results of your study. Dr. DeBakey has been kind enough to review it briefly with me in my office before I came here to the Cabinet Room.

On behalf of all of the American people, I want to express a deep sense of appreciation to the members of the Commission and particularly to the members of the Commission's staff. You have performed what I consider is a critically important public service and you have done it superbly.

Today, I call upon all our people—our doctors and our laymen, our citizens in and out of the Government, our people organized on the Federal, State, and local levels—yes, even the members of the press who are here this morning—to ponder the materials that we have had presented to us and to consider with a full sense of urgency the recommendations that this distinguished group of Americans has made.

Above all, I urge the American people to heed the conclusions of this Commission. Speaking from your great knowledge, you Commission members tell us the profoundly stirring fact: we stand at the threshold of a historic breakthrough. Heart disease, cancer, and stroke *can* be conquered—not in a millennium, not in a century, but in the next few onrushing decades.

If I remember correctly, Dr. DeBakey told me that these diseases cost us now $30 billion, and he also told me that he even thought during my lifetime that the progress we make would be startling and staggering and highly satisfactory.

During the recent decade, we Americans have found our way to many striking areas of agreement in public affairs. But a consensus can produce varied results. Consensus can become a comfortable cushion on which a nation simply goes to sleep. Consensus can also be an active, dynamic, rolling credo. Consensus can be a springboard, providing a takeoff for resolute action toward generally agreed upon goals.

So, I want to compliment and I want to congratulate you ladies and gentlemen who have rendered this faithful service to your country. I want to thank you for your dedicated labors and thank you for summoning us to put the American consensus to work in the most basic of all efforts—the preservation of life itself.

In the days ahead, we are going to ask the Congress and we are going to ask the country to lend us a hand in helping us to fight the ancient enemies of mankind—disease, poverty, and ignorance.

We are going to try to make education available to more of our people and have a better educational system in this country.

We are going to try to extend a helping hand to those whose economic lot has not been as good as our own and try to improve conditions where we will minimize poverty in this country.

We are going to not just establish a Commission on Heart Disease, Cancer and Stroke to recommend steps to reduce the incidence of these diseases; we are going to reduce them.

Two months after I spoke to the Congress, in February 1964, the Commission first convened here at the White House. I observed in the introductory statement on the first page of this report the President said at that time: "Unless we can do better, two-thirds of all Americans now living will suffer or will die from cancer, from heart disease, or stroke"—two-thirds of all Americans. "I expect you to do something about it." We said that to the Commission on that day.

They have done something about it, and with these guideposts and with these goals, we will begin this year in the Congress and in the country to make a concerted drive on these three enemies to the health of two-thirds of all Americans.

I am so proud that the men and women who represent the great in our country were willing to give their time, their talent, and their money to this effort, and I know that in their lifetime great satisfaction will come to each of them for knowing in their heart that they have saved millions of lives.

Thank you very much.

NOTE: The President spoke at 1:13 p.m. in the Cabinet Room at the White House. His opening words referred to Dr. Michael E. DeBakey, Chairman of the President's Commission on Heart Disease, Cancer and Stroke. The establishment of the Commission and the membership was announced by the President at his news conference of March 9 (see Item 211 [6]).

The Commission's report, entitled "A National Program To Conquer Heart Disease, Cancer and Stroke," is dated December 1964 (Government Printing Office, 114 pp.).

799   Remarks at a Reception for the New Democrats in Congress. *December 9, 1964*

I AM PROUD to welcome you tonight to your house—the house of all the people.

You are welcome here, not as partisans but—always and only—as Americans. I confess, however, that it is gratifying that the American people, in their wisdom, have chosen to send to the Congress so many able, outstanding, forward-looking Americans who happen also to be Democrats.

You have had a busy day. I am sure you are ready now to relax and enjoy your evening. But I must inform you now that is not the purpose of this meeting.

When the cherry blossoms are in bloom, we hope to have you and your wives here with us for a sociable evening. Tonight, however, we have planned a working session—because you and I and all of us are here to work, to work for 190 million American people and free men everywhere.

In coming to Washington, as you are now, you are tracing steps I myself once walked—as a 27-year-old new Member of the House. From that experience, under President Franklin Roosevelt, I acquired a lasting insight into the great importance and value of close associations and understandings between the newest Members of the House and their President.

I am hopeful that from this night forward many strong and warm friendships will grow between us—that we here at the White House and in the executive branch will be able to help you in an understanding way—and that you might be of some understanding help to us, from time to time.

Will Rogers once made a very wise observation. He said: "We are a funny people. We elect our Presidents, be they Republican or Democrat, and then go home and start daring 'em to make good."

That has been true in the past. I hope that is less true now. I believe all of us—whether public servants or private citizens—recognize that we are all on the same team together, that the issue of our times is not what a President accomplishes but whether America succeeds or fails.

Today our system, our society—and our Government, of which you are soon to be part—stand as the most successful in the history of man.

Our task—yours and mine—is to assure the continuation of that success, for all times to come.

This is no small challenge. Small men with small horizons could never be adequate to that challenge. For the times we are entering require of us all a largeness of vision, a largeness of spirit, a largeness of goals and aims that have not been required since the first Americans.

On January 20th, when I shall be privileged to take the oath of this office, we will be closer to the year 2000 than to the year 1929. Through most of my career—and through most of your adult lives—the thrust of our public policies and attitudes has been dominated by memory of the stock market crash, the great depression, and the events of the 1930's that led back to recovery.

In the next session of the next Congress, I believe our thrust and emphasis must change—and will change. We must begin to think about the future—about the year 2000—about the foundations we must put in place for a larger, more complex, more challenging America for our children and our children's children.

Your first Congress will be an historic Congress.

You—as much as any legislators since this Republic began—will be part of vital history for this land.

As Woodrow Wilson said, in his first inaugural, we shall not be writing on a clean sheet of paper. We have trusts to keep. We have obligations to honor. We have continuity to preserve. But, at the same time, we cannot fulfill our trust merely as trustees and executors of decisions made before by other Americans in other times.

We shall need to be—as Americans have always been—prudent and practical in what we undertake. But we shall also need those qualities always so much a part of American success—the qualities of courage, adventure, confidence, and a willingness to explore new domains.

For we shall not always be able to walk along marked trails or follow guideposts others have put in place for us. In a new day of new dimensions and new opportunities, we shall need to be trailblazers and pioneers—in the oldest and finest of our society's traditions.

I welcome this opportunity to work with you in this historic period. I hope this will be the first of many useful, profitable, and friendly meetings we shall have together— and that the separation of powers under our Constitution will not apply to our personal relations and understandings.

If I may quote him again, Will Rogers also said that "A Democrat never adjourns—he is born, becomes of voting age and starts right in arguing over something, and his political adjournment is his date with the undertaker."

So I don't want to adjourn this meeting of Democrats, but before I conclude, let me repeat for you a viewpoint which I think is a classic in the history of the House you are soon to enter.

More than 50 years ago, on May 6, 1913, a new Congressman from the State of Texas stood in the well of the House and spoke for the first time. The journal of that day records his words as follows: "It is now my sole purpose here to help enact such wise and just laws that our common country will by virtue of these laws be a happier and a more prosperous country. I have always dreamed of a country which I believe this should be and will be, and that is one in which the citizenship is an educated and patriotic people, not swayed by passion and prejudice, and a country that knows no East, no West, no North, no South, but inhabited by a people liberty-loving, patriotic, happy and prosperous; with its lawmakers having no other purpose than to write such just laws as shall in the years to come be of service to humankind yet unborn."

That philosophy served that Member well—and served this country greatly. For the man who spoke those words was the man who meant so much to me, to Speaker Mc-Cormack, to John Kennedy, and to many generations of American leaders. That man was the gentleman from Bonham, Tex.—the late beloved Speaker Sam Rayburn.

NOTE: The President spoke early in the evening in the East Room at the White House.

800   Remarks at the National Urban League's Community Action Assembly.   *December* 10, 1964

My longtime friend, Whitney Young, ladies and gentlemen:

It is more than 100 years since Abraham Lincoln charged the living to dedicate themselves to the unfinished work of the dead at Gettysburg.

Even Lincoln, with his deep sense of man's imperfections, could not know that a century later we would still be striving to abolish racial injustice.

No task is more deeply rooted in the complexities of American life. Poverty and tradition, fear and ignorance, the structure of our society and the workings of our economy, all converge on this enormous wrong which has troubled the American conscience from the beginning. Its just solution is essential, not only to give the full blessings of freedom to Negroes, but to liberate all of us.

There are those who say: It has taken us a century to move this far. It will take another hundred years to finish the job.

Well, I am here to say to you tonight that I do not agree.

Great social change tends to come rapidly in periods of intense activity and progress before the impulse slows. I believe we are in the midst of such a period of change.

So, it is our task to carry forward nothing less than the full assimilation of more than 20 million Negroes into American life. This is not to be an assimilation of bland conformity. Our object is not to make all people alike. It is, as it has always been, to allow ready access to every blessing of liberty, while permitting each to keep his sense of identity with a culture and tradition. In this way we enlarge our freedom and we enrich our Nation.

We have just passed a milestone in this task.

The Civil Rights Act of 1964 extends the protection of the law to many of the demands of justice.

This act, of course, is not the whole answer. But tonight I ask each of you to think for a moment what an enormous setback the failure to pass it would have been.

When I picked up after our beloved leader had been taken from us, I did not know and few in my vicinity knew that we would ever get as far as we have.

Now, your Government must and will move rapidly to carry out this legislation. I have come here tonight to tell you and I expect you to tell those that you counsel with and those you lead that we intend to give new vigor to our many activities in the field of equal opportunity.

The Congress, in title VI of the Civil Rights Act, established the principle that race or color can be no criteria for participation in Federal programs.

Last week I approved the first set of regulations to implement that principle. Those regulations are designed to provide a just and prompt and reasoned resolution of all disputes. Our first objective will always be to assure nondiscriminatory operation rather than to put an end to programs which are vital to the welfare of all Americans.

The widespread voluntary support, in all parts of the country, of the public accommodation title is proof of the educational value of law, and the great reservoir of good will among Americans. I believe this title, too,

will find wide acceptance. It is simple justice that all should share in programs that are financed by all and that are directed by the Government of all the people.

Within your Government there are many programs dedicated to the goal of equal opportunity. They range from the Civil Rights Division of the Justice Department, the Civil Rights Commission and the President's Committee on Equal Opportunity in Housing to the Community Relations Service, the President's Committee on Equal Opportunity in Employment, and the soon to be created Equal Employment Opportunity Commission.

Each of these groups has a distinct and a very important mission. Those now in existence have done a difficult task in an impressive way.

But really they all aim toward the same general objective. And really they must pursue that objective through cooperation among themselves and with private groups such as the distinguished members of this organization who have helped us so much for so long. With so many groups in a single field, there is always the danger of duplication, overlap, or unnecessary delay. As long as I am your President, I want the Government of all of the people to speak with a single voice on this single question.

Therefore, I am delighted to tell you tonight that I have asked Vice President-elect Hubert Humphrey, and he has agreed, to assume the responsibility for working with all of these groups, assisting in coordination of their efforts, and helping them to build toward an energetic pursuit of equal opportunity for all people in this Nation.

These are some of the steps that we are taking, and there are going to be a good many more. For, as the problem of civil rights has grown in urgency, it has also grown in complexity. We must open the doors of opportunity. We must equip our people to walk through those doors. Thus, programs to eliminate poverty, to improve education, to provide housing by enlarging the opportunities of all Americans assure new opportunities for Negro Americans.

There are those who predict that the struggle for full equality in America will be marked by violence and hate; that it will tear at the fabric of our society.

Well, for myself, I cannot claim to see so clearly into that future. I just do not agree.

I know that racial feelings flow from many deep and resistant sources in our history, in the pattern of our lives, and in the nature of man.

But I believe there are other forces that are stronger because they are armed with truth which will bring us toward our goal in peace.

These are our commitments to morality and to justice which are written in our laws and, more importantly, nourished in the hearts of our people.

These commitments carried forward by men of good will in every part of this land will lead this Nation toward the great and necessary fulfillment of American freedom.

In this way our peoples will once again prove equal to the ideals and the values on which this our beloved Nation rests.

This has been a long and somewhat exacting week. We have met and heard the problems of the Prime Minister of Malawi.

We have met and visited at some length with the Prime Minister of Great Britain, the United Kingdom.

We have met and discussed the problems of free men in southeast Asia.

We have reviewed the lot of the people on the continent of Africa, and particularly the Congo.

But in each and every one of these studies, we have tried to put the interest of the individual and the dignity of the person first and foremost in our minds.

In a doubtful period in 1957, 85 years since the Congress acted on the subject of civil rights and protecting the constitutional rights of all of our people, I sat down with the leaders of the Urban League, and with their guidance and with their help and with their support, for the first time in 85 years, we passed the first Civil Rights Act through the Congress of the United States.

That was a small step forward. We were just learning to walk, but by 1960 it was possible for us to implement that statute and to contribute some constructive improvements.

Then, a new administration came to power in 1961 and at the end of 4 years we had passed the most comprehensive legislation— and signed it—ever to be put on our statute books in this field.

Now, the lights are still on in the White House tonight—preparing programs that will keep our country up with the times, and it will keep our feet on the ground.

We have a Great Society. We do not have to begin one; we just have to keep it, retain it, improve it, and develop it.

We know that the education of our citizens, the employment of our people, the health of their bodies, the freedom they enjoy, the security that is theirs are all uppermost in the minds of those charged with the responsibility of leadership.

I would not be human if I did not say that under your leadership and the leadership of other conscious, concerned people in this country, you have placed upon me a terrifying responsibility and an obligation that it will be my determination to deserve every waking moment of my term of office.

Your faith in the future of your land and the future of the leadership that has been chosen has already been expressed, but I wanted at the end of a long day to come here and tell you of my faith in you.

There are many things I want for my people and a few things I want for my little girls. I am going to do what I can in the time allotted me to help bring those about.

One of the Presidents that I admire most signed the Emancipation Proclamation 100 years ago. But emancipation was a proclamation and was not a fact. It shall be my purpose and it is my duty to make it a fact.

Until every qualified person regardless of the house where he worships or the State where he resides or the way he spells his name or the color of his skin—until he has the right unquestioned and unrestrained to go in and cast his ballot in every precinct in this country, I am not going to be satisfied.

The finest compliment that I can pay to the Negroes of America is to say that if their constitutional rights are protected as mine are protected, if they have the privilege of voting as I am privileged to vote, then all these other problems will take care of themselves.

Now, I want to say one word before I leave. I must be careful not to be commercial. But you people have been trusting me for a long, long time. A good many of you

have been among my closest friends since I came here in 1937. There is just one thing I want to say to you.

I want to thank each and every one of you who has spent an hour or a dollar with the Urban League, because it is through efforts that you have made and others like you that the shackles of bondage have been removed from your fellow man. There are men who are dying tonight in Viet-Nam to preserve the freedom of us all, and the least that you can do, until you are called upon to give your life, is to give your support, give your talent, and give your heart to organizations like this and to leadership of men like Whitney Young.

NOTE: The President spoke at 8:40 p.m. in the Main Ballroom at the Sheraton-Park Hotel in Washington. In his opening words he referred to Whitney M. Young, Jr., Executive Director of the National Urban League.

For the President's approval of departmental and agency civil rights regulations, referred to during his remarks, see Item 792.

The theme of the National Urban League's Community Action Assembly, held in Washington December 9–11, was "Lifeline to Equal Opportunity." Its purpose was to bring together Federal officials and Negro leaders in order "to open pipelines of self-help for poverty-struck Harlems from New York to Seattle."

801 Remarks to Members of VISTA—"Volunteers in Service to America." *December 12, 1964*

Mr. Shriver and ladies and gentlemen:

I want to welcome you here today, the first frontline volunteers in our war against poverty. You have come from every part of this country, from every age group, from every background. You have come to serve the poor and the unfortunate of American society, and to open the door of American opportunity to all of our American people.

Your pay will be low; the conditions of your labor will often be difficult. But you will have the satisfaction of leading a great national effort, and you will have the ultimate reward which comes to those who serve their Nation and who serve their fellow man.

You are the first, as Sargent Shriver said, of the 3500 Volunteers in Service to America who will go into the field during this first year. No aspect of the war against poverty will be more important than the work that you do. New programs and new ideas, institutions, and administrators all will be fruitless unless we can reach—directly and personally—those that we are all trying so hard to help.

This is your job—to guide the young, to comfort the sick, to encourage the downtrodden, to teach the skills which may lead to a more satisfying and a more rewarding life. On your idealism and on your success rests much of our hope for the final elimination of poverty in our American life.

You bring to this task many varied skills. You have been trained in educational institutions of every level. Many of you bring a lifetime of experience and of fruitful labor for this country that we all love. All of you are willing to share the privation of the poor. And ultimately you will share the greatest victory in the life of any nation.

It is characteristic of America that we meet our great challenges. We meet them in war and we meet them in peace, through calling on the idealism and the love of country of all of our people. They have always responded, and the challenge has always been met.

Your presence here this morning, and the many who will follow, testifies to the fact that this basic strength of America is always equal to any task.

The initials of your organization spell VISTA. It is an appropriate name, for you will be opening up new vistas of hope for the poor, achievement for yourself, greatness for your Nation, the Nation you serve.

VISTA volunteers stand ready to serve at the request of every community and every neighborhood, every organization and institution, which joins the war against poverty.

I believe—I know—that you will receive the support of all Americans. And I hope that all those with skills and dedication to offer will come and join with you in this most extraordinary force for good in our country.

It is a pleasure to welcome you here in the White House, and it is with great pride that I welcome you in this new undertaking.

NOTE: The President spoke at 12:23 p.m. in the Theater at the White House. His opening words referred to Sargent Shriver, Director of the Office of Economic Opportunity, Chairman of the Economic Council, and Director of the Peace Corps, who introduced the group of 20 VISTA volunteers meeting with the President.

A White House release dated December 16 listed 162 new war on poverty projects announced by the President that day and noted that VISTA, the domestic version of the Peace Corps, was under the direction of the Office of Economic Opportunity. The release stated that 99 volunteers, the first of the 3,500 planned for the opening year, "would help teach, train, and counsel impoverished Americans in migrant worker communities, big-city slums, and hill towns of Appalachia." The group, the release further stated, would work on 12 separate projects in 28 communities.

802 Remarks to the Members of the Economic Opportunity Council. *December 12, 1964*

I LOOK to this body as a domestic national security council for the war on poverty.

Your job is to help me in making policy and program decisions in waging this war.

This Council of Cabinet officers and heads of agencies was established by the Economic Opportunity Act to advise on "the coordination of antipoverty efforts by all segments of the Federal Government."

As provided for by statute, Sargent Shriver will serve as Chairman of this Council and will have responsibility for its operation.

I am also asking Vice President-elect Humphrey to take a leading role in the war on poverty. I want Mr. Shriver to work with him to be sure that this is a well-coordinated, concentrated attack on poverty throughout the country. I have also requested him to serve as honorary chairman of the Advisory Council set up by the Economic Opportunity Act.

The membership of this group of distinguished private citizens will be announced shortly.

I hope the Vice President-elect will assume a role similar to the one I filled as Chairman of the Peace Corps National Advisory Council.

There are four broad areas in which I expect you to exercise initiative and take particular responsibility:

First, to review major policy issues that arise in conducting the war against poverty.

Second, to weigh national priorities for program needs in the war on poverty, and to assess the ability of existing programs to meet those needs.

Third, to support an information system which will provide local officials and private groups with the facts they need in working with us in this effort to eliminate poverty.

Fourth, to make certain that the antipoverty programs respond to local needs and encourage the full development of community action.

Vice President-elect Humphrey and I will look to the Economic Opportunity Council for advice and support in each of these areas and I will rely heavily upon his and your recommendations.

I call upon the members of this Council to meet as often as necessary, to recommend whatever actions need to be taken, and to carry out whatever tasks must be done to wage this war effectively. Our objective is total victory—and we are going to attain it.

NOTE: The President spoke at 12:40 p.m. in the Cabinet Room at the White House.

A White House release, dated January 28, 1965, announced the President's appointment that day of the members of the National Advisory Council. The release, giving the names and brief biographical sketches of the 14 members, noted that the Council would hold its first meeting February 3, 1965.

As printed, this item follows the prepared text released by the White House.

803   Letter to the Chairman, Federal Power Commission, in Response to the National Power Survey Report. *December 14, 1964*

[Released December 14, 1964.   Dated December 12, 1964]

Dear Mr. Chairman:

I have your letter of December 11 with which you transmitted the report of the National Power Survey undertaken by the Federal Power Commission in cooperation with all of the segments of the nation's electric power industry.

It seems to me that the survey represents a very constructive step in directing the at-tention of the government and of all of the various interested industry groups to our greatly increasing power needs of the future. A doubling or tripling of the electricity requirements in this country by the year 1980 presents a challenge to the nation that can and must be met.

It is obvious that the building of the Great Society rests, in part, on an abundant supply of low cost energy. The experience of the past few decades demonstrates conclusively how the standard of living of American citizens has continued to rise as we have developed greater supplies of electrical energy.

I think it is most significant that the Commission's survey was a cooperative effort between the Commission and the industry it regulates. The encouragement of greater cooperation and coordination among the nation's 3600 individual electric power systems should result in the economies of large-scale operation benefiting the consumer in every section of the country without regard to whether they are served by privately-owned companies, by municipally-owned systems or by cooperatives.

The Commission is to be congratulated for its initiative in undertaking the survey, and I share the Commission's hope that the results of the survey will benefit the nation, the nation's consumers and the nation's power industry.

Sincerely,

LYNDON B. JOHNSON

[Honorable Joseph C. Swidler, Chairman, Federal Power Commission, Washington, D.C.]

NOTE: The Commission's report, entitled "National Power Survey," consists of two volumes: The first (296 pp.) is the main report of the Commission, the second (423 pp.), a compilation of 24 advisory committee reports and an interim report on the defense implications of the survey (Government Printing Office, 1964).

The text of the Chairman's letter of December 11 was also released.

804   Remarks to the Members of a Delegation of Industrial Research Leaders Upon Their Return From the Soviet Union. *December* 15, 1964

Dr. Hornig, gentlemen:

I am very happy to have heard your impressions of Soviet science and technology, based on your 2-week visit to Soviet Russia. I am especially grateful to you men from industry who gave so much of your time to make this trip and to prepare for it and present your conclusions. This is another fine example of the willingness of American businessmen and scientists to give of themselves for the public good.

I am especially glad that you got to meet so many people in Russia and had such lengthy conversations with them. It is important for us to know the people and to understand as much as we can about their economic development. It is good to hear that the people you met in the research laboratories, factories, and schools throughout

the country showed such a lively interest in America and wanted to enter into contact with Americans by visits and correspondence. I was especially interested to hear that this was as true of people out in the middle of Siberia as it was in Moscow and Leningrad.

Visits like yours help us to get to know the Russian people better, to know their country and see their accomplishments and problems at first hand. We are hoping to cooperate with them in water desalting and perhaps other specific fields of technology that benefit mankind. I hope there will be more trips like yours, in both directions, and I am asking all agencies of the Government on our side to make sure that we're going as far as we can to extend this hand of peaceful contact to the Soviet people, without in any way endangering our security.

NOTE: The President spoke at noon in the Cabinet Room at the White House. His opening words referred to Donald F. Hornig, Special Assistant to the President and Director of the Office of Science and Technology, who headed the six-member industrial research delegation which visited the Soviet Union in November.

A White House release of the same day listed the members of the delegation. The release, reporting on the group's meeting with the President, stated that the members of the delegation gave the President an account of their discussions with the Soviet Vice Premier, the President of the Soviet Academy of Sciences, and other Soviet leaders, and also described their visits to factories, engineering design institutes, and laboratories in Moscow, Leningrad, Novosibirsk, and other cities.

805   Letter Accepting Resignation of Luther H. Hodges as Secretary of Commerce.   *December 16, 1964*

Dear Luther:

I am personally reluctant to accept your resignation. Your achievements as Secretary of Commerce have been a continuation of the selfless, patriotic dedication you have exhibited throughout your long service to your State and your Nation.

Your leadership in the Commerce Department has been marked by prudence and progress. You have given of your wisdom and your tolerance not only to your own Department, but to the entire Cabinet as well.

Under your leadership, our country has entered into a new era of international trade, increased cooperation between government and industry, and technological advance-ment for the industrial and commercial segments of our national life.

Good and wise men, sympathetic to the needs of the people, ready to work around the clock to meet those needs—these men are rare and precious. You are one of that scarce breed. You leave this government with my affection and my warmest best wishes.

Sincerely,

LYNDON B. JOHNSON

[Honorable Luther H. Hodges, Secretary of Commerce, Department of Commerce, Washington, D.C.]

NOTE: Mr. Hodges served as Secretary of Commerce from January 21, 1961, through January 15, 1965. His letter of resignation was released with the President's reply.

806   Remarks at a Televised Ceremony Marking the Change in Leadership at the Department of Commerce.   *December 16, 1964*

THIS IS a day of some personal sadness for me. I have in my hand the resignation of Luther Hodges who is departing his post as Secretary of Commerce.

Secretary Hodges is a distinguished American who has served his State and his Nation and has in his entire lifetime given to the American people the best that is in him always for the benefit of his beloved country. His stewardship of the Commerce Department was both progressive and prudent.

I have accepted Secretary Hodges' resignation with deep regret because he is not only a good and wise American but he is my longtime trusted personal friend. But the American system that produced a

Luther Hodges has within its gifts the capacity to produce a man to take his place.

I have elected to ask the Senate to give their advice and consent to my nomination of John T. Connor of New Jersey to be Secretary of Commerce.

I truly believe that John Connor is an authentic example of what the American educational and free enterprise system can create. Until yesterday he was the president of Merck & Company, one of the Nation's leading pharmaceutical firms. He was on the board of directors of General Motors and General Foods, and other leading boards. He is a leader on the Committee for Economic Development and the Business Advisory Council.

He is not unacquainted with the ways of Washington. In 1942 he was the General Counsel for the Office of Scientific Research and Development, at that time headed by the distinguished American, Vannevar Bush. In 1945 he became counsel to the new Office of Naval Research, and later special assistant to the late, respected James Forrestal. In between times he served as a rugged Marine and reached the rank of captain.

He graduated from Syracuse University in 1936 *magna cum laude,* and from Harvard Law School in 1939. I might add that he was not backward in his studies. He was elected to Phi Beta Kappa.

John Connor is the kind of man I am proud to have serve in the Cabinet. He is smart and he is loyal and he is patriotic. He will never discard a principle nor despair of doing what is right and ought to be done. I think the credentials that he bears in his heart and in his mind are the kind of credentials that will make his Nation proud and will cause great achievements to be his legacy in the country that he has served so well and in the Nation that he loves.

I now present to you Mr. Connor.

[*Responding, Mr. Connor stated that his appointment as Secretary of Commerce was quite a challenge to him and his family. "From a human point of view," he said, "of course, a change like this is never an easy one to make. . . . You know," he continued, "the President is often accused of being quite an arm twister. Well, I can testify that at least in this case he didn't even put a hand on my arm, much less twist it, but he did appeal to my mind and to my heart, and particularly to my patriotism, so here I am, and I will do my best." The President then resumed speaking.*]

I have asked the new Secretary of Commerce to meet and work with the Secretary of Labor and the voice of American labor in this country, Mr. George Meany. We have had some preliminary meetings, and I hope to see the relationship between business and labor continue in the years ahead as it has in the months behind us.

I know that the distinguished Secretary of Labor, Mr. Wirtz, will be anxious to cooperate, and I expect the Secretary of Commerce and the Secretary of Labor to work very closely in leading the business community and the labor community to a record of alltime harmony and mutual respect in this country.

I thank Mr. Meany for meeting with us this morning, and Secretary Wirtz. I now want to ask Mr. Hodges if he will say a word to you. George Reedy will have available for you Mr. Hodges' letter of resignation and my reply, together with biographical data concerning Mr. Connor.

Secretary Hodges.

[*Secretary Hodges responded by expressing his appreciation to the President for the cooperation and confidence he had exhibited toward him. Pointing to the fact that his letter of resignation was written in October he added, "I want to carry out a long-term plan of mine of finishing up at the end of a 4-year term, because I will be approaching 67 before very long. It has been an exhilarating experience," he concluded, "particularly the last year, sir, with you." The President again resumed speaking.*]

One final statement before we leave. We will try to make this transition effective on January 15th. We will send the nomination to the Senate at an early date. We have completed the necessary details and investigations and they are behind us and we hope that the takeover can be January 15th.

Secretary Wirtz, did you want to say something?

[*Secretary of Labor W. Willard Wirtz expressed his personal satisfaction at having worked with Secretary Hodges in bringing together the interests of American management and American labor and said he looked forward to the opportunity to work with Mr. Connor as he had worked with Secretary Hodges "in bringing forward those elements of unity which are so important to the national interest." The President then concluded his remarks.*]

I have asked Mr. Meany to meet with me and other members of American labor before we leave for the Christmas holidays to discuss our program for the coming years.

I have already met with the Economic Council and the Business Council, and I will be conferring from time to time with leading educators, businessmen, and labor men here at the White House, and perhaps at the ranch before the new session.

Thank you very much.

NOTE: The President spoke at 11:09 a.m. in the Theater at the White House.

For the President's reply to Secretary Hodges' letter of resignation, see Item 805. Mr. Connor's nomination as Secretary of Commerce was confirmed by the Senate on January 15, 1965.

807   Statement by the President on the Launching of the Italian San Marco Satellite.   *December 16, 1964*

A SIGNIFICANT milestone in cooperative international space efforts was achieved yesterday with the successful launching of the Italian San Marco satellite.

This marks the first time a launch crew of any nation other than the United States or the Soviet Union has put its own scientific payload into orbit.

My congratulations to the Italian people for their initiative and perseverance in the San Marco project. It is a source of particular satisfaction to me that I participated in the signing of the Italian-American agreement for this project in Rome in 1962.

I look forward to continued success in the next phase of the San Marco project when the Italian Space Commission will attempt the difficult operation of launching a similar satellite from an ocean platform near the equator.

NOTE: The U.S.-Italian agreement which led to the launching of the San Marco satellite was effected by an exchange of notes at Rome, September 5, 1962. The U.S. note was signed by Vice President Johnson, the Italian note, by Minister of Foreign Affairs Attilio Piccione. The agreement is printed in Treaties and Other International Acts Series (TIAS 5172; 13 UST 2120).

808   Remarks Upon Accepting a Ceremonial Pass to the 10th International Games for the Deaf.   *December 17, 1964*

THANK YOU very much. This is very attractive and I am happy and proud to accept this pass. When I accepted earlier the honorary chairmanship of the 10th Interna-

tional Games for the Deaf, I was hopeful that it might at least assure me a seat for these events which we were all anticipating with such great pleasure.

All Americans are very proud and pleased that after 40 years the Deaf Olympics will be held in the United States next summer, will be held here in Washington. One hundred years ago, President Lincoln signed the charter establishing here in Washington the beginnings of Gallaudet College which still stands as the only institution of higher learning of its kind anywhere in the world.

I have been personally much interested in and I have been rather closely associated with the inspiring work being done there to afford young people afflicted with deafness a broadening horizon of opportunity. As a Member of Congress, I followed very closely all the legislation affecting Gallaudet and did all I could to advance it.

As we can all be proud of the humane and intelligent progress our society has made in the attitudes toward those suffering this affliction, I am ever mindful of the inspiration the deaf themselves provide us. Despite the great handicap that they all must endure, the deaf are occupying ever-widening roles of leadership and usefulness in all the segments of our society and our American life.

Since the beginning in 1924, the Deaf Olympics have served effectively to awaken the world to the potential of the deaf for full participation in our affairs. I would express the personal hope that the presence of the games in this country next year will focus more attention upon the still unfulfilled potential of what we could and what we should be doing in this field.

We are coming into an age in the life of man when we do not need to accept with resignation the consequences of afflictions and illnesses which have plagued the human race since time began. There is undoubtedly much that we can still learn and much that we can do that is not now being done to advance medical research in preventing or relieving deafness.

Even more immediately, however, there is much we can do to improve the educational opportunities and the employment opportunities for those who presently suffer deafness. And it is my earnest hope that the games, which will bring together 700 star athletes from 27 participating nations, will be remembered as the start of a new race to overtake this affliction and all of its consequences.

Thank you very much for coming here. It is an honor to receive you in the White House and you know that these events will have my genuine interest and I assure you, again, of the concern of all of us in this country for helping one of the most worthy projects.

NOTE: The President spoke at 12:05 p.m. in the Cabinet Room at the White House. The ceremonial pass, a gold medal, was presented to the President by Milton J. Salzberg, chairman of special events for the International Games for the Deaf, at a ceremony attended by the IGD officers. At the close of the ceremony Jerald Gordon, IGD chairman, invited the President to open the games, to be held in June 1965 in the stadiums of the University of Maryland, College Park, Md., and Gallaudet College, Washington, D.C.

809 Remarks on the Decision To Build a Sea Level Canal and To Negotiate a New Treaty With Panama. *December 18, 1964*

THIS GOVERNMENT has completed an intensive review of policy toward the present and the future of the Panama Canal. On the basis of this review I have reached two decisions.

First, I have decided that the United States

should press forward with Panama and other interested governments, in plans and preparations for a sea level canal in this area.

Second, I have decided to propose to the Government of Panama the negotiation of an entirely new treaty on the existing Panama Canal.

These decisions reflect the unanimous judgment of the Secretary of State, the Secretary of Defense, the Joint Chiefs of Staff. They are based on the recommendations of Ambassador Robert Anderson, Secretary Stephen Ailes, Secretary Thomas Mann, and our Ambassador in Panama, Ambassador Jack Vaughn. They have the full support of Mr. Truman and General Eisenhower. They have been reported to, and in most instances sympathetically received by the leadership of the Congress.

These two steps I think are needed now— needed for the protection and the promotion of peaceful trade, for the welfare of the hemisphere—in the true interests of the United States and in fairness and justice to all.

For 50 years the Panama Canal has carried ships of all nations in peaceful trade between the two great oceans—on terms of entire equality and at no profit to this country. The canal has also served the cause of peace and freedom in two world wars. It has brought great economic contributions to Panama. For the rest of its life the canal will continue to serve trade, and peace, and the people of Panama.

But that life is now limited. The canal is growing old, and so are the treaties for its management, which go back to 1903.

The Panama Canal, with its limiting locks and channels, will soon be inadequate to the needs of our world commerce. Already more than 300 ships built or building are too big to go through with full loads.

Many of them—like our own modern aircraft carriers—cannot even go through at all.

So I think it is time to plan in earnest for a sea level canal. Such a canal will be more modern, more economical, and will be far easier to defend. It will be free of complex, costly, vulnerable locks and seaways. It will serve the future as the Panama Canal we know has served the past and the present.

The Congress has already authorized $17 million for studies of possible sites and of the other practical problems of a sea level canal. There seem to be four possible routes—two in Panama, one in Colombia, and one which goes through Nicaragua and possibly Costa Rica as well.

I have asked the Secretary of State to begin discussions immediately with all the governments concerned with these possible new routes. In these discussions we will be prepared to work on the terms and the conditions of building and operating a new canal, and if preliminary arrangements can be reached, we will be ready to go ahead with selected site surveys.

Last January there was violence in Panama. As I said then, "Violence is never justified and is never a basis for talks."

But while the people of the United States have never made concessions to force, they have always supported fair play and full respect for the rights of others. So from the very first day, as your President, I made it clear that we were ready to sit down and to seek answers, to reason together and to try to find the answers that would be just, fair, and right, without precondition or without precommitment on either side.

On that basis, relations between our two countries were resumed in April, and on that basis I chose Mr. Robert Anderson, the distinguished former Secretary of the Treasury under President Eisenhower, to be my special Ambassador on this problem. Since then Ambassador Anderson has been working with the American Ambassador, Mr. Vaughn, with the Secretary of the Army, Mr. Ailes, and with Secretary Mann of the State Department. They have recommended that we should propose a new treaty for the existing canal. After careful review with my senior advisers, I have accepted this recommendation.

Today we have informed the Government of Panama that we are ready to negotiate a new treaty. In such a treaty we must retain the rights which are necessary for the effective operation and the protection of the canal, and the administration of the areas that are necessary for these purposes. Such a treaty would replace the treaty of 1903 and its amendments. It should recognize the sovereignty of Panama. It should provide for its own termination when a sea level canal comes into operation. It should provide for effective discharge of our common responsibilities for hemispheric defense. Until a new agreement is reached, of course, the present treaties will remain in effect.

In these new proposals we will take every possible step to deal fairly and helpfully with the citizens of both Panama and the United States who have served so faithfully through the years in operating and maintaining the canal.

These changes are necessary not because of failure but because of success; not because of backwardness but because of progress. The age before us is an age of larger, faster ships. It is an age of friendly partnership among the nations concerned with the traffic between the oceans. This new age requires new arrangements.

The strength of our American system is that we have always tried to understand and meet the needs of the future. We have been at our best when we have been both bold and prudent in moving forward. The planning of a new canal and the negotiation of a new treaty are just such bold and prudent steps. So let us today in friendship take them together.

NOTE: The President spoke at 4:45 p.m. in the Theater at the White House. He approved the bill providing for the site studies on September 22, 1964 (Public Law 88–609, 78 Stat. 990).

810   Remarks at the Lighting of the Nation's Christmas Tree. *December 18, 1964*

Mr. Secretary of the Interior, Reverend Clergy, Vice President-elect Humphrey, ladies and gentlemen:

Once again, we come here to keep an old and cherished tradition—the lighting, here in Washington, of the Nation's Christmas Tree.

For all of us—of all ages—the lights of Christmas symbolize each year the happiness of this wonderful season.

But this year I believe that the lights of Christmas symbolize more than the happiness of the moment. Their brightness expresses the hopefulness of the times in which we live.

These are the most hopeful times in all the years since Christ was born in Bethlehem.

Our world is still troubled. Man is still afflicted by many worries and many woes.

Yet today—as never before—man has in his possession the capacities to end war and preserve peace, to eradicate poverty and share abundance, to overcome the diseases that have afflicted the human race and permit all mankind to enjoy their promise in life on this earth.

At this Christmas season of 1964, we can think of broader and brighter horizons than any who have lived before these times. For there is rising in the sky of the age a new star—the star of peace.

By his inventions, man has made war unthinkable, now and forevermore. Man must, therefore, apply the same initiative, the same inventiveness, the same determined effort to make peace on earth eternal and meaningful for all mankind.

For nearly 200 years of our existence as a nation, America has stood for peace in the world. At this Christmas season—when the world commemorates the birth of the Prince of Peace—I want all men, everywhere, to know that the people of this great Nation have but one hope, one ambition toward other peoples: that is to live at peace with them and for them to live at peace with one another.

Since the first Christmas, man has moved slowly but steadily forward toward realizing the promise of peace on earth among men of good will. That movement has been possible because there has been brought into the affairs of man a more generous spirit toward his fellow man.

Let us pray at this season that in all we do as individuals and as a nation, we may be motivated by that spirit of generosity and compassion which Christ taught us so long ago.

Now it is my great privilege to do as Presidents have done for 40 years—to press this button and light the Christmas tree for all the Nation. As I do so, may I take this opportunity to express to the distinguished Representatives, the Ambassadors of foreign countries, to our official family, to each home and each family in our glorious Nation the wishes of our family—Mrs. Johnson, Lynda, Luci, and myself—for a happy holiday season and years of peace and success to come.

Thank you and God bless all of you.

NOTE: The President spoke at 6:40 p.m. just before lighting the National Community Christmas Tree at the 11th annual Pageant of Peace ceremonies on the Ellipse near the White House. His opening words referred to Secretary of the Interior Stewart L. Udall, the Most Reverend William J. McDonald, Rector, Catholic University of America, the Most Reverend Archbishop Iakovos, Primate, Greek Orthodox Church of North and South America, the Right Reverend William F. Creighton, Bishop, Episcopal Diocese of Washington, and Vice President-elect Hubert H. Humphrey.

811 Statement by the President on the New Level of Personal Income in the United States. *December 18, 1964*

I AM HAPPY to announce a historic milestone in the economic progress of the United States. Personal income rose $3.3 billion in November to a seasonally adjusted annual rate of $502 billion, crossing the half trillion dollar mark for the first time.

This is a tremendous achievement for the American people and for our free enterprise system. Never before in our history or in the history of any other country has there been such an outpouring of the means to buy the good things of life. And never before have so many people shared in this wealth.

Most of the November rise in personal income occurred in private wages and salaries, reaching a seasonally adjusted annual rate of $340 billion. This represents a 25 percent increase over the 1960 level for wages and salaries and for total personal income.

While we still face the challenge of eliminating poverty from our society, this great income gain in the last 4 years clearly demonstrates that we have the means to achieve a decent standard of living for all Americans. It shows what American business, labor, agriculture, and the Government can accomplish by working together for the common good.

812   Statement by the President in Response to Report Reviewing Gains in Government Employment of Minority Groups. *December 21, 1964*

THIS PROGRESS is the result of affirmative and persistent efforts by the Federal agencies to hire, train, and promote on the basis of merit alone, without consideration of irrelevancies such as race or ancestry. It shows that it is possible to sweep away the customs and practices that have denied productive lives to many minority Americans. It demonstrates that there are, in truth, qualified persons from all races and regions who are available to fill posts of responsibility with dignity and competence. Our continued strength depends on our redoubled efforts to insure that the skills and potential of all our people are utilized effectively in the pursuit of our national goals.

NOTE: The statement was part of a White House release summarizing the report of the President's Committee on Equal Employment Opportunity. The report, a series of related studies in tabular form with the overall title "Study of Minority Group Employment in the Federal Government," was prepared for the Committee by the U.S. Civil Service Commission (109 pp., Government Printing Office, 1964).

The release stated that the report disclosed that minority Americans were increasingly being utilized in the Federal civil service. For the third successive year the annual minority census taken in June showed major changes in the number of Negroes and other minorities in middle and upper grade jobs. These advances were made despite a drop in overall minority employment in line with the general cutback in Government employment. Similar gains occurred in Negro employment in the upper levels of the blue collar, postal, and other pay categories. The release concluded by stating that the pattern of progress was quite similar for other minority groups, Mexican-Americans, Puerto Ricans, Indians, and Oriental-Americans.

813   Christmas Message to the Americans in Viet-Nam. *December 23, 1964*

TO MY fellow Americans in Viet-Nam, and to their wives, children, and parents, I send warmest Christmas greetings.

Those of us who are at home, full of joy and thoughts of peace, are ever mindful of, and grateful to, those thousands of you who toil today where there is no peace.

You are in Viet-Nam, far from the places and people you love, because the forces that have given our Nation strength and wealth have also placed upon it the burden of defending freedom—even in remote and distant villages.

In every generation the burden of protecting liberty has fallen to a few stouthearted men. We Americans celebrate this holy season in liberty because our forebears had the courage, the determination, the will to sacrifice, that was equal to the challenges before them. Future generations in many lands will spend Christmas days in freedom because there are men everywhere who are equal to this grim challenge in our time.

You who carry freedom's banner in Viet-Nam are engaged in a war that is undeclared—yet tragically real. It is a war of terror where the aggressor moves in the secret shadows of the nights. Murder and kidnaping and deception are his tools. Subversion and conquest are his goals. It is a war waged with political, social, economic, and psychological weapons as well as guns and bombs. Thus every American

in Viet-Nam, whether soldier, embassy secretary, or AID official, whether in the jungle, in the mountains, or in the cities, is on the frontlines of this struggle.

Those of you who are helping the Vietnamese people to defend themselves against this insidious warfare may serve in places with names that ring strange to American ears: Long Khot, Kien Tuong, Binh Gia. But your sacrifices are known and honored in American towns and cities more familiar to you, for you are meeting your country's commitment to a world of justice.

All Americans join me in sending thanks—and not at Christmas only, but around the clock, and around the year.

LYNDON B. JOHNSON

814 Statement by the President on the Appointment of John E. Horne as Chairman, Federal Home Loan Bank Board. *December 26, 1964*

THE SAVINGS and loan industry of the United States is one of the most rapidly growing institutions in our national economy. In selecting Mr. Horne, Chairman of the Home Loan Bank Board, the agency most directly concerned with the savings and loan industry, I am purposely placing the regulatory responsibility of this industry in the hands of an experienced public official. In his service with the Home Loan Bank

Board during the past 18 months and during his 2 years' service as Administrator of the Small Business Administration, Mr. Horne has demonstrated his commitment to the public service and his concern for a strong and growing economy throughout the United States.

NOTE: Mr. Horne's appointment as Chairman of the Federal Home Loan Bank Board became effective on January 26, 1965.

The statement was released at Austin, Tex.

815 Statement by the President on the Appointment of William J. Driver as Administrator of Veterans Affairs. *December 26, 1964*

I AM particularly pleased to announce Mr. Driver's appointment since he is the first career official to administer the affairs of America's veterans. He is being promoted

to this important position on the basis of outstanding achievement and demonstrated ability over a period of 16 years in the Veterans Administration.

I hope that the recognition accorded Mr. Driver for his effective and dedicated service will serve as an example to others in Government service. In the search for talent in this administration, I will fully consider the records of those who have made Government service their career as well as outstanding men and women in other walks of life.

NOTE: Mr. Driver's appointment as Administrator of Veterans Affairs was confirmed by the Senate on February 2, 1965.

The statement was released at Austin, Tex.

816 Letter to Secretary McNamara Transmitting Final Report of the President's Committee on Equal Opportunity in the Armed Forces. *December* 28, 1964

[Released December 28, 1964.   Dated December 26, 1964]

Dear Mr. Secretary:

Enclosed is a copy of the final report submitted by the Committee on Equal Opportunity in the Armed Forces. The report deals with the special problems of discrimination faced by American servicemen serving abroad and by those who serve in National Guard units.

The Committee has devoted considerable time and effort to its studies, and its recommendations obviously warrant prompt and thorough consideration within the Federal Government.

The Defense Department has, I believe, done an excellent job in resolving many aspects of the general problem of discriminatory treatment of those who serve in the Nation's Armed Forces. I would hope that the momentum already achieved in moving toward the Nation's objective of equality of treatment and opportunity for all servicemen would continue until every vestige of the problem has been eliminated.

The recent progress in securing integration of National Guard units is encouraging, and I urge that every effort be made to continue this movement toward a National Guard in every State in which there will be no barriers against participation based on race, color or creed. The cooperation that has been obtained between the Defense Department and the Governors of the various States in striving for this objective should be maintained and strengthened. I will appreciate receiving periodic reports from you on the progress made in this regard.

Because the Committee's report discusses the assignment of military personnel to United States Missions in other countries, I am also sending a copy of the report and of this letter to the Secretary of State.

Sincerely,

LYNDON B. JOHNSON

[The Honorable Robert S. McNamara, Secretary of Defense, Washington, D.C.]

NOTE: The Committee's report, dated November 1964 and entitled "Final Report: Military Personnel Stationed Overseas and Membership and Participation in the National Guard" (mimeographed, 24 pp. and tables) was released with the President's letter.

The initial report of the Committee was submitted to President Kennedy in June 1963 (see 1963 volume, this series, Item 251).

The letter was released at Austin, Tex.

817 Message to Giuseppe Saragat Upon His Election as President of Italy. *December 28, 1964*

ON BEHALF of the American people, I extend to you warm congratulations upon your election as President. I look forward to a continuation of the close friendship between our two countries in these times which present not only great problems but also great opportunities. Mrs. Johnson joins me in sending our personal best wishes.

Sincerely,

LYNDON B. JOHNSON

[His Excellency Giuseppe Saragat, Rome, Italy]

NOTE: The message was released at Austin, Tex.

818 The President's News Conference of *December 28, 1964*

THE PRESIDENT. I don't have any important news for you. I understood that some of you hadn't had a chance to come out and visit and you might like to do that before you went back. I know I am going to be here for at least the next couple of days.

[1.] I have a few brief announcements that will be of interest to you and I'll make them, and I have a comment I want to make about the state of the Union so that we can get it in the proper perspective. Then I'll go on "deep background" for you and answer freely and fully as I can anything that your editors may be interested in or that you may be interested in.

I have been poring over these thousands of pages from some 50 agencies regarding matters that they would like to have the President consider before drawing his pattern for his message to Congress this year. Obviously, the State of the Union Message will be brief and cannot deal with all these subjects.

We will give a general outline and emphasize some of the immediate, repeat immediate, recommendations that we would like to see promptly acted upon. The other parts of the administration's program will be dealt with during the next 4 years in a series of messages from time to time, and

they will be timed based upon when the Congress is ready to receive them and when the committees can act upon them and when the administration has completed its studies in the respective fields.

So I want to point out to you that the message that I will give on the evening of the 4th will not be a complete or final summation of all that we hope to achieve in this 4 years. That program will evolve over a period of time through various messages.

I don't want to leave the impression that we expect to build a Great Society and develop it overnight, or in any 1 day or in any 1 week or in any 1 month or in any 1 session. There will be, as I want to emphasize, a series of legislative proposals, and these will be brief and considered very carefully.

[2.] Now George [1] will give you details of these biographical sketches.

Mr. Frederick Lewis Deming will be the new Under Secretary of the Treasury, succeeding Mr. Roosa who will leave us the first of the year. Mr. Deming was born in Des Moines, Iowa, September 12, 1912; A.B. degree from Washington University, St. Louis, Mo.; has an M.A. degree from Wash-

---

[1] George E. Reedy, Press Secretary to the President.

ington University, St. Louis, Mo.; has a Ph. D. from Washington University, St. Louis, Mo. He has been since 1957 president of the Federal Reserve Bank of Minneapolis. He first went to work for the Federal Reserve Bank in 1941 as assistant manager of the research department. By 1953 he had served as economist, manager of the research department, assistant vice president, vice president, and finally first vice president. He continued to serve the St. Louis bank until 1957 when he became president of the Minneapolis bank.

From April to June 1956, Mr. Deming served as chief of Banking Advisory Mission to the Republic of Honduras, and from November to December 1960, served as consultant to the Central Bank, Government of the Republic of China. He was recommended by Secretary of the Treasury, Mr. Dillon, and by most of the—well, he is first on nearly everyone's list, and he is the only person that I have approached about it. I talked to him several weeks ago in Washington and he has now been cleared and he will give notice out there and be leaving shortly.

We are naming Mr. Sheldon S. Cohen, the General Counsel of the Internal Revenue Service, as the new Commissioner of Internal Revenue. Mr. Cohen is a Washington boy, finished Calvin Coolidge High School in Washington, D.C., has an A.B. degree from George Washington University with special honors in 1950; doctor's degree, with distinction, A average, and he completed it in 2 years in 1952; had special honors in accounting at George Washington University, where he was first in his school class. He is the recipient of Charles W. Dorsey Scholarship. He was editorial and business secretary, George Washington Law Review; he was case notes editor, George Washington Law Review; United

States District Court for the District of Columbia Bar; United States Court of Appeals Bar; United States Supreme Court, the Tax Court Bar; and Certified Public Accountant, Maryland, since 1953.

He has been associate professorial lecturer of George Washington University from 1958 to date; Howard University Law School lecturer in 1957 and 1958; 20th New York University Institute on Federal Taxation lecturer; and in 1957, American University Tax Institute.

He has been Chief Counsel of the Internal Revenue Service since January 6, 1964. He was formerly associated with the legal firm of Arnold, Fortas and Porter; of Stevenson, Paul, Rifkind, Wharton and Garrison. He was Legislative Attorney to the Chief Counsel's Office of Internal Revenue in 1952 to 1956. He was an accountant in a CPA's office in 1950 to 1952. He was former treasurer and member of the board of directors, Lane Manor Citizens Association; assistant treasurer, director, and membership chairman of the Jewish Community Center of Greater Washington; second vice president, director, and chairman of the legal committee, Jewish Social Service Agency. He had military service, U.S. Naval Reserve, 1945 and 1946.

He will be succeeded by a career man whom I am naming today, Mr. Mitchell Rogovin, presently Assistant to the Commissioner of Internal Revenue; born in New York, December 3, 1930; has an A.B. from Syracuse, Maxwell School of Citizenship; LL.B. from the University of Virginia, Du Pont Scholarship; has an LL.M. from Georgetown University, master's degree in taxation.

His career from 1954 to 1958, officer-in-charge, trial section, base legal office, Camp Pendleton, handling over 300 general courts-martial; 1958 to 1961, Office of Chief

Counsel, IRS, trial attorney; 1961 to 1964, Assistant to the Commissioner of the Internal Revenue Service. He received a Treasury Department Special Service Award in 1964. And he has got various memberships which George can give you.

He has taught at the University of Virginia Law School, 1958 to 1964, as a guest lecturer, and at Palomar College, 1956 to 1957, was an instructor in English and business law.

A note on Mr. Cohen may be of interest to you. During the last 12 months as Chief Counsel, from which position he is going to Commissioner, he inaugurated, in cooperation with the Commissioner, new procedures for the handling of rules and legislative proposals which will result in annual savings in excess of a million dollars. These new procedures, involving the elimination of duplication, will also mean faster service to the public and better administration of the tax laws.

He also developed the use of electronic data processing equipment to coordinate the work of field offices so as to provide similarity of treatment for taxpayers and to make the experience of individual field offices readily available to all of them.

Mr. Cohen streamlined the organization and operation of the Chief Counsel's office, which includes approximately 1,350 employees stationed in 32 offices throughout the Nation, with notable improvements in morale and efficiency.

Q. Do you have his birthdate, sir?

THE PRESIDENT. Yes, it is June 28, 1927. But that data will be available to you. I won't take any more of your time on them.[2]

[3.] We have a report today for the 5 months, July through November, of this fiscal year. Total expenditures of the Federal Government are down $1.2 billion over the same period of last year. The first 5 months of the present fiscal year's expenditures came in this afternoon, 39.3. The first 5 months of last fiscal year they were 40.5.

[4.] Secretary Rusk and Mr. Bundy will arrive at the ranch tomorrow. They will review with me international developments, various personnel matters in the department in Washington and ambassadors throughout the world, and we will finish up on the final study of the budget for the State Department.

I expect Mr. Gordon to be returning to review some extra data with us.

Q. Mr. President, may I interrupt? You mentioned Mr. Bundy. There are two of them. I assume this is McGeorge?

THE PRESIDENT. McGeorge Bundy. On Wednesday I expect Mr. George McGhee. He is home for consultations. I will ask him to come here and review developments in West Germany.

I have, in the last 24 hours, talked to Secretaries Rusk and McNamara, Mr. McCone, Mr. Bundy, and Mr. Moyers several times on the state of the Union; messages back and forth to the Chairman, Council of Economic Advisers and the Budget Director. I think that is about it. Now tomorrow will be Rusk's day primarily, and next day we will spend a good deal of time with Gordon and with Ambassador McGhee and others.[3]

---

[2] A biographical sketch of each of the appointees was released at Austin, Tex., on the same day.

[3] The President referred to Dean Rusk, Secretary of State, McGeorge Bundy, Special Assistant to the President, Kermit Gordon, Director of the Bureau of the Budget, George C. McGhee, U.S. Ambassador to Germany, Robert S. McNamara, Secretary of Defense, John A. McCone, Director of the Central Intelligence Agency, Bill D. Moyers, Special Assistant to the President, and Gardner Ackley, Chairman of the Council of Economic Advisers.

Q. Mr. Gordon on Wednesday, did you say, Mr. President?

THE PRESIDENT. I'm not quite sure; I think tomorrow, if they can get that many seats on the plane. I don't see beyond that.

[*The remainder of the news conference consisted of "deep background" briefing.*]

NOTE: President Johnson's thirty-fifth news conference was held at the LBJ Ranch, Johnson City, Tex., at 5:35 p.m. on Monday, December 28, 1964.

819   Statement by the President on the Appointment of Lloyd N. Hand To Succeed Angier B. Duke as Chief of Protocol. *December 29, 1964*

AMBASSADOR Duke's service as Chief of Protocol since 1961 has been outstanding. Mrs. Johnson and I, as well as all of official Washington, will very much miss Angier and his charming wife, Robin. In November 1963, Mr. Duke agreed to remain as Chief of Protocol for 1 year beyond his original plans. The country is fortunate that Mr. Duke's experience and ability will be utilized in the important assignment which will be announced soon.

Mr. Hand is an outstanding young lawyer and businessman who has worked closely with Mr. Duke on occasions during the past year. I look forward to this opportunity to work again with a trusted and respected friend and associate.

NOTE: Mr. Hand's appointment as Chief of Protocol became effective on January 21, 1965.

On January 27, 1965, the President announced his intention to nominate Mr. Duke as United States Ambassador to Spain. Mr. Duke's nomination was confirmed by the Senate on March 9, 1965.

820   New Year Greetings to Leaders of the Soviet Union. *December 30, 1964*

Dear Mr. Chairmen:

Personally, and on behalf of the American people, I extend to you and the Soviet people greetings and best wishes for the New Year.

The year just ending has produced significant accomplishment in some areas of endeavor. But major international problems are unresolved and the most urgent business for all of us remains strengthening the foundation of world peace. In this task, our two governments bear great responsibilities and it is my earnest wish that in the coming year we can make substantial progress.

Arms control remains especially urgent; nothing can contribute more to the hopes of mankind for the future. During the months ahead I hope we can work for practical agreements to this end. We can and should move to limit the spread of nuclear weapons; to achieve a verified worldwide comprehensive test ban; to make a cut-off of fissionable material production for weapons coupled with measures to safeguard the peaceful uses of nuclear power; and to agree on a verified freeze in existing offensive and defensive strategic nuclear delivery systems.

By progress in this critical area, our governments can help to make this a happier and safer world for all peoples. You may be certain that the American people and their government will never be second in this effort.

    Sincerely yours,

LYNDON B. JOHNSON

[Anastas Mikoyan, Chairman of the Presidium of the Supreme Soviet of the U.S.S.R., and Aleksei N. Kosygin, Chairman of the Council of Ministers]

NOTE: The message was released at Austin, Tex.

Appendix A—White House Press Releases

NOTE: Includes releases covering matters with which the President was closely concerned, except announcements of Presidential personnel appointments and approvals of legislation with which there was no accompanying statement.

Releases relating to Proclamations and Executive orders have not been included. These documents are separately listed in Appendix B.

For list of Press and Radio Conferences, see subject index under "News conferences."

In many instances the White House issued advance releases of addresses or remarks which differ from the text as actually delivered. These have been noted in brackets, thus: [2 releases].

1675

Appendix A

Appendix A

13 Letter to the Chairman, Civil Service Commission, on coordination of Federal activities in the field

14 Remarks of welcome at Union Station to President Segni of Italy

14 Toasts of the President and President Segni

14 White House announcement of the acceptance of a professorship by Brooks Hays

14 Telegram to Governor Sanford on his attack on poverty in North Carolina

15 Remarks to leaders of organizations concerned with the problems of senior citizens

15 Remarks to the members of the Davis Cup Team

15 Toasts of the President and President Segni at the Italian Embassy

15 Letter accepting resignation of Theodore C. Sorensen as Special Counsel to the President

15 Joint statement following discussions with the President of Italy

16 White House announcement following the President's meeting with William C. Foster on the eve of his departure for Geneva

16 Remarks by telephone for the keel-laying ceremony of the first automated cargo ship

16 Remarks to new participants in "Plans for Progress" equal opportunity agreements

16 Letter to the President of the Senate and to the Speaker of the House on appropriations for the Peace Corps

16 Memorandum on the observance of Brotherhood Week

16 Statement by the President upon appointing the Chairman of the Citizen's Advisory Council on the Status of Women

17 Statement by the President in response to a report on immigration

17 Letter to Dr. Jerome B. Wiesner as to the need for public institutions of higher learning in the District of Columbia

17 Letter to Teodoro Moscoso on his new assignments in the field of Latin American affairs

18 Remarks at the dedication of the National Geographic Society Building [2 releases]

18 Farewell message to President Segni of Italy

18 White House release concerning steps to relieve unemployment in Anaconda, Mont.

20 Remarks upon receiving a United States Army flag from senior commanders of the Army

20 Remarks to members of the National Congress of American Indians

20 Remarks to members of the Budget Bureau staff at the signing of the 1965 budget

20 Letter to Chairman Khrushchev on the eve of the reopening of the Geneva disarmament conference

20 Message to the first conference of the Catholic Inter-American Cooperation Program

20 Annual message to the Congress: The Economic Report of the President

21 Letter accepting resignation of Edward R. Murrow as Director, USIA

21 Statement by the President upon nominating Carl T. Rowan as Director, USIA

21 Remarks to the members of the President's Advisory Committee on Labor-Management Policy

21 Remarks at the presentation of the Distinguished Service Medal to Gen. David M. Shoup

21 Remarks of welcome at the White House to Prime Minister Pearson of Canada

21 Message to the 18-nation disarmament conference in Geneva

21 Statement by the President on the reopening of the Geneva disarmament conference

21 Radio and television remarks on the reopening of the Geneva disarmament conference

21 White House announcement of settlement of the airline labor dispute

21 White House announcement of supplemental appropriations requests for fiscal year 1964

21 Annual Budget Message to the Congress, fiscal year 1965

21 Annual message to the Congress, the District of Columbia budget

22 Remarks with Prime Minister Pearson at the signing of the Columbia River Agreement with Canada

22 Joint statement with Prime Minister Pearson on the Columbia River Agreement

Appendix A

1964
January

30 Letter to the President of the Senate and to the Speaker of the House transmitting proposed amendments to the Fair Labor Standards Act

30 Statement by the President on voter registration in the District of Columbia

31 Statement by the President on recent advances in Federal personnel management

31 Statement to members of the Business Group for Latin America

February

2 White House announcement of the President's acceptance of the honorary chairmanship of the Committee To Salvage Talent of the National Scholarship Service and Fund for Negro Students

4 Remarks upon witnessing the certification of the 24th amendment to the Constitution

4 White House release concerning the John F. Kennedy half dollars

4 Letter to the President of the Senate and to the Speaker of the House concerning Eximbank guarantees for U.S. sales to Yugoslavia

4 Letter to the President of the Senate and to the Speaker of the House concerning Eximbank guarantees for U.S. sales to the U.S.S.R., Bulgaria, Czechoslovakia, Hungary, Poland, Rumania

4 Letter accepting resignation of Timothy J. Reardon, Jr., as Special Assistant to the President

5 Remarks at the 12th annual presidential prayer breakfast [2 releases]

5 Special message to the Congress on consumer interests

5 Remarks in New York City at the Joseph P. Kennedy, Jr., Foundation awards dinner

6 Remarks in New York City at the dinner of the Weizmann Institute of Science [2 releases]

9 Statement by the President upon making public the report of the President's Council on Aging

10 Special message to the Congress on the Nation's health

10 Statement by the President upon making public his report to the Congress on communications satellites

11 Remarks upon signing bill amending the Library Services Act

11 Remarks to key officials of the Internal Revenue Service

1964
February

12 Letter to Sargent Shriver on his appointment to direct the program to eliminate poverty

12 Remarks of welcome at the White House to Prime Minister Sir Alec Douglas-Home

12 Remarks at the Lincoln Memorial [2 releases]

12 Letter accepting resignation of August Heckscher as Special Consultant on the Arts

13 Joint statement following discussions with the Prime Minister of the United Kingdom

13 Announcement of supplemental appropriations request for the John F. Kennedy Center for the Performing Arts

13 Announcement of supplemental appropriations request for the District of Columbia

13 Toasts of the President and of Prime Minister Sir Alec Douglas-Home

14 Remarks at St. Louis University

14 Remarks at the St. Louis bicentennial dinner [2 releases]

14 Announcement of the presentation of a painting by Joshua Meador of California's Big Sur area

17 Announcement of appointment of a committee for the celebration of the 400th anniversary of Shakespeare's birth

18 Announcement of membership of a special committee to study the operations of NIH

19 Remarks to a delegation of students from Seton Hall University

19 Message to the sixth plenary session of the U.N. Economic Commission for Africa

21 Remarks at the 96th Charter Day observance of the University of California at Los Angeles

22 Joint statement following discussions with the President of Mexico at Palm Springs, Calif.

22 Remarks in Los Angeles at a Mexican fiesta given in his honor by President López Mateos

25 Telegram to the President, AFL–CIO, concerning the union refusal to load wheat for Russia

25 Letter accepting resignation of Roger Hilsman as Assistant Secretary of State for Far Eastern Affairs

25 Letter to the Chairman, House Ways and Means Committee, endorsing the interest equalization tax on foreign securities

1964
February

26 Radio and television remarks upon signing the tax bill [2 releases]

27 Remarks at the ground-breaking ceremony for the Florida Cross-State Barge Canal [2 releases]

27 Remarks at Miami Beach at a Democratic Party dinner [2 releases]

28 Remarks at the swearing in of Carl T. Rowan as Director, United States Information Agency

28 White House statement on the signing of the Small Business Investment Act

March

1 Announcement of plans for an agency to make available information as to Federally-sponsored research

1 Remarks recorded for the opening of the Red Cross campaign

2 Remarks at the swearing in of Nicholas Johnson as Maritime Administrator

2 Table showing estimated distribution by States of the reduction in tax withholding

2 Announcement of appointment of members of the Public Advisory Committee for Trade Negotiations

3 Remarks to the winners of the Federal Woman's Award

3 Announcement of the President's request for a Tariff Commission study of imports of unmanufactured lead and zinc

3 White House statement on employment of members of minority groups in the Federal Government

4 Statement by the President following adoption of the Security Council resolution on Cyprus

4 Remarks at the swearing in of Frederick C. Belen as Deputy Postmaster General and William McMillan as Assistant Postmaster General

4 Remarks upon presenting the first Eleanor Roosevelt Memorial Award to Judge Anna M. Kross [2 releases]

5 Announcement of members of U.S. delegation to the inauguration of President Raul Leoni of Venezuela

6 Letter to Chairman Khrushchev on the situation in Cyprus

9 Remarks upon receiving the Secretary of Labor's manpower report

1964
March

9 Annual message to the Congress: The Manpower Report of the President

9 Letter to the President of the Senate and to the Speaker of the House proposing a National Commission on Automation and Technological Progress

9 White House statement announcing cutbacks in Federal civilian employment

11 Remarks upon signing bill extending the Federal Airports Act

12 Statement by the President upon approving bill authorizing appropriations for the Coast Guard

13 Remarks upon arrival in Cincinnati after aerial inspection of the Ohio River basin flood [2 releases]

15 Transcript of television and radio interview conducted by representatives of major broadcast services

16 Special message to the Congress proposing a nationwide war on the sources of poverty

16 Remarks on the third anniversary of the Alliance for Progress

16 Remarks to the Labor Advisory Council to the President's Committee on Equal Employment Opportunity

16 Letter accepting resignation of Steuart L. Pittman as Assistant Secretary of Defense

17 Letter to the Speaker urging House action on Federal pay legislation

17 White House statement on the situation in South Viet-Nam

17 Remarks in New York City at a dinner of the Friendly Sons of St. Patrick

18 Telephone conversation with the President of the National Farmers' Union

18 Letter to Secretary Dillon on the need for coordinating Federal actions in the field of bank regulation

19 Special message to the Congress on foreign aid

19 Remarks at the 1964 Democratic congressional dinner

19 Letter accepting resignation of Pierre Salinger as Press Secretary to the President

19 Letter to the President of the Senate and to the Speaker of the House transmitting reports on oceanographic research

1681

1964
March

20 Remarks upon signing bill authorizing appropriations for defense procurement and for research and development

20 Letter to the President of the Senate and to the Speaker of the House transmitting report on the water resources program

21 Statement by the President on Panama

23 Remarks in Atlantic City at the convention of the United Auto Workers [2 releases]

23 Letter to Secretary Hodges on highway safety

23 Veto of bill relating to a claim of R. Gordon Finney, Jr. (Congressional Record, Mar. 24, 1964, p. 5904)

23 White House announcement of supplemental appropriation requests

24 Remarks to the legislative conference of the Building and Construction Trades Department, AFL–CIO [2 releases]

24 White House announcement of amendments to the budget for economic and military assistance

25 Message to the U.N. Conference on Trade and Development

25 Remarks to members of the Southern Baptists Christian Leadership Seminar

25 Remarks upon accepting the Big Brother of the Year Award

26 Letter to the Speaker reporting on reductions in the cost of operating the Government

28 Statement by the President on the earthquake in Alaska

April

1 Letter to the President of the Senate and to the Speaker of the House proposing a study of the food industry

2 Message to the new President of Brazil

3 Remarks on the 15th anniversary of the signing of the North Atlantic Treaty [2 releases]

3 Remarks following the signing of a joint declaration with Panama

3 White House statement concerning the report to Congress on the food for peace program

3 Message to the Congress transmitting the 19th semiannual report under Public Law 480

1964
April

4 White House announcement of Federal disaster relief funds for Alaska

5 Statement by the President on the death of General MacArthur

7 Remarks to the Cabinet Committee on Export Expansion

9 Statement by the President following House action on the wheat-cotton and food stamp bills

9 Remarks to new participants in "Plans for Progress" equal opportunity agreements

9 Statement by the President on the eve of a national railroad strike

9 Radio and television statement announcing a moratorium in the railroad labor dispute

10 Statement by the President on the occasion of the beginning of negotiations in the railroad dispute

10 Remarks at the opening of final negotiations in the railroad dispute

10 Statement by the President: National Library Week

11 Remarks upon signing the wheat-cotton bill

13 Remarks at a reception for recently appointed women in Government

14 Letter from the Chairman, Federal Reconstruction and Development Planning Commission for Alaska

14 Remarks of welcome at the White House to Hussein I, King of Jordan

14 Toasts of the President and King Hussein I

14 Statement by the President on the death of Gen. Melvin J. Maas

14 Memorandum in response to a progress report on the joint financial management improvement program

14 White House announcement of disaster assistance for Del Norte County, Calif.

15 Statement by the President following a meeting with railroad management and union representatives

15 Remarks following a meeting with railroad management and union representatives

15 Remarks in support of a fundraising drive for a Winston Churchill Memorial Library at Westminster College, Missouri

15 Remarks upon signing order establishing the President's Committee on Manpower

15 White House announcement of investigation of tariff on cylinder, crown, and sheet glass

15 Joint statement following discussions with the King of Jordan

17 Remarks to a group in connection with the Montana territorial centennial

17 Remarks to the President's Commission on Heart Disease, Cancer and Stroke

17 Remarks to a group of Argentine Senators

17 Remarks at a reception for members of the American Society of Newspaper Editors

20 Remarks on foreign affairs at the Associated Press luncheon in New York City [2 releases]

20 Remarks at the swearing in of Dr. W. Randolph Lovelace as Director of Space Medicine for the Manned Space Flight

20 Remarks on introducing Secretary Rusk to the press following his return from the Far East

20 Message to the 73d Continental Congress of the Daughters of the American Revolution

20 White House statement following a review of implementation of the limited test ban treaty safeguards

21 Remarks to a group of Treasury Department officials on equal employment opportunity

21 Remarks to the members of the Public Advisory Committee on Trade Negotiations

21 Remarks upon receiving a citation from the Disciples of Christ Historical Society

21 Remarks to a group of editors and broadcasters attending a national conference on foreign policy

21 Statement by the President following the visit of Governor Connally of Texas

22 Remarks at the opening of the New York World's Fair [2 releases]

22 Remarks at the United States Pavilion, New York World's Fair

22 Radio and television statement announcing the settlement of the railroad dispute

23 Letter to the President of the Senate and to the Speaker of the House proposing additional aid for Alaska

23 White House announcement of amendment to appropriation request for airport construction and improvement

23 Remarks in Chicago at a fundraising dinner of the Democratic Club of Cook County [2 releases]

24 Remarks at the Lulu V. Cline School, South Bend, Ind.

24 Remarks in Pittsburgh to the League of Women Voters

24 Remarks in Pittsburgh at the Steelworkers Union Hall

24 Remarks at Mayo State Vocational School, Paintsville, Ky.

24 Remarks at the Johnson County Courthouse, Paintsville, Ky.

24 Remarks at the airport, Huntington, W. Va., upon departing for Washington

27 Remarks to the members of the U.S. Chamber of Commerce [2 releases]

27 White House statement in response to a task force report on the balance of payments problem

27 Remarks in response to a task force report on the balance of payments problem

27 Remarks to the members of the International Labor Press Association

28 Remarks to the Defense Advisory Committee on Women in the Services

28 Remarks on price stability at a White House dinner for business leaders

28 Letter to the President of the Senate and to the Speaker of the House transmitting the bill for the Appalachian Region

28 White House announcement concerning medallion to be presented to the Presidential Scholars

29 Remarks to a group of civil rights leaders

30 Remarks at a meeting of the President's Committee on Employment of the Handicapped [2 releases]

30 Remarks commemorating the 175th anniversary of the inauguration of George Washington

30 Remarks to the 1964 Campaign Conference for Democratic Women [2 releases]

Appendix A

1964
May

18 White House release concerning forthcoming visit of the King of Burundi

18 White House announcement of a further reduction in Federal employment ceilings

18 Special message to the Congress transmitting request for additional funds for Viet-Nam

18 Toasts of the President and Mayor Willy Brandt of Berlin

18 Remarks upon presenting "E" Awards for significant contributions to the export expansion program

20 Remarks at the presentation of the President's Safety Awards

20 Remarks to members of the Cooperative League of the U.S.A.

20 Statement by the President upon signing bill relating to fishing in U.S. territorial waters

20 White House announcement of forthcoming mission to Moscow by Dr. Jerome B. Wiesner

20 Letter to the Under Secretary of the Navy concerning the showing of a national anthem trailer film

21 Statement by the President in response to a report on the supersonic transport program

21 White House announcement of special Presidential citations for significant improvements in Government operations

22 Remarks upon arrival at Metropolitan Airport in Detroit

22 Remarks at the University of Michigan [2 releases]

22 Letter accepting resignation of Mortimer M. Caplin as Commissioner of Internal Revenue

22 White House release concerning revised budget receipts and expenditures

23 Remarks upon arrival at the airport, Roanoke, Va.

23 Remarks in Lexington, Va., at the dedication of the George C. Marshall Research Library [2 releases]

25 White House release concerning U.S. participation in the D-day ceremonies in France

25 Remarks at the swearing in of Mrs. Virginia Brown as Interstate Commerce Commissioner

1964
May

26 Remarks upon signing the International Development Association bill

26 Remarks upon presenting the Small Businessman of the Year Award

26 Remarks at the "Salute to President Johnson" dinner

26 White House announcement of decrease in appropriation request for the Internal Revenue Service

27 Remarks of welcome at the White House to President de Valera of Ireland

27 Statement by the President on the U.S.–Soviet consular convention

27 Toasts of the President and President de Valera

27 Letter to the President of India on the death of Prime Minister Nehru

27 Letter to the President of the Senate and to the Speaker of the House on the need for additional Alaskan reconstruction legislation

27 Message to the President of the Iran-America Society

28 Remarks in tribute to President Kennedy at a joint meeting of the Cabinet and the National Security Council

28 Response of Secretary Dillon to the President's tribute to the memory of President Kennedy

28 Statement by the President upon signing bill providing aid for Alaska

28 White House announcement of forthcoming meeting in Honolulu on southeast Asia

28 Remarks in New York City at the Young Democrats fundraising dinner [2 releases]

28 Remarks in Madison Square Garden at a New York Democratic gala [2 releases]

29 Remarks in Texas to the graduating class of the Johnson City High School [2 releases]

29 Remarks upon receiving a gift at the graduation exercises at the Johnson City High School

30 Commencement address at the University of Texas [2 releases]

30 Message to President de Valera

31 White House release concerning the report of the Council on Pennsylvania Avenue

1685

Appendix A

Appendix A

Appendix A

1964
July

29 Statement by the President on announcing a White House meeting of the presidents of State universities

30 Remarks upon presenting the Distinguished Service Medal to General McKee

30 Remarks to a group of State and local school officials

30 Statement by the President relating to the selection of a vice presidential candidate

30 Statement by the President following an agreement by certain civil rights leaders

30 Statement by the President on the anniversary of the Nuclear Test Ban Treaty

30 Statement by the President following the OAS decision on Cuban aggression against Venezuela

30 Statement by the President on the reduction of civilian employment in the Department of Defense

30 Statement by the President on receiving a progress report of the Council on Physical Fitness

31 Remarks upon signing a proclamation to commemorate the 20th anniversary of the Warsaw uprising

31 Statement by the President upon the successful flight of Ranger VII

August

1 Remarks following a briefing with space scientists on the successful flight to the moon

1 Statement by the President in response to a request for mediation in the shipping industry negotiations

1 Letter to Manlio Brosio on his appointment as Secretary General of NATO

2 White House statement on U.S. participation in the International Hydrological Decade

3 Remarks to foreign language newspaper publishers on their role in building American unity

3 Statement by the President upon instructing the Navy to take retaliatory action in the Gulf of Tonkin

4 Radio and television report to the American people following renewed aggression in the Gulf of Tonkin

5 Remarks at Syracuse University on the Communist challenge in southeast Asia [2 releases]

1964
August

5 Special message to the Congress on U.S. policy in southeast Asia

6 Remarks of welcome at the White House to the Secretary General of the United Nations

6 Toasts of the President and Secretary General U Thant

6 Veto of bill for the relief of Anthony F. Bernardo and Ambrose A. Cerrito (Congressional Record, August 6, 1964, p. 17748)

8 Statement by the President following House action on the economic opportunity bill

10 Remarks at a luncheon for businessmen

10 Remarks upon signing joint resolution for the maintenance of peace and security in southeast Asia [2 releases]

11 Remarks at a ceremony marking the issuance of the "register and vote" stamp [2 releases]

11 White House statement in response to a report on improving passenger transportation in the Boston–Washington corridor

11 White House announcement of supplemental appropriations request for the Department of Health, Education, and Welfare

11 Veto of bill for the relief of Catalina Properties, Inc. (Congressional Record, August 12, 1964, p. 18574)

11 Remarks to members of the National Association of Counties [2 releases]

12 Remarks upon signing the military pay bill [2 releases]

12 Remarks in New York City before the American Bar Association [2 releases]

12 White House announcement of the forthcoming Roosevelt-Campobello International Park ceremonies

12 White House release concerning supplemental appropriations request for various agencies

12 Letter to the Speaker transmitting appropriations request for activities authorized by the Economic Opportunity Act

13 Remarks upon signing the highway bill

13 Remarks at a luncheon for a group of State university presidents [2 releases]

14 Remarks upon signing the Government employees pay raise bill

1964
August

14 Remarks by telephone on the occasion of the commissioning of the U.S.S. *Casimir Pulaski*

14 White House release concerning supplemental appropriations request for the food stamp program

14 White House release concerning supplemental appropriations request for the Department of Health, Education, and Welfare (Office of Education)

14 White House release concerning supplemental appropriations request for the Department of Health, Education, and Welfare and the Selective Service System

14 White House release concerning supplemental appropriations request for the Housing and Home Finance Agency

14 White House release concerning supplemental appropriations request for the Department of the Interior

14 White House release concerning supplemental appropriations request for the Public Land Review Commission

15 Statement by the President concerning the development of a counter-insurgency aircraft

17 Remarks to members of the Communications Satellite Corporation Board

17 Statement by the President upon sending copies of the moon photographs to leaders of 110 nations

17 Statement by the President upon issuing memorandum on the staffing of international organizations

18 Remarks upon signing bill extending the Hill-Burton Act [2 releases]

18 Remarks to members of the National Citizens Committee for Community Relations [2 releases]

18 Remarks to the United States Marshals [2 releases]

18 Letter to the Speaker in support of the establishment of a National Council on the Arts

19 Remarks upon signing bill creating the National Commission on Technology, Automation, and Economic Progress

19 Remarks to the White House seminar students [2 releases]

19 Approval of recommendations as to radiation protection for Federal agencies

1964
August

19 Remarks at the President's Salute to the Congress [2 releases]

20 Remarks upon signing the Economic Opportunity Act

20 Special message to the Congress on U.S. participation in the United Nations

20 Remarks upon signing bill amending Securities and Exchange Act

20 Remarks at a reception for small businessmen

20 Statement by the President on the agreements for the establishment of a global communications satellite system

21 Remarks at the convocation of the National War College and the Industrial College of the Armed Forces [2 releases]

21 Statement by the President on the fifth anniversary of the statehood for Hawaii

22 Remarks upon awarding the Silver Star posthumously to Sgt. Harry A. Walling

22 List of Democratic Governors to meet with the President

22 Remarks to a group of Democratic Governors

22 Letter to the Attorney General on a program to combat juvenile delinquency in the District of Columbia

22 Figures on new durable goods ownership

24 White House release on management improvement in the Federal Government

24 Memorandum of disapproval of bill for the relief of the estate of Eileen G. Foster

25 White House statement on the labor dispute involving the non-operating railroad unions

26 Remarks upon signing bill permitting private ownership of nuclear materials

26 The President's medical report

26 Remarks before the National Convention upon recommending the nomination of Hubert Humphrey as Vice President

27 Remarks before the National Convention upon accepting the nomination [2 releases]

28 Remarks in Atlantic City before the Democratic National Committee

Appendix A

1964
September

16 Remarks with Prime Minister Pearson upon proclaiming the Columbia River Treaty [2 releases]

16 Remarks in Seattle on the control of nuclear weapons [2 releases]

17 Remarks in Sacramento on the steps of the State land saluting the Northwest-Southwest power transmission intertie [2 releases]

17 Remarks in Sacramento on the steps of the State Capitol [2 releases]

17 Statement by the President on reviewing California's plans under the Economic Opportunity Act

18 Remarks to the President's Advisory Council on Federal Reports [2 releases]

18 Remarks to members of the NATO parliamentarians conference

18 Remarks on immigration policy to a group interested in the Verrazano-Narrows Bridge commemorative stamp

19 Statement by the President upon the death of Professor J. Frank Dobie

20 Message to Prime Minister Olivier on the occasion of the independence of Malta

20 Remarks at the dedication of the Morgantown, W. Va., Airport [2 releases]

21 Remarks to a group of representatives of fraternal organizations

21 White House release concerning the 20th semi-annual report under the Agricultural Trade Development and Assistance Act

22 Remarks in Atlantic City at the convention of the United Steelworkers of America [2 releases]

22 White House statement on the work of the President's Commission on Heart Disease, Cancer and Stroke

22 White House announcement of appropriation request for carrying out the Farm Labor Contractor Registration Act

23 Excerpts from remarks at a meeting with the new panel of consultants on peace and national security

23 Remarks to the annual convention of the International Union of Electrical Workers [2 releases]

23 Message to the Congress transmitting Eighth Annual Report on the Trade Agreements Program

1964
September

23 White House announcement of appropriations requests for the Small Business Administration and for improvement of vocational education

24 Remarks upon presenting the Collier Trophy in aeronautics to Clarence L. Johnson

24 Statement by the President upon approving bill providing for a site study for a new interoceanic canal

24 Letter to the Chief Justice upon receipt of the Warren Commission report

24 White House announcement of appropriation request for the work of the Alaska Centennial Commission

24 White House announcement of appropriation request to cover U.S. participation in joint flood control projects with Mexico

25 Remarks in El Paso at a ceremony marking the settlement of the Chamizal dispute [2 releases]

25 Remarks in Oklahoma at the dedication of the Eufaula Dam [2 releases]

25 Remarks in Oklahoma City at the opening of the State Fair [2 releases]

25 Remarks in Texarkana at the dedication of John F. Kennedy Square [2 releases]

26 Statement by the President upon making public an FBI report on the recent urban riots

28 Remarks in Providence at the 200th anniversary convocation of Brown University [2 releases]

28 Statement by the President on the problems of the textile industry

28 Remarks in Hartford, Conn. [2 releases]

28 Remarks in Hartford to a group of business leaders

28 Remarks at the airport, Burlington, Vt. [2 releases]

28 Remarks in Portland, Maine, on the steps of the City Hall [2 releases]

28 Remarks in Manchester to the members of the New Hampshire Weekly Newspaper Editors Association [2 releases]

29 Toasts of the President and the Secretary General of NATO

29 Remarks upon arrival at Offutt Air Force Base in Omaha [2 releases]

1964
September

29 Remarks upon completing an inspection of SAC Headquarters, Offutt Air Force Base, Omaha [2 releases]

29 White House announcement of appropriation request for the Appalachian Regional Committee

29 White House announcement of nomination of Lt. Col. John H. Glenn, Jr., for promotion to the grade of colonel

30 Remarks at a meeting with representatives of veterans organizations

October

1 Remarks to the faculty and students of Johns Hopkins University [2 releases]

1 Remarks at the swearing in of Philip Nichols, Jr., and Linton M. Collins as judges

1 Letter to the Attorney General directing him to petition for an injunction in the maritime industry labor dispute

2 Remarks at the final meeting of the Alaska Reconstruction Planning Commission

2 Remarks upon proclaiming 1965 as International Cooperation Year [2 releases]

3 Special message to the Congress transmitting report on foreign assistance programs

3 Statement by the President on the effects of Hurricane Hilda

3 Statement by the President on the Department of Defense cost reduction program

3 Statement by the President on receiving progress report on a study of the draft system

3 Statement by the President on the first round-the-world cruise of a nuclear task force

3 Statement by the President announcing a change in the Foreign Service

3 Statement by the President on the cost of Government during July and August

3 Statement by the President reviewing the state of the economy

3 Statement by the President on Federal civilian employment

3 Remarks to a group of college student leaders [2 releases]

3 Statement by the President reviewing the work of the 88th Congress

1964
October

4 White House statement announcing the White House Fellows program

5 Remarks of welcome at the White House to President Macapagal of the Philippines

5 Statement by the President on the new labor contracts in the automobile industry

5 Message to the Second Conference of Nonaligned Nations meeting in Cairo

5 Toasts of the President and President Macapagal

6 Joint statement following discussions with the President of the Philippines

6 Remarks at the station at Alexandria, Va., at the start of Mrs. Johnson's trip through the South

6 Remarks at a meeting of "Scientists and Engineers for Johnson-Humphrey"

6 Remarks at a White House luncheon for businessmen

6 Remarks in Raleigh at North Carolina State College [2 releases]

7 Recorded statement marking the inauguration of television by communication satellite between the United States and Japan

7 Statement by the President at the beginning of a campaign trip

7 Remarks at the State Capitol in Des Moines [2 releases]

7 Remarks in Springfield, Ill., at the Sangamon County Courthouse [2 releases]

7 Remarks on the Courthouse steps in Peoria [2 releases]

7 Remarks in Peoria at the convention of the Illinois State Federation of Labor

7 Television address to the American people

8 Remarks at Washington High School, Lake County, Ind. [2 releases]

8 Remarks in Indianapolis at Soldiers and Sailors Square [2 releases]

8 Statement by the President upon signing bill extending the Agricultural Trade and Assistance Act

8 Remarks at a "Salute to President Johnson" dinner in Cleveland [2 releases]

1964
October

16 Message to President de Valera on the occasion of his 82d birthday

16 White House statement on high-speed rail transportation in the Northeast Corridor

16 Statement by the President upon signing Executive order "To Facilitate Coordination of Federal Education Programs"

16 White House memorandum on voting by Federal employees

17 Statement by the President upon signing bill relating to claims of U.S. nationals against the government of Cuba

17 Exchange of messages with the Secretary General of the North Atlantic Treaty Organization

17 White House announcement of appointment of delegates and alternates to the 13th session of UNESCO

18 Radio and television report to the American people on recent events in Russia, China, and Great Britain [2 releases]

19 Statement by the President following a meeting with congressional leaders

19 Statement by the President on the strike at General Motors

20 Remarks to members of the press following a meeting of the Cabinet

20 Statement by the President on the establishment of permanent task forces to assist communities faced with plant closings

20 Statement by the President on the death of President Hoover

21 Remarks in Memorial Hall, Akron University [2 releases]

21 Remarks in Belleville, Ill. [2 releases]

21 Remarks in St. Louis, Mo. [2 releases]

21 Statement by the President following a meeting with the panel of consultants on foreign affairs

22 Statement by the President upon making public a tabulation of major industry gains, 1961–64

23 Recorded remarks on the 19th anniversary of the United Nations

23 Recorded remarks congratulating the U.S. Olympic Team and the members of the U.S. Olympic Committee

23 Recorded remarks after further study of the report of the Council on Pennsylvania Avenue

23 Memorandum from Secretary Celebrezze on radiological surveillance following the detonation of the Chinese nuclear device

24 Remarks on the river front in Memphis [2 releases]

24 Remarks at an airport rally in Chattanooga [2 releases]

24 Informal remarks in Auxiliary Hall, Fifth Regiment Armory, in Baltimore

24 Remarks at the Fifth Regiment Armory in Baltimore [2 releases]

25 Letter to the President, Board of Commissioners, on crime in the District of Columbia

25 Statement by the President on the agreement with the Soviet Union for the exchange of weather information

25 Statement by the President: National First Voters Week

25 Statement by the President announcing a series of statements on economic issues

25 Presidential Statement No. 1 on Economic Issues: Maintaining Prosperity

25 Remarks in Boca Raton at the dedication of Florida Atlantic University [2 releases]

25 Remarks in Miami upon receiving a book relating to the Interama Cultural and Trade Center

25 White House statement announcing the establishment of the Federal Development Planning Committee for Appalachia

26 Remarks in Orlando, Fla. [2 releases]

26 Remarks at a rally in Hemming Park, Jacksonville, Fla. [2 releases]

26 Presidential Statement No. 2 on Economic Issues: Monetary Policy for Stability and Growth

26 Statement by the President upon making public a report on the desalting of sea water

26 White House statement on the joint team of experts report on the U.S.-Israeli water desalting program

26 Remarks at City Hall, Macon, Ga. [2 releases]

26 Statement by the President on the textile industry

1964
October

26 Remarks at a rally in Augusta, Ga. [2 releases]

26 Remarks on the steps of the State Capitol, Columbia, S.C. [2 releases]

26 Statement by the President on the occasion of a ceremony at the statue of Ukrainian poet Taras Shevchenko

26 Message to President Kaunda on the occasion of the independence of Zambia

26 Presidential Statement No. 3 on Economic Issues: Strengthening Our Balance of Payments

27 Presidential Statement No. 4 on Economic Issues: Responsible and Effective Fiscal Policy

27 Presidential Statement No. 5 on Economic Issues: Further Tax Reduction

27 Remarks at the presentation of a commission to Lt. Col. John H. Glenn, Jr.

27 Remarks to the members of the Inter-American Committee on the Alliance for Progress

27 Remarks in Boston at Post Office Square [2 releases]

27 Remarks at the Civil Center Arena in Pittsburgh [2 releases]

27 Remarks at an airport rally in Evansville, Ind. [2 releases]

28 White House announcement of members of U.S. delegation to the inauguration of the President of Chile

28 Presidential Statement No. 6 on Economic Issues: Strengthening State-Local Government

28 Presidential Statement No. 7 on Economic Issues: Improving the Tax System

28 Remarks in Albuquerque at the University of New Mexico [2 releases]

28 Remarks at City Hall in Los Angeles [2 releases]

28 Remarks at the Riverside, Calif., County Courthouse [2 releases]

28 Remarks at a rally in San Bernardino [2 releases]

28 Remarks at Lindbergh Field, San Diego [2 releases]

29 Remarks in Salt Lake City at the Mormon Tabernacle [2 releases]

29 Remarks recorded for the dedication of the Graduate Research Center of the Southwest

1964
October

29 Presidential Statement No. 8 on Economic Issues: Expanding World Trade

29 Presidential Statement No. 9 on Economic Issues: Promoting Price-Wage Decisions

29 Remarks at an airport rally in Wichita

29 Remarks in Convention Hall, Philadelphia [2 releases]

30 Presidential Statement No. 10 on Economic Issues: Achieving Full Employment

30 White House statement to accompany Presidential Statement No. 10

30 Statement by the President on the results of a survey of compliance with the Civil Rights Act

30 Remarks at an airport rally in Detroit [2 releases]

30 Remarks in Kosciusko Park, Milwaukee [2 releases]

30 Remarks at an airport rally in Rockford, Ill. [2 releases]

30 Remarks at the Chicago Stadium [2 releases]

31 White House statement on the attack on Bien Hoa Airfield in South Viet-Nam

31 White House announcement of allocation of disaster relief funds for use in California

31 White House announcement of additional funds for disaster relief in Florida

31 Remarks at the Old State House, Dover, Del. [2 releases]

31 Remarks at an airport rally in Wilmington, Del. [2 releases]

31 Remarks in Madison Square Garden [2 releases]

November

1 Letter to the Attorney General in response to a report on crime and law enforcement

1 Statement by the President making public a report on the balance of payments position

1 White House announcement concerning the issuance of a series of Presidential policy papers

1 Presidential Policy Paper No. 1: Education

1 Presidential Policy Paper No. 2: The Nation's Problems of Health

1 Presidential Policy Paper No. 3: Conservation of Natural Resources

1964
November

1 Presidential Policy Paper No. 4: Farm Policy

1 White House statement on the support during the campaign of the Student Body Presidents National Advisory Committee

2 White House announcement concerning the Veterans Day observance in Arlington Cemetery

2 Statement by the President announcing an expanded program to control cotton insect pests

2 Statement by the President on the fourth anniversary of the Peace Corps

2 White House release entitled "Economic News Note: A New Export Record"

2 Remarks at a rally in Houston [2 releases]

2 Remarks in Houston at Sam Houston Senior High School

2 Remarks at a rally in Pasadena, Tex.

2 Remarks at the State Capitol in Austin, Tex. [2 releases]

2 Radio and television address to the American people on election eve

4 Radio and television remarks to the American people at the close of election day

10 Remarks by telephone for ceremonies marking the 50th anniversary of the Port of Houston

12 Remarks of welcome at the LBJ Ranch to the President-elect of Mexico

12 The President's toast to Gustavo Diaz Ordaz, President-elect of Mexico

13 Statement by the President in response to report of the Inter-American Committee on the Alliance for Progress

14 White House statement on the appointment of the members of the National Commission on Technology, Automation, and Economic Progress

16 Remarks at the swearing in of Gardner Ackley as chairman and Arthur Okun as member of the Council of Economic Advisers

17 Remarks at the presentation of the White House Thanksgiving turkey

19 Remarks in the Cabinet Room at the unveiling of a bust of John F. Kennedy

19 Remarks at a luncheon of the Committee for Economic Development [2 releases]

1964
November

19 Statement by the President at a Cabinet meeting: The Great Society

19 Statement by the President at a Cabinet meeting: Personnel Appointments

20 Remarks at Southwest Texas State College, San Marcos [2 releases]

24 White House announcement of members of Cabinet Committee to plan U.S. participation in International Cooperation Year

24 Letter from Prime Minister Moro of Italy

25 Thanksgiving Day message to members of the Armed Forces

25 White House statement on the search for candidates for the White House Fellows program

27 White House announcement of the 1964 recipients of the National Medal of Science

28 Letter accepting resignation of Robert V. Roosa as Under Secretary of the Treasury for Monetary Affairs

28 Statement by the President on international cooperation in support of the pound sterling

29 White House statement upon making public a report on children's health

29 White House announcement of steps to speed up payment of GI insurance dividends

30 Message greeting Sir Winston Churchill on the occasion of his 90th birthday

30 Message congratulating the U.S. Olympic Team and the members of the Olympic Committee

December

1 White House statement following Ambassador Taylor's report on the situation in Viet-Nam

1 Remarks at a luncheon for the U.S. Olympic Medal winners [2 releases]

1 Remarks upon presenting the Distinguished Service Medal to Gen. Thomas S. Power [2 releases]

1 Citation accompanying Distinguished Service Medal awarded to General Power

2 Remarks at the ground-breaking ceremony for the John F. Kennedy Center for the Performing Arts [2 releases]

2 Remarks of the President at a luncheon for supporters of Radio Free Europe

1964
December

2 Remarks recorded for the commissioning of the U.S.S. *Sam Rayburn*

2 White House announcement concerning the Federal Employee Achievement Awards

2 Remarks to the members of The Business Council

3 Remarks at the 175th Anniversary Convocation of Georgetown University [2 releases]

3 Statement by the President on the supersonic transport program

3 White House announcement of Medal of Honor ceremony for Capt. Roger H. C. Donlon

3 White House announcement concerning the Lewis and Clark Trail Commission

4 Remarks at a ceremony marking the 10th anniversary of the Government Employees' Incentive Awards Act [2 releases]

4 Statement by the President on the November employment report

4 Statement by the President upon approving civil rights regulations covering the programs of Federal departments and agencies

4 White House announcement of forthcoming visit of the Prime Minister of Japan

5 Remarks at the presentation of the Medal of Honor to Capt. Roger H. C. Donlon, USA [2 releases]

5 Citation accompanying Medal of Honor awarded to Capt. Roger H. C. Donlon

7 Message to President Segni of Italy

7 Remarks of welcome at the White House to the new Prime Minister of Great Britain

7 Toasts of the President and Prime Minister Harold Wilson

7 Letter accepting resignation of Eugenie Anderson as Minister to Bulgaria

7 Letter accepting resignation of C. Allan Stewart as Ambassador to Venezuela

8 Joint statement following discussions with the Prime Minister of Great Britain

9 Remarks upon receiving report of the President's Commission on Heart Disease, Cancer and Stroke [2 releases]

9 Remarks at a reception for the new Democrats in Congress

1964
December

10 Remarks at the National Urban League's Community Action Assembly [2 releases]

12 Remarks to members of VISTA—"Volunteers in Service to America" [2 releases]

12 Remarks to the members of the Economic Opportunity Council

14 Letter to the Chairman, Federal Power Commission, in response to the National Power Survey Report

15 Remarks to the members of a delegation of industrial research leaders upon their return from the Soviet Union

15 White House announcement of the President's meeting with a delegation of industrial research leaders following their return from the Soviet Union

15 White House announcement of second annual Presidential Scholars program

16 Letter accepting resignation of Luther H. Hodges as Secretary of Commerce

16 Remarks at a televised ceremony marking the change in leadership at the Department of Commerce

16 Statement by the President on the launching of the Italian San Marco satellite

16 White House announcement of 162 approved war on poverty projects

17 Remarks upon accepting a ceremonial pass to the 10th International Games for the Deaf

18 Letter accepting resignation of Burke Marshall as Assistant Attorney General, Civil Rights Division

18 Remarks on the decision to build a sea level canal and to negotiate a new treaty with Panama [2 releases]

18 Remarks at the lighting of the Nation's Christmas tree

18 Statement by the President on the new level of personal income in the United States

21 Statement by the President in response to report reviewing gains in Government employment of minority groups

23 Christmas message to the Americans in Viet-Nam

1964
December

26 Letter accepting resignation of J. S. Gleason, Jr., as Administrator of Veterans Affairs

26 Letter accepting resignation of Joseph P. McMurray as Chairman, Federal Home Loan Bank Board

26 Statement by the President on the appointment of John E. Horne as Chairman, Federal Home Loan Bank Board

26 Statement by the President on the appointment of William J. Driver as Administrator of Veterans Affairs

1964
December

28 Letter to Secretary McNamara transmitting final report of the President's Committee on Equal Opportunity in the Armed Forces

28 Message to Giuseppe Saragat upon his election as President of Italy

29 Responses by the President's physician to questions concerning the President's health

29 Statement by the President on the appointment of Lloyd N. Hand to succeed Angier B. Duke as Chief of Protocol

30 New Year greetings to leaders of the Soviet Union

Appendix B—Presidential Documents Published in the Federal Register

PROCLAMATIONS

Appendix B

Appendix B

EXECUTIVE ORDERS

Appendix B

Appendix B

Appendix B

PRESIDENTIAL DOCUMENTS OTHER THAN PROCLAMATIONS AND EXECUTIVE ORDERS

Appendix C—Presidential Reports to the Congress

Subject	Published	Sent to the Congress	Date of White House release
National Aeronautics and Space Administration:		*1963*	*1963*
8th Semiannual	H. Doc. 179	Dec. 5	. . . .
		1964	*1964*
9th Semiannual	H. Doc. 314	July 1	. . . .
10th Semiannual	H. Doc. 355	Aug. 21	. . . .
Economic Report	H. Doc. 278	Jan. 20	Jan. 20
U.S. Aeronautics and Space Activities	H. Doc. 207	Jan. 27	Jan. 27
National Science Foundation	H. Doc. 209	Jan. 29	Jan. 27
U.S. Civil Service Commission	H. Doc. 263	Jan. 31	. . . .
U.S. Arms Control and Disarmament Agency	H. Doc. 219	Feb. 4	. . . .
United States Participation in the International Atomic Energy Agency	H. Doc. 226	Feb. 10	. . . .
Communications Satellite Corporation	H. Doc. 225	Feb. 10(H)	. . . .
		Feb. 17(S)	
Surgeon General, Public Health Service	H. Doc. 230	Feb. 17	. . . .
Office of Minerals Exploration:			
11th Semiannual	. . . . .	Mar. 9	. . . .
12th Semiannual	. . . . .	Sept. 8	. . . .
Federal Disaster Relief Program	H. Doc. 249	Mar. 18	. . . .
P.L. 480 (83d Congress):			
19th Semiannual	H. Doc. 294	Apr. 3(S)	Apr. 3
		Apr. 6(H)	
20th Semiannual	H. Doc. 365	Sept. 21	Sept. 21
National Capital Housing Authority	. . . . .	Apr. 6	. . . .
Special International Exhibitions	. . . . .	Apr. 6	. . . .

Appendix C

Subject	Published	Sent to the Congress	Date of White House release
Railroad Retirement Board	H. Doc. 277	Apr. 6	. . . .
Government Employees Training Act	. . . . .	Apr. 6	. . . .
Commodity Credit Corporation	. . . . .	June 12(S)	. . . .
		June 15(H)	
Alien Property, Office of	. . . . .	June 30	. . . .
St. Lawrence Seaway Development Corporation	H. Doc. 332	Aug. 3	. . . .
Lend-lease Operations	. . . . .	Aug. 6	. . . .
United States Participation in the United Nations	H. Doc. 188	Aug. 20	. . . .
Corregidor-Bataan Memorial Commission	H. Doc. 360	Sept. 8	. . . .
Trade Agreements Program	H. Doc. 366	Sept. 23	. . . .
Foreign Assistance Program	H. Doc. 357	Oct. 3	. . . .

Appendix D—Rules Governing This Publication

[Reprinted from the Federal Register, vol. 29, p. 11792, dated August 18, 1964]

TITLE 1—GENERAL PROVISIONS

Chapter I—Administrative Committee of the Federal Register

PART 32—PUBLIC PAPERS OF THE
PRESIDENTS OF THE UNITED STATES

PUBLICATION AND FORMAT

Sec.
32.1 Publication required.
32.2 Coverage of prior years.
32.3 Format, indexes, ancillaries.

SCOPE

32.10 Basic criteria.
32.11 Sources.

OFFICIAL DISTRIBUTION

32.15 The Congress.
32.16 The Supreme Court.
32.17 Executive agencies.
32.18 Governmental requisitions.
32.19 Extra copies.

PUBLIC SALE

32.22 Sale of annual volumes.

AUTHORITY: The provisions of this Part 32 issued under sec. 6, 49 Stat. 501, as amended; 44 U.S.C. 306. Sec. 6, E.O. 10530, 19 F.R. 2709; 3 CFR 1954–1958 Comp.

PUBLICATION AND FORMAT

§ 32.1 *Publication required.* There shall be published forthwith at the end of each calendar year, a special edition of the FEDERAL REGISTER designated "Public Papers of the Presidents of the United States." Ordinarily each volume shall cover one calendar year and shall be identified further by the name of the President and the period covered.

NOTE: This program started with the year 1957.

§ 32.2 *Coverage of prior years.* After conferring with the National Historical Publications Commission with respect to the need therefor, the Administrative Committee may from time to time authorize the publication of similar volumes covering specified calendar years prior to 1957.

NOTE: The committee has approved the publication of volumes starting with the year 1945.

§ 32.3 *Format, indexes, ancillaries.* Each annual volume, divided into books whenever appropriate, shall be separately published in the binding and style deemed by the Administrative Committee to be suitable to the dignity of the office of President of the United States. Each volume shall be appropriately indexed and shall contain appropriate ancillary information respecting significant Presidential documents not published in full text.

SCOPE

§ 32.10 *Basic criteria.* The basic text of the volumes shall consist of oral utterances by the President or of writings subscribed by him.

§ 32.11 *Sources.* (a) The basic text of the volumes shall be selected from: (1) Communications to the Congress, (2) public addresses, (3) transcripts of press conferences, (4) public letters, (5) messages to heads of state, (6) statements released on miscellaneous subjects, and (7) formal executive documents promulgated in accordance with law.

(b) In general, ancillary text, notes, and tables shall be derived from official sources.

Appendix D

OFFICIAL DISTRIBUTION

§ 32.15 *The Congress.* Each Member of the Congress, during his term of office, shall be entitled to one copy of each annual volume published during such term. Authorization for furnishing such copies shall be submitted in writing to the Director and signed by the authorizing Member.

§ 32.16 *The Supreme Court.* The Supreme Court of the United States shall be entitled to 12 copies of the annual volumes.

§ 32.17 *Executive agencies.* The head of each department and the head of each independent agency in the executive branch of the Government shall be entitled to one copy of each annual volume upon application therefor in writing to the Director.

§ 32.18 *Governmental requisitions.* Legislative, judicial, and executive agencies of the Federal Government may obtain, at cost, copies of the annual volumes for official use upon the timely submission to the Government Printing Office of a printing and binding requisition (Standard Form 1).

§ 32.19 *Extra copies.* All requests for extra copies of the annual volumes must be addressed to the Superintendent of Documents, Government Printing Office, Washington, D.C. 20402. Extra copies must be paid for by the agency or official requesting them.

PUBLIC SALE

§ 32.22 *Sale of annual volumes.* The annual volumes shall be placed on sale to the public by the Superintendent of Documents, Government Printing Office, Washington, D.C. 20402, at prices determined by him under the general direction of the Administrative Committee.

*   *   *   *

This revision of Chapter I of Title 1 of the Code of Federal Regulations shall become effective 30 days after publication in the FEDERAL REGISTER.

ADMINISTRATIVE COMMITTEE OF
THE FEDERAL REGISTER,

WAYNE C. GROVER,
*Archivist of the United States,
Chairman.*

JAMES L. HARRISON,
*The Public Printer,
Member.*

CHARLES F. SIMMS,
*Representative of the
Attorney General, Member.*

APPROVED:
ROBERT F. KENNEDY,
Attorney General.

BERNARD L. BOUTIN,
Administrator of General Services.

[F.R. Doc. 64–8366; Filed, Aug. 17, 1964; 8:49 a.m.]

INDEX

[Main references are to items except as otherwise indicated]

Index

Index

Index

Index

[Main references are to items except as otherwise indicated]

Index

[Main references are to items except as otherwise indicated]

Index

Index

[Main references are to items except as otherwise indicated]

Index

[Main references are to items except as otherwise indicated]

[Main references are to items except as otherwise indicated]

Index

Index

[Main references are to items except as otherwise indicated]

Index

Index

[Main references are to items except as otherwise indicated]

Index

Index

[Main references are to items except as otherwise indicated]

[Main references are to items except as otherwise indicated]

[Main references are to items except as otherwise indicated]

Index

Index

Index

Index

Index

Index

[Main references are to items except as otherwise indicated]

Index

Index

Index

Index

Index

Index

[Main references are to items except as otherwise indicated]

Index

Index

[Main references are to items except as otherwise indicated]

Index

Index

Index

Index

Index

Index

[Main references are to items except as otherwise indicated]

Index

[Main references are to items except as otherwise indicated]

[Main references are to items except as otherwise indicated]

[Main references are to items except as otherwise indicated]

Index

[Main references are to items except as otherwise indicated]

Index

Index

Index

Index

Index

Index

[Main references are to items except as otherwise indicated]

Index

Index

Index

Index

Index

Index

Index

Index

○